International Directory of

COMPANY
HISTORIES

International Directory of

COMPANY HISTORIES

VOLUME 28

Editor

Jay P. Pederson

ST. JAMES PRESS

AN IMPRINT OF THE GALE GROUP

DETROIT • SAN FRANCISCO • LONDON
BOSTON • WOODBRIDGE, CT

STAFF

Jay P. Pederson, *Editor*

Miranda H. Ferrara, *Project Manager*

Laura S. Berger, Joann Cerrito, David J. Collins, Steve Cusack,
Nicolet V. Elert, Jamie C. FitzGerald, Kristin Hart, Laura S. Kryhoski,
Margaret Mazurkiewicz, Michael J. Tyrkus, *St. James Press Editorial Staff*

Peter M. Gareffa, *Managing Editor, St. James Press*

Library of Congress Catalog Number: 89-190943

British Library Cataloguing in Publication Data

International directory of company histories. Vol. 28
I. Jay P. Pederson
338.7409

ISBN 1-55862-387-6

Printed in the United States of America
Published simultaneously in the United Kingdom

St. James Press is an imprint of The Gale Group

Cover photograph: Chicago Board of Trade
(courtesy of Chicago Board of Trade)

10 9 8 7 6 5 4 3 2 1

CONTENTS

Company Histories

PREFACE

The St. James Press series *The International Directory of Company Histories (IDCH)* is intended for reference use by students, business people, librarians, historians, economists, investors, job candidates, and others who seek to learn more about the historical development of the world's most important companies. To date, *IDCH* has covered over 3,800 companies in 28 volumes.

Inclusion Criteria

Most companies chosen for inclusion in *IDCH* have achieved a minimum of US$50 million in annual sales and are leading influences in their industries or geographical locations. Companies may be publicly held, private, or nonprofit. State-owned companies that are important in their industries and that may operate much like public or private companies also are included. Wholly owned subsidiaries and divisions are profiled if they meet the requirements for inclusion. Entries on companies that have had major changes since they were last profiled may be selected for updating.

The *IDCH* series highlights 10% private and nonprofit companies, and features updated entries on approximately 45 companies per volume.

Entry Format

Each entry begins with the company's legal name, the address of its headquarters, its telephone, toll-free, and fax numbers, and its web site. A statement of public, private, state, or parent ownership follows. A company with a legal name in both English and the language of its headquarters country is listed by the English name, with the native-language name in parentheses.

The company's founding or earliest incorporation date, the number of employees, and the most recent available sales figures follow. Sales figures are given in local currencies with equivalents in U.S. dollars. For some private companies, sales figures are estimates and indicated by the abbreviation *est.* The entry lists the exchanges on which a company's stock is traded and its ticker symbol, as well as the company's principal North American Industry Classification codes.

Entries generally contain a *Company Perspectives* box which provides a short summary of the company's mission, goals, and ideals, a list of *Principal Subsidiaries, Principal Divisions, Principal Operating Units,* and articles for *Further Reading.*

American spelling is used throughout *IDCH*, and the word ''billion'' is used in its U.S. sense of one thousand million.

Sources

Entries have been compiled from publicly accessible sources both in print and on the Internet such as general and academic periodicals, books, annual reports, and material supplied by the companies themselves.

Cumulative Indexes

IDCH contains two indexes: the **Index to Companies**, which provides an alphabetical index to companies discussed in the text as well as to companies profiled, and the **Index to Industries**, which allows researchers to locate companies by their principal industry. Both indexes are cumulative and specific instructions for using them are found immediately preceding each index.

Suggestions Welcome

Comments and suggestions from users of *IDCH* on any aspect of the product as well as suggestions for companies to be included or updated are cordially invited. Please write:

The Editor
International Directory of Company Histories
St. James Press
27500 Drake Rd.
Farmington Hills, Michigan 48331-3535

ABBREVIATIONS FOR FORMS OF COMPANY INCORPORATION

A.B.	Aktiebolaget (Sweden)
A.G.	Aktiengesellschaft (Germany, Switzerland)
A.S.	Atieselskab (Denmark)
A.S.	Aksjeselskap (Denmark, Norway)
A.Ş.	Anomin Şirket (Turkey)
B.V.	Besloten Vennootschap met beperkte, Aansprakelijkheid (The Netherlands)
Co.	Company (United Kingdom, United States)
Corp.	Corporation (United States)
G.I.E.	Groupement d'Intérêt Economique (France)
GmbH	Gesellschaft mit beschränkter Haftung (Germany)
H.B.	Handelsbolaget (Sweden)
Inc.	Incorporated (United States)
KGaA	Kommanditgesellschaft auf Aktien (Germany)
K.K.	Kabushiki Kaisha (Japan)
LLC	Limited Liability Company (Middle East)
Ltd.	Limited (Canada, Japan, United Kingdom, United States)
N.V.	Naamloze Vennootschap (The Netherlands)
OY	Osakeyhtiöt (Finland)
PLC	Public Limited Company (United Kingdom)
PTY.	Proprietary (Australia, Hong Kong, South Africa)
S.A.	Société Anonyme (Belgium, France, Switzerland)
SpA	Società per Azioni (Italy)

ABBREVIATIONS FOR CURRENCY

DA	Algerian dinar	M$	Malaysian ringgit
A$	Australian dollar	Dfl	Netherlands florin
Sch	Austrian schilling	Nfl	Netherlands florin
BFr	Belgian franc	NZ$	New Zealand dollar
Cr	Brazilian cruzado	N	Nigerian naira
C$	Canadian dollar	NKr	Norwegian krone
RMB	Chinese renminbi	RO	Omani rial
DKr	Danish krone	P	Philippine peso
E£	Egyptian pound	Esc	Portuguese escudo
Fmk	Finnish markka	SRls	Saudi Arabian riyal
FFr	French franc	S$	Singapore dollar
DM	German mark	R	South African rand
HK$	Hong Kong dollar	W	South Korean won
HUF	Hungarian forint	Pta	Spanish peseta
Rs	Indian rupee	SKr	Swedish krona
Rp	Indonesian rupiah	SFr	Swiss franc
IR£	Irish pound	NT$	Taiwanese dollar
L	Italian lira	B	Thai baht
¥	Japanese yen	£	United Kingdom pound
W	Korean won	$	United States dollar
KD	Kuwaiti dinar	B	Venezuelan bolivar
LuxFr	Luxembourgian franc	K	Zambian kwacha

International Directory of

COMPANY
HISTORIES

AAR Corp.

One AAR Place
1100 N. Wood Dale Road
Wood Dale, Illinois 60191
U.S.A.
(630) 227-2000
Fax: (630) 227-2019
Web site: http://www.aarcorp.com

Public Company
Incorporated: 1955 as Allen Aircraft Radio Inc.
Employees: 2,700
Sales: $782.12 million (1998)
Stock Exchanges: New York
Ticker Symbol: AIR
NAIC: 42186 Transportation Equipment & Supplies
    (Except Motor Vehicles) Wholesalers; 421860
    Aircraft Wholesaling; 336411 Aircraft Overhauling

A leading aftermarket support company to the aviation industry, AAR Corp. trades aircraft parts and whole planes, overhauls engines and airframes, and manufactures certain components. It has maintenance facilities in New York, London, The Netherlands, Oklahoma, Connecticut, and Miami. Containers and cases and mobile military shelters are a few of the company's newer product lines.

Origins

Ira Allen Eichner, born during the Depression, started his career dealing used electrical parts in Chicago. The end of World War II and the Korean War produced a glut of used aircraft that formed the basis for many an airline; it also produced a cheap supply of airplane parts. Trade in military surplus radios introduced Eichner to aviation; he went into business while an undergraduate at Roosevelt University in 1951 with a few hundred dollars borrowed from his fiancée. In 1955 Eichner formed Allen Aircraft Radio Inc., naming himself CEO. He became chairman in 1973.

In 1970 the name was changed to AAR Corp. AAR by this time was distributing Cessna aircraft. The general aviation market collapsed in the late 1970s, however. AAR dropped its general aviation business altogether by 1986.

AAR organized its Aircraft Turbine Center, Inc. in 1979 after future CEO David P. Storch, Eichner's son-in-law, joined the company. The unit maintained a broad variety of Pratt & Whitney and GE engines. By this time, its Allen Aircraft airframe parts subsidiary had become a leader in its field.

Deregulation and Its Aftermath: 1980s–90s

In 1981 AAR acquired the assets of Brooks and Perkins Corp., which would form the basis of its manufacturing group. Brooks and Perkins, founded in 1950, specialized in cargo handling systems.

AAR bought Circament Coating Technology Inc., a New York firm repairing turbine engine parts, in 1984. Fiscal year 1985 saw revenues of $219 million.

The 1980s and deregulation were good to AAR. New airplane purchases demanded enormous amounts of capital, as did parts inventories. Many carriers still possessed them and did their own maintenance, a service AAR had begun supplying. Still, as air traffic increased at a clip of eight percent per year in the last half of the decade, AAR's earnings increased even faster.

AAR was still dwarfed by Ryder System's $1 billion aviation services business. Eichner characterized AAR as a niche-oriented operation involved in a variety of unique projects.

Storch was named president in 1989, shortly before earnings began to falter, deflating AAR's long-expanding stock price. Among the causes were turnover problems at facilities in Oklahoma and Florida. Some of the Oklahoma staff subsequently received a raise. It lost customers such as Braniff Airways, which broke up in the chaotic atmosphere of deregulation. Still, the company managed a profit of $25.6 million on sales of $444.8 million for fiscal year 1989–90. Employees now numbered 2,500 at 25 facilities worldwide.

Company Perspectives:

AAR is the premier supplier of products and services to the worldwide aviation/aerospace industry. Founded in 1951, the Company has grown by anticipating and preparing for this dynamic environment, developing innovative products and programs, and delivering on a commitment to do things right for our customers. Today, comprised of more than 2,600 employees at 40 facilities strategically located in 12 countries, AAR is one of the world's largest and most diverse aviation aftermarket support companies.

AAR prided itself on anticipating customers' needs. It upgraded its computer system in 1990, allowing it to track parts going through its shops. One of AAR's new businesses proved highly lucrative. It leased four Boeing 737s and had bought eight Boeing 727s from Air France, leasing six of them to cargo giant DHL.

A worldwide recession in the early 1990s constricted the civil aviation market. High fuel prices and stiff fare competition furthered the damage. A war in the Middle East did not foster air travel. AAR's sales and profits declined accordingly; it only earned $283,000 in fiscal 1993.

The airlines' competitive situation resulted in keeping older planes working longer, which kept up demand for maintenance and parts. It also encouraged the outsourcing of maintenance operations, as the airlines sought to concentrate on their profit-making core activities. A flood of new budget carriers gave AAR potential new customers across the world. Some of these start-ups were not the best credit risks, however.

Competition for airframe maintenance resulted in more short-term contracts, a trend AAR resisted. Ten percent of its sales were from long-term agreements. It also faced serious price competition.

Under deregulation, purchasing had become more professional, and more professionalized, as more MBAs joined procurement departments. Parts supply became more competitive. Buyers demanded not just low prices, even if combined with fast, reliable service. They sought a process of constant refinement within the vendors to ensure consistent efficiency in the future. They also sought to reduce the numbers of vendors they used, sowing the seeds of eventual consolidation in the industry.

AAR still was able to make big deals. Sabena World Airlines hired AAR to manage its inventory in 1990. AAR had already been stocking the carrier's maintenance center in Brussels. When Eastern Airlines, a former client, went out of business, AAR was able to acquire its inventory of 45,000 parts for Boeing 757 and 727 aircraft. In 1993 AAR landed a $20 million-per-year inventory management contract at General Electric Co.'s engine maintenance facility in Wales, which it had taken over from British Airways. AAR staffed 18 employees there.

In spite of this entrée to the European market, the company's prospects in Asia remained dim. AAR did expand its Singapore plant and discussed a joint venture with Japan Airlines and Cathay Pacific to be based in Xiamen, China.

The company earned a profit of $9.5 million in fiscal 1993–94 on revenues of $407.8 million. It employed about 1,900 at the time. The federal government accounted for about a sixth of AAR's revenues. The U.S. military needed AAR to maintain its forces in the Persian Gulf and Bosnia.

About 70 percent of airlines performed their own maintenance in the mid-1990s. Aircraft orders also were down, which hurt AAR's fastener business. In addition, Delta, Singapore Airlines, and Swissair formed the DDS World Sourcing buying consortium in August 1995. Consolidation among airlines, however, was expected to reduce world fleet size, produce a supply of used parts, and induce a demand for outside inventory management, following the example of wildly successful Southwest Airlines.

AAR sought to develop its inventory management business as carriers became less involved in this function. It bought the spare parts inventory from carriers such as Lufthansa and Northwest, which freed their capital. Global spare parts inventories were valued at $25 billion, with 80 percent owned by the carriers. The top six airlines accounted for 40 percent of the engine maintenance market. They accounted for 80 percent in certain engine types.

Late 1990s Recovery

The airline industry recovered in the late 1990s, producing a great demand for new aircraft. By this time, outsourcing was a firmly established cost-cutting concept in both civil and military circles. Storch, who was named president and CEO in 1996, predicted 15 percent sales growth.

Long-term contracts now accounted for 30 percent of sales. AAR supplied GE's engine unit in Brazil, as well as those for such carriers as Northwest Airlines, Sabena, Lufthansa, and KLM. United and Delta were two of AAR's biggest clients for aircraft and engine leases, but it also served the military, regional airlines, and business operators.

Trading of parts and leasing aircraft and engines accounted for more than half of AAR's revenues. Overhaul work accounted for a quarter, and manufacturing cargo equipment and other products added the remaining fifth.

In February 1997 AAR resold some stock it had bought during the dark days of the recession, garnering $50 million. Revenues reached $589.3 million in 1996–97, while profits soared 44 percent to $23 million.

AAR picked up contracts left and right in the late 1990s. It began servicing planes for U.S. marshals. FedEx hired it to install cargo handling systems in its new Airbus aircraft. Grupo TACA, an alliance of Central American airlines, chose AAR for inventory management services valued at $10 million per year. It also won a new $25 million Department of Defense contract.

In the summer of 1997 AAR bought 14 747s from British Airways for $22 million. In general, the planes it bought did not have much service life left. After they had been leased for a year or two, AAR could disassemble them for parts, or lease them again depending on the market. AAR also leased DC-10s and Boeing 737s. AAR began building a new hangar in Oklahoma City in 1997.

While streamlining its own operations, it sought other companies to acquire. In June 1997 AAR bought Cooper Aviation Industries, a $45 million supplier of aviation components. In 1998 AAR bought Tempco Hydraulics, AVSCO Aviation Service Corporation (previously a division of Aerospatiale), and composites structure manufacturer ATR International Inc., aided in part by a weak stock market. AAR also entered into joint ventures, including one with General Electric known as Turbine Engine Asset Management LLC. Another joint venture with GE Capital Aviation Services formed Aviation Inventory Management Co. Meanwhile, AAR had diversified into industrial products such as floor cleaners, which it marketed under the PowerBoss brand. It sold this unit in November 1998.

With air traffic rising, sales boomed in fiscal 1997–98, up 30 percent. Foreign sales accounted for about a third of sales, down a little from the early 1990s.

Troubles at Boeing frightened AAR investors, although it accounted for less than one percent of the company's business, as Storch pointed out. Boeing also had announced in 1997 that it was entering the aircraft maintenance business. On a related note, the uncertain Asian market accounted for only three percent of AAR revenues. There remained concerns that certain Asian airlines might collapse, flooding the market with parts.

Revenues and profits continued to rise impressively in late 1998. Earlier in the decade, AAR had set a target of $1 billion in revenues by 2000. At the close of 1998, that goal seemed well within reach.

Principal Subsidiaries

AAR Aircraft Group, Inc.; AAR Allen Group, Inc.; AAR Allen Services, Inc.; AAR Engine Group, Inc.; AAR Engine Services, Inc.; AAR Financial Services Corp.; AAR International, Inc.; AAR Manufacturing Group, Inc.

Principal Divisions

Aircraft and Engine Group; Airframe and Accessories Group; Manufacturing Group.

Further Reading

Berss, Marcia, "You Need It, We Got It," *Forbes,* May 20, 1996, pp. 236–38.
Byrne, Harlan S., "A Smoother Flight," *Barron's,* May 5, 1997, p. 28.
Donoghue, J.A., "The Art of the Deal," *Air Transport World,* October 1995, pp. 67–71.
Dubashi, Jagannath, "Hired Hangar," *Financial World,* May 16, 1989.
Flint, Perry, "Lease 'Em, Sell 'Em or Scrap 'Em," *Air Transport World,* January 1998, p. 21.
Gubernick, Lisa, "Sky King," *Forbes,* February 24, 1986, p. 151.
Keefe, Lisa M., "AAR Facing Turbulence Ahead, But Eyes Clear Skies Long Term," *Crain's Chicago Business,* November 5, 1990, p. 38.
——, "Long-Time High-Flier AAR Corp. Loses Altitude," *Crain's Chicago Business,* August 6, 1990, p. 52.
Lefer, Henry, "Aviation Services Supermarket," *Air Transport World,* February 1991.
Murphy, H. Lee, "AAR's Military Work Shores Up Revenues," *Crain's Chicago Business,* October 24, 1994, p. 35.
——, "Deals, New Business Send AAR Soaring," *Crain's Chicago Business,* October 20, 1997, p. 28.
——, "Potential Downturn Doesn't Worry AAR," *Crain's Chicago Business,* October 26, 1998.
Nelms, Douglas W., "Man Over Machine," *Air Transport World,* November 1995, pp. 87–88.

—Frederick C. Ingram

A.B.Dick Company

7400 Caldwell Avenue
Niles, Illinois 60714
U.S.A.
(847) 779-1900
(800) 422-3616
Fax: (847) 647-6940
Web site: http://www.abdick.com

Wholly Owned Subsidiary of Paragon Corporate
Holdings, Inc.
Incorporated: 1884
Employees: 1,200
Sales: $268.62 million (1998 est.)
NAIC: 333293 Printing Machinery & Equipment
Manufacturing; 333315 Photographic & Photocopying
Equipment Manufacturing; 421420 Office Equipment
Wholesaling; 42183 Industrial Machinery &
Equipment Wholesalers

A.B.Dick Company is still going strong after 114 years in business and, after the turn of the new millennium, will be one of only a handful of companies who can say they have witnessed, and driven, change in three separate centuries. Owned by Paragon Corporate Holdings, Inc., a division of Nesco Inc., A.B.Dick continues as a leading worldwide supplier to the graphic arts and printing industry, manufacturing and marketing equipment and supplies for all stages of document creation— pre-press, press, and post-press—as well as continuing service and support.

Albert Blake Dick and
Thomas Alva Edison, 1884–1900

A.B.Dick Company was founded in 1884 in Chicago, Illinois, by a young lumberman named Albert Blake Dick, and was incorporated in that state on April 11. Offices were located at 720 W. Jackson Blvd. Business then was still predominantly done on a handwritten basis. Because there was no such ma-

chine as a mimeograph, it became necessary to invent one. How that invention came about is well documented and so is the fact that Thomas Alva Edison's ideas and his "electric pen" were key in the amalgamation of concepts that determined the form of the world's first duplicator, the "Edison-Dick Mimeograph." This simple machine created an industry.

In 1876 Thomas Alva Edison patented his "Edison Electric Pen." A few years later, experimenting with a file and waxed wrapping paper, Dick discovered the mimeograph process. The invention initiated the era of modern printed communications; formerly, documents were reproduced by the hand of a scribe. In 1887 the company released the Model "0" Flatbed Duplicator, which sold for $12. It was the original Edison Mimeograph and the company's first commercial product. Later that year, the Edison Mimeograph No. 4 came out, with a nameplate bearing the Edison patent from August 8, 1876. Over the rest of the 19th century, more products were developed: in 1894, the Edison Mimeograph Typewriter #3; in 1895, the Edison Mimeograph No. 51 "New Automatic"; in 1896, the Planetary Pencil Pointer; and in 1900, the Edison Diaphragm Mimeograph No. 61 (Rotary); the Edison Oscillating Mimeograph No. 71.; and the A.B.Dick No. 1 Folder, an automatic circular letter folding machine.

The Roaring Twenties, the Great Depression,
and World Wars

By the turn of the 20th century, A.B.Dick Company was flourishing. The A.B.Dick Model 75 Rotary Mimeograph was released in 1904. Capable of producing 50 copies a minute, it set the stage for ever increasing capacity in Dick products. The Edison Rotary Mimeograph No. 76 followed in 1909, as well as the A.B.Dick Company Adding Machine and the "Dermatype Wet Stencil," which replaced stiff wax stencil and revolutionized the industry. The Edison Mimeograph 77A came out in 1913. It is believed that the A.B.Dick mimeograph produced every copy of every single order of U.S. military personnel during World War I.

The ability to make 100 copies a minute was quite high-tech for the time, and the owner of the company knew that he had

Company Perspectives:

Our mission is to provide our customers with everything they need to succeed in the production of high quality rapid response printing. We further commit to the development of quality equipment and supplies which will assist our customers in their need to advance to a digital printing environment.

scratched only the surface of what potential existed. The flatbed mimeograph was replaced with the oscillating model, and soon the rotary had an electric motor added, which became the Model 77 and then the Model 78. The company's thrust had evolved from revolutionary to evolutionary. New stencil technology was converging continually with new equipment developments, allowing the company to expand and succeed at will. As the world changed and demands for copies grew, it almost seemed as though A.B.Dick was waiting for the needs to catch up with its vision of the future of duplicating. The company was always among the leaders of Chicago organizations.

A.B.Dick's visionary mimeograph process became part of the lexicon of the U.S. vocabulary. Nearly all needs for duplicated copy was done on the mimeograph. As technology became more available, the mimeograph continued to evolve around the basic ideas of the process. Throughout the Great Depression, two world wars, and other major changes taking place in a dynamic society—A.B.Dick Company grew by meeting the needs of a market it had created, and by continued research and development.

In 1924 stencil was improved again, and the "hill" dry stencil was introduced. It was the basic stencil, which changed only in minor detail all the way through the modern era. During these years, many tools (i.e., the stylus, shading plate, and lettering template) were perfected to allow free imagination to reign during stencil preparation. In 1932 A.B.Dick of Canada was established, representing the company's first international foray. Two years later, Albert Blake Dick, Sr., died and was replaced by his son Albert Blake Dick, Jr. His other son, Edison (so named because of his esteem for Thomas Alva Edison), became a board member and was intricately involved in the success of the business.

The company started building military hardware in 1939, as well as commercial products, including the A.B.Dick Portable Rotary #72; Mimeoscope #1; Model 96 Mimeograph; Edison Dick Mimeograph #30 (the simplest and smallest hand-operated mimeograph at the time); Model 100 Mimeograph; #9 Mimeoscope; Photomechanical Printer #67; Model 91 Mimeograph (17,874 units manufactured); and the Model 100 Chrome Mimeo (made as a one-of-a-kind showpiece at the 1939 World's Fair).

Through this period the company enjoyed the unusual growth of the "Roaring '20s" and fared through the Great Depression without laying off a single employee. In 1934 it announced a retirement plan for all employees, who, in grateful

appreciation, soon had a bronze plaque made for display at the headquarters building. When A.B.Dick Company opened the Niles Plant in 1949, that plaque was the centerpiece of a magnificent new lobby. The lobby, like the "keyhole," was among the many design contributions of Walter Dorwin Teague, the pre-eminent industrial designer of the era.

Beginning in 1941 and lasting through World War II, the company manufactured only products needed to support the war effort, focusing on key defense needs by manufacturing the esteemed Norden Bombsight for long-range bombers. Other products included spark plug bodies and aircraft landing gear. The following year A.B.Dick Company began publishing *Mimeographic,* a comprehensive company newspaper aimed at keeping military personnel informed of working family and vice-versa.

Post-World War II

Following the war, land was acquired in Niles, Illinois, to build a new factory. Ground was broken there on October 13, 1948. Also that year, the first postwar Mimeograph, the Model 400 Series, was released.

All operations moved to Niles on October 22, 1949. The complex there was dedicated on September 26, and A.B.Dick III locked the doors for the final time at 720 W. Jackson Blvd. In 1951 the new building added a west wing.

In 1952 the company began to expand, entering the offset business by acquiring Lithomat Corporation in Massachusetts, which made paper masters. The company's first offset machine, the Model 350, was manufactured in 1955. An International Division was added to the organization in 1956.

More products came out, including the first photocopier, the Model 110 DTR Unit, in 1957, and the Tabletop Offset Model 320 in 1959. Also in 1959, videograph research was completed and the first high-speed videograph became available. It would, in later years, become the cornerstone of Videojet Company, a leader in inkjet printing and bar code marking.

Through 1958 the company had known only three presidents: the founder, A.B. Dick; his son, Jr.; and his grandson, A.B. Dick III. Their strong reliance on family was the cornerstone of their approach to managing the business and its employees. They recognized then, as the company does now, that shared loyalty and teamwork in achieving mutual goals was an irreplaceable ingredient in success.

Outside the Family, 1960

In 1960 Karl Van Tassel took over as president, the first non-Dick family member to do so, and served until 1971. During this time the company began to serve the banking industry for MICR check printing. New products included the Mimeoscope #10, #5, and #4; Mimco-Introduced graph 410 and 450; and Spirit Duplicator M-210. The company historian, George Smith, noted that "this period was one of dynamic growth as the company changed location and started up in Offset, Videograph, Spirit, Azograph, MICR, and photocopiers, as well as continuing to develop new Mimeograph models, and furnish supplies for all the above." In September 1964 the Action

Offset Line was introduced at an elaborate presentation at McCormick Place in Chicago, Illinois. In all, nine new models were shown, of which the main ones were the Model 367A and the Tabletop Model 325.

A.B.Dick Company has remained at the forefront of the graphic arts and printing industry. As change accelerated in the 1970s, 1980s, and 1990s, the company's key products went through fast transitions in an attempt to continue to meet a growing and globally involved world.

John Stetson took over as president in 1971. The following year, in February, the company announced plans to go public with a listing on the New York Stock Exchange in September, selling shares at an opening price of $27. In 1974 the company entered a joint venture with Scott Paper to develop the System 200 Updatable Microfiche System. The company would buy out Scott Paper in 1978 to form the Record Systems Division (RSD). Major product lines were established, and there was more thrust at developing new products for all lines than announcements of new technology. Stetson left the company in 1978 to become secretary of the Air Force, and Van Tassel came out of retirement to serve again until April 8, 1979.

New Owners, 1979

The following day, April 9, 1979, General Electric Company (GEC) of England purchased the A.B.Dick Company for $104 million. Shares were returned to company ownership at $17 per share, and Geoffrey R. Cross became president and CEO.

After Cross shortly departed, Norman J. Nichol served as president for one year until David Powell assumed the office for GEC. He served twice in this capacity, with an interim nine months under the leadership of Jim Bast. During this period the company entered the microfilm/microfiche business. Word processors were introduced and the company was up and running in this technology. Smith noted that "the company changed radically with the new owners, GEC of The United Kingdom. Cross made it known early on that he saw computers and word processors as the future of the company. Soon, major efforts to develop and support these products was underway."

The K Series Copiers were introduced in 1986. Two years later the company acquired Itek Graphix in Rochester, New York, to expand its product lines in the pre-press arena. In 1989 the 2000 Series Copiers were introduced. Videojet became a separate company from A.B.Dick, spun off in 1991. Located in Elk Grove Village, it was wholly owned by GEC. In 1993 the Century 3000 Two-Color Press was introduced, and the Colorstar digital color printer was produced in 1995. Also that year, the company launched Micap Technology Corporation.

In 1996 Gerald J. McConnell was appointed president and CEO. That year, the company received a GATF Award for the DPM2000 and introduced the 3500 Series presses and the 9900 Series Offset Duplicators.

Another New Owner, 1997

Paragon Corporate Holdings, Inc., an investment firm and affiliate of Nesco Inc. of Cleveland, Ohio, assumed ownership of A.B.Dick Company in 1997, retaining McConnell as president. In 1998 the company purchased an operation in Holland, opened a supply distribution center in Sparks, Nevada, and announced its intention to move the manufacturing facility to Touhy Avenue and its worldwide headquarters to Caldwell Avenue, both in Niles, Illinois. GEC sold the old sites to Wal-Mart and Sam's Club.

A.B.Dick Company's potential continued to be considerable. Certainly the digital revolution impacted on its product mix as much as it did on society at large. The company saw digital capability as a power to be exploited in making things compact, user-friendly, fast, and versatile. It was impossible to say where it would lead, but safe to say that A.B.Dick Company, under former Chief Financial Officer Ed Suchma, who was appointed president and CEO in 1999, would be right alongside whatever new technology developed.

Principal Subsidiaries

A.B.Dick Contract Manufacturing; American Grafix Service.

Further Reading

"A. B. Dick Co.," *Crain's Chicago Business,* July 22, 1991, p. 26.

Arnott, Nancy, "Printing Money," *Sales & Marketing Management,* February 1995, p. 64.

Chapman, Bert, "Duplicators Offer Fast, High Quality Copy Reproduction for Small Printers," *Graphic Arts Monthly* and *The Printing Industry,* July 1982, p. 43.

Curtis, Carol E., "Ovonics—Has Its Time Come?," *Forbes,* August 4, 1980, p. 35.

Deady, Tim, "Datametrics Stands to Win Big in Printer Distribution Arrangement," *Los Angeles Business Journal,* April 3, 1995, p. 4.

Gillam, Carey, "A.B.Dick Transfers Execs," *Atlanta Business Chronicle,* August 27, 1993, p. 1A.

Higgins, Kevin T., "Personalized Ads Boon to Magazines: 'What Offset Was to Printing, Selectronics Will Be to Binding,' " *Marketing News,* June 20, 1986, p. 1.

"HPS Printing Products," *Orlando Business Journal,* September 6, 1991, p. 10.

Tieman, Ross, "AB Dick Sale Furthers GEC Streamlining," *Financial Times,* January 7, 1997, p. 16.

"Two-Color Press for Short-Run Work," *American Printer,* December 1992, p. 74.

—Daryl F. Mallett

ⅩAJINOMOTO

Ajinomoto Co., Inc.

15-1, Kyobashi 1-chome
Chuo-ku
Tokyo 104-8315
Japan
(03) 5250-8111
Fax: (03) 5250-8293
Web site: http://www.ajinomoto.co.jp

Public Company
Incorporated: 1909
Employees: 5,145
Sales: ¥835.97 billion (US$6.33 billion) (1998)
Stock Exchanges: Tokyo Osaka Nagoya Kyoto Hiroshima
    Fukuoka Niigata Sapporo
NAIC: 311423 Dried & Dehydrated Food Manufacturing;
    311421 Fruit & Vegetable Canning; 311411 Frozen
    Fruit, Juice, & Vegetable Processing; 311412 Frozen
    Specialty Food Manufacturing; 311225 Fats & Oils
    Refining & Blending; 31192 Coffee & Tea
    Manufacturing; 311991 Perishable Prepared Food
    Manufacturing; 325412 Pharmaceutical Preparation
    Manufacturing; 325414 Biological Product (Except
    Diagnostic) Manufacturing

Ajinomoto Co., Inc., the world's first and still-largest producer of monosodium glutamate (MSG), is one of Japan's largest food-processing companies. In addition to seasonings, Ajinomoto produces edible oils, frozen and processed foods, beverages and dairy products, amino acids, pharmaceuticals, and other specialty chemicals. Although the company has operations in 20 countries, it derives nearly 80 percent of its revenues in its domestic sphere.

Origins and Postwar Activities

MSG, the company's mainstay for more than 80 years, was discovered in kelp by Kikunae Ikeda at the University of Tokyo in 1908. With help from Ikeda, Saburosuke and Chuji Suzuki—two brothers who had been extracting iodine from seaweed since 1890—formed Ajinomoto to produce the substance commercially. They began marketing it in 1909 as ''AJI-NO-MOTO,'' which translates literally as ''essence of taste.''

The company focused on international sales and established a strong base in chemical development at its inception. A New York office was opened in 1917, and between the wars production and sales offices were opened throughout Asia, giving the company a global position decades before other Japanese companies. During this time the company began to produce MSG from soybean protein, which eventually led to the production of cooking oils. World War II halted MSG production, but between 1947 and 1953 AJI-NO-MOTO became available in the United States and Europe, and the company also began to sell cooking oil. In 1954 Ajinomoto opened offices in São Paulo, Paris, Bangkok, and Hong Kong.

Emphasis on chemical research culminated in the creation of the Central Research Laboratories in 1956. Research during the 1950s brought about not only different biological and synthetic methods of MSG production, but an entry into the pharmaceutical industry. The development of crystalline essential amino acids, used for intravenous solutions, introduced Ajinomoto to pharmaceuticals. Amino acids were found to have a wide variety of applications, and before the end of the decade they were being used in the company's seasonings and animal-feed additives.

Food Processing in the 1960s

The company took larger strides toward internationalization in the 1960s. Most overseas growth was limited to expanded production of seasonings in Asia and South America. However, through joint ventures and licensing agreements with U.S. and European companies, Ajinomoto increased its presence on those continents and at the same time expanded its product line domestically. The first large-scale licensing agreement came in 1962 when it began marketing Kellogg's breakfast cereals in Japan. A similar agreement with CPC International Inc. to manufacture and market Knorr soups was reached in 1965. These ventures established the company as a food processor and not just a seasonings producer. After 1965, the company applied its research to the development of new seasonings, soups, margarine, mayonnaise, frozen foods, and flavored edible oils. In 1973 Ajinomoto formed yet another joint venture, with General Foods, to produce coffees, instant coffees, and soft drinks.

The oil crisis led most companies to consolidate in 1973 and 1974, and internal development of food products increased during the 1970s. By 1978 seasonings accounted for only 22 percent of sales and processed food had boomed to 31 percent from 3 percent in 1965. In 1970 the company created Ajinomoto Frozen Foods and also began to collaborate with the NutraSweet Company of the United States. A 1979 joint venture with Dannon introduced dairy products for the first time to the company's product line.

Expanding Pharmaceutical Operations in the 1980s

Ajinomoto's new focus on products derived from its amino acids research proved well-timed as the company entered the 1980s. Growth in the Japanese food industry slowed significantly. Although MSG sales overseas increased, the domestic market was mature. Food-related products, which made up 80 percent of the company's sales, could no longer be relied on for large-scale or long-term growth. Management initiated a plan to expand its fine chemicals divisions further while diversifying the food products made by its overseas subsidiaries.

Pharmaceutical product sales were ¥20 billion in 1980; U.S. medical institutions and pharmaceutical manufacturers purchased half of the company's output. Although the reliance on exports would prove damaging to many Japanese companies as the yen appreciated in the late 1980s, Ajinomoto's extensive research investments in the 1970s gave it prominence in the field and made the division less vulnerable to international cycles.

The diversification into the pharmaceutical business was not easy. The complexity of the pharmaceutical market called for completely different marketing techniques as well as lengthy approval processes from various governments. In order to defray these high research-and-development costs, Ajinomoto typically used other companies to market its drugs or used licensed companies to produce them.

In 1987 the joint Ajinomoto-CPC International venture was altered, with Ajinomoto taking full control of the Japanese joint venture firm, Knorr Foods Co., Ltd. At the same time, Ajinomoto purchased from CPC a 50 percent equity stake in

CPC's seven Asian subsidiaries located in six countries. In 1990 Ajinomoto joined with the Calpis Food Industry Co., Ltd. in an agreement whereby beverages and dairy products manufactured and marketed by Calpis would be distributed by Ajinomoto.

Ajinomoto's new venture department was established in 1987 with a focus on new markets and cooperative producers in the life-sciences area. The department symbolized the company's commitment to the industry, and earnings showed why. In 1988 sales rose only 0.5 percent, but earnings grew 15.4 percent—due largely to the much higher margins the company earned on life-science products. In 1989 Ajinomoto ventured further into the area of fine chemicals through the US$92.4 million acquisition of S.A. OmniChem N.V. of Belgium, a maker of intermediate chemical products for the pharmaceutical and food industries.

Although the international market for research and development in pharmaceuticals made Ajinomoto less vulnerable to currency valuation cycles, a strong yen hurt the company nonetheless. In response to a reduced export market, the company turned to domestic food sales in the late 1980s, becoming more active in restaurants and foodservice and entering the fresh vegetable and fish market for the first time. The food-processing division was the only one in 1988 to show an increase in sales—to 40.6 percent of the company total—reflecting the influence of the difficult export market. Ajinomoto hoped to increase its overseas food production by taking advantage of the strong yen to acquire companies and diversify the product lines of its foreign subsidiaries.

The company continued to spend a higher percentage (3.3 percent) of sales on research than most food processors did, reflecting its interest in the fine chemical and pharmaceutical industries. In addition to this money, the Japanese government funded research on problems such as AIDS, and in the late 1980s university research became available to commercial developers. Funding from the MIT Cancer Research Institute, for example, helped support research and provide a wider variety of potential developments.

1990s and Beyond

In the 1990s Ajinomoto expanded rapidly in the increasingly open market of China, establishing seasoning, food, and pharmaceutical operations there. The company also continued to pursue joint venture opportunities. In 1992 Ajinomoto joined with Calpis and the French food conglomerate Danone Group to form Calpis Ajinomoto Danone Co., Ltd., a Japanese-based marketer of chilled desserts, most of which were made from dairy products. In the pharmaceuticals sector, Ajinomoto expanded its research in the areas of immune diseases and diabetes. In 1994 the company licensed to Sandoz AG of Switzerland a diabetes treatment. Moreover, in 1996 the U.S. Food and Drug Administration recommended as a first-line therapy for AIDS a drug called dideoxyinosine that Ajinomoto had developed.

The 1990s also saw the company struggle through a number of difficulties. The prolonged Japanese economic downturn led to only moderate increases in net sales during the early and mid-1990s and stagnated profits. Results improved during the later years of the decade, with net sales increasing from ¥750.84

billion in 1996 to ¥788.4 billion in 1997 to ¥835.97 billion in 1998, while net income rose from ¥10.49 billion in 1996 to ¥15.33 billion in 1997 to ¥17.98 billion in 1998. Other troubles included a U.S. investigation into allegations of international price fixing in the food and feed additive business. The investigation led to a criminal felony case brought in August 1996 against Ajinomoto and two other Asian companies charging them with conspiring to illegally fix the worldwide price of lysine—a livestock feed additive—in concert with Archer-Daniels-Midland Co. of the United States. In November 1996 Ajinomoto pleaded guilty to one conspiracy count and agreed to pay a $10 million fine. In early 1997 two Ajinomoto executives were indicted on charges of paying ¥6 million (US$47,500) to *sokaiya* gangsters. The *sokaiya* were Japanese mob extortionists who blackmailed companies by threatening to disrupt annual shareholder meetings. This scandal led to the resignation of the president of Ajinomoto, Shunsuke Inamori, who took personal responsibility for the alleged payoffs.

The new president, Kunio Egashira, announced in early 1999 that Ajinomoto would adopt a holding company system by the year 2002 and integrate 130 domestic and overseas group companies into about 90 firms. The company also planned to reduce its overall number of employees from 5,200 to 4,800 by 2005, and to cut its 150-person administrative staff in half by 2002. Through these moves to consolidate and streamline operations, Ajinomoto hoped to improve its early 21st century profitability.

Principal Subsidiaries

Knorr Foods Co., Ltd.; Toyo Oil Mills Co., Inc.; Ajinomoto-Takara Corporation; Ajinomoto Fresh Foods Co., Ltd.; Sanpuku Co., Ltd.; Sanmix Corporation; Sanpo Unyu Co., Ltd.; Daimi Co., Ltd.; Kumazawa Seiyu Sangyo Co., Ltd.; Ajinomoto Finance Inc.; Ajinomoto Service Co., Ltd.; Chubu Knorr Foods Co., Ltd.; Ajinomoto System Techno Corporation; Shin-Nippon Commerce, Inc.; Takara-Daimi Co., Ltd.; Ajinomoto General Foods, Inc. (50%); Charles River Japan, Inc. (50%); Ajinomoto U.S.A., Inc.; Ajinomoto Interamericana Indústria e Comércio Ltda. (Brazil); Ajinomoto del Perú S.A.; Ajinomoto Europe Sales GmbH (Germany); Ajinomoto Co., (Thailand) Ltd.; Ajinomoto (Malaysia) Berhad; A.I.F. Investment Pte. Ltd. (Singapore); S.A. OmniChem N.V. (Belgium); Heartland Lysine, Inc. (U.S.); EUROLYSINE (France); P.T. Ajinex International (Indonesia); Ajinomoto (Singapore) Pte. Ltd.; Ajitrade Pte. Ltd. (Singapore); Forum (Holdings) Ltd. (U.K.); Forum Products Ltd. (U.K.); Britannica Pharmaceuticals Ltd. (U.K.); Britannica Health Products Ltd. (U.K.); Forum Products Inc. (U.S.); Quantum Generics Ltd. (U.K.); Forum Products (Ireland) Ltd.; Ajinomoto Co., (Hong Kong) Ltd.; S.A. Ajinomoto Coordination Center N.V. (Belgium); Lianhua Ajinomoto Co., Ltd. (China); CPC/AJI (Thailand) Ltd. (50%); CPC/AJI (Malaysia) Sdn. Berhad (50%); CPC/AJI (Asia) Ltd. (Hong Kong; 50%); CPC/AJI (Hong Kong) Ltd. (50%); CPC/AJI (Singapore) Pte. Ltd. (50%); CPC/AJI (Taiwan) Ltd. (50%); Ajinomoto Tong Hsing Foods, Inc. (Taiwan; 65%).

Further Reading

Abrahams, Paul, "Japanese Drug Group Licenses Treatment," *Financial Times,* January 20, 1994, p. 28.

Burton, Thomas M., "Archer-Daniels Faces a Potential Blow As Three Firms Admit Price-Fixing Plot," *Wall Street Journal,* August 28, 1996, p. A3.

Dawkins, William, "Ajinomoto Profits Static for Year," *Financial Times,* May 26, 1995, p. 25.

——, "Tradition on a Knife-Edge," *Financial Times,* March 13, 1997, p. 21.

Kilman, Scott, "Ajinomoto Pleads Guilty to Conspiring with ADM, Others to Fix Lysine Price," *Wall Street Journal,* November 15, 1996, p. A4.

Lander, Peter, "Mob Scene," *Far Eastern Economic Review,* March 20, 1997, p. 58.

Nakamoto, Michiyo, "Ajinomoto Head Quits over Scandal," *Financial Times,* April 12, 1997, p. 21.

Tanzer, Andrew, " 'We Have Our Eyes Open'," *Forbes,* September 4, 1989, pp. 57 + .

—updated by David E. Salamie

Allou Health & Beauty Care, Inc.

50 Emjay Boulevard
Brentwood, New York 11717
U.S.A.
(516) 273-4000
Fax: (516) 273-4003

Public Company
Incorporated: 1962 as Allou Distributors, Inc.
Employees: 240
Sales: $301.8 million (fiscal 1998)
Stock Exchanges: American
Ticker Symbol: ALU
NAIC: 42221 Drugs & Druggists Sundries Wholesalers;
    42249 Other Grocery & Related Product Wholesalers;
    45439 Other Direct Selling Establishments

Allou Health & Beauty Care, Inc. distributes brand name health and beauty aid products, fragrances and cosmetics, nonperishable packaged food items, and prescription pharmaceuticals, primarily to independent retailers in the New York, New Jersey, Connecticut, Philadelphia, and Miami areas. The fragrance and cosmetic products were also being marketed nationally to discount chain stores, independent retail stores, and pharmacies, and directly to the public through Internet web sites. Allou also was distributing about 50 health and beauty aid products under the trademark ''Allou Brands'' and manufacturing and distributing generic hair- and skincare products. The distribution of branded prescription pharmaceuticals was through a wholly owned subsidiary, M. Sobol, Inc.

Allou Health & Beauty Care to 1994

Founded in 1962, Allou Distributors, Inc. was an obscure, privately owned, New York-based wholesale distributor named for its owners, Al Wexler and Lou Gastnay. It was providing such consumer items as toothpaste and shampoo to small mom-and-pop stores that had neither the capital nor warehouse space to buy goods directly from manufacturers. The company, which

was sold to Victor Jacobs in 1985 for $1.2 million in cash, lost $586,000 in fiscal 1986 (the year ended March 31, 1986), on revenues of $34 million. In the words of a company executive, Allou at that time had ''one foot in the grave and the other on a banana peel.''

The Hungarian-born Jacobs was a Holocaust survivor who came to New York City after World War II. He operated a small company that assembled first-aid kits before he purchased Allou. Jacobs made Allou profitable again mainly by cutting costs and then adding more products to the company's distribution stock. The new owner decided to handle only brand name goods advertised and recognized nationally, because sales of such products could subsist on consumer loyalty even in a recession. In fiscal 1987 the company had net income of $201,000 on revenues of $38.9 million. Profit remained under $1 million a year although revenues climbed each year, reaching $71.3 million in fiscal 1990.

Under its new name of Allou Health & Beauty Care, the company went public in 1989, raising $3.6 million by selling common stock at $10 for three shares. At the time the company was distributing national brand name health and beauty aid products, as well as fragrances and cosmetics, to independent retailers in the New York metropolitan area. Health and beauty aids was the chief source of revenue, accounting for 76 percent in fiscal 1988, while fragrances and cosmetics accounted for 22 percent and the company's own brands for two percent. Allou was leasing offices and warehouse space in an industrial park in Brentwood, New York. It was also, by fiscal 1990, publishing and distributing a fragrance catalogue quarterly. Victor Jacobs was chairman and chief executive officer of the company. Nonperishable food was added to Allou's roster of products in fiscal 1990 and two years later accounted for 12 percent of company revenues.

Allou passed the $1 million mark in net income on $88.7 million of sales in fiscal 1991. It had become one of the largest distributors of health and beauty aids and fragrances and cosmetics in the Northeast and was marketing about 50 health and beauty care products under the ''Allou Brands'' trade name. The company had hired managers experienced in the distribution business and had installed a new computer system to keep current on inventory in order to reorder merchandise before it sold out. Salespeople were being urged to initiate business instead of just taking orders. And growing sales volume had given the company the muscle to drive a harder bargain with its suppliers.

By mid-1993 Allou was distributing 15,000 products to some 8,500 retailers, who were now located in the Philadelphia and Miami metropolitan areas as well as New York City and its suburbs. It was also selling to 120 national merchandisers, including Wal-Mart Stores, Inc. The roster of goods under the Allou label had reached 75. Also in 1993, the elder Jacobs again became chief executive officer after yielding the title to his son Herman for about two years, and the company purchased M. Sobol, Inc., a wholesaler of branded pharmaceutical products doing $21.6 million in annual sales, for $1.6 million. Founded in 1928, Sobol was distributing pharmaceuticals to about 200 independent pharmacies in the Northeast.

Even before the acquisition of M. Sobol, Allou was diversifying its lines of business, with health and beauty aid products accounting for only 44 percent of revenues in fiscal 1993, fragrances and cosmetics for 37 percent, and nonperishable foods for 15 percent. With the acquisition of M. Sobol, the proportions in fiscal 1994 were: health and beauty aids, 36 percent; fragrances and cosmetics, 34 percent; nonperishable foods, 20 percent; pharmaceuticals, eight percent; and private-label products, two percent. Net income reached $3.7 million in fiscal 1994 on revenues of $205.5 million.

Seeking Higher Profit Margin: 1994–95

When a *Forbes* reporter visited the Allou premises in 1994, he found an operation that bore little resemblance to other companies doing more than $200 million worth of business a year. Except for Victor and Herman Jacobs, all the other company executives, including Herman's brother Jack, sat ''in shabby offices with worn carpeting, water-stained ceilings, and flickering fluorescent lights.'' They were doing every kind of job, including picking up orders and loading trucks. The elder Jacobs wandered around the warehouse, asking workers, ''So, what's news?'' The Jacobses, as members of an ultraorthodox Jewish sect, were forbidden not only from eating, but even from owning, leavened foods during Passover, so each year at this holiday season they turned over their shares to a Christian executive. ''Don't tell the SEC,'' joked Herman Jacobs to *Forbes*.

Idiosyncrasies aside, the Jacobses kept a very close eye on the bottom line. Unlike some wholesalers, Allou was not interested in high volume unless such sales resulted in a high profit margin. The company's 30 salespeople calculated, on computers, the gross margins of every transaction made. Although they were authorized to offer price discounts, their commissions were cut if the average gross margin fell below set guidelines. Constant vigilance had reduced losses from theft or damage from 40 cartons of merchandise a week to one a month, according to a company executive. A stock analyst, quoted in *Forbes*, said, ''This company is so unerringly focused on their business and the service they provide to their customers that they simply outhustle their big competitors.''

By 1995, however, Allou's gross profit margin had slumped from a high of 14 percent to almost as low as ten percent when the company was purchased a decade earlier. Confronted with increasing competition in pharmaceuticals, nonperishable foods, and brand name personal care products, the Jacobses decided to concentrate on areas that offered the possibility of higher profit margins. In September of that year the company began selling ''designer fragrances'' such as Elizabeth Arden's White Diamonds on the Internet at discounted prices. Shortly before the end of the year, Allou announced plans to manufacture several skin creams that would sell for less than prestige brands such as Estée Lauder's Fruition.

For the Internet, Allou established a new subsidiary called The Fragrance Counter, Inc. to sell such products by means of America Online Inc.'s computer links. Although prospective customers could not sample the products in cyberspace, Eli Katz, the subsidiary's chief operating officer, cited company findings that only half of the clients who purchase a fragrance ever smell it first in a store. The Fragrance Counter was only available through America Online, which received a commission on sales, until Allou established a web site in 1997, open to anyone with Internet access.

In October 1995 Allou purchased, for $2.2 million, selected assets of Russ Kalvin's, Inc., a privately owned manufacturer and distributor of professional haircare products. This acquisition enabled the company to manufacture and distribute salon quality hair- and skincare products through a subsidiary, Allou Personal Care Corporation, which in 1997 introduced a new Russ Kalvin Generic Brand Skin Care line. Like other health and beauty items Allou was hoping to develop, this line was a less expensive imitation of popular brand-name products.

Allou in 1998

In June 1998 Allou announced the acquisition of selected assets of Direct Fragrances Inc., a Miami-based fragrance telemarketer. This company was distributing fragrance products through more than 20,000 independent retailers in rural areas of the United States. Its customers were receiving catalogues six times a year and could place orders through a toll-free number.

In October 1998 The Fragrance Counter web site was offering a selection of 1,200 brands of perfume or cologne, including fragrances made by (or representing) such designers as Ralph Lauren, Calvin Klein, Versace, Estée Lauder, Chanel, and Giorgio Armani, ranging in price from $30 to more than $100. The Fragrance Counter was also operating The Cosmetics Counter, a web site introduced in June 1998 that was offering more than 1,000 items, including lipsticks, moisturizers, and tweezers. Katz said that within a year the cosmetics web page would include a section enabling viewers to sample a lipstick shade by filling in the color on the faces of models of different ethnic groups. Both sites offered gift cards, free shipping, money-back guarantees, and advice sections.

The Fragrance Counter subsidiary had sales of $671,000 in the quarter ending September 30, 1998, but was not yet profitable because of heavy spending for promotion. The commission arrangement with American Online was replaced in 1998 by a $12 million payment over four years that committed AOL to prominently display The Fragrance Counter to its subscribers. Allou also was paying Yahoo! Inc., Excite Inc., and Lycos Inc. to promote the cyberspace store on their portal sites and in December 1998 reached an agreement with Microsoft Corporation's MSN shopping site. The Fragrance Counter's products were being sold online only at full price in order not to compete with Allou's wholesale distribution of the same goods to retailers.

Allou's net income peaked in fiscal 1995 at $4.7 million on revenues of $237.5 million. Net income was $4.3 million in fiscal 1998 on revenues of $301.8 million. That year the company was distributing goods to more than 4,200 retail outlets, including small discount chains, individual health and beauty aid suppliers, and nonchain supermarkets. Fragrance and cosmetic products were also being distributed nationally to discount chain stores such as Wal-Mart and Sears, Roebuck, independent retail stores, and pharmacies, or directly through company catalogues. The company also was distributing about 50 health and beauty aid products under the trademark "Allou Brands." In addition, through Sobol, Allou was serving as a direct manufacturers' distributor of branded prescription pharmaceuticals.

Fragrances and cosmetics, which displaced health and beauty aids as Allou's leading product line in fiscal 1997, accounted for 39 percent of company revenues in fiscal 1998. The fragrances distributed by Allou included those produced by Fabergé, Inc., Chanel, Inc., and Revlon, Inc. Among the cosmetic products were eyeshadows, lipsticks, mascaras, and skincare products produced by Revlon, Inc., Coty, Lancôme, and Estée Lauder, Inc.

Health and beauty aids accounted for 35 percent of Allou's revenues in fiscal 1998. The company was distributing about 8,000 national name brand products in this area, grouped under 76 categories, from manufacturers such as Procter & Gamble Company, Johnson & Johnson, and The Gillette Company. Sales of Allou's own brands, manufactured for the company under contract, accounted for only one-half of one percent of revenues. Nonperishable packaged food items, purchased almost exclusively at discount prices from the major food companies, accounted for about nine percent of revenues. Allou reported that revenues from sales of Russ Kalvin's generic brand products were "not material."

Sobol was distributing about 4,000 branded pharmaceuticals from such manufacturers as Eli Lilly and Company, Glaxo Holdings p.l.c., Burroughs Wellcome Company, and Merck Sharp and Dohme, Inc. to about 700 independent pharmacies in the Northeast. In addition, Allou was distributing 3,000 generic prescription pharmaceutical products, purchased from manufacturers such as Schein Pharmaceuticals, Inc., Barre National, Inc., and Sidmak Laboratories, Inc. Pharmaceuticals accounted for 15 percent of Allou's revenues in fiscal 1998.

Allou Health & Beauty Care was leasing 143,894 square feet of space in Brentwood, New York, and also 80,000 square feet of space in Saugus, California, to manufacture Russ Kalvin's products. In July 1997 Jacobs family members owned 4.6 percent of the company's Class A common stock and 90 percent of the Class B stock, which entitled holders to five times as many votes per share as Class A stock. Heartland Advisors, Inc. owned 17.4 percent of the Class A shares.

Principal Subsidiaries

Allou Distributors, Inc.; Allou Personal Care Corporation; The Fragrance Counter, Inc.; M. Sobol, Inc.

Further Reading

"Allou Health to Stress Knock-Off Cosmetics," *Wall Street Journal,* December 29, 1995, p. B3B.

Feigenbaum, Randi, "Allou Net Surges," *Newsday,* June 24, 1997, p. A36.

Furman, Phyllis, "Allou's Products Have Allure, But Stock Lagging," *Crain's New York Business,* July 15, 1991, p. 17.

Gerena-Morales, Rafael, "Perfume Seller Sniffs Out More Customers Online," *Newsday,* October 5, 1998, p. C5.

Norton, Leslie, "Allou Winning Big Investors," *Crain's New York Business,* September 13, 1993, p. 31.

Schifrin, Matthew, "Shh! Don't Tell the SEC," *Forbes,* November 21, 1994, pp. 125–26.

Scully, Tara A., "Allou Teams Up with Perfume Telemarketer," *Newsday,* June 25, 1998, p. A58.

Weber, Thomas E., "Nothing to Sniff At," *Wall Street Journal,* December 7, 1998, p. R18.

—Robert Halasz

American Coin Merchandising, Inc.

5660 Central Avenue
Boulder, Colorado 80301
U.S.A.
(303) 444-2559
Fax: (303) 443-2264
Web site: http://www.skill-crane.com

Public Company
Incorporated: 1988
Employees: 790
Sales: $97.7 million (1998)
Stock Exchanges: NASDAQ
Ticker Symbol: AMCN
NAIC: 45421 Vending Machine Operators; 421920 Toys
    Wholesaling

American Coin Merchandising, Inc., which does business as SugarLoaf Creations, Inc., is the only publicly traded business of its kind. Along with its franchisees, it owns and operates more than 12,600 coin-operated skill-crane machines, called "Shoppes," throughout the United States. These machines are marked with the SugarLoaf logo, named after a mountain west of Boulder, Colorado; they dispense stuffed animals, plush toys, watches, jewelry, and other items. The company's Shoppes are placed in major supermarkets, mass mechandisers, bowling centers, bingo halls, bars, restaurants, warehouse clubs, and other high-traffic locations, including AMF Bowling Centers, Bonanza Steak Houses, Brunswick Bowling Centers, Cub Foods, Denny's, Flying J Truckstop, Fred Meyer Stores, Kmart, Kroger, Ponderosa Steak House, Safeway/Vons, 76 Truckstop, Truckstops of America, and Wal-Mart. The company sells the products vended in the machines to its franchisees, from whom it collects two to five percent of the gross machine revenue. The stores where the shops are located also get roughly 25 percent payment on the gross. American Coin Merchandising also operates bulk vending equipment and kiddie rides.

Early Growth Through Franchising

American Coin Merchandising Inc. was formed in Colorado in July 1988 by a group of four businessmen, who among them owned Southwest Coin, Omaha Coin, Colorado Coin, and T.R. Baron & Associates. Under the leadership of Richard Jones and J. Gregory Theisen, the goal of the new company was to support and add to the license, sale, and setup agreements of its predecessor businesses. Shortly thereafter, American Coin began to combine the buying power of its affiliated businesses to purchase products and skill-crane machines at lower prices. By 1990 it was creating its own territories and, in 1994, it hired Jerome M. Lapin, cofounder in 1958 of International House of Pancakes, to be its chief executive officer. It was reincorporated in Delaware in 1995. When Lapin became chairman in 1995, he brought all the companies under one roof and took the company public, raising net proceeds of $10.1 million. To expand operations, the company subsequently purchased substantially all of the inventory, property, and equipment of its original affiliated entities for a purchase price of $9 million.

Skill-crane machines have been in operation since the 1920s in the United States, but the new company sought to invent something different and better: to offer an alternative way to sell retail products, to sell toys instead of time. It incorporated what it considered to be several improvements and refinements into its Shoppes, increasing the size of its machines to enhance their visibility and to display and vend more products; creating bright and distinctive signage to attract customer attention; improving the exterior and interior lighting of machines to focus customer attention on the products in the Shoppes. In addition, the company upgraded machine operating mechanisms to achieve consistency of play and reliability of performance.

The SugarLoaf Toy Shoppe, in operation since the company's inception, featured a play price of 50 cents and dispensed stuffed animals, plush toys, and other toys. In 1993 the company introduced the SugarLoaf Fun Shoppe, which featured a play price of 25 cents and dispensed small toys, novelties, and candy. The SugarLoaf Treasure Shoppe came along in 1994 and, for a play price of 50 cents, dispensed jewelry, watches, bolo ties, and belt buckles. Between 1994 and 1996 American

Coin Merchandising increased the number of machines it owned from 168 to 3,800 and controlled another 3,200 machines operated through franchises. In 1994 total profit for the company was $1.1 million. During 1995 overall revenues totaled $25.7 million on the company's net income of $2.6 million. In that year, approximately six million stuffed toys were dispensed from SugarLoaf machines. The SugarLoaf Treasure Shoppe dispensed approximately 250,000 watches and 500,000 bracelets, necklaces, and other items.

As the defining force in its market—"We are the market," Jerry Lapin liked to boast of American Coin Merchandising— the company installed 856 new crane machines and opened seven new offices during the first six months of 1996. Revenues for the first half of 1996 increased 37.8 percent over the same period a year earlier; by the end of the year that number was up to 50 percent. In the summer of [final quarter of] 1996, the company gained its first major contract and established itself as Wal-Mart's principal skill-crane supplier, a move that brought another 700 Shoppes on board by November with more installations planned for 1997. This step was only a first in the direction of developing customer accounts in new markets, such as the chain restaurant industry. In 1997 American Coin Merchandising signed a three-year agreement with Safeway that made it the supermarket chain's domestic skill-crane operator and another three-year contract with AMF Bowling, Inc. to service approximately half of the latter's locations.

Buying Back the Franchises in the Mid-1990s

At about this point, the company changed its approach, instituting a strategy of buying back the remaining franchise offices around the country so that profits would stay within the company. American Coin Merchandising realized only about three cents on the dollar in the form of franchise royalties, whereas it made about a 29 cent profit per dollar for every machine it owned. The first buyback occurred in January 1996 with the $500,000 purchase of the Indiana-based operations and territory of Hoosier Coin Company, responsible for generating about $1.4 million in revenue in 1995. In July it added its Utah territory to its operations with the $938,000 purchase of SugarLoaf of Utah, which had 1995 revenue of $1.9 million. In September, for $1.65 million, it acquired SugarLoaf, Inc., which operated 202 machines in Louisiana and Oklahoma and

parts of Missouri, Illinois, and Texas. American Coin Merchandising rounded out the year with the December purchase of Creative Coin of Arizona for $1.46 million, bringing its Arizona territory back to the fold.

American Coin Merchandising was now five times larger than its largest competitor, and its vending machine empire continued to grow by the quarter [1997]. With just 14 percent of the skill-crane market under its control, the possibilities for its future growth loomed large. By September 1997 the company had added another 2,000 machines to its roster and its share price had risen to a 52-week high of almost $18. It sold off another one million shares at $15 per share, increasing its outstanding shares to 18 percent, and used the money raised to repay debt, purchase additional skill-crane machines, and fund acquisitions of other companies. *Business Week* named American Coin Merchandising 54th in its list of Hot Growth Companies for 1997, based on its three-year results in sales growth, earnings, and return on invested capital. *Forbes* ranked American Coin Merchandising 13th in 1997 in its list of the 200 best small companies—companies with sales of at least $5 million but not more than $350 million—based upon its 44.7 percent five-year average return on investment and revenues of $48 million for its latest 12 months.

The company's acquisition trend continued into 1998 with the addition of the Texas-based operations of Tejas Toy Corporation and control of American Coin Merchandising's Texas territory for $2.23 million; R&T Marketing, Inc., with its 370 skill-crane machines in ACMI's northern California territory for $2.14 million; and NW Toys Co., Oregon Coin Company, and Suncoats Toys, Inc. for an aggregate purchase price of approximately $30 million. The latter three purchases brought the Washington, Oregon, and central Florida territories of American Coin Merchandising under company control and added another 1,300 skill-crane machines to its inventory. In a move to no longer limit itself to the skill-crane business, American Coin Merchandising also acquired McCathren Vending Corporation, a Colorado-based bulk vending business that operated close to 5,000 pieces of vending equipment in Colorado, Utah, and Wyoming. The company had earlier bought Quality Amusement Corp. and Quality Entertainment in late 1997, part of a natural expansion, since those locations that housed SugarLoaf skill-crane machines often housed bulk vending machines and kiddie rides as well. The new direction came after Wal-Mart stores suggested that American Coin Merchandising put other kinds of machines in its stores. With the number of remaining franchisees down to 16, Jerry Lapin announced in the *Rocky Mountain News* that his company's growth strategy would not depend upon its ability to buy out its franchisees; it would go after new markets and its competition.

The Move to Related Acquisitions in the Late 1990s

American Coin Merchandising operated more than 10,000 skill-crane machines by the middle of 1998. Its share price was in the upper teens after a setback analysts regarded as temporary when it missed its earnings projections by a few cents. As a result, its stock tumbled 23 percent from its previous high of almost $23. The company, which earlier had been laughed at by analysts, was receiving high recommendations and experiencing great potential for growth as a result of the expansion of the big national chains with which it was allied. *Business Week* again named it to its list of the "Top 100 Companies," although this time it ranked only 90th. *Forbes* placed it 60th, down from its former ranking as 13th, in its list of the 200 best small companies.

American Coin Merchandising's next purchase enabled it to branch out into the amusement video and simulator game business, an industry with late 1990s revenues in excess of a billion dollars. For a purchase price of $4 million, the company acquired the privately held Chilton Vending Co. in mid-1998, thereby gaining a significant presence in Kansas and Missouri and expertise in the amusement video business. The acquisition added approximately 1,800 simulator and traditional video game machines, as well as some skill-crane and redemption equipment. Chilton, which had installations at Family Golf Centers, Inc., AMF Bowling Centers, and Worlds of Fun Amusement Park, had 1997 revenues of $4.5 million. Randy Chilton, third-generation management of Chilton, came on board with the acquisition to become American Coin Merchandising's new vice-president of Amusement Games Development.

In October 1998, with the acquisition of Plush 4 Play, American Coin Merchandising obtained placement agreements with Shoney's, Inc. and Friendly Ice Cream Corporation. The purchase, which cost American Coin $6.8 million plus a contingent earn-out of up to $2.7 million, was part of its plan to branch further into the restaurant industry. Plush 4 Play also sold prepackaged plush toys and animals to the skill-crane industry.

Future Plans

As American Coin Merchandising closed out 1998, it claimed about 23 percent of the more than 50,000 skill cranes in retail outlets in the United States, of which it owned 10,671, an increase of about 73 percent from the end of 1997. Since 1995 it had averaged greater than a 50 percent increase in annual revenues. It had completed ten acquisitions since October 1997 and had expanded into complementary vending operations, adding approximately 6,800 other vending and amusement machines at retail operations. Its revenues for the year rose 65.4 percent to a record $97.7 million, although net earnings decreased 12 percent to $3.9 million. This was due in part to higher interest and administrative costs related to the 1998 acquisitions.

As it entered 1999, American Coin Merchandising expected to acquire at least four more companies and had its sights on another ten to 12 related businesses. The immediate goal of the company was to integrate its acquisitions into its national network. Its larger goal was to consolidate the industry as a whole, a goal at which management judged itself increasingly successful.

Further Reading

Barrett, William P., "Brotherly Love," *Forbes,* July 28, 1997, p. 74.

Eaton, John, "Little Cranes, Big Bucks," *Denver Post,* October 14, 1998, p. C-01.

Narvaes, Emily, "Toying with Success," *Denver Post,* September 2, 1996, p. F-01.

Romero, Christine L., "Boulder, Colorado-Based American Coin Grabs 'Hot' Listing," *Daily Camera,* June 19, 1998.

—Carrie Rothburd

Live in the outside.

American Skiing Company

Sunday River Access Road
Bethel, Maine 04217
U.S.A.
(207) 824-8100
Fax: (207) 824-5158
Web site: http://www.peaks.com

Public Company
Incorporated: 1994 as LBO Resort Enterprises Corp.
Employees: 7,826
Sales: $ 340.42 million (1998)
Stock Exchanges: New York
Ticker Symbol: SKI
NAIC: 721110 Ski Lodges & Resorts with
    Accommodations; 713920 Ski Lift & Tow Operators

Bethel, Maine-based American Skiing Company (ASC) is a holding company that operates through various subsidiaries in two business segments: ski resorts and real estate. As the largest operator of alpine resorts in the United States, ASC owns and operates nine resort facilities, including two of the five largest resorts in the United States and at least one resort in each major skiing market. These resorts include: Sunday River and Sugarloaf/USA in Maine; Attitash Bear Peak in New Hampshire; Killington, Mount Snow/Haystack, and Sugarbush in Vermont; The Canyons, adjacent to Park City, Utah; Steamboat in Colorado; and Heavenly, near Lake Tahoe, California. In addition to offering skiing at its alpine resorts, ASC develops mountainside real estate that complements the expansion of its on-mountain operations. The company also owns and manages six Grand Summit Resort Hotels: two at Sunday River and one hotel each at Attitash, Mount Snow, Sugarloaf/USA, Killington, The Canyons, and Steamboat. Furthermore, ASC operates golf courses and conducts other off-season activities, including a program of Grand Summer Vacations in New England, and the Trail 66 Mountain Bike Race Series and Festival. These activities accounted for about 9.5 percent of the company's resort revenues for fiscal 1998. During the 1997–98 season, skier visits to ASC resorts increased 8.1 percent, compared to the industry average of 2.5 percent.

The Early Years: 1980–93

The founder of American Skiing Company, Leslie B. Otten, was the son of a successful steel magnate in prewar Germany. After the Nazi government seized the elder Otten's business in 1937, he immigrated to Canada and then moved to New Jersey where he started Albot Industries, a scrap-steel business. Leslie, Otten's only child, fell in love with skiing during his first ski trip. While a business student at Ithaca College, Otten worked as a part-time ski instructor at nearby Greek Peak and, as a class project, planned the creation of a small local ski area on Danby Mountain near Ithaca, New York. Meanwhile, his father was schooling him "in the basics of business every night at the dinner table," according to Bill Meyers in *USA TODAY*. In that article, Otten remarked that his father taught him "to think long term. And everything we've done in the company is for long-term gain'."

A ski industry consultant convinced Otten that Danby was too steep to support a successful ski area, but he got an "A" for the class. After graduation, Otten joined the Management Training Program at Vermont's Killington ski resort, owned by Sherburne Corporation. In 1972 Otten was sent to Bethel, Maine, to work at Sunday River Resort, another Sherburne-owned ski resort. Several bad-snow years, an energy crisis, and the acquisition of the Mount Snow resort led Sherburne to focus its capital resources on its Vermont areas, stall development of the Sunday River Resort, and then put it up for sale. In October 1980, Otten borrowed $840,000 from Sherburne and bought the resort.

The early years were not easy for the young entrepreneur. At the time of purchase, run-down Sunday River's fixed assets included one double chairlift, four surface lifts, and a small lodge at the base of the mountain. There were about 70 acres of trails, approximately one-third of which were covered by machine-made snow. To support his family and raise capital for Sunday River, Otten sold scrap, copper wire, and old bulldozer blades. The year-round staff of four became jacks of all trades, painting lifts, mowing the trails, and welding snowmaking pipe. "And to attract skiers," according to the *USA TODAY* story, "Otten sent a truck down to Boston, where it dumped mountains of snow on the Common. The message: 'The skiing is great at Sunday River, so come on up'."

Well schooled in business in his youth by his father, Otten knew that investment in flashy lodges and high-end hotels would tie up his limited capital; he based his plan for growing the company on snow quality and enhanced opportunities for skiing. Since Sunday River could easily access an exceptional amount of water, Otten made the resort River into a testing ground for snowmaking technology. Thus began the manufacture of what became known as "guaranteed quality snow." In order to increase sleeping quarters on the mountain, Otten built and sold more than 600 simple, cozy, and attractively priced condominium units. A 50 percent pre-construction sales policy (a permanent operating policy) ensured that the company would not be trapped in a quick economic downturn after the real estate boom of the mid-1980s. Innovative marketing and original programs increased sales and drew skiers to the resort; concomitantly came the creation of more trails and construction of additional lifts and lodging.

For the fiscal year ending July 1, 1980, the resort posted a $235,000 loss against total sales of $541,000. From 1980–90, the Sunday River Resort developed and introduced many ski programs that remained in use throughout the winter season and were expanded over the years. For instance, in 1985 the Edge Card was created for the nation's first-ever frequent skier program, and in 1990 the Perfect Turn Skier Development Program blended state-of-the-art ski techniques with leading-edge learning theory. In 1989 *Inc.* magazine, citing the success of Sunday River, recognized Leslie B. Otten as "Turnaround Entrepreneur of the Year." In 1992 Sunday River opened its first Grand Summit Resort Hotel. "Sunday River shot from being a torpid backwater with 40,000 skier visits in 1980–81, to the Northeast's second most popular resort, boasting more than 500,000 visits in 1997–98. After delivering goods, Otten focused on services. Here, his inspiration was enticing middle-class families to participate in 'quartershare' condos enclosed in Grand Summit Hotels near the base lodges," wrote Paul McHugh in the December 17, 1998 issue of the *San Francisco Chronicle*.

After more than a decade of continuing prosperity, for the fiscal year ending July 31, 1994, the company posted sales of $33.23 million and net income of $4.87 million. Otten thought the time had come to create the area's—and the nation's—largest operating company of ski resorts: "I'm in a business where I happen to be able to combine my avocation and my vocation. My office covers an expanse of 15,000 skiing acres,

1,000 trails and 176 lifts," he would later comment in a 1998 interview with *USA TODAY*.

Multi-State Expansion: 1994–98

In 1994 Otten formed LBO Resort Enterprises Corp. as a holding company of his resorts. In that same year he acquired Attitash Bear Peak Resort, located in New Hampshire's Mount Washington Valley, and began to expand onto the neighboring property of Bear Peak by creating long, wide, cruising terrain; by increasing snowmaking power; and by installing new chairlifts, such as the Abenaki quad and the Flying Bear high-speed quad which became operative in 1995. The Attitash Adventure Center housed the Discovery Center for beginning skiers and riders, provided space for all children's programs, adaptive programs, and snowboarders. Consequently, Attitash was recognized as a family-oriented resort and benefited from its location in the heart of New Hampshire ski country and its proximity to the Mount Washington Valley tourist area. In 1997 the second Grand Summit Resort Hotel opened at Attitash Bear Peak.

In April 1995, Otten completed the purchase of Sugarbush Resort in Warren, Vermont, and began to revitalize the 38-year-old resort. Because of its abundant natural snowfall and challenging terrain, Sugarbush was considered the best natural skiing mountain in New England. By early 1996, Sugarbush had seven new lifts, 300 percent more snowmaking, a 63-million-gallon snowmaking pond, newly expanded and redesigned base facilities, and the connection of its two areas (North and South) with the longest and fastest high-speed quad in the world. Sugarbush remained one of the few New England ski resorts to have kept its original-trail layout mostly intact. One of the most challenging trails was that of Castlerock, where experienced skiers ran head-on into deep powder, gnarly bumps, elevator shaft-like steeps, and more twists and turns than they could count. By year-end 1995, LBO also owned the two New Hampshire ski resorts known as Waterville Valley and Mount Cranmore.

In 1996, when LBO wanted to purchase S-K-I Ltd., the Department of Justice ruled that the company—at that time already the largest ski-resort operator in the region—had to sell its New Hampshire resorts at Waterville Valley and Mount Cranmore in order to preserve competition in New England. LBO agreed to do so and paid $137 million for the following S-K-I-owned resorts: Killington and Mount Snow/Haystack in Vermont; Sugarloaf/USA in Maine, and Waterville Valley in New Hampshire. LBO changed its name to American Skiing Company (ASC). The company then introduced its Edge card program as the industry's first multi-resort, frequent-skier program, and the Magnificent 7 card, which allowed guests to obtain lift tickets at a reduced rate when they purchased a seven-day package for skiing or riding. Later, these cards could be linked to all major credit cards accepted by ASC.

By year-end 1998, Killington was the largest ski resort in the northeast and the fifth largest in the United States, with over one million skier visits in the 1997–98 season. Killington was well-known for its diverse seven-mountain terrain which included the steepest mogul trail in the East, "Outer Limits," as well as the East's longest trail, the ten-mile "Juggernaut" slope. Killington

---

Company Perspectives:

Great snow, fast lifts, a wide range of terrain and outstanding services—these things skiers and riders demand. So we create these dynamic attractions that drive market share and increase revenues across all our businesses.

cleared and opened the first novice Snowshed Slope, and later developed the ''Graduated Length Method'' of learning to ski. Early on, the resort endorsed shaped skis and adopted the ''Perfect Turn'' Learn-to-Ski and Snowboard Programs. Of Killington's three halfpipes—the K-Pipe, the Peace Pipe, and the Pico Pipe—the most famous was the K-Pipe, frequently featured in major snowboard and lifestyle magazines, such as *Eastern Edge* and *Transworld Snowboarding.* The resort maintained the second largest snowboard coaching staff in this country.

Mount Snow/Haystack Resort, located in West Dover, Vermont, at the time of its purchase operated five separate mountain faces as well as nearby Haystack Mountain. After the 1992 opening of ''Un Blanco Gulch,'' the East's first snowboard park, Mount Snow became a mecca for riders from around the country. Mount Snow raised the bar for the fastest-growing winter sport in North America: snowboarding. The resort featured the 460-foot long halfpipe (dubbed The Gut) served by its own surface lift, while ''Belly Up'' became a site of major professional halfpipe events throughout the winter. Mount Snow also served as headquarters of the ASC-owned ''Original Golf School,'' which operated an 18-hole golf course and eight golf schools throughout the East Coast. At the close of the 1998 fiscal year, ASC had invested $15 million in capital improvements to the resort, including the installation of two high-speed chairlifts to make Mount Snow/Haystack the second largest ski resort in the Northeast.

Sugarloaf/USA (the Loaf), located in the heart of Carrabassett Valley in Maine's Western Mountains, was ranked as the number one overall ski resort in the East by the September 1997 *Snow Country* magazine. The mountain was famous for its Snowfields, beneath which lay terrain for skiers of all ability levels. Furthermore, each lift at the Loaf serviced a part of the mountain having its own special character and variety of terrain. For instance, the Timberline Quad, the only lift servicing ''above tree-line'' skiing and riding in the East, whisked skiers and riders up to the Snowfields at the summit of the mountain; the King Pine Quad brought skiers to the top of the King Pine Bowl where they could choose trails such as the Ripsaw Trail—maintained in its natural state—or the steep fall-line pitches of the Choker, Widowmaker, or Flume trails favored by the U.S. Ski Team as downhill training runs. Sugarloaf/USA operated a year-round conference center, a cross-country ski facility, and an 18-hole championship golf course (designed by Robert Trent Jones, Jr.) rated as one of the top 25 resort courses in the United States.

Expansion to the West: 1997–98

In July 1997, ASC made its first move westward with the purchase of Wolf Mountain Resort, an undeveloped ski resort located near Park City, Utah, in the heart of the Rocky Mountains. Otten, impressed by the area's seven canyons and 14 mountain peaks, perceived great potential for future operational and real estate development. Changing the resort's name to The Canyons, he dreamed of transforming it into one of the largest and most complete winter resorts in North America. Within less than two years ASC invested more than $30 million in improvements and expansion to make The Canyons the largest ski resort in Utah. Plans were made for construction of a Grand Summit Resort Hotel and Conference Center, and of The Sundial Lodge

(a condominium hotel), both projects to be completed by 2002 in the heart of The Canyons Vacation Village—in time for the Olympic Winter Games in Salt Lake City. The Canyons continued to be a haven for snowboarders and to offer a free-season pass to all honor-roll students in Utah, thereby assuring the loyalty of future ski and snowboard enthusiasts. The Utah Winter Sports Park, located immediately adjacent to the resort, was scheduled to serve as the venue for the ski jumping, bobsled, and luge events in the 2002 Winter Olympic Games.

For the fiscal year ending July 27, 1997, ASC posted sales of $175.39 million and a net income loss of $5.48 million, compared to sales of $73.42 million and a net income loss of $2.34 million for fiscal 1996.

In November 1997, ASC acquired two additional ski resorts from Kamori International Limited: Steamboat Ski Resort in northwest Colorado (close to the Continental Divide) and Heavenly Ski Resort, which straddled the California/Nevada state line near Lake Tahoe. As a result of these purchases, the company's Edge Card became the industry's first debit, direct-to-lift, frequent skier, and value-added card. Both the Edge and the Magnificent 7 card were now valid at ASC resorts from Maine to California.

Steamboat Ski Resort, covering a complete mountain range rising 10,568 feet up into the Colorado Rockies, earned the title of ''Ski Town USA'' for Steamboat Springs and its small ranching community. In keeping with Steamboat's western heritage there were many reminders of the Old West. For example, trails known as The Quickdraw, Buckshot, and Tomahawk were in the saddle of High Noon, near the Rendezvous Saddle Food Court; a coffee shop on the first floor of the Silver Bullet Gondola Building served hot cappuccino; and there were chairlifts with the colorful names of Tenderfoot, Colt, Rough Rider, and Bar UE. Steamboat's trail network consisted of 140 trails serviced by 22 lifts. More than one million skiers visited Steamboat each year of the 1991–97 seasons. During the summer of 1998, Steamboat built the new Pony Express quad detachable chairlift in Pioneer Ridge. Although Steamboat averaged annual snowfalls of 330 inches, ASC extended a snowmaking system to the mountain's summit, thereby insuring quality snow from the top of the mountain to its base.

Heavenly Ski Resort, situated at Tahoe's highest elevation on the south shore of Lake Tahoe, made it possible for skiers and riders to glide between California and Nevada on a mountain descent more than five miles long and, at every turn, glimpse the waters of Lake Tahoe. The resort operated two base lodges in Nevada, one lodge in California, four on-mountain lodges, and a full-service Monument Peak Restaurant located at the top of the tram and open to non-skiers and sightseers. When one of the Sierras' notorious snowstorms—known to dump up to seven feet of snow in 24 hours—ruled out a day on the slopes, guests could saunter through the brand-name outlets and quaint boutiques of the area's shopping plazas, visit some of the casinos, and decide at which of Lake Tahoe's 150+ south-shore restaurants they would dine. ASC's summer 1998 capital program included $7.8 million in proposed improvements at Heavenly, including two quad high-speed chairlifts, known as ''Gunbarrel Express'' and ''Stagecoach Express,'' and a fixed-grip three passenger chairlift known as the ''Perfect Ride.''

By November 6, 1997, the forsaken Sunday River Resort that Chairman, President, and CEO Leslie B. Otten bought in 1980 emerged as the flagship resort and home base of the American Skiing Company, the largest resort operator in North America. On that date ASC, with SKI as its ticker, began trading as a public company on the New York Stock Exchange at $18 a share.

Toward the 21st Century: 1998 and Beyond

Much of ASC's success had been generated from its commitment to the refinement and development of the snowmaking technology that, under the holding company's aegis, turned snowmaking into an art. "Snowmaking has been the single most important component in our success," said Otten in a 1998 interview for *Smithsonian* magazine. Indeed, by 1998 Sunday River operated New England's largest and most powerful snowmaking technology in a computer-driven system that turned on compressors and pumps capable of driving 65,000 cubic feet of air and 9,000 gallons of water per minute through 72 miles of steel pipe to produce snow. This system, developed in-house, was the world's largest high-pressured snowmaking system and was used exclusively at ASC's resorts.

The company's interval ownership product, the Grand Summit Resort Hotels, complemented the expansion of ASC's ski and snowboard operations. Otten shrewdly sold quartershare interval interest in these hotels, but ASC retained ownership of core hotel and commercial properties. Typically, the initial sale of quartershare units generated a high-profit margin; the company derived a continuing revenue stream from operating the hotel's retail, restaurant, and conference facilities as well as from renting quartershare interval interests when they were not in use by their owners. In prime locations within most of its resorts, ASC also developed Alpine Resort Villages designed to complement each resort's special characteristics.

During 1996–98, ASC quadrupled in size. For fiscal 1998, ASC's net revenue jumped to $340.42 million, and the company posted a $6.95 million income loss from operations, compared to fiscal 1997 revenue of $175.39 million and a loss from operations of $5.48 million. For two-and-one-half years, Otten laid out about $400 million to buy six additional ski resorts and "left American Skiing with $416 million in debt," according to Meyers in *USA TODAY*. Industry opinion was divided about whether or not Otten's decision was wise.

Otten did have some staunch supporters. *USA Today*'s Meyers expressed the confidence Chad Gifford, chairman of BankBoston, had in Otten: "Les has bitten off a lot," said Gifford, "but he'll see it through and see it through successfully." Although in an analysis of ASC's financial condition, Mark Thompson wrote in *MSN Money Central* that "Moody's

Investors Service raised a cautionary note" in its analysis of ASC's latest bond and did not expect the company to have the cash flow in 1999 to cover its fixed costs and capital expenses," Moody's added that the risks were "mitigated by a number of strengths." Owner of New England's six leading resorts and of three leading resorts in the West, ASC was, according to Moody's, "the most geographically diversified resort operator. The large number of presales of condominiums, which could be highly profitable by 2000, also bodes well for the future. And the company has surpassed its rivals in drawing skiers to the slopes, with an 8.5 percent increase last year, compared with a slight dip in skier visits to Vail."

Industry analyst Bill Meyers was of the same mind as Moody's: "If demographics are destiny," he wrote, "then American Skiing is in the right place at the right time. The company's mountains are a mecca for consumers age 40 to 59 and 10 to 24—two of the largest population segments in the USA." On the threshold of the 21st century, Meyers and others of like mind suggested that Otten had astutely positioned the American Skiing Company to glide into continuing prosperity.

Principal Subsidiaries

American Skiing Company Resort Properties, Inc,; ASC East, Inc.; ASC Leasing, Inc.; ASC Transportation; ASC West, Inc., ASC Utah, Inc.; Blunder Bay Development, Inc.; Killington, Ltd.; Killington West Ltd.; Mount Snow, Ltd.; Orlando Resort Corporation; Pico Ski Area Management Company; SKI Insurance Company; Steamboat Ski and Resort Corporation; Sugarloaf Mountain Corporation; Resorts Software Services, Inc.

Further Reading

"American Skiing Company Begins Trading on NYSE," *Business Wire,* November 6, 1997.
Hoffman, Carl, "Let It Snow: Ski Resorts Have Snowmaking Down to a Science—Now Sometimes the Real Stuff Gets in the Way," *Smithsonian,* December 1998, pp. 50–58.
"Justice Department Requires American Skiing Co. to Divest Two New England Ski Resorts," *Business Wire,* June 11, 1996.
McDonald, Michael, "Ski Empire Takes Fall on Wall Street: Investors Dump Shares of Otten's American Skiing Company," *Bangor Daily News,* July 31, 1998.
McHugh, Paul, "Master of the Ski Experience Has Given the Industry a Sweeping Lift," *San Francisco Chronicle,* December 17, 1998.
Meyers, Bill, "Ski Resort Mogul Maneuvers Success Despite Bumpy Ride: American Skiing Builds on Rec Boom," *USA TODAY,* December 28, 1998.
Thompson, Mark, "Vail Resorts, Intrawest and American Skiing Test All-Weather Strategies to Stop Downhill Stock Slides," *MSN MoneyCentral,* January 18, 1999.

—Gloria A. Lemieux

AmericanAirlines®

AMR Corporation

4333 Amon Carter Boulevard
Fort Worth, Texas 76155
U.S.A.
(817) 963-1234
Fax: (817) 967-9641
Web site: http://www.amrcorp.com

Public Company
Incorporated: 1934 as American Airlines, Inc.
Employees: 116,300
Sales: $19.21 billion (1998)
Stock Exchanges: New York Midwest Pacific Boston
   Cincinnati Zurich Basel Geneva
Ticker Symbol: AMR
NAIC: 481111 Scheduled Passenger Air Transportation;
   561599 Reservation Services

AMR Corporation is a holding company whose principal subsidiary is American Airlines, Inc., which was founded in 1934. American is the number two U.S. airline, trailing United Airlines, and provides scheduled service to more than 180 destinations throughout North America, the Caribbean, Latin America, Europe, and the Pacific Rim. American's hub cities are Dallas/Fort Worth, Chicago, Miami, and San Juan, Puerto Rico. The airline is a key component of the global oneworld alliance, which links certain operations of American, British Airways, Canadian Airlines, Cathay Pacific Airways, Qantas Airways, Finnair, Iberia, and LanChile. AMR also owns three regional airlines operating as American Eagle—American Eagle Airlines, Inc., Executive Airlines, Inc., and Business Express Airlines, Inc. In addition to its airline operations, AMR holds an 82.4 percent stake in the Sabre Group, which operates the leading computerized travel reservation system in the world.

Early History

American Airlines is a product of the merger of a number of small airline companies. One of these founding enterprises was the Robertson Aircraft Company of Missouri, which employed Charles Lindbergh to pilot its first airmail run in 1926. In April 1927 another of these small companies, Juan Trippe's Colonial Air Transport, made the first scheduled passenger run between Boston and New York City. The nucleus of these and the 82 other companies that eventually merged to form American Airlines was a company called Embry-Riddle, which later evolved into the Aviation Corporation (AVCO), one of the United States' first airline conglomerates. The conglomerate was headed by a Wall Street group led by Avrell Harriman and Robert Lehman that was not conversant with the new airline business.

In 1930 Charles Coburn formally united the various airlines under the name American Airways Company. American flew a variety of planes, including the Pilgrim 10A. In 1930 the company was granted control of the Southern airmail corridor from the East Coast to California. In 1934 the government suspended all private airmail contracts only to reinstate them a few months later under the conditions that previous contract holders were disqualified from bidding and companies could not have the same officers and directors. American Airways thus changed its name to American Airlines and, under the leadership of Lester Seymour, resumed its airmail business but due to the damage already caused by this interruption, was unable to maintain a profit.

During this period, a Texan named Cyrus Rowlett Smith was becoming a popular figure at American. Smith was originally the vice-president and treasurer of Southern Air Transport, a division later acquired by American. Seymour recognized Smith's ability and made him a vice-president of American in charge of the Southern Division.

In 1934 new American President Smith persuaded Donald Douglas, an aircraft manufacturer, to develop a new airplane to replace the popular DC-2. The company produced a larger 21-passenger airplane, designated the DC-3. Cooperation between the manufacturer and the airline throughout the project set an example for similar joint ventures in the future. American was flying the DC-3s by 1936 and, largely as a result of the successful new plane, went on to become the number one airline by the close of the decade. The DC-3 proved to be a very popular airplane; its innovative and simple design made it durable and easy to service.

Company Perspectives:

We will be the global leader in air transportation and related information services. That leadership will be attained by: setting the industry standard for safety and security; providing world class customer service; creating an open and participative work environment which seeks positive change, rewards innovation and provides growth, security and opportunity to all employees; producing consistently superior financial returns for shareholders.

During 1937, in reaction to a public scare over airline safety, American ran a printed advertisement that directly asked, "Afraid to Fly?" Citing the statistical improbability of dying in a crash, the copy discussed the problem in a straightforward and reassuring way. "People are afraid of things they do not know about," the advertisement read. "There is only one way to overcome the fear—and that is, to fly." The promotion succeeded in allaying passenger fears and increasing the airline's business.

Aided World War II Effort

When World War II started, American Airlines devoted over half of its resources to the army. American DC-3s shuttled the Signal Corps and supplies to Brazil for the transatlantic ferry. Smith himself volunteered his services to the Air Transport Command. American's president, Ralph Damon, went to the Republic Aircraft Company to supervise the building of fighter airplanes. After the war American returned to its normal operations, and Smith set out to completely retool the company with modern equipment. The modernization went smoothly and quickly. In 1949 American's archrival, United Airlines, was still flying DC-3s, while American had already sold its last DC-3s.

Following World War II, American Airlines purchased American Export Airlines (AEA) from American Export Steamship Lines. The steamship company was forced to sell AEA when the United States Congress decreed that transportation companies could not conduct business in more than one mode. It was an attempt to prevent industrial vertical monopolies from forming. American Airlines sold AEA to Pan Am in 1950.

In the late 1940s American suffered another financial crisis, caused mainly by the grounding of the DC-6. The airplanes were experiencing operational problems that led to crashes, and the federal government wanted all of them thoroughly inspected. Six weeks later they were back in service, but the interruption cost American a large amount of money. When banks restricted American's line of credit, Smith joined representatives of TWA and United on Capitol Hill to lobby for fare increases. Subsequently, as part of a compromise, American was awarded an airmail subsidy.

Still facing financial difficulties, company management attempted to raise cash by selling overseas routes served by the Amex flying boats. The sale was blocked by the Civil Aeronautics Board (CAB). American needed the cash, and Juan Trippe

at Pan Am actually wanted to purchase the overseas routes. As a result, they jointly lobbied the administration of President Harry S. Truman to overturn the CAB decision, but the timing was inauspicious. It was June 1950, and the president was focused on the war in Korea. A few weeks later, after the Korean situation stabilized, Truman did finally rule in favor of the airlines and American was allowed the sale. Thus the company avoided a debilitating financial crisis.

American made the first scheduled nonstop transcontinental flights in 1953 with the 80-passenger DC-7. In 1955 American ordered its first jetliners, Boeing 707s, which were delivered in 1959. With larger and faster aircraft on the drawing boards, American became interested in, and eventually purchased, jumbo B-747s in the late 1960s. The company also ordered a number of supersonic transports, but was forced to cancel these orders when Congress halted funding to Boeing for their development.

C.R. Smith left American in 1968 for a position in the administration of President Lyndon B. Johnson, serving as secretary of commerce. Smith was succeeded at American by a lawyer named George A. Spater, who changed the company's marketing strategy and attempted to make the airline more attractive to vacationers instead of to the traditional business traveler, a plan that ultimately failed. Spater's presidency lasted only until 1973, when he admitted to making an illegal $55,000 corporate contribution to President Richard Nixon's reelection campaign. Some believe the gift was intended to procure favorable treatment from the Civil Aeronautics Board for American. As a result, American's board of directors decided to fire Spater and draft Smith out of retirement at the age of 74 to head the company again.

Relocated HQ to Dallas/Fort Worth in 1979

Smith retired after only seven months when the board of directors persuaded Albert V. Casey to leave the TimesMirror Company in Los Angeles to join American. As the new chief executive officer, Casey reversed the company's fortunes from a deficit of $20 million in 1975 to a record profit of $134 million in 1978. To everyone's surprise Casey moved the airline's headquarters from New York City to Dallas/Fort Worth in 1979. Although some said Casey was unhappy with his inability to gain acceptance in New York's social circles, Casey reasoned that a domestic airline should be based between the coasts. Believing the company needed to be shaken out of its lethargy, he felt that American would benefit from the relocation.

Soon afterward, American introduced "Super Saver" fares during 1977 in an innovative attempt to fill passenger seats on coast-to-coast flights. TWA and United followed suit after they failed to persuade the CAB to intervene.

Also in 1977 American was forced to rehire 300 flight attendants who were fired between 1965 and 1970 because they had become pregnant. The award also included $2.7 million in back pay. Compounding these setbacks, on May 25, 1979, an American DC-10 crashed at Chicago's O'Hare airport. Later blamed on inadequate maintenance procedures, the crash resulted in 273 deaths and a fine of $500,000 by the Federal Aviation Administration (FAA). Although the company collected $24.3 million in insurance benefits, it was forced to pay wrongful death settlements averaging $475,000 per passenger.

The Airline Deregulation Act of 1978 had the effect of making the airline industry suddenly volatile and competitive. American could adjust to deregulation in one of several ways. First, it could sell its jetliners once they were written down, and move into other, more promising businesses. Second, it could scale down only partially, leaving a more efficient operation to compete with new airlines such as New York Air and People Express. A third option was to ask employees to accept salary reductions and other concessions as Frank Borman did at Eastern. In the end, American was not forced to take any of these measures. The company secured a two-tier wage contract with its employees and this new agreement reduced labor costs by as much as $10,000 a year per new employee. In addition, workers were given a profit-sharing interest in the company.

AMR Corporation Created in 1982

Robert Crandall, formerly with Eastman Kodak, Hallmark, TWA, and Bloomingdale's, joined American in 1973 and became its president in 1980. On October 1, 1982, Crandall oversaw the creation of a holding company, the AMR Corporation. According to the company's 1982 annual report, this move would not affect daily business, but would ''provide the company with access to sources of financing that otherwise might be unavailable.'' Known for his impatient and aggressive manner, Crandall may be credited with American's successful, but not completely painless, readjustment to the post-deregulation era. Crandall fired approximately 7,000 employees in an austerity drive, a decision that severely damaged his standing with the unions.

American updated its jetliner fleet to meet the new conditions in the industry during the 1980s by phasing in B-767s and MD-80s. The MD-80s had two major advantages over other aircraft: a two-person cockpit crew and high fuel efficiency. Crandall noted that American was developing a new, inexpensive airline inside the old one.

By the early 1980s, AMR had developed its Sabre computer reservations system into what was widely regarded as the best in the industry. The Sabre system allows agents to assign seats, reserve tickets for Broadway plays, book lodgings, and even arrange to send flowers to passengers. Extremely successful in filling space on American flights efficiently and inexpensively, the Sabre system eventually expanded by beginning operations in Europe.

As of 1982, American ran major hubs at Dallas/Fort Worth and O'Hare in Chicago. Secondary hubs in Nashville and Raleigh-Durham were intended to more firmly establish the airline in the Southeast. In addition to a multihub system and the reservations database, American contracted with smaller regional carriers.

American owned a number of subsidiaries when it created the AMR holding company. An airline catering business called Sky Chefs was started in 1942 and served American and several other air carriers. In 1977 American created AA Development Corporation and AA Energy Corporation. These subsidiaries—merged in 1984 to create AMR Energy Corporation—participated in the exploration and development of oil and natural gas resources,

many of which were successful. The American Airlines Training Corporation, created in 1979, serviced military and commercial contracts that provided training for pilots and mechanics. All three subsidiaries were sold in 1986.

In 1985 American surpassed United in passenger traffic and regained after 20 years the title of number one airline in the United States. Although the company had dealt reasonably well with disruptions in the industry, and despite its stated intention to grow internally, AMR announced in November 1986 that it would acquire ACI Holdings, Inc., the parent company of AirCal, for $225 million. This move came in response to announcements by American's competitors Delta and Northwest, which had entered into cooperation agreements with western air carriers. The addition of AirCal's western routes significantly increased American's exposure on the West Coast and gave it a base for expanding American services across the Pacific Ocean. The late 1980s also saw AMR delve further into the regional airline business, acquiring Nashville Eagle, establishing American Eagle, and buying additional regional airlines.

Late 1980s Challenges

As the decade of the 1980s ended, the airline industry was challenged by a weakening economy and such costly developments as the fuel price spike caused by the Persian Gulf War, which contributed to industry losses of $2.4 billion in 1990. American pursued a strategy of acquiring key overseas routes from troubled or failed airlines, cutting costs, and using its leading position to harry its opponents in price wars. In 1989 it purchased TWA's Chicago operations and London routes, to which it added, in 1991, six more TWA London routes at a price of $445 million. Also that year, American purchased from failed Eastern Airlines the routes to 20 Latin American sites. By the close of the 1980s American was purchasing planes at a rate of one every five days; its fleet stood among the world's newest. At the same time, Crandall cut executive perks and flight expenses in a general program of internal belt-tightening. The CEO once ordered the removal of olives from all salads served on American planes, saving $100,000 a year.

Throughout the late 1980s and early 1990s, Crandall's ruthless—and effective—competitive strategies were the focus of industry controversy. Smaller airlines, as well as such larger and financially troubled airlines as TWA, accused Crandall of using unfair, ''cannibalistic'' tactics to create a situation in which a few major carriers, having eliminated their competition, could agree to maintain high prices without fear of being undercut. Crandall countered, however, according to *Business Week,* that American's strategies were perfectly within reason in an ''intensely, vigorously, bitterly, savagely competitive'' industry. Any shifts within the industry, including the elimination of some weaker companies, he argued, were a necessary if painful part of restructuring an industry with a surplus of carriers. Further, he contended, many of American's ailing competitors brought their woes upon themselves by initiating fare wars, which forced all carriers to sell seats at losses that the smaller carriers ultimately could not afford. The airline industry, Crandall commented in an interview with *Time,* ''is always in the grip of its dumbest competitors.''

In April 1992 American introduced a new air fare system, designed to simplify rates that had been made complicated over the years by myriad restricted, cut rate fare specials. The new system included only four fares: first-class, coach, 7-day advance purchase, and 21-day advance purchase. Each price represented a cut in the fare for that category—up to 50 percent for first-class tickets—but the new system also eliminated the promotions that enabled vacation travelers to buy coach tickets at bargain rates. American held that the old discount fares were damaging the industry and that the new rates would be fairer to consumers. Detractors charged that the fares would benefit business travelers far more than tourists, and that the pricing system was designed to drive financially weak carriers out of business by forcing them to make fare cuts they could not afford. American's competitors soon matched its prices, then countered with a new wave of restricted, reduced fares.

After four straight years in the red from 1990 through 1993, AMR finally returned to profitability in 1994. The turnaround was at least in part an industrywide one as the excess capacity and intense fare wars in the U.S. airline industry during the early 1990s disappeared. Lower fuel prices also played a key role. In December 1995 American Airlines suffered its first fatal crash in 16 years when one of its planes crashed near Cali, Colombia. The following year AMR reduced its stake in its Sabre unit by about 20 percent through a public offering.

Alliances and Divestments Marked Late 1990s

Key developments in the late 1990s included alliances and divestments. One of the most important trends in the airline industry in the 1990s was that of global alliance building. In 1996 American Airlines and British Airways plc announced that they would form an alliance in which the two airlines would virtually operate as a single unit on North Atlantic runs. The plan, however, ran into severe regulatory problems, including a stipulation by the U.S. government that an "open skies" treaty between the United States and Britain precede any granting of antitrust immunity to the British Airways-American link-up. By late 1998 the open skies negotiations had ground to a halt. As it became more likely that the alliance with British Airways might never get off the ground, American Airlines shifted gears and announced in September 1998 the formation of the oneworld alliance. Oneworld initially included American, British Airways, Canadian Airlines, Hong Kong's Cathay Pacific Airways, and Australia's Qantas Airways, with the partners agreeing to link their frequent-flier programs and give each other access to their airport lounge facilities. Finnair and Spain's Iberia were slated to join oneworld in 1999, while Linea Aerea Nacional de Chile (LanChile) agreed to become the eighth member starting in 2000. American also entered into a separate bilateral marketing alliance with US Airways in April 1998, again involving linked frequent-flier programs and reciprocal airport lounge facility access.

In September 1998 AMR announced that it would sell three subsidiaries that had been part of the Management Services Group in order to focus on its core airlines businesses. By the end of the year the company had reached agreements to sell all three, with AMR Combs Inc., an executive aviation services company, going to BBA Group plc of the United Kingdom for $170 million; TeleService Resources, a telemarketing firm, sold to Platinum Equity Holdings; and AMR Services, a ground services and cargo logistics unit, bought by New York merchant bank Castle Harlan. These divestments left AMR with two main lines of business: the

Airline Group, which consisted of American Airlines and the American Eagle regional airline operations; and the Sabre Group, in which AMR held an 82.4 percent stake at the end of 1998.

American Airlines continued to be beset by labor troubles throughout the 1990s, including a brief strike by pilots in 1997 which ended after President Bill Clinton intervened, appointing a presidential emergency board to resolve the dispute through imposition of a new contract (under this pressure, the two sides soon reached their own agreement). When Crandall retired in May 1998, it appeared that better relations with labor might be on tap. Crandall's successor as chairman and CEO was Donald J. Carty, who had been president (a title he retained). Around the time of his promotion, Carty was quoted as having told union leaders that he planned to focus on employees because "happy employees make for happy customers, which make for happy shareholders." But trouble erupted following the December 1998 acquisition by AMR of low-cost carrier Reno Air, Inc. for $124 million. Reno Air had 27 planes in its fleet and hub cities in Reno, Nevada, and San Jose, California. Rather than operating it as a low-cost "airline-within-an-airline," AMR aimed to integrate Reno into American Airlines, thereby strengthening American's presence in the western United States. But when American attempted to integrate pilots from Reno Air without immediately giving pay raises to those Reno pilots moving into higher paying positions at American, members of the American Pilots Association (APA) began a sickout in early February 1999 that forced thousands of flight cancellations and crippled the airline. AMR sued the APA, winning a restraining order and an order for a return to work. After the pilots defied this order, a U.S. district judge found the union and its top two leaders in contempt of court for ignoring his order. This ended the sickout, but not before the eight-day action had cost AMR an estimated $150 million in lost business. In late February American and the APA agreed to attempt to resolve their dispute through nonbinding arbitration.

During 1999 American Airlines took delivery of 44 new airplanes, adding the Boeing 737 and 777 to its fleet. It was also in the midst of a $400 million program to overhaul the interiors of its 639-plane fleet, the first such change in 20 years. Sabre, meantime, rode the Internet wave of the late 1990s through Travelocity.com, its travel web site that was one of the leading sites for the purchase of airline tickets. These positive developments were tempered, however, by an antitrust lawsuit filed against American Airlines by the U.S. Department of Justice in May 1999. The Justice Department charged that the airliner in the mid-1990s had slashed fares upon the entry of low-cost rivals into its Dallas/Fort Worth hub, incurring losses in the process until the smaller competitors had been forced out. Following the departure of a rival, American would then raise fares and sometimes reduce service. American Airlines immediately responded with a vigorous denial of the charges, setting the stage for what could be a lengthy, contentious, and precedent-setting lawsuit—a lawsuit that was just one of the many challenges facing AMR at the end of the century.

Principal Subsidiaries

American Airlines, Inc.; AMR Eagle, Inc.; AMR Global Services Corporation; AMR Investment Services, Inc.; The Sabre Group Holdings, Inc. (82.4%).

Further Reading

"The Airline Mess," *Business Week,* July 6, 1992.

Baumohl, Bernard, Deborah Fowler, and William McWhirter, "Fasten Your Seat Belts for the Fare War," *Time,* April 27, 1992.

Castro, Janice, " 'This Industry Is Always in the Grip of Its Dumbest Competitors,' " *Time,* May 4, 1992.

Dwyer, Paula, Wendy Zellner, and Stewart Toy, "A Megadeal in the Skies," *Business Week,* June 3, 1996, pp. 50–51.

Goldsmith, Charles, and Julie Wolf, "EU Clears AMR/British Airways Alliance," *Wall Street Journal,* July 9, 1998, pp. A3, A10.

Jackson, Robert, *The Sky Their Frontier: The Story of the World's Pioneer Airlines and Routes, 1920–1940,* Shrewsbury, England: Airlife, 1983, 160 p.

Jennings, Mead, "If You Can't Beat 'Em," *Airline Business,* January 1995, pp. 22+.

Kindel, Sharen, "(Well) Grounded," *Financial World,* October 12, 1993, pp. 90–91.

Laibioh, Kenneth, "American Takes on the World," *Fortune,* September 24, 1990.

Lieber, Ronald B., "Bob Crandall's Boo-Boos: The Fiery American Airlines Chairman Faces Labor Strife That Could Create Long-Lasting Scars at His Company," *Fortune,* April 28, 1997, pp. 365+.

Mathews, Anna Wilde, and Scott McCartney, "U.S. Sues American Air in Antitrust Case," *Wall Street Journal,* May 14, 1999, pp. A3, A6.

McCartney, Scott, "American Air's Crandall, About to Retire, Is Flying High," *Wall Street Journal,* April 27, 1998, p. B4.

——, "American Turns Its Attention to Performance," *Wall Street Journal,* May 7, 1997, pp. B1, B4.

——, "AMR, Challenging UAL in West, to Buy Reno Air," *Wall Street Journal,* November 20, 1998, pp. A3, A8.

——, AMR, Forced to Cancel 22% of Flights, Threatens to Sue Pilots over Sickout," *Wall Street Journal,* February 9, 1999, pp. A3, A11.

——, "AMR Plans to Auction Three of Its Units to Focus on American Airlines Business," *Wall Street Journal,* September 30, 1998, p. A4.

——, "AMR Puts Pilot Costs Over $150 Million," *Wall Street Journal,* February 18, 1999, pp. A3, A12.

——, "At American Airlines, Pilots Trace Grievances to Deals in Lean Years," *Wall Street Journal,* February 11, 1999, pp. A1, A10.

——, "Tension at AMR Outlasts Fading Sickout," *Wall Street Journal,* February 16, 1999, pp. A3, A14.

Moorman, Robert W., "Eagle Preens Its Plumage," *Air Transport World,* April 1996, pp. 55–56, 59.

Reed, Dan, *The American Eagle: The Ascent of Bob Crandall and American Airlines,* New York: St. Martin's Press, 1993.

Serling, Robert J., *Eagle: The Story of American Airlines,* New York: Dial, 1980.

Tiburzi, Bonnie, *Takeoff! The Story of America's First Woman Pilot for a Major Airline,* New York: Crown, 1984, 299 p.

Turk, Paul, "American: Skills for Sale," *Airline Business,* March 1993, pp. 60+.

Woodbury, Richard, "How the New No. 1 Got There," *Time,* May 15, 1989.

Zellner, Wendy, "Portrait of a Project As a Total Disaster," *Business Week,* January 17, 1994, p. 36.

Zellner, Wendy, and Nicole Harris, "Where Are All Those Airline Tie-Ups Headed?," *Business Week,* May 11, 1998, pp. 32–33.

Zellner, Wendy, Mike McNamee, and Seth Payne, "Did Clinton Scramble American's Profit Picture?," *Business Week,* December 6, 1993, p. 44.

—John Simley
—updated by David E. Salamie

Arcadia Group plc

**Colegrave House
70 Berners Street
London W1P 3AE
United Kingdom
(0171) 636 8040
Fax: (0171) 927 1602
Web site: http://www.arcadiagroup.co.uk**

Public Company
Incorporated: 1917 as Montague Burton Limited
Employees: 20,000
Sales: £1.47 billion (US$2.28 billion) (1998)
Stock Exchanges: London
Ticker Symbol: BRTO
NAIC: 44811 Men's Clothing Stores; 44812 Women's
   Clothing Stores; 44814 Family Clothing Stores

Arcadia Group plc, previously known as Burton Group plc, is the second largest clothing retailer in the United Kingdom, with more than 2,000 outlets in downtowns and shopping centers throughout the country. With two exceptions, the group's store formats primarily sell private-label apparel. These formats are Evans, Principles for Women, Dorothy Perkins, and Top Shop (women's wear); and Burton Menswear, Top Man, Hawkshead, Racing Green, and Principles for Men (menswear). In mid-1998 Arcadia acquired Wade Smith, a retailer of designer brands, and launched SU214, a retailer of designer menswear, marking the group's first forays into the designer sector. The company also has ventured into home shopping via catalog marketing and Internet retailing and into overseas markets, with expectations for 200 outlets outside the United Kingdom by the end of 2000.

Founded Under the Burton Brand
in the Early 20th Century

It was at the beginning of the 20th century that the foundations of Arcadia Group were laid. In 1900, 15-year-old Meshe

David Osinsky joined the thousands of Jews fleeing westward from Russian persecution. Osinsky evidently opened his first store in Holywell Street, Chesterfield, England, in 1904. The merchandise offered for sale consisted of inexpensive ready-made suits for men and boys' wear under the name Burton. Men's suits "noted for hard wear and perfect fit," to quote a contemporary advertisement, were offered from 11 shillings and ninepence, boys' suits "in endless variety" were sold for one shilling and ninepence, caps were sold at one penny, and shirts of emerald green flannel with yellow stripes were sold to Irish farm workers. Advertisements also solicited orders for "bespoke" (made to order) suits. In 1908 a second Burton shop was opened in Mansfield and in 1909 a third shop was opened in Sheffield. Also in 1909 Osinsky, who was to change his name to Montague Burton, married Sophia Marks, daughter of a furniture dealer.

In the same year Osinsky also established the Progress Mills works in Leeds, setting up Elmwood Mills and the headquarters of the firm there in 1910. Between 1910 and the outbreak of World War I, 14 branches of the firm were created, mainly in the industrial towns of the Midlands and the North East. The number of branches had grown to 40 by 1919, including eight shops in Ireland. These were all to be stocked with clothing. There was also the mounting task of meeting the demand for uniforms, which the firm was under contract to supply—all this with a constantly changing labor force as men joined the war effort and were replaced by women. By the end of the war Elmwood Mills occupied five premises in Leeds, and the labor force had grown from 56 in 1914 to 500. Production was divided between civilian needs and contract requirements, which posed a problem. The firm either had to shelve half its productive capacity or expand the number of retail outlets. It chose the latter, and the number of shops grew from 40 in 1919 to 140 by 1922.

Rapidity of growth was accompanied by change in status: the company, Montague Burton Ltd., adopted limited liability in 1917 with a share capital of £5,002 increasing to £47,002 by 1924, all the shares but one—which belonged to Mrs. Burton—being held by Montague Burton. The firm by this time made almost entirely wholesale bespoke clothing, with the customer being measured in the branch shop and his requirements sent for translation into the appropriate garment. The advantage of the wholesale bespoke system to the customer was that he got exactly what he had ordered to suit his size and personal preferences, instead of the approximation he would be likely to get by buying ready-made. The benefits to the producer were not having to finance stocks of ready-made clothing and being able to avoid intermediaries. The success of the system lay in the speed with which the customer's order could be processed. This required organizational ability of a high degree and was of crucial importance in this highly competitive business. To this end, production was centralized at Hudson Road Mills, on a site offering plenty of scope for expansion, the first stage being opened in 1921.

Tremendous Growth Between World Wars I and II

The main force behind the move to the new factory was the growth in retail trade. Whatever the state of the national economy, there was no year between the wars in which the number of Burton shops failed to grow. From 140 in 1922, the number more than doubled to reach 291 by 1929 and doubled again by 1939. The early increase in the number of shops was in the older industrial areas of the country such as West Riding of Yorkshire, Lancashire, the Midlands, and the North East, accounting for 80 percent in 1919, but this had fallen by 1939 to 50 percent. This diversification of outlets was behind the firm's remarkable record. The shops themselves set new standards of excellence, reflected in the expenditure on fixtures and fittings. From 1917 to 1939 the average amount spent on these items rose from £123 to £1,834. The 1925 publication *Goodwill in Industry,* by J. Foster Fraser, produced to mark the years that the firm had been in business, contained the following description: ''Every Montague Burton shop has the same outward appearance, both in its window dressing and in the name of the firm uniformly presented in bronze lettering on the marble. The exterior stonework is always of emerald pearl granite with shafts of Scotch grey granite. The interior fittings of oak and gun-metal quiet and dignified are the same at every branch.'' This impression of quiet dignity was emphasized by the reception accorded to the customer. Each Burton shop received an instruction manual containing the following advice: ''Impress on staff (a) to offer customer a chair and an invitation to be seated (b) to greet customer with a cheerful 'Good morning' entering (or Good evening) (c) to wish the customer a pleasant 'Good day' when departing. The prefix 'Sir' after 'Good morning' or similar conversational courtesies appeals to the average man whether you're intellectual, social, economical superior or inferior. Make your customer feel he is welcome and that you are anxious to please him. Avoid the severe style of the income tax collector and the smooth tongue of the fortune teller. Cultivate the dignified style of the 'Quaker tea blender' which is the happy medium.''

The care and attention paid to the running of the branches was matched by that shown to the workforce, and the new factory building at Hudson Road facilitated this. Here it was possible to provide a fully equipped canteen for 2,000, serving a midday meal costing between four and ten pence, together with comprehensive welfare services. The motivation behind this provision was rooted in the belief that productivity and contentment of the workforce were positively related.

When the new canteen was opened by the Princess Royal in 1934 it seated 8,000 workers, indicating the firm's growth. In 1929 the company became a public limited liability company with a capital of £4 million, having been a limited liability company since 1917. Montague Burton was knighted in 1931. For the rest of the 1930s the story was one of uninterrupted expansion. The number of shops had reached 595 by the outbreak of World War II. The success of retailing brought pressure on the departments at Hudson Road that produced the ready-to-wear suits, and there was a shortage of female labor, which Burton's own success had helped to create. At first the labor surpluses of the Yorkshire coalfield area were tapped and female workers were bused in from places such as Castleford and Normanton. This source of labor proved inadequate, however, and the firm sought relief in the blighted cotton towns of Lancashire. Three factories were opened in the 1930s, including a custom-built one at Burtonville on the East Lancashire highway. Between them they employed 6,000 workers in addition to the 10,600 employed at Hudson Road.

The decade witnessed the beginnings of a move away from wholesale bespoke tailoring, which had been the mainstay of the firm's output, to the ready-made suit. According to the *Outfitter,* March 26, 1938: ''Montague Burton's are to make a definite and strenuous effort to popularise the ready to wear lounge suits throughout the British Isles. Some of the larger branches have always carried made-up suits, now a ready-to-wear department is to be part of every shop. For the first time a ready-made lounge suit is illustrated in the general spring catalogue issued from all branches. . . . The main branch in Tottenham Court Road, London W1 is the largest of its kind in Britain. Over 2,000 garments are always in stock in 250 different fittings.''

Change of this kind carried revolutionary implications that were far from complete by the outbreak of World War II. The firm threw itself wholeheartedly into the war effort. The float representing Burton at the London victory parade of June 6, 1946 bore the proud inscription ''13,642,169 Garments For The Fighting Services,'' and the importance attached to the factory by the Germans is illustrated by a map discovered in German archives, pinpointing it as a Luftwaffe target. Wartime shortages of materials, the disruption of the labor force in response to the demands of the armed forces, and clothes rationing continued into peacetime. Not until 1950 did the chairman's annual report to the shareholders refer to improved stocks commensurate with prewar standards. The unfortunate outcome of a policy of buying in stocks of raw material on such a scale in a rising market due to extraneous circumstances was revealed when those prices suddenly fell. In Burton's case it meant writing off stocks to the value of £1 million. This was followed in September 1952 by the sudden death of Sir Montague Burton.

Transformed into Burton Group, 1953–91

Measured in terms of turnover the £19.5 million that the firm achieved in 1953 had grown to almost £42 million by 1964. By 1990 this figure had been eclipsed by a turnover just short of £2 billion. Growth statistics, however impressive, conceal fundamental changes in the structure, organization, and purpose of the firm. By 1991 it had shed all its cloth and clothing manufacturing activities. The Hudson Road factory, which once housed thousands of workers, became a distribution center with the vast floor spaces carved up into smaller rooms. The Lancashire factories were gone, the one at Burtonville was demolished, and the two at Goole and Doncaster, acquired since the war, were vacated. The business became more diversified, ceasing to serve men only, with more than half its sales to women. The shops catered to different sectors of the market and carried a comprehensive stock of clothing. They consisted of Burton Retail, Dorothy Perkins, Top Man, Top Shop, Evans, Debenhams, Principles for Men, and Principles for Women, all together making up Burton Group plc.

The long march to achieve this position started in 1953 when Burton acquired the firm Jackson the Tailor, thereby seeking to strengthen the management by acquiring the services of Sidney and Lionel Jacobson, directors of the company Weaver to Wearer Ltd., who had built a reputation of successful trading and who became directors of Burton in 1953. It was due to them that the firm divested itself of its clothmaking activities. The acquisition of the Peter Robinson shops, which by 1967 had grown in number to 39, predated the arrival of the Jacobsons by six years and heralded the movement of the firm into the women's side of the market. A new departure was the introduction of credit facilities for customers in November 1958 to make the firm more competitive. In 1963 Burton set up in business in France, anticipating Britain's entry into the European Common Market by ten years. This was one strategy open to a firm that had saturated the home market. Ultimately it was a failure, notwithstanding the acquisition of the St. Remy company with 35 shops, which made Burtons one of the largest specialty clothing firms in France and which was finally sold in 1981.

Another venture that the firm tried was mail order. It was announced in 1964 that after much detailed organization and planning, the firm was ready to go ahead with the newly created Burton-by-Post venture. This was unprofitable and was sold in 1970. In spite of these schemes, aimed at diversifying the company's outlets and products, it remained dependent on sales of men's tailored clothing. With the exception of the small chain of women's shops doing business as Peter Robinson and the prestigious general outfitters Browns of Chester, the only women's clothing outlets were the Burton shops, hence the move into the women's trade with the purchase of Evans Outsizes in 1971. Sometimes the search for diversity led the firm in unaccustomed directions, as with the acquisition of Ryman's chain of shops specializing in office equipment, with a separate drawing office. This venture ended in 1981.

Another example of the search for diversity, announced by Ladislas Rice on joining the firm in 1969, was the purchase of Greens Leisure Centre with 41 branches specializing in photographic equipment. This was never a profitable enterprise and was disposed of in 1976. A venture more closely related to Burton's primary business was an attempt to break into the children's market with the establishment of the Orange Hand Shops. This development lasted just four years, and in 1976 the company decided that it could no longer justify further investment in the endeavor as it was unprofitable. More successful was the 1979 acquisition of the Dorothy Perkins chain of women's wear shops that featured mid-range prices.

In January 1972 the chairman's report, having declared the company's intentions to become known as a group in 1969, announced: "Our company is now on the way to becoming a group of specialist retail chains each with a clearly defined market and a distinctive face to the public. . . . We intend to maintain and develop our dominant position in the menswear market. However, we shall become less completely dependent on it as our newer retailing activities grow."

In conjunction with this strategy, Burton discontinued manufacturing on grounds of cost. The rationale of the process—probably the most important in its history—was outlined by Ralph Halpern (later Sir Ralph) in his chairman's report of December 1981. After detailing the reasons why Burton had fallen behind the British clothing retailers in general, he outlined measures to retrieve the situation. First was the curtailing of the company's manufacturing activity. Second was the application to other company chains of retailing methods evolved by the Top Shop sector, and third was the shedding of all the loss-making activities.

Draconian measures saw Burton emerge with its sights set on retail selling with different divisions specializing in different market areas. Two new chains of shops were added: Principles for Women in 1984 and Principles for Men in 1985, specializing in high-quality clothing, and Debenhams' chain of 67 stores and the shops of John Collier were acquired, also in 1985. Debenhams marked another departure in that it was a department store chain offering clothing for the whole family and housewares. The parent company changed its name to Burton Group plc in 1985. Principles for Women and Principles for Men merged to become Principles in 1990. November 1990 saw the retirement of Sir Ralph Halpern, the man who had transformed the firm of Burton almost beyond recognition. Laurence Cooklin, a company veteran, replaced Halpern as chief executive.

Difficulties in the Early 1990s Followed by a Turnaround

An ill-conceived move into property development, coupled with the negative effects of a policy of endless discounting of merchandise, led to declining fortunes for Burton in the early 1990s. The collapse of the U.K. property market left the group with unsalable property and a heavy load of debt. In 1991 Burton laid off 1,600 employees as part of a cost-cutting restructuring and also raised £161 million (US$262.9 million) through a stock offering to reduce debt, but it still posted a loss of £13.4 million (US$21.9 million) for the fiscal year ending in September. Revenues fell 7.1 percent in 1991 to £1.66 billion (US$2.71 billion). In February 1992 Cooklin resigned his position and was succeeded by John Hoerner. An American born in Lincoln, Nebraska, Hoerner was chairman and CEO of the L.S. Ayres division of the U.S.-based May Department Store Company before taking over as chairman and chief executive of Debenhams in April 1987, where he was credited with effecting a turnaround.

Hoerner moved quickly to reverse the entire group's fortunes. About 2,000 jobs were eliminated, including nearly 1,000 at the group's headquarters. All of the group's chains underwent wholesale revamping to reposition them for full price selling rather than the detrimental constant discounting of the past. This was accomplished by carefully selecting the target market for each format, then redesigning the stores and the merchandise. In 1993 Hoerner also launched a program called Townprint, which aimed to ensure that each outlet was located in the right place and properly distanced from each other. Townprint led to a major reorganization of the group's 1,600 stores, calling for the disposal of 380 units, the acquisition of 228 units, and the transfer of 354 units from one Burton Group format to another. By 1995 Burton was well on the road to recovery, posting aftertax profits of £73.8 million on turnover of £2.16 billion.

In July 1996 Burton made its first move into home shopping in decades with the acquisition of Innovations, a direct mail order company, for £44.9 million. Innovations itself was a catalog of gadgets, and this brand was sold to Great Universal Stores in November 1997 for £20 million. Burton retained Innovations' customer databases and the Hawkshead brand clothing catalog. Hawkshead sold outdoor clothing and casualwear for the entire family and, under Burton, began opening up retail shops as well. In October 1996 Burton ventured further into home shopping with the £19 million purchase of Racing Green, whose men's and women's apparel lines featured the ''smart-casual'' look. There were already a few Racing Green retail outlets, and the brand's retail side was significantly expanded soon after the acquisition by Burton. The group's home shopping endeavors widened with the fall 1997 launch of sales over the Internet. By 1999 the group claimed to have the largest Internet site in Europe. In December 1997 Burton formed an alliance with Littlewoods, the catalog and football pools group, to create a joint venture, Dial Home Shopping Ltd. The venture was charged with producing catalogs for all of the Burton brands.

Spun Off Debenhams, Became Arcadia in Early 1998

In July 1997 Burton Group announced that it would spin off the Debenhams department store chain to concentrate solely on apparel retailing. In January 1998 the demerger was consummated; simultaneous with this development, the group changed its name to Arcadia Group plc. Hoerner told the *Financial Times:* ''This name has a clear feel to it that we believe is appropriate to our future in stores, home shopping and the Internet—both in the UK and other countries—a real 'arcade' of brands.'' The change also meant that the group name would no longer be associated with only one of the company's many brands, even if that brand was the one on which the group was founded.

In July 1998 Arcadia added another brand to its collection through the purchase of Wade Smith for £17.3 million (US$28.7 million) in cash and £3.3 million (US$5.5 million) in debt. This acquisition marked another first for the group, as its existing formats all centered around private-label merchandise. Wade Smith, based in Liverpool, specialized in designer and branded sportswear. Arcadia was particularly interested in expanding the Wade Smith Jnr. subformat, which specialized in branded sportswear for customers aged 2 to 12. There were three Wade Smith Jnr. outlets at the time of the purchase, and Arcadia planned to expand it into a chain of up to 30 stores. In August 1998 the group launched a new format, SU214, selling

branded menswear and marking an additional commitment to the designer apparel sector.

For the fiscal year ending in September 1998, Arcadia Group posted strong results despite the spinoff of Debenhams. When considering only continuing operations, operating profits were £80.6 million (US$125.1 million) on revenues of £1.47 billion (US$2.28 billion). Arcadia had more than 2,000 outlets in the United Kingdom by 1999. In addition to seeking growth through the acquisition and launching of new formats and the forays into home shopping, the group intended to increase its overseas presence from the 57 outlets in 11 countries it had in late 1998 to 200 by the end of 2000. The Middle East and Europe were the two major areas of Arcadia overseas operation, and its European presence was slated to grow following the 1998 signing of a franchise deal with a partner for Iceland and Scandinavia.

Principal Subsidiaries

Arcadia Group Brands Ltd.; Arcadia Group Design & Development Ltd.; Arcadia Group Multiples (Ireland) Ltd.; Burton Retail Ltd.; Dorothy Perkins Retail Ltd.; Evans Ltd.; Hawkshead Retail Ltd.; Principles Retail Ltd.; Racing Green Ltd.; Redcastle Investments Ltd.; Redcastle Ltd.; Top Shop/Top Man Ltd.; Wade Smith Ltd.

Further Reading

''American Is New Chief of a Retailer in Britain,'' *New York Times,* February 14, 1992, p. D4.

Brown-Humes, Christopher, ''Burton Moves to Home Shopping with Innovations,'' *Financial Times,* July 20, 1996, p. 20.

Buckley, Neil, ''Burton More Than Doubles As It Breaks Off from Discounting,'' *Financial Times,* November 10, 1995, p. 17.

——, ''Pulling Its Socks Up,'' *Financial Times,* November 8, 1995, p. 19.

Edgecliffe-Johnson, Andrew, ''Burton to Change Name to Arcadia,'' *Financial Times,* October 13, 1997, p. 29.

——, ''Littlewoods Joins Burton in £15m Share of Brands,'' *Financial Times,* December 13, 1997, p. 18.

Fallon, James, ''Hoerner Using U.S. Savvy to Revamp UK's Burton,'' *Daily News Record,* January 13, 1993, p. 12.

——, ''UK's Arcadia Group Buys Wade Smith Retail Chain,'' *Daily News Record,* July 6, 1998, p. 22.

——, ''UK's Burton Joins Web Brigade,'' *Women's Wear Daily,* December 6, 1996, p. 12.

Fraser, J. Foster, *Goodwill in Industry,* Leeds: Burton, 1925.

Hollinger, Peggy, ''Arcadia Forced to Cut Prices by Competition,'' *Financial Times,* January 22, 1999, p. 18.

——, ''Burton Strengthens Mail-Order Side,'' *Financial Times,* October 22, 1996, p. 20.

——, ''Debenhams May Be Worth £1.5bn in Burton Demerger,'' *Financial Times,* July 9, 1997, p. 1.

——, ''Hoerner Looking tTo Cure All the Runny Noses,'' *Financial Times,* May 17, 1997, p. 20.

——, ''Hoerner's Excitement Leaves Market Anxious,'' *Financial Times,* July 9, 1997, p. 16.

Redmayne, Ronald, *Ideals in Industry,* Leeds: Burton, 1951.

Sigsworth, Eric M., *Montague Burton the Tailor of Taste,* Manchester: Manchester University Press, 1990.

—Eric Milton Sigsworth
—updated by David E. Salamie

Art Van Furniture, Inc.

6500 Fourteen Mile Road
Warren, Michigan 48092
U.S.A.
(810) 939-0800
Fax: (810) 939-3055

Private Company
Incorporated: 1959
Employees: 3,000
Sales: $440 million (1997 est.)
NAIC: 44211 Furniture Stores

Art Van Furniture, Inc. is the largest furniture store chain in the state of Michigan and the eighth largest nationwide, in terms of sales volume. Targeting the middle-class consumer, the company has achieved success by its emphasis on quick delivery, attentive customer service, and persistent advertising campaigns. In the late 1990s, the family-owned company employed five of founder Archie "Art" Van Elslander's ten children in key positions. Over the years, the chain has expanded to nearly 30 stores, most located in the metropolitan Detroit area.

Beginnings

Archie Van Elslander was born in 1930 on the east side of Detroit into a Belgian immigrant family. Van Elslander showed an interest in sales early on, hawking newspapers up and down Detroit's Gratiot Avenue as a youngster. During these years he also adopted his preferred name of "Art." After graduation from high school and a year in the U.S. Army, Van Elslander married and then began working for the Crown Furniture company, moving up to store manager within two years.

Desiring a business of his own, Van Elslander in 1959 mortgaged his house and borrowed from his insurance policies to finance the first Art Van Furniture store, a 4,000-square-foot outlet on Gratiot Avenue in East Detroit. As a salesman he had found it easier to omit the end of his last name when talking to customers, and it was this shortened form that he chose to use as the store's name. The early years were difficult, with Van Elslander, the store's sole employee, responsible for everything from opening in the morning to making deliveries after closing in the evening. As he would continue to do in the future, he involved his growing family in the business, bringing his wife and children in on Sundays to dust and sweep.

Key to the company's success was a policy of quick delivery. While most furniture stores required a customer to wait weeks or even months for an order to arrive from the manufacturer, Art Van maintained a warehouse that stocked a large backlog of goods, enabling prompt delivery of most items.

Strong automobile sales in the early 1960s boosted Detroit's economy, and sales of furniture were good. By 1964 there were a total of seven Art Van stores, Van Elslander having taken on several partners to help finance the expansion. However, an economic downturn that year caused sales to drop off, and the highly leveraged company faced the prospect of bankruptcy. Determined to pay off his creditors and remain in business, Van Elslander held a liquidation sale at the Michigan State Fairgrounds in a giant tent. Following the successful sale, he split the business with his three partners, giving each a store of his own and keeping four to himself. In the early 1970s he was able to buy the others out completely and again become sole owner. By this time Art Van had grown into a chain of 15 stores, all in the metropolitan Detroit area.

The early 1970s saw an increasingly competitive atmosphere as other furniture retailers such as Joshua Doore began to aggressively target Art Van's customers. Rather than bow to the competition, Van Elslander responded in kind, moving the company's headquarters and warehouse to a larger location and offering such new services as free immediate delivery. "I knew we had to expand or lose our business. Expand and keep up the advertising," said the company's founder.

Advertising had become a vital part of his strategy, and it would eventually make Art Van Furniture as well-known as McDonald's or Chevrolet to Detroit area residents. The company was one of the first in the area to use television spots to advertise furniture. Art Van commercials, which were changed

Company Perspectives:

Art Van Elslander opened his first furniture store in 1959. The 4,000-square-foot facility, located on Gratiot in East Detroit, featured Danish contemporary furniture and employed only its owner. The first Art Van store opened with a philosophy that is still the foundation of store operations today—provide area residents with quality furniture, at great prices, while implementing high standards of service.

weekly, stressed sale prices and the company's special services such as free delivery.

1970s and 1980s: Expansion During Recession

By the mid-1970s an economic recession began to cause a shakeout in the furniture business, and within the next few years over 80 furniture stores or companies in Michigan folded, including Joshua Doore, which at one time had operated over 300 showrooms. At the same time, however, Art Van was expanding its warehouse yet again and also opening its first stores outside of metropolitan Detroit, adding locations in Flint and Lansing in 1977. The year 1980 saw the company introduce an Art Van charge card and open an additional store, bringing the total count to 19 for the chain.

In 1983 the company named Gary Van Elslander, Art's son, to the position of president, while Art remained company chairman. In 1987 the Van Elslanders purchased an upscale furniture store, Scott Shuptrine, and soon bought three other independent stores and built a fourth, giving each the Shuptrine name. Scott Shuptrine's typical customer was 35 to 54 years old, with a household income of $50,000 and up, as compared to Art Van's 25- to 54 year-old, $25,000- to $30,000-a-year demographic. In 1989 Gary Van Elslander left Art Van to oversee the Shuptrine operation, which was run as a separate entity from Art Van Furniture. Profits remained elusive for Scott Shuptrine, however, due to strong competition from other high-end furniture retailers and the vastly different nature of its business. Unlike the more mainstream Art Van, which could sell couches or bedroom sets by the truckload, the high-end market was geared toward sales of expensive, custom-built pieces and relied upon the recommendations of interior design consultants. Showrooms were much more lavish and customers expected to be pampered. Thus, overhead was much higher than at an Art Van outlet. Over the next few years the number of Shuptrine locations declined to two.

In 1988 Art Van Furniture added a new service, Mattress Express, which guaranteed next-day delivery or the purchase was free, with free removal of mattresses that were being replaced. The company offered the mattresses it picked up to Detroit-area social service agencies, eventually purchasing a converted tire-shredding machine to dispose of the mattresses that were not reused. This massive, $200,000 device, the only one of its kind in the country, paid for itself quickly as shredded mattresses required only one-seventh the landfill space of intact ones.

Charitable Activities in the 1990s

In addition to running his furniture business, Art Van Elslander was also active in local community service organizations and was a frequent contributor to charities. One of his most public efforts involved rescuing a holiday tradition. The city of Detroit had enjoyed an annual, nationally televised, Thanksgiving Day parade for many years. However, in 1980 Hudson's department store ended its sponsorship, and in 1988 CBS dropped its national telecast, causing many other corporate sponsors to exit. The parade's budget immediately went into the red, and in 1990 the event was in danger of being canceled altogether. Reading in the newspaper of this possibility, Van Elslander quickly decided to make a contribution to keep the parade afloat. His $200,000 check enabled the parade to go on, and the next year he offered to match the contributions of other businesses up to $100,000. Charitable efforts were an ongoing activity for Van Elslander, who often donated money privately to local agencies. Over the years, other beneficiaries of his and the company's generosity included the St. Vincent de Paul organization, the National Cherry Festival, America's Walk for Diabetes, the Holland (Michigan) Tulip Festival, and many others.

By 1992 Art Van's annual sales had topped $220 million, and the company was still seeking new ways to reach customers. One successful idea was the introduction of clearance centers attached to many of the chain's stores. These centers sold damaged or overstocked merchandise at rates from 40 to 70 percent off retail, allowing the company to expand its penetration of the market to yet another price level. Art Van stores were also successful with sales of such accessories as lamps, area rugs, and wall art pieces. To increase sales of such items, products at the company's stores were arranged carefully into harmonious groupings that appealed to the eye. With research showing that customers who made a major furniture purchase often bought accessories to accompany it within 72 hours, the company put a great deal of effort into this category, which was a consistently profitable one.

Art Van Elslander's business acumen and community spirit led him to another new project in 1994, when he and a group of investors purchased the landmark Ponchartrain Hotel in downtown Detroit from the Resolution Trust Corporation. The purchase price was $4 million, and $7 million in renovations were planned. Van Elslander intended to turn the hotel's fortunes around, and immediately aligned the Ponchartrain with Holiday Inn's Crowne Plaza chain, enabling the hotel to benefit from that company's reservations network. The years following the city's deadly 1967 riots had seen Detroit's population drop precipitously, and some areas of downtown Detroit had come to resemble a no-man's land. With this and other major investments taking place in the area, it appeared that the city's badly damaged reputation might finally be on the mend.

A bitter strike at Detroit's two daily newspapers caused controversy for the company in 1995, as picketing union members targeted Art Van stores, which had continued to advertise in the two papers. Art Van filed charges with the National Labor Relations Board in October 1995, alleging that picketers had harassed customers at 11 of its Detroit area locations. The picketers withdrew after a Detroit NLRB official threatened to seek a federal injunction against the six unions involved.

An Upscale Redesign for the Late 1990s

By 1997, following a spurt of growth in the early to mid-1990s, the company had increased in size to a total of 26 stores with over 2,600 employees. An expansion of the flagship store in Warren, Michigan, was being planned at this time, based on company research into shopping patterns and lifestyles. The redesign, unveiled in August 1998, featured a two-story glass atrium entrance, a cappuccino bar, soft lighting, and a more upscale merchandise mix. The company was trying to attract more affluent patrons, while not alienating its core customers. Other stores in the chain were scheduled for similar upgrades, and the most recently built ones had incorporated the design changes from the outset. In November the company opened its 27th store, in northern Michigan's Traverse City. This 62,000-square-foot facility, which followed the new design, also featured a Kid's Castle, first introduced in the Warren makeover. The 1,400-square-foot play space featured climbing structures, a TV room, and a ball-play area. Art Van staff supervised the children while their parents browsed the store. The merchandise offered at Art Van now ranged from bedroom sets and mattresses to dinettes, entertainment centers, home office furniture, sofas, chairs, end tables, grandfather clocks, and children's furniture. Italian leather furniture and Amish-made oak furniture were displayed in specially designed sections of the stores to enhance their appeal.

Striving to distinguish itself for its customer service, Art Van stores not only offered free delivery and set-up of furniture, but also focused on the shopping experience itself, walking customers to their cars with umbrellas on rainy days, loading large purchases into their cars, washing their windshields, and presenting them with a flower. The company also offered a financing plan that required no money down, no interest, and no payments for two years. While competitors tried to match these terms, Art Van's policies proved the most generous.

The company's policies of attentive service, carefully designed stores, attractive financing plans, and heavily advertised sale prices proved an irresistible combination for several generations of Michigan furniture buyers. With its first 40 years in business largely a huge success, and the next Van Elslander generation actively involved in the company, Art Van Furniture seemed assured of continuing dominance of the Michigan furniture market.

Further Reading

Eberwein, Cheryl, "In the Vanguard," *Corporate Detroit Magazine,* October 1, 1992, p. 22.

Jackson, Kathy, "Retailers Open New Stores, Battle for Local Spending," *Crain's Detroit Business,* January 6, 1986, p. 1.

"Newspaper Picketers Agree to Leave Stores," *Cleveland Plain Dealer,* October 14, 1995, p. 2C.

" 'Pay Later' Becomes Business Mantra," *Grand Rapids Press,* December 30, 1998, p. B5.

Pepper, Jon, "Art Van Takes a Risk, Goes Higher Scale to Draw Customers," *Detroit News,* September 18, 1998, p. B1.

Preddy, Melissa, "Art Van Has Solution for a Downturn: Expand," *Detroit News,* April 9, 1996, p. B1.

——, "Michiganian of the Year: Art Van Elslander," *Detroit News,* April 5, 1998, p. E2.

Santorelli, Dina, "The Art of Accessories," *HFN,* September 25, 1995, p. 24.

Tompor, Susan, "The Art Van Man: Low-Key Founder Sets High-Powered Business Pace," *Detroit News,* September 30, 1990, p. 1.

Wilson, Melinda, "Art Van Owner Goes After Upscale Furniture Market," *Crain's Detroit Business,* February 6, 1989, p. 1.

——, "Runaway Van," *Detroit News,* July 29, 1991, p. 3F.

Wray, Kimberly, "Art Van Slates State-of-the-Art Store," *HFN,* May 18, 1998, p. 25.

—Frank Uhle

ASDA Group plc

ASDA House
Southbank
Great Wilson Street
Leeds LS11 5AD
United Kingdom
(113) 243 5435
Fax: (113) 241 8666
Web site: http://www.asda.co.uk

Public Company
Incorporated: 1949 as Associated Dairies and Farm
    Stores Limited
Employees: 48,072
Sales: £7.62 billion (US$12.73 billion) (1998)
Stock Exchanges: London
Ticker Symbol: ASDA
NAIC: 45211 Department Stores; 44511 Supermarkets &
    Other Grocery Stores; 45299 All Other General
    Merchandise Stores

In the late 20th-century race to fill Great Britain with large, brightly decorated supermarkets, ASDA Group plc has the unique distinction of being both an innovator and a latecomer to the field. ASDA introduced the concept of the ''superstore'' as early as 1965 and has never operated anything but these behemoths of the food-retailing world (a superstore is defined as one with 25,000 square feet or more of selling area). But it was not until the mid-1980s that ASDA began upgrading its warehouse stores to meet the standards of design appeal and fresh-food selection set by its major competitors. By the late 1990s the group had approximately 220 superstores, with the average size of these units on the increase as ASDA moved toward, larger formats—Market Hall superstores and hypermarkets. ASDA by that time had also completed a 70-year metamorphosis from dairy cooperative to supermarket giant—the United Kingdom's third largest food retailer on a market share basis. But in early 1999 ASDA and Kingfisher plc—a major European multicategory retailer, based in the United Kingdom—announced that the two companies would merge, an event that would bring to a close ASDA's existence as an independent firm.

Dairy Origins

The origins of the ASDA Group are to be found in the efforts of English dairy farmers to protect themselves from falling milk prices after World War I. When wartime price controls were lifted and England began once again to import large quantities of European dairy products, local milk prices fell sharply and showed every sign of continuing to do so. Various legislative remedies were devised, but in the meantime a Yorkshire dairy farmer named J.W. Hindell led a number of his fellows in the creation of Hindell's Dairy Farmers Limited, a 1920 partnership whose purpose was to acquire or build both wholesale and retail outlets for their milk, in that way securing for themselves a steady market and a floor price.

During the next 25 years, Hindell's assembled a wide variety of dairy businesses, founding or purchasing a total of nine operating companies involved in everything from the raising of dairy cattle to the processing and distribution of milk and milk products, as well as the promotion of numerous cafés, retail milk shops, and bakeries.

By the time of World War II, Hindell's, headquartered in Leeds, had extended its interests across the Midlands and diversified as far as meatpacking and even the quarrying of lime. The partnership became a public company in March 1949, as Associated Dairies and Farm Stores Limited, which included some 26 farms, three dairies, two bakeries, 42 retail shops, and pork-butchering facilities. With 1,200 employees, Associated was already an important part of the relatively quiet economy of northern England.

Entered Retailing in 1965

The next 20 years saw a veritable blizzard of further acquisitions by Associated. Dairies and creameries too numerous to mention became part of the rapidly growing northern conglomerate, but beyond expanding profits, little changed at the company until 1965, when Associated created a subsidiary called ASDA Stores Limited. In that year, the parent company, by then known

Company Perspectives:

Our mission is to be Britain's best value fresh food and clothing superstore, meeting the weekly shopping needs of ordinary working people and their families who demand value.

as Associated Dairies Limited, with sales of £13.5 million, was highly profitable and probably did not much concern itself with the tiny food-stores division, which at best could be expected to fill one more niche in the company's overall business plan.

As it turned out, however, the stores were an immediate and immense success. Associated had come up with a merchandising concept entirely new to England, and well-tailored to the working-class cities in which it chiefly operated: the company opened extremely large, rather spartan stores in abandoned warehouses or mills, offering to the public a limited selection of goods at the lowest possible prices. These ''edge-of-town'' stores depended for their success on the rapid proliferation of the automobile in Great Britain and the accompanying decline in local consumer loyalties. As in the United States, the British public soon decided that it cared less about neighborhood vendors than low prices, and the automobile allowed them to act on their preference. Associated's warehouse stores were an enormous success, and the company quickly set about the program of expansion that would make it one of the leading retailers in the country.

The company thus found itself milking two kinds of cows, dairy and cash, and the latter naturally proved the more attractive as time went on. Associated continued to add to its dairy holdings, but it was apparent by the early 1970s that the ASDA Stores division would soon dwarf its parent. At that time, the stores were still operated in a rudimentary fashion, with little centralized administration, primitive marketing, and no attempt at attractive floor displays. But ASDA had pioneered not one but two new ideas in British food retailing, the edge-of-town location and the superstore size, and for a long time had the market to itself.

The company opened stores in Scotland and Wales, and began casting about for opportunities to invest its growing cash reserves. In 1972 ASDA entered the travel agency business, in 1977 it had a go at furniture with its purchase of the Wade's stores, and at various times in the decade it tried its hand at a number of other diversions, none of them successful and all of them eventually disposed of. But longtime chairman Noel Stockdale could hardly be concerned about these minor setbacks; quite reasonably, he did not try to fix what was not broken, but continued building more superstores across the northern half of the country. By 1978 ASDA had 60 of these, and two years later they passed the £1 billion sales mark.

Increased Competition Led to Mid-1980s Overhaul

However, the rest of the marketplace had not stood still in the meantime. With ASDA's runaway success as a model, the established grocery chains began building similar superstores at out-of-town locations, while London-area stores discovered that low prices were not enough to please more sophisticated shoppers. These shoppers wanted pleasant surroundings as well as low prices, and they soon got both in the more luxurious superstores opened by ASDA's rivals. As a result, by the early 1980s the ASDA format of high volume, low price, and no frills had come to seem dated and unappealing. Customer loyalty, never strong in the economy store sector, shifted away from ASDA toward the chains more in tune with the new wave of unabashed materialism in Thatcher's England, leaving the Yorkshire firm in danger of an early death. In a period when everyone had a superstore, ASDA's were decidedly less ''super'' than the rest.

Such, at any rate, was the diagnosis of John Hardman when he became managing director of stores in June 1984. Though the company was in the midst of a profitable, £1.76 billion sales year, Hardman understood that the market had moved ahead of ASDA and would soon leave ASDA floundering in its wake. Hardman therefore proposed a radical repositioning of the ASDA chain, to include several improvements. First, ASDA would adopt a completely new look for all of the stores, replacing their stacked-carton, industrial brown decor with a new, appetizing green palette, dramatic lighting, dropped ceilings, and imaginative display racks. Second, the chain would introduce its own ''ASDA Brand'' line of foods, since private-label merchandising generally yields substantially higher gross margins. Third, the stores would install an EPOS system—electronic point of sale registers—to provide more efficient records and inventory control. Fourth, the company would build a centralized network of distribution warehouses, eliminating the scores of trucks that arrived each day at store loading docks. Fifth and last, ASDA would push toward the more affluent population in southern England and the London area, where relatively few superstores had as yet been built.

Around the same time Hardman was revamping its stores, ASDA made its largest acquisition to date. In 1985 the company purchased the leading retailer of furniture in the United Kingdom, a company known as MFI, which had sales of about £300 million a year. Company spokesmen at the time pointed to the two concerns' similar positions in the marketplace, since MFI also operated large, edge-of-town stores that sold low-price goods; but financial analysts from the beginning doubted the wisdom of the merger, and in this case they were correct. After only two years of an up-and-down marriage, ASDA sold its partner in the largest management buyout in British history, receiving £453 million in cash plus 25 percent of the newly formed ''Maxirace.''

Indeed, ASDA decided at that time to sell practically everything: under Hardman, now chairman, the company realized that its future resided in superstores and nothing but superstores, and therefore sold off not only MFI but also Associated Fresh Foods, the modest dairy company which at one time had been Hindell's Dairy Farmers Limited—that is, ASDA's own parent. ASDA would henceforth focus solely on its newly revamped and expanded line of food stores, with the single exception of Allied, a chain of carpet and drapery stores that the Group was unable to sell.

The superstore facelift and expansion program succeeded, at least initially. ASDA stores became known in the late 1980s for their innovative design, large selection of fresh foods, and equally extensive nonfood offerings, the latter accounting for some 25 percent of total store sales. Profits in the new and redecorated stores were significantly higher than in the older ones, due in part to the ever-increasing number of ASDA brand items on the shelves and the more efficient distribution system. The company continued its southern assault, opening an average of 12 to 15 new superstores each year, many of them in the crowded urban areas of the south. And, in the most dramatic proof yet of its commitment to the grocery business, ASDA in 1989 acquired 62 of rival Gateway's superstores for £705 million. This mammoth purchase, in a single stroke, increased ASDA's selling area by 50 percent, from five million to 7.5 million square feet, and further solidified its position as the largest operator of superstores in the United Kingdom.

Near-Collapse in Early 1990s, Then Turnaround

Unfortunately, as the company would later admit, it had paid too much for Gateway. Even worse, ASDA had funded the purchase by borrowing heavily, with its debt load ballooning to £1 billion. Compounding the situation was ASDA's move upmarket in the later 1980s, which had pushed up costs and thereby prices, resulting in the loss of many customers. With profits flagging and the company needing to service its burdensome debt, ASDA verged on bankruptcy by 1991. In June of that year Hardman was forced out by the company board, replaced as chairman by Patrick Gillam. In October 1991 ASDA appointed Archie Norman, age 37 at the time, as chief executive. Norman had been group finance director at U.K. retailer Kingfisher plc. In November 1991 ASDA completed a rights issue that raised £357 million (US$629.7 million) and cut debt to £668 million, but ASDA remained on the brink.

The new leadership at ASDA quickly began a three-year turnaround program. Prices were restored to the company's traditional five to seven percent below the competition. Costs were slashed, including the elimination of 500 management positions, a move announced in May 1992. ASDA stores' bolstered their selections of fresh foods and clothing. The clothing lines were sold under the George brand, which ASDA gained full control of in 1995 when it bought out its joint venture partner. To improve the company balance sheet, ASDA sold off additional peripheral businesses, including the Allied chain, which was sold to Carpetland in 1993, with ASDA gaining a 40 percent stake in the resulting company. ASDA also sold some property and large stores to its competition and returned its Gazeley Properties subsidiary to a more conservative role of property management, rather than the speculative property development it had ventured into. The company was also able to complete a second rights issue that raised an additional £347 million. By fiscal 1995 ASDA had returned to the black, posting pretax profits of £246.2 million on sales of £5.29 billion. The company's debt situation was finally under control. Results continued to improve, through fiscal 1998, when pretax profits hit £404.9 million (US$676.4 million) on sales of £7.62 billion (US$12.73 billion). In late 1996 with the turnaround complete, Gillam retired, Norman was named chairman, and Norman's deputy, Allan Leighton, became chief executive.

By the end of the 1990s ASDA began experimenting with new, larger formats, including the Market Hall superstores which featured more than 40,000 square feet of selling space and increased selections of fresh food and a larger area for the George clothing line. Thirty-five percent of the chain's units, at the close of fiscal 1998, were in the Market Hall format. ASDA also established a Hypermarkets division, which soon had 15 stores that exceeded 50,000 square feet. In 1998 the company tested the addition of small pharmacies to some of its stores and at its Canterbury unit opened the first hot and cold takeout restaurant in a U.K. superstore.

Meantime, ASDA was much in the news. Merger discussions between ASDA and Safeway in late 1997 and between ASDA and Kingfisher in the spring of 1998 both collapsed without an agreement being reached. A year later, however, ASDA and Kingfisher reached an agreement on a £5.4 billion merger that would create the largest multicategory retailer in the United Kingdom and one of the top ten retailers in the world. Kingfisher operated a number of chains in Europe, including variety shops, hardware centers, drug stores, electronics outlets, and music, video, book, and multimedia stores. Combining ASDA's strength in food, clothing, and household goods with Kingfisher's many areas of retailing experience would enable the combined company to create hypermarkets throughout Europe selling all manner of goods under one very large roof. It thus appeared likely that the 1990s trend toward ever-larger stores would lead to the end of ASDA's independent existence.

Principal Subsidiaries

ASDA Stores Limited; Gazeley Properties Limited; McLagan Investments Limited; The Burwood House Group Plc.

Further Reading

Blackwell, David, ''Asda and Kingfisher End Talks,'' *Financial Times,* May 18, 1998, p. 21.
Davidson, Andrew, ''Allan Leighton,'' *Management Today,* September 1997, pp. 38–40, 42.
Edgecliffe-Johnson, Andrew, and Peggy Hollinger,'' *Financial Times,* April 20, 1999, p. 21.
Hollinger, Peggy, ''Asda/Kingfisher Could Save up to £100m a Year,'' *Financial Times,* April 19, 1999, p. 24.
Hunt, Julian, ''If—Or When?,'' *Grocer,* November 29, 1997, p. 14.
Kellaway, Lucy, ''The Boss Who Calls His Workers 'Colleagues,' '' *Financial Times,* September 25, 1998, p. 13.
''The Norman Conquests,'' *Marketing,* January 4, 1996, p. 13.
Parker-Pope, Tara, ''Asda, Back from Brink of Bankruptcy, Continues Drive Against Fixed Pricing,'' *Financial Times,* November 27, 1995, p. B7D.
Price, Christopher, ''Norman to Become Asda Chairman,'' *Financial Times,* August 28, 1996, p. 19.
Pring, Andrew, ''The Best Chain We Never Had'','' *Grocer,* October 4, 1997, pp. 32–34.
Thornhill, John, ''Realism Impresses More Than Magic,'' *Financial Times,* January 16, 1992, p. 23.
Van de Vliet, Anita, ''Asda's Open Plan,'' *Management Today,* December 1995, pp. 50–54.
Wighton, David, ''Asda Boss Set to Speak His Mind,'' *Financial Times,* September 21, 1996, p. 6.

—Jonathan Martin
—updated by David E. Salamie

Atlas Copco AB

SE-105 23 Stockholm
Sweden
(08) 743 8000
Fax: (08) 644 9045
Web site: http://www.atlascopco.com

Public Company
Incorporated: 1873 as AB Atlas
Employees: 23,393
Sales: SKr33.74 billion (US$4.28 billion) (1998)
Stock Exchanges: Stockholm London Frankfurt
    Düsseldorf Hamburg
NAIC: 33312 Construction Machinery Manufacturing;
    333131 Mining Machinery & Equipment
    Manufacturing; 333991 Power-Driven Handtool
    Manufacturing; 333912 Air & Gas Compressor
    Manufacturing; 532412 Construction, Mining, &
    Forestry Machinery & Equipment Rental & Leasing;
    53249 Other Commercial & Industrial Machinery &
    Equipment Rental & Leasing; 54133 Engineering
    Services

Atlas Copco AB is one of the world's leading producers of compressors, mining and construction equipment, power tools, assembly systems, and motion control products. The company is also active in the rental equipment and service sector. Atlas Copco has gone through several transformations since its founding in 1873 as AB Atlas. It was initially a specialized manufacturer of railway equipment but switched at the beginning of the 20th century to diesel engines and pneumatic products. The production of diesel engines was abandoned after World War II, allowing the company to concentrate on the pneumatic equipment sector and erect an extensive international sales network that has made Atlas Copco into one of Sweden's biggest multinational concerns. Closely connected to the Wallenberg banking dynasty, Atlas Copco had to call on its financial support to weather several severe crises during its existence prior to World War II. In the postwar period, the profitability of Atlas Copco has improved greatly, despite a few temporary setbacks.

19th-Century Beginnings

AB Atlas was established in 1873 to supply equipment for the Swedish railways, with two factories located in Stockholm and Södertälje. Atlas was the brainchild of Eduard Fränckel, the chief engineer for Swedish State Railways (SJ), who became the company's first managing director. A second key figure behind Atlas was D.O. Francke, a Gothenburg industrialist and financier who headed the banking enterprise Göteborgs Handelskompani. The biggest shareholder in Atlas was André Oscar Wallenberg, the founder of Sweden's first commercial bank, Stockholms Enskilda Bank. Wallenberg had involved the bank in financing a number of railway construction projects and his interest in Atlas was a natural extension of this activity.

Atlas was soon the largest manufacturing company in Sweden in terms of production capacity. The large size of Atlas's planned operations reflected the optimistic outlook for the country's economy. The industrial revolution was gaining momentum in Sweden in the early 1870s and engineering firms were enjoying their first sustained period of profits. Atlas was entering a crowded field when it came to transportation equipment. Although it was profitable until 1877, Atlas then plunged into a deficit due to falling orders from Swedish state and private railways as the country entered a recession in the late 1870s.

Atlas's losses mounted during the 1880s as economic growth remained weak. Göteborgs Handelskompani, which was suffering financial reverses, gradually reduced its stake in Atlas, while Stockholms Enskilda Bank kept the company afloat through loans and consequently increased its control. A solution to Atlas's financial problems was difficult since the company was saddled with large and costly production facilities and faced fierce competition in the market for railway equipment and other heavy industrial goods at a time of economic slowdown. The company's situation revealed that "the initial investment in Atlas had not only been made at the wrong time but also in the wrong industry," corporate historian Professor Torsten Gårdlund concluded.

Company Perspectives:

The long-term goal of the Atlas Copco Group is to become the world's leading company within its specialist areas of business. The Group's business concept is to provide a broad range of products and services, which meet the needs of customers in the areas of: air and gas compression, as well as air treatment; industrial manufacturing and the automotive after-market; rock excavation, light construction and demolition; installation, repair and service.

Burdened with excess production capacity, Atlas had to find other business besides making railway carriages. It produced steel and wrought-iron parts for bridges and other structures and made an unsuccessful diversification into marine steam engines and boilers by buying a shipyard in Gävle in a drastic attempt to develop more profitable product lines. When these efforts produced poor results, the Södertälje and Gävle facilities were closed and activity was concentrated in Stockholm. In 1887 the Wallenbergs ousted company president Fränckel, who had been criticized for lax management, and replaced him with Oscar Lamm, a mining engineer.

With Atlas continuing to suffer losses and Stockholms Enskilda Bank having a significant part of its assets tied up in the company, Knut Wallenberg, who had become head of the bank on his father's death in 1886, decided at the end of 1890 to allow Atlas to be liquidated. The shareholders lost their investment, and the bank suffered heavy losses as its creditor. A new company named Nya AB Atlas (New Atlas Company) took over its assets, with Stockholms Enskilda Bank subscribing for the major part of the share capital. Under the firm control of the Wallenbergs, Nya AB Atlas became the cornerstone for the family's industrial empire, which now embraces most of Sweden's multinational corporations.

After the financial reorganization, the company developed a new specialty, heating ducts for buildings. It also began production of steam engines, steam locomotives, and machine tools. With the dawn of the 20th century it gradually phased out most of these products, including its original business of railway equipment, as it continued to change its product mix. It focused instead on two promising areas, oil-driven engines and air machinery and compressors. Production of compressed air equipment began in 1901, and, by the start of World War I, pneumatic products had become the company's dominant business area. Gunnar Jacobsson, who oversaw the development of this division, became the president of Nya Atlas in 1909, succeeding Lamm.

New Products and Corporate Structures in a New Century

In an attempt to improve the production and sales of oil-driven engines, its other main product area, Nya Atlas merged in 1917 with AB Diesels Motorer, which had been founded by the Wallenbergs in 1898 to acquire the Swedish patent rights for the engine developed by the German engineer Rudolf Diesel.

Atlas had cooperated with Diesels Motorer from the beginning in developing the engine for commercial use, while acquiring a minority stake in the engine concern. Diesels Motorer first developed a stationary engine for power generation, followed later by a marine engine. After several difficult years during which large investments were needed to perfect the engine, Diesel Motorer reported its first profit in 1906 and found growing export markets in both the United States and Russia as sales of the marine engine climbed.

The creation of the new company, Atlas Diesel, came at a time when demand for its products was strong due to World War I, producing good prices and profits, as neutral Sweden supplied both sides of the conflict. The merger also meant that Stockholms Enskilda Bank, which owned two-thirds of Nya Atlas and half of Diesels Motorer, could gain a profit from its long-term investment in the two concerns while retaining 40 percent of the share capital in the new company, which was now valued at two-and-a-half times the worth of the combined figures of its component companies. Nya Atlas President Jacobsson was appointed head of the new company.

Atlas Diesel began life with a healthy order book. The company's exports were dominated by diesel engines, which accounted for four-fifths of total foreign sales. These consisted mainly of marine engines supplied to the Allied nations to power their naval vessels. The end of the war brought with it a weakening in the business cycle. Deflationary policies were adopted in major export markets and deliveries to Russia were disrupted by revolution and civil war. By 1920, profits were practically nonexistent; during the next four years the company ran up heavy losses as the diesel engine business in particular suffered setbacks.

Debts mounted and Stockholms Enskilda Bank had to provide further credit. The company embarked on a cost-cutting program, selling its headquarters in Stockholm and reducing its workforce from a peak of 1,450 in 1917 to 240 in 1923. With the company regarded as overcapitalized, the share capital was drastically reduced from SKr 220 million to SKr 10 million in 1923 and SKr 5 million in 1925. To reduce the debt burden, most of the old Atlas facilities were then sold and the production of compressors and pneumatic products was moved to the southern Stockholm suburb of Sickla, where Diesel had its factories.

The completion of the financial reorganization and concentration of production at Atlas Diesel occurred as Sweden was emerging from the economic crisis of the early 1920s. Sales improved for both pneumatic products and engines, but interest payments and depreciation charges kept profits low. Moreover, Atlas Diesel was concentrating its resources on the diesel engine business, although sales of pneumatic tools were providing almost all of the profits. Management, dominated by engineers, favored investment in diesel engines because it was the company's most technologically advanced product group and therefore enjoyed great prestige. The company thus was in a poor financial position to withstand the effects of the 1930s Great Depression, which hit it with devastating effect. Atlas Diesel once again plunged into a deficit, and there were discussions about shutting down the company. Instead, Stockholms Enskilda Bank, the principal owner, decided to recapitalize the company.

The company's operations were modernized and rationalized under the strict supervision of the Wallenbergs, with emphasis placed on expanding the profitable pneumatic side of the business. Profitability recovered during the second half of the 1930s due to an improvement in the business cycle resulting from rearmament programs across Europe. Sales of pneumatic tools tripled between 1935 and 1939, while engine sales doubled. Dividends were paid to shareholders in 1935, for the first time since 1919.

In 1940 Gunnar Jacobsson, who had been president for more than 30 years, stepped down and was replaced by Walter Wehtje, a close friend of Marcus Wallenberg, Jr., the board chairman. Wehtje continued shifting the focus of the company from diesel engines, which had grown so technologically complex that their sales could not even cover their manufacturing costs, to the compressed air division, which had become the company's sales leader at the beginning of the 1930s and accounted for two-thirds of sales by the end of the decade. Nevertheless, the engine business was expanded during World War II as Atlas Diesel supplied motors for torpedo boats, and hydraulic gears used in other military equipment for the Swedish armed forces.

Postwar Developments

In the early postwar years, Wehtje decided that the company's manufacturing of diesel engines could not continue, and in 1948 the diesel engine division was sold to Nydqvist & Holm. Simultaneously, Wehtje decided to expand the air compressor division, sales for which had already doubled during World War II, by setting up a network of sales subsidiaries and agents around the world. This network was to be complemented by an expansion of production capacity in Sweden and the acquisition of manufacturing plants abroad. By this time, the company's compressed air tools had reached a high technical standard after years of research. It had pioneered a new technique of rock drilling, called the Swedish method, by combining a lightweight rock drill with a tungsten carbide bit. This product, developed in cooperation with Sandvik, would soon help Atlas Diesel penetrate international markets.

Manufacturing capacity was increased by purchasing several troubled factories in Sweden to ease the production bottleneck at the Sickla facility. Atlas Diesel also acquired its biggest manufacturing site abroad in 1956 when it bought the Belgian compressor company Arpic, in Antwerp.

Although it had disposed of the diesel engine business, the company retained the name Atlas Diesel until 1955 when it was changed to Atlas Copco AB. Copco stood for Compagnie Pneumatique Commerciale, the name of a Belgian subsidiary that had been adopted in its abbreviated form by a number of Atlas affiliates in other countries.

By the mid-1950s, Wehtje's strategy of international expansion was paying off with exports accounting for 65 percent of total sales. In 1957 Wehtje retired at the age of 60, having seen sales increase from SKr 20 million to SKr 315 million, the number of subsidiaries triple to 24, and the workforce expand from 1,500 to 6,000. His successor was Kurt-Allan Belfrage, a former diplomat and deputy managing director.

During the 1960s, the company's annual sales more than tripled from SKr 380 million to SKr 1.28 billion. As market demand grew, plants were acquired in Denmark, Italy, India, Brazil, Spain, and Mexico in addition to the existing facilities overseas in the United Kingdom, Finland, and Belgium. Popular products included portable compressors and new pneumatic hand tools in addition to rock drilling equipment. More than 80 percent of Altas Copco's sales were outside Scandinavia. Profits fluctuated during the 1960s due to increased costs, such as sharply rising wages, research and development investment, and marketing activity.

Atlas Copco underwent a reorganization in 1968 in an effort to promote decentralized management, with the company split into three basic groups: Atlas Copco MCT (mining and construction equipment), Atlas Copco Tools (industrial technology), and Atlas Copco Airpower (compressors). When Belfrage retired in 1970, the company's workforce had grown to 13,000 with a presence in 34 countries.

Erik Johnsson, the deputy manager for sales, was appointed the new president. He was replaced in 1975 by Tom Wachtmeister, who had held several senior positions in the company, including director of corporate planning. Strong global demand resulted in more than quadrupling sales during the 1970s. Atlas Copco reported a turnover of SKr 5.3 billion by the end of the decade.

Rationalized Operations in the 1980s

Atlas Copco was put to the test in the early 1980s when a worldwide recession left the company reeling with a sharp fall in profits in 1982 and 1983. Wachtmeister oversaw a stringent rationalization program that included shutting down one-quarter of the company's 46 factories and shedding one-fifth of the 20,000-strong workforce. He also decided to shift the product emphasis away from mining equipment, which had generated 65 percent of the turnover in the late 1970s but had suffered a sizable drop in sales during the recession.

Atlas Copco experienced a recovery in profits in 1984 and 1985 due to renewed demand in Western Europe as well as the devaluation of the Swedish krona in 1982, an important development for a company that generated 92 percent of its sales outside Sweden. Atlas Copco suffered another setback in profits in 1986 due to unexpected foreign exchange losses.

The company's results improved sharply in the late 1980s. Between 1987 and 1989, earnings climbed by 109 percent to SKr 1.53 billion. The upswing in the company's fortunes could be traced to its strategy of concentrating on its core product areas, unlike its more diversified rivals. The strategy reflected Wachtmeister's belief that Atlas Copco should dominate every market segment in which it was active. It also stemmed from the policy within the Wallenberg sphere that companies belonging to it should not compete with each other. This policy prevented Atlas Copco from expanding into the related area of robotics, which was the preserve of another Wallenberg concern, ASEA AB (later known as ABB AB, the Swedish half of ABB Asea Brown Boveri Ltd. and a major player in the worldwide power generation and electrical power transmission and distribution industries.)

Starting in 1987, Atlas Copco began acquiring other companies to build up its market position, particularly concentrating on widening the product line in the Atlas Copco Tools division, which was headed by Michael Treschow. Treschow adopted a strategy of acquiring top brands and by the early 1990s had transformed the Tools division into the multibrand Industrial division. The major acquisitions that shaped the Industrial division through 1991 were: U.S.-based Chicago Pneumatic Tool Co., which was acquired in 1987 and instantly made Atlas Copco the world's largest maker of compressed air tools and assembly systems; SA Ets Georges Renault—acquired in 1988—a French maker of industrial tools, primarily grinding/sanding machines and small assembly systems; and U.K.-based Desoutter Brothers plc, a manufacturer of a broad range of industrial tools and assembly units. In acquisitions outside of the industrial tools sector, Atlas in 1988 took over Secoroc, a manufacturer of rock-drill bits. This purchase led to a price war with the Swedish concern Sandvik, which formerly cooperated with Atlas Copco in marketing drill bits.

Recession and Acquisitions in the 1990s

In 1991 Treschow took over as chief executive from Wachtmeister. The new leader immediately had to contend with the deep recession of the early 1990s. He reacted with a massive restructuring, cutting the workforce by 30 percent, with the number of employees bottoming out at 18,104 in 1994. Treschow also gave each Atlas Copco division manager complete worldwide responsibility for his division, with profit and loss statements and balance sheets compiled for each so that each manager's performance could be measured. Through these steps, Atlas Copco remained in the black throughout the recession, despite a revenue decline of 25 percent from 1990 to 1993.

During and in the immediate years after the recession, Atlas Copco continued to aggressively pursue acquisitions. The Industrial division gained additional breadth through the acquisition of two makers of electric tools: AEG Elektrowerkzeuge of Germany and Milwaukee Electric Tool. The latter, a $550 million deal, was the largest purchase in Atlas Copco history and brought to the company a privately held group that claimed more than 20 percent of the U.S. electric tool market for industrial and professional use. Atlas Copco also created a number of joint ventures in the emerging nation of China from 1993 through 1997, encompassing construction machinery, compressors, and electric power tools.

In early 1997 Treschow left Atlas Copco to become chief executive at AB Electrolux, after that company had lost its chief executive to AB Volvo. Replacing Treschow was the head of Atlas Copco's Compressor division, Giulio Mazzalupi, a native of Italy. Mazzalupi wasted no time making his mark on the company, engineering another record acquisition, that of Prime Service, Inc., which was bought for $900 million in mid-1997. Acquiring Prime Service, the number two U.S. industrial equipment rental company, extended Atlas Copco into equipment rental, a rapidly growing sector in the United States, where increasing numbers of companies were renting equipment rather than purchasing it. Moving into rental provided Atlas Copco with a different method of reaching its same customers. Among Prime Service's rental products were air compressors, forklift trucks, mechanical loaders, light construction equip-

ment, and power tools. Following the acquisition and through the end of 1998, Prime Service acquired eight equipment rental companies in the United States and Mexico with aggregate annual revenues of SKr 900 million ($114 million). Initially part of the Compressor division, Prime Service became the core of the newly formed Rental Service division, which constituted a fourth business area for Atlas Copco.

Through the acquisitions of Chicago Pneumatic, Milwaukee Electric Tool, Prime Service, and other U.S. companies, Atlas Copco had significantly expanded its North American activities. In the early 1990s only about 15 percent of company revenues had been generated in North America, but that figure had increased to 37 percent by 1998, nearly equaling that of Europe (which stood at 40 percent). Thanks in large measure to the strongly performing Prime Service, Atlas Copco's revenues reached SKr 33.74 billion ($4.28 billion), a 12 percent increase over the previous year, and operating profits hit SKr 4.35 billion ($552 million), an increase of 14 percent. With the company's continuing focus on growth through acquisition, these figures were likely to continue their upward trajectory.

Principal Subsidiaries

Atlas Copco Rock Drills AB; Atlas Copco Craelius AB; Uniroc AB; Atlas Copco Berema AB; Atlas Copco Tools AB; Robbins Europe AB; Atlas Copco Controls AB; Atlas Copco Construction and Mining Export AB; Atlas Copco MCT Sverige AB; Atlas Copco Iran AB; Atlas Copco Compressor AB; Atlas Copco Ges.m.b.H. (Austria); Atlas Copco Brasil Ltda. (Brazil); Atlas Copco Tools spol s.r.o. (Czech Republic); Atlas Copco Chilena S.A.C. (Chile); Atlas Copco (Cyprus) Ltd.; Atlas Copco Kompressorteknik A/S (Denmark); Atlas Copco (India) Ltd. (40%); Atlas Copco KK (Japan); Atlas Copco Kenya Ltd.; Atlas Copco (Malaysia), Sdn. Bhd. (70%); Atlas Copco Maroc SA. (Morocco; 96%); Atlas Copco (Philippines) Inc.; Soc. Atlas Copco de Portugal Lda.; Atlas Copco (South-East Asia) Pte. Ltd. (Singapore); Atlas Copco (Schweiz) AG (Switzerland); Atlas Copco Venezuela S.A.; Oy Atlas Copco Ab (Finland); Atlas Copco France Holding S.A.; Atlas Copco Holding GmbH (Germany); Atlas Copco UK Holdings Ltd.; Atlas Copco Beheer b.v. (Netherlands); Atlas Copco S.A.E. (Spain); Atlas Copco Internationaal b.v. (Netherlands); Atlas Copco North America Inc. (U.S.); Atlas Copco Construction & Mining Technique AB; Industria Försäkrings AB; Atlas Copco Reinsurance S.A. (Luxembourg); Atlas Copco Fondaktiebolag.

Principal Divisions

Airtec; Portable Air; Industrial Air; Oil-Free Air; Atlas Copco Applied Compressor and Expander Technique; Atlas Copco Rock Drilling Equipment; Atlas Copco Craelius; Uniroc; Atlas Copco Construction Tools; Atlas Copco Wagner; Milwaukee Electric Tool; Atlas Copco Electric Tools; Atlas Copco Industrial Tools and Equipment; Alliance Tools; Prime Service.

Further Reading

Besser, Richard D., "Oh, to Be Bought by the Swedes," *Across the Board,* May 1990, pp. 39–41.
Brown, David, "Atlas Copco Changes Sales Tack," *Financial Times,* September 4, 1985.

Brown-Humes, Christopher, "Atlas Copco Buys US Tool Group for $550m," *Financial Times,* June 22, 1995, p. 30.

Burt, Tim, "A Tough Act to Follow," *Financial Times,* September 24, 1997, p. FTS2.

Burton, John, "Atlas Copco: Investor Faith Regained," *Financial Times,* July 3, 1990.

Gårdlund, Torsten, et al, *Atlas Copco 1873–1973: The Story of a World-Wide Compressed Air Company,* Stockholm: Atlas Copco, 1973.

Giertz, Eric, *The Atlas Copco Way,* Stockholm: Page One Publishing, 1998, 141 p.

McIvor, Greg, "Atlas Copco Buys US Equipment Hire Group," *Financial Times,* June 10, 1997, p. 30.

Moore, Stephen D., "Atlas Copco Will Acquire Prime Service for $900 Million in Bid to Spur Sales," *Wall Street Journal,* June 10, 1997, p. A4.

——, "Volvo CEO's Sudden Retirement Sparks Chain Reaction in Swedish Boardrooms," *Wall Street Journal,* January 28, 1997, p. A12.

"125 Innovative Years," anniversary issue of *Contact,* Stockholm: Atlas Copco, 1998.

Reed, Stanley, "The Wallenbergs' New Blood," *Business Week,* October 20, 1997, pp. 98, 102.

Verespej, Michael A., "Widespread Responsibility: Sweden-Based Buy Truly Global, Atlas Copco Finds That Universal Empowerment Can Be Highly Profitable," *Industry Week,* January 19, 1998, pp. 31+.

—John Burton
—updated by David E. Salamie

Bairnco Corporation

2251 Lucien Way
Suite 300
Maitland, Florida 32751-7037
U.S.A.
(407) 875-2222
Fax: (407) 875-3398
Web site: http://www.bairnco.com

Public Company
Incorporated: 1981
Employees: 816
Sales: $156.46 million (1998)
Stock Exchanges: New York
Ticker Symbol: BZ
NAIC: 322221 Coated & Laminated Packaging Paper &
   Plastics Film Manufacturing; 325211 Plastics Material
   & Resin Manufacturing; 32552 Adhesive Manufac-
   turing; 332213 Saw Blade & Handsaw Manufacturing;
   332211 Cutlery & Flatware Manufacturing; 332321
   Metal Window & Door Manufacturing; 333515
   Cutting Tool & Machine Tool Accessory
   Manufacturing; 334413 Semiconductor & Related
   Device Manufacturing; 334412 Circuit Boards,
   Printed, Bare, Manufacturing; 334220
   Communications Equipment, Mobile & Microwave,
   Manufacturing

Bairnco Corporation is a multinational company with sub-sidiaries operating in two business segments: engineered materials and components, and replacement products and ser-vices. Subsidiary Arlon, Inc. designs, manufactures, and sells engineered materials and components used in the electronic, industrial, and commercial markets. Its products include high-technology materials for printed circuit board industries, both commercial and military, in the United States, Europe, the Far East, and South America. Arlon also manufactures laminates providing high yields and high performance for microwave applications, such as in digital cordless telephones, direct broadcast satellite television systems, personal communications networks, and global positioning satellites. Finally, Arlon is also one of the most experienced vinyl film manufacturers in the world; under the Arlon brand name it markets specialty graphic films in a wide variety of colors, face stocks, and adhesive systems. Bairnco's other business segment, repre-sented by its Kasco Corporation subsidiary, manufactures and distributes replacement products and services to supermarkets; meat and delicatessen operations; and meat-, poultry-, and fish-processing plants throughout the United States, Canada, and Europe. These products and services are sold under several brand names: Kasco in the United States and Canada; Atlantic Service in the United Kingdom; and Bertram & Graf and Biro in continental Europe. In addition, Kasco distributes equipment to the supermarket and food-processing industries and also manu-factures small bandsaw blades for cutting metal and wood, as well as large bandsaw blades used at lumber mills.

The Early Years: 1967–89

Bairnco's origins may be traced to 1967, when Glenn W. Bailey bought a small company called Keene Packaging Com-pany, ''a producer of heat-sealed plastic packaging,'' according to Feder's story in the March 23, 1982 *New York Times*. Bailey previously had run 11 companies for Harold S. Geneen, the builder of the giant conglomerate that became known as the International Telephone and Telegraph Corporation. Using Geneen's growth strategy as a model, Bailey developed Keene by acquiring new companies in order to diversify into microcir-cuits, industrial bearings, fireproofing material, lighting fix-tures, and advanced composite materials. In 1968 he made his fourth acquisition, that of Baldwin-Ehret-Hill Inc., a manufac-turer of insulation with $30 million in annual sales, about $4 million of which was derived from asbestos products. That acquisition would become a nightmare for Bailey, who told news writer Feder that it was not until 1971 that he ''first heard there might be problems with asbestos.'' The problems materi-alized and then lingered for many years.

Although asbestos products were dropped from the Baldwin line in 1972 and the major part of that company's operations were eventually sold, Keene became an "asbestos victim": lawyers included Keene with other asbestos producers as defendants in thousands of lawsuits. "Partly because Wall Street was unenthusiastic about conglomerates and partly because of the asbestos cloud hanging over Keene, in the late 1970s the company's shares seldom edged above an unimpressive price/earning ratio of 6 during the late 1970s," according to Feder's story. However, despite a slump in sales during the 1974–75 recession, net income and sales grew steadily.

In an effort to draw the attention of Wall Street to the fact that Keene was a highly viable company, in April 1981 Bailey—with himself as chairman, president, and chief executive officer—established Bairnco (*bairn* is the Scottish word for child) as a holding company. His business plan, according to a case study in the July–August 1990 issue of *Harvard Business Review*, "was to acquire a family of separate companies with single or focused product lines, nurture them to the point where they may stand successfully on their own, and then spin them off to its shareholders—that is, to buy, build, and harvest." By implementing this strategy, Bailey rewarded investors and motivated entrepreneurship in the subsidiaries. He instituted basic management controls for all the 22 companies acquired since 1967, and Bairnco's slogan, "We grow companies," drew investors.

Over the long term, Bailey's strategy generated exceptional returns. For example, according to the *Harvard Business Review* case study, "an investor who held $1,000 worth of Bairnco shares on December 31, 1978, and who maintained the holdings in Bairnco plus its spinoff companies, would have held shares worth $14,551 ten years later—a 31 percent compound annual return—almost double the return from a similar investment in the Standard & Poor's '500'."

By year-end 1981, Keene—then a Bairnco subsidiary—had disposed of 2,425 of its asbestos cases, but the parent company remained questionably responsible for nearly 9,000 lawsuits. The other acquired companies were reorganized along specialty lines and grouped into five subsidiaries: Kaydon Corp. in Muskegon, Michigan; Genlyte Inc. in Secaucus, New Jersey; Kasco Corp. in St. Louis; Arlon Inc. in Rancho Cucamonga, California; and Shielding Systems Corp. in Norwalk, Connecticut. Kaydon and Genlyte were divested in 1984 and 1986, respectively.

In 1988 Bairnco generated revenues of close to $230 million, but the millions of dollars swallowed up by litigation penalized the company's earnings, with an estimated $260 million being paid for settlements from the mid-1970s to the late 1980s. While Keene's insurance companies covered all but $9 million, additional coverage remained in dispute. By year-end 1989, partly because of cutbacks in the U.S. defense budget, Keene and Shielding Systems reported losses of $1.9 million and $8.4 million, respectively. Still, the Arlon and Kasco subsidiaries cleared healthy profits. At the end of fiscal 1989 Bairnco's earnings were back in the black—a $7 million profit on sales of $196.6 million—and plans for another reorganization got underway.

Continuing Litigation in the Early 1990s

Chairman and President Bailey retired in May 1990. At that time, Luke E. Fichthorn III became chairman, and Richard A. Shantz took over as president. In June of that year Bairnco moved its headquarters from Manhattan to Maitland, Florida. Then the company spun off its Keene Corporation subsidiary, at a cost of $6 million. With these moves, Bairnco officials thought liability problems had ended, and Keene filed for relief under Chapter 11 of the Bankruptcy Code in 1993. However, on August 13, 1993, asbestos claimants filed a lawsuit against Bairnco and its five formerly or currently affiliated companies, accusing Keene Corporation of illegally spinning off key assets to its former parent company, a move, claimants asserted, made to avoid hundreds of millions of dollars in liability. Bairnco share prices tumbled to $4.125—from a high of $41 in 1987.

Maintaining that the claims against Bairnco were without merit and vowing to fight them, Fichthorn remarked in the August 14, 1993 issue of the *Orlando Sentinel* that "neither Bairnco nor any of its subsidiaries other than Keene ever produced or distributed asbestos products." Fichthorn further explained that Keene had ceased selling asbestos-related products before Bairnco had acquired it and that since 1990 Keene had operated separately from Bairnco.

Apart from its legal entanglements, Bairnco began focusing on its two core business segments—Arlon Engineered Materials and Components and Kasco Replacement Products and Services—and continued to divest itself of businesses not related to those two subsidiaries.

Refocusing Product Lines in the 1990s

Arlon's Electronic Substrates line included premium laminate products capable of sustaining the high temperatures needed in circuit boards for military electronics and sophisticated commercial applications, such as the surface-mount electronics for the Motorola worldwide satellite telephone system known as Iridium. The Microwave Materials product line produced the world's leading substrates for microwave applications. The business mix moved from a predominately military base to consumer products operating at microwave frequencies—digital cordless telephones, local and global cellular phone systems, direct-broadcast satellite television systems, global positioning satellite systems, and other personal communications equipment.

Under the Calon brand name, Bairnco also manufactured and marketed cast and calendered vinyl films for specialty graphics that were used by commercial sign manufacturers, graphic printing houses, and in other commercial and governmental-specification applications.

Under the Arlon brand name, Bairnco manufactured and marketed custom-engineered laminates and adhesives systems as well as a line of silicone-rubber materials used in consumer, industrial, and commercial products.

Through its multinational Kasco operations, Bairnco manufactured and supplied replacement products and services, principally to retail food stores, and to meat-, poultry-, and fish-processing plants throughout the United States, Canada, and Europe. Kasco made bandsaw blades for cutting and chopper plates and knives for grinding meat in supermarkets and packing plants; bandsaw blades for frozen-fish factories; small bandsaw blades for cutting metal and wood; and large bandsaw blades for lumber mills. During the fourth quarter of 1994, Bairnco decided to refocus Kasco's service-center program back to several selected market areas so that Kasco could provide cost-effective, value-added preventive maintenance and emergency service in confined geographical markets. Consequently, eight North American centers were closed.

Slow but Steady Progress in the Mid-1990s

Improvements in Arlon's results began to show the benefits of investing in the development of new markets as well as in expanding sales, marketing, and research efforts. During the first quarter, Kasco's reduced profits were disappointing, but by year-end a revised program was being implemented to make Kasco a value-added supplier of cost-efficient services to its customers. For fiscal 1994 Bairnco and its subsidiaries posted net sales of $145.52 million, compared to $135.58 million for 1992.

Bairnco's net sales increased 3.4 percent to $150.51 million in 1995. Arlon's sales of engineered materials and components increased 7.8 percent due to growing demand in the high-end and circuit board market but gross profit increased only 3.1 percent due to the impact of competitive pressures for lower-margin commercial products and attendant market erosion. Sales of Kasco replacement products and services declined 4.1 percent due to the reduction in Kasco's North American service-center revenues after the closing of eight centers. However, Kasco's gross-profit margin increased slightly due to an improved sales mix and reduced manufacturing costs.

Meanwhile, Keene Corporation emerged from Chapter 11 pursuant to a plan of reorganization approved in 1996. The Keene Plan provided for the creation of Keene Creditors Trust (KCT), a successor in interest to Keene. Bairnco and its subsidiaries remained entangled in legal battles, however, as the defendants in a lawsuit in which the KCT trustees, as plaintiffs, alleged "that certain sales of assets by Keene to other subsidiaries of Bairnco were fraudulent conveyances and otherwise violative of [New York State] law, as well as being violative of the civil RICO statute," according to the company's 1998 10-K annual report. It was not until the fourth quarter of 1998 that this legal matter approached a partial solution.

For 1996, Bairnco's sales of $150.23 million were slightly lower than those of 1995. Arlon's sales grew only 4.1 percent; however, sales to the graphics and electrical insulation markets continued to grow and more than offset lower sales to the electronics industry. Kasco's sales decreased 8.5 percent partly because of the program to refocus Kasco on its North American core business, partly because of decreased exports and reduced sales of equipment in Canada and France, and partly because of the severe impact of the "Mad Cow" disease on European meat consumption and the meat-processing markets.

During 1997, Arlon's Electronic Substrates and Microwave Materials product lines continued to implement lower-cost solutions in order to increase commercial sales and penetration of electronic applications in the consumer market. Significant investments in new equipment, product development, and research resulted in new lamination presses and expansion of the research and development laboratory, among other things.

Kasco remained the leading manufacturer and supplier of replacement products and services. The company had manufacturing facilities in St. Louis; Toronto; Gwent, Wales; and Pansdorf, Germany. In France, over and above producing replacement products, Kasco distributed equipment used in the supermarket and food-processing industries. Among the new products Kasco introduced in 1997 was the Predator Series of custom-splitter blades. These splitter blades reduced workplace noise, provided peak high-speed cutting, and lasted longer because of a unique Gold Tooth Hardening process. Kasco increased sales of its Mealtime Solutions seasoning program that allowed supermarkets to offer value-added products in their meat and delicatessen departments. The company moved its seasoning manufacturing plant from California to St. Louis, Missouri, and added a formulation lab and test kitchen.

During this time, Bairnco's board of directors authorized $5 million for ongoing repurchase of its common stock. Net sales for fiscal 1997 increased 5.6 percent to $158.71 million from $150.23 million in 1996. Arlon's sales increased 8.3 percent: all its markets experienced growth though there was substantial volatility within the electronics industry. Kasco's sales declined 0.2 percent: growth in the U.S. markets—especially in the seasonings for ready-to-cook foods for supermarkets and special products areas—was offset by the planned discontinuation of equipment sales in some Canadian markets. Furthermore, Kasco suffered from the negative impact of currency translation rates on sales of its European operations.

Toward the New Millennium: 1998 and Beyond

In 1998 Bairnco's board of directors authorized the repurchase of up to another $5 million of its common stock, in addition to the $3.5 million still unused from the $5 million authorized for this purpose in 1997. During 1998 Bairnco repurchased 737,400 shares for $6.2 million and was authorized to continue its stock repurchase program in 1999. At year-end 1998, $2.5 million remained available for additional stock repurchases.

Arlon introduced ProFleet, a pressure-sensitive vinyl product specifically designed for fleet and vehicle graphics. In September a new product line of electrostatic media was put on the market: the Imageburst electrostatic media line included StatPrint HP, StatPrint Intermediate, and StatPrint Promotional. Then, in November 1998 Bairnco purchased Northbrook, Illinois-based MII International, Inc., a manufacturer of adhesive-coated films for use in the graphics and industrial markets. MII's product lines complemented Arlon's vinyl product lines, expanded Arlon's coating and converting capacity, and provided additional brand recognition and new customer segments.

During 1998, Kasco improved several designs of its bandsaw blades, chopper plates, and knives. The company introduced a line of premium wood-cutting bandsaw blades for professional cabinetry and furniture makers. The Mealtime Solutions seasoning program continued to be popular for home-meal replacement items in supermarkets; several new product lines expanded the Mealtime Solutions program into delicatessen and seafood departments. Kasco placed greater emphasis on preventive maintenance, thereby increasing the value-added service given to its customers.

During the fourth quarter of 1998, the Transaction Lawsuit initiated in 1996 by KCT trustees against Bairnco and its subsidiaries again came to the fore. The plaintiffs alleged that Bairnco and others were derivatively liable for the asbestos-related claims against its former subsidiary, Keene Corporation, and wanted "compensatory damages of $700 million, interest, punitive damages, and trebling of the compensatory damages pursuant to civil RICO," according to Bairnco's 1998 annual report.

In a series of decisions that remained subject to appeal, the U.S. District Court for the Southern District of New York "dismissed plaintiff's civil RICO claims; dismissed 14 of the 21 defendants named in the complaint, and partially granted defendants' motions for summary judgment on statute of limitations grounds." All other claims were under investigation. These other claims included some against Bairnco, but company management believed that it had "meritorious defenses to all claims or liability purportedly derived from Keene and that it . . . [was] not liable, as an alter ego, successor, fraudulent transferee or otherwise, for the asbestos-related claims against Keene or with respect to Keene products." To that end, in the fourth quarter Bairnco set aside $7.5 million as a pre-tax provision for anticipated litigation costs.

Sales for fiscal 1998 decreased to $158.71 million in 1997 to $156.46 million in 1998. Operating profit before the provision for litigation costs was $12.03 million, down from $15.6 million in 1997. Weak demand in Bairnco's electronics markets was partly responsible for the dip in sales, while the lingering litigation about asbestos and other claims did not help the stock price. However, in a letter prefacing Bairnco's 1998 annual report, Chairman Fichthorn said that "the management development program, which is one of the keys to our future success, continued to make progress in all operations." He added that additional projects had been identified and that the outlook for 1999 was for improved sales and earnings." He expressed the belief that the company "would recover most of the ground lost in 1998" through the combination of growth from new products, higher growth in certain niche markets, and programs for continuing efficiency and yield improvement. At the approach of the 21st century, judging from Bairnco's past performance in overcoming obstacles, it did seem that the company was again headed for profitability.

Principal Subsidiaries

Arlon, Inc.; Kasco Corporation; Bairnco Foreign Sales Corporation (Barbados); Bertram & Graf Gmbh (Germany); Invabond Ltd. (Ireland); Atlantic Service Co. Ltd. (Canada); Atlantic Service Co. (UK) Ltd., (98.9%); EuroKasco S.A. (France).

Further Reading

"Asbestos Claimants File Lawsuit Against Keene," *New York Times,* International Section, August 14, 1993, p. 35.

"Bairnco Adopts a Reorganization," *New York Times,* January 25, 1990, p. D4.

"Bairnco Corp. Coming to Town," *Orlando Sentinel,* May 21, 1990.

Beall, Pat, "New Asbestos Suits Burn Bairnco on Friday the 13th," *Orlando Business Journal,* August 20, 1993, p. 20.

Burnett, Richard, "Making Corporate Juggling Pay, Bairnco Moves Act to Maitland, Spins Off Troubled Subsidiary," *Orlando Sentinel,* August 20, 1990, p. 21.

Feder, Barnaby J., "Bairnco: A Neo-Conglomerate," *New York Times,* March 23, 1982, pp. D1, D21.

Koenig, John, "Do These Central Florida Companies Deserve Stock Bashings?," *Orlando Sentinel,* March 4, 1999, p. B1.

Marcial, Gene G., "Will Bairnco Turn into a Comeback Kid?," *Business Week,* August 10, 1992, p. 63.

Snyder, Jack, "Investors Dump Bairnco Shares Over Asbestos Suit," *Orlando Sentinel,* August 14, 1993, p. D1.

Stewart, G. Bennett III, "Remaking the Public Corporation from Within," *Harvard Business Review,* July–August 1990, pp. 134–35.

—Gloria A. Lemieux

Baker and Botts, L.L.P.

One Shell Plaza, 910 Louisiana
Houston, Texas 77002-4995
U.S.A.
(713) 229-1234
Fax: (713) 229-1522
Web site: http://www.bakerbotts.com

Private Partnership
Founded: 1840 as Peter W. Gray
Employees: 1,300
Sales: $206 million (1998 est.)
NAIC: 54111 Offices of Lawyers

With branch offices in Dallas, Austin, New York, London, Moscow, Washington, D.C., and Baku, Azerbaijan, the Houston-based law firm Baker & Botts, L.L.P. ranks among the 50 largest law firms in the world, based on gross revenues and number of attorneys. It represents over half the *Fortune* 500 companies and many other clients, including charitable organizations, government agencies, estates, and individuals. Four generations of Bakers, including former U.S. Secretary of the Treasury and Secretary of State James A. Baker III, have been part of this firm that has played a key role in making Houston a modern city. From its historic representation of railroads, oil companies, utilities, and banks, the firm has diversified in the late 20th century to provide counsel to new kinds of companies, particularly those involving computers, telecommunications, biotechnology, and intellectual property issues. Baker & Botts's ability to serve its clients' overseas interests is strengthened by its affiliation with Lex Mundi, a global association of independent law firms.

Origins and Developments from 1840 to 1914

Baker & Botts began in 1840 when Peter W. Gray started practicing law. Assisting him was his father, William Fairfax Gray, who died just a year later. Peter Gray wrote the first Texas law codes after statehood in 1845. After he and "Colonel" Walter Browne Botts both served in the Confederacy during the

Civil War, they formed a partnership that in 1872 was joined by Judge James Addison Baker. After Gray joined the Texas Supreme Court in 1875, the firm became Baker & Botts. Other partners over several decades added to the firm's name, but in 1971 it returned to Baker & Botts as the permanent name.

For years most of the firm's work centered on serving mostly local clients. However, the firm began to change when it started representing railroads owned by Texans after the Civil War. Once those railroads expanded and consolidated and were taken over by northern and eastern investors, the law firm expanded its perspectives and practice. In 1893 it became general counsel for Southern Pacific, as all railroads dealt with the regulations from the federal Interstate Commerce Act of 1887.

Authors Lipartito and Pratt described Baker & Botts from 1866 to 1914 as "an elite firm in a colonial economy," meaning that the Texas economy, including railroads, oil, utilities, and other industries, were dominated by outside corporations that needed the help of local attorneys. Because of the hodgepodge of laws from state to state, well-connected local lawyers such as those at Baker & Botts played a key role in the expansion of large corporations in Texas.

During this time, Judge Baker's son "Captain" James A. Baker began his long, prominent career with Baker & Botts. One of his and the firm's most celebrated cases involved Houston's William Marsh Rice, a prominent businessman who first used the services of Peter Gray in 1840. Rice wanted a Houston institution of higher education to inherit his money, which Captain Baker helped make a reality. First, he contested a will of Rice's wife that funneled money to other causes. After Rice died suddenly in New York City in 1900, two men claimed his inheritance. Captain Baker traveled to New York City because of reports of foul play. It was soon discovered that Rice had been murdered and one of the murderers, a local attorney, had prepared a false will. That allowed Rice's money to finally fund Houston's Rice University.

Meanwhile, oil fever struck Texas, starting in 1901 with the major strike at Spindletop. Soon major firms established refineries on the Louisiana-Texas Gulf Coast and opened offices in Houston. Baker & Botts's first major oil client was the Texas

Company (Texaco), which paid the firm a retainer from 1914 through 1954. Although Texaco soon became a major national and international law firm, Baker & Botts's role for several years was to help Texaco deal with Texas laws.

A Growing Regional Firm, 1915–29

In 1914 Captain Baker presided over opening the Houston ship channel to the Gulf of Mexico, which allowed the city to bypass Galveston as the major port in that area. The channel tied Houston to the rest of the nation and helped the law firm become a leading regional law firm. Baker & Botts became a major law firm in the oil industry, but it continued to specialize in Texas law.

Baker & Botts also played a role in consolidating local utility companies during this period. The best example was its representation of Electric Bond & Share Company (EBASCO), the Chicago-based holding company. In the 1920s the firm helped EBASCO finance its acquisition of local power companies that did not have the resources to respond to Houston's growing need for electricity.

A National Practice, 1930–89

The Great Depression not only retarded the Texas regional economy; it also brought major new federal laws and regulations impacting many industries. For example, the Securities and Exchange Commission changed stock trading, and the Wagner Act increased the power of unions and changed labor laws. Lipartito and Pratt called it the "federalization" of corporate law. Responding to the New Deal legislation, Baker & Botts decided to move beyond Texas law and master the new federal legal requirements and thus become more of a national law firm akin to those on Wall Street.

In the 1930s Baker & Botts instituted an antinepotism rule to prevent family members from having undue influence in firm management. In its early decades several members of the Baker and Botts families ran the show, but becoming a national law firm required a more professional approach based simply on qualifications and experience.

After World War II, the booming Houston economy, led by the oil, natural gas, and chemical industries, brought the firm more nationally prominent clients. In the 1950s James A. Baker, Jr., began his career at Baker & Botts, following in his father's and grandfather's steps.

The firm increased from 47 to 132 attorneys between 1948 and 1968. Three years later it moved to new offices in One Shell Plaza, one of Houston's first modern skyscrapers.

In the 1970s and 1980s the firm began to add new attorneys who were not WASP (white-Anglo-Saxon-Protestant) males, including Jews, women, and blacks.

Baker & Botts added new offices in the 1970s and 1980s, starting in Washington, D.C., in 1972, in Austin a few years later, then in Dallas in 1985. This growth reflected expansion of clients' national and international business. It also resulted from growing competition within the legal profession, fueled by U.S. Supreme Court decisions that said professional restrictions on advertising violated the First Amendment and antitrust laws and

also by the publishing of financial data about law firms in the new 1979 magazine the *American Lawyer*. In addition, the newspaper *Texas Lawyer* began in 1987 to cover the finances of Texas law firms.

Such law firms as Baker & Botts grew rapidly in the last part of the 20th century partially because of the litigation explosion started in the 1960s. In 1964 the California Supreme Court in Vandermark v. Ford Motor Company ruled that a car dealership was liable for failed brakes on a car it had sold, "regardless of the obligations it assumed by contract." This and other cases led to what some have called the death of contracts and the rapid expansion of tort law and increased litigation. For example, Peter Huber in his well-documented 1988 book *Liability* wrote that, "The number of tort suits filed has increased steadily for over two decades. So has the probability that any given suit will conclude in an award. And the average size of awards has grown more rapidly still."

In one of Baker & Botts's major cases, close personal ties helped its client Pennzoil win over Texaco. Pennzoil had tried to acquire Getty Oil, but the deal fell through when Texaco purchased Getty. At that point Pennzoil sued Texaco for pressuring Getty to not complete its deal with Pennzoil. The jury decided that Texaco was guilty and should pay Pennzoil $10.5 billion. Texaco appealed and sought bankruptcy protection but finally in 1988 agreed to pay $3 billion in a cash settlement.

In 1988 Baker & Botts managing partner E. William Barnett said that Pennzoil v. Texaco had commanded his firm's attention more than any other in its long history. Several books resulted from this controversy, including James Shannon's *Texaco and the $10 Billion Jury* published by Prentice-Hall in 1988.

Challenges in the 1990s

In 1990 Baker & Botts's Dallas office hired about a dozen patent attorneys from the Dallas firm of Baker, Glast & Middleton. That "really represented a first step," said E. William Barnett in the May 21, 1990 *Houston Business Journal*. "The protection of intellectual property, technology, is more important than ever. That's particularly true in our part of the country. . . . The demand has grown enormously."

On November 1, 1997 the New York City firm of Brumbaugh, Graves, Donohue & Raymond merged with and became part of the New York Baker & Botts office. That merger resulted in Baker & Botts having over 100 attorneys specializing in intellectual property (IP) issues, the most in "any general firm in the country," according to Scott Partridge, the head of Baker & Botts's intellectual property practice in Houston, in the December 12, 1997 *Houston Business Journal*.

The rapidly growing IP specialty included patent lawsuits, which accounted for about 75 percent of all IP suits, and trade secrets theft, which were difficult to prove in court. Sometimes the cure for IP violations, namely litigation, was worse than the original problem because of huge legal fees. For example, Houston's Tanox Biosystems faced $500 million in attorney fees in one case. This excessive cost of litigation hurt not only companies but also consumers, for firms pass on their expenses to their customers.

Baker & Botts IP attorneys helped i2 Technologies become a public corporation in 1996. The Dallas-based software firm had a market capitalization of almost $1 billion. The law firm's other high-tech clients included Electronic Data Systems Corporation, Dell Computer Corporation, Lucent Technologies, and Texas Instruments.

In 1998 Baker & Botts represented Tele-Communications, Inc. (TCI) in its $65 billion merger with AT&T. Its telecommunications clients also included GTE Corporation, Cablevision, and Primestar.

Based on its work around the Caspian Sea starting in 1992 representing Pennzoil, Azerbaijan International Operating Company, and Howard Energy International, and building on its long history in the oil industry, in 1998 Baker & Botts opened a branch office in Baku, Azerbaijan, under the supervision of the firm's Moscow office. Due to increased interest in oil near the Caspian Sea, many oil companies needed extra legal counsel in gaining oil rights, setting up joint operations, building pipelines, and establishing oil tanker routes.

In 1999 Baker & Botts continued representing oil firms, such as Chevron Corporation, Conoco Inc., Exxon Corporation, Marathon Oil Company, Occidental Petroleum Corporation, and Shell Oil Company. In 1998 the law firm worked on 11 oil and gas mergers, acquisitions, or spinoffs that each were valued at more than $1 billion.

Clients in the chemical industry included Dow Chemical, Equistar Chemicals, Huntsman Petrochemical Corporation, and Lyondell Chemical Company. Columbia University and William Marsh Rice University were representative educational clients. Several banks and financial institutions received Baker & Botts's legal counsel, including Bank of America, Chase Bank of Texas, Lehman Brothers, Merrill Lynch, Salomon Smith Barney, the Federal Deposit Insurance Corporation, and Donaldson, Lufkin & Jenrette Securities Corporation.

Other miscellaneous clients in the 1990s included United Parcel Service, the Houston Rockets, Prudential Insurance, the Republic of Yemen, Deloitte & Touche, Global Marine, Ford, New York Life Insurance, Mitsubishi, HealthSouth, Grupo Mexico, Andersen Consulting, and American Airlines.

Because many of these and other corporate clients were multinational corporations, Baker & Botts over the years forged working relationships with many overseas law firms, and then in the 1990s became the only Texas law firm to join Lex Mundi, a worldwide association of about 150 independent firms created in 1989.

Joining Lex Mundi or one of the other global law firm associations contrasted with two other strategies. Some law firms became linked internationally through ties with one of the large accounting firms. The third and less common approach was for a large law firm to start its own offices in many nations. With branch offices in 35 countries, Chicago's Baker & McKenzie exemplified this third strategy.

In spite of major changes, Baker & Botts in the 1990s continued one firm tradition by having James A. Baker III affiliated with the firm. Most of his career had been spent with

another law firm and then in the 1980s President Reagan chose him as secretary of state.

The *Texas Lawyer* ranked Baker & Botts, with 410 lawyers, as the state's third largest law firm, based on its 1995 gross revenues of $171 million. Fullbright & Jaworski was the largest Texas law firm, with 615 lawyers and $227 million in gross revenues, while the 512-lawyer firm of Vinson & Elkins ranked number two, with $217 million in gross revenues. These three firms all were based in Houston, which along with Dallas firms dominated the state's legal profession.

In 1995 about 2,250 lawyers practiced in Houston and also in Dallas. However, by 1998 Dallas firms employed 3,061 lawyers, compared to Houston's 2,441 lawyers. Moreover, the *Texas Lawyer* 1998 survey showed that Dallas law firm revenues were increasing at almost twice the rate of those in Houston. Baker & Botts, of course, had a major office in both cities.

In November 1998 the *American Lawyer*, in its first survey of the world's largest law firms, ranked Baker & Botts as number 50 based on the number of its lawyers. Only two percent of its 496 lawyers were based outside the United States. Thirty of those top 50 firms had less than ten percent of their lawyers working outside their home country. Based on its gross revenue of $206 million, Baker & Botts was ranked as number 44 in the world. With $80.8 million in 1998 net profits, the firm enjoyed a prosperity fueled by a generally good U.S. economy.

As the new century and millennium approached, Baker & Botts faced plenty of competition and challenges. Many corporations hired inhouse lawyers to avoid paying high fees to outside attorneys. Some lawyers left Baker & Botts for greener pastures with other firms or to start their own businesses. Other lawyers left the profession or worked part-time to avoid stress and long hours and to have more flexibility and time for their families. A self-help consumer movement was stimulated by the availability of knowledge on the Internet and standard legal forms found in inexpensive software packages. Independent paralegals tested the boundaries of what it meant to practice law. The profession itself came under intense criticism from academics, journalists, and the general public.

Although Baker & Botts had changed over the decades, it remained cognizant of its long history, as seen by the fact that it commissioned two professionals to write the firm's history without any restrictions, except for client confidentiality. It also deposited its records in the Baker & Botts Historical Collection at Rice University's Woodson Research Center. That willingness to learn from its heritage helped the firm prepare for the future.

Further Reading

"Baker & Botts to Establish Office in Azerbaijan," *Business Wire*, May 28, 1998, p. 1.

Bundy, Stephen M., "Commentary on 'Understanding Pennzoil v. Texaco': Rational Bargaining and Agency Problems," *Virginia Law Review*, March 1989, p. 343.

Cook, Lynn J., "Diverse Industries Heat up Houston's IP Legal Market," *Houston Business Journal*, December 12, 1997, p. 2B.

"The Global 50," *American Lawyer*, November 1998, pp. 45–49.

Greer, Jim, "Baker & Botts Raids Dallas Law Firm," *Houston Business Journal*, May 21, 1990, p. 1.

Huber, Peter W., *Liability: The Legal Revolution and Its Consequences,* New York: Basic Books, 1988.

Lipartito, Kenneth, "What Have Lawyers Done for American Business? The Case of Baker & Botts of Houston," *Business History Review*, Autumn 1990, p. 489.

Lipartito, Kenneth, and Joseph Pratt, *Baker & Botts in the Modern Development of Houston,* Austin: University of Texas Press, 1991.

Naj, Amal Kumar, "Manufacturing Gets a New Craze from Software: Speed—Recent Applications Cut Supply-Line Guesswork and Expand Capacity," *Wall Street Journal,* August 13, 1996, p. B4.

Palay, Thomas, "Baker and Botts in the Development of Modern Houston [book review]," *Business History Review*, Summer 1992, p. 389.

"Texas Is New Wild West for Law Firms," *Salt Lake Tribune*, November 26, 1998, p. D2.

—David M. Walden

Barnett Inc.

Barnett Inc.

3333 Lenox Avenue
Jacksonville, Florida 32254
U.S.A.
(904) 384-6530
Fax: (904) 388-4566
Web site: http://www.bntt.com

Public Company
Incorporated: 1958 as Barnett Tube Fitting and Valve
    Company
Employees: 657
Sales: $199.6 million (1998)
Stock Exchanges: NASDAQ
Ticker Symbol: BNTT
NAIC: 421720 Plumbing Equipment Wholesaling;
    421710 Hardware (Except Motor Vehicle)
    Wholesaling

Barnett Inc. is a worldwide provider of plumbing, electrical, and hardware products distributing its goods to professional contractors, independent hardware stores, and maintenance managers. Through its six distinct comprehensive catalogs, and its wholly owned subsidiary, U.S. Lock Corporation, Barnett sells more than 12,000 brand name and private label brands, including Barnett (electrical), ProPlus (plumbing), Premier (plumbing and electrical), and Legend (hardware) to approximately 72,700 total active customers. The sales are supported by a nationwide network of 37 distribution centers and a sophisticated telemarketing staff of more than 100 people. The company's products are produced by more than 400 suppliers worldwide.

Tubes and Valves in the Beginning

The business was founded as a catalog distributor in 1958 by the Barnett family in Jacksonville, Florida. In the beginning the company was known as Barnett Tube Fitting and Valve Company and it supplied copper tubing to its customers. At that time Barnett served a specific market niche but as time passed, the family recognized the increased need for a wider variety of plumbing supplies and fixtures. As the company diversified over the years, they changed its name as well; in 1972 the company became known as Barnett Brass & Copper Inc.

As the number of products it offered grew, Barnett developed a business plan that included regional distribution centers so that customers could get faster turnaround on their orders. To be competitive, Barnett realized that a quick response time to their customers' needs would be critical. Waiting for parts or plumbing supplies meant holdups and cost excesses during construction. Consequently, in 1978 Barnett built its first remote distribution center, with more in the planning stages.

The Waxman Connection:
The Mid-1980s Through Mid-1990s

In 1984 Barnett Brass & Copper, Inc. was purchased by Waxman Industries, Inc., a building supplies company, for $12.5 million. The acquisition brought Waxman new distribution outlets, such as hardware cooperatives and supermarkets, and allowed it to enter the mail-order market. Barnett's mail-order products line doubled when it added Waxman products to its offerings. By 1989 Barnett reached the $50 million mark in sales and had expanded its national distribution center network to ten warehouses. In 1993 Waxman formed Barnett Inc. to take the company public, but held out on the initial public offering (IPO) until 1996. Barnett immediately expanded its operations by introducing its second catalog for maintenance professionals, an offering of more than 7,000 products, and further expanded its distribution center network, which now numbered 25 warehouses.

In 1995 Barnett Inc. reached $100 million in sales for the first time and, in addition to its professional and maintenance catalogs, introduced a third catalog directed to its hardware customers. Numbers of products sold by the company were increasing rapidly and sales were reflecting a solid base of committed customers. In April 1996 Barnett Inc. completed its IPO, marking the start of a new era for the growing company. For the five years prior to the IPO, the company had experienced a 15 percent yearly growth. After its IPO, Barnett managed to nearly double its catalog mailings from 2.5 million to

4.5 million, resulting in a growth of its customer base from 13,000 to nearly 51,000 in just one year. This turned out to be only the beginning for Barnett.

Acquisitions and Growth in the Mid-1990s

In 1997 Barnett Inc. purchased LeRan Gas Products from Waxman Industries. LeRan was a direct marketer of liquid propane gas products. In the same year the company added warehouse locations in Bayamon, Puerto Rico, and Milwaukee, Wisconsin, bringing the number of warehouse outlets to 32. In 1997 Barnett also added 1,800 new items to its product line, hired more telesales support staff, and stepped up its mailings from 2.5 million flyers in 1996 to 4.5 million in 1997. The company's success did not go without notice. On November 3, 1997 *Forbes* magazine ranked Barnett as 60th in its list of the "Top 200 Best Small Companies in America." The following spring, the magazine *Catalog Age* listed Barnett as one of the "100 Largest Business-to-Business Companies in the Nation." CEO William R. Pray attributed Barnett's success to the talent and dedication of its employees and to a simple strategy: "All the expansion is from our cash flow. We have no debt."

By 1998 Barnett boasted a customer base of 65,000 customers and Pray had aggressive goals of increasing the number of its mailings to seven million. Barnett also was making plans to expand dramatically into such new markets as hotels, hospitals, and schools. Effective telesales had proven to be an important aspect of Barnett's strategy. All of its telesalespersons were required to go through extensive product and skills training over a period of several months and then were assigned a specific customer database with whom to develop positive service-oriented relationships. This, coupled with Barnett's distribution center network, gave it the ability to respond personally and quickly to every customer need. The commitment to customer service resulted in a high customer retention rate of 84 percent for Barnett as compared with the 65 percent overall average in the direct mail industry.

The year 1998 proved to be the strongest ever for Barnett as it positioned itself for future growth. It moved into its new 39,000-square-foot international headquarters and call center on Jacksonville, Florida's west side in the LaVilla district. Barnett also expanded product lines by ten percent and recorded a net sales gain of 24.7 percent. By this time the company had a product line of more than 11,900 items being distributed to countries throughout North America, South America, and the Caribbean. "Barnett is a highly energetic, highly focused com-

pany," said Jeffrey Germanotta, an analyst with Robert W. Baird in Milwaukee. In 1998 he forecasted Barnett's earnings to rise from 87 cents a share to $1.10 in fiscal 1999 and $1.37 in fiscal 2000.

For the Home and the World: 1998 and Beyond

Barnett entered into a strategic alliance with the Hechinger Company, a leading retailer of products and services in the care, repair, remodeling, and maintenance of the home and garden. In 1998 Hechinger operated more than 200 stores under the names of Hechinger, Home Quarters Warehouse, and Builder's Square. With the combined catalog and telemarketing strength of Barnett and the outside sales force of Hechinger, customers would experience a full line of products along with next day delivery service to nearly 95 percent of the U.S. market.

By year's end 1998, Barnett also purchased all of the assets of U.S. Lock from Waxman Industries, Inc. for approximately $33 million. U.S. Lock was a leading distributor of security hardware to locksmiths and other security hardware installers, distributing more than 8,500 national brand name and private label products through its telesales operations, catalogs, and monthly promotional flyers throughout the United States. At the time of the acquisition, William Pray stated: "We believe the acquisition of U.S. Lock is a good strategic fit for Barnett, combining two direct mail, telesales businesses that have similar business models. We are excited about the opportunity to fortify U.S. Lock's solid growth strategies. With the continued leadership of Michael Gene Merber as President of U.S. Lock, together with his strong management team and infrastructure currently in place, we believe U.S. Lock is competitively positioned for continued sales and profit growth. This transaction will be a credit to our earnings and there are many synergistic opportunities for the businesses."

Success would not be limited to the home front, however. Barnett began to broaden its business plan and expand overseas. In 1997 international sales were at six percent. By 1998 the company saw an increase in worldwide sales to ten percent of its business.

As the millennium came to a close, Barnett was stronger than ever. Net sales for the nine months that ended March 31, 1999 totaled $174.4 million compared with $148.0 million in the prior year period, an increase of 17.8 percent. The company's net income totaled $11.3 million, an increase of 8.9 percent over the same period the previous year.

Commenting on the company's progress, Pray said, "The third quarter of our fiscal year generated a very impressive revenue increase in excess of 29 percent and once again reached record levels, however, our revenue growth did not meet our expectations. A slower than anticipated rate of new product introductions in the quarter, coupled with a disappointing roll-out of the Hechinger program were the primary reasons for our lower than expected performance. We are very encouraged by our internal growth rate versus our core growth rate indicating that we are getting increased market share. Our U.S. Lock subsidiary performance was very impressive and met our expectations."

During 1999 Barnett also had plans to add about 2,000 new products to its line and continue expansion overseas. The company also was continuing to develop more cost-effective direct mailing techniques to ensure the highest possible return on the millions of direct mail pieces sent annually. Its six separate catalogs targeted specific groups such as contractors, hardware stores, multifamily lodgings, LP gas dealers, and export/international customers. The catalogs averaged 900 pages in length and were being sent out two or three times a year. In addition to the catalogs, monthly promotional flyers were being sent out to existing and potential customers. Barnett also continued its strategy of establishing regional distribution centers. The company opened its 34th distribution center in Parsippany, New Jersey, and U.S. Lock opened its sixth distribution center in Dallas, Texas, and had plans to open new centers in Orlando, Florida, and Phoenix, Arizona, by the fall of 1999.

Principal Subsidiaries

U.S. Lock Corporation.

Further Reading

"Barnett Inc. Reports Fourth Quarter and Fiscal Year End Results," *PR Newswire,* August 24, 1998.

Basch, Mark, "Mild Winter Hurts Barnett Inc. Sales," *Florida Times-Union,* March 26, 1998.

Bennett, Jane, "Investor's Forum Combined Fun and Finance," *Jacksonville Business Journal,* November 17, 1997.

"Debt Plan's Success Sends Waxman Aloft," *Plain Dealer,* March 28, 1996.

"Seeking Even Faster Growth," *Catalog Age,* June 1998.

Shailaja, Neelakantan, "A Spin-off to Success," *Forbes,* November 3, 1997.

"Waxman Completes Sale," *Plain Dealer,* July 4, 1997.

"Waxman Hopes to Ease Debt with Barnett Stock Offering," *Plain Dealer,* February 7, 1996.

"Waxman Industries, Inc. Reports Fourth Quarter and Year End Results," *PR Newswire,* August 27, 1998.

—J. D. Fromm

Barney's, Inc.

575 Fifth Avenue
New York, New York 10011
U.S.A.
(212) 826-8900
(888) 222-7639
Fax: (212) 450-8492

Private Company
Founded: 1923 as Barneys
Employees: 1,700
Sales: $343 million (1998 est.)
NAIC: 44811 Men's Clothing Stores; 44815 Clothing
Accessories Stores; 44812 Women's Clothing Stores;
44819 Other Clothing Stores

Barney's, Inc. is a specialty retailer of high-quality men's and women's clothing and accessories, as well as gifts, cosmetics, fragrances, housewares, jewelry, antiques, stationery, and luggage. It leases and operates three large stores in prime areas of New York City, Chicago, and Beverly Hills, California and a few smaller stores in lower Manhattan and other U.S. communities, plus several discount outlet stores. For decades Barney's was a single Manhattan store for cut-rate men's suits. Beginning in the 1960s it went upscale, and by 1990 it had established a chain of stores stretching as far as Tokyo. Because of overspending, the family-run company fell deeply into debt and filed for bankruptcy protection in January 1996. It emerged from bankruptcy three years later under new ownership.

Seventh-Avenue Clothing Store: 1923–88

Barney Pressman started out in the business by pressing pants for three cents each in his father's clothing store. He founded Barneys in 1923 with $500 raised by pawning his wife's engagement ring in order to lease a 500-square-foot retail space at Seventh Avenue and West 17th Street in Manhattan, with 20 feet of frontage and an awning on which were printed the words "Barney's Clothes." Pressman stocked the store with 40 name-brand suits and soon added a big sign reading "No Bunk, No Junk, No Imitations." Barney's was able to sell tailored clothing by noted manufacturers at prices well below list by purchasing showroom samples, retail overstocks, and manufacturers' close-outs, sometimes at auctions and bankruptcy sales. It also offered free alterations and free parking. As business grew, floors above street level were added to the store, beginning in 1934.

Barney Pressman knew how to publicize his wares as well as fill his store. He claimed to be the first Manhattan retailer to use radio and television, beginning with "Calling All Men to Barney's" radio spots in the 1930s, a parody of the introduction to the Dick Tracy show. To advertise Irish woolens, he sponsored radio programs featuring Irish tenors and bands playing jigs. Women encased in barrels gave away matchbooks with the store's name and address. He even chartered a boat to take 2,000 of his customers from Manhattan to Coney Island.

Barney Pressman's son, Fred, joined the business in 1946. The company had sales of about $13 million in 1965, when its name was Barney's Clothes Inc. Beginning in 1964, the store started to shed its discount image. Fred Pressman said in 1973, according to *Business Week,* that he became "convinced that the discount route definitely was not for us. My father and I have always hated cheap goods. . . . I didn't want to sell low-end merchandise. Now, many of those who chose to are verging on bankruptcy."

In 1970 Barney's erected an adjacent five-story building called the International House and added another floor to the original four-level store, which was renamed America House. International House, Fred Pressman promised, would feature complete collections of European designers, "from denim pants to $250 suits," not just a watered-down "potpourri of fabrics and models." The renovated America House, he said, would hold merchandise from "manufacturers who are in effect designers." Together, the wings now constituted—according to Barney's—the world's largest individual men's clothing store, occupying the entire Seventh Avenue block between 16th and 17th streets, with 100,000 square feet of selling space and 20 individual shops.

By 1973 Barney's had annual sales of $33 million and sales per square foot about double the average men's specialty store.

The store was stocking 60,000 suits and employing 232 tailors for alterations. It was carrying full lines of such designers as Bill Blass, Pierre Cardin, Christian Dior, and Hubert de Givenchy. Barney's was the first U.S. clothing store to stock the full line of Giorgio Armani, with whom it signed an exclusive agreement in 1976. Its 13 buyers were free to reorder at any time of year. The twice-a-year warehouse sale, a Manhattan event for which prospective customers lined up outside the store, took care of overstocked inventory.

Barney's started carrying women's clothing for the first time in 1976, on the third floor of the international side, with fashions from more than 20 houses represented. Fred's son Gene, who was responsible for the plunge into women's wear, moved the women's area to a new top-level enclosure called The Penthouse the following year. Barney's also added housewares, cosmetics, and gifts to its inventory during this period. In 1977 The Pub, Barney's' restaurant in the store serving only carved roast beef, was renamed The Cafe and began offering salads, soup, and other sandwiches.

At Gene's behest, the apostrophe in Barney's' name was dropped by 1979, and about 1981 the company name became Barneys Inc. and the store Barneys New York. In 1981 the women's penthouse became a duplex. Some 80 percent of the women's merchandise was being imported, compared to 40 percent of the men's goods. In 1986 Barneys completed construction of a 70,000-square-foot women's store in a row of six restored townhouses and two larger adjacent buildings along 17th Street, two years behind schedule and at a cost of more than $25 million. The new store included a unisex beauty salon and restaurant, antiques, and accessories, gifts, and housewares boutiques. The *New York Times* article by Michael Gross on the opening called it "at least the equal of the best of its kind in New York, in terms of space, design, display and merchandise." It accounted for about one-third of Barneys' sales of some $90 million the following year.

Going National and International: 1988–95

In 1988 Barneys opened a 10,000-square-foot store for men in lower Manhattan's swank World Financial Center. Soon after, the company announced it would build a national chain of as many as 100 clothing stores, starting with three in Manhasset, New York; Short Hills, New Jersey; and Newton, Massachusetts. The proposed new stores would offer 75 percent women's apparel and 25 percent menswear, with the company's own private-label merchandise representing about 20 percent of sales. The stores were to be run by Barneys America, with Gene Pressman and his brother Bob as co-chief executives. (They later became co-presidents of the parent company; their father ascended to chairman, serving until his death in 1996.) To meet the ambitious goals, however, the parent company needed investors, and Wall Street looked askance at what Joshua Levine called "several sets of financial statements, depending on who was supposed to be looking at them."

Barneys found the financial partner it was seeking in 1989, when it announced a joint venture with Isetan Co., one of Japan's largest retailers. The agreement provided for Isetan to hold 80 percent and the Pressman family 20 percent in stores to do business in Asia under the Barneys New York name. The first of these, opened in Tokyo in late 1990, was the largest U.S. specialty store in Japan. Barneys would own 65 percent and Isetan 35 percent of Barneys America, with plans to open more small, upscale specialty clothing stores in malls. (The parent company reinserted the apostrophe in "Barney's" about this time.)

The original three Northeastern Barney's America stores were so intimidating to some women that a secretary visiting the Manhasset store (on Long Island's tony North Shore) called it "the kind of place you'd have to dress up to go shopping." A reporter covering this store's opening wrote that "Even the babies were dressed to the nines." The first U.S. branches under the new agreement were opened in 1990 in Dallas, Seattle, and Costa Mesa, California. Like the three Northeastern stores, they featured mostly women's merchandise and carried no men's suits. The goods at the Costa Mesa store included what *Forbes* writer Lisa Gubernick called "items the industry generally describes as 'fashion forward'—stuff that you tend to see more in magazines than on real people," such as skin-tight synthetics by the French designer Jean Paul Gaultier. Blouses in the Seattle store by the Italian designer Romeo Gigli ranged from $275 to $480.

By October 1990 Barney's America had opened a seventh store in Westport, Connecticut, and had added tailored clothing for men. It also opened stores in Houston and Cleveland in 1991. Meanwhile, a joint venture half-owned by Barney's and Isetan each was buying property for large new Barney's stores in midtown Manhattan, Chicago, and Beverly Hills, with Isetan committed to providing $236 million in acquisition and construction costs. The Chicago store opened on the city's fashionable Near North Side in 1992.

For the new 230,000-square-foot Manhattan Barney's—the largest new store in New York City since the Great Depression—the joint venture purchased an 11-story building on Madison Avenue between East 60th and 61st streets. This structure was gutted for a 22-story building with 14 floors of offices above the store. Extravagantly furbished with flooring made of exotic woods—and a marble mosaic on the lobby floor—gold-leaf ceilings, and lacquered walls, the new Barney's cost $267 million, according to one account. It opened in 1993. The following year Barney's New York also opened, at a cost of $120 million, a 125,000-square-foot store in Beverly Hills, including a five-story underground garage hastily built to meet an unforeseen zoning ordinance.

The Madison Avenue store did good business in spite of stiff competition in its posh locale, but some of the trade was at the expense of the downtown store. Sales in Beverly Hills suffered from the recession-gripped California economy. Barney's America also played poorly in the provinces, where women were put off by hipper-than-thou black-on-black fashions and styling for pencil-thin models, with larger sizes sometimes hard to find. In Dallas, a flap developed when a Barney's employee said the beauty salon would not style "big hair." The Cleveland store closed in 1993. Company sales came to about $180 million that year and operating income to about $19 million.

By 1994 there were indications that Barney's' finances were in serious disarray. Some of the company's more than 7,000 vendors were refusing to furnish the chain with goods because of late payments—often as tardy as six months. The company's obsolete inventory and distribution systems were only beginning to respond to the installation of state-of-the-art computerization. There were tales about how the Pressmans—eight of them on the company payroll—helped themselves to store merchandise without accounting for it, according to the *New York Times* article "Haughty Couture" and Joshua Levine's "Let Them Wear Black." To relieve its cash-flow problems, Barney's turned to insurance companies, which purchased about $45-million worth of unsecured long-term notes.

In and Out of Bankruptcy: 1996–99

In September 1995 Barney's received a letter from Isetan, seeking to take control of the company after having spent $616 million on Barney's-related affairs, including about $168 million in emergency loans, personally guaranteed by the Pressman brothers, to cover the cost overruns for the Madison Avenue and Beverly Hills stores. Barney's also owed banks nearly $170 million and others about $150 million. Instead of reaching an agreement with its creditors, Barney's filed for Chapter 11 bankruptcy in January 1996. It was later revealed that in fiscal 1995 (the year ended July 31, 1995) the company lost $120.8 million on sales of $338.7 million.

Isetan, whose claims came to $480 million, won a judgment against the Pressmans for the loans they personally guaranteed. It also won title to the three Barney's New York stores in New York, Chicago, and Beverly Hills. The original Barney's closed in 1997. Four Barney's America stores, including the ones in Houston, Dallas, and Troy, Michigan, also closed in 1997. "Basically," Thomas C. Shull, who was named president of the parent firm, told the *New York Times* in August 1998: "Barney's had taken a New York store and placed it in other cities without really appreciating the needs and wants by market." He concentrated on making the enterprise more customer-friendly, "hip but not haughty."

Barney's, in fiscal 1996, lost $71.9 million, including a charge of $29.4 million for reorganization costs, on sales of $366.4 million. In fiscal 1997 the company lost $95 million, including a charge of $72.2 million for reorganization costs, on sales of $361.5 million. In fiscal 1998 it lost $20 million on sales of $343 million but recorded operating earnings of $17.7 million, compared to an operating loss of $2.1 million the year before. By the end of the summer of 1998 only seven Barney's stores remained in existence. In addition, there were 11 to 13 discount stores in early 1999 and a distribution center in Lyndhurst, New Jersey. Gene and Bob Pressman stepped down as chief executives of Barney's in June 1998.

A bankruptcy plan was approved in December 1998. It acknowledged Isetan's ownership of the three big stores and also granted the company a small equity stake of around 7.3 percent, $23.2 million in cash, and $15 million in annual rent payments by Barney's for the three big stores. Some 70 percent of the stock was allotted to Whippoorwill Associates Inc. and Bay Harbour Management L.C., so-called vulture investors who had bought Barney's' debt at an average of 40 cents on the dollar. In August 1998 they held $133 million (and about $149 million in December) of the estimated $320 million in secured claims and had provided, or had promised to provide, Barney's with an equity infusion of $62.5 million. They paid $240 million for their stake in the company. The Pressman family retained about 1.5 percent of the stock. Remaining trade claims against Barney's were selling for about 15 cents on the dollar in February 1998.

Further Reading

Conant, Jennet, "Bringing Down Barneys," *Vanity Fair*, May 1996, pp. 74+.

Enrico, Dottie, "Barneys' Grand Opening," *Newsday*, August 21, 1989, Part III, p. 8.

Ettore, Barbara, "Barney's Seeks Uptown Image," *New York Times*, June 2, 1978, pp. D1, D11.

Gross, Michael, "Barney's Unveils Women's Store (at Least)," *New York Times*, September 2, 1986, p. B6.

Gubernick, Lisa, "So Where Are the Overcoats?," *Forbes*, June 11, 1990, pp. 178–79.

Hochswender, Woody, "Those Bold Pressman Boys," *New York Times*, December 2, 1990, Sec. 3, pp. 1, 10.

Levine, Joshua, "Let Them Wear Black," *New York*, March 1, 1999, pp. 21–29, 121.

Morrisroe, Patricia, "Dressing Up Downtown," *New York*, October 20, 1986, pp. 38–45, 47.

Sloane, Leonard, "New Barney's Wing to Open Today," *New York Times*, September 30, 1970, pp. 59, 63.

Steinhauer, Jennifer, "Barneys Is Seeking Bankruptcy, Citing Fight with Partner," *New York Times*, January 12, 1996, pp. A1, D3.

——, "Hip But Not Haughty at Barneys New York," *New York Times*, August 25, 1998, pp. D1, D6.

Steinhauer, Jennifer, and Strom, Stephanie, "Haughty Couture," *New York Times*, January 21, 1996, Sec. 3, pp. 1, 10–11.

Strom, Stephanie, "Barney Pressman, Retailing Legend, Is Dead at 96," *New York Times*, August 27, 1991, p. D23.

——, "Did Barneys Overextend Itself? Not Really, It Insists," *New York Times*, July 24, 1994, Sec. 3, p. 4.

"A $33-Million Men's Shop Tries Social Climbing," *Business Week*, September 1, 1973, pp. 48–49.

Turner, Richard, "Will the Pressmans Lose Their Shirts?" *New York*, May 13, 1996, pp. 34–39.

—Robert Halasz

Blue Diamond Growers

1802 C Street
Sacramento, California 95814
U.S.A.
(916) 442-0771
Fax: (916) 329-3335
Web site: http://www.bluediamondgrowers.com

Cooperative
Founded: 1910
Employees: 1,200
Sales: $434.5 million (1998)
NAIC: 311911 Roasted Nuts & Peanut Butter
   Manufacturing

Blue Diamond Growers is the world's largest tree nut marketer and also ranks as one of the largest agricultural cooperatives in the United States. Headquartered near the almond-producing areas of the Sacramento and San Joaquin Valleys, the 4,000-member grower cooperative is known especially for its name brand California Blue Diamond Almonds. The co-op also produces a variety of nuts in special cuts, sizes, and shapes as well as a growing list of nut-based products, which it sells to retailers, supermarkets, the foodservice industry, and confectioners worldwide. Operations are centered on a 180-acre complex featuring a 1.75-million-square-foot plant, with a production capacity of more than two million pounds of almonds daily.

The Blue Diamond Story, 1910s–70s

California almond growers once sold their crops to independent dealers, negotiating price individually. In 1910, dissatisfied with returns, 230 growers formed the California Almond Growers Exchange, and hired professionals to run the organization. Each member was paid according to the amount and quality produced, and the group's overall commitment was to find better ways of marketing California almonds, both domestically and internationally.

In 1914 the Blue Diamond label was introduced, and a small receiving and packing plant was built in Sacramento. In 1922 shelling and grading equipment were added, and in 1929 a five-story processing plant was erected to handle the increased business volume. Over 2,000 growers had joined Blue Diamond by the end of the 1930s, seeking better productivity and marketing capabilities. By 1940 8,000 tons of almonds were being processed annually, and that volume increased during World War II to supply the Armed Forces.

Concrete storage bins, cold-storage facilities, and automated equipment were added following the war. In 1955 the organization's marketing division branched out, additional sales agents were hired, and a worldwide advertising campaign was launched. Commercial airlines were persuaded to carry foil packets of Smokehouse Almonds, and passengers from all over the world asked where they could purchase the snack. In 1960 electronic sorting machines were installed, and cooking and packing facilities expanded. National advertising sparked consumer interest in almond recipes and growers steadily increased crop output from 1968 on. In 1973 Stanford graduate Walter F. Payne joined the co-op as planning and marketing director, bringing a unique combination of farsightedness and a penchant for "team-playing" to his task.

Moving Ahead, 1980s–90s

In 1986 almond prices seemed stuck at $1 per pound. CEO Roger Baccigaluppi began an aggressive overseas marketing campaign, tailoring his pitch to each country's needs. Yearly contracts with guaranteed prices were provided in West Germany, the almond's nutritional value was emphasized in Russia, and new almond dishes were developed for the Japanese market.

In spite of these efforts, a lag in profits continued until 1992, when Walt Payne stepped in as president and CEO. He established a management team that cut across departmental lines, encouraged employees to find practical solutions to difficult problems, and ordered $30 million in plant improvements over the next decade. The improved operating efficiency paid off.

Company Perspectives:

In 1910, 230 growers banded together to form an agricultural cooperative called the California Almond Growers Exchange. Their commitment was to find better ways of bringing California almonds to both domestic and international markets. From the beginning, we've been the leader in the industry, and today, as Blue Diamond Growers, we're the world's largest tree nut company.

Record returns were posted over the next three years, and members were paid an unprecedented $344 million on the 1994 crop. Board Chairman Howard Isom stated at the 1995 board meeting that the cooperative's real strength was, "the commitment of its members, belief in their product, and the company's financial strength, which give it credibility and staying power."

In 1996 Jilian Morley, Blue Diamond's transportation manager, blasted the International Longshoremen's and Warehousemen's Union (ILWU) as a primary obstacle to international transportation. Since the almond industry spends over $100 million annually on transportation, the complaint did not go unheard. Morley spoke out again in 1997, decrying centralized customer service centers with little knowledge of almonds. Ocean exports are subject to carrier conference rates, but Blue Diamond's domestic transportation bids are let several times a year, allowing more flexibility over the terms of shipper contracts. Morley was not necessarily looking for the lowest bid for her organization, she stated, but she was more likely to go with brand name carriers who were willing to ensure quality service.

Blue Diamond's snack sales had reached $16 million in 1996, when a marketing agreement with candymaker Brach & Brock for Almond Supremes was announced. In January 1997 the firm linked with Hornsby's Amber Hard Cider to provide Super Bowl tie-ins. In June 1997 Algernon Greenlee, Blue Diamond's business manager of retail products, announced that the company would enter nationwide test markets with Nut Thins, a specialty cracker produced by Sesmark Foods. In September 1997 almonds were added to International Home Foods' Crunch 'n Munch ready-to-eat popcorn. Smokehouse Almonds were featured in the 1998 film *Sphere*, with movie lobby samplings, couponing, and point-of-purchase offers at supermarkets and convenience stores. The almond's positive aspects were substantiated by research and heavily advertised. World almond consumption, led by an expanding U.S. market, was on the upswing.

Record Returns Followed by Bad Weather, 1997–98

The year 1997 was an excellent one for almond production, with an early harvest and record shipments. Domestic consumption climbed, retail sales revenues increased, and prices remained firm. Some $370 million in distributable pool proceeds were returned to the growers, representing 77 percent of the

overall 1997 crop sales value, attributed in part to Walt Payne's new management team. Payne noted in a members' report that selling prices "are the result of the balance or imbalance between supply and demand. Our job is to create a shortage for your product so that you will continue to receive profitable returns." Payne's expertise was recognized when he was named 1998 CEO Outstanding Communicator of the Year by the Cooperative Communicators Association (CCA).

Following the record 1997 returns, negative weather conditions dominated sales activity through 1998, the fourth wettest winter recorded for California since 1849. Almond trees require good weather to bring out the bees needed for pollination, explained Heidi Savage of the Almond Board of California (ABC) in *Traffic World*. Receipts and shipments were lower than expected, caused in part by the late crop coupled with conservative overseas buying. The market continued to weaken through the end of 1998, and almond prices traded down to $1.47 per pound for projected 1999 shipments. On the plus side, an agreement was reached with Diamond Walnut, guaranteeing each company's right to ownership of the brand name of their specific product.

Based upon new members and plantings, Walt Payne warned in his 1998 year-end message that the "optimum handle level," or most cost-effective processing level, for Blue Diamond would soon be reached. Consequently, he asked that grower membership be closed effective January 31, 1999. By doing so, the cooperative hoped to guarantee a home for all current members. While non-member contracts would be honored, conversion to full membership in the group by outside growers could no longer be guaranteed.

Future Prospects for World's Largest Tree Nut Marketer

During the 1990s, Blue Diamond planting acreage doubled and crop tonnage tripled. Blue Diamond's goal for the future was to increase retained earnings and decrease reliance on revolving reserves to finance working capital needs. Smaller unsold inventories held at the end of the year translated into accelerated payments to growers. Exciting, "cutting edge" projects were on the horizon, including enhanced farming techniques that would allow delivery of a fully sterilized product without the use of fumigants. Through the Almond Research Center (ARC), staffed with scientists and technologists who worked with consumers to develop nutritional products, increasingly versatile uses for the almond continued to be discovered. The ARC's efforts in the area of nutrition were validated by other research, including a five-year study conducted by the University of Nevada School of Medicine, which found that nut consumers were more likely to maintain or lose body weight, and since 90 percent of fat in almonds was unsaturated, frequent consumption could also help lower blood cholesterol levels. The ARC continued to create innovative uses for almonds, including in cosmetics, soaps, and pharmaceutical products. The blending of nature and technology which began in 1910, when the first delivery of almonds arrived at the California Almond Growers Exchange, now thrived as a proud tradition of providing customers with the highest quality almond products available anywhere.

Further Reading

Allen, Graham, "Team Talk," *Rural Cooperatives*, May/June, 1998, p. 22.

Blue Diamond Almonds: From the Valleys of California, Sacramento, Calif.: California Almond Growers Exchange, 1960.

"Blue Diamond Almonds Star in *Sphere*," *Rural Cooperatives*, January/February, 1998, p. 24.

Blue Diamond Update, Sacramento, Calif.: California Almond Growers Exchange, 1983–.

Bushnell, Peter G., and Gordon A. King, *The Domestic and Export Markets for California Almonds*, Oakland, Calif.: Giannini Foundation of Agricultural Economics, 1986.

Carnal, Jim, "California's Largest Almond Grower Signs Contract with Blue Diamond," *Knight-Ridder/Tribune Business News*, April 24, 1996, p. 4240243.

Fitzgerald, Kate, "Smokehouse Almonds Makes Star Connection with *Sphere*," *Advertising Age*, February 16, 1998, p. 32.

Graebner, Lynn, "Blue Diamond Fires Up Lawsuit Over Its Trademark," *Sacramento Business Journal*, September 18, 1998, p. 5.

——, "Blue Diamond Strikes Deal with Big Grower," *Sacramento Business Journal*, April 29, 1996, p. 14.

——, "Small Crop, Big Returns for Almond Growers," *Sacramento Business Journal*, December 16, 1996, p. 12.

Gross, Amy E., "Blue Diamond: Nuts About Marketing," *AdWeek's Marketing Week*, May 1, 1989, p. 29.

"Hornsby's Blue Diamond Tie In for Super Bowl Redux," *Brandweek*, November 10, 1997, p. 5.

Jenkins, Michael, "Gaining a Financial Foothold Through Public Warehousing," *Journal of Business Strategy*, May–June, 1992, pp. 53–57.

Lappen, Alyssa A., "Blue Diamond: Mother of Invention," *Forbes*, March 10, 1986, p. 156.

Lauerman, Kerry, "Green Harvest," *Mother Jones*, September/October, 1996, p. 63.

Mehegan, Sean, "Brach Continues Sub-Branding Push with New Blue Diamond Product," *Brandweek*, November 11, 1996, p. 16.

——, "Blue Diamond Expands into Cracker Business," *Brandweek*, June 9, 1997, p. 12.

Muller, E.J., "Almond Shippers Crack EDI's Hard Shell," *Distribution*, October, 1991, p. 50.

Payne, Walter F., Jr., "President's Corner," *Blue Diamond Growers Newsletter*, December 30, 1998.

Saccomano, Ann, "Birds, Bees and Trucks: When Mother Nature Gives Agriculture a Headache, Transportation Feels the Pain, Too," *Traffic World*, March 2, 1998, p. 40.

——, "Report Card for Carriers," *Traffic World*, April 28, 1997, p. 54.

Thompson, Stephanie, "Blue Diamond Puts Crunch in Munch," *Brandweek*, June 2, 1997, p. 4.

—Robert Reginald and Mary A. Burgess

Cameron & Barkley Company

P.O. Box 118007
Charleston, South Carolina 29423-8007
U.S.A.
(843) 745-6900
Fax: (843) 745-6973
Web site: http://www.cambar.com

Private Company
Incorporated: 1865
Employees: 1900
Sales: $610 million (1998 est.)
NAIC: 421830 Industrial Machinery & Equipment
    Wholesaling; 421610 Electrical Apparatus &
    Equipment, Wiring Supplies, & Construction Material
    Wholesalers

Cameron & Barkley Company is one of the oldest and best known providers of industrial and electrical supplies in the United States. It operates branches in 24 states and has a presence in Canada and Mexico. The entirely employee-owned company has grown significantly in the 1980s and 1990s, and its membership in the International Supply Consortium extends its reach even further.

Origins

Archibald Cameron was born in Scotland in 1813. After emigrating to the United States, he established the Cameron, McDermid and Mustard foundry in Charleston, South Carolina. An 1859 directory lists J. Johnson, Jr., and J.F. Taylor as partners in Cameron & Co. Foundry. The firm offered "stationary and marine engines, high and low pressure boilers, saw mills, threshers ... etc." The foundry was destroyed for the second time in a fire that ravaged Charleston in December 1861.

Among the foundry's products was equipment for the Confederate Army, including possibly the first rifled bore cannons made in the United States. Shortly after the Civil War ended,

Cameron went into business with Rufus Calvin Barkley, creating Cameron & Barkley Company on July 6, 1865. Both men had banking as well as manufacturing backgrounds. They established offices on the corner of Meeting and Cumberland Streets, a location that also stored oil, iron, and machinery.

Before the war Barkley had worked in Philadelphia's Baldwin Locomotive Works, and the new venture drew upon his machinery manufacturing experience. The company also supplied equipment to South Carolina's cotton mills, forming the basis of the industrial supply business. Railroad and steamship operators also patronized the company. Among its offerings were Studebaker horse-drawn wagons. After 20 years, Barkley bought out his partner, Archibald Cameron.

With the dawn of the new century, the company began dealing in light bulbs and lanterns, and phosphate mines in the South Carolina low country had become a major source of business. Cameron & Barkley opened an office in Tampa, Florida, in 1908 when its clients began mining phosphate in that vicinity. Lumber mills attracted Cameron & Barkley to Jacksonville in 1912 and an office was opened in Miami. These sites comprised its industrial supply network for many years.

The company (known by then as "CamBar") tried to put out top-quality catalogs and attempted to ensure that the manufacturers it represented were only the best. Its leather-bound 1926 catalog for mill supplies and machinery, contractors' equipment, and roofing material weighed in at nearly 800 pages. Other catalogs addressed heavy sawmill machinery; internal combustion engines; centrifugal sand dredges; pumping machinery; concrete, brick, and tile machines; irrigation outfits; motors and generators; machine tools; road building machinery; woodworking machinery; crate and veneer machinery; and locomotive cranes. CamBar had four locations at the time: Charleston, Jacksonville, Tampa, and Miami. Its "CamBar" logo incorporated the word "service" written on an underlining ribbon.

Rufus C. Barkley, the founder's grandson, joined the company in 1922 and became vice-president five years later. In 1933 he succeeded his father, Matthew B. Barkley, as president.

Company Perspectives:

Our Vision: Excellence in every aspect of our business. Our Mission: To exceed the requirements and expectations of our customers by empowering all employee-owners to provide superior value through quality service, innovation, continuous improvement, and strategic alliances with key suppliers. Our Principles: As a company responsible to our customers, suppliers, and shareholders, we will: expect integrity, professionalism, and ethical conduct from all employee-owners; be committed to continuous improvement in all areas of our business; be committed to superior service and satisfaction for all customers; create and sustain alliances with our customers, suppliers, and employee-owners; maintain a visible commitment to quality throughout our organization; create a participative work environment designed to empower all employee-owners to be innovative and creative; promote and encourage an attitude of cooperation and mutual respect.

New Postwar Ventures

Cameron & Barkley began distributing electrical supplies during World War II. Paper mills became major customers. It established branch offices in Savannah, Georgia, and Orlando in 1944. By 1946 it was opening its sixth store in Orlando, where the company helped develop spray irrigation systems for Florida citrus growers. CamBar also supplied the related packaging plants.

In 1950 CamBar employed 250 and had annual sales of $10 million. A fourth-generation descendant of one of the founders, Rufus C. Barkley, Jr., joined his father at the company in 1954. In the mid-1950s the company opened the retail lighting store that would bring it the most name recognition among Charleston residents.

In 1956, however, Cameron & Barkley moved its headquarters to Jacksonville and established a distribution center there. Barkley reasoned that site was geographically more central to the company's business and a better location to warehouse its stainless steel and specialty metal products.

Rufus C. Barkley was elected chairman in 1958 as Edward J. Fitzgerald, Jr., became president and general manager. Barkley took over when his father died in September 1959. He later explained to *Industrial Distribution* that many employees left the firm at the time, not having confidence in their new leader. Faced with poor results in most of the company's product lines, Barkley made what he later called one of his life's best decisions and bought Butt's Electrical Supply in Charleston.

Barkley also bought out the company's plumbing business with another employee. It became the Barkley Bilbro Supply Co. CamBar announced a move to a new headquarters in North Charleston, selling its site at Meeting and Cumberland Streets.

By October 1959 CamBar had moved its headquarters back to Charleston from Jacksonville. A new office also had been added in Bartow, Florida, while the Savannah branch closed.

Sales doubled between 1955 and 1965. The company invested in extensive renovation and construction to keep up with demand. It was now involved in construction (roofing, heating, and plumbing), agriculture (irrigation), and the automotive industry. The company's electrical supply business had five branches, all in South Carolina. At the time of its 100th anniversary, Cameron & Barkley employed 200.

New Owners and New Growth in the 1970s and 1980s

In 1975 the company was one of the first of its size to develop an employee ownership plan. Wary of takeover offers, Rufus Barkley wanted to keep the integrity of the company's heritage intact. The move also was credited as a great employee motivator. Sales were about $26 million in 1975. The company also sold its plumbing subsidiary that year.

Interestingly, to combat favoritism, an antinepotism provision was written into the Employee Stock Ownership Plan. This meant not even Barkley's own relatives could be hired. He reported that he was the last one interested in the family business anyway.

Sales passed $80 million in 1981. CamBar reopened a branch (industrial) in Savannah in 1982. The company named William G. Halbritter president and chief operating officer. By the next year, CamBar was entirely employee-owned.

CamBar Software, originally CamBar Business Systems, spun off of Cameron & Barkley's in-house MIS operation in 1981. IBM had been so impressed with CamBar's in-house order processing system that it asked the company to develop a version for others. A separate company owned by the employee trust, CamBar Software provided software for distribution and warehouse operations. In 1982 it became a sister company, owned by the Employee Stock Ownership Trust.

CamBar restructured in the mid-1980s after a decade of growth. Administrative, industrial, electrical, and national sales divisions were created. It preferred not to use offshore suppliers and created a "flexible manufacturing group" to equip the smaller, more automated plants that were becoming a trend. Customers began to expect more emphasis on service, including storeroom management.

Sales were more than $150 million in 1986. Industrial and electrical supplies were about equal in size. The full line industrial supply catalog had 800 pages, the electrical, more than 600. Cameron & Barkley, now with 40 branches, opened Florence Electronics in 1987 and purchased Raleigh's Southeastern Electronics in March 1989.

CamBar embraced Total Quality Management in the late 1980s. Many new clients were attracted to the company initially because it carried both industrial and electrical supplies. It pitched "one-stop shopping" to the point of selling the Gatorade drinks so popular with construction crews. The company, however, no longer carried roofing, plumbing, heating, automotive, or irrigation supplies.

Expanding Horizons in the 1990s

By 1990 Cameron & Barkley had 1,400 employee-owners. Operations stretched from Florida to North Carolina and its catalogs boasted more than 100,000 separate items. The founder's great-grandson and namesake was still chairman, and James R. Warren was president and CEO.

CamBar founded its Material Management and Services Inc. subsidiary in 1993. This provided staffing and support for warehouses. Its involvement in the role sometimes extended to the point of actually owning the clients' inventories.

Saturn Corporation, the offshoot of General Motors that set out to change the way cars were made, used Cameron & Barkley not only as an electrical and electronics vendor but also to manage 1,800 indirect suppliers. Supply chain management would be the central role in CamBar's relationships with large manufacturers.

A number of management philosophies urged multinational corporations in particular to reduce the amount of vendors while reducing costs. To this end, in June 1994 the company teamed with McJunkin Corp. to form McJunkin-CamBar and the International Supply Consortium. The pair's combined annual revenues topped $1 billion. Within a couple of months, Bearings, Inc. (later known as Applied Industrial Technologies) joined the venture. Bearings brought 300 branches and $800 million in annual sales to the consortium.

CamBar's revenues were more than $380 million in 1994. The company maintained a million square feet in warehouse space among 40 sites. It had embarked on an automation program incorporating radio frequency data communications and bar code scanning to improve efficiency and accuracy. It reported a 20 percent productivity increase while reducing costs dramatically. In 1995 CamBar had 1,640 employees and operations in ten states. Annual sales reached $540 million in 1996 and rose another $50 million the next year.

To position itself for the coming century, CamBar began to expand by acquisition into the Midwest. It bought Warner Industrial Supply Inc., a Minneapolis company nearly as old as CamBar itself. Warner's geographic reach extended as far as Washington state and Colorado. The purchase of Illinois-based Don E. William Co. soon followed. The acquisitions were expected to add more than $90 million a year to CamBar's revenues. CamBar Software also grew dramatically in the 1990s. Employment doubled to 100 in the 1990s and sales reached $8 million a year. Clearly, topping a billion in sales shortly into the new millennium was not out of the question for the venerable South Carolina company.

Principal Subsidiaries

Material Management and Services Inc.; McJunkin-CamBar (50%).

Principal Divisions

Administrative; Industrial; Electrical; National Sales.

Further Reading

"Cameron & Barkley and McJunkin Add Bearings, Inc. to Consortium," *Industrial Distribution,* September 1994, 12.

Cameron & Barkley Company, "1990: Celebrating Our 125th Anniversary," *CamBar Quarterly,* Fall 1990.

"Cameron & Barkley Offices Will Shift to Jacksonville," *News and Courier,* May 2, 1956.

"Company History," *Employee-Owner Handbook,* Charleston: Cameron & Barkley, 1995.

Ellenbogen, Milt, and Josephine Fiamingo, "Distributor of the Century: Cameron & Barkley Company," *Industrial Distribution,* December 1986, pp. 30–38.

Gardner, Fred, "Saturn's Better Idea: Outsource Purchasing," *Electronic Business Buyer,* September 1993, pp. 136–41.

Hatcher, Thurston, "Cameron & Barkley's a Heavyweight," *Post and Courier,* January 15, 1991.

"Making the Transition to World-Class Performance," *Automatic I.D. News,* March 1995, pp. 58–61.

McDermott, John P., "CamBar Continues Expansion," *Post and Courier,* December 30, 1998, p. 7B.

——, "CamBar to Buy Supplier," *Post and Courier,* January 12, 1999, p. B7.

"McJunkin-CamBar Deal Start of a Trend," *Industrial Distribution,* July 1994, pp. 9–10.

Parker, Jim, "Software Specialists," *Post and Courier,* January 24, 1994, pp. D1, D10–D11.

"Resume of the History of Cameron & Barkley," Charleston: Cameron & Barkley, c. 1965.

Williams, Charles, "Barkley State's Top Businessman," *Post and Courier,* November 13, 1995, p. C2.

—Frederick C. Ingram

Caribou Coffee Company, Inc.

615 North Third Street
Minneapolis, Minnesota 55401
U.S.A.
(612) 359-2700
(888) 227-4268
Fax: (612) 359-2730
Web site: http://www.caribou-coffee.com

Private Company
Incorporated: 1992
Employees: 1,800
Sales: $65 million (1998 est.)
NAIC: 722213 Coffee Shops, On Premise Brewing

Caribou Coffee Company, Inc. is a privately held, neighborhood-based, specialty retailer of high quality coffees, teas, bakery goods, and related merchandise. The Minneapolis-based company operated 125 stores in six states at the beginning of 1999 and was estimated to be the second largest company-owned and operated coffeehouse chain. Caribou Coffee is positioned to take the leap from regional operator to national player in the rapidly growing gourmet coffee industry.

The Saga Begins: 1992–93

The Caribou story begins, as legend has it, with an Alaskan wilderness vacation. Kimberly and John Puckett were inspired during the trip to do something larger with their lives and consequently formulated an idea for a business of their own.

Kim and John, both graduates of Dartmouth College's school of business, gained experience in finance and marketing prior to striking out on their own. Kim worked for General Mills, Dunkin' Donuts, and the Chase Manhattan Bank, and John served as a consultant with Bain & Company and as an investment banker for Merrill Lynch Capital Markets where he specialized in mergers, acquisitions, and leveraged buyouts.

The Pucketts, one-time regulars at the Coffee Connection, a small Boston chain, spent about a year researching the coffeehouse concept and looking for ways to improve on it. "What really interested us in coffee was, at the time, it was just booming in Boston, same thing that's happening in Minneapolis [now]," John Puckett said in a January 1994 *Twin Cities Business Monthly* article by Allison Campbell.

The pair moved to Minneapolis in the summer of 1992, following a six month analysis of potential markets. In addition to possessing positive demographics, the region was a known commodity: the home turf of Kim Puckett. Family, social, and school connections paved their way into the investment community and allowed the Pucketts to open their first coffeehouse that December.

In general, the gourmet coffee business was on an upswing. While overall U.S. coffee consumption had fallen during the 1960s, 1970s, and 1980s, the decline took the biggest bite out of the mass-produced ground variety of coffee sold in supermarkets. High gross profit margins on individual cups of specialty coffees, plus good return on investment, and relatively low start-up costs, drew scores of entrepreneurs such as the Pucketts to the business.

In the Twin Cities, the Pucketts' first shop, located in the affluent suburb of Edina, joined other coffee vendors already on the scene. They ranged from eclectic neighborhood hangouts with names like Muddy Waters to locally owned microroaster/coffeeshops such as Dunn Bros. Coffee Co. and franchise operations including Chicago-based Gloria Jean's Coffee Beans. On a larger scale, Folgers, Kraft General Foods, and Nestlé, entered the market with their own gourmet grinds, and the Seattle-based Starbucks coffeehouse chain went public in a push to become a national chain. The specialty coffee industry's annual sales were about $780 million in 1993.

Brewing Up a Storm: 1994–95

The Pucketts opened their second shop in the robust Uptown area of Minneapolis. Site selection was utmost on their mind. A key ingredient for the success of the coffeeshops was location, and the couple was determined to lock in good sites before Starbucks arrived on the scene.

Four Caribou Coffee shops marketed espresso drinks, baked goods, coffee beans, and branded merchandise as a new round of financing was put in motion in September 1993. Two earlier rounds netted $600,000, but in their third the company received commitments for $3 million, more than double the target figure of $1.2 million. Opening costs for a Caribou Coffee shop ranged from $175,000 to $200,000. In a short period of time, the company established itself as a top player in the Twin Cities market.

Unlike other locally based competitors Dunn Bros. and Kafte Inc., Caribou Coffee purchased rather than roasted its own beans, choosing instead to concentrate on service and quality control. The mystery shopper was one technique used to ensure good customer service: loyal customers trained to critique their Caribou experience regularly visited the shops. Kim, who was in charge of personnel, received the historically low score when she filled in for an ailing employee, according to the Campbell article.

While the Pucketts strived for product and customer service consistency from store to store, they also wanted each location to reflect the personality of the neighborhood. "All ours do now," said John Puckett in *Twin Cities Business Monthly*. "That's how we'll compete with what I'm sure will be ultra-deep pockets that come into this business, as the big chain companies see the growth." Neighborhood locations, preferably in older buildings, staffed by people with an affinity to the community helped create a unique feel at each location, according to Campbell.

As Kim managed the personnel aspects of the stores, John tended to coffee quality, real estate acquisition, and finances. A fourth self-managed private placement brought in $7.3 million in the spring of 1994. Some of the new capital was earmarked for expansion into a new market: Atlanta. Tennessee-native

John Puckett planned to capitalize on his knowledge of the Southeast, just as they had used Kim's knowledge of the Midwest as they built their Twin Cities market.

Bringing ten stores into operation in a relatively short period of time gave the couple ample learning opportunities. For example, they discovered downtown Minneapolis shops pulled in morning customers but slacked off over the rest of the day, thus proving to be poorer performers than the neighborhood shops. To facilitate growth the company made some internal adjustments, including the establishment of a central roasting facility and the hiring of a chief financial officer.

As expected, Starbucks came on the scene and opened shops in downtown Minneapolis in March 1994, providing competition for Caribou but also upping interest in specialty coffee. Kafte closed its Minneapolis locations a few months later, claiming competition among the larger players had inflated real estate prices for choice sites. Owner Joe Anderson, who established his first shop in 1985, also said in a November 1995 *Minneapolis/St. Paul CityBusiness* article, that Caribou Coffee had cornered the market on investment dollars as well.

The Pucketts continued to seek out opportunities which would strengthen their position in the market. In September 1994, Caribou Coffee entered into a joint agreement with Byerly's Inc. for shops in or adjacent to four of the upscale supermarkets—competitor Starbucks had similar arrangements with independent supermarkets in Seattle and Chicago. In addition to serving beverages to Byerly's shoppers, Caribou shelved branded coffee beans and merchandise. Caribou had other synergistic relationships with retailers, including bagel and bookstores.

Twenty-one Caribou Coffee shops pulled in a total of $6.45 million in sales in 1994, according to an April 1996 *Corporate Report Minnesota* article by Lee Schafer. The investment community, eager to send up the next Starbucks, continued to pump money into Caribou Coffee. The enterprise also drew interest, Schafer surmised in an earlier article, because of the caliber of investors already on board, such as John Puckett's uncle Dr. Thomas F. Frist, founder of the Hospital Corporation of America, and asset manager James R. Jundt, who was well-known on Wall Street. A round of funding in 1995 brought in about $18 million including the first institutional dollars. Oak Investment Partners of Newport, Connecticut, contributed $3.5 million.

Adjusting the Brew: 1996–97

A new look helped earn Caribou Coffee a spot on the 1996 "Hot Concepts!" list compiled by *Nation's Restaurant News*. An Alaskan lodge format replaced the slick urban look Caribou Coffee had cultivated. The change differentiated Caribou from Starbucks and brought the concept more in line with the experience that originally inspired Kim and John's enterprise. The Alaskan lodge concept, showcased in Caribou's larger shops, featured rough wood and stone decor, comfortable seating, cozy fireplaces, and live music for evening patrons. A running caribou continued to dominate the company's logo, and the Puckett's Alaskan photo hung in each store along with a request for outdoor vacation shots of customers wearing Caribou Coffee T-shirts.

On average, beverages pulled in 60 percent of revenue, food 20 percent, coffee beans 15 percent, and merchandise five percent. Total sales reached $15.46 million in 1995, but the developing company continued to lose money.

By May 1996, the Pucketts' grand adventure had spun off 58 units, including four Detroit-area Coffee Exchange stores acquired and converted to the Caribou Coffee format in 1995, but repeated rounds of financing had diluted their ownership to less than 20 percent. Board member James Jundt, who personally invested $1.65 million, held more than 10 percent of the company. Representatives of three venture capital firms, including Oak Investment Partners, also sat on the board.

The influx of funds from the investment firms put pressure on the Pucketts to reach the 100-store mark and take the company public, as had Starbucks at that watershed. Yet internal changes such as executive management turnover—the head of store operations and the chief financial officer departed—and the revamping of the concept slowed the growth rate. Predictions that the last round of funding would bring Caribou to the 100-store mark by the end of 1996 failed to pan out, and some investors expressed concerns regarding the Pucketts' ability to manage a larger company, reported Schafer.

Twenty-five store openings pushed the count to 89 by the beginning of 1997. In May, Jay Willoughby, a 24-year veteran of chain restaurant management, joined Caribou as president and partner. Willoughby previously headed the 1,000-plus Boston Market chain and PepsiCo restaurant ventures. Willoughby took command of all operations. Kim Puckett, as chair of the board, concentrated on corporate culture and communications, and John Puckett, as CEO, focused on raising funds.

Caribou's 89 units, located in the Twin Cities, Atlanta, Detroit, Chicago, North Carolina, and Ohio, placed the company in the number two spot among all U.S. company-owned coffee houses. Market leader Starbucks owned and operated 1,140 and San Francisco-based Pasqua Inc.'s held third place with 55. Two franchise operations, Gloria Jean's and Coffee Beanery, held the number two and three spots, respectively, behind Starbucks, when considering all U.S. coffeehouses.

Estimated to be the nation's fifth largest coffeeshop chain, Caribou Coffee ranked among the top 20 percent in the country among any business when it came to raising private funds. "Caribou might not have achieved that ranking if things had gone more smoothly," wrote Terry Fiedler for the *Star Tribune* in June 1997. "Because the company didn't have its cups in a row, it enlisted existing private investors for another round of financing—$12 million—this year instead of selling shares to the public." Caribou did finally top the 100-store mark in 1997, and total sales were about $40 million.

A deal with Delta Airlines in early 1998 promised the company some welcome exposure. Most of the Atlanta-based carrier's domestic flights would offer Caribou brand coffee. The coffee company already had a strong presence in the region: Caribou operated 18 Atlanta stores, second in number to the Twin Cities. Starbucks coffee had been aboard United Airlines flights since 1996, part of a growing trend in the airline industry to offer brand-name products.

The sheer number of tasting opportunities afforded by the airline deal outweighed anticipated sales gains: only about $4 million but for an estimated 60 million cups of coffee. Caribou Coffee sold just ten million cups in its stores on an annual basis but based on gross profit margins of up to 80 percent the stores earned the lion's share of revenues. Direct mail sales also got a boost when Caribou gained access to Delta's preferred customer list.

Another opportunity to build recognition as a national brand came by way of an agreement with Target stores. Caribou began test marketing bags of coffee beans in 20 Target stores across the country in July 1998 and then in all Target stores during the holiday season. A decision about a long-term deal was expected in 1999.

Pushing Toward the Peak: 1999 and Beyond

Caribou ads hit the airwaves for the first time in February 1999, beginning in the Atlanta area. Nationally recognized Twin Cities-based ad agency Carmichael Lynch handled the radio campaign which was slated for other major Caribou markets in the spring. Caribou used its "Life is short: Stay awake for it," slogan from print, outdoor, and direct mail ads in conjunction with slice of life scenarios.

The $3 billion gourmet coffee market steamed along but remained highly fragmented as the century wound down. Meanwhile, Caribou continued to position itself for the move from a regional to a national chain. Willoughby worked to create internal stability capable of supporting the leap. He brought the business to profitability for the first time by strengthening existing markets and working to retain and satisfy employees. Growth scheduled for 1999 was to be funded internally, but Willoughby had his eye toward that long-promised public offering as a vehicle to move Caribou to the next level.

Further Reading

Campbell, Allison, "Good As the Last Cup," *Twin Cities Business Monthly*, January 1994, pp. 32–36.
Carideo, Tony, "All Eyes on Piper Capital Fixed-Income Fund Losses," *Star Tribune* (Minneapolis), April 23, 1994, p. 3D.
——, "Rothmeier, 46, Suing Noel Rahn on Charge of Age Discrimination," *Star Tribune* (Minneapolis), September 28, 1993, p. 1D.
De Young, Dirk, "Caribou Coffee Gets Nice Perk—Test Rollout in Target Stores," *Minneapolis/St. Paul CityBusiness*, November 20, 1998, pp. 1, 44.
Fiedler, Terry, "Minneapolis-Based Caribou Coffee to Fly with Delta," *Star Tribune* (Minneapolis), January 8, 1998.
——, "Riding Herd on Caribou," *Star Tribune* (Minneapolis), June 22, 1997.
Finke, Gail Deibler, "An American Coffeehouse," *Visual Merchandising and Store Design*, November 1996.
Harper, Roseanne, "Caribou Coffee Bars Set to Bubble Up at Most Lunds Units," *Supermarket News*, January 19, 1998, pp. 27, 31.
Huber, Tim, "Caribou Sips $12M in Venture Financing," *Minneapolis/St. Paul CityBusiness*, May 9, 1997, pp. 1, 36.
"Industry Veteran Jay Willoughby Is Joining Caribou," *Star Tribune* (Minneapolis), May 3, 1997, p. 1D.
Khermouch, Gerry, "Caribou Goes Mellow in New Pitch," *Brandweek*, February 15, 1999, p. 9.
Maler, Kevin, "Caribou Drinks in $18M," *Minneapolis/St. Paul CityBusiness*, November 10, 1995, p. 10.

——, "Kafte Is Casualty in Local Coffee War," *Minneapolis/St. Paul CityBusiness*, June 17, 1994, p. 9.

Marcotty, Josephine, "Brewing Success," *Star Tribune* (Minneapolis), July 9, 1993, p. 1D.

McCartney, Jim, "The Buzz on Caribou Coffee," *St. Paul Pioneer Press*, March 14, 1999.

"NRN Names Eight to '96 Hot Concepts! Roster," *Nation's Restaurant News*, April 15, 1996, pp. 1, 82.

Schafer, Lee, "Caribou Runs with New York Banker," *Corporate Report Minnesota*, April 1995, p. 83.

——, "Coffee Clutch," *Corporate Report Minnesota*, August 1996, pp. 36–43.

Walkup, Carolyn, "Caribou Coffee: Taking the Coffeehouse 'On the Road,' " *Nation's Restaurant News*, May 20, 1996, pp. 56, 58.

——, "Drive-Thru Java Craze Hits the Ground Running, Heads East," *Nation's Restaurant News*, May 12, 1997, p. 6.

Waters, Jennifer, "Caribou Mugs It Up with Byerly's," *Minneapolis/St. Paul CityBusiness*, September 23, 1994, p. 2.

—Kathleen Peippo

Carmichael Lynch Inc.

800 Hennepin Avenue
Minneapolis, Minnesota 55403
U.S.A.
(612) 334-6000
Fax: (612) 334-6090

Wholly Owned Subsidiary of The Interpublic Group of
Companies, Inc.
Incorporated: 1962
Employees: 200
Gross Billings: $200 million (1997 est.)
NAIC: 54181 Advertising Agencies

Carmichael Lynch Inc., lauded for its recreation-related ads, was purchased by Interpublic Group in 1998. Propelled by cofounder Leland T. Lynch, the Minneapolis-based shop ranked as one of the largest independently owned agencies in the United States prior to the sale. The agency offers a wide range of marketing communication services, including advertising, direct marketing, sales promotion, research and account planning, media, and print and broadcast production. The firm also offers public relations through its division, Carmichael Lynch Spong Public Relations, founded in 1990, and design via Carmichael Lynch Thorburn, which was founded in 1996. Carmichael Lynch in general focuses on mid-sized clients, with annual billings ranging from $2 to $20 million, but also seeks out accounts with great brand names such as Schwinn, Formica, and American Standard.

Early Days in the Ad Biz: 1960s–80s

The Hamm's Beer bear was king of the "land of sky-blue waters" when Leland (Lee) Lynch and Jack Carmichael launched their Minneapolis advertising agency in 1962. Carmichael left the agency in 1969, and Lee Lynch fixed his mark on the business and the growing Twin Cities ad community. Carmichael Lynch earned Best of Show honors from The Advertising Federation of Minnesota in 1971 and in 1975 debuted in *Communication Arts*, a highly respected trade magazine.

The Twin Cities ad industry started making significant waves on a national level in the early 1980s. Rival agency Fallon McElligott & Rice's unconventional approach helped it earn Agency of the Year honors from *Advertising Age* magazine in 1984. The same year, Carmichael Lynch earned two Effie awards from the American Marketing Association—a feat confined to New York agencies until then. "And, unlike the creative awards," wrote Donna Dailey in a February 1985 *Corporate Report Minnesota* article, "only 31 Effies are awarded each year for demonstration of measurable results."

Despite growing popularity, Minnesota ad agencies were still viewed with some derision by their big-market counterparts, who sometimes referred to the advertising style coming from the region as "Minneapolis cute," according to Dailey. Furthermore, Carmichael Lynch and other Minneapolis/St. Paul-based ad agencies had trouble earning business from giant companies within their home state.

General Mills and Pillsbury, which ranked among the top U.S. advertising spenders, typically hired East Coast or Chicago ad agencies. Start-up companies willing to take advertising risks to break into the market kept the coffers of creative shops such as Carmichael Lynch full.

As the ad industry grew in Minnesota during the 1980s so did Carmichael Lynch. The agency's 1987 billings were $70.9 million compared with $46 million just four years earlier. Lynch acquired a string of smaller agencies, both within and outside of Minnesota, during the 1980s and into the 1990s.

Growth upped the agency's need for space, and Carmichael Lynch vacated the neighborhood mansions it occupied for nearly half of its 25 years in business. Lynch and Lou Bacig, president and partner, defied conventional wisdom and invested in a building located in a rundown area of downtown Minneapolis. They transformed the place into a symbol of the agency's creative energy and helped begin a revitalization of the area.

"Forty-one conference rooms are marked by bizarre decor reflecting parts of the agency's business. The cow room, with its udder-stated furnishings, represents agricultural clients. The urban-guerrilla room, with chain-link fence and tire tracks on

Company Perspectives:

Advertising with an Attitude.

You look, and you know. You feel something certain. You believe. That's advertising with an attitude.

Edge. Not somewhere in the middle. Tell the world where you stand. Shout it. Whisper it. Just don't mumble it.

Every ounce of what your product or service can be, that's what your advertising must be. There, in the style, the tone, the spirit, the conviction. Make a distinct impression. Build an image, become that image.

You cannot be all things to all people. Neither can Carmichael Lynch. This is our attitude. We're not looking for clients who keep pushing us to make the logo bigger; we're looking for clients who keep pushing us until the logo becomes a tattoo.

the wall, honors longtime client Harley Davidson,'' wrote Dan Wascoe, Jr., in an April 1988 *Star Tribune* article.

Carmichael Lynch was riding the wave of one of the fastest-growing industries in Minnesota, but the growth produced its share of challenges. The burgeoning marketplace created intense demand for creative talent. In 1989, Lynch and Bacig set up an employee stock ownership plan to try to counter the loss of employees in an industry plagued with a high turnover rate.

In addition to retaining talent, the company encountered other marketplace pressures. ''In the last year, more clients have demanded an answer to the question, 'Does this [advertising] really work?' '' said Lynch in a June 1988 *Corporate Report Minnesota* article by Bob Geiger. ''If it doesn't work you're looking at budget cuts,'' Lynch added.

Push for Continued Growth: Early 1990s

The American Association of Advertising Agencies (AAAA) named Carmichael Lynch agency of the year in 1991 on the strength of its sporting and recreational ads. Lynch, however did not want to see the agency pigeonholed in a single area. ''It's a daily struggle to overcome this image,'' said Lynch in a December 1991 *Corporate Report Minnesota* article. ''People used to say that the only thing we could do was long copy, fish ads, and print.''

Carmichael Lynch, in fact, spread its $100 million in billings among recreational and sporting goods accounts, business-to-business and technology, retail, services, and public relations activities. The agency added a public relations subsidiary, Carmichael Lynch Spong, in 1990 to handle increasing business in that area.

Lynch wanted the agency to continue growing, but big national accounts, particularly in the important auto industry, eluded them. ''Some feel that Carmichael-Lynch is at a disadvantage because it isn't well-known nationally; they point to Bacig's anti-press attitude as part of the problem. Others are convinced that Lynch himself is an obstacle to Carmichael-Lynch's growth. Yet, in the last decade, the agency has bounced

back and forth between Martin-Williams and Fallon McElligott in the hierarchy of Minnesota firms, no small accomplishment in a fiercely competitive climate,'' wrote Royer.

Even as controversy swirled around Lynch—ex-staffers were known to criticize the party atmosphere fostered by the exuberant CEO and the lack of a concrete plan for succession of leadership—the agency continued its award-winning ways and pulled in another AAAA award for creative excellence in 1993. On the year, the agency gained ten new accounts while losing only one. Carmichael Lynch's client list included Pentax Corporation, Korbel Champagne, Cargill Corporation, and Schwinn Cycling & Fitness.

Fifteen-year veteran Jack Supple was named president of the 170-employee agency in September 1994. Lynch continued in the capacity of chairman and CEO, and Bacig assumed the posts of vice-chair and managing partner. Supple had held the head creative post in the agency since 1989. ''Our mission is finding mid-sized clients who we feel offer the best opportunities for us to do good work, in terms of being able to actually make something happen—where you can really feel the impact,'' said Supple in a July 1995 *SHOOT* article by Kathy DeSalvo.

Under Supple's leadership, the agency brought in a number of key clients including Boston Beer Company and Minnesota-based National Car Rental, the fourth largest U.S. car rental company. Still, many in the industry and the press continued to think Lee Lynch when they thought of Carmichael Lynch.

Lynch, in turn, contended it was not merely his personality that shaped the climate of the agency, but the clients whom they served. ''You need to seek clients who want you to take risks,'' Lynch said in a June 1996 *Twin Cities Business Monthly* article by Russell Scott Smith. Schwinn Cycling & Fitness took a risk with an ad that read: ''Schwinns are red. Schwinns are blue. Schwinns are light and agile too. Cars suck. The end. . . . It took a great client to let us do that,'' Lynch said. The agency received the Stephen E. Kelly Award from the Magazine Publishers of America in 1994 for its Schwinn bikes campaign.

Change in the Air: Late 1990s

Supple weathered a volatile year in 1997, one marked by account turnover and the departure of prominent staff members. Fortunately, new accounts balanced out the losses, and the agency continued to show a profit. Nonetheless, the volatility raised questions regarding the future of the agency.

Advertising Age reported in January 1998 that Carmichael Lynch and Interpublic Group had been holding talks since October 1997 regarding the purchase of the agency. The New York-based holding company went on to purchase Carmichael Lynch for more than $30 million.

The premium price ''reflects the reputation earned by Carmichael Lynch for clever, effective work, particularly in print,'' wrote Stuart Elliott for the *New York Times*. The typical asking price for agencies was one times revenue: Carmichael Lynch's 1997 revenue was $24 million. Client billings had exceeded $200 million.

According to a February 1998 *Star Tribune* article by Ann Merrill, Carmichael Lynch had sought a buyer in order to finance growth and close out its employee stock ownership plan. Its affiliation with the world's third largest agency also would allow Carmichael Lynch to build an international presence.

Barry R. Linsky, senior vice-president for planning and business development at Interpublic Group spoke highly of the agency and its executives. "What attracts them to us," said Linsky to the *New York Times,* "is their terrific creative reputation, strong client list and defined and distinctive culture." The agency would continue to operate under its own name and retain a good deal of autonomy. Senior executives including Lynch, Supple, PR head Doug Spong, and design unit head Bill Thorburn continued in their posts.

The purchase was part of the consolidation trend in the slow growth advertising industry. Big holding companies pushed return on investment to the 15 to 20 percent range through new acquisitions, according to a June 1998 *Star Tribune* article by Merrill. In addition, the big players—Interpublic Group had billings of $21.1 billion—yearned for broad geographic coverage. Interpublic Group, which already held partial ownership of Minneapolis-based Campbell Mithun Esty, purchased Carmichael Lynch as part of its Midwest expansion.

During the months following the purchase, Carmichael Lynch expanded its available expertise through a strategic partnership with sister agency Weber Public Relations Worldwide. Weber was known for its technology clients such as Lotus and Digital Equipment Corp. Carmichael Lynch also acquired the Minneapolis office of Valentine-McCormick-Ligibel and gained Northwest Airlines Inc. as a client in the process. In early 1999, the agency's longstanding reputation for sports and recreation enthusiast ads helped lure its first ever auto manufacturer assignment: Porsche Cars North America.

Further Reading

Cardona, Mercedes M., and Pat Sloan, "Interpublic in Talks to Acquire Carmichael Shop," *Advertising Age*, January 12, 1998, pp. 1, 40.
"Carmichael Lynch Picks Jack Supple," *Star Tribune* (Minneapolis), September 27, 1994, p. 3D.
Daily, Donna, "Where Image Is King," *Corporate Report Minnesota*, February 1985, pp. 77–81.
DeSalvo, Kathy, "Serious Sports," *SHOOT*, July 14, 1995, pp. 34+.
Elliott, Stuart, "Advertising," *New York Times*," February 3, 1998.
Feyder, Susan, "Interpublic Group to Buy Shandwick's Parent Company," *Star Tribune* (Minneapolis), July 18, 1998, pp. 1D, 3D.
Fink, Laurie, "Advertising," *Corporate Report Minnesota*, June 1989, pp. 59–76.
Geiger, Bob, "Carmichael Lynch, This Bud's for You," *Star Tribune* (Minneapolis), February 6, 1995, p. 2D.
——, "Fallon McElligott May Land Philip Morris' Image Campaign," *Star Tribune* (Minneapolis), February 15, 1999, p. 2D.
——, "High Flying Advertising Agencies," *Corporate Report Minnesota*, June 1988, pp. 67–78.
——, "Interpublic Group Takes Over Minneapolis Shop Carmichael Lynch Today," *Star Tribune* (Minneapolis), February 2, 1998, p. 4D.
——, "Pentax Account Nice Present for Carmichael Lynch," *Star Tribune* (Minneapolis), December 27, 1993, p. 2D.
Merrill, Ann, "Carmichael Lynch Buys McGrath Buckley, Becoming Area's Third-Largest PR Firm," *Star Tribune* (Minneapolis), December 16, 1998, p. 3D.
——, "Carmichael Lynch Buys Minneapolis VML Office," *Star Tribune* (Minneapolis), December 17, 1998, p. 3D.
——, "Carmichael Lynch ESOP to Disappear in Deal," *Star Tribune* (Minneapolis), February 3, 1998, p. 3D.
——, "Carmichael Lynch Spong Joins Forces with Weber," *Star Tribune* (Minneapolis), October 1, 1998, p. 3D.
——, "Consolidation Is a Boon for 2 Ad Agency Execs," *Star Tribune* (Minneapolis), July 23, 1998, p. 1D.
——, "National Car Hires Carmichael Lynch," *Star Tribune* (Minneapolis), December 14, 1995, p. 3D.
——, "The Pitch for Consolidation," *Star Tribune* (Minneapolis), June 14, 1998, p. 1D.
Richard, Diane, "Carmichael Lynch Recovers Account Losses," *Minneapolis/St. Paul CityBusiness*, pp. 1, 40.
Royer, Mary-Paige, "He's Still the Lynch Pin," *Corporate Report Minnesota*, December 1991, pp. 48–55.
Smith, Russell Scott, "Lynch Pin," *Twin Cities Business Monthly*, June 1996, pp. 51–53.
Wascoe, Dan, Jr., "Carmichael Lynch Adds PR Branch," *Star Tribune* (Minneapolis), August 23, 1990, p. 1D.
——, "Cows in the Conference Room," *Star Tribune* (Minneapolis), April 17, 1988, p. 20SM.

—Kathleen Peippo

CBS Corporation

51 West 52nd Street
New York, New York 10019
U.S.A.
(212) 975-4321
Fax: (212) 975-1893
Web site: http://www.cbs.com

Public Company
Incorporated: 1927 as United Independent Broadcasters,
Inc.
Employees: 46,189
Sales: $6.80 billion (1998)
Stock Exchanges: New York
Ticker Symbol: CBS
NAIC: 51312 Television Broadcasting; 513112 Radio
Stations

The world's second oldest broadcasting network, CBS Corporation provides television programs to more than 200 affiliate stations in the United States. CBS Corporation was the name taken by Westinghouse Electric Corporation in 1997 after its 1995 acquisition of CBS Inc. Between 1995 and 1997, Westinghouse completed $25 billion in deals, including acquisitions and divestitures, to become a purely media-oriented company. During the late 1990s, CBS's CBS Television Network ranked as the most popular network. During the 1990s, the company began developing interests in cable television, following similar moves made by the other major networks. CBS's cable properties included The Nashville Network, Country Music Television, and a news and entertainment cable network called "Eye on People." The company also owned approximately 170 radio stations, which accounted for roughly 25 percent of total annual revenues.

Origins

In the late 1920s Arthur Judson, the impresario of the Philadelphia and New York Philharmonic orchestras, ap- proached the Radio Corporation of the National Broadcasting Company (NBC), then the only radio broadcaster in the United States, with an idea to promote classical music by airing orchestra performances; NBC declined. Undaunted, Judson founded his own broadcasting company, which he named United Independent Broadcasters, Inc. (UIB), in 1927.

Lacking the strong capital base NBC was afforded by its parent, RCA, UIB struggled to stay afloat for several months. In the summer of 1927, however, Judson found a rich partner in Columbia Phonograph, a leader in the phonograph record business. Columbia Phonograph bought UIB's operating rights for $163,000; the new company was named the Columbia Phonograph Broadcasting System.

Columbia Phonograph sold UIB's operating rights back to the broadcasting company in 1928, however, apparently because the phonograph company was frustrated by a lack of advertiser loyalty. The broadcasting company's name was then shortened to the Columbia Broadcasting System (CBS), and its finances were greatly enhanced that year when William Paley— the son of a Russian cigar company owner who eventually helped CBS earn its reputation as a classy network—invested $400,000 in the company's stock.

At the time of Paley's CBS stock purchase, the company consisted of only 16 affiliated radio stations and possessed no stations of its own. Paley, who was quickly elected president of the company, tripled earnings in his first year. This success was accomplished by offering to prospective affiliates the network's entire unsponsored schedule at no cost, in contrast to NBC, which charged affiliates for all programs. In return for free programs, affiliates gave CBS airtime for sponsored broadcasts, allowing the network to assure contracted sponsors that airtime would be available. Within a decade, CBS added nearly 100 stations to its network. Since the number of affiliates a network possesses determines the number of people it can reach, which in turn determines what a sponsor is charged, CBS was soon on firm financial ground. By 1930 CBS had 300 employees and total sales of $7.2 million.

Although CBS fared well, NBC continued to dominate the entertainment-oriented broadcasting industry. Paley, viewing news and public affairs as a quick way for CBS to gain respectability, decided to explore the potential for establishing its own network news. In 1930 he hired Ed Klauber to institute a news and public affairs section, and in 1933 the Columbia News Service, the first radio network news operation, was formed. By 1935 CBS had become the largest radio network in the United States.

In 1938 Edward R. Murrow began his career at CBS as head of the network's European division. The first international radio news broadcast was initiated later that year with Murrow in Vienna, Austria, William L. Shirer in London, and others reporting from Paris, Berlin, and Rome. With these newsbreaks, CBS began the practice of preempting regular programming. Interruptions were planned for prime listening time—8:55 to 9:00 p.m.—and were intended to give the network a "statesmanlike" image.

CBS entered the recording business in 1938 with the purchase of the American Record Corporation. Later called the Columbia Recording Corporation, it soon became an industry powerhouse.

By the beginning of World War II, CBS employed more than 2,000 people, had annual sales of nearly $36 million, and boasted more than 100 affiliate stations throughout the United States. In 1940 the world's first experimental color television broadcast was made from a CBS transmitter atop the Chrysler Building in New York City and was received in the CBS Building at 485 Madison Avenue. The following year marked the beginning of CBS's weekly broadcasts of black-and-white television programs. Also in 1941, the government ordered NBC to divest itself of one of its two networks, which eventually gave rise to the American Broadcasting Company (ABC).

Post-World War II Activity

Although CBS continued to expand after World War II, NBC was still the industry leader. Under Paley's direction, CBS lured stars away from NBC by devising a plan in which the celebrities could be taxed as companies rather than as individuals, greatly reducing the amount of income they were required to turn over to the government. Jack Benny was the first major star to leave NBC for CBS; soon Edgar Bergen and Charlie McCarthy, Amos 'n' Andy, Red Skelton, and George Burns and Gracie Allen followed. Within a year CBS took the lead from NBC in programming, advertising revenues, and profits—a lead it maintained as the two networks further expanded into television.

In 1946 CBS submitted its color television broadcasting system to the Federal Communications Commission (FCC) for approval. CBS was confident that its color system would be approved, even though existing black-and-white sets could not receive CBS's color broadcasts. The FCC did not approve the system, calling it "premature." In the meantime, RCA had developed a color system that was compatible with existing television sets. The CBS method produced a better picture, however, and in 1950, when both CBS and RCA submitted their systems to the FCC for approval, only the CBS system was approved. But RCA appealed the decision, preventing CBS from marketing its system and gaining time to improve the

quality of its own technique. In 1953 the FCC reversed and ruled in favor of RCA.

During the 1950s censorship became an issue in the broadcasting industry. The networks had always been sensitive to censorship pressure: the FCC was given authority to revoke a station's license if it did not serve the "public interest responsibly." In addition, advertisers were given permission to refuse to sponsor a program that they deemed offensive, and network affiliates could pressure the network into discontinuing a controversial program.

Censorship surfaced at all the networks during the early 1950s as U.S. Senator Joseph McCarthy's anticommunist campaign pressured networks and sponsors to blacklist certain actors and writers who were suspected of having left-wing associations. Although CBS was considered the most liberal of the networks, it required 2,500 employees to sign a "loyalty oath," which stated that they "neither belonged to nor sympathized with" any communist organization. In 1954 two CBS News commentators began to expose McCarthy's unethical behavior on the television show "See It Now." The program helped to discredit communist paranoia, but proved so controversial that CBS eventually canceled it.

By this time there were 32 million television sets in the United States, and television had become the biggest advertising medium in the world. The period was marred, however, by a 1956 TV quiz show scandal in which CBS's "$64,000 Question" was shown to be rigged.

In the late 1950s, Paley hired James Aubrey as president of CBS. Aubrey, who purportedly thought that television programming had become too "highbrow," introduced such shows as "The Beverly Hillbillies," "Mr. Ed," and "The Munsters." These series were extremely popular; in his first two years with CBS, Aubrey doubled the network's profits.

During the early 1960s, CBS embarked on a diverse acquisitions campaign. Before 1964 CBS had made only two acquisitions in its history, but from that year on the company made acquisitions almost every year. In 1964 the network purchased an 80 percent interest in the New York Yankees baseball team, which it sold ten years later. Acquisitions in the fields of musical instruments, book publishing, and children's toys were made throughout the 1960s.

By the end of the decade, CBS had 22,000 employees and net profits of more than $64 million. The network's most notable programming innovation of the decade came in 1968 with the debut of "60 Minutes," a television news magazine. The 1970s were a period of successful prime-time programming. In 1971 "All in the Family" debuted on CBS, and in 1972 both "M*A*S*H" and "The Waltons" were televised for the first time.

The 1970s, however, were also years of managerial turmoil. In 1971 Charles T. Ireland became the president of CBS but was replaced a year later by Arthur Taylor, who held the position for four years. Taylor was relieved of his duties when the network placed second in the Nielsen ratings for the first time in 21 years. John D. Backe, who had been president of the

CBS publishing division since 1973, was chosen as Taylor's replacement.

Meanwhile, in 1976 CBS relieved reporter Daniel Schorr of all duties after he leaked a secret House Intelligence Committee report on the Central Intelligence Agency (CIA) to the *Village Voice*. He resigned from CBS several months later. And in April 1979, in a case involving CBS and two employees—correspondent Mike Wallace and producer Barry Lando—the U.S. Supreme Court ruled that journalists accused of libel may be forced to answer questions about their "state of mind" or about conversations with colleagues during the editorial process. The decision was a victory for former Lieutenant Colonel Anthony E. Herbert, who contended that he was libeled in a "60 Minutes" broadcast that aired in 1973.

In 1979 CBS finally began to divest itself of some of its diverse holdings, selling at least one business every year for the next few years. The following year CBS regained dominance in the prime-time TV ratings, a position held by ABC since 1976. One week after CBS took the lead, however, President Backe was forced to resign. He was replaced by Thomas H. Wyman, who had been a vice-president at Pillsbury.

CBS went to court again in 1982 after it aired the documentary *The Uncounted Enemy: A Vietnam Deception.* The case was the beginning of a long-running battle between CBS and retired U.S. Army General William Westmoreland, who filed a $120 million libel suit against the network. The dispute ended several years later when Westmoreland withdrew his charges on a promise from CBS that the network would publicly attempt to restore his character.

By the early 1980s CBS operations had been divided into six main categories: the broadcast group, which was concerned with programming and production of shows for the network, theaters, home video, and cable TV; the records group; the publishing group; the toys division; the technology center, which was responsible for research and development of new technologies; and various corporate joint ventures, including CBS/FOX Company, a collaboration with Twentieth Century-Fox to manufacture and distribute videocassettes and videodiscs. In 1986 CBS sold its book-publishing business to Harcourt Brace Jovanovich, Inc., for $500 million, and that same year the company sold all of its toy businesses.

In 1983 CBS, Columbia Pictures, and Home Box Office (HBO) joined forces to form Tri-Star Pictures, a motion picture production and distribution company. By 1984 Tri-Star had released 17 full-length films, nine of which it also produced, and in 1985 CBS sold its interest in the company. Another experiment was Trintex, a commercial electronic service that allowed people access to news, weather, and sports information; financial and educational data; and home shopping and banking from a personal computer terminal. Initiated in 1984, Trintex—a project from which CBS withdrew in 1986—was the combined effort of CBS, IBM, and Sears, Roebuck & Co.

In 1985 Ted Turner, owner of Turner Broadcasting System (TBS), announced his intentions to take over CBS. In order to prevent this, CBS swallowed a $954.8 million poison pill by purchasing 21 percent of its own outstanding stock.

In September 1986 Larry Tisch replaced Tom Wyman as chief executive officer of CBS. Tisch had previously served as the chairman of Loew's Corporation, which owned nearly 25 percent of CBS stock at the time. Following a power struggle between Tisch and Wyman, who continued to serve as president of CBS, William S. Paley returned as chairman of the board and Wyman was forced to resign.

Although Tisch was originally to serve only as interim chief executive officer, within four months it was clear that the job was his. He immediately began cutting costs at the network. Trimming $30 million from the news division budget, Tisch tried to reduce programming costs, cut hundreds of jobs, and sold a number of CBS publishing concerns. He also sold CBS Records to the Sony Corporation in 1987 for $2 billion, even though the subsidiary, which boasted such top stars as Michael Jackson and Bruce Springsteen, had been a perennial moneymaker for the company.

Tisch was soundly criticized for selling the number one record company in the industry at a time when the music business appeared to be healthy, and for trying to cut television programming costs when cable TV and other pay services were seducing viewers with a broader and higher quality selection. CBS's prime-time hits were getting old; in 1987 the network came in last in the Nielsen ratings. To make matters worse, CBS viewers tended to be older than the audience advertisers were trying to reach.

In 1988 Tisch, under fire from the CBS board and affiliate stations for lacking any long-term strategy, appointed 38-year-old Kim LeMasters to head the network's entertainment division. LeMasters' task was to find new programming that would appeal to younger audiences.

CBS entered the 1990s absent Paley, who died in 1990. The company soon experienced a pleasant jump in the ratings but was still coping with slumping revenues. In 1990 CBS, like other companies dependent on advertising, saw its income drop precipitously as the country remained stuck in a recession, and prospects for an economic recovery seemed bleak as a war in the Persian Gulf threatened to erupt. Also contributing to the poor fiscal performance that year were the huge hits CBS took on major sports contracts, particularly on professional baseball: the company was forced to swallow $171.2 million in losses.

CBS enjoyed a moral, if not financial, surge in 1991, as the broadcaster's ratings—last among the networks for the previous four years—jumped to number one, the most dramatic recovery in television history. CBS boasted five of the top ten programs, including the number one "60 Minutes," which became the only show ever to rank first in three separate decades. Although executives from other networks claimed that special events, such as coverage of the World Series and the 1992 Winter Olympics, accounted for the coveted ratings trophy, CBS pointed out that it had beat the competition in regularly scheduled programming and had consistently led NBC and ABC in the weekly ratings races. Industry observers credited this victory to a better stock of shows on CBS as well as an aggressive self-promotional and marketing campaign that outpaced those of the rival networks. Even controversy played to CBS's favor. When U.S. Vice-President Dan Quayle accused the show "Murphy Brown," the third highest rated show on TV, of irresponsibly celebrating unwed mothers and the breakup of the traditional American family, CBS executives believed the political storm would only lead to greater viewer and advertiser interest.

But financial woes overshadowed these successes. Despite reducing its dividend, cutting $100 million in operating costs, and scaling back personnel by approximately six percent—the budgetary ax fell on the company's flagship news division particularly hard—CBS saw revenue fall eight percent and suffered a loss. Although the networks collectively did their worst business in 20 years, as total ad spending in the country declined for the first time in 30 years, 1991–92 was considered a banner period for television. American viewers were riveted by the Persian Gulf War, the confirmation hearings of Supreme Court Justice Clarence Thomas, and the dissolution of the Soviet Union.

However, CBS was not able to coast on these spectacles. As in 1990, the company racked up huge losses in its sports divisions, proving to some observers what had always been suspected: the network had grossly overpaid for its baseball and football contracts, which were to expire after their respective 1993 seasons. Despite projections of losses for its coverage of the 1992 Winter Olympics, CBS proudly revealed that it had broken even on the Games.

1995 Acquisition by Westinghouse

CBS lost the rights to NFC football games in 1993. This loss, combined with mounting financial losses and the lack of a move into cable, led to a vote of no confidence from one of CBS's top two institutional investors. In response, the beleaguered Tisch sold CBS to Westinghouse Electric Corporation in 1995 for $5.4 billion, marking the beginning of a dramatic era of change for the broadcasting company's new parent company.

Westinghouse, whose massive holdings included defense electronics, power generation, and nuclear engineering businesses, had experienced profound problems during the early 1990s. A lack of strategy, mismanagement, and a costly foray into the financial services business prompted the industrial giant's board of directors to recruit Michael H. Jordan, an executive from Pepsi, to lead the corporation to recovery. Initially, Jordan promised to restore Westinghouse to its former greatness as a technology-driven, industrial heavyweight, but he soon began to look toward other alternatives for the corporation's future. CBS, as it became apparent after Westinghouse acquired the broadcaster in 1995, represented Jordan's vision of Westinghouse's future, perhaps more so than anyone realized.

After abandoning a plan to split Westinghouse's diverse industrial holdings and CBS into two companies, Jordan decided to strip Westinghouse of all its industrial businesses and focus instead on broadcasting. Beginning in 1996, Westinghouse began transforming itself, in essence, into CBS, a process that required the industrial behemoth to peel away all its former strength and move headlong into television and radio broadcasting. In 1996, Westinghouse sold its Knoll Group furniture manufacturing operations, its defense electronics units, and its residential burglar alarm business. The following year, the company sold its Thermo-King business to Ingersoll-Rand for $2.56 billion and its power generation business to Siemens AG for roughly $1.5 billion.

By the end of 1997, Jordan had orchestrated $25 billion in deals to execute his strategy of turning Westinghouse into a broadcaster, a total that not only included the divestitures of the company's industrial holdings but also several important acquisitions. In 1997, Westinghouse paid $4.9 billion for Infinity Broadcasting Corporation, the second largest radio station network in the United States. Also in 1997, Jordan engineered CBS's belated push into cable by acquiring TNN (The Nashville Network) and the U.S. and Canadian operations of CMT (Country Music Television) from Gaylord Entertainment Co. for $1.55 billion. Additionally, CBS launched "Eye on People," a news and entertainment network expected to bolster the broadcaster's presence in cable.

On December 1, 1997, with much of Jordan's major transformation work completed, Westinghouse changed its name to CBS Corporation and moved its headquarters from Pittsburgh to New York City. Following the sale of its power generation business to Siemens, the only vestiges of the former Westinghouse were the company's nuclear power business and a unit that handled nuclear material for the U.S. government. Both of these businesses were divested in 1998, acquired by Morrison Knudsen and British Nuclear Fuels. What remained was the newly diversified CBS, whose strength during the late 1990s had grown amid the swirl of corporate activity surrounding it. Although the network continued to attract an older audience, CBS's television ratings were encouragingly high during the late 1990s, eclipsing all rival networks. As the broadcaster prepared for the 21st century, ready to begin an eight-year, $4 billion contract with the NFL (having outbid NBC for the rights), the company's new management hoped to engineer a return to the past, back to the years when CBS held sway.

Principal Subsidiaries

CBS Cable Networks, Inc.; Westinghouse Electric Corporation; TDI Worldwide, Inc.; Infinity Broadcasting Corporation.

Principal Operating Units

Infinity Media Broadcasting Corporation; CBS Entertainment; CBS News; CBS Sports; CBS Enterprises; CBS New Media; CBS Cable.

Further Reading

Boyer, Peter J., *Who Killed CBS? How America's Number One News Network Went Down the Tubes,* New York: Random House, 1988.

Carter, Bill, "CBS in First Place of Ratings Race for Year," *New York Times,* April 15, 1992.

"CBS Lays Off Hundreds to Cut Budget by at Least $100 Million," *Broadcasting,* April 8, 1991.

"Down to the Core," *Mergers & Acquisitions,* January–February 1998, p. 6.

Goldman, Kevin, "CBS Investors Entertain Disney Rumors, Drive Stock Up," *Wall Street Journal,* April 20, 1992.

——, "CBS Takes $322 Million Pretax Charge on Sports Contracts, Posts Quarterly Loss," *Wall Street Journal,* November 4, 1991.

Halberstam, David, *The Powers That Be,* New York: Knopf, 1979.

McClellan, Steve, "CBS to Break Even on Olympics," *Broadcasting,* March 2, 1992.

Metz, Robert, *CBS: Reflections in a Bloodshot Eye,* New York: New American Library, 1975.

Nelson, Carrington, "It's Official: TNN and CMT Networks Are Part of Westinghouse," *Knight-Ridder/Tribune Business News,* October 2, 1997, p. 1002B1255.

Paper, Lewis J., *Empire: William S. Paley and the Making of CBS,* New York: St. Martin's, 1987.

Slater, Robert, *This . . . Is CBS: A Chronicle of Sixty Years,* New York: Prentice Hall, 1988.

"Westinghouse RIP," *Economist,* November 29, 1997, p. 63.

—Mark Pestana
—updated by Jeffrey L. Covell

Champion Industries, Inc.

P.O. Box 2968
Huntington, West Virginia 25728-2968
U.S.A.
(304) 528-2700
Fax: (304) 528-2765
Web site: http://www.champion-industries.com

Public Company
Incorporated: 1922 as Chapman Printing Company
Employees: 907
Sales: $123.1 million (1998)
Stock Exchanges: NASDAQ
Ticker Symbol: CHMP
NAIC: 323117 Book Printing; 323114 Quick Printing;
   323110 Commercial Lithographic Printing; 42212
   Stationery & Office Supplies Wholesalers; 421210
   Office Furniture Wholesaling

Champion Industries, Inc. and its predecessor companies have been based in Huntington, West Virginia, since 1922. Champion was formed in 1992 when The Harrah and Reynolds Corporation spun off its printing division. Since that time Champion has grown through a series of acquisitions as well as internal growth. Its largest acquisition was that of Interform at the end of 1996. A business forms printer, Interform added substantially to the printing component of Champion's revenue. Prior to the acquisition, office products and furniture accounted for approximately 30 percent of Champion's revenue in 1994, with printing accounting for the rest. By 1998 office products and furniture accounted for approximately 23 percent of Champion's revenue, up from less than 19 percent in 1997.

Champion is organized into 21 divisions, 15 of which are operated as wholly owned subsidiaries. Ten of the divisions are devoted to commercial printing. Three divisions specialize in business forms. One division manufactures and sells tags used in a variety of industries. The company's office products, office furniture, and office design businesses are conducted by two

subsidiaries, Stationers, Inc., which primarily services customers located in West Virginia, Ohio, and eastern Kentucky, and Smith & Butterfield Co., Inc., which primarily services customers located in Indiana and western Kentucky.

Chapman Printing Founded, 1922

In 1922 John Osiola Costa Chapman founded Chapman Printing Company in Huntington, West Virginia. Operations there grew to include full-scale printing facilities, including web presses, and sales and customer service operations. Nearly 40 years later Chapman was acquired by Harrah and Reynolds in 1964 and became its printing division. Chapman had not grown substantially since its founding and reported net revenue of $3,000 on sales of $103,000.

Chapman Expanded Through Acquisitions, 1970–90

In 1972 Marshall T. Reynolds, president and general manager of Harrah and Reynolds, bought out his partner and became the sole shareholder in Chapman. In 1974 the Charleston division was established through the acquisition of the printing operations of Rose City Press. In 1977 the Parkersburg division opened and was expanded by the acquisitions of Park Press and McGlothin Printing Company. This division contained a large full-color printing facility and a state-of-the-art studio.

The company's Lexington division began operations in 1983 with the acquisition of the Transylvania Company. This location included a pre-press department, computerized composition facilities, a press room, and a bindery department, as well as customer service.

Expanded Office Furniture and Supplies Operation, 1987

Stationers, Inc., was acquired in 1987. It was an office products, office furniture, and retail bookstore operation. The company then consolidated its own office products and furniture operations with Stationers. In 1991 Stationers divested its retail bookstore operation.

From 1989 to 1992 Chapman reported relatively flat sales and gradually improving earnings. In 1989 it had a net loss of $100,000 on sales of $27.2 million. Sales hovered around $27 million for the next few years, with net income rising to $1.3 million in 1992.

Chapman Became Champion Industries, 1992

On July 1, 1992, Champion Industries was chartered as a West Virginia corporation. Prior to the company's initial public offering (IPO) in January 1993, it was operated as the printing division of The Harrah and Reynolds Corporation as Chapman Printing Company and Stationers, Inc. Following the IPO, Champion took possession of substantially all of the operating assets of Harrah and Reynolds's printing division, as well as its outstanding capital stock, in exchange for two million shares of common stock. Proceeds from the IPO were used to pursue an aggressive acquisitions strategy that sought to achieve dominance in specific regional markets in the eastern United States, especially in the South and Southeast.

Began Series of Acquisitions, 1993

In 1993 Stationers expanded through acquisition and began operating in Marietta, Ohio, under the name Garrison Brewer. In June 1993 the Bourque Printing division began operations with the acquisition of Bourque Printing, Inc. in Baton Rouge, Louisiana. Bourque expanded later in 1993 with the acquisition of Strother Forms/Printing of Baton Rouge, in 1994 with the acquisition of certain assets of Spectrum Press, Inc. of Baton Rouge, and then in 1996 with the acquisition of E.S. Upton Printing Co., Inc., of New Orleans. Upton, founded in 1889, was in bankruptcy at the time.

In September 1993 the Dallas Printing division began operation with the acquisition of Dallas Printing Co., Inc., in Jackson, Mississippi. In November Champion acquired Tri-Star Printing, Inc. Tri-Star was doing business as Carolina Cut Sheets, and Champion's subsidiary changed its name to Carolina Cut Sheets. It manufactured single-part business forms for sale to dealers.

For fiscal 1993 Champion reported net income of $2.1 million on revenues of $30.3 million. As a result of acquisitions made in 1993, revenues for fiscal 1994 rose to $43.2 million, and net income increased to 2.7 million. At this time office furniture and products accounted for 30.6 percent of the company's revenues.

In June 1994 Champion acquired certain assets of Premier Data Graphics, a distributor of business forms and data supplies in Clarksburg, West Virginia. In August the Dallas Printing division acquired certain assets of Premier Printing Co., Inc., of Jackson, Mississippi.

Acquired U.S. Tag and Ticket Co., 1995

In June 1995 Champion acquired U.S. Tag and Ticket Co., Inc., of Baltimore, Maryland, in exchange for 52,383 shares of common stock. U.S. Tag and Ticket manufactured tags used in a variety of industries, including shipping, postal, airline, and cruise. In November the company acquired Donihe Graphics, Inc., a high-volume color printer based in Kingsport, Tennessee, for $950,000 in cash and 66,768 shares of common stock. Revenues increased modestly in fiscal 1995 to $49.9 million, and the company reported net income of $3 million.

Four Major Acquisitions, 1996

In February Bourque acquired E.S. Upton Printing Co. for $750,000 in cash. In July Champion acquired Smith & Butterfield Co., Inc., an office products company with locations in Evansville, Indiana, and Owensboro, Kentucky, and made it a division of Stationers. Champion issued 66,666 shares of stock valued at $1.2 million in exchange for all of Smith & Butterfield's stock. In August Champion acquired The Merten Co., a commercial printer headquartered in Cincinnati, Ohio, for cash and assumed liabilities totaling about $2.5 million.

In its largest acquisition to date, Champion acquired Interform Corp., a business forms manufacturer based in Bridgeville, Pennsylvania, for $2.5 million in December. The acquisition gave Champion access to the large northeastern markets of Pennsylvania, New Jersey, and New York.

Revenues for fiscal 1996 increased 33 percent over the previous year to $66.4 million, and net income rose to $3.4 million. Office furniture and products continued to account for about 26 percent of revenues. However, the acquisition of Interform would increase printing's share of revenue in the coming years.

Continued Acquisitions Program, 1997–98

In May 1997 Champion acquired Blue Ridge Printing Co., Inc., of Asheville, North Carolina, and Knoxville, Tennessee, for 277,775 shares of common stock. Champion's revenues for fiscal 1997 were $108.4 million, an increase of 42 percent over the previous year. Net income rose modestly to $3.8 million. Office furniture and products accounted for only 18.8 percent of sales.

Champion made three acquisitions in 1998. In February it acquired the remaining office supply business of Rose City Press of Charleston, West Virginia, for 75,722 shares of stock valued at $1.25 million. In May it acquired Capitol Business Equipment, Inc., doing business as Capitol Business Interiors, of Charleston, West Virginia, for 72,202 shares of common stock valued at $1 million. Also in May Champion acquired Thompson's of Morgantown, Inc., and Thompson's of Barbour County, Inc., based in Morgantown, West Virginia, for 45,473 shares of stock valued at $600,000. Rose City, Capitol, and Thompson's were then operated as divisions of Stationers. For fiscal 1998, Champion reported net income of $4.2 million on sales of $123.1 million.

Outlook, 1999

Champion has acquired 12 printing companies and six office products and office furniture companies since its IPO in 1993. Through its program of acquisitions and internal growth it has been able to realize regional economies of scale, operational efficiencies, and exposure to new markets. It appears that Champion will continue its program of selective acquisitions in the printing and office products and furniture industries as it continues to achieve record profits and revenues.

Principal Subsidiaries

The Chapman Printing Co.; Bourque Printing, Inc.; Dallas Printing Co.; Carolina Cut Sheets; U.S. Tag and Ticket; Donihe Graphics, Inc.; Upton Printing Co.; The Merten Co.; Interform Solutions; Consolidated Graphic Communications; Blue Ridge Printing Co., Inc.; Stationers, Inc.; Garrison Brewer; Smith & Butterfield Co., Inc.; Champion-Clarksburg; Rose City Press; Champion-Morgantown; Capitol Business Interiors.

Further Reading

"Champion Industries, Inc.," http://www.champion-industries.com.

—David Bianco

CROWLEY AMERICAN TRANSPORT

Crowley Maritime Corporation

155 Grand Avenue
Oakland, California 94612
U.S.A.
(510) 251-7500
Fax: (510) 251-7788
Web site: http://www.crowley.com

Private Company
Incorporated: 1906 as Crowley Launch and Tugboat
Company
Employees: 5,000
Sales: $1.1 billion (1997 est.)
NAIC: 483111 Deep Sea Freight Transportation; 483113
Coastal & Great Lakes Freight Transportation; 48831
Port & Harbor Operations; 48833 Navigational
Services to Shipping; 48411 General Freight
Trucking, Local; 484121 General Freight Trucking,
Long-Distance, Truckload; 49311 General
Warehousing & Storage; 336611 Shipyard

Crowley Maritime Corporation is the largest operator of tugboats and barges in the world. The privately held company has two main operating subsidiaries. Crowley American Transport, Inc. provides ocean liner cargo services between the United States, Canada, Mexico, South America, and the Caribbean; its American Marine Transport, Inc. unit provides local, over-the-road, and commercial trucking services in the continental United States. Crowley Marine Services, Inc. provides worldwide contract and specialized marine transportation services, including petroleum product transportation and sales, tanker escort and ship assist, contract barge transportation and ocean towing, logistics and support services, marine salvage and emergency response services, spill-response services on the West Coast of the United States, and all-terrain transportation services. Crowley Maritime also has two other smaller subsidiaries: Crowley Petroleum Transport, Inc., which was formed in 1997 and operates petroleum tankers in the U.S. tanker trades; and Vessel Management Services, Inc., which was established

in 1996 and designs, engineers, constructs, and maintains ownership of new vessels for Crowley Maritime.

Founded in 1892

Thomas Crowley was 17 years old when he founded the business in 1892. Crowley purchased an 18-foot Whitehall boat for $80 and began a water-taxi service, delivering supplies, passengers, and crew members to and from ships that were anchored in the San Francisco Bay. By 1900 Crowley was running 36-foot and 45-foot gasoline-powered launches and a few years later he began to acquire gasoline- and steam-powered tugboats. With the motto "Anything, Anywhere, Anytime, on Water," the Crowley Launch and Tugboat Company was legally incorporated in 1906.

Over the next decade or so, Crowley continued to acquire more and larger vessels, adapting his equipment to meet the needs of his customers. In 1912 a shipyard, later known as the Pacific Dry Dock and Repair Co., was built in Oakland for repairing Crowley vessels. In addition, Crowley began operating San Francisco harbor tours on double-deck passenger boats he had built for the 1915 Exposition. Crowley also bought a 25 percent share of Shipowners and Merchants Tugboat Company, owner of the Red Stack tugs, in 1918. This investment was increased over the years until Crowley fully owned the company.

The Crowley fleet continued to expand after World War I, initiating tug and barge operations into Puget Sound and tugboat service into Los Angeles Harbor in the 1920s. Crowley purchased stock in two companies, Drummond Lighterage and the Cary-Davis Tug and Barge Company, and soon acquired a controlling interest in Drummond. In 1929 these two companies merged with two others, Pacific Towboat and Gilkey Bros., to form a new corporation, Puget Sound Tug and Barge Company with 48 barges and 27 tugs. Puget Sound later became fully owned by Crowley.

Crowley's growth and diversification continued through the 1930s. The company's launch and tug services reached all major ports on the West Coast, having expanded its harbor services to Long Beach and San Diego Harbors. In 1935 Crowley purchased the Bay Cities Transportation Company, expanding the company's capability in common carrier freight service, a business it had entered a few years earlier. Harbor Carriers was established about 1960 when the company began to operate ferry services, which are regulated by the California Public Utilities Commission. Before that, Crowley had operated nonregulated passenger services since its earliest years. Also in 1935, Harbor Tug and Barge Co. became a wholly owned Crowley company. Crowley added bulk petroleum transportation to its list of services in 1939, and by the onset of World War II, the company had purchased the entire petroleum barge fleet of Shell Oil Company in San Francisco and was delivering petroleum to Shell storage facilities throughout the Bay Area.

In the 1940s Crowley began ocean transportation of lumber along the West Coast using tugs and barges. Crowley achieved a major breakthrough in bulk barge transportation in 1948, when Crowley's United Transportation Co. began operating the first oceangoing bulk petroleum barge service on the Pacific Coast. The shipments, which were made in a brand new barge with a 14,000-barrel capacity, traveled between San Francisco and Coos Bay in North Bend, Oregon.

A second Oakland repair facility was acquired in 1953. The facility, the Martinolich Ship Repair Co. (later renamed the Merrit Shipyards), helped meet the increasing repair needs of Crowley's growing fleet. It was later merged into the Pacific Dry Dock and Repair Co.

Moved into Alaska in the 1950s and 1960s

In the mid-1950s Crowley began to establish services in the Arctic. In 1956 United Transportation Co. started shipping large amounts of asphalt between Portland, Oregon, and Anchorage, Alaska. The barges that made this trip were capable of carrying 12,000 barrels of asphalt. In 1958 Crowley began its longstanding relationship with the Military Sealift Command when it participated in the commercial resupply of the U.S. government's Distant Early Warning (DEW) Line installations. The DEW installations, part of a radar and defense communication system, were located in remote areas along the Alaskan coastline, in the Bering Sea and the Aleutian Chain.

Within the next few years common carrier service to Alaska was added to Crowley's line. Puget Sound Alaska Van Lines was formed in 1960, providing container and roll-on cargo service to

Alaska. This company was the predecessor of Alaska Hydro-Train, which began operating in 1963. Alaska Hydro-Train connected the railroad system of Alaska to that of the lower 48 states with container and ro-ro (roll-on/roll-off) railcar barge service between Seattle, Washington, and Whittier, Alaska.

During the remainder of the 1960s, Crowley played a major role in support of oil industry activities in Alaska. As oil drilling in the Arctic increased rapidly following the discovery of oil on Alaska's North Slope, so did Crowley's Arctic involvement. In 1966, in order to provide supply- and crew-boat services to oil companies attempting to set up offshore drilling operations in Cook Inlet, the Rig Tenders Company was organized in Kenai, Alaska. Then in 1968, Crowley successfully managed the first of its annual Arctic sealifts to Prudhoe Bay. Prudhoe Bay is on the North Slope of Alaska, and the voyage north from Seattle around Alaska's perimeter is close to 4,000 miles. The sealifts were made on 400-foot flat deck barges and carried oil industry cargo and plant modules, some of which were the size of an 11-story building. Crowley's 1970 sealift of 187,000 tons of cargo to Prudhoe Bay was the largest commercial sealift in the history of such endeavors.

Tremendous Growth and Diversification in the 1970s

Tom Crowley died in 1970 at the age of 95. His son, Thomas B. Crowley, Sr., had already been running the company, gradually assuming responsibilities since the 1940s. The 1970s were a decade of tremendous growth and diversification for Crowley. The company started its Marine Oil Pickup Service (MOPS) in 1970. MOPS was designed to clean up oil spills in Puget Sound. The same year, the company began passenger service between southern California and Santa Catalina Island with its Catalina Cruises. In 1971 Crowley created Gulf Caribbean Marine Lines, which was organized to carry cargo in warehouse barges from U.S. ports on the Gulf of Mexico to various locations in the Caribbean Sea. The company also began to focus on expansion into southeast Asia, establishing a company based in Singapore that provided offshore support services in that part of the world. In 1973 Crowley acquired an Alaskan trucking firm, Mukluk Freight Lines. Mukluk was the largest carrier of the 48-inch pipe used in constructing the 800-mile transAlaska pipeline.

Possibly the most important development of the 1970s occurred in 1974, with the acquisition of Trailer Marine Transport (TMT). TMT was a small tug and barge common carrier that had been operating since 1954. Crowley proceeded to transform TMT into the largest ro-ro barge operation in the world, ultimately using triple-deck barges that could carry more than 500 semitrailers. Also in 1974 came further involvement in southeast Asia, including an Indonesia-based joint venture tending drilling rigs and a second joint venture in offshore drilling services.

In 1975 Crowley Environmental Service evolved out of the earlier Puget Sound environmental operation, offering a broader range of services with offices all along the West Coast and Alaska. Upon the acquisition of the floating equipment of Pacific Inland Navigation Company, common carrier service extended to Hawaii. This acquisition also made APUTCO, previously a joint "cool barge" venture, a wholly owned Crowley subsidiary. Crowley All Terrain Corporation (CATCO), a company that specialized in transporting supplies and personnel in the Arctic, through all sorts of weather, over all sorts of terrain, was also organized in 1975. That was also the year of the worst ice conditions of the century faced by the Prudhoe Bay sealift flotilla, freezing in a number of the barges. Two additional Crowley companies were formed in 1975: Crowley Maritime Salvage and Global Transport Organization (GTO). GTO, formed jointly with two Canadian companies, was designed to perform tug and barge transportation services internationally, and was particularly active in the Arabian Gulf during Saudi Arabia's large-scale push toward industrialization.

In 1976 Crowley introduced a seasonal common carrier service to western Alaska from Seattle with the creation of Pacific Alaska Line-West. The following year, tanker-assist and escort services were initiated at the southern end of the transAlaska pipeline at Valdez, Alaska. In the late 1970s Crowley added to its fleet the *Arctic Challenger,* a 310-by-105-foot icebreaker barge followed by the salvage vessel *Arctic Salvor,* built through a vessel conversion in 1980. Among the companies formed or acquired during the 1970s was Salmon Carriers, an important Bristol Bay salmon industry hauler. During the 1970s Crowley developed the "float-on" loading technique, in which a barge is submerged in a controlled manner and cargo is floated into place.

Expansion Continued in the 1980s

Crowley's rapid expansion and emphasis on a more international focus continued through the 1980s. In 1981, in order to help meet the heavy lifting and hauling needs of its Alaskan land operations, Crowley acquired Shaughnessy and Company, based in Auburn, Washington. The company purchased Delta Lines from Holiday Inns Inc. in 1982. Delta, which operated 24 ships on five trade routes between the United States and South America, Central America, the Caribbean, and West Africa, was sold again just two years later. *American Shipper* estimated that in 1982 the company earned $42.5 million profit on revenues of $550 million.

Profits were cut in half in 1983, however, largely due to a severe drop-off in South American trade that caused Delta Lines alone to lose $20 million, but Crowley continued to expand. In 1984 TMT's Caribbean business benefited from the lengthening of five of its specially built triple-deck barges. These barges, formerly 400 feet long, were enlarged to 730 feet by the insertion of 330-foot sections into the middle of their bodies. By that year, Crowley controlled 35 percent of the barge business between ports on the Gulf of Mexico and Puerto Rico. At that point the company had about 500 vessels, and brought in about 70 percent of its sales revenues through its barge and tug operations. In 1985 Crowley established Pacific Alaska Fuel Services to serve western Alaska with the transportation and sale of petroleum products, through tank facilities located in Nome, Kotzebue, and Captain's Bay.

Further expansion took place over the next couple of years, as two major developments stretched Crowley's service area to include northern Europe, the entire Caribbean, and both coasts of South America. The first of these was the acquisition in 1986 of Coordinated Caribbean Transport, soon renamed Crowley Caribbean Transport (CCT). CCT had been in operation since 1961, when it consisted of two converted Navy landing vessels.

CCT's main role was to carry agricultural products north from the Caribbean and head south loaded with industrial equipment. Among the stops included on the route were Costa Rica, Panama, Jamaica, Haiti, the Dominican Republic, Ecuador, and Peru. Then in 1987, Crowley created American Transport Lines (AmTrans). AmTrans, organized as two separate ocean liner services to South America and Europe, quickly became the predominant American carrier to South America's East Coast. By the early 1990s AmTrans was carrying over 50 percent of the containerized cargo between the United States and Argentina, Brazil, and Venezuela. The company's "Sea Wolf" class containerships were equipped with their own cranes and were capable of carrying heavy-lift, ro-ro, and oversized cargoes. Crowley's revenues in 1987 were estimated between $700 million and $850 million. At the time, Crowley consisted of about 40 separate companies with approximately 4,000 employees.

By 1988 Crowley's share of the West Coast-Alaska market was about 18 percent. The company suffered through the worst financial year in its history, however, losing $30 million. Half of this loss was due to a Far East line, purchased from Pacific-Atlantic Navigation, that proved to be unprofitable. Catalina Landing, an unsuccessful real estate venture, and a strike by the Inland Boatmen's Union also contributed to the loss.

A remarkable turnaround occurred for Crowley in 1989, thanks in part to the $40 million the company grossed from the rescue of the *Exxon Valdez,* the oil tanker that ran aground in Alaska, spilling its cargo in Prince William Sound. Crowley was the primary contractor for the provision of cleanup support equipment and personnel. In the same year Crowley designed, built, and operated the Responder, the first barge in the world specifically geared for oil-spill contingencies for use in exploratory drilling operations. Crowley involved itself in other disasters that year as well, sometimes for profit, other times without financial gain. The Red and White Fleet transported 15,000 stranded commuters, at no charge, following the San Francisco earthquake. In addition, rebuilding projects that followed the destructive Hurricane Hugo increased cargo traffic, although the company also suffered damages from the storm.

In 1990 Crowley moved its headquarters from San Francisco—its base of operations for 98 years—to Oakland, California. By the beginning of the 1990s, the company had outposts throughout the world, with offices in over 100 major cities. During the crisis in the Persian Gulf, including both Operation Desert Shield and Operation Desert Storm, Crowley chartered several vessels to the U.S. Military Sealift Command. These ships, which supported the United Nations forces with transportation of personnel and supplies, included three ro-ro containerships, a tug, and a barge. After the conflict, Crowley was selected by the government of Saudi Arabia as primary contractor for the cleanup of oil spills covering 450 kilometers of Saudi Arabian coastline, brought about by the demolition of Kuwaiti oil tankers and facilities during the war. These various government contracts helped raise Crowley's 1991 revenues to an estimated $1.1 billion.

Reorganized in 1992

In 1992 Crowley underwent a legal reorganization. The 45 companies owned by Crowley were divided into two corporations based on the types of services they performed. Crowley American Transport, Inc. was created to encompass all companies that carry cargo on oceanliners or perform related services. The remainder of the companies, primarily those that provide marine contract services such as tugboat operations, were organized as Crowley Marine Services, Inc. The privately held Crowley Maritime Corporation would serve as a holding company maintaining full ownership of both corporations.

In mid-1994 the top leadership of Crowley Maritime changed for only the second time in company history; at age 28, Thomas B. Crowley, Jr., was elected chairman, president, and CEO following the death of his father from prostate cancer. Also in 1994 Crowley American Transport began scheduled service to the Bahamas from Port Everglades, Florida. Crowley Marine Services formed two joint ventures, Marine Response Alliance (established in 1994) and Clean Pacific (1995) to provide emergency service in accordance with the Oil Pollution Act of 1990.

In 1995 the San Francisco local of the International Longshore & Warehouse Union refused to allow Crowley Maritime to reduce crew sizes by one, prompting the company to pull its tugboats and ships out of its home port, after 100 years operating there. Crowley moved the vessels to Seattle and Los Angeles. Around this same time, an exhaustive study, dubbed Focus 2000, led to the identification of core activities for Crowley Marine Services: oil transportation, contract barge and towing services, marine fuel sales and distribution in western Alaska and Puerto Rico, docking and emergency response services for tankers, vessel salvage and spill cleanup services, western Alaska deck cargo services, and all-terrain transportation services. The study resulted in the divestment of several noncore operations, including the Red and White Fleet ferrying service as well as Catalina Cruises, both of which were sold in 1997.

In 1996 and 1997, Crowley American Transport greatly expanded its Central American operations, adding vessels and weekly fixed-day sailings. Crowley Maritime created a new subsidiary called Vessel Management Services, Inc. in 1996 to be responsible for the design, engineering, construction, and ownership maintenance of new company vessels. The following year another new subsidiary, Crowley Petroleum Transport, Inc., was

inaugurated with the purchase of two 658-by-100-foot, double-bottom oil tankers that would provide bulk oil transportation in the U.S. tanker trades. Also in 1997 Crowley American Transport expanded geographically, adding Chile to its U.S. East Coast-West Coast South America service. Estimated 1997 revenues for Crowley Maritime were in excess of $1.1 billion, and the company had about 5,000 employees that year.

Principal Subsidiaries

Crowley American Transport, Inc.; Crowley Marine Services, Inc.; Crowley Petroleum Transport, Inc.; Vessel Management Services, Inc.

Further Reading

Burstiner, Marcy, ''New Captain Preparing to Take the Helm at Oakland's Crowley Maritime,'' *San Francisco Business Times,* April 22, 1994, pp. 1, 16.

''Crowley Maritime Corporation: A Century of Service, 1892–1992,'' *Pacific Maritime,* May 1992.

''Crowley Maritime's Fight to Keep a Shaky Line Afloat,'' *Business Week,* August 20, 1984.

''Crowley Selling Passenger, Ferry Units,'' *American Shipper,* February 1995, p. 87.

Davies, John, ''Crowley Maritime: A Study in Diversity,'' *Journal of Commerce,* March 6, 1987.

Hauls of Fame, Vol. 10, Oakland, Calif.: Crowley Maritime Corporation, 1991.

Knee, Richard, ''Crowley's Next Generation,'' *American Shipper,* July 1994, p. 20.

——, ''Rebound for Crowley Maritime,'' *American Shipper,* November 1989.

''Leo Collar,'' *American Shipper,* October 1987.

March, Ann, ''Beating the Third-Generation Curse,'' *Fortune,* November 30, 1998, pp. 186–88.

Special Supplement, *Journal of Commerce,* November 10, 1988.

''Thomas B. Crowley,'' *American Shipper,* January 1984.

Tirschwell, Peter, ''Crowley's Brent Stienecker to Retire: Chairman Will Take on Larger Role,'' *Journal of Commerce,* July 14, 1998, pp. 1B, 3B.

—Robert R. Jacobson
—updated by David E. Salamie

CSR Limited

Level 24, 1 O'Connell Street
Sydney
New South Wales 2001
Australia
(02) 9235-8000
Fax: (02) 9235-8044
Web site: http://www.csr.com.au

Public Company
Incorporated: 1887 as The Colonial Sugar Refining
    Company
Employees: 19,700
Sales: A$6.96 billion (US$4.20 billion) (1998)
Stock Exchanges: Australian London New Zealand
NAIC: 212299 Other Metal Ore Mining; 212321
    Construction Sand & Gravel Mining; 311311 Sugar
    Cane Mills; 311312 Cane Sugar Refining; 321113
    Sawmills; 324122 Asphalt Shingle & Coating
    Materials Manufacturing; 326122 Plastics Pipe & Pipe
    Fitting Manufacturing; 327331 Concrete Block &
    Brick Manufacturing; 32739 Other Concrete Product
    Manufacturing; 32732 Ready-Mix Concrete
    Manufacturing; 32742 Gypsum Product
    Manufacturing; 331312 Primary Aluminum
    Production

CSR Limited is one of the world's largest building and construction materials companies, with operations in Australia, New Zealand, Asia, and the United States. The company is also Australia's largest manufacturer of raw and refined sugar products. Although CSR was established in 1855 to refine sugar and soon after diversified into raw sugar milling, its sugar activities represent only about one-fifth of CSR's annual sales. In an effort to change its image from that of solely a sugar producer, CSR has been promoting its increasingly strong position in the building and construction materials industry. The company has substantial operations in quarrying, concrete, cement products, bricks and tiles, plasterboard, insulation, and timber products, as well as investments in aluminum.

Early History

The Colonial Sugar Refining Company (CSR) was formed as a partnership in January 1855 under the chairmanship of Edward Knox, an ambitious 35-year-old entrepreneur. Having acquired some of the assets of the defunct Australasian Sugar Company, the partnership bought the Brisbane House sugar refinery in Sydney. Two years later, in 1857, a new holding company—the Victoria Sugar Company—was formed jointly by CSR shareholders and Victorian business interests, and a sugar refinery and molasses distillery were set up at Port Melbourne. Later that year, Knox sold his house and some of his shares in the company and left for Europe by ship. Before he reached Europe, he was bombarded with letters telling him the company was ruined. Knox returned to Australia immediately.

The company underwent serious financial difficulties following the depression in the world sugar trade from 1857 to 1858. CSR countered the potentially disastrous effects of the depression by diversifying into sugar milling. By 1869 the company had built a number of new mills in northern New South Wales. With the construction of the Chatsworth, Southgate, and Darkwater mills CSR entered the sugar milling industry. Darkwater Mill has since been renamed Harwood Mill and is the oldest continually working sugar mill in Australia. Knox's second son, Edward William, was put in charge of the project.

The 1870s saw further diversification within the sugar industry. CSR had by now established a network of mills and refineries on the Queensland coast and the purchase of a small freight ship—SS *Keera*—in 1873 gave the company an entry into the coastal shipping business. In 1874 the Victoria Sugar Company's refinery in Melbourne was destroyed by fire and then replaced by the newly built Joshua Brothers' refinery.

CSR continued its program of expansion throughout the next decade. On his retirement, Knox handed over management of the company to his son, writing to a friend, "I can only expect to leave a kind of smeary, sugary track behind me." Edward William Knox was an impetuous and autocratic manager, anxious to emulate his father's success. The milling operations were extended to Queensland, where new mills had been constructed in the early 1880s. In 1882 CSR embarked on its first overseas project, building a mill in Nausori, Fiji. The following year CSR formed the New Zealand Sugar Company to refine sugar in New Zealand, as an equal partnership with the Victoria Sugar Company and business interests in New Zealand. In the mid-1880s CSR's research team conducted the first sugar cane fertilizer trials.

Incorporated in 1887

On July 1, 1887, CSR was amalgamated with the Victoria Sugar Company and was incorporated as a public company, The Colonial Sugar Refining Company Limited. The new company merged the following year with the New Zealand Sugar Company, and CSR was established as a leader in the Australian sugar industry. As the 19th century drew to a close, CSR continued to acquire mills along the Queensland coast and set up a new refinery in Brisbane. Administrative changes, designed to make management of the spreading company more efficient, were introduced in the early 1890s: sugar cane estates in Queensland were divided into small farms for leasing—with the rights of purchase—to cane growers. In 1899 the company's investment in research and development allowed it for the first time to buy cane on the basis of its analyzed sugar content. Other sugar companies were less advanced in the research and application of chemical analysis, and CSR's commitment to research undoubtedly assisted its domination of the domestic sugar industry. In 1904 the company bred Australia's first successful commercial variety of sugar cane, which it christened Clark's Seedling.

Further expansion took place in the early part of the 20th century. An expedition in 1908 to New Guinea to collect samples of sugar cane and thereby improve breeding of new cane varieties for commercial use, gave rise to better cane and sugar yields. Two years earlier several Fijian plantations had been sold to a group of company officers who wanted to work for themselves. As World War I approached, CSR continued to consolidate its refining and milling businesses and sent another cane-gathering party to New Guinea. Trade in Australia benefited from the increase in the British government's demand for sugar and resources after World War I. In 1923 the commonwealth government transferred control of the sugar industry to the Queensland government, and CSR made its first annual refining and marketing agreement with the government. The worldwide Great Depression of the 1930s was threatening, however, and a downturn in demand was anticipated. In 1933 Edward William Knox retired, four months before his death. His son, Edward Ritchie Knox, took over as general manager.

Diversified into Building Materials and Construction Starting in the Late 1930s

The onset of World War II precipitated CSR's second major diversification. A pilot plant set up in 1936 to assess the feasibility of making wallboard from the residue fiber of crushed sugar cane provided CSR with what transpired to be a commercial method of disposing of its sugar millery byproducts. In 1939 CSR acquired shares in a chemicals plant in Sydney and opened a wallboard factory nearby, where the new product Cane-ite

was produced. To meet the needs of the Australian war effort, CSR reduced its sugar-based production activities from 1939 onward to manufacture war-related materials. A new plaster mill was introduced in Sydney in 1942. Two years later CSR began mining asbestos when it acquired Australian Blue Asbestos's mine in Wittenoom, Western Australia.

Although CSR was known mainly as a sugar producer, the postwar program of diversification changed the corporate profile considerably. The last year of the war marked CSR's first substantial entry into building materials and construction when the company bought an interest in Fletcher Holdings, a large construction and timber company based in New Zealand. During the late 1940s CSR introduced new building products—plasterboard and floor tiles—and expanded its factory stock in Sydney. The wave of expansion culminated in the formation of a new wholly owned subsidiary, CSR Chemicals, in 1948.

Over the next ten years, under the directorship of Edward Ritchie Knox, CSR continued to expand. The company's sugar operations were extended and facilities for bulk-loading raw sugar were introduced at two of the original Queensland mills and later extended to cover all 12 mills. In 1955 CSR was appointed coordinator for the Australian sugar industry's conversion to bulk handling. From the mid-1950s on, the company increased its involvement in the building materials industry. The acquisition in 1959 of the Bradford Insulation Group gave CSR a major share of the insulation products market throughout Australia. In the same year, the CSR Chemicals subsidiary spawned two new subsidiaries and a new product—particleboard—was introduced. Developments at this time included the takeover of Masonite Holdings, which manufactured hardboard.

The company opened new research centers in Brisbane in 1962 and in Sydney in 1963. The following year it joined American Metal Climax in a project to develop the Mount Newman iron ore deposits in Western Australia. From the mid-1960s until the early 1980s CSR increased its involvement in resources, including bauxite and alumina, tin, copper, coal, oil and gas, gold, aluminum, and minerals exploration. At the same time that CSR was increasing its investment in resources, it entered the concrete market for the first time. In 1965 it acquired a 50 percent share—with Blue Metal Industries—in Ready Mixed Concrete (RMC).

The 1969 takeover of Wunderlich Ltd., a large manufacturer of roof tiles, asbestos cement products, and architectural metal products, gave CSR its first significant entry into the Australian roof tile industry. The business was subsequently sold in 1983 to Monier. In 1972 the Fijian government bought CSR's Fijian sugar mills, ending the company's 90-year involvement in the Fijian sugar industry.

The resource ventures begun in the 1960s, during Australia's mineral boom, continued throughout the 1970s. The company began to invest in alumina and bauxite; various gold, tin, and copper ventures; and later, coal, oil, and gas. Extensive investments in a number of established coal mines made in the 1970s proved unsuccessful. The prices of coal and oil dropped almost immediately after the acquisitions had been made, near the peak of the energy cycle. A large proportion of loans made for the acquisition of coal and oil assets were in U.S. dollars. The repayments of these loans increased significantly with the fall in the Australian dollar exchange rate in 1983–84, coupled with falling energy prices.

Renamed CSR Limited in 1983

To reflect its diversification, and in an effort to modernize its corporate identity, the company dropped "Colonial Sugar Refining Company" from its original name and in 1973 it became CSR Limited. In the following year CSR entered the cement industry through the joint acquisition, with Pioneer International, of Australian and Kandos Cement. The managerial difficulties CSR was experiencing with such diverse business interests forced a strategic reorganization. The sugar division was formed in 1974 and the mineral division and the building and construction materials division were formed the following year.

Further diversification took place in 1977, when CSR bought AAR Ltd., an exploration company with natural gas, oil, and drilling contracts. Thiess, a large coal company, was acquired in 1979. When the resources boom of the 1970s and early 1980s petered out, CSR was left with a debt and interest burden that made the company vulnerable to takeover bids. Investors had lost faith in the company and CSR share prices plummeted. The company was surviving in large part on the activities of the sugar and building materials divisions, but the drop in world sugar prices in the early to mid-1980s made the situation worse. Until the extensive management and corporate restructuring that began in 1985, CSR was a struggling company. Bryan Kelman became general manager in 1983.

In 1981 the company significantly increased its investment in the oil industry when it bought an Australian-based, U.S.-owned oil and petroleum producer, Delhi International Oil Corporation. The major investments in coal, and particularly oil, were badly timed. The Delhi acquisition was hit with falling oil prices, lack of new oil discoveries, and a falling Australian dollar, while carrying extensive debt in U.S. dollars. As a result, the company began a process of repaying much of its debt through the sale of iron ore and some coal assets. This was followed in 1987 with the sale of Delhi for US$985 million, resulting in a loss of more than US$600 million.

In 1985 sugar profits fell dramatically. Growing public concern about the health risks associated with sugar consumption and a slump in world prices hit CSR badly. In 1985 sugar was at its lowest price in 200 years. Many cane farmers were living below the poverty line and accused CSR of mismanaging the industry in which it played a dominant role.

Shifted Away from Resources, Toward Manufacturing in the Late 1980s

In 1987 CSR began the process of changing the company from a diversified resources and industrial group to a diversified manufacturing company in building and construction materials and sugar—core activities in which the company had long years of experience, since 1855 in sugar and since 1939 in building materials. Between 1987 and 1989 the company sold more than US$2 billion of low-yielding and lossmaking assets in resources and reinvested these funds in building and construction materials and sugar operations, including large investments in the United States.

By the end of the 1980s CSR had sold all of its interests in tin, gold, and mineral exploration, its coal mines, and its oil and gas interests. The head office in Sydney, where the company had been based for 106 years, also was sold to compensate for falling profits. In addition, a more streamlined management structure was introduced. Ian Burgess took over as chief executive of CSR in 1987, and his ruthless approach to restructuring the flagging conglomerate was generally accepted as having saved CSR from takeover or collapse. Burgess had joined the company straight from school in 1950 and was anxious to change the antiquated management style. "It was a very conservative place," he told the *Wall Street Journal* on May 14, 1987, "you even had to get your wife approved. You had to go to your boss and say 'Please sir, can I get married?'" Under Burgess's guidance, each of CSR's divisions was transformed. The building materials division, for example, had employed 157 senior managers. After Burgess's reorganization, there were three. Burgess also dispensed with the CSR annual cricket match, a 94-year-old company tradition. By the end of 1989 the reorganization was complete.

The acquisition of the U.S. Rinker Materials Corporation in 1988 gave CSR a large proportion of the Florida concrete and quarry products market. In 1990 CSR acquired ARC America, a large quarry and concrete products operator with interests in 20 states including Ohio, Indiana, Michigan, Washington, California, Nevada, Texas, and Florida. By the end of 1990 the building and construction division made up 64 percent of total sales. CSR had grown into one of the largest quarrying and concrete operators in the United States and had more quarries there than in Australia. The same year CSR announced record profits. Against a background of high inflation rates and a weak Australian dollar in the mid-1980s, CSR's divestment policy appeared to have paid off. Further expansion in timber, when CSR bought Softwood Holdings in 1988, meant a quadrupling of profits for the timber products division. Despite slow growth in the construction industry, but with profits increasing by 65 percent in 1989, CSR began to focus on Europe and the United States for expansion. In 1987 the company bought a 49 percent share in Redland Plasterboard, a large British construction company with assets throughout Europe. Increasing competition in the United Kingdom and European plasterboard industry caused CSR to sell out its interest in 1990.

In 1989 controversy concerning the company's alleged negligence in its management of the Wittenoom asbestos mine, which it had sold in 1966, was settled. CSR paid out an estimated A$30 million in damages to more than 300 workers suffering from asbestos-related lung diseases. Australian newspapers referred to the event as "Australia's Bhopal."

A commercial development affecting CSR in the early 1990s was the deregulation of the domestic refined sugar industry, which began in 1989. CSR reassessed its refining capacity and locations in the face of greater competition, both from domestic sources and imports. Although profits as a commercial refiner were better than those earned as a toll refiner on behalf of the Queensland government, CSR lost about 20 percent of its market share within Australia—it stood at about 75 percent by mid-decade.

CSR continued its U.S. expansion in the 1990s, including the purchase of three U.S. building materials companies in 1996. By that time U.S. activities represented about one-third of CSR's total assets and 26 percent of its worldwide workforce. During the 1998 fiscal year more than 30 percent of CSR's revenues were derived from its North American operations and nearly 32 percent of its operating profit came from that continent.

With its North American operations continuing to grow, CSR also sought growth on another continent, that of Asia. With booming Asian markets located in CSR's own backyard, the company's growth there in the early and mid-1990s made much sense. Having already established a joint venture in Taiwan to build and operate a concrete products factory, CSR in 1994 formed a joint venture to supply premixed concrete in northern China, the company's first foray into that nation. Other joint ventures were formed in Hong Kong, Malaysia, Thailand, and Indonesia, with CSR entering the Asian market in four product areas: plasterboard, insulation materials, construction materials, and timber. In 1995 CSR combined its interests in these joint ventures within a new company called CSR Kuok Asia Ltd., which was 75 percent owned by CSR and 25 percent owned by the Kuok Group, an entity headed by Malaysian-Chinese businessman Robert Kuok. During fiscal 1998, however, CSR bought out the Kuok Group's interest and took full control of CSR Kuok Asia. From 1994 to 1997 CSR increased the number of plants it operated in Asia from 2 to 19. For the 1997 fiscal year, CSR's revenues from Asia increased more than 50 percent over the preceding year, reaching A$147 million. The Asian economic crisis that erupted during 1997 reversed this trend, however, as revenues from Asia for the 1998 fiscal year fell to A$132.8 million. That year CSR made no further investments in the region.

Late 1990s Restructuring

From the mid-1990s into the late 1990s, CSR was seeing a steady increase in revenues but a declining trend in operating profits. The company concluded that it was being dragged down by a number of underperforming units and that it would be to the company's advantage to reduce its interests to a narrower core through restructuring. During fiscal 1997 CSR closed 38 ''less efficient'' plants and generated A$240 million from the sale of noncore assets. The following year CSR sold American Aggregates Corporation, a U.S.-based operator of quarries and crushed stone plants, to Martin Marietta Materials Inc. for about US$235 million. Also during fiscal 1998 CSR took a A$398

million (US$240 million) after-tax charge to write down the value of a number of underperforming units. This charge led to a net loss for the year of A$109.8 million (US$66.3 million). CSR's restructuring efforts continued into 1999. The company announced in February 1999 that it had reached an agreement to sell its contract mining and civil contracting businesses to Downer Group Limited for about A$135 million (US$84.9 million). In April 1999 CSR announced that it would sell its South Australian and Victorian softwood plantations and sawmills to a U.S.-based timber partnership, RII Weyerhaeuser World Timberfund Pty. Ltd., for A$224 million (US$142.4 million). Through these divestments, CSR appeared to be securing itself a much more promising future as a highly focused building and construction material firm.

Principal Operating Units

CSR Construction Materials; CSR Building Materials; CSR America; CSR Timber Products; CSR Sugar; Aluminum.

Further Reading

Brooks, Geraldine, ''Australia's CSR Boosts Its Sagging Fortunes,'' *Wall Street Journal,* May 14, 1987.

Chow, Lotte, ''Go North: Like Many Australian Firms, CSR Sees Its Future in Asia,'' *Far Eastern Economic Review,* August 29, 1996, p. 60.

CSR: Building in Quality; Fact Book, Sydney: CSR, January 1990.

CSR Limited—130 Years, Sydney: CSR, 1986.

Lowndes A. G., ed., *South Pacific Enterprise,* Sydney: Angus & Robertson, 1956.

Sherwell, Chris, ''CSR Sheds Its Unloved Reputation,'' *Financial Times,* December 2, 1988.

——, ''CSR Works to a Sweeter Future,'' *Financial Times,* June 11, 1987.

——, ''Shifts in Australian Mining Row,'' *Financial Times,* August 24, 1988.

Tait, Nikki, ''CSR Settles 18,000 Asbestos Claims,'' *Financial Times,* April 30, 1996, p. 27.

——, ''Housing Weakness Drags Down CSR,'' *Financial Times,* May 13, 1997, p. 30.

——, ''Kuok and CSR in Construction Materials Deal,'' *Financial Times,* September 29, 1995, p. 27.

—Juliette Bright
—updated by David E. Salamie

Dale Carnegie Training, Inc.

1475 Franklin Avenue
Garden City, New York 11530
U.S.A.
(516) 248-5100
(800) 231-5800
Fax: (516) 248-5817
Web site: http://www.dalecarnegie.com

Private Company
Incorporated: 1945 as Dale Carnegie & Associates Inc.
Employees: 300
Sales: $50 million (fiscal 1997 est.)
NAIC: 61141 Business & Secretarial Schools

Based on Dale Carnegie's classic self-help book, *How to Win Friends and Influence People,* family-owned and -run Dale Carnegie Training, Inc. offers a path to successful living, with a heavy emphasis on success in business. In the late 1990s the company, both directly and through licensed sponsors, was instructing more than 3,000 students a week in about 70 countries, making it one of the world's largest adult-education operations. Its graduates included such noted entrepreneurs and business leaders as Tom Monaghan (Domino's Pizza), Mary Kay Ash (Mary Kay Cosmetics), Frank Perdue (Perdue Farms), and Lee Iacocca (Ford Motor Company and Chrysler Corporation).

The Carnegie Course: 1912–44

The son of a hardscrabble Missouri farm couple, Dale Carnegie found, while attending college, that training in public speaking enabled him to overcome shyness and raise his level of self-confidence and self-esteem. After a brief stint as a salesman, Carnegie moved to New York City to become an actor. He soon became discouraged, left show business, and returned to sales but did not find his niche until, in 1912, he offered to teach an evening course in public speaking at a Manhattan YMCA. Refused a $2-per-session salary, he negotiated payment on a commission basis instead and soon was earning $30 to $40 a night, teaching at YMCA's in Philadelphia, Baltimore, and Wilmington, Delaware, as well as New York City.

As Carnegie's course evolved, it broadened from public speaking to confidence building and increased personal effectiveness. By 1914 he was making $500 a week and hiring assistants to help him teach what he came to call the Dale Carnegie Course in Public Speaking and Human Relations. At first Carnegie simply posted rules or points for the 16-session course on a series of postcards he distributed to instructors. The postcards evolved into a series of booklets given both to instructors and to students taking the course. But despite Carnegie's hiring of instructors, his course remained essentially a one-man operation for many years, with average enrollment of fewer than 1,000 students a year. In 1935 he named his enterprise The Carnegie Institute for Effective Speaking and Human Relations.

Following the publication of Carnegie's 1936 book, *How to Win Friends and Influence People,* which more than 60 years later was still in print, the public flocked to his banner. A 1937 *New York Times* advertisement offering a free demonstration by Carnegie at the Hotel Astor promised 15 benefits in taking the course, among them the ability to think on one's feet, increase income, win more friends, improve one's personality, develop latent powers, and get to know intimately 40 ambitious men and women. It drew 2,500 people. According to a 1937 *Saturday Evening Post* article, the course consisted of 40 sessions over 16 weeks and cost $75. Classes were given such names as The Magic Formula Session, The Crashing-Through Session, The Heckling Session, and The Making-Your-Body-Talk Session. They were presided over by professional instructors paid $25 a night.

Other articles, written at various times, described the course in somewhat different ways. In order to master his techniques, Carnegie first required each student to seek a new approach to achieving his or her goals and then to share the results with the other students. In keeping with his maxim that "a man's name is to him the sweetest sound in any language," much of the first session was given to learning how to remember the names of the other participants. The fourth was a kind of show-and-tell session in which each class member was to bring "an exhibit that represents an achievement." The fifth, or "breakthrough" session was devoted to "coming out of your shell." In the seventh, the participants divided into smaller groups. The eleventh, like the fifth, was given to breaking down inhibitions, through role-playing exercises. Each student was expected to give at least one two-minute talk per session.

Training for Corporate Managers: 1945–90

In 1944 Carnegie began licensing certain territories to sponsors who agreed to pay a percentage of revenues to the home office and follow its instructional guidelines. Privately held Dale Carnegie & Associates, Inc. was established in 1945, with Carnegie as president and his wife Dorothy as vice-president. By 1949 the Dale Carnegie Course (now 14 rather than 16 sessions) was being offered annually to 15,000 students attending 300 classes in 168 cities in the United States, Canada, and Norway.

The annual number of Carnegie students had reached 60,000 by 1957, in 14 countries. License holders generally held classes in office buildings or hotels, but in some cases conducted sessions in conjunction with business or commercial colleges that they also operated. The staff of nearly 900 teachers was trained by a supervisory staff of 20 instructors from national headquarters. The course was for 14 weeks, with one four-hour session each week, generally from 6:30 to 10:30 p.m., with the tuition, including all books and materials, usually between $125 and $150. Subjects covered included developing poise, relaxation techniques, overcoming shyness, and displaying enthusiasm.

Although Carnegie's students sought personal growth and happiness, they commonly had more tangible goals, notably increasing their earning power. Business, in turn, was seeking enthusiastic, motivated, self-starting employees and middle managers who could motivate the people working for them. The Carnegie course instilled practical leadership skills based on cooperation rather than confrontation. General Motors Corporation began sending employees to Dale Carnegie & Associates in 1949, paying half the tuition. By 1959, 67 companies were sending staffers to Dale Carnegie, and some, such as The Coca-Cola Company, were paying the entire cost.

Dale Carnegie died in 1955 and was succeeded by his widow as head of Dale Carnegie & Associates. She was credited by Joseph Kahn of the *New York Times* with transforming the enterprise from " 'a Mom-and-Pop store' into a carefully managed commercial operation." She continued the policy of seeking enrollment from the ranks of corporate America and started a workshop for women that did not, however, prove financially successful. Although she remained the major stockholder of the closely held family corporation and had the title of chairwoman, her son-in-law, J. Oliver Crom, became president and chief executive officer of the enterprise in 1978.

Executives of Dale Carnegie & Associates said in 1983 that enrollment was at a record high and that they expected before the end of the year to graduate their three millionth student. The company now had its own "institutes" in 13 cities and 135 licensed sponsors in about 60 countries. There were now Carnegie courses on sales, customer relations, professional development, and executive presentations as well as the original one on public speaking and human relations—testimony to the overwhelming emphasis on business training.

Dale Carnegie & Associates also continued, however, to stress the founder's commonsense principles on how to win friends and influence people: smile, listen to others, make them feel important, encourage and praise good work, call attention to mistakes without violating Carnegie's first principle, "don't criticize, condemn or complain." Required reading, in addition to *How to Win Friends and Influence People,* included two more of Carnegie's books: one on public speaking, first published in 1926, and *How to Stop Worrying and Start Living* (1948).

The Dale Carnegie enterprise of the 1980s received renewed attention partly due to the efforts of Lee Iacocca, who, after reviving the fortunes of Chrysler Corporation credited, in his 1984 autobiography, the Carnegie course with transforming him from a "shrinking violet." By 1987 more than 400 of the nation's 500 largest companies had sent employees to take a Carnegie course at one time or another, and more than 75 percent of the 157,000 students enrolled annually were under corporate sponsorship. Licensed instructors were required to pay $750 and spend two years in part-time training. The basic course cost $700 to $1,000. Dale Carnegie & Associates celebrated the 75th anniversary of the original Dale Carnegie course in 1987 with a four-day convention in St. Louis.

The public-speaking course, based on Dale Carnegie's original seminar, remained by far the most popular of the eight different courses being given in 1989. This course was offered one night a week for 12 to 14 weeks. (The others were: sales, management, professional development, strategic presentations, customer relations, employee development, and executive image.)

Dale Carnegie in the 1990s

By 1990 Dale Carnegie & Associates had worldwide annual enrollment of more than 170,000—an increase of 60 percent since 1983—and 4,500 instructors. In that recession year, however, the enterprise suffered its first drop in enrollment since 1980 (during another recession). Even Chrysler eliminated its policy of paying the tuition (now $895 for the basic 14-session course) for any employee who wanted to take a course. Crom said in 1991 that the company was still profitable. However, it cut its courses from 14 to 12 weeks, updated the basic course, and added new business-related "modules."

There was no change nor need of change in Dale Carnegie's orientation. A *Los Angeles Times* reporter who attended a class in 1991 wrote, "Most enrolled because they want to do better on the job, though a few say they need help in family and personal relationships." In 1994 there were 4,000 Dale Carnegie instructors and 142 licensed sponsors in over 70 countries on every continent except Antarctica. The eight courses were being offered in 20 languages.

Stuart Levine succeeded Crom as chief executive officer in 1992, although he still reported to Crom, who remained president. Interviewed for *Newsday* in 1995, Levine told Drew Fetherston, "I have to tell you, this business was going south. . . . When income starts to drop, you take it personally." The problem, he felt, was that the company's offerings were out of date, with just one training course added in 15 years and a host of aggressive competitors nipping at the enterprise's heels. "We took a year and spent a large proportion of our advertising dollars on research," he continued. The result, according to Levine, was a greater emphasis on international sales—now responsible for 41 percent of revenue—new courses, and training companies to use workplace teams. The company also changed its name to Dale Carnegie Training and adopted a new logo and mission statement.

One result of the research effort was the creation of a short leadership program for middle- and upper-management people, titled "The Leader in You." Another was a book cowritten by Levine: *The Leader in You: How to Win Friends, Influence People and Succeed in a Changing World.* A quarterly newsletter, *The Leader,* was introduced in 1995. Levine, in October 1995, said the company's market share had increased eight to nine percent in the last year, on top of a three percent increase the year before, thereby reversing a three-year decline.

The flagship Dale Carnegie Course also underwent a revision during this period. It now began by asking participants to write a vision of how they would like to see themselves in the future. This vision became the anchor for the individual's course experience and was examined through what the company called "the five drivers of success," namely, self-confidence, human relations, communications, leadership, and controlling stress. These areas provided the framework of the course, leading to a four-phase continuous-improvement cycle, consisting of attitude change, knowledge, practice, and skill development.

Each of the 12 sessions now covered the following 12 subjects: laying the foundation for success, remembering names, building self-confidence, setting breakthrough goals, using the power of enthusiasm, crashing through barriers, strengthening relationships, using the power of recognition, becoming flexible, stating opinions, inspiring others, and identifying breakthrough results. Firms could also request a course tailored to their particular needs or problems.

By mid-1998 Crom again was chief executive officer, and Levine had departed. Crom indicated that the company, in which family members held all the stock, would remain private. "For us, the benefit of being private is more stability in terms of the people we have," he told James T. Madore of *Newsday.* "This is a very secure business. . . . We have certain strengths that we believe would be lost as part of a larger corporation." Dale Carnegie Training had offices in 70 countries and five million graduates in 1998. Annual revenues, including that of the licensees, came to $187 million in fiscal 1996 (the year ended August 31, 1996). The company reserved for itself operations in ten or more cities, including New York and Washington.

In addition to the basic Dale Carnegie Course, Dale Carnegie Training was, in early 1999, offering six other courses: sales advantage, leadership training for managers, high-impact presentations, leadership advantage, customer relations/employee development, and professional development.

Further Reading

Abrams, Garry, "All Smiles," *Los Angeles Times,* June 14, 1991, pp. E1, E16–E17.

Barron, James, "Old Ways Pay Off for Dale Carnegie," *New York Times,* August 8, 1983, pp. D1, D8.

Berry, Joe, "Dale Carnegie's Blues," *Adweek's Marketing Week,* February 17, 1992, p. 16.

Conniff, Richard, "The So-So Salesman Who Told Millions How to Make It Big," *Smithsonian,* October 1987, pp. 82–86, 88, 90, 92–93.

Fetherston, Drew, "Winning Friends, Influencing People," *Newsday,* October 9, 1995, pp. C1+.

Furio, Joanne, "His Own Success Story: He Knows How to Win in Business," *New York Times,* October 15, 1995, Sec. 13, p. 2.

Harriman, Margaret Case, "He Sells Hope," *Saturday Evening Post,* August 14, 1937, pp. 13–14, 30, 33–34.

Johnson, Dirk, "At 75, Carnegie's Message Lives On," *New York Times,* December 13, 1987, p. A28.

Kahn, Joseph, "Dorothy Carnegie Rivkin, 85, Ex-Dale Carnegie Chief, Dies," *New York Times,* August 8, 1998, p. A13.

Kelley, Bill, "How to Make Friends and Sell to People," *Sales & Marketing Management,* August 1989, pp. 40–42.

Kemp, Giles, and Claflin, Edward, *Dale Carnegie: The Man Who Influenced Millions,* New York: St. Martin's Press, 1989.

Madore, James T., "All in the Family for Most Privates," *Newsday,* June 8, 1998, p. C21.

Nelton, Sharon, "How to Win Friends—for Half a Century," *Nation's Business,* December 1986, pp. 40–41.

"Perk Up Your Personality," *Changing Times,* February 1957, pp. 15–17.

—Robert Halasz

De Beers Consolidated Mines Limited/
De Beers Centenary AG

36 Stockdale Street
Kimberley 8301
Republic of South Africa
(531) 80-7111
Fax: (531) 80-7230
Web site: http://www.edata.co.za/debeers

Langensandstrasse 27
6000 Luzern 14
Switzerland
(41) 403 540
Fax: (41) 444 468

Public Company
Founded: 1880 as De Beers Mining Company Ltd.
Employees: 25,000
Sales: R 24.85 billion (US$4.49 billion) (1998)
Stock Exchanges: Johannesburg London Paris Brussels
    Frankfurt Zurich Geneva Basel
Ticker Symbol: DBRSY
NAIC: 421840 Diamonds, Industrial, Wholesaling;
    421940 Diamonds (Except Industrial) Wholesaling;
    339913 Jewelers' Material & Lapidary Work
    Manufacturing; 42194 Jewelry, Watch, Precious
    Stone, & Precious Metal Wholesalers; 212399
    Precious Stones Mining; 421940 Precious Stones
    Wholesaling

The De Beers Group dominates the world market in rough diamonds. In 1990 it was split into two basic parts, De Beers Consolidated Mines Limited (De Beers Consolidated) and De Beers Centenary AG (Centenary). The first is a South African holding company controlling the group's South African assets. The second is a Swiss-registered holding company created to direct all the De Beers interests outside South Africa. The two share identical boards of directors and their stock is traded as a linked unit. De Beers Consolidated has a 9.5 percent interest in Centenary.

The combined group's main activities include: prospecting for and mining diamonds; the tightly controlled global marketing of its own rough—that is, uncut and unpolished—diamond production and that of cooperating producers via the Central Selling Organisation (CSO), the De Beers marketing arm; and, exceptionally (given that it does not retail the finished product), the worldwide advertising and promotion of diamond jewelry. It also manufactures synthetic diamond and abrasive products. In the late 1990s De Beers produced about half of the world's rough gem diamonds, and through the CSO, based in London, was marketing approximately 70 percent of the world diamond production.

Formed by Cecil Rhodes and others, De Beers is a close associate of the Anglo American Corporation of South Africa (Anglo), founded by Ernest Oppenheimer in 1917. Together they are often referred to as the Oppenheimer empire or ''greater group,'' forged by Ernest Oppenheimer. Since 1929 they have almost always shared the same chairman. De Beers Consolidated has held a large stake in Anglo, and Anglo has had large stakes in De Beers Consolidated and Centenary; these relationships, and De Beers's investment portfolio, were in the process of being significantly modified in 1999. The greater group wields significant influence within the South African economy. The vision and dogged determination of four chairmen—Cecil Rhodes, Ernest Oppenheimer, Ernest's son, Harry Oppenheimer, and Harry's son, Nicky Oppenheimer—have dictated the path taken by De Beers and the modern diamond trade over most of its existence.

1866 Diamond Discovery Led to
De Beers's Founding in 1880

The first authenticated diamond discovery in South Africa occurred in 1866, setting the modern diamond industry in motion. Prospectors came by the thousands to stake claims along the Orange and Vaal rivers. Between 1869 and 1871 six major diamond pipes or veins were discovered: Bultfontein, Kof-fiefontein, Jagersfontein, Dutoitspan, De Beers, and Kimberley, or the ''Big Hole,'' as it became known. Rhodes arrived at the New Rush settlement, renamed Kimberley in 1873. He began by supplying drinking water and ice to the community and contracting to pump water from the De Beers and Dutoitspan mines with a friend, Charles Rudd; the two bought a claim apiece, and from here Rhodes was to build his business empire.

De Beers Mining Company Ltd. was founded on April 28, 1880, by Rhodes and Rudd, with other partners. The company arose once the restrictions on the number of claims individuals could hold were lifted. Barney Bamato, Rhodes's main rival in acquiring dominant control of South African diamond production, meanwhile purchased claims in the center of the Kimberley mine and in 1885 merged with the Kimberley Central Mining Company. Rhodes, however, raised a £1 million loan from the London merchant bank N.M. Rothschild & Sons to outbid Bamato in 1887 to acquire the important Compagnie Francaise des Mines de Diamants du Cap claims adjacent to those of Kimberley Central. Rhodes and Bamato drained each other's profits by their rivalry through the mid-1880s. Bamato, however, eventually gave way to Rhodes's vision of a single controlling company and agreed to exchange his shares in the Kimberley Central mine for shares in De Beers.

De Beers Consolidated Mines was established on March 12, 1888, controlling around 90 percent of contemporary world diamond production. It owned the De Beers mine, three quarters of the Kimberley mine, and held controlling interests in the Dutoitspan and Bultfontein mines. The merger of the De Beers and Kimberley Central mines was contested in court by unhappy Kimberley Central shareholders. Rhodes and Bamato overcame this obstacle by liquidating Kimberley Central. De Beers paid the liquidators 5.34 million for Kimberley Central.

The move toward the consolidation of South African production was followed by a centralization in the control of sales of South African diamonds. Prior to De Beers Consolidated's creation, individual mines sold their production through different London dealers. In February 1890 De Beers concluded a sales contract with a new dealers' and brokers' syndicate, the London Diamond Syndicate. Ties between production and sales control were thus strengthened, several of the dealing firms having significant shareholdings in De Beers.

Fluctuation in demand, however, led to great ups and downs in these early days. In 1890, for instance, the company closed down operations at Dutoitspan, which was proving uneconomical. A new pipe, Wesselton in Kimberley, was discovered the same year. De Beers purchased it in 1891, determinedly continuing its policy of acquisition. De Beers, though, was deprived of the excitement of the discovery in 1893 of the Excelsior diamond at Jagersfontein, the second largest rough diamond ever found. The Jagersfontein mine would finally be acquired by De Beers in 1930.

The end of the century was marked in South Africa by political upheaval and the Boer War. Kimberley lay under siege by the Afrikaners between October 1899 and February 1900. Once the war was over, the great threat at the start of the new century came from the Premier (Transvaal) Diamond Mining Company, founded in 1902 following the discovery of diamonds near Pretoria. Its chairman was Thomas Cullinan, after whom the world's largest rough diamond, 3,106 carats, found at Premier in 1905, was named. The rich finds at the Premier mine opened a new period of bruising competition.

The U.S. financial crisis of 1907 to 1908 severely affected the demand for diamonds and, coupled with Premier's bid for independence of sales when it abandoned selling via the syndicate in 1906, had a crippling effect on trade. Premier soon recommended selling via the syndicate after the price it was receiving per carat had almost halved in a year, and the two companies agreed to limit sales. But De Beers had already had to reduce its mining activities considerably.

Still more significantly, diamonds were discovered in 1908 along the coast of then German South West Africa. Exclusive prospecting and mining rights were given to German companies. The Germans set up the Diamond Regie to regulate their production and marketing. For a brief period De Beers, with the London Diamond Syndicate, had an agreement to purchase diamonds from the Regie. But the latter moved to selling first to an Antwerp syndicate, then onto the open market by tender.

The discovery of diamonds in South West Africa heralded a great expansion in the areas of diamond production, further threatening De Beers's control. Alluvial diamond gravels were discovered in the Belgian Congo (now Zaire) in 1912. The Belgian Societé Internationale Forestière et Minière (La Forminière) began production in 1913. The year 1912 also saw the discovery of diamonds in Angola. The Companhia de Pesquisas Mineras de Angola (Pema) was created to exploit these finds.

The outbreak of World War I brought De Beers to a standstill. Mining was suspended in 1914, and the Diamond Syndicate stopped its contract. Only an essential core of workers remained, many others leaving to join the forces. In 1915 South Africa invaded South West Africa, defeating the German forces there and paving the way for the takeover of German diamond interests in the region.

Anglo Founded in 1917

Ernest Oppenheimer, who had arrived in South Africa in 1902—the year of Rhodes's death—to work as an agent for the diamond brokers A. Dunkelsbuhler & Co., founded Anglo in 1917. One of this company's primary aims was to mine gold on the eastern Witswatersrand. In 1919 it set about acquiring diamond interests in South West Africa previously belonging to the members of the German Diamond Regie, beating De Beers in securing them. These interests were transferred to the specially incorporated Consolidated Diamond Mines of South West Africa Ltd. (CDM) in 1920—the year in which the League of Nations mandated South West Africa to South African administration.

De Beers had secured a controlling share of its previous rival, the Premier mine, in 1917. At the time the purchase seemed important for maintaining its control of diamond production. Under Francis Oats, chairman of De Beers from 1908 to 1918, it was slow to respond to its encirclement by Ernest Oppenheimer, who continued busily acquiring diamond interests outside South Africa. Added to this, in 1918 the world's largest contemporary diamond deposits were found by a Belgian rail company in the Bakwanga region of the Belgian Congo.

While De Beers faced another depression in world markets at the beginning of the 1920s, exacerbated by the new government of the Soviet Union's sale of diamonds and jewelry confiscated during the Russian Revolution, Anglo continued buying into various areas of the southern African diamond industry. In 1923 it purchased a 16 percent share in Diamang, the new name given to Pema in 1917. Then in 1924 it was granted membership in the London Diamond Syndicate, only to rock the boat. Anglo and Dunkelsbuhler were asked to retire from the syndicate, having attempted to bid for the entire South African output.

The new Diamond Syndicate created in 1925 by Sir Ernest (Oppenheimer was knighted in 1921) quickly caused the London Diamond Syndicate's dissolution by offering better terms, and bought out its assets. Oppenheimer had been steadily building up his shareholding in De Beers and cementing a friendship with De Beers's largest shareholder, Solly Joel and his firm, Barnato Brothers. In 1926 Oppenheimer was elected to the De Beers board.

Spectacular new diamond discoveries were made in South Africa in 1926 and 1927, first in Lichtenburg, where hundreds of prospectors were allowed to rush off from a starting line to stake their claims, and then in Alexander Bay. By January 1927 Oppenheimer had secured a controlling interest in the Lichtenburg region and by 1929 he had bought out the remaining interests belonging to Dr. Merensky, the discoverer of the Alexander Bay deposits, for just over £1 million. The markets were flooded, however, by these massive discoveries, and De Beers suffered considerably. Through Oppenheimer's dynamic policies, his ever-expanding acquisitions of diamondiferous areas, and his control of the syndicate, he was elected chairman of De Beers in December 1929. He took the helm as the Great Depression began. Sales throughout the 1930s were poor to nonexistent; in 1932 mining came to a complete halt.

Predecessor of the CSO Formed in the 1930s

Important structural changes for De Beers and the diamond sales pipeline, however, were put in place during the decade. Oppenheimer felt the original purpose of a diamond syndicate to sell South African production was becoming too restricted. He envisioned a single organization for the producers and sellers of rough diamonds that would become, as far as possible, the exclusive marketing channel for world rough diamond production. The Diamond Corporation Ltd. was founded in 1930. De Beers, CDM, Premier, and other leading producers took a 50 percent holding, the Diamond Syndicate the other 50 percent. Sir Ernest became chairman. Anglo gave up its CDM holding for De Beers shares in the same year. This arrangement radically diminished the divergence of interests between the diamond producers and the sellers of rough diamonds, and effectively saw the start of a single central selling organization. The Diamond Corporation also established important financial resources to enable it to acquire further outside production. The Diamond Trading Company (DTC) was further formed as a subsidiary of the Diamond Corporation in 1934 to sell at "sights," the process by which boxes of rough gems prepared by the DTC (which painstakingly grades the individual diamonds and selects a percentage of the graded categories) are offered to the individual clients or "sightholders," diamond manufacturers and dealers it has carefully chosen from the world's cutting centers. The combined structures have become known as the CSO.

The concept behind the Diamond Corporation was expanded with the creation in 1934 of the Diamond Producers' Association (DPA), encompassing the members of the Diamond Corporation and representatives of the South African government and the administration of South West Africa. The DPA arose to create a pooling arrangement to enable the large producers to protect the market together. On the industrial diamond side, the Diamond Development Company Ltd. was created in 1934 to explore new uses for industrial diamonds. By 1936, a British company, Sierra Leone Selection Trust, entered into an initial marketing agreement with the Diamond Corporation.

World War II brought production to a halt. But just prior to the outbreak of the war, De Beers embarked on a significant new venture advocated by Harry Oppenheimer: its first advertising campaign, which was launched in the United States. Thus De Beers, selling the rough product, built a bridge of promotional support and solidarity with the jewelers, retailers of the final product. The De Beers campaigns, and in particular such catch phrases as "A Diamond Is Forever" and "Diamonds Are a Girl's Best Friend," have become something of a legend, promoting the romantic image of gem diamonds.

During World War II the company's production of industrial diamonds acquired greater importance. Sales of these rose to £4.3 million in 1942, representing nearly 40 percent of the total trade in diamonds. Surprisingly, the diamond market recorded record sales in 1943 (£20.5 million) and 1945 (£24.5 million). Conflict, however, arose with the U.S. government, which accused De Beers of being unwilling to loosen control of its diamond stockpile to help the war effort; it was further concerned about the shortage of industrial diamonds, and about Britain falling under enemy control. Sir Ernest denied the accusation and the shortage, and proposed the compromise of stockpiling in Canada. Industrial diamond sales were in fact supervised by the British government and prices were frozen. But Sir Ernest had angered the U.S. government, which pursued De Beers as an anticompetitive cartel. The U.S. Justice Department filed antitrust actions against De Beers in 1945, 1957, and 1974. De Beers did not take up the challenge of the U.S. courts and did not operate in the United States.

A further important discovery of diamonds had been made in Tanganyika (now Tanzania) at the beginning of the 1940s by a Canadian, Dr. John Williamson. Williamson first agreed to join the Producers' Association in 1947, but then changed his mind. He stockpiled his production and threatened to damage the CSO's position. Harry Oppenheimer eventually managed to negotiate a settlement. On Williamson's death, Oppenheimer negotiated with Williamson's heirs and secured a 50 percent share in the Williamson mine in 1958, the government taking the other 50 percent.

In 1952 De Beers was to benefit from a windfall profit of £40 million thanks to the sale of a stockpile of diamonds held since the Great Depression, helping to strengthen its financial base substantially. The unknown quantity for De Beers in the 1950s came from the production of synthetic diamonds by foreign companies. The Swedish Allmänna Svenska Elektriska Aktiebolaget was the first to successfully create synthetic diamonds. But it failed to secure the patent rights, taken up exclusively by the U.S. General Electric Company (GEC) in 1955. In response, De Beers set up its Adamant Research Laboratory in Johannesburg. By 1960 De Beers founded Ultra High Pressure Units Limited for the commercial manufacturing of synthetic diamonds. Only in 1966 would a lengthy and costly dispute with GEC over the patent rights be resolved. De Beers Industrial Diamond Division continues, with GEC, to be one of the main market leaders in synthetic industrial diamond production.

In 1955 De Beers began prospecting in the Bechuanaland Protectorate (now Botswana), and 1956 saw its founding of the Diamond Corporation Sierra Leone Limited (Dicosil). The Sierra Leone government granted it sole exclusive exporting rights. Outside De Beers control, Russia had been finding diamonds in the Urals and Siberia. In 1959 the first short-lived marketing deal was signed between the Diamond Corporation and the Soviet government for sales via the CSO. Diamond buying offices were established by the CSO across West Africa with the incorporation in 1961 of the Diamond Corporation West Africa Ltd. (Dicorwaf). The offices purchased diamonds from the independent individual alluvial diggers, helping to maintain market price stability.

That year independent prospectors discovered rich diamond deposits: Sammy Collins made a discovery on the coast off CDM's concessions, and Allister Fincham and William Schwabel (forming the Finsch mine) made a discovery in South Africa, northwest of Kimberley. By 1962 De Beers had secured a contract to prospect the latter; in 1963 it bought the rights to the Finsch pipe for £2.3 million, leasing the 70 percent state share. By 1965 it had taken a controlling stake in Sammy Collins's Marine Diamond Corporation by buying 53 percent of his Sea Diamonds Limited. De Beers's pursuit of rights may have been relentless, but certain smaller interests remained outside its control, for example in Ghana, the Central African Republic, Guinea, and South America.

Late 1960s Botswana Discoveries

A dramatic discovery, the Orapa pipe on the edge of the Kalahari desert in Botswana, was made in 1967 by De Beers geologists. De Beers Botswana Mining Company Limited (Debswana) was incorporated in 1969 as a joint venture between De Beers and the Botswana government. Further discoveries ensued at Letlhakane and Jwaneng, the latter—buried some 150 feet in the sand—hailed as a particular technological triumph. Debswana became a 5.27 percent shareholder in De Beers in 1987 in exchange for De Beers's acquisition of the diamond stocks built up by Debswana from 1982 to 1985.

Business cooperation did not always go so smoothly with the other African diamond-producing countries through the 1960s, 1970s, and 1980s. Newfound independence, political upheaval, vacillating policies, and illegal mining led to certain unstable relationships for De Beers. Sierra Leone declared an open market in 1974. Dicorwaf, which had superseded Dicosil,

lost its sole exclusive exporting rights. Its supposed monopoly had been undermined by theft from and illegal mining on Selection Trust's concessions.

For some 50 years, until the early 1970s, sales of Angolan diamonds by Diamang via the CSO went smoothly. The Portuguese withdrawal before the country's independence in 1975 and the civil war that raged afterwards saw this position collapse. Diamang's operations disintegrated, leaving a great deal of production to be smuggled out to Lisbon in Portuguese luggage and to Antwerp. The volume of this trade was so important that the CSO was forced to buy quantities of these diamonds when they came onto the open market in Belgium to maintain price stability. In 1977 the government took a majority interest in Diamang, later to become Endiama, and De Beers was left with a nominal shareholding. The government could not be seen to be dealing with a South African company, being officially at war with her neighbor. Thirty Cornish tin miners were recruited in London by Mining and Technical Services, a Liberian-registered company with several members of De Beers as directors, to go to Angola to advise and assist the state company. Endiama sold what diamond production there was by tender to Antwerp dealers. Following growth in production, however, Endiama signed an agreement with the CSO in 1991 for the marketing of all the diamonds from the important Cuango River region and for help in extending production.

After independence, the Tanzanian government fully nationalized the Mwadui (formerly Williamson) mine and set up its own sorting and valuing office. Production was run down and investment lacking, but the diamonds continued to be sold via the CSO. In Zaire, the CSO had set up a buying company, British Zaire Diamond Distributors Limited (Zaïrebrit, later Britmond) on the former La Forminière site, and from 1972 embarked on exploration. De Beers's involvement in Zaire underwent a serious crisis when the Zaire government broke off its contract (in operation since 1967) for the exclusive marketing of the Société Minière de Bakwanga (MIBA) diamonds by the CSO. Unhappy at being offered equal sales rights as one of four, the CSO withdrew from the country. The situation was resolved in 1983, first when the government allowed the CSO amongst others to buy the open-market production, and then when a new agreement was signed for the exclusive marketing of MIBA's production via the CSO. Elicit mining and black market buying have been even more rife here than in Sierra Leone.

In Namibia, De Beers's CDM enjoyed a remarkably stable position since the 1920s, only briefly troubled by Sammy Collins. To exploit the foreshore alluvial reserves of very high-quality gems, it developed sophisticated techniques, basically shifting sand dunes seaward, pushing the sea back by up to a quarter of a mile along ten miles. The area was said to have the most concentrated fleet of earth-moving equipment in the world. Security was high, though diamond theft was a problem. In the late 1960s and early 1970s, CDM production accounted for up to 40 percent of De Beers's total taxed profits. After 1974, no separate accounts were published. South Africa ignored the United Nations' lifting in 1966 of its Namibia mandate and the International Court of Justice's 1971 ruling that the territory be surrendered. Namibia finally achieved independence in 1989. De Beers was accused in the early 1980s by an ex-employee of deliberately overmining its Namibian territory before it might lose out with independence, and of transfer pricing. The Thirion commission supported allegations of overmining and tax evasion, but a government white paper later exonerated CDM on both counts. At present CDM remains 100 percent De Beers-owned and holds the lease on the area until 2010.

The largest diamond discoveries in the 1970s and 1980s were in Australia, which became the world's largest diamond producer in carats. The mainly Australian Katalumburu Joint Venture began prospecting in Kimberley, Northwest Australia, in 1972. Conzinc Riotinto of Australia Ltd. (CRA) joined the consortium in 1976, building up a 35 percent stake, which increased to almost 70 percent some years later. In 1977 it took over the management of the joint venture, later named Ashton Joint Venture (AJV). Ironically, De Beers had surveyed and dismissed the region in the 1960s. In 1982 CRA and Ashton Mining Ltd., holding 95 percent of the Australian production sales rights, approved a sales contract with the CSO until the end of the decade, the CSO guaranteeing its purchase of the entire production regardless of the state of the markets. This important contract was renewed in 1991.

In the late 1970s speculation by diamond traders, who had purchased and stockpiled large quantities of rough diamonds as a hedge against inflation, resulted in large numbers of diamonds in excess to jewelry demand later being released on the markets. Consequently, the early 1980s were adversely marked for De Beers. It had to limit its sales substantially so that the stocks that had built up in the cutting centers could be absorbed into the retail markets. Owing to De Beers's strict control over supply and thanks to the strength of its investments outside diamonds, it managed to ride out the severe recession.

The Soviet Union, which became one of the world's largest diamond producers, had abandoned official dealings with the CSO in 1963 because of De Beers's South African status, though it was revealed in the media that the Soviets were involved in covert dealings via a third party. Having developed their own cutting industry, though, the Soviets were able to sell certain stocks onto the open market independently. Occasionally they dumped large amounts onto the international market, for example in 1984. Once again, the CSO weathered the storm. In 1990 dealing between the two parties came back into the open, and Centenary concluded an extraordinary US$5 billion sales agreement with Glavalmazzoloto, the main precious metals and diamonds administrative body in the USSR, under which the CSO would market the USSR's rough diamond production for five years.

The acrimonious takeover bid by Minorco—an international mining investment house of the greater Anglo-De Beers empire in which Centenary later held 21 percent—for Consolidated Gold Fields (Consgold) brought De Beers unwanted publicity. Rudolph Agnew, chairman of Consgold, argued the undesirability of a South African group wielding such power over the gold industry, and attempted to discredit De Beers by asking the British Office of Fair Trading (OFT) to investigate the CSO as a "negative monopoly." In May 1989 Minorco's bid fell through due to legal obstacles, but in August 1989 the OFT announced that it would not mount an investigation into the CSO.

Controversial Dealings

It was not without controversy that De Beers exercised its formidable power over the diamond industry. It was frequently attacked as an anticompetitive, secretive cartel, a system De Beers referred to as a "producers' cooperative." De Beers was also attacked for profiting initially from exploitation through colonialism and then from the system of apartheid. Within South Africa, De Beers and Anglo were considered liberal. The greater group consistently opposed the government on its racial policy. Harry Oppenheimer served for many years as a member of parliament for the antiapartheid opposition, but progress in conditions for black workers was slow.

A fully integrated wage scale was established for all employees, regardless of race, in 1978. In 1981, for the first time in South African mining history, a recognition agreement with an established black trade union was signed, allowing for the representation of black employees in wage and other negotiations. At the end of the 1980s most of the black workers still migrated to the mines from neighboring states or South Africa's so-called homelands and lived in single-sex hostels away from their families. In 1988 the law was changed, giving blacks the right to acquire blasting certificates, opening the way for them to fill more skilled posts. Black workers' pay at the end of the 1980s was, on average, one-sixth that of white workers, who were generally skilled workers. De Beers, with Anglo, made major investments in social programs, calculated on a percentage of Anglo-De Beers dividend payments, via the joint Chairman's Fund. It embarked in 1987 on an employee share-ownership scheme to which 9,000 soon subscribed, and on a small-scale home-ownership scheme. It encouraged small black business enterprises by contracting out work to them and was a major contributor to the Urban Foundation for black housing. The greater group was recognized as a leader in South Africa in such initiatives, seeing its interest in encouraging the creation of a prosperous, capitalist black middle class.

New exploration and operations continued, with particularly important new developments for the 1990s at the Venetia mine in South Africa, at Elizabeth Bay, Auchas in Namibia, and in North Saskatchewan in Canada. Harry Oppenheimer stepped down as chairman in 1984 to be replaced by Julian Ogilvie Thompson, also chairman of Anglo and of Minorco, and Harry Oppenheimer's son Nicky became deputy chairman of De Beers and chairman of the CSO.

At the end of the 1980s sales soared to new heights, reaching a record $4.17 billion in 1988, almost four times what they stood at in the early 1980s. The massive De Beers advertising budget of around $172 million was spent on major campaigns in 29 countries. Twenty-five years ago, the tradition of the diamond engagement ring hardly existed in Japan; now 77 percent of Japanese brides receive one.

1990s and Beyond

In 1992 De Beers Marine recovered some 360,000 carats from CDM's offshore areas, and is developing the technology for sea-floor mining. But political, ethical, and economic problems plagued De Beers in the early 1990s. International calls for an end to apartheid in South Africa had repercussions for the country's largest conglomerates. The African National Congress (ANC) rallied for the unbundling of South Africa's largest conglomerates, including Anglo and De Beers. ANC leaders felt that the eventual dissolution of these companies would open big business to more blacks. More than 80 percent of the Johannesburg Stock Exchange was comprised of South Africa's six largest companies. Leaders of the ANC insisted that the country's economy was constricted by the conglomerates, and that the lack of competition inherent in the South African economy discouraged foreign investors. But De Beers and Anglo spokesmen saw their companies' strengths as a necessary attribute for world competition once South Africa became a fully accepted member of the community of trading nations.

In April 1992 De Beers's ethical standards came under the scrutiny of the U.S. Justice Department, which accused the diamond giant of price fixing in cooperation with General Electric Company. Although industrial diamonds fall outside the CSO's purview (and in any case bring only one percent of the price of gems), the Justice Department's lawsuit claimed that GEC and De Beers conspired to control over 90 percent of the worldwide market for high-grade industrial diamonds. In December 1994, however, a U.S. District Court judge threw the case out of court, having concluded that the Justice Department had failed to prove its case.

De Beers's control of the gem market was threatened in the early 1990s by the twin demons of recession and rogue diamond producers. The worldwide economic downturn depressed diamond sales in the United States and Japan, which together accounted for 66 percent of diamond jewelry sales. In response, De Beers cut back its purchases from diamond producers 25 percent in 1992 to adjust supplies according to demand.

Unfortunately, as De Beers limited its supplies, political upheaval in Angola resulted in more than 50,000 unauthorized diamond diggers in that country's rich diamond fields. De Beers was forced to spend an estimated $6 million per week on these illegal diamonds to guarantee a stable market. Add that to De Beers's contracts for $4.5 billion in diamonds and total rough sales at $3.5 billion, and a deficit situation was clearly at hand by September 1992. The company was forced again to reduce all its contracts by another 25 percent that month.

To make matters worse, Russian suppliers in the Sakha region began to demand more control over the sale of diamonds produced in that region. They based their demands on the fact that, by value, Russia had the world's largest diamond production as well as a stockpile of diamonds rivaling De Beers's own $3.3 billion reserves. In 1993 cash-strapped Russia began violating the 1990 marketing agreement signed between the CSO and former Soviet leader Mikhail Gorbachev. Russia began selling large quantities of low-quality diamonds outside the CSO, forcing the CSO to lower its prices for low-quality gems. This in turn prompted Argyle Diamond Mines of Australia, the leading diamond producer in the world, to leave the CSO in mid-1996 and sell still more low-quality diamonds outside the CSO. In response, De Beers and the CSO decided to concentrate on higher-quality stones.

In 1997 Nicky Oppenheimer took over as chairman of De Beers. That year the diamond industry was further rocked by the beginning of the Asian economic crisis, which collapsed demand in that region. Sales of rough gems in the first half of 1998 fell 41 percent, and revenues for De Beers Consolidated and Centenary fell from $6.42 billion in 1997 to $4.49 billion in 1998. De Beers also faced the prospect of potential new rivals in Canada, where Australia's largest company, BHP, and the world's largest mining company, U.K.-based Rio Tinto, were beginning to mine high-quality diamonds. On the positive side, after two years of contentious negotiations, De Beers and Russia finally reached a new diamond-trading agreement, a one-year pact, in late 1997. A year later the agreement was extended for three more years, with Russia agreeing to sell about half of its output to De Beers and gaining the right to sell five percent of its diamonds independently on the international market.

In the early years of the post-apartheid era, Anglo American had begun restructuring in part to protect its assets from possible nationalization. By the mid-1990s Anglo had transferred all of its non-African, nondiamond assets to an offshore affiliate, Luxembourg-based Minorco. Then, near the end of the decade, Anglo and Minorco reached an agreement to merge their businesses into a new U.K.-based company called Anglo American plc, which would have its primary listing on the London Stock Exchange with secondary listings elsewhere, including the Johannesburg exchange. At the same time, Anglo and De Beers agreed to rationalize their elaborate cross-holdings and common investment portfolios. In April 1998 De Beers acquired from Anglo its interests in the CSO and CSO affiliates, thereby bolstering De Beers position in diamonds. De Beers and Anglo also agreed to a scheme whereby De Beers would transfer the bulk of its noncore investment portfolio—which included interests in such firms as Anglo American Platinum Corporation Limited, Mondi Limited, Namakwa Sands Limited, and Samancor Limited—to Anglo, after which De Beers would hold a 42.1 percent stake in Anglo. De Beers would emerge from these maneuvers with, by and large, two main areas of operations: diamonds and its stake in Anglo.

By the late 1990s, the CSO marketed about 70 percent of the rough diamonds mined around the world, a decline from the 80 percent of the early 1990s. Nevertheless, and despite the defection of Australia and the difficulties in controlling the Russian and Angolan markets, the long-predicted demise of the De Beers diamond cartel had yet to materialize. In fact, De Beers was able to gain a long-sought foothold in the emerging Canadian diamond industry in early 1999 when it reached an agreement with BHP and Canada's Dia Met Minerals Ltd., who promised to sell 35 percent of their output to the CSO. It thus appeared likely that the De Beers stranglehold on the diamond industry would continue well into the new millennium.

Principal Subsidiaries

CDM (Proprietary) Limited; De Beers Industrial Diamond Division (Proprietary) Limited; De Beers Central Selling Organization (U.K.).

Further Reading

Barnes, William, ''De Beers Denies Branding Will Hit Diamond Market,'' *Financial Times,* July 31, 1998, p. 30.

Behrmann, Neil, "De Beers's Diamond Cartel Shows Flaws," *Wall Street Journal,* October 31, 1994, p. C1.

Carley, William M., "Fatal Flaws: How the Federal Case Against GE, De Beers Collapsed So Quickly," *Wall Street Journal,* December 28, 1994, pp. A1+.

Chilvers, Hedley A., *The Story of De Beers,* London: Cassell and Company, 1939.

Curtin, Matthew, "De Beers Faces Challenge to Its Power: Dominance in Diamonds Threatened by Russia, Canada," *Wall Street Journal,* August 22, 1994, p. A5B.

Dawley, Heidi, and William Echikson, "Cracks in the Diamond Trade," *Business Week,* March 2, 1998, p. 106.

"De Beers Is It," *Economist,* December 19, 1998, p. 89.

Frank, David, "Unbundling into Power," *Euromoney,* September 1992.

"Friends Again," *Economist,* March 2, 1996, pp. 59–60.

Fuhrman, Peter, "The Rough Trade in Rough Stones," *Forbes,* March 27, 1995, pp. 47+.

"Glass with Attitude," *Economist,* December 20, 1997, pp. 113+.

Gooding, Kenneth, "De Beers Digs Deeper into Its Resources," *Financial Times,* September 6, 1994, p. 32.

——, "Oppenheimer Connection Continues at De Beers," *Financial Times,* October 7, 1997, p. 25.

——, "Quiet Heir Apparent to a Mining Empire," *Financial Times,* August 19, 1996, p. 8.

——, "Steep Fall in Diamond Sales by De Beers," *Financial Times,* June 18, 1998, p. 32.

Green, Timothy, *The World of Diamonds,* London: Weidenfeld & Nicolson, 1981, 300 p.

Gregory, Theodore, *Ernest Oppenheimer and the Economic Development of Southern Africa,* Cape Town: Oxford University Press, 1962.

Hilzenrath, David S., and Steven Pearlstein, "U.S. Probing Possible Price-Fixing by GE," *Washington Post,* April 23, 1992.

Hocking, Anthony, *Oppenheimer and Son,* Johannesburg: McGraw-Hill, 1973, 526 p.

"Is It a Crack or a Scratch?," *Economist,* September 12, 1992.

Jamieson, Bill, *Goldstrike: The Oppenheimer Empire in Crisis,* London: Hutchinson Business Books, 1990.

Jessup, Edward, *Ernest Oppenheimer: A Study in Power,* London: Rex Collins, 1979, 357 p.

Kanfer, Stefan, *The Last Empire: De Beers, Diamonds, and the World,* New York: Farrar Straus Giroux, 1993, 409 p.

Kvint, Vladimir, "Sorry, Mr. Oppenheimer," *Forbes,* February 15, 1993, pp. 42–43.

McNeil, Donald G., Jr., "A Diamond Cartel May Be Forever," *New York Times,* January 12, 1999, pp. C1, C4.

Melcher, Richard A., and Deborah Stead, "Can De Beers Hold On to Its Hammerlock?," *Business Week,* September 21, 1992, pp. 45+.

Newbury, Colin, *The Diamond Ring Business, Politics and Precious Stones in South Africa, 1867–1947,* Oxford: Clarendon Press, 1989.

Pallister, David, Sarah Stewart, and Ian Lepper, *South Africa Inc.: The Oppenheimer Empire,* rev. ed., London: Simon & Schuster, 1987, 382 p.

"Prince of Diamonds," *Economist,* December 13, 1997, p. 60.

Reeve, Simon, "De Beers' Market Stranglehold Isn't for Ever," *European,* July 6, 1998, pp. 24+.

Schiller, Zachary, and Catherine Yang, "This Diamond Case Had Too Many Flaws," *Business Week,* December 19, 1994, p. 34.

Shor, Russell, "De Beers Versus the Bear Market: Who Will Win?," *Jewelers Circular Keystone,* June 1995, pp. 122+.

——, "Russia to De Beers: 'We Want More Control,'" *Jewelers Circular Keystone,* January 1993.

—Philippe A. Barbour and April Dougal Gasbarre
—updated by David E. Salamie

Debenhams Plc

One Welbeck Street
London W1A 1DF
United Kingdom
(44) 171 408 4444
Fax: (44) 171 408 3366
Web site: http://www.debenhams.co.uk

Public Company
Founded: 1778 as Flint & Clark
Employees: 27,187
Sales: £1.36 billion (US$2.29 billion) (1998)
Stock Exchanges: London
NAIC: 452110 Department Stores

Debenhams Plc is one of the United Kingdom's longest continuously operating clothing and goods retailers. The company owns and operates nearly 100 department stores, primarily in England. In the British market, Debenhams' annual sales of more than £1.3 billion place it among the country's top five retailers. Founded in 1778, Debenhams operated as an independent company until its hostile takeover by the Burton Group in the late 1980s. In 1998 Debenhams regained its independence when it was "demerged" from the Burton Group, which subsequently changed its name to Arcadia Group plc. Former Burton chief John Hoerner has taken charge of the new Arcadia Group, while the newly independent Debenhams continues to be led by CEO Terry Green.

18th-Century Origins

The first incarnation of what would later become known as Debenhams started up in 1778 as Flint & Clark, a London-based seller of clothing and other items. The Debenham (later Debenhams) name was added in the early 19th century, when William Debenham joined the company. The company, now known as Clark & Debenham, operated a store on London's Wigmore Street. Clark & Debenham would soon become a London fixture, expanding to operate stores throughout the city and into other parts of the United Kingdom as well. When a new partner joined the company, its name changed once again, to Debenham and Freebody. By the turn of the century, however, the company would become known simply as Debenhams.

Throughout its first 100 years Debenhams had grown to include not only a number of stores, but also its own manufacturing operations, producing the company's own clothing designs. In this capacity, Debenhams would build a strong—and somewhat exclusive—reputation; among its customers, Debenhams counted none other than Queen Victoria. The company would continue to build its reputation into the 20th century, especially with the opening of the first Debenhams department store in 1905. In the same year, the company incorporated under the Debenhams name.

Debenhams would convert its other stores to the department store format over the next decades. The company also expanded beyond its own stores, purchasing Harvey Nichols in 1913. The Harvey Nichols name, featured in Debenhams stores and in its own stores, would grow to become an exclusive, high-end label. In 1928 the ever-expanding Debenhams went public, listing its shares on the London Stock Exchange, just in time for the Great Depression.

By then Debenhams had been joined on the British retail scene by Montague Burton. That company had been founded in 1904 by Lithuanian tailor Moshe David Osinsky, who had changed his name to Montague Burton when opening his first shop in Chesterfield, England. The Montague Burton name apparently appealed to the British consumer: by the end of World War I the company operated some 40 shops. The company eyed still further expansion, going public in 1929. Marketing to the rising British middle class, offering quality clothing at affordable prices, Montague Burton weathered the Depression era in style. By the outbreak of World War II Montague Burton had grown to a national chain of more than 600 stores, with its own manufacturing facilities producing most of its goods. Founder Burton continued to run the company until his death in 1952; the company's name was simplified to the Burton Group in 1969.

In the post-World War II years Debenhams found itself playing catch-up in a marketplace featuring rising stars such as Marks and Spencer. One problem was the company's structure, which owed more to its 18th-century roots than to the modern commercial era. Although the company had continued to add new stores, each of its stores remained more or less independent while grouped under the Debenhams name. Purchasing, warehousing, and other functions were performed at individual locations, rather than through a centralized source. In addition, the positioning of some of the company's stores placed them in direct competition with other Debenhams stores, cannibalizing sales. Once a leader in the London department store market, Debenhams was soon outpaced by Marks and Spencer, among others.

Beginning in the 1950s, however, Debenhams began building a new, stronger, and more centralized management. The company took steps to streamline its operations, particularly in its purchasing program, reducing these expenses while strengthening consistency among the Debenhams stores themselves. The process of transforming Debenhams into a modern firm would continue into the 1960s.

Regaining Independence in the 1990s

As Debenhams continued consolidating its centralized operations, the Burton Group began to seek further expansion opportunities. In the 1970s that company would add new chains to its operations, creating a new format, the Top Shop, with women's fashions, and purchasing two existing chains, Dorothy Perkins and Evans, rounding out the company's women's fashions offerings. The Burton Group later expanded the Top Shop concept to include Top Man, seeking to appeal to a younger consumer group than the Burton Menswear stores. Closing out the 1970s, the Burton Group shut down its manufacturing operations, turning entirely to its retail stores. The appointment of Ralph Halpern as CEO and then chairman heralded a new era of expansion for the Burton Group. Under Halpern, a flamboyant figure who later would be knighted, the Burton Group would add a new store concept, Principles, and begin eyeing a new and greater extension of its operations.

By the 1980s Debenhams had grown as well. The company operated some 65 department stores. It also had attempted an expansion, buying up the Hamley toys retail chain. This acquisition was resold soon after; however, the Debenhams stores would continue to feature Hamley toys. Nonetheless, Debenhams was facing difficulties. The recession initiated by the oil crisis of the early 1970s had had lasting effects on the British economy, which continued in its slowdown into the 1980s. Debenhams revenues were slipping, as was its share price, making the company a ripe target for the hostile takeover rage of the 1980s.

That bid came in 1985, when the Burton Group launched a takeover of Debenhams. The department store company, independent for more than 200 years, fought to regain control, including seeking a white knight in competing retailers. In the end, however, the Burton Group won control of Debenhams, for a price of nearly US$900 million. Halpern brought in the

American John Hoerner, seconded by Terry Green, to revitalize the ailing Debenhams chain.

Hoerner and Green took Debenhams on a restructuring program, closing stores, reducing departments, cutting back on sales events, and introducing a series of company-owned brand names. Much of the new management team's efforts went toward repositioning Debenhams, which had slipped in prestige to the lower end of the market, toward a mid-range store concept.

By the end of the 1990s Debenhams was on its way to recovery—both in sales and profits. The Burton side, however, had run into difficulties, with a number of decisions made by the high-flying Halpern proving costly to the company. When Halpern resigned in 1990, his position was taken over by John Hoerner. The following year, Hoerner named Terry Green as CEO of the Debenhams operation. Green continued to expand the store-owned range of brands, bringing that number to around 40, each targeted to different market segments and product categories, by the mid-1990s. As Debenhams regained its profit and sales momentum, the company slowly began to seek new store openings.

The United Kingdom was hit by a new extended recession during the 1990s. As the effects of that economic crisis began to diminish in the second half of the decade, the Burton Group featured the successful Debenhams department store chain on the one hand and its portfolio of clothing retail chains, mostly struggling, on the other. In 1997 Hoerner announced that the Burton Group would ''demerge'' from the Debenhams chain, restoring the department store group to independence as a public company.

This move was taken at the beginning of 1998, at a cost of some £65 million. John Hoerner surprised analysts by remaining with the less profitable Burton Group. Terry Green remained as the Debenhams chief executive. In 1998, wishing to make a break with the past, the Burton Group renamed itself Arcadia Group plc.

Restored to independence, Debenhams featured more than 90 department stores, 118 restaurants, a growing wedding gift service, and a vibrant range of proprietary as well as internationally recognized brands. The company also had taken the first steps toward an international presence, entering a franchise agreement with the Middle East's MH Alshaya Group. The first two Middle East locations were opened in 1998, in Bahrain and Kuwait; two more Middle Eastern stores were scheduled to open in 1999, in Dubai and Jeddah.

Debenhams continued to expand its U.K. presence as well. In 1998 and 1999 the company embarked on an ambitious expansion plan, calling for the opening of 17 new stores and the modernization of some ten existing stores. Debenhams closed out its first year of regained independence with rising profits and rising revenues. The company could turn toward its third century as a mainstay of the British retail scene.

Further Reading

Bevan, Judi, ''Burton's Flying Ringmaster,'' *Daily Telegraph,* July 13, 1997, p. 4.

Cope, Nigel, ''Debenhams Plans New Stores,'' *Independent,* April 28, 1998, p. 21.

——, ''Debenhams to Be Spun Off As Burton Regroups,'' *Independent,* July 9, 1997, p. 17.

Gilbert, Nick, ''The Top Man and His Plan,'' *Independent on Sunday,* July 13, 1997, p. 3.

Koenig, Peter, ''Debenhams Gets a Brand New Image,'' *Independent on Sunday,* December 14, 1997, p. 2.

Larsen, Peter Thal, ''Debenhams Stays Bullish,'' *Independent,* October 28, 1998, p. 23.

Osborne, Alistair, ''Debenhams to Recruit 6,000 More Staff,'' *Daily Telegraph,* April 28, 1998.

Potter, Ben, ''Debenhams Passes High Street Test,'' *Daily Telegraph,* April 28, 1998.

—M. L. Cohen

Del Laboratories, Inc.

178 EAB Plaza
Uniondale, New York 11556-0178
U.S.A.
(516) 844-2020
(800) 953-5080
Fax: (516) 844-1515
Web site: http://www.dellabs.com

Public Company
Incorporated: 1961 as Maradel Products, Inc.
Employees: 1,480
Sales: $274.9 million (1998)
Stock Exchanges: American
Ticker Symbol: DLI
NAIC: 325412 Pharmaceutical Preparation
    Manufacturing; 32562 Toilet Preparation
    Manufacturing

Del Laboratories, Inc. manufactures, markets, and distributes cosmetics and proprietary over-the-counter pharmaceuticals. Its main cosmetics products are nail care and nail color products, color cosmetics, beauty implements, bleaches and depilatories, personal care products, and other related cosmetics items. These are marketed under such brand names as Sally Hansen and Naturistics. Its pharmaceutical products include oral analgesics (of which Orajel is the best known), acne treatment products, and ear drop medications.

The First Decade: 1961–71

Del Laboratories was founded as Maradel Products, Inc., with headquarters in New York City, to acquire going concerns in the health and beauty aid market and was incorporated in 1961. Martin E. Revson, former sales manager and executive vice-president of the giant cosmetics firm Revlon, Inc., was Maradel's largest single shareholder, with one-quarter of the stock, when he became its chairman in 1963. The younger brother of Charles and Joseph Revson, who founded Revlon, Martin Revson left the company in 1958 to strike out on his own. Revlon took a sizable stake in Maradel and held it until 1983. Martin Revson assumed the chairmanship after the expiration of a five-year agreement not to take an active part in a competing concern.

Maradel acquired The Theon Co., Inc. and an affiliate in December 1961 for $2 million. In 1962 it purchased M. Pier Co., Inc. and its subsidiaries for $3 million, Waval-Thermal Company and Beaute Vues Corporation for nearly $3 million, Sally Hansen, Inc. for $1.5 million, and Compstone Company Ltd. In 1963 it acquired Commerce Drug Co., Inc. and House of Tre-Jur, Inc. In all, Maradel acquired 11 companies in its first two years, for a total of $16 million.

The businesses that it purchased had sales of $8.1 million in 1961 and net income of $611,000. This grew to $9.1 million and $660,000 in 1962, the year the company went public, selling nearly 40 percent of its outstanding shares at $13 a share. More stock was offered the following year, at $20.50 a share.

With these purchases Maradel was manufacturing cosmetics; hair, bath, and dental preparations; and proprietary drugs and sundries. But the result, according to Dan K. Wassong, who joined the company in 1964 and became its president and chief executive officer in 1969, was "chaos. . . . No single acquisition was large enough to give Maradel the core of a cohesive executive team. Compounding this was the fact that many of the original owners who operated the acquired companies left before parent company management could be developed in depth. Additionally, these 11 enterprises had widely scattered manufacturing facilities, and the duplication in cost was staggering. Maintaining cost and quality control was virtually impossible."

Maradel lost $863,000 in 1963 and $44,300 in 1964 as a result of these problems and also its effort to franchise two newly conceived products. New management then took over, including former executives of other large companies in the cosmetics field. Most of the newer products were dropped and emphasis placed on product lines that had proven to be profitable. The eight manufacturing plants, plus warehousing and headquarters, were consolidated in Farmingdale, New York, except for packaging and components in Canajoharie, New York, the site of the Compstone subsidiary. By contrast, sales and marketing were decentralized. Four of the acquisitions were written off.

By the end of 1966, the year the company was renamed Del Laboratories, Maradel had regained its momentum. Net sales reached $12.1 million that year, and net income was $739,000.

In 1967 a third stock offering, at $11 a share, enabled Del to buy Rejuvia, Inc., which made eye makeup, nail polish, and lipstick retailed under the Flame-Glo (later Flame Glow) name. The company also acquired Blanchard Parfums Corporation, producer of popular priced fragrances; House for Men, Inc. (men's toiletries), and LaSalle Laboratories, Inc. (also men's toiletries) in 1967.

Del Laboratories' product line in 1967 included nail care products merchandised under the Sally Hansen label. Most prominent of these was Hard as Nails, believed to be the largest selling nail hardener on the market. About 30 eye makeup products, such as eye shadow and mascara, were being marketed under the Lashbrite name. The Tre-Jur division was making popular priced bath powder, soaps, and similar products, chiefly for Christmas. The Compstone division was producing sunglasses, with the main lines Oleg Cassini and Oculens.

The Nutri-Tonic division was making home permanents, hair lotions, shampoos, and related products, including Life hair conditioner and Go-Straight hair straightener. The Tiz division was distributing shampoos, hair colors, and eyelashes to the professional market. Commerce Drug Co., the proprietary medication unit, was carrying ophthalmic and pediatric preparations in addition to such popular items as Ora-Jel (later Orajel) for toothaches and Trialka for digestive problems.

Del Laboratories was in the red again in 1969, when it lost $2.1 million on net sales of $15 million. The company also lost money in 1970 before returning to profitability in 1971, when it had seven product lines in three marketing groups. Commerce Drug, the largest division, was contributing about one-third of the company's overall sales volume and a larger share of the profits. Its line of 60 proprietary drugs and 14 natural/organic vitamins included 13 nationally advertised products. Flame-Glo, according to Wassong, had been successfully transformed from a line oriented to "a mature audience" toward one "aimed at a youthful, contemporary market." The fragrance lines, accounting for about five percent of Del's cosmetics group sales, consisted of Parfums Blanchard and Parfums Schiaparelli, which was acquired in 1968 and imported fragrances from France.

More Products, Higher Sales: 1970–95

The 1970s was not a good decade for the U.S. economy, but Del Laboratories was solidly profitable. Sales grew by 13.7 percent for the 1970–74 period, compounded annually, while earnings increased at an annual rate of 7.4 percent during 1970–73. The company began paying dividends annually in 1973 and purchased a facility in Little Falls, New York, for production and warehousing in 1974. Sally Hansen, Flame-Glo, and Ora-Jel did particularly well in the late 1970s, though Lashbrite products were discontinued in 1978. That year Del acquired the LaCross division of A.R. Winarick, Inc. Based in Newark, New Jersey, La Cross manufactured manicure implements. The company also had, in 1979, a Rejuvia line that included Vitamin E skincare products, brush-on peel-off masks,

musk oil fragrances, and a Viganic line of medium-priced vitamins.

Del Laboratories had by far its best year yet in 1980, with net income of $3.6 million on net sales of $55.4 million. That year the company purchased the Propa pH acne care line from Ketchum & Company. Sally Hansen's Hard as Nails was doing particularly well in this period, accounting for half the $60 million-a-year nail care market in 1984 and holding third place in the $200 million-a-year nail polish market. The Sally Hansen division also was moving into facial cosmetics and by the end of the decade was turning out hair bleaches and depilatories as well.

During 1983–84 Del Laboratories introduced Natural Cold Wax, a depilatory; New Lengths, a fiber-based nail lengthener; and about 40 new Flame-Glo products or packages. The company acquired Chattem Inc.'s Quencher line of cosmetics in 1984 for about $5.5 million. Del's sales focus was the mass, rather than the middle, market, with Kmart Corporation its biggest customer. A *Business Week* article credited Wassong for the firm's success, quoting a company executive who said of him, "He knows what's selling and what's not. He makes a point of studying the competition." Revlon sold its 19 percent share of Del to Revson and Wassong in 1983.

After recording net income of more than $3 million in every year between 1983 and 1988, Del Laboratories stumbled in 1989, losing $1.8 million despite record net sales of $121.5 million because of a $2.5 million writeoff of unsold cosmetics inventory. Still especially lucrative was Commerce Drug, which accounted for 30 percent of sales volume and had a profit margin more than three times as high as the cosmetics lines. Its products now included Baby Orajel, Pronto lice shampoo, Propa pH skin astringent, Stye ointment, Boil Ease, Diaper Guard, Off-Ezy wart remover, and Arthricare arthritis cream. Del's sales remained flat in 1990, but the company earned $1.9 million.

Del Laboratories introduced Natural Glow, a line of 55 natural ingredient cosmetics, packaged with recyclable paper and plastics and supported by an expensive advertising campaign aimed at teenagers, in 1991. This line grew to 81 in 1992 and 111 in 1993. Naturistics, a new low-budget line of natural toiletries, also made its debut in 1991. In 1993 Del Laboratories sought to establish in-store boutiques in 250 mass-market outlets to house the company's bath and body products, color cosmetics, gift sets, and fragrances in a single 12-foot display. This promotion failed because retailers were unwilling to accept a combination of health and beauty aids and cosmetics in a single display. Nevertheless, Natural Glow displays were in 12,000 stores and Naturistics in 6,000 by mid-1996.

The Commerce Drug division changed its name to Del Pharmaceuticals in 1993. Sally Hansen introduced a professional line of its products during 1994–95 and had absorbed the Quencher line by the end of 1995. The LaCross line was integrated into the Sally Hansen line in 1994. The Flame Glow, Nutri-Tonic, Rejuvia, and Schiaparelli names apparently no longer were in use by 1996. In 1996 Del announced its fourth stock split since 1991 and the third consecutive year of dividend increases. Its net earnings had grown between 1993 and 1995 at a compounded annual rate of 28 percent on sales increases averaging 14 percent annually, thereby producing a three-year total return to investors of nearly 200 percent, counting stock appreciation as well as dividends.

Challenges and Changes: 1995–98

These results—and his 35 percent share of the company—enabled Wassong to survive the largest sexual-harassment monetary settlement in the history of the federal Equal Employment Opportunity Commission, by which Del Laboratories agreed in 1995 to pay nearly $1.2 million to 15 plaintiffs who had worked for the chief executive as assistants. At a press briefing, according to Dallas Gatewood of *Newsday,* 11 of the 15 women told reporters that Wassong grabbed their breasts or stroked their buttocks, spoke about his sex life, cast profane slurs on their appearance, and urinated in his office bathroom with the door open. Ten of the plaintiffs said they were fired or forced to quit because of his behavior. Nineteen other former employees also testified against Wassong but were not entitled to damages because of a statute of limitations. Wassong, who had taken the title of chairman as well as president of Del in 1992, denied any wrongdoing in statements issued through lawyers.

By 1997 retailers were willing to accept a single display of Natural Glow and Naturistics products, so Del Laboratories sent one, measuring six feet square and housing 400 stockkeeping units under the Naturistics banner, to 5,000 discount stores. These products encompassed skin, bath, and body care, fragrances, and color cosmetics. Some 16,000 to 18,000 stores were receiving the Natural Glow cosmetics line at this time. Del's pharmaceutical products included Orajel—the world's leading topical oral analgesic—and Tanac (oral analgesics), Propa pH (acne treatment), Pronto (pediculicides), Arthricare (topical arthritis treatment), and Auro-Dri (an ear remedy).

Del Laboratories expanded its cosmetics offerings by acquiring the Cornsilk brand of oil-control makeup from Chattem in 1998 for $10.75 million, plus the assumption of inventory and certain liabilities. Cornsilk, consisting of oil-control loose and pressed powders, liquid foundation, concealers, and a new light coverage makeup, was being distributed to some 15,000 mass-market retail stores. It was placed under the Sally Hansen banner. Also under this banner were the LaCross division's nail and beauty implements, lip color and skincare products, bleaches, and depilatories. Del established its distribution center in Rocky Point, North Carolina, in 1997 and moved its headquarters to Uniondale, New York, in that year.

In 1997 Del Laboratories enjoyed its eighth consecutive year of record sales and profits. Of Del's $263 million in sales, cosmetics accounted for 79 percent and pharmaceuticals for the remaining 21 percent. Net earnings came to $13.1 million, of which cosmetics accounted for 61 percent and pharmaceuticals for the remaining 39 percent. The company's long-term debt was $44.4 million. Sales rose to $274.9 million in 1998, but net income declined to $11.1 million because of about $4.9 million in sales returns and inventory write-downs. The latter appeared to be related to Del's decision to ask retailers to divide Naturistics' display units by category. The full-line display units "kind of limited the brand to large discount stores," said a Del executive.

In April 1998 Wassong owned or held options to 32.8 percent of the company's stock. Revson held 15.6 percent of the stock. Both Wassong and Revson had the right of first refusal for the other's stock.

The products of Del Laboratories were being sold principally in the United States and Canada to wholesalers (in the case of pharmaceuticals) and independent and chain drug, variety, and food stores. Wal-Mart Stores, Inc. was its chief customer in 1997, accounting for 22.7 percent of sales. Advertising its products on television and radio and in magazines and in-store displays and promotional activities was a major expense for Del, accounting for $33 million in 1997, or 12.5 percent of total net sales. Sales outside the United States and Canada came to only about two percent of the total.

Del Laboratories had its principal manufacturing facilities in Farmingdale, New York, for both cosmetics and pharmaceuticals in 1997. There were also manufacturing facilities in Newark, New Jersey, and Barrie, Ontario.

Principal Subsidiaries

Del Laboratories (Canada), Inc.; Del Pharmaceuticals, Inc.; Tipsco, Inc.

Principal Divisions

Cosmetics; Del International; Del Pharmaceuticals; LaCross Implements; Naturistics; Sally Hansen.

Further Reading

"Acquisitions Round Out Product Mix, Aid Upswing at Del Laboratories," *Barron's,* October 9, 1967, p. 31.

Allan, John H., "Brother of Revlon's President Elected Chairman of Maradel," *New York Times,* July 11, 1963, p. 27.

Brookman, Faye, "With Solid Bath, Nail Sales, Del Takes Aim at Top Tier," *WWD/Women's Wear Daily,* June 14, 1996, p. S18.

"Del Laboratories Goes After 'The Entire Market,' " *Business Week,* September 17, 1984, pp. 97, 100.

Falk, William B., "Them Vs. the CEO," *Newsday,* September 17, 1995, pp. A4–A5, A51.

Gatewood, Dallas, "$1.1M Bill in Sex Case," *Newsday,* August 4, 1995, pp. A5, A57.

Grover, Mary Beth, "Fire and Lice," *Forbes,* November 26, 1990, pp. 80, 82.

Kagan, Cara, "Del Gives Natural Glow to Naturistics," *Women's Wear Daily,* December 11, 1992, p. 6.

Rigg, Cynthia, "Del Searches for Fresh Look in Cosmetics," *Crain's New York Business,* February 11, 1991, p. 4.

Tode, Chantal, "Naturistics Melds HBA, Cosmetics," *WWD/Women's Wear Daily,* February 21, 1997, p. 10.

——, "Naturistics Pulls Back on Display Units," *WWD/Women's Wear Daily,* February 26, 1999, p. 11.

Troxell, Thomas N., Jr., "Success Formula," *Barron's,* July 16, 1979, pp. 32–33.

Wassong, Dan K., "Del Laboratories, Inc.," *Wall Street Transcript,* June 5, 1972, pp. 28,685–686.

—Robert Halasz

Dover Corporation

280 Park Avenue
New York, New York 10017-1292
U.S.A.
(212) 922-1640
Fax: (212) 922-1656
Web site: http://www.dovercorporation.com

Public Company
Incorporated: 1955
Employees: 23,314
Sales: $3.98 billion (1998)
Stock Exchanges: New York London
Ticker Symbol: DOV
NAIC: 332722 Bolt, Nut, Screw, Rivet, & Washer Manufacturing; 326199 All Other Plastics Product Manufacturing; 332313 Plate Work Manufacturing; 332116 Metal Stampings; 332618 Other Fabricated Wire Product Manufacturing; 333923 Overhead Traveling Crane, Hoist, & Monorail System Manufacturing; 333518 Other Metalworking Machinery Manufacturing; 333992 Welding & Soldering Equipment Manufacturing; 33321 Sawmill & Woodworking Machinery Manufacturing; 332991 Ball & Roller Bearing Manufacturing; 333412 Industrial & Commercial Fan & Blower Manufacturing; 333415 Air-Conditioning & Warm Air Heating Equipment & Commercial & Industrial Refrigeration Equipment Manufacturing; 3586 Measuring & Dispensing Pump Manufacturing; 333319 Other Commercial & Service Industry Machinery; 334412 Bare Printed Circuit Board Manufacturing; 334417 Electronic Connector Manufacturing; 334419 Other Electronic Component Manufacturing; 336211 Motor Vehicle Body Manufacturing; 334512 Automatic Environmental Control Manufacturing for Regulating Residential, Commercial, & Appliance Use

Dover Corporation is a diversified industrial manufacturing holding company composed of about 50 subsidiaries with about 200 product/market niches. Dover's management implements a distinctive approach: subsidiaries are allowed to operate with almost complete autonomy. Dover-subsidiary managers operate with great independence and are rewarded on the basis of long-term earnings growth and return on investment of individual businesses. The company is often thought of as a portfolio of companies rather than a conglomerate because of its hands-off organizational structure and philosophy of management. Dover-owned companies manufacture a wide range of industrial products, supplying the waste handling, bulk transport, automotive and automotive service, commercial food service, machine tool, fluid handling, petroleum, chemical, and electronics industries. With the early 1999 completion of the sale of Dover Elevator, the company is divided into four business segments—Dover Diversified, Dover Industries, Dover Resources, and Dover Technologies—each of which has its own president and CEO.

Early Years

Dover Corporation was formed in 1955, when New York stockbroker George Ohrstrom, Sr., recruited Fred D. Durham to manage four companies he had bought in the 1930s and 1940s. One of those companies was C. Lee Cook Company, a maker of seals and piston rings for compressors. C. Lee Cook had been built largely by its owner and president, Fred Durham, before being sold to Ohrstrom. Durham was made Dover's first president in 1955. The other three original companies were Rotary Lift, a manufacturer of automotive lifts; W. C. Norris, a maker of sucker rods for oil-well pumping; and Peerless, which was sold in 1977.

Dover's corporate offices, opened in 1955, were in Washington, D.C. In December of that year 930,000 common shares of Dover stock were listed on the New York Stock Exchange. The stock split three for two in 1965, and has split a number of times since.

Dover's corporate culture was molded by Durham, who felt that "business, like any other human enterprise, thrives best

101

Company Perspectives:

Dover's business goal is to be the leader in all the markets we serve. We earn that status by applying a simple philosophy to the management of our businesses. This requires us to: perceive our customers' real needs for products and support; provide better products and services than the competition; invest to maintain our competitive edge; ask our customers to pay a fair price for the extra value we add.

Service to our customers, product quality, innovation and a long-term orientation are implicit in this credo. Pursuit of this market leadership philosophy by all our businesses, plus value oriented acquisitions of companies that share this philosophy, plus a decentralized management style that gives the greatest scope to the talented people who manage these companies have combined to produce results featuring: long-term earnings growth; high cash flow; superior returns on stockholders' equity.

---

where creativity and initiative are encouraged in an atmosphere of maximum autonomy.'' Durham set out to give Dover an environment in which executives could work creatively and without the hindrance of bureaucracy. As Durham intended, autonomy, decentralization, and a minimal corporate staff became Dover's hallmarks. At the end of Dover's first year of operation the corporate staff consisted of three people, including Durham.

Each division functioned independently with its own president and board of directors. Between 1955 and 1979 Dover bought 14 companies, mostly privately owned or controlled. As part of Dover, the acquired companies retained much of their autonomy, and, in most cases, their preacquisition management, while benefiting from Dover's financial strength. At first Dover's corporate office assumed the role of central banker, monitoring subsidiaries' fiscal plans and overseeing capital spending in order to ensure high return on capital. Divisions were encouraged to keep cash flow heavy, in order to keep debt low and allow Dover to take advantage of acquisition opportunities and give divisions financial help when needed. The corporate office handled all financing.

The 1958 acquisition of the Shepard Warner Elevator Company gave Dover entry into the electric-elevator business. The purchase of Hunter-Hayes Elevator Company and Reddy Elevator Company in 1964 solidified Dover's position in that industry. For years Dover was number three in the U.S. elevator industry, behind Otis and Westinghouse.

In 1961 Dover bought Cincinnati, Ohio-based OPW, the leading U.S. maker of service station nozzles and other hazardous fluid handling equipment. When Fred Durham reached age 65 in 1964, OPW President Thomas C. Sutton was elected Dover's third president and chief executive officer. Dover's second president, Otto G. Schwenk, had served from 1961 to 1962. Schwenk was let go when Dover company presidents, united in opposition to his attempts to expand the corporate

staff, threatened to resign. Also in 1964, Dover's corporate headquarters were moved to New York.

Under Sutton's leadership Dover experienced tremendous growth. Sales leaped from $68 million in 1964 to $835 million in 1981. Sutton stuck closely to Durham's management philosophy, and eliminated the corporate position of internal auditor. To Dover's nucleus of well-managed companies many others were added, in accordance with a policy that required acquisitions to display such qualities as product excellence, market leadership, strong management, and high return on capital.

Expanded Through Acquisition in the 1960s and 1970s

Throughout the 1960s Dover's product base was expanded through acquisitions into a wide range of areas. Major purchases included De-sta-Co, a toggle clamps and flapper valves producer bought in 1962; the 1964 acquisition of Blackmer Pump Company, a maker of industrial pumps; Groen Manufacturing, a maker of steam-jacketed kettles and other equipment for the foodservice industry, purchased in 1967; and Ronningen-Petter, which produced filter-strainer units, bought in 1968. Also in 1968, Dover spun off its Dura-Vent subsidiary to employees. The Dura-Vent sale demonstrated another important facet of Dover's corporate strategy: divestiture of noncore businesses. Dover's 1966 acquisition of Turnbull, however, was not executed as seamlessly. The Turnbull acquisition negated corporate growth for two years as Dover's elevator division struggled to digest Turnbull.

During the 1960s the company began to export a broad range of its products through independent distributors and, later, through its own subsidiaries. During the 1960s and 1970s Dover operated primarily in the building industry—mostly elevators—the petroleum services equipment industry, and manufactured goods for various industrial uses.

In 1975 Dover acquired Dieterich Standard Corporation, a Denver, Colorado-based manufacturer of liquid-measurement instruments. Dieterich president Gary L. Roubos came to Dover with Dieterich. Roubos, with a background in chemical engineering and business administration, was elected Dover's president and chief operating officer within two years of the Dieterich purchase. In 1981 Roubos was named CEO, and in 1989 he became chairman. Roubos continued his predecessor's winning strategy. Acquisitions were typically small companies, mostly bought in exchange for cash. They were market leaders, or had proprietary lines that meshed with Dover's existing businesses and had good growth prospects. Dover acquisitions, almost without exception, had higher-than-average returns on invested capital. Beginning in 1963 and into the early 1980s the company averaged one non-elevator takeover a year. In the years Roubos served as president, from 1977 to 1989, sales doubled from $1 billion to a little over $2 billion. Difficulties in assimilating Weaver, an automotive lift company, caused that company to be shut down. Typically divisions that have been sold were not a good fit with Dover's other product lines.

In July 1979 Dover acquired Universal Instruments Corporation of Binghamton, New York. Universal, the world's leading manufacturer of automated assembly equipment for electronic circuitry, moved Dover into the electronics business. By 1989 Dover Technologies, Dover's electronics division, owned 12 companies. By 1980 the electronics market had become the second most important growth area for Dover, following petroleum-production products. During the 1980s, with the industry moving toward electronic-circuit miniaturization and cost reductions and quality enhancement through use of computer-controlled automation, Universal's sales soared.

Although petroleum-production and marketing equipment were Dover's fastest growing segments during the 1970s and 1980s, it was sensitive to the volatility of deregulation, environmental regulation, and pricing by the Organization of Petroleum Exporting Countries. The Norris division's sucker rods for lifting oil from wells were prey to the cyclical nature of the oil-drilling business and to the deregulation of the gasoline business. By the early 1980s, with the country in the midst of a recession, demand for oil-production equipment, an area that had comprised one-third of pretax profits, was sluggish. For instance, OPW, the leading supplier of gasoline-pump nozzles, had experienced rapid growth during the 1970s, with the installation of new pump nozzles for unleaded gasoline and the conversion of many gas stations to self-serve. Rotary Lift had done very well in the automobile-service industry during the 1970s; a number of mass-merchandisers were entering the automobile-service business and buying machinery from Rotary Lift. Recessionary pressures in the early 1980s, however, deterred purchases in the automotive service and repair industry. The diversity of Dover's product line, and moves into such areas as electronics, aerospace, and other growth areas, helped cushion the company against such economic swings.

Management Restructured in 1985

While Dover continued to grow under Roubos's leadership, its size and complexity began to hamper its approach. Thus, in 1985, Dover's management was restructured. The resulting arrangement created five major subsidiaries, each with between five and nine of its own related subsidiaries headed by a chief executive officer. The presidents of the approximately 40 companies that comprised Dover reported to the CEO of one of the five subsidiaries. The five subsidiary chiefs reported to the Dover CEO. Each subsidiary continued to seek to add complimentary acquisitions. The five subsidiaries were divided into four business sectors for reporting purposes. The sectors created in 1985 reflected the principal areas of market activity. They were building industries, comprised wholly of Dover Elevator International; the electronic products segment, representing Dover Technologies; the petroleum industry sector, representing Dover Resources; and industrial and aerospace products, comprised of the Dover Industries and Dover Sargent subsidiaries.

In 1989 Dover again revised its structure, into six sectors, to reflect shifts in market activity. Since the 1985 restructuring, distinctions created among petroleum, industrial, and aerospace companies had become increasingly blurred and decreasingly descriptive. The six sectors created in 1989 were Dover Elevator International, Dover Technologies, Dover Resources, Dover Industries, Dover Diversified, and Corporate Companies. All sectors except Corporate Companies are also subsidiaries in

their own right. True to character, each subsidiary office has three to five employees.

Dover bought about 25 companies between 1985 and 1988, for $460 million, but took on relatively little debt. In general, Dover's capital expenditures were financed with internally generated resources. The results were impressive, as evidenced by Dover's low debt, excellent long-term growth, and consistently above-average return on equity. In 1989 the company made no acquisitions, for the first time since 1980. The reason for this reticence was the inflated prices for acquisitions engendered by the leveraged buyout boom; Dover was following its traditional practice of not overpaying for the companies it acquired.

During the late 1980s and into 1990, market conditions in the defense electronics industry had been highly competitive, and performance of Dover's six defense electronics companies had been weak. At Universal Instruments 1989 profits declined 36 percent, and Nurad suffered an $8 million loss in the commercial radio market. Dover had responded to the flat market conditions by making management changes, ending Nurad's involvement in the commercial radio field, and trimming back operations. Beginning in 1988, Nurad was also the subject of a criminal investigation of its activities as a government contractor.

Dover was adversely affected by the recession of the early 1990s but remained profitable. Net sales stagnated, growing only from $1.95 billion in 1989 to $2.27 billion in 1992, while net earnings fell from $144 million in 1989 to $129.7 million in 1992. The company's return on average equity was also depressed by the recession, leveling at 15.9 percent for both 1991 and 1992—a better-than-average figure, but lower than the 20 percent or so that Dover typically reported. During 1991 Dover took charges totaling $37.3 million to sell or liquidate several underperforming businesses and to increase its insurance reserves for general liability and worker's compensation claims. Many Dover subsidiaries employed cost-cutting strategies during the recession, consolidating plants, reducing employment, freezing salaries, and reducing fringe benefits.

In May 1993 Thomas L. Reece was named president and chief operating officer of Dover; one year later he became president and CEO, with Roubos remaining chairman. Reece had joined the company in 1968 when it acquired Ronningen-Petter, of which he was marketing manager. He had risen through the ranks to become president and CEO of Dover Resources.

During 1993 Dover spun off its Dover Electronics Co. unit to shareholders because the unit was in direct competition with three other Dover Technologies equipment companies. Dover Electronics, a maker of electronic components for original equipment manufacturers, was renamed DOVatron International following the spinoff.

Acquisitions Increased in the Mid-to-Late 1990s

Starting in 1993, Dover also stepped up its acquisition activity in the friendlier postrecession environment. The company acquired the privately held Heil Company in 1993 for about $150 million in cash, making this one of the largest acquisitions in company history. The Chattanooga, Tennessee-based Heil, a manufacturer of garbage truck bodies and refuse equipment, had annual sales of about $165 million. In addition to seeking out larger acquisitions and more of them, Dover made another shift starting in 1994: encouraging the presidents of Dover subsidiaries to be on the lookout for ''add-on'' acquisitions—companies that could be merged into their own company, thereby strengthening its market position. For instance, Phoenix Refrigeration Systems, a maker of cooling units for supermarket display cases that Dover had acquired in 1993, itself acquired Hill Refrigeration Inc., a display case manufacturer, in 1994. The newly named Hill Phoenix, Inc. was then able to make complete display case units and thereby compete more effectively against its rivals. Dover's more aggressive approach to acquisition also began to be reflected in its financial statements. The company had typically held its debt to less than 15 percent of total capital. But, in part to fund acquisitions, long-term debt increased from $1.2 million in 1992 to $252.1 million in 1993, the latter translating into 81.9 percent of capital. From 1993 through 1997, the average long-term debt to capital ratio was 74.3 percent.

After acquiring ten companies in 1994, Dover spent $323.3 million in 1995 to make another nine acquisitions. The largest of these, and the company's largest purchase to date, also represented the company's increasing concentration on overseas growth. In September 1995 Dover paid $200 million for an 88 percent interest in Valance, France-based Imaje, S.A., one of the world's three largest manufacturers of industrial continuous ink-jet printers and specialized inks. Dover soon increased its interest to virtually 100 percent. In October 1995 the company ventured overseas again to buy the U.K.-based Hammond Engineering, Limited, a maker of rotary vane and screw compressors and hydraulic control units for the trucking industry.

Dover made ten more acquisitions in 1996, with an aggregate price of $281.7 million. The largest of these was the purchase of Pomona, California-based Everett Charles Technologies, Inc., a leading manufacturer of circuit board testing equipment. During 1997 Dover made 17 acquisitions, 15 of which were the add-on type, spending $261.4 million. The two stand-alone acquisitions made that year were not ''blockbusters'' like Heil, Imaje, and Everett Charles were; added to the Dover Resources group was Hydro Systems Company of Cincinnati, Ohio, a maker of cleaning chemical dispensing systems, while Dover Diversified gained Sanger, California-based Sanger Works Factory Holdings, Inc., the leading manufacturer of production equipment for making corrugated boxes in the United States.

Also in 1997 Dover divested its European elevator operations. In May of the following year, Dover announced that it would spin off its North American elevator operations—and its best-known brand, Dover Elevator—in early 1999. But, instead, Dover in early January 1999 sold Dover Elevator for $1.1 billion to the Thyssen Industries unit of Thyssen AG (which became Thyssen Krupp AG later in 1999 following a merger with Fried. Krupp AG Hoesch-Krupp). The divestment left Dover with four operating groups: Dover Diversified, Dover Industries, Dover Resources, and Dover Technologies. Meanwhile, 1998 was another record year for Dover Corporation as the company completed ten add-on acquisitions and four stand-alones, spending a total of $556 million, the most ever. Among the stand-alones was the largest acquisition yet in terms of price, namely the approximately $220 million purchase of pri-vately held Wilden Pump and Engineering Company, Inc. Wilden was based in Grand Terrace, California, and was the world leader in air-operated double-diaphragm pumps, a worldwide $250 million market. The other stand-alone companies acquired in 1998 were Salt Lake City-based Quartzdyne, Inc., the world leader in quartz-based pressure transducers, which are used in gas and oil drilling; Mentor, Ohio-based Wiseco Piston Company, Inc., the leading U.S. maker of high-performance pistons used in racing engines for autos, motorcycles, boats, and snowmobiles; and PDQ Manufacturing, Inc., a leading manufacturer of touchless car-washing equipment.

Despite the impact of the late 1990s Asian economic crisis, which hit the electronics sector—and consequently, Dover Technologies—particularly hard, Dover Corporation posted record revenues of $3.98 billion in 1998. Net earnings, however, fell from the 1997 total of $405.4 million to $378.8 million. With $800 million in aftertax proceeds in hand from the sale of Dover Elevator, the company planned to make additional acquisitions and repurchase stock. Dover could also be expected to use some of its cash to pay down its burgeoning debt, which ballooned to $610.1 million in 1998, thanks to the record acquisition activity.

Principal Subsidiaries

A-C Compressor Corporation; Avtec Industries, Inc.; Belvac Production Machinery, Inc.; Chief Automotive Systems, Inc.; Communications Techniques, Inc.; Conmec, Inc.; Davenport Machine, Inc.; DEK U.S.A., Inc.; Delaware Capital Formation, Inc.; Delaware Capital Holdings, Inc.; Dielectric Laboratories, Inc.; Dover Diversified, Inc.; Dover Europe Corporation; Dover Industries, Inc.; Dover Resources, Inc.; Dover Technologies International, Inc.; Dow-Key Microwave, Inc.; Duncan Industries Parking Control Systems Corp.; Everett Charles Technologies; The Heil Company; Hill Phoenix, Inc.; Hydro Systems Company; K&L Microwave, Inc.; Marathon Equipment Company; Mark Andy, Inc.; Midland Manufacturing, Inc.; Pathway Bellows, Inc.; PDQ Manufacturing, Inc.; Petro Vend, Inc.; PRC Corporation; Preco Turbine and Compressor Services, Inc.; Quartzdyne, Inc.; Randell Manufacturing, Inc.; Refrigeration Systems, Inc.; Revod Corporation; Robohand, Inc.; Ronningen-Petter; Sanger Works Factory Holdings, Inc.; Sonic Industries, Inc.; Texas Hydraulics, Inc.; Thermal Equipment Corporation; Tipper Tie, Inc.; TNI, Inc.; Tranter, Inc.; Tulsa Winch, Inc.; Universal Instruments Corporation; Vectron Laboratories, Inc.; Vectron Technologies, Inc.; Waukesha Bearings Corporation; Weldcraft Products, Inc.; Wilden Pump and Engineering Company, Inc.; Wiseco Piston Company, Inc.; The Wittemann Company, Inc.; atg test systems GmbH (Germany); DEK Printing Machines Ltd. (U.K.); Dover Corporation (Canada) Ltd.; Dover Europe Afzug GmbH (Germany); Dover Europe GmbH (Germany); Dover Exports, Ltd. (Barbados); Dover France Holdings SARL; Dover International Finance Services Ltd.; Dover UK Holdings Limited; HTT Heat Transfer Technologies, S.A. (Switzerland); Imaje S.A. (France); Imaje GmbH (Germany); Langbein & Englebracht, GmbH (Germany); Luther & Maezler GmbH (Germany); Soltec International, B.V. (Netherlands); SWEP International AB (Sweden); SWEP Technologies AB (Sweden); Universal Electronics Systems H.K. Ltd. (Hong Kong).

Principal Operating Units

Dover Diversified, Inc.; Dover Industries, Inc.; Dover Resources, Inc.; Dover Technologies International, Inc.

Further Reading

''Early History of Dover Corporation,'' New York: Dover Corporation, 1971.

Mendes, Joshua, ''Motivate and Get Out of the Way,'' *Forbes,* December 14, 1992, pp. 94+.

Smith, George David, and Robert Sobel, *Dover Corporation: A History, 1955–1989,* Cambridge, Mass.: Winthrop Group, 1991, 168 p.

Thackray, John, ''Diversification: What It Takes to Make It Work,'' *Across the Board,* November 1993, pp. 17–20.

Zweig, Phillip L., ''Who Says the Conglomerate Is Dead?,'' *Business Week,* January 23, 1995, pp. 92–93.

—Paula Cohen
—updated by David E. Salamie

Drew Industries Inc.

200 Mamaroneck Avenue
White Plains, New York 10601
U.S.A.
(914) 428-9098
Fax: (914) 428-4581
Web site: http://www.drewindustries.com

Public Company
Incorporated: 1962 as Drew Realty Corporation
Employees: 2,258
Sales: $330.6 million (1998)
Stock Exchanges: American
Ticker Symbol: DW
NAIC: 332321 Metal Window & Door Manufacturing;
    332322 Sheet Metal Work Manufacturing; 3446
    Ornamental & Architectural Metal Work
    Manufacturing; 42113 Tire & Tube Wholesalers

Drew Industries Inc. is a leading supplier of products for manufactured homes and recreational vehicles. Its Kinro, Inc. subsidiary manufactures and markets aluminum and vinyl windows for manufactured homes and aluminum windows and doors for recreational vehicles. Its Lippert Components, Inc. subsidiary manufactures and markets chassis and chassis parts for manufactured homes and recreational vehicles and galvanized roofing for manufactured homes. Its Shoals Supply, Inc. subsidiary manufactures and markets new axles and distributes reconditioned axles and new and reconditioned tires for manufactured homes.

Wide-Ranging Conglomerate: 1962–70

Drew Industries was founded in February 1962 as Drew Realty Corporation but very quickly was renamed Drew Properties Corporation. The revenues of the company's holdings in the 12 months prior to its founding were $2.9 million, with a net loss of $178,000. Assets came to $10.8 million. Drew Properties raised $1.6 million from the sale of stock in August 1962 for

the purpose of purchasing the Pickwick Hotel in San Francisco and Warren Apartments in Arlington, Virginia, and for working capital. The purchases were completed two months later. The company was based in New York City, and its chairman and president was Norman Elson. Harold Aibel was executive vice-president and treasurer.

Also in August 1962 Drew Properties, through an exchange offer, acquired interests in Phoenix Fifth Avenue Co., and stock of 14 corporations, including A & A Development, Elson-Aibel Development, and Aibel Corporation Properties, Hialeah, Florida, owners of an industrial park. The other companies owned 12 buildings in Manhattan; a shopping center in Daytona Beach, Florida; an apartment building in Phoenix; and leased office buildings in Atlanta, Louisville, Fort Lauderdale, and Miami Beach. In October 1962, along with the San Francisco and Arlington purchases, the company acquired the Dinkler-Andrew Jackson Hotel in Nashville and Belvedere Motel Hotel in Decatur, Georgia.

In 1964 Drew Properties acquired American Phoenix Corporation, another real estate investment company, through an exchange of shares. American Phoenix had assets of about $16.5 million and owned or operated eight properties, including motels in Dallas, Denver, St. Louis, and Asheville, North Carolina. American Phoenix shareholders received about 370,000 Drew shares of stock with a market value in excess of $2.9 million. Aibel, who was Elson's brother-in-law, succeeded Elson as president of the company in 1966.

With the acquisition of Plastimayd Corporation, a specialty plastics manufacturer, in 1968, Drew Properties ceased to be purely a real estate company and consequently changed its name to Drew National Corporation. Also in 1968, it acquired Irvins Inc., a Baltimore department store chain, and Public Furniture Sales Corporation, a New York City retailer of warehouse furniture. At the end of 1968 its real properties included, in addition to the aforementioned, Howard Johnson Motor Lodges in Charlotte and Fayetteville, North Carolina; a supermarket in Jacksonville, Florida; a shopping center in Anaheim, California; and an office building and other property in Beverly Hills, California. The Manhattan buildings and the Phoenix building apparently had been sold.

The February 1969 acquisition of Eve LeCoq, Inc. and its affiliate, Scarsdale Quilting Mills, Inc., also put Drew National into the manufacture of clothing for girls and young women and quilting. Four months later, the company established Summit Mortgage Investors, an enterprise that it intended to qualify as a real estate investment trust (REIT) under federal tax laws, transferring to Summit property appraised at about $10 million. The subsequent distribution of Summit shares to Drew shareholders and the company itself had advantages because REITs enjoyed tax-exempt status if, among other things, they distributed at least 90 percent of their taxable annual income to shareholders. Summit was made an unconsolidated subsidiary of Drew in 1970. Its holdings were sold to Madison Properties Inc. in 1971 for $4.4 million.

By the end of fiscal 1970 (the year ended August 31, 1970) Drew National was a conglomerate. The finance group consisted of Summit; Drew Equity & Funding Corporation, which was making mortgage loans; and Drew National Leasing Corporation, a 77 percent-owned unconsolidated subsidiary. The industrial group consisted of Plastimayd and two Florida-based companies making chemical compounds, housewares, and hardware. The consumer group was divided into six fields. In addition to Eve LeCoq, Drew had added two more women's wear firms, Ronnie Fashions, Inc. and Mr. Boots Ltd. Editions, Inc. Two Waterbury, Connecticut, retailers, Drew Metropolitan Corporation and Leopold's Furniture & Appliance Co., also had been added. Penn Valley Furniture Industries, Inc. had put the company into the manufacture of convertible sofas.

Drew National's biggest effort was being focused on door-to-door selling of furniture and major appliances in five states. The largest operation was Waterbury-based Drew-Albert Enterprises, Inc., which was covering 324 communities in Connecticut. Standard Distributors, Inc. was in charge of operations in Virginia. Acquired in 1968, Carsons of Fort Lauderdale, Inc., and Carsons of Atlanta, Inc., were active in Florida and Georgia, respectively. The M. Kovens Co., acquired in 1970, had headquarters in Baltimore and covered Maryland. Drew National had net income of $884,000 on net sales of $24.7 million in fiscal 1970. Direct sales of home furnishings accounted for about $9 million of that total.

Cutting Back Operations: 1971–80

By the end of 1972 it was clear that Drew National's appetite for acquisitions had outpaced its digestion, the company disclosing in later restatements a loss of nearly $1 million in fiscal 1971 and close to $1.3 million the following year. One of the biggest losers was Drew National Leasing. Drew National sold its stake in this subsidiary in 1971. However, annual reports for fiscal 1970 through 1973 were found by the Securities and Exchange Commission to overstate the earnings and prospects of both Drew National Corporation and Drew National Leasing Corporation, resulting in the sale of the latter at an inflated price of more than $2 million. The sale was rescinded, and Drew National in 1973 sold its interest for $115,000. Trading of Drew's stock on the American Stock Exchange came to a halt.

Drew National's real estate operations were almost as deficit-ridden as the leasing company. By the end of fiscal 1975 the company had rid itself of all such property except the Beverly Hills office building, an Anaheim restaurant and motel, and three mortgages. The sale of the company's leasehold interest in the Beverly Hills building in November 1976 put it out of the real estate business. The company disposed of its women's apparel division during 1973–74 because of poor sales and also sold Drew-cTi Inc., the industrial chemicals business, in 1973. It liquidated the Baltimore clothing chain and New York retailer of warehouse furniture during 1974–75, and Penn Valley, the sofa manufacturer, in 1975. Plastimayd, the plastics manufacturer, also was sold in 1975.

Slimmed-down Drew National now was pinning its hopes on door-to-door sales of home furnishings, which in 1973 had an annualized sales rate of $28 million from over 160,000 customers in 23 locations. The company made a small profit in fiscal 1973 but lost $3.4 million, including $1.7 million from continuing operations, in fiscal 1974. The following year it lost $7.5 million and, along with 22 of its subsidiaries, filed for Chapter 11 bankruptcy. It did not emerge from bankruptcy until 1979, when the company's unsecured Class II creditors received 12 percent of their claims, in the form of about $1.2 million and 929,716 shares of stock. Class I creditors earlier had accepted a cash payment of 20 cents on the dollar and 49,819 shares of stock. In addition, the company issued 500,000 shares of stock to certain banks and trade creditors.

Drew National narrowed its losses in fiscal 1976 and 1977 and became profitable again the following year, but only because of extraordinary credits, chiefly $5.4 million in tax credits carried over from the previous losses. Of $12.5 million in revenue in fiscal 1978, door-to-door merchandising of household furniture, appliances, and smaller household furnishings in eight cities accounted for 90 percent, with Scarsdale Quilting accounting for almost all the rest. In 1979 Bass Brothers Enterprises Inc. purchased 73 percent of the outstanding stock for $1.35 million, or ten cents a share.

Mostly Building Supplies: 1980–98

Drew National moved its offices from New York City to White Plains, New York, in 1980. Aibel resigned as president and was succeeded by Leigh J. Abrams, formerly president of Drew National Leasing and executive vice-president of the parent firm. E. W. Rose III, an investor, became chairman of the board. Also in that year, Drew National acquired manufacturer Horsman Dolls, Inc. for $6.5 million in cash and promissory notes. But the main event in 1980 was the purchase of Kinro, Inc. This company was producing aluminum-framed windows for the manufactured housing industry in four factories and had annual sales of $10 million. Beginning in 1982, Kinro acquired additional manufacturers of aluminum windows for manufactured homes and also developed a capacity to manufacture screens for its window products and, to a lesser extent, windows for minibuses.

Drew National was half-owned by Bass Brothers in early 1983, when it formed a subsidiary as part of a joint venture with Pratt Hotel Corporation, which had a majority stake in a company owning and operating the Sands Hotel & Casino in Atlantic City, New Jersey. State officials rejected the joint venture because the Bass brothers refused to file applications for a casino license and to undergo the state's extensive licensing investigation because of their reluctance to disclose information about their finances. Accordingly, Drew National was divided in 1984. The subsidiary, Bass Brothers Enterprises, Inc., merged with Pratt, but the Basses had no interest in the newly merged company. They maintained a 34 percent interest in the second new company, Drew Industries, Inc., which held all Drew National's non-gambling interests.

Drew Industries, in 1985, acquired Sandberg Manufacturing Co., producer of a line of wooden preschool toys, and Doolite, Inc., a manufacturer of doors for recreational vehicles. In 1987 it acquired Sun Valley Mobile Products, a purchase that enhanced its sales in the RV field. But its main acquisition, in 1985, was Leslie-Locke, Inc., a manufacturer of a diversified line of home improvement building products, with net sales of $32.3 million the previous fiscal year. Drew Industries paid 22 percent of its stock for this company. Also in 1985, the company liquidated Kupanoff Imports, Inc., an importer and distributor of Japanese-made kerosene heaters and related products that Drew National had purchased in 1982. Leslie-Locke acquired White Metal Rolling and Stamping Corporation, a manufacturer of aluminum ladders, in fiscal 1986 for $6.6 million in cash.

Merchandising operations still accounted for 14 percent of Drew Industries' sales in fiscal 1985, but the following year the company disposed of its three remaining direct-to-consumer divisions. It also liquidated Horsman Dolls and, in April 1987, sold Sandberg for $1.3 million. Drew Industries was now almost totally a building supplies company. Kinro was one of the two leading U.S. producers of windows for manufactured housing. Leslie-Locke, now the home improvements division, had an even higher sales level, but was not pulling its weight; in fiscal 1989, it actually lost money. The White Metal aluminum-ladder subsidiary was sold in 1990, despite annual sales of about $22.8 million. Scarsdale Quilting Mills, Drew's remaining nonbuilding supplies enterprise, disappeared about 1990.

Drew Industries' stock was selling as cheap as 20 cents a share in 1988 and (after a 1-for-10 reverse stock split in 1989) could still be had for under $1.50 a share at one point in 1991, the year certain company officers and directors bought all the Bass family holdings. In 1992, Drew had its best year yet, attaining record net income of $3.8 million on record revenues of $109.6 million. But the home-products segment produced only eight percent of company income in 1993 despite accounting for 49 percent of sales. In 1994 the company spun this unit off to its stockholders as Leslie Building Products, Inc. Drew Industries had net income of $8.1 million on net sales of $100 million in 1995.

Drew Industries acquired Shoals Supply, Inc. for stock valued at $7.5 million in 1996. This company was a supplier of products used to transport manufactured homes. It made new and used axles and chassis parts in five factories in four states and also distributed new and refurbished tires. In 1997 Shoals acquired Pritt Tire and Axle, Inc. for $4.45 million in cash and a small amount of stock warrants. With the acquisition of Shoals, Drew's net sales and income rose to $168.2 million and $12.6 million, respectively, in 1996.

By the end of 1996 Kinro had nine factories in the United States and an assembly operation in Juárez, Mexico. It had, in 1993, added high-quality vinyl windows to supplement its full line of aluminum primary windows, storm windows, and screens for manufactured homes. Its role in standardizing window sizes and styles for the once highly customized manufactured-housing industry had resulted in more timely deliveries and more dependable service at reasonable prices.

In 1997 Drew Industries purchased Lippert Components, Inc., a manufacturer and marketer of chassis and chassis parts for manufactured homes and recreational vehicles, as well as galvanized roofing for manufactured homes. The price was about $55 million in cash and stock. Lippert had revenues of about $99 million in fiscal 1997 and an operating profit of about $8.2 million. Drew had sales of $208.4 million and net income of $12 million in 1997. With the Lippert acquisition, these totals came to $330.6 million and $15.2 million, respectively, in 1998. The long-term debt rose, however, to $55.3 million at the end of the year.

Drew Industries owned 21 and leased 13 manufacturing and warehousing facilities at the end of 1997, all in the United States. Lippert accounted for 16 of these, Kinro for 12, and Shoals for six. Rose, still the company chairman, was Drew's largest stockholder in April 1997, with 19.1 percent of the common stock. FMR Corporation held 9.6 percent of the shares at the end of 1996.

Principal Subsidiaries

Kinro, Inc.; Kinro Holding, Inc.; Kinro Manufacturing, Inc.; Kinro Tennessee Limited Partnership; Kinro Texas Limited Partnership; Lippert Components, Inc.; Shoals Supply, Inc.; Shoals Supply Holding, Inc.; Shoals Supply Tennessee Limited Partnership; Shoals Supply Texas Limited Partnership.

Further Reading

''Drew Industries Plans to Buy Lippert for $55 Million,'' *New York Times,* July 23, 1997, p. D4.
''Drew National, Aides Accept Court Orders in Securities Case,'' *Wall Street Journal,* July 17, 1975, p. 17.
''Drew National Corp. Agrees to Sell Bulk of Its Common Shares,'' *Wall Street Journal,* June 19, 1979, p. 14.
''Drew National Says Creditors Committee Clears Settlement Plan,'' *Wall Street Journal,* February 2, 1978, p. 28.
''Drew National Sets Date for Distribution of Stock for Spinoff,'' *Wall Street Journal,* May 10, 1985, p. 45.
''Drew National Sets up an Investment Trust,'' *Wall Street Journal,* May 26, 1969, p. 14.
''Holders Approve Sale of American Phoenix to Drew Properties,'' *Wall Street Journal,* July 9, 1964, p. 7.
Kerfoot, Kevin, ''Kinro Begins Facility Construction in Rhea County,'' *Tennessee Manufacturer,* September 1996, p. 11.
''New Jersey Approves Plan to Remove Basses from Sands Ownership,'' *Wall Street Journal,* April 19, 1984, p. 44.

—Robert Halasz

E. & J. Gallo Winery

600 Yosemite Boulevard
Modesto, California 95354
U.S.A.
(209) 341-3111
Fax: (209) 341-3208
Web site: http://www.gallo.com

Private Company
Incorporated: 1933
Employees: 5,500
Sales: $1.5 billion (1997 est.)
NAIC: 31213 Wineries; 111332 Grape Vineyards

E. & J. Gallo Winery is the largest winemaker in the world, with production of nearly 900 million bottles per year. Gallo produces one in every three bottles of wine made in the United States. While best known for its inexpensive jug wines and such fortified varieties as Thunderbird, in the 1980s and 1990s Gallo has aggressively followed consumer preference into more expensive categories, notably cork-finished varietals (wines made wholly or predominantly from a single type of grape, such as Merlot). Many of these appear under brands other than Gallo, including Turning Leaf, Gossamer Bay, Indigo Hills, and Northern Sonoma. The winery, which remains privately owned by the Gallo family, has about 2,500 acres of prime Sonoma land in vine, making it the largest landowner in the region. It operates four California wineries. Gallo is also a market leader in sherry, vermouth, and port, marketed under the Gallo trade name; their other leading brands include André sparkling wine, E & J brandy, and Bartles & Jaymes wine coolers.

Early History

Gallo's phenomenal success rests on the shoulders of the brothers Ernest and Julio Gallo, who founded the winery in Modesto, California, in 1933. Ernest was regarded as the marketing and distribution expert, while Julio oversaw wine production. The Gallos' contribution to every aspect of their business is widely acknowledged throughout the industry. Ernest is credited with almost singlehandedly increasing domestic demand in the 1960s and 1970s, while Julio's technical innovations include the widespread adoption of stainless steel fermentation tanks to replace the traditional wood casks for all but the most expensive wines.

The growth of the Gallo winery parallels the emergence of California winemaking as a world-class industry. California had been successful in international competitions as far back as the early 1900s, but with the arrival of Prohibition in January 1920 the thriving industry was almost destroyed. Thousands of acres of carefully cultivated wine grapes were uprooted and replaced with cash crops such as apples and walnuts. When Prohibition was repealed on December 5, 1933, a mere 160 of California's original 700 wineries were intact, and federal and state taxation and legislation had decimated domestic wine consumption.

In 1933 Ernest and Julio Gallo, aged 24 and 23 years, respectively, entered the wine business. They had worked since childhood in the modest vineyards of their immigrant Italian father, and after the death of both their parents, they decided to start making their own wine. Their technical expertise was gleaned from two pre-Prohibition wine pamphlets in the Modesto Public Library. Ernest and Julio obtained the necessary government license, purchased winemaking equipment on credit, and leased a small Modesto warehouse for $60 a month. They then visited local growers, offering them a share of the profits in return for the use of their grapes. By the time of Prohibition's repeal in December 1933, Ernest had made his first sale of 6,000 gallons of wine to Pacific Wine Company, a Chicago distributor. Profit in the first year was $34,000, a sum that was immediately plowed back into the business.

The first Gallo winery was built at Dry Creek in Modesto and until the late 1930s sold table wine to local bottlers, who sold it under a variety of labels. In 1940, however, the first Gallo-labeled wine was introduced, and business increased substantially. Bottled in Los Angeles and New Orleans, the original selection consisted of the varietal wines Zinfandel and Dry Muscat, in addition to sherry and muscatel. It was during this early period that Ernest developed the strategic vision that would make him renowned throughout the industry. Realizing that consumption would never rise while wine was relegated to a secondary position behind hard liquor, he introduced the novel concept of salespeople who sold wine exclusively, a highly successful idea which was soon widely imitated. He recruited a team of zealous salespeople to push Gallo products and guarantee them high visibility on liquor store shelves. From the beginning, Gallo followed a strategy of expansion into new markets only when existing markets were conquered. Twenty-five years later, Gallo brands were available nationwide, and the company's distribution system was regarded as its greatest competitive strength.

Accomplishments in Winemaking, 1940s–70s

The company was also admired for its enological accomplishments. The Prohibition era had wreaked havoc on crops of better varieties of wine grape, which had been largely supplanted by inferior table and raisin varieties. The Gallo brothers addressed this problem with the purchase in 1942 of 2,000 acres of land in Livingston, California. Starting in 1945, they pursued an ambitious research and experimentation program that covered all aspects of viticulture, from rootstocks to irrigation methods. Grapes grown on the Livingston land were transported to a special research winery in Modesto for further testing. When a particular variable was determined to be beneficial, it was introduced into day-to-day winery operations. Many of the experiments, such as an innovative pest control system, were well ahead of their time and had far-reaching beneficial effects on the entire industry. In 1958 a research laboratory went into operation. By 1993 the research staff of 20 included chemical engineers, microbiologists, and biochemists, and a total of 50 research papers had been submitted by the winery to the American Society of Enology and Viticulture. The company also maintained a technical library designed to keep researchers and growers abreast of the latest developments in their respective fields.

In 1957 the Gallo brothers built a customized glass plant in Modesto, a step in the process of vertical integration which would eventually encompass the Fairbanks Trucking Company, an intrastate transportation company established in 1961; and Midcal Aluminum, an aluminum bottle cap and foil manufacturing plant founded the same year. In 1957 the company introduced Thunderbird, a citrus-flavored fortified wine that reflected consumer tastes of the period. Over the years, the brand began to sell particularly well in depressed neighborhoods because of its high alcohol content and low price. Although Thunderbird was undoubtedly one of Gallo's early marketing successes, it also contributed to the company's downmarket image. By 1989, in the face of public concern over alcoholism and internal family pressure, Gallo had asked distributors not to sell its flavored fortified wines to retailers in low-income neighborhoods.

Consumption of table wine in the United States increased more than sixfold between 1960 and 1980, corresponding to a period of great growth for the Gallo company. Production techniques were developed to provide high quality at lower cost than the competition. Wine industry experts unanimously praised Gallo's achievement in ''bringing new wine drinkers to the fold'' with their clean, consistent, and competitively priced product. As early as 1972 the wine critic of the *Los Angeles Times* identified Gallo Hearty Burgundy, priced at $1.25 a

bottle, as ''the best wine value in the country today.'' This wine was credited with influencing Americans to buy more California jug wines. In 1965 Julio Gallo established a Grower Relations staff of wine professionals who continue to work with growers, recommending new technologies and practices developed largely at Gallo's research facility. Among the most important developments of this period was a quality drive initiated by the company with California growers in 1967. In exchange for replacing existing grapes with grape varieties of Gallo's choice, growers were offered 10- to 15-year contracts guaranteeing them a fair price for their harvest. More than 100 growers signed contracts, thus ensuring the reemergence of such classic grapes as Chardonnay, Cabernet Sauvignon, and Sauvignon Blanc. As a result of the increasing supply of true wine grapes, Gallo was able to discontinue use of the inferior Thompson seedless grape in 1972.

In 1976 the Federal Trade Commission charged Gallo with unfair competition, and the winery signed a consent agreement restricting its ability to control its wholesalers. The consent order was designed to prevent Gallo from vertically integrating to a point where competitors would be unable to distribute their products effectively. In September 1982, Gallo successfully filed a petition to have the order set aside, arguing that ''dramatic changes in the wine industry,'' specifically the entry of conglomerates such as Coca-Cola and Seagrams, had rendered the terms of the original order obsolete.

Moved into Premium Wines in the 1980s

During the 1980s Gallo made a strong move into the premium wine market. In 1981 a premium Chardonnay was launched, to be followed one year later with a vintage-dated Cabernet from 1978. In late 1988, having dropped some of its original cork-finished varietals, Gallo introduced others, such as a successful new ''blush'' category of varietals. A vintage year was added across the Wine Cellars label, a trend the winery had resisted for many years. Given the company's production, marketing, and distribution expertise, no one in the industry was surprised when Gallo quickly took a leading role in the premium wine market. At the same time, Gallo was experiencing great success with the Bartles & Jaymes wine cooler, a beverage containing a mixture of wine, fruit juices, and carbonated water, and having less alcohol than table wine. The Bartles & Jaymes product was introduced in 1985 and within a year had become a market leader in a highly competitive and burgeoning segment. Many analysts attributed its success to an inspired ad campaign by Hal Riney and Partners, featuring a pair of eccentric characters named Frank Bartles and Ed Jaymes. The wine cooler phenomenon was short-lived, however; by 1993 demand had plummeted and Gallo and Seagrams were the only wine cooler producers left in the market. Advertising expenditure dropped accordingly. New introductions in the 1990s included the Eden Roc champagne brand, priced somewhat higher than the company's market leader, André champagne.

In April 1986, Ernest and Julio filed suit against their younger brother Joseph, charging him with trademark infringement. Joseph had begun to market cheese under the Gallo name. The case was important because it brought into question the right of an individual to use a personal name that had already been registered as a trademark by someone else. Several months later, Joseph filed a countersuit, claiming that he had been deprived of his rightful one-third share of their parents' winery, in effect a substantial share in the E. & J. Gallo Winery itself. Ernest and Julio's defense rested on the assertion that their winery was completely self-funded and had nothing to with their parents' estate. In September 1988 Joseph's counterclaim was dismissed. In June 1989 a U.S. District Court judge settled the trademark infringement case in favor of the plaintiffs, and Joseph Gallo was given 30 days to stop using the Gallo name on his cheese.

Second Gallo Generation Took Over in the 1990s

Ernest and Julio Gallo headed the winery they founded into their 80s. By the early 1990s the winery's leadership finally passed on to the second generation. Julio died in 1993 at the age of 83 from a broken neck he suffered when he overturned his jeep on a family ranch. Ernest, stricken by the loss, soon thereafter gave up day-to-day management, remaining involved only in long-range planning as Gallo chairman. Gallo was thereupon run by four copresidents: David Gallo, eldest son of Ernest, in charge of domestic marketing and advertising; Joe Gallo, also a son of Ernest, head of domestic and international sales; Bob Gallo, son of Julio, head of vineyards and winemaking; and Jim Coleman, Julio's son-in-law, responsible for warehouses and bottling plants. David died in March 1997 of a heart attack, leaving Joe Gallo fully in charge of sales. According to an article in the *Los Angeles Times Magazine,* 15 of Ernest and Julio's 20 grandchildren were employed by the winery in 1997, making it likely that Gallo family members would remain in leadership positions for years to come.

In the 1990s consumers continued to gravitate toward more expensive wines, and Gallo sought new ways to capture the mid-priced and premium categories. Despite the winery's efforts to escape its longstanding image, Gallo was still perceived as a low-end brand. To counter this, the Gallo winery began producing varietal wines under new brand names, with the Gallo name appearing nowhere on the label. In 1995 Turning Leaf made its debut, while Gossamer Bay debuted the following year. Gallo positioned both of these brands in the $5 to $10 per bottle range, the mid-priced area typical for supermarket-sold wine. By the fall of 1996 Turning Leaf had become one of the top 12 varietal wines sold in supermarkets.

Both Turning Leaf and Gossamer Bay were made at the Modesto winery; the inclusion of "Made in Modesto" on their labels was the only clue to their Gallo parentage. But Gallo was able to achieve an even greater distancing with wines produced in California's Sonoma County, where Gallo had been buying up vineyards and had a winery in Healdsburg. Gallo thereby began selling varietal wine vinted and bottled in Sonoma County; sold under a number of different brands, including Indigo Hills, Rancho Zabaco, Anapamu, Marcellina, and Northern Sonoma; and labeled "Made in Healdsburg." Some varieties sold for as much as $40 a bottle, placing them well into the premium category. Gallo wines finally began to receive serious attention from wine critics.

The move upmarket was not without its difficulties. Gallo was the object of a much-publicized lawsuit filed in April 1996 by Kendall-Jackson Winery Ltd., maker of Vintner's Reserve, the number one chardonnay brand in the United States. Kendall-Jackson contended that Gallo had copied the packaging of Vintner's Reserve for that of the Turning Leaf line of chardonnay and other varietals. Gallo prevailed in federal court in 1997 as well as in a federal court of appeals in 1998.

At the turn of the 21st century, Gallo Winery was well-positioned from the low to high ends of the wine market. Even under the direction of the second generation of Gallo family leadership, the winery was clearly following the direction of its founders—Ernest Gallo once said, "We don't want most of the business. We want it all."

Principal Divisions

Ballatore Champagne Cellars; E & J Distillers Brandy; E & J Gallo; Tott's Champagne Cellars.

Further Reading

"American Wine Comes of Age," *Time,* November 27, 1972.
Fierman, Jaclyn, "How Gallo Crushes the Competition," *Fortune,* September 1, 1986.
Fisher, Lawrence M., "The Gallos Go for the Gold," *New York Times,* November 22, 1992.
Gallo, Ernest, and Julio Gallo, with Bruce B. Henderson, *Ernest and Julio: Our Story,* New York: Times Books, 1994, 358 p.
Hamilton, Joan O'C., "Grapes of Wrath," *Business Week,* April 15, 1996, p. 50.
Hawkes, Ellen, *Blood and Wine: The Unauthorized Story of the Gallo Wine Empire,* New York: Simon & Schuster, 1993, 464 p.
King, Ralph T., Jr., "Grapes of Wrath: Kendall-Jackson Sues Gallo Winery in a Battle over a Bottle," *Wall Street Journal,* April 5, 1996, p. B1.
Laube, James, "Gallo Brothers' Growing Stake in Sonoma," *Wine Spectator,* May 31, 1991.
Prial, Frank J., "From the Top of the Barrel: Gallo Powers Its Way into the Premium Wine Market," *New York Times,* September 4, 1997, pp. D1, D4.
——, "Passing the Jug," *New York Times Magazine,* November 15, 1992.
Shanken, Marvin R., "Gallo's Dramatic Shift to Fine Varietals," *Wine Spectator,* September 15, 1991.
Stavro, Barry, "A New Vintage Gallo," *Los Angeles Times Magazine,* March 2, 1997, pp. 12–17, 28.
Stecklow, Steve, "Gallo Woos French, but Don't Expect Bordeaux by the Jug," *Wall Street Journal,* March 26, 1999, pp. A1, A14.
Steinriede, Kent, "New Gallo Brands Aim High," *Beverage Industry,* December 1998, p. 19.
——, "Technology Meets Tradition," *Beverage Industry,* December 1998, p. 22.

—Moya Verzhbinsky
—updated by David E. Salamie

Electronic Data Systems Corporation

5400 Legacy Drive
Plano, Texas 75024-3199
U.S.A.
(800) 474-2323
(972) 604-6000
Fax: (972) 605-2643
Web site: http://www.eds.com

Public Company
Incorporated: 1962
Employees: 110,000
Sales: $16.9 billion (1998)
Stock Exchanges: New York London
Ticker Symbol: EDS
NAIC: 51421 Data Processing Services; 541512
　　Computer Systems Design Services; 541513
　　Computer Facilities Management Services; 51121
　　Software Publishers

Electronic Data Systems Corporation (EDS) is a recognized leader in the management of information technology. The company designs, installs, and operates data processing systems for customers in the automotive, communications, energy, financial, government, healthcare, insurance, retail distribution, transportation, utilities, and manufacturing industries. An innovator in facilities management, EDS originated the concept of long-term fixed-price contracts for this industry. EDS owns the largest private digital telecommunications network in the world and conducts business in all 50 states and in 27 countries.

The Ross Perot Years, 1962–86

This multibillion-dollar corporation sprang from modest beginnings. At the age of 19, a young Texan named H. Ross Perot received a much desired appointment to the U.S. Naval Academy. Although he valued his time in the military, he found it too restrictive and decided against building a career in the Navy. In 1952, while still in the Navy, he was recruited to be a salesman by International Business Machines (IBM). Initially he found their business style comfortable, but became frustrated after a time.

In January 1962, Perot had already fulfilled his entire annual sales quota because of a recent change in IBM's commission structure. Not satisfied with the administrative job then offered him by IBM, he recognized an unmet need among IBM's many computer customers. Most companies had few knowledgeable personnel to operate their new computer equipment. Perot wanted to offer skilled electronic data processing management services to these companies. He presented his ideas to IBM executives, but they were not interested.

Perot left the company and, on June 27, 1962—his 32nd birthday—incorporated Electronic Data Systems in Dallas. EDS developed a business concept later termed ''facilities management.'' Companies would concentrate their energies on what they did best, leaving the computing and data processing tasks to EDS, who could do them more efficiently and economically.

Perot spent the first five months with his new business canvassing the East Coast and Midwest to find a first customer for his computer services company. He had bought wholesale computer time on an IBM 7070 computer installed at Southwestern Life Insurance in Dallas during the latter company's idle hours (EDS would not acquire its own computer until 1965). Once he sold this time at retail, he was in business. Collins Radio in Cedar Rapids, Iowa, became EDS's first customer, and launched a new industry called information services. In November, with money from that first sale, Perot hired IBM salesmen Milledge A. ''Mitch'' Hart and Thomas Marquez.

As EDS grew, Perot modeled employee behavior on the high standards of IBM. He demanded conservative dress, honesty with customers, and no alcohol consumption during business hours. He expected employees to stay sharply focused and highly disciplined. Although he ran the company with almost military precision, Perot established a management that listened to employee suggestions and ideas. According to an April 1969 article in the trade journal *Datamation,* Perot's goals were ''to create a climate of complete intolerance to company politics, to provide the finest personal and financial advantages for employees, to make EDS an exciting place to work . . . to promote from

Company Perspectives:

A sharp eye sees beyond what is and envisions what can be. Bringing that vision to life requires a wealth of insight, talent and resources. For clients around the world, Electronic Data Systems Corporation (EDS) is the bridge between vision and reality. We help clients see new ways to redefine their businesses or industries. Then we harness the power of information and technology to expand the horizons of innovation, productivity and service our clients deliver to their customers. The results we achieve speak to the value of a company that sees what the future can hold while helping its clients hold that future in their hands. That company is EDS.

within. . . .'' He believed in loyalty, but held duty at an even higher level. A motto over his office door read, ''Every Good and Excellent Thing Stands Moment by Moment on the Razor's Edge of Danger and Must be Fought for.'' Perot expected employees to fight for their ideas.

In 1963 EDS signed its first long-term commercial facilities management contract with Herman Lay of Frito-Lay. While other services companies offered short-term contracts of 60 or 90 days at hourly rates, EDS wrote five-year fixed-price contracts. EDS set up a customer's data processing system, provided the staff to run it, and, once the system was running smoothly, removed some personnel and reassigned them to new projects. Because EDS could cut expenses over the life of the contract by decreasing personnel costs, its profits increased. The customers benefited because they could budget long-term electronic data processing costs. The longer contracts also gave EDS stability.

The passage of Medicare legislation in 1965 gave EDS the opportunity to enter another lucrative market. Government agencies involved were about to take on a new mountain of paperwork. EDS organized Medicare and Medicaid claims processing systems in many states. By 1968, Medicare and Medicaid contracts provided about 25 percent of EDS revenues, and, by 1977, healthcare claims processing accounted for nearly 40 percent of EDS's sales.

In 1963, EDS executed its first insurance company contract with Mercantile Security Life and, by 1990, was the largest insurance data processor in the country. In 1968, it signed a Dallas bank as its first financial institution customer and later became the world's largest provider of data processing services to banks and savings and loans associations. Beginning with eight credit unions in 1974, EDS serviced more than 3,000 in 1990. While in 1978 EDS had only three employees in its Washington, D.C. office, in 1990, 6,000 people worked in EDS's government arena.

In 1968, prompted by an employee's question about the worth of the company's stock, Perot began to investigate the advisability of a public stock offering. He made the initial release small: 325,000 of his own shares and 325,000 new EDS shares—about seven percent of the company. The offering met

with phenomenal success, opening at $16.50 per share and closing at $22. Perot and EDS each received approximately $5 million. The stock traded over the counter until 1971, when the company was listed on the New York Stock Exchange. The shares climbed to a high of $160 in 1970; by April 1971, they had dropped to about $66, and in 1973, with a sharp decline in the stock market, EDS stock plummeted to $15 a share. But the company's revenues doubled almost every year between 1964 and 1970. Revenue increase slowed to 22 percent in 1971, with total revenues topping $100 million by the end of 1973, seven years ahead of the original goal set when the company was founded. Revenue growth slowed again in 1977 to 13 percent.

Perot served as president from the company's inception in 1962 until he appointed Hart to that position in 1970. Hart was president until his resignation in 1977. Perot stayed on as CEO and chairman of the board and resumed the presidency from 1977–79.

Pioneering Distributed Processing: The 1970s

EDS pioneered the concept of distributed processing, by which systems and terminals communicate with each other from remote locations. It developed computer systems set up to serve a specific industry. These systems could then be modified according to each customer's needs. In the 1970s, EDS developed Regional Data Centers, where customers could transmit their work to be handled by EDS's data processing equipment and personnel.

In the early 1970s, EDS bought Wall Street Leasing, a computer services subsidiary of DuPont Glore Forgan, Inc., one of the country's leading retail stockbrokers. Perot charged EDS Vice-President Morton H. Meyerson with the task of attempting to rescue the financially troubled firm. With encouragement from the Nixon Administration, which feared a financial disaster on Wall Street, Perot had begun by investing $10 million in DuPont. By 1973 he had invested further funds in Walston and Company, another retail brokerage house, and had proposed a merger between DuPont and Walston. By early 1974, Perot was defeated by the losses at DuPont and Walston and left Wall Street some $60 million poorer.

A lawsuit filed in 1976 by F. & M. Schaefer Corporation and F. & M. Schaefer Brewing Company, for whom EDS operated a data processing facility, contributed to the slowdown of revenue growth in the mid-1970s. Schaefer claimed that the EDS data processing system was inaccurate and deficient, resulting in inadequate and misleading information. EDS maintained that Schaefer filed the suit to avoid payment of more than $1.2 million owed to EDS. In the 1978 out-of-court settlement, EDS paid Schaefer Corporation $2.3 million and retained $1.3 million already paid by Schaefer. These kinds of lawsuits would continue to plague EDS to the end of the 20th century.

In 1975 the company began to aggressively pursue overseas business. Early the following year, EDS entered the international market by signing a contract with King Abdulaziz University in Saudi Arabia. Later that same year, EDS signed a three-year, $41 million contract with the government of Iran to provide computer services for their social security division and training for Iranian personnel. In December 1978, EDS suspended all operations because Iran was six months behind in payments. The scope of the Khomeini Revolution grew in Iran and, after the jailing of Iranian officials with whom EDS worked, Perot ordered EDS employees and their families home. A few employees remained, hoping the chaos would be resolved. The situation worsened with the "arrest" of EDS executives Bill Gaylord and Paul Chiapparone, with bail set at $12 million. Since diplomatic channels seemed closed, Perot took direct action. In early 1979, he organized a rescue team headed by Green Beret Colonel Arthur D. "Bull" Simons, whom Perot had previously hired to make private forays into Vietnam looking for servicemen missing in action. Although Gaylord and Chiapparone actually left the prison on their own when a rioting mob released all the inmates, they needed the EDS team to get them out of the country.

In the mid-1970s, EDS began a shift away from facilities management, since many companies were becoming interested in running their own data processing systems. In 1979 Meyerson became president, while Perot continued as chairman of the company. Under Meyerson, EDS diversified its business interests through acquisitions of turnkey systems for hospitals, small banks, and the small business field. With the purchase of Potomac Leasing in 1979, EDS moved into federal government contract work. The bulk of EDS business still remained in facilities management, with processing of healthcare claims a large percentage of the business through the 1970s and into the 1980s.

Always moving with the times, EDS became a systems integrator, sending in teams of experts to connect and coordinate a company's entire computer system, software, and telecommunications. In 1982 EDS celebrated its 20-year anniversary by winning a $656 million, ten-year contract for Project Viable, to streamline and update the U.S. Army's computerized administrative facilities and to build a network connecting 47 bases across the United States. The biggest contract in the information services industry at the time, the landmark agreement signified the start of the large systems integration market.

Under General Motors, 1984–96

On June 27, 1984, although the company never had a contract with an automobile manufacturer, EDS became a wholly owned subsidiary of General Motors Corporation (GM). GM needed EDS to coordinate and manage its huge, unwieldy data processing system and to cut its $6 billion annual data processing costs. Roger B. Smith, GM's chairman of the board, thought Perot's management style would be an asset to his giant corporation. The $2.5 billion purchase price was the largest ever paid for a computer services business. GM agreed to maintain EDS as a separate entity, keep key personnel, and issue a special class of common stock, called "Class E," which would be tied to EDS's performance, not GM's. Perot would retain managerial control of EDS and serve on GM's board of directors.

Problems surfaced within a year when the differences in management style between Perot and Smith became evident. The August 1984 issue of *Ward's Auto World* suggested "Mr. Perot is a self-made man and iconoclast used to calling his own shots . . . Roger B. Smith [is] a product of the GM consensus-by-committee school of management, never an entrepreneur."

EDS saw revenue increases as the result of the GM purchase. In 1985, the first full year after the acquisition, EDS revenues tripled to $3.4 billion. By 1986, personnel had grown to 44,000, almost triple the number from 1984. EDS also branched out into telecommunications and factory automation. Although EDS revenues increased substantially, profit margins fell to 5.5 percent in 1985. GM preferred contracts which stipulated a certain percentage for profit; EDS, on the other hand, wanted to continue the fixed-price contracts it had been using since inception. Additional problems arose as the result of the differing company cultures.

In 1986 GM management bought out Perot for more than $700 million and, for the first time in the 24 years since he started the company, Ross Perot was no longer in charge of EDS. Meyerson also resigned.

At that time, Lester M. Alberthal, Jr., became president and CEO. He had joined EDS as a systems engineer trainee in 1968. In June 1989, he was named chairman of EDS. Under Alberthal's leadership, EDS broadened its customer base and reduced its dependence on GM-generated revenues from 70 percent in 1986 to 55 percent in 1989. Revenues climbed to new highs. The company diversified, moving into energy, transportation, communications, manufacturing, and other new areas of business. Diversification included further expansion of international business. Administration of the company was reorganized through a leadership council, to spread responsibility and authority for daily operations to lower levels of the EDS hierarchy and allow the top executives to focus attention on development of long-range strategy.

Within the GM alliance, EDS developed the world's largest private digital telecommunications network: EDSNET. Consolidating the networks of both GM and EDS took three years, a staff of 2,000 people, and a cost of over $1 billion. In 1989 EDS opened its Information Management Center in Plano, Texas. The 153,000-square-foot facility served as the heart of EDS's extensive worldwide communications network and information processing centers where voice, data, and video transmissions travel to their destinations via state-of-the-art media. The center was the hub of operations for 15 North American and six international Information Processing Centers, allowing EDS to respond immediately to the needs of its thousands of customers, who were then able to take advantage of the leading edge of information technology.

Throughout the years, EDS contributed to the community and the nation as part of its company policy. In May 1989, and again in 1990, EDS supported Project JASON, which enabled 225,000 children around the country to witness live the undersea exploration of the Mediterranean Sea, led by Dr. Robert D. Ballard, the scientist who discovered the wreck of the *Titanic* in 1985. EDS provided satellite links and solved technological problems to ensure the success of the undertaking, created an Education Outreach Program for the communities where the company was located, and "adopted" several public schools and worked with teachers to help improve the quality of education.

In the early 1990s, the company won a string of big computer services contracts with regional and super-regional institutions in the banking industry. In 1992 total revenue reached

$8.2 billion, with net income at $636 million; the following year, revenue climbed to $8.6 billion, with a net income of $724 million.

In June 1994, the company signed a landmark $3.2 billion, ten-year outsourcing contract with Xerox Corporation. The company also discussed a merger with Sprint Telecommunications, and though nothing came of the talks, they were prescient of the convergence that occurred between telecommunications and computing over the next few years. Total revenue for 1994 reached $9.96 billion, with a net income of $821.9 million.

In January 1995, EDS signed a $350 million outsourcing agreement with American Express Bank Ltd. of New York and acquired A.T. Kearney, a global management consulting firm located in Chicago, for approximately $600 million. In addition, the company began working with Hong Kong-based CargoNet, a company which provided a comprehensive trade and transportation communication network designed to handle millions of trade-related documents each year, beginning a total transformation of the traditional trade cycle, using electronic commerce and logistics services to support Hong Kong trade and transport companies.

Also that year, the company created EDS Digital Studios and acquired Varitel Video, a midsized film-to-video transfer company. Two years later, the company spent $12 million to buy eight Quantel Dominos (of 15 existing on the West Coast at that time), high-resolution drawing pads and computer monitors used for film restoration, compositing, and creating digital special effects. Some of the subsidiary's products included *Post Paint* (an application which reduced "paint crawling," an animation problem which occurred when restoring animated films that were more than 20 years old in which the paint on individually painted frames tended to smear), *Post Camera* (which simulated a camera move after film had been shot), and *Post Rez* (which improved film resolution and produced a sharpness to the picture). New business consisted of 83 deals totaling more than $10.1 billion. Total revenue for the year reached $12.42 billion, with a net income of $938.9 million.

Self-Governing Again: 1996 Forward

In June 1996, the company was spun off from GM and became an independent company once again, triggering two years of restructuring, including related costs. The company struggled with a string of disappointing quarterly performances for a time, and the stock dropped to nearly half of what it had been trading at a year previously before bouncing back. In addition to a division pursuing multinational banking contracts, headed by Stephen R. Bova, the reorganization also spawned three other divisions—community banking, U.S. banking, and global securities services, headed by Louis Ivey, Michael Littell, and Michael T. Reddy, respectively. The company continued to do business with GM, after renegotiating their contracts, and ended up with $4.31 billion and $4.17 billion worth of business in 1997 and 1998, respectively, from the auto giant, in a ten-year $40 million agreement under which EDS would continue to be GM's principal provider of information technology (IT) services.

Early in the year, Rolls-Royce, one of the world's leading providers of aircraft and helicopter engines, engaged EDS and its management consulting firm, Kearney, and charged them with three goals: improve customer service, increase quality, and achieve significant business improvements. EDS created a "CoSourcing" relationship and improved many of Rolls-Royce's core business processes, including external purchasing, project management, product development and manufacturing, and information-handling and support systems. Rolls-Royce's U.S.-based subsidiary, The Allison Engine Company, later joined the agreement to improve global business process integration. Later that year, the relationship with EDS/Kearney was extended to Rolls-Royce's industrial power businesses, which provided systems in the naval power, oil and gas, electricity generation, transmission and distribution, and materials-handling market sectors encompassing Rolls-Royce's manufacturing capacity and support functions in Canada, Europe, Africa, and the Pacific Rim. *Integration Management* ranked the alliance as one of "Ten Deals That Shook the Globe" and praised both Rolls-Royce and EDS for a nontraditional approach in making the relationship work.

Also in 1996, the company began moving away from pursuing huge regional contracts in favor of smaller, more profitable ones with community banks (although in June the company signed a $250 million contract to manage desktop computer systems for Citigroup). As a result, in one larger deal EDS lost out in May to competitor Computer Sciences Corp. for part of a $2 billion, seven-year outsourcing contract with J.P. Morgan & Co., but signed 147 outsourcing contracts for a total value of $8.4 billion, including a ten-year, $75 million technology outsourcing agreement with Credito Emiliano, a private bank in Italy with 180 branches and 2,000 employees, EDS's first such contract with an Italian bank. Total revenue for the year reached $14.44 billion, but the company's profits declined for the first time since 1976, with a net income of $431.5 million, which included $895 million of restructuring charges, asset write-downs, and other related charges, as well as $45.5 million of one-time split-off costs, all before income taxes. On the up side that year, the company's stock began trading on the London Stock Exchange, and EDS became the first company to earn more than £1 billion in the U.K. computer services and software market.

By 1997 over 70 percent of the automated teller machines (ATMs) in the United States were manufactured by the company, making EDS the nation's leading designer and supplier of such. That year the company signed a record level of new business valued at more than $16.3 billion, including two mega-deals worth a combined $5.9 billion—one with The Commonwealth Bank of Australia Ltd.; the other with BellSouth in Atlanta, Georgia. Kearney's gross fees surpassed $1 billion for the first time, and new clients included market leaders such as British Airways, Chevron, and Mobil.

In June, the company merged its banking and securities unit with the credit services division, and the following month acquired all remaining outstanding equity interests in Neodata Corporation, a Colorado-based integrated marketing communications services company, for $61.7 million. The company's total revenue kept climbing, to $15.24 billion, with a net income of $730.6 million, outstripping the combined total revenue of its closest three competitors, Computer Sciences ($5.24 billion), First Data ($4.94 billion), and Vanstar ($2.01 billion).

Early in 1998, the company began working with Italy's Ministry of Education to help update their information technology infrastructure and help decentralize power and responsibilities from central government to peripheral offices. EDS allied with Ferrovie dello Stato (FS), the Italian State Railways, combining EDS's information technology expertise with FS's logistics know-how and existing infrastructure covering all of Italy. A distributed client/server system with 30,000 computers to link 14,000 institutions, from primary through high schools, with the Ministry's regional education offices throughout Italy, was designed.

In December 1998, Richard H. "Dick" Brown, former CEO of Vienna, Virginia-based Cable & Wireless, became the company's third CEO, replacing outgoing Alberthal, who also stepped down as chairman. During Alberthal's tenure, net sales grew from $4 billion to $16.9 billion, with a 1998 net income of $743.4 million. Also at the end of December, Vice-Chairman Gary Fernandes, a veteran EDS executive, retired, leaving industry analysts concerned about turnovers at the top of the company.

In January 1999, the company announced a joint venture with NCR Corporation, part of EDS's newly unveiled Business Intelligence Services (BIS) group. The arrangement would couple EDS's industry knowledge and consulting expertise with NCR's data warehousing capabilities. Together, EDS and NCR would help companies open up data warehouses linking employees, vendors, and business partners, a roughly $100 billion market. Such deals, coupled with a continuing emphasis on employee training and customer service, virtually guaranteed EDS's prominence within the information technology industry.

Principal Subsidiaries

A.T. Kearney Inc.; Bancsystems Association Inc.; Cummins Cash and Information Services Inc.; EDS Australia (65%); EDS Personal Communications Corp.; EDS Unigraphics; Energy Management Associates; Neodata Corp.; Scicon.

Principal Divisions

Credit Union Services; Health Care; Information Systems; Maintenance Systems Integration; Military Systems; Technical Products; People Systems.

Further Reading

Avery, Susan, "New Integrated Supply Raises Concerns," *Purchasing*, November 7, 1996, p. 71.

Black, George, and Toby Poston, "EDS's Global Reach to Win BP Deal," *Computer Weekly*, August 20, 1998, p. 2.

Callaway, Erin, "Xerox, EDS Try to Keep Spark in Outsource Deal," *PC Week*, September 9, 1996, p. 1.

Davey, Tom, "The Grass-Roots 6x86 Movement; Cyrix's EDS Deal Is Rooted in Desktop PCs," *PC Week*, March 18, 1996, p. 31.

Egodigwe, Laura Saunders, "EDS Insiders Post Stock Sales of $22.7 Million," *Wall Street Journal*, May 6, 1998, p. C1(W)/C1(E).

Files, Jennifer, "Shares of Electronic Data Systems Increase As Investors Applaud Changes," *Knight-Ridder/Tribune Business News*, August 9, 1998, p. OKRB9822005C.

Gabriele, Michael C., "Design Software Can Shorten Product Development Cycle," *Modern Plastics*, May 1996, p. 37.

Hausman, Tamar, "And the Finalists Are?" *Wall Street Journal*, November 24, 1998, p. B14(E).

Hudson, Richard L., "Two EDS Officers in Europe Defect to Philips Affiliate," *Wall Street Journal, Europe*, June 6, 1996, p. 3.

Jennings, Robert, "Card Firm, EDS in Dispute About 'Letter of Intent' for a Marketing Alliance," *American Banker*, January 16, 1996, p. 16.

Keenan, Charles, "EDS Is Testing Commercials on Teller Machines," *American Banker*, December 12, 1997, p. 11.

La Monica, Paul R., "EDS, IBM Promise Ways to Cut Costs," *American Banker*, May 2, 1997, p. 1.

Machlis, Sharon, "Electronic Data Systems Corp.," *Computerworld*, August 17, 1998, p. 1.

Nakamoto, Michiyo, "EDS to Take on 600 Yamaichi Staff," *Financial Times*, December 2, 1997, p. 26.

O'Sullivan, Orla, "Data Warehousing—Without the Warehouse," *ABA Banking Journal*, December 1996, p. 42.

Palmeri, Christopher, "Going It Alone," *Forbes*, December 16, 1996, p. 86.

Price, Christopher, "EDS-Led Group Wins 1.4BN Pounds Sterling Contract for Tube Ticketing," *Financial Times*, August 14, 1998, p. 16.

Radigan, Joseph, "EDS Nabs a Customer at Alltel's Expense," *US Banker*, January 1996, p. 17.

Sabatini, Patricia, "Mellon Hires Firm to Improve Bank's Software Development Practices," *Knight-Ridder/Tribune Business News*, September 19, 1997, p. 919B1028.

Talmor, Sharona, "Mine for Data," *The Banker*, April 1996, p. 93.

"$3.7B Outsourcing Deal for EDS in Australia," *American Banker*, August 14, 1997, p. 19.

Tucker, Tracey, "Nervous About PCs, Many Banks Go Halfway with Hybrid Systems," *American Banker*, August 21, 1996, p. 12.

Walton, Christopher, "Texas-Based Electronic Data Systems to Insure Its Gay Workers' Partners," *Knight-Ridder/Tribune Business News*, October 25, 1997, p. 1025B0910.

Warner, Melanie, "A Tale from the Dark Side of Silicon Valley," *Fortune*, April 13, 1998, p. 92.

Wighton, David, "EDS Among Bidders for Business," *Financial Times*, December 13, 1996, p. 10.

Wise, Peter, "EDS in Portuguese Venture," *Financial Times*, November 6, 1997, p. 5.

Zellner, Wendy, "EDS Is Learning the Price of Freedom," *Business Week*, May 5, 1997, p. 44.

—updated by Daryl F. Mallett

EQUIFAX

Equifax Inc.

1600 Peachtree Street, NW
Atlanta, Georgia 30309
U.S.A.
(404) 885-8000
Fax: (404) 888-5452
Web site: http://www.equifax.com

Public Company
Incorporated: 1913 as Retail Credit Company, Inc.
Employees: 14,000
Sales: $1.62 billion (1998)
Stock Exchanges: New York
Ticker Symbol: EFX
NAIC: 56145 Credit Bureaus; 514199 All Other
    Information Services; 52421 Insurance Agents &
    Brokerages; 56144 Collection Agencies; 54186 Direct
    Mail Advertising; 54191 Marketing Research &
    Public Opinion Polling

Equifax Inc. is the largest consumer credit bureau in the United States, providing information about consumers to clients in several industries, including insurance, finance, credit card, banking, retail, and telecommunications. In addition to consumer and commercial credit information services, Equifax has a diversified array of operations including payment services, software, modeling, analytics, consulting, and direct-to-consumer services. The company handles or facilitates more than ten million electronic transactions per day for 300,000 customers worldwide. Boasting operations in 18 countries and sales in more than 45, Equifax holds leading positions in consumer and commercial credit information in Canada, Argentina, Brazil, Chile, El Salvador, Peru, Portugal, Spain, and the United Kingdom. Equifax also holds the number one position in check guarantee and verification in the United States, Canada, France, Ireland, the United Kingdom, Australia, and New Zealand.

Late 19th-Century Beginnings

Equifax was founded in 1898 by two brothers, Cator and Guy Woolford. Cator Woolford got his start in the credit bureau business as a grocer in Chattanooga, Tennessee. There he supervised the compilation of a list of customers, with indications of their creditworthiness, for the local Retail Grocer's Association. To cover the costs of this effort, Woolford sold copies of the book to other merchants. Pleased with the success of his first listing, Woolford set out to make credit reporting his career.

With his brother Guy, a lawyer six years his junior, Cator settled on Atlanta as the site of his new venture. After several visits to the city, the Woolfords rented an office consisting of a single room on the fifth floor of the Gould Building, at 10 Decatur Street, and had the words "Retail Credit Company" printed on the door in large black letters. On March 22, 1899, the company opened for business.

Relying on his experience in Tennessee, Cator began by seeking out an alliance with the city's grocers. Using the ledger books of Atlanta's food retailers, the Woolford's copied out credit information on their customers on individual slips on paper, then arranged them into a book. After a month the task had grown so large that two additional men were hired to assist the Woolfords, and one week later a woman was employed as well. In June the pages of the book were run out on a mimeograph machine and bound between hard covers with the title "Merchant's Guide."

Merchants paid $25 a year to use the book and subsequent credit reports; grocers paid less. Although the company sold seven subscriptions rapidly after one of Atlanta's largest department stores bought the first, by the end of Retail Credit's first year only 37 merchants and 47 grocers had signed on board. The company posted a loss of $2,242.

In the following year, however, the number of customers increased and the company also branched out to other small, fast-growing commercial centers in Georgia. Credit books for Athens, Rome, Columbus, Macon, and Augusta were developed and marketed and a branch office was opened in Augusta. By the end of the company's second year, the staff had expanded to eight and the volume of sales was growing steadily.

Expanded into Insurance-Related Business in 1901

In June 1901 Retail Credit branched out into another industry, as it began providing so-called "moral hazard" information

---

Company Perspectives:

We don't create world commerce. We make it happen. And it happens two billion times a day. From an information kiosk in Chile to a bank in Nova Scotia. Yet, we are the part of the transaction you don't see. Bridging the gap between impulse and action. Connecting the buyer to seller in the blink of an eye. We are the technology that makes commerce easier. For merchants, banks, and credit unions. And for us all. We are the knowledge that drives commerce forward. Expanding further into emerging economies. Drilling deeper into databases. Discovering infinite new markets and opportunities. We are the power that changes the shape of global commerce. Adding speed, efficiency, and convenience to how the world does business. And introducing new possibilities in how people live their lives.

---

on potential policyholders to the Equitable Life Assurance Society. Insurance companies paid much more highly for the information they needed; Retail Credit quickly expanded operations into this lucrative area. In the fall of 1901, the company dispatched a salesman to the Northeast to drum up business in the home offices of the nation's largest insurance companies. Armed with a form showing the information that would be provided about each potential customer, the salesman pulled in a large number of new clients.

As a result of its growing insurance business, Guy Woolford opened a second company office in Dallas, Texas, in March 1902. Woolford relied on a large number of correspondents, primarily lawyers and merchants in small towns across the Southeast, to fill out reports on people trying to get insurance. The following year the company also opened a branch office in Cincinnati.

In April 1903 Retail Credit closed its Augusta office, after clearly noting signs that the branch would not become profitable. The same year, the company split operations between its two main clients, handling retail and insurance reports separately. Different inspectors carried out the two types of investigations. The company's retail credit reporting activities were restricted to the Atlanta area, while insurance activities were delegated a wider scope.

In 1904 a fourth office was opened in Kansas City, Missouri. Soon offices in Chicago and San Francisco came on line. Two years later the San Francisco office was entirely destroyed by earthquake and fire. Despite this setback, geographical expansion continued and New York premises were opened in 1907. Attempts to run facilities in Baltimore, Greensborough, and Philadelphia during this time failed, and the offices were closed.

Retail Credit set a pattern of aggressive development in the life insurance-related business that would later be applied when entering other fields. For instance, in 1908 the company began issuing reports for automobile liability insurers. With only seven branch offices in operation, Retail Credit proclaimed that it provided a "National Inspection Service," providing reliable reports of uniform quality for insurance purposes.

By 1913 Retail Credit had developed a special form for automobile insurance, to be completed by the investigator. The company started providing information to accident insurers and soliciting work related to fire insurance. With the company's sales running at $350,000, the Woolfords decided to incorporate. The enterprise was newly christened the Retail Credit Company, Inc., on December 29, 1913.

By 1915 Retail Credit's earliest work compiling lists of good and bad credit risks in the Atlanta area had dwindled to almost nothing. While this type of operation was inherently local, Retail Credit had become interested in activities that could be pursued on a broader scale. Towards this end, the company opened five new insurance-related offices in that year.

By the end of the company's second decade of existence, Retail Credit was thoroughly established as a significant partner in the life insurance business. The credit bureau had opened 34 branch offices in the United States and three in Canada, as well. In 1920, however, Retail Credit's insurance business suffered a serious blow when a consortium of insurance companies formed the American Service Bureau to provide members with investigative reports of the sort that Retail Credit supplied. Similarly an agency that had previously limited its activities to claims inspection also joined the fray. The increased competition resulted in a serious slump in Retail Credit's life insurance and credit reporting activities in 1921.

Retail Credit attempted to make up the slack by increasing automobile insurance reporting; by the following year, more than one-fifth of the agency's business was contributed by this division. The company also developed its first form containing questions relating to fire insurance. In the ensuing years, the volume of requests for this new service increased dramatically.

In 1923 Retail Credit spun off local consumer credit rating operations and formed a new corporation, Credit Service Exchange. These activities had long taken place at a different location under separate management; three years later, Retail Credit further severed its connection when the Exchange was sold to businessman L.S. Gilbert. By the end of the decade, however, Retail Credit had opted to reenter the consumer credit reporting business. In the early 1930s Retail Credit, having 81 branch offices at its disposal, began studying cost-effective means of getting back into the commercial credit report business. Gathering information by telephone, as well as simplifying forms for recording information, were two of the steps taken towards this end. Also proving helpful was the advent of credit bureau associations which had begun springing up as the exchange of information between fellow creditors became more common. In March 1930 Retail Credit established the Georgia Credit Exchange to provide services in cities across the state. In 1934 Retail Credit purchased a Brooklyn credit agency, Retailers Commercial Agency, Inc.

Retail Credit moved to professionalize operations in the 1930s, relying less and less on part-time correspondents for information and more often utilizing full-time, company-trained inspectors. By 1937 nearly three quarters of all the company's inspection forms were being filled out by full-time investigators, operating out of 96 Retail Credit offices in cities across North America.

The U.S. entry into World War II had a serious impact on Retail Credit's business. In 1941, when the war began for the United States, the company was providing 7.5 million reports a year; many of its inspectors, however, were drafted into the military and other employees left the enterprise to engage in war-related endeavors. In the first full year of U.S. military involvement, the company lost 1,200 workers. Pushed to the limit, Retail Credit finally allowed women to work as inspectors, in most cases permitting wives to take over their absent husbands' jobs. By 1944 the volume of reports produced had sunk to six million.

Significant Postwar Growth

With the robust recovery of the U.S. economy in the postwar years, however, Retail Credit's business revived and grew. The company continued expansion by opening new branch offices throughout the decades following the war. In 1950, 140 locations were providing services. The number grew to 258 over the next ten years.

By the mid-1960s, nearly 300 branch offices had been opened along with almost 1,400 sub-offices, employing roughly 7,400 inspectors. The company sold stock to the public for the first time in 1965. During this time, Retail Credit also took its first steps toward automation, converting files written on 3x5 index cards to electronic data systems. Eventually the company's ability to retrieve information by computer from vast data banks would prove one of Retail Credit's greatest assets.

In the early 1970s, Retail Credit purchased several competitors, buying credit bureaus in Oregon, Idaho, and California, and Credit Bureau, Inc., located in Washington, D.C. These purchases were subsequently challenged by the Federal Trade Commission (FTC), which claimed that they reduced competition. After a decade-long court battle, Retail Credit was allowed to retain the purchases.

Retail Credit's activities in the consumer credit business were regulated for the first time in 1971, when Congress passed the Fair Credit Reporting Act, effective in April. Under this law, consumers were given the right to gain access to their credit files and correct errors in them. The law also restricted the kinds of information credit bureaus could sell.

Three years later, Retail Credit ran afoul of the new federal regulations and was charged with violating the Fair Credit Reporting Act and the Federal Trade Commission Act. Among other directives given, the U.S. government ordered Retail Credit to stop rating employees by how much negative information they collected on consumers and to stop having investigators misrepresent themselves when conducting inquiries.

Began Diversifying in 1979

Retail Credit changed its name in 1979 to Equifax Inc., derived from "equitable factual information." The change symbolized the company's growing capabilities and prepared the way for further diversification of its activities, from operations centered in the insurance industry to wider marketing functions. In 1979 the company took a big step in that direction, acquiring Elrick & Lavidge, a Chicago firm that performed marketing surveys, and merging it into the company's Marketing Information Services subsidiary.

Also in the late 1970s, Equifax began strengthening consumer credit reporting operations by purchasing small, local credit reporting agencies and by affiliating with others. In doing so, the company expanded its computerized files enormously and paved the way for greater diversification. Likewise, Equifax gained the capability to provide additional types of information to clients.

Consolidation in the credit bureau industry continued throughout the 1980s, as Equifax and its two largest competitors, TRW Inc. and the Trans Union Corporation, divided up the nation's smaller credit bureaus amongst themselves. In a ten-year period, 104 smaller credit bureaus had been added to the Equifax network alone. By 1986 the company's files covered 150 million people in 28 states. In the following year, the company's capacity grew 40 percent, to cover all 50 states.

During this time, Equifax also continued to spend heavily on technological developments for the purpose of keeping data-processing equipment up to date and offering new products to customers with the equipment. Equifax moved into marketing databases, which allowed patrons to target their most likely customers. In April 1988 the company established a marketing services division, whose first project was to develop a direct-mail program to sell home mortgages for a Midwestern insurance company. The company planned to handle all phases of the operation, including selection of potential customers, production of mailing brochures, handling of telephone inquiries, verification of credit applications, and property appraisal. The marketing division had sales of $90 million in the first nine months in operation. Between 1983 and 1988, the company's overall revenues increased by nearly 60 percent, to $743 million, and earnings more than doubled.

In May 1989 Equifax formed a strategic alliance with the fifth largest credit bureau, CSC Credit Services, a division of the Computer Sciences Corporation; the yield was 65 additional bureaus, bringing Equifax's total number of bureaus to more than 300. The company's operations had already been divided into four divisions: insurance information services, its traditional strength; credit services; marketing services, the newest division; and Canadian operations, which were consolidated into one company, Equifax Canada Inc., in June 1989.

Moved into Europe in the Early 1990s

Equifax also divested itself of two unprofitable units in 1989, Equifax Insurance Systems and Enercon, Inc. As the 1990s arrived, the company strove to enter the European market. Equifax formed Wescot Decision Systems as a joint venture with marketer Next PLC in the United Kingdom. Late in 1991, the company bought out its British partner to form Equifax Europe.

In addition to formation of a technology division, brought about by the consolidation of the company's activities in that field, Equifax also acquired Telecredit, Inc., a Los Angeles credit bureau that provided check and credit card authorization services, for $457 million in 1990. The company's purchase of Telecredit was complicated by a sizable drop in the value of

Equifax stock during 1990, as investors grew concerned about the stability of the company's profits in an economic downturn.

Another concern was growing consumer dissatisfaction. In 1989 Equifax had commissioned a poll that showed that 71 percent of all Americans thought they had lost control over information concerning their lives and 79 percent considered privacy a basic right. Equifax was forced to confront growing consumer hostility in the early 1990s, as watchdog groups contended that credit bureaus' files were often inaccurate and were used in inappropriate ways. As an Equifax executive explained in *Business Week*, "People see the use of this information as a privacy problem if it goes beyond credit purposes." To make amends, Equifax announced in August 1991 that it would cease using credit information to compile lists for the purposes of direct marketing. The company would also no longer keep tabs on customers' buying histories for the purpose of placing shoppers in a range of categories from "luxury buyers" to "coupon clippers." Four months later, the company spent $9 million to open an elaborate consumer services center which provided information to callers about their credit file in eight languages.

Leaving the direct-marketing business enhanced Equifax's public image without too much sacrifice; the relinquished activities provided only $12 million, or one percent of Equifax's revenues. In addition, the company modified the processes for correcting mistakes in its files, making it easier for consumers to set the record straight. In 1991 Equifax also abandoned a planned joint database project with Lotus Development Corporation that would have made available to small businesses a wide array of demographic information at microneighborhood levels; a consumer outcry and negative media attention led to the project's demise. In mid-1992 Equifax agreed to provide consumers with a toll-free number and to begin investigating disputes within 30 days. By taking these steps to mollify the public, Equifax hoped to ward off federal legislation that would mandate costly measures to increase fairness. In addition, the company hoped to avoid the expensive class action suits over its activities that competitors had suffered.

Equifax's image-polishing moves came just as the company's net income had declined from $64 million in 1990 to $5 million in 1991; the general recession had held down demand for credit and credit reports, plus a restructuring that cut about 1,900 jobs resulted in a $19 million charge. Despite Equifax's flat earnings, the company moved past its main competitor, TRW, to seize the lead in market share among credit bureaus in the beginning of 1992. (TRW's credit bureau was spun off as Experian Inc. in 1996.)

Having already moved into check verification and credit card processing in the early 1990s, Equifax diversified again in 1992 through the acquisition of Health Economics Corporation, which moved the company into the field of healthcare information. By 1994 Equifax had acquired three more healthcare information firms, giving it a substantial presence in claims processing. With the 1993 acquisition of Integratec Inc., Equifax gained a leading provider of debt collection and other back-office services for credit card issuers and other lenders. In 1994 the company also greatly expanded its international operations through acquisitions and joint ventures, gaining a presence in 12 countries, including Argentina, Chile, Spain, the United Kingdom, and Australia. That year also saw Equifax introduce a record 25 new products. This heightened activity was fueled by the 1993 decision to subcontract the running of Equifax's computer operation to IBM, a move that freed Equifax's large technical staff to develop new ways of packaging the company's data in consultation with its customers.

Exited Healthcare and Insurance, Expanded Internationally, in Mid-to-Late 1990s

In an effort to focus on payment services, credit reporting, and risk management services, Equifax sold its healthcare information business in 1996, just four years after entering the field; then in the following year Equifax spun off its insurance information services group, which had been a part of the company for nearly as long as credit reporting had been. In August 1997 Equifax completed the spinoff of the new publicly traded ChoicePoint Inc.

During this same period, Equifax aggressively expanded overseas. In July 1995 Equifax acquired U.K.-based Infocheck Group Limited and TecniCob S.A., a French payment services firm. In June 1996 the company gained full ownership of Transax plc, the largest check guarantee company in the United Kingdom, while in March 1998 it acquired a leading U.K. risk and credit management firm, CCI Group Plc. In Canada, Equifax purchased Collective Credit Bureaus Ltd. and Creditel of Canada Limited, a credit reporting agency. With opportunities for expansion growing more limited in the developed world, Equifax turned to the Latin American and Asian markets, acquiring full or partial ownership of firms in Chile, India, Argentina, Peru, and El Salvador. During the second half of 1998 Equifax purchased an 80 percent stake in Segurança ao Crédito e Informações, the leading financial information company in Brazil; a 59 percent controlling stake in Unnisa-Soluções em Meios de Pagamento Ltda., Brazil's leading credit card processing firm; and a 34 percent interest in Proceda Tecnologia e Informática S.A., the second largest outsourcer of information technology in Brazil. Equifax had quickly built up a significant presence in the emerging Brazilian market through a total investment of more than $350 million.

As a new century dawned and the company entered its second century in business, Equifax was busy gaining a toehold in the burgeoning world of Internet commerce. Revenues had reached a record $1.62 billion by 1998, but the outlook was somewhat clouded by the economic uncertainties that had begun with the Asian financial crisis of 1997. Equifax's push into the Brazilian market was challenged by the economic difficulties there, especially the currency devaluation. As one of the key players in the increasingly electronic world of commerce, however, Equifax was likely to survive the thrive.

Principal Subsidiaries

1nfo Inc.; Acrofax Inc. (Canada); CBI Ventures, Inc.; Computer Ventures, Inc.; Credence, Inc.; Credit Northwest Corporation; Credit Union Card Services, Inc.; Equifax Asia Pacific Holdings, Inc.; Equifax Card Services (Madison), Inc.; Equifax Check Services, Inc.; Equifax Card Services, Inc.; Equifax Credit Information Services, Inc.; The Equifax Database Company Ltd. (Ireland); Equifax Decision Systems B.V. (Netherlands); Equifax de Mexico Sociedad de Informacion Creditica, S.A.; Equifax Europe Ltd.; Equifax Europe (U.K.) Ltd.; Equifax Healthcare Information Services, Inc.; Equifax Holdings (Mexico) Inc.; Equifax India Private Ltd.; Equifax Information Technology, Inc.; Equifax Investments (Mexico) Inc.; Equifax Investments (U.S.) Inc.; Equifax Luxembourg S.A.; Equifax Luxembourg (No. 2) S.A.; Equifax Mauritius Private Limited; Equifax Payment Services, Inc.; Equifax Properties, Inc.; Equifax-Rochester, Inc.; Equifax South America, Inc.; Equifax U.K. Finance Ltd.; Equifax U.K. Finance (No. 2); Equifax Ventures, Inc.; Financial Institution Benefit Association, Inc.; Financial Insurance Marketing Group, Inc.; First Bankcard Systems, Inc.; Global Scan Ltd. (U.K.); Global Scan (USA), Inc.; Goldleaf Technologies, Inc.; High Integrity Systems, Inc.; The Infocheck Group Ltd. (U.K.); Infolink Ltd. (U.K.); Light Signatures, Inc.; Market Knowledge, Incorporated; Stewardship, Inc.; Tecnicob S.A. (France); Transax Australia plc (U.K.); Transax France plc (U.K.); Transax (Ireland) plc; Transax Ltd. (New Zealand); Transax plc. (U.K.); Transax pty Ltd. (Australia); Transax S.N.C. (France); UAPT-Infolink, plc (U.K.).

Principal Operating Units

North American Information Services; Payment Services; Equifax Europe; Equifax Latin America; Knowledge Engineering.

Further Reading

"Building Credit Globally," *Institutional Investor*, April 1996, pp. 27–28.

Deogun, Nikhil, "Equifax Unveils Plan to Spin Off Insurance Line," *Wall Street Journal*, December 10, 1996, p. B4.

Fickensher, Lisa, "Credit Bureaus Reinvent Themselves for Kinder, Gentler, and Wider Role," *American Banker*, December 29, 1997, pp. 1+.

——, "Equifax Reshapes Itself to Leverage Its Strengths," *American Banker*, January 5, 1998, pp. 11+.

Frank, Robert, "Equifax Broadens Its Markets and Boosts Its Bottom Line: Credit-Reporting Firm Enters New Businesses and Spreads Its Global Wings," *Wall Street Journal*, September 22, 1994, p. B4.

Jakubovics, Jerry, "Jeff White Helps Equifax Fly High," *Management Review*, 1988.

Konrad, Walecia, "Credit Reports with a Smile," *Business Week*, October 21, 1991.

Kraus, James R., "Brazilian Deal Just a Step in Equifax's Push Abroad," *American Banker*, August 27, 1998, p. 5.

Kretchmar, Laurie, "How to Shine in a Sullied Industry," *Fortune*, February 24, 1992.

Lee, Shelley A., "Credit Equifax: Restructuring Pays," *Business Atlanta*, October 1992, pp. 122–24.

Maloney, Peter, "Credit Bureaus: An Oligopoly Raking in the Dollars," *United States Banker*, October 1989.

McNaughton, David, "Equifax Shifting Focus Away from Health Care," *Atlanta Journal and Constitution*, October 25, 1996.

Novak, Janet, "Lender's Best Friend," *Forbes*, December 18, 1995, pp. 198+.

Roberts, J.S., *The Spirit of Retail Credit Company*, Atlanta: Retail Credit Company, 1965.

Schwartz, Evan I., "Equifax' Exit May Not Tame the Consumer Backlash," *Business Week*, August 26, 1991.

—Elizabeth Rourke
—updated by David E. Salamie

The E.W. Scripps Company

312 Walnut Street, 28th Floor
Cincinnati, Ohio 45202
U.S.A.
(513) 977-3825
Fax: (513) 977-3721
Web site: http://www.scripps.com

Public Company
Incorporated: 1878 as Scripps and Sweeney Co.
Employees: 8,100
Sales: $1.44 billion (1998)
Stock Exchanges: New York
Ticker Symbol: SSP
NAIC: 51111 Newspaper Publishers; 51312 Television
     Broadcasting; 51321 Cable Networks; 51411 News
     Syndicates; 51211 Motion Picture & Video
     Production; 51114 Database & Directory Publishers

The E.W. Scripps Company is one of the largest media companies in the United States, with 19 daily newspapers, the Scripps Howard news service, nine television stations, and several cable-television interests, including full ownership of the Home & Garden Television network and the production company Scripps Productions and a majority interest in the Food Network. Through its United Media affiliate, it is also a worldwide syndicator of newspaper features and comics, including "Peanuts," "Dilbert," "Nancy," and "For Better and for Worse." E.W. Scripps also publishes independent Yellow Pages directories. Sixty percent of the company is owned by the Edward W. Scripps family trust.

"Penny Press" Origins

The E.W. Scripps Company began life in 1878 as Scripps and Sweeney Co. when 24-year-old Edward Willis Scripps, with his cousin John Sweeney and other family members, founded his first newspaper, the *Cleveland Penny Press*. Scripps had $10,000 in capital and owned 20 percent of the paper. The rest was owned by his half-brothers George Henry and James Edmund Scripps—each of whom received 30 percent stakes in the company—and other partners.

E. W. Scripps was a populist who thought that most newspapers were geared towards the rich. He wanted his newspaper to keep the poor informed through short, simple stories that could be understood by those without extensive education. He got many of these ideas from James E. Scripps, an English immigrant who started the *Detroit Evening News* in 1873. E.W. also added his interest in personal stories to the mix, later giving a raise to an editor who published the fact that he had been fined $10 for riding a horse while intoxicated.

At the time the *Cleveland Penny Press* was founded, most newspapers had a party affiliation. They also sold for more than a penny, and many contemporaries were skeptical that the *Press* would succeed. E.W. Scripps' formula proved successful, however, and within weeks the *Cleveland Penny Press* had a circulation of approximately 10,000. It was not a profitable operation, however, until James E. Scripps ordered E.W. to run the paper for $400 a week.

As soon as the *Penny Press* was making money, E.W. persuaded his brothers to buy the *St. Louis Chronicle*. He then spent a year in St. Louis managing the paper. E.W. bought a 55 percent interest in the *Penny Post*—part of which was already owned by James E.—went to Cincinnati to manage it, and changed the paper's name to the *Cincinnati Post*. He subsequently began taking on political corruption and winning circulation.

From 1887 to 1889 James E. Scripps was in Europe receiving medical treatment while E.W. managed the *Detroit News*. Although E.W. expanded advertising and circulation, James E. was angry with the changes his brother made; upon his return, James E. removed E.W. from every position he could. In 1890 E.W. started his own paper, the *Kentucky Post*, in Covington, across the Ohio River from Cincinnati.

Also in 1890 E.W. Scripps entered into a partnership with his business manager, Milton McRae; the two called their newspaper company the Scripps-McRae League. McRae handled day-to-day management of the papers and received one-third of the profits, while Scripps set editorial guidelines and long-term policy. In 1890, with his business running smoothly, Scripps began building a ranch outside of San Diego, California.

In 1894 George Scripps joined Scripps-McRae. This gave the group a controlling interest in the *Cleveland Press*. Later in the 1890s the group started the *Akron Press* and *Kansas City World*. As his chain expanded, E.W. Scripps chose young, growing towns to start new newspapers. He invested as little in machinery or plants as possible, usually buying old presses and renting run-down buildings. He would then hire young ambitious editors who were given a minority stake in their paper; many of them became rich if their newspapers succeeded. With E.W. Scripps spending most of his time in California, McRae often exceeded his authority and put editorial pressure on newspaper editors. Scripps would periodically venture out of California, discover what McRae was doing, and reverse it.

Scripps next began a series of West Coast newspapers unassociated with the Scripps-McRae League group. They included papers in Los Angeles, San Francisco, Fresno, Berkeley, and Oakland, California, as well as Seattle, Tacoma, and Spokane, Washington. In 1900 George Scripps died, leaving his stock to E.W. James E. Scripps contested the will, however, and James E. and E.W. settled out of court. E.W. was forced to give all of his stock in the Detroit newspapers to James E., who in return gave E.W. all of his stock in newspapers outside Detroit.

In 1902 Scripps started the Newspaper Enterprise Association (NEA), a service for exchanging and distributing illustrations, cartoons, editorials, and articles on such specialized subjects as sports and fashion. Newspapers in the Scripps chain paid a monthly fee and received information and illustrations none of them could have afforded individually. Although the NEA was originally only for Scripps papers, demand for its services was so great that it soon became available to any newspaper.

In 1906 Scripps entered another period of expansion, buying or starting papers in Denver and Pueblo, Colorado; Evansville and Terre Haute, Indiana; Memphis and Nashville, Tennessee; Dallas, Texas; and Oklahoma.

United Press Association Wire Service Formed in 1907

In 1907 Scripps combined the NEA, the Scripps McRae Press Association, and Publishers Press into the United Press

Association wire service in order to provide 12,000 words of copy a day by telegraph to 369 subscribers in the United States. A similar service, the Associated Press (AP), already existed and was far larger and better financed. Scripps viewed AP as monopolistic and too close to the establishment and deliberately set out to oppose it. AP was also geared toward morning newspapers, while most of Scripps's were evening newspapers. Scripps therefore had each of his papers send out stories from their area during the day and combined them with information gathered at offices set up in important news producing cities such as Washington, D.C., and other world capitals.

In 1908 E.W. Scripps retired from active management, appointing his son James G. Scripps chairman of the board. During World War I, E.W. was a passionate advocate of U.S. intervention on the side of the Allies and moved to Washington, D.C., to push his cause. Shortly thereafter, a family crisis erupted, during which Scripps's son James detached the five West Coast newspapers and the *Dallas Dispatch* from the chain. In 1918 United Press caused a storm of controversy when it reported the end of World War I four days before it actually ended. E.W. Scripps's health started declining during the war, and by its end he was largely living on his yacht. In 1920 he gave direct control of the chain to his son Robert and Roy W. Howard and in 1922 incorporated all of his stock, news services, and newspapers into the E.W. Scripps Company, based in Cincinnati. The profits went to the Scripps Trust, set up for his heirs.

Despite his semiretirement, Scripps had the energy to direct a last burst of expansion in the 1920s. He made Roy Howard chairman and business director in 1921. Howard had played an important role in building the United Press. By 1924, he was placed in full charge of both business and editorial by E.W.'s son Robert. The newspaper chain was renamed the Scripps Howard League. Beginning in 1921, newspapers were bought or started in Birmingham, Alabama; Indianapolis, Indiana; Baltimore, Maryland; and Pittsburgh. Sales for 1925 came to about $28 million. In 1926 the Denver-based *Rocky Mountain News* and *Times* were bought.

At the time of E.W. Scripps's death in 1926, the Scripps Howard League was the second largest newspaper chain in the United States, after William Randolph Hearst's. E.W. Scripps was one the most successful newspaper owners of the era of the so-called Press Barons. Because of his reclusive personality, though, he was one of the least known. He stood up for the working class but in many ways despised them. In addition, he encouraged his newspapers to crusade for female suffrage but considered women inferior to men.

In all, Scripps started 32 newspapers. Some of them did not stay in business long; some were unsophisticated but remained fiercely independent. Their emphasis on human interest stories was welcomed by new immigrants who had lost their former communities.

Roy Howard's stock holding in the company was small, but with his strong personality he influenced the Scripps heirs and took working control of the company, managing it as if it were his own and bringing his own family into the company hierarchy. In 1927, Scripps Howard bought the *New York Telegram*. Four years later, it purchased the *New York World* and merged the two newspapers into the *World-Telegram.* In 1936 Howard gave up his position as chairman of the chain and became president.

In the 1930s United Press built a network of bureaus in South and Central America and in the Far East, though its coverage was weaker in Europe, and it remained smaller than AP. Also that decade the newspaper chain began to shrink as less-profitable papers were sold or consolidated and six-day evening papers began to lose their appeal. During World War II Ernie Pyle came to fame as a Scripps Howard columnist reporting from the European battle theater, before losing his life on a Pacific battlefield.

Postwar Growth

After World War II Scripps Howard's sales grew dramatically, from nearly $50 million in 1940 to more than $100 million in 1948 and $140 million in 1952. Profits, however, were not increasing. Due to the rising cost of labor, newsprint, and printing machinery, profits were hovering around $10 million, according to *Forbes* magazine. In 1953 E.W. Scripps's grandson Charles E. Scripps became company chairman at the age of 33, and Roy Howard's son Jack R. became company president at the age of 42. By this time Scripps Howard had 19 newspapers with a total circulation of four million. The company was also expanding into broadcasting and owned radio and television stations in Cleveland and Cincinnati as well as in Knoxville and Memphis, Tennessee. The Scripps family trust still owned nearly 75 percent of the company. Management was decentralized with general operations conducted in New York, editorial policy in Washington, and finances in Cincinnati.

In 1958 United Press merged with the Hearst Corporation's troubled International News Service to become United Press International (UPI). Hearst gained five percent ownership of UPI, but most former International News Service employees were laid off. Also that year Scripps bought the *Cincinnati Times-Star* and merged it into the *Post,* giving the company control of all of Cincinnati's daily newspapers. The *Cincinnati Enquirer*—which had been acquired in 1956—was carefully kept separate from the other papers to diminish possible charges of a monopoly. In 1964, however, the U.S. Department of Justice accused Scripps Howard of owning a monopoly and ordered it to sell the *Enquirer.* The *Enquirer* was far stronger financially, but the trust's lawyers advised the firm that it would be better off selling it, rather than trying to sell the *Post.*

In the meantime, Scripps continued building its broadcast division, buying WPTV in West Palm Beach, Florida, for $2 million in 1961. In 1963 the broadcast properties were taken public under the name Scripps Howard Broadcasting Company. The initial offering quickly sold out, leaving the E.W. Scripps Company with two-thirds ownership.

Roy Howard died in 1964. One of the problems Jack Howard—who had succeed Roy Howard as president in 1953—faced was that the company was still run for the beneficiaries of the E.W. Scripps trust, and the trustees' lawyers sometimes had a large role in significant corporate decisions. More importantly, with the rise of television after World War II, evening newspapers across the United States found their circulations

declining: people read the newspaper in the morning and watched the news on television in the evening. In addition, management of Scripps had become so conservative that critics charged it had no long-range plans and did little beyond preserve its assets. More and more Scripps newspapers took advantage of a law that allowed newspapers in danger of failing to partially merge with stronger rivals, keeping only editorial departments separate. By 1980, 8 of the 16 remaining Scripps dailies were in such arrangements, a higher percentage than any other major chain.

In 1976 Jack Howard retired as president of E.W. Scripps but remained a director of E.W. Scripps and chairman of Scripps Howard Broadcasting. Edward Estlow became E.W. Scripps's first CEO who was not from the Scripps or Howard families; he had been the chain's general business manager.

Scripps slowly began to change in the 1970s. In 1977 the company bought for $29 million the 90 percent of Media Investment Co. that it did not already own. Media Investment had holdings in some of Scripps's newspapers and radio and television stations. The purpose of acquiring the investment company was to permit employees to own shares in the diversified E.W. Scripps Company.

Sold Cleveland Press *and UPI in the Early 1980s*

UPI losses were continuing to increase—$24 million between 1975 and 1980. In addition some of Scripps's newspapers were operating in the red, including the flagship *Cleveland Press.* In 1980 Scripps sold the *Press* for an undisclosed amount to Cleveland retailer Joseph E. Cole. The chain then had 16 daily newspapers, making it the seventh largest in the United States. Scripps continued a policy of not reporting financial data, but the *Wall Street Journal* cited its sales at approximately $550 million.

In 1981 the E.W. Scripps Company began looking for a buyer for UPI. Estlow said that part of the reason was the possibility that the beneficiaries of the Scripps trust fund might bring legal action forcing the closing or selling of the wire service. In 1982 the firm found a buyer for UPI: Media News Corporation, a private firm started for the purpose of buying UPI, which had 224 bureaus and 2,000 employees. The purchase price was not disclosed, but industry analysts felt it could not have been much more than the value of UPI's assets, which the *New York Times* estimated were worth about $20 million.

In the early 1980s Scripps began funneling money into its chain of weekly business journals. The publications were losing readership and advertising revenue, and some criticized them as lacking hard news. In 1985 Lawrence A. Leser became president of Scripps and quickly began making changes. He sold many of the weeklies, as well as a videotape publishing business, and concentrated on building the cable, broadcast, and daily newspaper operations, particularly in the rapidly growing South and West.

In 1986 the company bought two television stations from Capital Cities Communications and the American Broadcasting Co. Scripps paid an estimated $246 million for WXYZ in Detroit and WFTS in Tampa. The company was also building a string of cable television systems. In 1986 Scripps merged with the John P. Scripps newspaper chain, which was comprised of six California newspapers and one Washington newspaper.

Going Public in 1988

These purchases, along with a cable system being built in Sacramento, left the company with millions of dollars in debt. Partly in an effort to pay off this debt, the Scripps family members who controlled the Scripps trust fund decided to take the company public. In 1987, as a prelude to its stock offering, the firm officially released financial data for the first time, reporting operating income of $150 million on sales of $1.15 billion. It owned 20 daily newspapers and nine television stations and cable systems in ten states. The 1988 stock offering left the Scripps trust with approximately 75 percent ownership of the company.

In December 1988 the E.W. Scripps Company formed Scripps Howard Productions to produce and market television programs. In February 1989 it sold the six-day *Florida Sun-Tattler* for an undisclosed amount and bought Cable USA's system in Carroll County, Georgia. Profits for 1989 were $89.3 million on sales of $1.27 billion.

In 1990 Scripps began the SportSouth Network to provide regional sports programming on cable television in six southern states. Most of the firm's revenue continued to come from newspapers, but it believed that future growth would come from cable television. As of the early 1990s, the firm had 672,000 cable subscribers, making it one of the 20 largest cable system operators in the United States.

The E.W. Scripps Company also negotiated to buy WMAR-TV in Baltimore from Gillett Holdings for $154.7 million. Scripps backed out of the deal at the last minute and was sued by Gillett. The firms settled out of court, and Scripps bought the station for $125 million in cash. In late 1991 the company announced a modernization of the *Pittsburgh Press* delivery systems. The modernization, which would cause hundreds of layoffs, resulted in a crippling strike that lasted well into 1992; the newspaper was sold on December 31, 1992.

Increased Emphasis on Television Content in the Mid-to-Late 1990s

In 1993 the E.W. Scripps Company sold its Pharos Books and World Almanac Education units to K-III Communications and also sold its four radio stations, its television station in Memphis, Tennessee, and newspapers in Tulare, California, and San Juan, Puerto Rico. These moves occurred at the same time that the company was shifting to an increased emphasis on television and specifically on television content—as opposed to simply broadcasting. In March 1994 the E.W. Scripps Company purchased Cinetel Productions, a leading independent producer of cable-television programming. Ownership of Cinetel helped the company launch a new cable network, Home & Garden Television (HGTV), in late 1994. HGTV, which was available in 48.4 million cable homes by early 1999, marked the beginning of the company's cable narrowcasting strategy—what it called "category television." The aim was to become the predominant player in particular cable television categories.

HGTV's category was that of home decorating, improvement, and maintenance; landscaping; and gardening.

In 1994 Charles E. Scripps retired as company chairman, having served in that position since 1953, and was succeeded by Lawrence A. Leser. Two years later, William R. Burleigh was named president and CEO. Meantime, the E.W. Scripps Company continued to deemphasize its broadcasting side when it sold its cable systems to Comcast Corporation in November 1995 for $1.58 billion. On the newspaper side, the company divested its Watsonville, California, daily in 1995 and spent $120 million in 1996 to acquire the *Vero Beach Press Journal,* a daily. In August 1997 the E.W. Scripps Company traded its daily newspapers in Monterey and San Luis Obispo, California, to Knight-Ridder, Inc. for the *Daily Camera,* a newspaper in Boulder, Colorado. In October of that same year the company paid $775 million in cash—the firm's largest acquisition in history—for the media assets of Harte-Hanks Communications Inc., which included five daily newspapers in Texas and one in South Carolina, a group of a community newspapers in Texas, and a television and radio station in San Antonio.

This purchase immediately led to the company's acquisition of a second cable category network as the television and radio station were traded for a 56 percent controlling interest in the Food Network, a cable network featuring programming on food and nutrition. In early 1999 the E.W. Scripps Company sold the community newspapers it gained via Harte-Hanks to Lionheart Holdings LLC, a community newspaper group based in Fort Worth, Texas.

In May 1998 the company sold Scripps Howard Productions, and later that year Cinetel Productions changed its name to Scripps Productions. E.W. Scripps Company launched its third cable category network, Do-It-Yourself, in 1999. The company's category television unit was its fastest-growing operation, with revenues reaching $148.6 million in 1998, an increase of 76.5 percent over the previous year. Although this unit continued to operate in the red, it was clearly considered a key to the company's future.

Principal Subsidiaries

BRV, Inc. (Boulder Daily Camera, Bremerton Sun, Redding Record Searchlight, Ventura County Newspapers); Birmingham Post Company (Birmingham Post Herald); Channel 7 of Detroit, Inc. (WXYZ); Collier County Publishing Company (The Naples Daily News); Denver Publishing Company (Denver Rocky Mountain News); Evansville Courier Company, Inc. (91.5%); Force V Corporation (Destin Log); Independent Publishing Company (Anderson Independent Mail); Knoxville News-Sentinel Company; Memphis Publishing Company (The Commercial Appeal) (91.3%); New Mexico State Tribune Company (The Albuquerque Tribune); Scripps Acquisition L.P. (Corpus Christi Caller-Times, Abilene Reporter-News, Wichita Falls Times Record News, San Angelo Standard-Times); Scripps Howard Broadcasting Company (WMAR, Baltimore; WCPO, Cincinnati; WEWS, Cleveland; KSHB, Kansas City; KNXV, Phoenix; KJRH, Tulsa; WPTV, West Palm Beach, Home & Garden Television, Scripps Productions); Stuart News Company (Stuart News, Jupiter Courier, Vero Beach Press Journal); Tampa Bay Television (WFTS); The Television Food

Network, G.P. (56%); United Feature Syndicate, Inc. (United Media, Newspaper Enterprise Association).

Principal Operating Units

Newspapers; Broadcast Television; Category Television; Licensing and Other Media.

Further Reading

Abrams, Bill, "Capital Cities, ABC to Sell 2 TV Outlets to Scripps Howard," *Wall Street Journal,* July 29, 1985.

Astor, David, "Scripps Decides to Keep United Media," *Editor and Publisher,* August 21, 1993, pp. 34–35.

Baldasty, Gerald J., *E.W. Scripps and the Business of Newspapers,* Urbana: University of Illinois Press, 1999, 217 p.

Brendon, Piers, *The Life and Death of the Press Barons,* New York: Atheneum, 1983, 288 p.

Casserly, Jack, *Scripps: The Divided Dynasty,* New York: Donald I. Fine, 1993, 236 p.

Cauley, Leslie, "Scripps Quickly Proves an Outsider Can Start a Cable-TV Network," *Wall Street Journal,* November 13, 1998, pp. A1 +.

Cochran, Negley D., *E.W. Scripps,* New York: Harcourt, Brace and Company, 1933.

Garneua, George, "Scripps Buys Six Dailies," *Editor and Publisher,* May 24, 1997, pp. 6–7, 29.

Gilbert, Nick, "E. W. Scripps: Purring Without Garfield," *Financial World,* May 24, 1994, pp. 14 +.

Jessell, Harry A., "E. W. Scripps: Building, Growing with HGTV," *Broadcasting and Cable,* March 2, 1998, pp. 18–22.

Katz, Richard, "Scripps Tills Lush Niche Cable Garden," *Variety,* August 24, 1998, p. 18.

King, Michael J., "Weakened Chain," *Wall Street Journal,* November 28, 1980.

Lipin, Steven, "Scripps to Acquire Harte-Hanks's Media Assets," *Wall Street Journal,* May 19, 1997, pp. A3, A4.

Pace, Eric, "U.P.I. Sold to New Company," *New York Times,* June 3, 1982.

Phillips, Stephen, and David Lieberman, "Extra! Extra! Get Yer Share of Scripps," *Business Week,* July 11, 1988.

Robichaux, Mark, "Comcast to Buy E.W. Scripps's Cable Systems," *Wall Street Journal,* October 30, 1995, p. A3.

"Roy W. Howard, Publisher, Dead," *New York Times,* November 21, 1964.

"Scripps and Howard," *Forbes,* October 1953.

Trimble, Vance H., *The Astonishing Mr. Scripps: The Turbulent Life of America's Penny Press Lord,* Ames: Iowa State University Press, 1992, 547 p.

——, ed., *Scripps-Howard Handbook,* 3rd ed., Cincinnati: E.W. Scripps, 1981, 400 p.

—Scott M. Lewis
—updated by David E. Salamie

Featherlite Inc.

P.O. Box 320
Cresco, Iowa 52136
U.S.A.
(319) 547-6000
(800) 800-1230
Fax: (319) 547-6100
Web site: http://www.featherliteinc.com

Public Company
Incorporated: 1988
Employees: 1,737
Sales: $190.87 million (1998)
Stock Exchanges: NASDAQ
Ticker Symbol: FTHR
NAIC: 33621 Motor Vehicle Body & Trailer Manufacturing; 336212 Truck Trailer Manufacturing; 336214 Travel Trailer & Camper Manufacturing; 336211 Bus Bodies Manufacturing

Featherlite Inc. is an innovative leader in the design, manufacture, and marketing of aluminum specialty trailers and luxury motorcoaches. Through a dealer network encompassing the United States and Canada, as well as other parts of the world, Featherlite offers more than 400 standard and custom-made trailers. The company, headquartered in Iowa, serves the horse, livestock, utility and cargo, drop deck and flatbed semi, snowmobile, car, and race car trailer/transporter markets.

Moving from Earth to Aluminum: 1988

In 1988 the Clement family acquired the assets of an El Reno, Oklahoma-based business that had been manufacturing trailers since the early 1970s under the Featherlite brand name. "I was in the farm and construction equipment business, the auction business and real estate for 20 years before that," said President and Chief Executive Officer Conrad Clement. "When my two sons, Tracy and Eric, and I bought the company in 1988, it had 72 employees and annual sales of under $20 million." The Clements immediately moved the business to Grand Meadow, Minnesota. At first, the company almost exclusively manufactured horse and livestock trailers, but soon decided to change the mix of its trailer business by diversifying its product lines and developing higher-end products. The sales of the company grew steadily with this diversification

These early years of the company were characterized by great expansion as well as diversification of the product line. When the Clements first took over, there were only two plants totaling 160,000 square feet of space. By 1992 the company had nearly doubled its manufacturing space with the addition of the Nashua, Iowa plant, and increased from 72 to 460 the number of workers employed.

Featherlite's next move quickly propelled them into the fast lane toward success. The company decided to expand its line to build car transporters. Conrad Clement looked at the racing industry and saw potential not only for attracting new customers but for enhancing the visibility of the company brand. Thus, he contacted Richard Childress and Dale Earnhardt, both well-known on the NASCAR circuit at the time, and struck a deal to build them new race car transporters. These first trailers were completed in 1992. Then the company built a third trailer for Richard Petty, whose family name was synonymous with professional racing. Clement was a master at involving the drivers in the development process to win their approval. Both Childress and Petty flew to the plant to oversee the designs, and Clement even enlisted Petty to conduct an autograph session with his employees.

Building on this success, Featherlite quickly established itself as a leader in innovative specialty trailer designs by building race car transporters and other types of specialty trailers for motor racing's biggest stars. Featherlite's customer list soon began to look like a virtual "Who's Who" of racing greats, including NASCAR Winston Cup champion Jeff Gordon; CART Champion Alex Zanardi; NHRA Funny Car champion John Force; NASCAR Busch Series champion Dale Earnhardt, Jr.; NASCAR Craftsman Truck Series points champion Jack Sprague; and World of Outlaws sprint car champion Steve Kinser.

Company Perspectives:

Headquartered in Cresco, Iowa, Featherlite is a leader in designing and manufacturing high-quality aluminum and specialty trailers.

Going Public, 1994

In 1993 the company moved its corporate headquarters to a new 50,000-square-foot facility in Cresco, Iowa, to be closer to its manufacturing plants at Cresco and Nashua. By this time, the company employed 530 workers in all its plants. In September of the following year, the company raised $10.4 million in new capital through an initial public offering of common stock. About $4.2 million went into the construction of a 140,000-square-foot manufacturing space in Cresco in anticipation of future growth. The company also quickly increased the number of its employees to 800. In addition, Featherlite signed an agreement with Polaris Industries in 1994 to produce private label snowmobile, ATV, and personal watercraft trailers.

Race car transporters continued to fuel the growth of the company. In 1995 the 100th race car transporter was built for famous race car driver A.J. Foyt. That same year, Featherlite built its third plant, adding 101,000 square feet to its manufacturing capacity, and also constructed an addition to its interiors facility, increasing its size by 40,000 square feet.

In October 1995, Featherlite acquired the assets of Diamond D Trailer Manufacturing, a nationally recognized steel trailer manufacturer in Shenandoah, Iowa, in order to provide customers and dealers with a high quality, but less expensive alternative to all-aluminum trailer models. The acquisition included Diamond's 117,000-square-foot facility and added 75 Diamond D dealers to Featherlite's distribution system, while further augmenting the workforce by 985 employees. The innovative leader in the steel trailer industry, Diamond D trailers were designed to insure maximum structural integrity and cosmetic longevity while maintaining affordability to discriminating consumers.

As the company continued to diversify its product line, it also gained in popularity. By 1996 the company had 1,030 employees on the payroll and could have coasted. Instead it raced ahead. In January 1996, Featherlite entered the luxury motorcoach market with the acquisition of the assets of Vantare International, Inc. of Sanford, Florida. The Vantare acquisition enlarged the company's total workforce to 1,150 employees and added another 52,000-square-foot facility to its manufacturing capacity. Featherlite fully integrated Vantare's new luxury motorcoach division into its operations, contributing approximately $35 million in revenues to the company. Very quickly, Featherlite became a leading manufacturer and marketer of luxury motorcoaches.

In 1997 Featherlite completed a 20,000-square-foot addition to the Vantare plant, constructed a 20,000-square-foot addition to its employee Work Center, and raised its workforce to 1,200.

By that year, revenues had grown to over $135 million. In October 1997 the company signed a joint venture agreement with GMR Marketing to form Featherlite/GMR Sports Group, LLC. The goal of this joint venture was to develop promotional events and implement marketing strategies in the rapidly evolving motorsports industry. The company believed that a clearer marketing infrastructure was needed to support its growing brand name.

Having embraced the motorcoach line with the Vantare acquisition, Featherlite took a further step to secure its lead in the marketplace. The company reasoned that many of its established racing car transporter customers would also want luxury coaches. Consequently, in May 1998 Featherlite acquired the assets of Mitchell Companies, the manufacturer of Vogue luxury motorcoaches and bus conversion vehicles including its 90,000-square-foot manufacturing facility. Featherlite made changes in the Vogue line and introduced the 5000 Series (formerly the Vogue V) and Le Mirage Prevost conversion. Once again, Featherlite applied its now famous high quality craftsmanship to the Vogue.

The company also acquired the marketing and distribution system of Mitchell Motorcoach Sales, from which Featherlite was able to successfully market its now increased price point range in luxury motorcoaches and thereby broaden its market coverage. With the Featherlite Vogue, the company's presence in the recreation and leisure markets established Featherlite as the pacesetter for high-end luxury motorcoaches in the United States.

By 1998 when Featherlite marked its 25th anniversary, it boasted 1,737 employees. Featherlite's dealer network consisted of 240 full-line and approximately 900 limited-line dealers throughout the United States and in selected Canadian markets, further strengthening Featherlite's market penetration. The company implemented extensive training for all its dealers to improve their knowledge, experience, and productivity, and designed new, attractive marketing tools and reference materials to assist in closing sales. In addition to this network, the company had 75 Diamond D dealers nationwide and 30 regular and 1,500 part-time vendors in its vendor network throughout the Midwest. Another marketing strategy was its decision to take part in trade shows, fairs, and exhibitions annually. In 1998 alone, Featherlite's dealers worked 1,200 fairs with an additional 300 major exhibitions covered directly by Featherlite employees. Featherlite also made a major commitment to national advertising programs, including both print media and television.

Land, Sea, and Sky: 1998 and Beyond

In 1998 Featherlite decided to extend its penetration into an important niche market by establishing a formal agreement with Yamaha Motor Corporation USA to supply its line of recreational trailers to Yamaha dealers throughout the United States. The sales of motorcycle, snowmobile, ATV, and personal watercraft trailers through Yamaha dealers nationwide opened an important new distribution channel for Featherlite in this expanding recreational market.

Featherlite also began to venture into the aviation industry by starting a consulting and brokerage company, called Featherlite Aviation Company. The new company specialized in Beech and Cessna twin engine and turbine-powered product lines, offering professional aircraft brokerage and consulting primarily to existing clients wanting to purchase or sell quality aircraft. The company made a commitment to the city of Cresco, Iowa, to construct a hangar facility at a cost of approximately $300,000 as part of an airport expansion project.

By the late 1990s Featherlite trailers had a strong lead on competitors and orders for trailers were backed up. The company built a warehouse facility for raw material storage at its Cresco location at an approximate cost of $1.8 million financed with new borrowings and began a long range expansion of its Vantare facilities. At this time the company was using approximately one million pounds of aluminum per month. The availability and cost of aluminum, needless to say, was critical to the company. Therefore, Featherlite took a very aggressive stance in negotiating long-term commitments from its suppliers to provide, at a fixed price, substantially all of its total aluminum requirements on an established schedule into the future. The company estimated that even at a minimum increase of about four percent in the cost of aluminum it was money ahead.

Orders for specialty trailers continued to grow. By this time Featherlite produced over 400 custom order and standard model specialty trailers. Products included horse trailers, stock trailers, carhaulers, truck beds, utility trailers, commercial trailers, vending trailers, hospitality trailers, dry freight trailers, race car transporters, customized drop frame vans, ATV trailers, snowmobile trailers, watercraft trailers, and motorcycle trailers. Each year, the company produced approximately 8,000–10,000 trailers. Retail trailer prices ranged from approximately $1,000 for the small utility trailers to $250,000 for the most elaborate race car transporters to $650,000 for luxury coaches. The average trailer price was approximately $9,000.

Featherlite began investing more in promotions, developing such products as golf shirts, oxfords, jackets, T-shirts, sweatshirts, and collectibles that were displayed by sales department personnel and dealers at over 1,200 fairs, trade shows, races and other events throughout North America each year. The company also started to branch out into other recreation sport niches. In 1999 Featherlite held its first Featherlite Vogue Golf Tournament. The company donated a utility trailer that was positioned on the fairway of the second hole, giving players the opportunity to be the first to hit the trailer and take it home. Featherlite also became more involved in sponsorships that garnered recognition and publicity for its trailers. Sponsorships over the years of horse shows alone included: The Equine-All American Quarterhorse Congress, the National Cutting Horse Association, the National High School Rodeo Association, the Paso Fino Horse Association, the United States Team Roping Championships, the Livestock-Black Hills Stock Show, the Iowa State Fair, the National Finals Rodeo, the National Western World Pork Expo, the World's Toughest Rodeo, and the Professional Bull Riders.

The manufacturer also continued to dominate in the race car transporter business, with an estimated 80 percent of all drivers on the NASCAR Winston Cup series and many other teams hooked up to Featherlite race car transporters. For years it held the coveted title of "Official Trailer" of NASCAR, CART, IRL, NHRA, and the World of Outlaws sanctioning bodies, as well as the Indianapolis Motor Speedway and the Las Vegas Motor Speedway. Its race sponsorships included SPORTSCAR, the Featherlite Southwest Tour, the NASCAR Featherlite Modified Tour, the Eagle River Snowmobile Derby, and the Super Boat International Productions, Inc.

Throughout the growth and development of Featherlite, innovation, industry leadership, and top-notch products have been recognized as the company's key strengths. With a virtual lock on its core markets, and legions of loyal customers, Featherlite would likely remain a heavyweight in its industry well into the 21st century.

Principal Subsidiaries

Featherlite Aviation Company.

Further Reading

"Featherlite Announces Management Appointments: Continued Company Growth Results in Management Team Expansion," *PR Newswire*, October 27, 1997.

"Featherlite Completes Acquisition of Vogue's Luxury Motorcoach Manufacturer," *PR Newswire*, May 5, 1998.

"Featherlite Named Official Trailer and Luxury Motorcoach of the National Hot Rod Association," *PR Newswire*, June 6, 1998.

"Featherlite Reports Record Net Income and Sales for Fiscal Year," *PR Newswire*, February 17, 1999.

"Featherlite to Supply Trailers to Yamaha Dealers," *PR Newswire*, November 7, 1997.

"History in Motorsports and Customer Base: A History of Quality and Innovation," *PR Newswire*, January 1999.

"Light Heavyweight: At 25 Featherlite Rules Among Specialty Trailers," *PR Newswire*, November 1998.

—J. D. Fromm

Fellowes

Fellowes Manufacturing Company

1789 Norwood Avenue
Itasca, Illinois 60143
U.S.A.
(630) 893-1600
(800) 945-4545
Fax: (630) 893-9770
Web site: http://www.fellowes.com

Private Company
Incorporated: 1917 as The Bankers Box Company
Employees: 1,500
Sales: $400 million (1998 est.)
NAIC: 322211 Corrugated & Solid Fiber Box
Manufacturing; 42213 Industrial & Personal Service
Paper Wholesalers; 337214 Office Furniture (Except
Wood) Manufacturing; 421420 Office Equipment
Wholesaling

Fellowes Manufacturing Company is a leading global manufacturer of home and office organizational products, including computer accessories, consumer electronic accessories, paper shredders, and records storage boxes. Founded in 1917 by Harry Fellowes, the privately held, family-owned and -operated company is headquartered in Itasca, Illinois. Originally known as The Bankers Box Company, Fellowes has been responsible for creating innovative, leading-edge products such as the Disk Clip, introduced in the 1990s, the first device that allowed users to attach a 3.5″ diskette to a hardcopy document without damaging the diskette, as a banker's clip would.

Top competitors have included CompX International Inc., General Binding Corporation, and Tab Products Co., among others. By 1999 the company employed more than 1,500 people and operated seven wholly owned subsidiaries in Australia, the Benelux countries, Canada, France, Germany, Japan, and the United Kingdom. Fellowes' U.S. division operates from five plants located in Itasca, Illinois; Atlanta, Georgia; Belcamp, Maryland; Plano, Texas; and Cerritos, California.

The Bankers Box Company, 1917

A chance meeting in an elevator between Harry Fellowes and Walter Nickel in 1917 is where the Fellowes story begins. The two gentlemen were small businessmen who worked in the same office building. Harry learned that Nickel had been called up for duty in World War I and needed to sell his business, a start-up company that made inexpensive corrugated boxes used for storing bank records. Harry found the idea intriguing because of the recordkeeping requirements brought about by the newly enacted federal income tax. Consequently, before the elevator had reached the lobby, Harry Fellowes had purchased the company for a whopping $50. Thus The Bankers Box Company was born. Harry assembled the sturdy file-like boxes on his kitchen table at night and went out to peddle them during the day.

In May 1938 Harry's sons, John E. and Folger Fellowes, joined the company, traveling to the West Coast on sales calls. Some 20 years later, during the 1950s, John and his brother took over the management of the business from their father, with the goal of building the company into a strong national manufacturer. While Folger established the company's customer base and was in charge of sales and marketing, John managed the internal operations of purchasing, manufacturing, and administration, overseeing new product developments and new locations, increasing production and efficiency with each move, tailoring each new manufacturing location to regional customer needs, culminating in Fellowes' current one million-square-foot location just outside of Chicago, Illinois.

John recognized the company's global opportunities and led the company through a decade of overseas expansions during the 1960s and 1970s, opening subsidiaries in the United Kingdom, Australia, and Canada, as well as four regional U.S. manufacturing plants, which were added to provide faster service and lower freight costs for customers across the country. Building upon this foundation, the company later developed businesses in Germany, Belgium, the Netherlands, Luxembourg, France, and Japan, including exports to more than 60 additional countries. By 1972 the company was a major manufacturer of office products. As of 1998, John was still involved with Fellowes as vice-chairman, as an active member of the board, and as its principal stockholder, though he had turned the reins over to his two sons, James and Peter.

Third Generation, 1969

In 1969, when third-generation Fellowes family member James began working for the company, total revenues were somewhere around $4 million per year. Under his guidance as CEO—along with brother Peter as chief operating officer—the company increased its revenues at an estimated 14 percent annually from 1980 to 1994, with total revenue somewhere around $220.4 million in 1994 and a net income of about $9.2 million.

Industry Change and Paper Shredders in the 1980s

By 1980 total revenues reached approximately $31 million. During that decade, the office products industry changed radically. Manufacturers were challenged as office technology advancements changed the way people worked and the products they needed to support that work. In addition, increased foreign competition, consolidation within distribution channels, and rapid expansion of retail outlets began to present remarkable challenges to the manufacturers who supplied the distribution channels. Fellowes Manufacturing's answer to those challenges was to devote its energy and resources to planning carefully for the future. For example, early on Fellowes envisioned the computer as being the center of workplace activity. That led Fellowes to envision many products that related to the computer-based work environment of the 1990s. Consistent with the company's vision of the computer-based work environment, noticing that the computer environment was information-intensive and realizing that information in the wrong hands represented a significant risk for businesses and individuals, James Fellowes led his company into the paper shredder business.

In 1982 the company started selling, as an original equipment manufacturer (OEM), five general office shredders, which were manufactured by other companies, under their own brand name with moderate success. But competition soon sprang up, and the large, expensive ($1,500–$4,500) shredders quickly faced a shrinking market share. By the end of the decade the Fellowes line of general office shredders had evolved to eight machines with sales of more than $7 million per year. Nevertheless, although it was a thriving business for Fellowes at the time, the company was learning that its products, and those of its competitors, were not meeting consumers' needs effectively.

Listening to its customers complain about the inconvenience and distraction of leaving their workstation to shred documents,

the company's vision changed. The new plan: to design and manufacture a shredder so inexpensive that anyone handling sensitive information could shred documents at their workstation and to decentralize the shredding function in the same way that computers were being decentralized in the 1980s through PCs. In 1990 Fellowes introduced the world's first "personal shredder," making it convenient and affordable (starting at about $149) for the first time for anyone to have one at their workstation. The company also began marketing its products through the office "superstores" that were sprouting across the United States, such as Office Depot, OfficeMax, and Staples, as well as in chains such as Kmart, Target, and Wal-Mart, rather than through the big office machine dealers or wholesalers traditionally used in the industry. Prices for personal shredders continued to fall (by more than 60 percent from 1990 to 1999), creating stronger demand for shredders. By mid-1999 Fellowes was the leading brand of shredders in the world, growing from $8 million in sales in 1990, to account for 18 percent of the company's total sales in 1994, and to some $40 million in 1995, which represented more than half of the estimated $75 million market.

The company shipped more than 1,300 interbranch shipments with a total weight in excess of 32 million pounds in 1990. Looking for a more efficient way to provide better service and to meet the needs of its plants and its customers, the following year the company changed its distribution system from rail to trucking, employing carrier CRST Inc. of Cedar Rapids, Iowa, to handle the load.

Other Products in the 1990s

While the shredder lent prominence to the Fellowes name, and the company's original business—record storage equipment—accounted for 45 percent of sales during 1994, the new market was in computer accessories. In December 1994 the company introduced several new organizational products and computer accessories, including its new "Wild Things" line of multicolored computer accessories, its "Box Options" line of multipurpose corrugated storage products, and "Neat Ideas" portable organizers, all at the School and Home Office Products Association show in New Orleans. Computer accessories accounted for nearly 37 percent of the company's total revenue in 1994.

In January 1995, in an effort to continue to expand beyond office organization products and to increase its strength in new business segments, Fellowes acquired C-2 Office Gear Inc., a $21 million Chicago-based manufacturer of computer covers, mouse pads, wrist rests, keyboard protectors, laptop carrying cases, and molded products, as well as a license for a line of Looney Tunes products, for an undisclosed price.

At the 1997 Consumer Electronics Show, the company introduced a handheld computer input device, called "Tracker." The device was a result of a joint venture between Fellowes and Fujitsu Takamisawa, a Japanese producer of high-end technology. The Tracker used Fujitsu's proprietary Non-Contact Magnetic Field Detection method for "effortless and accurate" cursor control. The device, which contained no moving parts, was designed for both righthanded and lefthanded operation. The two-button device was released in both IBM PS/2 and Microsoft compatible formats.

In October 1998, to take advantage of its brand equity in the Fellowes name, the company unified the packaging of its products under a newly redesigned black, white, and yellow corporate logo. That year, the company, which was ranked 469th on *Forbes* "Private 500" list, expanded its product line by 147 new products, including such breakthrough products as the first Memoflex gel for ergonomic support, as well as new media storage products, glare filters, copyholders, licensed mouse pads, dust covers, and computer cables, all of which were added to enrich the company's offerings. In addition, the company expanded its line of Looney Tunes licensed computer accessories and audio storage products, including an embroidered CD player case, Tweety-at-the-Beach mouse pad, and character-themed CD jewel cases. By May 1999 the company offered the industry's most extensive line of computer accessories, with roughly 350 unique products and more than 2,000 SKUs (storekeeping units) within 17 different product categories. Also early that year, the company completed the acquisition of French binding and laminating company Lamirel.

In April 1999 the company received a 1998 Sears Partner in Progress Award. The award was given each year by Sears, Roebuck and Co. to a select group of vendor companies who supplied Sears with quality products and services on several levels and for various achievements.

By the end of the 20th century Fellowes Manufacturing remained a family-run firm as Harry's grandsons, James and Peter Fellowes, continued to build the global business, driven by a strong commitment to excellence. In mid-1999 the company had 1,500 employees worldwide, and seven foreign subsidiaries, marketing products in more than 60 international markets. As it had in the past, the office products industry would continue to evolve, and the company fully anticipated adapting new strategies to prepare for the future. The company cited as an example the trend toward increased mobility in the workforce. New product lines would accurately reflect this development as Fellowes continued to heed the most important voice in the industry, that of the consumer.

Principal Subsidiaries

Fellowes Australia; Fellowes Benelux; Fellowes Canada; Fellowes, Lynx S.A. (France); Fellowes GmbH (Germany); Fellowes U.K.; Fellowes Manufacturing Japan Ltd.

Further Reading

"Anti-Glare Screens Get Rave Reviews," *Modern Office Technology,* May 1990, p. 26.

Brindza, Stephen, "Inactive Filing Seems Valuable," *Modern Office Technology,* July 1988, p. 88.

Crown, Judith, "Office Products Firm Likes High-Tech Fallout," *Crain's Chicago Business,* April 24, 1995, p. 45.

"Fellowes," *Discount Store News,* October 26, 1998, p. 41.

"Fellowes Accessories Bow," *HFD,* December 6, 1993, p. 83.

"Fellowes' Looney Tunes Office Accessories," *HFN,* October 16, 1995, p. 100.

"Fellowes: New Swivel Arm Holder," *HFD,* September 21, 1992, p. 168.

"Fellowes Readies Instant-Win Promo," *HFN,* September 14, 1998, p. 62.

"Fellowes Receives Sears 1998 Partner in Progress Award," *PR Newswire,* April 19, 1999, p. 3136.

"Fellowes Screens to Cut Glare Set," *HFD,* August 2, 1993, p. 76.

"Fellowes Targets Home Offices," *HFD,* June 7, 1993, p. 80.

"Fellowes Unveils Work Station Line," *HFD,* June 8, 1992, p. 124.

"Fellowes Upgrades Shredder," *HFD,* July 20, 1992, p. 87.

Fondiller, David S., "Better Shred Than Read," *Forbes,* September 11, 1995, p. 186.

Garbato, Debby, "Fellowes Refocusing on Home Office Market," *HFD,* November 30, 1992, p. 58.

——, "Fellowes Sells Closet Mates," *HFD,* November 30, 1992, p. 56.

Greenberg, Manning, "Fellowes Finds Own Path to Home Office Profits," *HFD,* November 2, 1992, p. 107.

Hill, Dawn, "Fellowes Acquires C-2 to Add Clout in Computer Accessories," *HFN,* January 23, 1995, p. 51.

Nelton, Sharon, "The Benefits That Flow from Quality," *Nation's Business,* March 1993, p. 71.

"New Fellowes Finance Chief," *HFN,* February 10, 1997, p. 46.

Scelsi, Paul, "A Mode Change for the Better," *Chilton's Distribution,* May 1991, p. 56.

"The Scoop," *HFN,* January 16, 1995, p. 204.

Shear, Barbara, "Color and Variety Add Luster to Accessories: Manufacturers Are Striving to Produce Desktop Products That Are Attractive and Functional," *Office,* October 1991, p. 16.

Stankevich, Debby Garbato, "Fellowes to Unveil File Organizer That Fits into RTA Shelving Units," *HFD,* August 2, 1993, p. 65.

Sterngold, Mark, "Fellowes Manufacturing Inc.," *New York Times,* October 26, 1998, p. C9.

Troy, Terry, "Fellowes Inks Dan River Pattern Pact," *HFD,* January 27, 1992, p. 81.

"WARNING: Is Your Tax-Time Garbage a Buffet for Identity Thieves? Timely Advice for Anyone Filing Taxes in 1998," *PR Newswire,* April 7, 1999, p. 5323.

"Wrapper Doubles Output of Office Products," *Packaging Digest,* January 1994, p. 72.

—Daryl F. Mallett

First Alert, Inc.

3901 Liberty Street Road
Aurora, Illinois 60504-8122
U.S.A.
(630) 851-7330
Fax: (630) 851-8221
Web site: http://www.firstalert.com

Wholly Owned Subsidiary of Sunbeam Corporation
Incorporated: 1967 as BRK Electronics, Inc.
Employees: 3,142
Sales: $186.9 million (1997)
NAIC: 334290 Smoke Detectors Manufacturing; 339999
   Fire Extinguishers, Portable, Manufacturing; 332999
   Safes, Metal, Manufacturing

For more than 25 years, First Alert, Inc., along with its subsidiaries, has been a leading worldwide manufacturer and marketer of a line of home safety products. The company is one of the largest manufacturers of smoke detectors in the United States, a market in which it is estimated that more than 90 percent of all homes have at least one smoke detector. The "First Alert" brand name is one of the most widely recognized consumer brands in the home safety industry. Capitalizing on that brand name and its leading market share in the smoke detector segment, the company has developed and marketed a broad range of residential safety products, including carbon monoxide detectors, child safety products, electronic and electromechanical timers, fire escape ladders, fire extinguishers, fire safes and chests, motion sensing lighting controls, night lights, radon gas detectors, and rechargeable flashlights and lanterns.

Smoke Detectors, 1967

Up until 1969 Americans did not sleep as soundly as they might have. Then, as now, most fire deaths occurred during sleeping hours, usually before the flames even reached the victims, according to the National Fire Protection Association (NFPA). There was no such thing as a readily available warning device to guard against such tragedies. But in 1969, BRK Electronics of Aurora, Illinois, began marketing a product that would change fire safety forever: the smoke detector.

For three decades, BRK and its smoke detectors and related home safety products have helped millions protect their homes and families from fires. Originally designed for commercial use, the BRK smoke detector was redesigned for residential use in 1967. Two years later BRK model #S5679H became the first self–contained, battery–powered unit to pass stringent Underwriters Laboratories (UL) tests. It quickly attracted the attention of fire fighters nationwide, who were among the first to put smoke detectors in their homes. Through an intense development program, the company began to produce a series of more advanced, less expensive detectors in battery–powered and AC-powered models. BRK also entered the new construction and mobile home smoke detector markets.

In 1970 Pittway Corporation purchased BRK Electronics from the original owners. As a division of Pittway (itself incorporated in 1925 as Standard Power & Light Corp.), BRK Electronics flourished. During the early 1970s, through ongoing research and development, the company produced a series of high-quality, affordable, battery- and AC-powered and system smoke alarms. BRK Electronics used these successes to enter the new construction and mobile home markets and increase its share of the commercial system smoke alarm market.

Sears, Roebuck and Co. began selling BRK smoke detectors in 1974 under the Sears brand. Sales were so successful that other companies, including General Electric, Norelco, Water Pik, Gillette, and Honeywell, soon followed. In 1976 BRK introduced the First Alert brand battery-operated residential smoke alarms and entered the home safety market. Consumers responded enthusiastically and sales of smoke detectors soared. By 1980 First Alert brand products had become the most recognized name in smoke detection. First Alert, together with BRK brand alarms, sold primarily to electrical contractors, combined to make BRK Electronics the leading manufacturer of residential alarms; in 1990 First Alert sold its 100 millionth smoke detector.

BRK Electronics did not rest on its laurels. Through the years, BRK and First Alert continued to reinvest in research and

---

Company Perspectives:

To continue to further improve and broaden the entire home safety category—developing innovative products that continue to keep homes safe and sound.

---

development. The result was a series of technological breakthroughs (such as the dual–chamber ionization unit and Light Test Direct battery plug contacts) as the division built a comprehensive line of home safety and security products, including rechargeable lanterns in 1982, rechargeable flashlights in 1985, disposable fire extinguishers in 1986, a line of home security lighting products in 1992, and a carbon monoxide alarm in 1993. Other developments that have led to improved fire safety products over the years included a combination photoelectronic/ionization smoke detector; an AC smoke detector with battery backup; a smoke detector with an Escape Light that provided emergency lighting when the alarm sounded; a kitchen smoke detector with a silencer button; the Exclusive Light Test smoke detector, which could be tested with a flashlight beam; an AC–powered smoke detector for the hearing impaired, featuring a 177 candela strobe in conjunction with an 85 decibel alarm; a fire escape ladder; fire security safes and portable fire safes; the breakthrough technology ten-year smoke detector, which operated for ten years without a battery change; and the revolutionary new SureGrip trigger fire extinguisher design.

As First Alert helped the industry grow, the company also led a marketing charge to raise fire safety awareness and promote the First Alert brand. Key to this effort were aggressive consumer fire safety education campaigns in which First Alert worked with other organizations, including McDonald's, the United States Fire Administration, the national SAFE KIDS campaign, and local fire departments to promote fire safety awareness and smoke detector use.

In 1992 a major change in company ownership occurred when the net assets of the BRK Electronics division of Pittway were purchased by a newly formed corporation, now known as BRK Brands, Inc., a wholly owned subsidiary of First Alert, Inc.

Carbon Monoxide Detectors, 1993

The company's broad range of products, brand name strength, and its longevity in the smoke detector market allowed it to easily enter the carbon monoxide (CO) detector manufacturing business in September 1993, when it introduced the first battery-operated CO detector. The detector featured a unique SensorPack Module using biomimetic technology to imitate the body's response to CO. Sales soared, but some critics of the company bashed First Alert for creating the market for CO detectors with ''scare tactics,'' citing the company's ''colorless, odorless 'silent killer' [which] threatens your family while you sleep'' advertising campaign. However, following several highly publicized incidents involving accidental carbon monoxide poisonings (including tennis star Vitas Gerulaitus) and the enactment of an ordinance in Chicago effective October 1, 1994 requiring homes to have a CO detector installed, sales went up again.

In 1994 the CO detectors accounted for 35 percent of the company's total sales, which jumped 250 percent to $248 million. Also in 1994, First Alert, Inc., the holding company of BRK Brands, Inc., became a public company when shares of its common stock were sold to the public and began trading on the NASDAQ in March. Much of the money earned in the IPO, which offered 6.6 million shares of common stock for $19 per share, was used to pay off indebtedness. Following its spinoff from Pittway in 1992, BRK Brands, Inc. introduced several new products in addition to the carbon monoxide alarm, including a fire escape ladder, a line of fire security safes, and child safety and independent living products. First Alert declared a 2-for-1 split of common stock in November 1994.

In June 1995, James Amtmann, a 25-year veteran of Stanley Works Inc. in New Britain, Connecticut, joined the company as president and chief operating officer, a position that had remained open for the previous two years.

Two months later, market leader First Alert continued to grow with the introduction of two new CO detectors. A new self-powered carbon monoxide detector with a reformulated biomimetic sensor and a new plug-in detector utilizing tin dioxide semiconductor technology were introduced to offer consumers a choice in protection. The company also began lobbying for a home safety aisle in stores to help promote the protection of homes and families. That year, total revenue dropped less than one percent to $246.3 million, with net income dropping 35.1 percent to $11.4 million, while competitor Nova Systems Ltd. dropped out of the CO detector market.

Although First Alert manufactured more than half of the 5.2 million total carbon monoxide units shipped in 1995 in the industry, sales became sluggish even for the market leader, due in part to the seasonal nature of CO detector sales. Amidst financial problems, Amtmann resigned ''to pursue other interests'' in March 1996, being replaced briefly by Chairman and CEO Malcolm Candlish during the new executive search, and then, in September 1996, by Joseph Messner as president and CEO. In addition, a major shareholder, The Thomas H. Lee Co., was looking to divest itself of its holdings. By April, the company still faced approximately 30 competitors in the CO detector market—such as AIM Safety of Austin, Texas—as compared to just about six in the larger smoke-alarm marketplace. Vice-President and CFO Gary Lederer also resigned in July 1996 to jump over to First Alert's previous parent company, Pittway. He was succeeded by Michael Rohl, formerly First Alert's controller.

In August 1996 First Alert introduced yet another new plug-in CO detector, which featured a digital readout display to visually indicate levels of CO sensed by the detector. The growth potential of the new category of life-saving detectors was tremendous, and increased public awareness of this silent killer continued to fuel sales for a market that was still in its infancy. Also that month, the company launched a line of products targeting home safety for infants and small children. The 16-SKU product line included such items as an appliance lock, a balcony guard, bed rails, cabinet latches, a cord windup, electrical outlet covers, an expandable child bath seat, night lights, a nursery monitor, a roller shade, safety gates, a toilet lock, and a VCR lock, all of which began retailing between

$1.99 and $49.99, competing in an $80 million annual market. Before releasing the products, the company surveyed mothers and worked in conjunction with C. Everett Koop's National Safe Kids Campaign. The three different kinds of fire security safes for home and office use featured rounded corners for added safety, adjustable shelves and drawers, easy-to-read combination locks, a single-hinge door, and double security combination key and lock, and were UL listed.

In April 1998 the company was acquired by Sunbeam Corporation, who purchased First Alert's stock for $5.25 per share. The durable consumer goods giant picked up First Alert in a $2.5 billion acquisition that included Coleman Co. (the Wichita, Kansas-based manufacturer of outdoor recreation and hardware products) and Signature Brands USA Inc. (a Glenwillow, Ohio-based manufacturer of housewares, including the "Mr. Coffee" line). Coleman, however, unloaded its Coleman Safety & Security Prods. Inc. to U.K.-based Siebe PLC for $105 million, leaving a competitor to First Alert outside the fold.

That October, First Alert became one of the first CO alarm manufacturers to comply with Underwriters Laboratories' new testing standards for AC-powered, plug-in residential CO alarm standards, which are effective for products manufactured after October 1, 1998. The company's digital CO alarm also received UL approval.

At the end of the 20th century, the manufacturer continued to be a leader in many markets, distributing its products in more than 30 countries. First Alert was the leading brand of smoke alarms and carbon monoxide alarms in the United States, and the company's products continued to have strong consumer recognition as a result of three solid brand names: First Alert, Family Gard, and BRK Electronics. The company continued to improve and broaden its entire home safety product line, developing innovative products that would continue to keep homes safe and sound into the 21st century.

Principal Subsidiaries

BRK Brands, Inc.; BRK Brands Europe Ltd.; Electronica BRK de Mexico S.A. de C.V.; BRK Brands Pty. Ltd.; BRK Brands Canada.

Further Reading

Abdeddaim, Michelle Nellett, "Firms Offer Safety Guidelines for the Consumer and Retailer," *HFN*, October 23, 1995, p. 82.

——, "First Alert New President Is Part of Growth Strategy," *HFN*, June 12, 1995, p. 45.

Andreoli, Tom, "Alarmed by First Alert," *Crain's Chicago Business,* December 12, 1994, p. 34.

Bas, Ed, "CO Detectors May Be Next 'Must Have' Safety Device," *Air Conditioning, Heating & Refrigeration News,* December 13, 1993, p. 28.

Chandler, Susan, "Red Alert at First Alert: It Faces a PR Disaster Over Its Highly Sensitive CO Detectors," *Business Week,* January 9, 1995, p. 44.

Fondiller, David S., and John R. Hayes, "Silent Killer," *Forbes,* September 22, 1997, p. 16.

"For First Alert, Low-Profile Conveyors End Production Jams," *Modern Materials Handling,* June 1998, p. 77.

Halverson, Richard, "Fire Safes' Sales Potential Has Yet to Be Unlocked," *Discount Store News,* January 15, 1996, p. 65.

Hayes, John R., "False Alarms: First Alert Is Trying to Scare You into Buying Its Carbon Monoxide Detectors. Trouble Is, They Don't Work Well," *Forbes,* January 13, 1997, p. 52.

Howell, Debbie, "Home Security Products Grow As Consumers Put Safety First," *Discount Store News,* March 8, 1999, p. 29.

Laing, Jonathan R., "Into the Maw: Sunbeam's 'Chainsaw Al' Goes on a Buying Binge," *Barron's,* March 9, 1998, p. 13.

Lipin, Steven, "Sunbeam Purchases Signal New Phase: Three Firms Will Cost $1.8 Billion Plus Debt," *Wall Street Journal (Europe),* March 3, 1998, p. 3.

Murphy, H. Lee, "Carbon Monoxide Detector Biz Setting Off Alarms at First Alert; President Leaves, Majority Owner Seeking a Buyer," *Crain's Chicago Business,* April 22, 1996, p. 36.

——, "First Alert Sets Off Alarms: Carbon Monoxide Poisoning News Lifts Stock," *Crain's Chicago Business,* September 26, 1994, p. 62.

"Personnel Changes," *Do-It-Yourself Retailing,* July 1996, p. 83.

Porter, Thyra, "Sunbeam Trifecta: Buys 3 Big Brands," *HFN,* March 9, 1998, p. 1.

Ratliff, Duke, "Carbon Monoxide Alarms Get Hot," *HFD,* October 24, 1994, p. 73.

——, "First Alert Defends Detectors," *HFD,* December 12, 1994, p. 58.

——, "First Alert Stresses Variety of Goods," *HFD,* July 4, 1994, p. 54.

Schonfeld, Erick, "Smoke Signals Over Illinois," *Fortune,* July 24, 1995, p. 167.

"Sunbeam Buys Coleman, Signature Brands, First Alert for $2.5 Billion," *Knight-Ridder/Tribune Business News,* March 3, 1998, p. 303B0993.

"Sunbeam Plans to Acquire Three Companies," *Knight-Ridder/Tribune Business News,* March 3, 1998, p. 303B0924.

"Sunbeam Sets Tone for Expansion Campaign," *Do-It-Yourself Retailing,* April 1998, p. 100.

"Vendors Aim to Smoke Out More Sales," *HFN,* July 29, 1996, p. 44.

Waters, Richard, "Dunlap Turns from Cost Cuts to Mergers," *Financial Times,* March 3, 1998, p. 32.

Zbar, Jeffrey D., "First Alert Rings Up Sales with Carbon Monoxide Detector," *Advertising Age,* November 7, 1994, p. 12.

—Daryl F. Mallett

Florists' Transworld Delivery, Inc.

3113 Woodcreek Drive
Downers Grove, Illinois 60515
U.S.A.
(630) 719-7800
(800) SEND-FTD; (800) 736-3383
Fax: (630) 719-6170
Web site: http://www.ftd.com

Private Company
Incorporated: 1910 as Florists' Telegraph Delivery
Employees: 430
Sales: $161.3 million (1998 est.)
NAIC: 561422 Floral Wire Services; 453110 Florists

Florists' Transworld Delivery, Inc., better known as FTD, is the world's largest flowers-by-wire company, linking approximately 20,000 retail florists in the United States and Canada, which then handle the orders of customers who want to send flowers to recipients in distant cities. Outside North America, FTD links another 32,000 independent florists in 140 countries across the globe. The company operates an 800 number, so that customers can call from home to order flowers, and also handles transactions through its member retail shops. Using an advanced computer network to link its affiliates, FTD handles more than 12 million orders annually, down from over 22 million in 1987, a slump largely attributed to intensifying competition. From its founding in 1910 until 1994, FTD operated as a nonprofit cooperative. A merger with Perry Capital in 1994 set FTD up as a for-profit private company with a highly recognizable branded product, the FTD bouquet.

Early Years

FTD was organized on August 18, 1910, as Florists' Telegraph Delivery, by a group of 15 retail florists who agreed to exchange their out-of-town orders, signalling the orders to each other by telegraph. Even during its early years, Florists' Telegraph Delivery, or FTD, effected highly successful national advertising campaigns. In 1914, a Boston advertising executive coined the phrase ''Say It with Flowers'' for the company, a tag line which stuck with FTD for virtually the rest of the century. Also in 1914, FTD began using the Mercury Man logo, comprised of the Greek god Mercury in a winged cap and winged sandals striding along with a bouquet of flowers held in his outstretched arm. The logo became prominent in FTD advertising and endured as one of the most recognizable logos in the United States.

FTD also began to use well-known personalities to advertise its services. In 1933 the company launched National Shut-In Day, a day to remember invalids, and hired to advertise the event actress Mary Pickford, gossip columnist and celebrity radio commentator Walter Winchell, and singer Kate Smith. Moreover, Winchell also added a routine to his radio show in which he presented ''real orchids to real heroes.'' The orchids were provided by FTD, thus giving the florists' group prominent weekly exposure on a popular national broadcast.

Growth After World War II

FTD grew as a national retail member network, and after World War II it expanded abroad as well. On November 1, 1946, FTD established International Florists, Inc., to sell its flowers by wire all over the world. This allowed customers to send elaborate floral gifts across the ocean, and, in some cases, florists went to great lengths to keep up FTD's reputation for reliability. In one instance, a Spokane, Washington, businessman went on an around-the-world cruise, and his company ordered flowers sent to him at a dozen foreign ports of call. FTD handled the order with no problems, though it reported that its Kenyan member florist had to take a four-hour canoe trip downriver to make its delivery to the businessman's cruising steamer. The company was similarly proud of a British affiliate florist. Given the task of delivering a bouquet to a lighthouse keeper on a stormy day, the florist made four attempts by rowboat. Unable to land, the florist finally caught hold of a rope thrown out from the lighthouse and attached the box of flowers. The customer gratefully hauled it in.

Because of its growing international presence, Florists' Telegraph Delivery changed its name in 1965 to Florists' Transworld Delivery. The well-known initials stayed the same, and Transworld emphasized the company's expertise in delivering flowers across the globe. By 1969, FTD was processing more than 12 million orders annually. By 1974, the florists' cooperative had about 13,500 members. FTD's headquarters were in Southfield, Michigan, a suburb of Detroit, while its member retail florists were all across North America. Its international affiliates comprised approximately 40,000 florists in 130 countries, including countries behind the Iron Curtain.

With so many members to keep track of, FTD used computer tapes to handle records of its credits and debits, and such extensive computer files sometimes proved useful in unique applications. According to a 1974 article in *Nation's Business,* the FBI routinely paid visits to FTD's headquarters whenever a reputed mobster died. The FBI reportedly scanned FTD's records to keep tabs on who was sending flowers to the funeral. Because of the number of daily orders, and the importance of speed and accuracy to its business, FTD had to have the latest and best in computer equipment. From the computer tapes in use in 1974, the company finally launched its own computer network system in 1979, called the FTD Mercury Network. FTD delivered 6,500 computer consoles to member florists soon after adopting the system, allowing for faster and more reliable communication between retailers. In its first year of use, the FTD Mercury Network handled approximately 11,000 electronic orders every day.

Brand Development in the 1980s–90s

A prominent national advertiser since its inception, FTD employed the Detroit ad agency of D'Arcy Masius Benton & Bowles in the 1980s. This agency focused on strengthening the identity of FTD as a brand by inventing memorable names for particular flower arrangements, including the FTD Pick-Me-Up Bouquet and the FTD Tickler Bouquet. In 1983, FTD began using former NFL Hall of Fame football star, sports announcer, and actor Merlin Olsen as a spokesperson in its television ads.

By 1990, FTD was spending somewhere between $20–$25 million annually on advertising. The company ran ads on television and radio, as well as in newspapers and magazines, continuing to use its longtime spokesman, Merlin Olsen. The advertising campaigns emphasized sending gift bouquets as a "kind, convenient, and above all, fun" activity, according to a 1990 *Advertising Age* report, which added that FTD strove to make available "the perfect bouquet for all occasions." Ads were targeted toward different audiences at different times of year, aiming at men for Valentine's Day, and women for Thanksgiving and Christmas, for example. Beginning in 1990, FTD tried to reach a younger audience, too, placing ads in such magazines as *Vogue, Rolling Stone,* and *Sports Illustrated.*

The company also launched promotions centered on new floral arrangements that featured the products of partner companies. For example, in 1991 FTD ran a cooperative venture with Gerber Products Co., the renowned baby food and baby products manufacturer. The FTD Bundle of Joy bouquet came attached to an assortment of Gerber products, including a baby bottle and a toy. In other joint ventures, FTD sponsored an international sweepstakes with credit card company American Express in 1991 and conducted a similar contest with the Pontiac division of Detroit automaker General Motors.

The year 1993 saw the debut of the Chicken Soup Bouquet, a joint venture with Campbell's Soup Co. to combine a get-well floral bouquet with a Campbell's mug and a packet of instant chicken soup. Get-well bouquets already made up approximately 14 percent of FTD member florists' business, and the new product was intended to boost that already large segment of the market. All the advertising for these various new products was overseen by the advertising agency FTD had long been associated with, D'Arcy Masius Benton & Bowles.

Competition Intensifies in the 1990s

However, in spite of all the money FTD was spending on advertising, and the energy it was putting into creative marketing tie-ins with other companies, the company met with evidence of intensifying competition. Beginning in 1988, FTD experienced dropping market share and sales. From 1988 to 1994, FTD's share of floral orders fell from 80 percent to 58 percent, in part because of growing competition from cheaper flower outlets. Supermarket sales ate into the retail florists' market, and competing floral telephone order companies also stole some of FTD's traditional business.

One such competitor was 1-800-Flowers, a company that had been losing money in 1987 when it was bought by Jim McCann, a former social worker. By 1993 McCann had turned 1-800-Flowers around, and the company was reporting $100 million in annual sales. FTD launched its own toll-free number for use by the public in 1993: 1-800-Send-FTD. However, this move not only managed to take orders away from FTD member retail florists but also lost an estimated $13 million in the process.

In the flower market as a whole, flower-by-wire sales dropped more than 13 percent from 1990 to 1994, and nonflorists accounted for almost half the flower sales in the United States. Consumers were also increasingly exposed to other flower venues, such as catalogs and online services. All this was bad news for FTD, made worse by the fact that FTD's advertising was clearly not getting its message across. The company conducted a focus group in 1992 in Atlanta, surveying 18-to-25-year-old women who had recently used a florist for their weddings. FTD's marketing department asked each of these women if the florist they had used was an FTD member. Not one of the women in the focus group either knew or cared. In response to this eye-opening news, FTD started a new advertising campaign. Instead of emphasizing a particular holiday or bouquet, the new ads sought to reinforce the image of FTD florists as high-quality and reliable vendors.

Still, advertising alone did not seem likely to turn the floral cooperative around, and in July 1994 FTD announced its interest in accepting a merger offer from a New York banking firm, Perry Capital Corp. Perry Capital was run by Richard Perry, formerly an executive with the investment firm Goldman Sachs & Co. Perry offered to buy FTD for $112 million, with the intention of converting it into a for-profit business.

FTD's cooperative structure was cited as one element in its failure to compete in the 1990s. With the company governed by a board and a series of committees, change took a lot of time to implement. For example, FTD had explored instituting a toll-free number in the early 1990s, but by the time the idea was approved and implemented, 1-800-Flowers and several other companies already had thriving businesses and significant market share.

Richard Perry brought in a marketing consultant, Jerry Siano, to help convince FTD members that the cooperative would do well to accept the merger. Siano had worked with N.W. Ayer, a New York advertising firm that had masterminded the ''reach out and touch someone'' campaign for AT&T. Perry used AT&T as a model for what he would like to do with FTD: emphasize the company's reliability and great service. The new company would ''sell relationships, not just flowers'' according to a September 26, 1994 report in *Advertising Age.*

FTD's board accepted Perry Capital's proposed merger, but only by a vote of ten to nine. While FTD members were mulling over the proposal, Roll International Corp., a privately held company that owned both commemorative platemaker Franklin Mint and the flower delivery service Teleflora, offered $140 million for the company. However, ultimately, FTD members opted for Perry Capital's deal. The new for-profit company, FTD Inc., organized in November 1994. At the same time, the company launched a nonprofit trade association called FTD Association.

One of the first things the new company did was to change its advertising agency, hiring Grey Advertising in 1995 to handle its account, worth an estimated $35 million. FTD also worked to improve its computer network. In 1996 FTD florists were relying on outdated monochrome PCs which simply listed the different kinds of bouquets available. The company upgraded to a faster network that was able to transmit visual images of floral arrangements. The new computers were also capable of running CD-ROM versions of books important to florists and their customers, such as Emily Post's *Complete Guide to Weddings* and a dictionary of flowers and plants. Though the new system was expensive, it seemed to significantly enhance the service that individual FTD florists could offer their customers.

Competition continued to be fierce in the floral market. In 1997 two of FTD's rivals, Teleflora Inc. and Redbook Florists Service, announced that they would merge. Moreover, FTD experienced some challenges in the marketing department, as the company's vice-president for advertising left in 1997 and his duties were given to an outside consultant. Just two years after switching its advertising account from D'Arcy Masius Benton & Bowles to Grey Advertising, the company switched again, selecting W.B. Doner & Co. of Southfield, Michigan.

The company's advertising budget had gone up, from $12 million the year of its merger with Perry Capital to $35 million when Grey got the account, but ad spending had fallen to $16 million by 1996. The budget for new agency W.B. Doner was said to be in the broad range of between $20 million and $40 million.

The Late 1990s and Beyond

In 1997 FTD consolidated its corporate headquarters, combining the operations of its Michigan offices with its Boston offices at a centrally located office in Downers Grove, Illinois, a suburb of Chicago. At this time, the company was handling approximately 12 million orders a year, down from around 22 million orders ten years earlier. Still billing itself as the leader in the flowers-by-wire business, FTD strove to counter the changing business conditions and increased competition that had hurt sales and market share in the past.

As a private company, FTD showed signs of trying to adapt to a more competitive floral market, witnessed by new advertising campaigns and a better computer network. With regard to technology, FTD announced an agreement in 1998 with Dell Computer Corp. to buy more than 20,000 Dell desktop computers, workstations, and servers. That year FTD also announced it was upping its ad spending, planning to spend $30 million on a new campaign, likely influenced by Richard Perry, focused on ''selling relationships, not just flowers.'' The new 1998–99 campaign theme stressed that FTD was ''The place to find quality.''

Further Reading

''Campbell Joins FTD Bouquet,'' *Advertising Age,* January 11, 1993, p. 17.

Cortez, John P., ''FTD Plans Blossom,'' *Advertising Age,* October 7, 1991, p. 65.

——, ''Olsen Still in Blooms,'' *Advertising Age,* December 3, 1990, p. 51.

''FTD Announces That It Will Merge with Perry Capital,'' *Wall Street Journal,* November 8, 1994, p. B4.

''FTD Names Grey,'' *Wall Street Journal,* April 3, 1995, p. B12.

Hayes, Frank, ''Electronic Commerce: No Place for Wallflowers,'' *Computerworld,* May 26, 1997, p. 117.

''How Kmart's Former CIO Had Bloomed Anew at FTD,'' *Chain Store Age Executive,* February 1996, p. 156.

Johnson, Stephen S., ''Flower Power,'' *Forbes,* July 4, 1994, p. 144.

Louviere, Vernon, ''Say It with Flowers, and the FBI Listens,'' *Nation's Business,* March 1974, p. 41.

Mahoney, Jerry, ''Texas-Based Dell Computer Corp. Wins Two Big Orders,'' *Knight-Ridder/Tribune Business News,* November 3, 1998.

Petrecca, Laura, ''FTD's Selection of Doner Surprises DiNoto Agency,'' *Advertising Age,* June 30, 1997, p. 2.

Rickard, Leah, ''FTD Fights Back in $16M Image Ads,'' *Advertising Age,* September 27, 1993, p. 12.

——, ''FTD Nurtures Plans for Healthy Growth,'' *Advertising Age,* September 26, 1994, p. 4.

Steinmetz, Greg, ''FTD to Look at Bids to Make It Bloom Again,'' *Wall Street Journal,* November 2, 1994, p. B1.

—A. Woodward

Foley & Lardner

777 East Wisconsin Avenue
Milwaukee, Wisconsin 53202
U.S.A.
(414) 271-2400

Private Partnership
Founded: 1842 as Finch & Lynde
Employees: 1,452
Sales: $240 million (1998 cst.)
NAIC: 54111 Offices of Lawyers

Foley & Lardner is one of the oldest and largest law firms in the United States. From its 1842 origin as a two-man partnership focusing on local Milwaukee issues, the firm has grown to play an important role in the Midwest as its attorneys have successfully counseled corporations on how to flourish in the face of new laws and government regulations. For decades the firm numbered relatively few lawyers, but mergers with seven other law firms starting in the 1970s increased Foley & Lardner's national presence. In the 1990s the firm represents a growing number of clients in new practice areas, such as healthcare, environmental regulation, sports, and intellectual property issues concerning computers and telecommunications. It also works closely with other law firms in the GlobaLex Alliance to represent clients' interests in Europe and Asia.

Origins and Growth in the 1800s

In 1842 Asahel Finch and William Pitt Lynde created the partnership of Finch & Lynde in Milwaukee, then a town of just 2,500 with unpaved streets. Like Abraham Lincoln and many other lawyers of that era, Finch studied law as an apprentice. Lynde, however, graduated from Harvard Law School and then moved west. Initially they kept busy with local litigation, some from business failures after the Panic of 1837.

Both Finch and Lynde became heavily involved in civic and political matters, the former as a Whig and later a Republican and the latter as a Democrat. The partnership represented local railroad interests that competed with the growing railroad hub of Chicago. The firm also represented maritime companies shipping goods on the Great Lakes.

As Milwaukee's economy grew after Wisconsin became a state in 1848, Finch & Lynde provided legal services to manufacturing, banking, insurance, transportation, and utilities clients, and invested as businessmen in some of those companies. In addition, as more German immigrants moved to Milwaukee in the 1850s and started breweries, the law firm gained clients in that new industry which became an important part of the city's heritage.

In 1856 the partnership added Benjamin K. Miller, Sr., and Matt Finch, a nephew of Asahel Finch, and changed its name to Finches, Lynde & Miller. Both new attorneys had studied the law as apprentices.

During the Civil War, the practice continued to serve farming clients, an important area since Wisconsin led the nation in producing wheat for the Union armies. Litigation remained the partners' main forte, helping clients in diverse industries resolve problems from the Panic of 1857 and the chaos of the war years.

In the postwar era, Asahel Finch spent more time as a leading Milwaukee businessman, especially as president of the Milwaukee Gas Company. Lynde, between 1865 and 1879, served in the Wisconsin assembly and senate and in Congress, while representing clients in the federal district court and before both the Wisconsin and U.S. Supreme Courts. Since the lumber and timber products industry was the state's leading manufacturing field, the firm worked on some important cases involving lumber firms.

After the war the law firm also represented the Western Union Company as the telegraph expanded across the nation. Several pork producing companies used the firm's attorneys. By 1971 Milwaukee ranked fourth in the nation's meat-packing industry. Railroad consolidation and regulation provided plenty of problems for clients in that growing field as well.

During the Gilded Age, more corporations relied on attorneys counseling them how to avoid what author Ellen D. Langill in her history of Foley & Lardner called the "costly luxury'' of litigation. Partner B.K. Miller, who was handling much of the firm's routine work in the 1870s, provided such counsel and also handled estate and probate matters as more company leaders gained huge fortunes in the late 1800s. Miller was the incorporator and charter stockholder for the new Milwaukee Telephone Company, later renamed Wisconsin Bell. In the 1890s he helped start the Milwaukee Trust Company, whose successor, First Wisconsin Trust Company, became an affiliate of the First Wisconsin Corporation, later renamed Firstar Corporation. Not surprisingly, he served as a Milwaukee Chamber of Commerce trustee.

Between 1883 and 1885, partners Asahel Finch, Matt Finch, and William Pitt Lynde died, leaving Miller to run the firm with a few other attorneys and staff. Major clients around the turn of the century included the Northern Pacific Railroad, the Wisconsin Central Railroad, the First National Bank, Wisconsin Marine and Fire Insurance Company, American Express, Western Union, plus the telephone and transit companies. Foley & Lardner also served Marshall Field, the Chicago Board of Trade, the Continental Bank of Illinois, the Schlitz Brewery and other breweries, and several firms in the lumber, cement, steel, and clothing manufacturing industries.

Law firms helped corporations deal with more federal laws about this time, starting with the 1887 Interstate Commerce Act that regulated railroads. Other laws included the 1890 Sherman Antitrust Act and the 1903 Elkins Act authorizing federal judges to penalize railroads for rebates. It was the Progressive period when reformers set out to curb the dangerous power of trusts and protect consumers.

The Early 20th Century

After the death of B.K. Miller in 1898 and the departure of other partners, the law firm in 1906 was renamed Miller, Mack & Fairchild, a name it retained for 45 years. George P. Miller was one of B.K. Miller's sons. Edwin S. Mack was one of the few Jewish law partners in the early 20th century. Arthur Fairchild, the son of a prominent Wisconsin lawyer and politician, used his outgoing personality to attract new clients.

New clients chose Miller, Mack & Fairchild as their legal counsel, including Briggs and Stratton, Federal Rubber, West Bend Aluminum, Oscar Mayer and Company, and the Kresge retail store. Wills and estates also kept the firm busy. For example, George Miller for years represented the New York estate of Robert Graham Dun of Dun & Bradstreet fame.

During World War I, the firm represented railroads in their lawsuits against the federal government's regulatory efforts. The three main partners bought war bonds and supported the war effort, which antagonized Milwaukee's antiwar Socialist politicians and many in the German community.

In the 1920s Milwaukee's prosperity brought new business to the law firm. Edwin Mack played a key role in creating Wisconsin's Children's Code to cover juvenile lawbreakers, social programs for children, and child custody rules. He also promoted state legislation in 1927 that required Wisconsin attorneys to have at least two years of college.

In 1921 Leon Foley joined the firm. He had served in the Navy during World War I and then graduated first in his class at the University of Wisconsin's law school. Fred Sammond, who joined the firm in the 1920s, was the last partner who served an apprenticeship instead of going to law school. George Miller died in 1931, leaving the law firm under the leadership of Edwin Mack and Arthur Fairchild.

The Great Depression, World War II, and Early Postwar Period

By 1933 Miller, Mack & Fairchild had grown to eight partners and 20 support staff. During the Great Depression, the firm helped banking clients deal with New Deal legislation, such as the Glass-Steagall Act and the Federal Deposit Insurance Corporation in 1933. It also helped many of the state's banks that failed during the Depression. Because of the 1935 federal Wagner Act that empowered unions, the law firm developed expertise in labor law as a way to help their corporate clients.

World War II resulted in several partners and associates leaving the law firm to serve in the military, while others received deferments for providing technical or managerial assistance to clients producing war goods.

Lynford Lardner, Jr., joined the firm in 1940 at age 25 after earning both a business and law degree from Harvard. In 1942 Edwin Mack died, just a few months before the firm celebrated its centennial.

As soon as World War II ended, Miller, Mack & Fairchild began recruiting new lawyers. Under Foley's leadership, the partnership decided to recruit more attorneys from nationally ranked schools and develop practices in other areas. By 1958 the firm had grown to 18 partners and 20 associates. In the 1950s the firm gained several new clients in the movie industry, including RKO, Paramount, Warner Brothers, and Twentieth Century Fox that faced antitrust allegations.

In 1960 the firm's name became Foley, Sammond & Lardner. It was shortened in 1969 to just Foley & Lardner after the death of Sammond in 1966. In 1964 the Milwaukee Braves baseball team decided to leave the city, so Milwaukee County hired the law firm to try to keep the Braves from moving. That attempt failed, but years later the firm helped bring the Milwaukee Brewers to the city.

Expansion in the 1970s and 1980s

Foley & Lardner in 1971 became the first Wisconsin law firm to open an office in another state when it founded its Washington, D.C. branch. That office grew in 1974 with the merger of Hollabaugh & Jacobs, a five-lawyer Washington, D.C. firm specializing in antitrust and trade regulation.

In 1975 the firm began its second expansion office in Madison, Wisconsin, where it initially represented the First Wisconsin National Bank and the Wisconsin Housing Finance Authority, an agency the firm had helped create to borrow money for public housing.

In 1986 the Madison office expanded with the merger of Walsh, Walsh, Sweeney & Whitney, which helped make the Foley & Lardner branch office the largest law firm in Wisconsin's capital.

Foley & Lardner began its Florida operations in 1981 and then in 1985 merged with the Orlando firm of van den Berg, Gay, Burke, Wilson & Arkin, P.A. Three years later it merged with the Tampa firm of Hill, Hill & Dickenson, P.A. Finally, in 1991, the Jacksonville law firm of Commander Legler Werber Dawes Sadler & Howell, P.A. merged with Foley & Lardner.

The firm's expansion into Florida reflected the increasing population from migrating workers and retirees and the economic growth of the so-called sunbelt, at the same time many states in the rustbelt of the northeastern states suffered job losses and declining industries.

Foley & Lardner started new practice specialties as well as new geographical offices. After the federal government passed the 1970 Clean Air Act and the 1972 Clean Water Act, the firm began a small environmental law practice that later increased as new environmental laws and regulations were implemented. In 1983 the firm started its intellectual property practice and five years later merged with a firm of 14 attorneys who specialized in that area: Schwartz, Jeffrey, Schwaab, Mack, Blumenthal & Evans in Alexandria, Virginia. The firm's health law practice also began in 1983 in response to hospital clients dealing with federal laws that created Medicare and Medicaid in the 1960s and other state and federal legislation.

Foley & Lardner's major expansion in the 1970s and especially the 1980s was part of a nationwide trend as many law firms became more business-oriented. Two developments helped create this business atmosphere. First, the U.S. Supreme Court ruled that professional associations' restrictions against advertising violated the First Amendment's guarantee of free speech and also antitrust laws. From then on, more professionals, including lawyers, increased their advertising and marketing.

That competition was enhanced by the second event. Steven Brill in 1979 began publishing the new magazine the *American Lawyer,* spotlighting attorney salaries and other internal operations of various law firms. With that added information, law firms increased hiring of experienced attorneys from other firms instead of simply hiring new law school graduates and keeping them throughout their careers. This new trend was called lateral hiring or raiding other law firms. Lateral hires often took their clients with them to the new law firms.

During most of the 1980s general economic health and many acquisitions and mergers also stimulated the growth of law firms such as Foley & Lardner. Many corporations expanded nationally and overseas, thus increasing the need for law firms with national and international capabilities.

The 1990s

To deal with its clients' overseas concerns, Foley & Lardner in 1990 organized GlobaLex, a strategic alliance with two other full-service firms: Nicholson Graham & Jones in London and D. de Ricci-G. Selnet et Associes in Paris, with branches in Singapore and Taipei. In early 1991 Stuttgart's Thummel Schutze & Partner joined GlobaLex, which totaled over 550 attorneys in 20 offices in six nations.

By the early 1990s, law firms faced a slowing economy, and one study concluded that large corporations in 1991 cut spending on outside attorneys by 24 percent. Meanwhile, the nation's largest law firms, including Foley & Lardner, continued becoming more business-oriented by hiring communications or marketing directors and publishing firm brochures, tax guides, and newsletters, and sponsoring speakers and seminars on legal issues. Founded in 1986, The National Association of Law Firm Marketing in Northbrook, Illinois, grew to 1,100 members by 1993.

The Chicago Stock Exchange (CSE) in July 1993 dissolved its inhouse legal department and retained Foley & Lardner to be in charge of its legal matters. However, in 1998 the U.S. Securities and Exchange Commission ruled that the CSE had allowed the law firm to develop a conflict of interest involving Chicago-based Scattered Corporation. Using for the first time civil court principles instead of federal securities rules, the SEC decided that Foley & Lardner could not act impartially as the CSE's investigator in its disciplinary actions against Scattered while at the same time defending the stock exchange in a lawsuit filed by Scattered. The firm remained an outside counsel to the CSE but was no longer its general counsel.

In 1995 Circuit Court Judge Lawrence Kirkwood ruled that lawyers for Foley & Lardner and Chicago's Winston & Strawn should receive ten percent of the $188 million they won from the state of Florida in a class-action lawsuit filed for 650,000 drivers who complained the state had discriminated against them by charging excessive fees for registering out-of-state cars. Kirkwood's decision, based on the Florida Supreme Court's 1994 decision that the fees were unconstitutional, was appealed by the government to the state Supreme Court.

Foley & Lardner in late 1995 began its merger with the 75-lawyer Los Angeles law firm of Weissburg and Aronson Inc., specialists in counseling hospitals, nursing homes, and healthcare providers. With more mergers and acquisitions involving operations in the Midwest and East, Weissburg and Aronson needed the help of another law firm. On the other hand, Foley & Lardner wanted to expand its healthcare practice and have offices in California to serve its clients in Japan and South Korea, most of whom needed help with intellectual property issues. "They like to have lawyers accessible on the West Coast. Milwaukee or Washington, D.C., where a lot of the intellectual property work is done, is too far away," said Foley & Lardner Chairman Michael Grebe in the November 7, 1995 *Sacramento Bee.*

The completed merger with Weissburg and Aronson in 1996 created the nation's 15th largest law firm with 550 attorneys. Foley & Lardner's combined healthcare practice included over 100 attorneys.

In 1998 Foley & Lardner opened its 14th office in Denver. Originated to focus on medical organizations in the Denver area, the new office was located in the same building as one of the law firm's clients—Catholic Health Initiatives.

In 1998 Bud Selig, the recently elected commissioner of Major League Baseball, and Paul Beeston, baseball's president and CEO, chose Foley & Lardner partner Robert A. Du Puy as the sport's chief legal officer and executive vice-president for administration. Du Puy for about 20 years had worked in commercial law, notably in real estate investments for the then First Wisconsin Bank, JI Case's acquisition of International Harvester's farming equipment division, and the AllisChalmers Corporation bankruptcy. In the 1990s he helped baseball executives deal with various controversies, such as antitrust charges and removing Commissioner Fay Vincent in 1992.

Du Puy also had served as counsel to the Milwaukee Brewers when Selig was the team's president; that close association was crucial in Du Puy accepting the position with Major League Baseball. After that appointment, Du Puy moved to New York City where baseball was headquartered, but he also remained a Foley & Lardner partner. In case of any conflict of interest between the Brewers and Major League Baseball, Du Puy said he would stop representing the Brewers.

Also in 1998, the law firm created a new lobbying and public affairs section. In response to client demands, the firm hired two top individuals to head this effort to influence state and federal lawmakers: Scott Klug, a nonlawyer and former Wisconsin congressman, and John Matthews, Wisconsin Governor Tommy Thompson's chief of staff. To make this new effort bipartisan, Foley & Lardner in January 1999 hired three Democrats, including former state Representative Rosemary Potter.

Although Foley & Lardner changed in many ways over the years, it remained focused, as the new millennium approached, on serving business clients, the firm's original purpose when it was created in 1842.

Further Reading

Burke, Sue, "Foley Trains 'Zero Tolerance' for Sexual Harassment," *Business Journal-Milwaukee*, April 15, 1995, p. 8A.

Buss, Dale D., "Goin' South: Wisconsin Service Firms Make Forays to Warmer Climes with Mixed Success," *Corporate Report Wisconsin*, October 1993, p. 15.

Deutsch, Glenn, "Full-Service Law Firms Tap New Arsenal to Defend Their Turf," *Business Journal-Milwaukee*, May 1, 1993, p. 9.

Ferraro, Cathleen, "2 Giant Law Firms May Join Practices," *Sacramento Bee*, November 7, 1995, p. E1.

Freyer, Tony, "Foley & Lardner, Attorneys at Law, 1842–1992," *Business History Review*, Winter 1993, p. 664.

Gallagher, Kathleen, "SEC Decision a Disappointment to Foley; Ruling Involves Dual Roles in Law Firm's Work for Chicago Stock Exchange," *Milwaukee Journal Sentinel*, November 12, 1998, p. 1.

Hoeschen, Brad, "Baseball's Barrister," *Business Journal-Milwaukee*, January 1, 1999, p. 3.

Langill, Ellen D., *Foley & Lardner: Attorneys at Law, 1842–1992*, Madison, Wis.: The State Historical Society of Wisconsin, 1992.

"Lawyers in License Fee Case to Get $18-Million Series: Around Florida," *St. Petersburg Times*, July 14, 1995, p. 5B.

Mayers, Jeff, "Klug Will Lobby for Law Firm; Foley & Lardner Adds Two Other Republicans," *Wisconsin State Journal*, November 17, 1998, p. 1A.

Olson, Walter K., *The Litigation Explosion: What Happened When America Unleashed the Lawsuit,* New York: Truman Talley Books-Dutton, 1991.

Romell, Rick, "Partner at Foley Named Baseball's Chief Legal Officer," *Milwaukee Journal Sentinel*, September 30, 1998, p.1.

—David M. Walden

Foodarama Supermarkets, Inc.

922 Highway 33
Building 6, Suite 1
Freehold, New Jersey 07728
U.S.A.
(732) 462-4700
Fax: (732) 294-2347

Public Company
Incorporated: 1958
Employees: 4,550
Sales: $697.4 million (fiscal 1998)
Stock Exchanges: American
Ticker Symbol: FSM
NAIC: 311812 Commercial Bakeries; 311821 Cookie & Cracker Manufacturing; 311615 Meat Products; 44422 Nursery & Garden Centers; 44511 Supermarkets & Other Grocery Stores; 44531 Beer, Wine, & Liquor Stores

Foodarama Supermarkets, Inc. was operating 21 grocery stores, two liquor stores, and two garden centers in central New Jersey in 1998, all licensed under the ShopRite name. Most of the supermarkets were significantly larger than conventional ones, with in-store premium departments such as salad bars, snack bars, and pharmacies. Foodarama also owned a central meat- and food-processing facility and a bakery. It was a member of Wakefern Food Corporation, the largest retailer-owned food cooperative in the United States and the owner of the ShopRite name.

Foodarama Supermarkets to 1980

The business began as a single grocery store in 1916. It was owned by Joseph Saker's parents when he graduated from high school in 1946. He took an entry level job at a local Nescafé factory, loading and unloading coffee beans. According to Saker, after two years of hard work he was demoted in favor of a brother-in-law of the supervisor, an experience he called his "first lesson in politics." Saker then joined the family store, which was grossing about $900 a week. He got his parents to spend $3,000 to remodel the store and, in 1950, to lay out $20,000 for a self-service "superette" employing about 12 people. He also helped found Wakefern Food Corporation, which made it possible for its members to compete with the superchains by providing purchasing, warehousing, and distribution services on a cooperative basis.

Saker opened his first supermarket, ten times the size of the superette, in 1956, and incorporated Foodarama Supermarkets in 1958. By August 1965 the company was operating 14 stores—two of which it owned—within a 30-mile radius of headquarters in Freehold, New Jersey. These stores operated under the Shop-Rite (later ShopRite) name and carried nonfood items such as housewares and health and beauty aids as well as a full range of groceries. The company also owned seven parcels of land in central New Jersey and one parcel in Warmington, Pennsylvania, and it was leasing office and storage space in Freehold and Manville, New Jersey. Sales came to $43.3 million in fiscal 1963 (the year ended February 2, 1964), and net income was $387,000. These totals rose to $48.4 million and $653,000 in fiscal 1964.

Foodarama Supermarkets became a public corporation in 1965, when it collected about $2 million by selling stock at $12.75 a share. Joseph and his brother John, the treasurer, retained almost 56 percent of the shares. The infusion of fresh funds enabled Foodarama to acquire seven Shop-Rite stores in the next two years, one of which was closed, and also to open seven new stores. By October 1967 the company had 22 stores, in Pennsylvania, Connecticut, and Maryland as well as New Jersey. The following year it acquired four more supermarkets in New Jersey and Pennsylvania, plus a fifth under construction, for $3 million in cash and notes. Sales volume increased by more than fourfold between fiscal 1962 and 1968, and earnings rose by 750 percent. In 1968 the company raised over $40 million by selling more stock at $23.50 a share.

Foodarama Supermarkets, during 1969–70, acquired Big Apple Supermarkets, a chain of 48 stores mainly on Long Island. With the defection of Supermarkets General Corporation in 1968, which took the Pathmark name for its stores,

Foodarama now was the largest member of Wakefern. A number of its units had in-store pharmacies, and it also had successfully opened tobacco and record shops in a few stores. The 78 Foodaramas were large suburban stores in the range of 20,000 to 35,000 square feet. Net income reached $2.5 million in fiscal 1970 (the year ended November 1, 1970) on sales of $302.9 million. There were plans not only for more supermarkets but also for chains of private-brand gas stations and discount drug stores adjacent to the supermarkets.

Foodarama Supermarkets' sales volume reached a record $321 million in fiscal 1971, but its profit dropped by about 50 percent. By 1972 it was clear that the company had swallowed more than it could comfortably digest. Fourteen stores were sold in fiscal 1972 and 11 more during the three months ended January 31, 1973, leaving Foodarama with 41. The company also was operating six Shop-Rite gas stations contiguous or close to its supermarkets. It lost $8.2 million in fiscal 1972, including a charge of $5.3 million for discontinued operations, and then returned to profitability. It acquired two liquor stores and two garden centers adjacent to its stores in 1975 and 1976, respectively, and disposed of the gasoline stations in 1975.

Foodarama Supermarkets also was locked in a bitter dispute with Wakefern in the 1970s, filing lawsuits in 1971 alleging that certain of Wakefern's directors and members had illegally removed stock purchased from Supermarkets General from the cooperative's treasury, an action that led to the ouster of the existing officers, including Saker, who was secretary. Because of the change in control, Saker contended, nonmembers of Wakefern were barred from using the former Big Apple warehouse in Central Islip, New York, and as a result the warehouse lost money and was eventually sold. Saker lost his lawsuit in 1979 but remained the largest shareholder in Wakefern.

Competitive Challenges: 1980–92

Foodarama Supermarkets had 38 supermarkets in four states in fiscal 1980. Sales came to $412.9 million that year, but net income was only $1.3 million. The company's stock dipped as low as $3.25 a share in 1981, the first of three years out of the next four in which its net income fell below $1 million. Foodarama began paring its holdings, disposing of some of its smaller stores. Others were renovated and enlarged, with service centers added for specialties such as salad bars and cheese counters. In December 1982 the company opened the first of what it called World Class stores, in Bricktown, New Jersey.

After a strong fiscal 1985 Saker who, with close allies, controlled 48 percent of Foodarama Supermarkets' stock, proposed a leveraged buyout of the company. The offer of $20.50 in cash and notes was scorned as inadequate by other shareholders, however, and only passed by a narrow margin. A December 1986 New Jersey court decision voided the proposal. Foodarama disposed of its Connecticut stores in 1987, reducing the number of its units to 24. It acquired a processing facility for prepared foods, however, in 1986 and was fielding eight World Class stores in early 1988.

Foodarama Supermarkets had record net income of $3.7 million on sales of $482 million in fiscal 1987 and made almost as much profit the following year. Its stock rose to more than

$38 a share in 1989, the year the company purchased four stores from Hilltop Supermarkets Inc., a New Jersey operator, for $24 million. The acquired stores had annual volume of $120 million. In 1990 Foodarama was operating 26 supermarkets, plus the two adjacent liquor stores and two adjacent garden centers. Nineteen of the 26 were in New Jersey, five on Long Island, and two in Pennsylvania. They ranged in size from 26,000 to 75,000 square feet. Eighteen of the 26 had in-store pharmacies. Foodarama also was operating a bakery in Eatontown, New Jersey.

The acquisition of the Hilltop stores enabled Foodarama Supermarkets' sales to reach $673.1 million in fiscal 1990, but net income was only a little more than $1 million. The company's long-term debt reached a troublesome $71.7 million in early 1991. Although Foodarama's revenues reached a peak of $695.3 million in fiscal 1991, the company lost $553,000 and also lost money for two of the next three years. At the company's annual meeting the following spring, Saker said that the recession had continued to "cast a cloud over shoppers' buying habits last year."

In order to increase its profits, Foodarama Supermarkets now was counting on its 11 World Class stores, which were placing an emphasis on service and nonfood departments and on upscale goods that would allow higher markups than the chain's bread-and-butter grocery items. Among the specialty nonfood items at some of the 11 were expensive watches and perfumes and gourmet kitchen utensils. At the same time, Foodarama was discounting such items as greeting cards and paperback books as well as selling high-ticket goods such as television sets at promotional prices to draw in shoppers.

In order to meet competition from the spreading number of deep discounters and price-club operators, Foodarama also had begun adding warehouse-outlet units of 3,000 to 7,000 square feet to some stores. Space for these units was found in the back rooms of ten stores and stocked with some 1,500 grocery, perishable, and nonfood items at prices matching those of the clubs. In addition, in September 1992, all 182 ShopRite supermarkets in five states cut prices on more than 3,000 health and beauty care items.

The competitive challenge of the price clubs also led Foodarama to establish bigger stores, especially a 113,000-square-foot outlet in Neptune, New Jersey, that replaced an earlier 28,000-square-foot one. To lure shoppers farther away from this store than the usual two- or three-mile radius, the new superstore began, in 1993, to offer a rabbi-supervised "Kosher Experience." Building on Foodarama's ten years in ultra-Orthodox Lakewood, New Jersey, the Neptune store offered thousands of stockkeeping units of fresh, frozen, and shelf-stable kosher items, including a delicatessen island.

So large was Foodarama's Neptune store that its 30,000 square feet of selling space for nonfoods products was larger than most conventional supermarkets. It included sections for sporting goods, books and magazines, consumer electronics and camera equipment, automotive needs, flowers, and clothing and accessories. The health and beauty care section included 65 feet for hair care and 43 feet for vitamins. The warehouse store in back "could easily fill a basketball court," wrote Frank

Hammel. Its stock included stereos, radios, microwave ovens, and television sets. A leased video store was to open in the front of the store. Foodarama officials saw this gigantic unit as an attraction for every consumer in Monmouth County.

But in the face of an impending $2 million loss on reduced revenues in fiscal 1993, Foodarama Supermarkets was forced to sell its five Long Island stores to Grand Union for a total of $18.3 million. In February 1994 the company announced that it had defaulted on $35.2 million of loans and disclosed increasing operating losses. A restructuring of the company was made possible a year later, when it received a credit and loan facility of $38 million in order to pay three bank creditors and certain senior noteholders a total of $32.9 million. A year later Foodarama sold its two Pennsylvania stores to Wakefern for $8.3 million.

Two World Class Foodarama ShopRite stores opened in 1996, in Marlboro and Montgomery, New Jersey. Another opened in February 1998 in East Windsor as a replacement for an older, smaller unit in Highstown. A fourth opened in late 1998 in Bound Brook, and three more were expected before the end of 2000. Three leases had been signed by April 1998 for replacement locations, with additional plans to expand one existing store and the expansion of the chain's Long Branch store also under way.

After putting its finances in order Foodarama Supermarkets returned to the black, but its profit remained thin, with net income of only $1.1 million in fiscal 1997 on sales of $636.7 million. These totals improved to $1.8 million and a record $697.4 million, respectively, in fiscal 1998. Of the 1998 sales, groceries accounted for around 40 percent; dairy and frozen foods, 16.5 percent; meats, poultry, and seafood, 11 percent; nonfoods, ten percent; produce, 8.5 percent; appetizers and prepared foods, six percent; pharmacy, four percent; bakery, two percent; and liquor, floral, and garden centers, two percent. Products under the ShopRite label came to 17 percent of sales in fiscal 1997.

All of the company's 21 stores were being leased in 1998 and ranged in size from 30,000 to 101,000 square feet. The 15 World Class supermarkets were significantly larger than conventional ones and featured such premium services as fresh fish on ice, prime-meat departments with butcher service, imported cheese cases, salad and snack bars, bulk foods, and pharmacies. Many of these services were also available in the other stores. Foodarama's bakery was now in Howell, New Jersey. Its facility for meat and prepared foods was in Linden, New Jersey.

Joseph Saker, still chairman and president of Foodarama Supermarkets, owned 30 percent of the company's common stock in February 1998. Saker family members collectively owned 43 percent. The company's long-term debt was $50.7 million at the end of fiscal 1998. Foodarama held a one-eighth share of Wakefern.

Principal Subsidiaries

New Linden Price Rite, Inc.; ShopRite of Malverne, Inc.; ShopRite of Reading, Inc.

Further Reading

Barr, Stephen, ''CEOs: Masters of NO Degree,'' *Business Journal of New Jersey,* April 1992, pp. 30+.

Duff, Mike, ''Ready for a Fight,'' *Supermarket Business,* September 1991, pp. 187–89.

Elson, Joel, ''Foodarama Develops Format to Fight Clubs,'' *Supermarket News,* April 20, 1992, p. 42.

——, ''Foodarama Sets Growth by Construction,'' *Supermarket News,* April 13, 1998, p. 4.

Hammel, Frank, ''Now, Here's an Unorthodox Instore Service!'' *Supermarket Business,* January 1994, pp. 65–66, 71.

Lewis, Leonard, ''Foodarama's Final Round: Long Wakefern Fight Lost,'' *Supermarket News,* December 3, 1979, pp. 1, 12.

Mendelson, Seth, ''Foodarama's Nonfoods Smorgasbord,'' *Supermarket Business,* March 1994, pp. 88–89, 92.

Norris, Floyd, ''Why Not Shop Around?'' *Barron's,* August 4, 1986, p. 30.

Wahlgren, Gary, ''Foodarama Supermarkets, Inc.,'' *Wall Street Transcript,* March 8, 1971, p. 23,419.

—Robert Halasz

Fountain Powerboats Industries, Inc.

P.O. Drawer 457
Washington, North Carolina 27889
U.S.A.
(252) 975-2000
Fax: (252) 975-6793
Web site: http://www.fountainpowerboats.com

Public Company
Incorporated: 1979
Employees: 331
Sales: $50.6 million (1998)
Stock Exchanges: NASDAQ
Ticker Symbol: FPWR
NAIC: 336612 Boat Building; 326199 Boats, Inflatable
   Plastics, Manufacturing

Fountain Powerboats Industries, Inc., through its wholly owned subsidiary Fountain Powerboats, Inc., is one of the premier designers and manufacturers of ultra high-performance speed boats, sport cruisers, sport boats, and sport fishing boats. However, the company is no ordinary recreational powerboat manufacturer. As Ferrari and Lamborghini are to the automotive world, so Fountain is to the world of powerboats—a firm that is at the pinnacle of its industry. Having produced and sold some of the most expensive powerboats in the world to such customers as the late King Hussein of Jordan, the company recently has entered into numerous defense contracts with the U.S. Navy, U.S. Customs, and the U.S. Coast Guard to make high-quality, custom-designed rigid inflatables. In addition, the company has gone on an acquisitions campaign to vertically integrate its production process. Although the company's state-of-the-art production plant and headquarters are located along the Pamlico River in Washington, North Carolina, its network of distributors is worldwide.

Early History

The founder and owner of Fountain Powerboats, Reggie Fountain, was born and educated in Tarboro, North Carolina,

and from his early childhood he was fascinated with speedboats. He entered his first boat race at the age of 14, and from that time onward was increasingly involved in competitive speedboat racing. Yet he found time to earn both an undergraduate degree and a law degree from the University of North Carolina while he developed his skills as a speedboat racer. In 1970 Fountain entered into professional competition and, one year later, was honored as the Outstanding New Driver at one of the most prestigious speedboat racing events of the time, the Lake Havasu World Championships.

The skills he had developed during his earlier years paid off immediately in professional competition. In the second year of his career, Fountain set two world records and earned three national closed-course championships in one day at Marine Stadium in Miami—thus assuring himself a place in boat racing history. As his skills improved and the accolades continued, Fountain was soon a dominant force in speedboat racing. One of the most admired and vaunted teams in speedboat racing, the Mercury Factory Team, asked him to drive with legends Bill Seebold and Earl Bentz, and by 1972 the three men had become the winningest team in the history of tunnel outboard racing.

Fountain's success continued unabated during the entire decade of the 1970s. In 1973 he won an astounding 20 out of 31 races entered, and in 1975 he won a total of ten out of 19 racing events entered. In 1976 Fountain reached the top of his career in tunnel racing, when he won 15 out of 23 races, the most important including the famous St. Louis OZ World Championships. In 1978 the now legendary speedboat racer once again won the St. Louis OZ World Championships, among numerous other prestigious races around the globe. When he retired from active competition in 1979, Reggie Fountain had achieved a reputation and status in speedboat racing comparable to Babe Ruth and Joe DiMaggio in baseball and Mario Andretti in automobile racing. In short, it was not likely that another speedboat racer would equal Fountain's record-setting accomplishments for a long time.

The 1980s and Corporate Success

After retiring from active competition, Fountain contracted with Mercury Marine to design and manage a comprehensive research and development testing program. Before he could actually start the testing program, however, Fountain required a high-performance boat. He decided to purchase a 31-foot V-Bottom speedboat from Bill Farmer of Excalibur Boats located in Florida. As he became more and more involved in the testing program, Fountain came up with the idea of altering the boat to suit his purposes. At first the changes were relatively simple and small, like sandpapering the running surface to increase the overall speed of the boat. But as time went on, Fountain's alterations became noticeable and dramatic, such as the hand-crafted putty strakes added to improve handling and control of the boat, and the redesign and improvement of the stern drive height meant to improve acceleration.

Within a short time, Fountain had significantly improved the performance of his test speedboat. Recognizing that he could enhance its performance even more, he devoted himself to redesigning and improving both the hull and deck configurations. By the time he was finished, Fountain's alterations had changed the boat so much that it was virtually a new boat. As this alteration and testing process continued, Fountain discovered that there was a clearly identifiable market for the highly customized test boats that he was producing. A little marketing research, mostly consisting of discussions with speedboat enthusiasts and other speedboat retailers, convinced him that he could design, produce, and market his own boats, with less overhead and more customization than anyone thought possible.

With his own money earned from real estate investments over the years, the enthusiastic entrepreneur opened his business, Fountain Powerboats, Inc., in late 1979. Situated in an abandoned used car dealership in Washington, North Carolina, near the shores of the Pamlico River, Fountain's new firm grew rapidly. The first year of operation began with a 10,000-square-foot facility, eight employees, and sales amounting to $515,000. One year later, although his design and manufacturing facility remained the same size, both the number of employees and sales figure doubled. Fountain had discovered a niche in the recreational boat market, one that emphasized highly customized designs without concern for the price.

Throughout the decade of the 1980s Fountain Powerboats flourished. The success of the company was in large part due to the hands-on management style of its owner and the meticulous attention Fountain gave to the quality of his boats. From the beginning of the design and production process, Fountain insisted on using the best materials available for their construction. His company was one of the first in the boating industry to use space-age laminates, heralding a breakthrough in boat design and performance. Fountain was also a pioneer in using bidirectional, tridirectional, and quad-directional glass to improve and enhance performance, as well as paving the way for the use of lightweight coring material in constructing speedboats. One of his most impressive revolutionary designs involved the reconfiguration of the underneath of his boats by utilizing a notch transom, pad keel running surface that significantly improved the handling and performance of his speedboats. By the time the decade had come to a close, Fountain Powerboats employed more than 100 people and was selling millions of dollars worth of boats to people around the world, including some of the most notable celebrities and personalities in the United States, Europe, and the Middle East.

The Challenges of the 1990s

During the early and mid-1990s Fountain Powerboats was confronted with a series of challenges that tested the commitment and talent of its owner. A recession affected the fortunes of the company adversely, with many of the customers to which Fountain would ordinarily sell his boats unable to pay his higher prices because of setbacks in their investment portfolios. Compounding the matter was the government's imposition of a ten percent luxury tax placed on all boats, airplanes, and cars with a sticker price of more than $100,000. Consequently, the demand for Fountain's speedboats and new line of fishing boats dropped precipitously. To keep his boats before the public eye, and to raise money to sustain his company through this difficult time, Fountain decided to return to the professional offshore racing circuit.

Fountain's return to the racing circuit was an enormous success. He designed, built, and drove his own boat, the only V-bottom boat in most of the offshore races he entered, and dominated the competition. In 1990, at the start of his return, Fountain overcame overwhelming odds and predictions to the contrary to beat the entire field of unusually designed catamarans operated both by professionals and celebrities. Fountain was particularly vindicated by his victory, since it was widely regarded that V-bottom boats were not competitive with catamarans in smooth water. In 1992 Fountain won the OPT World and National Championships in open V-bottom boats, as well as the APBA World Championship. From the time he returned to the end of 1992, Fountain remained undefeated in all major offshore racing competitions.

In 1992 Fountain introduced a revolutionary design for his high-performance boats: the Positive Lift, a new type of boat bottom that increased acceleration, improved handling and cornering agility, and reduced consumption of fuel. With the government's repeal of the luxury tax in 1993, Fountain Powerboats seemed poised for a financial recovery. Yet the company's capital expenditure for retooling its production line to incorporate the new configurations for the Positive Lift boat bottoms, in concert with a complete overhaul of the firm's production process and facility, delayed prospects for an immediate and full economic recovery. By 1995, however, Fountain Powerboats was in the driver's seat, so to speak, with sales increasing dramatically and demand for the company's powerboats skyrocketing.

The year 1997 was a mixed one for Fountain Powerboats and its owner. Fountain had set eight world speed records in offshore racing competition since his return to the professional circuit in 1990 and was at the peak of his ability and performance as a speedboat racer. Fountain formed a partnership with Fabio Bruzzi, another veteran racer, and the two men designed and developed a unique surface drive for high-performance speedboats that was soon incorporated into many of the designs used for boats at Fountain's company. During the same time, however, Fountain had decided to merge with Mach Performance, Inc., a manufacturer of propellers for speedboats and various other types of boat designs. Unfortunately, the deal went sour when Fountain brought suit against the owner of Mach Performance, Gary Garbrecht, for fraud. Fountain argued that he had arranged a merger with Garbrecht in good faith, but that Garbrecht hid the true nature of his company's financial situation and prevented auditors from inspecting its inventory, consisting of equipment at the time of the merger that was obsolete and even defective. Even more distressing to Fountain was the suit brought against him and his company by the most famous basketball player in the world, Michael Jordan. Jordan and his lawyers accused Fountain of infringing on his trademark ''Air Jordan'' by using the phrase ''Air Reggie'' as part of an advertisement showing a powerboat surging in the air above the water.

Luckily, both of the lawsuits resulted in favor of Fountain Powerboats. The merger with Mach Performance was rescinded by the courts, at no loss to Fountain Powerboats or its operations. The suit brought by Michael Jordan against Fountain Powerboats for trademark infringement was settled out of court, also at no cost to the company, since there was a mutual agreement that the company would not use the particular phrase under discussion again in an advertisement.

As of mid-1999, Reggie Fountain maintained a 55 percent ownership of the company and was the driving force behind its continued success. Sales exceeded $50 million in 1998 and showed no signs of slowing down. Clearly, Reggie Fountain's hands-on management of the company, including his ability to incorporate revolutionary designs for the improved performance of his boats, placed Fountain Powerboats in a class by itself.

Further Reading

Reggie Fountain: A Biography, Washington, N.C.: Fountain Powerboats, Inc., 1997.

Sherman, John, ''Jump at the Chance,'' *Boating Magazine,* April 1998, p. 138.

Siedman, David, ''Flying Fortress,'' *Boating Magazine,* February 1999, p. 117.

Steele, Randy, ''Driving Ambition,'' *Boating Magazine,* February 1998, p. 44.

Stern, Richard L., ''Full Throttle, Damn the Shorts,'' *Forbes,* June 1, 1987, p. 80.

''A Stock Sinks,'' *Forbes,* December 28, 1987, p. 8.

Williams, John Page, ''One Helm, United,'' *Boating Magazine,* January 1999, p. 154.

—Thomas Derdak

Furon Company

29982 Ivy Glenn Drive
Laguna Niguel, California 92677
U.S.A.
(949) 831-5350
Fax: (949) 363-6276
Web site: http://www.furon.com

Public Company
Incorporated: 1955 as The Fluorocarbon Company
Employees: 3,315
Sales: $485 million (1998)
Stock Exchanges: New York
Ticker Symbol: FCY
NAIC: 339112 Catheters Manufacturing; 326113 Plastics
    Film & Unlaminated Sheet Manufacturing; 325991
    Plastics Resins, Custom Compounding; 326199 All
    Other Plastics Product Manufacturing

Furon Company is the world's leader in the design and manufacture of specialized polymer components and parts for a wide range of applications in many fields, including the process, transportation, electronics, healthcare, and industrial equipment industries. Seals and bearings, fluid handling components, tapes, films, coated fabrics, hose, tubing, and plastic-formed components are among the products manufactured for various industries. Many of Furon's products are custom manufactured for specific needs. Furon's medical products include catheters, fluid and drug delivery parts, patient monitoring, and infusion systems, primarily for critical care and catheter lab use. The company focuses on niche markets and applications that provide its customers value-added product solutions. Brands developed by Furon include CHR, Dekoron, Felsted, Fluorglas, Medex, Meldin, Omniseal, Rulon, Synflex, and Unitherm. Some of the company's largest customers for industrial products include The Boeing Company, Coca-Cola Company, and Navistar International Corporation. In addition to its offices throughout the United States, the company has expanded operations into Belgium, Italy, England, and Germany.

The 1950s: Teflon Processing

Founded by George Angle in 1955, Furon was initially named The Fluorocarbon Company. The company began by producing Dupont's Teflon—or polytetrafluoroethylene—a product used primarily as a nonstick coating for kitchen utensils. Teflon is capable of being molded, machined, and fabricated into many shapes and components, including miniature solenoid valve bodies. The Fluorocarbon Company developed Teflon spring-energized seals in order to handle extreme temperatures and strong forces for commercial aircraft use. The coating could withstand expansion, contraction, flexure, and angular movement. After thorough testing, the material received military approval for its aircraft applications. The Fluorocarbon Company continued to develop and produce a wide variety of resins made of exclusive compounds. The company's production process began with the purchase of standard polymer resins from a variety of chemical companies. At Fluorocarbon, engineers added to or modified the resins to impart the special properties suitable for specific application needs. Sometimes such additives as nylon were added to impart extra strength, or graphite for lubrication.

Following its initial public offering in 1962, Fluorocarbon grew rapidly, soon becoming the world's largest processor of Teflon. The company began then with five small manufacturing plants, 20 employees, and $600,000 in sales, but expanded to over 2,900 employees and more than $300 million in sales under the leadership of Peter Churm, who assumed the Fluorocarbon presidency in 1963. His style allowed a decentralization of management, with decision-making located at individual operating units, complemented by strategic direction provided by a veteran senior management team.

The 1970s–80s: Plant Expansion and Growth

In 1988 Fluorocarbon acquired all of the outstanding common stock of Reynolds & Taylor, Inc., a fabricator of high performance composite materials for the aerospace, aviation, and defense industries. For a space shuttle experiment Fluorocarbon introduced a special flawless, thin-walled gas-permeable membrane. Specifications required that the membrane be translucent and perfected to assure uniform gas and light diffusion.

Other thermoplastic developments included fiber optic cables and pressure-formed instrumentation packaging. Also in 1988, Fluorocarbon acquired the fixed assets and inventory of Parker Hannifin's gasket division, located in Sulfur, Louisiana. In addition, it purchased Dixon Industries Corporation from CHR Industries, Inc. and Bunnell Plastics Inc. from the Bundy Corporation, which was a wholly owned subsidiary of the Delaware-based TI United States, LTD.

In 1989 The Fluorocarbon Company responded to negative publicity arising from new information concerning the environmental hazards involved in the release of fluorocarbons into the atmosphere. As a diversionary tactic, it adopted Furon Company as its new name. Furon established its World Class Performance program in order to accomplish an objective of becoming number one or two in the market niches it served. The program emphasized a new formalized cost reduction program and instituted a performance measuring system, called Economic Value Added, or EVA. By 1990, following Management's primary emphasis on increased materials development, Furon's Advanced Polymers Division developed Meldin 2000, a versatile, high-temperature material, first introduced at the National Design Engineering Show. The material offered long wear, low friction, and superior compression strength properties. The resulting components produced ranged from hydraulic hoses to wire and cable products. For the heating, ventilation, air conditioning, and power generation industries, Furon offered Dekoron tubing, wire, and cable, which were mainstays in chemical processing applications. For other markets such as agriculture, trucking, construction equipment, paint equipment, and beverage dispensing, Furon developed the special family of products labeled Synflex.

The company's reputation for problem solving expertise was especially strong in its materials technology and systems design. Its diverse assortment of custom-tailored products necessitated extensive fabrication and manufacturing capabilities, a focus which contributed to further expand company product goals. Components were created to provide seals and o-rings for automobiles that were flexible enough to withstand extreme conditions in low temperatures and meet tight emission standards. Pressure-sensitive tapes and coated fabrics were developed from elastomers including silicone, fluorosilicone, Neoprene, natural rubber, butyl, polyurethane, and others. The special properties of these materials protected critical components from heat, electrical interference, chemicals, conformal coatings, shock, and vibration. Silicon foam, polyisocyanurate and polyimide foams were developed to provide non-toxic fire blocking capabilities. In 1991, Furon's business segments included the areas of Engineered Products, Fluoropolymers, Fluid Sealing, Extrusion Technologies, and Furon Europe (where the company manufactured and sold a variety of products using technologies specifically designed for the requirements of the European market). Furon recognized a strong demand for its products in Europe, and moved the CHR operations, previously housed in the Netherlands, to Gembloux, Belgium, bringing manufacturing facilities closer to markets. New offices were also opened in Germany, France, and the United Kingdom, with further expansion scheduled for Japan and the Pacific Rim. Sales plans were developed for exportation to the Arabian Gulf, Central and South America, Eastern Europe, and Africa. Despite Furon's expansion and technological efforts, 1991 sales had decreased from $327 million to $306 million, due largely to a lagging worldwide economy.

Restructuring in 1992

Furon executives decided to focus attention on those businesses showing higher profit margins and the ability to sustain internal growth rate objectives. Seven of the company's divisions were consolidated into other business units as a means of reducing expenses, and a new materials technology center combining research, development, and production, was established in Aurora, Ohio (the Macromeric Division). Its purpose was to serve internal needs, and to facilitate sales of proprietary polymer materials to businesses outside the company in certain noncompetitive situations. Furon incurred a restructuring charge of $32 million, attributable to the selling of six businesses, management reorganization, consolidation, discontinuance of certain product lines, revision of certain employee benefit plans, and the write-down of a prior discontinued business investment. In 1992 the major markets Furon served, especially the petrochemical, aircraft, aerospace, defense, construction, and pulp and paper markets (comprising about 30 percent of sales), faltered, and the European market suffered even more than the domestic economy. The company responded by implementing rigorous new marketing strategies, continuing to cut costs and accelerating product development efforts by capitalizing on materials and processing technologies. Sales were brighter in the heavy duty truck, electronic, and medical markets, which at that time made up approximately 25 percent of sales.

By 1994 an upturn in the global market was reflected in a 14 percent rise in Furon sales, from $266 million in the previous year to $302 million. Bolstered by the positive outlook, capital projects increased and numerous opportunities in electronics and medical products were targeted. The company purchased Custom Coating and Laminating in Worcester, Massachusetts, a company that manufactured release films and tapes. In March 1995, Furon switched from the NASDAQ to the New York Stock Exchange due to the perception that the company's access to capital markets would be enhanced by the NYSE in the long-term. Price spreads and volatility were additional considerations.

Sales and earnings rose to record highs in fiscal 1997. Anticipating that healthcare industry sales would rise to about a quarter of the company's total, Furon acquired Medex and its subsidiaries—a company with annual sales in the $100 million range—for approximately $160 million. Previously, Furon's medical products had been sold primarily to other device manufacturers, but Medex concentrated on sales of polymer-based medical devices to end users, hospitals, and alternate care sites. Medex offered a full line of products for neonatal and pediatric intensive care and adult critical care uses, including disposable transducer kits for pressure monitoring, IV sets for fluid and drug delivery, and inflation devices of the catheterization lab. It was a leading provider of syringe pumps and related disposable sets for infusion therapy. In 1997 The U.S. Food and Drug Administration approved the marketing clearance for a reusable pressure transducer to monitor blood pressure during surgical procedures, items well received by physicians and nurses who noted the high standards of performance. The company also acquired Scientific Device Manufacturers, Inc. (SDM), which began operating as a part of Medex, adding products to the existing medical products platform. Since nearly 39 percent of Furon's sales in the medical sector were derived outside the U.S. market, the Furon acquisitions, including AS Medical GmbH, enabled the company to expand its healthcare base in Europe and the United States.

Excluding Medex, approximately 27 percent of Furon's sales were generated by new products during this period, reflecting a strong commitment to developing business through the introduction of new product lines. By 1998 Furon's medical devices sector comprised approximately 24 percent of total sales for the year and 32 percent of the company's operating income. Demographics indicated that the aging of the U.S. population, heightened concern over the spread of infectious diseases, and a shift toward less invasive surgical procedures would assure continued global growth in the medical device sector.

The year 1998 was an excellent one for Furon, with sales up 24 percent, and earnings up 25 percent, increases attributed in large part to the Medex acquisition. Furon escaped the direct effects of the economic problems in the Far East where it had not yet gained a foothold, though the company had plans for future expansion into the region. While Furon experienced lower than expected demand for medical devices in the United States in 1998, European acquisitions and sales continued to grow.

Principal Subsidiaries

Fluorocarbon Components, Inc.; Sepco Corp.; Fluorocarbon Foreign Sales Corp.; CHR Industries, Inc.; Dixon Industries Corp.; Bunnell Plastics, Inc.; Ashfield Medical Systems, Ltd.; Medex.

Further Reading

Bissell, Ron, "Furon Introduces New Blood Pressure Monitoring System," *Bacon's*, August 15, 1998.
"Furon and GenCorp Report Increased Earnings," *Bacon's*, June 29, 1998.
"Furon Flying," *Forbes*, October 24, 1994, p. 312.
"Gridiron Wiring to Counter Lake Erie Winds," *WJI Industry News*, July 1, 1998, p. 16.

—Terri Mozzone

Furr's Supermarkets, Inc.

1730 Montano Road NW
Albuquerque, New Mexico 87107
U.S.A.
(505) 344-6525
Fax: (505) 761-0866

Private Company
Incorporated: 1904 as Furr's, Inc.
Employees: 5,600
Sales: $1 billion (1997 est.)
NAIC: 44511 Supermarkets & Other Grocery Stores;
   311812 Bakery Products, Fresh

Furr's Supermarkets, Inc. operates 68 grocery stores in New Mexico and west Texas under the names Furr's, Furr's Emporium, Bag 'n Save, and So:Lo. All boast "everyday low prices"; some stores also offer a video rental department, pharmacy, bank, or post office in addition to a full range of food items. Windward Capital Partners is the majority owner of the company in which grocery supplier Fleming Cos., Inc. has a 30 percent stake and management has six percent.

Foreign Ownership in the 1980s and Sellout in 1990–91

When West German-based Rewe-Liebbrand invested in Furr's, Inc. in 1979, it was one of several German companies seeking to find a safe haven for its money. The Texas-based chain, originally founded in 1904, had been on the brink of bankruptcy, but under its new ownership, it purchased an additional 13 stores from Safeway in 1987, bringing its total number of units to approximately 140. Of these, 55 were among the first supermarkets to have video departments, 15 were superstores known as Furr's Emporiums, and seven were Bag 'n Save warehouses.

When new opportunities opened up in Europe after the reunification of East and West Germany in 1990, Rewe-Leibbrand decided to move its investments back home. It began to liquidate its Furr's stores in the Texas panhandle and sought a buyer for the remainder of its operations in New Mexico and west Texas. Jan Friederich and Stuart Rosenthal, U.S.-based Liebbrand executives, seized upon the opportunity to orchestrate a management-led leveraged buyout. In March 1991 Furr's managers, led by Friederich and Rosenthal—and backed by Lubbock-based Fleming Cos., Inc., wholesalers—purchased about 75 stores, including the 13 former Safeways, and split off from Furr's, Inc. to become the new Furr's Supermarkets. Ibero American Bank of Hamburg, Germany, still owned 54 percent of the company and Fleming owned 40 percent, with management now in charge of the remaining six percent.

Chairman and CEO Friederich and President and COO Rosenthal immediately moved the company's headquarters from Lubbock, Texas, to Albuquerque, New Mexico, and began to change the focus and the look of the new chain's stores, emphasizing growth throughout existing locations via aggressive merchandising. Furr's, Inc. already enjoyed strong market penetration; historically, however, it had had fewer customers per store and fewer sales per square foot than its major competitors, Albertson's and Smith's. The late 1980s, during which an economic depression hit west Texas, had been a period of stagnation for the old Furr's. The company had continued nonetheless to use the same unsuccessful ad formats and display programs on which it had long relied. It also had been slow to carry new items. The new Furr's merchandising effort and look were thus part of an overall plan to update the store. In leaving the legacy of the old company behind, Rosenthal and Friederich set out to convince consumers to shop Furr's Supermarkets as their primary store and thereby to increase its same-store sales.

As part of this effort, Furr's began to remodel its stores. By mid-December 1991 the management team had completed 11 major and 24 minor remodels of units and plans were afoot to remodel 15 more units in 1992. There were also chainwide attempts to promote new items via in-store television monitors, newspaper ads, and shelf signage as well as through "Smart-Buy" in-store circulars in which products appeared at a deep discount for a two-week period. After finding out that customers' had an unfavorable perception of the chain's pricing, management opted to lower prices across the board and institute an "everyday low price program," which put it in more direct competition with other supermarkets. The chain also undertook merchandising changes to upgrade the quality and variety of goods and to create the impression of abundance. As one example, produce was displayed in open shipping crates in an attempt to create the feeling of a bustling farmers' market. In addition, it placed greater emphasis on volume-oriented merchandising, expanded grocery assortments, and switched from self-distribution to outside suppliers—Fleming for grocery and nonfood products and R.C. Taylor for tobacco and candy items.

Taking on the Competition in the Early 1990s

Repackaging itself continued to be a way of life for Furr's Supermarkets throughout 1992. After the successful farmers' market approach helped sales of fresh produce to rise, Furr's introduced its Kitchen Cupboard, a 48-square-foot boutique section located in a high traffic area of several stores, as a bid to cash in on the impulse-driven, high-margin kitchenware market. The chain's intent behind the introduction was to "group the [kitchenware] category into a cohesive presentation that says to shoppers this is where they can expect to find all these items, along with realistic price points," according to Jay Goble, vice-president of Furr's Supermarkets nonfood and pharmacy. Soon after the boutique was in place in the first few stores, initial reports showed "dramatic sales increases" in kitchenware sales and led to its incorporation chainwide. The chain also piloted 200 private-label items in categories such as baby care, feminine hygiene, oral hygiene, vitamins, and cough and cold care, which contributed to an increase in chainwide sales. In fact, sales of Furr's' own cough and cold products and analgesics increased during the 1993 nationwide slowdown in such items.

However, the nation's 73rd largest chain was not content to compete only with other supermarkets in its class. In 1992 Furr's Supermarkets opened So:Lo Fresh Mart, a new warehouse-type banner positioned against club stores, such as Wal-Mart's Sam's Clubs. The So:Lo format, which featured an expanded assortment of perishables and a wide variety of institutional-sized packaged goods and club-style packs, debuted in a 40,000-square-foot space that had previously housed a Furr's Bag 'n Save unit.

The chain also deepened its assault against the service sector with its 1993 introduction of 49-cent rentals on videos and the development of its in-store bakeries. Its "every video, everyday" low pricing on rentals was accompanied by the revamping and enlargement of five of its 27 existing video rental departments and the construction of seven new, larger video sections in selected stores. These new, self-enclosed, security protected departments housed up to 5,000 tapes as well as other value-added services including a micro lab to provide one-hour photo finishing, the sale of film and batteries, steam cleaner rentals, money orders, and lottery tickets. During the months following the changes in its video departments, Furr's video rentals increased fourfold, leading local video specialty retailers to picket the stores, claiming Furr's' pricing strategy was unfair and anticompetitive.

In Furr's bakery departments, changes also came in the direction of providing more service, although here the strategy was to eliminate items that did not meet the desired gross profit level in favor of those that did. The chain installed cookie depositors in each of its bakeries, and the percentage of store sales derived from bakery sales rose to well above three percent. Spurred on by the success of its bakery, Furr's next moved to expand its hot food program, taking on the fast-food industry and responding to the increasing trend in the United States toward buying prepared meals for consumption at home.

An Emphasis on Small, Neighborhood-Based Stores in the Early 1990s

Furr's Supermarkets were doing well across the board. Having sold two stores and purchased three since the 1990 buyout, Furr's' typical store began to see more customers. Although units' average transaction size continued to run several dollars below the company's big chain competition, Furr's saw real growth overall. According to Friederich, as early as 1992 Furr's Supermarkets were outperforming the industry, with sales gains in the double digits. Estimates for 1992 revenue were in the $900 million range.

Management attributed much of Furr's Supermarkets' success to its strategic plan, which called for responsiveness to consumers' needs. Viewing the relative smallness of Furr's stores when coupled with the fact that there were more Furr's per major market areas as a source of strength, the chain seized upon the opportunity to become a neighborhood convenience store as well as a primary store to customers. The chain began a concerted effort to serve its Mexican-American shoppers better by installing tortillerias in its larger Emporium stores and offering a range of Hispanic products in all stores in the early 1990s. Beginning in October 1991, Furr's began its "Education First" initiative in an effort to get involved in the communities it served, pledging more than $1 million in aid to schools in New Mexico and west Texas. It arranged to donate computers to schools that saved its cash register receipts on an ongoing basis; sponsored an afterschool "Homework Hotline" that provided free study assistance to New Mexico students; organized a "Stay-in-School" program encouraging Albuquerque youth to complete high school; and, in association with the American Heart Association, sponsored a health education program, "The Heart Treasure Chest."

In an unusual and highly successful move to incorporate consumers' preferences into its planning efforts in 1993, management of the Furr's Albuquerque store solicited area resident input prior to beginning its remodeling effort. It sent out a series of three letters mailed to about 8,000 households in which it asked what departments, products, and changes shoppers wanted to see in the remodeled 33,500-square-foot store. Drawing upon the 2,000 responses it received, Furr's Albuquerque added a scratch-and-mix bakery and a deli department and also expanded its seafood selection. Sales at the remodeled unit almost doubled after a block party was thrown for neighborhood residents. Although these sales figures later dropped to a 48 percent increase, Furr's attributed the continued increase to its efforts.

Changes in Management and FTC Woes in the Mid-1990s

It thus came as a surprise in July 1993 when Rosenthal resigned as the company's president, announcing as the reason for his resignation his desire to pursue other business plans. Furr's' concurrent act of excising five corporate staff positions and closing four stores in west Texas led to speculation that Rosenthal's departure was, in fact, part of a company move to reduce administrative costs. W.R. Buz Doyle, who assumed the position of president and chief operating officer eight months later in March 1994, immediately undertook the job of searching out new sources of revenue and new routes to expand the chain that was then enjoying annual sales of more than $1 billion.

Shortly before Doyle came on board, Furr's paid $400,000 in civil penalties to the FTC for violation—when it purchased a store it had formerly leased—of a 1988 order that required it to seek FTC approval prior to making any new acquisitions. The order levied against the old Furr's after it obtained the 13 Safeways had been intended to protect against any anticompetitive effects that would result from Furr's' increased presence in El Paso. As part of this ruling, Furr's was required to seek FTC approval prior to making any new acquisitions. If Furr's was to grow as planned, however, management felt that it needed to be able to add to its number of stores. Thus in April 1994 Furr's sought and was granted FTC approval for the purchase of four new stores and the retroactive purchase of one additional property. In April 1995 Furr's asked and was granted FTC approval to release it from restrictions requiring that it seek agency approval before buying any of the 57 stores it leased.

That July, Furr's received the financial resources it required to end foreign involvement in its business and increase the stake of the company held by its senior executives. Windward Capital Partners, a privately owned New York investment firm, acquired a majority interest in Furr's from a German investor, and proceeds of the deal went to provide capital to fund the chain's future growth plans: around $1 million to be spent during the next five years to remodel the majority of stores and accelerate the growth rate of new stores. Plans for expansion were accompanied by plans for computerizing services: training cashiers at CD-Rom workstations, installing electronic shelf labels, and selling online by 1999.

Computerization of operations also reached into the supply side of the business in late 1998. Following settlement of the 1997 dispute between Furr's and Fleming, whereby Furr's accused its distributor of fraud and unfair trade practices—failure to pass along discounts from manufacturers and breaking the agreed-upon markup terms of its ten-year supply contract—the company settled out of court for the right to purchase

Fleming's El Paso-based distribution center. This move meant building the chain's buying department and making changes in its accounting and warehousing systems; it began the process of implementing supply-chain software to handle its warehouse operations as well as its buying functions and billing and reconciliation processes. The system, which used radio frequency control on the forklifts, updated inventory levels and order status in real time; the buying system allowed buyers to see all available items as well as what deals were ahead or being terminated. The billing and reconciliation systems helped reduce use of paper and improved accuracy.

As Furr's headed into 1999, it launched an aggressive growth plan that included both continued remodels and new store development. It completed a six-month exploration of strategic alternatives and a review of prospective new investors with plans to open a Hispanic-format group of stores under the name La Feria.

Principal Divisions

Bag 'n Save; Furr's Emporium; So:Lo.

Further Reading

''Furr's Gets Go Ahead for 1993 Acquisition,'' *FTC Watch,* October 10, 1994.
Garry, Michael, ''Battle of the Networks,'' *Progressive Grocer,* February 1994, p. 69.
——, ''Chains: Starting Over,'' *Progressive Grocer,* February 1992, p. 111.
Gurin, Rick, ''Six Months to Supply Chain Management,'' *Automatic I.D. News,* January 1999, p. 13.
Ingram, Bob, ''Blinded by the Light,'' *Supermarket Business Magazine,* November 1993, p. 99.
Krumrei, Doug, ''Bet on the Spread: Furr's Supermarkets Inc.'s In-Store Bakery Program a Success,'' *Bakery Production and Marketing,* January 24, 1994, p. 22.
''Oops: Furr's Seeks Prior Post-Acquisition Approval,'' *FTC Watch,* June 6, 1994, No. 414.
Schwartz, Steve, ''Furr's Supermarkets Kicks Off Video-Expansion Plan,'' *Video Business,* February 5, 1993, p. 23.
Zwiebach, Elliot, ''Remaking Furr's,'' *Supermarket News,* December 16, 1991, p. 1.

—Carrie Rothburd

The Go-Ahead Group Plc

Level 16
Cale Cross House
Pilgrim Street
Newcastle upon Tyne NE1 6SU
United Kingdom
(44) 191 232 3123
Fax: (44) 191 221 0315
Web site: http://www.go-ahead.com

Public Company
Incorporated: 1913 as Northern General Transport
    Company
Employees: 8,464
Sales: £414.3 million (US$691 million) (1998)
Stock Exchanges: London
NAIC: 485210 Bus Line Operation, Intercity; 485113
    Bus Services, Urban & Suburban; 485112 Suburban
    Commuter Rail Systems; 485111 Suburban Transit
    Systems, Mixed Mode

From tiny regional bus company to a growing presence on the European urban transport scene, The Go-Ahead Group Plc is riding smoothly into the next century. Go-Ahead, based in northeastern England, has built a strong collection of bus and train transport services subsidiaries and has focused especially on London, one of the world's most active urban transport markets. The European market has been targeted for the company's future expansion, however. In 1998 Go-Ahead formed a strategic partnership with France's Via-Générale de Transport et d'Industrie SA (Via-GTI, a subsidiary of Compagnie Générale des Eaux), making a successful bid to take over operations of London's Thameslink train service. Go-Ahead also has joined in a consortium with other Europe-based transport providers. This consortium was awarded the contract for the operation of the Stockholm Commuter Railway in Sweden in early 1999. Go-Ahead holds a 39 percent share in this consortium. Go-Ahead's expansion ambitions have taken it beyond the urban transport market and into the broader transport market with the 1998 acquisition of London-based aviation services company GHI.

The centerpiece of Go-Ahead's urban transport services division is its two London bus subsidiaries, London Central and London General. The two bus lines operate more than 1,100 vehicles—the largest fleet of the famed red London buses, including the largest number of the world-renowned Routemaster double-decker buses. The two London subsidiaries, which employ more than 3,500 people and operate from ten garages, provide transportation to the Central and South London districts for more than 220 million passengers per year. Go-Ahead's London-based bus divisions, which operate under five-year contracts with that city's central transport authority, provide some 18 percent of the city's total passenger bus needs. As the Routemaster buses—some of which have been in continuous operation for more than 40 years, with more than one million road miles—are scheduled to be phased out by the year 2001, Go-Ahead has invested in modernization of its London fleet, including the purchase of some 200 new vehicles for 1999.

Go-Ahead's other bus operations include its predecessor company's former Northern bus line in the company's Tyne & Wear base; the Oxford Bus Company, serving that city; the Wycombe Bus Company; and the Brighton & Hove Bus and Coach Company. Go-Ahead's bus subsidiaries operate a combined fleet of more than 2,400 buses, with more than 8,700 employees serving nearly 400 million passengers per year.

Deregulated Transport in the 1980s

The introduction of motor-driven vehicles, including steam-powered, electric-powered, and internal combustion engines, and the creation of a network of paved roads gave rise to new forms of urban transportation. Tramways, at first steam-powered and later electric-powered, were developed by the 1880s, and the first vehicles serving as the forerunners to the modern bus concept appeared shortly after. Urban transport began as a private business concern. An early urban transport company was the Gateshead and District Tramways Company, which began operations in that northeastern area of England in 1883. Gateshead and District Tramways Company was taken

---

Company Perspectives:

Go-Ahead's corporate goal is to become: One of Europe's leading urban passenger transport providers. This will be measured in terms of: meeting customer needs; recognition of high quality standards; sensitivity to environmental issues; efficiency of operation and the generation of profits to support reinvestment. Go-Ahead will be a symbol of value, service, and quality against which all others in urban transport are judged, whilst caring for its customers and staff and being known as a quality partner for local authorities, communities and other operators.

---

over by the British Electric Traction Company in 1897. The company soon added electric-powered trams to its operations.

Developments in the internal combustion engine, and particularly of the diesel engine type, opened the way to new and larger types of vehicles. The motor bus, more flexible than the rail-limited tram, soon made its appearance on England's city streets and highways. The British Electric Traction Company added its own bus operations, through subsidiary Northern General Transport Company. This predecessor to the later Go-Ahead Group started operation in 1913.

The Northern General Transport Company quickly established itself as a leading public transport concern in the northeastern region. The company's expansion gave it the economies of scale to enable it to adopt an aggressive ticket pricing program. Northern General's competitors, unable to meet the company's prices due to their smaller fleets and lower passenger numbers, abandoned their routes to Northern General. At the dawn of World War II, Northern General had successfully established itself as the sole bus company in the Gateshead district.

Northern General's position would be further enhanced following the war. The British government chose to encourage development of the nation's bus routes, adopting laws that called for the substitution of buses for the country's remaining tram lines. By the 1950s all of the country's tram lines had been shut down. In that area, a new type of bus was introduced, one which would become famous the world over.

The Routemaster, as the red double-decker bus was called, was developed by Bill Shirley, who was named general manager of London's Park Royal company in 1953. The Routemaster featured a so-called "monocoque" design, in which the body and chassis were of one piece, making the bus both safer and more reliable. The first Routemaster entered service in 1956. In all, more than 3,000 of the double-decker buses were built before the end of production in 1970. Despite being more expensive to build than the standard type bus, the Routemaster sold well in London, so well that the distinctive red double-decker bus quickly became a symbol of London itself. Designed to last only 15 years, many Routemasters continued to provide service into the 1990s. By then, however, the aging of the fleet and the prohibitive cost of building new models caused the city to call for a phasing out of the Routemaster soon after the year 2,000.

The Routemaster would achieve success in part because of a major shift in urban transportation. In the 1950s the British government began taking control of the country's public transportation system. The United Kingdom's bus and train companies were nationalized. Bus transport was grouped under the government-run National Bus Company. The formerly independent bus companies were regrouped as some 70 regional subsidiaries.

In the 1970s, as the Arab Oil Embargo and resulting world economic crisis deepened, the British government began seeking ways to increase public transportation ridership and reduce the country's dependence on automobiles. Increasing the integration of the country's bus and train systems offered the prospect of attracting greater numbers of passengers. The Gateshead bus subsidiary would be among the pioneers of such an integrated approach, linking the areas bus routes with its Metro train and subway system, not only by introducing travel cards and transfer tickets good for both bus and train travel, but also by coordinating the two systems' schedules so that each could feed passengers to the other.

The move would help the Gateshead unit to maintain a healthy balance sheet into the 1980s. During that era the conservative government under Margaret Thatcher sought to privatize the many nationalized British industries. One of the first to be targeted was the country's public transport system. Express bus coaches, serving the interregional and rural markets, were privatized in 1980. The next step in deregulation was the opening of the country's urban bus routes to private ownership. This step was accomplished in 1985, for all British cities except London. The National Bus Company would be broken up entirely by the early 1990s, with its regional subsidiaries transformed into private companies, including several serving the London area.

The Gateshead district's Northern General Transport Company was taken over in a management buyout led by general manager Martin Ballinger in 1987. Northern General then changed its name to Go-Ahead Northern. The company continued to focus on its northeastern district, while developing greater ambitions.

Major Transport Player in the 1990s

Ballinger and the other buyout partners looked forward to bringing Go-Ahead Northern public to ease their debt load and see a return on their investment. To achieve a public listing, however, the company saw the need to expand and, especially, to gain a presence in England's crucial southern region. In 1993 Go-Ahead saw its opportunity, buying up the Brighton and Hove Bus and Coach Company, serving those southern communities. This purchase was followed by the acquisition of the Oxford Bus Company, including its Wycombe Bus Company subsidiary. Go-Ahead's focus, however, remained inevitably fixed on the London market, one of the world's busiest urban transportation markets.

Go-Ahead would continue to hover around London itself until 1994, when it acquired the London Central bus company and its important routes. In that year Go-Ahead went public on the London Stock Exchange, taking on the new name of The Go-Ahead Group. The London Central purchase was followed by the acquisition of London General, for £46 million, in 1996.

London General, one of the capital city's most important bus companies, gave Go-Ahead a commanding 18 percent share of the London metropolitan market. The company's routes served primarily the city's southern areas, which were poorly served by the London Underground. The London General acquisition also would give Go-Ahead one of the largest fleets of Routemasters.

Seeking to increase the integration of its services, as well as to enter new areas for expansion, Go-Ahead next turned its attention to the city's passenger railroads as these were being deregulated. In 1996 the company was awarded the contract for the operation of the Thames Trains regional franchise, serving the line between London and outlying areas. The franchise was to be held by Victory Railway Holdings, a joint venture established between Go-Ahead and Thames Trains management. The Thames Trains venture would get off to a rocky start, as technical problems and poor coordination with the railroad authority brought on a high percentage of train delays.

These difficulties did not deter Go-Ahead from going ahead with its railroad expansion plans. In 1997 the company was awarded the franchise for the Thameslink train system, operating between Bedford and Brighton and London, in partnership with the French company Via-GTI. The GoVia partnership also suggested The Go-Ahead Group's interest in international expansion.

This would follow quickly. In 1998 Go-Ahead announced that it had won the franchise for the operation of the Stockholm commuter rail network, in consortium with Via-GTI and the Sweden-based BK Tag. By now, Go-Ahead's ambitions extended to a new area of transportation services, that of airline services. In 1998 the company acquired London-based GHI and its Gatwick Handling and other subsidiaries, providing ground-handling, baggage, transport, and other airline support services to Gatwick and other airports. Under Go-Ahead, GHI secured a number of new contracts; several produced losses, however, and in February 1999 Go-Ahead announced that it was restructuring its GHI subsidiary and reducing its payroll.

Nonetheless, Go-Ahead as a whole continued to produce steady increases in revenue growth, as well as strong profits. The company began to take a leading role in antipollution and other environmental efforts, as well as efforts to reduce inner city congestion through guided bus routes, to counter criticism of buses in general while winning new ridership. As the United Kingdom's bus and rail market became settled in large part by the late 1990s, Go-Ahead's moves toward international expansion were seen as a strong play for making the company a major transportation provider for the 21st century.

Principal Subsidiaries

Brighton & Hove; London Central; London General; Oxford Bus Company; Wycombe Bus Company; Thames Trains; Thameslink; Go Northeast; Go Coastline; Go Gateshead; Go Northern; Go Wear Buses.

Further Reading

Clark, Andrew, "Go-Ahead Slams Railtrack Failings," *Daily Telegraph,* September 19, 1998.
"Go-Ahead Group Buys London General Bus Company for Pounds 46 Million," *Financial Times,* May 24, 1996.
"Go-Ahead On Track in Sweden," *Independent,* December 17, 1998, p. 18.
Grimond, Magnus, "Go-Ahead Buys Up London Bus Group for Pounds 46.1m," *Independent,* May 24, 1996, p. 23.
——, "Go-Ahead Keeps Motoring," *Independent,* May 24, 1996.

—M. L. Cohen

Golden Books FAMILY ENTERTAINMENT

Golden Books Family Entertainment, Inc.

888 Seventh Avenue
New York, New York 10106
U.S.A.
(212) 547-6700
Fax: (212) 547-6788
Web site: http://www.goldenbooks.com

Public Company
Incorporated: 1910 as Western Printing & Lithographing
    Co.
Employees: 1,200
Sales: $243.6 million (1997)
Stock Exchanges: NASDAQ
Ticker Symbol: GBFE
NAIC: 51113 Book Publishers; 323117 Book Printing;
    51211 Motion Picture & Video Production

Since 1996 when a new investor group took control of the company, Golden Books Family Entertainment, Inc., a leading publisher of children's books in the North American market, has been in a period of transition and restructuring that resulted in Chapter 11 bankruptcy filings in February 1999. Perhaps best known for its Little Golden Books line of children's books, which it began publishing in 1942, the company, under CEO Dick Snyder, was striving in the late 1990s to reach a broader audience as a producer of children's and family-oriented entertainment in all media. In the process, the company was restructured into three main business segments: Consumer Products, which included the Children's and Adult Publishing divisions; Entertainment, which included the Golden Books Entertainment Group (GBEG); and Commercial Products, which included the Commercial Printing division. In 1999, despite low sales and cash reserves, mounting losses, and a recent slump in stock value from $12 to 25 cents per share, a plan for emerging from its heavy debt load kept Golden Books afloat into the 21st century.

Early 1900s Origins

Golden Books can trace its beginnings to a printing operation begun in Racine, Wisconsin, in the early 1900s. In 1907

Edward Henry Wadewitz, with help from his brother, Al, purchased the West Side Printing Co. in Racine, Wisconsin. The following year Roy A. Spencer, a journeyman printer, joined West Side and together with the Wadewitzes developed a small firm, which was incorporated as Western Printing & Lithographing Co. in 1910.

In 1915 Western began printing books for the Hamming-Whitman Publishing Co., and when Hamming-Whitman defaulted on its bills, Western decided to liquidate the book stock itself. The next year Western acquired Hamming-Whitman's assets and formed a new subsidiary, Whitman Publishing Co. Soon the Whitman children's books were being sold on a grander scale at Woolworth Co. and other retail chains.

During the 1920s Western grew through a series of acquisitions. In 1923 it acquired the Broecker Box Co., which made boxed games and jigsaw puzzles, and purchased its first large press for high-volume book printing. Other acquisitions during this time included the Sheffer Playing Card Co. (1925) and the Stationers Engraving Co. (1929) of Chicago.

During the 1930s Western sought to establish a presence nearer the hub of the publishing industry, purchasing plant facilities in Poughkeepsie, New York, and opening two offices in New York City, one for Whitman Publishing Co. and the other for its Artists and Writers Guild Inc. (AWG) subsidiary, which was created to oversee new product development. AWG's presence in New York soon led to collaborative efforts with publishing giant Simon & Schuster, creating a relationship that would prove beneficial to Western. Also during this time, Western signed a contract with Walt Disney giving it exclusive book rights to all of Disney's licensed characters. Soon AWG and Simon & Schuster entered the juvenile book market together with the Walt Disney title *Bambi.*

The First Little Golden Books in 1942

While working on *Bambi,* executives at AWG and Simon & Schuster decided that a whole line of affordable books for American children might prove popular, and in 1942 the first Little Golden Books for children were published through a joint venture between Simon & Schuster and Western's AWG. Specifically, Simon & Schuster was the publisher of Little Golden

---
Company Perspectives:

The company owns one of the world's largest libraries of family entertainment copyrights and creates, publishes, and markets entertainment and educational products for children and their families through all media. Its extensive library includes Pat the Bunny, The Lone Ranger, Lassie, Underdog, Little Lulu, The Poky Little Puppy, Turok, *popular holiday animated programs, such as* Rudolph the Red-Nosed Reindeer *and* Frosty the Snowman, *and Shari Lewis'* Charlie Horse, Lamb Chop and Friends.

Books, AWG produced them, and Western printed them. The Little Golden Books represented a new direction in publishing for children in that they were inexpensive, easily available, and featured sturdy cardboard covers. According to former Western chairman Richard Bernstein, "They were the first books designed to be owned and cherished by children rather than borrowed from their parents."

The first 12 Little Golden Books titles to go on sale in October 1942 were priced at 25 cents apiece and included what would become enduring classics: *The Poky Little Puppy, Prayers for Children,* and *Three Little Kittens.* All 12 titles proved extremely popular, with an estimated 1.5 million copies printed within five months. By the mid-1940s, most of the 12 titles had gone into their seventh printings. The number of titles being offered by Little Golden Books increased rapidly; in January 1951, the 101st title, *Doctor Dan, the Bandage Man,* was released. In 1958 Western joined with Pocket Books Inc. to purchase Simon & Schuster's interest in Golden Books, and the new subsidiary was dubbed Golden Press, Inc.

Western established a reputation as an innovative publisher and printer. The company put out the first touch-and-feel book for children, *Pat the Bunny,* as well as the first scratch-and-sniff books and books that glowed in the dark.

Public Offerings and Acquisitions: 1960s–90s

In 1960 Western Publishing and Lithographing went public and shortened its name to Western Publishing. In 1961 it acquired Capitol Publishing, which made games, play kits, and other products. Western would enjoy great success in the late 1980s with its popular game *Pictionary.* By that time, however, Western had become a subsidiary of the toy manufacturer Mattel, Inc., which took over Western in 1978 during an acquisition spree. For the next five years, Western would not turn a profit, as parent Mattel stumbled to keep its holdings together.

In 1984 Richard Bernstein and some senior Western executives acquired a controlling interest in Western. Bernstein, a major real estate manager in Manhattan during the 1970s and a candidate for New York City comptroller in 1981, was attracted to Western, which had very little debt and about $29 million in cash reserves.

In 1986 Bernstein took the Western Publishing Group, Inc. public again, raising $80 million from the stock offering. At that time, the company had two subsidiaries: Western Publishing

Co. and Penn Corp. Penn manufactured and marketed disposable paper tableware and party goods, stationery and advertising specialties, and promotional business products. These products typically featured characters from Western's books.

The following year Western came out with a blockbuster boardgame called *Pictionary,* a variation of charades in which players took turns depicting names and phrases with pencil and paper for their teammates to guess. Book production continued apace as well, and new management believed they had turned the company around, as earnings hit a record $30 million on revenues of $550 million in 1989. By fiscal 1991 Western's revenues had increased to $554.5 million.

In 1992 Western celebrated the 50th anniversary of Little Golden Books. It was estimated that Western had sold 1.5 billion books in those 50 years. Having concentrated on mass market retail outlets for its books, in 1992 the company committed itself to improving relations with independent bookstores. However, retailers such as Kmart and Wal-Mart would remain the company's chief distributors. Also during this time Western adopted a policy of never letting its books go out of stock. The printing plants in Racine began creating excess inventories. As a result, the companies profits began to decline, as inventories eventually had to be sold for as little as five cents on the retail dollar.

As a result of this move, as well as from alleged financial mismanagement in general, Western lost more than $140 million from 1993 through 1996. In fiscal 1994, Western lost $55 million on sales of $617 million. Toward the end of 1993 Moody's Investors Service downgraded Western's bonds.

In response, Western began selling off parts of its business. After launching 20 new adult and juvenile games in 1993, the company completed the sale of its games and puzzles group to Hasbro Inc. in 1994. Also sold were its school book club business to Troll Associates and its direct marketing continuity clubs to Reader's Digest. The company's advertising specialty divisions were also sold.

New Ownership in the Mid-1990s

In 1996 an investment group led by Richard Snyder and media mogul Barry Diller, with the backing of venture capital firm Warburg, Pincus Ventures, paid $65 million for a controlling interest in Western and changed its name to Golden Books Family Entertainment, Inc. Snyder, former chairman and CEO of Simon & Schuster, became chairman and CEO of the newly named Golden Books. The deal was approved by Western's shareholders on May 8, 1996. While Snyder's long-term strategy was to "build a focused family entertainment company that goes well beyond books," his immediate priority was to revitalize the company's core business, mass market children's books. At the time of the sale, Western was the largest children's book publisher with some 3,300 employees.

Acting quickly, Snyder fired most of the company's management team and began assembling a new one. The company adopted a new business strategy, namely, to build a leading family entertainment company that would publish, produce, market, and license children's and family-related entertainment products. The company planned to build on the highly recognized Golden Books brand to develop family-oriented content through multiple media.

One of Snyder's first moves was to bring in Bob Asahina, a former senior editor at Simon & Schuster, to head a new adult division that would publish nonfiction titles for the adult market. Snyder also lured Willa Perlman from Simon & Schuster to head Golden's children's book division. Her first assignment was to renew the company's Star Wars licenses with George Lucas, who had become disillusioned with Western under Bernstein. She also renewed the company's five-year licensing deal with Jim Henson Productions for the Muppet characters.

In August 1996 Golden Books acquired an extensive library of character-based properties from Broadway Video Entertainment, L.P. Golden reportedly paid $81 million in cash and $10 million in stock for the company's family video library. Broadway Video was founded by Lorne Michaels and held the copyright and licenses to a variety of characters, films, and television programs. With the acquisition, Golden Books formed the Golden Books Entertainment Group (GBEG), which would be headed by Eric Ellenbogen, president of Broadway Video Entertainment. GBEG would generate revenues by licensing properties from this library to third parties. Among the library titles were *Rudolph the Red-Nosed Reindeer*, *Frosty the Snowman*, *Santa Claus Is Coming to Town*, *Lassie*, *The Lone Ranger*, and selected episodes of *Felix the Cat* and *Abbott and Costello*, among other titles.

Also announced was a strategic alliance with greeting card giant Hallmark, in which Hallmark would acquire $25 million of Golden's common stock in September 1996 and invest another $25 million by the end of 1996. The two companies intended to work together to develop personal expression, family entertainment, and personal development products. Hallmark envisioned a Golden Books section in its Kid Zones kiosks being test marketed at its 8,000 stores. Hallmark's acquisition of Golden's stock for $25 million gave it a 9.3 percent interest in the company.

Golden Books also moved to get out of commercial printing and other noncore businesses. In November 1996 it sold its Penn Corp. subsidiary to Peacock Papers, Inc., and in December 1997 it sold its Cambridge printing operation. The company was then organized into three divisions: Children and Adult publishing, Golden Books Entertainment Group (GBEG), and Commercial Printing. Once the reorganization was completed at the end of 1996 (with 1997 to be a transition year), the company's editorial, creative, marketing, and licensing staffs of the children's publishing division were consolidated in Golden's New York office. These functions had previously been split between New York and Racine. The reorganization left only Golden's manufacturing business in Racine, along with other support functions such as its MIS, financial, human resources, and legal staffs, which would also be moved to New York eventually.

For the year 1996, Golden Books reported a net loss of $197.5 million on sales of $254 million. The loss, however, included restructuring and other one-time charges of $132.3 million, which included $36 million in extraordinary items.

At the end of 1996, Golden Books surprised some observers by opting to maintain its Racine printing plant. To entice Golden Books to stay in Racine, the city and state had put together a financial package worth an estimated $5 million. Moreover, the plant's printing unions made wage and benefit concessions and agreed to changes in certain work rules. The company planned to move its in-house printing operation to a more efficient facility in Racine and eliminate about 200 jobs. It would maintain a workforce there of about 500.

As the company's restructuring took place and its new business strategy was implemented, Golden signed new licensing agreements, launched new publishing initiatives, built the new facility in Racine, and reorganized its sales force. In September 1997 the company signed a new, five-year license agreement with Disney that allowed Golden to use all of Disney's animated characters in selected product categories.

The company also reorganized its Children's Publishing division sales force, with a goal toward strengthening ties with customers and expanding sales through new retail channels. Among its new publishing initiatives was the signing of an agreement to publish the very popular R.L. Stine *Fear Street* books starting in March 1998.

In July 1997 Golden established the Golden Value Books and Special Markets business unit within the Children's Publishing division. Its objectives were to develop lower-priced value products for all retail channels and to pursue other specialty publishing opportunities outside the traditional retail channels, including book clubs, direct mail, electronic retailing, and television shopping. These products would be published under the Merrigold Press imprint. In September of that year the company launched its Adult Publishing list. Stressing family-oriented titles, the list featured Stephen Covey's *The Seven Habits of Highly Effective Families,* a *New York Times* bestseller. One industry observer would later suggest that Golden Books had overpaid for the Covey title as well as for its licensing agreements, causing the company to lose money despite healthy sales of popular products.

Nevertheless, the focus on building Golden Books as a family entertainment empire continued. The entertainment division (GBEG) expanded its library and television production operations with the acquisition of Shari Lewis Enterprises, Inc., in July 1997. In non-book publishing areas, GBEG signed licensing agreements with Swat-Fame, Inc., a leading manufacturer of children's wear, and with Eden LLC, a leading creator and manufacturer of infant toys, to manufacture products based on characters from the company's library, including characters from *Pat the Bunny* and *The Poky Little Puppy*. GBEG also entered into a strategic alliance with Sony Wonder, a division of Sony Music, to develop children's home video and audio products. For 1997, its first full year of operations, the GBEG division's revenues were $29 million, up from $4.1 million for 1996.

In July 1997 construction began on a new $40 million state-of-the-art manufacturing facility in Racine. Through an arrangement with the developer, the building was erected to Golden's specifications, and Golden would lease it on a long-term basis from the developer. Manufacturing operations commenced in February 1998, but the new plant would soon come to be regarded as a costly mistake, as it could not handle the production required of it.

The company continued its strategy of disposing of noncore business assets by selling its printing operations in Cambridge, Maryland, for approximately $20.2 million. Also sold was the Racine building that had housed the company's main plant for $2.4 million. In an effort by Golden to streamline its distribution channels and supply chain, the distribution center in Coffeyville, Kansas, was scheduled to be shut down by June 1998 and consolidated into the company's distribution facility in Crawfordsville, Indiana.

Liquidity Crisis in 1998

While Golden Books continued to be a popular item, their profit margin became increasingly slim. Moreover, some critics alleged that the company was squandering money on executive pay raises and perks. Whatever the cause, toward the end of 1998 the company began to experience serious financial problems. On September 15, 1998, Golden Books deferred a $5.7 million interest payment on its senior notes for 30 days, after which it was in default. This resulted in the company being in default on two credit agreements totaling $55 million. In November of that year the company received a commitment from a lender to allow it to borrow up to $45 million to be secured by a lien against the company's inventory, receivables, trade name, and other intellectual property assets.

In mid-1998 filings with the Securities and Exchange Commission (SEC), Golden Books stated that its new strategy had not been fully implemented, and that it did not expect to generate positive net income until after 1999 at the earliest. For the second quarter of 1998, the company reported a net loss of $30.6 million on sales of $43.1 million.

Following the second quarter loss, Moody's Investors Service downgraded $150 million of the company's senior notes and $115 million of its convertible trust originated preferred securities. The bond rating service was concerned that Golden Books would be forced to seek a restructuring and even possibly a sale. It also noted that the company's stock price had gone down, reducing the possibility of further public investment as a possible source of funds.

At the same time the investment group Golden Press Holdings, which consisted of Barry Diller, Richard Snyder, and Warburg, Pincus Ventures, announced it would commit an additional $25 million in investment, if necessary, that could be used at the company's option.

In early 1999 the company was in the process of restructuring its financing in order to solve its liquidity deficiency. During the previous 12 months its stock had lost most of its value, and

in February 1999 NASDAQ suspended trading of Golden Books stock. Then it was announced that Golden Books had developed a prearranged Chapter 11 bankruptcy plan. Under the plan, holders of preferred stock would receive 60 cents on the dollar and a 42 percent interest in the company. This move was expected to reduce the company's debt load from $300 million to around $87 million. Opponents to the plan were the common stockholders, including former CEO Bernstein, whose shares were annulled, or rendered valueless. Snyder, his board of directors, and management team, some of whom have left since the bankruptcy filings, hoped that this financial restructuring would enable Golden Books to continue operations and eventually become a healthy company in the next century.

Principal Divisions

Consumer Products; Entertainment; Commercial Products.

Further Reading

Foran, Pat, "Nahikian Steers Western Publishing Beyond the Survival Stage," *Business Journal-Milwaukee,* March 19, 1990, p. S10.

Goddard, Connie, "Fifty Years of Books 'For the Masses'," *Publishers Weekly,* June 22, 1992, p. 28.

"Golden Books, Bondholders Agree to Bankruptcy Plan," *Bloomberg News,* February 24, 1999.

"Golden Books Family Entertainment Announces Restructuring Agreement and New Financing Facility," *Business Wire,* February 24, 1999.

"Golden: Possible Profits in 2000?," *Publishers Weekly,* August 31, 1998, p. 15.

Gubernick, Lisa, "The Best Revenge," *Forbes,* October 21, 1996, p. 104.

Maughan, Shannon, "Golden Books, Sony Wonder in Co-Venture," *Publishers Weekly,* February 9, 1998, p. 25.

McCormick, Moira, "Golden Books Pursues Partnerships," *Billboard,* August 22, 1998, p. 75.

Milliot, Jim, "Bernstein Explains Western's 'Most Difficult Period'," *Publishers Weekly,* October 10, 1994, p. 10.

——, "Golden Books Defining New Strategies," *Publishers Weekly,* August 5, 1996, p. 272.

——, "Golden Completes Its Publishing Reorganization; Nelvana Buy Is Off," *Publishers Weekly,* November 11, 1996, p. 10.

Reid, Calvin, "Golden to Publish New Series by R.L. Stine," *Publishers Weekly,* August 18, 1997, p. 10.

Samuels, Gary, "Sorry About That, Folks," *Forbes,* August 29, 1994, p. 53.

Schnayerson, Michael, "Dick Snyder's Tarnished Crown," *Vanity Fair,* May 199, pp. 110+.

"Snyder Group to Buy Control of Western Publ.," *Publishers Weekly,* September 11, 1995, p. 10.

"Western Publishing Launches More Than 20 Games," *Playthings,* February 1993, p. 79.

—David Bianco

The Grand Union Company

201 Willowbrook Boulevard
Wayne, New Jersey 07470-0966
U.S.A.
(973) 890-6000
Fax: (973) 890-6671

Public Company
Incorporated: 1916 as Jones Brothers Tea Co.
Employees: 15,000
Sales: $2.27 billion (1998)
Stock Exchanges: NASDAQ
Ticker Symbol: GUCO
NAIC: 44511 Supermarkets & Other Grocery Stores;
    44512 Convenience Stores

The Grand Union Company is a food retailer operating 222 Grand Union supermarkets in six states, including 123 in New York, 40 in Vermont, 41 in New Jersey, 13 in Connecticut, three in New Hampshire, and two in Pennsylvania. The stores, each of which is designed to meet local needs, range in size from 7,000 to 64,000 square feet and feature a wide variety of brand-name and private label groceries. Some units include cafes, pharmacies, and alcoholic beverage departments. The company also has begun experimenting with alternative formats in selected locations, including Hot Dot Foods Market, a limited-assortment store. Grand Union struggled mightily through the 1990s, losing money every year and twice entering into bankruptcy protection.

Early History

Cyrus, Frank, and Charles Jones founded what was to become Grand Union in 1872. They called the business the Jones Brothers Tea Co., starting with one store in Scranton, Pennsylvania, where the shelves were stocked with coffee, tea, spices, baking powder, and flavoring extracts. The brothers expanded the business steadily, branching out with new stores in eastern Pennsylvania, Michigan, and New York. By the time it built its headquarters and warehouse in Brooklyn, New York, the company was known as the Grand Union Tea Co.

In 1912 Grand Union was a 200-outlet chain store with operations across the country. In addition to its business establishments, the company supported a small army of 5,000 door-to-door salesmen and delivered goods in horse-drawn wagons. The brothers incorporated the Jones Brothers Tea Co. in 1916.

Grand Union used its financial strength through the 1920s to acquire other food businesses, including Progressive Grocery Stores, the Union Pacific Tea Co., and Glenwood stores. After merging with the Oneida County Creameries Co. in 1928, the Jones brothers reincorporated under the Grand Union name.

During the 1930s Grand Union grew to be one of the country's most thriving food chains. In 1931 the company had 708 small stores and $35 million in sales.

The next decade saw the development of the "supermarket" concept. The idea was to house a range of groceries, including meat, dairy products, and inedible packaged goods, under one roof. When Lansing P. Shield took over as Grand Union president in the early 1940s, he embraced the supermarket format and plunged the company forward into a new era of food marketing. Grand Union was one of the first companies to utilize the format.

Shield helped evolve the supermarket concept by demanding that the spacious supermarkets be designed carefully so as not to overwhelm customers used to smaller shops. Shield suggested breaking down the open spaces by building more walls and dispersing special product displays throughout the aisles. By the mid-1950s, Grand Union operated about half the number of stores it did in the 1930s, but the stores turned out nearly seven times the volume of sales. By then the company had outgrown its Brooklyn headquarters. It opened a new facility in Elmwood Park, New Jersey, in a red brick tower that was later to become a community landmark.

Launched New Formats, from 1956 Through the Early 1970s

When grocery stores became involved in the discounting business, Grand Union was again one of the first in the food business to welcome the idea. The first Grand Union general merchandise discount store, called Grand Way, opened in 1956 in

Keansburg, New Jersey. After the Keansburg store proved a success, the company opened another in Albany, New York. By 1962 Grand Union was operating 21 discount stores. To keep the stores running smoothly, Chairman Thomas Butler hired Joseph L. Eckhouse, formerly the head of the Gimbel Bros. department store in New York, to oversee them. Eckhouse envisioned the Grand Way stores as a place to buy quality goods and fashionable clothing at lower prices than department stores. Eckhouse died, however, before his vision could be fully realized.

Grand Union, which reached $1 billion in sales in 1968, continued to open additional Grand Way stores and enter new retail businesses, including convenience food stores, trading stamps, and catalog showrooms for discounted general merchandise. As competitive pressures increased in the early 1970s, Grand Union entered another phase of supermarketing: the so-called superstore. These shopping emporiums sought to provide customers with myriad products of every kind at one locale. A Grand Union superstore, for example, offered consumer items in such diverse areas as prescription drugs, auto parts, clothing, shoes, and household gadgets, as well as the usual mix of groceries. By 1973 Grand Union was operating ten such superstores. Although these new businesses were not failures, they did not contribute enough to the company's bottom line to justify their continued existence. By the early 1970s they had begun to lose their luster and Grand Union began divesting itself of many of them.

Taken Over by Cavenham in 1973

In 1973 Grand Union stock was trading at less than half of book value and the company seemed to be stagnating. The company's status attracted the interest of Cavenham Ltd., a British food conglomerate, which made a $19-per-share tender offer for control of the company. The move by Cavenham, which was owned by financier James Goldsmith, marked the first significant foreign investment in U.S. food retailing. When the $64 million deal was finalized in December 1973, Cavenham quickly appointed Englishman James Wood as president. Wood wasted little time in shaking up what was then the ninth largest supermarket chain in the country.

Wood sparked the divestment of Grand Union's nonfood businesses, reorganized its management structure, and established a new image for the store based on low prices. Wood oversaw a Grand Union that had 534 supermarkets in New York, New Jersey, Connecticut, Massachusetts, Vermont, New Hampshire, Pennsylvania, Maryland, Virginia, West Virginia, Florida, Puerto Rico, and the U.S. Virgin Islands. The company's nonfood operations consisted of 23 Grand Way stores, 18 Grand Catalog discount stores, 18 E-Z shop convenience stores, a food equipment subsidiary, and the Stop & Save Trading Stamp division. After only a year Cavenham stripped Grand Union of 31 supermarkets, pulled back its trading stamp operations, and closed nine Grand Way outlets. Grand Union's performance for fiscal year 1974 was $2.3 million in net income, down from $8.4 million the year before. Sales, however, climbed for the year from $1.4 billion in fiscal 1973 to $1.5 billion in fiscal 1974. The following year Grand Union sold its E-Z shop division and closed five of its catalog showrooms.

The divestitures did have their price. In 1975 Wood stated that phasing out trading stamps completely would result in a

$5.75 million charge against earnings. In addition, the elimination of the nine Grand Way stores cost the company a $10 million pretax write-off. By 1978, however, Grand Union was ready to expand again. The company started opening new stores and acquired several regional supermarket chains in the Southeast and Southwest, including Colonial Stores in 1978. Three years later Grand Union merged with J. Weingarten Inc., a Texas supermarket chain, which became an affiliate of the company. By 1982 the chain boasted 856 stores with outlets as far west as Texas, as far north as Canada, and as far south as Florida. The expansion was a gamble that eventually cost Grand Union more than it bargained for. In fiscal 1982 the company reported a record sales level of $4.1 billion, twice as much as what was recorded just three years ago. The drain on earnings proved to be drastic, however, with a drop of 30 percent to $24 million. "We screwed it up," said James Goldsmith in an article for *Business Week*.

After that calamitous financial performance, Grand Union again entered a phase of heavy consolidation. The biggest drop in the number of stores came in fiscal 1982, when it closed 150 stores. By November 1982 another 62 units were gone, leaving the company with just 671 supermarkets. The revamped organization was centered in New England and New York, with a few sites in Virginia, Georgia, and the Carolinas.

By ridding itself of money-draining nonfood operations and trimming the number of its outlets, Grand Union showed a renewed devotion to food marketing. In 1979 it introduced its Food Market prototype, a 45,000-square-foot supermarket with specialty departments featuring gourmet foods such as stuffed artichokes, specially blended coffees and teas, baked goods, and imported cheese. The company planned to spend the bulk of its $700 million capital improvement budget over six years to convert most of its units to the Food Market prototype.

Food Markets were a hit with shoppers. Imported wines and ready-to-cook dinners such as fish and poultry were finding steady buyers, but the conversion project proved to be very expensive. The average cost of turning a store into a Food Market was $1.5 million. By 1982 a total of 70 stores had been converted at a cost of $100 million. The project contributed to another poor performance for the fiscal year ended April 1983. The store reported operating losses of $20 million, although it posted a $226,000 bottom-line profit. As Goldsmith put it in the *Business Week* profile, "We managed to turn a dull but fairly profitable chain into an exciting loss-maker." Some rivals blamed Grand Union for not doing enough research before converting a store to a Food Market. The converted sites that did well were located in areas with higher incomes rather than working class neighborhoods.

Other supermarkets were selling gourmet foods, but they covered the cost with profitable general merchandise departments, a business Grand Union abandoned after Cavenham Ltd. bought the company. Nonetheless, Goldsmith hoped that the expensive luxury food items eventually would make the store some money.

Ever on the lookout to maintain and improve upon the slim profit margins of the supermarket industry, Grand Union introduced another marketing innovation in 1983 to help increase its business. To help convince shoppers they were getting the lowest prices at Grand Union, the store began publishing a free booklet listing prices on some 9,000 products. The company hoped that shoppers would use the booklet if they found themselves in a competitor's store; with the booklet, they could then determine that Grand Union's prices were cheaper. If a shopper found an item at a cheaper price, Grand Union promised to match it. Despite the expense of the new program, which cost about $80 million to create and promote, some stores reported an increase in sales as high as 25 percent.

Meanwhile, the company was still struggling in its efforts to return to profitability. In the fiscal year ended in April 1984, it posted a $115.2 million loss due to store closings concentrated in Florida, Washington, D.C., and Texas, a strike at its New Jersey stores, and the start-up costs of the new pricing program. Sales for the year dropped two percent from the previous year's $3.52 billion to $3.44 billion.

Taken Private in 1989

All efforts to put the supermarket giant back on track were not enough to keep Goldsmith from finally deciding to sell it. In 1989 Grand Union was bought for $1.2 billion by an investor group headed by Salomon Brothers Inc. and Miller Tabak Hirsch & Company, two New York investment banking firms. At the time, Grand Union was the 11th largest supermarket chain in the country with $2.7 billion in sales, 306 Grand Union and Big Star stores, and 21,000 employees. The two buyout partners each received a 40 percent interest in the company, with the remaining 20 percent held by senior management. The buyout of Grand Union added another $325 million to the company's $300 million in high-yield debt and another $545 million in bank loans.

Under its new owners, Grand Union set another course to improve its business. This meant offering more items in bulk and larger sizes and more competitive pricing through discounting, price freezes, and buy-one, get-one-free offers. In 1991 the company introduced its own line of environmentally sound paper products.

Three years after the 1989 deal Grand Union's ownership shifted again when Salomon Brothers sold its interest in the company to Miller Tabak Hirsch & Company's affiliate, GAC Holdings L.P., which owned 41 percent of the GND Holdings Corp., the parent company of Grand Union. In fiscal 1991 Grand Union's numbers were still disappointing, with a loss of $53.8 million on $2.92 billion in sales. Grand Union was sold again in 1992 when a group led by Gary Hirsch, a principal of Miller Tabak, bought GND Holdings and formed a new holding company, Grand Union Holdings Corp.

Filed for Chapter 11 Protection in 1995 and 1998

The crushing load of debt from the buyouts, coupled with heightened competition in the food retailing sector, left Grand Union to flounder during the entire decade of the 1990s. In pure numerical terms the nadir came in 1993 when the company lost $313 million. That year Grand Union sold 48 of its 51 Big Star stores to A&P for $20-$25 million in cash; soon thereafter, Grand Union was reduced to only one format—the Grand Union stores, with 251 units carrying that banner in the Northeast. In November

1994 the company announced that it would sell or close up to 25 of its underperforming units. At the same time the company was negotiating with its creditors about restructuring its $2.1 billion in debt. In January 1995 Grand Union filed for Chapter 11 bankruptcy protection in a prepackaged arrangement with its creditors. The company emerged in June of that year having reworked its capital structure and reduced its debt by $600 million. Hirsch was replaced as chairman of the company by Roger E. Strangeland, who had retired as chairman and CEO of the Vons Companies, Incorporated—an Arcadia, California-based food retailer—in May 1995. Joseph J. McCaig remained president and CEO of Grand Union, which emerged from Chapter 11 as a public company trading on the NASDAQ, with 231 stores in six northeastern states—New York, Vermont, New Jersey, Connecticut, New Hampshire, and Pennsylvania.

The company was hardly out of the woods yet. It continued to lose money every year and, with its balance sheet still overleveraged, was unable to expend the resources necessary to upgrade its many outdated stores and increase their size. Restructurings followed. In January 1996 Grand Union announced a plan to consolidate its administrative, support, and grocery marketing operations at the corporate headquarters in Wayne, New Jersey. In late 1996 the company received the first portion of a $100 million cash infusion from the sale of preferred stock to an investment group that included affiliates of Shamrock Capital Advisors, the Roy E. Disney family, and the General Electric Pension Fund. This investment group thereby gained majority control over Grand Union. Proceeds from the sale were earmarked to partially fund a $240 million, three-year capital spending plan that aimed to renovate, expand, replace, or add a total of 78 units. Just as this plan was being launched a series of executive departures rocked the company. By March 1997 CFO Kenneth Baum, COO William Louttit, and Executive Vice-President of Operations Darrell Stine had all resigned. Two months later McCaig resigned as president and CEO, citing philosophical differences with the board over the company's direction. McCaig was temporarily replaced by Strangeland; in August 1997 J. Wayne Harris, a former A&P and Kroger Company executive, was named chairman and CEO. Then in October of that year Gary Philbin joined Grand Union as president and chief merchandising officer, having previously worked as an executive at Cub Foods.

Meanwhile, in June 1997 Grand Union announced yet another restructuring, this one involving a reduction in operating divisions from four to two, a restructuring of the merchandising departments, and the elimination of about 80 jobs, mainly at company headquarters. Nonetheless, the company was still struggling to compete against its main rivals, Giant Foods and Stop & Shop, both of which operated stores that were newer and larger than those of Grand Union. The company neared bankruptcy again in August 1997 but was able to secure $250 million in credit that allowed it to stay out of default. In September 1997 the company's stock began trading on the NASDAQ SmallCap Market, after the price fell below $4.

By early 1998 the company remained weighed down by approximately $1 billion in debt. Sales were on the decline, and for the fiscal year ending in March 1998 Grand Union posted a net loss of $304 million. In February 1998 Grand Union defaulted on a loan payment and began negotiations with its creditors on another prepackaged Chapter 11 bankruptcy plan. In May of that year the company's stock was delisted from the NASDAQ SmallCap and began trading over the counter. Grand Union entered Chapter 11 protection in June 1998, emerging two months later having reduced its debt by $600 million. In October 1998 the company regained its listing on the NASDAQ national market. Grand Union then embarked on a program to open new stores and modernize its existing stores, adopting a more contemporary look. It also intended to experiment with alternative formats geared to specific marketing areas, such as the limited-assortment format christened Hot Dot Foods Market, the first of which opened in January 1999 in Winooski, Vermont. Whether these moves marked the beginning of Grand Union's resurrection remained to be seen.

Principal Subsidiaries

Grand Union Stores of New Hampshire, Inc.; Grand Union Stores, Inc., of Vermont; Merchandising Services, Inc.; Specialty Merchandising Services, Inc.

Further Reading

"The Bargain That Wasn't," *Forbes,* August 21, 1978.

Bartlett, Sarah, "$1.2 Billion Buyout of Food Stores," *New York Times,* April 11, 1989.

Bralove, Mary, "Grand Union Becomes a Much Tauter Ship Under British Captain," *Wall Street Journal,* January 31, 1975.

——, "Superstores May Suit Customers to a T: A T-Shirt or a T-Bone," *Wall Street Journal,* March 13, 1973.

Brennan, Robert J., "Salomon to Sell Grand Union Stake to Miller Tabak," *Wall Street Journal,* April 14, 1992.

A Brief History of the Grand Union Company, Wayne, N.J.: Grand Union Company, 1993.

DeMarrais, Kevin G., "Grand Union Supermarkets File for Bankruptcy, Try to Change Image," *Record* (Hackensack, N.J.), November 17, 1998.

Gattuso, Greg, "Grand Union Sets Capital Realignment, Chapter 11," *Supermarket News,* April 6, 1998, p. 1.

"Grand Union Converts to Full-Service," *Chain Store Age Executive,* November 1982.

"Grand Union Expects a $5,750,000 Charge from Stamp Phaseout," *Wall Street Journal,* June 19, 1975.

"Grand Union Gets Another Cash Infusion from Backers," *Supermarket News,* March 3, 1997, pp. 1+.

"Grand Union: Jimmy Goldsmith's Maverick Plan to Restore Profitability," *Business Week,* May 14, 1984.

"Grand Union's Grand Scheme," *Progressive Grocer,* October 1983.

"Grand Union's Loss More Than Doubled in Fiscal 4th Quarter," *Wall Street Journal,* June 11, 1984.

Klepacki, Laura, "Grand Union Unveils Plans for Tough Times," *Supermarket News,* October 14, 1991.

Lebhar, Godfrey M., *Chain Stores in America, 1859–1962,* 3rd ed., New York: Chain Store Publishing, 1963.

Orgel, David, "Grand Union Is Revamping Its Structure, Cutting Staff," *Supermarket News,* June 2, 1997, pp. 1+.

Tibbits, Lisa A., "Grand Union's Grand Visions Set to Boost Image, Sales," *Supermarket News,* February 19, 1996, pp. 1+.

——, "Restructuring Underway at Grand Union," *Supermarket News,* January 29, 1996, pp. 1+.

"Tough Times Lead to Tougher Posture," *Progressive Grocer,* October 1984.

Zimmerman, M.M., *The Super Market: A Revolution in Distribution,* New York: McGraw-Hill, 1955.

Zwiebach, Elliot, "A&P Agrees to Purchase 48 Big Stars," *Supermarket News,* February 15, 1993, pp. 1+.

——, "Chapter 11 Plan Filed by Grand Union Co.," *Supermarket News,* January 30, 1995, pp. 1+.

——, "Grand Union Bankruptcy Plan Gets Court's OK," *Supermarket News,* June 5, 1995, pp. 1+.

——, "Grand Union Contends Performance Improving," *Supermarket News,* November 3, 1997, pp. 1+.

——, "Grand Union Details Expansion Plan," *Supermarket News,* February 1, 1999, pp. 4, 55.

——, "Grand Union Exits Chapter 11: CEO Sees 'A Bright Future,' " *Supermarket News,* August 24, 1998, p. 1.

——, "Grand Union Names A&P Executive to Take Helm," *Supermarket News,* August 11, 1997, pp. 1+.

——, "Grand Union Poised for Challenges," *Supermarket News,* June 12, 1995, pp. 4+.

——, "Grand Union Reorganizing to Cut Costs," *Supermarket News,* August 1, 1994, pp. 1+.

——, "Planning to Be Grander," *Supermarket News,* January 18, 1999, pp. 1, 10–15.

—Julie Monahan
—updated by David E. Salamie

GreenPoint Financial Corp.

90 Park Avenue
New York, New York 10016
U.S.A.
(212) 834-1000
Fax: (212) 834-1711
Web site: http://www.greenpoint.com

Public Company
Incorporated: 1868 as The Green Point Savings Bank
Employees: 1,739
Sales: $1.06 billion (1998)
Stock Exchanges: New York
Ticker Symbol: GPT
NAIC: 52212 Savings Institutions; 522292 Real Estate
    Credit; 551111 Offices of Bank Holding Companies

GreenPoint Financial Corp. is a bank holding company whose bank subsidiary, GreenPoint Bank, had 73 branches in the New York City metropolitan area in 1998. Through its mortgage lending subsidiary, the company was the national lender in no-documentation residential mortgages. With a 1998 acquisition, Greenpoint also became the second ranking originator and servicer of manufactured home loans in the United States. In addition, it was operating a for-profit community development subsidiary in the New York City metropolitan area.

Green Point Savings Bank to 1990

Located at the northwest end of Brooklyn, Greenpoint was still a small, quiet community in 1868, when prominent local citizens received a state charter to establish The Green Point Savings Bank, a mutual thrift institution and the forerunner of GreenPoint Bank. It opened for business the following year and collected about $135,000 in deposits in the first year of operation. By 1880 its deposits had grown fivefold, and they tripled again by 1885. Deposits reached more than $5 million in 1905. After moving several times, the bank, in 1908, settled into its own newly erected granite-faced building at Manhattan

Avenue and Calyer Street. The bank's assets came to $12.4 million in 1918.

In 1928 Green Point opened a branch in another Brooklyn neighborhood, Crown Heights. After merging with the troubled Home Savings Bank in 1931, however, Green Point moved this branch to Flatbush. Green Point had 77,109 depositors and $65.1 million in assets at the beginning of 1940 and 105,546 depositors and $159.3 million in assets at the end of 1950. Net profits came to $3.35 million that year. The bank opened a branch in Canarsie in 1952. By the end of 1960 the number of depositors had grown to 132,813, assets to $296.7 million, and net profit to $10.2 million. Green Point opened a branch in Flushing, Queens, in 1967 and in Levittown in Nassau County in 1969.

Green Point Savings Bank had 168,765 depositors at the end of 1970, $588.6 million in assets, and $25 million in net profits for the year. The number of depositors was 218,856, and assets were $1.18 billion, at the end of 1980. In the 1970s and early 1980s, the bank opened three more Brooklyn branches, one in Queens, and four in Nassau County communities. In 1983 Green Point was making more mortgage loans in Brooklyn, Queens, and Nassau County than any other lender—even Citibank, which was 80 times bigger. The bank earned $7.6 million in 1982, a year in which 90 percent of all U.S. savings institutions were reporting losses because of high interest rates.

The corporation's success in this field was attributed to its willingness to make mortgage loans without requiring verification of such basic information as income or place of employment. Many of its clients were people who earned more money than they declared on their tax returns, said the bank's president, adding "We are not the I.R.S." Most of its borrowers were choosing an "automatic credit" mortgage, which only required checking the applicant's name with a credit bureau. Even if the credit report showed that the applicant was in arrears of bills or loans, Green Point might still approve the mortgage, though at a higher price. In some cases the bank would make the loan even if the customer could not meet the 25 percent down payment. In spite of its customer-friendly policies, Green Point was experiencing fewer foreclosures than most other mortgage lenders.

The bank also was making mortgage loans expeditiously. Its business in this field came 90 percent of the time from real estate brokers and lawyers, and within two days of the initial call from these sources, it was sending out an appraiser to inspect the property. Because of a simplified form, its personnel could process about 14 appraisals a day, compared to only three or four if they were using standard appraisal forms requiring depreciating every major item in the house individually.

In 1987 Green Point Savings Bank entered Westchester County for the first time and by mid-1988 had 16 branches. In 1987 the bank launched a highly successful referral network that encouraged real estate professionals to send it customers. "We rarely turn a loan down," bank president I. J. Lasurdo told Phil Roosevelt, "but we may charge extra fees or higher interest rates, depending on the problems surrounding the particular application." The bank's mortgage portfolio represented about 85 percent of its total assets, which had reached $3.2 billion in 1988. Its return on assets was among the highest of any thrift institution in the state of New York. The bank had net income of $78 million in 1989, a year in which *American Banker* ranked it third strongest among the nation's 100 largest thrifts and the strongest on the East Coast. Assets reached $5.12 billion in 1990.

From Bank to Holding Company: 1990–95

Green Point Savings Bank's high profile in the mortgage market was not without its hazards, however. During the recession of the early 1990s, in poor Brooklyn neighborhoods a number of dilapidated apartment buildings for which the bank held mortgages were abandoned. Although Green Point had built a reputation for helping residents and community groups in minority neighborhoods, it now was faulted for failing to respond to hazardous building conditions or provide heat, hot water, and other services, sometimes for months. The bank's explanation that it was not legally entitled to enter premises until the foreclosure process was completed did not deflect criticism. One city housing official told Barbara W. Selvin of *New York Newsday,* "Green Point has stood in the way of our getting [our] administrators in buildings, or our getting services restored in buildings they've had put under receivership." In 1993 the bank established a subsidiary to help low- and moderate-income persons in the metropolitan area find affordable housing.

With one of the highest capital-to-assets ratios in the thrift industry, Green Point was still in robust health in 1992, It ranked first in the dollar amount of residential mortgages in Brooklyn, Queens, the Bronx, Staten Island, and Long Island. The core customer remained a heavy saver in a blue-collar neighborhood. Green Point's chairman and president said that,

though the bank had tightened its credit standards, it was still more liberal than most banks. It could afford to be so because it restricted itself mainly to lending money on houses in neighborhoods where its appraisers kept a sharp eye on appropriate values, with a maximum mortgage of $400,000. Although Green Point's level of nonperforming loans was higher than the thrift industry's average, it also received higher yields in order to compensate for higher risk.

Green Point Savings Bank bought four branches in Westchester and Rockland counties from CrossLand Federal Savings Bank in early 1993, raising the number of its branches to 25. It moved its headquarters to Flushing around this time. With 246,000 depositors and $6.5 billion in deposits, Green Point was the nation's largest mutual savings bank when, in December 1993, its depositors approved a plan to convert it from mutual to stock ownership. The conversion received state sanction the following month, but the state rejected a provision that called for the bank's top officials and trustees to receive a financial package of an estimated $30 million and ordered the company to add three new independent trustees to monitor the bank's affairs.

The company raised $786 million in its initial public offering by selling a majority of its common stock at $15 a share. In 1995 the bank purchased 60 New York branches of Home Savings of America, FSB, with $8.3 billion in deposits, from H.F. Ahmanson Inc. for some $600 million. This acquisition brought Green Point into Manhattan and Suffolk County for the first time as well as enhanced its presence in Brooklyn, Queens, and Westchester County. Also in 1995, the bank's holding company acquired the national wholesale residential mortgage lending operation of Barclay/America/Mortgage Corp., a subsidiary of Barclays Bank PLC. This operation remained based in Charlotte, North Carolina. A subsidiary of the bank, it took the name GreenPoint Mortgage Corp. The bank itself, which dropped "Savings" from its title in 1995, was now a subsidiary of GreenPoint Financial Corp., a holding company established in May 1995.

National Mortgage Lender: 1996–98

The Barclay acquisition enabled GreenPoint Financial to take its mortgage loan business nationwide, at a pace of $2.4 billion in 1996, a 140 percent increase from the previous year. Most of these loans—offered in 10 markets outside New York City by early 1997—were no documentation, or "no-doc," loans that the mortgage subsidiary offered to home buyers who were having trouble meeting the usual income and credit standards. In return for the loans, they put up larger down payments—at least 25 percent—and paid higher interest rates and loan fees. (GreenPoint also offered low documentation, or "low-doc," mortgage loans, with a reduced rate for the provision of certain income documentation. The low-doc product was discontinued in February 1997.) Unlike many other thrift institutions, the company was holding on to all its mortgages instead of reselling them.

Skeptics said GreenPoint Financial's no-doc mortgage loans were producing results only because property values were growing significantly due to boom times, allowing the mortgage subsidiary virtually to recover its investment when borrowers defaulted. But Thomas S. Johnson, GreenPoint's chairman and president, said its secret was "management discipline," according to Karen Talley, with checks and double checks, instead of the scattershot approach he said produced volume for other lenders but also led to lax standards. Johnson said that because appraisals had to be dead accurate, GreenPoint Mortgage was maintaining its own corps of appraisers instead of, as most other lenders, farming the work out. It was lending no more than 75 percent of a property's appraised value or purchase price. The company frequently was choosing to foreclose rather than renegotiate or restructure a nonperforming loan and was collecting 97 cents on the dollar when it did foreclose.

GreenPoint Financial entered another field in 1998, when it purchased BankAmerica Housing Services, which it renamed GreenPoint Credit Corp., for $703 million. The acquired company was originating and servicing manufactured housing loans for BankAmerica Corp. through a sales and service network of 45 offices with more than 5,000 dealer relationships in 48 states. It ranked second in such mortgages in 1996, with 16 percent of about $12.6 billion originated in the manufactured housing sector. When BankAmerica closed NationsCredit Manufactured Housing Corp., the nation's fourth largest manufactured housing lender, in December 1998, GreenPoint said it would buy the unit's dealer contacts for an undisclosed amount.

Also in December 1998, GreenPoint Financial moved to double its lending capacity by purchasing Headlands Mortgage Co. for $473 million. Headlands was a specialist in "alt-A" loans to borrowers who did not quite meet the guidelines of Freddie Mac and Fannie Mae, names given to government-sponsored enterprises purchasing the bulk of mortgage loans. Headlands, whose sales force was strongest in the West, while GreenPoint's was strongest in the East, had originated more than $6.8 billion in loans in 1998 by early December.

GreenPoint Financial Corp. in 1997

GreenPoint Financial's revenues remained steady at $1.03 billion in 1997, but its net income rose to $147.6 million. A share of stock traded as high as $75.50 during 1997, leading to a two for one stock split in March 1998. Mortgage originations reached $2.85 billion in 1997, and the company was offering mortgages in 25 cities by March 1998. Nonperforming assets were remaining at a steady rate of 2.9 percent of the company's total assets, which were $13.1 billion in 1997. The long-term debt was $399.5 billion at the end of 1997. Revenues and income rose only slightly in 1998, to $1.06 billion and $149.5 million, respectively.

At the end of 1997 GreenPoint Mortgage was servicing about 95,000 residential mortgage loans with outstanding principal balances of $9.6 billion, including $8.9 billion in its own portfolio. In addition to no-doc loans, which had a maximum amount of $1 million, it was offering full-doc ones (those in accordance with Federal National Mortgage Association guidelines). Both fixed and adjustable rates were being offered, with terms of 10 to 30 years for fixed rates and terms of up to 30 years for adjustable rates. The mortgage subsidiary also was originating real estate loans in the New York City metropolitan area for larger residential, mixed use, and commercial properties. Of total loans of $8.9 billion in 1997, 86 percent were designated for one- to four-family homes; seven percent to apartments; six percent, commercial; and one percent other.

GreenPoint Financial also was offering student and personal-savings loans. GreenPoint Community Development Corp. was offering lending programs, development opportunities and assistance, consulting, and other activities to foster greater access to affordable housing for low- and moderate-income persons residing in the New York City metropolitan area. GreenPoint Bank had 74 full-service offices, all in the metropolitan area. The holding company maintained operating centers and mortgage lending centers in Lake Success, New York, and Charlotte, North Carolina; a mortgage lending center in Englewood Cliffs, New Jersey; and a servicing center in Columbus, Georgia. The company also had hub offices in eight other states. It moved its headquarters to Manhattan in 1996. An employee stock ownership plan controlled 19.1 percent of the shares at the end of 1997. Fidelity Management & Research Corp. owned 8.5 percent.

Principal Subsidiaries

Greenpoint Bank; GreenPoint Mortgage Corp.; GreenPoint Capital Trust I; GreenPoint Community Development Corp.

Further Reading

Bennett, Robert A., "Unorthodox Savings Bank," *New York Times,* July 5, 1983, pp. D1, D7.

Croghan, Lore, "GreenPoint's Thrifty Quest," *Crain's New York Business,* March 21, 1997, pp. 1, 29.

Cwiklik, Robert, "GreenPoint Financial Agrees to Acquire Unit of BankAmerica for $703 Million," *Wall Street Journal,* April 14, 1998, p. C21.

Dugas, Christine, "Green Point Brass Lose Windfall," *Newsday,* January 25, 1994, pp. 31. 33.

Isidore, Chris, "GreenPoint Takes 'No' for Answer," *Crain's New York Business,* March 16, 1998, pp. 23–24.

Leuchter, Miriam, "Capital Albatross," *Crain's New York Business,* May 15, 1995, pp. 1, 32.

——, "Thriving Queens S&L Ready to Expand," *Crain's New York Business,* February 1, 1993, pp. 3, 22.

"Our History," *http://www.greenpoint.com/aboutus.html.*

Prins, Ruth, "Want a Mortgage? Show Us the Cash," *USBanker,* June 1997, pp. 45–46, 48.

Radigan, Joseph, "A Bank Grows in Greenpoint," *USBanker,* July 1995, pp. 8–9.

Roosevelt, Phil, "I.J. Lasurdo: Hard Act to Follow," *American Banker,* August 19, 1988, pp. 6–7.

Selvin, Barbara W., "Reluctant Landlord," *New York Newsday,* February 23, 1991, pp. A36–A37.

Talley, Karen, "GreenPoint Head Has Lowdown on No-Doc," *American Banker,* June 6, 1997, p. 10.

Timmons, Heather, "GreenPoint Entering New Loan Niche in $473M Deal," *American Banker,* December 10, 1998, pp. 1, 5.

—Robert Halasz

Gulfstream

Gulfstream Aerospace Corporation

P.O. Box 2206
500 Gulfstream Road
Savannah, Georgia 31402-2206
U.S.A.
(912) 965-3000
Fax: (912) 965-4333
Web site: http://www.gulfstreamaircraft.com

Public Company
Incorporated: 1978
Employees: 7,700
Sales: $2.43 billion (1998)
Stock Exchanges: New York
Ticker Symbol: GAC
NAIC: 335411 Aircraft Manufacturing; 481211
    Nonscheduled Chartered Passenger Air
    Transportation; 532411 Aircraft Rental & Leasing

Gulfstream Aerospace Corporation, a medium-sized company located in Savannah, Georgia, is a world leader in the design, development, manufacture, and marketing of business aircraft. Its product line includes the Gulfstream IV-SP, which has a range of 4,220 nautical miles, placing Frankfurt in reach of New York; and the Gulfstream V, introduced in 1997, which has a range of 6,500 nautical miles, placing Tokyo within reach of New York. In addition to its aircraft, Gulfstream also offers such services as financing, leasing, charters, management, and maintenance.

Began As Grumman Project

The history of Gulfstream began in the 1950s, when the huge Grumman Corp. of New York, largely a manufacturer of military aircraft and parts, evolved an airplane for the use of big business as well as government. In 1959 the company unveiled the world's first business plane, the Gulfstream I. Two hundred of them sold quickly. When Grumman introduced the Gulfstream II in 1966, a record 256 of them were sold quickly at home and abroad. The GS II could fly faster than commercial jets and was the first business aircraft capable of carrying a full crew and seating up to 16 passengers. This unique business jet caught the imagination of the monied public. Soon versions of the corporate jet were created by other companies, including Canada's Canadair and France's Dassault-Breguet, Gulfstream's chief competitors. In 1967 Grumman set up an assembly plant in Savannah, Georgia, for the manufacture of GS IIs.

Despite the popularity of the corporate jet, the business jet fell on hard times during the recession of the late 1970s, prompting Grumman to sell off its business jet assets and concentrate on its main industry, the manufacture of military aircraft. Allen E. Paulson, head of his own holding company in California, American Jet Industries (a company that converted planes into propjets), had longed for the moment when he could become owner of his own aircraft manufacturing company. Paulson had grown up in humble circumstances. As an adult he became an aircraft mechanic for TWA and eventually learned enough about aviation to do business in aircraft parts, the basis of his early fortune. In 1978 he seized the opportunity to buy the Gulfstream plants and offices from Grumman for $52 million, forming the Gulfstream Aerospace Corporation. Despite recessionary times, plans were in the works to create an even better, more sophisticated business jet, the Gulfstream III.

Paulson's entrepreneurial daring paid off, and the early years of his company were surprisingly profitable. Revenues climbed from $187 million in 1980 to $582 million two years later. Under its dynamic new owner, Gulfstream transformed itself in the first year and a half from what had been largely an aircraft assembly plant to a major manufacturing center. Aircraft parts that had formerly been purchased from numerous vendors were manufactured by Gulfstream, increasing the company's production capacity. Paulson saw to it that the company transformed itself into a high-tech establishment with state-of-the-art manufacturing equipment and the latest computers. The company also expanded outside of Savannah, acquiring in 1981 a large (400,000-square-feet) plant in Oklahoma City, the Gulfstream Aerospace Technologies. Company morale was high, and the new GS III had a backlog of sales that the company raced to meet. The new corporate jet was in such demand that produc-

---

Company Perspectives:

Founded in 1958, Gulfstream Aerospace is the world leader in business aviation. The Company has produced over 1,000 aircraft for corporate, government, private, and military customers around the world. The Company's flagship products—the Gulfstream IV-SP and the Gulfstream V—are the world's most technologically advanced business aircraft. More than one-quarter of Fortune *500 companies operate Gulfstream aircraft to gain a competitive edge and expand their business horizons.*

---

tion continued until 1987. Its popularity was due to many factors, including its long flight capability. The GS III earned the distinction of being the first business jet to fly over both poles nonstop.

Times were changing for aircraft manufacturers, however. Over the previous ten years, the cost of developing a new jet had risen ninefold, and competition from foreign companies—whose aircraft industries were often government subsidized—was keen. In the mid-1980s, despite boom economic times, the aviation industry stagnated; 1982 was perhaps the worst year in the industry. Gulfstream's profits shrank, and Paulson offered eight million shares of the company's common stock for sale (out of 33 million shares, 70 percent of which he still owned). These were quickly snapped up, raising $152 million for the company.

Purchased by Chrysler in 1985

At the same time, the domestic auto industry was experiencing flush times. The nation's third largest automaker, Chrysler Corporation, headed by Lee Iaccoca, was casting about for ways to diversify. Chrysler Corporation bid $637 million for ownership of Gulfstream Aerospace in 1985, keeping Allen E. Paulson as chair of the new subsidiary. That same year, General Dynamics Corporation acquired Cessna Aircraft (an even bigger company than Gulfstream), which had been suffering financially for some of the same reasons.

Production of the GS III was brisk and plans were in the works for the premier business jet of the 21st century, the GS IV, yet Paulson chafed under what he considered to be Chrysler's ignorance of the aviation industry. Nonetheless, Chrysler's purchase of Gulfstream enabled the subsidiary to move forward and prosper, establishing record profitability in the years of Chrysler ownership. In 1987 production of the GS III ended and the GS IV was on the market, sleeker, faster, and practically noiseless, with a $15.8 million price tag ($3 million more than its predecessor). In that year the GS IV set a world record for speed as it flew around the world. Gulfstream Aerospace had a backlog of 100 orders for the new GS IV, the biggest backlog in company history. In 1986 the company again expanded, acquiring a plant at Long Beach, California.

With the onset in 1990 of another recession, however, Chrysler decided to divest its non-automaking subsidiaries. A

major effort had to be made to streamline the company to counter the onslaught of Japanese automobile competition, which had resulted in a $664 million loss in revenue for Chrysler that year. Once again, Gulfstream was for sale to the highest bidder, and Paulson was eager to repurchase the company and develop it.

Taken Private Again in 1990

With the assistance of Forstmann Little & Company, Paulson purchased all 25 million shares of Gulfstream's common stock from Chrysler, an investment of some $825 million. Gulfstream Aerospace Corporation once more was an independent private company under Paulson's ownership, and again he purchased the company, as in 1978, at the height of a recession.

Paulson had big plans for the now independent company. He envisioned the development of a supersonic world class corporate jet (which could reduce flying time from New York to California to less than three hours) in cooperation with the Sukhoi Design Bureau of the Soviet Union, as well as successors to the GS IV: the GS V and the "expanded" version of the GS IV, the GS IV-SP). William C. Lowe was named president and CEO of the company, while Paulson retained his position as chair of Gulfstream.

Whereas the joint project with the Soviet Union fell through and the supersonic jet was placed on the back burner, Paulson's other plans materialized under Lowe's management. Lowe was highly experienced, having served more than 25 years as a manager at IBM and as president for development and manufacturing at the Xerox Corporation. At Gulfstream, Lowe endeavored to diversify and streamline the company, though aircraft and aircraft parts continued to be Gulfstream's chief manufactures. It entered the international military market in its production of the SRA, or Special Requirements Aircraft. The company also concentrated on upgrading its older GS IIs and IIIs, for the more cost-conscious customer, to comply with Federal Aviation Administration (FAA) noise regulations, and to extend their life span into the 21st century. The international market became increasingly important to Gulfstream Aerospace; by the fall of 1991, well over 60 percent of GS sales were abroad.

Gulfstream evolved after its inception in 1978 from an aircraft assembly plant in Savannah, Georgia, to a major manufacturer of highly sophisticated jet aircraft, a world pacesetter. The company downsized in terms of employees from 5,500 to 4,900 while at the same time expanding its facilities considerably. It grew to include not only the original plants in Savannah, but also its engineering support center, Gulfstream Technologies in Oklahoma City, and assembly plants in Long Beach, California. In the fall of 1992, the new Gulfstream V, complete with computer workstation aboard and state of the art telecommunications, was unveiled at the National Business Aircraft Association Conference in Dallas; featured also was the upgraded GS IV-SP (Special Performance) business jet, production of which began in 1993. Both aircraft were designed with advanced collision-avoidance features.

Nevertheless, Gulfstream had more than its share of problems in the early 1990s. Marketing luxury business jets in a time of budget cutting and recession proved extremely difficult and challenging. The company continued to be cash strapped. An attempt in the spring of 1992 to duplicate the sale of common share stock of ten years earlier fell through, with few buyers. Skepticism about Gulfstream's ability to pay its huge debt of nearly $1 billion was a chief factor in the lack of interest to buy stock in the company.

New Management Team Sparked Mid-1990s Turnaround

Soon thereafter, Paulson announced his retirement. His shares in the company were purchased by Forstmann Little. Additional management changes ensued as the company's struggles continued. In April 1993 Fred A. Breidenbach, an executive at General Electric Company (GE) with a background in manufacturing, was named president and chief operating officer. Lowe remained CEO and became chairman as well in May 1993, replacing Paulson. Soon after these changes were made, Gulfstream came close to violating the covenants on $400 million in bank loans. Another new executive, CFO Chris A. Davis, a former colleague of Breidenbach's at GE, worked to persuade lenders to grant Gulfstream a reprieve while Breidenbach moved quickly to slash costs, cutting the workforce by 750, or 16 percent, by the end of 1993, and scrapping plans to add three new buildings to the Savannah production complex. In November of that year Lowe was pushed out, and Theodore Forstmann, senior partner at Forstmann Little, became chairman (the CEO slot remaining vacant).

By late 1993 the new management team had staked the company's future to that of the G V, which was touted as an ultra-long-flight business jet with a maximum range of 6,500 nautical miles, 54 percent more than the G IV-SP, and with a slightly roomier cabin. Gulfstream took a $204 million charge against earnings in 1993 to write off the balance of its investment in the G IV-SP, which the managers considered obsolete. As a result, the company posted a $275 million loss for the year. Gulfstream's future was still in grave doubt, as its G V had potential head-to-head competition from Bombardier, which in late 1993 decided to proceed with the development of its own ultra-long-range model, the Global Express.

Providentially, the surging U.S. economy—which reignited the market for corporate aircraft—provided Gulfstream with a huge boost starting in 1994, as sales increased, company debt fell, and back orders climbed steadily. While the G V remained under development, the G IV-SP proved to be far from obsolete and its sales rebounded. By the end of 1994 the company also had in hand 41 firm orders for the G V. By year-end 1996, this backlog had reached 67, representing about $2.4 billion (at an average per-plane price of $36 million). In October 1996 the reinvigorated Gulfstream was able to sell a larger-than-expected $888 million in shares through an initial public offering, one of the largest of the year. Meanwhile, in 1995 the company launched the Gulfstream Shares program in a joint venture with Executive Jet, Inc. The program allowed customers to purchase partial ownership in Gulfstream aircraft in return for a certain number of hours of flying time per year. The intent of the program was to expand the extremely limited market for business jets.

On April 11, 1997, the Gulfstream V received final and full certification from the FAA, easily beating the Global Express to

market. The G V had been developed at a cost of more than $250 million, a sum that was soon seen to be more than justified. By the end of 1997 Gulfstream had been able to deliver 29 of the new jets and had a backlog of 45 orders. Company revenues thereby nearly doubled, to a record $1.9 billion, while net income soared from $47 million in 1996 to $243 million in 1997. During 1998 a record total of 61 G Vs and G IV-SPs were delivered, helping to increase revenues to $2.43 billion. At year-end 1998 56 G Vs and 50 G IV-SPs were on back order, representing about $3.3 billion in sales. Meantime, Gulfstream received the 1997 Robert J. Collier Trophy, aviation's most prestigious award, from the National Aeronautical Association for the Gulfstream V.

In part to keep up with its increasing backlog and to bolster its aircraft maintenance and parts business, Gulfstream in August 1998 acquired K-C Aviation, Inc. from Kimberly-Clark Corporation for around $250 million. K-C Aviation had facilities in Texas, Wisconsin, and Massachusetts, which included the capacity to complete 21 additional aircraft interiors each year. Gulfstream further expanded its service offerings through the launch in 1998 of a central clearinghouse to facilitate charter transportation on Gulfstream aircraft. Also debuting in 1998 were a short-term lease program, which operated through a joint venture with GATX Capital, and Gulfstream Management Services, a joint venture with Chrysler Pentastar Aviation, Inc., which offered owners of Gulfstream aircraft flight crew, dispatch, and maintenance management services. In December 1998 the company announced a new management structure to take it into the next century. A three-person Office of the Chief Executive was formed, consisting of Forstmann, chairman and CEO; Bill Boisture, president and COO; and Davis, executive vice-president and chief financial and administrative officer. With two aircraft models sporting heavy backlogs and a growing array of services, Gulfstream Aerospace appeared headed for smooth sailing for the foreseeable future.

Principal Subsidiaries

Gulfstream Delaware Corporation; Gulfstream International Corporation; Gulfstream Aircraft Incorporated; Gulfstream Financial Services Corporation; Gulfstream NetJets, Inc.; Gulfstream Aerospace Technologies; Gulfstream Aerospace Corporation of Texas; Gulfstream Aerospace (Middle East) Ltd. (Cyprus); Gulfstream Aircraft Corporation (Hong Kong); Interiores Aereos S.A. De C.V. (Mexico).

Further Reading

Anders, George, "Gulfstream Drops Proposal to Offer Stock to the Public," *Wall Street Journal,* April 2, 1992.
Baldo, Anthony, "Barrier Breaker," *Financial World,* April 18, 1989.
Bianco, Anthony, and William C. Symonds, "Gulfstream's Pilot," *Business Week,* April 14, 1997, pp. 64–69, 72, 74, 76.
"BMW Venture with Rolls-Royce Nets Gulfstream Order," *New York Times,* September 9, 1992.
Brown, David, "Sukhoi, Gulfstream to Study Supersonic Business Jet," *Aviation Week & Space Technology,* June 26, 1989.
Clow, Robert, "Gulfstream Sets Reverse LBO Despite Lagging Projections," *Investment Dealers Digest,* February 10, 1992.
Cole, Jeff, "New Business Jets Take Wing with Style," *Wall Street Journal,* April 7, 1997, p. A9B.
Deutschman, Alan, "Flying Free?" *Fortune,* January 29, 1990.

Goldsmith, Charles, ''Gulfstream and Bombardier Stage Business-Jet Dogfight,'' *Wall Street Journal,* June 20, 1997, p. B4.

Goldwater, Leslie, ''Gulfstream Aerospace: Smooth Flight from Role of Assembly to Total Manufacture,'' *Production,* July 1987.

Hawkins, Chuck, ''Can a New Bird Get Gulfstream Flying?,'' *Business Week,* February 15, 1993, pp. 114, 116.

Laws, Margaret, ''Poised for Take-Off: The Clouds Are Finally Lifting for Private Plane Makers,'' *Barron's,* April 11, 1983.

Levin, Doron P., ''Gulfstream to Be Sold by Chrysler,'' *New York Times,* December 7, 1989.

Marcial, Gene G., ''Gulfstream May Be Ready to Soar Again,'' *Business Week,* September 10, 1984.

''New Gulfstream IV-Special Performance Announced at Farnborough,'' Savannah, Ga.: Gulfstream Aerospace Corporation, 1992.

Phillips, Edward, ''Gulfstream Offers Business Jet Owners Upgrades to Meet Expanding Noise Limits,'' *Aviation Week & Space Technology,* November 12, 1990.

——, ''Service, International Sales to Spur Business Flying in '90's,'' *Aviation Week & Space Technology,* March 18, 1991.

Risen, James, ''Chrysler Sells Unit After Loss of $664 Million,'' *Los Angeles Times,* February 14, 1990.

''The Story of Gulfstream Aerospace,'' Savannah, Ga.: Gulfstream Aerospace Corporation, 1992.

''Super Long Range Gulfstream V Mockup Shown at NBA 1992,'' Savannah, Ga.: Gulfstream Aerospace Corporation, 1992.

Symonds, William C., and David Greising, ''A Dogfight over 950 Customers,'' *Business Week,* February 6, 1995, p. 66.

''Takeovers,'' *Industry Week,* October 14, 1985.

Ticer, Scott, ''Why Gulfstream's Rivals Are Gazing Up in Envy,'' *Business Week,* February 16, 1987.

Warwick, Graham, ''Business Builder,'' *Flight International,* June 30, 1993, p. 19.

——, ''Long-Range Rivals Compete,'' *Flight International,* October 18, 1995, pp. 40+.

Wilson, J.R., ''Long-Range Bizjets Battle for Markets,'' *Interavia Business and Technology,* April 1995, pp. 11+.

—Sina Dubovoj
—updated by David E. Salamie

Harpo Entertainment Group

110 N. Carpenter Street
Chicago, Illinois 60607
U.S.A.
(312) 633-0808
Fax: (312) 633-1111
Web site: http://www.oprah.com

Private Company
Incorporated: 1986 as Harpo Productions, Inc.
Employees: 175
Sales: $150 million (1997 est.)
NAIC: 51211 Motion Picture & Video Production;
    512110 Television Show Production; 512120
    Television Show Syndicators

Based in Chicago, and with additional offices in Los Angeles, Harpo Entertainment Group is one of the most successful production companies in the history of entertainment, one of the largest black-owned companies in the world, and the brainchild of one of the television industry's highest-paid performers ever, Oprah Winfrey (Harpo is Oprah spelled backwards). With productions ranging from made-for-TV movies and miniseries, to feature films and books, videotapes and CDs, Winfrey's reign as the Queen of Entertainment has extended almost from the inception of the company, winning both her and her company and show numerous awards.

Child Prodigy, 1957

Oprah Winfrey was already a budding public speaker in 1957, at the age of four, when she toured churches in Nashville, where she would recite the sermons of James Weldon Johnson. However, she had a rough start. Born in 1954 out of wedlock to teenage parents in Kosciusko, Mississippi, Winfrey lived in terrible poverty on her grandmother's farm. From the age of six to 13, she lived with Vernita Lee, her mother, in Milwaukee, Wisconsin, where she was sexually molested and abused by male relatives; at the age of 14, Winfrey gave birth to a premature baby, who died shortly afterwards. After running away and being kicked out of a juvenile detention home because

all the beds were filled, she was finally sent to Nashville, Tennessee, to live with her father, Vernon Winfrey. A barber and businessman, Vernon provided the discipline that was lacking in his daughter's life, instituting a strict curfew and stressing the value of education. Under his firm guidance, Oprah quickly changed her life's direction.

Broadcasting Start, 1973

In 1973, at the age of 19, Winfrey was hired as a reporter by WVOL, a radio station in Nashville, and her broadcasting career was off and running. During this time, she went to Tennessee State University, where she majored in Speech Communications and Performing Arts. In her sophomore year (1975), she moved to WTVF-TV in Nashville, becoming the first and youngest African American woman anchor at the station.

In 1976 Winfrey went to Baltimore, Maryland, where she joined the staff of WJZ-TV news as a news co-anchor. Two years later, she became, in addition to her duties as reporter and anchor, the host of that station's program "People Are Talking." In January 1984, Winfrey moved again, to Chicago, Illinois, where she would host WLS-TV's program "AM Chicago," a local half-hour talk show with sagging ratings, scheduled opposite Phil Donahue's top-rated show. One month after Winfrey became the host, the program had become the number one show in the city, and the producers gave Winfrey an extra half-hour for the show. In September 1985, they renamed it "The Oprah Winfrey Show." Also that year, Winfrey would costar, along with Whoopie Goldberg, Danny Glover, and Rae Dawn Chong, in Steven Spielberg's movie *The Color Purple*, based on the novel of the same name by Alice Walker. Her poignant performance (and her first-ever acting experience) as Sofia would win her a nomination for an Academy Award and a Golden Globe Award for Best Supporting Actress. The following year, she would costar with Matt Dillon in *Native Son*, the second movie adaptation of Richard Wright's 1940 classic novel.

Harpo Productions, Inc., 1986

Winfrey's love for the screen and her desire to bring quality entertainment projects into production were what prompted her to form her own production company, Harpo Productions, Inc.,

Company Perspectives:

Oprah Winfrey is most interested in concentrating on those topics that can actually help people improve their lives—shows on battered women and alcoholism, for example, or on building relationships with family members. This will both increase the power of the show and make people feel better about their lives.

in 1986, with Winfrey as the chairman and Winfrey's agent, Jeffrey Jacobs, as the president and COO. Early that year, Jacobs managed to buy the syndication rights to the show and began distributing it through King World Productions. On September 8, 1986, "The Oprah Winfrey Show" was televised nationwide. Less than a year later, the program was ranked the top syndicated talk show in the United States, pushing out long-time leader "Donahue." In June 1987, the show received three Daytime Emmy Awards for Outstanding Host, Outstanding Talk/Service Program, and Outstanding Direction. In June 1988, "The Oprah Winfrey Show" was awarded its second consecutive Daytime Emmy Award as Outstanding Talk/Service Program. The show would remain the number one talk show for 12 consecutive seasons, receiving a total of 32 Emmys, seven of which went to the host. Also in 1988, Winfrey received the International Radio and Television Society's "Broadcaster of the Year" Award, making her the youngest person and only the fifth woman ever to receive the honor. At the conclusion of the 1995–96 television season, Winfrey was honored with the most prestigious award in broadcasting, The George Foster Peabody Individual Achievement Award. Winfrey also was recognized by *Time* magazine as one of "America's 25 Most Influential People of 1996."

Harpo's first coproduced project was *The Women of Brewster Place*, a film released in 1989, in which Winfrey costarred with Paul Winfield, Robin Givens, and Moses Gunn, followed by a miniseries of the same name during the 1996–97 season, which recounted the lives of the female denizens of an inner-city brownstone, adapted from the Gloria Naylor novel. Other productions, such as *Kaffir Boy*, Mark Mathabane's autobiography of growing up under apartheid in South Africa, followed, as well as the 1998 feature film, *Beloved,* based on the Pulitzer Prize-winning novel by Toni Morrison. Winfrey would spend ten years producing and would star in the film, directed by Jonathan Demme.

In October 1988, Harpo Productions made television history when it announced that it had assumed ownership and all production responsibilities for "The Oprah Winfrey Show" from Capitol Cities/ABC, making Oprah Winfrey the first woman in history to own and produce her own talk show. That year, the company spent $20 million to buy and renovate a huge, 100,000-square-foot television and film production facility located in downtown Chicago to house its headquarters, where "The Oprah Winfrey Show," as well as other Harpo Entertainment productions, would be produced. When originally purchased, the old complex featured three stages, screening rooms, production offices, a darkroom, kitchen facilities, and indoor parking. The renovation added office space, a gym, a larger stage for Winfrey's daily show, and an updated look for the exterior of the old building.

In 1991 Winfrey initiated The National Child Protection Act and testified before the U.S. Senate Judiciary Committee to establish a national database of all convicted child abusers. On December 20, 1993, U.S. President William Jefferson Clinton signed into law the "Oprah Bill." Also that year, after eight years in syndication, Winfrey was at a crossroads both personally and professionally and began to think about retirement from the cockfighting ring the talk show industry had become. Instead, Winfrey changed the focus of her show, featuring poetry, music, literature, authors, and actors, as well as human issues such as dealing with the loss of a child, weight loss topics, and the like. The following year, Winfrey signed an unprecedented contract with King World, extending her show through the end of the 20th century. Winfrey also became one of King World's largest shareholders, with more than a million shares to her name.

By 1996 Winfrey was only the third woman in history (along with Mary Pickford and Lucille Ball) to own a major studio, and was personally worth an estimated $98 million. She also topped *Forbes*'s list of the highest paid entertainers in the United States, replacing Bill Cosby. In September 1996, Winfrey announced the start of Oprah's Book Club, an on-air reading club, created with the idea to get the country more inspired about reading. All of the books Winfrey selected for the program became instant bestsellers, averaging over a million copies sold each.

At the start of the 1997–98 television season, Winfrey announced the creation of Oprah's Angel Network, a national effort targeted at her viewers with the goal of having them open their hearts and share with those in need the bounty and blessings in their own lives. One of the hallmarks of the Angel Network was The World's Largest Piggy Bank, a campaign that encouraged viewers to save their small change for a national fund to provide scholarships for college students; another was the volunteer work with Habitat to Humanity to build homes for the poor. Total revenue for 1997 reached $150 million, a 7.1 percent growth over the previous year. Also in 1997, Winfrey was named *Newsweek*'s "Most Important Person" in books and media, and *TV Guide*'s "Television Performer of the Year." She was also awarded a People's Choice Award for "Favorite Television Performer."

In 1995 ABC and Harpo Films announced a three-year agreement under which Harpo would produce six made-for-TV movies for the network under the "Oprah Winfrey Presents" banner, extending the relationship between ABC and Harpo, which had already produced a number of miniseries, movies, and primetime specials for the network, including "The Women of Brewster Place," *Overexposed* (1992), and *There Are No Children Here* (1993). The first title in the "Oprah Winfrey Presents" program was *Before Women Had Wings*, followed by the four-hour miniseries *The Wedding,* based on the Doubleday novel by Dorothy West, the last surviving member of the Harlem Renaissance. The company also optioned the rights to *The Keepers of the House*, a Pulitzer Prize-winning novel (1964) written by Shirley Ann Grau, chronicling the lives of a wealthy white Southern landowner, his black housekeeper, and their three children from the 1930s to the 1960s. Other projects in the pipeline for the company included adaptations of

Their Eyes Were Watching God, based on a novel of the same name by Zora Neale Hurston; *Paradise*, another novel by Toni Morrison; and *Katherine*, a novel by Anchee Min.

In 1998 a group of Texas cattle owners filed a lawsuit against Winfrey for libel due to comments she made on her show about "Mad Cow Disease," claiming it adversely affected the market. Winfrey won the suit, which was watched closely by First Amendment rights advocates worldwide, when the jury determined she did not bad-mouth the beef industry. While the lawsuit was ongoing, Winfrey took over a local theater in Amarillo, Texas, turning it into an impromptu set for several months.

In October of that year, the company launched oprah.com, an online web site codeveloped by ABC Internet Group and Harpo Productions to allow more input from Winfrey's huge following of fans. In December 1998, Winfrey announced the creation of Oxygen Media, a new cable channel targeted at women. Joining the venture were big hitters in the entertainment world, such as Geraldine Laybourne, formerly president of Nickelodeon and the founder of Oxygen Media, as well as Marcy Carsey, Tom Werner, and Caryn Mandabach, producers of "Roseanne." Other backers included America Online and ABC. Also in 1998, King World Productions paid Harpo Productions $150 million to renew the contract for "The Oprah Winfrey Show," extending the talk show through at least the 2001–02 TV season; the show has historically represented approximately 40 percent ($200 million or so) of King World's annual revenue for several years. By the end of the 20th century, "The Oprah Winfrey Show" was the class act on the block, in a neighborhood riddled with smarmy talk shows, with a viewership of some 20 million throughout the world.

Principal Subsidiaries

Harpo Films, Inc.; Harpo Productions, Inc.; Harpo Video, Inc.

Further Reading

"ABC Internet Group," *ADWEEK Western Advertising News*, October 26, 1998, p. 34.
Borden, Jeff, "A Secret Not Even Oprah Will Air: Declining Ratings," *Crain's Chicago Business*, August 14, 1995, p. 1.
——, "A *West Side* Story: Oprah As Producer," *Crain's Chicago Business*, March 26, 1990, p. 19.
——, "When Money Can't Cut It: Next on 'Oprah'!" *Crain's Chicago Business*, January 11, 1993, p. 9.
Coe, Steve, "Winfrey Signs Film Deal with Disney," *Broadcasting & Cable*, November 6, 1995, p. 58.
Flint, Joe, "Winfrey's Harpo, ABC Pact for 6 Pix," *Variety*, May 29, 1995, p. 23.

Freeman, Michael, "Oprah Winfrey's," *MEDIAWEEK*, March 21, 1994, p. 16.
"Hamdon Entertainment Has Secured Exclusive International Distribution Rights to All Made-for-TV Movies from Harpo Films," *Broadcasting & Cable*, September 29, 1997, p. 88.
"Harpo Films, Oprah Winfrey's Production Division, Has Optioned the Rights to 'The Keepers of the House' " *Broadcasting & Cable*, August 14, 1995, p. 56.
"Harpo Scores First Non-Oprah TV Deal," *Crain's Chicago Business*, July 2, 1990, p. 1.
"King World Agrees to Pay $150 Million in 'Oprah' Deal," *Wall Street Journal*, September 25, 1998, p. B7.
"King World Productions Has Agreed to Give Oprah Winfrey Until Oct. 6 to Decide Whether to Continue Her Top-Rated Talk Show," *Broadcasting & Cable*, September 18, 1995, p. 80.
Lloyd, Fonda Marie, "Footprints in Time: 25 People Who've Blazed an Indelible Trail of Black Business Progress Since 1970," *Black Enterprise*, August 1995, p. 108.
McClellan, Steve, "Upheaval at Harpo?" *Broadcasting & Cable*, October 31, 1994, p. 14.
Melcher, Richard, "Next on Oprah: Burned-Out Talk-Show Hosts?" *Business Week*, October 2, 1995, p. 64.
Melcher, Richard, and Kelley Holland, "What Women Really Want?" *Business Week*, December 7, 1998, p. 50.
Nathan, Paul, "The Right Backup," *Publishers Weekly*, September 25, 1995, p. 16.
——, "Two Black Novels," *Publishers Weekly*, April 10, 1995, p. 17.
Nicholson, Gilbert, "FOX6 Quits on 'Oprah,' and 'Wheel,' " *Birmingham Business Journal*, November 9, 1998, p. 1.
Noglows, Paul, "Oprah: The Year of Living Dangerously," *Working Woman*, May 1994, p. 52.
"Oprah, ABC Extend Pact," *Broadcasting & Cable*, October 23, 1995, p. 24.
"Oprah Reups with King World; Syndicated Talk Show Host Extends Her Agreement with Syndicator," *Broadcasting*, August 8, 1988, p. 37.
"Oprah: The Winner Who's Taking It All," *Broadcasting*, March 27, 1989, p. 35.
" 'Oprah' Staying at King World," *New York Times*, September 25, 1998, p. C17.
"Oprah Winfrey's Harpo Films Will Produce Six Made-for-TV Movies," *Broadcasting & Cable*, May 29, 1995, p. 32.
"Oxygen Media," *Wall Street Journal*, November 25, 1998, p. B12.
Schlosser, Joe, "King World Locks in Oprah," *Broadcasting & Cable*, September 28, 1998, p. 6.
Shahoda, Susan, "Oprah Winfrey Buys Historic Chicago Film & Television Complex," *Back Stage*, Sept 30, 1988, p. 4.
"Standby Line for Oprah Winfrey Show in Amarillo, Texas, Still in Place," *Knight-Ridder/Tribune Business News*, February 6, 1998, p. 206B0937.
"Tim Bennett," *Broadcasting & Cable*, July 11, 1994, p. 70.

—Daryl F. Mallett

⊠ HAZELDEN

Hazelden Foundation

P.O. Box 11, C03
Center City, Minnesota 55012-0011
U.S.A.
(651) 257-4010
(800) 257-7810
Fax: (651) 257-1055
Web site: http//www.hazelden.org

Nonprofit Company
Incorporated: 1949
Employees: 850
Sales: $53.4 million (1998)
NAIC: 621420 Drug Addiction Treatment Centers & Clinics; 623220 Alcoholism Treatment Centers and Clinics; 62322 Residential Mental Health & Substance Abuse Facilities; 51130 Book Publishers

A pioneer in its field, Hazelden Foundation is widely considered the most influential chemical dependency treatment center in the nation, claiming about 40,000 alumni. Hazelden's $20 million publishing business and $25 million endowment fund make it one of the wealthiest as well. In addition to the Center City, Minnesota complex, treatment locations include Florida, New York, Chicago, and Texas.

A.A., the Bedrock of Hazelden Foundation: 1940s–50s

A writer, a lawyer, and a priest, all alcoholics who had been helped by Alcoholics Anonymous (A.A.), were among those who laid the groundwork for Hazelden. The original concept, a treatment facility for priests, was formalized in 1947 with backing from a prominent Minneapolis businessman and the archbishop in St. Paul, Minnesota. But personality conflicts and philosophical disagreements nearly scuttled the venture entirely. In 1948, the planning group reorganized. The concept was reworked as a treatment center for professional men: the clergy-only aspect of the original program had been a sticking point for important funders.

In December 1948 Richard Coyle Lilly, a well-known Midwest banker and financier purchased the Power Farm (known as Hazelden) in Center City, Minnesota, for $50,000, via the Coyle Foundation. The property, located about 45 miles north of the Twin Cities, consisted of 217 acres of farm and woodland. The 17-room house, later known as the Old Lodge, would serve as the main treatment center. Hazelden Foundation was incorporated as a not-for-profit agency on January 10, 1949.

Lynn Bernard Carroll, a well-respected speaker on the A.A. circuit and a member of the original planning group, was named the first director. The first patient arrived in the spring of 1949; Hazelden was set up as a hospital corporation which would operate a sanatorium for curable alcoholics. During the first three years of operation, Carroll was the only full-time counselor. The rest of the staff included "Ma" Schnable, who served as cook and nurse, the groundskeeper for the estate, and a series of utility men whose tasks included tending to men going through alcohol withdrawal.

"Looking back years later after he had departed from Hazelden, Carroll reflected that when the program opened there was no model to follow. He wanted the men to stay three weeks, and to provide them with an environment where, once they were dry, they could be educated to the A.A. program," wrote Damian McElrath in *Hazelden: A Spiritual Odyssey*.

In addition to Carroll and Lilly, a third man, A.A. Heckman, one of the original incorporators, was central to the formative days of Hazelden, according to McElrath. As a board member, Heckman laid out a vision for the future which touched on concerns ranging from a strong fiscal policy to careful patient evaluations.

The early days were not without peril, with the patient census low and fundraising efforts lagging, Hazelden failed to make payments on its contract for deed and Lilly foreclosed in 1951. The Butler family, owners of Butler Brothers Mining located on the Iron Range of northeastern Minnesota, purchased the option from Lilly. Lawrence Butler had been Hazelden's first patient and later joined the board. His brother Patrick had been treated at Hazelden twice. The two men and their father were committed to helping other alcoholics. The board of trustees reorganized in 1952 with Patrick Butler as president. Patrick's wife, Aimee Mott Butler, would also contribute her time and talents to the success of the venture.

For the first decade or so, simplicity was the hallmark of the program at Center City. Patients attended lectures and groups, and were expected to behave responsibly. "For its part, Hazelden provided a beautiful, wholesome, and clean environment, excellent food, and an A.A. counselor," wrote McElrath. In 1953, a halfway house, the Fellowship Club, was established in St. Paul, providing a haven for homeless men attempting to recover from alcohol addiction. Patients were expected to pay for their stay in both programs. The Center City rate was $100 for the first week and $85 for any additional weeks. The Fellowship Club charged $21 per week for room and board. Grant money was procured for those in need.

Butler played an active role in ensuring the success of Hazelden. Early on, he set up an advisory committee to educate employers about the impact of alcoholism on the workplace and to promote the treatment program in Center City. He also established connections with Yale's alcohol studies program and served on the National Council on Alcoholism. The publication arm of Hazelden took hold in 1954 when Butler purchased *Twenty-Four Hours a Day,* a meditation book for alcoholics. Literature such as the Hazelden newsletter and several brochures had already been in print.

Carroll, in the meantime, was splitting his time between counseling duties and speaking engagements in the Midwest and Canada. "Carroll's cultivation of both the alumni and A.A. groups produced excellent results. In 1954 A.A. members referred 28 percent of Hazelden's patients, while 41 percent were referred by former patients—an astonishing total of almost 70 percent," wrote McElrath. Hazelden was a harbor for those suffering from alcoholism.

Considered "hopeless cases" during the years following the repeal of Prohibition, alcoholics often were refused even basic medical care, but in 1954 the American Hospital Association recognized alcoholism as a disease. The action opened the way for the development of new treatment models in that arena. Dr. Nelson Bradley and psychologist Daniel Anderson brought

changes to the treatment of alcoholics at Willmar State Hospital, which was designated one of Minnesota's "inebriate asylums." Patrick Butler would bring their innovations to Hazelden.

New Treatment Methods Bring Big Changes: 1960s–70s

By 1960, a multidisciplinary approach to treatment was in place at Willmar: physicians, nurses, psychiatrists, psychologists, social workers, recreation directors, clergy, and recovering alcoholics serving as counselors teamed together to treat alcoholics. Anderson had already begun consulting at Hazelden. Longtime counselors, committed to the A.A. philosophy, objected to psychological aspects of the program Anderson brought with him from Willmar. But change was in the air, and Anderson was appointed vice-president and CEO of Hazelden in 1961.

The ideas and methods developed at Willmar included a detoxification program, a primary care program, a combined aftercare and outpatient program, as well as a multidisciplinary approach to alcoholism treatment. Anderson modified and adapted Willmar's program at Dia Linn, Hazelden's treatment facility for women located in White Bear Lake, Minnesota, a suburb north of St. Paul.

Dia Linn, established in 1956, drew women from around the country. While the attitude toward male alcoholics had begun to soften somewhat, women alcoholics continued to be viewed as moral degenerates. As Anderson integrated the Willmar model into Hazelden's Dia Linn program, the demand for beds at Center City continued to climb. The patient population doubled in six years, topping 500 in 1963. Hazelden purchased a nearby hotel to handle the overflow.

With a significant number of patients coming from the Chicago-Milwaukee area, Hazelden considered opening a facility in that region, but instead decided to expand at Center City. The larger facility would house the women's program as well. Even though Dia Linn's patient count was on the rise, the facility was operating in the red. The Fellowship Club also failed to earn money, but the proceeds from the sale of *Twenty-Four Hours a Day* balanced the books in St. Paul.

The million-dollar project resulted in residential buildings that accommodated 18 to 22 patients and a counselor. The units included such features as meeting and coffee rooms, a chaplain's office, and a library. A new main building housed kitchen and dining rooms plus a 160-seat meeting room. The construction, which included an infirmary and administration building, was completed in 1966.

With Anderson in place as director and the multidisciplinary approach about to be implemented at Center City, old counselors, including Carroll, began to depart, signaling an end to an era. The remainder of the decade, according to McElrath, was "marked by a relentless flow of ideas and endless experimentation." Hazelden developed a repeater's program, an extended care program, various training programs (up until this time there was no formal counselor training), a family program, and a research and evaluation department. Administratively, Hazelden was divided into three divisions: Treatment, Business, and Operations.

Hazelden's continued success at drawing patients led to another space shortage by the end of the decade. With a debt of nearly $2 million on the books, the organization launched a fundraising drive. An additional rehabilitation unit, a multi-purpose building, and a 316-seat auditorium were completed in 1970. Since opening its doors, the Hazelden complex grew to include facilities ranging from a detoxification unit to a driving range. Over 11,000 patients were admitted to the program.

The 1970s proved to be a time of internal change following the rapid expansion in the 1960s. The board reorganized in 1971 with Patrick Butler as president and director. Operations were structured under two divisions, Administrative Services and Rehabilitation. In 1978, four more divisions were added: Education and Consultation; Personnel; Research and Evaluation; and Training.

Publication Boom, Treatment Bust: 1980s

The publication end of the business had become the largest revenue producer by the mid-1980s thanks to sales of such books as *Codependent No More*. First offered through Hazelden's direct-mail catalog in 1985, the Melody Beattie offering became a fixture on the *New York Times* bestseller list after hitting the bookstores. Hazelden sold an estimated $16 million in Beattie books and tapes in 1990. Total revenue climbed from $15.4 million in 1982 to $48.9 million in 1990.

While the publication business was peaking, the outlook for Hazelden's treatment program, which drew patients from among the ranks of the rich and famous, began to change. A 1986 article in the *American Psychologist* kicked off a debate questioning the effectiveness of standard treatment programs. Hazelden's $7,000, 28-day residential program began experiencing a decline in occupancy as insurers moved to shorter residential stays and more outpatient treatment coverage.

The number of chemical dependency beds in the United States had doubled between 1978 and 1984, days of liberal insurance coverage, but by 1992 half those beds were unoccupied. Hazelden's Center City occupancy rate remained above the national average at 80 percent, but a youth residential treatment program was down to 60 percent, and a Florida-based program slipped under 40 percent. An expanded fundraising program helped Hazelden's financial picture: endowments rose from $5.2 million in 1987 to $12.2 million in 1990.

New Leadership: 1990s

Hazelden turned 40 in 1989. That same year Patrick Butler stepped down as chairman of the board of trustees, a position he had held for nearly two decades. Under his guidance Hazelden established itself as the leading purveyor of the "Minnesota Model" of chemical dependency treatment, but that model was under the gun and revenue was declining.

Hazelden implemented a voluntary employee separation program in the spring of 1991. The organization also cut back on programs and sold the Employee Assistance Services division and its research consultation operation that year. While other treatment programs adapted to the changing attitude among third-party payors, Hazelden held fast to its tried and true measures. "We won't back off from what we've been doing," said Harold Swift, Hazelden's president, in a 1992 *Corporate Report Minnesota* article. "To do so would hurt our success rate."

The nationwide scale-back in the chemical dependency treatment industry hurt Hazelden's educational materials sales. An estimated 60 percent of the books and tapes were sold to treatment centers, hospitals, and professionals in the field. In addition, Hazelden faced increased competition. The self-help literature boom of the 1980s had drawn huge commercial publishers into the segment—the market peaked at about $60 million in the mid-to-late 1980s. Stellar sale producer Melody Beattie, in fact, switched to Simon & Schuster, Inc. in 1991. Furthermore, while other publishers pushed the envelop of the "bibliotherapy" category with books on topics such as sex addiction, Hazelden lagged behind the pack in broadening its offerings.

With for-profit hospitals and mental healthcare providers shutting down their chemical dependency units, Hazelden brought a new leader on board. Jerry Spicer was named president and CEO in July 1992. He introduced a shorter in-patient treatment option and new services such as a five-day smoking-cessation program. Spicer also initiated discussions with local service provider networks and insurers regarding future treatment offerings.

Hazelden was facing changing attitudes among the public at large as well. According to a 1993 *Star Tribune* article by Susan Feyder, a shift in public opinion regarding substance abuse was keeping some people from seeking help. Chemical dependency was again being viewed as moral weakness or criminal behavior rather than an illness as Hazelden and the medical profession at large maintained. In 1993, 35 staff members were laid off. The total number of employees was about 600, down from over 800 in 1992.

Hazelden added to its publications division in 1994 with the purchase of CompCare Publications and The Parkside Publishing Program, both established marketers of chemical dependency books. The introduction of a national sales force targeting treatment centers, schools, and prisons, helped boost revenues and counter the ongoing decline in interest in self-help books. To cut costs, the company closed its Ireland-based European distribution office in 1994 and shifted the operation back to Center City.

Thanks to increased marketing, shorter residential programs, and fewer competitors, patient occupancy rates rose. Treatment services regained its position as the largest revenue maker by 1994. In response to concerns regarding third-party payments, which accounted for about 50 percent of treatment revenues, Hazelden escalated its formal outcomes research efforts. Total revenues for 1995 reached $54.3 million. Patient count increased from 7,280 in 1995 to 7,837 in 1996. An increase in outpatient numbers counterbalanced a drop in the inpatient count.

In 1997, Melody Beattie returned to the Hazelden fold, and in 1998 the publications and training programs of Minneapolis-based Johnson Institute were acquired. Also in 1998, Hazelden expanded its program offerings to include treatment for chronic conditions such as eating disorders, pain, and diabetes. About 20 new related products were expected to be added in the publications area, boosting the number of titles from 80 to 100. Hazelden also planned to delve into the area of complementary medicine and other healing modalities, thus broadening its approach to treatment.

Preparing for the New Millennium

As Hazelden neared its half-century mark, scientific developments were altering how drug treatment would be carried out in the future. "The new research is a mixed blessing for Hazelden and other A.A.-based treatment centers. On the one hand, neuroscientists using advanced imaging equipment to observe changes in the regions of the brain that are known to govern addictions have provided evidence that addicts do not simply lack willpower or character," wrote David Samuels in a 1998 *New Yorker* article. If addiction can be treated through therapeutic drugs, programs like Hazelden, Samuels speculated, could become obsolete. Hazelden had already integrated the use of antidepressants and other therapeutic drugs in their program, an action from which some other well-known treatment centers such as the Betty Ford Clinic had abstained.

While Hazelden depended on its stellar reputation to carry it through much of its first 50 years, the organization had become more aggressive about promoting its agenda as it headed toward the next millennium. Hazelden lobbyists worked for legislative changes on a national level to bring insurance coverage for chemical dependency treatment in parity with other major diseases. William Cope Moyers, who had been treated for crack cocaine addiction at Hazelden, was director of public policy. A PBS series on addiction, narrated by his father, television journalist Bill Moyers, aired about the same time Congress began the 1998 hearings on parity legislation.

Further Reading

Borger, Judith Yates, Sandra Earley, Tom Fredrickson, and Kevin Maler, "Healing Themselves," *Minneapolis/St. Paul CityBusiness*, August 13, 1993, pp. 5.

"Briefs," *Star Tribune* (Minneapolis), September 28, 1998, p. 2D.

Draper, Norman, and Allen Short, "Hazelden: Even an Elite Treatment Program Has Many Failures," *Star Tribune* (Minneapolis), June 27, 1993, p. 11A.

Earley, Sandra, "Hazelden to Pack Up in Ireland," *Minneapolis/St. Paul CityBusiness*, August 26-September 1, 1994, p. 2.

Feyder, Susan, "Fiscal Therapy," *Star Tribune* (Minneapolis), January 25, 1993, p. 1D.

Gale, Elaine, "Author Melody Beattie Will Return to a Position at Hazelden Publishing," *Star Tribune* (Minneapolis), October 23, 1997, p. 4E.

"In Brief," *Star Tribune* (Minneapolis), April 22, 1994, p. 5D.

Manning, John, "Hazelden Broadens Conditions Treated," *Minneapolis/St. Paul CityBusiness*, April 10, 1998, p. 13.

——, "Larger Treatment Facilities Buck Admissions Downturn," *Minneapolis/St. Paul CityBusiness*, June 6, 1997, p. 10.

McDowell, Edwin, Twin Cities Area Fuels Explosion in Self-Help Books," *Star Tribune* (Minneapolis), September 11, 1989, p. 1E.

McElrath, Damian, *Hazelden: A Spiritual Odyssey*, Center City, Minn.: Hazelden Foundation, 1987.

Meier, Peg, "State Emerged 20 Years Ago As Major Center for Treatment," *Star Tribune* (Minneapolis), April 21, 1991, p. 4E.

Nissen, Todd, "Economics Spurs a New Outlook on Mental Care," *Minneapolis/St. Paul CityBusiness*, September 11–18, 1992, pp. 1, 32.

Pokela, Barbara, "New Hazelden Chief Searches for Priorities," *Star Tribune* (Minneapolis), June 26, 1989, p. 2D.

Samuels, David, "Saying Yes to Drugs," *New Yorker*, March 23, 1998, pp. 48–55.

"The Star Tribune Nonprofit 100," *Star Tribune* (Minneapolis), November 4, 1996, p. 4D.

Wieffering, Eric J., "Hazelden Is Recovering," *Corporate Report Minnesota*, September 1994, p. 10.

——, "Trouble in Center City," *Corporate Report Minnesota*, January 1992, pp. 43–46.

Youngblood, Dick, "Drug Treatment Suffering As Companies Cut Back," *Star Tribune* (Minneapolis), November 4, 1991, p. 2D.

—Kathleen Peippo

Heidrick & Struggles International, Inc.

Sears Tower
Department CSP
233 S. Wacker Drive
Suite 4200
Chicago, Illinois 60606-6303
U.S.A.
(312) 496-1200
Fax: (312) 496-1200
Web site: http://www.h-s.com

Public Company
Incorporated: 1953
Employees: 750
Sales: $329 million (1998)
Stock Exchanges: NASDAQ
Ticker Symbol: HSII
NAIC: 56131 Employment Placement Agencies

Heidrick & Struggles International, Inc. is one of the largest executive search firms in the world, and the largest operating within the continental United States. The company provides its services to the entire range of industries, and focuses on identifying, evaluating, and recommending highly qualified candidates for senior executive positions in companies around the world. Heidrick & Struggles operates a network of 59 offices in the United States, Europe, Asia, Africa, the Middle East, and Latin America, and has formed strategic partnerships with search firms in both Germany and the Republic of South Africa. With the demand for talented senior executives increasing at a dramatic rate, the company since 1995 has grown significantly, with worldwide revenues increasing at a compounded rate of 25 percent annually.

Early History

What has developed into the one of the most successful international executive search firms was founded by two men in 1953, Gardner Heidrick and R. Struggles. Both had served in a number of executive level positions, and had worked their way up the corporate ladder. Yet the two men were dissatisfied with their careers, and longed for a new and exciting challenge. As the corporate environment and culture began to change during the late 1950s, Heidrick and Struggles recognized the need for a firm that would identify and recommend highly suitable candidates for specific positions at the highest level of corporate management. Incorporating their company in 1953 and locating their headquarters in Chicago, the two young entrepreneurs decided to use their own names to identify the company.

Heidrick & Struggles soon garnered a reputation for personally identifying and placing candidates in the banking, insurance, and accounting industries. Many of the firm's placements during its early years were in management and marketing. While the company prospered, its operations grew at a relatively slow pace until the arrival of Gerard Roche. Roche was a graduate of the University of Scranton, located in Pennsylvania, having received his B.A., and he also earned an M.B.A. from New York University, working for it at night while he toiled away during the day. Gardner Heidrick identified Roche, who was working as the vice-president of marketing at a division within Mobil Corporation, as the best candidate for a position with Milprint, a subsidiary of Philip Morris located in Milwaukee.

Heidrick was so impressed with Roche that, rather than placing him with Milprint, convinced him to work at Heidrick & Struggles in the New York office. Heidrick had hired Roche not only for his display of intelligence and aggressiveness, but also for his charm and engaging personality. Little did Heidrick and Struggles know that their firm would never be the same after Roche's arrival. Much to his credit, Roche personally changed the way headhunting was done in the United States. From the very first day, Roche began his job with a methodical search for job openings. He would search tirelessly for positions that needed filling in major corporations, and then convince their management that he was the person who deserved to be entrusted with the responsibility for finding that individual. Then he would search Heidrick & Struggles' data bank for possible candidates, and use his extensive list of corporate contacts to put together an initial list of 50 or 60 names. After having narrowed down the list to between three and five individuals, he would then present them to the prospective employer for evaluation. A meeting between the candidate and employer then occurred, and before long a contract was signed. Using this method, Roche claimed a success rate of nearly 85 percent.

Working at Heidrick & Struggles during the mid- and late 1960s was easy for Roche. A natural-born salesman, he easily persuaded rising young executives to change jobs and loyalties at a moment's notice. The offer of a $5,000 to $10,000 raise enticed many executives to accept a new job offer even though their old job was just as promising. One of the secrets to Roche's success at this time was his willingness to meet with people on a one-to-one basis over dinner, at breakfast, for a game of golf, or even by entertaining clients at his own home in Chappaqua, New York. This personal touch, along with the unbridled enthusiasm and respectful professionalism he brought to his job, made Roche one of the most trusted and respected headhunters within the industry.

Growth and Expansion During the 1970s and 1980s

Roche was clearly the rising star in the company's firmament, and his success during the 1970s continued unabated. Roche regarded everyone he met as either "a prospect, a candidate, a reference or a client." This attitude enabled him to fill over 150 positions during the decade of the 1970s alone, with approximately one-fourth of them presidential or CEO positions. By 1978 the company's board of directors was convinced that Roche should be appointed the chief executive of Heidrick & Struggles. Yet even after this appointment, Roche continued to carry a full search load for two years. At the beginning of the 1980s, he was poised to personally place some of the major talents in the corporate world, including: Thomas Vanderslice, who was convinced to leave General Electric in order to head GTE; Edward Hennessy, who jumped from his position at United Technologies to assume the top job at Allied Corporation; and Robert Frederick, a GE employee enticed to become president at RCA.

As the 1980s progressed, Roche began to expand the number of employees in both the Chicago and New York offices, as well as initiate a grand strategy to make Heidrick & Struggles more of an international executive search firm. He opened numerous offices throughout Europe, and established a reputation for the company as one of the more aggressive and successful executive search firms in countries such as England, France, and The

Netherlands. The company's board of directors, however, decided that Roche could not maintain a full client search schedule while also managing the operations of the company, so they promoted him to the position of chairman both as a reward for his success and as an attempt to help him manage his time better.

Although Roche did in fact reduce his client search responsibility, due to the economic recession that hit the American economy during the early 1980s, Heidrick & Struggles fell on some difficult times. In 1980 the company placed approximately 600 high-level executives, but by 1982 that figure had fallen to just around 500. In addition, Roche was forced to reduce his staff from 100 to 82, thus putting the brakes on Roche's strategy for expansion, at least for the short term. With these setbacks, the executive search firm of Russell Reynolds surpassed Heidrick & Struggles both in revenues and in ranking within the industry. Nonetheless, the company continued on, and Roche somewhat resumed his client search schedule to place George M.C. Fisher at Eastman Kodak, Stanley C. Gault at Goodyear Tire & Rubber, and Michael C. Jordan at Westinghouse Electric. These placements not only helped revive the fortunes of Heidrick & Struggles, but enhanced Roche's reputation as one of the preeminent figures in the industry.

Resurgence During the 1990s

As the fortunes of the company were revived, Roche renewed his efforts to transform Heidrick & Struggles into one of the leading executive search firms in the world. Building upon what had already been developed during the 1980s, an extensive network of offices were established around the globe, including such major international cities as Hong Kong, New Delhi, Tokyo, Singapore, Amsterdam, Berlin, Barcelona, Geneva, Milan, Moscow, Paris, Prague, Warsaw, Buenos Aires, Lima, São Paulo, Capetown, and Johannesburg, not to mention many cities throughout the United States. By the mid-1990s, the company counted 59 offices located in 30 countries that were dedicated to serving the employment needs of major multinational corporations. By 1998 the company's offices in Europe generated over $125 million in revenues, second only to its network of offices scattered throughout the United States.

Roche recognized that the continued growth of Heidrick & Struggles depended not only upon expanding its international presence, but on refining its core business and becoming the leading executive search firm for senior level positions. Under Roche's guidance, the company began to concentrate on seven core industry practice groups, including international technology, industrial manufacturing, consumer products, financial services, healthcare, professional services, and the higher education/nonprofit sector. Heidrick & Struggles consultants were trained in building relationships with job candidates as well as with corporate clients. To better understand the needs of their clients, company consultants were encouraged to conduct thorough investigations into clients' corporate cultures, operations, business strategies, current personnel, and overall strengths and weaknesses. Roche regarded this type of research as the only successful way to place candidates that would meet the needs of its clients. At the same time, Roche emphasized placement at the highest levels of corporate management, thus leading the company to focus on the recruitment of chief executive officers, presidents, chief financial officers, chief operating officers, members of boards of directors, and a small section of additional management positions such as departmental and division heads. By the end of fiscal 1981, over 80 percent of the company's searches were placements for the above positions.

During the late 1990s, the company's success continued without interruption. Heidrick & Struggles had expanded its client base from 1,800 in 1995 to over 3,100 by the end of 1998. The company employed 346 executive search consultants worldwide, with an average of nine years experience for each individual. Most significantly, however, was the company's emphasis on a strategic acquisitions plan to continue its expansion, including the purchase of Fenwick Partners, Inc., an executive search firm based in Boston, Massachusetts, specializing in computer software, medical electronics, and engineering placements; Mulder & Partner GmbH & Co. KG, the largest executive search firm in Germany; and Redelinghuys & Partners, an executive search firm based in Capetown and Johannesburg, South Africa. All of these moves resulted in a dramatic increase in revenues, from $161 million in 1995 to $329 million by the end of fiscal 1998.

With Roche still in the driver's seat, and with his personal involvement still at the forefront of the company's highest level of executive searches, an even brighter future seemed likely, particularly if the firm adhered to its trademark strategy, that of combining an extraordinary degree of professionalism and know-how with a warm and engaging personal touch.

Principal Subsidiaries

Fenwick Partners, Inc.; Mulder & Partner GmbH & Co. KG; Redelinghuys & Partners.

Further Reading

Byrne, John H., ''Can Tom & Jerry Find a Big Cheese for Big Blue?,'' *Business Week,* February 22, 1993, p. 40.

——, ''Headhunter to the Stars,'' *Forbes,* June 20, 1983, p. 106.

''Gerald Roche: High-Powered Headhunter,'' *Management Review,* July 1994, p. 60.

''High Tech's Headhunters,'' *Forbes ASAP,* October 7, 1996, p. 68.

Lublin, Joan S., ''Heidrick & Struggles Likely to Announce Intent to Acquire Rival Fenwick Partners,'' *Wall Street Journal,* March 30, 1998, p. A4(E).

——, ''The Right Image,'' *Wall Street Journal,* December 29, 1998, p. B10(E).

Quick, Rebecca, ''Heidrick Holders Vote to Offer Stake in Firm to Public,'' *Wall Street Journal,* March 2, 1998, p. C22(E).

Rose, Frederick, ''Star Wars: Headhunting Firms Angle for Each Others' Top Recruiters,'' *Wall Street Journal,* May 12, 1998, p. A1(E).

—Thomas Derdak

Helene Curtis Industries, Inc.

325 North Wells Street
Chicago, Illinois 60610
U.S.A.
(312) 661-0222
Fax: (312) 661-2250

Wholly Owned Subsidiary of Unilever plc
Incorporated: 1927 as the National Mineral Company
Employees: 1,900
Sales: $1.31 billion (1997 est.)
NAIC: 32562 Toilet Preparation Manufacturing

Helene Curtis Industries, Inc. manufactures and markets personal care products, primarily shampoo and conditioners, hand and body lotions, and deodorants and antiperspirants. Shampoo constitutes Helene Curtis's primary strength—Suave is one of the top shampoo brands in the United States. Helene Curtis was run by the original founding family from its founding until Unilever, an Anglo-Dutch conglomerate, acquired the company in 1996.

Origins on Eve of Great Depression

Helene Curtis was founded in Chicago in 1927 as the National Mineral Company by Gerald Gidwitz and Louis Stein. The company started out manufacturing just one product, the Peach Bloom Facial Mask. Made of special clay mined in the hills of Arkansas, the facial mudpacks were packaged and sold to beauty salons nationwide. At a time when personal care products were becoming increasingly sophisticated, Gidwitz and Stein recognized that their sole product could not sustain the company with its limited market. The partners soon shifted the company's emphasis to haircare products, beginning a long history of producing successful, innovative personal care products.

The Great Depression years, ironically, turned out to be among the company's most successful. As the straight hairstyles of the 1920s gave way to a rage for waves, Gidwitz sensed opportunity in haircare. At the time cumbersome electric

waving machines took hours to wave hair and were extremely expensive for beauticians to purchase. Thus, such haircare was usually only available to the well-off. This changed when researchers at the National Mineral Company developed ''machineless'' waving pads and designed a machine that could mass produce them. The pads created a revolution in the haircare industry, drastically simplifying the permanent wave process, and consequently allowing people to have professional beauty care at an affordable price.

Gidwitz determined that there was another aspect of haircare that could provide an opportunity for the company. Until that time most people washed their hair with laundry or plain soap, since the products available specifically for use on hair were harsh and overpriced. The company developed Lanolin Creme Shampoo, one of the nation's first detergent-based shampoos, introduced in the mid-1930s. The popularity of the shampoo, available only in beauty salons, prompted National Mineral Company to follow it up with Suave Hairdressing in 1937. The demand for the hair tonic became so great, the company began manufacturing small retail sizes for salon resale.

Turning its attention to wartime production during World War II, the company's name changed to National Industries, Inc., and factories were converted to manufacture aircraft gun turrets, electric motors, radar equipment, and motion picture sound projectors for the military. The company also maintained its presence in the haircare industry with the introduction of Empress, a further innovation for permanent waves. A revolutionary nontoxic chemical perm, Empress utilized a cream oil solution wrapped on wooden rods. National Industries also branched off into the manufacture of hair dryers and other professional beauty supplies. Gerald Gidwitz, in the meantime, became president and CEO during the war years.

The Helene Curtis Name Following World War II

After the war National Industries shifted its focus back to the manufacture of personal care products. The renewed emphasis on this industry prompted a name change, and the company became Helene Curtis after Louis Stein's wife and son. It was at this time that Suave Hairdressing and Lanolin Creme Shampoo were introduced for retail sale in department and drugstores, and quickly began outselling the competition. In 1948, reflecting the company's growth, Helene Curtis moved to a new corporate headquarters and manufacturing facility.

In 1950 Helene Curtis developed the generic term hairspray for its new aerosol product, Spray Net. Other successful, and effective, products introduced during the 1950s included the spray-on deodorant Stopette and a nonprescription dandruff shampoo called Enden. These two products were advertised on television during such shows as ''What's My Line?'' and ''Oh! Susanna,'' helping to make Stopette the bestselling deodorant on the market, a position it maintained for several years.

In addition, the company expanded its product line with several acquisitions, including Kings Men male toiletries, Lentheric fragrances, and Studio Girl cosmetics. By the mid-1950s Helene Curtis products were being manufactured and sold in 25 countries. Another milestone occurred in 1956 when Helene Curtis went public after 32 years of private ownership, selling 375,000 shares of Class A stock for $10 per share.

Helene Curtis further broadened its line of personal care products in 1960, when Tender Touch, the first popularly priced bath oil, was marketed. In addition the company began to build on the success of its Suave brand, introducing shampoos, creme rinses, and wave sets. Other innovative products launched during the 1960s were Quik-Care hair conditioner, the synthetic hair oil First Time, and Secure, a pressed, powder-dry deodorant with a patented formula.

In 1961 Helene Curtis's stock was accepted on the New York Stock Exchange, and by the middle of the decade the company had licensed its products in 81 countries. Capitalizing on a consumer hair trend, the Professional Division of Helene Curtis launched the Wigette line of small hairpieces made of human hair, as well as synthetic versions under the Nature Blend brand name.

The 1970s saw Helene Curtis making further advances in permanents. UniPerm became the first compact machine to give perfect permanent waves, while the Professional Division introduced Moisture Quotient and the One Better permanent—the first perm to combine the advantages of alkaline waving and conditioning. In addition, a shampoo called Everynight, designed for frequent use and targeted at teens, was exclusively advertised by tennis star Chris Evert. In the meantime the Suave brand, which had sold its billionth bottle, expanded its selection of fragrances and formulas, and in 1977 Suave became the highest-selling shampoo in the United States. A Suave brand roll-on antiperspirant/deodorant was launched, marking the company's first entry in that category. By the end of the decade Helene Curtis was represented in more than 110 countries.

Helene Curtis joined the *Fortune* 500 group of companies in the 1980s, and established itself as the growth leader in the personal care industry. During a time when many of the company's competitors were growing through acquisition, Helene Curtis instead kept to its longstanding strategy of fueling growth through continued innovation and further brand extensions. Also, the company was making significant strides in its international markets, especially Japan, one of the first international markets in which Helene Curtis established a presence during the 1950s. By

the mid-1990s the Japanese market accounted for more than 20 percent of the company's annual sales.

Introducing New Products in the 1980s

Building on Suave's name and reputation—the brand held fast to its position as the top daily haircare brand in the United States—Helene Curtis entered the skincare lotion sector with several different formulas. In addition, a new line of Suave antiperspirant/deodorants strengthened the company's presence in that category. A new brand was launched in 1982, however, with a $35 million investment and the introduction of Finesse conditioner. The product, with its patented, time-activated formula designed to give both light and deep conditioning as necessary, proved so popular that the premium-priced brand was expanded to include shampoo and hairspray, as well as the Finesse Nutricare line of haircare items.

Helene Curtis followed up on the success of Finesse with the $40 million launch of the Salon Selectives brand of shampoos, conditioners, and hairsprays. By offering customized products that combined the company's salon heritage with a mid-range price, first-year sales reached $40 million, recouping Helene Curtis's initial investment. By 1988 both Salon Selectives and Finesse had joined Suave as leaders in their market segments, and the brands' success in the United States was matched by their popularity in international markets. Meanwhile the Professional Division strengthened its lead position in the salon category with the introduction of such products as Post Impressions, a waving system that eliminated post-perm odor and dryness, and the Attractions line of haircare products with collagen. The Quantum brand was also launched with the Quantum Acid Perm that quickly became, as it continues to be, the bestselling permanent wave brand.

The company's product lines were not alone in their expansion during the 1980s—as business had boomed, so had the need for additional manufacturing capacity. In 1982 Helene Curtis completed construction of a plant in City of Industry, California. This was followed in 1989 by a $32 million, state-of-the-art distribution center that, at 376,000 square feet, had double the capacity of the former facilities. In addition, the company's corporate headquarters had been relocated in 1984. Ronald J. Gidwitz, son of Gerald Gidwitz, took over as CEO in 1985.

New Products and Parentage in the 1990s

In 1990 Helene Curtis introduced Degree antiperspirant/deodorant, at that time the company's most successful new product launch. With a formula activated as body heat rises—and aided by a $50 million advertising campaign—Degree quickly garnered a large share of the market, achieving the company's market share goal for the brand's first year in only eight months. This success was followed by yet another entry into the haircare market with the introduction of the Vibrance brand; Vibrance was priced higher than other Helene Curtis shampoos and sales were slow, leading to its repositioning as an organic brand. By the end of fiscal 1992 Helene Curtis had attained the billion dollar mark with total sales of $1.02 billion.

However, as the 1990s continued it became increasingly clear that Helene Curtis's smaller size in comparison with its competitors put it at a significant disadvantage. As more and more emerging markets were opening up and the personal care industry was becoming increasingly global, Helene Curtis simply did not have the resources to compete on an international scale with such giants as the Procter & Gamble Company and Unilever. The company began seeking a partner, finding one in Unilever, and announcing in February 1996 that it had agreed to be acquired by Unilever for about $770 million. Helene Curtis thus joined a company that derived about 20 percent of its revenues from personal care products, including such brands as Elizabeth Arden and Calvin Klein cosmetics, Vaseline, Pond's facial cleansers, Q-tips, Cutex nail-polish remover, and Pepsodent toothpaste.

Following the acquisition, Unilever made a number of moves to strengthen Helene Curtis. In November 1996 Unilever sold the North American side of Helene Curtis's professional haircare line to Shiseido Company Limited of Japan. Unilever then in 1997 sold Helene Curtis's Japanese professional haircare business, also to Shiseido. Helene Curtis's workforce was cut nearly in half, its operations were consolidated, and a product streamlining initiative cut the company's line of products by about 20 percent by mid-1997. In October 1997 Unilever merged three U.S. personal care businesses—Helene Curtis, Chesebrough-Pond's, and Lever Brothers—into a new Home & Personal Care North America unit. The three businesses continued to operate independently, however. Ronald Gidwitz remained president and CEO of Helene Curtis in the immediate aftermath of the acquisition but resigned in 1998 to concentrate his attention on his venture capital company.

In February 1998 Helene Curtis made its first major product introduction as a Unilever subsidiary. That month marked the debut of ThermaSilk shampoos, conditioners, and styling aids, which were backed by an $85 million advertising campaign, one of the largest in company history. The new line was based on heat-activated technology that was designed to improve the condition of hair with the use of a blow dryer. The company predicted that ThermaSilk would generate $120 million in sales during its first year, and that figure was exceeded. In 1999, therefore, the brand was pushed through a $100 million marketing effort and the line was extended through the debut of three more products. This successful launch provided solid evidence of the renewed strength of Helene Curtis thanks to the deep pockets of its new parent.

Principal Subsidiaries

Helene Curtis Australia Pty. Ltd.; Helene Curtis Europa B.V. (Netherlands); Helene Curtis International Italia S.p.A. (Italy); Helene Curtis Japan Inc.; Helene Curtis, Ltd./Ltee. (Canada); Helene Curtis New Zealand Ltd.; Helene Curtis Scandinavia AB (Sweden); Helene Curtis UK, Inc.

Principal Operating Units

Helene Curtis International; Helene Curtis North America; Helene Curtis U.S.A.; Helene Curtis U.S.A. Professional.

Further Reading

Anderson, Veronica, "What's Ahead at Helene Curtis?," *Crain's Chicago Business,* February 19, 1996, pp. 3+.

Byrne, Harlan S., "Prettier Prospects," *Barron's,* July 10, 1995, p. 18.

Crown, Judith, "Selling Brands Abroad," *Crain's Chicago Business,* Feb. 24, 1992, p. 13.

Dubashi, Jagannath, "Shampoo," *Financial World,* December 8, 1992, pp. 68+.

Edgecliffe-Johnson, Andrew, "Unilever to Merge Three US Units," *Financial Times,* September 26, 1997, p. 22.

Freeman, Laurie, "Using Finesse: Helene Curtis Looks Overseas," *Advertising Age,* March 6, 1989, p. 36.

Gallagher, Patricia, "Why Helene Curtis Should Be Sweating," *Crain's Chicago Business,* June 20, 1994, pp. 1, 52.

Gibson, Richard, "Unilever Cut Bid for Curtis After Projection," *Wall Street Journal,* February 23, 1996, p. A7.

Gibson, Richard, and Sara Calian, "Unilever to Buy Helene Curtis for $770 Million," *Wall Street Journal,* February 15, 1996, pp. A3, A4.

Helene Curtis: Beauty Innovations Around the World Since 1927, Chicago: Helene Curtis Industries, Inc., 1978.

"Helene Curtis Enters a New Era of Innovation," *Drug and Cosmetics Industry,* August 1996, pp. 34–37.

"Helene Curtis Industries, Inc.," *The Market for Toiletries and Cosmetics,* New York: Business Trends Analysts, 1989, pp. 515–19.

Kalish, David, "Personal Care: Salon Selectives—Cheap Chic," *Marketing and Media Decisions,* March 1989, pp. 95–98.

Mehegan, Sean, "Lean, Mean Helene Shapes Up for P&G," *Brandweek,* June 17, 1996, pp. 1+.

Rejtman, Jack, "Degree Antiperspirant Has Scent of Success," *Wall Street Journal,* August 12, 1993, p. B8.

Rewick, C. J., "A Model Makeover: New Parent Unilever Adds Bounce to Helene Curtis Brands," *Crain's Chicago Business,* March 22, 1999, p. 13.

Schellhardt, Timothy D., "Tossing Its Head at P&G, Helene Curtis Styles Itself No. 1 in the Hair-Care Market," *Wall Street Journal,* November 19, 1992, p. B1.

"Skin Care Market Shows New Signs of Vitality," *Drug and Cosmetic Industry,* August 1992, pp. 28–29.

Sloan, Pat, "Degree Makes Leaders Sweat," *Advertising Age,* December 10, 1990, p. 16.

—Sina Dubovoj
—updated by David E. Salamie

Herman Goelitz, Inc.

2400 North Watney Way
Fairfield, California 94533
U.S.A.
(707) 428-2800
Fax: (707) 423-4436
Web site: http://www.jellybelly.com

Private Company
Incorporated: 1898 as Goelitz Confectionary Company
Employees: 400
Sales: $100 million (1998 est.)
NAIC: 31134 Nonchocolate Confectionery
    Manufacturing; 31133 Confectionery Manufacturing
    from Purchased Chocolate

Herman Goelitz, Inc. is a privately held candy company known primarily for its phenomenally successful "Jelly Belly" jelly beans. The gourmet beans rocketed to fame during the first presidential campaign of Ronald Reagan, and Reagan's passion for the sweet treats encouraged sales of Jelly Bellies around the world. The company makes a full range of candy products, but Jelly Bellies account for about 70 percent of sales. Herman Goelitz also manufactures candy corn, licorice candies, assorted gummy candies such as bears and worms, and chocolates such as chocolate mints and chocolate-covered nuts. The company operates out of headquarters in Fairfield, California, plus manufacturing facilities in Fairfield and in North Chicago, Illinois. Goelitz also runs one freestanding retail store to sell its candies, as well as stores attached to its manufacturing plants. A new plant is in development near Kenosha, Wisconsin, that will feature a store and restaurant as well as expanded production facilities. Herman Goelitz candies are sold across the United States and in 35 countries worldwide.

Early Years

The company that became Herman Goelitz, Inc. was begun by two immigrant brothers from the Harz Mountain region of Germany. Gustav and Albert Goelitz came to the United States shortly after the Civil War, and settled in Illinois with an uncle who had emigrated earlier. The brothers went into business in 1869 in Belleville, Illinois, making and selling candy. Elder brother Gustav, who was 24 at the time, made the candy in the back room of their store, and handled retail sales up front. Albert, who was 21, sold their candy in neighboring towns, traveling tirelessly in a horsedrawn wagon.

The business prospered, and the two brothers married and raised families. Gustav's sons eventually joined the business. By about 1890, the business had moved into a handsome brick building on Main Street in St. Louis. But the candy company was hard hit by the depression that gripped the country a few years later, the infamous Panic of 1893. Economic turmoil, combined with labor unrest, unmoored the previously successful confectionary, and the brothers were forced to sell the business in order to satisfy debts. Gustav Goelitz was apparently shattered by the loss, and he died in 1901, when he was only 55 years old. Albert, on the other hand, lived to be 80, and worked until his death as a traveling candy salesman, selling another company's products.

By 1898, with the Panic behind them, Gustav's sons decided to restart the family business. Adolph Goelitz moved to Cincinnati and opened the Goelitz Confectionary Company there. He was joined by a friend and neighbor, William Kelley, and eventually by Kelley's cousin Edward and by the younger Goelitz brothers Gus, Jr., and Herman. These families became more closely tied when Edward Kelley married one of the Goelitz sisters, Joanna. This second start for the Goelitz candy empire was a good one. The candy industry in the United States was growing overall, and by 1912 Goelitz Confectionary had so much business it had to turn down new orders. In order to expand production, the company moved to North Chicago, Illinois, a factory town with low land costs and easy access to railroads. Goelitz built a new plant in North Chicago, and specialized in the types of candy known as butter creams or mellocremes. Goelitz's bestseller was candy corn, a soft, three-color candy that was made by a painstaking pouring process.

Through the World Wars

The years of World War I were apparently difficult for Goelitz Confectionary. Anti-German sentiment was strong in the United States, and this may have led to problems at the company. At this time, no one could decide who should lead the company, and each of the family members took a turn. Soon Gus, Jr., left the company, and brother Herman departed for California to found his own business. He set up Herman Goelitz Candy Company in Oakland in 1922, and carried on with his family's famous recipe for candy corn. Because of the difficulty of shipping candy long distances, the industry of that era was strictly regional, so Herman's new company was not in competition with the North Chicago Goelitz Confectionary.

Both Goelitz companies did well throughout the 1920s, a time of great growth and prosperity in American industry. Then, just as the whole country suffered through the Great Depression of the 1930s, so, too, did the candy companies. But unlike many other candy companies, the Goelitz companies remained in business. Candy corn, the staple of both companies, had sold for 16 cents a pound in the 1920s, and during the Depression the price was almost half that, at 8½ cents. But the Goelitz companies kept going, and eventually a third generation of the family joined the business. Aloyse Goelitz, Herman's daughter, married Ernest Rowland, and Rowland too became part of the confectionary company. In Illinois, descendants of the Goelitz and Kelley families joined the business.

Hard times for the candy industry ended with the advent of World War II. Candy consumption rose nationwide. Although sugar was rationed and the war caused labor shortages, the Goelitz companies worked at top capacity. Because chocolate was also rationed, and most of it was consigned to soldiers fighting overseas, non-chocolate candy such as the Goelitz companies specialized in saw something of a resurgence. After the war, growth in candy consumption jumped up an astonishing 60 percent, and the companies did quite well.

A New Direction in the 1970s

The high tide that had lifted the Goelitz companies through World War II and after subsided by the 1970s. Other manufacturers began producing candy corn, long the Goelitz specialty, cutting into market share and competing on price. Both Goelitz companies relied almost exclusively on mellocremes, soft candies made by the candy corn method. This restricted product line hurt the companies. Aloyse and Ernest Rowland, who were running the California Herman Goelitz Candy Co., came up with an idea for a new candy while driving across the desert after a trade show in Las Vegas in 1972. This was a chocolate-covered mint, called the Dutch Mint, the first chocolate the company had ever manufactured. The Dutch Mint became one of the best-selling Goelitz products, but it alone was not enough to get the company out of financial trouble. It was clear to both William Kelley, who ran the Illinois Goelitz Confectionary, and to the Rowlands in California, that the companies would have to diversify their product lines in order to continue to compete with bigger national confectioners. But expansion was particularly difficult in the mid-1970s because of escalating sugar prices. By 1975, the sugar market was in a crisis, as unusually high prices forced many sugar-dependent companies out of business. William Kelley shut down the North Chicago Goelitz plant for some months, hoping to reopen when the sugar market settled down. Rowland in California borrowed heavily to stay in business, and energetically branched into more non-mellocreme candies.

The most significant year for the Goelitz companies came in 1976, when the Jelly Belly was born. Herman Goelitz Candy Co. had been making traditional jelly beans since 1965. These candies were made with a clear center of pectin, and covered with a hard sugar casing of different fruit flavors. There was nothing particularly novel about the Goelitz jelly beans, though the governor of California, Ronald Reagan, did fancy them. He had turned to jelly beans as an oral fix after he quit smoking. In 1976 David Klein, a Los Angeles candy distributor, approached Goelitz's president Herman Rowland with an idea for a ''Rolls Royce'' of jelly beans, a pungently fruit-flavored bean made with natural ingredients. Rowland's company took on Klein's idea, and developed eight varieties of a small, intensely flavored jelly bean.

Whereas traditional jelly beans had flavoring only in the sugar coating, these new beans had a strong flavor in the center as well. They were gourmet jelly beans, much more exciting to the palate than the old Easter standby. The first eight flavors debuted in the summer of 1976, and immediately attracted attention. The company sold its Jelly Bellies in bags of a single flavor, a marked departure from the traditional assorted mix. Each flavor was so intense that it needed to be savored individually. The taste caused a sensation, and production had to be stepped up at Herman Goelitz. Within a year, 25 flavors of Jelly Bellies had been developed, and demand was growing. Herman Rowland proposed that his California company formally join the other branch of the family, and buy into Goelitz Confectionary in Illinois. The two companies reunited in 1978, becoming Herman Goelitz, Inc.

Jelly Bellies had many celebrity fans, including such stars as Barbra Streisand, Jerry Lewis, Jack Lemmon, and Glenn Ford. But the Jelly Belly aficionado who really put the candy on the map was Ronald Reagan. He had been eating regular jelly beans for years, and when Goelitz sent him the new Jelly Bellies, he was hooked. While Reagan was governor of California, Goelitz supplied his administration with two dozen one-pound bags of jelly beans every month. During his campaign for president in 1980, the press commented on Reagan's jelly bean habit, and Jelly Bellies suddenly got enormous exposure. Goelitz came up with a new flavor, blueberry, in order to provide red, white, and blue Jelly Bellies for Reagan's inauguration, and Herman Rowland donated three-and-a-half tons of beans for the festivities. Jelly Bellies became an integral part of the Reagan administration, as the president had a jar of them on the table for all his meetings. Herman Goelitz, Inc. supplied a standing order for up to 60 cases of Jelly Bellies every month, which were distributed throughout the White House, Capitol Hill, and numerous government agencies. By 1981, the company was netting about $6 million from Jelly Bellies, and sales had started to go international. The Goelitz plants in both Illinois and California were running round-the-clock shifts, and they still could not keep up with orders.

Continued Growth in the 1980s and 1990s

Goelitz executives worried that Jelly Bellies was just a fad, but the bottom did not fall out. The company opened a new plant and corporate headquarters in Fairfield, California, in 1986. By 1992, the company had to double the size of the plant. Though Jelly Bellies sold for three to four times the price of traditional jelly beans, devoted customers were willing to pay the price, and the brand found new adherents every year. Jelly Bellies occupied a niche market, and Goelitz thought it might be able to expand sales by placing the candy in supermarkets and other mass market outlets. The company set up a mass market division in 1991. However, this effort proved unsuccessful, apparently because Goelitz did not want to pay the so-called slotting fees that supermarkets required for new products.

Despite the failure of this initial push, by 1997 approximately 15 percent of Jelly Bellies sales came from mass outlets. Other big candy makers had begun to encroach on Jelly Belly territory, as both Hershey and Mars came out with new jelly bean recipes. Sales at Herman Goelitz had grown by about 15 percent annually since 1985, and the candy maker searched for new ways to continue its expansion. In 1996, the company opened its first retail store. The store, in a factory outlet mall not far from the company's headquarters in Fairfield, California, sold the whole Goelitz line of candies in addition to all the 40 official Jelly Belly flavors and ''Belly Flops''—beans the factory had rejected because of imperfect shape. The retail store was an outgrowth of the stores the company ran attached to its factories. Goelitz factory tours were increasingly popular, drawing 175,000 people to the Fairfield factory in 1996. In 1997, the company tried again to reach mass markets, hoping to expand its sales in that category from 15 percent to 25 percent. Because Jelly Bellies were perceived as a gourmet item, the company had to be careful to keep up this effect even while reaching into supermarkets and chain stores. Goelitz chose its mass outlets carefully, venturing into ones that were well-respected in their regions. These included Dominick's Freer Foods in Illinois, Albertson's on the West Coast, the Alabama-based Bruno's, and Wegman's in upstate New York. Goelitz hired brokers and distributors to keep up its Jelly Belly displays and bulk bins in these chains, so there would be no sloppy or poorly maintained displays that could bring down the fine image of the brand.

The company marketed Jelly Bellies in innovative ways, spending little on conventional advertising but relying on word of mouth from lots of giveaways. Goelitz provided 350,000 free sample bags of Jelly Bellies a month to Southwest Airlines in the late 1990s, and gave away numerous samples through sports events such as golf tournaments and boat races. When the company came up with a new flavor, it relied on lots of sampling and feedback to determine if it had a good one. For 1997, the company projected it would give away more than 10 million bags of samples.

The company also tried to expand its export sales in the late 1990s. Because of Jelly Bellies' popularity with Ronald Reagan, the candy had been introduced around the world during his years in office. International orders comprised about seven percent of sales by 1998, with sales concentrated in six countries. The company used the same advertising techniques abroad as at home, that is, principally sampling, to try to reach more customers abroad. Goelitz president Herman Rowland aimed to grow the company's international sales to at least ten percent over the next few years.

To keep up with its enormous growth, the company invested $40 million in a new factory in Wisconsin that was set to open in the year 2000. The new plant was to have a 375,000-square-foot ground floor production area, with a second story devoted to a visitors center. The company also started construction on a new visitors center at its Fairfield plant, to handle the burgeoning crowds that took Goelitz's Candyland tours. In addition, the company attempted to bolster its non-Jelly Belly brands in the late 1990s. To spread the gourmet cachet to its other products, Goelitz repackaged some of its other candies, such as Jordan Almonds, Licorice Pastels, and Dutch Mints, in gift boxes imprinted with the line ''from the makers of Jelly Belly.'' Though Jelly Bellies made up about 70 percent of the company's $100 million sales in 1998, Goelitz wanted to emphasize that it had many other products, all made with the same care that went into its flagship brand.

Principal Subsidiaries

Goelitz Confectionary Co.; Herman Goelitz Candy Co.

Further Reading

''Hill of Beans,'' *Time*, February 23, 1981, p. 122.
Ledford, Dave, ''Goelitz's Fortunes Set by Employee Loyalty,'' *Candy Industry*, June 1998, pp. 30–32.
Mehegan, Sean, ''Brand Builders: Seeding New Ground,'' *Brandweek*, June 2, 1997, p. 20.
Slater, Pam, ''Maker of Jelly Belly Candy Takes Retail Leap with California Store,'' *Knight-Ridder/Tribune Business News*, October 10, 1996, p. 1010B0236.
Tiffany, Susan, ''Herman Goelitz's Sweet Fortunes Overflow,'' *Candy Industry*, June 1998, pp. 22–28.
Wilhelm, Maria, ''If the Reagan Administration Is Full of Beans, Blame Jelly Belly Baron Herman Rowland,'' *People*, February 23, 1981, p. 103.

—A. Woodward

Hewlett-Packard Company

3000 Hanover Street
Palo Alto, California 94304
U.S.A.
(650) 857-1501
(800) 752-0900
Fax: (650) 857-7299
Web site: http://www.hp.com

Public Company
Incorporated: 1947
Employees: 124,600
Sales: $47.06 billion (1998)
Stock Exchanges: New York Pacific Frankfurt London
     Paris Tokyo Zürich
Ticker Symbol: HWP
NAIC: 334111 Electronic Computer Manufacturing;
     334112 Computer Storage Device Manufacturing;
     334119 Other Computer Peripheral Equipment
     Manufacturing; 333313 Office Machinery
     Manufacturing; 334413 Semiconductors & Related
     Device Manufacturing; 334613 Magnetic & Optical
     Recording Media Manufacturing; 334519 Other
     Measuring & Controlling Device Manufacturing;
     334510 Electromedical & Electrotherapeutic
     Apparatus Manufacturing; 811212 Computer & Office
     Machine Repair & Maintenance

Hewlett-Packard Company (HP) is the second largest computer company in the world, behind only International Business Machines Corporation (IBM). Its offerings in the computer area include hardware ranging from palmtops through personal computers to supercomputers, software, networking products, printers, scanners, and support and maintenance services. In 1998 HP derived 84 percent of its revenues from its computer sector. The remainder came from test and measurement products and service, medical electronic products and service, electronic components, and chemical analysis and service. In March 1999 the company announced that it would spin off these operations as an independent company by mid-2000 in order to sharpen its focus on its computer operations.

Began As Maker of Test and Measurement Products

William Hewlett and David Packard, graduates of Stanford University's electrical engineering program, were encouraged by Professor Frederick Terman to start their own business in California. The two men worked in the garage behind Packard's rented house in Palo Alto, California. Starting with only $538, the men began work on a resistance-capacity audio oscillator, a machine used for testing sound equipment. After assembling several models—baking paint for the instrument panel in Packard's oven—they won their first big order, for eight oscillators, from Walt Disney Studios, which used them to develop and test a new sound system for the animated film *Fantasia.*

On January 1, 1939, Hewlett and Packard formalized their venture as a partnership, tossing a coin to decide the order of their names. Hewlett won. In 1940, with a product line of eight items, the two men moved their company and its three employees to a building in downtown Palo Alto.

During World War II, Terman, who was then in charge of antiradar projects at Harvard, contracted his former students to manufacture microwave signal generators for his research. When the war ended, HP took full advantage of the growth in the electronics sector, particularly in the defense and industrial areas. The founders also decided at that time what their respective roles would be in the company: Hewlett would lead technological development, and Packard would be in charge of management. Hewlett-Packard Company was incorporated in 1947. By 1950 the company had 70 products, 143 employees, and revenues of $2 million.

HP introduced a revolutionary high-speed frequency counter, the HP524A, in 1951. This device, which reduced the time required to measure radio frequencies from ten minutes to about two seconds, was used by radio stations to maintain accurate broadcast frequencies, particularly on the newly established FM band.

Company Perspectives:

Our basic business purpose is to create information products that accelerate the advancement of knowledge and improve the effectiveness of people and organizations.

The company maintained stable and impressive growth through the end of the decade. In November 1957 Hewlett-Packard offered shares to the public for the first time. It also moved into a larger complex in the Stanford Research Park.

In 1958, with revenues of $30 million, HP made its first corporate acquisition: the F.L. Moseley Company of Pasadena, California, a manufacturer of graphic recorders. The company's expansion continued in 1959 with the establishment of a marketing office in Geneva, and a manufacturing facility in Boeblingen, West Germany. After adding another factory in Loveland, Colorado, in 1960, Hewlett-Packard purchased the Sanborn Company, a medical instruments manufacturer based in Waltham, Massachusetts, in 1961.

The company gained wider public recognition when it was listed on the Pacific and New York stock exchanges in 1961 and in the *Fortune* 500 a year later. In 1964 Hewlett-Packard developed a cesium-beam "flying clock," accurate to within one-millionth of a second. Company engineers embarked on a 35-day, 35,000-mile world tour to coordinate standard times.

In 1963 Hewlett-Packard expanded its presence in Japan through a joint venture with the Yokogawa Electric Works, and in 1965 it acquired the F & M Scientific Corporation, an analytical-instruments manufacturer, based in Avondale, Pennsylvania. In 1966 the company opened its central research laboratory, which became one of the world's leading electronic research centers.

Moved into Calculators and Computers in the Late 1960s and 1970s

Though primarily a manufacturer of instruments for analysis and measurement, Hewlett-Packard developed a computer in 1966. The HP-2116A was developed specifically for HP's own production control; the company had no plans to enter the computer market. Two years later, however, HP introduced the HP-9100A, the first desktop calculator capable of performing scientific functions. In 1969 David Packard was appointed deputy secretary of defense in President Richard Nixon's administration. Packard returned to his company as a director in 1972.

During this time, HP developed a handheld scientific calculator called the HP-35, known as the "electronic slide rule." Designed partially by Bill Hewlett, it was introduced in 1972. When Texas Instruments entered the market in 1973, Hewlett-Packard's device, which retailed at $395, was forced into the high end of the market.

Hewlett-Packard made its first decisive move into business computing, a field dominated by IBM and Digital Equipment Corporation, with the HP3000 minicomputer, introduced in 1972. This signalled a major change in company strategy. In the spring of 1974 Hewlett and Packard decided, despite record earnings, that the company was growing too fast. Refocusing on product leadership, the founders established a new, highly decentralized structure, letting each of the company's divisions conduct its own research and development.

In 1977 Bill Hewlett relinquished the presidency to John Young, a career HP man determined to make the company successful in the computer market. Although he was chosen by Hewlett and Packard, Young was virtually unknown to the company's customers and 37,000 employees. Nonetheless, he replaced Hewlett as chief executive officer a year later.

Introduced Personal Computers and Printers in the 1980s

Hewlett-Packard introduced its first personal computer, the HP-85, in 1980. The market's initial reaction was cool, causing Young and other managers to investigate new, IBM-compatible designs, which were introduced in the mid-1980s. HP's broad move into information processing proved successful; the company quickly established itself as a leading computer vendor. Like other vendors, however, HP had designed each of its major computer lines for a specific use, making each model incompatible with the others. This resulted in redundant research and development and product support costs, and limited expansion capabilities for customers. In response to these problems, HP began a six-year program to develop architecture and software that would be compatible with existing programs. In the meantime, HP introduced a number of other products, including the HP9000 technical workstation (1982), the HP150 touchscreen PC, the HP ThinkJet inkjet printer (1984), and the HP LaserJet printer—a phenomenally successful product which came to dominate the printer market soon after its 1984 debut.

In 1986 the company introduced its new family of Spectrum computer systems, developed at a cost of $250 million. The project was based on a concept called RISC—Reduced-Instruction-Set Computing. RISC enabled programs to run at double or triple conventional speed by eliminating many routine instructions. In spite of critics' claims that the stripped-down instruction set made the program less flexible and overspecialized, other computer companies soon began developing their own RISC chips.

While market projections for Spectrum were good, and the system itself was state of the art, HP initially failed to capitalize on its technology because of the company's strategy of focusing on markets rather than product lines. Sales efforts, however, were soon redoubled on every level. The company even began joint marketing with telecommunications and peripherals companies previously regarded as competitors.

John Young's leadership of Hewlett-Packard was highly regarded. The Precision Architecture line gained wider acceptance after a problematic introduction, and came to be seen as a bold gamble. By 1988 Young had restored the company's momentum, with net earnings rising 27 percent during that year. Directors Hewlett and Packard were no longer involved in the day-to-day running of the business, and in 1987 Walter B.

Hewlett and David Woodley Packard, the sons of the founders, were elected to the board. In 1988 the company's stock began trading on the Tokyo stock exchange—its first listing outside the United States—then the following year gained listings on four European exchanges: London, Zürich, Paris, and Frankfurt.

In April 1989 Hewlett-Packard paid $500 million for Apollo Computer, a pioneer in the design, manufacture, and sale of engineering workstations. Integrating the two companies and eliminating unnecessary engineers and salespeople proved more time-consuming than anticipated, and as sales dropped, Hewlett-Packard slipped back to second position in late 1989. The company faced a further setback when Motorola Inc. delayed introduction of the advanced microprocessor chip it had promised HP for a new line of workstations.

Following a trend that developed in the information processing industry in the late 1980s and early 1990s, HP forged alliances with a number of companies that had previously been competitors. These included Hitachi, a microchip company; Canon, which provided the engines for HP's bestselling laser printer line; and 3Com, with which HP had a marketing and research agreement. Purchases during this period included Eon Systems, a manufacturer of equipment that monitored computer networks; and Hilco Technologies, a maker of factory software in which HP obtained a 25 percent stake.

Early 1990s Difficulties Led to Restructuring

In spite of the new focus on workstation technology and cooperative trade agreements, HP began 1990 with sagging profits and a lackluster consumer response to its new product line. Like many of its larger competitors, it had fallen victim to an unwieldy bureaucracy that discouraged entrepreneurial decision-making on the part of group managers. In 1990 earnings fell 11 percent to $739 million, down from $829 million in 1989. David Packard, the retired cofounder of the company, returned to his office to take a more active role in running the business.

John Young, president and CEO, responded to the crisis by undertaking a thorough restructuring of Hewlett-Packard. He eliminated excess layers of management and divided computer products into two main groups: those sold directly to big customers (workstations and minicomputers) and those sold through discount dealers (printers and PCs). In a deliberate move away from the consensus style of management, he set up a virtually autonomous design group within the computer division, and put it in charge of developing a new workstation based on the RISC technology that Digital had helped pioneer. The results were impressive. After only a year of development, the Series 700 workstations were introduced in 1991 to universally favorable reviews. The machines were considered several years ahead of their time, a crucial advantage in an industry where the constant development of new technologies makes products obsolete almost as soon as they reach the market.

HP's 95LX palmtop personal computer, also introduced in 1991, established an important new market in information devices. The 95LX, which retailed for $699, contained built-in Lotus 1-2-3 spreadsheet software, and immediately became a hot seller. Realizing its potential as the wave of the future,

Hewlett-Packard quickly began to look for alternative markets for the palmtop, including navigation software and real estate applications.

The resurgence of the company was not achieved without a price. Reluctantly violating its no-layoff policy, HP cut 3,000 positions in 1990 and a further 2,000 positions in 1991. While executives agree that downsizing was a necessary evil, the staff reductions, together with a more aggressive advertising stance, changed the company's image. When John Young announced his retirement in July 1992, he presided over a dynamic, if less paternalistic, company. His successor, Lewis E. Platt, an executive vice-president and head of the company's computer systems organization, took over in November 1992. Following Packard's retirement as chairman in 1993, Platt was named chairman, president, and CEO of HP.

Aggressively Expanded in PCs in the Mid-1990s

When Platt took over as CEO in 1992, Hewlett-Packard's share of the personal computer market was a mere one percent. Moreover, PCs accounted for only 5.7 percent of the company's overall revenues of $16.4 billion. By 1995 HP was the fastest-growing maker of PCs in the world, having initially targeted corporate customers. In August 1995 HP went after the home PC market with the launch of the Pavilion line. Throughout this revitalization of the company's PC lines, HP adopted a much more aggressive pricing policy. It had traditionally charged a premium price for its personal computers, but began pricing them no higher than five percent above the lowest-priced comparable models on the market. Its market share consequently soared, with the company leaping all the way to third place in mid-1997, edging out Dell Computer and trailing only Compaq Computer Corporation and IBM. By 1998 Hewlett-Packard derived 19.1 percent of its total revenues of $47.06 billion from the sale of personal computers.

Hewlett-Packard's pursuit of personal computer prominence was problematic given that sector's relatively low margins, but Platt felt the company had to be a major player in PCs in order to remain one of the top computer companies in the world. Although Platt did not want HP to be ''just'' a peripherals company, the firm continued to churn out successful products in that area: the HP Color LaserJet printer and the HP OfficeJet multifunction machine (a combined printer, fax machine, and copier), both introduced in 1994; and the HP OmniGo 100 handheld organizer, which debuted in 1995. With the Internet and electronic commerce burgeoning, HP in mid-1997 paid nearly $1.2 billion to acquire VeriFone, Inc., a maker of in-store terminals used to verify credit card transactions. HP hoped to combine a personal computer or other electronic device with a VeriFone-derived card reader and appropriate software to create a system providing consumers with additional payment options for their electronic commerce purchases. Also in 1997 HP was added to the companies that comprise the prestigious Dow Jones Industrial Average. Meantime, cofounder David Packard died on March 26, 1996.

Hewlett-Packard's revenues had been growing at an annual 20-percent-plus clip from 1993 through 1996, but in 1997 these increases began to shrink. Sales increased from $38.42 billion in 1996 to $42.9 billion in 1997, or 11.6 percent, then to 47.06

billion in 1998, an increase of 9.7 percent. Net income fell from $3.12 billion in 1997 to $2.95 billion in 1998. Among the reasons for these declining fortunes was the Asian economic crisis, which began in July 1997; HP's slow response to the opportunities presented by the explosion of the Internet; and falling prices for personal computers and computer peripherals. In addition, HP's printer lines, especially in the inkjet area, were being buffeted by competition from new, low-cost rivals and declining margins in the PC and printer areas were dragging down the profitability of HP as a whole.

1999 Plan to Spinoff Noncomputing Lines

In late 1998 the company launched a comprehensive review of its operations. It announced in March 1999 that as a result of this review it intended to spin off into a separate firm its non-computing segments: test and measurement products and service, medical electronic products and service, electronic components, and chemical analysis and service. These segments generated about $7.6 billion in revenues during 1998, or 16 percent of the total. Hewlett-Packard hoped this major divestment—which included the company's original lines of business—would sharpen the firm's competitive instincts, energize its workforce, and enable it to become a more aggressive player in the increasingly important sphere of the Internet. The company also announced that upon completion of the spinoff by mid-2000, Platt would step down as chairman and CEO. A search committee was formed by the company board to find a successor; this person might be an outsider, which would be a company first. In any event, it was clear that the turn of the millennium marked the end of an era, and the beginning of a new one, for Hewlett-Packard.

Principal Subsidiaries

Hewlett-Packard Puerto Rico; Hewlett-Packard World Trade, Inc.; Heartstream, Inc.; Microsensor Technology, Inc.; VeriFone, Inc.; Hewlett-Packard Asia Pacific Ltd. (Hong Kong); Hewlett-Packard Caribe Ltd. (Cayman Islands); HP Computadores (Brazil); Hewlett-Packard Computer Products (Shanghai) Co., Ltd. (China); Hewlett-Packard de Mexico S.A. de C.V.; Hewlett-Packard Espanola, S.A. (Spain); Hewlett-Packard Europe B.V. (the Netherlands); Hewlett-Packard France; Hewlett-Packard GmbH (Germany); Hewlett-Packard Holding GmbH (Germany); Hewlett-Packard (India) Software Operation Pte. Ltd.; Hewlett-Packard Italiana S.p.A. (Italy); Hewlett-Packard Japan, Ltd.; Hewlett-Packard Korea Ltd.; Hewlett-Packard Ltd. (U.K.); Hewlett-Packard (Malaysia) Sdn. Bhd.; Hewlett-Packard Malaysia Technology Sdn. Bhd.; Hewlett-Packard (Manufacturing) Ltd. (Ireland); Hewlett-Packard Medical Products (Qingdao) Ltd. (China); Hewlett-Packard Microwave Products (M) Sdn. Bhd. (Malaysia); Hewlett-Packard Penang Sdn. Bhd. (Malaysia); Hewlett-Packard S.A. (Switzerland); Hewlett-Packard Shanghai Analytical Products Co., Ltd. (China); Hewlett-Packard Singapore Pte. Ltd.; Hewlett-Packard Singapore Vision Operation Pte. Ltd.; BT&D Technologies Ltd. (U.K.); CoCreate Software GmbH (Germany); Shanghai Hewlett-Packard Company (China); Technologies et Participations S.A. (France).

Principal Operating Units

Chemical Analysis Group; Components Group; Consumer Products Group; Enterprise Computing Solutions Organization; HP Labs; Information Storage Group; LaserJet Solutions Group; Medical Products Group; Personal Systems Group; Test and Measurement Organization.

Further Reading

Arnst, Catherine, "Now, HP Stands for Hot Products," *Business Week,* June 14, 1993, p. 36.

Buell, Barbara, "Hewlett-Packard Rethinks Itself," *Business Week,* April 1, 1991.

Burrows, Peter, "Lew Platt's Fix-It Plan for Hewlett-Packard," *Business Week,* July 13, 1998, pp. 128–31.

——, "The Printer King Invades Home PCs," *Business Week,* August 21, 1995, pp. 74–75.

Clark, Don, and George Anders, "After Split, Outsider May Be Hired As Next CEO, Breaking Tradition," *Wall Street Journal,* March 3, 1999, pp. A3 + .

Goldgaber, Arthur, "The Teflon Tech Company: How Long Will Wall Street Give Hewlett-Packard the Benefit of the Doubt?," *Financial World,* July/August 1997, pp. 90–93.

Hamilton, David P., and Scott Thurm, "H-P to Spin Off Its Measurement Operations: Sharper Focus on Computing Will Emerge," *Wall Street Journal,* March 3, 1999, pp. A3 + .

Hof, Robert, "Hewlett-Packard Digs Deep for a Digital Future," *Business Week,* October 18, 1993, pp. 72–75.

——, "Suddenly Hewlett-Packard Is Doing Everything Right," *Business Week,* March 23, 1992.

Hof, Robert, and Peter Burrows, "Hewlett-Packard Heads for the Home," *Business Week,* May 8, 1995, p. 102.

"HP Fact Sheet," Palo Alto, Calif.: Hewlett-Packard Company, 1998.

Hutheesing, Nikhil, "HP's Giant ATM," *Forbes,* February 9, 1998, pp. 96 + .

Klein, Alec, "As Cheap Printers Score, H-P Plays Catch-Up," *Wall Street Journal,* April 21, 1999, pp. B1 + .

Linden, Dana Wechsler, and Bruce Upbin, "Top Corporate Performance of 1995: 'Boy Scouts on a Rampage,' " *Forbes,* January 1, 1996, pp. 66 + .

Nee, Eric, "Defending the Desktop," *Forbes,* December 28, 1998, p. 53.

——, "Lew Platt: Why I Dismembered HP," *Fortune,* March 29, 1999, p. 167.

——, "What Have You Invented for Me Lately?," *Forbes,* July 28, 1997, pp. 76 + .

Packard, David, *The HP Way: How Bill Hewlett and I Built Our Company,* edited by David Kirby with Karen Lewis, New York: HarperBusiness, 1995, 212 p.

Pitta, Julie, "It Had to Be Done and We Did It," *Forbes,* April 26, 1993, pp. 148–52.

Stross, Randall E., "What's a High-Class Company Like Hewlett-Packard Doing in a Lowbrow Business Like PCs?," *Fortune,* September 29, 1997, pp. 129 + .

Wiegner, Kathleen K., "Good-Bye to the HP Way?," *Forbes,* November 26, 1990.

Zell, Deone, *Changing by Design: Organizational Innovation at Hewlett-Packard,* Ithaca, N.Y.: ILR Press, 1997, 180 p.

—John Simley
—updated by David E. Salamie

Hexcel Corporation

Two Stamford Plaza
281 Tresser Boulevard
Stamford, Connecticut 06901-3238
U.S.A.
(203) 969-0666
Fax: (203) 358-3993
Web site: http://www.hexcel.com

Public Company
Incorporated: 1948 as California Reinforced Products
    Company
Employees: 5,597
Sales: $1.09 billion (1998)
Stock Exchanges: New York Pacific
Ticker Symbol: HXL
NAIC: 332116 Metal Stamping; 31321 Broadwoven
    Fabric Mills; 335991 Carbon and Graphite Product
    Manufacturing; 325211 Plastics Material & Resin
    Manufacturing; 32552 Adhesive Manufacturing;
    31332 Fabric Coating Mills

Hexcel Corporation is the worldwide leader in the manufacture of advanced structural composites. These materials, which include honeycomb-cell reinforced structures, resin-coated woven fiber sheets, and other types of composite products, are used in a variety of applications where light weight and strength are required. About half of the company's sales are to aircraft manufacturers, while another tenth are to space and defense contractors. The remainder of Hexcel's customers include makers of athletic equipment, such as tennis racquets and running shoes, manufacturers of printed circuit boards, and the construction industry. The company also manufactures specialty chemicals that are used in such products as cough syrup and mouthwash. Since emerging from bankruptcy in 1995, Hexcel has begun acquiring companies that add to its strengths. A merger with the composite division of the Swiss chemical giant Ciba-Geigy in 1996 gave that company almost half of Hexcel's stock. Wary of its longtime reliance on the aerospace and defense industries, Hexcel has been seeking diversification to give it greater stability, completing a series of major acquisitions

following the merger that have given the company a wider range of products than ever before.

Early Years

In 1946 two engineers working at the University of California-Berkeley, Roger Steele and Roscoe Hughes, decided to explore the possible commercial uses of a variety of new plastics and construction technologies developed during World War II. Working initially out of Hughes's basement, Steele refined a product called expanded honeycomb over the next two years. In 1948, following a successful demonstration of expanded honeycomb at a government-sponsored plastics conference, the newly christened California Reinforced Plastics Company was awarded its first contract, for research and development of honeycomb materials for use in radar domes on military aircraft. The company was incorporated in September of that year. In 1949 California Reinforced Plastics gambled, submitting an intentionally low bid to produce fuel cell support panels for the B-36 bomber; the bid was accepted, further cementing the new company's ties to the defense industry.

The early 1950s saw continued growth, and in 1954 the company's name was changed to Hexcel Products, Inc., which was derived from the hexagonal cell-shaped honeycomb materials which it manufactured. These cellular structures, made from galvanized fiberglass or aluminum and other materials, were lighter in weight and stronger than a comparable amount of steel, and were ideal for use in aircraft where any weight that could be saved in construction could be allocated to payload or fuel.

By the late 1950s a national recession and a series of military cutbacks were affecting Hexcel's sales. In 1961 the company chose a new president, William S. Powell, who subsequently restructured the company's operations, exiting several unprofitable lines of business. Soon after this the military buildup of the Vietnam War era caused the company's sales to climb again, with record sales to profits ratios between 1962 and 1967. A new manufacturing plant was begun in Arizona in 1965, and in 1967 Hexcel's first overseas operation came on line, in Welkenraedt, Belgium. In 1968 Hexcel purchased one of its major suppliers, Coast Manufacturing, and that company's three manufacturing plants. Hexcel products were now being used in military and

Company Perspectives:

Hexcel's operating principles are: Customer Satisfaction— Customer satisfaction is our highest priority. We will provide the highest quality materials and services to make our customers' products stronger, lighter, better; Continuous Improvement—We will always strive to improve and we will pursue continuous improvements in all of our activities through measured performance in a fact-based culture; Simplicity and Speed—In all that we do, we seek to simplify the task by identifying what is essential and then to implement with efficiency and speed; Employee Commitment and Pride—The strength within Hexcel is its employees. Our success depends on hiring, developing and retaining employees who are knowledgeable, committed to teamwork and proud of what they do. We will provide them with an open, creative and safe workplace, communicating to them frequently and honestly; Honoring Commitments—We will live up to the commitments we make to our customers, employees, suppliers, shareholders and the communities in which we do business.

commercial aviation as well as the United States space program. The landing pads on the lunar module that carried the first men to the moon were built from Hexcel honeycomb materials. The company's revenues in this period were still almost exclusively derived from honeycomb products.

Another sales slump at the start of the 1970s saw Hexcel implement further changes. Harvie M. Merrill, who had become CEO and president in 1969, began to seek markets outside of the company's traditional aerospace and defense areas. One such venture was the introduction of skis made of composite materials. The company brought these to market in 1971, the first time it had made something for direct retail sale. Unfortunately Hexcel's lack of experience in this field doomed the effort, despite positive responses to the product's quality, and the ski operation was eventually sold. In 1975 Hexcel acquired a company that specialized in graphite weaving technology and in 1977 it purchased Tower Scientific, a manufacturer of replacement knee, hip, and shoulder joints. Other efforts to diversify at this time included development of different types of composites and increasing the company's production of specialty chemicals and resins. By 1978 the company's sales of honeycomb materials were split 50/50 with other composites, though the bulk of sales were still to defense and aerospace manufacturers. Hexcel stock, which had previously traded on the Pacific Stock Exchange, was listed on the New York Exchange in 1980.

1980s: Financial Challenges

By the late 1970s economic recession had forced Hexcel to retrench yet again. Returning to a focus on its core technologies, the company sold its medical products line soon after its exit from the ski market in 1981. Efforts to reach European customers were broadened during this time with the purchase of half of Stevens-Genin S.A., a French maker of glass-fiber and woven industrial materials, and the acquisition of Seal Sands Chemical Co. Ltd. of England, a specialty chemicals manufacturer. The remainder of Stevens-Genin was acquired five years

later. Hexcel-produced composites were used in several high-profile ways during this decade, with the space shuttle Columbia and the Voyager aircraft both making extensive use of the company's products. In the latter case, Hexcel composites comprised some 80 percent of the structural space, but only 20 percent of the weight of the aircraft that made the world's first non-refueled circumnavigation.

In 1986 CEO Merrill stepped down, to be replaced by COO Robert L. Witt. The company also began building a new plant in Chandler, Arizona, to facilitate the company's participation in building the U.S. military's B-2 "Stealth" bomber. This top-secret project reportedly used Hexcel composites to improve the radar-evading capabilities of the plane. Unfortunately for the company, the easing of the Cold War and the resulting changes in military priorities caused delays in orders for the planes just as the Arizona facility was coming on line. As it had done several times before, Hexcel did some belt-tightening and laid off a small number of employees, also redirecting the company's new Arizona operations toward producing materials for commercial aerospace, which was in a growth period. Sales had peaked in fiscal 1988 at $399 million, but dropped off the following year, though Hexcel still posted a profit. The company had a total of 17 manufacturing facilities worldwide at this time.

In 1990 Hexcel announced the formation of a joint venture with a Japanese company, Dainippon Ink & Chemicals, to manufacture honeycomb composites in Japan, with a late 1991 start-up date projected. The company also began working with Reebok, the shoe manufacturer, to develop honeycomb arch supports for its shoes, which it began to manufacture in Casa Grande, Arizona. Hexcel materials were also used in the high-speed trains that ran through the English channel "Chunnel" tunnel, in fishing rods, golf clubs, baseball bats, bicycle frames, and many other civilian, non-aerospace goods. The company also manufactured chemicals which were used as ingredients in Alka-Seltzer tablets, Scope mouthwash, and Vicks Formula 44 cough syrup. These specialty chemicals accounted for as much as nine percent of the company's sales at this time. Nevertheless, the company still realized most of its profits from sales to the commercial aerospace business.

As competition among airlines heated up following the Reagan administration's deregulation of the industry, and profit margins began to tighten or disappear, airplane manufacturers soon found orders for new planes delayed or canceled. Hexcel's two biggest customers, Boeing and Airbus, both cut back their orders for composites, resulting in a severe reduction in income for the company. While sales to aerospace firms had accounted for some 40 percent of Hexcel's revenues, they were responsible for almost 70 percent of profits. As a result of the downturn, losses for fiscal 1992 stood at $17.3 million, and the company was forced to take drastic action. A restructuring was announced in late 1992, with a 20 percent reduction in the company's workforce, and sales or closings of more than a third of its facilities. An attempt to ward off competitor BASF, by buying the German company's main U.S. plant, failed in early 1993 when the two concerns could not agree on a price. In July 1993, CEO Bob Witt resigned, to be replaced by the team of John Lee and John Doyle, both company directors.

Bankruptcy Protection in 1993

Despite its best efforts, including a second restructuring plan announced in September 1993, Hexcel could not stop the losses, and the company decided to enter Chapter 11 bankruptcy protection in December of that year. The following August the company announced that it would sell its Chandler, Arizona, plant to Northrop Grumman, builder of the B-2 bomber, for $30 million. Hexcel sold a vacant plant in Los Angeles in November for $2.6 million and its European resins business for $9 million at year's end. In early February 1995 the company emerged from Chapter 11, having arranged $45 million in exit financing from Citicorp. Another $50 million was obtained from a stock offering arrangement with Mutual Series Fund, Inc.

Soon after it left bankruptcy protection, the company announced a merger with the composites division of Ciba-Geigy, the Swiss chemical and pharmaceuticals giant. The Anaheim, California-based Ciba Composites had 1994 sales of $293 million, just slightly lower than Hexcel's $313.8 million. The unusual arrangement, in which Hexcel gave Ciba-Geigy 49.9 percent of its stock and over $70 million to pay off long-term debt, strengthened Hexcel's presence in the aerospace market, and particularly in Europe. Ciba Composites specialized in composite resins and structural materials, but did not manufacture honeycomb. It supplied many of the same industries as Hexcel, and the European jet maker Airbus was a major customer. Ciba also brought to the merger Heath Tecna, a company which manufactured composites-based aircraft interior furnishings. The combined companies retained the name of Hexcel. John Lee took the post of CEO, while Ciba Composites President Juergen Habermeier was named Hexcel president and chief operating officer. Following the merger Hexcel consolidated some of its facilities, announcing the closing of its U.S. Materials site in Anaheim and a layoff of some 156 workers. The expanded company now employed 4,700 people at 19 plants located in seven countries.

In June 1996 another major competitor, the Composites Products Division of Hercules, Inc., was acquired. This purchase strengthened Hexcel's efforts to increase the company's vertical integration by adding a carbon fiber plant outside of Salt Lake City. Soon thereafter another major acquisition was thwarted, as Hexcel's plan to purchase Fiberite, Inc., the second leading U.S. composites maker, was threatened with an antitrust investigation by the Federal Trade Commission. The company backed off, purchasing only Fiberite's satellite-materials business and the rights to certain technologies.

In February 1998 Hexcel announced the formation of a joint venture with Boeing and two Malaysian aviation firms to be called Asian Composite Manufacturing Sdn. Bhd. The new company would build a plant in Malaysia to make composite parts for aircraft. Final assembly would be completed at Hexcel's Kent, Washington, facility. Another joint venture with Boeing was to be located in China. BHA Aero Composite was to be a three-way venture that also involved Aviation Industries of China. In addition to these aerospace-related moves, Hexcel also formed an alliance with Sika Finanz AG of Switzerland, a maker of construction chemicals and adhesives, to develop and market composite products for the construction industry. In the fall of 1998, the company completed acquisition of most of Clark-Schwebel, Inc., a maker of glass fiber fabrics which were used in printed electronic circuit boards. The $463 million deal gave Hexcel Clark-Schwebel's U.S. operations and its stake in three joint ventures, with acquisition of the company's European unit expected to follow. Hexcel Chairman John Lee announced that this would boost Hexcel's non-aerospace sales from 35 percent to 50 percent of the company's total revenues.

Further consolidation of operations occurred in March 1999, when Hexcel announced the closing of a Clark-Schwebel plant in Cleveland, Georgia. Since 1997 the company had been following the "Lean Enterprise" philosophy, which held that elimination of waste and redundancy in a business led to reduced costs, improved quality, and greater customer satisfaction. The company anticipated further consolidation to occur throughout 1999.

As Hexcel began its second 50 years of business, it had reached the position of global leader in the manufacture of composites. Through a series of acquisitions it had also achieved the diversification it had long been seeking. While the company was still in the process of consolidating its new acquisitions to promote greater efficiency, it was riding the crest of a wave of aircraft construction, and, with its new Clark-Schwebel acquisition, was positioned to capitalize on the increasing demand for electronic products that used printed circuit boards.

Principal Subsidiaries

Hexcel Beta Corporation; Hexcel Far East, Inc.; Hexcel Pottsville Corporation; Hexcel Technologies, Inc.

Principal Divisions

Heath Tecna Aerospace.

Further Reading

Barnum, Alex, "Hexcel Files for Chapter 11," *San Francisco Chronicle,* December 7, 1993, p. B3.
Beauchamp, Marc, "The Right Stuff? (Hexcel Corp.)," *Forbes,* November 3, 1986, p. 100.
Calbreath, Dean, "Hexcel Restructures: Aerospace Makes Room for Sport," *San Francisco Business Times,* July 16, 1993, p. 5.
Fairclough, Gordon, "Cytec to Acquire Most of Fiberite, After Rival Hexcel Drops Its Bid," *Wall Street Journal,* August 26, 1997, p. B4.
Granelli, James S., "Hexcel to Phase Out Anaheim Facility, Lay Off 156 Workers," *Los Angeles Times,* February 7, 1996, p. 6.
"Hexcel Closing Texas Plant, Cutting Staff," *San Francisco Chronicle,* April 14, 1993, p. C3.
"Hexcel Completes Clark-Schwebel Acquisition," *Aerospace Daily,* September 18, 1998, p. 456.
"Hexcel Expects Cuts in Defense Contracts," *San Francisco Examiner,* January 31, 1990, p. C4.
"Hexcel, Japanese Company Form Joint Honeycomb Manufacturing Venture," *Aerospace Daily,* April 23, 1990, p. 131.
"Hexcel Returns to Le Bourget," *Aerospace Daily,* June 23, 1997, p. 478.
Howe, Kenneth, "Hexcel to Merge with Swiss Giant/$220 Million Deal for Pleasanton Firm Is Complex, Unusual," *San Francisco Chronicle,* July 13, 1995, p. B1.
Pelline, Jeff, "Honeycomb Material Maker's Outlook Isn't All Sweetness," *San Francisco Chronicle,* June 1, 1989, p. C1.
Pollack, Andrew, "Hexcel Flying High on Honeycomb/Its Profitable Product Not Taken Lightly," *San Francisco Chronicle,* October 17, 1986, p. 37.
Siegmann, Ken, "Hexcel's Aerospace Sales Plummet As Aircraft Builders Cut Production," *San Francisco Chronicle,* December 17, 1992, p. C1.

—Frank Uhle

Holme Roberts & Owen LLP
Attorneys at Law

Holme Roberts & Owen LLP

1700 Lincoln Street, Suite 4100
Denver, Colorado 80203-4541
U.S.A.
(303) 861-7000
Fax: (303) 866-0200
Web site: http://www.hro.com

Private Partnership
Incorporated: 1950 as Holme, Roberts, More, Owen & Keegan
Employees: 463
Sales: $60 million (1998 est.)
NAIC: 54111 Offices of Lawyers

Holme Roberts & Owen LLP has grown from a small partnership into one of the largest law firms in Colorado's Rocky Mountain area. From its main Denver office, the company operates branch offices in Boulder, Colorado Springs, Salt Lake City, and, internationally, in London. Holme Roberts & Owen (HRO) provides legal counsel in a wide variety of areas, from mining, energy, and banking, three traditional practice areas, to more recent fields such as environmental and intellectual property law that have expanded due to more government regulations and innovative technology. HRO's largest practice concentration is in litigation.

Origins and Early Practice

HRO can trace its earliest history to 1898, when William McKinley was in the White House and two Denver attorneys began a partnership in Colorado. At that time, Tyson Dines, Sr., a prominent trial lawyer who had come from St. Louis teamed up with Elmer F. Whitted, the lawyer for Colorado and Southern Railroad, to form Dines and Whitted. After Dines's cousin Orville Dines and Peter Hagner Holme joined, in 1906 and 1908, respectively, the firm became known as Dines, Dines, and Holme, remaining under that name until 1950.

In the early years, the partnership concentrated much of its practice in mining, oil, and railroad issues. For example, Dines, Sr., represented Verner Reed, a prominent Denver citizen, in his oil claims in the Salt Creek fields of Wyoming. The law firm was also involved in mining litigation in Cripple Creek, a mining community west of Colorado Springs, as well as in railroad litigation in the early 1900s.

In 1919 Harold D. Roberts joined the firm and one year later became the main draftsman of the Mineral Leasing Act that guided the ways in which the federal government leased oil, gas, and other mineral rights to companies. This Act would remain in effect in 1999.

Dines, Sr., died in 1928, but his son, Tyson Dines, Jr., remained a partner for many years. J. Churchill Owen, Sr., also integral to the firm's early growth, joined the law firm in 1926. Owen, Sr., was born in Cripple Creek, where his father practiced law in the mining boom times from 1894 to 1906. Attorneys Robert E. More and Milton J. Keegan also started working for the firm in 1926.

In the 1920s the firm became more involved in banking issues and in representing Denver's stock brokerage firms. For example, Holme and Dines, Jr., helped found the U.S. National Bank of Denver in 1921 and served on that entity's board of directors. The stock market crash of 1929 did not hurt Denver as much as it affected other areas of the nation, and the law firm, comprised of about ten lawyers, stayed active with oil and banking issues throughout the 1930s. During World War II, Owen, Sr., left the firm to serve on the federal government's War Production Board, while a staff of eight attorneys kept the firm running.

Postwar Expansion

In 1950 the firm's name was changed to Holme, Roberts, More, Owen & Keegan. Keegan died in 1954, and More retired in the late 1950s, so the firm then became Holme Roberts & Owen. Two sons of name partners joined the firm after World War II. Peter Holme, Jr., had come onboard by 1955, about the same time his father died. In 1957 James C. Owen, Jr., joined the firm. The son of name partner J. Churchill Owen, Sr., James Owen was born in 1926, graduated from Yale with a B.S. degree in 1954, and two years later received an LL.B. degree cum laude from the University of Denver. Partner Ted Stockmar also joined the growing firm in the mid-1950s. With a degree in petroleum engineering from the Colorado School of Mines, as well as a law degree, Stockmar proved integral to the law firm's oil practice.

James E. Bye joined HRO in 1957 and went on to become one of the firm's top attorneys dealing with tax issues, natural resources, and international law. Bye would push for passage of the North American Free Trade Agreement (NAFTA) in the 1990s and worked with other HRO attorneys to aid clients doing business in the United States, Mexico, and Canada.

With about 17 lawyers and six partners by 1955, the firm was ready for a new office, moving from its original offices in the old First National Bank Building to become the first tenant in a new building on the corner of 17th and Broadway. Denver was booming and so was HRO.

Harold Roberts and other HRO attorneys played a major role in Denver's struggle for adequate water supplies in the 1950s. In 1952 The Denver Water Board retained Roberts in the fight to gain water from the Blue River on the Western Slope of Colorado and bring it over the mountains to Denver on the Eastern Slope. After several years in court, Denver won this struggle against Western Slope interests and also the federal government that claimed prior rights to the supply in question. The city honored Roberts by naming the diversion tunnel that brought water to Denver "The Harold D. Roberts Tunnel." Unfortunately, Roberts died soon thereafter of a heart attack in 1956.

HRO expanded from 17 to 26 attorneys between 1955 and 1965, and its staff increased from 23 to 32. More companies moved to Denver; new buildings were constructed; and the oil and mining industries remained vital. By 1965 HRO was among Denver's top three largest law firms.

Denver's and HRO's growth continued in the decade from 1965 to 1975. New mining and oil discoveries and a booming real estate market kept HRO busy. The firm increased to 61 lawyers and 79 staff members, and it opened its Colorado Springs branch office during those ten years. The firm recruited female partner Pat Clark to gain her expertise in the real estate field, but she soon accepted an appointment as a federal bankruptcy judge. Another partner, Dick Matsch, left to join the federal district court.

Meanwhile, HRO helped the United States National Bank merge with the Denver National Bank to create the Denver U.S. National Bank and later helped it to organize a bank holding company. Soon the names became the United Bank of Denver and the United Bank of Colorado.

Rapid Growth in the 1970s and 1980s

From 1975 to 1985, HRO saw tremendous growth, from 61 to 170 attorneys. By 1985 the firm also employed 44 paralegals. This expansion occurred as the nation suffered extreme inflation from the Arab oil embargo and the energy crisis of the 1970s. Such events increased the need for U.S. oil firms to search for new oil deposits; major oil firms, who were potential clients, started regional offices in Denver during those years. New high-tech firms in Denver also needed legal services, and HRO grew accordingly. During this time, HRO opened an office in Boulder.

In 1980 HRO opened its Salt Lake City office, the first out-of-state firm to do so. Since it was larger than any of the historic Utah law firms, which had at most about 100 attorneys, HRO offered higher salaries; the lateral hires began.

HRO's expansion from 1975 to 1985 coincided with the nationwide growth and transformation of many firms. Previously most partners came up through the ranks and were paid on a seniority "lockstep" method. However, after U.S. Supreme Court rulings opened the way for professional advertising, *American Lawyer* magazine began in 1979 to feature information about partner salaries in different firms. Lateral hires, or raiding other firms for experienced partners who usually specialized in one area of the law, became standard practice at HRO and other large firms.

Still, some older generation HRO attorneys bemoaned the resulting loss of collegiality and tradition that lateral hires engendered. For example, in the January 17, 1999 *Denver Rocky Mountain News* James C. Owen, Jr., after 42 years at HRO, remarked: "We had great camaraderie. We've grown so large now that it's much less so. . . . Many young lawyers here know nothing about our history, or they don't care."

The 1990s

As the decade began, HRO continued to grow. In 1991 the firm opened a new office in London. Senior partner Bruce R. Kohler, a Harvard Law School graduate with 18 years of experience at HRO in international business transactions, headed the new office. In an interview published in the July 31, 1991 *Deseret News,* Kohler explained that "It's a general phenomenon of the Rocky Mountain region. . . . Companies in our area are now becoming active internationally and this move (to open a London office) is our response to that." Kohler also pointed out that both small and large firms, such as U.S. West, were taking advantage of these new business opportunities, but in any case they usually needed outside advice from consultants, trade experts, and of course attorneys. Previously, only large law firms in the East or West could afford such overseas offices, added Kohler.

HRO's London office maintained strong ties to affiliated law firms in France, Belgium, Germany, Ireland, Italy, The Netherlands, Switzerland, and Spain. HRO attorneys helped its corporate clients deal with changing European laws and trends. New business was generated, for example, in the early 1990s, when the treaty for European unity was signed and ratified by 12 nations, leading to the European Union introducing a common currency called "the euro" by the end of the decade.

Following the collapse of the Soviet Union in 1991, several U.S. law firms started offices in Moscow, as did HRO in 1993, to help businesses take advantage of new opportunities. For example, HRO represented Interfax, the former Soviet Union's largest independent business and news agency, as it increased operations in Western Europe and North America.

However, Moscow office rentals in the 1990s ran four times the rates as those in downtown Manhattan. In the November 1998 issue of *American Lawyer,* HRO partner David Goldberg said the firm's Russian practice was profitable. However, in February 1997 the firm closed its Moscow office due to high business expenses and political dangers. In addition, competition from huge law firms, some with 1,000 lawyers or more, prompted HRO to exit Moscow. The erratic Russian economy, where government employees sometimes went months without being paid and even food was hard to buy, caused other law firms to reduce their staffs and pare down for long-term survival.

At the same time, back in Salt Lake City, HRO's Mark Buchi, the branch office's managing partner, played a key role in what became known as the landmark ''AMAX case'' that impacted all Utah property owners. It started in 1986 when several Utah companies, including AMAX Magnesium, later renamed MagCorp, represented by Buchi, asked the State Tax Commission for a 20 percent property tax discount. Buchi argued that state-assessed properties of AMAX should receive the same rate as county-assessed properties. The commission refused, so the case went to the Utah Supreme Court, which in 1990 ruled that the discount should apply to AMAX. After more disputes on this issue, in 1993 Utah's Court of Appeals ordered the State Tax Commission to strictly follow the 1990 ruling by the Utah Supreme Court.

In 1997, HRO's Salt Lake City office merged with the firm of Haley & Stolebarger, a commercial litigation firm. Five attorneys joined HRO as a result of the merger, including partners George M. Haley and Robert L. Stolebarger, and also Frank E. Moss, Utah's U.S. Democratic senator from 1959 to 1977, who was ''of counsel'' to HRO. Moss, aged 88, still spent a couple of hours a day in 1998 at the firm's downtown office. He also served as the senior counsel for the Washington, D.C.-based humanitarian group called The Caring Institute.

Two HRO attorneys made significant contributions as Utah tax lawyers. Mark Buchi, who had served as chair of the Utah State Tax Commission, was honored by the Utah State Bar's Tax Section as the outstanding tax attorney of 1997. Buchi spent three years developing a new state tax court system that was implemented on May 1, 1997, only to be rejected by the Utah Supreme Court. However, an amendment to the Utah Constitution allowed the new tax court to finally be implemented.

In 1998 Utah Governor Mike Leavitt appointed HRO's R. Bruce Johnson to the tax commission. Johnson had worked as a trial attorney for the U.S. Department of Justice's Tax Division before joining HRO.

HRO employed about 25 attorneys in its Salt Lake City office. Its lawyers authored Utah's Limited Liability Company Act and represented major clients such as U.S. West Communications, Intermountain Health Care, Flying J, The Williams Companies, Amalgamated Sugar Company, Brigham Young University, Chase Manhattan Bank, Morris Travel, and the Northwest Pipeline Company.

Diversity issues influenced HRO in the 1990s. Not only did the firm represent clients hit with discrimination issues, the firm itself tried to hire as many lawyers with different backgrounds as it could. By 1999, the firm employed 19 women partners and 40 women associates. However, few minorities joined HRO.

HRO attorneys demonstrated a wide diversity of political views. Some in the firm backed Republican partner Don Bain when he ran for Denver mayor in 1987, while others backed the successful candidate, Federico Pena. Some HRO attorneys represented lesbian and ACLU clients.

In contrast, partner John R. Wylie in the Colorado Springs branch office headed a conservative Christian lawyers association. Wylie oversaw HRO's representation of some major religious organizations based in Colorado Springs, including The Navigators, a nondenominational organization that by 1990 had 3,000 staff members in over 70 nations working to build lay discipleship. HRO's religious clients also included the Promise Keepers, World Vision, Young Life, and the Christian and Missionary Alliance.

In the late 1990s, HRO employed about 50 attorneys involved in some form of litigation practice, the firm's largest concentration of legal expertise. The following cases were notable.

In 1997, HRO represented plaintiffs in the two largest jury verdicts in Colorado's history. First, HRO helped Arapahoe County cable TV company United International Holdings Inc. win a $153.5 million civil lawsuit against Wharf Holdings Inc., a Hong Kong firm. Wharf was convicted of breaking an oral agreement to United International that the latter would have a ten percent share in creating Hong Kong's first cable television system.

In the second case, HRO represented Boulder-based Storage Technology Corporation that won a $67.8 million award from Array Technology Corporation and its parent, Tandem Computers Inc., for selling flawed computer devices and not delivering the equipment on time.

In 1997 Tele-Communications Inc.'s founder Bob J. Magness died and left a $1 billion estate, the largest in Colorado history. HRO represented the estate's two executors, Director Donne Fisher and University of Denver Chancellor Dan Ritchie, in a complicated court battle that finally was settled in April 1998.

HRO attorneys also represented defendant Martin Marietta Corporation (MMC) in one of the nation's major age discrimination lawsuits. In the early 1990s, MMC's Astronautics Group laid off approximately 5,000 workers at its Denver facilities. Almost 200 of those workers alleged that the firm discriminated against them because they were over 40 years old. In Marvin D. Wilkerson et al v. Martin Marietta Corporation, Judge Wiley Daniel in 1997 decided that the consent decree agreed to by the federal Equal Employment Opportunity Commission and MMC was ''fair, adequate and reasonable.''

After litigation, HRO's second largest practice area was its corporate and securities practice, which involved about 20 percent of its business. Representative clients included ACX Technologies, the Adolph Coors Company, and the Anschutz Corporation. In the 1990s, HRO's corporate attorneys played key roles in the merger of Southern Pacific with Union Pacific to create the nation's largest railroad firm.

HRO's third major practice area in the late 1990s was environmental law. HRO helped its clients comply with numerous federal and state environmental laws that began to be passed around 1970. HRO's attorneys wrote the *Colorado Environmental Law Handbook,* published by Government Institutes, Inc., and represented such clients as Shell Oil Company, Southern Pacific, Sundstrand Corporation, Cotter Corporation, and Meridian Oil in complex environmental cleanup and personal-injury cases.

With so many new lawyers graduating from law schools, the 1990s saw even more aggressive rivalries in the legal services industry. Just as HRO moved to Salt Lake City to challenge smaller firms, large national firms came to Denver to compete with HRO and other local firms. At the same time, big accounting firms hired hundreds of attorneys. Many corporations beefed up their own internal law departments to avoid paying the high costs of outside counsel. In addition, independent paralegals provided some limited services and computer software programs allowed consumers to help themselves using standardized legal forms in simple transactions. The self-help movement impacted most professionals, not just lawyers.

In the January 17, 1999 *Denver Rocky Mountain News,* HRO's Executive Committee Chairman Dean Salter described HROs future plans. Despite the consolidation of small firms into huge firms, he observed, "we are not looking for a merger partner." He added, "There will be a place for us—a good strong regional firm—for a long time." Other than increasing the firm's intellectual property practice and adding more attorneys to its London office, HRO said it had no other expansion plans.

On January 2, 1999, the death of HRO partner James C. Owen, Jr., marked the end of an era at the law firm. Owen was the last partner whose surname was part of the firm's identity. For over four decades he had worked as an HRO attorney representing key clients, including the United Bank and the Gates Rubber Company, which was acquired by the British firm Tompkins plc for $1.6 billion.

Beyond his legal work, Owen set a great example of community service for his HRO colleagues. For years he served the Boys and Girls Club of Metro Denver, which his father had founded in 1961. Owen also sat on the boards of the Denver Zoo, the Botanical Gardens, the Museum of Contemporary Art, and the Denver Public Library. Owen conceded that such civic activities gained HRO contacts, and thus clients, but he maintained that they were still important and worthy causes in their own right.

Chairman Dean Salter in the January 17, 1999 *Denver Rocky Mountain News* recognized Owen as "a repository of so many traditions of the firm," and HRO attorneys strove to continue Owen's heritage of community service. For example, in 1999 HRO announced that attorneys Manuel L. Martinez, Matt A. Mayor, and Nancy J. Gegenheimer had been elected, respectively, to The Children's Hospital Foundation Board of Trustees, the Opera Colorado Board of Directors, and the board of the Boys & Girls Clubs of Metro Denver.

HRO attorneys thus tried to balance their legacy of serving local and regional organizations with their firm's more recent focus on international clients and issues in an era of rapid change for both society and the legal profession.

Further Reading

Funk, Marianne, "Local Opportunities Blossom As National Law Firms Branch Out," *Deseret News,* April 3, 1994, pp. M1, M2.

Hansen, Susan, "Lost in the Ruble," *American Lawyer,* November 1998, pp. 80–85.

Hoback, Jane, "Hallowed Halls," *Denver Rocky Mountain News,* January 17, 1999, pp. G1, G8-G10.

Knudson, Max B., "New Law Office in London Offers Utah Firms a Gateway to Europe," *Deseret News,* July 31, 1991.

Owen, J. Churchill, Sr., "History of Holme Roberts & Owen," Denver: Holme Roberts & Owen LLP, 1985.

Rayburn, Jim, "Suit Could Jeopardize AMAX Pact," *Deseret News,* May 23, 1992.

Roberts, Harold D., *History of the Salt Creek Oil Fields,* Denver: Holme Roberts & Owen, n.d.

Walden, David M., "Holme Roberts & Owen LLC," in *Centennial Utah,* edited by G. Wesley Johnson and Marian Ashby Johnson, pp. 70–71, Encino, Calif.: Cherbo Publishing Group, 1995.

—David M. Walden

⇔ ICF KAISER

ICF Kaiser International, Inc.

9300 Lee Highway
Fairfax, Virginia 22031-1207
U.S.A.
(703) 934-3600
Fax: (703) 934-3740
Web site: http://www.icfkaiser.com

Public Company
Incorporated: 1914 as Kaiser Engineers, Inc.
Employees: 5,000
Sales: $1.21 billion (1998)
Stock Exchanges: New York
Ticker Symbol: ICF
NAIC: 54133 Engineering Services; 23493 Industrial
    Nonbuilding Structure Construction; 54171 Research
    & Development in the Physical, Engineering, & Life
    Sciences; 54172 Research & Development in the
    Social Sciences & Humanities; 54152 Computer
    Systems Design Services

ICF Kaiser International, Inc. is one of the largest engineering, construction, program management, and consulting services companies in the United States. Headquartered in northern Virginia, the company has 70 offices around the world. In 1998 projects included the U.S. Department of Energy's Rocky Flats Closure Project, the Nova Hût steel minimill in the Czech Republic, the Metro Manila Light Rail Transit System in the Philippines, expansion of an alumina refinery in western Australia, and facilities management support at the Kennedy Space Center and nearby rocket launch sites. Until 1999, three operating companies comprised ICF Kaiser: ICF Kaiser Engineers and Constructors, ICF Environment and Facilities Management Group, and ICF Kaiser Consulting Group. In March 1999 the company announced the sale of both the consulting group and the facilities management unit.

Early History

The "Kaiser" in ICF Kaiser International traces its roots to 1914, and the founding of the Henry J. Kaiser Company, Ltd., a construction company in Spokane, Washington, and the forerunner of Kaiser Aluminum & Chemical Corporation. Henry Kaiser's philosophy was "Do it faster, cheaper, and better," and he encouraged innovation among his employees. One early product of The Hobby Lobby (the company's research department) was the rubber-tired wheelbarrow. Kaiser's first big job, in 1927, was as a subcontractor building 200 miles of highway through the mountains and jungles of Cuba. The company finished a year ahead of schedule.

In the early 1930s the federal government began huge public works jobs to counter the Great Depression. In the West, this meant building dams to supply water for irrigation and power. Henry Kaiser and his engineers took part in building Bonneville (Hoover), Boulder, and Grand Coulee Dams. Even while working on the last of these giant projects, the company also was building a section of the Oakland-San Francisco Bay Bridge, tunnels, smaller dams, and a new set of locks for the Panama Canal. In 1939, when he lost out on the bid for building the Shasta Dam in northern California, Kaiser expanded into manufacturing. He designed and built the Permanente Cement Company in just seven months and provided the gravel to the Shasta builders.

When the United States entered World War II, Kaiser moved crews and equipment from Grand Coulee to San Francisco Bay and built a shipyard that eventually produced 1,490 merchant (Liberty) ships, aircraft carriers, and other warships. He built a second shipyard in Oregon, and his engineers, according to a company publication, "designed an entire city for 35,000 people and built it in three months." Kaiser also built planes and ship engines, and his engineers built airfields and other military installations. To supply steel plate, Kaiser built a steel plant and began production. During the war, Kaiser Industries had 300,000 people working for it. Before the war ended, the engineering department decided to seek projects outside Kaiser. This was the beginning of Kaiser Engineers, Inc.

Going International: 1950–76

During the 1950s, Kaiser Engineers increasingly took on jobs abroad, including designing and building a car factory in Argentina to produce Willys Jeeps and Kaiser automobiles. As the lead company in a seven-firm consortium, Kaiser took on the Snowy Mountains Hydroelectic Power project in Australia, a 25-year project, with Kaiser Engineers finishing their portion on time and under budget. Domestic projects included the dual-purpose reactor at Hanford, Washington. By 1965 *Engineering News-Record* ranked Kaiser Engineers as the number one contractor in the world. When Henry Kaiser died in 1967, Kaiser Engineers was operating in 21 states and 14 countries. The company continued designing and building, including steel-producing plants; cement plants; rapid transit projects in Baltimore, Maryland, and Washington, D.C.; aluminum and alumina factories; and the Great Plains Coal Gasification project in North Dakota.

A Part of Raymond International: 1977–86

In 1977 Kaiser Industries dissolved. In June, Raymond International Inc., a Houston-based construction company, paid $30 million for Kaiser Engineers, which had $172 million in revenues. Raymond, with $254 million in revenues, was shifting from big public works projects to concentrate on private jobs. With the purchase of Kaiser Engineers, it gained the management and design capabilities it lacked to compete in the increasingly complex construction business.

In 1983 Raymond went private in a leveraged buyout, borrowing about $200 million from nine banks to pay the purchase price. When the bottom fell out of the oil and gas market soon afterward, the company began defaulting on its loans.

A Separate Company: 1986–88

In 1986 the bank consortium split Kaiser Engineers from Raymond International, forming a separate company with some $60 million of debt. At the time, Kaiser Engineers had just started building the largest copper mine in the world, the Neves-Corvo project in Portugal. Because Portugal had so little industry, almost everything for the project had to be imported. This required 680 purchase orders from 16 countries on five continents, as Kaiser built, in addition to the copper mine itself, roads, a railroad, four dams, a copper concentrator, a 40-kilometer water pipe, and a port facility. To accomplish this, the company used its Kaiser Engineers Management System

(KEMS), a computerized system for planning, monitoring, and cost control of huge projects.

When the company completed Neves-Corvo two years later, the bank consortium split Kaiser Engineers in two. It sold Kaiser's operations in Australia and Asia to the Australian conglomerate Elders Group IXL Ltd. The rest of Kaiser, including 2,000 employees and 1987 revenue of $300 million, was sold to tiny American Capital and Research Corp. (ACR) of Fairfax, Virginia. James O. Edwards, the chairman and president of ACR, developed the complicated transition in partnership with Elders.

American Capital and Research Corp.: 1969–88

ACR was a new private holding company established in 1987 and run by former top federal officials. Its primary business was ICF Inc., an energy, health, and environmental consulting company founded in 1969. ICF started life as Inner City Fund, a venture capital fund that helped minority-owned businesses raise money and win government contracts. The company reorganized itself as ICF in the mid-1970s and, following the passage of the first real hazardous waste disposal bill in 1976, grew by winning government contracts for energy and environmental policy analysis. Over the years ICF expanded to include subsidiaries handling economic analysis, biotechnology and risk assessment, defense analysis, and a computer group. In the process, it attracted senior government officials from energy, environmental, and health-related agencies. Critics complained that this created an unfair advantage in winning federal contracts, particularly in the hazardous waste field.

In the mid-1980s ICF began buying other consulting firms as part of a strategy to shift its primary business from analysis to field activities, particularly in the environmental field, and to increase its revenues to $100 million by 1990. Recent amendments to the hazardous waste disposal bill established "cradle to grave" liability for waste generators and required reams of documentation. "Big money was coming not from studying toxic waste dumps, but from cleaning them up," an ICF official recalled in a 1990 interview with *Diablo Business*.

Among its purchases was Clements Associates, Inc., a specialist in environmental risk assessment; K.S. Crump & Co., another risk assessment firm; SRW Associates, a small engineering firm; Buc & Associates, an economic consulting firm; and the Naisbitt Group, a trend analysis company. The purchase of Lewin and Associates Inc. made ICF the largest consulting practice in the healthcare and energy fields. In 1987 the company set up the ICF Defense Group to go after contracts in the national security and intelligence fields and established ACR.

Turning Around Kaiser Engineers: 1988–89

The Kaiser acquisition in 1988 greatly strengthened ACR's (and ICF's) engineering capabilities. Kaiser's current contracts included cleaning up Boston Harbor, construction and services work at the federal government's Hanford nuclear site in Washington state, and several highway and transit projects. Yet while Kaiser added some $300 million to ACR's annual revenues, it also brought ACR between $20 and $30 million in financial liabilities.

In less than a year, ACR trimmed Kaiser's debt through individual negotiations and slashed the company's overhead. Instead of losing $1 million a month, ICF Kaiser Engineers was profitable. ACR merged Kaiser with ICF Inc. in 1989, to form ICF Kaiser Engineers, a subsidiary of wholly owned ICFcorp International.

Later that year ACR bought CYGNA Group, a $30 million California firm that provided hazardous waste cleanup and plant reengineering services to the nuclear power industry. ACR was becoming an environmental conglomerate, providing government and industry with a single place to go for handling environmental problems.

ACR also strengthened its non-environmental subsidiaries. Its computer systems division, for example, acquired four local firms in barely more than a year, increasing its revenues to $37 million. The acquisitions left ACR with some $40 million in long-term debt, and in December 1989 it went public, raising about $26 million. Most of that was used to reduce the debt.

A Busy Year: 1990

ACR continued to expand into other markets, such as air-quality modeling services and negotiation and mediation services for big government and private contracts. By mid-1990 ACR owned 18 companies. In September 1990 ACR acquired International Waste Energy Systems, a design firm specializing in waste incineration systems. That same month it became one of the first U.S. companies to enter the huge pollution control market in the former Soviet Union and Eastern Europe, helping design systems to monitor pollution at Soviet coke plants. The company also purchased Kaiser Engineers Australia Pty Ltd. and Kaiser Engineers International from Elders Resources NZFP Ltd., recombining the original Kaiser Engineers. ACR had revenues of $503.9 million in fiscal 1990. Meanwhile, ICF Kaiser Engineers won a five-year, $50 million contract from the U.S. Air Force to design cleanup solutions for potentially hazardous waste sites on military bases around the world and was constructing Asia's largest high-speed railroad in Taiwan.

ICF Kaiser Engineers was one of the nation's top engineering firms specializing in toxic waste cleanup, with more than two-thirds of its contracts dealing with environmental projects. In addition to developing systems to actually clean up or destroy waste at a site, the subsidiary offered front-end services to determine the extent and nature of contamination at a site and conducted studies of alternative corrective actions.

Times of Trouble: 1991–93

Between 1989 and 1991, ACR's gross revenue more than doubled. The company began 1991 with a name change. To reflect both its roots and its growing international presence, the company became ICF International Inc. As it prepared for a $46 million stock offering in June, though, the fast-growing company ran into trouble. Known for its tight management controls, ICF International suddenly discovered that several of its non-core subsidiaries were performing poorly.

It appeared that the company tried to duplicate its successful shift in the environmental field to managing contracts and providing services without understanding the new fields into which it was moving. Providing services in areas such as health and information technology often meant developing products to be sold to new markets at a later date. Yet the subsidiaries continued to bill on ICF International's hourly model. As a stock analyst told the *Washington Post* in November of that year, "The company proved not particularly good at managing product-oriented businesses."

That discovery caused the company to cancel the stock offering and resulted in a first-ever quarterly loss. Its stock prices slumped, lenders demanded renegotiations, and over the next two years ICF International sold off 14 subsidiaries, although usually at a profit.

By 1993 ICF International had returned to profitability. It was now a company focused on its core business of environmental and transportation/infrastructure consulting and engineering. It had laid off employees and restructured both its credit agreements and its management, moving the president of ICF Kaiser Engineers (now called the Engineering & Construction Group) from Oakland, California to Fairfax, Virginia.

In June the company again changed its name, becoming ICF Kaiser International to underscore that it had integrated its California engineering firm with its Washington, D.C. consulting business, and in September it began trading on the New York Stock Exchange. But 1993 was a tough year for environmental markets, particularly for hazardous waste contracting, which saw a nine percent drop in billings by consulting firms. ICF Kaiser International registered a loss for the fiscal year.

The Mid-1990s

In 1994 ICF Kaiser focused increased emphasis on its domestic consulting services and set up an international company in Mexico to provide environmental consulting and engineering services in Mexico. It sold most of its Cygna Energy Services subsidiary and began unsuccessful talks to acquire a Pennsylvania-based hazardous waste cleanup company. Revenues in fiscal 1995 rose 32 percent from the previous year, but the company again reported a net loss of $1.66 million, down from $12.5 million for fiscal 1994.

The following year it won a $3.5 billion contract from the U.S. Department of Energy to clean up the Rocky Flats nuclear weapons plant in Colorado. In August, it bought EDA Inc., a Maryland engineering consulting firm, and later that year obtained the license to market a new process of making steel from steam coal, iron ore, and scrap.

In 1996 nearly 69 percent of the company's revenue came from contracts with the U.S. Department of Energy. But that year ICF Kaiser lost the Hanford nuclear waste contract, which it had had for 14 years and which represented approximately $10 million a year. At the same time, Congress failed to reauthorize the Superfund cleanup law and federal projects were on hold until the Republican leadership decided the direction it would take rewriting major environmental legislation and regulations. Among the contracts ICF Kaiser won in 1996 was that with a Czech steelmaker to build a minimill and another with the U.S. Army Corp of Engineers to clean up federal installations in its Southern Pacific region. Following the

ICF Kaiser International, Inc.   203

Hanford loss, the company took severe cost-cutting steps that continued into 1997.

The company's news coverage during 1997 had little to do with its work. First the media focused on the selection of former Energy Secretary Hazel O'Leary to ICF Kaiser's board and then on CEO James Edwards's name on a list of some 150 potential contributors Vice-President Al Gore was to call for the Democratic National Committee.

Financial Troubles: 1998 to the Present

In 1998 ICF Kaiser acquired ICT Spectrum Constructors Inc., one of the country's largest builders of semiconductor plants, in a move to broaden its construction services. ICT Spectrum had been spun off from its parent, Micron Technology Corp., in 1997. Later in the year ICF Kaiser announced a $35 million loss in the second quarter due to cost overruns at four nitric acid plant projects. The loss wiped out any hopes for a profit that year. ICF Kaiser replaced the company president and the president of the engineers and constructors group. At the same time, the company lost its contract to manage the upgrade of the Bath Iron Works in Maine, although it kept the contract for engineering work on the project.

In November, James Edwards, chairman and CEO since 1985 and a member of ICF Inc. since 1974, resigned. "I've had enough of difficult times and stress and no capital for growth," Edwards told *Engineering News-Record*. Keith Price, appointed president earlier in the year, was named CEO, and board member and former Congressman Tony Coelho was elected chairman.

Rumors about parts of the company being on the block soon proved true. On March 9, 1999, the company announced it was selling its consulting group, which accounted for about ten percent of company revenues, for $75 million. The new owners would be the group's management and CM Equity Partners L.P., a private, New York-based equity investment fund. The next day, ICF Kaiser announced that the IT Group, formerly known as International Technology Corp., was buying its environmental and facilities management group for $82 million. That sale was completed in April, just days before ICF Kaiser reported that its losses for 1998 totaled $100.5 million, compared with $5 million in 1997, and just days after naming James Maiwurm chief executive and president, the company's third head in five months.

With two of its three operating groups sold and the problems with the four nitric acid plants corrected, ICF Kaiser prepared to focus on and expand its engineering and construction business. As the new CEO stressed when he assumed office, "Our traditional expertise and our current book of business in the transit, water, alumina/aluminum, iron, steel, and mineral industries are real strengths. We believe transportation and infrastructure management, particularly when focused on large-scale public projects, including Rocky Flats, are all areas where Kaiser has an outstanding reputation, and we intend to strengthen these lines of business."

Principal Subsidiaries

ICF Information Technology, Inc.; Clement International Corp.; Cygna Group, Inc.; ICF Kaiser Holdings Unlimited, Inc.; ICF Kaiser Development Corp., Inc.; ICF Kaiser Engineers Group, Inc.; Monument Select Insurance Co.; Tudor Engineering Co.; Systems Applications International, Inc.; Systems Applications, Inc.; EDA, Inc.; K.S. Crump Group, Inc.

Further Reading

"ACR to Buy Elders Stake in Kaiser Australia Unit," *Journal of Commerce,* September 14, 1990, p. 5A.
"American Capital and Research Corp. to Acquire Cygna Group," UPI, June 20, 1989.
Berselli, Beth, "ICF Kaiser Ousts President," *Washington Post,* August 8, 1998, p. D1.
Bettelheim, Adriel, "Flats Cleanup Firm on Gore 'Call Sheet,' " *Denver Post,* September 11, 1997, p. A21.
Bredemeier, Kenneth, "ICF Kaiser Names New President," *Washington Post,* April 6, 1999, p. E3.
Chandler, Clay, "Consulting Firm Agrees to Acquisition," *Washington Post,* August 27, 1987, p. E1.
Cloud, John, "The Trouble with Hazel," *Time,* September 29, 1997, p. 28.
"A Contractor Buys Some Brains," *Forbes,* October 15, 1977, p. 32.
"Edwards Out As ICF Chair," *Energy Daily,* November 6, 1998.
"Environmental Markets Are Off, But Firms Aren't Down or Out," *Engineering News-Record,* April 4, 1994, p. 41.
Gellene, Denise, "Kaiser Engineers Merging with Unit of Its Virginia Parent Firm," *Los Angeles Times,* March 2, 1989, p. D11.
Hamilton, Martha, "Clean Doesn't Always Mean Green," *Washington Post,* September 29, 1996, p. H2.
——, "Cleaning Up on Environmental Concerns," *Washington Post,* July 23, 1990, p. E1.
——, "ICF Gets a New President to Lead It Through Expansion," *Washington Post,* December 6, 1993, p. F9.
——, "ICF Kaiser Plans Sale of Second Main Unit," *Washington Post,* March 10, 1999, p. E3.
——, "ICF Kaiser Reports Loss of $27 Million for Quarter," *Washington Post,* April 17, 1999, p. E2.
——, "ICF Kaiser's Consulting Unit Is Being Sold," *Washington Post,* March 9, 1999, p. E3.
——, "ICF Kaiser Sports a New Name and Attitude," *Washington Post,* September 27, 1993, p. F5.
——, "ICF Rebuilds After Effects of Stock Debacle," *Washington Post,* November 11, 1991, p. F1.
——, "Va. Company, Soviets Form Joint Venture," *Washington Post,* September 11, 1990, p. C1.
"Henry J. Kaiser: The Legacy Continues," Fairfax, Va.: ICF Kaiser International, Inc., June 1995.
"ICF Kaiser Announces New Management Team," Corporate Press Release, ICF Kaiser International, April 5, 1999.
"ICF Kaiser Changes Leaders But Problems Still Abound," *Engineering News-Record,* November 16, 1998, p. 14.
"ICF Kaiser Growing As Acquisitions Mount," *Engineering News-Record,* April 12, 1990, p. 22.
"ICF Kaiser Remains in Red," *Washington Times,* April 29, 1995, p. C4.
"ICF Kaiser to Buy Chip Plant Builder," *Engineering News-Record,* February 23, 1998, p. 16.
"ICF to Market Romelt Process Utilizing Steam Coal in Steelmaking," *Coal Week International,* October 24, 1995, p. 10.
"The IT Group Completes Acquisition of ICF Kaiser's Environment and Facilities Management Group," *PR Newswire,* April 12, 1999.
"James Edwards," NBC Business Video, NBC Desktop, Inc., September 17, 1997.

"Kaiser Contract Delayed; Company Is Up for Sale," *Engineering News-Record,* April 7, 1988, p. 17.

Laux, Emily, "Acquisition Campaign Changing Face, Nature of ICF's Consulting Business," *Business Review,* August 5, 1985, p. 13.

Litvan, Laura M., "Fairfax Company Out Front in Efforts to Save the Earth," *Washington Times,* May 11, 1990, p. C1.

Menninger, Bonar, "ICF: Making of a Megafirm," *Washington Business Journal,* July 3, 1989, p. 1.

"Pension Plans," *National Journal,* June 15, 1985, p. 1441.

Rubin, Debra K., "Industry Veteran Keith Price Now President of Troubled ICF Kaiser," *Engineering News-Record,* August 17, 1998, p. 15.

Shaw, Jan, "Stock Offering Enabling Firm to Pay Debts," *San Francisco Business Times,* December 25, 1989, p. 1.

Sugawara, Sandra, "D.C. Consulting Firm Is Engineering Increasingly Big Deals," *Washington Post,* November 21, 1988, p. F5.

"Waste Incinerator Design Firm Sold," *St. Louis Post-Dispatch,* September 21, 1990, p. 3B.

Webb, Margaret, "American Capital Renamed ICF," *Washington Post,* January 23, 1991, p. C11.

Weiss, Shari, "One Man's Poison . . . Is Another Man's Profit," *Diablo Business,* June, 1990, p. 39.

Zonana, Victor F., "Banks Sell Kaiser Group to 2 Bidders," *Los Angeles Times,* June 17, 1988, p. D2.

—Ellen D. Wernick

Imax Corporation

2525 Speakman Drive
Sheridan Science and Technology Park
Mississauga, Ontario L5K 1B1
Canada
(905) 403-6500
Fax: (905) 403-6450
Web site: http://www.imax.com

Public Company
Incorporated: 1967 as Imax Systems
Employees: 493
Sales: $190.4 million (1998)
Stock Exchanges: NASDAQ Toronto
Ticker Symbol: IMAX
NAIC: 51211 Motion Picture & Video Production; 42141
   Photographic Equipment & Supplies Wholesalers;
   512131 Motion Picture Theaters, Except Drive-in;
   71399 All Other Amusement & Recreation Industries;
   33431 Audio & Video Equipment Manufacturing

Imax Corporation, founded in 1967 and headquartered in Mississauga, Canada, is the pioneer and leader of giant-screen, large-format film entertainment, as well as the industry leader in the creation and production of high-end rides and attractions. Successful products include IMAX Simulator Rides and IMAX Ridefilm Systems. These breakthrough innovations combine IMAX projection technology with sophisticated motion programming and digital sound to create a truly unique and captivating experience. The following three subsidiaries are fundamental to the activities of Imax: Ridefilm Corporation, which manufactures and produces motion simulation theaters or movie rides; Sonics Associates, a world leader in sound system design and manufacturing, which manufactures headsets for shutter glasses at Imax theaters; and David Keighley Productions, a leader in the field of image quality assurance and laboratory postproduction, based in Los Angeles.

In 1999 there were more than 180 permanent IMAX theaters operating in 24 countries, of which only four in North America were owned and operated by IMAX: Vancouver, Calgary, and Winnipeg in Canada; and Scottsdale, Arizona. The rest are licensed to zoos, aquariums, shopping malls, theme parks, and related venues. A key focus for Imax is the production of high-quality films for the exclusive IMAX theater network. The organization has extensive in-house experience in producing critically acclaimed and broadly appreciated films. By 1999 films produced or distributed included *Africa's Elephant Kingdom, Blue Planet, Cosmic Voyage, Destiny in Space, Fires of Kuwait, The Hidden Dimension, The IMAX Nutcracker, Into the Deep, L5: First City in Space, Mission to Mir, Mountain Gorilla, Primiti Too Taa, Race the Wind, The Secret of Life on Earth, Special Effects, Survival Island, Titanica,* and *T-REX: Back to the Cretaceous,* just to name a few.

Young Filmmakers, 1965–67

Founded in 1967 by a group of five filmmakers and inventors who wanted to show off the beauty of the medium, Imax Systems, as it was known then, has since consistently delivered the world's premiere cinematic experiences on huge screens. However, the company had inauspicious beginnings. Independent filmmaker Graeme Ferguson had attended Galt Collegiate Institute in Galt, Ontario, Canada, where he met Robert Kerr and Bill Shaw, and the three men founded a student newspaper together. Ferguson went on to the University of Toronto, where he began making films. One summer, he was selected to be an intern at the National Film Board of Canada (NFB), and he went on to become an independent filmmaker, eventually working in New York. In 1965, Ferguson was asked by the Canadian Expo Corporation to do a film for Expo '67 in Montreal, but it had to be produced by a Canadian company. Kerr was at the time serving as mayor of Galt and still managing the printing company he had sold. Ferguson approached him about setting up a film production company. Kerr agreed, and they produced the film *Polar Life* for Expo '67.

Meanwhile, film producer Roman Kroitor had also been a summer intern at NFB. He began working there full-time after finishing college. In 1965 he suggested the board form a committee to produce a multiple-image, experimental film for the 1967 Expo. Kroitor's concept was selected, and he produced *Labyrinth.*

Expo '67 proved to be the birthplace of big-screen movie production. Other forerunners in big-screen production were in attendance there, including Colin Low, Kroitor's codirector on *Labyrinth*; Christopher Chapman; Francis Thomson; and Alexander Hammid, all of whom Ferguson would turn to as Imax Corporation developed.

A New Company, 1967

In 1967 Fuji Bank of Japan asked Kroitor to produce a film for Expo '70, to take place in Osaka, Japan, with partial financing provided by Fuji. Kroitor turned to Ferguson and Kerr to help him do it. Multiscreen Corporation was created, with Ferguson as the president. In order to showcase the new film, the company would have to create new technology for it, including a new camera to shoot images on a film frame ten times larger than the normal 35mm format, new equipment to project those larger frame images onto a six-story-high screen, and other accoutrements such as new lenses, sound equipment, lighting, and seating arrangements.

Norwegian-born inventor Jan Jacobson, located in Copenhagen, designed a new camera to use 65 mm film horizontally, in less than three months. But the projector proved to be a tougher issue to handle. The company acquired a patent for a Rolling Loop projector from Ronald Jones, a machine shopowner in Brisbane, Australia, but it needed to be adapted to handle the larger size film. The partners turned to old friend Bill Kerr. Kerr had gone to work for Ford Motor Company for a few years as an engineer, eventually moving on to CCM, a sporting goods and bicycle manufacturing company. Kerr and Jones worked together via airmail across two continents to develop the projector. Meanwhile, Kroitor moved to Japan, along with Canadian director Donald Brittain and cameraman Georges Dufaux, to work with Asuka Productions to develop the movie they would show. Despite drawbacks, cash flow problems, and bouts of frustration, the projector and film were finished, and *Tiger Child* played on the big screen at Expo '70, while the audience was carried through the theater continuously on a large rotating platform, each observer viewing the endless film from a different starting point.

In 1971 Ontario Place, a government-sponsored theme park in Toronto, included Cinesphere, a theater showcasing new technology. Ontario Place bought the Expo '70 projector, which was brought back from Japan, refined a bit, and installed in the spring of 1971. That first IMAX projector was still running at Ontario Place at the end of the 20th century. The first film shown there, *North of Superior*, was produced by the company, which quickly gained a reputation for its projectors and sound systems, as well as for showing educational films created by institutions such as The Kennedy Space Center and Grand Canyon National Park. Over the next decade, the company would not only change its name several times, but change leadership and ownership as well, nevertheless while building more Imax theaters and creating more movies for the medium.

Competition Grows, 1983

In 1983 special effects wizard (*2001: A Space Odyssey*; *Close Encounters of the Third Kind*; *Star Trek: The Motion Picture*) and director (*Brainstorm*) Douglas Trumbull, along with restaurant and hotel mogul Robert Brock (Brock Hotels,

Park Inns International Inc.), founded Showscan Film Corporation, a competitor of Imax. Showscan revolutionized the industry, releasing a new cinematographic technique in February 1984 that offered three-dimensional picture without viewers having to wear the infamous blue-and-red glasses. Showscan began showing films at 60 frames per second, rather than the normal 24 frames per second. The company built four prototype theaters, including one in Dallas, connected with Brock's Showbiz Pizza Place restaurant outlets, and began showing a movie called *New Magic*. In August 1990, the company changed its name to Showscan Corporation. Meanwhile, in 1986, Iwerks Entertainment Inc. sprang up in California, reincorporating in Delaware in October 1993 under the same name. A year later, Iwerks acquired Omni Films International Inc. for approximately $19.17 million.

At Expo '90, also held in Osaka, the company unveiled its new 3-D technology, Imax Solido, which gave new life to a medium plagued with terrible 3-D renditions. The film shown there, the first of many to be produced eventually by the company, was *Echoes of the Sun*, a mostly computer-generated picture coproduced with Japanese company Fujitsu, and shown on a wrap-around screen and viewed with battery-powered goggles. The first 3-D Imax theater was built in Vancouver that year.

New Owners, 1994

In August 1994, competitor Showscan changed its name to Showscan Entertainment Inc. to reflect its more comprehensive focus. That year, WGIM Acquisition Corporation (made up of investment group Wasserstein Perella & Company, owned by Bruce Wasserstein and Joseph Perella, both formerly of First Boston; Cheviot Capital Advisors, led by Bradley J. Wechsler and Richard L. Gelfond; and some private investors such as Douglas Trumbull), bought out IMAX's five original owners and The Trumbull Company Inc. for approximately $100 million. Later that year, the company went public, selling its stock for $13.50 per share.

With the acquisition of Trumbull, Imax also acquired Trumbull subsidiary Ridefilm Theaters, a motion simulator company known for its creation of rides based on movies. Douglas Trumbull was the creative mastermind behind the design of IMAX Ridefilm, described by the company as "the most immersive, dynamic and realistic simulation product available." The 18-person modular system featured 180-degree, spherically-curved screens; proprietary orthogonal-motion base technology; high-speed, high-resolution projector technology; and six-track DTS sound. The attraction remained unparalleled by the end of the century, leaving Imax as the industry leader over competitors such as Iwerks and Showscan, with more than 20 ride locations throughout the world, including the United States, China, France, Japan, Korea, the United Kingdom, Thailand, Norway, Canada, Brazil, Argentina, and the Philippines. Entertainment produced on the rides included features such as *Asteroid Adventure*; *Crashendo*; *Dolphins—The Ride*; *Fun House Express*; *In Search of the Obelisk*; and *ReBoot: The Ride* and *ReBoot: Journey into Chaos*, based on the computer-animated television program of the same name.

Using the most advanced motion picture and special effects technology, IMAX HD Dome and motion simulation, IMAX Simulator Rides revolutionized the attractions industry. In 1997 the company built its first motion simulator theater ride in Thailand, at Major Cineplex's entertainment complex on Sukhumvit Road, near the city of Ekamai. By this time, the company already featured simulator rides in Germany, at Caesar's Palace in Las Vegas, and at Universal Studios in both Los Angeles and Orlando, showing such features as *Race for Atlantis*, *Asteroid Adventure*, and *Back to the Future—The Ride*. Meanwhile, in July 1997, Showscan Entertainment acquired 15 percent of Reality Cinema Pty. Ltd. in Darling Harbour, Sydney, Australia.

Also in 1997, in order to allow more than one theater to open per year, the company hired Toronto-based Young & Wright Design Architects to design a prototype theater which could be duplicated across the country, a move many other companies were preparing as well. Additionally that year, the company was awarded the only Oscar Award given for Scientific and Technical Achievement by the Academy of Motion Picture Arts and Sciences. Total revenue for 1997 reached $158.5 million.

In January 1998, despite the Asian economic crisis, interest in the entertainment industry in that region of the world was increasing. Early in the year, Imax Corporation entered into an agreement to build a 600-seat IMAX 3D theater in Bangkok, Thailand (the first in that country). The theater was to be operated by Cinema Plus Limited, Imax's Australian licensee, and Major Cineplex Company Limited, a 40-year-old company operating in the areas of entertainment, retail, and real estate, with 75 screens in Thailand.

That March, the company revolutionized three-dimensional cinema again with a new prototype theater, the IMAX 3D SR, located at the Arizona Mills shopping mall in Tempe, Arizona. It was the first of 12 3D screens to be built by the joint venture between IMAX Theater Holdings Inc. of Canada and Ogden Film & Theater Inc. of New York. The addition of the $7 million, 59- by 82-foot screen and 22,000-square-foot theater made the greater Phoenix area the only marketplace supporting two IMAX theaters; the other, a regular IMAX screen, was located in Scottsdale, Arizona, another suburb of Phoenix. Two other 3D screens opened that year in Nyack, New York, and Miami, Florida, marking another milestone for the company: the first time it had featured multiple-screen openings in one year. The new technology offered both two-dimensional, regular movie format, and three-dimensional features requiring the use of a headset and cordless ski-goggle type headsets containing liquid-crystal lenses which worked in sync with the projector lenses.

As of early 1999 there were more than 180 permanent IMAX theaters in 25 countries, with a backlog of more than 75 theater systems scheduled to open in 15 new countries during the next few years. Over 500 million people had seen an IMAX presentation since the medium premiered in 1970, and the company had forged strategic alliances and relationships with some of the most prominent corporations in the world, including The Walt Disney Company, Famous Players Inc. (a subsidiary of Viacom Inc.), and Loews Cineplex Corporation, to name a few. The agreement with Famous Players included building IMAX 3D theaters in ten of Famous Players' new and existing theaters in Canada. For fiscal 1998, total revenue climbed again, reaching $190.4 million, with a net income of $1.8 million.

At the beginning of 1999, the company estimated that more than 65 million people worldwide were expected to attend an IMAX theater during the calendar year, and with more theaters opening around the world, the company moved into the 21st century with lots of potential to continue dominating its niche markets, especially since it signed a deal with Disney subsidiary Buena Vista Pictures for the exclusive giant-screen release of *Fantasia 2000,* a remake of the classic animated feature.

Principal Subsidiaries

David Keighley Productions 70 MM Inc.; Ridefilm Corporation; Sonics Associates, Inc.

Further Reading

Booth, Cathy, "IMAX Gets Bigger (by Getting Smaller): The Megamovie Company Is Downsizing into Lesser Burgs," *Time,* June 29, 1998, p. 48.

Carrns, Ann, "Atlanta on Short List for Ridefilm Site," *Atlanta Business Chronicle,* October 6, 1995, p. 5A.

Creno, Glen, "New Arizona Imax Theater Goes After Mall Crowd," *Knight-Ridder/Tribune Business News,* July 22, 1996, p. 7220185.

Dries, Mike, "On Track to 500 Screens, Marcus Theaters Teams with IMAX," *Business Journal-Milwaukee,* May 1, 1998, p. 5.

Elmer-DeWitt, Philip, "Grab Your Goggles, 3-D is Back! Eye-Popping Realism Gives New Life to an Old Craze," *Time,* April 16, 1990, p. 77.

Graves, Jacqueline M., "These Movies Are Going to Be Big, Really Big," *Fortune,* June 12, 1995, p. 24.

Howard, Bob, "San Bernardino, Calif., Officials to Set Policy on Big-Screen Theaters," *Knight-Ridder/Tribune Business News,* May 21, 1996, p. 5210312.

Johnson, Ted, and Diane Goldner, "Bigscreens Make Mainstream Breakout Bid," *Variety,* January 27, 1997, p. 5.

Keating, Peter, Jim Frederick, Susan Scherreik, and Penelope Wang, "Word on the Street," *Money,* February 1999, p. 65.

La Franco, Robert, "The Biggest Show on Earth: Siegfried & Roy Grab IMAX Riches by Their Tigers' 3-D Tails," *Forbes,* September 21, 1998, p. 228.

McCollum, Brian, "Myrtle Beach, S.C., Theater Builder Signs Big-Screen Deal with IMAX," *Knight-Ridder/Tribune Business News,* July 7, 1995, p. 7070029.

Messinger, Rob, "Large-Screen Cinema Battle Takes Shape in Ontario, Calif.," *Knight-Ridder/Tribune Business News,* April 30, 1996, p. 4300004.

Netherton, Martha, *Business Journal—Serving Phoenix & the Valley of the Sun,* November 21, 1997, p. 1.

O'Brien, Tim, "Joint Venture Strengthens Imax's European Presence," *Amusement Business,* February 13, 1995, p. 26.

Olson, Eric J., "Giant Screens Poised for Big Impact," *Variety,* January 4, 1999, p. 9.

Ray, Susan, "Giant-Screen Theaters Riding Wave of Increased Interest, Sales," *Amusement Business,* September 12, 1994, p. 22.

——, "IMAX, Trumbull Co. Joining Forces," *Amusement Business,* January 17, 1994, p. 26.

——, "Leisure Technology: Location Based Entertainment Leads the High-Tech Charge," *Amusement Business,* September 12, 1994, p. 17.

Russell, John, "Cinemark Considers 24-Screen Theater in Akron, Ohio," *Knight-Ridder/Tribune Business News,* November 4, 1998, p. OKRB9830804.

——, "Imax Expands Its Large-Format Movies into Commercial Theater Complexes," *Knight-Ridder/Tribune Business News,* January 6, 1999, p. OKRB9900607.

Serino, Joseph, " 'Signature Entertainment' Gaining Ground in Urban Development Field," *Amusement Business*, July 8, 1996, p. 26.

Smith, Elliot Blair, "California's Edwards Theaters Circuit Has Big Plans for IMAX," *Knight-Ridder/Tribune Business News*, July 8, 1997, p. 708B0971.

Tillson, Tamsen, "Imax Beefs up Network with Eye on Hollywood," *Variety*, February 23, 1998, p. 30.

Turner, Dan, "Iwerks Sues Competitor over Unfair Practices," *Los Angeles Business Journal*, March 4, 1996, p. 10.

Turnis, Jane, "Cinemark Plans Megaplex, IMAX Theater in Colorado Springs, Colo.," *Knight-Ridder/Tribune Business News*, February 22, 1999, p. OKRB990530AB.

Waal, Peter, "The Plot Quickens," *Canadian Business*, June 26, 1998, p. 52.

Wadley, Jared, "San Bernardino County, Calif., May Get Giant-Screen Theater," *Knight-Ridder/Tribune Business News*, February 21, 1996, p. 2210010.

Whitelaw, Kevin, "At the Movies: 3-D Comes to the Giant Screen," *U.S. News & World Report*, September 16, 1996, p. 68.

Zoltak, James, "Cinema Plus Deal to Give Imax Corp. Presence in Australia, New Zealand," *Amusement Business*, January 15, 1996, p. 22.

——, "Imax Lands Five Theater Orders for Hammons Projects," *Amusement Business*, July 24, 1995, p. 34.

—Daryl F. Mallett

JACOB LEINENKUGEL BREWING COMPANY
CHIPPEWA FALLS, WISCONSIN

Jacob Leinenkugel Brewing Company

1 Jefferson Avenue
Chippewa Falls, Wisconsin 54729
U.S.A.
(715) 723-5558
(800) LEINIES; (800) 534-6437
Web site: http://www.leinie.com

Wholly Owned Subsidiary of Miller Brewing Company
Founded: 1867
Employees: 75
Sales: NA
NAIC: 31212 Breweries

Jacob Leinenkugel Brewing Company is a prominent regional and specialty beer brewer. Leinenkugel's core market is the upper Midwest, which used to be the only place consumers could buy the beer. Since linking with Miller Brewing Company in 1988, Leinenkugel's brands have reached broader markets across the United States. The company's core product is its Leinenkugel's Original, a beer first brewed in 1867. This accounts for about 40 percent of the company's sales. Leinenkugel also produces a variety of seasonal and specialty beers, and these make up the remaining 60 percent of sales. Within the Miller Brewing Company, Leinenkugel operates as part of a division called the American Specialty and Craft Beer Company. This division promotes Leinenkugel and other small breweries owned by Miller, to capture the small but growing specialty beer segment of the U.S. beer market.

Early Years

The company was founded by Jacob Leinenkugel, an immigrant from Bavaria who descended from a family of brewmasters. Leinenkugel picked out the northwoods town of Chippewa Falls, Wisconsin, to start a brewery. In 1866, when Leinenkugel arrived there, the town was a remote place unserviced by railroads. Almost all Chippewa Falls' 2,500 inhabitants worked in the timber trade, logging in the forests or working the huge sawmill on the Chippewa River. The town had few female inhabitants, and the loggers typically worked 12- to 16-hour shifts. This then seemed like a community ripe for a brewery. Chippewa Falls also had another essential ingredient for a brewery: a good source of pure water in its rivers and the Big Eddy Springs. Jacob Leinenkugel went into business in 1867, brewing inside a 24-by-50-foot building. His beer was packed in wooden barrels and delivered by wagon to Chippewa Falls saloons. By 1890 the brewery was doing so well that Leinenkugel invested in new facilities. He built a new brewery, a three-story malthouse, a barn to house the delivery horses, and several other buildings. When Jacob Leinenkugel died in 1899, the business passed to his son Matt.

Leinenkugel remained a strictly regional beer for a long time. Chippewa Falls was not easily accessible, and beer was a fragile beverage that did not do well when shipped long distances. So the company confined its sales to northern Wisconsin. When Prohibition made beer sales illegal in 1918, the company made do by producing a line of soda water. But it kept its brewing equipment in place, and when Prohibition was repealed in 1933, the company started up again with its original recipes. At that time it made its flagship brand, called simply Leinenkugel's, as well as a bock beer. When the United States entered World War II, rationing and labor shortages caused other breweries to raise their prices. But Leinenkugel steadfastly kept its prices the same. After the war, the company invested again in new equipment. In 1955 Leinenkugel installed glass-lined fermentation tanks at its brewery, and these were the first of their kind in use in the United States.

Greater Distribution in the 1970s

Since the company's founding in 1867, Leinenkugel's beer had been sold only in the northwoods area of Wisconsin known as the Chippewa Valley. Sales had been steady enough to allow the company to expand its facilities, but it was not until 1970 that Leinenkugel began to reach out to bigger markets. The company began selling its beer in Minnesota that year, and in 1972 also reached into the Upper Peninsula of Michigan market. The president of the company was still a family member, Bill Leinenkugel. In a March 29, 1982 article in *Advertising Age*, Bill Leinenkugel noted that one of the advantages of being a small, regional brand was that he felt no need to change the company's recipes in order to please a mass market palate. The company did add a light beer in 1972, but otherwise the product remained the same, brewed with the old equipment by a workforce of only about 30 people. Through the 1970s, Leinenkugel expanded only gradually into neighboring markets; by 1982, the beer could still be found in just four states. The company sold Leinenkugel's in northern Illinois, upper Michigan, Minnesota, and Wisconsin, and only in markets that were within 300 miles of its Chippewa Falls plant. The company spent comparatively little on advertising, though it did have a presence on local radio and television stations. Its spokesman was a prominent Minnesota sports broadcaster, Ray Scott. Leinenkugel also occasionally ran print ads in regional magazines such as the *Wisconsin Business Journal*. The company sometimes sponsored special events such as a Pure Water Day, too.

One barrier to greater distribution of Leinenkugel's was that the beer was made with no chemicals, unlike most national brand beers. This gave it a short shelf life, and so it was difficult for the company to imagine it could penetrate into wider markets. But the beer was becoming known outside its limited Midwestern market. In 1978 *Newsweek* magazine lauded Leinenkugel's, labeling it "The Pride of the Northwoods," and in 1982 *Advertising Age* featured the brand in an article about regional breweries. President Bill Leinenkugel thought that the company might grow by finding more creative ways to reach people within its geographic market area. The company opened a hospitality center in 1980, with a small museum and gift shop, and began offering tours of the brewery. Northern Wisconsin attracted a lot of tourists in the summer, and the hospitality center was devised to bring them to Chippewa Falls and introduce them to the taste of Leinenkugel's. Besides tourists, the company also thought it could reach out more to college students. A number of small colleges dotted the upper Midwest, and by 1982, Leinenkugel was planning ways to appeal to these young drinkers. The company also planned to start selling its beer in Iowa in the early 1980s. But that was as far as the company's expansion plans went.

Under Miller After 1988

By 1987, Leinenkugel was a profitable company, comfortable in its geographic niche. The brewery produced 60,000 barrels of beer that year, and sales in its four-state market had been growing impressively. The company had made few changes in the late 1980s. It introduced Leinenkugel's Limited (Northwoods Lager) in 1986, a new product based on an original Leinenkugel family recipe. Its Original brand, the core product, won a gold medal in 1987 at the Great American Beer

Festival, more evidence of the beer's great appeal. Still a small, family-controlled company, Leinenkugel seemed to be making the most of its regional market without straining for greater growth. But in some ways the company was trapped. While it was doing well in its region, the company did not have the resources in terms of marketing and distribution to get its beer beyond the Midwest. The company wanted to branch out in a different way, too. Specialty brewing—small-scale production of "hand-crafted" special recipe beers—was a market category that was just starting to boom in the late 1980s, and Leinenkugel wanted to get in on it. But the company did not have the cash to finance a switch to a new product. In the meantime, Miller Brewing Company, one of the American beer giants, was experiencing stagnant sales. It was also locked into its core product, and was having difficulty breaking into new areas. Miller first approached Leinenkugel about a sale in 1987. According to Leinenkugel family legend, the father of current company president Jake Leinenkugel thought Miller wanted Leinenkugel to buy *it*. But it came to pass the other way around. Leinenkugel became a wholly owned subsidiary of Miller Brewing Company on April 1, 1988.

The sale was a shock for many Leinenkugel fans and employees, who feared the giant beer company would adulterate the Leinenkugel recipe and perhaps close down the historic brewery. Despite company president Jake Leinenkugel's assurances that Miller had no intent to mess with a successful product, the brand lost an estimated ten percent of its core customers in the year following the sale. After that, however, sales took off as Miller's marketing expertise and deep pockets allowed the smaller company to branch out. Although sales were still primarily in the four states Leinenkugel had traditionally sold in, Miller managed to get the brand distributed in Michigan, Indiana, Ohio, Nebraska, and Colorado by 1994. Sales in the upper Midwest market grew by double digits, and soon after the sale to Miller, Leinenkugel began producing new beers.

Its first venture into the small batch specialty beer category was its Northwoods Lager, introduced in 1986, before the sale to Miller. Leinenkugel's next attempt was Leinenkugel's Red Lager, first brewed in 1993. This was a direct attempt to counter the popularity of a Coors brand, Killian's Irish Red. The company also started brewing seasonal beers, such as an Autumn Gold specialty and a dark Winter Lager. Success with specialty brews was important to Leinenkugel. Though only two percent of the U.S. beer market was held by specialty brews in the early 1990s, this category was growing faster than anything else. Growth in the specialty beer niche grew 40 percent in 1995 alone, while sales of mass market beer were flat. Leinenkugel's first attempts to get in on the "hand-crafted" market were not as successful as they might have been, and in 1995 Miller formed a new division to better focus its specialty brands. It formed a unit called the American Specialty and Craft Beer Company (Absco.), and placed Leinenkugel under this division, along with the Celis Brewery in Austin, Texas, and another affiliate called The Shipyard Brewing Company, of Portland, Maine. The purpose of Absco. was to let the small brewers do what they knew best—that is, make their particular beers. Though they had the support of Miller's research and development teams, particularly important in making a new product consistent, as well as Miller's vast financial backing, marketing and distribution was handled by managers who really understood the smaller beer market. Aptly put in a May 1996 article in *Beverage Industry*, Leinenkugel and the other small brewers under Absco. had the opportunity to "link up to Miller's resources without being 'Millerized.' "

Marketing of Leinenkugel's brands under Absco. stressed the northwoods Wisconsin background of the beer. To make sure that all the people handling the brand really understood this, the Leinenkugel brothers Dick, vice-president of sales, and John, a brand assistant, started what they called "Camp Leinenkugel" in the mid-1990s. They invited sales representatives from parent company Miller to Chippewa Falls to see the Leinenkugel brewery in action, and to brush up on the selling and merchandising of Leinenkugel's brands. Sales of all Leinenkugel's brands rose precipitately in the early 1990s, from 85,000 barrels in 1988 to almost 270,000 barrels in 1996. The old Leinenkugel's brewery worked double shifts, and some of the Leinenkugel's Original brand was made at Miller's plant in Milwaukee. Also in September 1995 Miller bought a Milwaukee brewery formerly owned by Blatz, and used this facility to develop new specialty beers for Leinenkugel. By 1996, Leinenkugel had quite a line of specialty beers. It made Auburn Ale, the company's first ever ale, a Creamy Draft, another English-style ale, and a Bavarian-style wheat beer called Leinenkugel's Hefeweizen. Then it had a year-round complement of seasonal beers, from its Big Butt Doppelbock, available only from January through April, to its Berry Weiss, a fruit flavored summer beer. For fall there was the Autumn Gold, and winter had been covered since 1993 by Leinenkugel's Winter Lager. Because it had a beer for every season, Leinenkugel was able to command retail shelf space for its craft products year-round.

Since the sale to Miller, Leinenkugel's production capacity nearly tripled, and the brand began appearing in markets as far from the Wisconsin northwoods as California and Florida. The company managed to do this without sacrificing its historic brewery or modifying the recipe for its Leinenkugel's Original brand. By the late 1990s, Leinenkugel's was in places it would hardly have imagined ten years earlier. In 1998, Leinenkugel opened a brew pub in the unlikely location of the new baseball stadium in Phoenix, Arizona. Though beer brewers had traditionally been barred by law from also owning or operating bars, there were exceptions for brew pubs, where beer was made and sold on the same premises. Although the law's loopholes were apparently intended to keep small brewers in business, there seemed to be nothing prohibiting Miller from opening Miller's Leinenkugel Brewing in the Phoenix Bank One Ballpark. It was far removed from the Chippewa Valley, but the foray into retail venues was happening at other big breweries, as well as smaller ones such as Samuel Adams. It was this kind of creative marketing and latching onto new niches that Leinenkugel had been unable to finesse when it was a stand-alone private company. So the match-up with Miller seemed a successful one. Leinenkugel was still run by fifth-generation descendants of Jacob Leinenkugel, with three brothers in top positions, including president. The recipe for the Original brand beer had not been changed. Yet the company was very different in the late 1990s than it had been ten years earlier. Sales were growing, and it had penetrated into many regions beyond the Midwest. Leinenkugel was bigger, more flexible, producing more volume, and more varieties of beer. The combination of the mainstream Miller and the small regional brewer seemed to be working to the advantage of both companies.

Further Reading

Causey, James E., "Leinenkugel Brewing Co. Taps into Craft Beer Market," *Knight-Ridder/Tribune Business News*, September 6, 1996, p. 909B0292.
Holleran, Joan, "Leinenkugel Brews Up New History," *Beverage Industry*, May 1996, p. 28; "Macro Goes Micro," *Beverage Industry*, May 1996, p. 24.
Kermouch, Gerry, "Leinie's Heir Brewing Miller Sales," *Brandweek*, September 13, 1993, p. 20.
"Miller Keeps the Mystique, Adds Employees at Leinie's," *Corporate Report-Minnesota*, June 1994, p. 72.
"A Miller Unit Buys Brewery," *New York Times*, September 21, 1995, p. D19.
Ortega, Bob, "How Big Brewers Are Sidling into Retail," *Wall Street Journal*, May 18, 1998, p. B1, B11.
Tait, Nancy, "Specialty Markets Give Small Operators a Taste of Success," *Advertising Age*, March 29, 1982, p. M46.

—A. Woodward

Johnson Publishing Company, Inc.

820 S. Michigan Avenue
Chicago, Illinois 60605
U.S.A.
(312) 322-9200
Fax: (312) 322-0179
Web site: http://www.ebony.com

Private Company
Incorporated: 1942 as Negro Digest Publishing Co.
Employees: 1,500
Sales: $361.1 million (1997 est.)
NAIC: 51112 Periodical Publishers; 511130 Book
Publishers; 56151 Travel Agencies

Johnson Publishing Company, Inc. is the world's largest black-owned publishing company. It is the home of *Ebony*, *Jet*, and *EM* magazines, as well as Fashion Fair Cosmetics, Supreme Beauty Products, *Ebony* Fashion Fair, and the Johnson Publishing Company Book Division.

Humble Beginnings, 1942

Johnson Publishing Company was founded in November 1942 by John H. Johnson—who was working part time as an office boy for Supreme Life Insurance Company of America, located in Chicago, Illinois—and his wife, Eunice. Johnson's job was to clip magazine and newspaper articles about the black community. As he clipped, the idea for a black-oriented magazine came to mind. Using his mother's furniture as collateral, he secured a loan of $500. He then mailed out $2 charter subscription offers to potential subscribers. Over 3,000 replies came in, and the $6,000 was used to print the first issue of *Negro Digest*, a magazine based on the popular *Reader's Digest*.

Negro Digest Publishing Co. was born. Immediately facing obstacles such as finding a landlord willing to rent him office space in a not-yet-desegregated United States, Johnson managed to secure a room in the private law office of Earl B. Dickerson, on the second floor of his employer's building, the

Supreme Life Insurance Company. In 1943 Johnson purchased a building at 5619 South State Street, to house the fledgling company. In 1949 the company converted a funeral parlor at 1820 South Michigan Avenue into office space and moved there, a location which would remain the company's headquarters to the end of the 20th century, although it would grow to be 11 stories tall. Along the way, *Negro Digest*, which had a circulation at one time of 100,000 subscribers, was renamed *Black World*. In the 1970s, the readership dwindled, and the magazine was finally canceled in 1975.

However by that time, the company was going strong with other products. In 1945 Johnson launched *Ebony*, a magazine patterned after *Life*, but focusing on the black community, culture, and achievements. It was an immediate success and remained the company's flagship publication into the 21st century, with a readership at one point of over 1.3 million. In 1951 Johnson created another magazine, called *Jet*, a celebrity-oriented magazine focusing on black entertainers and public figures. For nearly 20 years, these two magazines were the only publications for blacks in the United States.

Unable to obtain advertising in those years, Johnson created the Beauty Star mail-order company and began advertising its products, such as haircare products, wigs, and vitamins in his own magazines. In 1947 the company picked up its first major advertising account in Zenith Radio and, after sending a salesman to Detroit every week for nearly ten years, finally managed to sign Chrysler Corporation in 1954. The magazine drew the talents of many people, including author Era Bell Thompson (1905–1986), who served as associate editor of *Ebony* from 1948 to 1951, and comanaging editor from 1951 to 1964, before becoming international editor for the company thereafter.

In 1957 *Ebony* Fashion Fair blazed a trail of fashion excellence that has endured the test of time. Four gorgeous black models brought fashion excitement to audiences in ten cities—Chicago; Indianapolis; New Orleans; Baltimore; Los Angeles; Dayton, Columbus, and Cleveland, Ohio; Philadelphia; and Washington, D.C.—where they displayed an array of dazzling American designer fashions. The late Freda DeKnight, *Ebony* magazine's home service director and *Ebony* Fashion Fair's first commentator, paraded fashions in homespun rhetoric weaving imaginary tales about each model and fashion. The 41st annual tour took place in the 1998–99 fashion season, with audiences still experiencing lively commentary, enriched with synthesizer programming, a drummer, a bassist, R&B, jazz, and song and dance routines performed by talented members of the troupe. Thirteen models moved swiftly down the runways and across stages in 1998–99, emphasizing elegance and excitement as they displayed American and European fashions brilliant with color, detail, and pizzazz. At the conclusion of the 40th annual tour, funds raised since inception by sponsors of the show had reached $45 million, all designated for various charities and scholarships. By then the show had given 540 young people and 112 wardrobe assistants the opportunity to visit cities and countries of many cultures, and had been sponsored by over 180 prestigious social and civic organizations, including the United Negro College Fund, the NAACP, and the Urban League.

Johnson quickly soared to fame. By the early 1960s, he was one of the most prominent black men in the country. In 1963, he and John F. Kennedy posed together to publicize a special issue of *Ebony* which was celebrating The Emancipation Proclamation. In 1972, U.S. magazine publishers gave him accolades as Publisher of the Year. He would also go on to become chairman and CEO of Supreme Life Insurance Company, his first employer.

In 1973 the company began publishing *Ebony Jr!* (now defunct), a magazine designed to provide "positive black images" for pre-teens. Johnson branched out into new media formats when he began buying radio stations, including WJPC, Chicago's first black-owned station. The following year, the company purchased WLOU in Louisville, Kentucky, and in the mid-1980s, the company acquired WLNR in Lansing, Illinois, which was merged with WJPC in 1992; the combined station was sold in 1995. Also in 1973, Fashion Fair Cosmetics was founded by the company in answer to the problems that women of color had in finding shades to match their skin tones. The company would go on to compete successfully against such huge competitors as Revlon and Johnson Products of Chicago, an unrelated company. Fashion Fair would grow to become the world's number one cosmetics company for women of color, with annual sales in 1982 reaching over $30 million, and the products being sold in over 2,500 stores throughout the United States, Canada, Europe, Africa, and the Caribbean.

In the early 1980s, Johnson began to groom his daughter Linda, who received her M.B.A. at Northwestern University's J.L. Kellogg School of Management, to take over the business.

Linda started working summers for the company at the age of 15, eventually becoming fashion coordinator for both magazines and cosmetics. Linda Johnson Rice would go on to become president and chief operating officer of the company, as well as a director for such companies as Bausch & Lomb. In 1981 Johnson's adopted son, John E., a staff photographer for the company, died of sickle-cell anemia, at age 25. That year, the company's total revenues reached $81 million. The following year, the company's revenue grew to $102 million.

In 1985 the company launched a new magazine called *EM (Ebony Man)*, targeted mainly at the growing ranks of increasingly affluent buppies (black urban professionals). Like a black version of *GQ (Gentlemen's Quarterly)*, the inaugural November issue was chock-full of photos of immaculate male models bedecked in the latest fashions of clothing, with a healthy dollop of fashion and grooming tips, and filled with articles on health, fitness, personal finance, and shopping techniques.

In 1988 Johnson was inducted into the Publishing Hall of Fame, along with such other luminaries as Harold K. Guinzburg, founder of Viking Press and The Literary Guild; Maxwell Perkins, editor at Charles Scribners Sons; Richard Leo Simon and Max Lincoln Schuster, founders of Simon & Schuster, Inc.; and William Randolph Hearst, founder of Hearst Publishing Corporation. That year, the company had total revenues of $215 million, making it the second largest black-owned business in the United States, behind Reginald Lewis's TLC Beatrice International Holdings. By this time, Johnson was also on the boards of Greyhound and two of his first advertisers, Chrysler and Zenith. The following year, Johnson was the recipient of IABC's Excellence in Communication "EXCEL" Award. That year, he was also the only black man on the *Forbes* list of the 400 wealthiest people in the United States. Johnson was also awarded the U.S. Presidential Medal of Freedom in 1996.

Also in 1989, Johnson wrote his autobiography, *Succeeding Against the Odds*, with assistance from longtime *Ebony* editor Lerone Bennett, Jr. In the autobiography, Johnson explained how he got started. "In organizing the staff [of my first magazine], I reached out to everybody, for I knew nothing about magazine publishing and editing. . . . When all else failed, I looked in the phone book and called an expert. Since I had nothing to lose, I always started at the top. I received valuable advice from Henry Luce of Time-Life and Gardner Cowles of *Look*. . . . It was hard to get through to Luce, but . . . I used a simple approach that almost always worked. I simply told the secretary or aide that I was the president—I stressed the word president—of my company. 'It is,' I said, 'a small company but I am the president, and I want to talk to your president. . . If the president of the smallest country in the world comes to Washington, our president, as a matter of public policy and protocol will see him. So it seems to me that your president, in the American tradition, will see me for a few minutes if you pass this request on and tell him that I don't want a donation or a job.' I used that on Henry Luce's secretary, and I got in to see him."

In 1991 the company sold its controlling interest in the last minority-owned insurance company in Illinois, Supreme Life Insurance, Johnson's first employer, to Chicago-based Unitrin, a life, health, and property insurance company. Total revenues for 1991 climbed to $281 million. Also that year, the company entered into a joint venture with catalog company Spiegel Inc. to develop a fashion line and mail-order catalog aimed at black women, launching a mail-order catalog called *E Style* to that effect in 1993. An accompanying credit card with the "E Style" imprint appeared in 1994.

In October 1992, the company introduced "Ebone," a new line of cosmetics for women of color, as well as a three-part videotape series called *The Ebony/Jet Guide to Black Excellence*, which profiled black leaders, entrepreneurs, and entertainers to help provide positive role models for young people.

In November 1995, the company expanded its operations with the launch of *Ebony South Africa*, a counterpart to the U.S. version of the magazine. Because trade tariffs on incoming products to South Africa were taxed at 100 percent of the cost, Johnson Publishing subsidiary EBCO International teamed up with five South African companies, with Johnson holding 51 percent of the joint venture, in order to avoid losing money on the project. The company invested $2–$3 million on facilities, equipment, and staffing, opening editorial offices in Sandton, near Johannesburg. In the inaugural November 1995 issue, Bishop Desmond Tutu related the story of when he saw his first issue of *Ebony*, which had Jackie Robinson on the cover, when the cleric was nine years old and living in a ghetto township located some 30 miles outside of Johannesburg.

Total sales for 1997 reached $361.1 million, a 10.9 percent growth over the previous year, in which the company ranked 28th overall in magazine publishing companies by advertising revenue, with $26.8 million for the first half of 1996. However, competition in the black-oriented magazine industry finally began to catch up with Johnson Publishing Company. With a plethora of new titles appearing, such as *Black Enterprise*, and the rise of other black-oriented entertainment and informational vehicles such as Black Entertainment Television (BET), circulation of *Ebony* dropped seven percent.

Still, the company bounced back without noticeable difficulty: all three major magazines (*Ebony*, *Jet*, and *EM*) continued to draw advertisers and readership, as the company entered the 21st century poised to sustain its long history of leadership within the black-oriented publishing industry.

Principal Subsidiaries

Ebony Fashion Fair; Fashion Fair Cosmetics; Mahogany Travel Service Inc.; Supreme Beauty Products; EBCO International (South Africa; 51%).

Principal Divisions

Johnson Publishing Company Book Division.

Further Reading

Alpert, Mark, "*Jet* Powered," *Fortune*, July 31, 1989, p. 266.

"B.E. Industrial Service 100," *Black Enterprise*, June 1996, p. 117.

Cyr, Diane, "Ten Inducted into Publishing Hall of Fame; Scholars, Risk Takers, Writers and Empire Builders Constitute This Year's Honorees," *Folio: The Magazine for Magazine Management*, January 1988, p. 43.

Dingle, Derek T., "Doing Business John Johnson's Way," *Black Enterprise*, June 1987, p. 150.

——, "New Directions for Black Business," *Black Enterprise*, August 1985, p. 67.

"EXCEL Award Winner John H. Johnson Communicates Success," *Communication World*, May 1989, p. 18.

Falkof, Lucille, *John H. Johnson, The Man from Ebony*, Ada, Okla.: Garrett Educational Corp., 1991.

Greenberg, Jonathan, "It's a Miracle," *Forbes*, December 20, 1982, p. 104.

Johnson, John H., *Succeeding Against the Odds: The Autobiography of a Great American Businessman*, New York: Amistad Press, 1989.

"Like Father, Like Daughter," *Fortune*, October 3, 1983, p. 180.

Mangelsdorf, Martha E., "Succeeding Against the Odds: The Autobiography of a Great American Business," *Inc.*, October 1993, p. 58.

"The Silent Strength of Family Businesses," *U.S. News & World Report*, April 25, 1983, p. 47.

Wellemayer, Marilyn, "A Gym of One's Own," *Fortune*, February 21, 1983, p. 149.

Whigham-Desir, Marjorie, "Forging New Frontiers: Never Ones to Shy Away from New Ventures, B.E. 100s Companies Are Making Their Mark—and Market—Internationally," *Black Enterprise*, May 1996, p. 70.

——, "Marathon Men: 25 Years of Black Entrepreneurial Excellence," *Black Enterprise*, June 1997, p. 104.

—Daryl F. Mallett

Johnson Worldwide Associates, Inc.

1326 Willow Road
Sturtevant, Wisconsin 53177
U.S.A.
(414) 884-1500
Fax: (414) 631-4426
Web site: http://www.jwa.com

Public Company
Incorporated: 1985
Employees: 1,366
Sales: $303 million (1997)
Stock Exchanges: NASDAQ
Ticker Symbol: JWAIA
NAIC: 33992 Sporting and Athletic Goods
   Manufacturing; 314912 Canvas & Related Product
   Mills; 315999 Other Apparel Accessories & Other
   Apparel Manufacturing; 314991 Rope, Cordage &
   Twine Mills; 335312 Motor & Generator
   Manufacturing; 334514 Totalizing Fluid Meter &
   Counting Device Manufacturing; 339920 Fishing
   Tackle & Equipment Manufacturing; 421910 Sporting
   & Recreational Goods & Supplies Wholesalers

Johnson Worldwide Associates, Inc. manufactures, markets, and distributes a wide range of its own brand-name recreational products, including Minn Kota and Neptune battery powered boat motors, Mitchell fishing rods, Johnson reels and spoons, Beetle Spin lures, Eureka! and Camp Trails camping tents and backpacks, Silva field compasses, Jack Wolfskin outdoor gear, Old Town canoes and high-performance kayaks, and Scubapro and SnorkelPro underwater diving gear. Although the company headquarters is located in Mount Pleasant, Wisconsin, a rather sleepy and quaint small town in the heart of the American Midwest, recently the firm has made a commitment to expand its operations, and presently counts a growing number of manufacturing facilities and distribution centers not only in the United States, but in such countries as England, France, Spain, Belgium, Canada, Hong Kong, Italy, Switzerland, Germany, Sweden, Austria, Australia, Mexico, and Japan.

Early History

During the late 1960s and early 1970s, Johnson Wax (S.C. Johnson & Son, Inc.) initiated a diversification strategy similar though not identical to the diversification programs being carried out by many *Fortune* 500 companies. The plan was to acquire a group of small to medium-sized firms that were manufacturing recreational products with recognizable brand names, and form them into a recreational products division. Based largely on the fact that Samuel C. Johnson, the owner of the $2 billion Johnson Wax empire, was known as a sports enthusiast, the company initially purchased a small electric motor boat and fishing reel manufacturer located in Minnesota. Yet, even though the new recreational products division grew due to the help provided by the marketing network and management ability of Johnson Wax, as the division prospered it came into competition with consumer and institutional products groups for a larger share of the parent company's resources.

Confident that the recreational products division could stand on its own, company management and the Johnson family decided in the mid-1980s that it was time for the division to function as an independent company. The newly named Johnson Worldwide Associates was spun off from parent company Johnson Wax by means of a leveraged buyout to Samuel C. Johnson and the Johnson family. The buyout amounted to just over $66 million, with the Johnson family maintaining a 42 percent investment interest, but a 72 percent majority voting interest. Within two years, the company had firmly established itself in the fishing equipment and camping equipment markets, and the Johnson family thought an IPO was the next step in the firm's growth. Thus in 1987, just a short time after its spinoff from Johnson Wax, the small but growing Johnson Worldwide Associates went public in order to have access to the capital market and to establish a market value for the company's stock.

Having received an enthusiastic welcome from the traders and investors on Wall Street, Johnson Worldwide stock was

Company Perspectives:

JWA will be an entrepreneurial company engaged in outdoor recreation markets. As such, we will be end-user focused and decisive in action. JWA will bring innovation to the marketplace in increasingly rapid fashion; will concentrate on remaining lean in structure, yet be flexible enough to move quickly to respond to competitive actions; and will continue to deal ethically in all aspects of our business.

initially offered to the public at $15.50 per share. Almost overnight, the company raised $25 million, which was used quite wisely to pare down its debt. Unfortunately, the stock market crash of October 19, 1987 occurred one week after the company's initial public offering and sent its share price spiraling downward out of control. The company lost 50 percent of its share value within a few days. Yet management decided to make another offering of common stock available a short ten months later and, with its solid product line in fishing gear and camping equipment, Johnson Worldwide Associates soon recovered.

Growth and Expansion

By the end of the 1980s, the company was making its brand-name Johnson fishing reels, Minn Kota electric fishing motors, Old Town canoes, Eureka! Tents, and Camp Trail backpacking gear. The company was so successful that its Minn Kota electric fishing motors had captured a 70 percent share of the entire market within the industry, with sales of approximately $80 million for 1989. In addition, the firm's diving equipment, sold under the brand name Scubapro, had achieved record sales and, as a result, management at Johnson Worldwide Associates decided to invest heavily in the manufacture, distribution, and sale of diving gear and marine equipment throughout Europe. From the company's spinoff in 1985 to 1990, operating profits increased at an annual rate of 35 percent. With $232 million in sales for 1989, Johnson Worldwide Associates was named one of the best small companies in the United States by *Forbes* magazine.

During this time, the company made one of its first overseas acquisitions, a fishing reel manufacturer in Cluses, France, named Mitchell Sports, S.A. Mitchell Sports was one of the most revered manufacturers in the sporting goods industry, mostly due to the regard with which serious fishermen held the company's Mitchell 300 fishing reel. First introduced in the early 1950s, the reel had never fully taken advantage of its popularity among fishermen in the United States, but Johnson Worldwide immediately developed new brochures, television commercials, and displays to market an updated version of the Mitchell 300 fishing reel. Not surprisingly, the product became one of the bestselling items in the company's history.

By 1992, the company's net sales had increased to $334 million, with 43 percent of the total resulting from sales outside the United States. The purchase of Jack Wolfskin one year

earlier, a German firm that manufactured backpacks, camping tents, and outdoor clothing, was a large part of the company's rising fortunes in Europe. New models of its camping tents, fishing reels, and canoes were soon warehoused at a new Wolfskin facility in Germany, and sales began to increase at a dramatic rate. Old Town Canoes, one of the firm's most successful product lines throughout North America, was just as popular in Europe. The diving and marine businesses of Johnson Worldwide Associates produced over 70 percent of their sales outside the United States, and new models for diving masks and rubber goods sold particularly well throughout Europe's Scandinavian countries.

Augmenting the company's recreational products line was its development of a marking products business, which included such items as hand stamps, ink rolls, ink jets, and other office equipment. In 1989, management had made a significant investment in developing technology for bar coding systems, equipment for check processing, highspeed addressing, and postal coding. By the early 1990s, this strategic investment began to pay dividends, with sales increasing at a rate of ten percent annually, and marking products totaling approximately 20 percent of the company's overall sales. Once again, European operations played a major role. The largest hand stamp facility of the company was located in Sweden, with the majority of sales in that and neighboring countries.

The Mid-1990s

Unfortunately, the company's strategy for growth was flawed, and resulted in major financial repercussions during the mid-1990s. Seeking to expand its operations and revenues quickly through a series of acquisitions, management had overextended itself. Earnings dropped precipitously, and management was forced to make drastic decisions. Many of the companies purchased during this time were sold off. In addition, the company made a strategic decision to streamline its operations, thus requiring the sale of its entire marking products business.

Since Samuel C. Johnson, the owner of Johnson Wax, was involved in establishing the company and running it, he had incorrectly assumed that it could be developed in much the same fashion as his first entrepreneurial effort. What this meant was that a core business would provide a steady flow of cash and additional investment and expansion capital, while other businesses could be added or sold depending on their profitability. But the corporate sector had changed enormously since Samuel Johnson had established Johnson Wax, and the same strategies for growth and expansion were no longer applicable. After going through a number of different CEOs and presidents, the old warrior was still smart enough to recognize his mistakes and change course.

What this meant was that Johnson Worldwide Associates required a comprehensive restructuring from a holding company with numerous but unrelated businesses working mostly independently of one another to an efficiently run operating company whose core business was the manufacture and marketing of a complete line of recreational sports products and clothing. By 1995 earnings had rebounded, and company management was focusing on the development of new products, such as electronic diving equipment and camping gear. A new president and chief executive officer, Ronald Whitaker, was hired to guide the company's product development, and to implement a long-term, but more cautious, acquisitions program that would enhance its position in many of the recreational products markets.

By the end of 1997, the company's focus had been narrowed to five core product markets, including fishing rods, reels, and lures; electric boat motors, speedometers, marine and automotive compasses, and weather instruments; diving equipment and accessories such as regulators, masks, fins, wet and dry suits, gloves, dive belts, dive computers, snorkels, and buoyancy compensators; outdoor equipment such as camping tents, backpacks, commercial tents, bicycling gear, sleeping bags, field compasses, and outdoor clothing; and watercraft, including canoes, kayaks, paddles, and oars. Although sales were holding steady, amounting to just over $300 million at the end of fiscal 1997, management was optimistic that a few well-chosen, strategic acquisitions would increase that figure. To this end, in July 1997 management purchased Plastiques L.P.A. Limitee, a privately owned firm located in Canada that was widely regarded as one of the premier makers of high-quality kayaks in the country; Uwatec AG, a German-based manufacturer of diving computers and other electronic equipment; and Ocean Kayak, Inc., another Canadian-based producer of kayaks which had been identified as one of the fastest-growing recreational products firms throughout North America.

Johnson Worldwide Associates regarded itself as a well-integrated, global outdoor recreational products company; nonetheless, management was still searching for just the right product mix to ensure its continued growth. Johnson did, however, think it had found the right leadership in the person of Helen Johnson-Leipold, who came on board as chair and CEO in March 1999. Johnson-Leipold had most recently served as vice-president for worldwide consumer marketing under S.C. Johnson & Son.

Principal Subsidiaries

Airguide Instrument Co.; Johnson Camping, Inc.; Johnson Fishing, Inc.; Old Town Canoe Co.; Seaco/Elliot, Inc.; Under Sea Industries, Inc.

Further Reading

Balin, Kim Thuy, "Eschler's Fashionable Performance," *Sporting Goods Business,* April 16, 1999, p. 22.

Byrne, Harlan S., "Johnson Worldwide," *Barron's,* March 2, 1992, p. 37.

——, "Johnson Worldwide Associates, Inc.," *Barron's,* July 10, 1989, p. 35.

Carpenter, Kristin, "Backwoods Showdown," *Sporting Goods Business,* January 6, 1998, p. 44.

"Johnson Worldwide Names Helen Johnson-Leipold Chairman and CEO," *PR Newswire,* March 9, 1999.

Koselka, Rita, "More Fun Than Selling Floor Wax," *Forbes,* November 12, 1990, p. 222.

McEvoy, Christopher, "Acquiring Mind," *Sporting Goods Business,* August 1995, p. 44.

——, "Despite Slow Start, Retailers Still Bullish on Outdoor Boom," *Sporting Goods Business,* August 1995, p. 22.

Young, Kevin, "Standard Operation," *Sporting Goods Business,* August 1995, p. 48.

—Thomas Derdak

JPS Textile Group, Inc.

555 North Pleasantburg Drive, Suite 202
Greenville, South Carolina 29607
U.S.A.
(864) 239-3900
Fax: (864) 271-9939

Public Company
Incorporated: 1988
Employees: 2,900
Sales: $389.2 million (1998)
Stock Exchanges: NASDAQ
Ticker Symbol: JPST
NAIC: 313210 Broadwoven Fabric Mills

JPS Textile Group, Inc. manufactures textile products for a diverse range of applications. Its yarn is used principally in the manufacture of apparel, while its woven materials and specialty extruded materials can be found in commercial and institutional roofing, reservoir and landfill liners and covers, printed circuit boards, advanced composite materials, tarpaulins, awnings, athletic tapes, wallboard tapes and tile backings, security glazing, athletic shoes, as well as medical, automotive, and industrial components. The company was formed from some of the assets of the venerable J.P. Stevens & Co., which were acquired in a leveraged buyout in 1989. Since that time, JPS has reportedly met with difficulty in keeping up payments to holders of high interest bonds and has filed for bankruptcy protection twice. According to some industry analysts, the company's main business seems not to focus on spinning textiles so much as on navigating a web of debt.

Origins: Bidding War

JPS was formed from some of the assets of J.P. Stevens & Co., one of the giants of the textile industry with a history dating back to 1813. In the mid-1980s Stevens ran 59 textile plants employing 27,800, 10,000 of whom were in South Carolina, where it based its operations center, making it the state's third largest employer. Stevens had also become renowned for its opposition to unions, and its intractability in labor negotiations was met with a well-publicized consumer boycott. Struggles at one Stevens plant were dramatized in the 1979 Academy Award-winning movie *Norma Rae*.

The textile business was booming in 1988, and a takeover quest begun by Stevens's own management in the twilight of the acquisitive 1980s cost them control of the company. Specifically, a group of J.P. Stevens managers led by Whitney Stevens, a descendant of the founder, offered $696 million for the company, or $43 per share, when stock was trading at $33. However, the company's shareholders rebuffed the offer, as Odyssey Partners Group, a diversified New York investment partnership, as well as textile rival West Point-Pepperell, both made higher offers. Odyssey's bid of $953 million was soon countered by West Point. After more rounds of feverish bidding, the attorneys general of New York and the Carolinas and the Federal Trade Commission voiced their concerns about job losses and antitrust implications.

Following their reassurance that there would be no plant closings, West Point finally bought the company in May 1988 for $1.2 billion, or $68.50 a share. West Point sold Stevens's aviation and towel businesses to the NTC Group, while Odyssey Partners Group bought the remaining businesses for $615 million, renaming the collective operations JPS Textile Group, Inc.

Soon thereafter, the attorneys general investigated possible collusion in the takeover. Some industry observers characterized the Odyssey Group as corporate raiders who had no interest in textile operations. Odyssey had been formed in 1982 by former Oppenheimer & Co. partners; two of that company's directors had in fact pioneered the practice of leveraged buyouts. However, JPS was not the group's only holding in that industry, and some analysts praised Odyssey's ability to compete during difficult times.

Odyssey Partners owned 37.5 percent of the new company. William J. DeBrule, Grant Wilson, and Joe Schneider together owned an equivalent share, while Drexel Burnham Lambert Group Inc. owned the rest. The buyout cost $579 million, financed with high interest (16–19 percent) junk bonds. The new company's total liabilities were $650 million. Textile executive DeBrule served as the first chief executive officer at JPS.

The operations Odyssey acquired accounted for $796 million of Stevens's $1.6 billion in sales for 1987. Employees numbered 9,584. Although operating income held steady at about $35 million per year between 1988 and 1989, the previously profitable divisions' net losses mounted from $10 million to $57 million.

The new JPS Textile Group, ranked in the *Fortune* 500, produced a wide array of fabrics: rayons for apparel, cotton fabrics for book binding, carpet and headliners for automobiles, elastics for apparel, golf balls, and roofing. JPS also held the license to use the J.P. Stevens brand name until the year 2013.

In 1989, to offset some of its debt, JPS sold some plants, raising $20 million in the process. The company lost $10 million, however, on the sale of a fiberglass fabrics plant in Walterboro, North Carolina. Overall, the company lost $57 million in 1989, when its debt payments were $93 million. In 1990, when JPS employed 9,000, annual sales were $822 million. Still, its net worth had only risen to $46.8 million by July, putting it in threat of default on its loans with Citibank N.A. of New York, which required that JPS reach a minimum net worth of $55 million. (This requirement was subsequently amended.) Still the company had some evidence that its situation might be improving during the course of the year, though it had not yet attained profitability.

1991 Bankruptcy

During this time, slackening demand in the company's key markets limited its potential for recovery. A U.S. economic recession slowed auto sales to the point of stopping some production lines, while dismal housing starts paralyzed the home furnishings market.

Bondholders rejected several restructuring offers in 1990, but when JPS filed for bankruptcy in February 1991 they had agreed to lower payments in exchange for 49 percent of the company's stock (up from the $80 million and 30 percent of shares offered before). The novel "prepackaged" reorganization was approved by the court in only a couple of months. The company's debt was reduced from $531 million to $481 million and it would save $180 million in payments through 1995.

In 1991 the firm successfully lobbied South Carolina for a break on property taxes worth $950,000. At this time, JPS employed 3,900 of its 8,000 workers in that state. After DeBrule departed, Jerry Hunter, who had been an executive with the original J.P. Stevens, became president and chief operating officer at JPS, while Odyssey investor Steve Friedman became CEO.

JPS's sales fell seven percent in 1991, but the company expected to recover as the U.S. economy lifted out of its recession. Still, although sales did improve, particularly in the auto division, interest payments obliterated any profit.

JPS's automotive divisions employed 2,267 and produced carpet and other fabrics, with a turnover of about $300 million per year. In 1994 JPS sold this subsidiary to Rhode Island-based

Foamex International Inc., a Fortune 500 producer of automotive polyurethane foam, for $283 million. JPS spent $213 million of the proceeds to reduce debt to about $290 million and focused its attention on the remaining apparel fabrics and home fashions businesses. Also during this time, JPS sold its JPS Carpet Corp. subsidiary, owners of the Gulistan brand, for $27 million to a group of existing managers, who formed Gulistan Holdings Inc. to buy the operation.

Increasing competition from cheaper imported fabrics hurt U.S. demand in the women's apparel market, the company's primary business. At the same time, however, demand for fiberglass fabrics rose. JPS sold its elastics apparel business for $5 million during this time, and spent $14 million closing its Dunean apparel fabrics plant in Greenville, South Carolina.

The *Greenville (South Carolina) News* reported the company paid an average of $66 million a year from 1988 to 1996 simply on interest for its public bonds. In 1996, JPS lost $67 million on sales of $449 million.

1997 Bankruptcy

JPS defaulted on its bonds in December 1996. The company sought the advice of a New York investment bank, the Blackstone Group, when it realized it would be unable to make the huge principal payments coming due. With total liabilities of $464 million, JPS filed for Chapter 11 bankruptcy on August 1, 1997.

The bankruptcy plan was to reduce bond debt from $278 million to $186 million. The company still owed $85 million to lenders such as Citibank and General Electric Capital Corp. In return for the lowered obligations, bondholders' equity in the company increased to 99 percent. The deal brought five new members to JPS's seven-member board, and the reorganization allowed the company to make $23 million a year in capital expenditures with the hopes of attaining higher margins. Investments in automation were critical to compete with cheaper labor abroad, and many of JPS's mills were built before World War I. Some analysts suggested that management problems would also need to be addressed as well.

Hunter voiced relief in the debt reduction that would allow more focus on normal operations. Even though JPS had managed to eke out an operating profit in all of its units in 1997, its debt servicing resulted in yet another net loss. WestPoint Stevens, which had acquired other parts of the J.P. Stevens empire, refinanced its own $1 billion debt in 1998 by selling new bonds.

The Asian economic crisis of the late 1990s portended a strong start to 1998 for JPS, which manufactured fiberglass fabrics used in circuit boards and had even founded a Technical Services Center at its Slater fiberglass products facility to research new technologies. Still, JPS lost $10.7 million on sales of $389.2 million for the year. The company sold its home furnishing business to Virginia-based Belding Hausman Incorporated for $11.4 million, a purchase that included the Boger City plant in Lincolnton, North Carolina, which had produced most of its home fashion textiles. In February 1999 the company announced plans to close the Angle apparel fabrics plant in Rocky Mount, Virginia.

After Jerry Hunter retired in February 1999, Michael L. Fulbright replaced him as JPS chairman, president, and CEO. Fulbright had lead The Bibb Co. before it had merged with the Dan River Co. in October 1998. At JPS, he hoped to expand the company's industrial product segment, which accounted for half its sales. Fiberglass fabric sales were up in the first quarter of 1999. However, flat sales in other segments gave JPS a net loss, albeit a relatively small one ($288,000). Perhaps the company's narrowing of focus would lead it to that most desirable of products: profit.

Principal Subsidiaries

JPS Elastomerics; JPS Converter and Industrial Corporation.

Further Reading

Bray, Chad, "JPS Feels Asian Fallout," *Greenville (South Carolina) Business,* February 12, 1999, pp. 1D-2D.

DuPlessis, Jim, "Diversity the Fabric That Keeps JPS an Industry Giant," *Upstate Business (Greenville News),* November 14, 1993.

——, "JPS Out from Court's Thumb," *Greenville News,* April 3, 1991, p. 4D.

——, "JPS Ownership to Change with Bankruptcy," *Greenville News,* May 17, 1997, p. 8D.

——, "JPS Refinancing Plan at Critical Juncture," *Greenville News,* August 13, 1990, pp. C1–C2.

——, "JPS Textile Group Expects to Rebound with the Economy," *Greenville News,* February 24, 1992, pp. 1C, 4C.

——, "JPS Textile May Reshuffle Debt—Again," *Greenville News,* February 28, 1997, pp. 1A, 9A.

——, "Lifting a Heavy Load," *Upstate Business (Greenville News),* August 31, 1997.

——, "Merger May Spare Some White-Collar Stevens Jobs," *Greenville News,* April 26, 1988, pp. 1A, 9A.

——, "Stevens Takeover Left Legacy of Debt," *Greenville News,* February 26, 1990, pp. 1C-2C.

——, "Sweetened Offer Gets Cold Shoulder from JPS Investors," *Greenville News,* September 10, 1990, pp. 1C, 3C.

——, " '21' Club Owner to Buy JPS Division," *Greenville News,* April 29, 1994, 8D.

Elliott, Suzanne, "Odyssey Officers Called 'Corporate Raiders,' " *Greenville News,* March 18, 1988, p. 2C.

Flach, Tim, "JPS Gets Last Minute Tax Break," *Greenville News,* July 20, 1991, p. 1A.

Fladung, Thom, "Stevens' Strategy Opened Door to Takeover," *The State,* April 26, 1988.

——, "Tables May Have Turned on West Point-Pepperell," *The State,* May 26, 1988.

Keenan, Tim, "Strategic Foam," *Ward's Auto World,* June 1995, pp. 45–46.

Mildenberg, David, "Stevens Leaves Legacy of Anti-Unionism," *Charlotte Observer,* April 26, 1988.

—Frederick C. Ingram

Kendall-Jackson Winery, Ltd.

421 Aviation Blvd.
Santa Rosa, California 95403
U.S.A.
(707) 544-4000
Fax: (707) 544-4013
Web site: http://www.kj.com

Private Company
Incorporated: 1982 as Kendall-Jackson Vineyards and
    Winery, Ltd.
Employees: 1,100
Sales: $250 million (1997 est.)
NAIC: 312130 Wineries

One of the few remaining family-owned wineries in the nation, Kendall-Jackson Winery, Ltd. is one of California's largest and fastest-growing wine companies. Kendall-Jackson and its sister wineries comprise the 13th largest wine operation in the United States. The company produces approximately 1.7 million cases of wine annually from the fruits of its more than 10,000 acres of vineyards, and exports to at least 40 countries worldwide. According to company documents, Kendall-Jackson's four separate wineries house what is possibly the single largest barrel fermentation project in the world. *Wine and Spirits* magazine ranked Kendall-Jackson wines as the "Number one brand of the fifty top selling brands" by owners and sommeliers (wine waiters) from the nation's top restaurants for three years in a row (1995–98). Kendall-Jackson's award-winning Vintner's Reserve line includes Chardonnay, Cabernet Sauvignon, Sauvignon Blanc, Pinot Noir, Zinfandel, and Merlot varietals.

In 1982 Kendall-Jackson Vineyards and Winery was founded by California native Jess Stonestreet Jackson. Jackson was born in 1930 and grew up in San Francisco where he was informally introduced to wine and family winemaking by Italian neighbors he befriended. Academically, Jackson's ranking earned him a scholarship to attend college at the University of California at Berkeley, where he studied law while working at the San Francisco docks to pay living expenses. He also worked as a Berkeley policeman and as a legal researcher for then California Attorney General Pat Brown, who later became governor. Jackson passed his bar exam in 1955 and became a respected attorney specializing in land use and property rights issues. In one of his most famous cases, he helped represent Joe Gallo against his winemaking brothers, Ernest and Julio, in a "failed attempt to gain a third of the world's largest winery, E. & J. Gallo," according to Kim Marcus of *Wine Spectator*.

Establishing a Vineyard in the 1970s

Jackson and his family owned 80 acres of pear and walnut orchards in Lakeport, the Clear Lake region of northern California, but Jackson's perennial interest in grapes and winemaking motivated the family to remove the trees and convert the crops to vineyards. The vineyards flourished and for seven years the family sold the grapes to local wineries such as Fetzer, until the market shifted in 1981, leaving most of their crop unsold. In Jackson's words, "I never intended to go into the winemaking business," adding "but I was forced to. We couldn't sell our grapes for what it cost us to grow them. So we did the only thing we could do—we made wine." The first two Chardonnays were bottled under the Chateau du Lac label. For almost a decade, Jackson had experimented with different styles of wine, growing several varieties of grapes and supplementing them with grapes grown in vineyards throughout California's cool coastal regions. Most California wineries emphasized making wines from a single vineyard, but Jackson blended grapes grown in locations such as Santa Barbara, Monterey, Sonoma, and the Lake counties. He and his first wife established the Kendall-Jackson Winery (Kendall was Jackson's first wife's maiden name) when they discovered a market niche for reasonably priced Chardonnay wine.

Under the supervision of Jedidiah Steele, the winemaker recruited to oversee processing, the Kendall-Jackson Chardonnay became an instant success thanks to a mishap involving unfermented sugar. The fermentation became "stuck," meaning that there was too much sugar left in the wine. Several winemakers were recruited to help save the wine, but their methods could not accomplish the degree of dryness they de-

Company Perspectives:

To make truly exceptional wines, we work to control the countless details inherent in the selection of our vineyards, the quality of our barrels, and the delicate balance of assembling the final blend. Ultimately, the fate of each bottle is in the hands of our winemakers. Since nothing has ever surpassed the caliber of wine classically crafted through hands-on techniques, we will remain devoted to artisan winemaking.

sired, which as it turned out, created a flavor much appreciated by consumers. The Chardonnay became one of California's most popular wines—before long 60 percent of American consumers would choose sweet and fruity Chardonnays as their wine of choice. The first Kendall-Jackson Chardonnay vintage, introduced in 1983, was named the Vintner's Reserve Chardonnay, and won the American Wine Competition's first-ever Platinum Medal. The wine, described in company documents as "rich, round, flavorful" was made at the Vinwood winemaking facility with "hand-crafted methods, including small oak barrel fermentation, malolactic fermentation and aging on the yeast lees (wine sediment)." The Vintner's Reserve line was expanded to include Sauvignon Blanc, Cabernet Sauvignon, Pinot Noir, Merlot, Zinfandel, and Riesling. Following on the footsteps of those successful introductions—and further experimentation—Kendall-Jackson soon introduced a new collection of wines, the Grand Reserve line, made from the finest of their grapes from the finest vineyards, including Chardonnay, Cabernet Sauvignon, Pinot Noir, Zinfandel, and Merlot. The Grand Reserve line was committed to producing a product only in years when the company's highest criteria for quality could be met, according to company accounts.

Growing a Company in the 1980s

Following the initial success of the Kendall-Jackson Vintner's Reserve wines, Jackson decided to give up his law practice in order to devote all of his time and energy to winemaking. His competitors credit him with having a keen sense of the consumer's perspective. "He's been creative when the industry's been lethargic," according to a Kim Marcus interview in *Wine Spectator* with Michael Mondavi, president and CEO of Robert Mondavi Winery. His wines appealed to the consumer's palate, especially the slightly sweet Vintner's Reserve Chardonnay, a wine suited for most any occasion. Jackson, savvy in the field of real estate dealing, continued to buy prime vineyards at bargain prices and proceeded to hire the best winemakers he could find. According to Marcus, Jackson sometimes relied on the advice of another Napa Valley winemaker, Ric Forman, who described Jackson as "a hard-bargaining businessman." He continued, "He's outrageous. He thrives on the game. It's not the money for him, it's the game." His talents have earned him a reputation as a cunning dealmaker with high energy and entrepreneurial skill, evidenced by his enormous production and relatively fast ascension within the industry. While wine purists have sometimes dismissed the quality of the sweeter Kendall-Jackson wines, Jackson insists that his wines are made

from the finest grapes and provide a product desired in the marketplace. Virtually all of the grapes (99 percent) that go into making Kendall-Jackson's intensely flavored fruity wines come from two climatic zones in California, on land that stretches from Mendocino in the north to Santa Barbara in the south. Wines such as Chardonnay, Pinot Noir, Syrah, and Zinfandel taste best when the grapes are grown from coastal vineyards, influenced by the cooling breezes of the Pacific Ocean. A second, more temperate zone is suited to varietals such as Cabernet Sauvignon, Merlot, Sangiovese, and Sauvignon Blanc. Soils within zones also vary—as do influential altitudes—which is why a Chardonnay from the Santa Maria Bench-area tastes tropical, like guavas and mangos, while the more northern-grown grapes produce a Chardonnay that has more of a pear and citrus flavor—considerations that Jackson and his vintners appreciate before buying and planting grapes, and before blending. Jackson told Kim Marcus that "All good grapes are mountain grapes, because of natural selection. Because the first vinfera vines grew in the Caucasus Mountains of the former Soviet Georgia, grapes bear the best fruit in thinner, but well-drained soils," which explains Jackson's tendency, says Marcus, to grow grapes on small slopes with drainages that mimic mountain conditions.

The fruitful 1980s gave way to the birth of traditional values in winemaking. An awakening had occurred as consumers and vintners recognized the taste and consistency advantages of designating certain vineyards for particular wines. In 1995 Jackson structured eight of his smaller wineries into an organization called Artisans & Estates, made up of his start-up wineries: Stonestreet, Cambria, Camelot, and Lakewood; plus the acquired wineries of Edmeades, La Crema, and Robert Pepi. Separate expert winemakers were set up to run each winery, each specializing in making wines from single vineyards and viticultural regions. Among the top winemakers hired were veterans such as Charles Thomas formerly from Robert Mondavi, John Hawley formerly from Clos du Bois, and Tom Selfridge formerly from Beaulieu. Soon after their formation, the organization launched a sparkling wine called Kristone from the Santa Maria region. They also introduced a tenth label, Hartford Court, specializing in Russian River Pinot Noir. In a *Wine Spectator* interview, Jackson told Marcus: "I have been intrigued by the concept of a given vineyard that could give great results. The reason why I went up and down the coast was to find that perfect vineyard. But in any given year, a particular vineyard will let you down," he explained. His strategy combined the blending of wines for the Kendall-Jackson label, to assure a reliable product, and added specialty wines from particular vineyards to enhance the company's reputation for producing what he referred to as "hand-crafted" wines, presented by Artisan & Estates. Through the purchase of what he considered the best vineyards from each grape-growing region, the Artisan & Estates wines were intended to encompass a more exclusive image, a production concept described by the company as a "flavor domain," an exceptional flavor indigenous to each area.

Expanding into Italy, Jackson purchased Villa Arceno, a 110-acre Tuscan estate with vineyards suited to Chianti, Cabernet Sauvignon, and Chardonnay wines. Within 18 months, several other properties were added to the list, including a 200-acre Merlot vineyard in the Carneros district of Napa County, the 67-acre Veeder Peak vineyard in Napa, known for its Cabernet Sauvignon, a portion of the Durell Vineyard in Sonoma Valley with prime grapes for Chardonnay and Syrah wines, among others. One of his largest purchases was the 5,500-acre, $8 million Gauer Ranch in Sonoma County, followed by the acquisition of the 1,200-acre, $12 million portion of the Tepusquet Vineyard, a source of grapes for the fruity-tasting Vintner's Reserve wines. He also expanded southward into Chile and Argentina. Jackson observes a basic investment strategy: buy low and sell high. New players within the California wine industry in the 1980s and into the early 1990s increased competition which forced many of the smaller wineries into extinction. Jackson took advantage of opportunities to expand through the purchase of bargain properties without highly leveraging his winery, as profits were routinely reinvested in the business. He also began planting vineyards in the lower-priced southern California coastal regions (compared to Sonoma and Napa Counties), a region relatively new to the production of large-scale vineyards.

The 1990s: Barrel Manufacturing

Vintner John Hawley oversaw all of the Kendall-Jackson wine production. He emphasized the advantages of handling the grapes as little as possible during the winemaking process, choosing not to fine, filter, or manipulate the wine needlessly. At the Vinwood facility, grapes were fed whole into the presses on a conveyer system, allowing for more free-run juice and less sediment in need of filtering. The initial fermentation took place in 20,000-gallon stainless steel tanks before being transferred into small oak barrels where the major fermentation occurred before aging and finally, bottling. The barrels imparted a spicy—sometimes compared to vanilla or butterscotch—toasty-oak flavor to wine and allowed a slow evaporation of water and alcohol, which intensified as the wine aged. The shape of the barrels, grain density, oak source, thickness of stave, and level of toasting were some of the variables in the manufacturing process that contributed to a particular wine's taste. After determining that the high cost of oak wine barrels—considered by Jackson to be a significant flavor component in crafting quality wine—cut into profits, Jackson, in partnership with the Independent Stave Company of Missouri, bought a wine barrel making operation in Beaune, France, called Merrain International. Typically, the French oak barrels cost in the range of $650 each. By controlling his supply, Jackson cut the cost of producing the tens of thousands of needed barrels in half and gave his winery an assurance of source, quality, and handling of the oak.

Viticulturist Randy Ullom became Jackson's winemaker for Camelot Vineyards in 1993. He soon was responsible for heading the company's winemaking production at Vina Calina in Chile, and also helped establish the Argentinean Mariposa label while overseeing the Argentinean production. Prior to employment with Jackson, the wines Ullom had produced while working for De Loach's Vineyards in Sonoma County were consis-

tent gold medal winners at wine competitions. Jackson eventually invited Ullom to become winemaster for the Kendall-Jackson Winery, a job he accepted with trepidation. According to company documents Ullom commented, "Sometimes I look at all of the vineyards we own, and all of the individual lots of wines that we make, and the thousands of barrels we have sitting in our cellar and I think, *You gotta be kidding me.* After I've sufficiently recovered from my daily panic attack, I just take off my coat, dig in my heels and take it one barrel at a time."

In 1995 *Wine and Spirits* magazine named Kendall-Jackson "Winery of the Year." In the following year Kendall-Jackson focused on marketing and signed a distribution contract with Regal Wine Company, a direct sales concern, making it the predominant California distributor for Kendall-Jackson wines, an account which was previously handled by Southern Wine and Spirits. In that year Jackson sued E. & J. Gallo, the world's largest winemaking operation, for trademark infringement, citing the similar bottles and "colored leaf" logos used by Gallo, but the jury rejected the claim which was later affirmed in a federal appeals court ruling.

Jackson maintained that controlling growth—and avoiding the fate of many smaller wineries, who during the 1980s expanded too rapidly and then were forced to sell out to larger operations—was paramount to being successful. He was determined to remain a family-owned business, along with his wife who served as president of Cambria, two daughters who worked at the winery, and six other relatives. Committed to further developing the Artisans and Estates wines, Jackson also continued to focus on how consumers thought about California wine. "Wine is entirely different from liquor or beer, and I'd like to see our industry free itself from the images that are used to sell those products," he stated. "Wine is a part of our cultural heritage. It has always been the traditional partner with food. Wine celebrates friends, family, love—all of the best things in life!"

Principal Subsidiaries

Kendall-Jackson Vineyards and Winery, Ltd.; Majestic Marketing Group, Ltd.; Regal Sales Co.

Further Reading

Frost, Bob, "Action Jackson," *San Jose Mercury News (West Magazine),* October 19, 1997.
Marcus, Kim, "California's Mystery Vintner," *Wine Spectator,* July 31, 1995, pp. 1+.
"Regal to Distribute Kendall-Jackson," *Nation's Restaurant News,* September 30, 1996, p. 82.
"Wine and Spirits 9th Annual Restaurant Poll," *Wine and Spirits,* April 1998, pp. 73+.

—Terri Mozzone

Royal Dutch Airlines

Koninklijke Luchtvaart Maatschappij, N.V.
(KLM Royal Dutch Airlines)

55 Amsterdamseweg
PO Box 7700
Amstelveen 1117 ZL
Netherlands
+31 020 649 9123
Web site: http://www.klm.com

Public Company
Incorporated: 1919
Employees: 26,000
Sales: NLG 13.3 billion (1998)
Stock Exchanges: New York Amsterdam
NAIC: 481111 Passenger Carriers, Air, Scheduled

Koninklijke Luchtvaart Maatschappij, N.V., translated as KLM Royal Dutch Airlines, and best known simply as KLM, is the world's oldest scheduled airline. As the national flag carrier, KLM is the most visible commercial ambassador for the Netherlands, serving 163 destinations in 75 countries on six continents.

Regal Beginnings

KLM was organized by a young aviator lieutenant named Albert Plesman. In 1919 Plesman, with the financial support of an Amsterdam shipping company, sponsored the ''Elta'' aviation exhibition in Amsterdam to satisfy the public's fascination with the airplane. Over half a million people attended the air show. When it closed, several Dutch commercial interests decided to establish a Dutch air transport company, and Plesman was nominated to head the company.

The Royal Dutch government lent its support to Plesman's project by offering to allow him use of the title *Koninklijke,* meaning ''Royal,'' in the company's name. On October 7, 1919, the Koninklijke Luchtvaart Maatschappij, or ''KLM,''

was founded in The Hague. It was one of the world's first commercial airline companies.

In its early years KLM transported passengers, freight, and mail to a growing number of European destinations linking Dutch cities with London, Paris, Oslo, and Athens. At that time the Netherlands had a worldwide empire with colonies in Asia and the Caribbean. Soon KLM was charting routes to link these colonies with Holland. Services to Curacao and Trinidad were opened, and in 1927 KLM established a route from Amsterdam to Batavia (later Djakarta) on the island of Java in Dutch Indonesia. The 8,700-mile trip took 11 days.

At the start of World War II German armies invaded the low countries and closed KLM operations. Plesman was understandably upset by the occupation and frustrated with his inability to convince the Germans to relax their grip on the Netherlands. One summer night Plesman's determination to take action led him to awaken one of his house guests, a Swedish KLM pilot named Count von Rosen. Plesman reportedly asked the Count, ''What can I do to stop this?,'' and Von Rosen replied, ''You could talk to my Uncle Hermann.'' Suddenly Plesman realized he was speaking to the nephew of the German Reichmarschall Hermann Göring. A few days later Plesman was in Berlin discussing the possibility of a peace treaty between England and Germany with Göring.

Plesman formulated a document which was later forwarded to Churchill's office in London. The peace terms would leave the British Empire intact but give Germany control of the European continent and the United States control of the Americas. The matter was ''studied with much interest'' and receipt of the document was acknowledged by Lord Halifax. Göring, however, became displeased with Plesman's initiative and later had him jailed. Plesman was released in April 1942 and told to remain at his house in Twenthe in the woods of eastern Holland until the end of the war. During this time he kept himself occupied by formulating strategies for the postwar operation of KLM.

Company Perspectives:

KLM wants to excel in the quality of its connections, by linking as many cities as possible. KLM's goal is to participate in one of the leading global airline systems as an independent and financially strong European partner. KLM aims to sustain passenger preference and provide a stimulating and stable working environment for its employees. Targets also include a structural increase in shareholder value and a mutually profitable relationship with its partners.

Postwar Expansion

When the war ended in the spring of 1945 Plesman was largely forgiven by the public for his attempts to make peace with the Germans earlier in the war. Soon afterwards he traveled to the United States to negotiate the purchase of surplus warplanes for KLM. The company wasted no time rebuilding its network, but since the Dutch East Indies were in a state of revolt, Plesman's first priority was to reestablish KLM's route to Batavia. By the end of the year KLM was again flying to Indonesia. By 1948 services were opened to Africa, North and South America, and the Caribbean. Also during the immediate postwar period, the Dutch government expressed interest many times in gaining a controlling stake in KLM. Plesman, however, was a fiercely independent man and kept the company under private control while conceding only a portion of KLM's ownership to the government.

Indonesia (formerly the Dutch East Indies) gained its independence from the Netherlands in 1949. The following year the Indonesian government established its own national airline called Garuda. KLM assisted Garuda from the time of its inception and continued to aid the company with technical and financial assistance until 1982. KLM later helped to establish several other airlines in developing nations, including Philippine Airlines, Nigeria Airways, Viasa (Venezuela), Egyptair, and Aerolineas Argentinas.

In 1950 KLM entered into an agreement with Swissair and Belgium's Sabena airlines which led to the establishment of a spare parts pool. The BeNeSwiss agreement laid the ground for a future maintenance pool called the KSSU group, which included KLM, Scandinavian Airlines, Swissair, and the privately operated French airline UTA. KLM also continued to modernize and expand during the 1950s. It was the first European airline to fly new versions of the Lockheed Constellation and Electra. In addition, several destinations in western North America were added to KLM's route structure. In 1954 the company created KLM Aerocarto N.V., an aerial survey and photography service.

Albert Plesman died on December 31, 1954, at the age of 64. Praised and decorated as a hero of the Netherlands, Plesman also received decorations from Denmark, Belgium, Sweden, Czechoslovakia, Greece, Tunisia, Lebanon, and Syria. The company he left behind was entering a difficult period in commercial aviation history. A sudden and unexplained decline in ridership caused financial reverses at KLM and most of the world's other airlines. The company also faced the burden of financing a costly conversion to jet airplanes. Moreover, by this time the government had increased its ownership of the company to two-thirds by purchasing new KLM stock issues. The board of directors, however, remained under the control of the private shareholders.

Weathering the Jet Age

In 1961 KLM reported its first year of losses. The company's president, I.A. Aler, resigned and was replaced by Ernst Hans van der Beugel. Yet the change in leadership was not enough to reverse the company's financial difficulties. Aler returned to active participation and enlisted McKinsey & Company, an airline consulting firm, to make recommendations for restoring the company to profitability. Their study concluded that KLM should reduce its staff and number of airplanes. Aler, however, had already reduced the staff by one-seventh and refused to release any more personnel. In January 1963 Aler left KLM and later, suffering from exhaustion, checked into a hospital.

KLM's board of directors then elected Horatius Albarda to the company's presidency. Albarda initiated a reorganization of the company which involved further cutbacks in staff and air services. Unfortunately, Albarda's tenure of presidency ended when he was killed in a private plane crash during 1965. Albarda was succeeded by KLM's Deputy President Gerrit van der Wal, who would adopt Albert Plesman's attitude toward government involvement in KLM. Before his appointment to KLM Van der Wal reached an agreement with the government in that, despite its major financial holding in the company, KLM would be run as a private enterprise without interference from the government. By 1966 the Dutch government's interest in KLM had been reduced to 49.5 percent.

In 1965 the airline created a subsidiary called KLM Helicopters to transport oil workers to and from oil drilling rigs in the North Sea. The division was eventually expanded in its range of operations to include specialized and chartered airlift services. KLM created another subsidiary in 1966 to operate domestic passenger air services in the Netherlands. KLM Dutch Airlines connected a number of smaller Dutch cities with the nation's international airports in Rotterdam and Amsterdam. KLM later included flights to other European cities, and in 1976 the division's name was changed to KLM CityHopper.

In an attempt to better utilize its facilities at Amsterdam's Schiphol Airport, KLM initiated a promotion called Distrinet, in conjunction with some Dutch shipping and transport companies. Distrinet was intended to coordinate these various Dutch companies in order to establish Amsterdam as the primary continental port of entry and distribution for European cargo.

KLM was a regular customer of the McDonnell Douglas Corporation during this time. When the airline introduced jet service in 1960, it decided to employ the Douglas DC-8 rather than the Boeing Company's 707, and in 1969 the company purchased DC-9s rather than Boeing's similarly configured three-engine 727. In 1971, however, KLM purchased the first of several Boeing 747 jumbo jets. McDonnell Douglas campaigned very hard to prevent KLM from purchasing more Boeing products, but KLM opted to remain neutral, preferring to recognize the unique qualities of each company's product and avoid becoming the exclusive customer of any one company.

McDonnell Douglas's response to Boeing's production of the 747 was to manufacture the DC-10, which became available shortly after the 747. The DC-10 was smaller than the 747 and somewhat more efficient at lower passenger load factors (when a number of seats remained empty). In 1972 KLM purchased the first of several DC-10s to provide the airline with a more flexible fleet. Boeing and McDonnell Douglas, however, soon had more than just each other for competition. Several airlines, most of them European and including KLM, placed orders for a new airplane being developed by Airbus, the European aerospace consortium. KLM ordered ten Airbus A-310 passenger jetliners scheduled for delivery beginning in 1983.

Difficult economic conditions caused by the oil crisis in 1973–74 forced KLM to seek government assistance in arranging debt refinancing. In return for the government's money, KLM issued additional shares of stock to the government. By the late 1970s the government held a 78 percent majority of KLM stock. Company management, however, remained under the control of private shareholders.

Sergio Orlandini (his father was Italian and his mother Dutch) became KLM's president in 1973. Upon taking office he was confronted with a problem common to all international carriers at that time: overcapacity. KLM was flying planes with too many empty seats. The solution at other airline companies was to offer discounted fares in the belief that some income from a given seat was better than none at all. Orlandini chose another approach. His idea was to reconfigure KLM's 747s (with their huge capacity for passengers) so that they could carry a combination of passengers and freight. A partition separated the passenger cabin from the cargo hold in the rear of the airplane. Later 747s delivered to KLM (called ''combis'') were specifically designed for combinations of passengers and freight. KLM competed with Federal Express and DHL by specializing in high-end operations such as shipping live horses and global sourcing.

In the mid-1980s, one-sixth of KLM's earnings came from non-airline operations, which included management consulting, technical services, staff training, hotels, duty-free shops, catering, and ground handling. Under the terms of the KSSU agreement, KLM performed maintenance on 747s and overhaul of CF6 engines. The company's diversity enabled it to survive difficult periods in the airline passenger market.

The Dutch government's share of KLM was reduced to 54.8 percent in 1986, a figure that was expected to be reduced even further as the decade progressed. Also during this time, KLM began cooperating with British Airways and several American airline companies in lobbying to relax airline regulations in Europe.

Liberalization in the 1990s

Airlines worldwide were hurt by the Persian Gulf crisis and sluggish economy that opened the 1990s. In order to survive the decade's Pyrrhic competition, KLM aimed for at least a ten percent share of the markets served by itself and its affiliates.

KLM invested heavily in its fleet, bringing its debt and lease obligations to the $2 billion level. In the short term, the carrier configured its combis to carry more freight. However, KLM still lost money as the dollar and yen fell in value and was unable to turn a profit for 1990–91.

KLM started a three-year restructuring plan in 1990. The plan eliminated about 1,000 staff positions and focused the company on its core operations, with hopes of cutting expenses 15 percent a year. However, productivity increases were the most important component of the regimen. Pieter Bouw, a longtime KLM veteran, became its chairman in 1991. The reforms begun under Bouw were estimated to improve productivity by 60 percent within a few years. *Business Week* noted that passenger traffic rose by half without a further loss of jobs.

As the European market liberalized, KLM developed its Amsterdam hub, feeding it with traffic from 50 affiliated airlines. The most newsworthy of its partnerships was that with Northwest Airlines (NWA). KLM owned a 20 percent equity holding in NWA and though the two reaped significant benefits from their cooperation, the relationship proved notoriously difficult at times, culminating in an aborted takeover attempt on the part of KLM. Still, the relationship gave KLM the global reach it found necessary for survival in the deregulated international environment. An ''open skies'' agreement between the United States and the Netherlands allowed KLM and NWA to operate virtually as a single airline. The pair cut transatlantic fares and offered U.S. passengers discounts and easy connections to KLM's European and North African destinations. Even so, profits were not instantaneous for NWA, which would suffer numerous labor crises, and KLM was compelled to write off its original $400 million investment made in 1989.

KLM had its own labor concerns as well. Pilots made some concessions in 1993 in the face of further losses, when management contemplated moving back office operations from The Hague to a lower-cost area such as India.

KLM finally saw another profit in 1993–94, of $42 million on revenues of more than $5 billion. Cargo operations contributed $800 million. In 1993–94, KLM was 38.2 percent owned by the Dutch government but received no subsidies, unlike other European counterparts such as Air France, which received nearly $4 billion that year.

Meanwhile, KLM's partner NWA had posted an even larger profit—$296 million—surpassing even American Airlines. Combined, KLM/NWA would have been the world's third largest airline in 1994, prompting notice from other U.S. carriers resentful of the pair's antitrust exemption. The partnership brought in an extra $300 million per year to the two carriers. KLM increased its stake in NWA to 25 percent—the legal limit.

In December 1995, KLM successfully bid for a 26 percent share of newly privatized Kenya Airways. The two shared codes, as Kenya Airways implemented KLM's customer service procedures and benefited from new economies in purchasing and other areas.

An operating loss of $86.8 million in 1996–97 followed high fuel prices and weak Dutch currency. The next year, however, brought reported income of $389 million. KLM's internal regimen appeared to be working under CEO Leo van Wijk. KLM's 1998 contract with its seven unions would allow for three bonuses and a permanent pay raise.

In 1997, KLM agreed to sell its shares back to NWA for $1.1 billion, an investment that was originally worth $400 million. The takeover issue put aside, the two signed a ten-year extension to their mutually beneficial arrangement.

Into the New Millennium

KLM entered into another close partnership with Alitalia SpA in December 1998. The deal was expected to particularly benefit the pair's cargo operations. KLM also teamed with Eurowings, Braathens, Malaysia Airlines, Nippon Cargo Airlines, and others during the late 1990s. Air Engiadina and Air Alps Aviation operated flights under the brand ''KLM Alps.'' KLM Cargo formed an alliance with EAC Logistics, based in Beijing.

Nearly 15 million passengers flew KLM in 1998, more than double the number carried ten years earlier, and the company ordered $1.2 billion of Boeing aircraft to meet the new demand. Faced with finite capacity at its Schiphol hub, KLM aimed to develop Europe's first multi-hub system.

Principal Subsidiaries

KLM Cityhopper B.V.; KLM UK.

Principal Divisions

KLM Cargo; KLM Systems Services.

Further Reading

''Airline of the Year,'' *Air Transport World,* February 1998, pp. 39–40.

Allen, Roy, *Pictorial History of KLM, Royal Dutch Airlines,* London: Ian Allen, 1978.

Cottrill, Ken, ''KLM, Alitalia Join Forces,'' *Traffic World,* December 7, 1998, pp. 37–38.

Feldman, Joan M., ''Potential Realized,'' *Air Transport World,* December 1996, pp. 44–47.

McKenna, James T., ''Northwest/KLM Package Challenges Competition,'' *Aviation Week and Space Technology,* February 15, 1993, p. 31.

Morais, Richard C., ''They Ship Horses, Don't They?'' *Forbes,* November 7, 1994, pp. 45–46.

Ott, James, ''KLM Boosting Productivity and Debt to Survive Airline Wars of 1990s,'' *Aviation Week and Space Technology,* May 27, 1991, pp. 81–82.

——, ''Top Airline Competitors Share Growth Strategy,'' *Aviation Week and Space Technology,* August 10, 1998, pp. 53–58.

Samuels, David, ''You Also See the Ugly Side,'' *International Commercial Litigation,* May 1998, pp. 10–13.

Shiffrin, Carole A., and Pierre Sparaco, ''European Carriers Regroup As Alcazar Hopes Fizzle,'' *Aviation Week and Space Technology,* November 29, 1993, pp. 29–30.

Toy, Stewart, et al., ''Flying High,'' *Business Week,* February 27, 1995, pp. 90–91.

Tully, Shawn, ''Northwest and KLM: The Alliance from Hell,'' *Fortune,* June 24, 1996, pp. 64–72.

—updated by Frederick C. Ingram

Lafarge Corporation

11130 Sunrise Valley Drive, Suite 300
Reston, Virginia 20191-4329
U.S.A.
(703) 264-3600
Fax: (703) 264-0634
Web site: http://www.lafargecorp.com

Public Company
Incorporated: 1909 as Canada Cement Company
Employees: 10,000
Sales: $2.44 billion (1998)
Stock Exchanges: New York Toronto Montreal
Ticker Symbol: LAF
NAIC: 32731 Cement Manufacturing; 327331 Concrete Block & Brick Manufacturing; 327332 Concrete Pipe Manufacturing; 32739 Other Concrete Product Manufacturing; 32732 Ready-Mix Concrete Manufacturing; 32742 Gypsum Product Manufacturing; 212312 Crushed & Broken Limestone Mining & Quarrying

Lafarge Corporation, a U.S. holding company, is the largest construction materials company in North America. With more than 500 facilities in 44 states and all provinces of Canada, the company's three operating groups produce and distribute products ranging from cements and fly ash to concrete pipes and bricks to gypsum wallboard. A Lafarge subsidiary, Systech Environmental Corporation, supplies fuel-quality waste for burning in cement kilns and alternative raw materials used in producing cement. Paris-based Lafarge S.A. owns approximately 52 percent of Lafarge Corporation.

Mergers in Canada: 1909–70

In the early part of the century the cement business in Canada was fiercely competitive, with companies producing more cement than was needed. In 1909 Max Aitken, a businessman, suggested that ten companies merge to try to stabilize the industry. The result was the Canada Cement Company. Based in Montreal, the new enterprise went on to dominate the Canadian market, manufacturing and selling cement.

Cement, a fine powder, was first processed in 1824. It got the name portland cement because it looked like the gray stone found on the island of Portland off the coast of England. Cement was a critical ingredient in the making of concrete, used in residential and commercial buildings as well as roads, dams, and other public works.

All cement contained four elements: calcium, silica, aluminum, and iron. To make its cement, Canada Cement Company quarried stone, usually limestone because it had a lot of calcium, and crushed it into pieces no bigger than two inches in size. Those pieces were blended with sand, bauxite, or other additives to get the correct mixture of elements, ground more finely, and cooked in a kiln, using coal or coke to reach temperatures of up to 2700 degrees Fahrenheit. In the kiln, small cement pellets called ''clinker'' formed, which, after cooling, were ground into fine cement powder. Depending on the properties needed for the concrete it would be used to make, fly ash or gypsum might be added to the cement. It was then shipped out to the buyer, who combined it with water and aggregates (crushed stone, sand, and gravel) to make ready-mix concrete.

In 1956, nearly 50 years after Canada Cement was formed, Ciments Lafarge, a French company founded in 1833, came to Canada. It built a cement plant near Vancouver, British Columbia, and formed Lafarge Cement North America. In 1970 the Lafarge operation merged with Canada Cement (still the largest cement producer in the country), creating Canada Cement Lafarge Ltd. (CCL), with 11 plants coast-to-coast.

Entering the U.S. Market: 1971–82

In addition to its cement business, the new company was increasingly producing and supplying its own ready-mix concrete and aggregates. The year 1972 saw the creation of a new subsidiary, Canfarge Ltd., to oversee its concrete-related, construction materials business.

In 1973 CCL moved south into the U.S. market. With Lone Star Industries Inc., a U.S. company based in Texas, CCL established Citadel Cement Corporation, a joint venture to distribute cement in the southeastern part of the United States. Citadel began operations in January 1974, in Atlanta, Georgia. When the joint venture dissolved in 1977, CCL kept Citadel and two cement plants in the southern United States, incorporating the wholly owned subsidiary as Citadel Cement Corporation of Maryland.

The 1982 recession in the United States slowed housing and other construction activity to a 20-year low, and CCL reported a net loss of $25 million on revenues of $900 million. Despite the difficult times, CCL borrowed money to buy General Portland Inc., the second largest U.S. cement producer, for $326 million. The Dallas-based company, with ten plants and the capacity to make six million tons of cement a year, traced its roots to the Southwestern States Portland Cement Company, established in 1907.

Lafarge Corporation: 1983–85

In 1983 CCL underwent a major reorganization. In February, Citadel's name was changed to Lafarge Corporation, and in April, Lafarge Coppée, the company's French parent, made it a U.S. holding company. What had been a CCL subsidiary was now CCL's parent, having received 69 percent of CCL in a stock exchange with Lafarge Coppée and five French banks. The move was made primarily to make it easier for the company to raise money in U.S. equity markets. "We just couldn't raise enough equity in Canada," Lafarge's vice-president of investor relations told *Fortune* in a 1984 article.

The new company, the largest cement manufacturer in North America, was headquartered in Dallas, with General Portland and CCL becoming wholly owned subsidiaries. Later that fall, Lafarge Corporation issued common and convertible stock in a $44 million offering. The money raised was used to refinance some of the debt incurred in the General Portland purchase.

The construction economy began improving in the United States during 1983, with a slower recovery in Canada. Lafarge Corporation benefited from the increased cement consumption and stabilization of cement prices, although it still operated at a net loss of $13.1 million for the year. The reason for the price stabilization, and one of the domestic cement industry's biggest problems, was that as construction picked up, foreign producers poured concrete into the U.S. market, taking advantage of the high dollar and low shipping rates to get rid of an excess overseas. The company sold some of its nonessential properties in both Canada and the United States as it began taking cost-cutting measures. "We realized that we had entered a new world in which pricing patterns were going to be different than

in the past," the company's chief financial officer reflected in a 1988 *Washington Post* article.

It also began cutting labor costs, which led to a six-month strike during 1984. At the end of the year it operated 19 cement manufacturing plants with an annual capacity of some 13 million tons of cement. In Canada, where the company also manufactured ready-mix concrete and concrete products, its markets spread across the country. In the United States, the company's markets were primarily across the South and Southwest.

By 1985 the company was again operating in the black, with net sales of $944.5 million. In Canada, cement consumption grew by 13 percent during the year, evidence of a strong construction recovery. In the United States, the company saw its cement shipments increase by ten percent and operating income grew despite lower cement prices due to more imports. That year Lafarge Corporation opened a new research and technical center in Montreal, the largest private laboratory in the North American cement industry.

Acquisitions, Restructuring, and a Move: 1986–87

During the latter part of the decade, Lafarge Corporation began buying other companies. In 1986 its U.S. subsidiary, General Portland, bought East Texas Stone Co. That acquisition increased Lafarge's aggregates resources in the United States, which then included operations in Louisiana, New York, and Washington. Later that year Lafarge Corporation bought Systech Environmental Corporation, a company that processed industrial waste to fuel cement kilns, 14 cement distribution terminals along the Great Lakes, and a closed cement plant in Alpena, Michigan, which it reopened a few months later.

The Systech purchase was an important factor in the company's attempt to cut its fuel expenses. Cement makers began testing the burning of hazardous waste in their kilns during the 1960s, and Systech first began supplying Lafarge Corporation (then CCL) in 1979. The fuels were the byproducts of plants, producing items such as paints, inks, cosmetics, and electronics, as well as auto and truck assembly operations. During the mid-1980s the alternative fuel business boomed; Systech's sales grew from $1.8 million gallons in 1980 to approximately 51 million gallons in 1988.

Early in 1987 Lafarge Corporation reorganized its operations, combining the activities of CCL and General Portland under a single management, and creating four regional operating groups covering cement manufacturing and marketing in both the United States and Canada and a fifth unit responsible for other construction materials products. Bertrand Collomb, who had been the head of General Portland and, previously, president and CEO of Ciments Lafarge France, became vice-chairman and chief executive officer. Robert Murdoch, formerly head of Canada Cement Lafarge, was named president and chief operating officer. In a company press release, Collomb explained the move, "This restructuring will permit us to take a more integrated perspective to our overall North American operations and their development opportunities."

In the fall of 1987 the company moved to Reston, Virginia, outside Washington, D.C., to be closer to its Canadian offices and French parent and more central to its markets. The company decorated the halls of its new corporate offices with framed cement bags, presenting an honor roll of small companies that were now part of Lafarge. Effective January 1988, CCL changed its name to Lafarge Canada Inc. in recognition of the growth of its construction materials business as well as its cement operations, and General Portland was merged into the company.

The move and the reorganization occurred as the company was undergoing "a remarkable turnaround," according to the *Washington Post*. For 1987, Lafarge Corporation reported profits of $75 million on sales of $1.22 billion, a 27 percent increase over 1986 sales. Cement accounted for 55 percent of 1987 sales, with the remaining 45 percent coming from construction materials. Canadian operations contributed 57 percent of sales and 78 percent of the company's operating income.

Vertical Integration: 1988–92

In 1987 the Federal Trade Commission (FTC) issued a new ruling permitting vertical integration in the construction materials industries. The FTC decision overturned an 18-year-old ruling in a move that would quickly change the face of the cement industry in the United States and make it more similar to overseas cement industries. Lafarge Corporation, which held minority stakes in two ready-mix concrete companies, soon increased its shares to full ownership. The acquisitions added Bryco Inc., a Texas ready-mix concrete company and its 12 plants and 75 ready-mix trucks, and Jimco, a large ready-mix concrete company in New Orleans. Later in 1988, Lafarge bought Centurion Products Co., a small Pennsylvania company specializing in producing pre-blended colored masonry cement and colored portland cement.

Business was continuing to improve, and Lafarge Coppée had no interest in selling its North American subsidiary, despite an unsolicited bid by a group of anonymous stockholders of $1.47 billion in cash. At the end of 1988 Bertrand Collomb assumed new duties with Lafarge Coppée in Paris and Robert Murdoch, a former summer intern and the current president and COO, was appointed president and CEO.

The company continued to buy, diversifying both vertically and horizontally. In 1989 it acquired seven subsidiaries of the Standard Slag Holding Company, becoming one of the largest aggregate producers in the United States. The next year, it purchased National Minerals Co., a fly ash company in Wisconsin, and Beyer's Cement Inc., a wholesale cement distributor in North Dakota, acquiring terminals in key cities as well as a fleet of 170 trailers and semi-trailers.

In 1991, despite a downturn in the construction industry, Lafarge Corporation added the Missouri Portland Cement Company and Davenport Cement Company, expanding Lafarge's presence along the Mississippi River. The purchases included three cement plants, 15 terminals, two quarries, and more than 30 ready-mix, aggregate, and concrete paving operations, and increased Lafarge's clinker capacity by nearly one-quarter. As part of the transaction, the company also acquired ProChem Technology Inc., a chemical admixture firm based in Denver. In mid-1992 Robert Murdoch resigned, and Michel Rose, a Lafarge Coppée executive, assumed the positions of president and CEO.

An Improving Market and Gypsum Wallboard: 1993–96

By 1993, demand for cement was slowing, having fallen more than 11 percent since its peak in 1987. Things were better for domestic producers, after U.S. companies shut out low-priced imports with the implementation, in 1990, of antidumping trade actions against international firms.

Lafarge Corporation reorganized again in 1993, consolidating its operations into three cement regions and three construction materials regions, and began selling off its assets in Texas and Alabama. The plants there were considered too far from their markets and unable to meet profitability objectives, even though two were the company's lowest cost manufacturing plants.

However, selling its assets was not the only way Lafarge Corporation regained its profitability. By 1994 nearly all of its 15 full-production cement plants were increasingly recycling industrial byproducts to use as raw materials in making their cement. One plant in British Columbia, for example, used mill scale from a local manufacturer for 90 percent of its iron requirements. The mill scale cost $2 (Canadian) per metric ton, whereas magnetite, which the plant used to use, cost $40 per metric ton. Other alternative materials included glass bottles for silica; waste calcium carbonate, which provided pure lime, from pulp mills; sand from foundries; and fly ash from coal-burning power plants.

By mid-1994 the company's sales were up more than seven percent, and net income had risen 71 percent. In 1995 Lafarge bought National Portland Cement's cement grinding plant in Florida, followed, in 1996, by the acquisitions of Tews Company, Wisconsin's largest ready-mix concrete producer, and two gypsum wallboard plants from Georgia Pacific. With the latter purchase, the company established Lafarge Gypsum to produce and distribute wallboard and related products. Also in 1996, president and CEO Michel Rose returned to France for a new position with Lafarge S.A., and John Piecuch, who joined Lafarge Corporation in 1987, was appointed president and CEO.

1997 to the Present

Lafarge Corporation continued to make acquisitions, including 125 North American operations that were part of Lafarge S.A.'s purchase of the British construction materials company Redland PLC. These increased the company's annual aggregates sales by 75 percent and its ready-mix concrete sales volume by one-third and added more than six million tons of asphalt sales annually.

Through its Canadian subsidiary, the company purchased another wallboard manufacturing plant and gypsum quarry, a manufacturer of joint compounds, and, in January 1999, announced it would build a fourth wallboard plant, a $90 million facility in Kentucky. The company continued construction of two state-of-the-art cement plants, replacing older plants in Kansas City, Missouri, and Richmond, British Columbia, and acquired a cement plant in Seattle, Washington.

The company's 1998 acquisitions, combined with the strong construction economy, boosted net income of 29 percent over the previous year, and revenues of 33 percent to $2.45 billion, a new high for Lafarge Corporation. In the United States, low interest rates were expected to support high levels of building activity. That situation, along with the 1998 federal highway bill, and its six-year, $215 billion in transportation funding, could expect to keep Lafarge Corporation busy producing its cement, aggregates, concrete-related materials, and gypsum wallboard.

Principal Subsidiaries

Lafarge Canada Inc.; Cement Transport, Ltd.; Friday Harbor Sand & Gravel, Inc.; International Atlantins Ins. Co.; National Mineral Corp.; Systech Environmental Corp.; Walter N. Handy Co., Inc.

Further Reading

Biondo, Brenda, "Rounding Up Replacements: Lafarge Corp.'s Use of Alternative Raw Materials," *Pit & Quarry,* May 1994, p. 20.

Boyer, Edward, "Corporate Border Crossers," *Fortune,* April 30, 1984, p. 332.

"Canada Cement Lafarge Ltd. and Lone Star Industries Complete Separation," *Wall Street Journal,* November 2, 1977, p. 45.

"Citadel Cement Corp Names President," *New York Times,* September 29, 1973, p. 41.

Gladstone, Rick, "Cement Giant Gets $1.47 Billion Cash Offer, Rejects It," *Associated Press,* September 20, 1988.

Hall, William, "Lafarge Plans to Raise $50 Million in U.S. Market," *Financial Times* (London), September 20, 1983, p. 21.

Hinden, Stan, "Reston-Based Lafarge Corp. Hardens Grip on Domestic Cement Market," *Washington Post,* April 25, 1988, p. E5.

"How Cement Is Made," http://www.lafargecorp.com/prd_cmth .htm.

Huhta, Richard S., "Another Look at Vertical Integration," *Rock Products,* February 1990, p. 15.

"Lafarge Acquires Cell-Tex," Reston, Va.: Lafarge Corporation, April 15, 1999.

"Lafarge Corp. Announces Major Construction Materials Acquisition," Reston, Va.: Lafarge Corporation, March 17, 1998.

"Lafarge Corp. Announces Purchase of National Gypsum's Plant in Alpena," *UPI,* December 23, 1986.

"Lafarge Corp. Completes Acquisition of Systech Corp.," *PR Newswire,* December 29, 1986.

"Lafarge Corporation Announces Purchase of East Texas Stone Co.," *PR Newswire,* August 29, 1986.

"Lafarge Corporation Board Appoints New CEO," *PR Newswire,* August 5, 1996.

"Lafarge Corporation History," http://www.lafargecorp.com/hist.htm

"Lafarge Corporation Reports 1983 Operating Results," *PR Newswire,* February 3, 1984.

"Lafarge Corp. Reports Record Fourth-Quarter Earnings, 29% Improvement for Year," Reston, Va.: Lafarge Corporation, January 27, 1999.

"Lafarge Expands Grasp on Midwest Market," *Engineering News-Record,* January 7, 1991, p. 13.

"Lafarge Invests $230 Million in State-of-the-Art Cement Plants," *Industrial Specialties News,* November 13, 1995.

"Lafarge Posts Significant Earnings Improvement Paced by Record Canadian Operating Results," *Southwest Newswire,* January 29, 1986.

"Lafarge to Acquire Atlantic Group Limited," Reston, Va.: Lafarge Corporation, December 17, 1998.

"Lafarge to Build North America's Largest Wallboard Production Line," Reston, Va.: Lafarge Corporation, January 27, 1999.

Leepson, Marc, "Doing Business: Profiles of Three Companies in the County," *Regardies: The Business of Washington,* December 1988, p. 170.

Menninger, Bonar, "Billion-Dollar Cement Producer Sets Up in Reston," *Washington Post,* March 28, 1988, p. 10.

Sansbury, Tim, "Cement Makers Provide Market for Hazardous Waste, As Fuel," *Journal of Commerce,* December 8, 1988, p. 4B.

Setzer, Steven W., "Higher Prices on the Way," *Engineering News-Record,* December 21, 1992, p. 28.

Singletary, Michelle, "Lafarge Corp. Chief Resigns," *Washington Post,* June 10, 1992, p. F1.

Wyman, Stephen H., "From Summer Intern to Chief Executive: In 23 Years, Robert Murdoch Rises to Top of Reston-Based Lafarge Corp.," *Washington Post,* November 14, 1988, p. F16.

"U.S. Construction Boom Boosts Cement, Aggregate Sales," *Industrial Specialties News,* August 8, 1994.

—Ellen D. Wernick

Lennox International Inc.

2100 Lake Park Boulevard
Richardson, Texas 75080
U.S.A.
(972) 497-5000
Fax: (972) 497-5292
Web site: http://www.lennox.com

Private Company
Incorporated: 1904 as Lennox Furnace Company
Employees: 11,700
Sales: $1.82 billion (1998)
NAIC: 333415 Air Conditioning & Warm Air Heating
    Equipment & Commercial & Industrial Refrigeration
    Equipment Manufacturing; 333414 Heating
    Equipment Manufacturing, Except Warm Air
    Furnaces; 333994 Industrial Process Furnace & Oven
    Manufacturing; 336322 Other Motor Vehicle
    Electrical & Electronic Equipment Manufacturing;
    42173 Warm Air Heating & Air Conditioning
    Equipment & Supplies Wholesalers

Lennox International Inc., through its four main subsidiaries—Lennox Industries Inc., Heatcraft Inc., Armstrong Air Conditioning Inc., and Lennox Global Ltd.—produces and markets a broad range of residential and commercial heating, air conditioning, and refrigeration equipment and components. Prior to a proposed initial public offering that the company announced in April 1999, Lennox International was owned almost entirely by members of the Norris family, which has controlled the company since 1904; John W. Norris, Jr., is chairman of the board and chief executive officer. About 110 descendants of founder D.W. Norris own shares of Lennox.

Lennox Industries Inc. is the core business of Lennox International. This subsidiary is a North American manufacturer of residential and commercial heating and air conditioning equipment. Lennox products are marketed directly to its network of 5,000 independent dealers located throughout the United States and Canada, a unique setup in the heating, ventilating, and air conditioning (HVAC) industry. Lennox Industries' facilities include three factories in Marshalltown, Iowa; Stuttgart, Arkansas; and Toronto, Canada, as well as numerous sales and distribution centers, dealer service centers, and a large research and development laboratory located in Carrollton, Texas. Lennox Industries is also the parent company of Hearth Products Inc., which was established in 1998 and produces fireplaces, fireplace inserts, and other hearth products. About half of the parent company's revenue is generated by Lennox Industries. Heatcraft Inc. has been part of Lennox International since 1973. Heatcraft, with headquarters in Grenada, Mississippi, has three divisions: the Heat Transfer Division, which produces heat transfer surfaces, including coils and copper tubing, as well as other components; the Refrigeration Products Division, which manufactures refrigeration conditioning units, unit coolers, air-cooled condensers, and cooling towers; and the Electrical Products Division, which makes electrical controls, package humidifiers, and electrical heating elements. Armstrong Air Conditioning Inc. is based in Bellevue, Ohio, and manufactures a broad range of residential furnaces and air conditioners. Lennox Global Ltd., based in Richardson, Texas, was formed in 1995 to expand Lennox's presence outside North America and has since formed several joint ventures that make and distribute HVAC products in Europe, Australia, Singapore, Mexico, and Brazil.

Coal Furnace Beginnings

Lennox got its start in Marshalltown, Iowa, in the last years of the 19th century. Two inventors, Ernest Bryant and Ezra Smith, patented a design for a riveted-steel sheet metal coal furnace, a significant improvement over the cast iron furnaces of that time. Bryant and Smith hired Dave Lennox, who operated a machine shop in Marshalltown, to build the equipment necessary to manufacture their furnace. Bryant and Smith did not have adequate financial backing for the project, however, and when they could not pay Lennox for his work, Lennox took over the furnace patents, altered the design, and set out to market the furnace himself. Shortly thereafter, Lennox decided to sell the furnace business. It was purchased in 1904 by D.W. Norris, editor and publisher of the local newspaper. He incorporated the operation as Lennox Furnace Company, and proceeded to sell 600 furnaces in the company's first year. The Lennox method of distribution, selling, and delivering products directly to authorized dealers was established in the company's first years of operation. Company president Norris established a direct link to dealers using newspaper advertising, his area of expertise.

The superiority of the Lennox sheet metal furnace over the cast iron models commonly in use quickly became apparent. Cast iron furnaces were prone to warping after years of continual heating and cooling. This often caused the shell to crack, and smoke and coal gas could leak into a living space. The Lennox model solved this problem, since no warping occurred. By 1923, the company had expanded enough to open a warehouse in Syracuse, New York. Two years later, a factory was built in that city. In 1927 Lennox acquired the Armstrong Furnace plant in London, Ohio. The Armstrong facility, which produced steel coal furnaces, was moved to Columbus, Ohio, the following year.

John W. Norris, son of company president D.W. Norris, went to work for Lennox in 1927 following his graduation from Massachusetts Institute of Technology. By the early 1930s, the younger Norris had set up a research department in the back part of a warehouse. Several important industry developments came about as a result of Norris's research. Among these developments was the addition of blowers to furnaces in the mid-1930s. Around the same time, oil- and gas-burning furnaces were introduced as well. The appearance of oil and gas forced-air furnaces completely changed the face of the residential heating market. During this period Norris developed a line of smooth, porcelain-enameled cabinets in which to house the furnaces, revolutionizing furnace design for years to come. This marked the first time aesthetics were taken into account in the design of heating equipment, in recognition of the increasing use of the American basement as a living area. A gas forced-air furnace specifically designed for attic or crawlspace installation went into production in 1939.

As the demand for Lennox equipment increased, new facilities were added. In 1940 a new and larger factory was built in Columbus. This plant was also a center for sales, distribution, and product service support for parts of the country that the Marshalltown and Syracuse facilities could not support. By the onset of World War II, Lennox held an important place in the heating industry. During the war the company's production included not only heating equipment for military use, but also parts for aircraft and bombs. A precision machine shop in Lima, Ohio, was purchased for that purpose in 1942. Demand for Lennox products soared when the war was over. By the end of the 1940s, several new divisions were added, including a factory in Fort Worth, Texas, and sales centers in Atlanta, Los Angeles, and Salt Lake City. In 1949 D.W. Norris died, and John W. Norris, Sr., became president of Lennox.

Expanded into Air Conditioning in the 1950s

Lennox continued to expand quickly in both its product line and geographical scope in the 1950s. In 1952 Lennox began manufacturing air conditioning systems. Its first model was a three-ton water-cooled air conditioner, produced at the newly expanded Fort Worth plant. Within the next couple of years, compressors and air conditioning systems for industrial and commercial use went into production as well. Lennox went international in 1952, with the creation of Lennox Industries (Canada) Ltd.

In 1955 the Lennox Furnace Co. changed its name to Lennox Industries Inc. in order to better reflect the broader range of products being manufactured. Further innovations created by Lennox during that decade included commercial air conditioning systems that saved energy by using outside air whenever possible; and modular systems for high-rise buildings, in which each floor was heated and cooled separately from the others.

Lennox expanded the scope of its operations in 1962 with the creation of an International Division. A full-production facility was established in Basingstoke, England (outside of London), and sales offices and warehouses serving most of Western Europe were opened in the Netherlands and in West Germany. By this time, the Canadian operation included a manufacturing plant in Toronto, Ontario, as well as a sales and distribution facility in Calgary, Alberta. Among the products introduced by Lennox during the 1960s were the Duracurve heat exchanger, which eliminated noise and cracking in gas furnaces, and multizone rooftop units for heating and cooling.

Acquired Heatcraft in 1973

In 1971 Norris was succeeded as president by Ray C. Robbins. Under Robbins, Lennox continued to expand at a rapid pace during the 1970s. In 1973 Lennox acquired the Tennessee-based Heatcraft Inc. from PEP Industries. Heatcraft, a manufacturer of electric heating and cooling components such as coils, condensing units, and copper tubing, became a wholly owned subsidiary of Lennox. The following year Lennox began construction of a new factory for the production of commercial heating and air conditioning equipment in Stuttgart, Arkansas. Later in the decade, Lennox began to outgrow some of its facilities, and a migration to the Dallas area began. The company's Marshalltown Research and Development Laboratory and the heat pump research facility in Fort Worth were consolidated into a larger, more modern location in Carrollton, Texas, in 1977.

The following year the company's corporate headquarters were relocated from Marshalltown to Dallas. The Midwest Division sales headquarters and manufacturing plant located in Marshalltown remained intact. The year 1978 also marked the debut of the LOGIC (Lennox Objective Guide to Installation Comparisons) computer program for the analysis of HVAC designs, and the opening of a computerized corporate data center. In 1979 testing was completed on a home-sized solar-powered air conditioning system, produced by Lennox in cooperation with Honeywell under government contract.

John W. Norris, Jr., became president and CEO of Lennox in 1980. Robbins stayed on as chairman of the board. By 1981, the company's unique distribution system boasted a total of 6,000 dealers throughout the United States and Canada, supplied by a network of 31 warehouses. That year, Lennox controlled 17 percent of the residential market for gas forced-air furnaces. The company did nearly as well in the central electric heating and unitary air conditioner markets, with 14 percent and 15 percent shares, respectively.

Introduced Pulse Furnace in 1982

In 1982 Lennox made a major gain in the home heating industry with the appearance of the first Pulse combustion gas furnace, a high-efficiency forced-air unit that marked the first major improvement in home heating in 20 years. The G14 Pulse furnace operated with no open flame, igniting tiny bursts of gas and air at a rate of about 60 bursts a second and at over 90 percent fuel efficiency, a significant improvement over the 55 percent energy efficiency of most furnaces in use at that time. With the introduction of the Pulse, sales at Lennox reached an estimated $600 million for 1982.

In 1983 Lennox built a copper tube plant in Bossier City, Louisiana. The following year, the company introduced the Power Saver air conditioner, the first two-speed air conditioner to achieve a 15.0 Seasonal Energy Efficiency Ratio (SEER). The expansion and consolidation of company facilities continued in the mid-1980s. In 1985 Lennox began an expansion program at its National Parts Distribution Center in Urbandale, Iowa, just outside of Des Moines. The compressor research lab in Fort Worth was integrated into the Carrollton research and development complex that year as well. A year later Lennox International Inc. was formed as the parent company for Lennox Industries and Heatcraft. Around the same time, Heatcraft acquired the Grenada, Mississippi, coil manufacturing and copper mill facility of SnyderGeneral Corp. This facility was expanded in 1987 to include the production of precision tools and dies for making heat transfer products. Lennox began offering limited lifetime warranties on its Pulse furnaces in 1987, prompting its competitors to come up with similar warranty programs of their own. In 1988 Heatcraft acquired another of SnyderGeneral's facilities, a refrigeration products manufacturing plant in Wilmington, North Carolina.

Two important technological developments occurred at Lennox in 1988: the introduction of the first heat pump to use a scroll-compressor; and a licensing agreement with Powell Energy Products to develop and market thermal energy storage systems using Powell technology. The year also marked the reacquisition of Armstrong Air Conditioning. Lennox had owned Armstrong from the mid-1920s into the 1950s, when it was sold off. Armstrong was purchased by Johnson Corporation in 1962, which was in turn acquired by Magic Chef in 1971. Magic Chef became a division of Maytag in 1986, and its name was lengthened to Magic Chef Air Conditioning. It was this division that Lennox International purchased from Maytag in 1988 and subsequently renamed Armstrong Air Conditioning Inc.

Reorganized in 1989 and 1990

Early in 1989, Lennox announced a reorganization of its corporate structure, in which each of its three operating subsidiaries would have its own president and chief operating officer. Donald W. Munson was named to head Lennox Industries; Robert L. Jenkins became president of Heatcraft; and Robert E. Johnson was named to lead Armstrong. Other developments that year included the opening of a new Lennox Industries sales and distribution center in Wilmington, Massachusetts, to serve dealers in New England and eastern New York. Also, the Research and Development Laboratory in Carrollton, Texas, was approved by the American Gas Association as an accredited lab for certification testing.

In 1990 work was completed on a new corporate headquarters for Lennox International and Lennox Industries in Richardson, Texas, a suburb of Dallas. The following year the company launched another reorganization plan, in which its sales management, marketing, and product ordering teams were united in the new headquarters, a change from the previous arrangement of five semi-autonomous regional divisions. At the same time, production was consolidated into four locations, meaning the closing of the Fort Worth facility. Also in 1991, Norris was voted in as chairman of the board. Robbins's title was elevated to chairman emeritus. Donald Munson retired in July 1992, and Thomas J. Keefe, a member of the Lennox International board, took over as president and chief operating officer of Lennox Industries. Later that year, a ten-year anniversary celebration for the Pulse furnace took place in Marshalltown, Iowa, the company's birthplace and furnace manufacturing location, during which the one millionth Pulse furnace was dedicated. Meanwhile in Europe, the company's Basingstoke, England, facility, operated by Lennox for over 30 years, was closed. Its operations were moved to a new, 100,000-square-foot plant in Northampton.

Lennox introduced its new "Diplomat" line of central air conditioners, heat pumps, and gas furnaces in early 1993. The Diplomat line was developed as a means of gaining a stronger foothold in the residential new construction market, an area that Lennox had often been priced out of in previous years. Also in 1993 the Columbus, Ohio, plant was closed, with the manufacturing operations there consolidated into the Marshalltown, Iowa, factory. In 1994 Lennox introduced CompleteHeat, the industry's first high-efficiency space heating/hot water system. Lennox also became the first HVAC company to manufacture gas fireplaces in North America that same year.

In 1995, the year the company celebrated its centennial anniversary, Robert Schjerven was named president and COO of Lennox Industries after having served as head of Armstrong Air Conditioning; Ed French took over as president of Armstrong, following a stint as head of Heatcraft's Refrigeration Products Division. That year Lennox announced its intention to ultimately go public, offering no more than a 20 percent interest through an IPO. This plan appeared to have been at least temporarily scuttled, however, after it became widely known that a possible flaw in a key component of the 400,000 Pulse furnaces made before 1988 could, in rare cases, lead the furnaces to leak poisonous carbon monoxide gas into the homes. In September 1995 a $1 billion class-action lawsuit was filed against Lennox in Dallas, a case that the company won in January 1998. Prior to that victory, Lennox began a furnace inspection program in late 1997, and had inspected 130,000 furnaces by early 1998. To pay for the program the company took a $140 million pretax charge in 1997, which led to a full-year net loss of $33.6 million (compared to net profits of $54.7 million in 1996). Although it appeared that the company would survive this setback, its reputation had suffered from being probed by the Consumer Product Safety Commission and being the subject of media scrutiny including coverage by a national prime-time news show.

Formed Lennox Global in 1995

Perhaps the most important event of 1995 came in May when Lennox added a fourth main subsidiary, Lennox Global Ltd., to its organizational chart. Lennox Global was created to expand the manufacturing and sales operations of Lennox Industries, Armstrong, and Heatcraft in areas outside the United States and Canada. In addition to its manufacturing facility in the United Kingdom, Lennox International had established joint ventures in France and Mexico which market refrigeration products and had gained full control of an Australian concern. These operations were consolidated under the banner of Lennox Global, which aimed for additional overseas growth through the formation of more joint ventures. The first of these came in 1996 when Lennox joined with the Brancher group of France to form HCF-Lennox, which combined several of the two companies operations into an entity with $160 million in annual sales and the number one position in Europe for rooftop air conditioners in addition to leading positions in chillers, precision air conditioners, process cooling, and commercial refrigeration systems. Other joint ventures were soon formed in Spain, with Refac, and in the Latin American region, with Strong. In September 1998 Lennox spent $20.5 million to acquire a majority interest in Brazil-based McQuay do Brasil S.A., a specialist in commercial refrigeration and heat transfer products, which it marketed in Brazil and surrounding countries. The addition of Lennox Global increased Lennox International's sales outside the United States and Canada from $28.5 million in 1996 to $244.5 million in 1998. The 1998 figure represented 13.4 percent of the company's overall sales of $1.82 billion, and the company aimed to increase that to 50 percent by 2005.

In September 1998 Lennox began a new strategy of acquiring heating and air conditioning dealers in the United States and Canada in order to distribute Lennox products directly to consumers and thereby gain a portion of the revenues and margins available at the retail level. Lennox also hoped to take advantage of the growth opportunities available in what was a highly fragmented market, with more than 30,000 dealers in the U.S. retail sales and service market alone. By the end of 1999's first quarter, Lennox had spent about $55 million to acquire 37 dealers in Canada and was making plans for U.S. acquisitions.

Having entered the hearth products market in 1994, Lennox expanded upon that initiative in 1998 when it formed Hearth Products Inc. as a Tustin, California-based wholly owned subsidiary of Lennox Industries. Following the 1998 acquisitions of Marco Mfg., Inc. of Lynwood, California; Pyro Industries Inc. of Burlington, Washington; and Superior Fireplace Company of Fullerton, California, and the early 1999 purchase of Security Chimneys International, Ltd.—for a total of $120 million—Hearth Products was one of the largest makers of hearth products in the United States and Canada, offering a full line of products including gas and wood-burning fireplaces, fireplace inserts, free-standing stoves, and gas logs. Also in 1998 Lennox International and Lennox Industries agreed to settle a lawsuit brought by 11 former sales managers, who charged they had been fired or demoted, at the ages of 41 to 58 years old, as a result of a practice or pattern of age discrimination at Lennox. Although the company admitted no wrongdoing, it agreed to pay the plaintiffs a total of $6.2 million, undergo 42 months of Equal Employment Opportunity Commission monitoring, and change its personnel practices.

By early 1999, Lennox had built up about $115 million in debt as a result of its hearth products acquisitions, its international expansion, and its dealer acquisition program. To pay down some of this debt—as well as to fund further expansion—Lennox decided to resurrect the idea of an initial public offering. In early April 1999 the company announced that it intended to sell an unspecified stake in the company to the public through an IPO. Following the offering, the 110 descendants of D.W. Norris who owned the company's stock would still be in firm control of the company, but they would have an increased ability to sell their stock holdings. It appeared that Lennox International was going public at a time of exciting company initiatives and excellent prospects for 21st-century growth.

Principal Subsidiaries

Armstrong Air Conditioning Inc.; Heatcraft Inc.; Lennox Global Ltd.; Lennox Industries Inc.

Further Reading

A Century of Comfort: Lennox: The First Hundred Years, 1895–1995, Richardson, Tex.: Lennox International Inc., n.d., 44 p.

Consdorf, Arnold P., and Charles W. Behrens, ''A Combination of Change and Stability,'' *Appliance Manufacturer,* November 1977, pp. 40–47.

Duffy, Gordon, ''Lennox Gears Up for Expansion in New Home and World Markets,'' *Air Conditioning, Heating, and Refrigeration News,* January 25, 1993, pp. 102–04.

Dworkin, Andy, ''Furnace Flaw Keeps Texas' Lennox Industries in Hot Seat,'' *Dallas Morning News,* March 2, 1998.

——, ''Texas-Based Heating, Cooling Firm Plans for Small Public Offering,'' *Dallas Morning News,* April 6, 1999.

''Gas Furnaces: Lennox Is Hot in Ownership Now and in the Future,'' *Appliance Manufacturer,* July 1983, p. 38.

Kunde, Diana, "Richardson, Texas-Based Lennox Agrees to Settle Age Bias Suit," *Dallas Morning News,* May 12, 1998.

"Lennox Link to Dealers Thrives on Direct Communication," *Appliance Manufacturer,* October 1981, p. 54.

"Lennox Moving Corporate HQ to Dallas Area," *Air Conditioning, Heating, and Refrigeration News,* March 20, 1978, p. 1.

"Lennox Reorganizes," *Air Conditioning, Heating, and Refrigeration News,* April 8, 1991, pp. 1–2.

"The Lennox Story," *Appliance,* February 1982, special section.

"Lighting a Fire Under Furnace Sales," *Business Week,* October 25, 1982, p. 82.

Mahoney, Thomas A., "Lennox Celebrates 100 Years in Business," *Air Conditioning, Heating, and Refrigeration News,* July 17, 1995, pp. 3+.

"Multifaceted Lennox International," *Appliance Manufacturer,* July 1996, special section.

"Special Section: Lennox International," *Appliance Manufacturer,* August 1990.

"Sun-Powered Home Air Conditioner," *Machine Design,* June 21, 1979, p. 8.

—Robert R. Jacobson
—updated by David E. Salamie

Leprino Foods Company

1830 West 38th Avenue
Denver, Colorado 80211
U.S.A.
(303) 480-2600
(800) LEPRINO; (800) 537-7466
Fax: (303) 480-2605

Private Company
Incorporated: 1946
Employees: 2,300
Sales: $1.25 billion (1998 est.)
NAIC: 311513 Cheese Manufacturing; 311412 Frozen
Specialty Food Manufacturing; 311999 All Other
Miscellaneous Food Manufacturing; 42241 General
Line Grocery Wholesalers

Leprino Foods Company, owned by the Leprino family, is the largest producer of mozzarella cheese in the United States. The company holds more than 20 patents and makes more than 700 pounds of cheese each year in its seven cheesemaking plants, including a mozzarella plant in New Mexico that is the world's biggest. Leprino supplies cheese to most of the United States' nationwide pizza chains, including Domino's, Little Caesars, and Pizza Hut, and uses five to seven percent of the nation's total milk supply, which it receives from the nation's largest dairy cooperatives, including the Dairy Farmers of America. Leprino revolutionized cheesemaking with its "continuous extrusion" process. The company also makes sweet whey, whey protein concentrate, and lactose for use in baby formula, as well as ice cream and baked goods.

A Family-Owned, Family-Run Business: Beginnings in 1946

Leprino Foods was founded in 1946 by Michael Leprino, Sr., who had emigrated to Denver, Colorado from his native Italy in the early part of this century. First a truck farmer, then a grocer, Mike Leprino began his career as a cheesemaker when his daughter, Ange, who was building her own business preparing Italian foods, needed a better quality ricotta for the cheese ravioli she and her husband, Frank, were marketing under the label Frangi's. Inspired by his cheesemaking success, Mike Leprino also started to make scamorze, a form of mozzarella molded into pear-shaped balls, which he sold to local neighborhood grocery stores. Helped by his young son, Jim, the family-owned, family-run business began to operate out of the family's home on 38th Avenue in Denver, a site it still occupied when Jim took over as chairman and chief executive officer of the company in 1972 upon Mike Leprino's death.

The newly founded business was a local success, and Mike Leprino, sensing pizza's potential for growth, prepared his company for expansion. In the 1960s, while mozzarella production paralleled the rise of pizza as the national dish, Leprino went to Wisconsin to learn how to make mozzarella in 20-pound blocks. There, he linked up with Les Kielmeier, a cheesemaker, who joined Leprino Foods and introduced it to many of the technological advances that enabled it to begin production of its value-added items. From 1970 to 1993 domestic production of cheese was on an upswing: cheddar cheese went from about one billion pounds annually to 2.4 billion; mozzarella production increased from 245 million pounds to two billion.

During this time, Leprino Foods became an innovator in the world of cheese production and the company experienced continued growth. Chief among the innovations developed at Leprino was its "continuous extrusion" process. At its highly automated plants, milk was first tested for acidity, butterfat content, and other characteristics, then pasteurized and piped to tanks where some of its fat content was skimmed and shipped to a butter plant for production. Whey protein was sent down a separate track to produce animal feed, additives for food companies, or ingredients used in pharmaceuticals. In enclosed vats, the remaining curd was cooked, mixed, cut, and stretched to a taffy-like consistency, then extruded from the mixer in a continuous ribbon that traveled through an ice-cold brine bath before it was cut into smaller slabs, shredded, and "quick frozen." The advantage of this process was time saved: conventional mozzarella had to be aged for one to two weeks, but Leprino produced its mozzarella in a matter of hours. In 1988 the company added "quality locked" cheese, a frozen, free-flowing shredded form of mozzarella, which constituted its second major innovation. In 1989 a new line of enhanced cheeses, including varieties of part-skim mozzarella that mimicked the taste, appearance, and melting properties of other cheeses, such as muenster or provolone blends, was added to Leprino Foods' line of offerings.

Specializing in Foodservice Distribution: Late 1970s Through Early 1990s

Leprino's manufacturing capacity grew steadily throughout the 1980s. In 1988 it partnered with the Michigan Milk Producers' Association, which put up 80 percent of the necessary capital to build a cheese manufacturing plant that Leprino then leased and operated. The plant, at an estimated cost of $30–$40 million, was hailed as a boon to Michigan dairy farmers. Leprino, however, was involved in more than just cheese production. In the late 1970s the company became a specialist foodservice distributor, servicing primarily pizza operations. By the mid-1980s it was supplying an average of 700 items, had eight distribution centers, and served an expanded product mix that included tortillas, pinto beans, meat, spices, and paper products shipped to Mexican food restaurants. The company enjoyed approximately $248 million worth of sales as a distributor in 1983, 6.3 percent or $15 million of which came from its new Mexican food business.

By the early 1990s Leprino Foods had nine distribution centers in Colorado, California, Arizona, Texas, Missouri, Florida, and Pennsylvania, carried a mix of 1,800 items, and supported a staff of about 40 district salespeople, four national account representatives, and 27 customer service people. The company served 4,850 different drop locations. Its sales totaled $379 million in 1989, with about half that amount derived from pizza operations, such as Pizza Hut, and 20 percent from its own manufactured cheeses, chief among them its Quality Locked Cheese products. The remainder of Leprino's sales came from other fast-food chain operators, such as Manchu Wok, Miami Sub, and Subway. In 1990 the company's revenue deriving from distribution sales rose to $401.7 million; in 1991 sales were at $414.1 million. In 1993 Stouffer Foods Corporation selected Leprino Foods as its first Certified Supplier, becoming Leprino's largest industrial customer and increasing distribution-derived revenues yet further.

Then, in 1994, in a sudden narrowing and focusing of operations, the company sold off both the assets and business of its restaurant supply distribution operation to International Multifoods Corporation, leaving it with only its cheese manufacturing business. Though neither company ever revealed the purchase price, industry analysts estimated that Multifoods paid from $100 to $125 million for Leprino Foodservice Distribution. The acquisition included seven warehouses, the lease on two others, a fleet of trucks, and the contract for a second, leased fleet.

Overseas Speculation in the Mid-1990s

It appeared that Leprino Foods had decided to pinpoint its efforts on its growth overseas. In association with Pizza Hut, for whom Leprino was the sole U.S. supplier, the company began to speculate about expanding into Europe. In 1994 the company attempted a joint venture with the Irish dairy cooperative Golden Vale, whose Northern Ireland Leckpatrick subsidiary was one of the largest single milk buyers in all of Ireland. Leprino had similarly attempted to establish its presence in Europe in 1993, but plans to base its manufacturing operations in the Republic of Ireland were shot down when Irish dairy companies protested that the move would put too much pressure on milk supplies available for Irish cheese production. The new Leprino production unit, which was to have an initial capacity of 18,000 tons a year, was scheduled to begin operations in 1996.

As plans for the plant went ahead in 1994, however, opposition to the proposed development once again became intense. The Irish-dominated European Association of Mozzarella Manufacturers threatened European court action if the British government granted aid to the foreign facility. The Association claimed that there was already excess capacity in the industry and that the use of government funds to create jobs would simply displace existing jobs elsewhere. Finally, after six months of speculation, the European Commission officials gave the project state aid approval, and the Industrial Development Board, the government grants agency in Northern Ireland, confirmed that it would formally offer Leprino Foods aid on a par with two other existing mozzarella manufacturers in Northern Ireland. However, plans for the plant were aborted suddenly when Pizza Hut would not guarantee its European market to Leprino Foods.

The following year, an attempt to expand sales into Canada also ended abruptly in failure when the Canadian government refused to waive a 300 percent tariff levied against shipments of cheese from the United States into Canada in excess of an annual quota of 45 million pounds. Pizza Hut of Canada, which had had hopes of cashing in on the success of its parent company's "Stuffed Crust" promotion in the United States, requested a shipment from Leprino Foods worth about $30 million to import 20 million pounds of a special string mozzarella produced exclusively by Leprino, only to find out that the annual Canadian-American quota had already been met.

Success Nationally, Strained Ties Locally: The Late 1990s

This setback notwithstanding, *Dairy Foods* magazine ranked Leprino Foods third—behind only Kraft and Suiza Foods in its third annual listing in 1995 of North America's largest dairies, both private and public. In addition, although Leprino Foods dropped one position to number four in the magazine's 1997 tally, it was still among the top 100 companies as calculated by dairy sales totals at the retail and foodservice levels. In 1996 Leprino was 158th in *Forbes* magazine's listing of the nation's 500 largest private companies; it had climbed to 140th two years later in the magazine's 1998 tally.

Leprino Foods was without question the world's largest mozzarella cheese manufacturer by the late 1990s. In June 1998 the board of directors of Dairy Farmers of America approved a letter of intent to sell a total of six of its cheese plants—one in Wisconsin and five in Nebraska—as well as its interest in a seventh New York plant to Leprino Foods as part of an ongoing business relationship between the two. In announcing the alliance, according to a report in *Dairy Market's Weekly,* Dairy Farmers of America's board chairman praised Leprino's record of growth and innovation from 1988 to 1998.

Back at home on 38th Avenue in Denver, however, the relationship among neighbors was less than convivial. Leprino was still located at its original, albeit significantly modified and enlarged site, which housed office space and a research center and laboratory. The company hit the press in 1998 when a September report released by the Colorado Public Interest Research Group ''Troubled Waters'' placed it at the top of a list of corporate polluters discharging toxins into Colorado's streams. In addition, a simmering land use battle involving the company, which had begun in 1996, went forward to the full city council in June 1998 after city-sponsored mediation between residents and Leprino Foods failed to reach an accord. Neighbors complained that Leprino's continued expansions were ruining their neighborhood and blighting their streets with traffic, noise, and a sour, cheesy odor. They also said that the company had not honored past promises to landscape some parking areas, avoid converting a vacant lot into parking, and curtail heavy truck traffic through the neighborhood. The discord was resolved eventually after the company threatened to pull out of Denver if the city vetoed its expansions, and the council voted unanimously to rezone to allow the company another expansion. In return, Leprino agreed to reduce the bulk of its buildings and to restrict truck traffic.

Further Reading

Flynn, Kevin, ''Cheese Dispute Growing Ripe; Upset Neighbors Say 'No Whey' to Company's Research Plans As Rift Continues to Soar,'' *Denver Rocky Mountain News,* June 25, 1998, p. 5A.

''Green Light for Leprino/Golden Vale Joint Venture,'' *Dairy Markets Weekly,* June 8, 1995.

Leib, Jeffrey, ''Denver's Big Cheese,'' *Denver Post Magazine,* April 16, 1995, p. 10.

''Leprino Foods Co.; Top 25 Specialized Foodservice Distributors,'' *Institutional Distribution,* February 1990, p. 93.

''Leprino Foods to Buy Cheese Plants from DFA,'' *Dairy Markets Weekly,* June 25, 1998, p. 6.

''Leprino Foods to Set Up Mozzarella Production Plant in Europe,'' *Dairy Markets Weekly,* December 15, 1994, p. 3.

—Carrie Rothburd

LodgeNet Entertainment Corporation

3900 West Innovation Street
Sioux Falls, South Dakota 57107
U.S.A.
(605) 988-1000
(888) 563-4363
Fax: (605) 988-1532
Web site: http://www.lodgenet.com

Public Company
Incorporated: 1983 as Satellite Movie Company
Employees: 739
Sales: $166.4 million (1998)
Stock Exchanges: NASDAQ
Ticker Symbol: LNET
NAIC: 513220 Cable Program Distribution Operators;
513210 Pay Television Networks; 33429 Other
Communications Equipment Manufacturing

LodgeNet Entertainment Corporation is a leading entertainment company providing network-based video games, movies-on-demand, cable television programming, and other services to more than 4,000 hotels worldwide. The company also provides Super Nintendo video games and PRIMESTAR satellite television to corporate-managed hotel chains and individually owned franchise properties, including Budgetel Inns, Delta Hotels and Resorts, Doubletree, Embassy Suites, Harrah's Casino Hotels, Hilton, Holiday Inn, Inter-Continental, ITT Sheraton, La Quinta Inns, Marriott, Outrigger, Prince, Radisson, Red Roof Inns, The Ritz-Carlton Company, Starwood Hotels & Resorts, and Westin.

The company pursues its strategic goals in the lodging industry through the design, assembly, installation, and servicing of two types of guest room entertainment and information systems. ''Guest Pay'' systems are those that deliver on-demand movies, games, and information services to the guest on a pay-per-view or pay-per-use basis, generating recurring revenue for the company. ''Free-to-Guest'' services involve satellite-delivered programming such as HBO and CNN, using PRIMESTAR compressed digital technology. LodgeNet con-

nects consumers with content using a proprietary broadband local-area network (b-LAN) system architecture. The company designs, builds, programs, and operates these systems.

Satellite Movie Company: 1980–91

The company was founded in 1980 by Tim C. Flynn as Satellite Movie Company. The company's initial business was providing satellite television systems to hotels and motels, including satellite earth stations, master antennae, and on-property signal distribution systems, plus programming and related marketing support materials. Programming sources included such services as ESPN, Cable News Network, Showtime, The Movie Channel, and national superstations WTBS and WGN.

Satellite Movie Company, which was originally incorporated in South Dakota in February 1983, began offering pay-per-view (PPV) movie systems to the lodging industry in 1986. The company's initial PPV offering was a scheduled system, offering newer movies than those available on cable, broadcast at preset times over the guest room television system.

LodgeNet Entertainment Corporation, 1991–96

In September 1991 the company adopted the name LodgeNet Entertainment Corporation to reflect the evolution of its services from satellite-based programming to a broader network distribution model. This move anticipated the introduction of the LodgeNet Guest Scheduled video-on-demand service in 1992, the company's initial interactive service. A significant advancement in guest room entertainment services, the Guest Scheduled video-on-demand system generated more movie buys and revenue because it responded instantly to the guest's order rather than forced the guest to wait for the movies' next scheduled broadcast. It also was capable of offering a much larger movie selection than a scheduled system, which expanded revenue by increasing the chance that a guest would find an appealing title to view. Finally, the enabling technology behind Guest Scheduled—two-way digital communication between each guest room and LodgeNet—also opened the door to additional interactive services.

Company Perspectives:

LodgeNet will be the leading distributor of interactive, multimedia entertainment and information services to the lodging industry. Our intent will be to provide these services using our advanced, cost-effective b-LAN and Internet technologies. Distribution of these services will take place in North American and selected international markets where it is both economically and technically feasible. We will succeed by providing innovative, demand-driven services in these selected markets. We will differentiate ourselves through excellence in system design, content marketing, and customer and technical support.

In March 1993 the company, in a joint venture with NTN Communications of Carlsbad, California, began testing of the hotel room interactive television in approximately 5,000 guest rooms over a period of five months. The full capability was demonstrated in late 1993 with the introduction by LodgeNet of network-based Super Nintendo Entertainment System video games for the guest room, which proved to be exceedingly popular with hotels and guests and, by mid-1999, was installed in more than 530,000 LodgeNet guest rooms. Subsequently, LodgeNet introduced additional interactive services, including Guest Satisfaction Survey, the HotelGuide interactive hotel directory, HotelTour interactive property tour, Room Service Menu Display, Internet Site Promotion, and Video Check-Out with Guest Room Printers.

The company incorporated in Delaware during 1993 via a merger as a successor to Satellite Movie Company. In October of that year the company went public, offering some 4.5 million shares in its initial public offering and bringing in $56.48 million in proceeds, which were used to redeem outstanding preferred stock, reduce bank debt, and provide working capital.

In 1994 LodgeNet partnered with Sony Corporation, which made a series of Trinitron televisions compatible with LodgeNet's interactive systems. Meanwhile, competitors Spectradyne and COMSAT Video Enterprises were not idle. Dallas-based Spectradyne formed an alliance with Ross Perot's former company, Electronic Data Systems (EDS), for using compressed digital video to program scheduled movies to hotel rooms, calling their offering "SpectraVision"; and Bethesda, Maryland-based COMSAT Video Enterprises, a subsidiary of COMSAT Corp., allied with Silicon Graphics and Bell Atlantic to target two segments of the lodging business: traditional satellite programming combining channels free to the guest with for-pay movies and live special events and On Command Video, a paid entertainment and information system. Smaller competitors also were offering movies in hotel rooms. Peoria, Illinois-based SVI Systems offered movies with its Instant Entertainment or Super Video Cinema programs, but its technology relied on portable videocassette players rather than high-speed, high-tech telecommunications equipment.

Early in 1995, Santa Clara, California-based 4th Network began working on an interactive shopping and guest services system. Total revenue for LodgeNet in 1995 reached $63.2 million.

In January 1996 LodgeNet forged an agreement with PRIMESTAR Partners L.P., making LodgeNet the exclusive provider of PRIMESTAR products and services to the lodging industry. PRIMESTAR agreed to provide LodgeNet with access to its digital satellite technology, and the Philadelphia-based company featured more than 1.6 million sites installed throughout the United States. PRIMESTAR by LodgeNet (PbL) was formed as a division of LodgeNet to handle the alliance and, almost immediately, hotel owners and operators seized upon the programming, customer service, and low per-room cost offered by PbL. By the end of 1998 PRIMESTAR by LodgeNet was serving nearly 380,000 rooms with Free-To-Guest programming.

Also that month, the company formed ResNet Communications Inc. to extend its b-LAN system architecture and operational expertise into the multiple dwelling unit (MDU; apartment/condo/townhouse) market. In October, TCI Satellite MDU, Inc., an affiliate of Tele-Communications Inc. (TCI), agreed to invest up to $40 million in ResNet in exchange for up to a 36.99 percent interest in ResNet and agreed to provide ResNet with long-term access to the digital DBS signals provided by TCI Satellite for the MDU market on a nationwide basis via the PRIMESTAR satellite signal. Approximately $5.4 million in cash was paid to LodgeNet, with the remainder of the $34.6 million to be provided in the form of available financing.

By April 1996 the company had more than 200,000 hotel rooms set up to play Super Nintendo Entertainment System games via interactive network. Total revenue for the year reached $97.72 million, with a net loss of $3.25 million.

1997 and Beyond

Prior to 1997, the company focused its marketing efforts on the 150- to 300-room and the more than 300-room segments of the hotel market, which represented about 26 percent and 12 percent of the lodging industry's 3.5 million rooms, respectively. In 1997 the company, in an effort to target an area of the industry not as saturated with competitors, began to market to the less than 150-room market.

June 1997 found the company announcing a strategic alliance with SkyMall Inc. to deliver a video version of the latter company's in-flight airline catalog. The service allowed hotel guests to browse and shop from an interactive video catalog in their room. Because of LodgeNet's position as number two in the industry, a new interactive addition for the year was the presence of advertising "banners" on the video screens in the hotel rooms, similar to Internet-based ad banners, which provided a significant new revenue source for the company.

International sales efforts for the company expanded in 1997, with LodgeNet signing agreements with Panama-based Five Star Entertainment Inc. to bring, via the latter company, LodgeNet's services to Central America. Five Star began installing systems in Panama and began looking into the markets of Belize, Costa Rica, Guatemala, El Salvador, Honduras, and Nicaragua. In addition, the company inked deals with TCI NetVision for the Venezuelan market, Roombar S.A. in the Dominican Republic, and InfoAsia for the Indonesian, Philippine, Thai, Singaporan, and Malaysian markets.

The company added approximately 100,000 rooms to its guest pay base in 1997, bringing the total to 511,000, as well as 126,000 new Nintendo rooms. The company's core lodging business was bolstered in 1997 by contract renewals and such new clients as Carefree Resorts and Prime Hospitality, as well as the addition of several high-profile ownership/management companies to its corporate roster. The company's Canadian branch did well also, installing interactive systems in more than 125 hotel properties throughout that country, including Delta Hotels and Resorts, ITT Sheraton Canada, Centennial Hotels, Coast Hotels Limited, Westmont Hospitality Group, and Canadian Niagara Hotels Inc., as well as numerous independent properties. However, while total revenue that year reached $135.7 million, a 38.9 percent growth over the previous year, net losses continued to mount, reaching $25.41 million for the year.

In 1998 a number of changes occurred. May found the company moving to its new headquarters location on West Innovation Street in Sioux Falls, South Dakota. In July the company promoted Scott C. Petersen from executive vice-president and chief operating officer to president and chief executive officer, replacing Flynn, who moved up to become chairman of the board. By this time, LodgeNet was the second largest provider of interactive entertainment and information services to the lodging industry.

In June the company acquired Connect Group Corporation in a stock swap. The acquisition gave the company the ability to deliver a comprehensive solution to cost-effectively enable plug-and-play high-speed Internet access for hotel guest rooms and meeting spaces as well as the technology to allow guests with laptop computers to connect to the Internet from their rooms at more than 50 times the speed of conventional modems and bypass the hotel's PBX system.

In November 1998 the company completed the merger of its subsidiary ResNet with Interactive Cable Systems Inc. and Shared Technologies Communications Corporation, to form Global Interactive Communications Corporation, a company designed to provide video, voice, and Internet services to the MDU market. At start-up, the new company (owned 30 percent by LodgeNet) had in excess of 650 properties, 125,000 passings, and 55,000 subscribers in 28 states from coast to coast. The new Richardson, Texas-based company also featured customer service and field operations in Tampa, Florida, and construction and warehousing activities in Sioux Falls, South Dakota.

Also in 1998, LodgeNet signed agreements with the Red Roof chain and Carefree Resorts. The company added approximately 84,000 rooms to its guest pay base in 1998, bringing the total to 596,806. Still, while revenue continued to climb, net losses mounted as well, with the company bringing in a total $146.48 million, while losing $39.91 million in 1998.

In March 1999 AT&T—the world's premier provider of voice and data communications and the nation's largest direct Internet service provider—and LodgeNet entered an agreement to provide high-speed Internet access to hotels across the country. With the world's largest, most powerful long distance network and the largest wireless network in North America,

AT&T would supply high-speed Internet access to guest rooms equipped with OnLine by LodgeNet. The service also would supply the hotels themselves with connectivity to their meeting rooms, back offices, and public areas. Wingate Inns International Inc. announced in January that it would be the first hotel chain to deploy LodgeNet's services with Internet connectivity to some 23,000 rooms nationwide that year. By this time, partners in PRIMESTAR included TSAT, Time Warner Entertainment, Comcast Corporation, Cox Communications, MediaOne, and GE Americom.

The company's primary focus at the end of the 20th century was on the two million guest rooms in North America located at hotels, motels, and resorts containing 100 or more rooms. By mid-1999 LodgeNet served some 700,000 rooms at more than 4,500 lodging properties in the United States, Canada, Japan, South Korea, Brazil, Panama, Venezuela, and Peru. As the lodging industry propelled itself into the 21st century, LodgeNet, a specialized communications company, would continue to invest in its internal resources and pursue complementary partnerships to ensure hoteliers the technology and programming that guests demanded.

Principal Subsidiaries

Global Interactive Communications Corporation.

Principal Divisions

PRIMESTAR by LodgeNet.

Further Reading

''AT&T and LodgeNet to Provide Hotels and Guests with High-Speed 'Plug and Play' Internet Access,'' *PR Newswire,* March 10, 1999, p. 2382.

''AT&T Inks Net Access Deal with LodgeNet,'' *Content Factory,* March 11, 1999, p. 1008069u3464.

''Daniel Brooking,'' *Television Digest,* February 17, 1997, p. 19.

''Denver Votes to Subsidize Adam's Mark Hotel Enhancement,'' *Travel Weekly,* August 21, 1995, p. 20.

''Hotel Room Interactive TV,'' *Television Digest,* March 29, 1993, p. 18.

''Internet Inn,'' *PC Magazine,* May 27, 1997, p. 9.

''John M. O'Haugherty,'' *Broadcasting,* January 6, 1992, p. 116.

McConville, Jim, ''TCI Takes Stake in LodgeNet; Will Invest $40 Million in DTH Service to Apartments,'' *Broadcasting & Cable,* October 28, 1996, p. 86.

Veilleux, C. Thomas, ''Primestar's Extending Its Service,'' *HFN,* January 15, 1996, p. 191.

Waxler, Caroline, ''Movie Blues,'' *Forbes,* June 16, 1997, p. 270.

Weinstein, Jeff, ''Will Guests Have Time to Sleep, Too?,'' *Hotels,* February 1995, p. 46.

Whitford, Marty, ''High-Speed Access Gains Ground,'' *Hotel & Motel Management,* February 15, 1999, p. 3.

Wolff, Carlo, ''A Garden of Digital Delights,'' *Lodging Hospitality,* December 1994, p. 87.

Worcester, Barbara A., ''Saying Good-Bye to Industry Giants,'' *Hotel & Motel Management,* April 20, 1998, p. 26.

—Daryl F. Mallett

Logitech International SA

Moulin du Choc D
CH-1122
Romanel-sur-Morges
Switzerland
(41) 21 863 5111
Fax: (41) 21 863 5311
Web site: http://www.logitech.com

Public Company
Incorporated: 1981 as Metaphor Inc.
Employees: 2,700
Sales: $390.2 million (1998)
Stock Exchanges: Zurich NASDAQ
Ticker Symbol: LOGIY
NAIC: 334119 Mouse Devices, Computer Peripheral
   Equipment, Manufacturing

Logitech International SA is the world's leading manufacturer of computer input and interface products, ranging from computer mice to joysticks and computer keyboards. Logitech supplies original equipment manufacturer (OEM) products to 18 of the 20 leading computer manufacturers, including Apple, Hewlett Packard, Dell, Packard Bell, Acer, IBM, Toshiba, Compaq, Vobis Microcomputer, and Siemens Nixdorf Information Systems. Logitech is based in Switzerland, where the company operates its research and development facilities and financial operations; a second headquarters, in Fremont California, keeps the company close to the Silicon Valley scene.

Some 90 percent of Logitech's sales come from its range of control devices. These include the company's line of computer mouse devices, trackballs, and touchpads, as well as joysticks and other gaming interface equipment for the consumer and OEM markets. The company also manufactures and/or distributes 3D controllers for both professional and consumer/entertainment markets, including its 6DOF (''six degrees of freedom'') controller—a product originally developed for the computer-aided design (CAD) market, but that, with increasing processing power available to consumer computers, is being adapted to the computer gaming market. Another 3D device is the Magellan mouse (known as the Space Mouse in Europe), developed by Germany's Space Control GmbH; in 1998 Logitech, which had distributed Space Control's 3D controller to the CAD/CAM/CAE market in the United States since 1993, acquired a 49 percent equity stake in Space Control, with an option to increase its ownership position to 100 percent by the year 2001. Logitech also manufactures computer keyboards, especially in conjunction with its cordless mouse, to provide a wireless desktop.

Pointing the Way to the Future in the 1980s

One of the most important inventions for ''personalizing'' computers was that of the computer mouse. Developed by computer visionary and pioneer Douglas C. Engelbart, a new computer input device made its debut in 1963 at the Stanford Research Institute. Engelbart continued to refine the concept, and by 1968 Engelbart's team made the first public presentation of the device—by then dubbed the ''mouse''—at the 1968 American Federation of Information Processing Societies' Fall Joint Computer Conference at San Francisco.

Engelbart's mouse would change the course of computing history and would launch Logitech as a company a decade later. The first commercial presentation of the mouse also would present the first ''windows''-type graphical user interface, which, controlled by the mouse, would enable the computer to become accessible for individual and home use, and not the private domain of highly trained programmers. In conjunction with the mouse, Engelbart would introduce such basic computer concepts as the onscreen combining and manipulating of text and graphics, hypertext and hyperdocuments (which would become extremely important for later Internet development), and videoconferencing. Engelbart's place in the computer industry of the 1960s and 1970s was highlighted by his office's position as the second node of the ARPAnet, which would later become the Internet.

Engelbart also proved an inspiration for a new generation of engineers and computer industry developers, including two

---

Company Perspectives:

Logitech's objective is to become the leading provider of human interface devices in the growing mass consumer market. As computing, communications and consumer electronics continue to create new product categories, the Company intends to provide affordable, user-friendly interface solutions, supplying consumers with maximum comfort and control. Logitech intends to meet these objectives by capitalizing on its technological innovations, brand image, customer relationships and manufacturing capabilities.

Stanford University engineering students, Daniel Borel, from Switzerland, and Pierluigi Zappacosta, from Italy. Inspired by the burgeoning Silicon Valley scene, Borel and Zappacosta decided to set up their own company to produce software products. The partners hoped to bring the same sense of entrepreneurship that they had found in California to the European computer industry.

In contrast to the United States, where high-tech companies could find a vast pool of venture capital and other financial backing, especially for the development of computer technology and products, the European situation in the late 1970s remained fixed on an older corporate model. Unable to find the venture capital that they needed, and with no banks willing to risk a multimillion-dollar load, Borel and Zappacosta were forced to place their dream of starting their own software company on hold.

Engelbart's invention would change the pair's direction. As Zappacosta told *Fortune:* "We didn't want to be in mice. They seemed to be beneath our intelligence. We wanted to be a software company—like Microsoft." Nonetheless, it was with the computer mouse that Borel and Zappacosta finally would go into business. In 1981 the pair acquired the U.S. distribution rights for a mouse designed in Switzerland. Hardware proved an easier investment sell than the pair's software dream. With the backing of a number of Swiss investors, Borel and Zappacosta set up the company that would later become known as Logitech. Originally operating from a "garage" shop, the company was established with headquarters in Switzerland, but with a strong U.S. presence from the start.

Borel and Zappacosta's timing was fortuitous. In 1982 Steve Jobs, of the rising computer star Apple, made the decision to incorporate Engelbart's mouse in the company's computer systems. The decision would revolutionize the computer industry, paving the way for the first truly "personal" computers. Other computer designs would soon adopt the mouse as well. Borel and Zappacosta, originally scornful of the mouse, quickly discovered the device's interest, as well as its possibilities. They continued to make improvements in the design and manufacturing methods.

Logitech (the company would not adopt this name until 1988) at first produced mice for the Apple computer systems. As other manufacturers began producing mice-controlled com-

puter interfaces, Logitech's mice were adapted for these systems, too. For the distribution of its products, Logitech was unable to afford the retail path. Instead, the company took out ads in the growing number of computer and other electronic technology magazines, newspapers, and trade journals.

Logitech also would find a new boost as an OEM. In the early 1980s the company was contracted by Hewlett Packard (HP) to produce mice for that company's computer systems. The HP contract placed Logitech—then known as Metaphor—on the computer peripherals map. Soon after, the company signed contracts with AT&T, Olivetti, Convergent Technologies, DEC, and others. Apple, which was in the process of launching the breakthrough Macintosh computer systems, soon would turn to Logitech for its computer mouse needs as well. Around this time, Logitech also introduced the first "cordless" mouse, a product that would forecast the growing demand for the wireless desktop in the late 1990s.

Logitech expanded rapidly. In the mid-1980s it began increasing its manufacturing capacity, with plants in California and Ireland, and in 1988, a new plant in Taiwan. The launch of production in that facility enabled Logitech to take on its largest client to date: IBM and its personal computer range, which had already succeeded in defining an industry standard for personal computing. In that year, Logitech incorporated under the name Logitech International SA, trading on the Zurich stock exchange.

Market Leader in the 1990s

By then Logitech had moved into the retail channel, with the launch of its C7 mouse. A square-shaped mouse in marked contrast to the "ergonomic" designs of the late 1990s, the C7 nonetheless featured the three-button design that would become something of a Logitech hallmark. Throughout the late 1980s and early 1990s Logitech continued to build its position in the computer market. A 1991 joint venture agreement brought the company to mainland China, reinforcing its manufacturing position, while also bringing additional funding from both the Chinese government and from Hong Kong.

Logitech also was branching out. A 1990 deal gave the company a share of Canada's Advanced Gravis, a maker of joysticks as well as pointing devices, including a Mouse Stick, for the variety of computer systems available at the time—including the Amiga, Atari, Tandy, and other systems. In 1991 Logitech increased its share in Advanced Gravis to 58 percent, giving Logitech seats on Advanced Gravis's board of directors.

In that same year Logitech made another significant acquisition, buying up 50 percent of Gazelle Graphics Systems, of California. The company would acquire full ownership of Gazelle in 1993, giving Logitech control of Gazelle's innovative trackball technology, which soon would become an important feature of the growing portable computer market. The introduction of new three-dimensional pointing technology, initially developed by NASA, brought Logitech into the high-end graphics market, with its Magellan 3D pointer for Silicon Graphics and other high-end CAD/CAM/CAE workstations. The Magellan, developed in conjunction with Germany's Space Control, would be dubbed the Space Mouse for the European market.

Not all of Logitech's investments were successful. In 1993, for example, the company joined with cable television giant TCI in an investment in Virtual I/O, a Seattle-based maker of a three-dimensional computer display headset. This product, however, proved to be a bit ahead of its time. The company also attempted to enter the soundcard market, with, among other products, its SoundMan speaker system. The company's sound products failed to move the computer industry, which was just beginning to adopt another soundcard technology, the Soundblaster, as a de facto standard.

Meanwhile, Logitech had begun to look beyond the pointing device and joystick market. In the mid-1990s the company attempted to enter two more promising markets: scanners and digital cameras. Logitech would achieve some early success in the scanner market, with its handheld and sheetfed scanner designs. Yet Logitech was far from alone in entering this market, which soon was flooded with products from a large number of competing businesses. A price war broke out, severely cutting into Logitech's profit margins. Worse for Logitech, the market clearly shifted away from the sheetfed design to the flatbed design. By the late 1990s Logitech's scanner division was losing money heavily. The company faced a similar situation in the digital camera market. The entry of such major manufacturing names as Sony, Philips, and others into the digital camera market forced Logitech into the niche player position of that market.

The company's financial troubles, exacerbated by an extended economic crisis both in the United States and in Europe, forced Logitech to reorganize its operations in 1995. The company closed its U.S. and Ireland manufacturing facilities, moving production entirely to China and Taiwan, while cutting some 500 jobs.

Logitech, which had posted revenues of more than US$300 million in 1994, also was facing new competition in its core product line—and from the most fearsome competitor of all. In the mid-1990s the Microsoft Corporation was branching out into computer peripherals, launching its own mouse products and joysticks. Given its near-monopoly position in the worldwide personal computer market, Microsoft was able to impose itself quickly on the pointer market, taking some 40 percent of it. Logitech, which had been earning margins up to 50 percent on its pointing products, was forced to cut its prices to compete with the software giant. Nonetheless, Logitech was able to maintain its leadership position, particularly as the leading OEM mouse supplier, with customers including 18 of the world's 20 largest computer manufacturers.

Logitech's restructuring would cost the company some US$20 million in 1995; by 1996, however, the company had once again been restored to profitability—in time to celebrate the production of its 100 millionth mouse. Once again regrouped around its pointing devices, Logitech would quickly double that figure, announcing the production of its 200 millionth mouse in December 1998. The company's scanner division was sold off in 1997 to Storm Technology, a deal that also gave Storm a ten percent investment in Logitech.

Since its origins, Logitech had been headed by Daniel Borel and Pierluigi Zappacosta, who had shared CEO and other duties. In 1998, however, Borel retired to the position of company chairman. Logitech brought in Guerrino De Luca, a former executive at Apple Computer and architect of Apple's Claris division's success. De Luca, who had served as CEO of Claris and had once been pegged for the top Apple spot as well, resigned from Apple with the return of company founder Steve Jobs to its leadership. De Luca moved quickly to enhance Logitech's image beyond that of a mouse and joystick maker to that of the leading computing interface company.

One of De Luca's first acts was the acquisition of the QuickCam digital camera division from Connectix Corporation. The QuickCam had been one of the first digital video cameras designed for easy incorporation into a personal computing system. Introduced in the mid-1990s, the distinctive QuickCam—shaped much like an eyeball—had captured the industry's lead. The rise of the Internet—and the appearance of faster modem and other data transfer technologies, including satellite and cable internet access—had made videoconferencing technology viable. Many industry analysts expected to see a boom in digital video camera sales for the end of the century.

In addition to the QuickCam purchase—which, by late 1998, resulted in three new Logitech-signed QuickCam products—Logitech purchased a ten percent interest in Immersion Corporation, pioneer of "force feedback" technologies, designed to enhance user interactivity with games, Internet, and other computer applications. In early 1999 Logitech also debuted several new products, including its next-generation mouse designs, such as the Gaming Mouse, developed specifically for computer strategy and FPS (first-person shooter) games. Logitech continued to make revenue advancement, topping the US$400 million mark for 1998. Although mouse sales continued to represent some 75 percent of these sales, Logitech's moves into the broader interface market were expected to maintain its position as one of the world's leading computer peripherals manufacturers.

Further Reading

Buckler, Grant, "Advanced Gravis, Logitech Complete Deal," *Newsbytes News Network,* May 9, 1991.

Joseph, Cliff, "De Luca's Peripheral Vision," *Independent,* September 21, 1998, p. 14.

"Logitech: 40 million de mulots," *Les Echoes,* May 18, 1998, p. 67.

"Logitech Mice Reach 100 Million," *Newsbytes News Network,* April 15, 1996.

Nulty, Peter, "Logitech International," *Fortune,* November 11, 1994, p. 116.

Olenick, Doug, and Steve Koenig, "Connectix Opts Out of Videoconferencing Market—Logitech Moves to Acquire QuickCam Line for $25 Million," *Computer Retail Weekly,* August 17, 1998, p. 2.

—M. L. Cohen

MacAndrews & Forbes Holdings Inc.

35 East 62nd Street
New York, New York 10021
U.S.A.
(212) 688-9000
Fax: (212) 572-8400

Private Company
Incorporated: 1984
Employees: 29,854
Sales: $6.07 billion (1997 est.)
NAIC: 32562 Toilet Preparation Manufacturing; 333991
Power-Driven Handtool Manufacturing; 335211
Electric Housewares & Household Fan
Manufacturing; 336612 Boat Building; 33992
Sporting & Athletic Goods Manufacturing; 52212
Savings Institutions; 555112 Offices of Other Holding
Companies

MacAndrews & Forbes Holdings Inc. is the company that holds the assets of Ronald Owen Perelman. Starting in 1978 with a loan of less than $2 million, Perelman assembled a portfolio that, in little more than a decade, made him one of the wealthiest individuals in the country. Perelman used the tools so popular in the 1980s—including hostile takeovers, leveraged buyouts, and junk bonds—to establish and expand his personal empire. He continued dealing at a frenetic pace in the 1990s, most prominently in collecting and then disposing of media companies. In 1998 he held, through MacAndrews & Forbes, substantial interests in a number of operating companies, including Revlon Group Inc., First Nationwide Holdings Inc., and Sunbeam Corporation.

Erecting an Empire: 1978–89

The eldest son of a wealthy Philadelphia businessman, Perelman studied business administration at the University of Pennsylvania's Wharton School before becoming an executive in his father's company, Belmont Industries. Working for this conglomerate proved an ideal training ground for what the younger Perelman would do so well: create personal wealth by purchasing undervalued companies, paying for the acquisitions by selling underperforming segments of these businesses.

Since his father showed no foreseeable desire to retire, Perelman, at the age of 35, resigned his post in 1978 to pursue his career in New York City. He brought with him his first wife's fortune as well as his own considerable savings. Perelman's initial move was to purchase, for $1.9 million borrowed from a bank, a 40 percent interest in Cohen-Hatfield Industries, a jewelry business. He sold all the company's operations except the most profitable one, its wholesale watch distribution division, and, after repaying the purchase price, pocketed a $15 million profit.

Next Perelman purchased, in 1980, MacAndrews & Forbes Co., a firm dating from 1850 that was the world's leading manufacturer of licorice extract, sold principally to the tobacco industry for flavoring in cigarettes. The company also was a bulk chocolate wholesaler. The purchase, for about $45.7 million, was made through Cohen-Hatfield, which was then merged into what became MacAndrews & Forbes Group Inc. A consortium of banks provided $35 million for the acquisition and was repaid with the proceeds from selling high-yield company bonds. Perelman sold the chocolate part of the business in 1986 for about $45 million.

In January 1983 Perelman purchased Technicolor Inc., the company whose photo color process had long been used in motion pictures, for $102 million plus the assumption of $17 million in debt. This acquisition challenged MacAndrews & Forbes's own creditworthiness, but Perelman quickly sold five divisions, reducing the cost of the purchase by $68 million. Aided by the advent of multiplex theaters, Technicolor, like other film processors, soon entered a boom period; in 1988 Perelman sold his controlling interest in the company to Carlton Communications for $780 million. Perelman bought 20 percent of a similar firm, Compact Video Inc., in 1983 for $12.5 million realized from the sale of Technicolor divisions and by the end of 1987 had raised the MacAndrews & Forbes stake in this company to 40 percent.

Perelman's first wife sued for divorce in 1983, claiming part ownership of everything her husband owned. To protect his assets, Perelman announced he would take MacAndrews &

Forbes Group private by making it a subsidiary of newly formed MacAndrews & Forbes Holdings Inc. The new company, installed in Perelman's East Side Manhattan townhouse, borrowed against its assets to buy the 66 percent of the shares of MacAndrews & Forbes Group that Perelman did not own. Nine separate shareholder suits were fielded against the plan, but the company became fully his in March 1984.

To finance the assumption of $52.7 million in debt, Perelman turned to Michael Milken, the Drexel Burnham Lambert financier who would soon become famous as Wall Street's junk-bond king. Since angry MacAndrews & Forbes shareholders were unwilling to accept company bonds—even high-yield ones—for their stock, Milken agreed to sell the bonds to Drexel clients for cash that was used to pay off the stockholders. It was a tactic that Perelman and Milken would use over and over again.

MacAndrews & Forbes Holdings quickly took on new debt by purchasing Consolidated Cigar Holdings Ltd., the largest U.S. cigar producer, from Gulf & Western Industries in 1984 for $124 million, only $15 million of it in cash. Also in 1984, Perelman bought a controlling interest in Video Corporation of America, a tape duplication and stage rental firm, for $33.3 million, putting it under the Technicolor banner.

Perelman next took aim on Pantry Pride Inc., a poorly run retailer whose attraction was tax-loss carryovers totaling at least $330 million that could be used to offset income from profitable MacAndrews & Forbes holdings. A $60 million purchase of preferred stock gave him effective control of this company in June 1985. Within months, all three chains under the corporate umbrella were liquidated, leaving Pantry Pride a corporate shell for Perelman's biggest target yet: Revlon.

Assembling $761 million worth of high-interest bonds underwritten by Milken and a $500 million bank loan, Perelman attempted, through Pantry Pride, a takeover of the world famous cosmetic company, which was also engaged in pharmaceuticals and health and eye care. Revlon's management fought the offer furiously but eventually capitulated, in October 1985. The price was heavy: at least $2.7 billion, when factoring in debt refinancing, income taxes, severance pay, and compensation for lawyers and investment bankers. Pantry Pride disappeared in 1986, becoming Revlon Group, Inc. The following year Perelman took the company private, selling newly issued MacAndrews & Forbes junk bonds through Drexel Burnham Lambert to buy out the other shareholders for $784 million.

While keeping the cosmetics division intact, Perelman already had sold two Revlon divisions for a total of more than $1 billion. In 1987 he sold Revlon's vision care business for $574 million more. Another Revlon division, National Health Laboratories, became a separate public company in 1988. Perelman also beefed up Revlon by purchasing cosmetic lines such as Max Factor in 1987 for a total of $500 million and Betrix, a German firm, for $170 million in 1989. The cigar-smoking magnate sold a division of Consolidated Cigar for $45 million in 1986 and the rest of the company for $128 million in 1988.

His appetite whetted by the Revlon acquisition, Perelman attempted a hostile takeover of The Gillette Company in 1986, offering $4.12 billion for the company. After pocketing a profit of at least $34 million in selling back to management his 16

percent share of its stock (a payoff critics called ''greenmail''), Perelman made three more offers for Gillette in 1987, raising his bid to $5.7 billion before giving up in the face of management's continued resistance. Perelman also made unsuccessful bids for TV Services and CPC International, then quit attempting hostile takeovers. Instead he began refinancing his junk-bond debt with lower-cost bank loans. Writing in 1990, syndicated columnist Allan Sloan, a persistent critic, acknowledged, ''Perelman . . . was smart enough to use junk bond financing to make his fortune and also smart enough to jump off the junk bandwagon before it crashed.''

MacAndrews & Forbes Holdings entered a new area in December 1988, when it agreed to invest $315 million (of which only $171 million was its own cash) in five troubled Texas savings and loan association units. The deciding factor for Perelman was a federal government guarantee of $5 billion to cover future losses over the next ten years. The transaction also allowed him to apply the net operating losses (estimated at $900 million to $1.2 billion) of the acquired institutions, which were consolidated as First Gibraltar Bank, to reduce the taxes of any of his profitable businesses. A sixth Texas savings and loan was added in 1990. MacAndrews & Forbes held 80 percent of First Gibraltar in 1991.

Perelman, who had created Andrews Group Inc. from the corporate shell of the former Compact Video, used this private holding company to purchase Marvel Entertainment Group, holder of such comic book titles as Spiderman and The Incredible Hulk, for $82.5 million in January 1989. Not long after, Andrews bought Marvel's parent, film and television producer New World Entertainment Inc., for Andrews Group for between $120 million and $145 million. Andrews, according to Sloan, arguably was being used as a ''corporate toxic waste dump for unwanted and overpriced businesses.'' The company, 57 percent owned by MacAndrews & Forbes Holdings, lost $14.8 million in 1989 and had a negative net worth of $10 million. Three shareholders suits accused him of fraud when, in 1990, he successfully pushed through a buyback plan in which shares were repurchased with junk bonds as payment.

Also in 1989, MacAndrews & Forbes acquired The Coleman Company, Inc., maker of stoves, lanterns, and camping and other recreational equipment, for $545 million. Perelman reduced the debt for this purchase by selling the heating and air-conditioning divisions. By the end of 1990 he had sold everything except Coleman's camping equipment and boat businesses, plus added power tool and recreational vehicle businesses. Between 1993 and late 1995 he bought seven more companies for Coleman.

Institutional Investor's May 1989 issue featured Perelman on its cover and called him ''the richest man in America,'' with a personal fortune approaching $5 billion. *Forbes* ranked him third, estimating his worth at about $3 billion. But Perelman's empire was shaky, according to some writers. *Forbes's* Gretchen Morgenson estimated in 1990 that the assets of MacAndrews & Forbes Holdings exceeded its debts by only $1.3 billion.

Focus on Media Companies: 1990–95

Perelman enhanced his financial position in 1991 by selling Revlon's Max Factor line and Betrix label to Procter & Gamble

Company for $1.14 billion, taking Marvel Entertainment public (and selling about 30 percent of the stock), and selling most of his National Health Laboratories stock. In 1995 National Health Laboratories, in which Perelman still held 24 percent of the stock, was merged with Roche Biomedical, another large clinical laboratory, to become Laboratory Corporation of America.

By mid-1992 Perelman was shopping for more companies. In September of that year he purchased, for Andrews Group, trading card and bubblegum company Fleer Corporation, for $265 million. The following year he purchased 46 percent of Toy Biz, Inc. for $7 million. Also folded into Andrews Group, in 1993, was SCI Television, a bankrupt station owner with $1.3 billion in debt for which Perelman paid $100 million in cash in return for a 54 percent stake. Half-ownership of Genesis Entertainment, a television syndicator, was placed into Andrews Group's New World Entertainment unit.

After MacAndrews & Forbes sold 130 First Gibraltar Bank branches to BankAmerica Corporation for $110 million in 1992, Perelman's profit on his savings and loan transactions may have exceeded $1.2 billion. In 1994 Perelman used nearly $500 million in tax credits to buy California's First Nationwide Bank, the nation's fifth largest savings institution, in a deal valued at $1.1 billion. The transaction was made through Dallas-based First Madison Bank, a savings and loan association founded by Perelman in 1993 with assets left over from the First Gibraltar sale.

Boston Whaler Inc., a boat builder, was sold in 1993 to MacAndrews & Forbes by Reebok International Ltd. for $20 million. Perelman added Coleman divisions and boating brands MasterCraft and Skeeter, plus O'Brian water skis, to this acquisition and created Meridian Sports Holdings as the corporate umbrella for these companies. Also in 1993, Mafco Holdings, Inc., a recently created Perelman company, purchased Consolidated Cigar again, this time for $180 million (of which only $30 million was cash).

New World Entertainment and SCI Television were merged in late 1993 to form New World Communications Group. This merger into a company 54 percent owned by Perelman in mid-1994 and still reporting to Andrews Group allowed New World Entertainment, the television-producing arm, access to the cash generated by the now profitable TV stations. The communications group also included now wholly owned Genesis Entertainment, and Guthy-Renker Corporation, the leading "infomercial producer" in the United States, in which Perelman had bought a minority interest the previous year. Perelman also bought four more TV stations from Great American Communications for $360 million and four from Argyle Television Holdings for $716 million, financing the purchases with the aid of $205 million from a rights offering and $300 million in credits from a group of banks. Since New World now exceeded the legal limit of 12 TV stations, several were sold.

The reorganization of New World included a deal struck with Rupert Murdoch switching nearly all of the New World stations from CBS affiliation to affiliation with Murdoch's Fox Broadcasting Network. Murdoch agreed to invest $500 million in New World in exchange for 20 percent of the stock, to consider New World-produced programming for Fox's lineup,

and to form a joint syndication arm with New World to supply both station groups with programming.

Another Perelman holding company, named Mafco Consolidated Group, was formed to acquire Abex, a manufacturer of aerospace and industrial products, in 1994 for about $200 million. Since Abex was selling its brake friction division to Cooper Industries for $207.4 million, Perelman got the company essentially for nothing. It joined Consolidated Cigar and Mafco Worldwide "Flavors" (previously MacAndrews & Forbes Co.) as divisions of Mafco Consolidated Group, which was at least 80-percent owned by Perelman.

Business Week in 1995 calculated that Perelman had bought, since 1978, 44 companies, creating a highly leveraged empire with a net value of $4.93 billion. According to this magazine, the use of separate holding companies limited the overall enterprise's legal liability in issuing debt, because the debt was secured by the operating companies. The enterprise at the apex of Perelman's pyramided assets was Mafco Holdings, according to *Business Week* and a biography of Perelman, but MacAndrews & Forbes, according to the *Wall Street Journal* and *Barron's*. The operating companies, according to Perelman's critics, were being milked systematically for the benefit of the holding companies. While Perelman was said to pay his top executives well—each reportedly earning $10 million a year—they were receiving no equity, leaving Perelman in total control.

Still Buying and Selling: 1996–98

After years of floundering, Revlon Inc.'s operating income, in 1995, finally exceeded the interest payments on its debts. This enabled Perelman to take the company public in 1996, raising $180 million by selling 15 percent of the shares. New World, on the other hand, was losing money and close to $1 billion in debt. In 1996 Perelman arranged to sell his 37 percent stake in the enterprise to Murdoch's News Corporation for about $2.48 billion in stock and the assumption of $590 million in New World debt. (He had previously sold two stations to NBC for $425 million.) Also in 1996, First Nationwide Holdings Inc. purchased California Federal Bank for $1.2 billion, enabling First Nationwide to create the country's fourth largest savings and loan association, with 242 branches in California, Florida, and Texas. In addition, Perelman sold Mafco Consolidated's licorice and flavorings business for $180 million. Consolidated Cigar went public in that year, but Mafco Consolidated retained 65 percent of the shares.

Perelman's reputation as a manager suffered serious damage from the end of 1996 bankruptcy of Marvel Entertainment. Swelled by lucrative licensing deals, the company's stock was trading at $35 a share at the end of 1993, raising Perelman's stake to a value of $2.8 billion on an original cash investment of $10.5 million. In 1995, however, Marvel went into a nosedive, and the following year it lost $464.4 million. Perelman's attempt to refinance the company was frustrated by its bondholders, notably rival entrepreneur Carl Icahn, who rejected the reorganization plan, which called for the creditors to take a substantial loss. Perelman then walked away from his investment (which included a 26 percent stake in Toy Biz), allowing it to fall into bankruptcy. Icahn, who won court approval to take it over, in turn lost control of the company and joined the angry Marvel shareholders and bondholders who were suing Perelman.

According to *Barron's,* Perelman's Revlon Worldwide holding company had, in May 1997, almost $2 billion in long-term debt and negative stockholders' equity of almost $1 billion. Nevertheless, Perelman had raised $900 million in February to refinance Revlon debt coming due, and in May he raised $470 million in loans for Coleman. Other debt payments were reported to have been pushed back beyond 2000, leaving Perelman with more than $1 billion available for another acquisition. Revlon, California Federal, and Consolidated Cigar were said to have generated more than $600 million in profits in 1996 yet apparently paid little or nothing in federal tax due to what *Barron's* writer Jacqueline Doherty called "skillful use of holding companies and tax laws."

Mafco Holdings announced in December 1997 that it was acquiring about 72 percent of Panavision Inc., the leading manufacturer and supplier of cameras to the film industry, for about $610 million. Two months later, Perelman's California Federal Bank agreed to purchase Golden State Bancorp Inc. for stock and warrants valued at as much as $2.8 billion. The combined firm, now the nation's third largest thrift institution, would be known as Golden State Bancorp but operate under the name California Federal Bank, with Perelman holding a stake of 30 to 33 percent.

In March 1998 Perelman sold his 82 percent share of Coleman to Sunbeam Corporation for stock valued at $590 million to $643 million, plus $160 million in cash. To protect his 14 percent investment in the troubled appliance manufacturer, whose stock value dropped 80 percent on news that it might have overstated its 1997 sales, he took over management of the company in June. By mid-August, Perelman's stock was worth only $72 million. Sunbeam owed creditors about $2.2 billion, including $500 million to one of Perelman's holding companies.

The Marvel and Sunbeam fiascos clearly took a toll on Perelman's fortune. In *Forbes'*s October 1998 ranking of the richest Americans, he dropped out of the top 10, with an estimated $6 billion, compared to $6.5 billion in the October 1997 listing, when he was ranked in eighth place. Before the year was out, Perelman again sold Consolidated Cigar, this time for $531 million, almost three times what he paid in 1993. The buyer was a French company, Selta S.A.

Further Reading

Bryant, Adam, "Pow! The Punches That Left Marvel Reeling," *New York Times,* May 24, 1998, Sec. 3, pp. 1, 10.

Doherty, Jacqueline, "Bulletproof Billionaire?" *Barron's,* May 19, 1997, pp. 18, 20.

Furman, Phyllis, "Perelman's Tangled Web," *Crain's New York Business,* April 28, 1997, pp. 1, 40–44.

Hack, Richard, *When Money Is King,* Los Angeles: Dove Books, 1996.

Harris, Kathryn, "Broadcasting's Creators of a New World," *Los Angeles Times,* June 18, 1994, pp. D1–D2.

Laing, Jonathan R., "Now It's Ron's Turn," *Barron's,* October 12, 1998, pp. 31–32, 34–35.

Morgenson, Gretchen, "The Perils of Perelman," *Forbes,* December 10, 1990, pp. 218–20, 222.

Nathans, Leah J., "Perelman Is No Superhero to Investors at Andrews," *Business Week,* July 23, 1990, pp. 57–58.

Pollock, Ellen Joan, and Brannigan, Martha, "The Sunbeam Shuffle, or How Ron Perelman Wound Up in Control," *Wall Street Journal,* August 19, 1998, pp. A1, A8.

Ramirez, Anthony, "The Raider Who Runs Revlon," *Fortune,* September 14, 1987, pp. 57–63.

Sloan, Allan, "How Perelman Pocketed a Cool $1.2 Billion on Sale of S&Ls," *Los Angeles Times,* September 27, 1992, p. D5.

——, "Perelman Deal on Andrews Is for Brave Only," *Los Angeles Times,* May 28, 1990, p. D5.

Smith, Randall, and Wessel, David, "New Look: The '80s Are Over, and Ron Perelman Positions Himself As an Industrialist, Not a Raider," *Wall Street Journal,* March 27, 1990, pp. A1, A10.

Spiro, Leah Nathans, and Grover, Ronald, "The Operator," *Business Week,* August 21, 1995, pp. 54–60.

—Robert Halasz

⋀⋁ Mail-Well

Mail-Well, Inc.

23 Inverness Way East, Suite 160
Englewood, Colorado 80112-5713
U.S.A.
(303) 790-8023
Fax: (303) 397-7400
Web site: http://www.mail-well.com

Public Company
Incorporated: 1994
Employees: 13,000
Sales: $1.50 billion (1998)
Stock Exchanges: New York
Ticker Symbol: MWL
NAIC: 322232 Envelope Manufacturing; 322233
   Stationery, Tablet, & Related Product Manufacturing;
   323110 Commercial Lithographic Printing; 323119
   Other Commercial Printing

Within what it calls the "highly fragmented printing industry," Mail-Well, Inc. has been a leading consolidator. From its incorporation as Mail-Well in February 1994 through early 1999, the company made more than 40 acquisitions, increasing its revenues from $260 million to $1.5 billion. Through these purchases, Mail-Well has built up significant businesses in four areas: commercial printing, in which it offers printing products and services within the general printing market; envelopes, in which it is the largest maker and printer of envelopes in North America, serving the direct mail, corporate, and retail office product markets; labels, in which it is a leading supplier of glue-on paper labels and graphic services to the food, beverage, and household products industries in North America; and printing for distributors, in which it is the top supplier of custom business documents, pressure-sensitive labels, envelopes, and commercial printing to the U.S. distributor market. Mail-Well has more than 110 printing plants in the United States, Canada, and Mexico, and has, since mid-1999, established a presence in Europe.

Rocky Mountain Roots

The roots of Mail-Well's main predecessor company can be traced back to the 1919 founding in Denver, Colorado, of Rocky Mountain Envelope Co., which was the first consumer envelope manufacturer in that city. The cofounders were Carl L. Tucker and Willett R. Lake, transplanted Missourians, who led the company into the 1960s. During the 1920s, when Denver experienced rapid growth, the company changed its name to Rockmont Envelope Co. in order to distinguish itself from the growing number of firms that had included "Rocky Mountain" in their names. Early on, Rockmont began branding its envelopes with the trademark "Mail-Well."

Rockmont grew steadily over the years, and by the late 1950s had a 100,000-square-foot manufacturing plant in Denver, as well as additional plants in Houston, Los Angeles, and Portland, Oregon. Rockmont also had scattered around the country seven warehouses which served the company's customers in the entire continental United States. With a workforce exceeding 500, Rockmont made all manner of envelopes, ranging from an inch square to a yard wide by 45 inches long. The company had also made modest moves into the manufacture of low-cost stationery, which was sold in supermarkets and drugstores, and of specially designed paper bags for department stores.

In 1960 Rockmont diversified into the production of school supplies, offering a full line of typing paper, filler paper, notebooks, spiral-bound theme books, memo pads, and tablets. By this time the company was one of the largest manufacturers of envelopes in the United States. The company structure had also changed by the early 1960s, as Rockmont Envelope became a subsidiary of Pak-Well Paper Industries, Inc., a Colorado holding corporation headed by Tucker and Lake. In early 1963 Pak-Well was taken public through the sale of 153,620 shares of common stock at $11.50 per share. Pak-Well had revenues of more than $13 million in 1962, and operated plants in Denver, Portland, Houston, Phoenix, Los Angeles, Salt Lake City, and Honolulu.

By the early 1970s, sons of the cofounders had taken over management of Pak-Well, with Richard B. Tucker serving as president and Willett R. Lake, Jr., in the position of chairman. The company posted net earnings of $1.74 million on sales of $53.8 million in 1973.

The road from the early 1970s to the emergence of Mail-Well in 1994 is a rather sketchy one, but Pak-Well eventually fell into the hands of paper company Great Northern Nekoosa Corporation. Pak-Well then became part of Georgia-Pacific Corporation when that paper giant acquired Great Northern for $4.5 billion in 1990. By the early 1990s what was once the diversified Pak-Well had become strictly an envelope maker operating under the Mail-Well Envelopes and Wisco Envelopes names.

Creation of Mail-Well, Inc., 1994

The early 1990s saw many paper companies exit from the envelope business because profits in that sector had been eroded by postage increases, new technologies, and changes in the customer base. Around this same time, Gerald F. Mahoney had entered the world of entrepreneurship by purchasing a small, one-plant manufacturer of envelopes called Pavey Envelope and Tag Corp. Mahoney had previously served as CFO and in other positions at a number of companies, including a one-time *Fortune* 500 firm that grew very fast through acquisitions before downsizing itself through the spinning off of a number of operations. Mahoney joined with some partners with leveraged buyout experience to form the Houston-based Sterling Group Inc. After Georgia-Pacific decided to exit from envelope making, it reached a deal with Sterling to sell its envelope business for $155.1 million. Sterling also purchased—for $4.4 million—Pavey, which it merged with the Georgia-Pacific envelope business in February 1994 to create Mail-Well, with Mahoney serving as chairman and CEO.

Mail-Well was launched with 16 manufacturing plants that had produced about 13 billion envelopes during 1993. It also began with debt of $142 million and equity of only $17 million. Mahoney's plan for Mail-Well was clear from the start: he aimed for it to be a major consolidator within a highly fragmented industry. Envelope makers typically served customers within local or regional areas. By growing through acquisition and gaining additional manufacturing and distribution operations, Mail-Well would still be able to serve regional customers

but would benefit from economies of scale. Mahoney also reasoned that larger corporations with operations in different regions of the country might prefer dealing with a single envelope supplier that had plants located in each of those regions, rather than having to contract with several different suppliers.

Mahoney's first major acquisition came in December 1994 when Mail-Well paid $97.4 million to purchase American Envelope Company, which had annual revenues of $180 million, from CC Industries. The purchase increased the number of plants to 29 and the number of employees to 4,200, and made Mail-Well the largest envelope manufacturer in the United States. Next, Mail-Well gobbled up Supremex, Inc. for $65.5 million in July 1995. Supremex was the largest envelope maker in Canada, with revenues of $90 million and 11 manufacturing facilities.

Mail-Well's next move was to create a second leg for the company to stand on. In August 1995 it entered the field of commercial printing through the $82.6 million acquisition of Graphic Arts Center, Inc., a leading West Coast-based printer of "high-impact" documents, such as car brochures and annual reports. By this time the company's debt load had reached $370 million, while equity had increased only to $33 million, so Mahoney in September 1995 took the company public on the NASDAQ, raising $64 million through the IPO. Mail-Well's debt was thus reduced to $310 million, while its equity grew to $100 million. For 1995 the company posted net income of $8 million on net sales of $596.8 million.

The acquisitions in 1996 were more modest ones, but fit into the company strategy of pursuing small commercial printers and envelope printers in geographic areas not already served by Mail-Well. In April 1996 Mail-Well spent $28 million for Quality Park Products, Inc., a Pennsylvania-based printer of envelopes for the office products market, a fast-growing segment and a new area for Mail-Well. In November of that year the company increased its share of the Canadian envelope market to more than 50 percent with the $20 million acquisition of Ontario-based Pac National Group Products, Inc. And one month later, Mail-Well's high-impact commercial printing sector was bolstered through the $20 million purchase of Indianapolis-based Shepard Poorman Communications Corporation, a specialist in calendars and computer instruction books. Net sales increased by more than 30 percent in 1996, reaching $778.5 million, while net income more than doubled to $16.9 million. In December 1996 Mail-Well's stock moved from the NASDAQ to the New York Stock Exchange.

Added Third and Fourth Legs in 1997 and 1998

During 1997 Mail-Well spent about $87 million to acquire six more companies, including envelope maker Griffin Envelopes Inc., based in Seattle, and several firms in the commercial printing field—Seattle-based Allied Printers, Atlanta-based National Color Graphics, Inc., and Western Graphics Communications, headquartered in Cambridge, Maryland. The most significant acquisition of the year, however, was that of Murray Envelope Corporation of Hattiesburg, Mississippi. The addition of Murray provided Mail-Well with a third leg, that of printing services for the distributor market. Among the items that Murray supplied to distributors were envelopes, secure documents, pressure-sensitive labels, index tabs, and mailers. Revenues stood at $897.6 million in 1997, with net income growing to $22.2 million.

In January 1998 Paul V. Reilly was named president and chief operating officer of Mail-Well, having previously served as CFO. Also in early 1998 Mail-Well improved its equity base through a secondary stock offering that raised $90 million in capital. During 1998 the company stepped up its acquisitions activity, purchasing 23 more companies for an aggregate $369.5 million in cash, stock, and assumed debt. Three of these acquisitions were particularly significant. The addition in January of Fairhope, Alabama-based Poser Business Forms, Inc., which had annual revenues of $90 million, enhanced Mail-Well's printing for distributors sector. In March Mail-Well gained a fourth leg through the purchase of the label division of Lawson Mardon Packaging Inc. This division, which was based in Toronto, had annual sales of $81 million and was the second largest supplier of glue-on labels in North America, with a special focus on the food and beverage markets. Mail-Well's new label group was bolstered in May with the acquisition of the label division of International Paper, which included one of the most advanced label printing facilities in the United States. The company's third major acquisition of 1998 also came in May when it acquired Los Angeles-based Anderson Lithograph, a $135 million in revenue firm with a reputation as one of the top commercial printers in the country. Also in May Mail-Well merged with seven commercial printing companies through the exchange of common stock worth about $118 million. The largest of these companies was St. Louis-based Color Art, Inc., which had revenues of about $75 million in 1997. In June 1998 Mail-Well's stock split two for one. The host of acquisitions helped push revenues up to $1.5 billion for 1998, a 68 percent increase. Net income, however, fell to $21.7 million, reflecting a $21.8 million charge taken late in the year to restructure the envelope and commercial printing operations, including the closure of three facilities and resulting staff reductions.

Mail-Well was able to smoothly integrate this many companies within a short period mainly because of its hands-off, decentralized management style. Mahoney told the *Denver Business Journal:* "We let them pretty much run the business as they were before and over a period of time the culture evolves as they get to know how we operate." One key imperative eventually absorbed by the acquired companies was Mail-Well's keen attention to cost-containment, particularly through an emphasis on productivity gains.

While the acquisition pace slowed in 1999, Mail-Well made a significant move in the middle of the year when it gained a European beachhead through the $102 million acquisition of Porter Chadburn plc, a publicly traded London-based label manufacturer. Porter Chadburn had revenues of $126 million, 70 percent of which came from the United States, where ten of its 13 plants were located. But the purchase did give Mail-Well its first European operations and moved its label division into the number two position in North America. The company's workforce grew to more than 13,000, while the number of printing prints increased to 110.

By the dawn of the new millennium, Mail-Well had quite rapidly gained top positions within four separate sectors of the $98 billion printing industry. With about 50,000 commercial printers in the United States, more than 7,600 of which had sales in excess of $3 million, Mail-Well still had plenty of opportunities for acquisitive growth. The European printing market was likewise fragmented, and the company was poised to become a key consolidator on that continent as well.

Principal Subsidiaries

Mail-Well I Corporation; Mail-Well Canada Holdings, Inc.; Supremex Inc.; PNG Inc.; Classic Envelope Plus, Ltd (75%); Innova Envelope; Mail-Well Trade Receivables Corp.; Murray Envelope Holdings, Inc.; Murray Envelope Corp.; Barkley, Inc.; N-M Envelope Co., Inc.; Atlantis Index, Inc. (50%); Consolidated Converting Services, Inc. (20%); Graphic Arts Center, Inc.; Mail-Well West, Inc.; Wisco Envelope Corp.; Wisco II, LLC; Wisco III, LLC; Poser Business Forms, Inc.; Mail-Well Label Holdings, Inc.; Mail-Well Label Company (Canada); Mail-Well Label USA, Inc.; Mail-Well Commercial Printing, Inc.; National Graphics Co.; McLaren Morris and Todd Company (Canada); Mail-Well Mexico Holdings, Inc.; Graphic Arts Center de Mexico.

Further Reading

Aven, Paula, "Mail-Well Seals Acquisitions," *Denver Business Journal,* February 26, 1999, pp. 20B+.

Eaton, John, "Investors Take Shine to Mail-Well," *Denver Post,* April 30, 1998, p. C1.

"Growth Story," *Wall Street Corporate Reporter,* January 19–25, 1998.

Haselbush, Willard, "Denver-Made Envelopes Carry America's Mail," *Denver Post,* September 15, 1957, pp. 1E, 3E.

——, "Rockmont Envelope Moving to New Plant," *Denver Post,* June 30, 1963, p. 1D.

——, "Rockmont Only Tip of Pak-Well Iceberg," *Denver Post,* March 24, 1974, p. 67.

"Mail-Well Buys Label-Making Unit," *Pulp and Paper,* April 1998, pp. 19+.

Marsh, Virginia, "Mail-Well Bids £47m for Porter Chadburn," *Financial Times,* March 17, 1999, p. 22.

Mayer, Olivia, "Pushing the Envelope," *Colorado Business Magazine,* March 1998, p. 40.

Narvaes, Emily, "Englewood's Mail-Well, Under New Ownership, Is Buying Other Companies and Expanding Quickly," *Denver Post,* September 7, 1996, p. D1.

"Rockmont Envelope Opens New Building," *Denver Post,* November 6, 1963, p. 35.

Schwartz, Jerry, "Paper Maker Is Selling Off a Major Unit," *New York Times,* December 9, 1993, p. D4.

Smith, Jerd, "Sealed Deal Creates Local Giant: At American Mail-Well, Low Profile Belies Rank As Top Envelope Maker," *Denver Business Journal,* January 13, 1995, p. A1.

Svaldi, Aldo, "Buying Binges Buoy Mail-Well Stock Price," *Denver Business Journal,* May 2, 1997, pp. 3A, 63A.

——, "Mail-Well's Proceeds Will Go to Retire Debt," *Denver Business Journal,* October 13, 1995, p. A10.

—David E. Salamie

Management and Training Corporation

3293 Harrison Boulevard
Ogden, Utah 84403
U.S.A.
(801) 626-2000
Fax: (801) 621-2685
Web site: http://www.mtctrains.com

Private Company
Incorporated: 1980
Employees: 6,000
Sales: $254 million (1998 est.)
NAIC: 62431 Vocational Rehabilitation Services; 561210
    Correctional Facility Operation on a Contract or Fee
    Basis

Management and Training Corporation (MTC) provides an at-risk population with job training programs that include vocational, academic, and social skills. As the largest contractor for the U.S. Department of Labor, MTC runs 27 Job Corps centers and sites that offer vocational training in a variety of programs, such as auto mechanics, office skills, and welding. It also operates job placement services, helping some 9,500 persons find jobs every year. MTC uses its experience in job and academic training to manage ten jails and correctional facilities, mostly in Texas. There inmates may learn English as a second language, anger management, vocational skills, and how to overcome substance abuse problems. The company works with state and local governments to make sure both inmates and communities benefit from their private prison programs. MTC is the nation's third largest company operating private correctional facilities.

Preliminary Developments in the 1960s and 1970s

In the early 1960s many people changed their thinking about poverty in the United States, especially after reading Michael Harrington's 1962 book *The Other America,* which argued that about 50 million ignored Americans were more or less stuck in poverty. "What emerged in the mid-1960s was an almost un-

broken intellectual consensus that the individualist explanation of poverty was altogether outmoded and reactionary,'' wrote Charles Murray in 1984. "Poverty was not the fault of the individual but of the system.''

With that consensus President Lyndon Johnson in 1964 began his War on Poverty with legislation that provided job training and other antipoverty programs. The Job Corps was authorized by the Job Training Partnership Act. In 1965 Morton Thiokol, a Utah-based company most famous for making rocket boosters, became involved in the job training business when it began managing the Clearfield Job Corps Center in Clearfield, Utah.

Entrepreneur Robert Marquardt, Ph.D., headed Morton Thiokol's training effort. He was born in Dayton, Ohio, to two teachers. By the age of eight he was working and learning skills from talented individuals in many fields. He cleaned and repaired furnaces, did yard work, took care of farm animals, raised vegetables and sold them door-to-door, and followed his parents' advice always to work hard and read many books. While in high school in World War II, he hired 17 other students to help in his tree cutting company. In 1944 he volunteered for the Navy and became a gunnery officer/navigator.

In 1950 Marquardt entered Denison University to earn a business degree. Meanwhile, he continued his business ventures, selling sporting goods, sweaters, and perfume. After graduating from Denison, he joined the U.S. Air Force Procurement team as an aerospace salesman/technical representative, which gave him knowledge of contracts, electronics, weapons, and salesmanship. Then he left Air Force Procurement to start his own technical consulting firm representing various companies in their sales negotiations and contracts with the Air Force.

In 1958 Thiokol recruited Marquardt to move from Ohio to Utah to head its sales organization as the company's first vice-president of Thiokol Aerospace Marketing. He traveled widely selling Thiokol products and programs, including propulsion systems used in the Minuteman ICBM and, eventually, the Space Shuttle.

In 1965 Marquardt started Thiokol's Economic Development Operation to run Job Corps centers. He expanded the firm's educational programs for state governments and the federal government's Department of Labor, Bureau of Indian Affairs, Commerce Department, Office of Economic Opportunity, Department of Housing and Urban Development, and Office of Education. In an interview, Marquardt said he was happy to promote education and training, instead of selling weapons systems that could destroy millions of people.

The Job Corps programs targeted disadvantaged youth aged 16 to 24 who needed assistance so they could get a job and be self-sufficient citizens. According to *The United States Government Manual 1997/98,* Job Corps provided ''diagnostic testing of reading and math levels; occupational exploration programs; world of work training; basic education programs; competency-based vocational education programs; counseling and related support services; work experience programs; social skills training; intergroup relations; recreational programs; meals, lodging, and clothing; health care; and child care.''

In addition to the Clearfield center, by the 1970s Thiokol managed the Atlanta, Georgia Job Corps Center; the Charleston, West Virginia Job Corps Center; and the Turner Job Corps Center in Albany, New York. Then a major turning point occurred.

Forming MTC in 1980

In 1980 Morton Thiokol decided to end its Job Corps programs and other low-profit ventures to emphasize its rocket motor production. Dr. Marquardt and others in the firm's Education and Training Division persuaded Morton Thiokol executives to sell the division.

Three others cofounded the Management and Training Corporation, incorporated on December 11, 1980, under the laws of Delaware. Samuel T. Hunter worked nine years with Thiokol before becoming MTC's vice-president in 1980. In 1999 he continued to serve as the company's executive vice-president in charge of training and a member of the Inside Board of Directors. Bernie R. Diamond helped Dr. Marquardt in Thiokol's education division before serving as an MTC vice-president from 1980 to 1998. He also worked as the national director of community relations for Job Corps. In 1999 he remained on MTC's Outside Board of Directors. Jane A. Marquardt, a part-

ner in the Ogden, Utah law firm of Marquardt, Hasenyager & Custen since 1977, served as an MTC director and legal counsel from 1980 to 1999.

In the September 13, 1998 *Salt Lake Tribune,* Bernie Diamond recalled, ''After we convinced them to sell it to us we mortgaged everything to buy it. We were making a big gamble. The government could have cancelled funding for the Job Corps program that year.'' But it did not.

MTC early on organized a distinguished group of directors, including Dr. Terrel H. Bell, President Ronald Reagan's Secretary of Education. Others included Rodney H. Brady, Ph.D., the assistant secretary of the U.S. Department of Health, Education and Welfare from 1970 to 1972 and president of Ogden, Utah's Weber State College from 1978 to 1985. Later Brady became the president/CEO of the Mormon church's Deseret Management Corporation. Another original board member was Robert T. Heiner, who retired in 1991 after ten years as the president, CEO, and chairman of Utah's First Security Bank.

On December 3, 1980 Lynn W. Merrill and Larry Merrill incorporated Meridian Publishing Company, Inc. in Utah. In 1984 its name was changed to Meridian Publishing, Inc., a wholly owned subsidiary of MTC. Scott Marquardt, the son of Robert Marquardt, served as Meridian's president and then in 1991 became MTC's president. MTC spun off Meridian as an independent firm based in Ogden. It published the *Utah Report* for The Economic Development Corporation of Utah.

MTC's Job Corps Operations in the 1990s

Management and Training Corporation in the late 1990s operated 27 Job Corps centers or satellites. In addition to its original four centers, it ran other centers or satellites in Edinburgh, Indiana; Sedro-Wooley, Washington; Chicago; Cincinnati; Cleveland; Dayton, Ohio; Denison, Iowa; Manhattan, Kansas; Honolulu; Makawao, Maui, Hawaii; Kwajalein, Marshall Islands; Indianapolis; San Bernardino, California; Drums, Pennsylvania; Kittrell, North Carolina; Philadelphia; Portland; Washington, D.C.; Lopez, Pennsylvania; Shreveport, Louisiana; Reno, Nevada; Troutdale, Oregon; and Astoria, Oregon.

About 90 percent of Job Corps students lived in center dormitories during their training. MTC offered its students vocational training in accounting, auto mechanics, business and clerical skills, construction trades, culinary arts, welding, health occupations, retail sales, and surveying, as well as training to become opticians and computer service technicians. Some students received academic instruction, whether in English as a second language, high school classes to prepare them for the General Education Development (GED) exam, or local college classes. MTC daily offered more than 6,200 hours of classroom instruction.

In August 1998 President Clinton signed into law the Workforce Investment Act that contained ''all the new rules under which Job Corps will operate,'' according to an article in the Winter 1999 *Job Corps in Action,* a periodical published by Management & Training Corporation. Based on the new law, Job Corps National Director Mary Silva then issued a series of specific challenges. By the year 2000, Job Corps was expected to cut the dropout rate by 20 percent, involve 50 new national and regional employers, and have 75 percent of all graduates earn at least $8 an hour at a full-time job within six to 12 months after their initial placement. Silva also stated, "There is no question that outreach and admissions staff need to reach Hispanics, the fastest growing segment of our population and the one with the largest percentage of youth. The current number of Spanish-speaking staff within Job Corps is insufficient."

Starting in the Private Prison Industry in the 1980s

In 1983 the Corrections Corporation of America (CCA) in Nashville, Tennessee, became the nation's first for-profit company to build and manage prisons and other corrections facilities for local, state, and federal government agencies. For example, CCA in 1984 built a 68,000-square-foot detention center in Houston for far less money and much quicker than typically done by the Immigration and Naturalization Service.

Because of a general crime increase starting in the 1960s, it was not surprising that prisons were busting at the seams by the early 1980s. By June 30, 1985, for example, the nation's federal, state, and local prisons housed 490,000 inmates. The decade of the 1980s would record a 9.1 percent overall growth rate in the number of prisoners.

Thus by late 1985 about two dozen facilities, out of a total of more than 4,000 U.S. jails and prisons, were owned or managed by private firms as a way to relieve the burden on public correctional agencies. "We get so many calls that we don't even have to do any marketing," said an American Corrections Corporation executive in the October 30, 1985 *Financial World*.

That huge demand for prison services led Management and Training Corporation in 1987 to enter the new industry by managing the Eagle Mountain Community Correctional Facility in Desert Center, California. MTC's leaders felt that their experience in job training was a great background that could be used to rehabilitate inmates and prepare them for life after prison.

Some, however, criticized private prisons. For example, the American Bar Association (ABA) in 1986 passed a resolution to halt what it called the "rush toward total privatization" of government facilities until complicated constitutional and economic issues were resolved. In the March 17, 1986 *Fortune*, the ABA's Laurie Robinson expressed her concerns about the possibility of private prisons declaring bankruptcy and abusing prisoners.

MTC Correctional Work in the 1990s

By 1992 state and federal prison overcrowding resulted in courts ordering 45 states to reduce the number of inmates in at least some of their prisons. About this time MTC began operating its second prison: the Marana Community Correctional Treatment Facility in Marana, Arizona.

In August 1995 the company opened its third such facility, the Promontory Community Correctional Center in Draper, Utah, designed to prepare inmates for parole. That prison's 240 inmates arrived within 90 days of their parole dates. At Promontory, inmates received driver's licenses, wrote resumes and found jobs, and started checking accounts.

"I've been very anxious to try it (privatization)," said Utah's Governor Mike Leavitt about his state's first private prison. "It's met all my expectations." The governor pointed out in the September 16, 1995 *Deseret News* that it cost MTC $37 a day to house, train, and feed the Promontory prisoners, but the state would charge $55 to $58 for the same services.

Soon MTC opened four other correctional facilities: Bradshaw State Jail in Henderson, Texas; Dawson State Jail in Dallas, Texas; Garza County Regional Juvenile Center in Post, Texas; and Gregg County Detention Center in Longview, Texas.

In 1998 MTC won a bid in which it replaced CCA as the manager of two Texas prisons, a contract worth $61.5 million over five years. Effective January 1, 1999, MTC managed the Diboll, Texas Correctional Center and the Billy Moore Correctional Center in Overton, Texas. Both were prerelease facilities with at least 500 beds. With the addition of those two Texas prisons, MTC ran ten private prisons across the nation.

In December 1998 Utah state officials sent a request for proposals to four private prison firms that earlier had prequalified to bid during a failed attempt to turn a state women's prison over to the private sector. The four firms—MTC, CCA, Wackenhut, and Cornell Corrections—submitted their bids by March 1999 to build a 500-bed prison.

Meanwhile, the Utah Legislature in 1999 debated several bills concerning private prisons. All four prison firms hired prominent local lobbyists to represent their interests in this public policy dispute.

The need for more Utah facilities came from a 250 percent increase in the state's prison population from 1984 to 1999. FBI statistics indicated Utah's crime rate had risen to ninth in the nation, so the state scrambled in the 1990s to find somewhere to house its mushrooming prisoner population.

In 1999 MTC operated no overseas prisons, although one had been approved but not yet funded in South Africa. MTC also had done some research and consulting work for Canada and New Zealand, but Dr. Marquardt said his firm's focus remained on serving clients in the United States.

Further Reading

Becker, Craig, and Amy Dru Stanley, "The Downside of Private Prisons," *Nation,* June 15, 1985, p. 728.

Burton, Greg, and Judy Fahys, "Lawmakers See Privatized Prisons in the Correction System's Future," *Salt Lake Tribune,* March 3, 1999, p. A8.

Collins, Chris, "Job Corps Successes 'Dubious,' Report Says," *Detroit News,* November 20, 1998, p. A8.

Donaldson, Amy, "Facility Gives Parolees a Chance," *Deseret News,* September 16, 1995.

Edwards, Alan, "Advisers Vote to Unionize at Job Corps," *Deseret News,* March 23, 1996, p. B1.

——, "Discipline Giving Corps Better Image," *Deseret News,* September 30, 1996.

Fields, Gary, "Privatized Prisons Pose Problems Not a Panacea, States Discover, Despite Savings," *USA Today,* November 11, 1996, p. 3A.

Gehrke, Robert, "Legislature Holds the Key to Easing Prison Problems," *Salt Lake Tribune,* February 24, 1999, p. D3.

Mitchell, Lesley, "Ogden Firm Private Prison Innovator," *Salt Lake Tribune,* September 13, 1998, pp. E1, E4.

Murray, Charles, *Losing Ground: American Social Policy, 1950–1980,* New York: Basic Books, 1984.

Mylar, Frank D., "Utah Should Give Private Prisons a Chance," *Deseret News,* February 3, 1999.

Nielsen, John, and H. John Steinbreder, "Second Thoughts on Private Slammers," *Fortune,* March 17, 1986, p. 10.

Seligman, Daniel, "Making Crime Pay," *Fortune,* June 29, 1992, p. 111.

Stevens, Catherine, "Are We Ready for This Growth Industry?," *Financial World,* October 30, 1985.

—David M. Walden

Marie Callender's Restaurant & Bakery, Inc.

1100 Town and Country Road
Suite 1300
Orange, California 92668-4626
U.S.A.
(714) 542-3355
Fax: (714) 542-8078
Web site: http://www.mcpies.com

Private Company
Incorporated: 1964 as Marie Callender's Pie Shops, Inc.
Employees: 10,000
Sales: $270 million (1997 est.)
NAIC: 72211 Full-Service Restaurants; 722211 Limited-
    Service Restaurants

Marie Callender's Restaurant & Bakery, Inc. is one of the largest restaurant and bakery chains in the western United States. Recognized as a premier pie making enterprise, the company's 156 restaurants, 56 franchises, and several smaller operations are located in 13 states and Mexico, namely Arizona, California, Colorado, Idaho, Illinois, Minnesota, Nevada, New Mexico, Oregon, Texas, Utah, Washington, Wisconsin, and Mexico City. Marie Callender's offers customers over 30 varieties of pies, which are baked fresh daily at each restaurant. The company stresses the high level of quality in their products, using real whipped cream, farm-fresh eggs, fruits, and chocolate. The company also offers full dining menus for breakfast (at limited locations), lunch, and dinner.

1948: All-American Pie

Marie Callender's was founded in Long Beach, California, in 1948 when Marie Callender was encouraged by husband, Cal, and son, Don, to pursue the American dream and roll her prodigious pie-making skills into profits. Marie was a South Dakota native who had moved to southern California and married at the age of 17. She worked in the food service industry at a delicatessen prior to making the decision to sell the family car for $700, using the funds to rent a converted World War II Quonset hut that would become the site of the first Marie Callender's bakery. The remaining cash funded a down payment on a small oven, refrigerator, rolling pin, and various baking utensils. Marie was soon in business, baking whole pies for wholesale customers. Seats were removed from a 1936 Ford sedan to make room for the stacks of pies that would be delivered to local restaurants. All three family members worked 13-hour shifts once orders that originally numbered ten per day soon swelled to 40 per day—and within two years, the business had grown to 200 pie requests per day, a volume which necessitated the purchase of a truck and a mixer.

Fifteen years later, the business had grown substantially to the extent that several thousand pies per day were created for several restaurants. Although production had grown considerably by 1963, profits were less than desirable, prompting Don Callender to begin formulating plans for the construction of a retail pie and coffee shop in Orange, California. In that same year the company incorporated and was renamed Marie Callender's Pie Shop, Inc. The retail business at that time sold only whole pies that were made fresh daily, priced at 95 cents apiece. By offering free slices of pie and coffee the new restaurant enticed many new customers. The Marie Callender's formula proved so successful that soon a second small retail shop was opened in La Habra, then another in Anaheim, California.

The company expanded into other menu items in 1969, beginning with hamburgers, ham stacked sandwiches, salads, chili and cornbread, and grew to include a wide variety of homestyle meals. A year later the family-owned business had grown to a chain of 26 restaurants located primarily in southern California. Then a franchise restaurant was opened in Houston and another in Las Vegas. Cal became the full-time financial manager, while Don continued with expansion plans. Don was concerned with creating a comfortable, homey image for the company, one in keeping with the associations people made with home-baked pie. Stylistically, the restaurant interiors imitated a cozy English country decor. Don expressed concern for the integrity of Marie Callender's architectural design, emphasizing that their restaurants should not have a ''cookie cutter'' look or feel, and opted to build businesses that were varied in their architectural ambiance, reflecting a niche between the

Company Perspectives:

Our dedication remains to deliver the freshest and best tasting pies this side of the Mississippi, to each and every customer that passes through our doors. A primary goal for the future is centered around the ongoing expansion of the chain and the gradual evolution of the menu and foods to meet the tastes of today's customers while maintaining the commitment to made-from-scratch, high quality foods that has been the cornerstone of tradition for the past 50 years.

casual and family dining sector. Finally, in 1986, having fulfilled goals and imminent expansion plans, Don negotiated the sale of the family chain to Ramada International for over $80 million.

Investment Bankers Go for the Dough, 1989

According to Kelly Barron of the *Orange County Register*, following Ramada's buyout of Marie Callender's, "the hotel operator did little to build upon the chain's homespun image and 25 varieties of fresh-baked pies." Don Callender sued Ramada and the management at Marie Callender's contending that "they breached a contract allowing him to stay in operations," according to Barron. The suits were settled in 1994, ending Don Callender's involvement in the chain. Following unsuccessful attempts to develop the company, Ramada sold its share of the debt-laden chain to the Wilshire Restaurant Group, a shell company made up of insurance companies and individuals, who added another $60 million to the debt load. The Wilshire Group prudently began to concentrate efforts on improving employee training and service. Despite their efforts, interest payments overwhelmed profits and the company defaulted on its loans. Management began courting investors to either buy or recapitalize it. In 1993 Saunders, Karp, and Megrue, LP, a New York-based firm, bought a majority interest (68 percent) in the company with an investment of $30 million. Existing management owned 15 percent, leaving a 17 percent ownership by other investors. The firm had other resources with additional holdings in Mimi's Cafe and the apparel retailer Charlotte Russe. Marie Callender's restructured its debt after obtaining a new $15 million credit line.

Under the new leadership, Leonard H. Dreyer was promoted to president and chief executive of Marie Callender's, which at that time consisted of 145 units. Launching an effort to repair the damaged chain, Dreyer closed several underperforming stores and opened no new ones. According to Melinda Fulmer of the *Orange County Business Journal*, at the point when Wilshire Restaurant Group bought the chain from Ramada, industry onlookers commented that "Marie Callender's had the smell of death" about it, due in part to bad franchisee relations, erratic store density, and heavy debt from the leveraged buyout. Streamlining operations, the new management sold its frozen food line to Conagra Inc. for about $140 million. Dreyer implemented ways to cut costs, tightened quality controls, and strengthened relations with franchisees. He focused on what made the restaurant work in the early days and added menu items to keep up with

evolving tastes and trends. Under its newly focused direction, Marie Callender's once again maintained its market share with reported 1993 revenues of $240 million.

In homage to the quality of products originated by "the" Marie Callender, Dreyer continued to endorse and use her original pie recipes for most of the 33 varieties of pies it made. Fulmer of the *Orange County Business Journal* reported that "Dreyer never met the lady who spawned the chain of restaurants, who died of cancer last year (1995) at age 88." The company kept their core menu but added new items in an attempt to attract a broader customer base, recognizing that competitors were offering extensive menus, including specialty desserts. Marie Callender's expanded its pie line in time for the 1994 holiday season, with the introduction of its superpremium pies, satin pies described by the company as "one up on silk pies." Offering desserts not readily available at home or elsewhere, they unveiled a "superpremium" pumpkin version on a white chocolate base, and a peanut butter pie on a dark chocolate base. Sales heated up when the company began offering fresh-roasted and carved-to-order turkey, rather than the precooked turkey previously offered. The company attempted to offer something for everyone: veggie burgers for vegetarians, low-fat items for the weight-conscious, and traditional fare for average consumers. They added sliced turkey breast sandwiches with choices including roasted sweet peppers, romaine lettuce, and roasted garlic mayonnaise on focaccia; turkey Caesar salad; and turkey luncheon with apple-walnut stuffing, giblet gravy, mashed potatoes and vegetables.

The company continued to grow at a steady pace, boosted by customer loyalty and the home-cooked image. Fulmer reported in the *Orange County Business Journal* that "the chain comes closer to white tablecloth restaurants than competitors Coco's, Carrows, and Denny's, with their made-from-scratch foods and ambiance . . . but customers are reluctant to pay the price associated with this quality." The company found it difficult to exceed the $10 price point, though overhead costs, particularly real estate prices, continued to rise. As part of its new marketing strategy the company began to explore the advantages of building smaller units. Some of the larger flagship units were built 15,000 square feet in size, but the newer prototypes were designed at an average of 5,000 square feet. In addition to scaling down their regular formats, the company also began operating their even smaller format, Best of Marie's concept in food courts which were typically located in malls and universities. The food court concept was an attempt to expand the market base to include 20-year-olds. Although the Best of Marie's were not widely profitable, they functioned as a marketing tool for the larger restaurants.

Expansion: A New Flavor for the 1990s

As part of their major expansion plan Wilshire Restaurant Group purchased the restaurant chain East Side Mario's from PepsiCo in 1997. Gerald Tanaka, president of Mario's, became senior vice-president of Marie Callender's and helped implement a restaurant concept he termed as "lighter, brighter, more casual than our traditional dining rooms," according to Don Nichols of *Restaurant Business*. Attempting to attract younger clientele, the company modernized its "look" and opened ten new locations in California, Nevada, Oregon, and Texas. The newer units could seat approximately 175 people, with one-third of the space sectioned in a cafe setting. Geographic locations in smaller markets with less competition, such as Waco, Texas, were considered. Also, in addition to the regular Callender's menu items, the cafes served beer, wine, gourmet coffees, and espresso. A food-to-go counter was expanded to attract young double-income families, which immediately produced an average 20 percent of revenue, including pie takeouts. Tanaka told Don Nichols of *Restaurant Business* that "East Side Mario's is newer and sexier, but it wouldn't make sense for us to focus all of our attention on it." He added that "Marie Callender's is a stable concept with a long history of success that we can grow nationally and internationally."

Marie Callender's unexpectedly came into the limelight in connection with a sensationalist news story. It was discovered that prior to their mass suicide, members of the San Diego-based Heaven's Gate cult had apparently eaten their last meal at a Carlsbad, California Marie Callender's, which landed the company on popular national television shows such as "Jenny Jones" and "Extra." The national coverage coincided with the largest expansion undertaken by Marie Callender's in a decade.

Management continued to assess the company's position and the reasons for its steady but relatively slow growth of five to ten percent since 1995, despite the fact that surveys showed that 85 percent of consumers recognized the Marie Callender's name. One of the internal challenges facing the chain involved the lack of an advertising agreement among its franchisees, making funding and approval for advertisements unnecessarily difficult. Also, the differing designs in restaurant layout complicated the uniformity of menu presentation, especially in locations with counter seating, which limited menu options. Dreyer began spending a great deal of time visiting restaurants and talking to employees in order to get a ground-level perspective. In order to remain competitive the company continued searching for smaller regional chains that could be converted to Marie Callender's restaurants, particularly in the Midwest and Southeast.

Complementing his strategic financial aptitude, Dreyer's unique personal style served as an inspiration to company employees. Dreyer told Fulmer of the *Orange County Business Journal*: "I believe that from the top down it's got to be an environment that nurtures the employee," adding, "If they're not happy, the customer won't be happy." Known for his offbeat humor, Dreyer has built a reputation in the industry for his antics. He occasionally dresses up in strange outfits such as a serape and a sombrero for company sales contests. Once, while still working for Denny's, he was given a camcorder at a finance managers conference and asked to film a commercial for the chain. He produced a "commercial" dealing with the unlikely theme: Why ax murderers like to eat at Denny's, complete with props. Every Fourth of July, according to Fulmer, Dreyer wears a T-shirt decorated like a Marine Corps uniform and marches from his home, leading his neighbors in a parade down the street to the tune of "The Halls of Montezuma," which he blasts from his home stereo. Distasteful or not, he became a company icon of energy, leading the chain from stagnation into a new era. The company celebrated its 50th anniversary in 1998, while planning for 12 more full-service stores in the Pacific Northwest, Texas, and in the Southeast. Adapting to the times, Marie Callender's developed homestyle takeout meals targeting busy two-job families. For the future, Dreyer has indicated the possibility of raising additional capital by taking the company public. The company would like to see annual revenue growth rise to the ten to 15 percent level. According to Fulmer, Dreyer said that an offering "would be the exit strategy majority-owner Saunders, Karp & Megrue, L.P. eventually is looking for. If they could find a buyer out there that would make sense to buy Marie Callender's, they might," he continued, "But the more likely strategy would be an initial public offering. We realize that the public marketplace is where you get the most value out of the company."

Further Reading

Barron, Kelly, "Going Sky-High with Pie," *Orange County Register*, May 6, 1997, p. 1.

——, "Marie Callender's Restaurant Chain Enjoys Strong Recovery, Expansion," *Knight-Ridder/Tribune Business News*, May 6, 1997, p. 506B1025.

Fulmer, Melinda, "No Pie in the Sky," *Orange County Business Journal*, April 22–28, 1996.

Goldfield, Robert, "Marie Callender's Prowls Metro Area for Restaurant Sites," *Business Journal—Portland*, January 31, 1997, p. 8.

Hardesty, Greg, "Orange, Calif.-Based Marie Callender's Restaurant Chain Is Up for Sale," *Knight-Ridder/Tribune Business News*, September 18, 1998, p. OKRB982610B3.

Liddle, Alan, "Marie Callender's Concern Mulls Sale, Alternatives," *Nation's Restaurant News*, September 28, 1998, p. 3.

Marie Callender's Corporate History, Long Beach, Calif.: Marie Callender's Restaurant & Bakery, Inc., 1998.

"Marie Callender's Exec. Dreyer Feted for His Spirit of Giving," *Nation's Restaurant News*, May 19, 1997, p. 39.

Nichols, Don, "Checking the Callender: A 29-Year-Old Concept Gets an Update," *Restaurant Business*, May 1, 1997, p. 26.

Thompson, Stephanie, "Marie Callender's: CME Takes a Homey Brand on the Board," *Brandweek*, March 9, 1998, p. R11.

Walkup, Carolyn, "Winter Sellers Warm Season's Profits," *Nation's Restaurant News*, November 21, 1994, p. 63.

—Terri Mozzone

Mark IV Industries, Inc.

One Towne Centre
501 John James Audubon Parkway
Post Office Box 810
Amherst, New York 14226-0810
U.S.A.
(716) 689-4972
Fax: (716) 689-6098
Web site: http://www.mark-iv.com

Public Company
Incorporated: 1970 as Mark IV Homes, Inc.
Employees: 16,000
Sales: $1.95 billion (1999)
Stock Exchanges: New York
Ticker Symbol: IV
NAIC: 32622 Rubber & Plastics Hoses & Belting Manufacturing; 326199 All Other Plastics Product Manufacturing; 334113 Computer Terminal Manufacturing; 333415 Air-Conditioning & Warm Air Heating Equipment & Commercial & Industrial Refrigeration Equipment Manufacturing; 336321 Vehicular Lighting Equipment Manufacturing; 335129 Other Lighting Equipment Manufacturing; 336211 Motor Vehicle Body Manufacturing; 336413 Other Aircraft Parts & Auxiliary Equipment Manufacturing; 334513 Instruments & Related Product Manufacturing for Measuring, Displaying, and Controlling Industrial Process Variables; 334515 Instrument Manufacturing for Measuring & Testing Electricity & Electrical Signals; 33995 Sign Manufacturing

Mark IV Industries, Inc. is a manufacturing conglomerate with two main operating units. Mark IV Automotive makes automotive systems and components, including power transmission systems, air intake systems, fuel systems, and fluid-handling systems. The automotive unit is also involved in the automotive aftermarket, producing belts, hoses, and acces-

sories. Mark IV Industrial manufactures power transmission, fluid power, and fluid transfer products for various industrial applications; provides mass transit and traffic management systems; and makes specialty filtration products. Mark IV's greatest asset, however, may be chairman and CEO Salvatore H. Alfiero's propensity for finding and acquiring small technical or industrial companies that are undervalued but are leaders in specialized or niche markets. Mark IV owns more than 70 plants in the United States and abroad.

Early Years

Alfiero, with an undergraduate degree in aerospace engineering from Rensselaer Polytechnical Institute and an MBA from Harvard, and Clement R. Arrison (Mark IV's longtime president), a graduate of the University of Michigan with a degree in electrical engineering, met in 1967 when they both worked for Radatron, a Buffalo company manufacturing automatic radar detectors.

After two years, they invested in Glar-Ban International, a small company in Cheektowaga, New York, that manufactured nonglare instrumentation panels for aircraft. Both Alfiero and Arrison took leadership positions with the company. At the same time, Alfiero and a partner started Mark IV Homes, Inc., a mobile-home manufacturer in Pennsylvania. They were planning to call the company Cardinal Homes but they needed an alternate name in case their first choice was taken. Alfiero's associate happened to notice a cigar box on the desk; the name on the box was Mark IV. When they found out that the name Cardinal was, indeed, already in use, Mark IV Homes, Inc. was born.

In 1970 Glar-Ban bought Radatron, Alfiero's and Arrison's former employer, for $400,000. Glar-Ban continued to buy small companies for the next few years: in 1971, T. James Clarke Box & Label Corp., a drug and healthcare packaging manufacturer in Jamestown, New York; in 1972, E.N. Rowell Co., another box and packaging manufacturer in Batavia, New York; in 1974, Metal Awning Components Inc., in Clawson, Michigan; and in 1975, Nuclear Radiation Developments (NRD), a manufacturer of smoke detection and static elimination equipment in Grand Island, New York.

Mark IV Homes grew steadily from 1969 to 1973, building six plants and acquiring Roycroft Industries, Inc., a mobile home manufacturer in Chesaning, Michigan. Then a recession hit and the company's sales dropped from $29 million in 1973 to $19 million the next year. Interest rates were too high for potential buyers to finance housing purchases, and to make matters even worse, consumers were also turning away from mobile and manufactured homes. Mark IV showed a loss of almost $2 million in 1974 and posted losses for the next two years as well. Alfiero knew he had to get out of the mobile home business.

Mark IV Industries Emerged in 1976

In 1976 Alfiero bought out his Mark IV Homes partner. Alfiero and Arrison merged Glar-Ban and Mark IV, moved their headquarters to Williamsville, near Buffalo, and changed the name of the company to Mark IV Industries, Inc. In 1977 Mark IV, now the owner of several small, diverse manufacturing companies, showed a profit of $787,000, its first profit in four years, and sales increased from $18 million to $30 million. Still, it took several years for the company to find its direction. Alfiero and Arrison bought a few more small companies, but as Alfiero told the *New York Times*, "we were a company looking for what we wanted to be."

In the early 1980s, they knew they wanted to become a miniconglomerate and play the acquisitions game. They sold unprofitable or marginal enterprises, including Rowell, Radatron, and their remaining mobile home plants. They bought polystyrene foam producer Toyad Corporation of Latrobe, Pennsylvania, for more than $5 million and Pacemaker Plastics, Inc. for a quarter of a million dollars.

The two chief officers felt confident about their company because they had a solid base and a healthy balance sheet, but they still did not have a firm sense of where they were going until 1983, when they bought Protective Closures, the nation's

top manufacturer of plastic caps, seals, and plugs. Arrison told *Western New York* magazine, "Over the years, we have become more sure of the areas where we do well and the areas we should avoid. In the beginning, we would try most anything. Today, we are much more selective in the industries where we'll participate and the types of companies we'll let go."

Acquisition of Protective Closures did not come easily. Mark IV finally acquired it for $10 million only after a bidding war with another company. But Protective was a clear moneymaker. With the addition of Protective Closures Mark IV's sales shot up from $21.5 million in 1983 to almost $39 million in 1984, and the company earned close to $2 million, nearly doubling its profits in a year. E. Maclin Roby, Mark IV executive vice-president and former chair of Gulton Industries, told the *New York Times* that the purchase of Protective Closures "was a pivotal event." He called it the "cash machine that allowed them to go off on a wider acquisition program." Not only was the purchase of Protective Closures a monetary success, but Mark IV finally found its direction: it would buy small undervalued companies that were already the leaders in their own specialized markets.

Alfiero and Arrison called this first phase of the new Mark IV its "build and prune" phase. The company was using debt to buy manufacturing companies in three core areas, and acquired companies had to be leaders in their niche markets. If some operations of the acquired company did not fit the product or profitability objectives of Mark IV, they were sold, enabling Mark IV to buy other companies or buy down its debt.

Following this "build and prune" strategy, in 1985 Mark IV bought LFE Corporation of Clinton, Massachusetts, a manufacturer of hydraulic, process control, and environmental control products. It also happened to be almost twice the size of Mark IV. Mark IV borrowed $37 million to buy LFE, and this acquisition also paid off in a big way. Mark IV's annual sales tripled to $120 million with the purchase of its first diversified company. In 1986 Mark IV purchased Gulton Industries Inc., a New Jersey company making electronics products for defense, audio, graphic display, and industrial uses.

Both LFE and Gulton perfectly fit Mark IV's criteria for acquisition. As Alfiero outlined in the *New York Times*, Mark IV's strategy was to target companies with a strong market position, a wide array of proprietary products, and less than 25 percent of sales to aerospace or military industries. Perhaps most importantly, company insiders could not be in control of a substantial share of the company's stock.

Acquisition of both LFE and Gulton started as hostile takeovers since neither company probably would have taken Mark IV's acquisition quest seriously because of its relatively small size. But after Mark IV began to purchase a substantial number of shares, it got the attention it wanted. Before long, hostile takeovers turned into friendly acquisitions.

Mark IV allowed a great deal of autonomy to the divisions it bought. Although management remained decentralized and division managers continued to run their own companies without day-to-day interference from Mark IV, the Mark IV corporate staff grew quickly, and in 1986 the company moved from its cramped offices in the Buffalo suburb of Williamsville to the nearby town of Amherst.

Mark IV did not have to worry about not being taken seriously after buying LFE and Gulton. According to *Financial World,* Mark IV was the fastest-growing company in the United States in 1986. Mark IV continued to follow its "prune and build" strategy, buying Conrac Corp., an electronics displays manufacturer; Eagle Signal Controls, a traffic signal manufacturer; and Cetec and Electronic Counters and Controls, both audio equipment manufacturers. In five years, Mark IV's assets had skyrocketed from $19 million to $612 million. Investors who had paid less than $2,000 each in 1969 owned stock worth more than $2 million in 1987.

Acquired Armtek in 1988

In the fall of 1988 the company paid $625 million for Armtek of Jamestown, New York, a manufacturer of automotive and industrial products, in the biggest acquisition in Mark IV's history. Alfiero told *Forbes* magazine, "The biggest thing we had going for us was that nobody thought we could pull it off."

With this purchase of another company twice its size, Mark IV's debt was more than $1 billion, and Alfiero and Arrison sought to reduce that debt quickly. Within a year, Mark IV sold two of Armtek's divisions—Copolymer, a chemicals producer, and Blackstone, a manufacturer of original equipment heat exchange systems for cars. Using those net proceeds, Mark IV paid off money borrowed to finance the Armtek purchase and ended up paying only $37 million for Dayco Products, which had been responsible for half of Armtek's sales and profits. Dayco was a definite moneymaker. With sales of $425 million, it was the nation's leading supplier of original equipment automobile accessory drive systems and the second leading supplier of aftermarket accessory drive systems.

Alfiero also began buying Mark IV's junk bonds at a heavily discounted rate when the government began pushing companies to put them on the market. Alfiero eliminated another $250 million in debt this way.

In 1991 Mark IV purchased F-P Electronics, a Canadian manufacturer of electromagnet information display devices; Anchor Swan, maker of garden hoses and flexible hoses for cars; Vapor, the world's largest maker of door systems for trains and buses; and two foreign companies, Dynacord of Germany and Klark-Teknik of the United Kingdom, both adding to Mark IV's audio line.

The company's largest core business in 1992 was Power Transfer and Fluid Handling. Mark IV's Dayco was the leading manufacturer of industrial belts and hoses used in home appliances, diesel engines, snowmobiles, and gardening, and a leading supplier of coolant hoses, power steering hoses, fuel hoses, transmission oil cooler hoses, and belts to the U.S. Big Three automakers. This core business also benefited in the 1990s from increased public concern about the environment since Dayco manufactured gasoline dispensing hoses, including the vapor recovery hose used at gasoline pumps to return gas fumes. This hose was also introduced in Europe in response to the European Clean Air Act.

In 1992 the Mass Transit and Traffic Control division worked with AT&T to develop and distribute an automatic electronic toll collection system that would allow drivers to pay their tolls with their AT&T "Smart Card" without stopping at toll booths. Mark IV also supplied traffic lights, electrical controls, interior lighting, and passenger information systems for buses, trains, and airplanes. The Americans with Disabilities Act also brought new opportunities to Mark IV, which had developed information display systems with enhanced audio and video display. Mark IV also looked forward to increased sales related to more government funding of mass transit systems.

Mark IV's third core area, professional audio equipment, produced recording studio equipment, systems for live performances, and products for permanently installed sound systems. Its products included amplifiers, microphones, mixing consoles, signal processors, and loudspeakers. Consolidation of the audio industry in the early 1990s was a boon to Mark IV because it could acquire companies that were well known and respected. Mark IV's audio equipment was sold under its division names, Electro-Voice, Altec, Vega, Dynacord, Gauss, Klark Teknik, and University Sound. Mark IV sound systems were used in the 1991 "Monsters of Rock" tour in England, Europe, and Russia, as well as at Euro Disneyland, which had the largest computer-controlled sound system in the world when it opened in 1992.

Mark IV retained several companies, particularly instrumentation companies, that did not strictly fit into its core areas but were leaders in niche markets in the aerospace, defense, and plastics industries. It also kept one of its earliest acquisitions, Clarke Container, a maker of child-resistant prescription bottles.

Shifted to Slower Growth in Recessionary Early 1990s

Mark IV had spent $1.25 billion from 1985 to 1991 buying 40 companies, an acquisition spree that increased company revenues from $38 million in fiscal 1985 to more than $1 billion in fiscal 1992. This phenomenal growth also landed Mark IV on the *Fortune* 500. When the economic climate shifted in the early 1990s into recession, the company shifted as well, focusing on debt reduction, operational improvement, and much more selective acquisition.

During the recession, Mark IV sought companies that could bolster its core businesses rather than establish core businesses. A prime example of this came in June 1993 when Mark IV acquired the European and North American assets of Pirelli S.p.A.'s power transmission belting business for about $105 million. The business fit well with the Dayco unit; it also significantly increased Mark IV's presence in Europe, as the company also aimed for international growth. Dayco's European operations were further bolstered in September 1994 through the purchase of Hevas Tube Systems AB, a Swedish maker of automotive rubber tubing and tube assemblies. Also in 1994 Mark IV purchased Mexico-based Citla, a producer of industrial and automotive tubes and tube assemblies.

The early 1990s also saw Mark IV prune some of its noncore units. In June 1993 the company sold four units—LFE Instruments, Graphic Instruments, Eagle Industrial Products, and the U.K.-based Mark IV Instruments Ltd.—to Washington, D.C.-

based Danaher Corporation for $35 million. The divested units were manufacturers of microprocessor and computer-based instruments and controls. Mark IV's traffic management unit, Mark IV IVHS Inc. (for Intelligent Vehicle Highway System), received a significant boost in early 1994 when it won a potentially huge contract for the electronic collection of tolls. Within a few years, IVHS had developed a toll collection system called E-ZPass for an interagency group of 11 transportation authorities in New York, New Jersey, Pennsylvania, Delaware, and Maryland. Through E-ZPass, vehicles could be equipped with electronic devices called tags that the system could read electronically as a vehicle passed through a toll area, with the toll then charged to the motorist's account.

In November 1994 Mark IV completed a $286.3 million acquisition of Purolator Products Inc., a leading manufacturer of automotive and industrial filtration products. This was the second largest acquisition in company history and added to the company's existing product lines in the automotive aftermarket, original equipment, and industrial markets. During fiscal 1996 Mark IV paid $24.4 million for FitzSimons Manufacturing Company, a manufacturer of fuel system components for the North American automobile and truck industries. The company acquired the Imperial Eastman division of Pullman Co. in March 1996 for about $78 million. Imperial Eastman specialized in thermoplastic hydraulic and pneumatic hose assemblies, couplings, adapters, and fittings.

Major Restructuring Began in 1996

Also in 1996 Mark IV began a major reorganization and restructuring. The company reorganized itself into two market-defined operating units: Mark IV Industrial and Mark IV Automotive. Mark IV also took a $112.5 million restructuring charge in fiscal 1997 for the closing of all or parts of 12 manufacturing and distribution facilities in the United States and Europe, and a workforce reduction of about 1,000 employees, or six percent. The company also began divesting a number of noncore units: Vapor, sold in September 1996 to Westinghouse Air Brake Company for $66.4 million; Interstate Highway Sign, sold in October 1996 to a Baton Rouge-based privately held company for about $12 million; Automatic Signal/Eagle Signal, sold to Siemens Energy & Automation Inc., a unit of Germany's Siemens AG, in January 1997 for $16.6 million; the Mark IV professional audio unit, sold to an affiliate of Greenwich Street Capital Partners, Inc. in February 1997 for $156.4 million; Gulton Data Systems, sold to BFGoodrich Co. in March 1997 for about $23 million; and LFE Industrial Systems, sold to U.K.-based Eurotherm PLC also in March 1997 for $12.5 million. When added with other sales, these divestitures generated gross proceeds of about $313 million, some of which was used to fund acquisitions to bolster the company's automotive and industrial units. In October 1997 Mark IV spent about $60 million for LPI Systèmes Moteurs S.A., a French maker of plastic air admission systems, including air intake manifolds and cooling modules, for automotive applications.

In December 1998 Mark IV announced that it planned to reposition its automotive aftermarket business, which accounted for about 20 percent of overall revenue. This business had been hurt by changes in the market, most notably improvements in the quality and performance of automotive OEM com-

ponents and systems, which lessened the demand for replacement parts. The repositioning effort aimed at consolidating distribution facilities; cutting low-margin, slow-selling product lines; reducing inventory levels; rationalizing the customer base; and reducing the workforce. An aftertax charge for this repositioning of $38.7 million was taken during fiscal 1999, leading to a reduction in net income from $98.6 million in fiscal 1998 to $47.6 million in 1999. Net sales increased from $1.84 billion in 1998 to $1.95 billion in 1999.

During 1999 Mark IV continued to seek ways to strengthen its two core units through divestments and acquisitions. In February 1999 the company sold its Purolator automotive filter business to Arvin Industries, Inc. for $276 million, a move intended to allow Mark IV Automotive to concentrate on power transmission and air intake systems, along with fluid-handling and fuel systems. The sale did not include Purolator's specialty filters operation, which remained part of Mark IV Industrial. In March 1999 Mark IV sold Eaglemotive Corporation, a maker of automotive fan clutches and oil coolers, to Standard Motor Products, Inc. for about $13.4 million. One month later, Mark IV Industries expanded in Europe through the $148 million purchase of Italy-based Lombardini FIM S.p.A., a leading European manufacturer of small diesel engines with manufacturing plants in Italy, France, and Spain and distribution throughout Europe and North America.

Principal Subsidiaries

Dayco Products, Inc.; Purolator Filter Products; Facet International, Inc.; Purolator Products Air Filtration Company; Mark IV Holdings, S.A. (Belgium); Mark IV PLC (U.K.); Pietranera S.r.l. (Italy); F-P Technologies Holding Corp.; Gulton-Statham Transducers, Inc.; F-P Displays, Inc.; Mark IV Holding AG (Switzerland); Mark IV France S.A.S.; Armtek International Holding Company, Inc.; Mark IV Industries GmbH (Germany); Eagle Funding Corporation; Clarke Container Company, Inc.; Glar-Ban Incorporated; Mark IV Holdings Inc.; Aerospace Sub, Inc.; Mark IV Industries Ireland; Mark IV IVHS, Inc.; NRD, LLC; Lum-Eag Holdings (Ireland); Mark IV Automotive do Brasil Ltda. (Brazil); Dayco Argentina; Lombardini FIM S.p.A.

Principal Operating Units

Mark IV Automotive; Mark IV Industrial.

Further Reading

Baker, M. Sharon, "Alfiero: Mark IV on Course for More Growth, Debt Reduction," *Business First of Buffalo,* July 13, 1992, p. 11.
——, "Call It Whatever You Want, but Mark IV Is Always Changing," *Business First of Buffalo,* May 11, 1992, p. 20.
Davis, Bruce, "Mark IV to Buy Pirelli Belt Unit," *European Rubber Journal,* June 1993, pp. 12+.
English, Dale C., "Profile: Sal H. Alfiero, Clement R. Arrison," *Western New York,* August 1989.
Hartley, Tom, "Mark IV Collects Huge Toll Road Contract," *Business First of Buffalo,* March 28, 1994, p. 15.
——, "Purolator Products Is Mark IV's 2nd Largest Acquisition," *Business First of Buffalo,* October 10, 1994, p. 5.
Magnet, Myron, "This Gang Finally Shot Straight," *Fortune,* January 10, 1994, pp. 104+.

Mehlman, William, ''Asset Juggling Skills Keep Mark IV on High Curve,'' *Insiders' Chronicle,* January 29, 1990.

Norman, James R., ''Quick Reflexes,'' *Forbes,* March 2, 1992.

Norton, Erle, ''Mark IV to Cut Work Force 6%, Take a Special Charge, Post Loss for Quarter,'' *Wall Street Journal,* October 2, 1996, p. A4.

Robinson, Karen, ''Mark IV Looks to Expand Core Businesses to Europe,'' *Business First of Buffalo,* August 23, 1993, p. 7.

Wiener, Daniel P., ''Mark IV: The Making of a Miniconglomerate,'' *New York Times,* August 9, 1987.

Williams, Fred O., ''Mark IV of Amherst, N.Y., to Sell Part of Purolator Auto Filter Business,'' *Buffalo News,* February 9, 1999.

Zremski, Jerry, ''Mark IV Industries Is Growing into Big Conglomerate,'' *Buffalo News,* June 15, 1986.

—Wendy Stein
—updated by David E. Salamie

Mesaba Holdings, Inc.

7501 26th Avenue South
Minneapolis, Minnesota 55450
U.S.A.
(612) 726-5151
Fax: (612) 726-1568
Web site: http://www.mesaba.com

Public Company
Incorporated: 1944 as Mesaba Aviation, Inc.
Employees: 2,634
Sales: $277.22 million (1998)
Stock Exchanges: NASDAQ
Ticker Symbol: MAIR
NAIC: 481111 Air Passenger Carriers, Scheduled

Mesaba Holdings, Inc., through its wholly owned subsidiary Mesaba Aviation, Inc. (Mesaba Airlines), is one of the Midwest's largest regional airlines. With a fleet of 86 jet and jet-prop aircraft, Mesaba handles more than 700 daily departures to 91 cities in Colorado, Illinois, Indiana, Iowa, Kentucky, Michigan, Minnesota, Montana, Nebraska, New York, North Dakota, Ohio, Pennsylvania, South Dakota, Tennessee, Virginia, West Virginia, and Wisconsin and the Canadian provinces of Ontario, Quebec, and Saskatchewan. Under a reservation code-sharing agreement with Northwest Airlines, Mesaba has operated as Northwest Airlink since 1984, serving the hub airports of Detroit and Minneapolis/St. Paul. Mesaba and Northwest coordinate their flight schedules to provide connections to air travelers. Mesaba's headquarters are located at the Minneapolis/St. Paul International Airport.

"The Mighty Eagle": 1944–83

Mesaba Aviation, Inc. was founded by Gordy Newstrom in 1944 in Coleraine, Minnesota. The company first operated with a single J3 Cub airplane as a Fixed Base Operator, chartering flights and giving flying lessons. Mesaba Aviation took the name "mesaba" from the name of the geographic iron ore range in northern Minnesota. The word "mesaba" is the Native

American word for "mighty eagle" and "giant of the hills." In 1950, Newstrom moved the company to Grand Rapids, Minnesota, to be closer to the Blandin Paper Company and a larger customer base.

In 1973 the company and all its assets were sold to a Duluth-based business that operated a scheduled airline service. Holdings at that time included 15 aircraft and several aircraft hangars. Mesaba Aviation then initiated scheduled service to Spencer, Iowa, as well as Ely, Virginia, and Duluth, Minnesota.

The airline was sold to the Swenson family in 1978, who under CEO Rob Swenson was already operating a small carrier in Thief River Falls, Minnesota. As a result, Mesaba Airlines expanded to several markets in Minnesota and Iowa, as well as North and South Dakota. At that time the airline operated a fleet of Beech 99 turboprop aircraft.

In 1983 Mesaba became a publicly held company when it sold two million shares of common stock in the company. The company began trading on the NASDAQ under the ticker symbol MAIR. The airline offered a second public offering of 900,000 shares in 1985. After forging a partnership with Republic Airlines in 1983 to connect mutual passengers and offer joint fares, Mesaba continued to grow and acquire additional aircraft. The Fokker F-27 and later the Fairchild Metro III aircraft became the backbone of the Mesaba fleet.

The Northwest Connection: 1984–90s

In 1984 Mesaba Airlines began operating under a Part 121 Air Carrier Certificate from the U.S. Department of Transportation, the same type of certificate as that held by the major airlines. The carrier was then flying to 13 cities in five states and had relocated its corporate offices to the Minneapolis/St. Paul International Airport. Also that year, Mesaba discontinued its relationship with Republic and signed a code-sharing agreement with Twin Cities-based Northwest Airlines. This marked the beginning of a very long-term relationship between the two companies. The agreement called for Mesaba to operate as Northwest Airlink, so all of the airline's flights would carry the familiar "NW" computer reservation code. Additionally,

Company Perspectives:

By keeping our focus firmly on serving our guests' needs, we will provide safe, reliable, convenient and comfortable air transportation that will set the standard for all regional airlines, while providing a secure and positive environment for our associates, and a market-driven return on investment for our shareholders.

Mesaba's schedule would be coordinated with Northwest's, offering convenient connections and competitive joint fares.

In 1985 Mesaba Airlines purchased seven new Fairchild Metro III aircraft to replace its 15-passenger Beech 99 aircraft. The carrier also added three Fokker F-27 aircraft to its fleet. Northwest Airlines and Republic Airlines merged in 1986, causing Mesaba to realign its route structure, discontinuing service to five markets and initiating service to three more cities. At that time, the airline was carrying about 20,000 passengers every month.

Mesaba soon outgrew its facilities and, in 1988, built a new corporate headquarters at the airport. This new 80,000-square-foot facility housed the airline's corporate offices and a maintenance hangar. During the summer of the same year, Simmons Airlines, the Northwest Airlink partner at the Detroit hub, was purchased by American Airlines. This move left Northwest Airlines without a regional partner at its Detroit facility. So, in August Northwest Airlines selected Mesaba Airlines from several other regional airlines to operate as the Airlink affiliate at the Detroit hub. This was a tremendous boost to Mesaba. The transition from one partner to another was accomplished by late fall of that same year with Mesaba adding 325 new employees. The new operation nearly doubled the airline's route structure, increased passenger traffic over 73 percent and solidified the corporate relationship they had with Northwest Airlines.

To manage its growth and define its operations further, the shareholders of the company approved the formation of a holding company to be called AirTran, with Mesaba being its only subsidiary. (In 1994 the holding company's name was changed to Mesaba Holdings, Inc., at which time Northwest made a 29.7 percent investment in the carrier. A year later, Minneapolis investor Carl Pohlad assumed chairmanship of Mesaba.)

On December 1988, the airline initiated service to four new markets out of the Detroit hub, including Cleveland, Dayton, and Akron, Ohio, and Erie, Pennsylvania. This was accomplished with the addition of nine Fokker F-27s and seven Fairchild Metro III aircraft. In January 1989, the airline expanded service to four additional markets in Michigan: Pellston, Traverse City, Flint, and Wausau. Further expansions took place in February 1989 when the carrier expanded into Houghton, Marquette, and Toledo, Ohio. By June 1989, the carrier had doubled its traffic and had added 30 cities to its entire system as the result of the Detroit expansion.

To maintain its growing business, more aircraft were needed as well as new, modernized facilities to house the aircraft. In 1991 the airline built a new hangar facility at Detroit Metro International Airport to service the Detroit aircraft. The carrier also acquired a hangar in Wausau, Wisconsin, which had been owned by Midstate Airlines. That year, Mesaba Airlines also entered into an agreement with Northwest Airlines, which called for Northwest Airlines to lease 25 deHavilland Dash aircraft on behalf of Mesaba Airlines. These 37-passenger aircraft would be delivered from 1991 through 1993.

In November 1995, Mesaba Airlines in connection with Northwest Airlines opened the new ''G'' concourse at Detroit Metro International Airport. The new world-class facility offered expanded and improved passenger seating, convenient shuttle trips to the aircraft, and significant reduction in distance the passengers had to walk to the other Northwest concourses. Four months later, in March 1996, Mesaba announced the purchase commitment of 50 34-passenger Saab 340 aircraft with the option of purchasing 22 additional aircraft. The order included a mix of new and pre-owned aircraft, including 20 pre-owned Saab 340A and 30 new Saab 340Bplus aircraft.

To accommodate the increased passenger traffic and aircraft in use, Mesaba began a major facility upgrade at its Minneapolis hub in May 1996. The upgrade included improved passenger seating and the addition of workstations with telephone and modem hookups for business travelers. Improved lighting and signage was also included in the refurbishment. In the next month, Mesaba began taking delivery of the Saab aircraft at the rate of two per month.

By October 1996, Mesaba executed a separate agreement with Northwest Airlines for the operation of 12 new Avro RJ85 aircraft, which allowed the company to be the first regional airline in the United States to offer its passengers a first-class cabin.

Mesaba moved into its new 9,000-square-foot regional terminal at the end of the Green concourse at Minneapolis/St. Paul International Airport in May 1997. The new terminal was modeled after the successful Detroit regional terminal, whose design to support expansion of service proved valuable over time. In June 1997, Mesaba successfully introduced its first two Avro RJ85 aircraft.

By mid-July, the last of the Fairchild Metro III aircraft were retired from the Mesaba fleet, allowing Mesaba to offer an all cabin-class fleet. This same year, Mesaba announced that it signed an agreement to fly six additional Avro RJ85 regional jets for Northwest Airlines which brought the total number of RJ85s to 18. In addition to this, Mesaba and Northwest announced plans to amend their existing regional jet agreement to increase from 18 to 36 the number of Avro RJ85 aircraft that would be operated by Mesaba on the behalf of Northwest over a ten-year period.

On August 1, 1997, the airline expanded its operation to include services to 14 markets that were previously served by Express Airlines, Inc., another Airlink affiliate. In December, Mesaba inaugurated regional jet service to Aspen and Steamboat Springs, Colorado, as well as Montreal, Canada. These additions alone broadened the airline's route map over 1,600 miles. The same year, Mesaba added summer service between Minneapolis/St. Paul and Aspen/Snowmass, Colorado.

Bozeman and Kalispell, Montana service was also added to the route system, stretching Mesaba's service to western Montana.

In October 1998, Mesaba began nonstop service from Duluth, Minnesota, to Detroit, Michigan, with the Avro RJ85 aircraft. The company retired the last ten of its older deHavilland Dash 8 aircraft in December 1998. By the end of 1998, Mesaba boasted a fleet of 80 state-of-the-art jet and jet-prop aircraft, offering over 800 daily departures to 91 cities in 18 states and three Canadian provinces.

Facilities continued to keep up with the expansion as well. In June 1998, Mesaba opened a new maintenance facility at the Rhinelander-Oneida County Airport in Wisconsin. The facility was designed to house up to four Saab 340 aircraft. Mesaba also planned the facility to provide temporary housing for its Rhinelander crew. By December of the same year plans were underway to construct a $12.5 million, 126,000-square-foot aircraft maintenance facility and crew base at the Cincinnati/Northern Kentucky International Airport in early 1999 and the company was also reviewing expansion possibilities at its Detroit and Minneapolis/St. Paul facilities.

A Quarter Century and Still Going Strong

Throughout 1998 Mesaba celebrated its 25th anniversary of scheduled commercial service. To mark the occasion, the airline placed in service a new Saab 340Bplus aircraft with a special commemorative paint scheme. The aircraft was named The Silver City Flyer. That year the airline's president and CEO, Bryan K. Bedford, was named Regional Airline Executive of the Year by *Commuter Regional Airline News* and the Allison Engine Company. In addition, Mesaba was named "Regional Airline of the Year" by *Air Transport World* magazine. This was the first time in five years that a U.S.-based regional airline had been selected for the honor by the highly respected aviation journal. Finally, *Forbes* magazine listed Mesaba as one of the "Top 200 Small Companies in America." The company was listed 41st in *Forbes*'s annual ranking and was the only airline to be included in the listing that year.

As it headed into the next century, Mesaba was a prominent regional airline poised for a bright future. Building on a 46 percent increase in air traffic and reportedly high consumer satisfaction, the company slogan announced: "Mesaba, An Airline To Call Your Own." The carrier remained committed to quality service, leading edge technology, sound training protocol, and ongoing aircraft development and maintenance. Net income for fiscal 1999 was expected to reach $24.3 million on overall revenue of $348 million.

Principal Subsidiaries

Mesaba Aviation, Inc.

Further Reading

"Carrier to Expand Role As Feeder to Northwest," *Wall Street Journal*, October 10, 1996.
Hess, Amerada, "U.S. Equity Preview," *Bloomberg Review*, December 7, 1998.
"Mesaba Airlines Announces Construction of New Maintenance Facility," *PR Newswire*, December 3, 1998.
"Mesaba Aviation, Inc.," *Aviation Week & Space Technology*, January 1, 1998.
"Mesaba Holdings, Inc. Announces $30 Million Stock Repurchase Proposal," *PR Newswire*, November 19, 1998.
"Mesaba Makes Push for Quality," *USA Today*, June 22, 1998.
"Mesaba Shift," *Flight International*, May 5, 1996.
"Northwest Mesaba," *Flight International*, March 3, 1995.
"The Top 200 Small Companies in America," *Forbes*, October 21, 1998.

—J. D. Fromm

Mikasa, Inc.

20633 S. Fordyce Avenue
Long Beach, California 90810
U.S.A.
(310) 886-3700
Fax: (310) 763-0625

Public Company
Incorporated: 1936 as All Star Trading
Employees: 3,460
Sales: $397.2 million (1997)
Stock Exchanges: New York
Ticker Symbol: MKS
NAIC: 421220 Chinaware, Household-Type,
   Wholesaling; 442299 Chinaware Stores

A fast-growing retailer and wholesaler, Mikasa, Inc. sells causal and formal dinnerware, displaying its greatest strength in the casual segment of the market (settings that retail for less than $130). Mikasa sold its dinnerware and decorative accessories through wholesale accounts in the United States and abroad and through a network of approximately 150 U.S.-based factory outlet stores. Unlike many of its competitors, the company did not own manufacturing facilities. Instead, Mikasa contracted out designs to approximately 175 factories in 25 countries. Production was concentrated in Germany and Austria, where 30 percent of the company's merchandise was manufactured. The flexibility engendered by contracting out production enabled Mikasa to introduce numerous patterns into the market each year and quickly expand production of designs that proved popular. During the 1990s, the company increasingly broadened its product categories, experimenting with cookware, bath accessories, and other decorative accessories for the home—all patterned after its popular dinnerware designs. The company was partly controlled during the late 1990s by chairman emeritus George Aratani, the son of Mikasa's founder.

Founded in the 1930s

Mikasa's predecessor was a company named All Star Trading, founded in 1936. The ties that connected All Star Trading

and Mikasa were familial—the business legacy of the Aratani family. Setsuo Aratani, a Japanese-American, started All Star Trading as an import-export enterprise specializing in trade with Japan. When hostilities between Aratani's source country and his supply country erupted on December 7, 1941, the business abruptly closed, but following World War II, Setsuo's son George and a partner named Alfred Funabashi revived the trading company. The younger Aratani and Funabashi sold flash-frozen tuna and developed the company into one of the largest importers of toys, distributing its merchandise through a half-dozen department store chains on the East Coast. Before the end of the 1950s, the pair began concentrating on importing china made in Japan, using the trademark they adopted in the 1950s—"Mikasa," Japanese for "three umbrellas."

The gradual move into the chinaware business evolved into the company's exclusive occupation by the early 1960s. In 1965, the company's path crossed with a young department store merchandiser named Alfred Blake, who was impressed by the Mikasa designs he saw while working with Hudson's Bay stores in Canada. Blake's interest was sufficient to prompt a career move. He joined Mikasa as a commissioned sales representative for western Canada in 1965, when the California-based company was collecting $5 million a year in sales. Blake's esteem for Mikasa's merchandise translated into high sales, fueling his promotion within the company's sales ranks. When Alfred Funabashi died in 1976, the impressive Blake was named president and began working alongside George Aratani.

Expansion Begins in the 1970s

Under Blake's operational control, Mikasa flowered into a vibrant enterprise. He made wholesale changes with alacrity. Blake broadened the company's line of merchandise, adding crystal stemware and new, less expensive brands to buttress the company's flagship Mikasa brand. For housewares departments in department stores, Blake created "Studio Nova," which sold for roughly 40 percent less than Mikasa brand china. For mass merchants and discount stores, Blake created a more affordable brand, dubbed "Home Beautiful." Blake's innovative approach also broadened the awareness of the Mikasa name and its assorted brands. He opened a showroom in New York City, where the company's tableware was showcased in mid-

Company Perspectives:

Mikasa's multiple brand strategy allows us to target our diversified product line to consumers through a number of distribution channels. Our four proprietary brands of Mikasa, Christopher Stuart, Studio Nova and Home Beautiful are marketed in North America through 152 Company-owned and operated stores and the Company's retail account base of over 7,000 accounts. These retail accounts represent traditional and non-traditional channels of distribution and include major department stores in North America as well as catalog showrooms, corporate and incentive award accounts, home shopping television, hotels, mass, merchants, military base exchanges, restaurants and warehouse clubs.

Manhattan, and in 1978 he directed the company's foray into the retail sector, establishing an outlet store in a warehouse in Secaucus, New Jersey—the first of many more to follow. Blake's influence on the maturation of Mikasa was profound, evidenced in the robust financial growth of the company during his first decade of control. When Blake was named to the presidential post, Mikasa was collecting $26 million a year in sales; by 1985, the company was generating $137 million in annual sales.

By the mid-1980s, confidence at the company's headquarters was running high. Blake and a group of senior executives, who each held small investment stakes in the company, were ready to significantly increase their financial investment in the company. In 1985, the management group initiated a leveraged buyout (LBO) of the company, offering $1 million in cash and borrowing $31 million to obtain ownership from George Aratani. The LBO, completed in 1985, was a sign of the executives' faith in Mikasa's future, but to their chagrin, outside influences conspired against the new owners shortly after the deal was concluded.

Mid-1980s Crises Alters Strategy

In 1986, Japan's currency began to appreciate quickly against the U.S. dollar, making goods produced in Japan more expensive in the United States. To make matters worse, U.S. department stores were struggling with their own ills, forcing some retailers to close stores and others either to consolidate or to streamline their operations. The net effect was fewer china departments within department stores nationwide, delivering a second pernicious blow to Mikasa's business. After their first year of ownership, the new owners had little to celebrate: losses for the year amounted to a numbing $3.6 million. The future would have looked even bleaker had Mikasa's group of executive-owners known the tableware industry was destined for a decade-long slump. Between the mid-1980s and mid-1990s, the "tabletop" industry, which included flatware, cups, saucers, plates, crystal, serving platters, and Christmas plates, recorded little growth.

Although the company did not escape the 1980s without experiencing several difficult years, strident growth arrived as the 1990s began, thanks in large part to the measures taken by Blake. His response to the growing strength of Japanese currency was

crucial to the company's trend-bucking success. Blake moved some of Mikasa's production out of Japan to low-cost, contract operations in Malaysia, Thailand, and Yugoslavia, essentially doing what Nike did during the early 1980s to record prolific growth in a lackluster industry. While other chinamakers struggled to make money in the face of rising labor and operating costs incurred from their own factories, Mikasa thrived mainly because it owned no factories. The company contracted its designs to other manufacturers and prospered, while many of its competitors were held in check by escalating overhead.

The cost-savings realized from outsourcing production also gave Mikasa another important advantage, namely, flexibility. The company could quickly increase production volume on popular patterns and quickly abandon designs that failed to impress customers. Additionally, enhanced flexibility in production enabled Mikasa to churn out a greater diversity of patterns than many of its competitors. With a larger number of designs introduced into the market each year, the company's odds for success increased, frequently putting Mikasa on the leading edge of emerging trends. Blake also began to emphasize the expansion of the company's outlet stores, which reduced the reliance on department stores and strengthened Mikasa's brand identity.

Blake's meaningful operational changes began to pay substantial dividends by the beginning of the 1990s, as the company strove to shrug aside the industrywide malaise affecting its competitors and effectively market tableware to what Blake referred to as the "McDonald's/microwave generation." To accomplish this goal, the company moved in three general directions. The first relied on Mikasa's production flexibility. When the company identified a popular design from one of its numerous pattern introductions in a given year, it would quickly orchestrate the production of the particular design on a number of supplementary products, such as servers, carafes, napkin rings, and butter dishes—occasionally branching far afield by adorning the popular pattern on non-tableware items such as picture frames. "Customers," Blake remarked, "are treating dinnerware like sportswear, and accessorizing," so the company followed suit and began broadening and diversifying its product lines and product categories. The other two areas of emphasis that fueled the company's rise were international expansion and the expansion of its network of retail stores. In 1991, Mikasa formed a joint marketing venture named Mikasa Europe Distribution with a German partner to market the company's products in Europe. As the 1990s progressed, Mikasa intensified its efforts overseas, adding a relatively small yet growing facet to its operations. A greater contributor than international sales to the company's revenue growth during the 1990s was the company's chain of factory outlet stores. As their numbers grew, providing a means to dispose of excess inventory, the retail stores became increasingly important to Mikasa's well-being, accounting for roughly half of the company's total sales by the early 1990s.

Between 1989 and 1993—years that encompassed a nationwide economic recession—Mikasa's sales increased at a compound annual rate of 14.2 percent, from $175 million to $299 million, and its net income grew at a compound annual rate of 34.4 percent, swelling from $7.7 million to $25.2 million. By this point, Mikasa sold its cups, saucers, plates, crystal, and other dinnerware items through independent distributors in eight countries. The company owned its own buying agency in

Japan, controlled its joint marketing venture in Germany, and operated retail outlets in more than half the country. Much had been achieved since the troubled months following the LBO, but more was yet to come. To fund expansion, the company filed with the Securities and Exchange Commission in April 1994 for an initial public offering (IPO). Blake was hoping to raise $27 million for the expansion of the factory store network and for international expansion. The IPO was completed in June 1994, yielding an estimated $23.7 million in net proceeds, providing Blake with a bankroll to fund Mikasa's expansion.

1994 Public Offering Spurs Expansion

At the time of the IPO, Mikasa operated 75 retail stores. The company planned to open between 20 and 25 new stores during the remaining six months of 1994, and another 50 stores in 1995 and 1996. The stores, which averaged 7,500 square feet, generated nearly half of Mikasa's sales, with the balance derived from 8,000 wholesale accounts supplying approximately 40,000 locations in the United States. To further expose the company's range of merchandise, Mikasa sold its products through mail-order catalogs, striving to tap into demand through a variety of marketing formats. "Families," noted Blake, "aren't instilled with a tradition of dining elegance and butlers scurrying around with silver trays." It was the company's objective to instill a need for tableware, but not necessarily tableware that evoked dining elegance. In the formal segment of the market—settings that retailed for more than $130— Mikasa ranked fifth in the nation, but in the casual segment the company ranked as the market leader, controlling 40 percent of the market. Mikasa's strength in the casual segment and its ability to roll out a range of ancillary merchandise in support of a popular design dictated its business strategy. Instead of limiting itself to marketing fine tableware, the company pursued a much larger customer base. "We're not just competing against other chinamakers," explained the company's president, Raymond Dingman, Jr., whose prominence at Mikasa increased during the 1990s, "We are competing for the decorating dollar."

Over the course of the next three years, Mikasa nearly doubled the number of factory outlet stores it operated. By 1997, after recording $372.3 million in sales for the previous year, the company had 140 stores in 40 states and contracted the production of its products at 150 factories in 22 countries. To stimulate further growth, the company began using its stores in 1997 as a testing ground for expanding its product categories. A line of cookware and a line of bath accessories debuted in some of the stores, representing one aspect of Mikasa's growth strategy for the late 1990s and the years to follow. Dingman explained the three-part strategy: "First, we'll work closely by extending existing product lines. We're also looking to expand existing product categories. We think we can grow through acquisitions," he remarked, unveiling a new potential method for expansion. "We expect to be a consolidator, not a consolidatee."

As the company pursed the objectives of its growth strategy, it completed work on the infrastructure to support future expansion. In discussions dating back to 1993, company executives had evaluated the distribution and service needs of Mikasa,

attempting to determine what the company would need in the future. From these discussions, an ambitious project was born for a new distribution facility to improve the company's existing capabilities, which relied on distribution centers in Secaucus, New Jersey, and Laguna Beach, California. Mikasa broke ground on the project in March 1996, when construction began in Charleston, South Carolina. When completed in October 1997, the $60 million facility typified a state-of-the-art distribution center. Inside were 60,000 square feet of office area, 270,000 square feet of warehousing space, and 263,000 square feet set aside for shipping and receiving. At the dedication ceremony for the building, South Carolina's governor was in attendance, the state's Secretary of Commerce, and Charleston's mayor, personages testifying to the momentous nature of the event. "Merchandising and marketing is changing," Blake remarked, referring to the company's new complex. "This is the future of the company; the new face of the company." The advantages gained in service and distribution efficiency from the Charleston facility were expected to be realized as the company entered the 21st century. Other potential developments included acquisitions and a new breed of retail stores patterned after a prototype named Mikasa Home Store, which sold merchandise without the sharp discounts offered at the factory outlet stores. With these avenues of growth on the horizon, Mikasa prepared for the future, holding sway as the dominant designer and marketer of casual dinnerware.

Principal Subsidiaries

American International, Incorporated; Christopher Stuart Galleries, Inc.; Houseware Merchandisers, Inc.; Mikasa Licensing, Inc.; Tabletop Merchandisers, Inc.; Mikasa Nagoya Holdings, Inc.; Mikasa International, Inc.

Further Reading

Campbell, Laurel, "Tableware Company Opens Memphis, Tenn., Factory Outlet Store," *Knight-Ridder/Tribune Business News*, March 5, 1997, p. 305B0948.
Darlin, Damon, "Accessorizing the Dinner Table," *Forbes*, December 19, 1994, p. 288.
Kehoe, Ann-Margaret, "Mikasa Growth Plan: Acquire and Extend," *HFD*, October 20, 1997, p. 45.
——, "More Factory Stores for Hot Mikasa," *HFD*, June 20, 1994, p. 63.
Martin, Karen E., "Mikasa Offers Upscale Look with Outlet Prices," *Chain Store Age Executive with Shopping Center Age*, August 1994, p. 48.
"Mikasa Factory Store in N.H.," *HFD*, September 12, 1994, p. 76.
"Mikasa: Factory Stores in Hawaii, Ind.," *HFD*, September 19, 1994, p. 64.
"Mikasa Inc. Slates IPO of 3.125 Million Shares," *HFD*, April 25, 1994, p. 126.
Parker, Jim, "China Maker Mikasa Dedicates Berkeley County, S.C., Distribution Center," *Knight-Ridder/Tribune Business News*, July 15, 1998, p. OKRB9819602C.
——, "Mikasa's New Distribution Center Can Be Traced to 1980s Retail Scene," *Knight-Ridder/Tribune Business News*, July 20, 1998, p. OKRB9820102F.

—Jeffrey L. Covell

The Minute Maid Company

Post Office Box 2079
Houston, Texas 77252
U.S.A.
(713) 888-5000
(800) 888-6488
Fax: (713) 888-5959
Web site: http://www.cocacola.com

Division of The Coca-Cola Company
Incorporated: 1945 as Florida Foods, Inc.
Employees: 1,900
Sales: $2 billion (1997 est.)
NAIC: 311311 Frozen Fruit, Juice, & Vegetable
 Processing; 31193 Flavoring Syrup & Concentrate
 Manufacturing

The Minute Maid Company claims to be the world's leading marketer of juices and juice drinks. In the $3 billion U.S. orange juice market, however, the company trails market leader and archrival Tropicana Products, Inc. (which is itself a division of PepsiCo, Inc., Coca-Cola's archrival)—Minute Maid holding 24 percent of the overall market, Tropicana 33 percent. Minute Maid dominates the $550 million frozen concentrate sector, with 44.7 percent market share (while private labels hold 39.4 percent and Tropicana 5.4 percent); but in the $2.45 billion chilled juice sector, Tropicana claims 39.8 percent market share, private labels 22.5 percent, and Minute Maid only 19.3 percent. In addition to the flagship Minute Maid Premium brand orange juice, the company also sells Minute Maid lemonade drinks, fruit punches, and apple, cherry, grape, and other juices. Other brands include Hi-C fruit drinks, Five Alive citrus drinks, Bright & Early grape and orange breakfast beverages, and Bacardi mixers. Minute Maid International markets the company's branded juice products in more than 80 foreign countries, aided by processing and packaging plants in Canada, Puerto Rico, South Africa, France, Spain, the Netherlands, and Japan. Minute Maid Danone, a 1996-created joint venture with Groupe Danone of France, sells Minute Maid Premium juices in

several European countries, holding the number one position in refrigerated juices in Spain and Portugal. Other partners include Brazil-based Sucocitrico Cutrale Ltda., the largest grower and processor of oranges in the world and one of Minute Maid's major orange suppliers, and Minneapolis-based Cargill Inc., which distributes Minute Maid products to the foodservice industry.

World War II Research Led to Company Founding

During World War II the Boston-based National Research Corporation (NRC) developed high-vacuum evaporation processes for dehydrating penicillin, blood plasma, and streptomycin for use in the U.S. war effort. The U.S. Army wanted to extend this technological advance into the area of providing its troops nutritious food, especially orange juice. Previous attempts to concentrate orange juice through boiling the water out of the juice failed because the boiling process destroyed the flavor. When NRC scientists employed, on orange juice, the high-vacuum process used to dehydrate penicillin, they were able to create a concentrated powder that made flavorful orange juice when reconstituted.

In early 1945 NRC organized Florida Foods Corporation, with John M. Fox as its head, and built a plant in Plymouth, Florida. The company aimed to win a contract for 500,000 pounds of powdered orange juice, which the Army had offered. Through Fox's persistence, Florida Foods was awarded the contract in the spring of 1945 for $750,000 worth of orange powder. Fox next secured $2.7 million in capital from investors, but the end of the war led the Army to cancel the order.

Undeterred, Fox shifted the company's focus to the consumer market. In need of a brand name, Florida Foods hired an advertising agency based in Boston, a city whose rich history included the famous Minutemen. The agency thereby created the Minute Maid brand, a name connoting convenience and ease of preparation. Concluding that the orange powder would not constitute a viable consumer product, Fox also led his company to market an "intermediate step" in the vacuum process—that of frozen orange juice concentrate. Through experimentation, the company settled on a process that eliminated 80 percent of

271

the water in orange juice, forming a frozen concentrate that when reconstituted created orange juice richer and more flavorful than that created from the powder.

The first shipment of Minute Maid concentrate—the first concentrated orange juice brand—took place on April 15, 1946, from the Plymouth plant. That same month the company changed its name to Vacuum Foods Corporation. Lacking funds for advertising and promotion, Fox went door to door in his hometown of Hingham, Massachusetts, offering free samples out of the ice- and can-filled trunk of his car. The product quickly caught on, and grocery stores in the area found it difficult to keep their freezers stocked with Minute Maid.

Once funds became available for marketing, ads stressed the superior taste of Minute Maid compared to canned orange juice, as well as the time savings in preparation compared to squeezing fresh oranges. It was the 1948 launch of the Bing Crosby radio campaign, however, that set Minute Maid on the road to national prominence. The extremely popular Crosby began endorsing the product during his daily radio program; his pitch was so strong that some consumers concluded—errantly—that he owned the company. This very successful campaign increased sales tremendously and led to a nearly 30-year promotional relationship between Minute Maid and Crosby and his family. Meanwhile, in October 1949 the company incorporated its brand into its company name, when it adopted the name Minute Maid Corp.

Acquired by Coca-Cola in 1960

The precipitous growth of Minute Maid during its early years was evident in the company's revenue figures. During its first year of operation in 1946, the company recorded sales of $374,500. Just five years later, sales reached $29.5 million. In 1958 the company developed centrifuge equipment that removed water from the concentrate through freezing rather than evaporation, thereby improving the concentration process. By 1960 Minute Maid had gained the attention of soft drink king Cola-Cola Company, which late that year acquired the company through a stock swap, marking the firm's first venture outside of soft drinks. Five days after the purchase was consummated, Fox—president of Minute Maid at the time—left the company. Benjamin H. Oehlert, Jr., who had helped shepherd the purchase through, was named president of Minute Maid Company, which was set up as a division of Coca-Cola. By the time of the acquisition, Minute Maid had expanded beyond orange juice and was also marketing the Hi-C line of canned fruit drinks.

In the initial years under Coca-Cola, much stayed the same at Minute Maid, most notably the distribution, as channels for frozen juices and soft drinks were markedly different. But Coke reacted aggressively when the citrus industry encountered one of its periodic freezes in December 1962, a freeze that destroyed more than one-third of the orange crop in Florida. As usual, prices shot up and consumption dropped. The amount of orange concentrate shipped dropped by 50 percent, remaining at the reduced level for several years.

In the aftermath of the 1962 freeze, Coca-Cola officials were determined to secure a steady supply of oranges outside of Florida, particularly as a hedge against future freezes. The company helped a Brazilian orange wholesaler, Jose Cutrale, Jr., enter the orange growing business by providing him with planting and cultivation advice and with technical assistance in the area of juice production. Cutrale's company, Sucocitrico Cutrale Ltda., eventually became the largest grower and processor of oranges in the world and one of Minute Maid's major suppliers. The relationship between Minute Maid and Cutrale, one that Minute Maid typically played down so as not to antagonize its Florida suppliers, continued into the late 1990s.

Not unexpectedly, Minute Maid's packaging and advertising became more sophisticated within the Coke marketing empire. In 1965 Minute Maid changed its packaging, which had consisted of a white, orange, and green scheme and had been imitated by competitors. The new design was most notable for its unusual black background, which provided a strong contrast with competitors' packaging and helped the brand retain its loyal customers. On the advertising front, Minute Maid ads by this time no longer touted orange juice as strictly a health drink for preventing colds and the ''Asian flu.'' Instead, ads emphasized Minute Maid's ''natural sweetness'' and ''natural freshness,'' and attempted to position—mostly unsuccessfully—orange juice as a drink that was not just for breakfast. Also, in 1968 the company began airing prime-time television commercials featuring Bing Crosby and his family; this remarkably successful campaign continued until Crosby's death in 1977. Minute Maid in 1969 introduced a 16-ounce frozen concentrated orange juice package, the largest such package in the industry. Eventually the Minute Maid division was renamed Coca-Cola Foods, with Minute Maid remaining the centerpiece brand.

''Orange Juice Wars'' Began in 1973

The so-called ''orange juice wars'' were most heated during the 1980s and 1990s, but the fierce rivalry between Minute Maid and Tropicana began as early as 1973. That year, Coca-Cola Foods boldly targeted Tropicana's dominance of the chilled juice sector with the introduction of Minute Maid chilled juice made from reconstituted frozen concentrate. Coca-Cola Foods not only went after Tropicana in the New York metropolitan area where Tropicana's market share was around 40 percent, it also quickly rolled out its new product nationwide, becoming the first company to market chilled juice nationally. Both companies claimed production of the superior product. Coca-Cola Foods argued that it could overcome seasonal variations in the taste and quality of oranges through the concentrating process, which allowed for the blending of the juice of oranges picked at various times of the year. Tropicana countered, contending that its not-from-concentrate chilled juice was inherently better because it was bottled right out of the orange (after pasteurization). The Minute Maid-Tropicana rivalry grew more heated in 1975 when the latter reentered the market for frozen concentrate. Tropicana gained deeper pockets in 1978 when it was acquired by Beatrice Foods Co.

Around this same time, Coca-Cola Foods launched a new brand, Bright & Early, a breakfast beverage sold in frozen concentrated form. This was just one of a host of new products introduced from the mid-1970s through the mid-1980s. The Five Alive brand made its national debut in 1979 with the launch of a fruit drink composed of 60 percent fruit juice from oranges, grapefruit, lemons, tangerines, and limes. This product—initially available in frozen concentrate but later offered chilled as well—marked the beginning of an industry trend toward high-juice-content fruit drinks that were lighter than typical fruit juices and therefore accepted by consumers as an all-day refreshment. In 1982 a second Five Alive flavor was added, one that combined apple, grape, lemon, pineapple, and cherry juices. The Minute Maid brand itself meanwhile extended in all directions. By mid-1984 Minute Maid frozen concentrates included the flagship orange juice, reduced-acid orange juice, orange juice with more pulp, pineapple orange juice, tangerine juice, grapefruit and pink grapefruit juice, apple juice, grape juice, pineapple juice, lemonade, pink lemonade, limeade, and fruit punch. Also developed was a line of all-natural Minute Maid crystals—powdered drink mixes available in lemonade, pink lemonade, lemon-limeade, and fruit punch flavors. In the chilled segment, Coca-Cola Foods similarly expanded beyond orange juice, adding lemonade, pink lemonade, fruit punch, and grapefruit juice to its stable. In 1983 the division became the first American firm to nationally market a single-serving fruit drink in an aseptic Tetra Brik package, the so-called and soon to be immensely popular "drink box." Debuting that year in the new packaging were the three most popular Hi-C flavors: orange, grape, and fruit punch. By 1984 Coca-Cola Foods held the top spot in orange juice, with 22 percent of the $3 billion market, but it was much more than simply a maker of orange juice.

Two key 1983 events shook the orange juice industry and intensified the "orange juice wars." The Procter & Gamble Company (P&G) launched the Citrus Hill brand, offering both frozen concentrate and from-concentrate chilled juice. By 1984 the marketing power of P&G had quickly made Citrus Hill into a fairly strong third player. That year the declining frozen concentrate sector was led by Minute Maid's 25 percent share, with Citrus Hill holding seven percent and Tropicana four percent. Tropicana still held the top spot in the rapidly growing chilled juice sector at 28 percent, with Minute Maid claiming 18 percent and Citrus Hill nine percent. The second key event of 1983 was an orange freeze which forced Tropicana to raise the price of its not-from-concentrate chilled juice three times in quick succession. Amazingly, the company saw no dropoff in purchasing, as customers were clearly willing to pay a premium for what they perceived to be a superior product—the not-from-concentrate juice. With funds from the higher prices, Tropicana began to expand outside its strongholds in the northeast and southeast; by the late 1980s Tropicana was a national brand for the first time. Minute Maid was hurt further by the continuing erosion in sales of frozen concentrate. In 1986 U.S. sales of chilled orange juice surpassed those of concentrate for the first

time, as consumers continued to seek out more convenient foods.

Minute Maid struck back with several product introductions: Minute Maid Calcium Rich, a calcium-fortified orange juice, in 1987; Minute Maid Premium Choice, a not-from-concentrate chilled orange juice aimed squarely at Tropicana, in 1988; Minute Maid Pulp Free orange juice, in 1989; and Minute Maid Juices to Go, a line of single-serve juices and juice drinks, in 1990. Premium Choice found some initial success, gaining 11.7 percent of the not-from-concentrate juice market by 1990, but not before Tropicana had sued Coca-Cola Foods over the use of the phrase "straight from the orange" in its packaging and advertising. Coca-Cola Foods decided to drop the slogan rather than contest the lawsuit. Despite the new products, the company was losing its battle with Tropicana, as that company—which had been acquired by The Seagram Company, Ltd. in 1988—edged past Minute Maid in 1990 in the overall orange juice market, claiming a 22.3 percent share to Minute Maid's 22.2 percent. Despite P&G's marketing strength, Citrus Hill became a casualty of the orange juice wars when P&G pulled the plug on the brand in September 1992, unable to compete with the two industry giants. The Minute Maid-Tropicana rivalry grew even more intense in the wake of Citrus Hill's departure, with Tropicana gaining the initial upper hand. By 1993 Tropicana had extended its lead in the overall orange juice market to a somewhat comfortable 30.1 percent vs. 25.9 percent. By 1996 the gap had grown even larger, 32.4 percent vs. 24.3 percent.

Mid-1990s Turnaround Effort

Coca-Cola Foods was its parent company's only division to post an operating loss in 1995. In the summer of that year Ralph Cooper took over as CEO and president from Timothy Haas. Under Cooper's leadership, Coca-Cola Foods made a number of moves in 1996 and early 1997 aimed at turning its fortunes around. To emphasize its main brand name, it changed its name to The Minute Maid Company. It also gave itself an ambitious goal—to become the "Coca-Cola Company of juices worldwide." To this end, Minute Maid aimed to aggressively expand overseas. In 1996 the company entered into a 50-50 joint venture with Groupe Danone of France, whereby the two companies would sell refrigerated juice under the Minute Maid and Danone names throughout Europe and Latin America. In late 1996 Minute Maid decided to abandon its foray into the not-from-concentrate sector, and focus on revitalizing its from-concentrate chilled juice and frozen concentrate offerings. The company in January 1997 launched a new orange juice formulation called Minute Maid Premium through a $50 million promotion and advertising campaign—the largest marketing campaign in company history. Minute Maid claimed that this was "the first orange juice to deliver the taste sensation of eating a fresh, ripe orange, every time."

Minute Maid returned to profitability in 1997 and had begun to close the gap between itself and Tropicana (which Seagram sold to PepsiCo, Inc. in August 1998). Although its turnaround was not yet complete, the company appeared to have been revitalized through the Minute Maid Premium launch as well as from its rapid international expansion. Although it was no longer number one in the United States, the company lay claim to the top spot in juices and juice drinks worldwide. Minute

Maid had perhaps been wounded in the initial skirmishes of the orange juice wars, but had survived to fight another day.

Further Reading

"Can Orange Juice Fill Pause That Refreshes?," *Business Week,* July 25, 1964, pp. 100, 102.

"Coca-Cola Invades Tropicana's Market," *Business Week,* December 1, 1973, pp. 26, 28.

Dagnoli, Judann, and Jennifer Lawrence, "P&G Squeezed: Minute Maid Premium Makes Gains," *Advertising Age,* January 30, 1989, pp. 6, 90.

Deogun, Nikhil, and Vanessa O'Connell, "Storming the OJ Wars, Pepsi to Buy Tropicana," *Wall Street Journal,* July 21, 1998, pp. B1, B6.

Gleason, Mark, "Minute Maid Pares Prices," *Advertising Age,* October 23, 1995, pp. 1, 8.

Groden, Louise L., "Minute Maid," *Encyclopedia of Consumer Brands,* volume 1, edited by Janice Jorgensen, Detroit: St. James Press, 1994, pp. 376–79.

Harris, Nicole, Gail DeGeorge, and Mia Trinephi, "It's Zero Hour for Minute Maid," *Business Week,* December 2, 1996, pp. 87–88.

Khermouch, Gerry, "Pulp Wars: The Squeeze Is on As OJ Rivals Minute Maid and Tropicana Expand into Other Juice Categories," *Brandweek,* April 11, 1994, pp. 28+.

Lavin, Douglas, "Coke in Venture with France's Danone to Distribute Orange Juice Overseas," *Wall Street Journal,* September 25, 1996, p. B8.

Lawrence, Jennifer, "Big Squeeze: Minute Maid Adds Calcium," *Advertising Age,* July 27, 1987, pp. 3, 66.

——, "Coca-Cola to Shake Tropicana Juice," *Advertising Age,* May 23, 1988, pp. 3, 89.

McCarthy, Michael J., "Squeezing More Life into Orange Juice: Premium Juice Is Focal Point of Fierce Battle," *Wall Street Journal,* May 4, 1989, p. B1.

Morris, Betsy, "Coca-Cola Foods' Teasley Focuses Marketing on Minute Maid Juices," *Wall Street Journal,* June 23, 1988, p. 38.

——, "Shaking Things Up at Coca-Cola Foods," *Wall Street Journal,* April 3, 1987, p. 36.

Pollack, Judann, "Minute Maid Ad Budget Will Triple to Boost Brand," *Advertising Age,* November 25, 1996, p. 29.

Prince, Greg W., "Ready to Stir," *Beverage World,* December 1995, pp. 25, 28.

Roush, Chris, "Coca-Cola's Minute Maid Unit Has Turned Around, with Big Plans on '98 Agenda," *Knight-Ridder/Tribune Business News,* August 13, 1997.

Schiller, Zachary, and Gail DeGeorge, "What's for Breakfast? Juice Wars," *Business Week,* October 5, 1987, pp. 110, 115.

Shapiro, Eben, "Tropicana Squeezes Out Minute Maid to Get Bigger Slice of Citrus Hill Fans," *Wall Street Journal,* pp. B1, B10.

"Stacy, John D., "Coke Foods Energizes Juice Market," *Beverage World,* August 1984, pp. 41–42, 44.

Tenser, James, "Minute Maid Gets Its Juices Flowing," *Supermarket News,* June 7, 1993, p. 10A.

Theodore, Sarah, "Minute Maid Bites Back," *Beverage Industry,* January 1997, p. 33.

"This Is Coca-Cola?," *Business Week,* October 8, 1960, pp. 80, 85.

—David E. Salamie

Mirage Resorts, Incorporated

3400 Las Vegas Boulevard South
Las Vegas, Nevada 89109
U.S.A.
(702) 791-7111
Fax: (702) 792-7676
Web site: http://www.mirageresorts.com

Public Company
Incorporated: 1949 as Golden Nugget, Inc.
Employees: 17,085
Sales: $1.52 billion (1998)
Stock Exchanges: New York Pacific
Ticker Symbol: MIR
NAIC: 72112 Casino Hotels

Mirage Resorts, Incorporated is one of the largest developers and operators of casinos in the world, with a focus on the upper end of the market. Mirage's Las Vegas holdings include the flagship Mirage resort, the ultra-luxurious Bellagio, Treasure Island, the Holiday Inn Casino Boardwalk, and (through a joint venture with Circus Circus Enterprises Inc.) the Monte Carlo, all located on the Strip; and the Golden Nugget, the largest hotel in downtown Las Vegas. Outside Las Vegas, the company runs the Golden Nugget-Laughlin in Laughlin, Nevada; and in Biloxi, Mississippi, the Beau Rivage, the largest casino in the United States outside of Nevada. In the works is the company's return to the Atlantic City market.

Golden Nugget Origins

Mirage got its start as the Golden Nugget casino, which opened in downtown Las Vegas in August 1945. The town's largest gambling hall at the time, with 5,000 square feet of gaming floor, the Golden Nugget was decorated in a Victorian San Francisco-Barbary Coast style and was owned by a group of Las Vegas businessmen headed by Guy McAfee. McAfee had been a police captain in Los Angeles who ran a gambling operation on the side in the 1930s. When a reform mayor was elected in 1938, McAfee was forced out of southern California, and he and other gamblers migrated to Nevada, where gaming was legal. McAfee purchased a roadhouse called the Pair-O-Dice Club (a pun on Paradise Valley, the name of the area where it was located). The club was located on Highway 91, the road to Los Angeles south of town, which would later become known as the Las Vegas Strip. The new owner scheduled the club's reopening, under the name 91-Club, to exploit the burst of publicity generated by the Las Vegas divorce of movie star Clark Gable and his wife on March 7, 1939.

With the advent of World War II in late 1941, Las Vegas became a center of war-related industry, since it was considered far enough inland to be safe from the enemy bombers that were presumed to menace the coasts. The defense boom flooded Las Vegas with thousands of fliers, soldiers, and defense workers, which stimulated the local economy, in particular the prostitution and casino industries. In 1942 McAfee expanded his gambling operation when he purchased the Pioneer Club, near other casinos on glitzy Fremont Street in downtown Las Vegas. In 1945 he purchased an additional Fremont Street casino, the Frontier Club. McAfee invested the profits from this club in parcels of adjacent land, which became the site of the Golden Nugget, completed in late 1945. Both the Frontier Club and the Golden Nugget were partly owned by organized crime leader Benjamin ''Bugsy'' Siegel in the mid-1940s, until he was killed in 1947.

In 1948 the Golden Nugget unveiled a 100-foot-high electric sign to call attention to itself and compete with the lavish structures being built out of town on the Las Vegas Strip. With the sign, McAfee billed his casino as ''the brightest night spot in the world.'' In the following year, the Golden Nugget company was incorporated.

Steven A. Wynn Took Over in Early 1970s

During the 1950s and 1960s, Las Vegas underwent spectacular growth, and the Golden Nugget profited, along with the rest of the hotel industry, from that growth. By the early 1970s, however, management of the casino had become lax, and it was losing money. The Golden Nugget had degenerated into a dingy, lackluster, somewhat sleazy operation by 1973, when Steven A. Wynn, a Las Vegas liquor wholesaler who had previously owned a portion of another casino property, began buying stock in the company. By the middle of the year, Wynn had acquired more than five percent of the outstanding shares, and he was able to persuade the company's leaders to put him on its board in June. Shortly thereafter, he presented members of the board with evidence of waste in the casino's operations and embezzlement by employees, and asked to be allowed to run the company. On August 1, 1973, Wynn was appointed chairman and president of Golden Nugget.

When Wynn took over, Golden Nugget owned just one casino in downtown Las Vegas, which generated annual revenues of $19 million. The casino was known as a place for low rollers, but its new president soon brought his own flashy style to the operation, repositioning the Golden Nugget as a haven for big spenders. Wynn liked to hobnob with celebrities, and he brought high-profile acts to the Golden Nugget to entertain. In addition, he provided a corporate jet to ferry high rollers to the casino. In the late 1970s, Wynn defied conventional wisdom about the viability of his casino in a somewhat run-down area, far from the glitzy Strip or the center of Las Vegas, by constructing a luxury high-rise hotel with 579 rooms, including lavish suites, for Golden Nugget patrons. Under its new leadership, the made-over casino began to turn a profit.

Turned Attention to Atlantic City in Late 1970s

In addition to its Las Vegas operations, Golden Nugget turned its attention eastward. When New Jersey became the second state after Nevada to legalize casino gambling, the company acted quickly to get in on the ground floor of this potentially lucrative market. In October 1978, Golden Nugget completed its purchase of a one-square-block property occupied by a motel on the Atlantic City Boardwalk, and announced plans to build a hotel-casino complex on the site. With 500 rooms, the project was slated to cost $75 million. In the next several months, Golden Nugget struggled to raise the money it needed to build its Atlantic City project. Coming off a year of low profits, with a money-losing fourth quarter, the company's stock price was not high enough for

it to generate the necessary income through the sale of additional shares. Finally, under the tutelage of investment bankers from Drexel Burnham Lambert, who had pioneered the use of junk bonds, Golden Nugget was able to put together a package of debt and equity financing that made it possible for the company to raise funds equaling its current assets twice over. With this money, Golden Nugget broke ground on its Atlantic City development on September 5, 1979.

While it was making rapid progress in construction in the East, the company ran into legal difficulties in Las Vegas in 1980, when a Nevada grand jury subpoenaed company records to determine whether insider trading of Golden Nugget stock had taken place. As a result of this investigation, Wynn was forced to resign temporarily as head of the company's New Jersey subsidiary in order to expedite Golden Nugget's petition for a temporary license to operate its Atlantic City casino.

Fifteen months after construction began, on December 12, 1980, the Golden Nugget-Atlantic City opened its doors, becoming the sixth operating casino in town. The project's final costs totaled $160 million. Although it was somewhat smaller, the casino replicated the Las Vegas original in its decor and its appeal to high-rolling customers. Its lounge featured such A-list performers as Frank Sinatra and Dean Martin, and the company ferried favored customers from New York to Atlantic City in its own fleet of helicopters.

By January 1981 the Atlantic City casino was doing well, racking up a $2 million pretax profit, twice that of the Las Vegas casino, in that month alone. It had become the most profitable casino in Atlantic City almost overnight. Unlike some other casinos, Golden Nugget was able to make money despite the strict New Jersey regulatory environment, which raised costs for casino operators. The company reaped the advantages of its casino's design, which allowed a high density of gambling equipment per square foot and utilized the fewest number of employees possible under New Jersey law.

Building on this initial success, Golden Nugget announced in February 1981 that it would purchase 48 acres of real estate on the Las Vegas Strip, on which it would build a massive new casino and $430 million resort. In the ensuing months, however, the Las Vegas gambling industry was hit by a recession, and the company canceled its plans for the new development in December.

Six months later, in June 1982, Golden Nugget announced that it would indeed expand, but in New Jersey. The company put forth a proposal to purchase a 17-acre site outside Atlantic City that held a discount department store and was located far away from the congestion of the Boardwalk. This would allow extensive parking facilities and room for expansion. One obstacle, however, was the need to obtain a zoning variance to construct a casino at that location. When this proved insurmountable, Golden Nugget purchased instead, for $25 million, a 15-acre parcel of land in Atlantic City previously owned by MGM-Grand Hotels, in early 1983. The company announced plans for a 500-acre hotel and casino complex, on which it would begin construction later in the year.

By early 1984, industry watchers had become intrigued as Golden Nugget proceeded with plans for its $300 million Atlantic City project in secrecy. In an unusual move, all workers were asked to sign contracts forbidding disclosure of any aspect of the project to outsiders. By that fall, however, increasing competition in the Atlantic City market had slowed growth in the company's profits, and Wynn decided that the market was not strong enough to merit what was by then a $400 million investment. Golden Nugget took a $15.3 million loss when it canceled its plans for the second Atlantic City casino, contributing to an 86 percent drop in net income for the year.

In addition to falling profits in 1984, Golden Nugget faced regulatory difficulties as a result of the organized-crime connections of Edward M. Doumani, a Las Vegas businessman who was its second largest shareholder after Wynn. The Doumani stake had first attracted attention three years earlier, and the family was now ordered to sell its holdings in the company.

In April 1985 Golden Nugget made a move to expand in another fashion when it offered to buy more than a quarter of the much larger Hilton Hotels Corporation, as a first step toward taking it over entirely. The move, which was ultimately blocked by Hilton, seemed designed to enhance the image of Wynn as a gambler not just in casinos, but in the world of corporate takeovers as well. Under the tutelage of his friend Michael Milken, the Drexel Burnham Lambert junk-bond king, Wynn used Golden Nugget's casino earnings to purchase stakes in companies ripe for takeover, and then sold those holdings at a profit. In addition, Golden Nugget made a stab at the takeover of the Dunes Hotel and Casino, another Las Vegas property, which was also rejected.

Sold Atlantic City Hotel in 1987

Throughout the 1980s, Golden Nugget's Atlantic City casino remained profitable, contributing a large portion of the company's profits. Nevertheless, in anticipation of increasing competition and declining profits in New Jersey, Golden Nugget sold its Atlantic City casino to the Bally Manufacturing Corporation, which owned other nearby gaming properties, in March 1987 for $440 million, resulting in a $170 million pretax profit. The Golden Nugget-Atlantic City had been a gold mine, and in its seven years of operation in New Jersey, the company had gone from being a minor, single-property operation in Las Vegas to a major contender in the casino industry, largely on the strength of the windfall profits it reaped in the early days of legalized gambling in New Jersey.

After pulling out of the East Coast market, Golden Nugget turned its full attention to its operations in Nevada. As it was finalizing the lucrative Atlantic City sale, the company put the finishing touches on a major expansion and renovation of its flagship property in downtown Las Vegas. Now more opulent than ever, the renovated Golden Nugget included additional hotel rooms; several restaurants, including one reserved for high rollers; a pool with a computerized misting system to simulate tropical humidity in the desert; a spa, beauty salon, and gym; meeting rooms; and a display featuring a huge nugget of gold, weighing 61 pounds.

Golden Nugget found itself on the other side of the corporate takeover game in mid-1987, when it attracted the unwelcome attention of casino owner Donald Trump. Trump, who had made no secret of his desire to move into the Las Vegas market, purchased 4.9 percent of the company's outstanding stock in a tentative bid to take control of Golden Nugget. Although the attempt ultimately failed, the move earned Trump the lasting enmity of Wynn.

In November 1987 Golden Nugget broke ground on a massive project on the Las Vegas Strip next to the top-of-the-line casino Caesars Palace. The new project was designed to expand the company's presence in the Las Vegas market, push it into the top tier of casino operations, and position Golden Nugget in the front of the race for the future of Las Vegas, in which the city would be marketed as a resort destination that offered much more than mere gambling. Golden Nugget planned to make its new hotel one of the world's largest, with 3,030 rooms.

The following year, Golden Nugget made a somewhat belated and modest entry into the booming casino market of Laughlin, Nevada, a town located on the bank of the Colorado River, which formed the border with neighboring Arizona. The company purchased an old casino, called the Nevada Club, which it renamed the Golden Nugget, and a small related hotel across the river in Bullhead, Arizona. The cost of the properties was $40 million. Subsequently, the company expanded and upgraded the casino and added a parking garage.

In 1989 the company increased its Nevada property holdings when it opened the Shadow Creek golf course, designed as a perquisite for high rollers at its casinos. At a cost of $37 million, the course featured 10,000 pine trees brought in by truck to disguise the arid nature of the course's true landscape.

Mirage Opened in 1989, Treasure Island in 1993

On November 22, 1989, Golden Nugget opened its spectacular new Las Vegas attraction, called the Mirage, after two years of construction. The cost of the project was reported to be $620 million, but some in the industry felt it was closer to $700 million. The company had risked a large portion of its capital to complete the project and taken on large debts, floating a $540 million bond issue through Drexel Burnham Lambert and the soon-to-be-jailed Milken. Observers predicted that the Mirage would need to take in $1 million a day just to break even. To justify the expense, the project included a host of unique features. The most eye-catching of these was a five-story manmade volcano that erupted on schedule every 15 minutes. In addition, there were lagoons, a waterfall, abundant palm trees, an aquarium of sharks and stingrays, and a dolphin pool surrounded by bars, restaurants, and stores. Guests could also see live white tigers behind a glass wall, a preview of the entertainment in the hotel's showroom, and a magic and tiger-taming act by Siegfried and Roy, the most popular entertainers on the Strip.

To prevent the Mirage from infringing on the business of the Golden Nugget casino across town, the company attempted to shift the older casino's clientele base downward slightly, adding more slot machines and reducing the prices of drinks to bring in crowds, making up for the loss of the highest rollers, particularly the most coveted players from Asia, the Middle East, and Mexico. In further efforts to woo these essential players to the Mirage, the company hired well-connected employees from other casinos to market the Mirage overseas, and made two private jets available to ferry high rollers to Nevada. Golden

Nugget badly needed capital from the new resort, since it had posted losses of $7.6 million in 1988, and $11.4 million over the first nine months of 1989.

In addition to the various attractions at the Mirage, Golden Nugget set out to attract gamblers by staging boxing matches at the hotel. In February 1990 the company tried to woo Buster Douglas, who had just defeated Mike Tyson to win the World Heavyweight title, away from his promoter Don King, promising him $50 million and $2 million in stock for two title bouts at the Mirage. This move quickly resulted in a flurry of lawsuits to prevent the fighter from switching promoters. Nevertheless, Douglas fought Evander Holyfield at the Mirage in 1990. Although the company lost $2 million promoting the fight, the increased revenues to the casino made up the difference.

In 1991 Golden Nugget sponsored additional matches at the Mirage, including two bouts between Tyson and Razor Ruddick, though the company did not promote the match or receive any portion of the gate receipts. The addition of the Mirage helped the company's net income to jump 57 percent in 1991, enabling the company to pay off one-third of the debt it had taken on to build the project. The tropical resort's success came at the expense of the older Golden Nugget casino, however, as its revenues slipped by more than one-fifth during this time. To emphasize Golden Nugget's transformation from a casino operator to an entertainment company, its name was changed to Mirage Resorts, Incorporated.

In October 1991 Mirage announced its intention to construct a second lavish resort on the Las Vegas Strip, adjacent to the Mirage. To be called Treasure Island, this project was designed to appeal to middle-class customers. With a cost estimated at $300 million, which would soon rise to $430 million, the hotel was slated to have 3,000 rooms. In front, to attract attention, stuntmen dressed as pirates and British sailors would stage mock gun battles on exploding ships floating in an artificial lagoon dubbed Buccaneer Bay. "Customers will be caught in the crossfire," noted the company's promotional literature. Construction began on the project in March 1992, and Treasure Island opened in October 1993. The addition of the Mirage and Treasure Island helped Mirage Resorts increase its net revenues from $299.8 million in 1989 to $1.25 billion in 1994.

In February 1992 Mirage completed improvements to its Laughlin property, which included an atrium with foliage and a waterfall, similar to the one so prominently featured at the Mirage, and additional restaurant and lounge facilities. The company constructed a 300-room hotel on the site, completed in late 1992.

Monte Carlo, Bellagio, and Beau Rivage Added in the Mid-to-Late 1990s

In the early 1990s Wynn was finally able to effectuate the purchase of the Dunes Hotel, which he then had demolished in 1993 and 1994. On the site, Mirage Resorts planned to develop two additional properties. June 1996 saw the opening of the first, the Monte Carlo, a 3,000-room resort catering to middle-class clientele through an atmosphere of "casual elegance." Jointly owned by Circus Circus Enterprises Inc., the Monte Carlo was developed for $350 million.

A much larger undertaking was the Bellagio, adjacent to the Monte Carlo and connected to it by a monorail system. Opened in October 1998, the 3,005-room Bellagio was considered the most expensive casino ever built, with a $1.6 billion price tag. It was also considered the most elegant casino ever, featuring a Northern Italian village theme, complete with an artificial eight-acre lake, 1,200 fountains, gardens, and red-tile-roofed Tuscan villas. The Bellagio also featured a botanical conservatory; an art gallery with a $300 million collection of works by such artists as Van Gogh, Monet, and Renoir; a collection of high-end shops and restaurants; and a water-oriented Cirque de Soleil spectacle. The art gallery provoked controversy even prior to Bellagio's opening, with some Mirage shareholders objecting to the lavish spending; consequently, in January 1998 Wynn bought four of the works of art for a total price of $25.6 million. Bellagio's art gallery therefore included paintings owned both by Mirage Resorts and Wynn. Bellagio's initial months of operation were highly successful, with the casino pulling in more than $3 million per day in gross revenues, a record-setting pace.

In June 1998 Mirage Resorts added to its Las Vegas Strip holdings through the $112 million purchase of Boardwalk Casino, Inc., whose assets included the Holiday Inn Casino Boardwalk, a 653-room casino located between the Monte Carlo and Bellagio. The acquisition also brought additional undeveloped land to the company, giving Mirage Resorts 40 acres and 817 feet of frontage on the Strip for possible development.

At the same time that it was bolstering its Las Vegas presence, the company was also pursuing expansion elsewhere, including a return to Atlantic City and an entrance into the burgeoning gambling town of Biloxi, Mississippi. In Atlantic City, Mirage Resorts initially entered into a joint agreement with Circus Circus and Boyd Gaming Corporation to develop a complex of three gambling resorts. In early 1998 the City of Atlantic City conveyed to Mirage Resorts 125 developable acres of land in the Marina area—the largest potential casino site in the city—in exchange for the company agreeing to clean up the site (a former municipal landfill) and to develop a hotel-casino there. Shortly thereafter, Mirage Resorts pulled out of the agreement with Circus Circus and Boyd Gaming, saying it would proceed on its own. Its former partners sued Mirage. But in July 1998 Mirage and Boyd entered into a new 50-50 joint venture for the development of a $750 million, 1,200-room hotel casino on a 25-acre portion of the site. Construction of the Borgata (Italian for "village"; the Borgata would be somewhat similar to the Bellagio in regard to its Italian village concept) was slated to begin in the fall of 1999. At the same time, Mirage Resorts was proceeding on its own to develop the $1 billion Le Jardin luxury casino resort, to be built adjacent to the Borgata.

In Biloxi—located on the Mississippi Gulf Coast, the third largest U.S. gambling market after Las Vegas and Atlantic City—Mirage Resorts developed the $680 million Beau Rivage casino resort, which opened in March 1999. With 1,780 rooms, the Beau Rivage was the largest casino-hotel in the United States outside the state of Nevada. It was also one of the most elegant casinos in the region, and even featured a deluxe marina able to accommodate yachts of up to 125 feet in length.

With the company's tremendous 1990s expansion, net revenues reached $1.52 billion by 1998. For 1998, however, net income fell from the $207.6 million figure of 1997 to $81.7 million, thanks in part to the $88 million spent on the extravagant opening of the Bellagio. But this was likely a short-term setback, as Mirage Resorts was on a roll in developing and running increasingly elaborate, and profitable, entertainment resorts.

Principal Subsidiaries

AC Holding Corp.; AC Holding Corp. II; Atlandia Design and Furnishings, Inc.; Beau Rivage Resorts, Inc.; Bellagio; GNL, Corp.; GNLV, Corp.; GNS Finance Corp.; Golden Nugget Aviation Corp.; LV Concrete Corp.; MAC, Corp.; MH, Inc.; The Mirage Casino-Hotel; MRGS Corp.; Treasure Island Corp.

Further Reading

Christensen, Jon, ''The Greening of Gambling's Golden Boy,'' *New York Times,* July 6, 1997, pp. F1, F9.

Grover, Ronald, ''Steve Wynn's Full House,'' *Business Week,* April 1, 1996, pp. 55–57.

——, ''Tigers, a Volcano, Dolphins, and Steve Wynn,'' *Business Week,* November 20, 1989.

——, ''Wynn's World: White Tigers, Blackjack, and a Midas Touch,'' *Business Week,* March 30, 1992, pp. 75+.

Johnson, Bill, ''Golden Nugget Chairman Wynn Takes His Biggest Dice Roll in Bid for Hilton,'' *Wall Street Journal,* April 11, 1985.

Labich, Kenneth, and Joe McGowan, ''Steve Wynn: A $2.5 Billion Wager,'' *Fortune,* July 22, 1996, pp. 80+.

Littlejohn, David, ''Bellagio: Italy Never Had It Like This,'' *Wall Street Journal,* October 29, 1998, p. A20.

Martin, Frances, ''Stephen A. Wynn,'' *Hotels,* November 1994, p. 48.

Martin, Richard, and Alan Liddle, ''Wynn's New Mirage in the Desert: $1.6B Bellagio Hotel,'' *Nation's Restaurant News,* November 2, 1998, p. 1.

Metz, Robert, ''Golden Nugget: Surprising Gain,'' *New York Times,* February 3, 1981.

Millman, Joel, ''Can Steve Win?,'' *Forbes,* May 28, 1990.

Moehring, Eugene P., *Resort City in the Sunbelt: Las Vegas, 1930–1970,* Las Vegas: University of Nevada Press, 1989, 329 p.

Painton, Priscilla, ''The Great Casino Salesman,'' *Time,* May 3, 1993, pp. 52+.

Phalon, Richard, ''Zero-Sum Game,'' *Forbes,* March 23, 1987.

Posner, Bruce, and Cunningham, Sheila, ''Golden Nugget's Slow Roll to the Boardwalk,'' *Business Week,* April 30, 1979.

Pristin, Terry, ''Mirage Resorts Is Accused of Breaking Joint Agreement to Build Project in Atlantic City,'' *New York Times,* January 21, 1998, p. B8.

Purdum, Todd S., ''Nugget's Long-Shot Hilton Bid,'' *New York Times,* May 12, 1985.

Smith, John L., *Running Scared: The Life and Treacherous Times of Las Vegas Casino King Steve Wynn,* New York: Barricade Books, 1995, 352 p.

Stevenson, Richard W., ''Golden Nugget's Roll of the Dice,'' *New York Times,* November 16, 1989.

—Elizabeth Rourke
—updated by David E. Salamie

Mitsui & Co., Ltd.

2-1 Ohtemachi 1-chome
Chiyoda-ku
Tokyo 100-0004
Japan
(03) 3285-1111
Fax: (03) 3285-9819
Web site: http://www.mitsui.co.jp

Public Company
Incorporated: 1947 as Daiichi Bussan Kaisha, Ltd.
Employees: 10,861
Sales: ¥17.52 trillion (US$131.7 billion) (1998)
Stock Exchanges: Tokyo Osaka Nagoya Kyoto Hiroshima
    Fukuoka Niigata Sapporo Luxembourg Amsterdam
    Frankfurt NASDAQ (ADRs)
Ticker Symbol: MITSY
NAIC: 551111 Holding Companies, Bank

Part of the Mitsui group, Mitsui & Co., Ltd. is the largest of Japan's general trading companies, known as *sogo shosha*. It was also the first such company, having been founded in 1876, and created the model for other *sogo shosha* that were formed later. These companies are general in nature both in that they handle a wide range of products and services in nearly every industry, and in that they can handle a broad range of functions. General trading companies specialize in bringing together—on a global level—buyers and sellers of a variety of products and services and handling finance and transport of the resulting transaction; the companies derive most of their revenues from commissions earned through these transactions. In addition to this more traditional *sogo shosha* activity of facilitating trade flows, Mitsui also works with clients to create new trade flows and new business through identifying new business opportunities, assisting in technology transfers, and organizing joint ventures—what the company calls "enterprise investment." In the late 1990s, in response to the implementation of Japan's financial "big bang"—the long-anticipated deregulation of the country's financial sector—Mitsui added a third main area of

activity, that of financing. Mitsui has a global network of about 225 offices and more than 1,000 subsidiaries and associated companies in 90 countries.

Early History of Mitsui Group

The Mitsui family traces its ancestral lineage to about 1100 A.D., and for its first several hundred years produced successive generations of samurai warriors. By 1650, however, the role of the samurai had changed. Sokubei Mitsui, head of the family, became a *chonin,* or merchant. He established a soy and sake brewery whose products first became popular in the red-light district of Edo (Tokyo). The business, which passed to his son Takatoshi, later expanded to include a dry-goods store, a pawnshop and a currency exchange which later evolved into a bank. The dry-goods store (named Echigoya in honor of an ancestor) operated on an innovative "cash only" basis with nonnegotiable prices. The bank introduced the concept of money orders to Japan. The various Mitsui business ventures continued to grow through the end of the 17th century, particularly the bank, which was selected by the Tokugawa government to be its fiscal agent in Osaka. In the ensuing 150 years Mitsui enterprises prospered in the cities of Edo and Kyoto as well as Osaka.

During the 1860s the Mitsui financial reserve was nearly depleted. The family took the unprecedented step of hiring an "outsider" named Rizaemon Minomura away from another company in Edo. Minomura was a promising young executive who had demonstrated his talents and had a proven record of success. As an orphan and childhood drifter, he had no allegiance to family or prejudice to social status. Minomura also had a close personal relationship with Kaoru Inoue, a Japanese statesman with considerable influence in government circles. When Mitsui was forced to lend 350,000 ryo (the old Japanese currency) to the failing Tokugawa government, Minomura, through his government contacts, managed to secure a government remittance of 320,000 ryo. Having saved the company from ruin, Minomura was promoted to "head clerk," or chief executive, and given near dictatorial power.

Through an efficient information network, Minomura learned of the impending financial collapse of the Tokugawa government. He redirected support to the opposition Restoration party, a political movement that vowed to reinstate the Meiji government. In return for its support, Mitsui was appointed to manage the party's finances. After the battle of Tobu-Fushimi in 1868, the feudal government fell and the Meiji emperor Matsuhito was restored to power. Mitsui severed its ties with the Tokugawa rebels and continued to develop intimate relations with Meiji politicians. Mitsui became the official Meiji government banker, a position that greatly increased its influence and ability to expand.

Minomura urged that Mitsui relocate its headquarters from Kyoto to the new capital of Tokyo. He encountered strong resistance from the Mitsui family and the people of Kyoto. Arguing that the company needed to be located at the center of activity in order to survive, Minomura eventually won his point and moved the company to Tokyo in 1873.

In Japan at this time, capital and talented entrepreneurs were concentrated in the hands of a few large, well-diversified companies called *zaibatsu,* or "money cliques." The four largest *zaibatsu* were Mitsui, Mitsubishi, Sumitomo, and Yasuda, all of which controlled large banks. In turn, the banks were directed to provide low-cost capital for financing the *zaibatsu's* numerous industrial ventures. In 1874 Mitsui, as the de facto Ministry of Finance, held about ¥3.8 million and US$460,000 for the government, free of interest with no minimum reserve level.

The Meiji government initiated an extensive program of national modernization. Students were sent to the United States and Europe to study modern industrial production methods and bring them back to Japan where they would be applied to government-sponsored enterprises. The modernization program encountered difficulties because the government companies were unable to generate capital for investment and lacked managerial expertise. The *zaibatsu* companies, which had money and talent, were invited to participate in the modernization program by managing several of the various state enterprises. While still diversified, Mitsui remained primarily involved in banking, Mitsubishi established a shipping empire, and Sumitomo became a major copper producer.

During a Tokugawa rebellion at Satsuma the government commissioned Mitsui to provide about two-thirds of the army's provisions. Within a year the company's wealth had grown from ¥100,000 to ¥500,000. Hachiroemon Mitsui, the head of the family, was appointed by the government to at least 15 managerial positions in state enterprises. In the meantime, Inoue helped Minomura to consolidate his position in the company by informing him of impending changes in government policy. But while Hachiroemon Mitsui took credit for many of the company's new ventures, it was actually Rizaemon Minomura who planned and executed them.

It is not true that Mitsui was only as successful as it was because of its close relationship with the government. Two other wealthy families from the Tokugawa period, Ono and Shimada, encountered financial difficulties and later collapsed. Mitsui was successful because it was well organized and did not retain incompetent managers just because they were family members.

After Mitsui began to trade internationally in 1874, its business took a turn for the worse. It was unprepared to compete with larger foreign companies which had established trading networks and the benefit of protected colonial markets. By 1876 Minomura considered closing the international venture.

At this time Kaoru Inoue, who had previously left government service to pursue a career in industry, decided to return to politics. In order to avoid an explicit conflict of interest he was forced to sell Senshusha, the company he established in 1872. Senshusha did a great deal of business with the government, which was considered an excellent customer. It was also managed by a respected administrator named Takashi Masuda. Inoue offered to sell Senshusha to Mitsui (which was certain to continue funding his political aspirations). Finally, the sale was considered a personal favor to Minomura. Mitsui, after all, badly needed the talents of Masuda, who had gained considerable experience in international trade while working for an American company.

Mitsui Bussan Formed in 1876

In July 1876 Senshusha was merged with Kokusangata Karihonten, the Mitsui "temporary" head office for domestic trade located in Tokyo, and renamed Mitsui Bussan Kaisha (the Mitsui Trading Company). Takashi Masuda was placed in charge of the Bussan, and the following year took over as head clerk when Minomura died at the age of 56.

Shortly before Minomura died, Mitsui Bussan was appointed as marketing agent for high-grade coal from the government's Miike mine, which it later purchased. In order to facilitate the profitable export of coal to China, the Bussan established a small office in Shanghai, its first foreign outpost.

In 1877 Mitsui Bussan was asked to supply military provisions to government forces in Kyushu during another samurai rebellion called the Seinan War. The conflict generated a ¥200,000 profit for the company, which was later used to finance the opening of additional Bussan branch offices in Hong Kong (1878) and New York (1879).

In 1882 Takeo Yamabe, an agent for the Osaka Textile Company, chose Mitsui to handle a purchasing transaction with two British textile machinery companies. Over the next few years the Bussan continued to purchase British textile machinery, primarily from Platt & Company. It became the exclusive Japanese agent for Platt in 1886. The Bussan's imports of textile machinery (mostly spindles) averaged between ¥25,000 and ¥46,000 in the years 1885 to 1887, but rose to ¥270,000 in 1888.

In order to meet the sudden demand for cotton in Japan, Mitsui began to import cotton from Shanghai in 1887. When less expensive cotton of a higher quality became available from India, Mitsui dispatched an agent to Bombay, where a representative office was opened in 1892. By 1897 Mitsui accounted for over 30 percent of Japan's cotton imports. In 1900 the Bussan began to import American cotton through its New York office.

1880s Shipping Battle with Mitsubishi

Mitsui relied heavily on the shipping services of Mitsubishi. Since it operated a monopoly in maritime transportation, Mitsubishi was free to charge highly inflated rates for its services. Companies such as Mitsui, which were heavily dependent on shipping, suffered greatly at the hands of Mitsubishi. When Eiichi Shibusawa, an "enemy" of Mitsubishi's founder Yataro Iwasaki, decided that he would no longer tolerate the monopoly practices, he proposed to Masuda that Mitsui help him to establish a rival shipping company. What ensued has been described as one of the most publicized and deadly episodes of competition in Japanese economic history.

In 1880 Mitsui participated in the establishment of the Tokyo Fuhansen (Sailing Ship) Company. A year later it appeared that Mitsubishi had succeeded in driving Fuhansen out of business. Determined to prevail, Shibusawa enlisted additional support from Masuda and Kaoru Inoue. In 1882, they arranged the formation of a new company called Kyodo Unyu (United Transport) in which Fuhansen was merged with a number of smaller shipping companies. The previous year Mitsubishi lost its "protector" in the government, Count Okuma. Iwasaki's enemies in government seized upon the Count's death as an opportunity to retaliate against Mitsubishi. The government provided Kyodo Unyu with trained shipping crews and increased the company's capitalization by 75 percent. Over the next two years fares on the Kobe-Yokohama passenger route dropped from 5.5 to 0.25 yen.

By 1885 the resources of both Mitsubishi and Kyodo Unyu were almost completely depleted. It was at this point that Shibusawa proposed that the government impose regulation of the industry. Unknown to him, however, Yataro Iwasaki had secretly purchased over half of the shares of Kyodo Unyu. He merged the company with Mitsubishi and renamed it the Nihon Yusen Kaisha (Japan Shipping Company), or NYK. Both Shibusawa and Masuda, who remained major shareholders of NYK were denied managerial roles in the new company, and both felt humiliation from their failure to defeat Mitsubishi.

Mitsui Bussan also emerged from the battle with Mitsubishi financially exhausted. Once again Masuda approached Inoue, who managed to secure a government loan to the Mitsui Bank on the condition that Masuda would be replaced by Hikojiro Nakamigawa, a former English teacher at Keio College who had quickly risen to become president of the Sanyo Railway Company. Masuda accepted Inoue's conditions, but remained with the company.

In the meantime, Eiichi Shibusawa continued to challenge NYK by organizing subsequent shipping companies, all of which failed. However, the Oji Paper Company, which he established in 1875, had become quite successful. Shibusawa persuaded Nakamigawa to increase the Bussan's investment in Oji Paper until it acquired a majority in 1890. Almost completely by surprise, Nakamigawa had Shibusawa and his talented nephew Okawa removed from the company. Mitsui took over control of Oji Paper and Shibusawa, defeated a second time, retired.

Chosen to reform Mitsui, Nakamigawa had the company's charter amended in 1896 to include shipping. Two years later several other transport-related operations were added, including warehousing and insurance. Although Nakamigawa died in 1901, his plans for Mitsui to enter maritime transport continued under Masuda. In 1903 a separate division for shipping was established. By the time the Bussan was formally incorporated in 1910, it had entered a number of new businesses; it was no longer just a trading company.

Mitsui Bussan profited greatly during World War I. On several occasions the Mitsui Bank called in outstanding loans from other creditors in order to finance the Bussan's numerous ventures. In 1917 the company created the Mitsui Engineering & Shipbuilding Company which manufactured many ships for the transport division.

As a result of international treaties signed after the war, Japan became a more influential power in Asia. Only 50 years after the Meiji Restoration, Japan began to imitate the industrialized West in another way by "exporting" capital (or making large capital investments in its colonial possessions) to Formosa (Taiwan), Chosen (Korea), and Manchukuo (Manchuria). Mitsui was an active participant in the development of these areas by helping to establish an industrial infrastructure.

Takashi Masuda, who was advancing in age, relinquished his responsibilities to Takuma Dan, a former government engineer from the Miike coal mine. Although he was not trained as a businessman, Dan was a highly disciplined manager. During the 1920s the number of companies under the Bussan's control quadrupled. Toward the end of the decade, however, extreme right-wing militarists initiated a terrorist campaign against the traditional establishment. Mitsui, the largest *zaibatsu*, was frequently attacked because it came to symbolize the democratic capitalist establishment in Japan. In 1932 Takuma Dan was assassinated by a rightist "young officers" group.

Mitsui elected Seihin Ikeda to succeed Dan, but this did not prevent further attacks. Right-wing militarists subsequently assassinated hundreds more moderate politicians, industrialists, and military officers. Perhaps under threat, Mitsui ceased trading a number of agricultural products and offered a substantial amount of stock in its subsidiaries to the public. In 1933 the Bussan established a ¥30 million fund for the promotion of social services and relief of the "distressed." After the February Incident, an isolated but serious mutiny of rightist officers in 1936, the Mitsui family announced that it would cease to participate in the management of the Bussan.

In order to appease critics of "democratic industrialism" who were rapidly coming to power, many of the *zaibatsu* openly participated in the development of a *Junsenji Keizai,* or "quasi-war-time economy." As a result, several *zaibatsu* directly benefited from the government's increased investment in heavy industry. The military/industrial establishment grew rapidly after Japanese forces invaded China in 1937. That year Mitsui launched the Toyota Motor Corporation and Showa Aircraft Industry Company. Mitsui Bussan had become the largest and most powerful conglomerate in the world, employing 2.8 million people.

Like nearly all Japanese companies, Mitsui played an active role in the Japanese war effort, helping to develop shipping, railways, mining, chemical and metallurgical industries, and electrical generation. The company was active in every country under Japanese occupation. By 1943, however, it was realized that Japan had no chance of winning the war. When the mainland of Japan became exposed to aerial bombings, major factories and industrial enterprises were primary targets.

Zaibatsu *Dissolved After World War II*

When the war ended in September 1945, Japan had been almost completely destroyed. All of Mitsui Bussan's major facilities were severely damaged. The entire nation was placed under the command of a military occupation authority, called "SCAP," for Supreme Commander of Allied Powers. Representatives of the *zaibatsu* convinced President Truman's envoy John Foster Dulles that, if properly administered, a "generous" peace treaty would ensure that Japan would become a reliable American ally in the Far East. Nonetheless, SCAP reorganized Japanese industry on the American model of organization and enacted an "Anti-Monopoly Law." Since they were considered monopolies, the *zaibatsu* were ordered dissolved. Mitsui Bussan was broken into over 180 separate companies, none of which were allowed to use the prewar Mitsui logo.

Mitsui Bussan was divided into the "new" Mitsui Bussan (called the Nitto Warehousing Company), Daiichi Bussan, Nippon Machinery Trading, Tokyo Food Products, and a dozen smaller firms. The Mitsui Bank, which during the war was merged with the Daiichi and Daijugo Banks to form the Teikoku Bank, was split into two banks, Mitsui and Daiichi. Mitsui Mining was reorganized and renamed Mitsui Metal Mining. Nettai Sangyo and Mitsui Wood Vessels were dissolved, and Mitsui Lumber was absorbed by the new Bussan. Affiliated companies such as Tokyo Shibaura Electric (later called Toshiba) and Toyota were made fully independent. Finally, all coordination of activities through a *honsha,* or parent company, was strictly prohibited.

Mitsui Bussan Reformed in the 1950s

Despite the various prohibitions, leaders of the former Mitsui *zaibatsu* companies remained in close contact; 27 of them formed a monthly luncheon group called the Getsuyo-kai (Monday Conference). The antimonopoly laws were subsequently weakened by Japanese acts of legislation in 1949 and 1953. After the Korean War (1950–53) the laws were further relaxed and many of the *zaibatsu*, including Mitsui, began to reform under the direction of their former subsidiary banks. Even the Mitsui logo (the Japanese character "three" surrounded by a diagonal square, representing "wellspring") came back into use. Nitto Warehousing began to absorb some of its former component companies in 1951, and in 1952 adopted the name New Mitsui Bussan. Daiichi absorbed the remaining companies between 1951 and 1957, and in 1958 was itself merged with the New Mitsui Bussan, which dropped "New" from its name.

The new *zaibatsu,* called *keiretsu* (banking conglomerates) or *sogo shosha* (trading companies), lacked the strict vertical discipline of the prewar organization. Mitsui completed its reassembly and transition into a *sogo shosha* by 1960.

As the Bussan's various subsidiary industries consolidated their operations, their quasi-*honsha* parent company began to establish offices in many foreign countries, even ones with which Japan had no formal diplomatic ties. As it did before the war, Mitsui's foreign offices functioned as unofficial Japanese consulates.

A second meeting group called the Nimoku-kai was established in 1960. Members of this group later included Toyota, Toshiba, and many of the Getsuyo-kai members. Together with the Getsuyo-kai, which included Toyo Menka Kaisha, Ishikawajima-Harima Heavy Industries, Showa Aircraft, and Oji Paper, among others, the Nimoku-kai enabled Mitsui to coordinate the activities of the former *zaibatsu* affiliates.

In order to expand its heavy industry sector Mitsui purchased the Kinoshita Sansho steel company in 1965. Kinoshita's operations were later merged with Mitsui's Japan Steel Works, Ltd., which was established in 1907. During the 1960s Mitsui helped to develop the Robe River mine in Western Australia, which provided most of the iron ore for the Mitsui steel mills in Japan. Other Australian ventures followed, including another iron ore mine at Mount Newman and a bauxite mine at Gove. These projects led to the creation of a larger joint venture with AMAX in 1973 called Alumax, which produced aluminum in the United States.

Several of Mitsui's former subsidiaries, while remaining associated companies, resisted amalgamation with the parent company because each company's management board wanted to avoid interference from Mitsui; they did not want to be placed into a larger industrial scheme that would reduce their independence. Associated companies, such as Onoda Cement, Toyo Manka, Sapporo Breweries, and Oji Paper, which permitted a more embracing relationship with Mitsui, found the amalgamation difficult to bear. Managers of these companies were given subordinate positions in Mitsui and their opinions carried significantly less weight. In 1973 three other companies, Toshiba, Mitsui O.S.K. Lines, and Mitsukoshi, rejoined Mitsui by accepting membership in the Nimoku-kai. Other larger and more successful associated companies, such as Toyota and Ishikawajima-Harima Heavy Industries, were not expected to join the Nimoku-kai as full members.

Involved in Troubled Iranian Petrochemical Complex in the 1970s and 1980s

Mitsui became a major petrochemical company in 1958. The chemical division, Mitsui Koatsu, sold not only its products, but its production technologies. In 1973 work began on the Iran Japan Petrochemical Complex at Bandar Khomeini (originally Bandar Shapur, or "The Shah's Port"), a US$3 billion joint venture between Mitsui and Iran's National Petrochemical Co. which was to be the largest chemical plant in the Middle East. By the time of the 1979 Iranian Revolution, the complex was 85 percent complete, but construction cost overruns of US$1 billion and the revolution brought construction to a halt. Work resumed after the Japanese government agreed to partially bail Mitsui out by anteing up US$100 million. But after war broke out between Iran and Iraq in late 1980, Bandar Khomeini became a target for Iraqi bombers, who heavily damaged the complex in air raids conducted from 1980 through 1984, forcing the suspension of construction once again. Wishing to rid itself of this embarrassing albatross, Mitsui reached an agreement with the government of Iran in 1989, whereby the Japanese firm paid Iran US$900 million in compensation for withdrawing from the project, as well as agreeing to provide up to US$500 million in long-term credits for Iranian imports of oil industry equipment and to purchase US$300 million in Iranian oil. (A first phase of the complex finally opened in 1990, with a second phase opening in 1994, and a third in 1996. The total cost of the complex ended up reaching US$5 billion.)

From the 1970s through the 1990s, with the company's traditional operations in such areas as steel and chemicals seeing slower growth rates, Mitsui sought to enter new industries and thereby broaden its activities. One of the key new areas for Mitsui was high tech—electronics, information technology, and the like. In 1984 the company entered the personal computer field for the first time, through a joint venture with Solana Beach, California-based Kaypro Corporation. In a first for Mitsui, which was normally a dealer in other companies' products, the company designed, arranged the manufacture, and arranged the distribution (through Kaypro) of a product, namely a notebook-size personal computer. By the end of the 1980s Mitsui had been involved in numerous other high-tech operations: satellite launchings, a fiber-optics communications system in Tokyo, the importing into Japan of state-of-the-art medical equipment, and office-automation software. Mitsui also entered the field of biotechnology, with company scientists working to develop new strains of hybrid rice.

Late 1980s Economic Slide

The bursting of the late 1980s Japanese economic bubble led to prolonged difficulties for most of the *sogo shosha*. As a byproduct of the stagnation of their core trading activities, nearly all of the *sogo shosha* had diversified aggressively into financial investments during the speculative bubble, which reached its peak in 1988–89. The trading companies built up large stock portfolios and became hooked on the revenues they could gain through arbitrage (or *zaiteku*, as it is known in Japan). Once the bubble burst, the *sogo shosha* were left with huge portfolios whose worth had plummeted; the companies were forced to eventually liquidate much of their stock holdings. Ironically, Mitsui was spared much of these difficulties because of its ill-fated involvement in the Bandar Khomeini project. The huge expenses the company incurred as a result of its Iranian debacle kept it from investing heavily in *zaiteku*.

The entire decade of the 1990s was a challenging one for the *sogo shosha* not only because of the lingering effects of their overzealous 1980s investments but also due to the stagnant Japanese economy of the early and mid-1990s, the Asian economic crisis that began in 1997, and the Japanese recession that followed the latter. Mitsui was heavily involved in such troubled nations as Thailand and Indonesia. While it attempted to contain the damage that the crisis—and the Japanese recession—inflicted upon it, Mitsui also laid plans for the development of a third company ''core competence'' (the first being the traditional trading activities of a *sogo shosha;* the second being ''enterprise investment, or the creation of new worldwide trade flows through investment in new enterprises and new industries). Mitsui was pursuing opportunities in financing, in order to take advantage of the Japanese ''big bang,'' the long-anticipated deregulation of the financial sector, a prime opportunity to secure new revenue sources.

Principal Subsidiaries

STEEL PRODUCTS: Mitsui Bussan Construction Materials Co., Ltd.; Mitsui Bussan Coil Center Co., Ltd.; Guangzhou Ribao Steel Coil Center Ltd. (China); Bangkok Coil Center Co., Ltd. (Thailand); Euro Mit-Staal B.V. (Netherlands); Mitsui Steel Development Co., Inc. (U.S.A.); P.T. Fumira (Indonesia). RAW MATERIALS: Mitsui Iron Ore Development Pty. Ltd. (Australia); Mitsui-Itochu Iron Pty. Ltd. (Australia); Caemi Minerão e Metalurgia S.A. (Brazil); Sesa Goa Ltd. (India); Mitsui Coal Holdings Pty. Ltd. (Australia); BHP Mitsui Coal Pty. Ltd. (Australia); Mitsui Gordonstone Investment Pty. Ltd. (Australia); MCDA Bengalla Investment Pty. Ltd. (Australia); Mitsui Bussan Carbon Energy Co., Ltd.; Mitsui Bussan Raw Materials Development Corp.; Mitsui Minerals Development South Africa (Pty) Ltd.; J M Alloys (Pvt) Ltd. (Zimbabwe); Advalloy (Pty) Ltd. (South Africa); Pacific Coast Recycling, LLC (U.S.A.). NON-FERROUS METALS: Mitalco Inc. (U.S.A.); Mitsui Bussan Commodities Ltd. (U.K.); The International Metals & Minerals Co., Ltd. (U.K.); Mitsui Bussan Futures Ltd.; Union Titanium Sponge Corp. (U.S.A.). PROPERTY, SERVICE, CONSTRUCTION, AND HOUSING BUSINESS DEVELOPMENT: Mitsui Bussan House Tech, Inc.; AIM Services Co., Ltd.; Bussan Real Estate Development Co., Ltd.; Mitsui Bussan Forestry Co., Ltd.; Mitsui Wood Systems, Inc.; P.T. Wisma Nusantara International (Indonesia); Singapore Cement Manufacturing Co. (PTE). PLANT AND PROJECT: Mitsui Bussan Plant & Project Corp.; Chlorine Engineers Corp. Ltd.; NEC Moli Energy (Canada) Ltd.; NEC Moli Energy Corp.; AMR Refractarios, S.A. (Spain). ELECTRIC MACHINERY: Nihon Dennetsu Co., Ltd.; Toyo Nuclear Services Co., Ltd.; MBK Power Plant Services Co., Ltd.; MBK Power Plant Engineering Co., Ltd.; Bussan Electric Machinery Trading Co., Ltd.; NGK Stanger PTY Ltd. (Australia). COMMUNICATIONS, TRANSPORTATION, AND INDUSTRIAL PROJECT: Furukawa Industrial S.A. Produtos Elétricos (Brazil); Sanyo Co., Ltd.; MBK Microteck Inc.; Mitrail Inc. (U.S.A.); Shibaura Technology Int. Corp. (U.S.A.); Shin-Nippon Air Technologies Co., Ltd.; Mitsui Bussan Machinery Sales Co., Ltd.; Toyo Valve Co., Ltd.; Echo Inc. (U.S.A.); Mitsui Machinery Distribution, Inc. (U.S.A.); P.T. Yanmar Diesel Indonesia; MBK Transportation Systems Co., Ltd.; The MBK Rail Capital Companies, Inc. (U.S.A.). MOTOR VEHICLES: Toyota Canada Inc.; Yamaha Motor (U.K.) Ltd.; N.V. Subaru Benelux S.A.; Subaru Deutschland GmbH (Germany); Yamaha Motor Deutschland GmbH (Germany); Thai Hino Motor Sales Ltd. (Thailand); Mitsui Bussan Automotive Inc. MARINE AND AEROSPACE: Orient Marine Co., Ltd.; Toyo Ship Machinery Co., Ltd.; Tombo Aviation Inc. (U.S.A.); Tombo Aviation Netherlands B.V.; Mitsui Bussan Aerospace Co., Ltd.; Mitsui Bussan Aerospace Corp. (U.S.A.); Nippon Koki Co., Ltd.; Asia Air Survey Co., Ltd. ELECTRONICS AND INFORMATION: Nihon Unisys Ltd.; Toyo Officemation Inc.; Adam Net Ltd.; Bussan System Integration Co., Inc.; Japan Satellite Systems, Inc.; Moshi Moshi Hotline Inc.; Mitsui Electronic Telecommunication Services Co., Ltd.; Nokia Mobile Communications K.K.; AOL Japan, Inc. PETROCHEMICALS AND POLYMERS: Global Octanes Corp. (U.S.A.); Intercontinental Terminals Co. (U.S.A.); Phalloy MTD B.V. (Netherlands); Alberta & Orient Glycol Co., Ltd. (Canada); Bangkok Polyethylene Co., Ltd. (Thailand); Mitsui Plastics Inc. (U.S.A.). SPECIALTY CHEMICALS AND PLASTICS: Honshu Chemical Industry Co., Ltd.; Mitsui Bussan Solvent & Coating Co., Ltd.; Seiki Corp.; Xeus Inc.; Novus International Inc. (U.S.A.); Palm-Amide SDN BHD (Malaysia); China Mitwell Pharmaceuticals Co., Ltd.; Dalian Nitto Plastic Molding Co., Ltd. (China). FERTILIZER AND INORGANIC CHEMICALS: Daito Chemical Industries, Ltd.; Santoku Chemical Industries Co., Ltd.; Mitsui Bussan Agro Business Co., Ltd.; Mitsui Salt Pty. Ltd. (Australia); Mitsui Denman (Ireland) Ltd.; Eurocel S.A. (France); Santoku Merck Pte. Ltd. (Singapore); Fertilizantes Mitsui S.A. Industria Comerc (Brazil); Anagra S.A. (Chile); Pacific Ammonia Inc. (Canada); P.T. Kaltim Pasifik Amoniak (Indonesia). lain ENERGY: Japan Australia LNG (MIMI) Pty. Ltd. (Australia); Mitsui Oil Exploration Co., Ltd.; Wandoo Oil Development Co., Ltd.; Arcadia Petroleum Ltd. (U.K.); Westport Petroleum Inc. (U.S.A.); Mitsui Oil (Asia) Pte. Ltd. (Singapore); Mobil Unique (Vietnam) Co., Ltd.; Jiangyin Changjiang Petrochemical Storage and Transportation Co., Ltd. (China); Mitsui Oil & Gas Co., Ltd. FOODS: Mikuni Coca-Cola Bottling Co., Ltd.; San-yu Shokuhin Co., Ltd.; Daiichi Broilers Co., Ltd.; MBK Ryutsu Partners Co., Ltd.; United Flour Mill Co., Ltd. (Thailand); United Grain Corp. (U.S.A.); Ventura Foods, LLC (U.S.A.); Mitsui Foods Inc. (U.S.A.). TEXTILES: Valentino Boutique Japan Ltd.; Gianni Versace Japan & Co., Ltd.; Black & White Sportswear Co., Ltd.; Max Mara Japan Co., Ltd.; Mitsui Bussan Inter-Fashion Ltd.; Alcantara S.p.A. (Italy); M.M.F. Co., Ltd. GENERAL MERCHANDISE: Takasaki Paper Mfg. Co., Ltd.; Rossignol Japan Corp.; Mitsui Bussan Sports Co., Ltd.; Nippon Brunswick Co., Ltd.; Nippon Sherwood Medical Industries Ltd.; Busslain an Promotion Co., Ltd.; Mitsui Bussan Digital Corp.; Bussan Lladro Co., Ltd. TRANSPORTATION LOGISTICS: Nitto Warehouse Co., Ltd.; Toshin Soko Kaisha, Ltd.; Insurance Company of Trinet Asia PTE Ltd. (Singapore); Intermodal Terminal Inc. (U.S.A.); Utoku Express Co., Ltd.; Airborne Express Japan, Inc.; Eastern Sea Development Co., Ltd. (Hong Kong); Thai Container Systems Co., Ltd. (Thailand).

Further Reading

"The Billion-Dollar Target," *Forbes,* November 10, 1980, p. 14.

Dawkins, William, "Japan's General Traders Double Growth in Profits," *Financial Times,* May 22, 1996, p. 35.

——, "Trading Houses Disappoint As Yen Takes Toll," *Financial Times,* May 19, 1995, p. 26.

Fairlamb, David, "The Sogo Shosha Flex Their Muscles," *Dun's Business Month,* July 1986, pp. 44+.

Glain, Steve, "Japan's Trading Giants Spark Venture-Capital Boom," *Wall Street Journal,* May 15, 1997, p. A18.

Iwao, Ichiishi, "Sogo Shosha: Meeting New Challenges," *Journal of Japanese Trade & Industry,* January/February 1995, pp. 16–18.

Marcom, John, Jr., "Mitsui, Giant Trading Firm, Plans to Enter Personal-Computer Field," *Wall Street Journal,* March 14, 1984.

Martin, Bradley K., "Japan's Trading Giants Look to Year 2000," *Wall Street Journal,* March 31, 1986.

"Mitsui: End-Run Strategy," *U.S. News & World Report,* August 24, 1987, pp. 42+.

Morikawa, Hidemasa, *Zaibatsu: The Rise and Fall of Family Enterprise Groups in Japan,* [Tokyo]: University of Tokyo Press, 1992, 283 p.

Nakamoto, Michiyo, "Japan Trading Groups in Tie-Up Talks," *Financial Times,* October 6, 1998, p. 32.

——, "Trading Groups Reveal Heavy Indonesian Exposure," *Financial Times,* May 28, 1998, p. 27.

Roberts, John G., *Mitsui: Three Centuries of Japanese Business,* New York: Weatherhill, 1973, 564 p.

Rosario, Louise do, "Lose and Learn: Japan's Firms Pay Price of Financial Speculation," *Far Eastern Economic Review,* June 17, 1993, pp. 60–61.

Sender, Henny, "Let Me Introduce You: The Shosha Are Making It Easier to Set Up in China," *Far Eastern Economic Review,* February 1, 1996, p. 51.

——, "The Sun Never Sets," *Far Eastern Economic Review,* February 1, 1996, pp. 46–48, 50.

"Traders' Duel: Mitsubishi-Mitsui Rivalry Heats Up," *Tokyo Business Today,* September 1995, p. 18.

Wiegner, Kathleen K., "Saving Skin but Losing Face," *Forbes,* October 15, 1979, pp. 74, 77.

Yonekawa, Shin'ichi, ed., *General Trading Companies: A Comparative and Historical Study,* Tokyo: United Nations University Press, 1990, 229 p.

Yonekawa, Shin'ichi, and Hideki Yoshi Hara, ed., *Business History of General Trading Companies,* Tokyo: University of Tokyo Press, 1987.

Yoshihara, Kunio, *Sogo Shosha: The Vanguard of the Japanese Economy,* Tokyo: Oxford University Press, 1982, 358 p.

Young, Alexander, *The Sogo Shosha: Japan's Multinational Trading Companies,* Boulder, Colo.: Westview Press, 1979, 247 p.

—updated by David E. Salamie

Morrison Knudsen Corporation

720 Park Boulevard
Post Office Box 73
Boise, Idaho 83729
U.S.A.
(208) 386-5000
Fax: (208) 386-7186
Web site: http://www.mk.com

Public Company
Incorporated: 1932 as Morrison-Knudsen Company, Inc.
Employees: 8,500
Sales: $1.86 billion (1998)
Stock Exchanges: New York Pacific
Ticker Symbol: MK
NAIC: 23332 Commercial & Institutional Building Construction; 23331 Manufacturing & Industrial Building Construction; 23412 Bridge & Tunnel Construction; 23491 Water, Sewer, & Pipeline Construction; 23499 All Other Heavy Construction; 212112 Bituminous Coal & Lignite Surface Mining; 33651 Railroad Rolling Stock Manufacturing; 54133 Engineering Services; 92411 Administration of Air & Water Resource & Solid Waste Management Programs; 55112 Offices of Other Holding Companies

Morrison Knudsen Corporation (MK) has long stood as one of the world's largest engineering and construction organizations. A 1954 feature article in *Time* identified cofounder Harry Morrison as "the man who has done more than anyone else to change the face of the earth." Such words reflect the magnitude and scope of the company's projects, ranging from work on the Hoover Dam to the construction of the then largest building in the world, the Vehicle Assembly Building at the Kennedy Space Center, to the building of portions of the transAlaska pipeline. Today, MK is active in more than 35 countries, serving the environmental, heavy civil, industrial, mining, operations and maintenance, power, process, transportation, and logistics markets.

Dams Marked Early Years

The company's origin dates back to Idaho's Boise Valley at the turn of the century, when Morris Hans Knudsen and Harry W. Morrison teamed up to exploit business opportunities introduced by the National Reclamation Act of 1902. The U.S. government was subsidizing projects to irrigate vast tracts of desert. Knudsen, a native of Denmark, moved to Idaho with his wife in 1905. He became well known for his skill using horses and basic scrapers to haul dirt. Morrison, a native of Illinois, moved to Idaho in 1904 as a concrete superintendent for water reclamation projects. In 1912 Morrison and Knudsen collaborated on their first job, a subcontract for approximately $14,000 worth of work at a pumping station along the Snake River near Grand View, Idaho. This and other early jobs generated little, if any, profit. The first financially successful endeavor for the duo was the 1914 construction of Three-Mile Falls Dam in Oregon. In addition to yielding a profit, the Three-Mile job established the company as a legitimate player in dam construction, which became one of the company's hallmarks. (By the 1980s MK had built more than 150 dams, including Brownlee, one of three dams erected across the Snake River in Hells Canyon for Idaho Power; Karadj, near Teheran, Iran; San Luis, in California, with a crest length of more than three miles; and Hungry Horse and Yellowtail, both in Montana.)

One of the most significant milestones in the growth of Morrison-Knudsen Company was, in fact, construction of yet another dam, the Hoover (Boulder) Dam, contracted in 1931. The magnitude of the job led to the 1932 incorporation of Morrison-Knudsen Company, Inc. The project was massive, drawing on 5,000 workers. It called for 4.5 million yards of concrete (enough to pave a four-lane highway from Seattle to Miami, according to company sources) and reached a height of 726 feet upon completion. To handle such a formidable task, Morrison brought together a consortium of different companies, Six Companies, Inc., thus introducing the now commonplace practice of joint-venture construction. The dam was completed in 1935, two years ahead of schedule.

Having survived the Great Depression, due, in part, to its success with the Hoover Dam project, MK was prepared to meet the business demands of World War II. The company joined other contractors in a joint venture known as Contractors, Pacific Naval Air Bases. Building airfield facilities on Midway and Wake islands in late 1941, more than 1,200 company workers were captured by the Japanese. On the Hawaiian island of Oahu, MK was also engaged in the construction of 20 huge naval fuel-storage vaults, each 250 feet high and 100 feet in diameter. MK launched its company magazine, the *eMKayan,* in March 1942, a strategic time to reinforce public relations.

These and other World War II projects established long-lasting ties for MK in the area of military contracting. In addition to extensive building contracts in Vietnam, the company procured a substantial amount of business outside of active battle zones. The Distant Early Warning (DEW) Line, a chain of bases and radar installations, was constructed and maintained across northern Canada, as was the ''White Alice'' communications system in Alaska. In the 1960s MK became a leading builder of missile facilities, including the first U.S. underground Titan missile installation at the Lowry Air Force Base in Colorado. The company sponsored a joint venture for the Aeropropulsion Systems Test Facility, an advanced jet engine center for the U.S. Air Force, which was completed in 1984. The company also was involved in the reconstruction of Kuwait following the 1991 Gulf War. According to *U.S. News and World Report,* such an expensive national reconstruction effort had not been launched since the Marshall Plan molded a new Europe after World War II.

Postwar Diversification

While World War II initiated new business, the war's end also brought reconstruction projects and expansion opportunities in new domains. In 1950 MK bought the Cleveland-based industrial builder H.K. Ferguson Company, which aided greatly in the trend toward rebuilding the American infrastructure. The 1950s also marked the establishment of the company's engineering subsidiary, International Engineering Company, Inc., which was designed primarily to implement public works in less industrialized nations (its first project was a dam in India). By the mid-1950s, the firm had been commissioned by ten foreign governments. The company had by this time established a notable presence in a number of international markets, working on projects in such distant lands as Afghanistan, China, Iran, and Saudi Arabia. A *Time* magazine article in May 1954 titled ''Builders Abroad—Ambassadors with Bulldozers'' emphasized the impact of the construction industry on world economy. The magazine cover featured a portrait of Harry Morrison with the subheading, ''To tame rivers and move mountains.''

The company further diversified in the 1960s, establishing itself as one of the major contractors to the developing space program. In addition to other contracts for the American space program, in 1966 the company contracted the Vehicle Assembly Building (VAB) in Florida. The world's largest building at the time, it was used to assemble the Apollo and Saturn V rockets, for which MK also constructed the launching pads.

The Vietnam War in the 1960s and early 1970s also stimulated business, when the U.S. government engaged the company as the sponsor of a joint venture—called RMK-BRJ—that consisted of MK International, Raymond International, Brown & Root, and J.A. Jones Construction Company. Under the command of the U.S. Naval Facilities Engineering Command, RMK-BRJ constructed bridges, highways, jet airfields, hospitals, deepwater ports, communications facilities, water supply systems, power plants, supply depots, and other facilities from 1962 to 1972. The venture, which employed more than 50,000 people, resulted in roughly $1.9 billion of business.

Tremendous Growth Under McMurren, 1970–84

The challenges of the Vietnam era forged the business skills of William H. McMurren, who was elected president and chief executive officer in 1970. McMurren served for 14 years and carried the company into the 1980s under a new program of expansion and diversification. McMurren first established his abilities as a manager while directing missile site construction during the early 1960s. From 1970 to 1984, when he died at the age of 57, McMurren enhanced the traditional construction abilities of MK and extended activities to engineering, construction management, mining, real estate, manufacturing, and shipbuilding.

Indeed, the late 1970s and early 1980s marked a period of unprecedented growth for MK. The company expanded into mining, a logical offshoot of its heavy civil engineering operations. MK explored for precious metals, coal, lignite, and limestone mines throughout the United States and in various foreign countries. Notable examples included the 1973 Rio Blanco Copper mine in Chile, hewn out of solid rock in the forbidding landscape of the Andes Mountains; the Cerrejon Coal Project, a $2 billion turnkey project in northeastern Colombia; and the 1989 joint venture with Eastmaque Gold Mines, Ltd. to operate and develop the Cargo Muchacho Project in southeastern California (known as the American Girl Joint Venture). MK also delved into shipmaking, acquiring full ownership of National Steel and Shipbuilding Company (NASSCO) of San Diego in 1979. One of its first projects was the construction of a fast-combat support ship for the Navy, with an open contract for further orders.

MK also moved into environment-related industries of hazardous waste handling and storage and energy plant repair, modification, and improvement. By 1987 the company had carried out design and construction management of remedial actions programs at 24 abandoned uranium processing sites nationwide for the Department of Energy. It also worked on waste-to-energy plants in Florida; Charlotte, North Carolina; and Fayetteville, Arkansas.

Also chartered to broaden MK's base was the new venture Morrison-Knudsen Services, designed to maintain and operate military facilities in Alabama, Arizona, and California. Finally, the company focused particular energy on its railroad business, rebuilding transit cars and, by the late 1980s, serving as the sole domestic manufacturer of the cars. By the early 1980s MK's varied initiatives, fostered by McMurren, had bolstered the company's potential on numerous fronts.

The firm's growth, however, was hampered by a harsh economic climate in the mid-1980s, prompting the company to restructure its operations. On May 3, 1985, stockholders approved a plan of reorganization and agreement of merger wherein Morrison-Knudsen Co., Inc. became a wholly owned operating subsidiary of Morrison Knudsen Corporation. Other subsidiaries included Morrison-Knudsen Engineers, Morrison-Knudsen International Company, and MK-Ferguson Company (National Steel and Shipbuilding Company remained a subsidiary of Morrison-Knudsen Company). The new company structure was designed to accommodate growing complexities in the engineering and construction industries. The short-term result of the reorganization bordered on disaster. In 1988 MK suffered a loss of $3.35 per share from continuing operations and an $8.17 per share loss from discontinued operations, in part because of a $42 million pretax loss on the disposition of its interest in the shipbuilding operation of NASSCO.

Agee Hired As Chairman and CEO in 1988

Due, in large part, to such slippage, the company initiated another round of reorganization in 1988, appointing William J. Agee to replace W.J. Deasy as chairman and CEO. Agee's principal responsibility was to reverse the negative trend in MK earnings while at the same time resuscitate his own business reputation, which had suffered in the media since the early 1960s.

As chief financial officer at Boise Cascade Corporation, Agee had been instrumental in heading the company in the direction of urban renewal, an area that was trendy, though not especially prudent, according to Richard Stern in a June 1992 *Forbes* article. Boise Cascade's financial woes, which included defaulted real estate sales and inadequate reserves for South American bonds owned by a subsidiary, did not reach their peak, however, until after Agee had left the company. In 1972 he joined Bendix Corporation as chief financial officer, becoming chairman in 1977. In 1980 he drew criticism for his relationship with a young protégée, Mary Cunningham, who rose to the position of vice-president of strategic planning at Bendix before the age of 30. In 1982 Agee and Cunningham married. In that same year, Agee launched a hostile bid to take over Martin Marietta Corporation, the missile and technology company. Marietta fought back by buying Bendix shares in what was called a "Pac-Man defense," a reference to the video-game character that defends itself by swallowing its enemies to become stronger. Finally, Allied Corporation intervened, absorbing Bendix and dismissing the Agee couple.

Upon joining MK, Agee effected an immediate strategy to rescue the company from debt and heavy losses. He cut the payroll, stopped bidding for small projects, and rebuilt the company's international business. He made MK's transportation-construction business the top-ranked company in the United States, while other main lines improved, but less dramatically. Agee also strengthened MK's balance sheet, cutting debt from $300 million to almost nothing and amassing $100 million in cash. Other financial figures also looked promising: in February 1990 the company reported 1989 net income of $32.2 million, or $2.81 per share, on revenue of $2.2 billion, representing an all-time record for net income from continuing operations of the engineering and construction and rail systems segments, and surpassing the 1981 record by over $3 million. Net income for 1990 rose to $34.5 million on revenue of $1.7 billion. By 1991 the company reported a second quarter backlog of $4.1 billion, up from $3.4 billion for the same period during the previous year. Agee's restructuring, however controversial, had dramatically transformed MK's financial fortunes.

A large part of the change was attributable to MK's emphasis on the transportation sector, especially design and construction of transit cars. Ken Fisher, president and CEO at Fisher Investments, identified excellent investment opportunities in a 1992 portfolio letter, recognizing that MK had built up its rapid transit system business from less than one percent of its total revenues to 40 percent. The company's success in its emphasis on the transportation industry was further illustrated by the position it assumed at the forefront of a revival of interest in rail transportation in the United States. Sensitive to current trends, Agee envisioned not only high-speed rail between cities, but also commuter transit in every major U.S. city.

To that end, the company won various contracts around the country. It contracted the construction of tunnels and substations for the Bay Area Rapid Transit system in northern California and tunnels and underground stations for the Washington, D.C. "Metro" subway system. In November 1991, MK was approved by the Honolulu City Council to design, build, operate, maintain, and supply vehicles for a $1.7 billion, 15.6-mile elevated rapid transit system serving Honolulu. In January 1992 the company became managing director for a consortium to develop a high-speed rail system linking Houston, Dallas-Fort Worth, Austin, and San Antonio. A less high-tech project was the Hornell plant, located near Elmira, New York, that started remanufacturing 750 transit cars in the early 1980s. The plant lost significant earnings that year, but subsequently managed to improve profits. In March 1992 MK announced an agreement with Caterpillar, Inc. to use state-of-the-art Caterpillar engines in its generation of new locomotives.

MK was also involved in the controversial bidding for a Los Angeles transit project in 1992. The bidding pitted MK and the Japanese-based Sumitomo Corporation against each other for a Los Angeles County transportation contract to build the $122 million Green Line Cars. Although the MK bid was approximately $5 million cheaper for the County of Los Angeles, Sumitomo won the bid, allegedly due to greater experience in the industry. Ray Grabinski of the transportation commission explained to ABC News that "this wasn't the difference between a Honda and a Ford Taurus. This was the difference between a Honda and a mechanic saying he can build you a car." A national uproar ensued, arguing in favor of American jobs and fueling a rash of anti-Japanese sentiments. In January county transportation officials canceled their contract and convened a special panel to standardize rail car design and build the vehicles locally, possibly drawing on a multicompany venture to implement it. Though MK did not win back that contract, it found business further north, in San Francisco, where it contracted with the Bay Area Rapid Transit (BART) to renovate an abandoned steel warehouse in the area as a manufacturing site for 88 Caltrans cars by 1994. The so-called "California car" was designed as a double-decker model for commuter systems and longer-distance routes inside the state.

A less controversial, though highly publicized, deal was also made with Metra, the Chicago area commuter rail agency, in January 1992. The contract called for MK to build 173 new rail cars and to refurbish 140 existing cars. The tab, worth $378 million, constituted the largest transit-car order for the company and one of the biggest in U.S. history. According to the contract, MK was to reopen one section of the Pullman freight car plant on Chicago's South Side and begin hiring in late 1992, with final deliveries scheduled for late 1995. Since employment was particularly low on the South Side, where USX Corp.'s South Works steel mill had recently closed, skilled workers were in abundance. Nevertheless, labor disputes erupted when MK won the contract over Montreal's Bombardier, Inc.; Bombardier had committed itself to a United Auto Workers' facility, while MK had not promised union ties.

Mass-Transit Contracts Led to 1996 Bankruptcy, Takeover by Washington Construction

Agee had correctly foreseen a resurgence of rail transit, but MK's mass-transit business quickly unraveled. After losing the Honolulu rapid-transit contract in 1992, the Texas high-speed rail project fell apart the following year because of financial difficulties. It also soon became clear that MK had gained its prominent position in the industry by seriously underbidding its contracts. This risky practice was compounded by the company's difficulties in fulfilling the contracts. By early 1995 MK was a year late in delivering 113 transit cars to the California Transportation Dept., and had encountered numerous production problems in attempting to fulfill its Chicago contract. Around this same time, the company announced a $310 million loss for 1994, largely as a result of the mass-transit unit's debacles; and with the red ink mounting and the company's creditors threatening to cut off its financing, MK's board fired Agee in early February 1995, citing in part alleged financial improprieties committed by Agee and accounting irregularities.

In early March 1995 the board named Robert A. Tinstman, who had been the head of MK's mining unit, the new CEO. To bolster the company's sinking credibility with lenders, clients, and the media, the board brought in Robert S. Miller, Jr., as the new chairman in April of that year. Miller had been a key financial architect of the early 1980s bailout of Chrysler Corporation. With $350 million in debt, MK appeared on the brink of bankruptcy and/or possible dismemberment.

Through astute maneuvering, however, Tinstman and Miller were able to keep MK largely intact, with one key exception—the railcar unit, the root of the company's difficulties, was offloaded to MK's creditors in late 1995. MK would once again concentrate on its historic core areas: heavy construction, environmental cleanup, engineering projects, and mining. Also in 1995 the company settled numerous shareholder lawsuits and reached agreement with its creditors on a rollover of debt into 1996.

Having gained some breathing room, Tinstman and Miller had enough time to convince Dennis R. Washington to rescue

Morrison Knudsen by acquiring it. Following a prepackaged bankruptcy filing that was filed in June 1996, MK emerged from bankruptcy in September of that year and was then acquired by Washington Construction Group, Inc. Originally known as Kasler Holding Company, Washington Construction was owned by Dennis Washington and was the largest builder of roads and bridges in California. After Washington Construction acquired the much larger MK, it then adopted the name of the acquired company, Morrison Knudsen Corporation. Washington held an initial 37 percent stake in the new MK. The deal also had MK swap its debt for equity, with the company's creditors emerging with 45 percent of the company. The remaining equity was held by people who had held shares in Washington Construction. Dennis Washington became chairman of the new MK, Miller was named vice-chairman, while Tinstman served as president and CEO.

Results for fiscal years 1997 and 1998 appeared to confirm that MK was safely on the road to recovery. Revenue increased from $1.68 billion in 1997 to $1.86 billion in 1998, while net income rose from $32 million to $37.6 million. In January 1999 the company announced a consolidation of two of its operating groups—Heavy Civil Construction (which worked on infrastructure projects) and Mining—into a new unit called the Morrison Knudsen Constructors Group. This left MK with two main units, the other being the Engineers and Constructors Group, which specialized in engineering, construction, maintenance, and environmental services. In February 1999 Tinstman retired from MK and Washington added the presidency and CEO position to his duties as chairman. The following month MK and British Nuclear Fuels Ltd. completed a joint acquisition of Westinghouse Electric Company from CBS Corporation. Westinghouse was a world leader in commercial nuclear power technology, was involved in the nuclear defense industry, and was involved in the development of new nuclear plant technology, including the under-design AP600, an advanced, passive nuclear power plant.

Principal Subsidiaries

Broadway Insurance Company, Ltd. (Bermuda); Centennial Engineering, Inc.; Industrial Constructors Corporation; MK Ferguson of Oak Ridge Company; Morrison Knudsen B.V. (Netherlands); Morrison Knudsen Deutschland GmbH (Germany); National Projects, Inc.

Principal Operating Units

Engineers and Constructors Group; Morrison Knudsen Constructors Group.

Further Reading

Aeppel, Timothy, and Steven Lipin, "CBS to Sell Nonmedia Lines to Consortium," *Wall Street Journal,* June 29, 1998, p. A4.
"Builders Abroad; Ambassadors with Bulldozers," *Time,* May 3, 1954.
Dobbs, Lou, "Interview with Morrison-Knudsen CEO William Agee," *CNN Moneyline,* January 21, 1992.
Einhorn, Cheryl Strauss, "Mountain Man's American Dream," *Barron's,* September 30, 1996, pp. 29–32.
eMKayan, Boise, Idaho: Morrison Knudsen Corporation, March 1987.
Fritsch, Jane, "Axing of Sumitomo Paints County into Corner," *Los Angeles Times,* January 24, 1992.

Greenwald, John, "The Wreck of Morrison Knudsen," *Time,* April 3, 1995, pp. 52–53.

Korman, Richard, "Award of Excellence," *Engineering News Record,* April 7, 1997, pp. 32–41.

Krueger, Bob, "Dream of Texas High-Speed Rail May Be Dying," *Houston Chronicle,* January 12, 1992.

Laing, Jonathan R., "Bigger and Better: Morrison Knudsen's Billionaire Rescuer Folds in the Fabled Anaconda Copper Mine," *Barron's,* September 1, 1997, p. 12.

——, "Boise Blues: At Morrison Knudsen, the Toughest Days May Lie Ahead," *Barron's,* May 29, 1995, pp. 15–16.

Levinson, Marc, "A High Roller Craps Out," *Newsweek,* February 20, 1995, p. 44.

Maturi, Richard, "Revived Morrison Knudsen Focuses on the Environment," *Denver Business Journal,* February 21, 1992.

Melcher, Richard A., Dori Jones Yang, and William C. Symonds, "The Morass Engulfing Morrison Knudsen," *Business Week,* April 3, 1995, p. 54.

O'Reilly, Brian, "Agee in Exile," *Fortune,* May 29, 1995, pp. 50+.

Phillips, Don, "Getting U.S. Back on Track; Transit Agency Uses Economic Muscle to Revive Pullman Rail Car Legacy," *Washington Post,* May 24, 1992.

Rigdon, Joan E., "Stealth Billionaire: Dennis Washington Buys a Lot of Firms, but Just Who Is He?," *Wall Street Journal,* June 6, 1996, pp. A1+.

Rigdon, Joan E., and Joann S. Lublin, "Call to Duty: Why Morrison Board Fired Agee," *Wall Street Journal,* February 13, 1995, p. B1.

Stern, Richard L., and Reed Abelson, "The Imperial Agees," *Forbes,* June 8, 1992.

Taub, Stephan, "Morrison Knudsen's Ticking Bomb Debt," *Financial World,* October 24, 1995, p. 18.

Yang, Dori Jones, and Kevin Kelly, "Why Morrison Knudsen Is Riding the Rails," *Business Week,* November 2, 1992.

—Kerstan Cohen
—updated by David E. Salamie

MOVADO GROUP

Movado Group, Inc.

125 Chubb Avenue
Lyndhurst, New York 07071
U.S.A.
(201) 460-4800
Fax: (201) 460-8384

Public Company
Incorporated: 1961 as North American Watch Company
Employees: 800
Sales: $237 million (1998)
Stock Exchanges: NASDAQ
Ticker Symbol: MOVA
NAIC: 334518 Watch, Clock, & Part Manufacturing

Movado Group, Inc. is a leading manufacturer, marketer and distributor of luxury watches. The company is an amalgamation of several historic fine watchmakers, including the Swiss Movado and Concord companies, and it also makes watches under the brand names Vizio and ESQ. It has a licensing agreement to make watches under the Coach brand, a name long associated with fine leather goods, and also distributes the top-of-the-line handmade Swiss watches of Corum and Piaget. The company operates several retail Movado stores, which not only sell its watches but home and office accessories and jewelry as well. Perhaps its most recognizable product is the Movado Museum Watch. The watch's black, numberless face is adorned only with a single dot at 12 o'clock. The company was formerly known as North American Watch Company.

Early Years

Several roots led to the current Movado Group. In the United States, the company dates back to 1961, with the founding of the North American Watch Company. This company was run by Gedalio Grinberg, an immigrant from Cuba. He owned 50 percent of the company, in partnership with a Swiss watchmaker and a consortium of three U.S. businessmen. In 1969, North American Watch became the parent company of Concord, an old Swiss watchmaker. It was the U.S. distributor for two other Swiss watches, Piaget and Corum, as well. Concord was founded in Bienne, Switzerland, in 1908. The company made fine luxury watches, and was especially noted for its skill in producing ultra-thin designs. Since its beginnings, Concord was associated with some of the world's leading jewelers, including Tiffany's and Cartier, for whom it designed private-label watches. Another unique design from Concord was a watch with a coin for a face. Its first coin watch premiered in 1946, and the company still makes these unusual and distinctive watches.

An even older company was Movado, which dated back to 1881. This company was at first the workshop of a young Swiss, Achille Ditesheim, who moved with his family from Alsace, France, to the village of La Chaux-de-Fonds in the Swiss Jura Mountains in 1876. In 1881 Ditesheim was 19, and he set himself up in business with six craftsmen to manufacture watches. His small workshop grew quickly, so that by 1897 it employed 80 watchmakers. It had become one of the largest watch manufacturers in all Switzerland, and was noted for its technological sophistication. Early for its time, Ditesheim's company used electricity and advanced machinery in place of the simple hand tools of other watchmakers. Achille Ditesheim gave his company the name Movado in 1905, choosing a word meaning "always in motion" in the then flourishing international language of Esperanto.

Movado was always an admired innovator in technology and design. In 1912 its Polyplan watch pioneered a curved design, with movements specially engineered to conform to an elongated case that followed the plane of the wearer's wrist. Movado's designs also won top awards at the Paris, Brussels, and Liege world expositions. The company became internationally prominent, and by 1920 Movado was making more than 700 different wristwatch models. Two of its most famous watches from the 1920s were the Valentino and the Ermeto. The Valentino was inspired by the glamorous star of the silent screen Rudolf Valentino. It was encased in sensuous snakeskin. The Ermeto was a handheld watch in a small box, the forerunner of the travel clock. Opening the case revealed the timepiece, and the motion automatically wound the watch. It was an ingenious design, which the company promoted with extensive advertising. Movado produced its Ermeto watch in a variety of styles, including etched gold or silver, and several enameled versions such as a striking black and white checkerboard design. The more luxurious Ermeto watches were trimmed with precious stones.

Movado continued to produce complicated and innovative watches in ensuing decades. In the 1930s the company manufactured one of the first digital watches, and as early as 1935 Movado was making water-resistant watches in both round and rectangular styles. In 1945 the company debuted the world's first automatic winding wristwatch. This was called the Tempomatic. By 1956 the Tempomatic had been retooled into the Kingmatic. This was an automatic watch designed to be extremely rugged, and it was one of Movado's best sellers in the 1950s and 1960s. Movado's signature Museum Watch was first manufactured for sale in 1962. An American artist, Nathan George Horwitt, designed the stark, black, numberless dial watch in 1947, and in 1960 Horwitt donated his prototype to the Museum of Modern Art in New York. Movado agreed to produce the Horwitt watch in 1962, and it went on to become one of the world's bestselling dial designs.

North American Watch in the 1970s

In 1969, Gedalia Grinberg's North American Watch Company purchased the Swiss watchmaker Concord. This was an interesting moment in the history of watch technology, because in 1968 Swiss watchmakers first developed the quartz watch. These watches combined an integrated circuit with a battery-powered quartz crystal which oscillated at thousands of vibrations per second. The resulting watch was more accurate than the meticulously handcrafted mechanical watches the Swiss were so famed for making. It took only a few years for the technology to spread to other countries. In the United States, Texas Instruments began selling plastic quartz watches for under $10. Though cheap and perhaps not fashionable, they were every bit as functional as an expensive mechanical watch. K. Hattori & Co., a Japanese company, began promoting its Seiko brand watches by 1972, cutting deeply into Swiss market share. While nearly 40 percent of watches on the U.S. market in 1971 were imported from Switzerland, by 1976 less than 20 percent were Swiss.

Consequently, North American Watch, which also distributed the Swiss Piaget and Corum brands, had rather limited corporate success in the early 1970s. Swiss watches were falling out of vogue. In 1976 North American Watch had sales of $8.1 million, and its net income was a measly $209,000. This led Grinberg to adopt a new marketing strategy in 1977. While other Swiss watchmakers had shied away from the new quartz technology, Grinberg asked that 90 percent of his watches have quartz works. By comparison, the prestigious Rolex company was making only about 15 percent of its watches with quartz works in the late 1970s. Thus the watches had the latest technological advantage, yet North American's products remained classic in other ways. They were gold, studded with diamonds, and had no alarms or calculators. They were the old-fashioned luxury Swiss watches in every way but the inside. Then Grinberg upped North American's ad spending. In 1977 the company spent $1.4 million on advertising, and by 1980 it was spending $6 million annually. In another unusual move, North American eschewed the standard print ads and went to television. The company wished to reach out to middle-income Americans, who would see owning a gold Swiss watch as both status symbol and investment. The watches were expensive, ranging from about $400 in 1980 to as much as $60,000 for the Concord Delirium, and North American tried to market them as hedges against inflation. Few middle-income Americans could plunk down $60,000 for a watch in 1980, but there were apparently many who would pay up to $10,000 for a model from the more moderate Concord Nine Line collection. Grinberg's revamping of North American was successful almost immediately. From the sluggish figures of 1976, sales went up almost sixfold by 1980. The company pulled in $45 million in sales for 1980, with profits of $3 million. Although previously not a serious competitor, it now found itself outselling some of the larger and better-known names in Swiss watches.

Expanding Product Lines in the 1980s

Though the percentage of watches imported from Switzerland to the United States continued to plummet, hanging just above six percent in 1981, North American Watch did not suffer. It spent more each year on advertising, dedicating some $14 million in 1982. Sales were still soaring in the early 1980s, reaching close to $86 million in 1982. North American competed with more than a dozen different brands that made up the luxury watch market in the United States in the early 1980s, and the company was recognized within the industry as the most successful Swiss watch distributor. In 1983 North American added another Swiss watch brand to its portfolio, Movado. After its great success earlier in the century, Movado was ailing. In fact the company was losing money at the time of the acquisition. But it was a good match for North American Watch, forming the least expensive end of its four brands. Movado watches were priced from around $200 to $2,500, while Concord watches ran from around $500 to $10,000. Piaget and Corum, the two brands North American distributed but did not own, were even more expensive.

North American Watch made the most of Movado. The black Museum Watch was already well known, and the company expanded the line to include dozens of variants. There were at least 24 different watches being sold under the name Movado Museum Watch in 1986, and some of these were a far cry from the gaunt simplicity of Horwitt's original design. One watch even had numbers on the dial, and it was ringed with diamonds. The name ''Museum Watch'' had a certain cachet that the company's advertising exploited as well as it could. The Museum of Modern Art, which displayed the original Horwitt watch, even put up a disclaimer in 1984, noting that "the Movado watch is not a Museum of Art watch, nor is there any connection between the Museum of Modern Art and the Movado Watch Corporation." Sol Flick, a lawyer for North American Watch countered that the "museum" in "Museum Watch" might refer to any museum. "It could be the Museum of Natural History," he said in a November 1986 *Consumer Reports* article.

Nevertheless, North American's advertising continued to make references to the Museum of Modern Art. Capitalizing on the name even further, the company set up a division in 1987 called Movado Museum Designs International Ltd. This was to develop products such as desk accessories, luggage, jewelry, leathergoods, and handbags for sale in department stores that also handled Movado watches. In 1988, the company opened its first freestanding Movado store, on Madison Avenue in New York City.

North American Watch made a move into another luxury category, luggage, in the late 1980s. In 1987 it bought Wings, a formerly chic luggage maker that was now losing money. Similar perhaps to Movado, Wings had been a glamorous brand through the 1950s and 1960s, but sales had sagged afterwards and the company had not been able to market itself effectively. North American bought the company and then went back into its design history and brought out new versions of old classics. In keeping with its retro feel, a Wings ad for 1988 was a re-shot version of one from 1953. North American Watch promoted its new line heavily, allocating approximately $1 million of its total ad budget in 1989 for Wings.

Under Movado Name in the 1990s

In the early 1990s North American Watch continued to promote its products heavily through advertising, both in print and on television. For years the company had relied on an in-house advertising agency, though by the late 1980s North American also used outside agencies. Romantic, virtually wordless television ads were designed by Ogilvy & Mather to appeal to a worldwide audience, because the company had growing sales in Asia, the Middle East, Latin America, and Europe.

In 1992 North American introduced a new line of high-performance watches geared for sports enthusiasts and active people. At first called Esquire, the company shortened the name to ESQ in 1995. The watches were less expensive than North American's other Swiss watches, and were different in design, with lots of features packed on the dial. This gave North American a good product spread, with watches in every segment of the market except for the very cheapest. Then on September 30, 1993 North American Watch Company raised cash by going public. The company wanted to expand more into retailing, among other things, and the stock offering was expected to bring an influx of money. Apparently, the company did not make as big a splash as it had expected. Though its sales and profits had been increasing at respectable rates, the name North American Watch was not well known. So in 1996 the company officially adopted the name of its best-known brand and became the Movado Group, Inc.

The newly named company rolled out plans to expand its product line and to court new markets, principally in Japan, Hong Kong, and Taiwan. Movado also signed an agreement with Coach, a well-known luxury luggage maker, to produce a line of Coach watches. In an interesting mix, this got the luggage maker's name on watches just as Movado was trying to extend its brand name onto luggage, jewelry, and accessories. The company intended to put the Movado name on a bigger variety of items for its stand-alone Movado boutiques. Although in 1997 Movado's sales were principally through independent jewelers, jewelry chains such as Zales, Helzberg, and Sterling, or through premium department stores, including Saks, Macy's, and Nieman-Marcus, it had opened a small line of retail outlet stores. These 16 stores across the United States sold its discontinued merchandise, as well as samples and factory seconds. The New York Movado boutique was still the only one of its kind, while a second store the company operated sold only Piaget watches and jewelry. In 1998 Movado announced that it would open three new boutiques, with plans for four more the next year. The stores sold Movado brand jewelry and accessories as well as watches, with 500 products at a range of price levels. The new stores aimed to draw in the kind of customers who bought Movado watches, though the boutiques were emphatically not merely watch shops. The famous black face of the Museum Watch was transferred onto a wall clock that faced the store entrance, and the kind of spare, modern design epitomized by the Museum Watch was meant to carry through to the whole store. The 1998 stores opened in malls in Short Hills, New Jersey, and in White Plains, New York, while the third, in Rockefeller Center in Manhattan, replaced the first retail space the company had opened in New York ten years earlier.

Financially, Movado was doing very well in the late 1990s. Sales climbed steeply, from $161 million in 1995 to $237 million in 1998. Net income also kept pace. Movado continued to spend heavily on advertising worldwide. The company's strategy for the future hinged on reaching farther into international markets with its core brands and expanding its move into retailing. By 1998, just under 17 percent of the company's sales were international, up from 14 percent in 1997. In the same period, its domestic sales grew almost 11 percent. Movado signed a new licensing agreement, expanding into clocks through the Linden company. Linden was a leading clock maker, and it agreed to develop, produce and distribute clocks with the Movado name. The company was anxious to refine and improve the stores it opened in 1998, viewing them as prototypes for future rollouts of boutiques in malls across the United States and then internationally. With surging sales and an increasingly recognized brand name and design style, Movado seemed ready to handle more growth and expansion into the next century.

Principal Subsidiaries

SwissAm Inc.; Concord Watch Company, S.A. (Switzerland); Montres Movado, S.A. (Switzerland); Movado Watch Company, S.A. (Switzerland); N.A. Trading Ltd. (Switzerland); North American Watch of Canada, Ltd.

Further Reading

Barmash, Isadore, "Fighting the Recession by Spotting Some Fads and Inventing Others," *New York Times*, November 17, 1991, p. F5.

"Battling for Luxury Watches," *New York Times*, June 5, 1984, p. D5.

"Coach, Movado: Timely Pair," *WWD*, December 1, 1997, p. 12.

Dougherty, Philip H., "Ogilvy Puts Romance in Concord Watch Ads," *New York Times*, April 21, 1987, p. D27.

——, "Ogilvy Turns Seductive for Watches," *New York Times*, May 2, 1988, p. D11.

Elliot, Stuart, "Movado Group Hires an Outside Agency to Reset the Luxury Face of Its Concord Watch," *New York Times*, October 27, 1998, p. C7.

Hessen, Wendy, "The Book on Movado," *WWD*, October 28, 1996, p. 11.

McLean, Bethany, "A Timely Move," *Fortune*, October 14, 1996, p. 296.

"Movado Group's Earnings Increase 41.7% in Quarter," *WWD*, April 6, 1998, p. 17.

"Movado Raises $32.2M," *WWD*, October 23, 1997, p. 22.

"Movado's Net Rose 13% in Latest Period, Helped by Strong Sales," *Wall Street Journal*, December 11, 1996, p. C19.

"Movado Strategies: Boutiques, Diversification, Sales Penetration," *Jewelers Circular Keystone*, December 1997, p. 28.

Neiss, Doug, "Movado Forms New Division to Develop Complements of Museum Watch," *HFD*, August 10, 1987, p. 48.

Newman, Jill, "Movado Opens First New York Unit," *WWD*, December 16, 1988, p. 6.

"North American Watch: Selling Jewelry Rather Than Time," *Business Week*, January 14, 1980.

Roman, Monica, "What's with the 10 Grand Watch?—Big Biz!" *Daily News Record*, March 25, 1983, p. 15.

Schuster, William George, "Movado: The New Jeweler," *Jewelers Circular Keystone*, June 1998, p. 328.

Simon, Ellen, "Movado Group Profit Rises 24 Percent," *Knight-Ridder/Tribune Business News*, March 31, 1997, p. 331B1236.

Stern, Aimee L., "Upgrading 'Wings' to First-Class Status," *Adweek's Marketing Week*, March 6, 1989, p. 74.

"What's in a Name? The Movado Museum Watch," *Consumer Reports*, November 1986, p. 694.

—A. Woodward

National Amusements Inc.

200 Elm Street
Dedham, Massachusetts 02026
U.S.A.
(781) 461-1600
Fax: (781) 461-1412
Web site: http://www.national-amusements.com

Private Company
Incorporated: 1946 as Redstone Management
Employees: 4,500
Sales: $235 million (1997 est.)
NAIC: 512131 Motion Picture Theaters, Except Drive-In

One of the ten largest U.S.-based movie theater chains, National Amusements Inc. operates more than 1,200 screens in the United States, the United Kingdom, and in South America. A privately held company owned by Sumner M. Redstone and his family, National Amusements operates as the parent company of Viacom Inc., which includes Paramount Communications, MTV Networks, Nickelodeon, VH1, Blockbuster Video, Simon & Schuster, Showtime Networks, Inc., and other major entertainment properties. National Amusements acquired Viacom in 1987, when the company was generating slightly more than $900 million in annual revenue. By the late 1990s, Viacom was collecting in excess of $12 billion in revenue each year.

Origins of Family Business

The mastermind behind National Amusements was and is Sumner Redstone, whose distinguished professional career represents a rags-to-riches transformation. He was born in 1923 and spent his childhood in a Boston tenement without a bathroom. His father, born Max Rohtstein, changed his name to Michael Redstone and supported his family by selling newspapers on the streets of Boston. Later, the elder Redstone worked as a linoleum salesman, eventually saving enough money to enter the nightclub business. He purchased Boston's Latin Quarter from Lou Walters, father of Barbara Walters, and did well enough as a nightclub owner to finance other entrepreneur-

ial ventures. Michael Redstone opened the third drive-in theater in the United States and expanded it into a chain that proliferated following World War II. It was a business—Redstone Management—over which his son would later assume control.

While his father created a career for himself as a business owner, Sumner Redstone distinguished himself as an exceptionally gifted student. At Boston Latin School, Redstone won all the academic prizes for his class and led the school's debating team. He enrolled at Harvard at age 17, becoming a member of the class of 1944, but finished his studies in two-and-a-half years, departing the Ivy League school at the height of World War II fluent in Japanese and conversant in Latin, French, and German. His skills as a linguist led to a position in an elite U.S. Army intelligence team responsible for breaking the Japanese military and diplomatic codes. After the war, Redstone entered Harvard Law School, where he finished his studies in 1947. For the next several years, Redstone practiced as an attorney, serving for three years as special assistant to U.S. Attorney General Tom C. Clark in Washington, D.C. In 1951, at age 28, Redstone was named partner of the Washington law firm Ford, Bergson, Adams, Borkland & Redstone, where he stayed for the next three years. By 1954, the highly successful Redstone was ready to pursue a different profession. "When I found out I wasn't going to make the world better by being a lawyer," he explained, "I decided I wanted to be in business for myself." His logical segue into the business world was joining his father, who, along with Sumner's younger brother Edward, was busy managing 12 drive-in theaters controlled by Redstone Management, a company later to develop into National Amusements Inc.

As part of Redstone Management, Sumner Redstone used his skills as an attorney to become an indispensable partner in the family business. At the time, motion picture studios wielded supreme authority over theater operators like Redstone Management. "We had to be combative," Redstone remembered. "These companies [the studios] were predators that didn't want us to get first-run product." Redstone flexed his litigative muscles and fought back, suing the studios for access to first-run films. He prevailed, earning recognition within the motion picture industry and proving to be an adept business operator. The theater chain he joined in 1954 and gradually took control of expanded to 59 screens a decade after his arrival and swelled to 129 screens after another decade. At the end of this 20-year expansion period in 1974, Redstone was 51 years old and financially independent, but his greatest fame and wealth still lay ahead. During the next 20 years, Redstone developed into a national figure in the business world and became one of the wealthiest individuals in the United States.

National Amusements served as Redstone's private investment arm and the parent company of a host of businesses acquired by Redstone. He gained the financial wherewithal to purchase the properties owned by National Amusements by demonstrating exceptional skill as an investor. Impressed by the movie *Star Wars,* Redstone began accumulating stock in Twentieth Century Fox in 1977. He eventually acquired five percent of the company, paying an average of $8 per share. When he sold his stake in 1981, Redstone's shares sold for $60 each, netting him at least $20 million. In 1980, Redstone began investing in another motion picture studio, acquiring ten percent of Columbia Pictures. Two years later, he recorded a $25 million profit when his shares were sold to the Coca-Cola Company. Redstone repeated his pattern of investment success with an interest in MGM/UA, which he sold to Kirk Kerkorian in 1985 for a $15 million profit.

1987 Acquisition of Viacom

Redstone orchestrated a number of other lucrative investment deals, giving him the financial clout to entertain the possibility of completing the biggest deal in his life. National Amusements, which was operating roughly 400 screens by the mid-1980s, served as the corporate entity through which Redstone made his bid to become a media mogul. On February 2, 1987, Redstone drew a hailstorm of national press when he made a tender offer for Viacom International, comprising cable, television, radio, and distribution properties that generated $919 million in 1986 revenues. Prior to making his bid for Viacom, which was in the midst of a management-led leveraged buyout, Redstone had accumulated 9.9 percent of Viacom's stock. During the five months preceding his offer for the company, Redstone increased his stake to 19.6 percent, just below the level Viacom's corporate bylaws would trigger defensive measures. In June 1987, Redstone completed the deal, acquiring 83 percent of Viacom in a transaction valued at $3.4 billion. With his majority stake in the company, Redstone gained control of a host of properties, including five television stations, eight radio stations, and cable systems serving more than one million customers in 150 communities. Redstone also assumed ownership of other Viacom properties, including Viewer's Choice, a pay-per-view network, basic cable networks in MTV, Nickelodeon, Showtime, and The Movie Channel, the syndication rights to the "Bill Cosby Show," and a worldwide television program distribution business.

With Viacom, Redstone had a sizeable foundation to build an even larger media empire, one that would be publicly held yet have National Amusements, a private company, as its parent company. The movie theater chain operated by National Amusements, meanwhile, continued to expand, but in a different direction. By the beginning of the 1990s, the company was operating approximately 600 screens, primarily located at major intersections in the urban Northeast. Real estate during the late 1980s had become a scarce commodity, however, forcing Redstone to look elsewhere to expand his theater chain. He began expanding internationally in England, where he focused on less economically robust cities such as Birmingham, Leeds, and Liverpool. Between 1988 and 1990, Redstone spent approximately $25 million to open seven massive movie theater complexes, housing more than 70 screens. From England, Redstone continued his overseas expansion into Scotland, Chile, and Argentina.

Although National Amusements ranked as one of the smallest components of Redstone's developing media empire, it represented an integral facet of his long-term objective of controlling filmed and recorded entertainment to be distributed through cable, broadcasting, retail outlets, and movie theaters. Around National Amusements, the more prominent components of Redstone's empire were added, particularly during the 1990s when Redstone took his skills as a dealmaker to the next level. In 1994, Redstone unleashed his acquisitive might in full force, spending nearly $20 billion in two, industry-shaking transactions. In July 1994, Viacom acquired Paramount Communications Inc., paying $10 billion for the movie studio and its numerous properties. Redstone wanted the movie studio and its expansive film library—the assets that prompted the deal—but he also gained ownership of a host of other properties, many of which he later sold. Paramount owned theme parks, television stations, book publisher Simon & Schuster, the USA television network, Madison Square Garden, the National Basketball Association's New York Knicks, and the National Hockey League's New York Rangers. Two months after closing the Paramount acquisition, Redstone paid $8 billion for Blockbuster Entertainment Corporation, the largest videotape retailer in the United States. As part of the Blockbuster acquisition, Redstone also acquired Spelling Entertainment Group, a publicly traded television production company.

By the time the two acquisitions were completed, National Amusements operated 950 movie screens worldwide, with the bulk of the expansion during the first half of the 1990s derived from new theater openings in the United Kingdom and South America. National Amusements' pace of expansion during the latter half of the 1990s equaled its growth rate during the first of the decade, enlarging the chain until it ranked as one of the ten largest motion picture circuits in the United States. Meanwhile, the assets majority-owned by National Amusements, which thoroughly dwarfed the theater chain's stature, underwent significant change. Viacom's stock reached its peak in 1995 and then began a two-year precipitous slide that saw it devalued by approximately 50 percent. "It was the bottom of a period of deep gloom," Redstone reflected. "We lost complete credibility."

Late 1990s Recovery of National Amusements' Companies

Viacom was laden with debt, which Redstone went to great lengths to reduce, divesting more than $7 billion worth of assets to buoy Viacom's financial position. He sold Madison Square Garden for slightly more than $1 billion, half of USA Networks for $1.7 billion, and most of Simon & Schuster, gaining $4.6 billion from the deal. The divestitures greatly reduced Viacom's debt, but the company was also burdened by the anemic performance of Blockbuster. To cure Blockbuster's ills, Redstone used his persuasive skills as a negotiator, taking an approach that harked back to his early years with Redstone Management.

The 6,000-store Blockbuster chain was suffering from profound problems. "The marketing was terrible. The T.V. ads were ridiculous. There weren't even enough tapes in the stores," Redstone told *Forbes* in June 1998, rattling off several of the chain's problems. At the heart of the difficulties, as Redstone saw it, was a power struggle between movie studios and videotape rental companies, similar to the dynamics involved in Redstone's fight to give his father's drive-in theaters access to first-run Hollywood films. "Year after year the studios kept raising the price of tapes to companies like Blockbuster," Redstone complained. "When the price of tapes got up to about $65 each, we realized we couldn't afford to buy enough tapes to sufficiently stock the shelves." After failing to obtain sharp discounts for Blockbuster's volume purchases, Redstone took another approach. Movie theaters, as he well knew, did not pay a flat price for the right to show movies; they shared the revenue they collected with the studio. Video stores, which served the same purpose as movie theaters by bringing entertainment products to consumers, should operate under a similar arrangement, as Redstone explained to movie studio operators. Warner Bros. disagreed, refusing to share revenue in return for selling Blockbuster its movies at greatly reduced prices. Redstone did succeed, however, in convincing Walt Disney's chairman, Michael Eisner, to agree to his proposal. Under the terms of the agreement, Walt Disney sold its videotapes to Blockbuster for roughly one-tenth their previous price in exchange for 40 percent of the rental revenue. After a particular movie's popularity waned and Walt Disney' share of the revenue diminished, Blockbuster sold the used videotape, generally recouping its original investment. The deal enabled Blockbuster to stock more copies of popular movies and started an industry trend. One by one, studios agreed to Redstone's proposal. "Blockbuster's happy," Redstone to *Forbes*, "the studios are happy, and the customers are happy because they get what they want."

The deal brokered with the movie studios turned Blockbuster's performance around, with the company's market share increasing from 25 percent to 30 percent by 1998. Before Blockbuster surged forward, however, Redstone displayed his shrewd investing talents again, having National Amusements purchase an additional $250 million of Viacom stock while it languished on the market. By the late 1990s, nearly everything under Redstone's control was performing admirably. Paramount had teamed up with Fox to produce *Titanic*, the greatest grossing film ever, and joined forces with DreamWorks SKG to produce two other late 1990s hits, *Deep Impact* and *Saving Private Ryan*. Viacom's cable systems had increased its household coverage from 15 percent to more than 24 percent and its various cable television networks were airing highly popular programming obtained from Paramount's vast library of entertainment. National Amusements had expanded as well, enlarging to more than 1,200 screens in 12 countries. As Redstone prepared for the 21st century, further growth of his dominant media empire was expected, with National Amusements serving as the privately held investment arm to facilitate future expansion.

Principal Subsidiaries

Viacom Inc.; Blockbuster Entertainment Group; Cinamerica Theaters; Computer Curriculum Corp.; Paramount Pictures Corp.; Spelling Entertainment Group; Paramount Parks; Silver Burdett & Ginn Co.; Hamilton Projects Inc.; Showtime Networks Inc.; World Vision Enterprises Inc.

Further Reading

Baldo, Anthony, "Now Redstone Wants Orion Pictures," *Financial World,* February 23, 1988, p. 16.

Button, Graham, "Sir Sumner?," *Forbes,* February 5, 1990, p. 178.

Lenzner, Robert, "The Vindication of Sumner Redstone," *Forbes,* June 15, 1998, p. 23.

Matzer, Marla, "Winning Is the Only Thing," *Forbes,* October 17, 1994, p. 46.

"More Bidding Action for Viacom," *Broadcasting,* March 2, 1987, p. 36.

"Redstone Ready to Sell to Buy," *Broadcasting,* August 8, 1988, p. 26.

"Viacom LBO Bid Imperiled," *Broadcasting,* February 9, 1987, p. 49.

—Jeffrey L. Covell

National Broadcasting Company, Inc.

30 Rockefeller Plaza
New York, New York 10112-0002
U.S.A.
(212) 664-4444
Fax: (212) 664-2648
Web site: http://www.nbc.com

Wholly Owned Subsidiary of General Electric Company
Incorporated: 1926
Employees: 5,510
Sales: $5.15 billion (1997)
NAIC: 51312 Television Broadcasting

A broadcasting giant, National Broadcasting Company, Inc., through the NBC Television Network, serves more than 200 affiliate stations in the United States. During the late 1990s, NBC ranked as the number one network in the country, attracting more viewers than rivals ABC, CBS, and Fox. In the early 1990s, NBC ranked as the third network, but the popularity of such shows as "Seinfeld," "Friends," "Frasier," "ER," and "Dateline NBC," fueled the company's rise to preeminence over its competitors. The decade also saw the company diversify into cable, new media, and global television broadcasting. NBC's 24-hour cable channel, CNBC, was used as a springboard to launch cable television business news channels in Europe and Asia, and its 1996 joint venture with Microsoft led to the launch of MSNBC, a 24-hour cable news network and Internet site. In addition to part ownership in cable channels such as A&E, NBC also owns 19 percent of Internet service provider Snap!. NBC's annual revenue of more than $5 billion accounted for roughly five percent of GE's annual sales volume.

NBC's Origins in Radio

The original owner of NBC was the Radio Corporation of America (RCA). RCA was formed after World War I by several large U.S. companies in order to keep "wireless" (radio) technology in American hands. At the time, it was the leading manufacturer of radio receivers in the world.

RCA's goal in forming NBC was to be able to provide a large number of quality radio programs so that, as one of its newspaper ads said, "every event of national importance may be broadcast widely throughout the United States." General Electric Company (GE) and Westinghouse also had ownership interests in NBC, but RCA bought them out in January 1930 and remained the sole owner until 1986, when General Electric acquired RCA for $6.3 billion.

NBC's first radio broadcast, on November 15, 1926, was a four-and-a-half-hour presentation of the leading musical and comedy talent of the day. It was broadcast from New York over a network of 25 stations, as far west as Kansas City. Close to half of the country's five million radio homes tuned in. The first coast-to-coast broadcast soon followed, on New Year's Day in 1927, when NBC covered the annual Rose Bowl football game in California.

The demand for a network service among local stations was mounting so rapidly that less than two months after its first national broadcast, NBC split its programming into two separate networks, called the "red" and the "blue" networks, to give listeners a choice of different program formats. By 1941 these two networks blanketed the country; there were 103 blue subscribing stations, 76 red, and 64 supplementary stations using NBC programs. The blue network provided mostly cultural offerings: music, drama, and commentary. The red featured comedy and similar types of entertainment. There were regular radio programs for children, as well as soap operas and religious programs. When the Federal Communications Commission (FCC) declared in 1941 that no organization could own more than one network, NBC sold the blue complex, which became the American Broadcasting Company (ABC).

Early radio provided a forum for the popular vaudeville entertainers of the day: NBC hired many of them—Rudy Vallee, Fred Allen, Jack Benny, Ed Wynn, Eddie Cantor, Al Johnson, Groucho Marx, Bob Hope, Jimmy Durante, Bing Crosby, Red Skelton, Edgar Bergen, and Charlie McCarthy, and George Burns and Gracie Allen, to name a few. These performers had their own shows and appeared on each others' as well.

From the first coast-to-coast broadcast of the Rose Bowl in 1927, sporting events were a radio mainstay. That same year, the red and blue networks tied in with a number of independent stations to broadcast the second Gene Tunney-Jack Dempsey heavyweight fight from Soldier Field in Chicago. Two years later NBC broadcast the Kentucky Derby. During the 1920s and 1930s, the network featured the World Series many times, as well as major football games, golf tournaments, and the Olympics in Los Angeles in 1932.

NBC's first special events broadcast was Charles A. Lindbergh's arrival in Washington on June 11, 1927, after his historic transatlantic flight. In 1928 the network began coverage of national political events, covering the Republican and Democratic national conventions; the inaugurations of presidents Herbert Hoover in 1929 and Franklin D. Roosevelt in 1933; the opening of the 73rd Congress on March 9, 1933; and Roosevelt's first ''Fireside Chat'' on March 12th of that year. ''NBC News'' was officially created in 1933. The first international NBC broadcast also occurred in 1928, when the network carried a pick-up of President Calvin Coolidge opening a Pan-American conference in Havana.

In 1923 David Sarnoff, the founder of NBC, wrote a memorandum to the board of directors of RCA about something he called ''television,'' or ''the art of distant seeing.'' ''Television,'' he said, ''will make it possible for those at home to see as well as hear what is going on at the broadcast station.'' The groundwork for his vision had been laid by the invention of the cathode-ray tube in 1906—the forerunner of the modern television picture tube.

RCA engineers began actively conducting television experiments in 1925, but it was not until 1939 that NBC began what is considered the first regular television service, with a telecast of President Roosevelt opening the New York World's Fair. The first television network broadcast occurred on January 11, 1940, when programming was transmitted from RCA's WNBT-TV New York City to General Electric's WRGT-TV, Schenectady, New York, via automatic radio relays.

In 1941, NBC obtained a commercial television station license from the Federal Communications Commission for WNBT-TV and officially became the world's first commercial television station.

Television programming was limited by World War II to four hours a day. In 1942 NBC Radio began featuring ''The Army Hour,'' an official weekly broadcast that provided on-the-scene reports from military bases and battle zones. On D-Day, June 6, 1944, the network canceled all commercial broadcasts to provide continuous news coverage of the invasion of Normandy. Although World War II slowed the growth of television, NBC continued to experiment with new broadcasting concepts, including color television. During the mid-1940s NBC began to build a television empire the same way it had built its radio network. Its first television network consisted of four stations that covered New York City, Philadelphia, Schenectady, and Washington, D.C.

Post-World War II Growth of Television and NBC

After the war, television began to expand news coverage, create new weekly variety and drama programs, and adapt popular radio shows to the screen. ''Meet the Press,'' a program featuring a panel of journalists interviewing important public figures of the day, debuted on NBC Radio in 1945. It switched to NBC-TV in 1947, destined to become the longest-running show on television.

By this time, two more stations had joined the NBC-TV network. In 1947 there were only 14,000 television homes: at the start of 1948 this number had swelled to 175,000, and by the end of the year, nearly a million sets had been sold. During this time the number of operating television stations had mushroomed from 19 to 47.

By 1951 NBC had installed regular coast-to-coast network television service. Its first venture was covering the signing of the Japanese peace treaty in San Francisco on September 4, 1951. Popular early coast-to-coast programs included the ''All Star Revue'' with Jack Carson and ''The Colgate Comedy Hour'' with Eddie Cantor.

As the 1950s progressed, NBC Radio focused on news, sports, and public affairs programming while NBC-TV implemented new programming formats, expanding its schedule from the late afternoon and evening formats prevalent at the time to include a new kind of show, the early morning weekly series. ''The Today Show,'' which began in 1952, was the pioneer among such programming, offering news, features, interviews, and entertainment in a two-hour, magazine-type format.

In 1953 NBC presented the first coast-to-coast transmission of a color broadcast. Later that year, the FCC approved the RCA-backed National Television System Committee's standards for color compatibility, which removed CBS's rival color system from competition. This new technology made it possible for viewers who did not own a color television set to receive all network programs on their old black-and-white sets, even if the programs were broadcast in color.

Television programming continued to expand. As equipment was improved and miniaturized, it became easier for television teams to cover fast-action news in the field. In 1956 NBC aired the first videotape, and in 1962 the launching of the ''Telstar'' communications satellite made it possible to relay live video sequences from continent to continent almost instantaneously.

By the 1960s television was big business, and NBC continued to expand its programming with such popular programs as ''The Virginian,'' Rowan and Martin's ''Laugh-In,'' ''The Man from U.N.C.L.E.,'' and ''Star Trek.'' The network also initiated and presented the 1960 presidential debates between John Kennedy and Richard Nixon. In 1964 it presented the first made-for-TV movie, establishing a new television format.

During the 1970s, though television programming was swelling to an all-time peak, radio was sagging. NBC tried, unsuccessfully, to buoy radio sales by introducing several new programs. In 1975 NBC Radio introduced an ambitious 24-hour radio news network, the National News and Information Service (NNIS), but it was discontinued two years later for lack of audience and station clearance.

NBC was so disheartened by its lack of success in the radio arena that in the early 1970s it developed a plan to sell all of its radio stations and exit the business. It never followed through, though, and by December 1983 the network had completed the conversion of its radio transmissions from landlines to satellite. In 1985 NBC established a radio-programming distribution arm called NBC Radio Entertainment, allowing it to get involved with a variety of musical programs such as country and jazz. With these changes, NBC's radio business became profitable again, but in 1988 NBC did finally decide to leave the business, and that year sold seven of its eight radio stations.

The early 1980s was a hard time for NBC Television. In 1983 none of NBC's nine new shows was renewed, and the network received low consumer ratings for the third year in a row. Some sources attributed this decline to poor management and a mishandled budget. The network quickly replaced low-rated programming and managed to bring its ratings up to second place by the 1984–85 season, and to number one by 1985.

In 1986 NBC facilitated the exchange of news between NBC-TV affiliates by launching the "Skycom" domestic and international satellite system. It became the only network to use satellites as its sole method of distribution. In the same year, General Electric Company acquired RCA for $6.3 billion and became NBC's parent company.

GE's early management of NBC coincided with the departure of chairman Grant Tinker, a well-respected executive who, along with programming chief Brandon Tartikoff, was generally given credit for the network's rise to first place during the 1980s with such hits as "Cheers," "The Cosby Show," "St. Elsewhere," and "Hill Street Blues." The naming of Tinker's successor, former president of GE financial services Robert C. Wright, was viewed as the inauguration of a new era at NBC, one in which the network's corporate culture was radically altered to reflect a primary concern with shareholder's profits. Tartikoff's 1991 move to head Paramount was a further signal that a new guard was in place.

NBC Under Wright: The 1990s

Wright's institution of budget and staff reductions helped NBC to realize an initial increase in revenues, but beginning in 1989 these figures began to decline along with operating profits. According to GE's 1991 annual report, the broadcasting subsidiary weathered "the worst network advertising market in 20 years." With a four percent decrease in revenues that year, NBC suffered an operating profit decrease of 56 percent. NBC still won the 1990–91 ratings wars, though "by its narrowest margin in six years," and was the recipient of 22 Emmy Awards.

The company entered 1992 having divested itself of RCA Columbia Home Video and acquired the Financial News Network, which it merged with its Consumer News and Business Channel. April saw the last episode of "The Cosby Show," a virtual goldmine with its continuing syndication; in May the company ballyhooed the long and colorful history of "The Tonight Show," starring Johnny Carson, with a final airing that was a resounding success.

After winning the May sweeps, the most important of three ratings months, NBC poised itself for coverage of the Barcelona Summer Olympics. Although Steve McClellan and Rich Brown reported that losses for the network and for its Triplecast venture with Cablevision (an expensive service providing subscribers with continued coverage of the games from beginning to end on three separate cable channels) "will total between $50 million and $100 million," Wright and others viewed NBC's coverage as profitable in other ways, not least of which was the showcasing of NBC talent. Despite Wright's prediction a year earlier that the outcome of 1992 would be "extremely questionable," NBC nonetheless appeared motivated to get the most for its programming dollar and intended to move in the direction of attracting younger viewers, a demographic group that in turn attracted the highest commercial fees.

As NBC sought to win over the coveted 18- to 49-year-old viewing audience, however, the broadcaster faltered. In selecting senior executives for several positions, Wright had erred, hiring individuals ill-equipped to manage the company's news and entertainment programming. The network slipped to the number three position in 1993, falling behind rivals ABC and CBS and barely managing to beat back the upstart FOX network. Wright bore the brunt of the criticism, as those inside and outside the industry belittled the ability of a GE-trained lawyer to steward the fortunes of an entertainment company. Wright could not be dissuaded from altering his strategy, however, an approach articulated by his boss, GE's chief executive officer, John (Jack) F. Welch. Said Welch, according to a February 1997 *Fortune* profile: "People say, 'Jack, how can you be at NBC, you don't know anything about dramas or comedies. . . .' Well, I can't build a jet engine either. I can't build a turbine. Our job at GE is to deal with resources—human and financial. The idea of getting great talent, giving them all the support in the world, and letting them run is the whole management philosophy of GE, whether it's in turbines, engines, or a network." With the support of Welch, Wright intended to manage NBC the GE way, despite mounting opposition to operating the network in the traditional corporate manner.

Wright turned his attention toward cutting costs and eliminating NBC's bureaucratic structure. The network's workforce was trimmed from 8,000 employees to fewer than 5,000, saving the company nearly $120 million in overhead. As Wright performed the tasks expected of a former financial services president, he also compensated for his initial hiring mistakes by recruiting creative executives with an entrepreneurial zeal, notably Don Ohlmeyer. Ohlmeyer, a sports and entertainment producer who ran his own production company, joined NBC in early 1993 to lead NBC Entertainment. The strategy developed in 1993 was to build a dominant Thursday night of programming. The popularity of shows such as "Seinfeld," "Friends," "Frasier," and the hour-long drama "ER" achieved this objective unequivocally, breathing new life in the network after the loss of "The Cosby Show" and "Cheers." Under Ohlmeyer, the broadcaster became an innovator, the first network to segue from one program to another without a commercial break (NBC's vaunted "seamless" programming) and the first to show previews of the upcoming program on half the screen while credits rolled on the other half. By 1995 NBC ranked as the number one network.

With the network again capturing the industry's highest ratings, Wright continued to broaden NBC's interests. Leading the pack, however, was not enough for Wright. "We have to be bigger than broadcasting," he told *Fortune*. "That worried me before I got here, that worried me the day I got here, and it's worried me every day since." Wright demanded NBC diversify into cable, new media, and global television, thereby providing opportunities for growth to compensate for the perennial decline in broadcast viewership. In 1996, the company teamed up with Microsoft to launch MSNBC, a 24-hour cable news network and Internet site, which was jointly owned by the two companies. That same year, Wright also began a push into overseas markets with the launch of CNBC Europe and NBC Asia.

By the beginning of 1997, Wright could point to strong evidence for managing NBC in the traditional GE manner. The network was still in the lead, and for the fourth consecutive year it had generated record revenues and earnings, recording more than $5 billion in revenue and an estimated $950 million in operating profit. As the network entered the late 1990s, it appeared to occupy solid ground, although it did not have NFL football on its schedule for the first time in more than 30 years. NBC did own the television rights, however, to the Olympics through 2008, having secured a $4 billion deal in 1995. In the future, NBC was expected to further its involvement in cable, new media, and international broadcasting, as it fought the capricious war to lead the nation in broadcast ratings.

Principal Subsidiaries

CNBC, Inc.; Living Music, Inc.; NBC Entertainment Corp.; NBC News Bureaus, Inc.; NBC News Worldwide, Inc.; NBC International Limited; NBC Subsidiary KCNC-TV, Inc.; Spectacular Music, Inc.; NBC Digital Publishing; NBC Online Ventures.

Further Reading

Auletta, Ken, *Three Blind Mice: How the TV Networks Lost Their Way,* New York: Random House, 1991.

Campbell, Robert, *The Golden Years of Broadcasting: A Celebration of the First 50 Years of Radio and Television on NBC,* New York: Charles Scribner's Sons, 1976.

Carter, Bill, "All the Networks Exult As Sweep Month Ends," *New York Times,* May 21, 1992.

Elliott, Stuart, "NBC Likes Young Viewers, Judging From Its Fall Plans," *New York Times,* May 13, 1992.

Gorowitz, Bernard, ed., *On the Shoulders of Giants: 1924 to 1946—The GE Story,* Schenectady, N.Y.,: Elfun Society, Territorial Council, 1979.

Gunther, Marc, "How GE Made NBC No. 1," *Fortune,* February 3, 1997, pp. 92+.

Huff, Richard, "Wright of Passage: NBC Prez Sees Rocky '92," *Variety,* August 12, 1991.

McClellan, Steve, and Rich Brown, "NBC Claims Silver (Lining) in Summer Olympic Effort," *Broadcasting,* August 10, 1992.

"Nets 'Yellow' with Envy," *Advertising Age,* November 9, 1998, p. 44.

Schatz, Ronald W., *The Electrical Workers: A History of Labor at General Electric and Westinghouse, 1923–60,* Urbana: University of Illinois Press, 1983.

Sharkey, Betsy, "Master of His Domain," *ADWEEK Eastern Edition,* June 1, 1998, p. S26.

"When the TV Going Gets Tough," *U.S. News & World Report,* May 13, 1991.

—Suzanne Leibundguth
—updated by Jeffrey L. Covell

National Discount Brokers Group, Inc.

10 Exchange Place
Jersey City, New Jersey 07302
U.S.A.
(201) 946-2200
(800) 888-3999
Fax: (201) 946-4510
Web site: http://www.ndb.com

Public Company
Incorporated: 1981 as The Sherwood Equity Group Ltd.
Employees: 572
Operating Revenues: $164.4 million (fiscal 1998)
Stock Exchanges: New York
Ticker Symbol: NDB
NAIC: 52312 Securities Brokerage; 55112 Offices of
    Other Holding Companies

National Discount Brokers Group, Inc. is a holding company for National Discount Brokers, a discount broker mainly serving individual investors, and Sherwood Securities, a wholesale market maker specializing in NASDAQ and small-cap over-the-counter stocks. The company also had a controlling interest in Equitrade Partners, a wholesale market maker specializing in New York Stock Exchange securities. (Market makers have an effective monopoly in the trading of certain stocks. In return for this monopoly, they have the obligation to maintain an orderly market and dampen price volatility in the stock by selling when the public is buying and buying when the public is selling.)

Wholesale Dealer Until 1987

Sherwood Securities was founded in 1968 by Richard Marino and Charles Sheils, with Marino's brother Dennis joining the firm the following year. It was incorporated in 1981 as The Sherwood Equity Group Ltd. and changed its name in 1983 to Sherwood Capital Group, Inc. In fiscal 1985 (the year ended May 31, 1985), Sherwood Capital Group registered a net loss of nearly $1.7 million on revenue of $13.7 million; the following year revenue grew to $28.7 million, and the company had net income of $3.1 million. Assets came to $39.3 million. Headquarters were in New York City.

Sherwood Capital Group's broker-dealer unit, Sherwood Securities Corporation, was a major market maker in over-the-counter stocks by 1987, when it was trading in about 2,600 securities. As a market maker, Sherwood Securities acted as a wholesale dealer in the execution of transactions. It was acting as principal in transactions through buying, selling, and maintaining an inventory in the securities in which it was making a market. About 1,800 of the securities in which Sherwood Securities was a market maker were being displayed in the electronic quotation medium referred to by the acronym NASDAQ. The firms that had elected to make a market in a security quoted on NASDAQ displayed the price at which they were willing to buy (bid) or sell (ask) these securities. The market maker adjusted its bid and asked prices in response to supply, demand, and other factors affecting the market for each security.

Private telephone lines connected the Sherwood Securities trading operations to the order-entry departments of about 275 brokerage firms and institutional customers. Sherwood was a leader in automated trading, which in 1987 accounted for more than half of its total volume. The company also was executing over-the-counter transactions for retail brokers, including certain clearing accounts. Most notable of these firms was Quick & Reilly, Inc., which accounted for 14.5 percent of all orders executed by Sherwood Securities in fiscal 1987.

Troubled Retail Acquisition and Aftermath: 1987–90

Sherwood Capital Group was seeking to become a retail broker in 1986, and shortly before the end of the year it paid $19 million to buy 33 retail brokerage offices from First Jersey Securities Inc. with a total annual revenue of around $70 million. The new unit was named Sherwood Capital Inc. and placed under Frederic Rittereiser, former chief executive officer of First Jersey.

First Jersey Securities had acquired, according to *Business Week,* the *Wall Street Journal,* and other sources, an unsavory reputation for stimulating trades in the small over-the-counter companies whose shares it underwrote by such alleged means as having one branch urge the sale of a stock while another recommended buying it. When Sherwood Capital Group went public in May 1987 as Sherwood Group, Inc., the hundreds of First Jersey brokers who had moved over to Sherwood quietly sold about $60 million of stock for about 54 percent of the shares outstanding. The offering was made available only to Sherwood's 300,000 customers, many of them former First Jersey clients. Sherwood officers and directors retained about 21 percent of the shares.

The acquisition of First Jersey's brokerage network proved a disaster for Sherwood Group when the stock market crashed in the fall of 1987. The network was sold in May 1988 at a loss of $19.7 million, with 15 offices purchased by Hibbard Brown & Co., 11 by F.N. Wolf & Co., and six by J.T. Moran & Co. The company also ceased underwriting securities, which had accounted for seven percent of its revenues in fiscal 1988. Sherwood Group lost $40.1 million in fiscal 1988 on gross operating revenues of $48.5 million. It lost another $10.4 million the next year on revenues of only $13.1 million and $8.4 million in fiscal 1990 on revenues of $15 million. In all, Sherwood lost about $60 million because of the First Jersey debacle.

Sherwood Group received some help in September 1988, when S.G.I. Partners, L.P., paid $2.7 million for about 15 percent of the company. The purchase price, however, was only a little more than $1 a share, compared to the $8.50 a share of the initial public offering the previous year. This partnership was said to be controlled by Arthur Kontos, managing director of the securities firm Spear, Leeds & Kellogg, the largest specialist (market making) firm on the New York Stock Exchange and also operator of an over-the-counter market-making unit competing with Sherwood Securities. Kontos became president and chief executive officer of Sherwood Group, while James Lynch, Jr., also a Spear, Leeds & Kellogg partner, became chairman.

Wholesale and Retail in the 1990s

In 1989 Sherwood Group purchased a 60 percent interest in Equitrade Partners, a specialist market maker on the New York Stock Exchange, for $3.6 million. S.G.I. continued to raise its stake in Sherwood Group, to nearly 40 percent in 1991 and more than 58 percent in 1992. When Sherwood Group earned about $100,000 on revenues of $21.7 million in fiscal 1991, it began six consecutive years of increased sales and profit. It was the only company making a market in NASDAQ International stocks for the overnight trading sessions initiated to coincide with trading in London. In 1993 Sherwood Group acquired Triak Services Corporation, a start-up brokerage that by the end of 1994 was making markets in 29 American Stock Exchange stocks. Sherwood Securities added an institutional research department for NASDAQ and small-cap over-the-counter securities in 1991.

S.G.I. Partners, according to a 1994 *Investment Dealers' Digest* article, was really controlled by Peter Kellogg, senior managing director of Spear, Leeds & Kellogg. The *IDD* article called Kellogg "the most powerful and feared man on Wall Street" and went on to claim that Kellogg held "a stake in every means by which shares and options trade on nearly every

major exchange in the US." Kellogg also personally held about a million shares of Sherwood stock, or about eight percent of the shares outstanding. Spear, Leeds & Kellogg was careful, however, to avoid formal authority over Sherwood.

In January 1994 a start-up firm called National Discount Brokers started advertising a flat fee of $25 for over-the-counter trades of up to 20,000 shares. Rival discount brokerages gradually learned that NDB was an operating arm of Triak. Although they were said to have "erupted in fury" and begun shifting some business away from Sherwood Securities in retaliation, according to Kontos "Sherwood Securities didn't lose one customer because of National Brokers." According to *IDD*, Troster Singer Co., Spear, Leeds & Kellogg's over-the-counter market-making operation, was expressly forbidden to seek any business lost by Sherwood Securities. National Discount Brokers also became the first major discount broker to sell stock over the Internet, in 1995.

Sherwood Group's revenues nearly doubled in fiscal 1996, reaching $180.2 million, while its net income rose to $20.1 million. The next two years were not as good. Revenues barely rose in fiscal 1997, to $181.1 million, and net income fell to $9.3 million. That year the company paid $9.2 million as its share of the settlement of a class-action lawsuit in which investors claimed that more than 30 of NASDAQ's market makers conspired to keep overly wide the spread between the prices at which they bought and sold 1,659 NASDAQ stocks. The company also was fined $1 million by the U.S. Securities and Exchange Commission in January 1999 in connection with alleged trading abuses.

Sherwood Group moved its head office and trading facilities to Jersey City in 1995 and its sales office to another downtown Manhattan location in 1996. In the latter year National Discount Breakers initiated a "supermarket" of no-load mutual funds that allowed consumers to choose for purchase from over 260 funds through a single provider without paying a fee, even when purchasing funds from different companies. In 1998, when NDB's standard trading fee was $14, it formed an alliance with Women's Connection Online, providing custom-made educational pages to the site and paying a fee in exchange for the service's online link to its own trading site.

Sherwood Group changed its name to National Discount Brokers Group, Inc. in December 1997. Although the firm's net income rose to $11.9 million in fiscal 1998, revenues fell to $164.5 million because of competition from better-financed rivals. By this time NDB no longer was one of the top ten Internet brokers and, in the words of one reporter, risked becoming "a niche player in an industry it helped to create."

National Discount Brokers' strategy in 1998 was to find new clients among the nine million people expected to begin investing online for the first time by 2002. The pact with Women's Connection Online was one facet of this plan. Another was a link to blackstocks.com, an Internet site aimed at African American investors. NDB's partnerships were said to account for 5,000 of the 20,000 customers added in 1998. Still another means of recruiting new clients was "NDB University," a new investor-education program the company had begun offering on its web site.

Sherwood Group in 1998

Sherwood Securities remained the subsidiary for making markets in NASDAQ and small-cap securities on a wholesale basis. Sherwood Securities was trading in about 3,400 securities in 1998 and also acting as a principal for its own account. It also provided limited retail brokerage services and from time to time was making venture capital investments. It had offices in Boston, Chicago, Denver, Los Angeles, and Minneapolis as well as Jersey City.

Triak was doing business as National Discount Brokers, which remained a deep-discount brokerage firm specializing in trade execution for individual investors through interactive voice response and Internet distribution channels. At the end of July 1998, National Discount Brokers had more than 120,000 customer accounts comprising over $5.3 billion in assets.

In 1997 Sherwood Group acquired DNY, a company engaged in specialist trading on the New York Stock Exchange, paying $15.3 million in cash to Dresdner Bank AG. The name of the company was subsequently changed to SHD Corporation. At the end of July 1998 National Discount Brokers Group and its SHD subsidiary owned about 72 percent of Equitrade Partners, which was a registered specialist in 157 equity securities on the New York Stock Exchange. Another subsidiary, MXNet Inc., was sold in 1998 to IPC Information Systems Inc. for $6.7 million.

Sherwood Group was no longer clearing trades for other retail brokers in 1998. Sherwood Securities was clearing its wholesale market making and customer transactions through Broadcort Capital Corporation. Equitrade was clearing its transactions through Spear, Leeds & Kellogg, and National Discount Brokers was clearing its transactions through the Pershing Division of Donaldson, Lufkin & Jenrette Securities Corporation. In August 1998 S.G.I. Partners, L.P. held 28.5 percent of the common stock of National Discount Brokers Group. Entities responsible to Arthur Kontos held 20.3 percent, and entities responsible to Peter R. Kellogg held 19 percent.

Principal Subsidiaries

The Ebercom Company; SHD Corporation; Sherwood Capital, Inc.; Sherwood Management Corporation; Sherwood Newco Corporation; Sherwood Properties Corporation; Sherwood Securities Corporation; Simcon Corporation; Triak Services Corporation; Equitrade Partners (72%).

Further Reading

Birger, Jon, "On-Line Brokerage Fights for Attention," *Crain's New York Business,* December 21, 1998, pp. 4, 19.

Engen, J., "NDB's Affinity Relationship Brings On-Line Trading to Professional Women," *American Banker,* May 12, 1998, p. 13A.

Hensley, Scott, "National Discount Fund 'Supermarket,' " *American Banker,* April 11, 1996, p. 19.

Huxley, Alex, "Automated OTC Market: Positioned for Growth," *Wall Street Computer Review,* August 1987, pp. 32, 34.

McMorris, Frances A., and Lohse, Deborah, "Sherwood Unit Plans to Settle Trading Case," *Wall Street Journal,* April 10, 1997, pp. C1, C11.

Schroeder, Michael, "Fines on 28 Securities Firms Mark End to Nasdaq Trading Inquiry," *Wall Street Journal,* January 12, 1999, p. B6.

Smith, Priscilla Ann, and Power, William, "Former First Jersey Salesmen Market $60 Million of Stock in New Employer," *Wall Street Journal,* June 3, 1987, p. 5.

Swartz, Steve, and Smith, Priscilla Ann, "First Jersey Securities to Sell Its Retail Lines," *Wall Street Journal,* December 24, 1986, p. 4.

Taub, Peter, "Peter Kellogg's Bet on Brokerages," *FW/Financial World,* February 18, 1992, pp. 14–15.

Welles, Chris, "Trying Not to Be a Second First Jersey," *Business Week,* January 12, 1987, p. 44.

Willoughby, Jack, "A Modern-Day Rockefeller," *Investment Dealers' Digest,* December 12, 1994, pp. 12–19.

—Robert Halasz

The Nature Conservancy

4245 North Fairfax Drive, Suite 100
Arlington, Virginia 22203-1606
U.S.A.
(703) 841-5300
Fax: (703) 841-9692
Web site: http://www.tnc.org

Nonprofit Company
Incorporated: 1951
Employees: 2,000
Sales: $326.23 million (1996)
NAIC: 813312 Environment, Conservation, & Wildlife
   Organizations; 525930 Real Estate Investment Trusts

The Nature Conservancy (TNC) is the star performer among environmental groups, in size, growth, effectiveness, and stature among government agencies and private donors. On average, 1,000 acres a day are added to its system of nature preserves, the world's largest. When TNC cannot buy desired property, it sometimes attains conservation easements restricting use of the land in return for tax benefits.

TNC traditionally has maintained a low profile, preferring to let its partners reap the media attention. It began pressing, however, for more publicity in this earth-friendly age, garnering numerous product sponsorship deals as its membership approached one million. Author Peter Drucker singled out the management skills of the group, whose MBAs and lawyers injected a powerful dose of high finance into a field better known for grass roots activism.

Origins

The Ecological Society of America, a scientific group, was founded around 1900. In 1917 it formed a study group, the Committee for the Preservation of Natural Conditions, that would split from the Society in 1946 to become The Ecologist's Union.

One of this group's members, engineer Dick Pough, learned of the Nature Conservancy of the British government while traveling to England. In 1951 The Ecologist's Union adopted the name The Nature Conservancy, although Pough envisioned private rather than state support for the group. Donations from Pough's wealthy connections—such as $100,000 from *Reader's Digest* cofounder Mrs. DeWitt Wallace—put TNC in business.

TNC bought its first 60-acre property, Mianus Gorge, in 1955, sparing it from the development that surely would have spread from nearby New York City. Other small preserves followed, and the group found itself in competition with the venerable Audubon Society, also soliciting property donations.

This year marked the beginning of TNC's Land Preservation Fund, which acted as a rotating credit account. From an initial $7,500 donated by the Old Dominion Foundation the fund blossomed to more than $100 million by 1990. Mining heiress Katharine Ordway donated more than $53 million.

TNC bought the entire island of St. Vincent off of Florida's gulf coast for $1 million in 1969. It became a 13,000-acre national wildlife refuge. The 40,000-acre Virginia Coast Reserve was even more ambitious. The Virginia Coast Reserve was first begun in 1969 to protect nesting shore birds in particular from a developer who wanted to continue the development in overcrowded Virginia Beach to the barrier islands. After TNC began making acquisitions, however, politicians scrapped plans for bridges connecting the islands to the mainland.

The Corporate 1970s

By the 1970s the character of the organization had shifted from that of a scientist's group to something more akin to that of a property management company. TNC had about 50 employees, including Pat Noonan, a determined MBA who served as director of operations.

The group began to court corporations, the scourge of many environmentalists, for land donations. Union Camp Corporation donated 50,000 acres of the Dismal Swamp, a gift worth

$12.6 million and believed to be the largest corporate donation at the time.

The Nature Conservancy employed a novel strategy in acquiring 35,000 acres of Mississippi swampland in 1973. When some of the shareholders of the Pascagoula Lumber Company vetoed a purchase offer of $15 million, it bought a controlling interest in the company. In 1976 TNC sold the land to the state of Mississippi for use as a state park. Mississippi, with its sportsmen-oriented approach to conservation, gave TNC a foothold in the Southeast.

In the case of Shelter Island, TNC bought all of a New York realty company's holdings, including property in Manhattan and Miami, to attain some Long Island osprey habitat. After the excess was resold, the land for Mashomack Preserve cost $5 million. Within 20 years, the osprey population had doubled.

Pat Noonan became president of TNC in 1974. At the insistence of its board of directors, TNC had developed a long-range plan. The United States was divided into regions, which would start the next level of organization: self-funding programs in each state.

Dr. Robert Jenkins, TNC's chief scientist, proposed a rescue mission for TNC: "The preservation of biotic diversity." He often alluded to Noah's Ark. TNC attempted to preserve specific species at risk by controlling specific habitats. The first of 50 State Natural Heritage Programs was established in South Carolina in 1974. After receiving initial support from TNC in identifying species at risk, the programs reverted to state funding.

An international program also was started. It eventually grew to include dozens of preserves in Latin America and the Caribbean, as well as projects centered in Canada, Palau, and Indonesia.

In 1978 TNC spent $2.8 million on its largest purchase at the time, buying nine-tenths of Santa Cruz, an isolated island off California whose rare native plant species had been severely threatened by feral pigs and 30,000 sheep, which TNC would have to eradicate. Fortunately, an ecologically savvy New England heiress supplied a quarter of the $4 million required to complete the project.

Thriving Under Reagan in the 1980s

Pat Noonan stepped down as president in 1980 but continued to serve as a consultant, as TNC required all the creativity it could muster. During the Reagan years, money for public programs of all kinds was scarce and Secretary of the Interior James Watt halted federal land acquisition. Nevertheless, TNC was able to persuade the state of Mississippi to support the launch of the Rivers of the Deep South program, which began with a massive $15 million grant from a private foundation.

By 1984 TNC had invested $25 million in the Virginia Coast Reserve, now expanded to include deepwater frontage along the eastern shore of the Virginia mainland. Since TNC could not sell the land to the federal government as a wildlife refuge during the Reagan administration, it was financed by an innovative charitable lead trust, which allowed the tax-free distribution of a foundation's real estate investment.

In 1984 TNC turned over to the federal government the 118,000 acres of North Carolina coastland that would become the Alligator River National Wildlife Refuge. Red wolves would be first reintroduced into the wild here. The same year, the largest privately held preserve, the 67,000-acre Panther Ranch, was given to TNC by the Harte family of Texas. Most of it became part of the Big Bend National Park straddling the Rio Grande. The year 1984 also marked the establishment of Coachella Valley Preserve, which helped keep 13,000 acres of expensive Palm Springs real estate habitable for creatures like the fringe-toed lizard.

While other environmental groups such as Greenpeace (which eschews any corporate support) made headlines by chasing whaling ships and blocking logging roads, TNC's less confrontational approach attracted a broad base of supporters. By 1985 membership stood at 300,000.

TNC began a unique program, surveying 25 million acres of Department of Defense property, in 1988. Another new partner was Ducks Unlimited, which it joined in buying $3.5 million of California farmland to be reverted to waterfowl habitat.

TNC began an extensive survey of 14,000 North American plant species and added an even more impressive purchase than the Santa Cruz property: nearly all of the Animas Mountain range in New Mexico—321,703 acres of diverse wildlife habitat formerly owned by the Gray Land and Cattle Company. Negotiations for the acquisition had begun in 1982. The Big Bend development protected marshland on a similar scale in the eastern United States. Big Bend soon was resold to the state of Florida.

In 1989 The Nature Company, a Berkeley, California catalog merchandiser, entered a partnership with TNC whereby it processed new memberships and donated a portion of its product sales. Income at the time was $168 million and in 1990 membership reached 600,000 as the last of 50 state chapters was added. With assets worth $620 million, TNC managed 1.5 million of the more than 5.5 million acres it had protected.

TNC promoted the concept of "greenways"—linear belts of wilderness connecting wildlife sanctuaries. Its philosophy grew to rely less upon acquisitions, preferring to convince existing owners to take care not to harm wildlife by using pesticides, and so forth.

TNC sometimes appeared the bane of property developers, resentful at being told how to use their land and at the millions spent to preserve unappealing species such as crocodiles and rats. In addition, land acquired by the Conservancy no longer generated property taxes for local communities.

TNC also faced charges of threatening reluctant property owners. Further, an audit questioned prices federal agencies paid for TNC properties from 1986 to 1991. Subsequent reviews factoring in donations and other losses concluded, however, that TNC actually lost money on the deals.

The Green 1990s

Realizing the importance of accounting for people themselves in populated landscapes, TNC began acquiring new properties around its Virginia Coast Reserve to be resold with permanent restrictions to encourage certain uses, specifically, farming rather than coastal property development. TNC created the for-profit Virginia Eastern Shore Sustainable Development Corporation to manage the project, which included job creation among its objectives.

TNC extended its approach of compromise and cooperation to big business. Corporate giving accounted for $2 million, or 16 percent, of TNC income in 1991. By the mid-1990s, 500 companies, such as Miller Brewing Company, Canon USA, Honda of America, Procter & Gamble, and Warner-Lambert, supported TNC with donations, some of them through cause-related marketing. This arrangement allowed the corporate partners to use the TNC name and logo in promotions. TNC also introduced its own credit card.

In 1992 TNC helped broker a compromise between the Walt Disney Company, which wanted to expand its Orlando theme park, and the state of Florida, which wanted to protect adjacent wetlands. Disney agreed to restore 8,500 acres of wilderness in central Florida and was allowed to proceed with its development. TNC also worked out an agreement with Georgia-Pacific concerning timber harvesting on certain property. Each party held one vote to decide whether particular parts of the area should be harvested.

TNC reassessed its performance measures—such as acreage protected—after the bog turtle population in Schenob Brook, a Massachusetts acquisition, continued to decline because of uses of the watershed beyond the site's borders. The organization began seeking out much larger areas to preserve, designated Last Great Places, such as the Fish Creek Project organized to save a population of freshwater mussels. In this case, TNC helped subsidize no-till farming technology to reduce the amount of silt in the water. TNC's vision of preserving entire biological systems actually had been pronounced as far back as 1975.

To restore 36,000 acres of tallgrass prairie in Oklahoma bought in 1989, TNC initiated a series of prescribed burns there in 1993. A small herd of bison then was reintroduced onto the restored landscape. Membership reached 766,000 in 1993, revenues were $280 million, and nearly eight million acres had been protected. Assets approached $1 billion.

The number of species found in tropical rain forests ensured TNC's interest in foreign countries. A dozen Conservation Data Centers cataloged this ecological diversity around the globe, and its "Parks in Peril" program assisted national governments in maintaining existing parks. At the end of the century, TNC had operations in more than 20 countries. TNC helped preserve 57 million acres outside the United States, compared to ten million within. In 1996 TNC counted 900,000 members and 1,850 corporate associates.

Further Reading

Blair, William D., Jr., *Katharine Ordway: The Lady Who Saved the Prairies,* Arlington, Va.: The Nature Conservancy, 1989.

Fabris, Peter, "Doing Good by Doing Well," *CIO,* April 1, 1995, pp. 42–50.

Grove, Noel, *The Nature Conservancy,* New York: Harry N. Abrams, 1992.

Howard, Alice, and Joan Magretta, "Surviving Success: An Interview with the Nature Conservancy's John Sawhill," *Harvard Business Review,* September-October 1994, pp. 108–18.

Kennett, Jim, "Land Donations: A Booming Business Option," *Environment Today,* April 1993, pp. 3, 12.

Morine, David E., *Good Dirt: Confessions of a Conservationist,* Chester, Conn.: Globe Pequot, 1990.

Osterland, Andrew W., "War Among the Nonprofits," *FW,* September 1, 1994, pp. 52–53.

Regan, May Beth, "No Nukes, No Logging, No Money," *Business Week,* July 24, 1995, p. 40.

Zbar, Jeffrey D., "Firms Go Green with Conservancy," *Advertising Age,* January 11, 1993, p. 16.

—Frederick C. Ingram

Nestlé S.A.

Avenue Nestlé 55
CH-1800 Vevey
Switzerland
(021) 924-2111
Fax: (021) 921-1885
Web site: http://www.nestle.com

Public Company
Incorporated: 1866 as Anglo-Swiss Condensed Milk
    Company
Employees: 225,808
Sales: SFr 71.7 billion (US$52.09 billion) (1998)
Stock Exchanges: Basle Geneva Zurich Amsterdam
    Brussels Frankfurt London Paris Tokyo Vienna
NAIC: 311514 Dry, Condensed, & Evaporated Dairy
    Product Manufacturing; 31152 Ice Cream & Frozen
    Dessert Manufacturing; 311511 Fluid Milk
    Manufacturing; 311421 Fruit & Vegetable Canning;
    311411 Frozen Fruit, Juice, & Vegetable Processing;
    311412 Frozen Specialty Food Manufacturing; 31123
    Breakfast Cereal Manufacturing; 311111 Dog & Cat
    Food Manufacturing; 31132 Chocolate &
    Confectionery Manufacturing from Cacao Beans;
    312111 Soft Drink Manufacturing; 31193 Flavoring
    Syrup & Concentrate Manufacturing; 31192 Coffee &
    Tea Manufacturing; 311823 Dry Pasta Manufacturing;
    311999 All Other Miscellaneous Food Manufacturing;
    325412 Pharmaceutical Preparation Manufacturing;
    32562 Toilet Preparation Manufacturing

Nestlé S.A. is the largest food company in the world. With about 500 manufacturing facilities on six continents, Nestlé has often been called "the most multinational of the multinationals," largely because less than two percent of its sales are made in its home country. About 37 percent of sales are derived from the overall European market, 32 percent from the Americas, and 19 percent from Africa, Asia, and Oceania (with the remainder not geographically categorized). Nestlé S.A. is a holding company for more than 200 subsidiaries and affiliates that manufacture and sell a wide variety of products, including coffee, mineral water, chocolate and malted beverages, chocolates and confectionery, culinary and refrigerated products, dairy products, baby food, breakfast cereal, frozen foods and ice cream, pet foods, pharmaceutical products, and cosmetics.

Early History

While serving as the American consul in Zurich, Charles Page decided that Switzerland, with its abundant milk supply and easy access to the whole European market, was the perfect location for a condensed milk factory. The first canned condensed milk had been produced in the United States by Gail Borden some ten years before, and originally Page planned to produce and sell "Borden Milk" in the European market as a licensee. The plan fell through, however, so in 1866 he established the Anglo-Swiss Condensed Milk Company as a limited company in Cham, Switzerland.

The company's name was meant to flatter the British, to whom Page hoped to sell a great deal of his condensed milk. Anglo-Swiss first expanded its operations beyond Switzerland's borders in 1872, when it opened a factory in Chippenham, England. Condensed milk rapidly became a staple product in European cupboards—the business downturn in 1872 and the depression of 1875 did not affect the firm's sales. Charles Page died in 1873, leaving the company in the hands of his brother George and Anglo-Swiss's other investors. The next year, Anglo-Swiss undertook further expansion in England by purchasing the Condensed Milk Company in London. By 1876 sales were almost four times their 1872 level.

Meanwhile, in Vevey, Switzerland, in 1867 Henri Nestlé began selling his newly developed cow's-milk food for infants who could not be breast-fed. Demand for his Farine Lactée Nestlé soared; between 1871 and 1873, daily production more than doubled, from fewer than 1,000 tins a day to 2,000. Nestlé's goal was to bring his baby food within everyone's reach, and he spared no effort in trying to convince doctors and mothers of its benefits. But while his energy and good intentions were nearly endless, his financial resources were not. By 1873, demand for Nestlé's product exceeded his production capabilities, resulting in missed delivery dates. At 61, Nestlé was running out of energy, and his thoughts turned to retirement. Jules Monnerat, a former member of parliament who lived in Vevey, had long eyed the business, and in 1874 Nestlé accepted Monnerat's offer of SFr 1 million. Thus, in 1875, the company became Farine Lactée Henri Nestlé with Monnerat as chairman.

In 1877 Nestlé faced a new competitor when the Anglo-Swiss Condensed Milk Company—already the leading manufacturer of condensed milk in Europe—decided to broaden its product line and manufacture cheese and milk food for babies. Nestlé quickly responded by launching a condensed milk product of its own. George Page tried to buy the competing company outright, but he was firmly told that Nestlé was not for sale. Turning his attention elsewhere, he purchased the Anglo-Swiss Company's first factory in the United States in 1881. The plant, located in Middletown, New York, was built primarily to escape import duties, and it was soon successful enough to challenge Borden's supremacy in the U.S. condensed milk market. It also presented a drawback: George Page spent so much time there that Anglo-Swiss began to lose its hold on Europe—much to the delight of Nestlé. After George Page's death in 1899, the Anglo-Swiss Condensed Milk Company decided to sell its American business to Borden in 1902 so that it could concentrate on regaining market share in Europe.

Until 1898 Nestlé remained determined to manufacture only in Switzerland and export to its markets around the world. But that year the company finally decided to venture outside Switzerland with the purchase of a Norwegian condensed milk company. Two years later, in 1900, Nestlé opened a factory in the United States, and quickly followed this by entering Britain, Germany, and Spain. Early in the 1900s, Nestlé also became involved in chocolate, a logical step for a company based in Vevey, the center of the Swiss chocolate industry. Nestlé became a partner in the Swiss General Chocolate Company, the maker of the Peter and Kohler brands. Under their agreement, the chocolate company produced the first Nestlé brand milk chocolate, while Nestlé concentrated on selling the Peter, Kohler, and Nestlé brands around the world.

Nestlé and Anglo-Swiss Merged in 1905

In 1905 Nestlé and the Anglo-Swiss Condensed Milk Company finally quelled their fierce competition by merging to create the Nestlé and Anglo-Swiss Milk Company. The new firm would be run by two registered offices, one in Vevey and one in Cham, a practice it continues today. With Emile-Louis

Roussy as chairman, the company now included seven factories in Switzerland, six in Great Britain, three in Norway, and one each in the United States, Germany, and Spain.

In response to an increase in import duties in Australia—Nestlé's second largest export market—the company decided to begin manufacturing there in 1906 by buying a major condensed milk company, the Cressbrook Dairy Company, in Brisbane. In the next few years production and sales continued to increase as the company began to replace sales agents with subsidiary companies, particularly in the rapidly growing Asian markets.

Most of its factories were located in Europe, however, and when World War I broke out in 1914, Nestlé's operations, particularly in such warring countries as Britain and Germany, were seriously affected. Although production continued in full force during the early months of the war, business soon grew more difficult. By 1916 fresh milk shortages, especially in Switzerland, meant that Nestlé's factories often sold almost all of their milk supplies to meet the needs of local towns. Shipping obstacles, increased manufacturing and operating costs, and restrictions on the use of production facilities added to Nestlé's wartime difficulties, as did a further decrease in fresh milk supplies due to shortages of cattle.

To deal with these problems and meet the increased demand for its products from governments supplying their troops, Nestlé decided to expand in countries less affected by the war and began purchasing existing factories, particularly in the United States, where it established links with several existing firms. By 1917 Nestlé had 40 factories, and in 1918, its world production was more than double what it was in 1914. Nestlé pursued the same strategy in Australia; by 1920 it had acquired a controlling interest in three companies there. That same year, Nestlé began production in Latin America when it established a factory in Araras, Brazil, the first in a series of Latin American factories. By 1921, the firm had 80 factories and 12 subsidiaries and affiliates. It also introduced a new product that year—powdered milk called Lactogen.

It did not take long for the effects of such rapid expansion to catch up with the company, however. Nestlé and Anglo-Swiss reported its first loss in 1921, to which the stock market reacted with panic, making matters worse. The company explained that the SFr 100 million loss was due to the rising prices of raw materials such as sugar and coal, and a trade depression that had caused a steady fall in consumer purchasing power, coupled with falling exchange rates after the war, which forced the company to raise prices.

To battle the storm, the company decided to reorganize both management and production. In 1922 it brought production in line with actual sales by closing some of its factories in the United States, Britain, Australia, Norway, and Switzerland. It also hired Louis Dapples, a banking expert, to put the company back in order. Dapples directed Nestlé with an iron fist, introducing stringent financial controls and reorganizing its administration. By 1923, signs of improvement were already evident, as Nestlé's outstanding bank loans had dropped from SFr 293 million in 1921 to SFr 54.5 million in 1923. Meanwhile in France, Belgium, Italy, Germany, and South Africa, production facilities were expanded. By consolidating certain operations and expanding others, Nestlé was also able to widen its traditional range of products.

Overall, the late 1920s were profitable, progressive times. In addition to adding some new products of its own—including malted milk, a powdered beverage called Milo, and Eledon, a powdered buttermilk for babies with digestive disorders—the company bought interests in several manufacturing firms. Among them were butter and cheese companies, as well as Sarotti A.G., a Berlin-based chocolate business that began manufacturing Nestlé, Peter, Cailler, and Kohler chocolate. In 1928, under the direction of Chairman Louis Dapples, Nestlé finally merged with Peter, Cailler, Kohler, Chocolats Suisses S.A.—the resulting company of a 1911 merger between the Swiss General Chocolate Company and Cailler, another leading firm—adding 13 chocolate plants in Europe, South America, and Australia to the growing firm.

Expanded During the Great Depression

Nestlé was becoming so strong that it seemed even the Great Depression would have little effect on its progress. In fact, its U.S. subsidiary, Nestlé's Food Company Inc. of New York, barely felt the stock market crash of 1929. In 1930 Nestlé created new subsidiaries in Argentina and Cuba. Despite the Depression, Nestlé added more production centers around the world, including a chocolate manufacturer in Copenhagen and a small factory in Moravia, Czechoslovakia, to manufacture milk food, Nescao, and evaporated milk. Factories were also opened in Chile and Mexico in the mid-1930s.

While profits were down 13 percent in 1930 over the year before, Nestlé faced no major financial problems during the Depression, as its factories generally maintained their output and sales were steady. Although Nestlé's New York-based subsidiary, renamed Nestlé's Milk Products Company, was more affected than those in other countries, U.S. sales of milk products were steady until 1931 and 1932, when a growing public frugality began to cause trouble for more expensive but established brands such as Nestlé's. Profit margins narrowed, prices dropped, and cutthroat competition continued until 1933, when new legislation set minimum prices and conditions of sales.

The markets, such as the United States, that were among the first to feel the effects of the Depression were also the first to recover from it. The Depression continued in Switzerland, however. Nestlé products manufactured there could no longer compete on international markets since Swiss currency exchanges were made especially difficult from the early 1930s, when many major countries devalued their currencies, until 1936, when Switzerland finally did likewise. The company decided to streamline production and close several factories, including its two oldest, in Cham and Vevey.

Decentralization efforts begun during the Depression continued to modify the company's structure gradually. By 1936, the industrial and commercial activity of the Nestlé and Anglo-Swiss Condensed Milk Company itself was quite limited in comparison with the considerable interests it had in companies manufacturing and selling its products. More than 20 such companies existed on five continents. In effect, the firm had become a holding company. Consequently, the Nestlé and Anglo-Swiss Condensed Milk Company Limited was established to handle production and marketing on the Swiss market; the parent company officially became a holding firm, called the Nestlé and Anglo-Swiss Holding Company Ltd.; and a second holding company, Unilac Inc., was created in Panama by a number of Nestlé's overseas affiliates.

Nescafé Instant Coffee Debuted in 1938

In 1937 Louis Dapples died, and a new management team, whose members had grown up with the organization, took over. It included Chairman Edouard Muller, formerly managing director; Carl J. Abegg, vice-chairman of the board; and Maurice Paternot, managing director. In 1938 Nestlé introduced its first nonmilk product: Nescafé. The revolutionary instant coffee was the result of eight years of research, which had begun when a representative of the Brazilian Coffee Institute asked Louis Dapples if Nestlé could manufacture "coffee cubes" to help Brazil use its large coffee surplus. Although coffee crystals and liquid extracts had been tried before, none had satisfactorily preserved a coffee taste.

Nestlé's product took the form of a soluble powder rather than cubes, allowing users to control the amount of coffee they used. Although Nestlé originally intended to manufacture Nescafé in Brazil, administrative barriers were too great, so Nescafé was first manufactured in Switzerland. Limited production capacity meant that it was launched without the elaborate marketing tactics usually used for products with such potential.

Nescafé quickly acquired a worldwide reputation, however, after it was launched in 1939 in the United States, where it did exceptionally well. Nestea, a soluble powdered tea, also made a successful debut in the early 1940s.

World War II had a dire effect on Nestlé. In 1939 profits plummeted to $6 million, compared to $20 million the year before. As in the last war, the company was plagued by food shortages and insufficient supplies of raw materials. To wage its own battle against the war, the company decided to split its headquarters at Vevey and transfer part of the management and executive team to an office in Stamford, Connecticut, where it could better supervise distant markets. Nestlé continued under control of dual managements until 1945.

But the war was not all bad for Nestlé. When the United States became involved in 1941, Nescafé and evaporated and powdered milk were in heavy demand from American armed forces. Nestlé's total sales jumped from $100 million before the war to $225 million in 1945, with the greatest increase occurring in North America, where sales went from $14 million to $60 million. With the end of the war, Nestlé's European and American branches were able to discuss future plans without fear of censorship, and the company could begin to face the challenge of rebuilding its war-torn subsidiaries. Nestlé also relaunched Nescafé and baby foods and began to research new products extensively. Researchers focused on the three areas Nestlé considered most likely to affect the food industry's future: an increase in world population, rising standards of living in industrialized countries, and the changing social and economic conditions of raw-material-producing countries.

Postwar Expansion Through Merger and Acquisition

In 1947 Nestlé merged with Alimentana S.A., the manufacturer of Maggi seasonings, bouillon, and dehydrated soups, and the holding company changed its name to Nestlé Alimentana Company. Edouard Muller became the first chairman of Nestlé Alimentana, but he died in 1948, before the policies he helped formulate put the company on the road to a new future. Carl Abegg assumed leadership of the board.

In 1950 Nestlé acquired Crosse and Blackwell, a British manufacturer of preserves and canned foods. Nestlé hoped its $24 million investment would serve as a marketing outlet for Maggi products, but the plan was less than successful, primarily because Crosse and Blackwell could not compete in the United Kingdom with H.J. Heinz Company. Similar setbacks occurred in 1963, when Nestlé acquired Findus frozen foods in Scandinavia for $32 million. Although the company performed well in Sweden, it encountered difficulties in other markets, where the British-Dutch giant Unilever reigned. While parts of the Findus operation eventually became profitable, Nestlé merged its German, Italian, and Australian Findus branches with Unilever. The development of freeze-drying in 1966 led to Taster's Choice, the first freeze-dried coffee, as well as other instant drinks.

In 1971 Nestlé acquired Libby, a maker of fruit juices, in the United States, and in 1973 it bought Stouffer's, which took Nestlé into the hotel and restaurant field and led to the development of Lean Cuisine, a successful line of low-calorie frozen entrees. Nestlé entered the nonfood business for the first time in 1974 by becoming a major shareholder in the French company L'Oreal, a leading cosmetics company. Nestlé diversified further in 1977 with the acquisition of Alcon Laboratories, a Fort Worth, Texas, pharmaceutical company that specialized in ophthalmic products. Then, two years later, Nestlé purchased Burton, Parsons and Company Inc., an American manufacturer of contact lens products. The company adopted its present name—Nestlé S.A.—in 1979.

Faced Boycott in Late 1970s and Early 1980s

The 1970s saw Nestlé's operations in developing countries increase considerably. Of Nestlé's 303 manufacturing facilities, the 81 factories in developing nations contributed 21 percent of Nestlé's total production. In the mid-1970s, however, the firm faced a new problem as a result of its marketing efforts in these countries, when a boycott against all Nestlé products was started in the United States in 1977. Activists claimed that Nestlé's aggressive baby food promotions made mothers in developing countries so eager to use Nestlé's formula that they used it any way they could. The poverty-stricken areas had high rates of illiteracy, and mothers, unable to read and follow the directions, often mixed the product with local polluted water or used an insufficient amount of the expensive formula, unwittingly starving their infants. Estimates of Nestlé's losses as a result of the boycott, which lasted until the early 1980s, ranged as high as $40 million.

In 1981 Helmut Maucher became managing director of Nestlé and made this controversy one of his top priorities. He met with boycott supporters and complied with the World Health Organization's demands that Nestlé stop promoting the product through advertising and free samples. His direct confrontation of the issue contrasted with Nestlé's earlier low-profile approach and was quite successful in allaying its critics' fears.

Series of Major Acquisitions in the Later 1980s

Maucher also reduced overhead by turning over more authority to operating units and reducing headquarters staff. In addition, he spearheaded a series of major acquisitions. In 1985 Nestlé acquired Carnation, a U.S. manufacturer of milk, pet, and culinary products, for $3 billion, at the time one of the largest acquisitions in the history of the food industry. This was followed in 1985 by the acquisition of Hills Brothers Inc., the third largest U.S. coffee firm, which added ground roast coffee to Nestlé's product line. In the late 1980s, as food companies around the world prepared for the integration of the European Community in 1992, Nestlé continued to make major acquisitions. In 1988 the company paid £2.55 billion (US$4.4 billion) for Rowntree Mackintosh PLC—a leading British chocolate manufacturer—marking the largest takeover of a British company by a foreign one to date. That same year Nestlé also purchased the Italian pasta maker Buitoni SpA.

Capital expenditures reached SFr 2.8 billion in 1991. Half was devoted to installation improvements, including data processing and automation, particularly in North America and Europe. The other half was spent expanding plants, primarily in Latin America and the Far East, areas where products were often based on local raw materials, tastes, and habits. That year Nestlé made 31 acquisitions, also adding a new factory in the People's Republic of China. Among the companies purchased were Alco Drumstick, a U.S. ice cream manufacturer with many European activities; Indra, a Swedish frozen-food maker; La Campiña, a Mexican evaporated milk producer; and 97 percent of Intercsokoládé, a Hungarian chocolate maker. The latter was Nestlé's first venture into the newly opened markets of Eastern Europe.

In September 1991 Nestlé and The Coca-Cola Company formed a 50-50 joint-venture, Coca-Cola Nestlé Refreshment Company, to produce and distribute concentrates and bases for the production of ready-to-drink coffee and tea beverages. With an initial capitalization of $100 million the products, to be sold under the Nescafé and Nestea brand names, would be marketed worldwide save for Japan, primarily through Coca-Cola's international network of businesses.

Nescafé, sold in more than 100 countries by 1991, was launched in the Republic of Korea—Coca-Cola and Nestlé's first joint endeavor—as was Nescafé Cappuccino in Europe. Hills Bros. "Perfect Balance," a 50 percent-decaffeinated coffee, began selling in the United States, as did Nestea in cans at the beginning of 1992. By early 1992, a joint venture allowed the company to obtain a majority interest in Cokoladovny, a Czechoslovakian chocolate and biscuit producer. In addition, Nestlé in 1992 battled for and won, with a bid of $2.3 billion in cash, the French mineral water producer Source Perrier, though European regulators forced Nestlé to sell off some Perrier brands. That same year Nestlé took nearly full control of another mineral water concern, Vittel; Nestlé had acquired a 30 percent stake in Vittel in 1969, a move marking the company's first foray into mineral water.

Reemphasis on Core Food Area in Later 1990s

As the 1990s continued, Nestlé recommitted itself to its core food products area, never having been able to grow its health-care and cosmetics sectors into significant parts of the overall business. The company sold off some of its health and beauty interests, retaining Alcon and the minority holding in L'Oreal—it still hoped to gain full control of the latter, which was privately controlled. Nestlé made other divestments as well, including Wine World Estates, a group of northern California wineries (sold in 1995); canned beans and pasta operations in Canada, a fresh meat business in Germany, and cold meat operations in Sweden (1996); Contadina canned tomato products in the United States, Sarotti chocolate and Dany sandwiches in Germany, and Locatelli brand cheeses in Italy (1997); and Libby's canned meat products, which were sold to International Home Foods for $126 million in 1998.

Acquisitions in the mid-to-late 1990s centered around mineral water, ice cream, and pet foods. In 1993 Nestlé purchased mineral water brands in the United States (Deer Park and Utopia) and Italy (Vera and San Bernardo), as well as ice cream brands in Italy, the Philippines, and South Africa. Added in 1994 were the Alpo pet food company in the United States and Warnke ice creams in Germany; the company also gained a majority stake in chocolate maker Goplana S.A. in Poland. Still further expansion of the ice cream sector came in 1995 with the purchase of Conelsa, the leader in the Spanish market; the chilled dairy products division of Pacific Dunlop in Australia; and Dolce S.A.E., the leading maker of ice cream in Egypt. That year Nestlé also acquired Ortega, a leading brand of Mexican food products in the United States. In 1997 Nestlé entered the Canadian ice cream market through the purchase of Ault and Dairy World, giving the company a 40 percent market share. In early 1998 Nestlé took full control of the San Pellegrino mineral water group and acquired Klim milk powders and Cremora coffee creamers from Borden Brands International. Also in 1998 the company secured the number two position in the European pet food market, trailing only Mars, through the £715 million (US$1.2 billion) purchase of the Spillers pet food business of Dalgety PLC.

Despite all of this activity, Nestlé's acquisition pace slowed during the late 1990s as the company shifted toward organic growth starting in 1996. The numerous acquisitions had enabled Nestlé to gain a presence in various product areas in various countries. The company now had fewer countries and products that it wished to add to its portfolio. Other reasons for the shift to organic growth included the increasing price of acquisitions and antitrust concerns. Meanwhile, in June 1997 Peter Brabeck-Letmathe was named chief executive, taking over the day-to-day management of Nestlé from Maucher. In September 1998 Nestlé announced that Maucher would retire as chairman by the spring of 2000, being replaced by Rainer Gut, then chairman of the Credit Suisse Group.

Nestlé's aggressive marketing of infant formula once again became an issue in 1997 when a report called *Cracking the Code* was issued by the Interagency Group on Breastfeeding Monitoring (IGBM), which had conducted research in Bangladesh, Poland, South Africa, and Thailand. The IGBM concluded that several companies, including Nestlé, were in violation of the World Health Organization's International Code of Marketing of Breastmilk Substitutes, which had been adopted in 1981. According to the report Nestlé's code violations included supplying pregnant women and health workers with materials that promoted formula feeding but did not emphasize the superiority of breastfeeding over formula, and distributing free samples. Nestlé countered by calling the report biased and flawed, and by eliciting a response critical of *Cracking the Code* from an independent marketing research consultant.

At the dawn of the 21st century, Nestlé, after more than 130 years in business, had about 500 factories in more than 78 countries, boasted sales exceeding SFr 70 billion, and was the undisputed leader in the food industry worldwide. Its portfolio included more than 8,500 brands. The company had set a goal of achieving four percent underlying sales growth each year, but failed to meet this target for 1998, largely because of economic downturns in southeast Asia, Latin America, and Eastern Europe. Although the worldwide economic difficulties led to questions about Nestlé's short-term prospects, the company seemed certain to maintain its preeminent position over the long haul.

Principal Subsidiaries

EUROPE: Nestlé Deutschland AG (Germany; 97.2%); Blaue Quellen Mineral- und Heilbrunnen AG (Germany; 90.6%); Trinks GmbH (Germany; 90.6%); Alcon Pharma GmbH (Germany); Alois Dallmayr Kaffee OHG (Germany; 48.6%); Heimbs & Sohn GmbH & Co. KG (Germany; 48.6%); Azul Kaffee GmbH & Co. KG (Germany; 48.6%); Nähr-Engel GmbH (Germany; 97.22%); Vittel Mineralwasser GmbH (Germany); Österreichische Nestlé GmbH (Austria); Nestlé Belgilux S.A. (Belgium); Perrier Vittel Belgilux S.A. (Belgium); Alcon-Couvreur S.A. (Belgium); Nestlé Sofia A.D. (Bulgaria; 99%); Nestlé Danmark A/S (Denmark); Premier Is A/S (Denmark); Nestlé España S.A. (Spain); Productos del Café S.A. (Spain); Davigel España S.A. (Spain); EYCAM Perrier S.A. (Spain); Alcon-Cusi S.A. (Spain); Helados y Congelados S.A. (Spain); Compañia del Frio Alimentario S.A. (Spain); Compañia Avidesa S.A. (Spain; 99.43%); Alimentos Congelados S.A. (Spain); Soumen Nestlé Oy (Finland); Nestlé France S.A.; France Glaces-Findus S.A.; Chambourcy S.A. (France; 99.9%); Herta S.A. (France); Davigel S.A. (France; 99.9%); Perrier Vittel France S.A.; S.A. des Eaux Minérales de Ribeauvillé (France; 98.3%); Société Conditionnement et Industrie S.A. (France; 77.9%); Eau Minérale Naturelle de Plancoët "Source Sassay" S.A. (France); Nestlé Coffee Specialties France S.A.; Nestlé Clinical Nutrition S.A. (France); Laboratoires Alcon S.A. (France); Nestlé Dairy Industry S.A.I. (Greece; 85.4%); Alcon Laboratories Hellas E.P.E. (Greece); Nestlé Italiana S.p.A. (Italy; 99.9%); SO.GE.AM S.p.A. (Italy); SO.GE.PLAST S.p.A. (Italy); Alcon Italia S.p.A. (Italy); Nestlé Hungaria Kft (Hungary); A/S Nestlé Norge (Norway); Nestlé Nederland B.V. (Netherlands); Alcon Nederland B.V. (Netherlands); Goplana S.A. (Poland; 76.97%); Nestlé Polska Sp. zo.o. (Poland); Naleczowianka Spolka zo.o. (Poland; 33.3%); Winiary S.A. (Poland; 83.28%); Nestlé Portugal S.A.; Longa Vida S.A. (Portugal); Sociedade das Aguas de Pisoes Moura S.A. (Portugal); Nestlé (Ireland) Ltd.; Nestlé Food S.r.o. (Czech Republic); Nestlé UK Ltd.; Perrier Vittel UK Ltd.; Buxton Mineral Water Company Ltd. (U.K.); Alcon Laboratories (U.K.) Ltd.; C.U. Rossiya (Russia; 93.21%); Nestlé Zhukovsky

Ice Cream LLC (Russia; 80.48%); Nestlé Food LLC (Russia); Nestlé Food S.r.o. (Slovakia; 99.9%); Svenska Nestlé AB (Sweden); Jede AB (Sweden); Zoégas Kaffe AB (Sweden); Société des Produits Nestlé S.A.; Nestlé Suisse S.A.; Frisco-Findus AG (99.8%); Perrier Vittel Suisse S.A.; Alcon Pharmaceuticals Ltd.; Nestlé World Trade Corporation; Food Ingredients Specialities S.A.; Nestlé Coffee Specialties S.A.; Nestlé Türkiye Gida Sanayi A.S. (Turkey). AFRICA: Nestlé (South Africa) (Pty) Ltd.; Alcon Laboratories Pty Ltd. (South Africa); Nestlé Cameroun (Cameroon; 99.6%); Nestlé Côte d'Ivoire (Ivory Coast; 80.9%); Dolce S.A.E. (Egypt); Industrie du Froid S.A.E. (Egypt); Société des eaux minérales Vittor S.A.E. (Egypt; 88.5%); Nestlé Gabon (90%); Nestlé Ghana Ltd. (51%); Nestlé Guinée (Guinea; 99%); Nestlé Foods Kenya Ltd.; Nestlé's Products (Mauritius) Ltd.; Nestlé Maroc S.A. (Morocco; 93.4%); Nestlé Foods Nigeria PLC (57%); Nestlé Sénégal; Nestlé Tunisie (Tunisia; 59.2%); Nestlé Zimbabwe (Pvt) Ltd. AMERICAS: Nestlé Argentina S.A.; Alcon Laboratorios Argentina S.A.; Nestlé Bolivia S.r.l.; Nestlé Industrial e Comercial Ltda. (Brazil); Companhia Produtora de Alimentos (Brazil); Tostines Industrial e Comercial Ltda. (Brazil); Perrier Vittel de Brasil Ltda. (Brazil); Alcon Laboratorios do Brasil S.A. (Brazil); Nestlé Canada, Inc.; Midwest Food Products, Inc. (Canada; 50%); Laura Secord, Inc. (Canada); The Perrier Group of Canada Ltd.; Alcon Canada, Inc.; Nestlé Chile S.A. (99.5%); Alcon Laboratorios Chile Limitada; Nestlé de Colombia S.A.; Laboratorios Alcon de Colombia S.A.; Nestlé Costa Rica S.A.; Nestlé El Salvador S.A.; Nestlé Ecuador S.A. (74.7%); Neslandia S.A. (Ecuador); Nestlé USA, Inc.; Nestlé USA - Food Division, Inc.; Nestlé USA - Beverage Division, Inc.; Food Ingredient Specialities, Inc. (U.S.A.); Great Spring Waters of America, Inc. (U.S.A.); Nestlé Puerto Rico, Inc. (U.S.A.); Alcon Laboratories, Inc. (U.S.A.); Alcon (Puerto Rico), Inc. (U.S.A.); Nestlé Guatemala S.A.; Nestlé Hondureña S.A. (Honduras); Nestlé-JMP Jamaica Ltd.; Cremo Ltd. (Jamaica); Compañáa Nestlé S.A. de C.V. (Mexico); Alimentos Findus S.A. de C.V. (Mexico); Industrias Alimenticias Club S.A. de C.V. (Mexico); Manantiales La Asuncion, S.A. de C.V. (Mexico); Alcon Laboratorios S.A. de C.V. (Mexico); Productos Nestlé (Nicaragua) S.A.; Nestlé Panamí S.A.; Nestlé Caribbean, Inc. (Panama); Nestlé Perú S.A. (93.1%); D'Onofrio S.A. (Peru; 80.6%); Sociedad Dominicana de Conservas y Alimentos S.A. (Dominican Republic; 75.7%); Compañia Dominicana de Alimentos Lacteos S.A. (Dominican Republic); Helados Nestlé S.A. (Dominican Republic); Nestlé Trinidad and Tobago Ltd.; Nestlé del Uruguay S.A.; Nestlé Venezuela S.A.; Chocolates Nestlé S.A. (Venezuela); Caramelos Royal C.A. (Venezuela). ASIA: Saudi Food Industries Co. Ltd. (Saudi Arabia; 51%); Nestlé Bangladesh Ltd. (60%); Nestlé Ice Cream L.L.C. (United Arab Emirites; 49%); Nestlé Hong Kong Ltd.; Nestlé Dairy Farm Hong Kong Ltd.; Nestlé India Ltd. (51%); P.T. Nestlé Indonesia (57.6%); P.T. Nestlé Confectionery Indonesia; P.T. Nestlé Asean (Indonesia) (60%); P.T. Supmi Sakti (Indonesia; 97%); OSEM Investments Ltd. (Israel; 39.7%); Nestlé Japan Ltd.; Nestlé-Mackintosh K.K. (Japan; 66%); Perrier Japon K.K. (Japan); Alcon Japan Ltd.; Nestlé Jordan Trading Co. Ltd. (49%); Nestlé Kuwait General Trading Co. W.L.L. (49%); Société pour l'Exportation des Produits Nestlé S.A. (Lebanon); Nestlé (Malaysia) Bhd. (52.7%); Nestlé Foods (Malaysia) Sdn. Bhd. (51%); Nestlé Products Sdn. Bhd. (Malaysia; 51%); Malaysia Cocoa Manufacturing Sdn. Bhd. (51%); Nestlé Asean (Malaysia) Sdn. Bhd. (60%); Nestlé Cold Storage (Malaysia) Sdn. Bhd. (51%); Milkpak Ltd. (Pakistan;

56.2%); Nestlé Philippines, Inc.; Nestlé Foods Korea Ltd.; Nestlé Shuangcheng Ltd. (People's Republic of China; 90%); Nestlé Dongguan Ltd. (People's Republic of China; 60%); Maggi Dongguan Ltd. (People's Republic of China); Nestlé Tianjin Ltd. (People's Republic of China); Nestlé Qingdao Ltd. (People's Republic of China); Nestlé Dairy Farm Tianjin Ltd. (People's Republic of China; 75%); Nestlé Dairy Farm Qingdao Ltd. (People's Republic of China); Nestlé Dairy Farm Guangzhou Ltd. (People's Republic of China; 60%); Nestlé Singapore (Pte) Ltd.; Nestlé Asean Singapore (Pte) Ltd. (60%); Nestlé Lanka Ltd. (Sri Lanka; 90.8%); Nestlé Taiwan Ltd.; Nestlé Distributors Ltd. (Taiwan); Foremost Foods (Taiwan) Ltd.; Alcon Pharmaceuticals Ltd. (Taiwan); Nestlé Products Thailand, Inc.; Nestlé Asean (Thailand) Ltd. (60%); Quality Coffee Products Ltd. (Thailand; 49%); Nestlé Foods (Thailand) Ltd.; Nestlé Trading (Thailand) Ltd. (49%); Nestlé Manufacturing (Thailand) Ltd.; Nestlé Ice Cream (Thailand) Ltd. (46.3%); Nestlé Vietnam Ltd.; Long An Mineral Water Joint Venture Company (Vietnam; 42.7%). OCEANIA: Nestlé Australia Ltd.; Petersville Australia Ltd.; Nestlé Echuca Pty Ltd. (Australia); Alcon Laboratories (Australia) Pty Ltd.; Nestlé (Fiji) Ltd. (67%); Nestlé Nouvelle-Calédonie S.A. (New Caledonia); Nestlé New Zealand Ltd.; Nestlé (PNG) Ltd. (Papua New Guinea); Nestlé Polynesia S.A. (French Polynesia).

Further Reading

Hall, William, "Leading Swiss Banker to Be Nestlé Chairman," *Financial Times,* September 21, 1998, p. 26.

——, "Maucher Keeps His Claws in Nestlé," *Financial Times,* May 7, 1997, p. 26.

——, "Strength of Brands Is Key to Success," *Financial Times,* November 30, 1998, p. SII.

Harrisson, Pierre, *L'Empire Nestlé,* Lausanne, Switzerland: Editions P.-M. Favre, 1983, 493 p.

Heer, Jean, *Nestlé: 125 Years, 1866–1991,* Vevey, Switzerland: Nestlé, 1991.

——, *World Events, 1866–1966: The First Hundred Years of Nestlé,* Vevey, Switzerland: Nestlé, 1966.

Interagency Group on Breastfeeding Monitoring, *Cracking the Code,* UK Committee for UNICEF, 1997.

Maucher, Helmut, *Leadership in Action: Tough-Minded Strategies from the Global Giant,* New York: McGraw-Hill, 1994, 160 p.

"Nestlé Consolidating Its Chocolate Production," *New York Times,* February 5, 1993.

Oram, Roderick, "Nestlé's Portfolio of Possibilities," *Financial Times,* August 8, 1996, p. 24.

——, "Sweet Success for a Strong Leader," *Financial Times,* September 19, 1995, p. 53.

Rapoport, Carla, "Nestlé's Brand Building Machine," *Fortune,* September 19, 1994, pp. 147–48, 150, 154, 156.

Rohwedder, Cacilie, "Nestlé Goes on Investment Diet, Limiting Its Expansion: Emphasis Shifts to Strengthening Core Food Products in European Market," *Wall Street Journal,* September 27, 1994, p. B6.

Steinmetz, Greg, and Tara Parker-Pope, "All Over the Map: At a Time When Companies Are Scrambling to Go Abroad, Nestlé Has Long Been There," *Wall Street Journal,* September 26, 1996, p. R4.

Templeman, John, Stewart Toy, and Dave Lindorff, "Nestlé: A Giant in a Hurry," *Business Week,* March 22, 1993, pp. 50–51, 54.

Urry, Maggie, and William Hall, "Nestlé Buys Spillers for £715m," *Financial Times,* February 5, 1998, p. 21.

—Anne C. Hughes
—updated by David E. Salamie

Niagara Corporation

667 Madison Avenue
New York, New York 10021
U.S.A.
(212) 317-1000
Fax: (212) 317-1001

Public Company
Incorporated: 1993 as International Metals Acquisition
Corporation
Employees: 645
Sales: $207.5 million (1998)
Stock Exchanges: NASDAQ
Ticker Symbol: NIAG
NAIC: 331221 Rolled Steel Shape Manufacturing

Niagara Corporation was, in the late 1990s, the largest independent producer of cold-drawn steel bars in the United States, with annual output of 300,000 tons. It consisted of two subsidiaries: Niagara LaSalle Corporation, a manufacturer of such bars, and LaSalle Steel Corporation, a producer of specialized as well as standard cold-finished steel bars. Niagara's products were being used primarily in the U.S. and Canadian automotive and machine tool industries. The company was assembled in the 1990s by the acquisition of three separate manufacturing firms.

International Metals Acquisition: 1993–95

Niagara was founded in 1993 by Michael J. Scharf as International Metals Acquisition Corporation, with the objective of acquiring an operating business engaged in the metals processing and distribution industry or metals-related manufacturing industry. Scharf was chairman, president, and chief executive officer of the firm, which was based in New York City and raised $15 million in a public offering of stock that year. Scharf, who said in 1994 that he had $50 million in equity for a purchase, had been in the metals distribution business since 1970, when he founded Unimet Corporation, a specialty processor with initial capital of $450,000 that was sold in 1973 for at

least $14 million. In 1983 he took a one-quarter stake in Edgcomb Steel of New England Inc. for $4 million and, after the 1984 acquisition of a metals service center chain, turned it into the largest independent metals processor. Edgcomb's 1986 leveraged buyout netted its shareholders $150 million, and the 1989 sale of the company brought them another $100 million.

Scharf's objective in 1993 was to buy a metals service center as part of a planned chain of small metals distribution firms. Instead, however, he changed course and in 1994 offered at least $105 million to acquire New Jersey Steel Corporation, a producer of steel reinforcing bars used in reinforced concrete by the construction industry. After he tried to revise the deal by offering less cash and more International Metals stock, New Jersey Steel terminated the tentative agreement in early 1995. Scharf said he had changed his offer because he perceived a ''diminution of the company's value.''

Following the collapse of this proposed acquisition, Scharf purchased Niagara Cold Drawn Corporation in 1995. Niagara owned the property that had been the Buffalo steel plant of Bliss & Laughlin Industries Inc. from 1929 to 1971, when it was producing cold-finished steel bars for heavy equipment moving mechanically, such as automobiles, appliances, and construction and farm equipment. This 193,000-square-foot mill was closed by a strike in 1971 and was sold the following year to Ramco Steel Inc. for an undisclosed sum in cash. The owner in 1985, Ramco-Fitzsimmons Steel Co. Inc., went bankrupt that year, and the plant closed again. It reopened in 1986 under Niagara Cold Drawn Corporation, a company owned mainly by Allister Corporation, and continued to process hot-rolled steel bars into cold-finished flat steel bars between six and 48 inches wide for steel service centers and screw machine shops.

Niagara Cold Drawn was also leasing a smaller mill in Chattanooga, Tennessee, in 1992, when it was 80 percent owned by Adage Inc., which had acquired Allister. Adage sold Niagara Cold Drawn to International Metals Acquisition for $10.7 million in cash. ''I was attracted to Niagara for a variety of factors,'' Scharf told *American Metal Market* in June 1995, ''one being that it has a consistent record of growth. It has excellent management; it's a good facility; it has an excellent product, good potential for growth and is very service oriented.'' Scharf needed to make an acquisition because International Metals' charter required the company to dissolve and return the money raised from investors if it did not acquire a company within two years of the initial public offering of stock in August 1993. The purchase called for Niagara's senior managers to continue in their posts for five years. International Metals Acquisition then changed its name to Niagara Corporation.

Southwest and LaSalle Acquisitions, 1996–97

Niagara Cold Drawn, in early 1996, purchased Southwest Steel Co., Inc., a manufacturer of cold-drawn steel bars, for $3.1 million in cash and promissory notes and the assumption of $9.4 million in debt. This company had been producing cold-finished steel bars in Catoosa, Oklahoma, a suburb of Tulsa, for more than ten years under the name Sauk Southwest Steel Co. before it changed its name to Southwest Steel Co. Inc. in 1991. The company built a new cold-finished steel-bar plant in 1995 in Midlothian, Texas, across the road from Chaparral Steel Co., its main supplier of hot-rolled bars. This mill was expected, by 1998, to raise Southwest's annual output from about 25,000 to about 60,000 tons and also raised its size range to five-inch-diameter round bars. Sixty-five percent of its customers were service centers, which had been turning elsewhere to meet their larger size needs.

Southwest was merged into Niagara Cold Drawn and vacated its Oklahoma plant. Niagara Corporation's net sales rose from $17 million in 1995 to $74.8 million in 1996. Its net income increased from $344,000 to nearly $1.1 million.

Niagara Corporation, in 1997, purchased LaSalle Steel Co. from Quanex Corporation for $66.9 million in cash. LaSalle was making cold-finished bars in Hammond and Griffith, Indiana, and Spring City, Pennsylvania, when it was purchased in 1981 by Quanex Corporation for $52 million in cash and notes. LaSalle had sales of $158.5 million, operating income of $10.4 million, and earnings of $5.6 million in fiscal 1996 (the year ended October 31, 1996). Its two remaining Indiana plants were making cold-finished and chrome-plated steel bars for the automotive and durable-goods markets. The acquisition enabled Niagara's net sales to reach nearly $205 million in 1997. Its net income came to $1.9 million.

The LaSalle purchase made Niagara the largest independent producer of cold-drawn steel bars in the United States. These bars were being manufactured for a smooth and shiny surface, uniform shape with close size tolerance, enhanced strength characteristics, and improved machinability, characteristics essential for many industrial applications. The Hammond plant experienced a nine-week strike in 1998, but Scharf claimed that orders were not affected because of the hiring of about 100 replacement workers and boosted production by the other plants.

Niagara Corporation in the Late 1990s

Niagara Cold Drawn, now renamed Niagara LaSalle, was manufacturing round bars ranging from a quarter-inch to six inches in diameter and rectangular, square, and hexagonal bars in a variety of sizes, the majority of which were drawn, or pulled, in sizes of a quarter-inch to six inches thick and up to 15 inches wide. The length varied from ten to 20 feet, with most ten to 12 feet. Niagara LaSalle's products in 1997 included cold-drawn bars used in machining applications, automotive and appliance shafts, screw-machine parts, and machinery guides; turned, ground, and polished bars used in precision shafting; and drawn, ground, and polished bars used in chrome-plated hydraulic cylinder shafts.

LaSalle, a technological leader in the development of specialized cold-drawn steel products, had pioneered in the large drawbenches that were commonly used in cold finishing and had developed the principle of stress-relieving cold-finished steel bars. It was employing a number of advanced processing techniques in the manufacture of value-added steel bars, including thermal treatment and chrome plating. In addition to cold-drawn bars, LaSalle's products included custom-cut bars shipped on a just-in-time basis for steering columns and shock absorbers; stress-relieved bars used in high-strength shafting, gears, and drive mechanisms; quench and tempered bars used in high-strength bolting and high-impact rod cylinders; and chrome-plated bars used in hydraulic and pneumatic cylinders.

Steel service centers accounted for about 77 percent of Niagara's sales in 1998, with the balance coming from original equipment manufacturers (OEMs) and the screw machine industry. Steel service centers purchase and warehouse large amounts of standardized steel products for direct sale to OEMs. Of about 650 active customers in the United States and Canada in 1998, Niagara's three largest were Alro Steel Corporation, A.M. Castle & Co., and Earle M. Jorgenson Co. These three accounted for about 44 percent of sales.

Niagara LaSalle owned manufacturing facilities in Buffalo and Midlothian, Texas, in 1998 and was leasing a manufacturing plant in Chattanooga. LaSalle owned manufacturing facilities in Hammond and Griffith, Indiana. These five Niagara plants were operating at about 75 percent of capacity. Leased headquarters for the parent company were in New York City. Michael J. Scharf held a 12.7 percent stake of Niagara in June. His brother Gilbert, the company's secretary, held 5.6 percent. In 1998 the company posted sales of over $207 million.

Principal Subsidiaries

LaSalle Steel Corporation; Niagara LaSalle Corporation.

Further Reading

"Bankrupt Ramco-Fitzsimmons Is Reopened Under New Name," *American Metal Market,* July 25, 1986, p. 6.
Beirne, Mike, "IMAC Spurns Durrett for Niagara," *American Metal Market,* June 13, 1995, p. 2.
——, "N.J. Steel Finds a Buyer—at Last," *American Metal Market,* August 4, 1994, p. 2.
——, "Service Centers Seen As Purchase Candidates," *American Metal Market,* February 25, 1994, p. 5.
——, "Southwest Plans New Bar Mill," *American Metal Market,* November 29, 1994, p. 4.

"Bliss & Laughlin Sells Plant," *Wall Street Journal,* November 15, 1972, p. 12.

Hassler, Darrell, "9-Week Strike Ends at LaSalle," *American Metal Market,* July 21, 1998, p. 16.

"LaSalle Purchase Boosts Niagara Earnings, Sales," *American Metal Market,* August 11, 1997, p. 3.

Madore, James T., "Area Steel Firm Draws Fire on State Grant," *Buffalo News,* March 23, 1993.

Marcial, Gene G., "Niagara Goes Roaring On," *Business Week,* December 22, 1997, p. 92.

"Quanex Acquires LaSalle for $52M Cash and Notes," *American Metal Market,* November 17, 1981, p. 2.

"Quanex to Sell LaSalle Steel to Niagara," *Houston Chronicle,* January 24, 1997, p. C3.

"Tulsa Maker of Steel Bars Alters Name," *American Metal Market,* October 18, 1991, p. 3.

—Robert Halasz

Nintendo Co., Ltd.

60, Fukuine Kamitakamatsu-cho
Higashiyama-ku, Kyoto 605
Japan
(075) 541-6111
(800) 255-3700; (800) 422-2602
Fax: (075) 531-9577
Web site: http://www.nintendo.com

Public Company
Incorporated: 1889 as Marufuku Company, Ltd.
Employees: 1,002
Sales: ¥534.325 billion (US$4.04 billion) (1998)
Stock Exchanges: Tokyo
Ticker Symbol: NTDOY
NAIC: 339932 Games, Toys, & Children's Vehicle Manufacturing; 421920 Electronic Games Wholesaling

Nintendo Co., Ltd. is a toy and home entertainment concern that is famous worldwide for its popular home video games. Nintendo's products arose in the mid-1980s from the relative obscurity of the amusement arcade to change the concept of home entertainment in both Japan and the United States. Nintendo's main U.S. product, the Nintendo Entertainment System (NES), and its Japanese counterpart, the Family Computer (Famicom), were embraced by consumers of both nations, but increased competition in the early 1990s from a new generation of video machine competitors loosened Nintendo's commanding hold on the market. The company's commitment to quality and innovation, as represented by its Nintendo 64 machine and software, kept Nintendo in the game as it advanced through the increasingly competitive environment. In the late 1990s, the revitalization of its hand-held, portable Game Boy system by way of the Pokemon game concept proved to be one of the company's—and the $15 billion industry's—biggest successes of the period.

Playing Card Company: 1880s–Early 1960s

Nintendo was founded as Marufuku Company, Ltd., in Kyoto, Japan, in 1889 by Fusajiro Yamauchi, the great grandfather of the current president of Nintendo. Marufuku made playing cards for the Japanese game of Hanafuda, which is said to have had its origin in Tarot cards. In 1907 Marufuku introduced the first Western-style playing cards in Japan. Marufuku initially made the cards for Russian prisoners of war during the Russo-Japanese War of 1904–05 when the soldiers wore out the decks they had brought from Russia.

Between 1907 and World War II Marufuku solidified its status in the playing-card business. World War I, in which Japan fought on the side of the Allies, did not affect business in any remarkable way. In 1925, however, Marufuku began exporting Hanafuda cards to Japanese emigré communities in South America, Korea, and Australia. The years 1925 to 1928 also saw Marufuku developing a new, more effective marketing strategy that placed its products in tobacco shops. These marketing moves were complemented by Marufuku's aggressive advertising, as Japan's business practices became more Westernized.

World War II devastated the Japanese economy and delivered a hard blow even to the previously modest but stable home amusement market. The playing card industry and Marufuku, though, fared far better than most. In the austere postwar climate, when entertainment had to be cheap and simple, the demand for playing cards only decreased slightly. Marufuku, whose physical plant had not been damaged much in the war, thrived in the years following the war.

Hiroshi Yamauchi became Marufuku's president in 1949, embarking on a wide-ranging program to modernize and rationalize the way his family's company was run. In 1952 Marufuku consolidated its factories, which had been scattered throughout Kyoto. In 1951 Yamauchi changed the company name to one more appropriate to the leisure industry; he called it the Nintendo Playing Card Company, Ltd. In Japanese, the word "Nintendo" has a proverbial meaning that loosely translates as, "You work hard but, in the end, it's in heaven's hands."

Business boomed in the postwar era. In 1953 Yamauchi responded to a shortage in playing-card-quality paper by challenging his company to develop plastic playing cards. After initial difficulties in printing and coating the plastic cards, Nintendo started mass-production. In 1959 Nintendo first showed its sharp eye for the children's market when it released playing cards in Japan that were printed with Walt Disney cartoon characters. By 1962 business was so good that Nintendo decided to go public, listing stock on the Osaka and Kyoto stock exchanges.

Diversification: 1960s-Early 1980s

A year later Nintendo began the drive towards diversification and innovation that eventually led it to the late 1980s boom that made its name a household word. First, in 1963, Nintendo augmented its product line by marketing board games as well as playing cards. By 1969 the game department was so successful that a new game production plant was built in Uji city, a suburb of Kyoto. The year 1970 saw Nintendo introducing electronic technology for the first time in Japan with its Beam Gun Series. An especially popular example of this technology was the laser clay-pigeon shooting system, introduced in 1973, in which arcade players aimed beams of light at targets projected on a small movie screen. By 1974, Nintendo was exporting this and other projection-based games to the United States and Europe.

In the next few years, arcade game technology made remarkable strides, with Nintendo in the vanguard. In 1975, in cooperation with Mitsubishi Electric, Nintendo first developed a video game system using a video player—a technology made more complex the next year when a microprocessor was added to the system. By 1977 this technology was being marketed as part of the first, relatively unsophisticated generation of home video games.

In the amusement arcade Nintendo's games were beginning to feature higher levels of technology. In 1978 Nintendo developed and started selling coin-operated video games using microcomputers. This innovation, which in 1981 resulted in such arcade hits as Donkey Kong, gave to arcade video games the complex graphics and stereo sound that Nintendo would later market for home use.

As the 1980s began, Nintendo started selling the Game and Watch product line—a handheld series of electronic games, such as football, with liquid crystals and digital quartz microhardware. By this time, Nintendo found that its export business required a firmer foothold in the United States and established

Nintendo of America, Inc., a wholly owned subsidiary, in New York City. In 1982 the U.S. office was moved to Redmond, Washington, and established there with an operating capital of US$600,000. As the 1980s progressed, the company focused on the development and marketing of home video technology. A new plant was built in 1983 in Uji city to meet the production requirements of Nintendo's new flagship product, the Family Computer. Famicom, which allowed arcade-quality video games to be played at home, came to be played in more than 35 percent of Japan's households.

With Famicom swiftly selling in Japan, Nintendo began exporting it to the United States. In 1985, however, when Nintendo was ready to enter U.S. homes, the home video market there seemed all but tapped out. The United States had experienced a dramatic home video boom in the late 1970s and early 1980s, but by mid-decade this boom had ended, leaving the U.S. industry with hundreds of millions of dollars in losses. The sales of the U.S. home video industry had plummeted from a $3 billion peak in 1983 to a $100 million trough in 1985. These figures did not daunt Nintendo, which quietly test marketed its games during the darkest depths of the U.S. slump. The response was enthusiastic. Nintendo concluded that the problems in the U.S. home video market were caused by an excess of uninspiring, low-quality games with which an undisciplined industry had flooded the market, losing the trust and patience of its customers as it went after quick profits.

Seizing Opportunity: Mid-1980s

Nintendo came to the United States in full force in 1985 with its American version of the Famicom, renamed the Nintendo Entertainment System. First year profits were astounding, and the skillfully managed demand of the U.S. market showed few signs of softening from its introduction to the end of the decade. According to Yamauchi, Nintendo owed its success to its ability to control the quality and amount of game software being sold for its NES systems. The NES hardware was similar to its Japanese precursor, the Famicom, consisting of a Nintendo control deck, hand controls, and the game cartridges themselves. The control deck sported an eight-bit computer that generated stereo sound and images in 52 colors. It hooked up with the purchaser's television set to allow the viewer to play a complex video game—which could take up to 70 hours to complete—by manipulating a joystick that controlled movement in two dimensions.

The NES control deck was sold at close to cost, about US$100, to place it in as many homes as possible. Nintendo then made a profit by selling its own game cartridges at US$25 to US$45 apiece, and by arranging lucrative licensing agreements with the numerous computer software manufacturers who were eager to get a piece of Nintendo's pie by creating software for Nintendo's games.

From the very beginning of its U.S. home video foray, Nintendo gained customer loyalty and enthusiasm by producing or licensing sophisticated, challenging, and surprising software for its NES. By 1989, this practice had translated into a 75-80 percent share of a US$3.4 billion home video game market. But the business strategies that brought Nintendo to its position of dominance soon came under intense scrutiny. Stymied competitors, the U.S. government, and Nintendo's own licensees—who found that Nintendo's mode of granting licenses for game software could soak up as much as 50 percent of their profits—all came to regard Nintendo's trade practices with a suspicion that led to widely publicized litigation.

Nintendo and most industry analysts maintained that a lack of quality control killed the first home video craze in the early 1980s. To avoid making the same mistake, Nintendo erected a demanding series of market controls. Each of its licensees was limited to developing only six new game titles a year. Nintendo manufactured its own patented game cartridges and required would-be software programmers to buy the cartridges in batches of 10,000 and then to assume full responsibility for reselling the game cartridges after they had been programmed by the licensee. To make certain that hardware competitors and software licensees would not try to circumvent Nintendo's control, Nintendo included a security chip in each game cartridge. Games programmed on cartridges lacking this microchip appeared scrambled when one tried to play them. Nintendo reserved the right to modify games or to forbid a licensee's attempts to market a game that had been deemed unsatisfactory in evaluations conducted by the company. When a licensee's game gained approval, the developer had to wait two years before selling a version of its game to Nintendo's competitors. Because of these safeguards, the quality of Nintendo-compatible software remained high. Yet dissatisfaction developed in the U.S. industry with Nintendo's control.

In December 1988 Tengen Incorporated, a subsidiary of Nintendo's archrival Atari and a Nintendo software licensee, filed an antitrust suit. Tengen wished to make games that would run on Nintendo's NES without having to go through Nintendo's series of quality-control measures. Having cracked the code programmed into the microchip in Nintendo's cartridges, Tengen released a game without Nintendo's approval. Nintendo filed a countersuit in February 1989 claiming patent infringement. By then Tengen's parent company, Atari, had jumped into the fray, filing a separate US$100 million antitrust suit against Nintendo. As the litigation piled up, it became apparent that cultural differences in business practices were near the heart of the conflict.

Playing the Market: Late 1980s

The 1980s were otherwise a successful decade for Nintendo. The company concentrated on popularizing its existing products and developing new ones. In Japan Nintendo developed and started to sell a Family Computer Disk Drive System, which hit the mature Japanese market in 1986. The way this new product expanded communications capabilities of the Famicom was dramatically showcased in 1987, when Nintendo in Japan organized a nationwide Family Computer Golf Tournament. Players throughout Japan used modems, public telephone lines, and disc facsimile technology to compete against each other from their own living rooms in Nintendo's home video game version of golf. Nintendo looked to the day when nationwide tournaments could be conducted with contestants comfortably ensconced in their living rooms. The network, which Nintendo soon hoped to duplicate in the United States, allowed people throughout Japan not only to play Nintendo games against each other but enabled people to download information from stock companies and trade in stocks, shop, or make ticket reservations.

In 1989 Nintendo announced a deal with Fidelity Investment Services, Boston, to bring this technology to the United States. For about US$200, American owners of Nintendo's NES could buy a modem, a controller/joy stick, and a Fidelity-designed software cartridge that would allow the use of their home entertainment hardware for a more serious purpose: managing stock portfolios. A US$3 million grant in 1990 to MIT's Media Lab was earmarked for researching the possibility of making video games more educational.

Despite such serious uses of its equipment, Nintendo remained synonymous with high-technology home fun, largely due to its expert marketing techniques and customer support. In 1988 Nintendo began publishing *Nintendo Power* magazine for its U.S. customers. This magazine, aimed at adolescents, was filled with game-playing tips and announcements concerning recently developed games and hardware. For those times when Nintendo Power could not help a frustrated game player, Nintendo introduced a 20-hour telephone bank with advice from 300 game counselors.

Further public relations efforts included a deal with Ralston Purina Company in May 1989 to market a citrus-flavored Nintendo Cereal System, featuring edible versions of the heroes from Nintendo's video games. In 1989 Nintendo also teamed up with PepsiCo and the nationwide toy retailer Toys 'R' Us for special joint promotions and in-store displays. Nintendo spent $60 million on U.S. advertising that year.

In 1989 Nintendo also returned to the handheld electronic game market it had created a decade earlier. The battery-operated Game Boy, about the size of a paperback book, featured interchangeable game cartridges, stereo sound, and complex dot-matrix graphics. In Japan Nintendo unveiled a new 16-bit advanced version of the Famicom, dubbed the Super Family Computer. Its more complex electronics meant more challenging games, more interesting graphics, and more realistic sound. Nintendo waited to release the U.S. version of the 16-bit machine until it felt the market was ready.

The company's leader, Yamauchi, one of the richest men in Japan, did not own a car or a television. He professed a disinterest in electronic games, saying he preferred chesslike board games. A frugal and cautious businessman, Yamauchi had a reputation for a reserved demeanor. His personality was compared to the minimalist architecture of the company's headquarters in Kyoto. Despite Yamauchi's disciplined management style, the company was still able to create an environment in the research and development division that was conducive to creativity.

In reality, only ten percent of Nintendo's games originated under Nintendo's roof. The bulk of the company's products were created by independent designers, some of whom became millionaires in their own right in spite of Nintendo's strict guidelines. Designers built games on speculation, paid Nintendo to produce the game cartridge, and then paid for the necessary marketing and advertising. These rules and Nintendo's near-monopoly of the video game market led many in the industry to characterize Yamauchi as a tyrant.

A New Game Forming: Early 1990s

Developments in the early 1990s appeared foreboding to Nintendo's hold on the market. Several antitrust cases, including one brought by a U.S. Senate subcommittee and one brought by Time Warner's Atari Games, threatened to change the look of the video game industry. Moreover, the continued success of Sega Enterprises, Ltd. gave Nintendo its first real competitor. It was Sega's 16-bit Genesis System that led Nintendo to upgrade its eight-bit machinery. Sega's growing product line and state-of-the art programs rivaled those of Nintendo and offered buyers an alternative video game system.

Nintendo was not to be easily vanquished, however. Indeed, many industry observers saw Nintendo as the "next Disney," and a survey of school children found that the Mario character was more popular than Mickey Mouse. Although video game sales slowed in 1990, growing less than half as fast as they had the previous year, Nintendo's sales increased by 63 percent. When U.S. videogame sales reached $4.2 billion by 1991, Nintendo products accounted for $3.2 billion.

In the summer of 1992 Japan's Capcom Co. released Street Fighter II for Nintendo, and the game met with immediate success. Also in 1992, Nintendo produced Super Mario Paint, a drawing program featuring the company's star character, a game based on the Road Runner cartoon character, and the long-awaited "Zelda" sequel, *The Legend of Zelda: A Link to the Past*. Nintendo hoped eventually to raise its U.S. household penetration rate from 17 percent to the 35 percent it had achieved in Japan and mirror in the United States the profit-producing ten-to-one software-to-hardware ratio that Nintendo had achieved in its home country.

Nintendo's exports to the United States had grown eightfold from 1987 to 1991, and the company held 60 percent of the 16-bit U.S. market at the end of 1992. Yet Sega's comparative advertising, begun in 1990, pried open Nintendo's grip on consumers. Sega branded Nintendo's games as children's toys, and Nintendo of America failed to respond to the ploy. Nintendo's U.S. market share fell to 37 percent by the end of 1993. Jeopardy continued into 1994 when a new generation of machines hit the market.

Sega's and Sony's new game consoles were 32-bit systems utilizing CD-ROM disk drives. Sega's Saturn and Sony's PlayStation had inherently large storage capacities, thanks to the CD-ROMs, but were considered sluggish. Nintendo, on the other hand used much faster but more expensive silicon storage cartridges. Instead of matching the moves of its competitors, Nintendo concentrated on developing, in partnership with California-based Silicon Graphics, Inc., a 64-bit processor with superior capabilities.

Faced with consumer desertions to the 32-bit machines, Nintendo tried to extend the life of its 16-bit Super Nintendo System by bringing out hot games. Donkey Kong Country, which had been designed for the 64-bit system, was released in a 16-bit format and became the bestselling game of 1994.

The video game machine makers spent millions each year on software development. Independently produced games continued to generate the bulk of Nintendo's revenue in this important area: in-house software brought in around 35 percent of sales. In 1995, pressed by the need to produce software for its new machine, Nintendo purchased 25 percent of Rare Ltd., a U.K.-

based developer. This was Nintendo's first investment in a software maker outside of Japan.

Nintendo's promise of a cheaper and more exciting video system by early 1996 dampened Saturn and PlayStation sales somewhat during the 1995 Christmas season. Nevertheless, Sega passed Nintendo in terms of total sales for the first time in the fiscal year ending March 1996. Nintendo's consolidated sales fell 15 percent and operating profits fell 24 percent. The 32-bit machines, the economic recession in the important Japanese market, and the defection of independent software producers to the competition contributed to Nintendo's downward spiral.

Nintendo 64 (N64) finally hit the market in 1996. Japanese consumers were eager to check out the new system. "With preordering rampant and queues outside the stores, some 300,000 Nintendo 64 machines were snapped up by eager addicts on the first day," according to an August 1996 article in the *Economist*. Anticipating the U.S. release, Sega and Sony cut the prices on their 32-bit units.

The N64 Japanese launch got off to a fast start but stalled just as quickly: only a few games were ready for the format. Nintendo had backpedaled on the N64 release date a number of times, a situation that served to frustrate many independent software makers and led to the defection of some important developers to Sony.

Further complicating matters was the complexity of programming required for the N64 software and programmers' frustration with the limited storage capacity of the cartridges as compared to the CD-ROMs used by the competition. Another factor in the mix, one which was not there during Nintendo's glory days, was the personal computer (PC). PC makers were fabricating increasingly sophisticated games, drawing talent from the software developer pool and eating into the market.

Difficulties aside, Nintendo continued to live up to its reputation for quality software and produced another blockbuster game. "This is probably the most perfectly crafted video game ever," wrote Neil Gross in *Business Week*. Shigeru Miyamoto, the designer of the original 8-bit Mario game, scored big with Super Mario 64.

Mario's fluid movements through dazzling three-dimensional graphics set the game apart from earlier versions and from competitor's 32-bit games. Sony and Sega, on the other hand, were not just waiting for Nintendo to rack up points. Sega was the first to release a web-browsing device, and Sony was way ahead of the pack in number of games available. Nintendo continued to feel the pinch and recorded its third straight year of declining financial results in the fiscal year ending March 1996.

In the first half of 1996, sales of the 16-bit Super Nintendo machines and related software plummeted. Sales generated by the new system, due in part to the lack of software, did not pick up all the slack. In September 1996 N64, with eight titles on hand, hit North American shelves; by June 1997, 2.6 million machines had been sold, capturing 50 percent of the market. An additional 2.7 million had been sold elsewhere in the world. Revenue for fiscal 1997 were up 18 percent to $3.5 billion. Earnings increased nine percent to $54 million.

Sony, the market leader, had more than 11 million PlayStations in the hands of consumers worldwide and carried 150 game titles. Nintendo 64 offered just 17 titles for play. The importance of the software lay most clearly in its profitability. Nintendo's margins for hardware were one to five percent while software yielded margins of nearly 45 percent. Software produced more than 50 percent of the company's profits. Aware of the dilemma it faced, Nintendo of America's chairman personally solicited the services U.S. software developers.

In an effort to boost capacity, a sticking point with the game makers, Nintendo put an N64 peripheral in the pipeline. The DD64, a magnetic disk drive, was to also contain a communications device. ''Still,'' wrote Seanna Browder in *Business Week*, ''there are risks even to this. Historically, add-on devices don't go over big with gamers, who make one initial hardware investment and call it a day. There's also the chance that Nintendo could split its market into two camps—N64 and DD64. Then, game developers will be scratching their heads, wondering which to support.''

Nintendo was headed in the right direction, but the progress was not entirely smooth. Sales and profits were boosted in 1997 by Pokemon or Pocket Monsters, a new game played on Nintendo's handheld Game Boy machines, but the year was marked by a delay in the launch of the new hardware platform, DD64, and the botched delivery of *Yoshi's Story*, a much ballyhooed software title.

Nintendo came back in early 1998 with the introduction of the Game Boy Camera, a digital offering that sold for $50 and attached to the Game Boy machine. Nintendo sold more than 700,000 of the units in its first five weeks on the Japanese market.

Solidifying its dominance in the handheld market, Nintendo also released Game Boy Color and Pokemon Pikacu, a virtual pet. (The Pokemon game had spawned a multibillion-dollar industry of related merchandise.) In late 1998, Nintendo spent millions on the rollout of *The Legend of Zelda: Ocarina of Time* and achieved record pre-sales on the game.

The Future Is Now: 1999, 2000, and Beyond

The next generation of video game machines appeared on the horizon late in 1998, when Sega introduced its 128-bit Dreamcast machine to Japan. The system processed data more quickly than both PlayStation and Nintendo 64 and thus was capable of producing more lifelike graphics. Dreamcast was scheduled to hit the United States in the fall of 1999.

Not to be outdone for long, both Sony and Nintendo planned for a year 2000 release of their new machines. Sony said its PlayStation II, which it categorized as a home entertainment system, was even faster than Dreamcast and would produce images with graphic quality similar to animated movies. No longer just a game machine, PlayStation II would accommodate movies and games recorded on digital video disks (DVD). Breaking with industry convention, the machine would also play games produced for the original PlayStation. Nintendo, in a $1 billion partnership with IBM, said its next generation console, code named Dolphin, would also use DVD and exceed the speed of even Sony's offering. Hype aside, Nintendo faced another unsettled transition period as it again maneuvered from one generation of game systems to the next.

Principal Subsidiaries

Nintendo of America, Inc. (U.S.A.); Nintendo of Australia Pty, Ltd.; Nintendo of Canada, Ltd.; Nintendo Espana, S.A.; Nintendo of Europe GmbH (Germany); Nintendo France S.A.R.L.; Nintendo Hong Kong Limited; Nintendo Netherlands B.V.

Further Reading

Abrahams, Paul, ''Nintendo's Errors Could Well End Up Costing It the Game,'' *Financial Times*, October 17, 1998, p. 21.

Alexander, Steve, ''The New 128-Bit Consoles: A Whole New Game,'' *Star Tribune* (Minneapolis), May 14, 1999, pp. D1–D2.

Brandt, Richard, ''Clash of the Titans,'' *Business Week*, September 7, 1992.

Browder, Seanna, Steven B. Brull, and Andy Reinhardt, ''Nintendo: At the Top of Its Game,'' *Business Week*, June 9, 1997, pp. 72–73.

Carlton, Jim, ''U.S. Retail Sales of Video Games Up 32% for Year,'' *Wall Street Journal*, November 6, 1998, p. B6.

Dawley, Heidi, and Paul M. Eng, ''Killer Instinct for Hire,'' *Business Week*, May 29, 1995, pp. 91–92.

Gross, Neil, '' 'Infinitely Cool' in 64 Bits,'' *Business Week*, October 14, 1996, p. 134.

Gross, Neil, and Robert D. Hof, ''Nintendo's Yamauchi: No More Playing Around,'' *Business Week*, February 21, 1994, p. 71.

''Hasbro to Handle Pokemon in U.S.,'' *Advertising Age*, June 1, 1998, p. 44.

Jackson, David S., ''The Spielberg of Video Games,'' *Time*, May 20, 1996, p. 53.

King, Sharon R., ''Mania for 'Pocket Monsters' Yields Billions for Nintendo,'' *New York Times,* April 26, 1999, pp. A1 +.

Konish, Nancy, ''Video Game Giants Are Neck and Neck for the Profit,'' *Electronic Design,* September 14, 1998, p. 32A.

Krantz, Michael, ''Super Mario's Dazzling Comeback,'' *Time,* May 20, 1996, pp. 52–54.

Kunii, Irene M., ''Sega: We're Going to Blow Them Out of the Water,'' *Business Week,* December 7, 1998, p. 108.

——, ''Smile, You're on Candid Game Boy,'' *Business Week*, April 27, 1998, p. 8.

Lefton, Terry, ''Zelda Returns with $10M,'' *Brandweek*, October 19, 1998, p. 8.

McGill, Douglas C., ''Nintendo Scores Big,'' *New York Times*, December 4, 1988.

Moffat, Susan, ''Can Nintendo Keep Winning?,'' *Fortune*, November 5, 1990.

Nakamoto, Michiyo, ''Competition Continues to Squeeze Nintendo,'' *Financial Times*, May 23, 1996, p. 36.

——, ''Move to New Technology Hurts Nintendo,'' *Financial Times*, November 6, 1996, p. 34.

——, ''Sales of New Game Lift Nintendo,'' *Financial Times*, November 14, 1997, p. 22.

''Nintendo Wakes Up,'' *Economist*, August 3, 1996, pp. 55–56.

''Now, the Latest Beepings from Video-Game Land,'' *Money*, July 1991.

Takahashi, Dean, ''Nintendo Is Top Scorer in Game Sales, But Sony Sees Bigger Hardware Growth,'' *Wall Street Journal*, January 19, 1999, p. B6.

—Rene Steinke and Mary McNulty
—updated by Kathleen Peippo

NKK Corporation

1-1-2, Marunouchi
Chiyoda-ku
Tokyo 100-8202
Japan
(03) 3212-7111
Fax: (03) 3214-8400
Web site: http://www.nkk.co.jp

Public Company
Incorporated: 1912 as Nippon Kokan K.K.
Employees: 15,613
Sales: ¥1.11 trillion (US$8.42 billion) (1998)
Stock Exchanges: Tokyo Osaka Nagoya
Ticker Symbol: NKKCY
NAIC: 331111 Iron & Steel Mills 331221 Rolled Steel
   Shape Manufacturing; 23499 All Other Heavy
   Construction; 334111 Electronic Computer
   Manufacturing; 334413 Semiconductor & Related
   Device Manufacturing; 334613 Magnetic & Optical
   Recording Media Manufacturing; 336611 Ship
   Building & Repairing; 23331 Land Subdivision &
   Land Development

NKK Corporation is one of the world's largest steelmakers and Japan's second largest. In addition to steelmaking, the company is active in engineering, urban development, and electronics. NKK's engineering sector is involved in designing and building such projects as pipelines, power plants, water supply and sewage treatment systems, bridges, ships, and offshore structures. The urban development unit designs and constructs condominiums, office buildings, amusement parks, golf courses, and other facilities. The electronics group develops automation design systems, advanced computer software, and integrated circuits, as well as computers.

Early History

In Japan, as in other areas of the world, the growth of the steelmaking industry has often been associated with the needs created by warfare. From ancient times, the Chinese had forged weapons from iron-bearing stones by heating them in charcoal fires. By the sixth century A.D., when Chinese technology and cultural influences began to be adopted in Japan, processes were being developed to prolong and heighten the heating of iron ore and to remove impurities. By medieval times, Japanese steelmaking had become a high art. Knights wore loose armor made of three- or four-inch pieces of thin steel, linked by colorful thongs. The knights took particular pride in their exquisitely designed, long, curved, laminated steel swords. The swords, reportedly the finest in the world, were in particular demand throughout east Asia, and thousands were exported.

Japan's supply of iron ore was poor. While steelmaking technology developed rapidly in the iron-rich countries of Europe and the United States, Japan's steelmaking stagnated. With the waning of knighthood, and Japan's virtual isolation from the rest of the world during the Tokugawa shogunate, little steel was made.

During the 19th century, the Tokugawa shogun gradually lost control over Japanese commercial interests. Although the surface aspects of Japanese life appeared to be as firmly in place as they had been throughout the shogun's rule, discontent with the limitations imposed by the government began to escalate.

Disenchanted with the Tokugawa shogun, many of the people began to become optimistic about their prospects under a restoration of imperial rule. The presumptive heir to the throne promised progress in "catching up" with the rest of the world—economically, technologically, and culturally. Upon assuming the throne in 1868, the new Meiji emperor proceeded to do just that. Actually, the reforms were not so much the work of the individual on the throne as they were the work of a group of young men—fewer than 100—who supported the regime as an opportunity to introduce Western-style efficiencies and power into Japan. Educated abroad, they had a vision of a stronger Japan that could result from applying Western technologies and political and cultural concepts to the economic and other problems the Japanese people faced. That vision became a reality as Japan became the first Asian nation to achieve world power status through the use of Western concepts.

Japan's economic problems had arisen through the inefficiency and corruption that had gradually crept into industries the Tokugawa shogunate owned. The supporters of a return to imperial rule under a progressive Meiji regime were sometimes referred to as an oligarchy of commercial and political interests as they gathered power to influence government decision-making. They were credited with persuading the government to sell its factories to private individuals and groups. Eventually only the manufacture of munitions remained under the government's direct ownership.

By 1881 new shipyards were operating under private ownership. Government support of the shipyards, provided through subsidies and the awarding of contracts, cushioned the early years, but strict regulation of business and industry was enforced from the start.

The need for iron and steel to support a military and naval buildup heightened as Japan waged war with China in 1894 and 1895. The shipbuilding industry, for example, was hampered by the fact that most of Japan's iron and almost all of its steel had to be imported. In 1896 the government decided to establish an iron and steel industry. The Yawata works opened in 1901. Processing plants were needed, however, to turn the Yawata works' pig-iron and steel into products that shipbuilders, engineering companies, and other heavy industries required. Pipe, for example, was in increasing demand. As conflicts with Russia and China engendered greater military buildup, and an influx of Japan's population into urban areas created new needs for private housing and public works projects, the demand for pipe, particularly strong steel pipe, grew.

Nippon Kokan K.K. Established in 1912

Conscious of the growing market for pipe, Ganjiro Shiraishi, an independent businessman, began in 1911 to gather the financial support and Western-developed technical expertise to produce what would become an innovation—Japan's first seamless steel pipe. After more than a year of initial research and organizational development, Nippon Kokan K.K. began operations in mid-1912 with ¥2 million in capital. During its first few years, the company was occupied with the complex process of setting up an open-hearth furnace for refining steel scrap and pig iron. The first steel was tapped from that furnace in 1914.

The seamless steel pipe that Nippon Kokan produced proved to be stronger, longer-wearing, and easier to install than pipe parts that had to be fitted and welded together. The market for it grew larger as Japan prepared to enter World War I in 1916, and

naval vessels and military installations created new demands. The success of Nippon Kokan's first years led to the opening of a subsidiary in 1917—Electric Iron and Steel.

Along with the other Allied nations that joined forces to defeat Germany in World War I, Japan emerged from the conflict as a victorious world power. This created ties that encouraged international trade. Japan's militarists, who favored future expansion through military aggression and colonialism, began to meet strong opposition from the merchants and manufacturers who favored maintaining peaceful relations and fostering expansion through international trade.

For about a decade, those who favored expansion through international markets prevailed. Both the import and export businesses flourished, as Western fashions, sports, and other novelties captured the public fancy in Japan, and Japanese products became widely sought by other nations.

The domestic market for pipe underwent a sudden surge through a national disaster. The Great Kanto Earthquake, September 1, 1923, leveled half the buildings in Tokyo and most of those in Yokohama. Rebuilding factories and office buildings, private residences, and public buildings took several years—and many miles of pipe. The new buildings, incorporating some of the world's most advanced designs and products, reflected the Western influences popularized through the postwar years.

In 1929, however, a worldwide depression began that brought an abrupt halt to much of the international trade activity that Japan had enjoyed. Japan's militarists began to look toward colonizing areas rich in natural resources as a way of renewing expansion efforts. The nation's population had grown beyond the means of its own resources to provide adequate food and housing.

Manchuria, a disputed territory, became a target, and was annexed to Japan in 1931. Steel products were again in increased demand as plans for further military action called for the buildup of new installations and vessels. To smelt iron directly from ore, Nippon Kokan built a 400-ton blast furnace, completing it in 1937. A 600-ton blast furnace was completed in 1938. Even the fact that Japan was poor in iron ore operated to Nippon Kokan's advantage. Because there was no need to situate its plants near a mountainous source of ore, the plants were located close to Tokyo's waterfront, convenient both for receiving ore from other countries and for efficient shipping of steel products to customers.

Entered Shipbuilding in 1940

Through a merger, Nippon Kokan went into the shipbuilding business in 1940, acquiring the Tsurumi Steelmaking and Shipbuilding Company. As Japan went to war with the United States the following year, plans for a 5,000-ton capacity shipbuilding berth at the company's Shimizu shipyard went forward; the project was completed in 1943. At that time, Ryozo Asano had been in office as Nippon Kokan's president for six months. Until 1945 when bombing raids and the consequent fires destroyed many of Tokyo's buildings and caused the populace to flee, Nippon Kokan's plants were in full operation, supplying many steel products needed in the war effort. Japan's defeat was a shock to many of its citizens who had been told only of its victories; it demoralized many such as Asano, who saw the results of years of concerted effort go up in smoke. He resigned.

Although business was at a standstill for many months as the Supreme Council of the Allied Forces (SCAP) took over governing the country and preparing it for future self-government, Nippon Kokan survived. In April 1946 a new president, Masato Watanabe, began the task of rebuilding the company's facilities and customer base. The constitutional reforms and financial support that SCAP introduced created a new climate for business recovery and growth that helped Nippon Kokan and other businesses progress rapidly.

Along with the legislative and economic aids to recovery of business and industrial facilities and markets came new ideas for improving organization and product quality. In 1950, 45 leading industrialists in Tokyo met with W. Edwards Deming, a U.S. statistician who taught a quality-centered approach to manufacturing involving all employees in decision-making, for continuous improvement and responsiveness to consumer needs. An annual Deming Prize was awarded to the company best exemplifying the success of these methods. Nippon Kokan was the winner in 1958.

Postwar International Expansion

International expansion was already underway. The company acquired an interest in the Ujiminas Steel Works in Brazil in 1957 and, the following year, opened offices in New York. In 1959 Düsseldorf, Germany, became Nippon Kokan's European headquarters. The company was on an ascendant growth curve that was to extend well into the next quarter-century. Offices were opened in Singapore, Los Angeles, and London between 1961 and 1963.

Nippon Kokan K.K. also worked to expand the number of operations within its mills to include the full range of activities from handling ore to production and distribution of a complete product line, in other words to become an integrated steel manufacturing company. The company consolidated a group of works it had acquired in the Mizue area to form the Mizue steel works. In 1963 its engineering and construction division began the first of five successive stages of work at Fukuyama to build the world's largest integrated steel mill. The project was completed in 1973. Another large-scale operation was created in 1968 by consolidating the company's Kawasaki, Tsurumi, and Mizue plants into one entity: the Keihin steel works.

The company continued to expand abroad, acquiring a 62.7 percent interest in the Sermani steel finishing business in Indonesia in 1970, and opening offices in Rio de Janeiro, Brazil, in 1975. A Houston, Texas, office was opened one year later.

At home, the Keihin steel works was expanded between 1975 and 1979 by constructing the world's most modern steel-making facilities on a man-made island, Ohgishima. Upon completion of the first stage of this project, the Japan Society of Civil Engineering awarded Nippon Kokan K.K. its 1975 Technology Prize.

The company reorganized its divisions in 1979. Initially, the shipbuilding division, including the ten-year-old Tsu shipyard, was combined with the engineering and construction division.

The following year, however, a further reorganization of the heavy industries division resulted in a three-division system: energy, heavy industries, and shipbuilding.

Steelmakers in Japan, like those in the United States, faced the problem of maintaining plant efficiency while keeping overhead to a minimum, and using resources effectively to make a profit while meeting worker and consumer expectations. In general, U.S. steelmakers, with older plants to maintain, neglected maintenance needs and the development of new technologies, while the Japanese, though equally cost-conscious, did not. As a result, Japanese steelmakers, such as Nippon Kokan K.K., moved ahead in productivity product quality. Market demand for high-quality raw steel and for steel products was high. By the 1980s, it was evident that Nippon Kokan K.K., among other Japanese steelmakers, held the competitive edge.

Nippon Kokan K.K. had formed joint ventures with companies throughout the world—in the United States and Canada; in Indonesia, Thailand, and Singapore; and in Belgium, Brazil, Saudi Arabia, Nigeria, and Australia. Sachio Hatori, the company's executive vice-president, opposed such solutions, stating, "Joint ventures are low-risk, but they cannot improve the whole process. If the steel itself is bad, it doesn't matter how good the galvanizing is."

Purchased Interest in National Steel in 1984

Instead, in 1984, Nippon Kokan K.K. purchased a 50 percent interest in National Steel Corporation, the sixth largest steel works in the United States. This purchase provided the opportunity to exert a positive influence on product quality. Although Nippon Kokan sent managerial talent to National Steel's site near Detroit, the company resisted any attempt to diminish the independence of National Steel's operations. The immediate result of the purchase was to double National Steel's annual capital investment to $200 million and to infuse new and advanced technology into the U.S. firm. By 1990 Nippon Kokan K.K. owned 70 percent of National Steel. Although productivity increased, National Steel's profits continued to decline. Nippon Kokan entered into a joint venture with another U.S. company, Martin Marietta Corporation, in 1984, forming the International Light Metals Corporation.

Yoshinari Yamashiro became president of Nippon Kokan K.K. in 1985, a time when fluctuations in the value of the yen and other factors were beginning to flatten the 25-year upward curve of prosperity and profits for many Japanese companies. He introduced a new note of informality and desire for closeness to company operations as he asked employees to address him as they would one another—as mister, rather than to use his title.

To cope with problems arising as markets matured and consumer demands changed, the new president initiated a restructuring of the corporation. In 1988 the company name was changed to NKK Corporation, a name that had often been used informally. Divisions were created to reflect the increased diversity of company interests, products, and services. Steelmaking, still the core of the company's business, was strengthened by adding facilities to produce materials and parts for special needs. For example, a continuous galvanizing line at the Keihin and Fukuyama works helped meet high domestic demand for a number of steel products. The reorganization also resulted in converting some of NKK's operating units into subsidiaries.

In 1992 Yamashiro was named chairman of NKK, with Shunkichi Miyoshi promoted from executive vice-president to president. Shunkichi, a metallurgist by training, was the first technical person in the presidential post in company history.

Having already entered the field of electronics in the areas of computer hardware and software, minisupercomputers, and communications network systems, NKK in 1992 began making microchips at a new factory outside Tokyo. NKK thus followed in the footsteps of fellow Japanese steelmakers Kawasaki Steel and Kobe Steel into the world of semiconductors.

1990s Difficulties

Throughout the 1990s NKK was beset by numerous difficulties. Following the collapse of the Japanese financial bubble of the 1980s the Japanese economy entered into a prolonged state of stagnation, at the same time that a strong yen made Japanese imports less desirable. Simultaneously, Japanese steelmakers, like their counterparts in North America, were facing increasing competition from upstart operators of minimills, whose state-of-the-art equipment and minimal workforce requirements resulted in a lower-cost operation. Compounding the situation was falling demand for steel.

To make matters worse, NKK's entrance into the U.S. steel market through National Steel turned nearly disastrous. NKK had poured $2 billion into National Steel by the mid-1990s to modernize the steelmakers outdated facilities, but management difficulties, poor relations with labor, a bloated workforce, and a product line consisting mainly of cheaper steels all contributed to a consistently unprofitable operation. National Steel's losses led in turn to losses at NKK, including net losses of ¥26.79 billion in 1994 and ¥35.37 billion in 1995.

To stem the red ink, NKK aggressively restructured its operations, making a number of moves more typical of a U.S. company rather than one located in Japan. The company steadily cut its workforce, mainly through an early retirement plan, reducing the number of employees from 22,214 in 1994 to 15,613 in 1998. It consolidated its facilities, most notably by combining two of its large-scale steel mills, the Keihin Works and the Fukuyama Works. NKK also sold off some of its noncore assets and reduced its capital spending by one-third. Through these efforts the company returned to profitability from 1996 through 1998.

In mid-1997 Miyoshi became chairman of NKK, while Yoichi Shimogaichi was appointed president, having joined the company in 1958. Shimogaichi almost immediately faced additional difficulties. The Asian financial crisis, which began in 1997, and the subsequent fall of the Japanese economy into recession combined to collapse demand for steel from the automobile and construction sectors to a 30-year low. Japanese steelmakers were also hurt when their export markets were further curtailed following the filing of dumping charges against them by U.S. steelmakers in September 1998 and by the February 1999 U.S. Department of Commerce preliminary ruling that imposed antidumping duties on them. In addition, NKK had to contend with the failure of its minimill affiliate, Toa Steel. With Toa expected to post a pretax loss for the fiscal 1999 year of about ¥25.5 billion (US$184.8 million), the company was forced to liquidate with its assets being taken over by NKK. In late 1998 NKK announced additional workforce cuts of 3,300, or more than 20 percent, which would reduce its workforce to about 12,000. With NKK, as well as other Japanese steelmakers, expected to post a huge loss for the 1999 fiscal year, speculation was rife about possible consolidation among the big five integrated steelmakers.

Principal Subsidiaries

Tokyo Shearing Co., Ltd.; Nippon Kokan Light Steel Kabushiki Kaisha; Kokan Drum Company, Ltd.; Kokan Kenzai K.K.; Kawasaki Kokan Co., Ltd.; NKK Marine & Logistics Corporation; Nissan Senpaku Ltd.; Kokan Mining Company, Ltd.; Galvatex Corporation; Kokan Kikai Kogyo K.K.; Fukuyama Kyodo Power Co., Ltd.; Fukuyama Kyodokiko Corporation; NKK Trading Inc.; Nichiei Unyu Soko K.K.; Fuji Kako Co., Ltd.; NK. Coal Center Co., Ltd.; Nippon Kokan Pipe Fitting Mfg. Co., Ltd.; Japan Casting Co., Ltd.; Nippon Chutetsukan K.K.; NK Forge Co., Ltd.; IROX-NKK Co., Ltd.; Ishibashi Kosan Co., Ltd.; Nippon Kokan Koji K.K.; NKK Plant Engineering Corporation; Nippon Rotary Nozzle Co., Ltd.; NKK Design & Engineering Corporation; Kokan Densetsu Kogyo K.K.; NK Home Co., Ltd.; Kokan Construction Corporation; NKK Credit Corporation; Adchemco Corporation; NK Techno Service Co., Ltd.; NK Management Center Co., Ltd.; Japan Adcoating Co., Ltd.; NKF Corporation; NK-EXA Corporation; NKK Europe Ltd. (U.K.; Germany); NKK Netherlands B.V.; NKK America Inc. (U.S.A.); National Steel Corporation; NKK Titanium U.S.A.; NKK-Steel Engineering, Inc.; NKK Corporation de Mexico, S.A.

Principal Divisions

Steel Division; Engineering Division (Energy Industries Engineering Division; Environmental Industries Engineering Division; Plant Engineering Division; Steel Structure, Machinery, and Construction Division; Shipbuilding and Offshore Structure Division; Concept Engineering Center); Urban Development Division; LSI Division; Information Processing System Department.

Further Reading

Awanohara, Susumu, "Nerves of Steel," *Far Eastern Economic Review,* November 11, 1993, pp. 56–59.

Baker, Stephen, "Down and Dirty in the Steel Belt," *Business Week,* June 20, 1994, p. 44.

Baker, Stephen, and Nancy Pieters, "How National Steel Got So Bent out of Shape," *Business Week,* September 2, 1996, p. 42.

Cramb, Gordon, "NKK Sheds 1,300 Jobs by Transferring Staff," *Financial Times,* August 9, 1994, p. 4.

Dawkins, William, "Steelmaker That Re-invented Itself," *Financial Times,* March 29, 1995, p. 5.

Furukawa, Tsukasa, "Business As Usual for Japan's Toa Steel—Until March," *American Metal Market,* September 18, 1998, p. 3.

———, "NKK Restructures to Improve Steel Earnings," *American Metal Market,* March 25, 1994, p. 3.

Glain, Steve, "NKK Breaks Some of Japan Inc.'s Rules: Steelmaker's Aggressive Restructuring Pays Off," *Wall Street Journal,* April 10, 1996, p. A9.

Harney, Alexandra, "NKK Warns of Further Fall in Profit," *Financial Times,* February 10, 1999, p. 35.

Johnstone, Bob, "Crucibles for Chips," *Far Eastern Economic Review,* July 23, 1992, p. 58.

Klamann, Edmund, "NKK Still Seeking Payoff for U.S. Venture," *Japan Economic Journal,* September 8, 1990.

Milbank, Dana, "Changing Industry: Big Steel Is Threatened by Low-Cost Rivals, Even in Japan, Korea," *Wall Street Journal,* February 2, 1993, pp. A1 + .

"NKK Today," Tokyo: NKK Corporation, 1989.

Norton, Erle, "National Steel's Dream Team Dissolves: Ex-President, an Assistant Chosen by NKK, Seemed to Be Well-Matched," *Wall Street Journal,* August 22, 1996, p. B4.

——, "National Steel's President Steps Down After NKK Takes Away His CEO Title," *Wall Street Journal,* August 21, 1996, p. B4.

—Betty T. Moore
—updated by David E. Salamie

N.V. Koninklijke Nederlandse Vliegtuigenfabriek Fokker

P.O. Box 7600
1117 ZJ Schiphol
The Netherlands
(020) 605 2730
Fax: (020) 605 2929
Web site: http://www.fokkernl.com

Public Company
Incorporated: 1919
NAIC: 336411 Aircraft Manufacturing

Few names evoke the romance of flight like that of Fokker. Even fewer can lay claim to participating in so many colorful and pivotal moments in aviation history. Although N.V. Koninklijke Nederlandse Vliegtuigenfabriek Fokker, Europe's oldest civil aircraft maker, went out of business in 1997, many Fokker planes are still operated by the world's regional airlines. In addition, a new company, Rekkof Restart NV, has been formed to resume production of Fokker 70 and 100 aircraft.

Fokker and the Birth of Air Warfare

Anthony H.G. Fokker was born in 1890 on a coffee plantation on the island of Java in the Dutch East Indies, presently the Republic of Indonesia. At the age of 20 he taught himself to fly on a small home-made monoplane which he had constructed in an abandoned zeppelin hanger in Baden-Baden, Germany. With newer, improved aircraft, he won a military competition in St. Petersburg (now Leningrad). Fokker was a poor student but had an unusual talent for aviation. He intermittently attended an engineering school in Frankfurt, and in 1912 was asked by the German government to teach military aviation.

Fokker failed to gain the interest of the Italian and British governments in his aircraft. The Germans, however, were more intrigued, purchasing a number of airplanes for their air corps. When World War I broke out, Fokker was involuntarily conferred German citizenship and given orders to continue building airplanes for the Kaiser. Nonetheless, Fokker still regarded himself as a patriotic citizen of neutral Holland.

When the French pilot Roland Garros was shot down on October 5, 1918, the Germans noticed that his airplane's propeller was fitted with steel deflectors. The deflectors allowed the pilot to operate his machine gun, oblivious to the obstruction of the propeller; bullets would ricochet off the blades rather than damage them. The propeller was taken to Berlin and shown to Fokker. Three days later Fokker returned from his factory at Schwerin with a device which synchronized the firing of a machine gun to the passing of the propeller blades. In effect, the airplane's engine operated the gun, firing bullets between the blades rather than at random. By the end of the war Fokker had produced more than 40 types of airplanes for the Germans, including the Triplane preferred by the infamous Red Baron.

Stateside Between the Wars

Fokker was later invited to the United States by the Army Air Corps. He shipped airplanes to the Air Corps and Navy until 1922, when he established a factory at Hasbrouck Heights, New Jersey, just across the river from New York. The company was called the Atlantic Aircraft Corporation and its sales were handled by Hamilton Standard, which later became a division of United Aircraft.

In 1925 Anthony Fokker brought a new tri-motor (three-engine airplane) to the United States from his factory in the Netherlands and won the Ford Reliability Tour. Later named the "Josephine Ford," this airplane was used by Admiral Richard Byrd and Floyd Bennett on their flight to the North Pole. Another Fokker airplane, the Southern Cross, was used by the aviator Sir Charles Kingsford-Smith for his historic trip across the Pacific and around the world.

The company changed its name to the Fokker Aircraft Corporation of America on December 3, 1927. In May 1929 Fokker was merged with Dayton-Wright, a subsidiary of General Motors. In the summer of 1930 Fokker was reorganized, becoming a wholly owned subsidiary renamed the General Aviation Corporation. However, in compliance with the provisions of the Air

Mail Act of 1934, General Motors was forced to dissolve General Aviation.

Fokker left General Motors because of differences in opinion over company policy. He subsequently returned to Holland where he maintained his company, the Nederlandse Vliegtuigenfabriek, which produced a variety of military and civilian aircraft. KLM (Royal Dutch Airlines) developed an air route to the Netherlands Indies for the Dutch government, using Fokker aircraft. In 1929 a U.S. Army Fokker C-2A established a duration record of 150 hours and 40 minutes. In that same year, however, Fokker lost both his second wife and his test pilot, Bertus Brase. These losses depressed him so much he admitted that he no longer enjoyed flying and preferred instead to spend time either on his yacht or driving.

In March 1931 a Fokker tri-motor crashed and killed the popular Notre Dame coach Knute Rockne. The accident was widely reported and resulted in a sudden loss in popularity of and confidence in Fokker airplanes. An investigation revealed that a rotten wooden joint in the wing assembly caused the wing to rip off during flight. Fokker favored building airplanes with wood, but his customers demanded that they be made of metal. When Douglas unveiled its all-metal DC-2, Fokker negotiated an arrangement to manufacture the airplane in Europe. He later won an agreement to build the DC-3 and Lockheed Electra, though neither one was ever built in Holland. As an agent for Douglas, Fokker sold almost 100 DC-2s and DC-3s in Europe.

World War II and Cold War Competition

On December 23, 1939, after a three week battle with pneumococcus meningitis, Anthony Fokker died. He was survived only by his mother. The company remained in business until the following May when it was confiscated by the invading armies of Nazi Germany. Friedrich Seekatz, who had been arrested by the Dutch authorities because of his German sympathies, was reinstated by the Germans and placed in charge of the factory, which was converted to repair German military aircraft operating from Dutch air bases. For this reason the factory was heavily bombed by the Royal Air Force.

By the end of the war the factory had been looted by the German army and almost completely destroyed by Allied bombings. However, Fokker's technical staff survived the war and within a year the factory was completely rebuilt. The company's new S-series designs entered production soon after the war, some of which were produced in the United States by Fairchild and in South America by the company's Brazilian subsidiary.

Fokker developed a 44-passenger turboprop airplane called the F-27 Friendship in 1956. Development costs and an initially weak market for the F-27 depressed profits, but after a slow recovery hundreds were sold to airlines all over the world. The Soviet aircraft company Antonov produced an aircraft called the An-24 which was strikingly similar to the F-27. This led many to believe that Antonov merely reverse-engineered an F-27 for its own purposes. Over 1,100 An-24s were built by Antonov during Fokker's production run of the F-27.

On March 21, 1960, Republic Aviation Corporation of Long Island, New York, acquired a sizeable minority interest in Fokker. The two companies concluded a number of cooperative agreements involving the production and sale of their airplanes. At this time Fokker also began production of Lockheed F-104 Starfighters in collaboration with German and Belgian companies. In association with the Dutch electronics company Philips, Fokker manufactured parts for the Hawk missile. During the 1960s Fokker also produced parts for Northrop's Canadian-built F-5 fighter.

In 1964 Fokker's airframe division developed a 60- to 85-passenger jetliner called the F-28 Fellowship, which was designed for short to medium range airline routes. The F-28 entered service in 1969. An agreement between Fokker and Fairchild-Hiller of America to build a shorter version of the F-28 called the F-228 resulted in a production run of over 100 of these airplanes.

Fokker's aerospace division was formed in 1967. Its expertise in thermal control, maneuvering, electronics, and structures gave the division important roles in the development of the ANS and IRAS scientific satellites and spacecraft with the European Space Agency (ESA) and the National Aeronautics and Space Administration (NASA). Some of its later contributions were to the ESA Giotto Halley's Comet probe and the Ariane rocket program.

Emerging into the 1970s

In 1969 Fokker merged with the Vereinigte Flugtechnische Werke GmbH (VFW) of West Germany. The new company, which comprised the entire Dutch aircraft industry, was named VFW-Fokker B.V. Fokker continued to manufacture the F-27, F-28, and VFW614 (the first postwar German jet) in addition to various parts for other aircraft. VFW-Fokker was also chosen to manufacture a significant portion of General Dynamics' F-16 fighter jets sold to NATO.

After heavy financial losses the partnership with VFW was dissolved in 1980 and Fokker was once again brought under direct private ownership. Seventeen percent of the company's stock was acquired by the Dutch ABN-Bank, an additional 17 percent was acquired by VMF machining industries, 20 percent was acquired by the Northrop Corporation during the 1960's, and the remaining 46 percent was divided among a number of private investors.

During the 1970s the company developed improved designs of its F-27 and F-28. The market for small fuel efficient turboprops and jets was still quite lucrative, but now Fokker was facing stronger competition from other small airplane manufacturers such as de Havilland and British Aerospace in the United Kingdom.

Frans Swarttouw assumed leadership of Fokker in 1978 and undertook the mission of making the company more competitive with its larger rivals. He devoted a great deal of the company's financial resources to development of the F-50 and F-100. It was regarded by many as a risky gamble, but the company's commitment to technological superiority, product versatility, and reliable product support rewarded it with a solid market share.

The Fokker 50 propjet was the successor to the F-27 turboprop. The F-50 had many of the same dimensions as the Friendship with the exception of its engine nacelles and windows. The F-50 incorporated improved electronic systems and featured a new cabin layout and interior. It was also capable of carrying more passengers than its predecessor.

Finding a Niche in the 1980s

In the early 1980s, after the new jets from Boeing and McDonnell Douglas were announced, Fokker recognized a gap in the airliner market for jetliners capable of serving the world's many short-haul routes. To fill that gap Fokker began development of a new jetliner designated the F-100. Fitted with more efficient Rolls-Royce Tay engines and capable of carrying 100 passengers, Fokker's new plane had the lowest break-even load factor of any jet available. It had the potential to deliver a profit with only 30 percent of its seats filled. Impressive statistics such as these led a number of major airlines, including Swissair, KLM, ILFC, and USAir, to order the F-100. Because of its advanced electronic systems, the F-100 became known as one of the easiest commercial jets to pilot. Fokker built its F-100 in collaboration with Britain's Short Aircraft Company, Rolls-Royce, and Dowty Rotol; Germany's Messerschmitt Bolköw-Blohm; the U.S. companies German and Collins; and others.

The company manufactured airplane wings for Britain's Short 330 and 360 aircraft in addition to wing components for the Airbus consortium's A-300 and A-310. Fokker began preliminary work on a fuel-efficient prop-fan airplane designated the FXX, designed to challenge the Boeing 7J7 and McDonnell Douglas MD-91 prop-fan airplanes. Fokker also assembled missiles and worked on the European space program.

Original plans to coproduce a new, larger Fokker jet—the MDF-100—with McDonnell Douglas were canceled when the latter company decided to concentrate instead on building an improved version of its DC-9 called the MD-80. This 150-seat niche would subsequently be exploited by the Airbus A320 program.

The Fokker 50 and 100 proved much more expensive to develop than planned. The project had been funded by a revolving credit account established to rebuild the Dutch aviation industry after World War II. The $500 million loan was expected to be paid off in the mid-1990s. While competitors Airbus and DASA both had access to state capital, they did not have to pay interest on their loans.

In 1987 Fokker lost $87 million, forcing the company to borrow another $96 million from the government and increase its outstanding shares from 5.3 million to 33.3 million. It raised another $144 million from selling bonds in Germany and Holland. The Dutch government then owned 33 percent of the company.

However, in spite of the company's poor financial returns, its Fokker 50 turboprops and Fokker 100 jets were storming the small airliner market. Both competition among air carriers for newer planes and more extensive route networks increased demand for regional aircraft. There was a three-year wait for Fokker 100s and one year for Fokker 50s—a backlog worth $6 billion. In 1989 *Financial World* noted the company landed the largest export order in Dutch history—$3 billion worth of planes for American Airlines. However, the massive demand strained Fokker's relatively small facilities. Ironically, KLM Royal Dutch Airlines canceled their own order around the same time.

Swarttouw stepped down as chairman in June 1989 for health reasons. Martin Kuilman was tapped as his interim replacement, followed by Eric Jan Nederkoorn. Nederkoorn invited other companies to buy the company to fit in with the global restructuring. He dismissed Japanese suitors, however, due to their inexperience in the aerospace industry.

Falling in the 1990s

Fokker announced profits of 83 million guilders ($44 million U.S.) in 1990. Still it planned to cut 1,000 workers from its workforce of 13,000. Although the manufacturer considered having Lockheed assemble its planes in the United States, Fokker eventually decided opening a second production line would be less efficient. At the same time, it planned expanded versions of its two popular aircraft, to be known as the Fokker 80 and the Fokker 130. A smaller version of its Fokker 100 jet was conceptualized.

Meanwhile, the Deutsche Aerospace (DASA) consortium was preparing to compete with Fokker head-on from scratch in this market, a mindset analysts viewed as uneconomical. The project would require a $2.5 billion investment while stretching the Fokker 100 would require a fraction of the effort. Oddly, DASA's Messerschmitt-Boelkow-Blohm was at this time a partner in the Fokker 100.

In the early 1990s, a war in the Persian Gulf and a global recession caused an industrywide crisis that hit Fokker hard. Sales fell to $1.92 billion in 1993 from $2.13 billion the previous year.

DASA took over a 51 percent stake in Fokker in 1993 since the Dutch government no longer wanted to subsidize the company. After Nederkoorn resigned in February 1993, Daimler-Benz executive Ben J.A. van Schaik was designated his successor. In spite of its massive backlog before the crisis, Fokker was left with dozens of unsold aircraft which it unloaded at bargain prices.

As Fokker entered its 75th anniversary, it contemplated alliances with British Aerospace and other airframe makers while DASA pitched the concept of a 120-seat FA-X twinjet collaboration to Chinese and Korean agencies. Further restructuring followed, including a $350 million loan from DASA, and the sale of aerospace technology to Rabobank for $234 million. Fokker planned to cut its workforce further to 8,500. By this time, the new Fokker 70 aircraft had received about a dozen orders. Still, the company lost $305 million in 1994. The low value of the U.S. dollar compounded Fokker's difficulties.

1996 Bankruptcy

After failing to agree with the Dutch government on financing, DASA withdrew support for its struggling affiliate altogether on January 22, 1996. DASA had offered $620 million in additional funding but wanted $800 million from the government. Fokker immediately approached British Airways, in the market for 100 regional craft, for business which ultimately never came.

On March 15, Fokker applied for protection from creditors. The company continued to manufacture planes and had a backlog of about 75 aircraft, though growing competition in its sector depressed prices. DASA reaffirmed its commitment to service Fokker aircraft. Stork NV subsequently acquired the rights to the maintenance business, which operated under the name Fokker Aviation.

Serious suitors included Bombardier, whose Short Brothers subsidiary was a major Fokker supplier. Samsung and Yakovlev also attempted to save the manufacturer. However, Fokker ceased producing planes in May 1997.

Rekkof Restart

In 1998, Dutch entrepreneur and regional airline executive Jaap Rosen Jacobsen founded Rekkof Restart NV in order to resume production of Fokker 70 and 100 aircraft. Rekkof (''Fokker'' in reverse) acquired tooling from Fokker trustees and began negotiating with former suppliers. The new company hoped to employ 500, a shadow of the former workforce. However, it expected lean assembly techniques to bring production to comparable levels.

Rekkof was backed by Swiss investors. Advantages to the restart included the absence of development costs and a jump on potential competitors in the market. However, the volatile economic climate of the late 1990s postponed production. The Dutch civil aviation authority approved Stork-owned Fokker Services to build the first 40 aircraft, after which it would share the license with Rekkof.

Principal Subsidiaries

Fokker Aircraft B.V.; Fokker Administration B.V.

Further Reading

''Fokker at 75,'' *Air Transport World,* November 1994, p. 144.

Fokker, H.G. Anthony, and Bruce Gould, *Flying Dutchman: The Life of Anthony Fokker,* New York: Arno Press, 1931.

Grigsby, Jefferson, ''The Red Baron Flies Again,'' *Financial World,* September 19, 1989, pp. 30–34.

De Leeuw, René, ''In Homage to Fokker,'' *Airways,* January 1999, pp. 59–63.

Mecham, Michael, ''Incoming Fokker Chief Dares Competitors to Buy Company,'' *Aviation Week and Space Technology,* April 15, 1991, pp. 28–29.

Moorman, Robert W., ''A Diamond Jubilee with Hope,'' *Air Transport World,* November 1994, pp. 90–91.

Postma, Thijus, *Fokker: Aircraft Builders to the World,* London: MacDonald and Jane's, 1980.

Reed, Arthur, ''Fokker on the Crest of a Wave,'' *Air Transport World,* March 1991, pp. 37–41.

''Rekkof Proceeds with Fokker 100 Despite Gloom,'' *Aircraft Value News,* December 7, 1998.

Sparaco, Pierre, ''Daimler-Benz Abandons Fokker,'' *Aviation Week and Space Technology,* January 29, 1996, pp. 34–36.

——, ''Money-Losing Fokker Faces Deep Cuts,'' *Aviation Week and Space Technology,* August 21, 1995.

Taverna, Michael A., ''Fokker 70/100 Restart Decision Looms,'' *Aviation Week and Space Technology,* October 5, 1998, p. 89.

—updated by Frederick C. Ingram

Omron Corporation

Karasuma Nanajo
Shimogyo-ku
Kyoto 600-8530
Japan
(075) 344-7000
Fax: (075) 344-7001
Web site: http://www.omron.com

Public Company
Incorporated: 1948 as Tateisi Electric Manufacturing
    Company
Employees: 18,800
Sales: ¥611.80 billion (US$4.63 billion) (1998)
Stock Exchanges: Tokyo Osaka Kyoto Nagoya Frankfurt
Ticker Symbol: OMRON
NAIC: 334111 Electronic Computer Manufacturing;
    334119 Other Computer Peripheral Equipment
    Manufacturing; 333313 Office Machinery
    Manufacturing; 33422 Radio & Television
    Broadcasting & Wireless Communications Equipment
    Manufacturing; 334413 Semiconductor & Related
    Device Manufacturing; 334418 Printed Circuit
    Assembly (Electronic Assembly); 334419 Other
    Electronic Component Manufacturing; 334511 Search,
    Detection, Navigation, Guidance, Aeronautical, &
    Nautical System & Instrument Manufacturing; 334514
    Totalizing Fluid Meter & Counting Device
    Manufacturing; 339112 Surgical & Medical
    Instrument Manufacturing; 541512 Computer Systems
    Design Services; 561110 Business Management
    Services

Omron Corporation is a world leader in the field of automation. The company has six main divisions. The largest, accounting for about 51 percent of overall sales is the Industrial Business Group, which manufactures and distributes control components—such as printed circuit board relays, security sys-tem sensors, and seismic sensors—and is a leading provider of factory automation systems. The Social Systems Business Group, which accounts for about 23 percent of sales, is a leader in the field of service automation, manufacturing automatic teller machines, point-of-sale systems, electronic cash registers, vending machines, airport automated check-in systems, automatic ticket gates, and traffic information and management systems. The Healthcare Division generates about seven percent of revenues; makes and markets healthcare products used by consumers and professionals, including digital blood pressure monitors, digital thermometers, body-fat meters; and offers medical systems and services. Omron's Specialty Products Division, responsible for about eight percent of sales, is active in three product areas: computer peripherals, such as modems and scanners; automotive electronic components, such as power window switches and air bag pressure sensors; and highly specialized sensors, such as the bill recognition unit installed in photocopiers to prevent paper currency counterfeiting. Generating another eight percent of sales is the Open Systems Division, which develops message and telemarketing systems for the public and private sectors. The final division is the Creative Service Business Division, which contributes less than four percent of Omron's overall sales; this division offers professional business services to corporate clients in such areas as logistics, information systems, communications, human resources management, and financial management.

Early History

Kazuma Tateisi, born in 1900, was graduated from the electrical engineering department of what is now Kumamoto University. Tateisi worked briefly as an electrical engineer for the government on a Hyogo hydroelectric plant, and then began working for the Inoue Electric Manufacturing Company in 1922.

The New York stock market crash of 1929 triggered the "Great Showa Depression" in Japan. When Tateisi became part of Inoue's reduction in its labor force, he rented a factory and began to manufacture household appliances. Sales on his knife grinder and pant press, items Tateisi developed himself, were low. But in 1932 Tateisi used the knowledge of induction relays he had acquired at Inoue to invent and develop a timing device that limited X-ray exposure to $\frac{1}{20}$ of a second. He began production of the timer through a joint venture with Dai Nippon X-ray Inc., using Tateisi Medical Electronics Manufacturing Company as a label.

Early in 1933 Tateisi moved to Osaka to be nearer to Dai Nippon. The Tateisi Electric Manufacturing Company began operations on May 10 that year, the date that is celebrated as the founding anniversary of Omron.

Lack of capital and contractual limitations with Dai Nippon hampered the young company, but in early 1934 Tateisi began to market an induction-type protection relay, which was an essential component of the timer. The component found a large market and successfully raised revenue.

Later that year a typhoon struck Japan's western coast, causing extensive damage to factories there. Hitachi, the chief manufacturer of induction-type protection relays, could not meet the immediate demand, and orders for repair or substitution of relays overwhelmed Tateisi's small factory. The company quickly transferred the manufacturing of its timers to Dai Nippon and concentrated on the relay. The timer would be the last device made by Tateisi for several decades; the transfer marked the beginning of Tateisi's focus on components.

Demand for the relay devices continued after the recovery from the typhoon as Japanese industrial development increased overall, allowing Tateisi to expand his output and facilities. In 1937 Tateisi built a larger factory with offices and a warehouse. He also established a branch office in Tokyo and purchased another factory, where parts from the Osaka plant were assembled.

Research conducted during World War II led to the development of a product line that would become an area of extensive postwar growth for the company. At the request of Tokyo University, Tateisi began to research microswitches, also known as precision switches, in 1941; in 1944 the company supplied 300 microswitches to the university.

During World War II, Tateisi produced flap switches for aircraft and acted as a subcontractor to Mitsubishi Heavy Indus-

tries. In 1944 Tateisi converted a movie studio into the Kyoto branch factory. A year later the Tokyo branch office and the main factory were destroyed in air raids, forcing all production to the Kyoto branch, which remained the company's headquarters until 1968.

Since Japan's hydroelectric plants were largely intact after the war, electricity at least was not scarce. The company's initial peacetime production centered on small household consumer appliances under the name Omlon (which later became Omron), an independent subsidiary.

In 1947 the government, seeking to prevent the frequent electrical overloads common at the time, asked appliance manufacturers to develop a current limiter. Production for the government required incorporation, which Tateisi completed on April 14, 1948. Although the company was once again part of the component industry, postwar prosperity was still several years away. In 1949 the allied powers enacted the Dodge Line, requiring the Japanese government to take anti-inflationary action. These measures revoked the funds that had provided the market for Tateisi's limiter.

This action struck a serious blow to Tateisi's 33 employees, who had devoted all production capability to the limiter. Debt forced reductions in operations and reorganization in the company's subsidiaries. Sales dropped 57 percent that year, to the company's record low.

Efforts to rebuild amid economic instability continued until the intervention of the United Nations in the Korean War stimulated the economy and increased demand for relay devices. This renewed demand allowed Tateisi to reopen the Tokyo branch office and to build a new office in Osaka.

Entered Automation Field in the 1950s

By 1953 the company employed 65 people and Korean wartime demand had boosted the Japanese industrial economy. Kazuma Tateisi had taken an interest in cybernetics—automatic control systems. After a tour of U.S. companies, he felt sure that an automation revolution was at hand in Japan and reorganized the company accordingly.

Development of new products had assumed a rapid pace, and a centralized company could not efficiently administer market-oriented production. Tateisi introduced the "Producer System" (P-system), which delegated individual products to independent companies. Under the P-system, the managers of individual factories and subsidiaries were responsible for production and labor relations while the head office retained all other decision-making. This decentralization allowed a varied product line and profitability on items with slim margins. The company continued to pursue this approach to production, creating separate sales and research subsidiaries in 1955.

In 1958 Omron became a registered trademark and began to be used on all the company's products. But more importantly, the company developed its first control system, which combined several of its components. The following year a P-system company began production of control systems. With these and other innovations, the company saw sales increase tenfold between 1955 and 1959, to ¥1.3 billion.

With the help of government financing, Tateisi completed his Central Research Institute in 1959, which helped speed the development of new items, especially the contactless switch of 1960. This switch's tremendous success solidified the company's future commitment to research and development and gave it prominence in the area of high-tech research.

Entered Health Field in Early 1960s

In 1961 Tateisi introduced a stress meter, the first of many low-cost cybernetic devices for medicine and biology. Instead of establishing a subsidiary, however, health engineering remained part of the parent company as a department.

Complex vending machines, introduced in 1963, were also a long-term success for the company. Capable of dispensing several different items and accepting a variety of currencies, the machines' currency calculation and detection equipment soon found applications in areas beyond food vending. The device proved to be a major breakthrough for the company, as it offered electronic processing of financial transactions, an enormous area of growth in the decades to come.

During the mid-1960s, international sales grew through long-term export contracts. Tateisi opened a representative office in New York, and began to earn the respect of U.S. buyers as a quality producer of vending machines and other electronically monitored control devices just as market demand for such items intensified.

When the company went public in 1962 it had to consolidate the management and financing of the P-system companies in order to be traded on commodities markets, a process that was completed in 1965. Although this sacrificed many of its cost advantages, Tateisi took advantage of its public status. Thanks in part to a period of national economic growth, the company now had the means to invest more heavily in its structural facilities and established eight new factories, four offices, and seven retail branches.

During the eight-year period ending in 1967, annual sales increased almost tenfold again, to ¥10 billion. In 1968 the company built new headquarters in Kyoto and changed its name to Omron Tateisi in celebration of its 35th anniversary.

Omron established the first Japanese research center in the United States in 1970, benefiting from reduced funding for NASA, which made more technically trained employees available. The research and development center in California met with some hostility from people who saw it as another example of the growing economic threat Japan's booming economy represented. The center eventually helped to develop large-scale integrated circuits and liquid crystals, further advancing Omron in the area of electronics research.

The late 1960s and early 1970s were a healthy time for Omron; the company set a five-year sales goal in 1969 of ¥100 billion, and increased its international presence.

The pace of product development grew. During the 1960s, technology advances, including devices pioneered by Omron, created the possibility of universal electronic controls, as opposed to the control devices of the 1950s, which were developed individually as needed. In 1968 Omron introduced a contactless pinboard sequence programmer, which allowed systems flexibility and increased the number of individual tasks to which they could be applied. Four years later, Omron introduced a programmable sequence controller.

Reorganized in the Mid-1970s

The oil crisis in 1973 sparked a period of slow growth nationwide. The mid-1970s were the most stagnant years since the Dodge Line of 1949. Omron was caught expanding its production once again, and was forced to lay off workers and cut production in the P-system companies. In an attempt to build immunity to such fluctuations, the company pruned management and restructured. While many Japanese companies increased their export drive to overcome this economic shock, Omron delayed such efforts until its reorganization of 1976 was completed.

The reorganization was expensive but successful. Sales decreased and the company reported negative net profits for 1975-76, but after three years it was back on course. In 1978, four years behind its original goal, Omron's sales reached ¥101.1 billion. In 1979 Takao Tateisi succeeded Kazuma Tateisi as president, and a new sales goal of ¥500 billion was set for 1990.

Two years later the goal still looked reasonable. Demand for control systems increased 20 percent each year and overall sales grew steadily. But the next decade was an unstable one for Omron, and many changes were eventually required.

Growth slowed substantially in 1981 and actually reversed in 1982. Sales slowly increased but it was six years before the company was fully recovered. Although still sensitive to the global economic climate, Omron had satisfactory returns in many areas. Exports had slowed due to yen appreciation, but overall sales of ATMs, switches, relays, office automation equipment, and medical devices increased rapidly, while control systems continued to increase more moderately.

The brisk pace of 1984-85 hinted at recovery, and the corporation set record net profit levels. But sales of control systems, Omron's largest sector, did not increase and electronic funds transfer systems (EFTS), the second largest sector, actually decreased. Further frustration came from the appreciating yen, which limited export potential.

By 1987 international sales accounted for only 17 percent of sales, down from 25 percent at the beginning of the decade. Yet Omron's limited vulnerability to fluctuations in the exchange rate did offer opportunities, and the company mobilized to capitalize on them. The strong yen led many companies in Japan to reinvest in their manufacturing facilities and information systems, which improved Omron's domestic sales. Omron also invested in itself, nearly doubling its long-term debt during the decade to ¥34.8 billion, and lowering its earnings for 1985 and 1986. The exchange rate also allowed the company to increase overseas production and buy more components from Taiwan and South Korea. In 1988 these investments finally improved earnings, which nearly doubled in one year, while sales, only slightly behind schedule, jumped to ¥315 billion.

Transitioned to Systems Development in Late 1980s

Omron had also used the slow growth period to restructure. Its most important move was its transition from a component manufacturer to a producer of integrated control systems. As it entered the late 1980s, Omron relied on research and development and its expertise in combining cybernetic technology, advanced controls, computers, and telecommunications technology to position all of its sectors for the next growth period.

Such flexibility in applications was crucial as customers' needs grew more complex. The retail industry, for instance, increased its demand for faster seller recognition, order placement, and stock control. Other industries interested in EFTS technology included insurance and securities companies wishing to gain rapid access to markets.

Omron's most significant move toward systems development came in 1988, when the company integrated the Control Components (65 percent of sales) and the EFTS divisions (19 percent), believing that technical integration of the company's two largest divisions would be vital to future growth. These divisions were regrouped as Industrial-related Strategic Business Units (SBUs) and Social-related SBUs. The latter was certain to employ the company's Office Automation and Information Systems divisions, which made up ten percent of sales in 1988.

Following the collapse of the 1980s Japanese financial bubble, Omron and other high-tech Japanese companies faced a much more difficult operating environment in the 1990s. The bleakest period for Omron came from 1992 to 1994, when net income dropped to ¥6.17 billion (1992), ¥4.57 billion (1993), and ¥4.69 billion (1994). The figure for 1991 was ¥21.47 billion, while the company recovered in 1995 to ¥12.15 billion. Cost-cutting measures taken by Omron to improve the results included sharply reducing capital spending, streamlining operations—including the reduction of products offered by more than 30 percent—and cutting the workforce by 1,500 through attrition, over a three-year period starting in 1994. The company also stepped up its efforts to develop higher value-added products.

With domestic demand stagnant, Omron looked for opportunities for growth through export. The rapidly emerging nations of southeast Asia were particularly targeted both for potential sales and as an area where manufacturing could be carried out more cheaply than in Japan. Likewise, China became a key for overseas growth and Omron established a regional headquarters there in fiscal 1995. During fiscal 1996, Omron expanded its facilities in Indonesia and also opened three new factories in Shanghai. In early 1997 the company announced plans to double its presence in Asia, outside Japan, by 2001. Omron had already become a much more export-oriented firm, increasing its sales outside of Japan from 16.5 percent in 1990 to 25.6 percent in 1997. The company aimed to further increase export sales to 30 percent by 2001. Another goal was to raise the overseas procurement rate from ten percent to 30 percent during the same period.

The beginning of the Asian financial crisis in mid-1997 and the subsequent fall of the Japanese economy into recession wreaked havoc upon Omron's plans. During the 1999 fiscal year ending in March 1999, Omron saw its export of control components fall due to weak global demand and a strong yen. Revenues fell for the year, as did net income, which declined from ¥18.3 billion in 1998 to ¥2 billion in 1999. In March 1999 Omron announced another restructuring plan, this one to lower the company's workforce from 18,800 to 16,800 by March 2002 and to reduce the number of directors from 30 to less than ten.

Principal Subsidiaries

EUROPE: Omron Europe B.V. (Netherlands); Omron Telford Ltd. (U.K.); Omron Manufacturing of the Netherlands B.V.; Omron Electronics Manufacturing of Germany G.m.b.H.; Omron Electronics Ges.m.b.H. (Austria); Omron Electronics N.V./S.A. (Belgium); Omron Electronics A.G. (Switzerland); Omron Fabrikautomation G.m.b.H. (Germany); Omron Electronics A/S (Denmark); Omron Electronics S.A. (Spain); Omron Electronics S.a.r.l. (France); Omron Electronics S.r.L. (Italy); Omron Electronics Norway A/S; Omron Electronics B.V. (Netherlands); Omron Electronics Lda. (Portugal); Omron Electronics A.B. (Sweden); Omron Electronics O.Y. (Finland); Omron Electronics Ltd. (Turkey); Omron Electronics Ltd. (U.K.); Omron Electronics, Kft. (Hungary); Omron Electronics Spol. S.r.o. (Czech Republic); Omron Electronics SP.Z.O.O. (Poland); Omron Electronics G.m.b.H. (Germany); Omron Systems Europe G.m.b.H. (Germany); Omron Systems U.K. Ltd.; Omron Retail Systems France s.a.r.l.; Omron Healthcare G.m.b.H. (Germany); Omron Medizintechnik Handelsgesellschaft G.m.b.H. (Germany). NORTH AMERICA: Omron Management Center of America, Inc. (U.S.A.); Omron Advanced Systems, Inc. (U.S.A.); Omron Manufacturing of America Inc. (U.S.A.); Omron Electronics, Inc. (U.S.A.); Omron Canada, Inc.; Omron Dualtec Automotive Electronics, Inc. (Canada); Omron Automotive Electronics, Inc. (U.S.A.); Omron Systems, Inc.; Omron Healthcare, Inc. (U.S.A.); Omron Office Automation Products, Inc. (U.S.A.). SOUTH AMERICA: Omron Componentes Eletrô Eletrônicôs da Amazonia Ltda. (Brazil); Omron Eletrônica do Brasil Ltda. (Brazil); Omron Business Sistemas Electrônicos da América Latina Ltda. (Brazil). ASIA PACIFIC: Omron Asiapacific Pte. Ltd. (Singapore); Omron Malaysia Sdn. Bhd.; PT Omron Manufacturing of Indonesia; Omron Electronics Sales and Service (Malaysia) Sdn. Bhd.; Omron Electronics Pty. Ltd. (Australia); Omron Electronics Ltd. (New Zealand); Omron Korea Co., Ltd.; Omron Electronics Co., Ltd. (Thailand); Omron Mechatronics of the Philippines Corporation; Omron Automotive Electronics Korea Co., Ltd.; Omron Business Systems Singapore (Pte.) Ltd.; Omron Business Systems Malaysia Sdn. Bhd.; Omron Healthcare Singapore Pte. Ltd. CHINA AND TAIWAN: Omron (China) Group Co., Ltd. (Hong Kong); Omron (China) Co., Ltd.; Omron Trading (Shanghai) Co., Ltd. (China); Omron Shanghai Computer Corp. (China); OTE Engineering Inc. (Taiwan); Shanghai Omron Automation System Co., Ltd. (China); Shanghai Omron Control Components Co., Ltd. (China); Omron (Shanghai) Co., Ltd. (China); Omron Electronics Asia Ltd. (Hong Kong); Omron Taiwan Electronics Inc.; Yamron Co., Ltd. (Taiwan); Beijing GOT Business Computer System Co., Ltd. (China); Omron (China) Co., Ltd.; Omron Dalian Co., Ltd. (China).

Principal Divisions

Industrial Business Group; Social Systems Business Group; Healthcare Division; Specialty Products Division; Open Systems Division; Creative Service Business Division.

Further Reading

Baker, Gerard, "Restructuring Helps Omron to Rise 42%," *Financial Times,* November 9, 1994, p. 33.

Dawkins, William, "Omron Shrugs Off Domestic Doldrums," *Financial Times,* November 7, 1995, p. 27.

Fifty Years of Omron: A Pictorial History, Kyoto: Omron Tateisi Electronics, 1985.

" 'Fuzzy' Profits for Omron," *Industry Week,* September 3, 1990, p. 56.

Johnstone, Bob, "Mechatronic Marvels," *Far Eastern Economic Review,* July 29, 1993, p. 30.

Robinson, Gwen, "Omron Set to Expand in Asia," *Financial Times,* January 22, 1997, p. 32.

Wagstyl, Stefan, "Omron Fights to Retain Competitive Edge," *Financial Times,* February 25, 1992, p. 27.

—updated by David E. Salamie

The Orvis Company, Inc.

Historic Route 7
Manchester, Vermont 05254-0798
U.S.A.
(802) 362-1300
(800) 548-9548
Fax: (802) 362-0141
Web site: http://www.orvis.com

Private Company
Incorporated: 1856 as C.F. Orvis Company
Employees: 1,200
Sales: $200 million (1997 est.)
NAIC: 454110 Mail-Order Houses; 339920 Fishing
  Tackle & Equipment Manufacturing; 713990 Fishing
  Guide Services; 713990 Hunting Guide Services;
  721214 Hunting Camps With Accommodation
  Facilities; 721214 Fishing Camps With
  Accommodation Facilities

Founded in 1856, The Orvis Company, Inc. is the nation's oldest mail-order company. Through yearly mailings of more than 40 million catalogs—resulting in 70 percent of its sales—the company sells premium fly-fishing tackle, hunting gear, and shotguns, as well as clothing, artwork, and gift items for the country life. Orvis operates 16 retail stores in the United States and four in the United Kingdom, claims over 500 dealers worldwide, and offers fly-fishing and shooting schools as well as chartered vacations and lodging.

Charles F. Orvis and the Beginning of the Mail-Order Industry

In 1831, when Charles Frederick Orvis was born, life in Vermont still bore a strong flavor of frontier days. Children were trained to be ruggedly self-reliant. Charles Orvis developed an uncommon practical inventiveness along with an unusual business acumen. By the age of 20 he was skilled with hand and machine tools and had mastered the basics of mechanical engineering. Charles, like many rural boys, also developed an interest in field sports early in life. However, his love was not just for "the kill," but for the whole outdoors. He was eager to learn. As a boy he once watched an older gentleman who was an experienced fly fisherman demonstrate such artistry with the rod that it left Charles awestruck. That day Charles learned the value of experience and proper tools that he would carry with him all his life.

Charles carefully examined the best rods of the day and was soon building his own rods. It became a growing hobby for him. Both Charles and his brother Franklin became aware of the increasing tourism in Vermont and decided to reel in some business. In 1853 Franklin opened a hotel that later would become the famous Equinox House. Their lodging venture was profitable enough for Charles to turn his hobby of rod building into a business as well. In 1856 he formed the C.F. Orvis Company, with sales rooms in a small stone building next to the hotel. The Orvis family prospered as trains brought ever increasing numbers of tourists from New York and other cities to Manchester. These customers were great advertisements for the new fishing tackle company. The well-made rods and flies that were carried home by wealthy sportsmen generated repeat orders by mail. Building on his successful business, in 1861 Charles erected the Orvis Hotel on the same street as his brother's establishment. The brothers also invested in and promoted the resort industry which brought support to Charles's interests in the fishing tackle business. The community of Manchester, surrounded by the Green Mountains, gained recognition as a fine resort area. By 1861 and the beginning of the Civil War, Orvis had firmly established itself as a manufacturer of solid wood rods of superior quality. It also was becoming noted for its wide selection of flies, and had started a promising mail-order business.

The war temporarily halted expansion, but by the 1870s the company's prospects had brightened. With a growing network of railroads, thousands of sportsmen began to travel to faraway lakes and streams. Increased orders for fishing tackle prompted Orvis to relocate his business to the now historic white frame building on Union Street. He began to explore the ways to improve his business and his products. As yet fly reels were not invented.

Most people simply used casting reels. Orvis studied what was needed and what emerged was his first great innovation: the first ventilated narrow-spool fly reel to be mounted upright. In 1874 Orvis received a patent on his new design in fly reels regarded as a landmark in American fishing tackle history. The perforations on the side plates, which lightened the reel considerably, permitted air circulation through the line when it was on the spool. The reel was first offered in the trout model, followed later by a second model which was a bass reel with a wider spool, and a line capacity of 70 to 80 yards, compared to the trout reel's 40 or 50. The two models, trout and bass, remained standard items for 40 years. Around 1900 the same reel was also offered in aluminum. Orvis was always conscientious about customer service, even when his product was not at fault.

From 1870 to 1900 Charles Orvis faced some very stiff competition. Hiram Leonard was producing fishing masterpieces, as were Shipley and Krider, Abbey & Imbrie, and Spalding. What Orvis did was excel in his production and marketing strategy. He made many personal contacts and received strong endorsements by well-respected sportsmen of his time. By the second half of the 19th century many woods were available to innovative rod builders. By 1870 the bamboo rod was being used in the United States as well. Although the split bamboo rod was recognized as superior to its solid wood forebears, no manufacturer could ignore the traditional materials. So Orvis experimented, well into the 1880s, with a wide assortment of materials. He eventually settled on lancewood rods and, after about 1876, bamboo rods. According to "The Orvis Story," "his rods were reliable, his service and repairs were widely known, and his prices were reasonable. As one Vermont Yankee put it, 'God made poles . . . . Charlie Orvis makes fishing rods.' "

Orvis rods received many unsolicited endorsements by leading anglers of the day, all of which helped the business to flourish. Orvis's contribution was not in producing large numbers of rods, but in producing a quality product and offering it at a surprisingly low price. He was getting testimonials at a time when some of his competitors were charging three times as much for their rods. Quality was critical to Charles Orvis. Every Orvis rod bore the seal of the master's hand.

The Real Ferguson: Standardizing Fly Tying in the Late 1800s

By the last decades of the 1800s, the expanding American frontier invited many anglers to explore new waters. As fly fishing became popular, new fishing flies were in demand. Yet there was no recognized standard, no way anglers could know that the fly they ordered would be what they wanted. It was at this time that Charles Orvis's daughter Mary Ellen began to make what would become a major contribution to the company. In 1876 Orvis hired one of the best fly tiers in the city to come teach his skill to Mary and the five to seven women that formed her Orvis fly production unit. Soon they were filling orders of flies made to exacting specifications. Mary, however, saw the deeper need for standardizing the fly tying industry. She heard from so many fishermen who were frustrated with being unable to get what they wanted. What one called a "grizzly king" was often far different from another's idea. One fisherman lamented, "I can't seem to get the right Ferguson." Meeting his need, the man wrote back gratefully, saying, "You are the first I have met in a long time who knew the real Ferguson." Over time, Mary would help many anglers find "the real Ferguson;" and in so doing she would give her father's company a great boost in prestige and secure herself a permanent place in angling history.

By 1890 a full line of Orvis Superfine Flies were listed in the catalog under several classifications. They also offered standard as well as flies less generally known and not kept in stock. There were floating may-flies, and caddis flies made to order in any size desired. Bass flies were available in 80 patterns, along with richly dressed salmon flies. Fifty-six Halford dry flies completed the listing. In total, 434 patterns graced the catalog. Soon another catalog was needed. Mary's catalog or book, which appeared in 1892, immediately became the one source for fishing ties. *Favorite Flies and Their Histories* was the world's first illustrated classification and standardization of fishing flies. In 1893 she directed the assembly of an exhibit of Orvis flies and fishing photographs, taken by the nation's leading photographers in many states, for the World's Columbian Exposition in Chicago. With the renown of the Orvis line of fishing rods and Mary Orvis's reputation for fishing ties, Orvis commanded a solid market share into the 20th century. The company expanded its mail-order catalogs into geographic areas as their tourism and resort business grew. The company also began advertising more in the major outdoor magazines and journals of the time.

The "Duckie" Years: 1939–65

The crash of 1929 and the Great Depression brought disaster to all the Orvis enterprises. The lathes and milling machines were silenced. By 1939 Orvis was down to two employees, "Bert" Orvis and Hallie Galaise, the last of Mary's fly tiers. Little inventory remained, and day-to-day money came in from repairing bicycles and tennis rackets. The romantic great outdoors was not accessible to most Americans. By the 1930s, north woods hotels were rotted and empty and few streams were visited by sportsmen. One by one the names of the old prestige tackle makers disappeared from the advertising pages of the sporting magazines. Orvis was well on its way to becoming a memory when Dudley "Duckie" C. Corkran arrived on the scene.

Corkran was an enthusiastic angler and golfer who had frequented the Manchester area over the years. In 1939 he learned of the Orvis operation and its struggles and arranged to purchase the company. What Corkran bought was a building, some well worn machinery, and a time-honored name. His first step was to hire Wesley D. Jordan as plant manager. Jordan, a veteran of the rod-building business, had started with the Cross

Rod Company in 1919. Jordan shopped for good cane, rebuilt the Orvis milling machine, and developed a plan to improve the finish and durability of fly rods. However, just as Jordan nearly had the company on its feet, World War II began.

The surprise attack on Pearl Harbor on December 7, 1941, turned the nation's businesses to war production. Within days, Corkran received a three a.m. telephone call from the Boston Procurement Office of the Army, ordering ski poles made from Orvis split bamboo sticks. The poles were painted white for camouflage and shipped to the West Coast and Alaska, where the first U.S. ski troops were in training and engaged in Aleutian Island patrols. While the war brought the ski pole contract, it also brought new orders for the old Orvis Glass Minnow Trap. Because of food rationing and the harassment of the saltwater fishing fleet by German U-boats, commercial freshwater fishing was in peak production along the Mississippi. The popularity of the trap carried over well into the 1960s, but it was during the war that it played a crucial role in the company's survival.

Up to the 1940s, fishing rods were built of various woods and varnished for protection. The varnishes were easily chipped or cracked, and exposed wood could rot and weaken quickly. Bamboo also cracked and split. Wes Jordan sought for a way to treat the bamboo deeper than its surface, to actually impregnate the fibers. After many tries, Jordan succeeded by sawing the cane poles in half, then tempering and impregnating them before gluing them together again and curing them. In 1946 the Orvis team led by Jordan patented the world's first impregnated bamboo rod, making rods completely waterproof and warp-proof.

Over the next two decades, Orvis experienced steady growth and, with the help of its expanding mail-order business, became a brand name in outdoor sports. In 1956, the company celebrated its 100th year of operation by entering the retail market with the opening of its flagship store in Manchester, Vermont. The store at that time boasted over 10,000 flies and a casting pool for testing rods. By 1965 the company had grown to annual sales of about $500,000.

New Ownership Under Leigh Perkins: 1965–92

As Duckie Corkran approached 70 years old he began to look for a buyer for his company. Through a friend he met Leigh H. Perkins. Corkran was very concerned with how the new owner would run Orvis. But Leigh Perkins was already an Orvis man. He had bought his first Orvis rod in 1948 while in college. As a businessman, Leigh Perkins was fascinated with mail-order marketing and its challenges, so he immediately began to explore the possibilities. The venerable firm, renamed The Orvis Company, Inc., grew rapidly as it increased its offerings. Its catalog doubled in size and then doubled again as new customers discovered Orvis. Perkins decided to broaden his base of customers further by moving into the training business. In 1966 Orvis opened the first U.S. fly fishing school in Manchester, Vermont. He planned to not only sell the rods, but teach people how to use them. He also continued the Orvis tradition of innovation. In 1967 Orvis designed and produced the world's first "Zinger" (pin-on reel) for anglers. As Orvis became a well-known brand name, the company experienced greater success. Perkins made the Orvis name synonymous with a way of life: a style of country living.

Perkins soon brought Baird Hall, an advertising executive, into the company to establish a company newspaper. Hall's enthusiasm for fly fishing and country life were matched by his business sense. Having ties to the forests of Georgia in its rod-making capacity, Orvis in 1970 started a line of firewood known as Georgia Fatwood Kindling. The company expanded its lines of apparel the following year and introduced the world's first brown camouflage hunting gear. Perkins and his staff insisted that the same uncompromising quality that was demanded of Orvis fly rods be present in the company's tweed jackets, Irish sweaters, and carbon steel cutlery. Innovation continued as well. In 1972 Orvis developed the first modern exposed-rim, skeleton frame, superlight fly reel, and named it the "CFO." Two years later, Orvis developed its first series of graphite rods. Perkins wanted to lure in the hunters as well. In 1973 he opened the country's first dedicated wingshooting school at its facilities in Manchester, Vermont.

By the late 1970s, with fly fishing enjoying a resurgence in popularity, Orvis started a program to broaden its retail presence. Orvis made agreements with retailers to become Orvis outlets, remain independent and, for a relatively small investment, profit by merchandising the complete Orvis line. By 1977 there were few sporting magazines and publications, commercial or nonprofit, that did not have an Orvis Shop advertisement in their pages. In 1982 Orvis established its mail-order and retail business in southern England near the legendary trout rivers. To support this expansion and overall growth, Orvis realigned its servicing centers, and opened a new major customer service and distribution center in Roanoke, Virginia, in 1987. By 1988 Orvis had developed an effective worldwide distribution system with 400 dealers worldwide.

To keep the public abreast of all its new products and services, The Orvis Company launched its own newspaper. The *Orvis News* grew out of the Record Catch Club, serving as an outlet for the growing number of photographs being submitted by customers. It included sporting and conservation features, worldwide sporting and travel stories, and advertisements for merchandise.

The 1980s were also marked by further research and product development. In 1984 Orvis introduced sporting clays to the United States through its Houston store. In the mid-1980s, the Orvis rod shop unveiled the Ultra Fine, the world's first two-weight graphite rod. By 1986 gross sales of the company reached $50 million. In 1987 Orvis introduced the first one-weight rod. A year later Orvis became the first in the industry to introduce a 25-year, unconditional fly rod guarantee. In 1989 Orvis rods were named the "No.1 Best Made Product of the United States in the 1980s" by Tom Peters, author of *In Search of Excellence*.

Leigh Perkins's son, Leigh "Perk" Perkins, Jr., came to the company just as Baird Hall retired. After his stint as editor of the *Orvis News* he directed the opening of Orvis's new retail store in San Francisco, and moved there in 1980 to become its first manager. Perk's younger brother David also entered the family business soon afterward, first as an instructor in the fishing and shooting schools, and then moving up to the dealer department, which coordinated business between Orvis and its many shops. To become a more important source for all the furnishing of country life, Orvis in the late 1980s purchased Gokey Company, a leading manufacturer of fine hunting boots, shoes, and luggage since 1850. In 1986 the company began its Orvis-Endorsed Lodges, Outfitters, and Guides Program as a recreational sporting outlet for a growing customer base. It defined and set the standard of quality and responsibility for sporting people that carried well into the next decade.

Education and Commitment: The 1990s

If the 1980s were characterized by expansion and innovation, the keywords for the 1990s would be education and commitment. The company went beyond selling products to promoting sporting traditions and the outdoor way of life. Orvis's mission was embodied in Leigh Perkins's words, "If we are to benefit from the use of our natural resources, we must be willing to act to preserve them." Orvis announced a challenge grant to benefit wetlands in the United States and raised more than $200,000 in two years. In 1991, Orvis raised $110,000 to benefit the South Fork of the Snake River in Idaho. The following year Orvis raised $163,000 in a challenge grant to benefit the Big Blackfoot River in Montana. Soon afterward, Orvis conducted a $100,000 challenge grant to aid in the restoration of Florida Bay. This, of course, generated a good deal of positive publicity for Orvis, whose sales continued to be strong. By 1993, gross sales exceeded $100 million.

In 1992 Leigh H. Perkins named his son "Perk" Perkins as president and CEO of Orvis. A year later Orvis purchased British Fly Reel, the largest single producer of fly reels in the world, securing its international leadership. The Orvis CFO III disc fly reel won the "Best in Show" at the International Fly Tackle Dealer Show. Orvis introduced the Trident series, the first fly rod to use MVR (Maximum Vibration Reduction) technology in 1995. That same year, the company bought and reopened the famed Sandanona Shooting Grounds in Millbrook, New York. In 1997 Orvis acquired a majority share in Redington Fly Rods & Reels of Stuart, Florida, best known for its value-priced, quality rods. Also in 1997, the company reached its $200 million mark in gross sales. The following year, Orvis introduced the Flex Index system to fly rod design, reaffirming its leadership in product design. To expand its influence, the company started a travel business in 1988, offering its customers Fishing Vacations ranging from fly fishing the Chalk Streams of England to salmon fishing on the Kola Peninsula in Russia. The Orvis Wingshooting Lodges offered customers the opportunity to hunt everywhere on the continent, from the Barton Ridge Plantation in Rockford, Alabama, to the Diamond J Guest Ranch in Ennis, Montana.

It also persevered in its mission to promote the preservation of the environment through its funding and restoration projects.

The company raised public consciousness and taught deeper responsibility to its customers through its newspaper, the *Orvis News*, and its catalogs reaching over 40 million customers annually. In its growing fishing and wing shooting schools, nearly 3,000 students every year were taught not only the techniques and gear of fishing and shooting, but also the code of ethics and a high standard of sporting philosophy and resource conservation. The schools have been credited with being a major force behind the formalization of an American sporting code.

Throughout its long history, Orvis has stayed the course set by its founder: that of providing quality products to the outdoor sporting world. It also continued in its commitment to the environment. The company was named an "Environmental Leader" by the Direct Marketing Association and regularly donated five percent of its pretax profits to conservation efforts. Along with customer matching programs, this amounted to nearly $1 million raised annually for a wide variety of habitat restoration projects. Orvis also continued to forge partnerships with other conservation groups, including Trout Unlimited and The Nature Conservancy. As the 21st century approached, it could confidently be said that Orvis was as serious about educating sporting men, women, and children to maintain quality fish and wildlife habitat as it was about growing its business. After all, the two went hand in hand.

Further Reading

Dee, Libby, "Kinsley & Co. Adding Women's Clothing, Expanding Orvis Shop," *Boulder County Business Report,* August 1, 1998.

Fraser, Laura, "The Lure of Fly-Fishing, *HealthDate,* March-April 1995, p. 42.

Gill, Kathy, "Three Companies Forced to Halt Sales of Knock-off Products," *PR Newswire,* February 22, 1999.

"Is the Trident True?," *Outdoor Life,* December 1995, p. 80.

"Orvis Freezes Salaries, New Hires: Poor Pre-Holiday Mail-Order Sales Blamed on Global Uncertainty," *Florida Times-Union,* October 25, 1998.

"The Orvis Story," http://www.orvis.com/detail.asp?subject = 9&index = 1.

"Orvis Will Promote Octoraro Campaign: National Firm Raising Money for Watershed," *Lancaster New Era,* December 17, 1997.

"Redington and Frisby Top Offer 'Smart' Headwear to Global Fishing Market," *PR Newswire,* September 10, 1998.

Towle, Michael D., "Pounding Swords into High-Tech Playthings: Cold War Gadgetry Goes Civilian," *Fort Worth Star-Telegram,* December 5, 1998.

Wagner, Wendy, "James Fishing's Fine River's Variety Can Please Anyone from Master to Novice," *Richmond Times-Dispatch,* August 2, 1998.

Zheutlin, Alan, "Columbia Sportswear Continues Aggressive Campaign Against Copycats," *CPA Journal,* December 1998, p. 58.

—J. D. Fromm

Otis Spunkmeyer, Inc.

14490 Catalina Street
San Leandro, California 94577
U.S.A
(510) 357-9836
(888) ASK-OTIS; (888) 275-6847
Fax: (510) 357-5680

Private Company
Incorporated: 1977 as Otis Spunkmeyer, Inc.
Employees: 1,500
Sales: $200 million (1998 est.)
NAIC: 422490 Bakery Products Wholesaling; 422420
    Bakery Products, Frozen, Wholesaling; 311821
    Cookie & Cracker Manufacturing

A rising contender in the foodservice industry, Otis Spunkmeyer, Inc. produces frozen cookie dough, muffins, bagels, brownies and other baked goods to more than 100,000 wholesale customers. Otis Spunkmeyer excelled largely because of its distribution system, comprising roughly 60 distribution centers and a fleet of freezer trucks. During the late 1990s, the company operated manufacturing plants in San Leandro, California; Pittsburgh, Pennsylvania; and Columbia, South Carolina. Internationally, Otis Spunkmeyer operated sales centers in the United Kingdom, Mexico, and in Canada. In 1999 First Atlantic Capital, Ltd., a private investment firm, acquired a majority interest in the company.

Origins of a Retailer Turned Wholesaler

Kenneth B. Rawlings and his wife, Linda, who opened their first fresh-baked cookie store in Oakland in 1977, founded Otis Spunkmeyer. For the name of their business, the Rawlings took the suggestion of their 12-year-old daughter, Kimberly, who came up with the Otis Spunkmeyer name, but their choice of what type of business to open was decidedly less whimsical. The Rawlings did their research, reading various marketing studies that consistently rated cookies as one of the most stable food items. Fresh-baked cookies, as a retail concept, also ex-

uded another strength. They were highly popular, trendy food items, the appeal of which helped the Rawlings transform their Oakland store into a chain. By 1983, there were nearly two dozen Otis Spunkmeyer stores in operation, composing a thriving, fast-growing chain. Despite the signs of a regional chain about to spread its presence across the country, there were no more Otis Spunkmeyer stores opened after 1983. Rawlings was discouraged mainly by the high overhead costs that hobbled what otherwise would have been strident progress. His belief in the market strength of fresh-baked cookies, however, had not weakened, so he decided to approach the business from another angle. His strategic change in stance produced a far more powerful company than the retail chain that existed between 1977 and 1983.

Rawlings decided to abandon the retail market and moved headlong into wholesale. He sold the retail outlets and began marketing frozen cookie dough to hospitals, convenience stores, and corporate and school cafeterias, tapping into the demand for fresh-baked cookies by enabling his wholesale customers to tap into the demand. By 1985, the change in strategy had produced an entirely different sort of company than the Otis Spunkmeyer of the early 1980s. The company generated $8.5 million in sales in 1985, a total collected from the 5,000 wholesale accounts Rawlings had assembled. Nearly all of the company's customers were in California, with the balance divided between customers in Texas and Washington, but immediate plans called for penetration into the Midwest, and from there to regions in the eastern United States.

During the 1980s, Otis Spunkmeyer quickly emerged as one of the leaders in its industry, but the prolific rise of the company was not merely because of Rawlings's decision to switch from retail to wholesale. His move from one sector of the market to the other also came with an innovative approach to marketing frozen cookie dough to wholesale customers, making Rawlings an industry pioneer—later to be copied by competitors—and Otis Spunkmeyer distinctly different from other frozen cookie dough manufacturers. Rawlings supplied more than dough to his customers. His fresh-baked cookies program included the loan of a small, pre-set-temperature oven, pre-portioned frozen cookie dough, and branded displays and point-of-sale

Company Perspectives:

Otis Spunkmeyer is never in a holding pattern. The research and development team is always creating and testing new flavors, recipes and ingredients, always looking to enhance Otis Spunkmeyer products. We are dedicated to providing our customers with delicious baked goods.

materials—the marketing tools that fueled impulse purchases of cookies.

By the end of the 1980s, the effectiveness of Rawlings's approach could be discerned by comparing the stature of Otis Spunkmeyer to its size in 1985. Sales were up from $8.5 million to $37 million. The number of wholesale customers had increased from 5,000 to more than 40,000. The true strength of the company, however, was not reflected in either of these remarkable increases. Underpinning the vitality of Otis Spunkmeyer was its distribution system, another unique characteristic of the company that distinguished it from its competitors. Unlike other frozen cookie dough manufacturers who relied on distributors to deliver their products, Otis Spunkmeyer operated a direct-store-delivery system (DSD) that gave it greater abilities in customer relations and service and greater control over the supply of its frozen cookie dough. Otis Spunkmeyer's DSD system included its own fleet of freezer trucks and, most importantly, a network of distribution centers that served as company sales centers. The effect of this distribution system on the company's success during the 1980s and its evolution during the 1990s was of paramount importance, representing the true strength of Otis Spunkmeyer. The first distribution center, fittingly, had opened during the company's turning point year in 1983, established in Sacramento, California. By the end of the 1980s, there were 41 distribution centers supporting the company's operation.

Product Diversification Begins in 1990

The value of Otis Spunkmeyer's distribution system was demonstrated during the 1990s, as the company used its established network to market products other than frozen cookie dough. The first such use of the company's vaunted distribution system occurred as the 1990s began, when Rawlings acquired Sweet Happenings, a $1-million-in-sales, Modesto, California-based muffin company, in January 1990. After the acquisition, muffins were fed into the same sales and distribution network that previously had marketed only frozen cookie dough. Otis Spunkmeyer tripled the sales volume recorded by Sweet Happenings management during the first year of muffin sales. By the end of 1991, muffin sales had swelled to $10 million, a total that was expected to jump threefold again after the construction of a new muffin plant in Dallas in January 1992.

As work was underway to introduce muffins into the company's distribution network, Otis Spunkmeyer added another product, acquiring a wholesale specialty coffee-roasting company based in Mountain View, California called Peter James Coffee Ltd. in 1991. The company began selling coffee in four

flavors, with plans to introduce another 36 flavors at a later date, but while the development of these ancillary products was underway, Rawlings had not diverted his attention away from promoting the sale of Otis Spunkmeyer frozen cookie dough. In 1992, Rawlings made the ambitious leap into the international arena, introducing the company's frozen cookie dough into Mexico and Europe. Through a joint venture—Otis Spunkmeyer de Mexico—with a local pizza parlor operator, Otis Spunkmeyer opened a distribution center outside Mexico City in June. Overseas, the company leased office and warehouse space near Heathrow Airport in London, expecting to distribute cookie dough in England from its manufacturing plant in Pittsburgh. Once established in the United Kingdom, Rawlings planned to expand cookie dough distribution into mainland Europe, with muffins and coffee to follow, until eventually a manufacturing plant could be opened in Europe.

By the time international expansion was underway in 1992, Rawlings's confidence was at a new high. His sales goal for the end of the decade was nothing less than $1 billion, a lofty objective whose basis was predicated on the strength of the company's distribution system—an asset Rawlings was fully aware of. "We are no longer a cookie company," Rawlings proclaimed in the *San Francisco Business Times* in mid-1992. "We intend to be a distribution company that makes our own products and distributes them." There was ample evidence for adopting such a perspective. Muffin sales were expected to reach between $60 and $90 million in 1993, with further increases anticipated after another muffin manufacturing plant was opened, slated to be located in Atlanta. Similar growth was expected from the acquisition of Peter James Coffee, which had debuted as the company's newest product line, christened "Otis Spunkmeyer Classic Collection Coffee." The profits gleaned from funneling frozen cookie dough, muffins, and coffee through the company's DSD system had enabled the Rawlings, who shared adjoining desks at the company's San Leandro headquarters, to branch out into other businesses. The couple owned a burrito shop, a limousine shuttle, and their most visible property, 2 DC-3 airplanes that provided sky tours of the San Francisco Bay Area under the name "Otis Spunkmeyer Air." Each of the Rawlings was committed to expanding their business empire further. "We have no desire to take off and go to Tahiti," Linda Rawlings explained. Kenneth Rawlings underscored his wife's comment, saying, "Linda and I own 100 percent of the company, and that's the way it will be in our lifetimes. Our goal is to build a very big company."

At the time Rawlings articulated his goal to create a massive foodservice company, Otis Spunkmeyer already ranked as the world's largest manufacturer of gourmet frozen cookie dough, producing more than 2.5 million cookies per day. Sales, since the switch to wholesale in 1983, had grown at a robust pace, averaging 50 percent annual increases for the ensuing eight years. Rawlings wanted far more than being the world's largest producer of frozen cookie dough, however. He wanted to use the company's distribution network to market a host of other baked food products and thereby achieve $1 billion in sales, but the company had a difficult time making the transition from a fast-growing cookie dough producer into a diversified heavyweight in the foodservice industry. By the mid-1990s, sales had essentially flattened, despite steady increases in muffin sales. By the beginning of 1996, Rawlings was ready to look for help in lifting Otis Spunkmeyer to what he referred to as ''the next level.''

1996 ''Baking a Difference'' Marketing Campaign

Rawlings recruited a friend he had known socially for 15 years named John S. Schiavo. A senior vice-president of J&J Snack Foods Western Division, Schiavo joined Otis Spunkmeyer in March 1996, becoming the company's president and chief operating officer. Rawlings, who remained chairman and chief executive officer, saw his partnership with Schiavo as complementary, saying, ''I have a management background. John knows production. He knows foodservice sales [and] brings several unique talents to the company.'' It was Schiavo's responsibility to identify growth areas for the concept Rawlings had created and to exploit the potential of the company's distribution system. ''In watching the company,'' Schiavo explained, ''I felt there were many opportunities that Otis Spunkmeyer had not fully realized. I felt the name Otis Spunkmeyer, in and of itself, was crying out for some fresh marketing.''

Schiavo's influence on Otis Spunkmeyer materialized in the company's ''Baking a Difference'' marketing campaign, a program aimed at taking Rawlings's concept an evolutionary step forward. The inspiration for the campaign struck Schiavo during his first few weeks with the company, when he was grappling with how all the pieces of Otis Spunkmeyer fit together and how the cohesive whole could be marketed with an integrated plan that maximized the company's potential. One facet of the Otis Spunkmeyer portfolio that Schiavo initially perceived as particularly incongruous was Otis Spunkmeyer Air. Rawlings had purchased the two DC-3 aircraft as a promotional vehicle for Otis Spunkmeyer, but Schiavo felt the two vintage planes did not fit into the core operation plan he was attempting to develop. His mind changed in an instant, however, one day while he was passing by photographs of vintage airplanes at Otis Spunkmeyer's headquarters. ''I stopped dead in my tracks,'' Schiavo recalled in the January 1997 article ''Cleared for Take-Off,'' ''and said, 'Name. Plane,' and I thought about the Goodyear blimp . . . maybe there's something we can do here.''

The company hired The Laux Agency, a Wisconsin-based marketing firm, to flesh out Schiavo's idea into a creative and comprehensive marketing program. The Laux Agency took the image of the DC-3 and introduced a character, never to be seen, named ''Otis Spunkmeyer,'' as the airplane's peripatetic pilot, perpetually in search of the greatest recipes and best ingredients in the world. Aside from developing an aeronautic theme that was extended throughout the Otis Spunkmeyer product line, The Laux Agency also developed new product ideas and marketing programs targeted to specific foodservice segments, such as schools, restaurant chains, and other wholesale customers. The ''Baking a Difference'' program was introduced to the Otis Spunkmeyer sales staff in November 1996 and to customers in January 1997, representing Schiavo's attempt to take the company ''to the next level,'' which he identified as achieving an annual growth rate ranging between 15 and 20 percent. As part of the program launch, Otis Spunkmeyer introduced five new lines of cookies and a line of par-baked bagels marketed under the ''Barnstormin' Bagels'' banner. After this initial product

expansion, the company planned to introduce at least two new major product lines annually.

Although Otis Spunkmeyer fell well short of Rawlings's goal to reach $1 billion in sales by the end of the 1990s, the company did achieve encouraging progress with its ''Baking a Difference'' program. Sales increased to $170 million in 1997, and by March 1998 the company had recorded double-digit sales growth every month since September 1996. Sales eclipsed $200 million in 1998, prompting company officials to aim toward doubling sales during the next three years. To achieve such growth, the company was concentrating on new baked goods, including breakfast pastries, rugelah, and miniature cakes, as well as looking to expand through the introduction of products to be baked on-premises for sit-down restaurants.

As Otis Spunkmeyer prepared for the future, hoping to exploit the strength of its distribution system, the company fell under new ownership and, with it, gained the financial wherewithal to actualize its expansion plans. In January 1999, First Atlantic Capital, Ltd., a private investment firm known for acquiring and expanding mid-size companies, acquired a majority interest in Otis Spunkmeyer. First Atlantic's majority stake led to management changes, with the private investment firm's managing director, Joseph Haviv, becoming chairman of Otis Spunkmeyer, Rawlings named vice-chairman, and Schiavo appointed as chief executive officer. As First Atlantic took charge of stewarding Otis Spunkmeyer's fortunes, it hoped to accomplish what Rawlings and Schiavo had been trying to achieve throughout the 1990s. The expansion of product lines and the possibility of future acquisitions provided the two avenues of potential growth as Otis Spunkmeyer entered the 21st century.

Principal Subsidiaries

Otis Spunkmeyer Air; Otis Spunkmeyer Plastics.

Further Reading

Carlsen, Clifford, ''Sweet Dreams: Spunkmeyer Hopes New Products and Plans Can Help Its Cookie Dough Rise,'' *San Francisco Business Times,* March 6, 1998, p. 3.

''First Atlantic Capital Acquires a Majority Interest in Otis Spunkmeyer, a Leading U.S. Manufacturer of Dough and Muffins,'' *Business Wire,* January 5, 1999, p. 1.

Keyser, Christine, ''San Leandro's Otis Spunkmeyer No Longer Just Another Cookie Maker,'' *San Francisco Business Times,* July 24, 1992, p. 6A.

Malovany, Dan, ''Cleared for Take-Off,'' *Snack & Bakery Foods,* January 1997, p. 22.

''Otis Spunkmeyer Buys Coffee-Roasting Co.,'' *Nation's Restaurant News,* September 23, 1991, p. 30.

''Otis Spunkmeyer Expanding,'' *Supermarket News,* June 22, 1992, p. 47.

''Otis Spunkmeyer Tries Coffee,'' *Supermarket News,* October 26, 1992, p. 63.

Reiss, Evette, ''Doughmaker Plans to Move into Retail Cookie Market,'' *San Francisco Business Times,* April 16, 1990, p. 9.

''Spunkmeyer Names President,'' *Supermarket News,* June 17, 1996, p. 42.

—Jeffrey L. Covell

Pacific Sunwear of California, Inc.

5200 East La Palma Avenue
Anaheim, California 92807
U.S.A.
(714) 693-8066
Fax: (714) 701-4298
Web site: http://www.pacificsunwear.com

Public Company
Incorporated: 1979
Employees: 3,161
Sales: $227.1 million (1998)
Stock Exchanges: NASDAQ
Ticker Symbol: PSUN
NAIC: 44811 Men's Clothing Stores; 44814 Family
    Clothing Stores

A fast-growing specialty retailer, Pacific Sunwear of California, Inc. sells casual apparel, footwear, and accessories designed for teenagers and young adults in more than 300 stores throughout 40 states. Pacific Sunwear operates two chains, its flagship Pacific Sunwear concept, which caters to suburban fashion tastes, and d.e.m.o., a concept influenced by urban fashion trends. Nearly all the company's stores are located in regional malls. During its relatively short history, Pacific Sunwear has undergone several transformations. The company started as a surf shop, broadened its merchandise to include casual young men's apparel in 1990, and began retailing young women's apparel and footwear in 1995. Against the background of these strategic alterations, the company expanded vigorously, increasing its store count from 21 units in 1988 to 344 units by the beginning of 1999. Annual sales during the decade swelled from $18 million to $321 million. The company was expected to open 108 stores in 1999, which included 25 units of its 15-unit d.e.m.o. chain. Merchandise brands carried in the company's stores include Quiksilver, Rusty, Stussy, Billabong, Doc Martens, Venus Girl Trap, and private-label brands Bullhead, Breakdown, Diversion, and Tilt. Pacific Sunwear generates 75 percent of its revenues from young men's merchandise and the balance from young women's merchandise. More than a quarter of total sales are derived from the sale of T-shirts and knit and woven tops.

1980 Surfing Origins

The roots of Pacific Sunwear's business originated in Newport Beach, California, where Tom Moore opened his first shop catering to surfers in 1980. The opening of another small surf shop in southern California was not a remarkable event, but the success of the Newport Beach store did lead to a novel development in surf shop history. Hoping to secure year-round business, Moore and his partners opened a second shop the following year in a mall—the exclusive domain of Pacific Sunwear stores for the next 17 years.

The location proved a winner, generating more than $1 million in sales in 1982. The success of the first mall store, located in Santa Monica Place, spawned the establishment of ten more stores, all in proximity to the coast and all situated in malls. With the financial backing of venture capitalists in 1987, the chain grew to 21 stores, collecting $18 million in sales in 1988.

By all measures, the concept was a success, thriving during a decade in which bright, neon shorts and shirts of the surfer lifestyle were popular, trendy apparel items among nonsurfers as well. Quick success, however, turned to quick failure when the company began to expand outside of California. Sales plunged sharply at stores on the East Coast and in Minnesota, for example, where a company store located in the Mall of America struggled to sell shorts when the thermometer outside read 17 degrees below zero. According to a company official, the typical customer reaction was ''this is a cool store, I'll be back when it's summer.'' In response, new management was brought in to inaugurate the new decade, led by Michael W. Rayden, whose chief task was to transform the chain into a profitable retailer able to expand outside of southern California.

Strategy Changes in 1990

A retail veteran, Rayden joined Pacific Sunwear in 1990 after working for Stride Rite, Eddie Bauer, and Liz Claiborne. During the early 1990s, Pacific Sunwear registered two money-

---

losing years and closed eight underperforming stores, as the company suffered along with the decline in popularity of the surfer ''look.'' Of the stores closed, four were in the company's mainstay California market and the other four were located in new markets—two units in Texas and two in Washington, D.C.

Pacific Sunwear had faltered in its first bid to become a national retailer, but the company did not make the same mistake twice. Rayden devoted his first years with the company to developing a new merchandising strategy and forming a more prudent real estate plan to support geographic expansion. Rayden's new merchandising strategy revamped the Pacific Sunwear concept. He broadened consumer appeal—thereby increasing the company's customer base—by adopting a new focus for the retailer. Instead of relying on shorts, shirts, and hats, Rayden shaped Pacific Sunwear into a young men's casual apparel retailer, a chain that carried fashionable brands such as Stussy, Mossimo, Quicksilver, Rusty, and Billabong. Rayden was trying to attract a specific customer: white, suburban, teenage males. The intense focus on attracting this type of customer proved successful. By early 1993, there were 60 Pacific Sunwear stores in operation, with 47 units located in California and the remaining 13 units spread among Arizona, Connecticut, Florida, Nevada, New Jersey, and Washington— all in regional malls Annual sales in 1992 were up more than 30 percent from the previous year's total, and profitability was sound. Profitability had been sustained for seven consecutive quarters, and Rayden was ready to expand in earnest.

The signal informing outside observers of Rayden's readiness to expand on a grand scale arrived in March 1993, when Pacific Sunwear filed with the Securities and Exchange Commission for an initial public offering (IPO) of stock. The company hoped to raise $14.4 million in proceeds from the IPO, and earmarked $4.2 million of the total to expand. News of the IPO arrived at the same time the company announced its expansion plans for the immediate future; between 18 to 20 store openings were planned for 1993, and 25 store openings were slated for 1994.

1993 Public Offering Fuels Expansion

In the wake of the IPO, Pacific Sunwear expanded at a vigorous pace, exceeding its own projections. By late 1994, there were 118 stores in 17 states, the result of 46 new stores added to the chain in 1994, which was nearly twice as many new store openings as announced in early 1993. On the heels of this prodigious growth spurt, plans were announced for the expansion of the chain by 35 percent, or 50 new stores, in 1995. In 1995, the square footage of the entire Pacific Sunwear chain increased 45 percent over the retail space occupied by the

company in 1994. Fifty-five stores debuted during the year for a total of 128 stores opened during the previous three years. Remarkably, profitability was sustained during this period of prolific growth, as Pacific Sunwear recorded positive net income for 15 consecutive quarters.

Amid the frenzied expansion activity in 1995, the first currents of a movement to fundamentally alter Pacific Sunwear's concept emerged. At a two-and-a-half day executive retreat in May 1995, Pacific Sunwear officials discussed broadening the chain's customer appeal again. The executives who had gathered at Rancho Valencia discussed introducing new types of merchandise into the stores, making the stores bigger to house the new merchandise, and increasing the percentage of private label merchandise within the stores. In the months following the executive retreat, footwear and junior women's apparel began appearing in Pacific Sunwear stores, as the stores themselves became larger. The square footage in new stores was increased 50 percent to 3,000 square feet. With these changes, the company began to stray from its tight focus on white, suburban, teenage males in order to embrace a broader customer base, thereby making the transition from a niche-oriented retailer to a more broadly defined specialty retailer.

As the company maneuvered through this transition—its most profound change since Rayden arrived in 1990— unexpected news took industry pundits and analysts by surprise. On January 30, 1996, Rayden announced his resignation from Pacific Sunwear, sending a shockwave through the financial community that caused the company's stock value to fall 15 percent. Rayden left the company to join Ohio-based women's apparel retailer The Limited, where he was named president of Limited Too, a division that sold casual sportswear for girls. While an executive search firm looked for a replacement for Rayden, Greg Weaver, Pacific Sunwear's chief operating officer, took over as president.

Weaver Era Begins in 1996

Weaver's temporary stewardship of Pacific Sunwear occurred at a critical juncture in the company's history and at a time of great opportunity for astutely managed, young men's apparel retailers. During the previous three years, more than 2,500 young men's stores were closed, as such retailers as Merry-Go-Round, Edison Bros., and Clothestime either exited the business or reduced the size of their chains. Fewer stores left more business for existing retailers to capture, business that Weaver estimated at $2 billion. Enticed by the potential, Weaver was intent on capturing the lion's share of the abandoned business. ''Our mission,'' he said in September 1996, ''is to become the dominant, national specialty retailer of teenage apparel, footwear, and accessories.'' A month after setting this lofty goal, Weaver was named chief executive officer of the company, having, according to Pacific Sunwear's chairman of the board, ''demonstrated great success since assuming operational control.'' The search for Rayden's successor was over; it was Weaver's responsibility to lead the company toward national dominance.

As Weaver set out in pursuit of his objective in September 1996, Pacific Sunwear operated 198 stores in 33 states. By the end of 1996, 30 new stores had been established during the year.

This was a relatively slow pace of expansion for the company, limited by the problems associated with its transition into a specialty retailer, but 1996 only proved to be a temporary lull. In 1997, 50 new stores were slated to open and another 50 stores scheduled for 1998, with expansion aided by a stock offering in June 1997 that raised $29 million.

As Pacific Sunwear began fulfilling its expansion goals, opening an average of two new stores each month, the company achieved additional growth in a new way. For the first time in its history, Pacific Sunwear completed an acquisition, purchasing a 15-unit, young men's and junior chain named Good Vibrations for $9.2 million in September 1997. Similar to Pacific Sunwear, Good Vibrations was a regional mall-based retailer of casual young men's apparel, accessories, and footwear, whose annual sales, collected from the company's stores in Florida, amounted to $17 million. Following the acquisition, the Good Vibrations name was retained, with Good Vibrations and Pacific Sunwear stores in many cases operating within the same mall.

Pacific Sunwear broke with tradition in another way in 1997, opening its first non-mall, freestanding store. Located in Greenwich Village, the 6,000-square-foot store was evidence of Weaver's conviction, as expressed to the *Daily News Record* in September 1997, that Pacific Sunwear "can take this store prototype anywhere in the country." The Greenwich Village store was the first of what was expected to be several Pacific Sunwear units in the lucrative New York City market. Following the debut of the Greenwich Village store, the company began researching other potential store locations in densely populated urban environments, specifically in Chicago and Boston.

As the company entered 1998, it announced plans to expand on another front. In February, Pacific Sunwear revealed its intentions to launch a second retail concept whose merchandise would duplicate Pacific Sunwear merchandise to a very limited extent. Named "d.e.m.o.," the new concept was expected to offer, according to the company, "popular and emerging cross-cultural brands," catering to urban fashion tastes rather than retailing the clothing trends of suburbia. After initial experiments proved positive, Good Vibrations stores were converted to the d.e.m.o. format. A majority of the 15 stores planned for the first wave of expansion were expected to be opened before the 1998 school season, with stores slated for malls in California, Florida, Illinois, Louisiana, New Jersey, New York, and Michigan. Between April and August, 15 d.e.m.o. stores were opened in time for the back-to-school season, recording sufficient success to prompt the company to expand further.

As Pacific Sunwear reached the end of a prodigious ten-year growth period, the company showed no sign of slowing its pace of expansion. In 1999, 108 stores were scheduled to be opened, including the 25 new d.e.m.o. units. To assist in this ambitious expansion, the company launched its first national advertising campaign in February 1999, placing advertisements in the *Sports Illustrated* swimsuit issue, *Teen People* magazine, and *Seventeen* magazine. Said Weaver, according to a February 1999 *Business Wire* report, "With our aggressive growth plans to add 108 stores in 1999 we felt it was the right time to aggressively step up our marketing efforts." On this note, Pacific Sunwear prepared for the work ahead, intent on becoming the dominant national retailer for the youth of America.

Principal Subsidiaries

Good Vibrations, Inc.

Further Reading

Barron, Kelly, "CEO Steps Down at California Retailer Pacific Sunwear," *Knight-Ridder/Tribune Business News,* January 31, 1996.
——, "Cool It," *Forbes,* November 2, 1998, p. 218.
——, "Pacific Sunwear's Future Looks Bright Despite Departure of CEO," *Knight-Ridder/Tribune Business News,* February 10, 1996.
D'Innocenzio, Anne, "Pacific Sunwear Chain Planning to Go Public," *Daily News Record,* March 3, 1993, p. 10.
"Greg Weaver Promoted to CEO of Pacific Sunwear of California," *Daily News Record,* September 26, 1996, p. 2.
Hardesty, Greg, "California's Pacific Sunwear to Expand Urban-Themed Clothing Stores," *Knight-Ridder/Tribune Business News,* September 15, 1998.
Kaplan, Don, "Pacific Sunwear, Gadzooks Drive to Nab $2B Void in YM Market," *Daily News Record,* September 12, 1996, p. 3.
La Franco, Robert, "Pacific Sunburn?," *Forbes,* May 5, 1997, p. 190.
"Pacific Sunwear Launches National Ad Campaign," *Business Wire,* February 3, 1999.
"Pacific Sunwear Launching New Chain," *Daily News Record,* February 13, 1998, p. 4.
"Pacific Sunwear of California Sets '95 Store Expansion Plan," *Daily News Record,* October 7, 1994, p. 4.
"Pacific Sunwear Stock Rises," *Daily News Record,* December 19, 1996, p. 10.
Palmieri, Jean E., "Fads Don't Fit Pacific Sunwear's Fashion Focus," *Daily News Record,* August 28, 1995, p. 14.
——, "Pacific Sunwear Acquires Good Vibration; $17 Million, 15-Unit Men's Chain Will Retain Name," *Daily News Record,* September 10, 1997, p. 16.
Smith, Elliot Blair, "Stock Sale Reaps Pacific Sunwear $29 Million to Fund Expansion," *Knight- Ridder/Tribune Business News,* June 12, 1997.
Zimmermann, Kim Ann, "Controlled Growth: Pacific Sunwear's New Network Will Keep the Company on the Expansion Path While Cutting Costs," *Footwear News,* February 23, 1998, p. 17.
——, "Pacific Sunwear Preps for E-Commerce," *Daily News Record,* January 13, 1999, p. 14.

—Jeffrey L. Covell

Parker Drilling Company

Eight East Third Street
Tulsa, Oklahoma 74103-3637
U.S.A.
(918) 585-8221
Fax: (918) 631-1341
Web site: http://www.parkerdrilling.com

Public Company
Incorporated: 1954
Employees: 3,500
Sales: $481.22 million (1998)
Stock Exchanges: New York
Ticker Symbol: PKD
NAIC: 213111 Drilling Oil & Gas Wells

Parker Drilling Company is a leading provider of contract drilling and drilling-related services—including land, transition zone, and offshore drilling—to major oil companies, independent oil and gas producers, and government-run oil companies. It has operated in 49 countries, primarily in the transition zones of the Gulf of Mexico, Nigeria, Venezuela, the Caspian Sea of Kazakhstan, and the offshore waters of the Gulf of Mexico, and in numerous on-land oil and gas producing regions throughout the world. Parker maintains a fleet of 75 international land rigs, 15 U.S. deep gas land rigs, 34 barge rigs, seven platform rigs, seven offshore jackup rigs, and specialized rental tools that it leases to other drilling companies. Parker Drilling Company has become the dominant operator in the heli-rig market, operating 80 percent of all rigs transportable by helicopter to otherwise inaccessible desert, jungle, and mountain locations. It is also a specialist in deep well, arctic, and geothermal drilling.

A Company Committed to Innovation Since 1934

Gifford C. Parker, an Illinois farmer, excited by the opportunities presented by the Oklahoma and Texas oilpatch, founded Parker Drilling Company in Tulsa in 1934. The following year, the new company pioneered the use of diesel electric powered drilling rigs and by 1945 was branching out into the interna-

tional market. During the next four years, Parker Drilling began to operate five rigs in Venezuela and 12 in Canada.

In 1954 the company was incorporated in Oklahoma. Robert L. Parker, Gifford's son, purchased the company and became its president, a role he retained until 1977 when he was elected chief executive officer. Robert L. Parker, Jr., Gifford's grandson, joined the company in 1973 and followed his father as president and chief operating officer in 1977. He later became chief executive officer in 1991. Under the direction of both men, the company committed itself to the exploration and practice of new drilling techniques. Starting in the 1960s in west Texas, Parker created its own niche by developing new deep drilling technology that has since become the industry standard. By the mid-1960s Parker had eight deep drilling wells—defined as those 18,000 feet and deeper—the oldest of these being one it drilled for Gulf Oil in west Texas. In 1969, the year Parker went public with shares sold on the over-the-counter market, the company landed a major contract with the United States Atomic Energy Commission to drill a series of holes up to 120 inches in diameter and 6,500 feet in depth in Alaska and Nevada for nuclear testing. Three years later Parker set a world record for deep well drilling with a 28,500-foot well, again in west Texas. In 1977, using the world's largest rig at the time, Parker drilled the deepest test to date in the Middle East in Kuwait.

During the second half of the 1960s the company began to pioneer the helicopter-transportable rig technology for which it eventually became well known. Parker engineers experimented with the design, later patented, of several series of rigs that could be disassembled, flown into remote or environmentally sensitive areas, and there reassembled for the operator's drilling program. During the 1970s and 1980s Parker technology also introduced a number of changes in the realm of arctic drilling, including new rig designs, innovative rig-moving systems, and improved drilling technology for arctic conditions. In 1975, the year the company was listed on the New York Stock Exchange, it acquired OIME, a design, engineering, and manufacturing firm located in Texas that evolved into Parker Technology, Inc., or Partech, Parker's research and development, manufacturing, and rig service center. In 1978 Parker Drilling pioneered arctic drilling technology using a winterized rig on wheels, designed and manufactured for an ARCO Alaska, Inc. drilling program in the Prudhoe Bay Field.

International Drilling Beginning in the Early 1980s

The early 1980s proved a time of dramatic change in the energy industry. Under President Reagan's direction, many of the restraints imposed upon companies during the previous decade, including such things as pestilent controls on industrial fuel burning, were dismantled by Congress as a part of the National Energy Plan II. As a result, there was a gradual increase in drilling activity, including a move to international drilling. In 1980 Parker was awarded a contract in the People's Republic of China to work in Xinjiang province, becoming the first American land drilling company to work in that nation. This contract was followed in 1984 by a second, for work jointly undertaken by Parker and China's National Oil & Gas Exploration and Development Corp. Elsewhere in the Asia-Pacific area, Parker signed on to its first operation in New Zealand and its second in Papua New Guinea. Parker also began operations in Somalia, Tanzania, the Sudan, and South America.

In the late 1980s, the Soviets began launching a new push to increase the output of their vast oil and natural gas reserves. Parker signed a protocol agreement with the Soviet Union's Ministry of Oil and Gas Industry in 1989 to act as exclusive project manager in negotiating a comprehensive contract to coordinate the planning, design, engineering, and implementation of deep well drilling on a remote desert location near the Caspian Sea. Parker became the first Western drilling contractor to work in the Siberian arctic when it entered into a contract in 1991 with White Nights Joint Enterprise to provide two state-of-the-art rigs and supervisory personnel for an improved-recovery and development-drilling program. This operation was followed by two others in 1993, one of these a contract to develop one of the world's largest oil fields, the Tengiz oil field in Kazakhstan; the other, to provide drilling services in western Siberia.

Throughout the early 1990s, Parker Drilling continued to develop its overseas operations. In 1992 it traveled to the Congo where it was hired to design hybrid rigs combining the drilling technologies of both the petroleum and solid minerals industries and to wireline core several holes for oil and gas exploration. In 1993 it returned to Argentina, where it had last worked in 1974,

before that country's oil industry was nationalized, and contracted to drill 48 wells. It also signed contracts in Colombia and in Peru to drill a total of up to seven wells. In 1995 Parker agreed to manage China's state-owned Great Wall Drilling Co.'s rigs as well as to train its crews, and to drill two wells south of Hanoi, Viet Nam, for an Australian company.

Acquisitions in the Mid-1990s

Parker Drilling's revenues for fiscal 1995 were $157.4 million with net income of $3.9 million. In 1996 revenues dropped to $156.7 million, but income increased slightly to $4.1 million. By fiscal 1997 those figures were at $311.6 million and $16.3 million, respectively. This significant increase between 1996 and 1997 reflected changes within Parker Drilling, specifically, the November 1996 acquisitions of Mallard Bay Drilling, Inc. and Quail Oil Tools. Mallard, a leader in transition zone barge and offshore platform drilling and the largest operator of barge rigs in the Gulf of Mexico, enabled Parker to expand into the offshore drilling market, moving away from its focus on large land rigs that drilled for natural gas and smaller rigs that were easily transported to remote locations. The addition of Quail Oil Tools, the second largest provider of tools and equipment to exploration, production, and service companies in the Gulf of Mexico, moved the company into equipment rental.

These changes also reflected a general upswing in the oil market. The year 1996 and most of 1997 were a time of high activity for oil and gas companies, during which they increased exploration and production budgets in response to demand and strong commodity prices. In July 1997 Parker acquired Bolifor S.A., a Bolivian drilling contractor. Hercules Offshore Drilling, along with its affiliate, Hercules Rig Corp., came on board in December 1997, purchased from a publicly owned Malaysian company for $195 million. These two purchases enabled Parker to expand into a unique industry niche, drilling and workover in waters 215 feet or less, at a time when rig day rates and utilization were approaching a 15-year high, with many segments of the industry near full utilization. Mallard, Quail, and Hercules, as subsidiaries of Parker Drilling, increased not only the size of the company, but also the percentage of its revenue generated domestically and made the company's U.S. operations more profitable.

The sudden upswing, however, was followed by just as abrupt a downturn. From the fall of 1997 to the spring of 1998, the price of a barrel of oil fell from $20 to $11, the lowest level in 25 years, once adjusted for inflation. This drop caused drilling to slack off and reduced spending by Parker's customers. A merger with Louisiana-based Superior Energy Services would have made Parker the second largest oil tool rental company behind Weatherford International, but plans to merge were called off in 1998 after both companies' stock prices fell in response to an oil price collapse.

Downturn in the Drilling Market in 1998

As 1998 progressed, reduced activity and lower rates throughout the industry resulted in a significant slowdown in activity for Parker Drilling. The market cooled to oil service stocks, and shares of Parker and its peer companies lost on average 70 percent of their value. Parker closed out 1998 as one of the New York Stock Exchange's four worst-performing stocks. At the same time, the financings related to acquiring Mallard and Quail combined with Parker's issuance of convertible notes in July 1997 and senior notes in 1998 substantially increased the company's debt. Parker Drilling went from having $3.4 million in debt in 1996 to $651.6 million in 1998.

In other ways, however, 1998 was a notable year for Parker Drilling. In a move to centralize its administration, the company completed its new 47-acre Mallard-Partech complex in New Iberia, Louisiana and made plans to move Hercules' Lafayette shore base to a building adjacent to Partech in the spring of 1999. A new central health, safety, and environment (HSE) team formed and launched a companywide HSE initiative. The new ParkerNET system, the company's globally accessible intranet, computerized new maintenance procedures via its preventive maintenance program. In addition, despite the general softness in industry conditions, drilling and service activities remained strong in the Caspian Basin, Nigeria, parts of South America, and the Gulf of Mexico. In 1998 Mallard Drilling completed the redesign, fabrication, and winterizing of a rig for arctic-style drilling conditions in the northeast Caspian Sea for a three-year Royal Dutch Shell-led drilling project and, in early 1999, entered into an alliance agreement for all of Texaco's domestic inland water drilling and workover requirements.

In fact, fiscal 1998 operations represented a significant improvement over 1997 due to the continued strength of barge drilling operations in the transition zones and most international land drilling markets and the addition of Hercules' shallow water and platform drilling operations. Year-end revenue was $481.2 million and net income was $28.1 million. Yet the improvement of the last six months of fiscal 1998 was followed by a further decline in the oilfield services industry combined with the most dramatic drop in energy prices since the 1980s. During the first quarter of fiscal 1999, Parker experienced a net loss of $7.7 million. As a result, management anticipated substantially less capital spending in 1999 and took moves to conserve cash, reduce operating and overhead costs, and consider the sale of certain assets. Hercules and Mallard were incorporated into the company as a division called Parker USA Drilling Company in early 1999, leaving only Quail Oil Tools and Partech as the company's subsidiaries.

Principal Subsidiaries

Parker Technology, L.L.C. (Partech); Quail Oil Tools, L.L.P.

Principal Divisions

Parker USA Drilling Company.

Further Reading

"Drilling Program Set in Russia's Far East," *Oil & Gas Journal,* July 3, 1995, p. 27.

Horovitz, Bruce, "Here Comes National Energy Plan II," *Industry Week,* May 4, 1981, p. 17.

—Carrie Rothburd

Penn Engineering & Manufacturing Corp.

P.O. Box 1000
Danboro, Pennsylvania 18916
U.S.A.
(215) 766-8853
Fax: (215) 766-7366
Web site: http://www.pemnet.com

Public Company
Incorporated: 1942
Employees: 1,368
Sales: $179.7 million (1998)
Stock Exchanges: New York
Ticker Symbol: PNN
NAIC: 332722 Bolt, Nut, Screw, Rivet, & Washer
    Manufacturing; 333513 Machine Tool Manufacturing;
    335312 Motor & Generator Manufacturing

When Penn Engineering & Manufacturing Corp. celebrated its 50th anniversary in 1992, it was on the way to becoming the leading manufacturer of self-clinching fasteners used by the computer, data communications, telecommunications, general electronics, automotive, and avionics industries. Between 1991 and 1995 the company's shipments of fasteners doubled to more than 1.8 billion annually. The company's growth continued during the second half of the decade, and in 1998 it was named to *Forbes* magazine's list of the ''200 Best Small Companies.'' Its second line of business is the manufacture of small high-performance DC (direct current) motors used in lightweight precision applications.

Company Founded in 1942

In 1942 K.A. Swanstrom, formerly president of Elastic Stop Nut Corporation, left the company and founded Penn Engineering & Manufacturing Corp. Penn began operations on Christmas Eve, 1942, in the rented corner of an old stocking mill located in a small Pennsylvania town. The next year Swanstrom obtained a license from RCA for a new type of clinch nut, which was a screw machined from square stock. RCA needed a new type of fastener when it switched from using thick cast metal sections to thin sheet metal for its military electronics enclosures. RCA held the patent, but Swanstrom was able to improve upon the original design and create Penn's first product, the original S-nut, which was screw machined from round stock. Later that year Penn developed a cold-headed clinch nut, known as the CL-type.

Swanstrom's self-clinching design was simple and solved RCA's need for reliable threads in thin sheet metal. As the fastener is pressed into a punched hole, the sheet material actually moves or ''cold flows'' into an undercut below the fastener head, locking the device securely into the sheet. The fastener provides a reliable threaded insert allowing other components to be assembled and disassembled with the thin sheet metal.

Penn built its business on self-clinching fasteners. These small devices allowed sheet metal fabricators to easily and cost-effectively provide strong threads in thin sheet metal. Self-clinching fasteners become an integral part of the material in which they were installed. Like other small manufacturers in the 1940s, Penn was creating a new technology that would lead to the future world of automation and electronics. Over the next 60 years its fasteners would be used in personal computers, computer cabinetry, power supplies, instrumentation, telecommunications equipment, and certain automobile parts such as air bags and windshield wipers.

Going Public: 1950s–60s

In 1952 the company purchased 15 acres in Danboro, Pennsylvania, for the construction of a 10,800-square-foot manufacturing plant. In 1956 the company officially registered its PEM and Triangle trademarks, which had been in use since 1946.

In 1966 Penn became a publicly traded company, first listing its stock on the over-the-counter market and then gaining admission to the American Stock Exchange. The Swanstrom family owned or controlled more than 50 percent of the company's stock, however, giving it effective control of the firm. In 1967 the Pemserter Series 1 press was introduced. The company's presses provided for rapid and accurate installation of fasteners.

Company Perspectives:

Invention is rooted in Penn Engineering's heritage. The original S-nut was the first self-clinching fastener that Penn Engineering produced when K.A. Swanstrom founded the company in a rented garage in 1942. Over the years, new product development and R&D efforts enabled the company to expand its product offerings from this single product to a product catalog of 28 fastener families and over 12,000 different line items. Today Penn Engineering ships over two billion fasteners to manufacturing companies worldwide— and the original S-nut still accounts for over 25 percent of that volume. All of which proves that "Today's Innovations are Tomorrow's Solutions."

Over the years the company would introduce new models of manual and automated presses for fastener installation to provide its customers with complete fastening systems.

Diversification and Expansion in the 1970s

Penn diversified by acquiring Pittman Company, based in Sellersville, Pennsylvania, in 1970 for $262,500. Pittman manufactured miniature DC (direct current) motors. As the motor division grew, its high-quality, high-performance, permanent magnet DC motors would be used in lightweight precision applications such as archival storage, printing, copying, robotics, and medical diagnostic equipment. The Pittman division made a broad range of products that were typically adapted to the specific requirements of individual customers.

The Danboro facility was expanded in the early 1970s, and the company established PEM International Ltd. as a subsidiary in Doncaster, England, to serve as a U.K. distributor.

In 1976 the Pittman motor operation moved to a new 30,000-square-foot facility located in Harleysville, Pennsylvania. Major expansions were completed in 1978 at plants located in Danboro, Harleysville, and Winston-Salem, North Carolina. In 1979 Ken Swanstrom, son of the founder, was named president of the company.

Solid Performance Continued As Manufacturing Capacity Increased in the 1980s

In 1980 the Pemserter Series III press was introduced, and the company manufactured its six billionth PEM fastener. In 1981 the Winston-Salem plant was expanded by 8,000 square feet, and a 45,000-square-foot manufacturing facility called Plant 2 was completed in Danboro. Four years later 40,000 square feet of space was added to Plant 2 and 23,000 square feet was added to the Winston-Salem facility.

In 1983 Pittman introduced the first line of brushless motors. Penn's engineering department acquired CAD (computer-assisted design) equipment, and Penn introduced the microprocessor-controlled Pemserter Series 100 press and the manual Series 4 press. In 1986 Penn paid $3.5 million in cash for Standard Insert Co., which became a division of the company in 1991.

Company sales for 1989 were about $66 million. Fasteners accounted for $48 million, and $18 million came from Pittman motors and controls. Net income was $6 million, a 60 percent increase over the previous year. International sales accounted for about 17 percent of revenue.

Manufacturing Capacity Increased to Meet Growing Demand in the 1990s

In 1990 Penn established its own export department to handle the world marketing of PEM fasteners. PEM International Ltd. became the company's master distributor for Europe. During the 1990s Penn's international distributor network would grow to include some 40 authorized distributors located in 30 countries, which were supplied from warehouses located in Doncaster, England, and in Singapore. The company's independent distributors carried their own inventories and sold other industrial components, but they could not sell fasteners that competed with Penn's.

Also in 1990, 16,000 square feet of space was added to the Pittman manufacturing facility in Harleysville and a new plant in Suffolk, Virginia, came on line. The Suffolk plant added 25,000 square feet of manufacturing space and was built at a cost of $3.5 million.

The company's new manufacturing resource planning system (MRP II) became operational in 1990. It linked the company's manufacturing operations to provide better coordination among its three facilities in Danboro, Winston-Salem, and Suffolk.

In 1992 the company celebrated its 50th anniversary, and the next year founder K.A. Swanstrom died. During the year a 25,000-square-foot addition to the Suffolk plant and a 6,300-square-foot addition to the Danboro plant were completed.

In 1995 the Pemserter Systems Division introduced the Series 2000 press and Pemserter Plus automatic feed module. Autospec product capabilities were introduced to meet the fastening needs of the worldwide automotive industry. For 1995 Penn reported net income of $13.8 million on net sales of $141.3 million.

Between 1991 and 1995 the company's fastener shipments doubled, from 896 million units to 1.8 billion units annually. Demand for the company's fasteners had increased faster than its manufacturing capacity, and in 1996 the Winston-Salem plant was replaced by a new 120,000-square-foot manufacturing facility there. With a 43,000-square-foot addition to the Danboro plant, Penn had 375,000 to 400,000 total square feet of manufacturing floor space in its facilities. During the year the company's stock was listed on the New York Stock Exchange. The Swanstrom family continued to hold about 52 percent of the firm's voting stock and remained in control of the company. Sales increased to $160.3 million, while net income remained relatively flat at $13.9 million. That year the fastener and motor divisions were awarded ISO 9001 certification.

Also in 1996 the company created a new, wholly owned subsidiary, PEM International Singapore Pte. Ltd., after acquiring the assets and inventory of a former authorized distributor for $2.9 million. This location would serve as a distribution center for the Pacific Rim and adjacent regions.

In 1997 Penn introduced R'Angle fasteners, which allowed panels to be clinched at right angles. For the year net income rose to $14.5 million and sales were $167.7 million. In 1998 the company introduced threaded steel R'Angle fasteners. A new LightStream infrared safety system was introduced for the Series 2000 press. Martin Bidart replaced Ken Swanstrom as president and chief operating officer, with Swanstrom remaining as chairman and CEO.

Penn was named to *Forbes* magazine's 1998 list of the "200 Best Small Companies." Companies were ranked based on growth and profitability. Penn had a five-year average annual sales growth of 14 percent and a five-year average annual growth in earnings per share of 13 percent. It was ranked 200th on the list. For 1998 Penn reported record net sales of $179.7 million and net income of $16.6 million. The fastener division accounted for $146.9 million of sales, or 82 percent, and the Pittman motor division accounted for 18 percent of sales with $32.8 million.

As a recognized leader in fastening solutions, Penn was in a strong position to continue setting record levels of sales and net income. It had good working relationships with original equipment manufacturers (OEMs) and their subcontractors, working with them early in the design process to provide fastener solutions. Moreover, it had supplied companies such as IBM, Hewlett-Packard, Pitney Bowes, and Xerox for more than 25 years.

Finally, it possessed a stable, experienced senior management team, and family control of the majority of the company's voting stock would protect it from hostile takeover attempts.

Principal Subsidiaries

PEM International Ltd. (U.K.); PEM International (Singapore) Pte. Ltd.; PEM Management, Inc.; PEM Investments, Inc.; PEM World Sales, Inc.

Further Reading

Colucci, Deana, "Basic Philosophy Yields Success with Basic Parts," *Design News,* June 23, 1997, p. 108.

"Fasteners Aim at Uninterrupted Laptop Performance," *Design News,* January 20, 1997, p. 45.

Harvey, Robert E., "Penn Opens Up $3.5M Fastener Factory in Va., Linking Operations with MRP II System," *Metalworking News,* August 14, 1989, p. 5.

Ozanian, Michael K., and Kurt Badenhausen, "Survival of the Fittest," *Forbes,* November 2, 1998.

Penn Engineering & Manufacturing Corp., New York: PaineWebber Inc., 1996.

"Penn Engineering & Manufacturing Corp.," *Philadelphia Business Journal,* October 3, 1988, p. 15.

"Penn Engineering Announces Sales and Earnings for Fourth Quarter 1998 and Declares Quarterly Cash Dividend," Danboro, Pa.: Penn Engineering & Manufacturing Corp., January 27, 1999.

Remich, Norman C., Jr., "Survival Kit for a Rugged Computer," *Appliance Manufacturer,* June 1997, p. 72.

—David Bianco

Phelps Dodge Corporation

2600 North Central Avenue
Phoenix, Arizona 85004
U.S.A.
(602) 234-8100
Fax: (602) 234-8337
Web site: http://www.phelpsdodge.com

Public Company
Incorporated: 1885 as Copper Queen Consolidated
    Mining Company
Employees: 13,924
Sales: $3.06 billion (1998)
Stock Exchanges: New York
Ticker Symbol: PD
NAIC: 212234 Copper Ore & Nickel Ore Mining;
    331411 Primary Smelting & Refining of Copper

One of the largest copper miners in the world, Phelps Dodge Corporation produces 30 percent of the copper in the United States and operates several manufacturing businesses to insulate the company from the cyclicality of copper prices. Phelps Dodge's copper business is conducted through the company's Phelps Dodge Mining Company subsidiary, which also produces silver, gold, and other minerals as a byproduct of its copper operations. The manufacturing side of the company's business operates through a division called Phelps Dodge Industries, which has expanded aggressively during the 1990s. The manufacturing businesses include a ten percent interest in Accuride Corporation, a truck wheel and rim manufacturer; Columbian Chemicals Company, one of the world's largest producers of carbon black (used in inks and tires); Phelps Dodge Magnet Wire Co., the world's largest producer of magnet wire; and Phelps Dodge High Performance Conductors, which manufactures specialty conductors used by the automotive, computer, and aerospace industries.

19th-Century Origins

In 1834 founder Anson Phelps, a New York entrepreneur thoroughly experienced in the import-export trade and well-

connected in his targeted British market, formed Phelps, Dodge & Co. Along with his junior partners, sons-in-law William Dodge and Daniel James, Phelps supplied his English customers with cotton, replacing it on the homeward journey with tin, tin plate, iron, and copper, for sale to government, trade, and individual consumers in the United States. Before long, Phelps started a manufacturing company in Connecticut called the Ansonia Brass and Battery Company, and in 1845 he helped organize the Ansonia Manufacturing Company, which produced kettles, lamps, rivets, buttons, and other metal items.

Phelps steered his fledgling empire grimly through a seven-year panic that began during 1837. His reward came during the following 14 years of national prosperity, when large numbers of his products went west with new settlers, accompanied travelers on the rapidly expanding railroads, and provided a modicum of comfort for miners at the recently discovered Sierra Nevada gold deposits in California. Even broader markets came from such inventions as the McCormick reaper and the electric telegraph, whose need for cable wire would swell Phelps Dodge coffers well into the next century. By 1849 the company was capitalized at almost $1 million, and its profits were almost 30 percent.

Phelps's death in 1853 gave his son and each of his two sons-in-law a 25 percent interest in the business, with 15 percent going to a younger son-in-law. This second partnership was scarcely five years old when Anson Phelps, Jr., died. On January 1, 1859, the partnership was revised again, to increase the firm's capitalization to $1.5 million and to give William Dodge and Daniel James each a 28 percent share. With reorganization complete, the company turned its attention to developing industries like mining.

An interest in timber had begun in the mid-1830s, when Phelps, Dodge accepted timberlands in Pennsylvania in lieu of payment for a debt. Later it built the world's largest lumber mill there, establishing a timber agency in Baltimore, Maryland, to send its products to domestic and foreign customers.

Despite these diversifications, the principal interests of the company were still mercantile; however, through the advice of James Douglas, a mining engineer and chemical geologist, Phelps, Dodge was persuaded to take a large block of stock in the Morenci copper mine in what was then the Arizona Territory. Morenci was owned by the Detroit Copper Company, which exchanged the stock for a $30,000 loan. Douglas was also enthusiastic about prospects for another claim called Atlanta, situated in Arizona's Bisbee district, about 200 miles southwest of Morenci. In 1881 the company bought the Atlanta claim for $40,000.

Two years later Phelps, Dodge had a chance to purchase the adjoining Copper Queen mine, which was then producing about 300 tons of ore monthly. The partnership decided to buy Copper Queen when Douglas hit the main Atlanta lode in 1884, at almost the same time that a Copper Queen tunnel penetrated the lode from a different spot. Arizona mining operations at the time stuck strictly to the "rule of the apex," according to which a claim owner could follow a vein of ore onto another claim, if the deposit had come closest to the surface on his land. This had occurred with Copper Queen, and Phelps, Dodge, rather than risk losing this strike to the Copper Queen owners, purchased the Copper Queen mine, merging it with the Atlanta claim.

In August 1885 Phelps, Dodge & Co. decided to streamline its operations by incorporating the subsidiary Copper Queen Consolidated Mining Company in New York, with James Douglas as president. Cautiously, Douglas made no major acquisitions for ten years. Then, he bought the Moctezuma Copper Company in Sonora, Mexico, from the Guggenheim family. Two years later he purchased the Detroit Copper Company.

20th Century: A Focus on Copper

A large increase in domestic iron production during the 1890s plus a two cents tariff on each pound of imported tin plate instituted in 1890 combined to make profitable metal markets hard to find. These factors and the fast growth of the company's mining interests forced it to withdraw from most ventures other than copper mining and selling by 1906.

Phelps, Dodge still retained its Ansonia Brass and Copper Company, however, which had become one of the largest U.S. manufacturers of copper wire for the new telephone industry. Other products included brass wire, sheet copper, and rolled brass.

The shift to mining interests led to a need for another reorganization. In 1908 the old Phelps, Dodge & Co. partnership was dissolved, to be replaced by a corporation called Phelps, Dodge & Co., Inc. Capitalized at $50 million, the new concern consolidated all the various Phelps, Dodge mining interests—Copper Queen Consolidated Mining Company; Moctezuma Copper Company; Detroit Copper Mining Company; and Stag Cañon Fuel Company, a subsidiary consisting of coal and timber properties near Dawson, New Mexico, purchased in 1905 to supply the mines and smelters with fuel.

By now there were 10,000 employees working in the mines, the smelters, the company railroads, and other ventures. There was also competition from other mining companies, which were able to mine copper, but lacked smelting facilities for processing. To provide these competitors with more efficient service while handling the smelting for its own copper mines, Phelps, Dodge abandoned its old Bisbee smelter and erected a new one some 23 miles away.

Following the 1917 entry of the United States into World War I, demand for copper for munitions and communications exploded. The company smelters turned out 600 to 700 tons daily. Also in 1917, Phelps, Dodge & Co., Inc. transferred its assets and subsidiaries to Copper Queen Consolidated Mining Company. Copper Queen became the operating company and changed its name to Phelps Dodge Corporation.

With all enterprises operating at capacity, the Bisbee miners went on strike in July 1917. One factor was the powerlessness of mine managers to make policy decisions on behalf of top management in New York. Another was the shrinking supply of experienced workers, who were going into the military or being lured away by higher salaries and better working conditions.

The International Workers of the World (Wobblies) easily caught the attention of the miners working for Phelps Dodge. At issue were better working conditions, a wage increase to $6 per day, and abolition of the unpopular physical examination to which all applicants were subjected before obtaining a job. Many suspected the exam was a filter to exclude prospective miners with unpopular political affiliations.

When the strike was two weeks old, Phelps Dodge director Walter Douglas instructed an employee of the El Paso & Southwestern Railroad to transport about 1,200 strikers to Columbus, New Mexico, where they were to be turned loose. After the commander of a nearby army camp refused permission to unload the cars, the workers were released in a small Mexican town called Hermanas, where they lived at starvation level until two carloads of food arrived from the U.S. Army base at nearby El Paso, Texas. Though 25 participants in the Bisbee deportation were indicted, no particular blame was attached to any individual and the matter petered out.

The end of World War I brought a need for downscaling of all operations. Government warehouses were packed with more than 800 million pounds of copper, and more was coming in from Chilean mines at low cost. To counter these new challenges, Phelps Dodge and other large U.S. copper mining companies cut production and formed the Copper and Brass Research Association to seek out and promote new uses for copper. At the same time, the companies founded the Copper Export Association, pooling 400 pounds of copper for exclusive sale in foreign markets.

Suffering acutely from the postwar slump in demand was the Arizona Copper Company, with holdings adjoining the Phelps Dodge Morenci properties. Part of this company's assets was a huge deposit of low-grade ore that it could not afford to develop. Phelps Dodge bought Arizona Copper and merged it with its Morenci holdings in 1921, in exchange for 50,000 shares of capital stock.

By 1925 business expansion was demanding record amounts of copper. In that year almost 1.75 billion pounds of refined copper were produced all over the country. Arizona's contribution to this total was more than 800 million pounds, a quarter of which came from Phelps Dodge mines. The stock market crash in 1929 brought the bonanza to an end, however. Demand for copper dwindled everywhere, the price falling to 18 cents per pound from a high of 23 cents. Effects of the crash were felt immediately. Sales, $46.1 million in 1928, were down to

$38.7 million in 1929, though net earnings were $4 million, up from $2.6 million the year before.

In April 1930 Walter Douglas resigned as chief executive of Phelps Dodge. In his stead came Louis S. Cates. Cates's first priority was to integrate the Phelps Dodge operations and to cut costs and allow for the Arizona tax of two cents on every pound of copper processed. Cates then, also in 1930, acquired the Nichols Copper Company, which had an electrolytic refinery on Long Island, New York.

In another important 1930 acquisition, Phelps Dodge bought National Electric Products Corporation, a large manufacturer of copper products for electrical and building purposes, with an annual capacity of more than 200,000 pounds of fabricated copper products and 150,000 pounds of steel. National Electric brought the company eight plants and a major interest in the Habirshaw Cable and Wire Corporation.

Cates reorganized all subsidiaries into two efficient organizations. The first, the National Electric Products Corporation, consisted only of the National Metal Molding division. This division's main interest was steel products, and it eventually reverted to its original owners by an exchange of stock. The second division was headed by a new subsidiary called the Phelps Dodge Copper Corporation. This division was charged with operating all the fabricating divisions including Habirshaw Cable and Wire.

Cates's next challenge was the long-operative Copper Queen mine, whose high-grade ore was becoming inaccessible and too expensive to mine. Phelps Dodge acquired the Calumet & Arizona Mining Company, a longstanding rival with Bisbee acreage adjoining Copper Queen. Overriding the objections of Calumet president Gordon Campbell, who resigned in April 1931, the purchase became final in September, giving Phelps Dodge title to a low-cost New Cornelia mine 150 miles away at Ajo, Arizona. Phelps Dodge consolidated the Calumet & Arizona and Copper Queen operations to reap economies of scale.

The Depression continued, however; the end of 1932 showed sales of just under $22 million, as opposed to $50.3 million in 1931. In an effort to pare costs and keep pace with lower demand, Cates cut production at the Copper Queen. He also suspended all operations at New Cornelia, and closed both the Stag Canyon coal operations and Morenci.

Nevertheless, Phelps Dodge bought the United Verde Copper Company despite a steep price of $20.8 million. With about 6,100 acres of claims in Arizona, United Verde proved its worth in 1937, when reserves of 6.9 millions tons of ore were produced. In 1937 the company went ahead with long-held plans to expand operations at Morenci, where a clay ore-body was prepared for open-pit copper mining, refining, and smelting, at a cost of $32.6 million.

By 1939 the Depression years were part of the company's history. Sales reached $75.5 million, yielding total income of $15.5 million, and the number of employees, recorded in mid-1938, reached about 9,000.

World War II once again found plants operating at maximum capacity. Stepping in for employees on military service,

women and Navajo Indians ran the Morenci mine, smelting facilities, and refining plant. Typical of pay rates was the wage for rock-shoveling—64 cents per hour.

Once again operating at full capacity, Phelps Dodge supplied condenser tubes for the navy and cables for communications and electric power. Other orders were harder to fill—notably a specialized lead pipe in 50-mile lengths, which was laid under the English Channel to supply Britain's troops with gasoline for the Normandy invasion.

Already looking towards the war's end in 1944, the company began to build the Horseshoe Dam on the Verde River, about 55 miles northeast of Phoenix, Arizona, to allow for water conservation while filling the needs of its Morenci operations. Year-end 1944 sales figures of $168.1 million more than doubled the $80 million figure for 1940.

Post-World War II Expansion

By 1950 Phelps Dodge was the second largest domestic copper producer, contributing 30 percent of the country's output. It was also one of the world's top three, its position as a purely domestic supplier made even more secure by a two cents per pound import duty. Characteristic of the 1950s was government activism in the industry, partly as a result of the Korean War. At the end of 1950, the government instituted price controls for copper, placing a cap of 24.5 cents per pound. Other moves came as a result of a 1947 Federal Trade Commission study, emphasizing the surprisingly low level of competition in the industry, and intimating the power was concentrated in the hands of too few groups.

Though not specified by the report, there was also a feeling that copper resources could be exhausted, because copper companies were doing little to find additional reserves, and that this situation should be remedied. Negotiations between the government and the mining companies followed. Over the next two years, the country's copper-mining capabilities increased by 25 percent, thanks to seven new mines.

Phelps Dodge's contribution to this effort was the Lavender Pit mine, opened in 1954 to develop an extension of the Bisbee operations known as the Bisbee East orebody. As was the case with most of the companies, terms of the agreement were that the open-pit mine should be developed and equipped with a smelter at a cost of $25 million, entirely corporate-sponsored. In return, the company asked for a guarantee that the government would buy its copper at protected prices. By 1956 Lavender Pit produced 80.3 million pounds of copper.

Another important development was the Peruvian Project, a joint venture between Phelps Dodge and three other mining companies intended to provide ownership of three southern Peru mines, together containing an estimated one billion tons of low-grade ore. Phelps Dodge's 16 percent share of the costs was $24.3 million. The peak sales year of the 1950s was 1956, when sales reached $540.3 million, yielding a total income of $153.9 million.

At the end of the 1950s, the company spread its wings beyond its Canadian subsidiaries, venturing into several developing countries. A 51 percent interest in a 1957 enterprise called the

Phelps Dodge Copper Products Corporation of the Philippines gave it a new source of insulated wire and cable for electrical use. Another venture blossomed in 1960, when the United States Underseas Cable Corporation was established jointly with several U.S. companies and a West German company. There was also a San Salvador affiliation called the Phelps Dodge Products de Centro America S.A., which manufactured electrical wire and cables for the Central American market.

Despite these overseas connections, however, Phelps Dodge kept its main activities in the United States. This policy protected its copper from politically inspired import tariffs, as well as from taxation, strike activity, and fluctuating prices found in foreign bases like Chile. By the end of 1963, this policy yielded $327 million in sales, from annual production reaching 261,400 tons.

Another advantage of domestic concentration was vertical integration. Now one of the country's three largest copper producers, Phelps Dodge through its fabricating subsidiaries provided outlets for its copper. This hedge against price swings also gave it immunity against purchasing at high prices to make sure that fabricating subsidiaries had an adequate copper supply.

By 1965 the price of copper rose from 34 cents to 36 cents per pound. Plastics, lead, aluminum, and zinc had advanced far enough to threaten long-term copper markets. Phelps Dodge president Robert Page felt it desirable to keep copper prices moderate enough to maintain demand for the metal.

Still, the new opportunities aluminum offered could not be ignored. In 1963 the company formed the Phelps Dodge Aluminum Products Corporation, offering aluminum wire and cable to complement the copper line. Though the aluminum enterprise produced 17 fabrication plants by 1970, the company foresaw little long-term profit in it, and therefore merged its company with the Consolidated Aluminum Corporation in 1971.

In July 1967 an industrywide strike began that lasted until the end of March 1968. The Phelps Dodge operations most affected were the Morenci, Ajo, and Bisbee mines, as well as the El Paso refinery. Run by a coalition of 14 unions led by the United Steelworkers of America, the strike called for company-wide bargaining for all operations, regardless of competitive and geographic differences. Eventually, an average increase of $1.13 per hour in wages and benefits sent workers back to their jobs after the administration of U.S. President Lyndon B. Johnson intervened. Post-strike operations recommenced without raw-copper shortages, since most refiners were able to reuse scrap copper to augment their reserves.

Company chairman Robert Page handed the helm to George Munroe in 1969. Still holding the presidency—the office of chairman was abolished—Munroe oversaw the establishment of a new mine at Tyrone, New Mexico. Formerly known as Burro Mountain, this was a low-grade ore deposit that previously had been too expensive to work. New technology made the mine economically feasible, boosting total capacity by 20 percent annually. The expansion brought its reward; the decade ended with sales of $672.1 million.

In 1969 Phelps Dodge swapped 800,000 of its own shares for a 26 percent interest in Denver, Colorado-based Western Nuclear, Inc., a company concerned with uranium mining, mil-

ling, and exploration. Initially, an open-pit uranium mine and mill were erected near Spokane, Washington. Three years later, Western Nuclear became a wholly owned subsidiary, undergoing a $71 million expansion and modernization program to improve its production capacity at other facilities in Wyoming.

With the Clean Air Act of 1970, environmental concerns came to the fore. The most critical problem Phelps Dodge faced was at Douglas, Arizona, where its smelter regularly processed seven percent of the nation's annual copper production. By 1973 Arizona anti-pollution laws required $17 million worth of emission-control adaptations to this smelter, although the Environmental Protection Agency (EPA) was still undecided about its requirements. This left a strong possibility of conflict between state and federal regulations. Fears of a clash were dispelled when federal standards proved to be lower than those of Arizona; state regulators were still dissatisfied, despite the money spent on emission control equipment. Phelps Dodge officials protested, claiming that these expensive standards would force the company to shut the smelter down, putting almost 2,000 people out of work.

Because of sluggish demand and foreign competition, production cutbacks followed at a new mine called Metcalf, and at Morenci, Ajo, and Tyrone. The shift showed up in net income figures—$121.7 million for 1974, $46.3 million by the following year, and $17.9 million by 1977. The smelters kept operating 24 hours a day, however, to cope with the large amount of ore that had accumulated during the shutdown for the installation of pollution controls.

By 1978 there were voluble industry complaints that piecemeal EPA regulations made long-term antipollution planning impossible. The $2 billion initially spent plus frequent updating added about ten cents per pound to production costs, bringing the consumer's price for copper up to about 75 cents per pound.

Coupled with cheaper foreign competition and sluggish demand, this brought a business-cycle trough to the industry. Company executives blamed the crisis on the waning uranium market—Western Nuclear had lost its biggest customer, the Washington Public Power Supply System—the demand slump caused by the slowdowns in the automobile and housing industries, and environmental protection woes. Many outsiders felt it was time to expand Phelps Dodge interests beyond copper.

In the first quarter of 1982 the company revenues showed a $19.1 million deficit. In April Munroe laid off 3,800 workers and closed all four mines and three out of four smelters. He also instituted salary cuts at all levels, and reluctantly took on short-term debt to cover operating costs.

The following year the United Steelworkers instituted an industrywide strike. Kennecott Corporation, the country's top copper producer, settled quickly, exchanging a three-year wage freeze for a cost-of-living allowance reaching $1.87 per hour at six percent inflation. Using this settlement as a model, the strikers then approached Phelps Dodge management. The company counteroffered abolition of the cost-of-living allowance, a three-year wage freeze, and lower wages for new workers.

By the end of August 1983 the stalemate had led many workers to cross picket lines, despite sharp harassment from hard-line strikers. At Morenci, the company called in the National Guard, fomenting more resentment. The strike ended uneasily the following fall, with the company refusing to budge on its position, and the miners voting to decertify the 13 unions that had long been present at the mines and the smelters.

Now, management turned its attention to reorganization. First on the agenda was a strategy to reduce production costs to less than 65 cent per pound, and lessen dependence on copper. The economy drive began with the 1982 move of company headquarters to Phoenix. At the same time, the Morenci, Ajo, and Douglas smelters were closed and replaced by a state-of-the-art, $92 million solvent extracting-electrowinning plant at Morenci that produced 100 million pounds of copper annually by mid-1987. Electrowinning is a process of recovering metals from a solution through electrolysis.

Electrowinning capacity grew further in 1986, when the company built a $55 million plant after buying a two-thirds interest in New Mexico-based Chino Mines Company from Kennecott. In the same year, the company sold a 15 percent interest in the Morenci mine for $75 million. Also sold was the uranium-mining business.

1980s and 1990s: Diversification into Manufacturing

The 1986 purchase of Columbian Chemicals Company for $240 million diversified Phelps Dodge interests to include the manufacture of carbon blacks, used to strengthen tires and to make toner for copiers. Also providing profitable diversification was Accuride Corporation, a manufacturer of steel wheels and rims for trucks and trailers, which merged with the company in 1988 at a cost of $273 million. That same year, all operations were divided into two new operating divisions, headed by the Phelps Dodge Mining Company and Phelps Dodge Industries.

By the end of 1989, the company had an income of $267 million, on sales of $2.7 billion. A year later, net income leaped to $454.9 million, on sales of $2.6 billion, partly with the help of a joint venture between Phelps Dodge and Sumitomo Electric Industries, to sell magnet wire in the United States.

Although Phelps Dodge continued to expand its copper activities during the 1990s—particularly overseas—an emphasis was placed on developing the manufacturing side of the company's business during the decade. The acquisitions of Accuride, Columbian Chemicals and Hudson International during the latter half of the 1980s were important forays into new fields, creating a foundation the company would build on during the 1990s as the manufacturing division, operated under the control of Phelps Dodge Industries, took shape. The largest segment of the company's manufacturing business was wire and cable production, governed by Phelps Dodge Magnet Wire Co., the largest magnet wire producer in the world. Expansion of this business was achieved through acquisition and expansion, beginning in 1992 with the purchase of three Venezuelan wire and cable manufacturers and the establishment of a wire and cable plant in Thailand. Two years later, two magnet wire production facilities were acquired, one in El Paso, Texas, and the other in Laurinburg, North Carolina, to serve regional demand not met by the company's Hopkinsville, Kentucky plant,

the largest magnet wire plant in the world. Capacity at the El Paso plant was doubled in 1996, followed by a commensurate increase in production at the Laurinburg facility in 1997.

The investment in the Phelps Dodge Industries division paid off handsomely in 1995, as the company's carbon black, truck wheel and rim, and wire and cable businesses each registered a record high in sales. For the year, record financial and production totals led to what Phelps Dodge's chairman, chief executive officer, and president, Douglas C. Yearley, described as "the best year in the 162-year history of our company." The progress achieved within the Phelps Dodge Industries division played an important part in engendering the banner year, but the company could not claim such a victory without realizing significant gains in its copper business, upon which it was heavily dependent. The average price of copper in 1995 surged to $1.35 per pound, 28 cents higher than the previous year, and Phelps Dodge reaped the benefits, registering record production totals at its Morenci, Candelaria, Chino, and Hidalgo mining facilities. On the heels of this resounding success, the company planned to focus its exploration efforts in South America, Africa, and the Far East, intending to increase its annual copper production total to two billion pounds during the ensuing five years.

In 1996, Phelps Dodge's manufacturing businesses continued to perform admirably, with the exception of Accuride Corporation, which suffered from weak demand for heavy wheels. Phelps Dodge's wire and cable business rallied forward, its progress highlighted by the company's first entry into the People's Republic of China through a joint venture called Phelps Dodge Yantai Cable Company that allowed Phelps Dodge to acquire, expand, and operate the power cable manufacturing facility in Yantai in the Shandong province. As this historic project began, the company initiated a three-year expansion program aimed at increasing Columbian Chemical's carbon black production capacity by 25 percent. Another notable development during the year was the acquisition of Nesor Alloy Corporation, which was combined with Hudson International Conductors to form Phelps Dodge High Performance Conductors, organized as the newest addition to the Phelps Dodge Industries division.

The late 1990s saw copper prices sag from 1995's level, but the company recorded meaningful progress in its manufacturing operations, helping to offset troubling developments in its mining activities. An uncertain regulatory environment concerning mining and exploration prompted Phelps Dodge to close its U.S. exploration offices. Falling copper prices forced the company to close a mine in Chile and another mine acquired in a $105 million hostile takeover of Cobre Mining Co. in 1998. Along with these closures, Phelps Dodge also sold 90 percent of Accuride to Kohlberg Kravis Roberts in 1998, gaining $480 million from the sale. On the positive side, Phelps Dodge opened a new wire magnet plant in Monterrey, Mexico, in 1998 and agreed to purchase the carbon black assets belonging to Brazil—based Copebras for $220 million. With these developments behind it, Phelps Dodge prepared for the 21st century, a company wed to its 18th-century roots in copper and consistently striving to expand its more modern aspect in manufacturing.

Principal Subsidiaries

Phelps Dodge Industries, Inc.; Accuride Corp. (10%); Columbian Chemicals Co.; Phelps Dodge High Performance Conductors; Phelps Dodge International Corp.; Phelps Dodge Magnet Wire Co.; Phelps Dodge Mining Company; Chino Mines Co. (67%); Compania Contractual Minera Candelaria (Chile) (80%); Compania Contractual Minera Ojos del Salado (Chile); Phelps Dodge Copper Products Co.; Phelps Dodge Exploration Corp.; Phelps Dodge Hidalgo, Inc.; Phelps Dodge Mining (Pty.) Ltd. (South Africa); Phelps Dodge Morenci, Inc. (85%); Phelps Dodge Refining Corp.; Phelps Dodge Tyrone, Inc.

Principal Divisions

Phelps Dodge Mining; Phelps Dodge Industries.

Further Reading

Cleland, Robert Glass, *A History of Phelps Dodge: 1834–1950,* New York: Alfred A. Knopf, 1952.

Durham, G. Robert, *Phelps Dodge Corporation: "Proud of Its Past, Prepared for the Future,"* New York: The Newcomen Society of the United States, 1989.

Navin, Thomas R., *Copper Mining & Management,* Tucson: University of Arizona Press, 1978.

"Presbyterian Copper," *Fortune,* July 1932.

—Gillian Wolf
—updated by Jeffrey L. Covell

Pioneer

Pioneer Electronic Corporation

4-1, Meguro 1-chome
Meguro-ku
Tokyo 153-8654
Japan
(03) 3494-1111
Fax: (03) 3495-4428
Web site: http://www.pioneer.co.jp

Public Company
Incorporated: 1947 as Fukuin Electric Works, Ltd.
Employees: 20,470
Sales: ¥559.84 billion (US$4.24 billion) (1998)
Stock Exchanges: Tokyo Osaka Amsterdam New York
Ticker Symbol: PIO
NAIC: 33431 Audio & Video Equipment Manufacturing;
334612 Prerecorded Compact Disc (Except Software),
Tape, & Record Producing; 33421 Telephone
Apparatus Manufacturing; 33422 Radio & Television
Broadcasting & Wireless Communications; 334613
Magnetic & Optical Recording Media Manufacturing;
334119 Other Computer Peripheral Equipment
Manufacturing; 334511 Search, Detection, Navigation,
Guidance, Aeronautical, and Nautical System &
Instrument Manufacturing; 512212 Motion Picture &
Video Distribution

Pioneer Electronic Corporation is one of the leading electronics firms in the world. The company divides its operations into several product groups, with the largest being car electronics, generating nearly 45 percent of net sales. Included in this grouping are Pioneer's car stereos, car CD players, car speakers, and car navigation systems. Pioneer's second largest product group, and the company's original arena, is that of home audio, which generates 20.5 percent of overall sales. Among the home audio products are stereo systems, receivers, CD players, cassette tape decks, and speaker systems. In the video product group, responsible for 13.4 percent of sales, are digital versatile disc (DVD) players, laser disc players, karaoke systems, and plasma displays, color screens that feature high picture quality and thin profiles. The ''other electronics'' group generates 14.5 percent of net sales and includes equipment for cable TV systems; multifunction, cordless, and cellular telephones; and digital direct-broadcast satellite decoders. Finally, accounting for about seven percent of net sales is the audio/video software group, which sells movies and animation, karaoke and game software, music, and car navigation software in the DVD, laser disc, videocassette, CD, CD-ROM, and other formats. Nearly two-thirds of Pioneer's overall net sales are generated overseas.

1930s Origins

Pioneer is largely a creation of the Matsumoto family. Nozomu Matsumoto was born in Kobe in 1906, the son of a Christian missionary. He inherited his parents' religious faith, which may have played a role in his early desire to bring ''technological innovation based on deep emotions'' to the Japanese people. Specifically, when Matsumoto heard a new, Western-built phonograph speaker in 1932, he was so struck by its superior tone that he immediately resolved to make such products available in Japan.

In 1936 Matsumoto founded a tiny company called Fukuin Shokai Denki Seisakusho, or Gospel Electric Works. From a workshop in Osaka, Matsumoto and a colleague struggled to devise a ''dynamic'' speaker like the Philco model Matsumoto had listened to, and after a year of experimentation the A-8 was brought to market in 1937. In recognition of its groundbreaking role Matsumoto christened the speaker Pioneer, and graced it with the corporate logo that was used for decades: the Greek letter omega—symbol of electrical resistance—and a tuning fork.

Matsumoto soon grew dissatisfied with his Osaka location, and in 1938 moved the company to Tokyo. In a factory above which his growing family lived, Matsumoto built and repaired radios and speakers and began to build a modest reputation as a reliable local craftsman. The founder's sons, Seiya and Kanya Matsumoto, helped run the production lines while their father was out making deliveries and sales. Matsumoto's wife Chiyo served as company chef, maintenance staff, and accountant. Before

Matsumoto's sons were old enough to take a hand in running the company, war swept over Japan. The Matsumoto family survived intact, as did Nozomu Matsumoto's commitment to bringing audio enjoyment to the Japanese. In 1947, as the national economy slowly regrouped under Allied supervision, Matsumoto incorporated Fukuin Electric and resumed his quest.

Soon after graduating from Chuo University with a business degree, Seiya Matsumoto joined his father's company as head of marketing and sales. Seiya Matsumoto was a natural salesman, remaining in charge of the company's sales division from that time until he was made president in 1982. His brother's talents were more mechanical, like his father's, and when Kanya Matsumoto was finally coaxed into joining the firm, he oversaw the technical and manufacturing aspects of the business.

Stereo Systems in the 1960s and 1970s

Fukuin made great strides in the postwar boom economy, with sales and profits climbing at a steady pace while the company continued to build its reputation as a maker of audio components, especially speakers. The Japanese electric industry as a whole enjoyed similar success, and by the mid-1950s Fukuin was selling a significant number of components to its bigger competitors. This was a profitable business but not likely to build the kind of mass brand-name recognition that would make the company a true audio giant. Achieving such recognition would require the production and effective marketing of complete stereo sets, and in the early 1960s Matsumoto and his sons set out to achieve that goal.

The company first changed its name, from Fukuin (Gospel) Electric to the nondenominational Pioneer. It next brought out, in 1962, the first stereo system with detachable speakers, a variation on the usual one-piece console design. This experiment, known as the PSC-5A, was extremely successful and became the stereo industry's standard format. Pioneer also committed itself to the production of full stereo component sets, hoping to share in the blossoming overseas trade with a full range of audio products.

Having thus raised the stakes by positioning Pioneer as a competitor with Japan's leading audio manufacturers, founder Matsumoto realized that his company would need executive experience on a scale greater than he or his sons could provide, and in 1963 Yozo Ishizuka was brought in from Toshiba as managing director. Ishizuka is generally credited with smoothing Pioneer's transition from family business to multinational concern, something that Nozomu Matsumoto made possible by his graceful withdrawal from the executive suite. Over a period of years Matsumoto gradually relinquished control, eventually

naming Ishizuka president in 1971, while he himself remained a rather distant chairman of the board.

In 1964 Pioneer brought out its S-71X modular stereo set, a runaway success that solidified acceptance of separable stereo equipment and put Pioneer on the audio map. The S-71X, introduced at a time when Japanese electronic goods were fast becoming the standard around the world, was instrumental in Pioneer's explosive growth in the 1960s. Under the careful guidance of Ishizuka, Pioneer expanded its range of products, opened the first of its overseas sales offices, and pared its debt burden to virtually nothing. Perhaps of greater significance was the company's decision to enter the nascent car stereo business. With Japan well on its way to becoming one of the world's leading automobile manufacturers, Pioneer was able to popularize the concept of quality stereo systems in even the most modestly priced cars. Car stereo quickly became an important part of Pioneer's overall sales and would remain so. In 1975 the company introduced the world's first component car stereo.

Early Development of the Laser Disc

Along with several other Japanese companies, Pioneer began research into the possibility of home video equipment as early as 1972. Within a few years, however, President Ishizuka and Chairman Matsumoto agreed that their company had fallen too far behind to continue competing in the development of video systems based on magnetic tape, and instead focused on the idea of optical discs that reproduced images by means of a laser beam. As the race for video technology continued, it became clear that Pioneer's technically superior disc equipment would succeed or fail in isolation; none of the competing companies followed Pioneer into laser disc manufacturing, choosing either tape or discs played with a needle similar to that used on a phonograph. Each year Pioneer's risk increased. If it was able to build a cheap, reliable laser disc machine the market would be won. However, it seemed more likely to most observers that the company was digging its own grave.

As befit its name, however, Pioneer persevered with its disc research, in 1978 announcing that it had perfected the first laser optical video-disc player and in 1981 introducing a similar machine for home use. Even if laser disc had immediately taken off, Pioneer would still have been years behind its chief rivals financially. Victor Company of Japan (JVC) had watched revenue from videocassette recorder sales climb from $36 million in 1976 to $1.4 billion in 1981, when Pioneer finally entered the market. As it turned out, disc sales did not take off at all. Pioneer's machine had several drawbacks. The laser disc player was far more expensive than its VCR counterpart; the discs themselves were to be sold, not rented, making them costly; and the discs could not be "rewritten," or recorded on at home.

Despite these formidable problems, Pioneer remained committed to the disc concept, making it its mission to "never let the LaserDisc be a failure," as stated in *The Spirit of Pioneer*. The company poured an enormous amount of money and effort into the disc program in the early 1980s, only to be greeted with a worldwide recession in audio sales compounded by the falling value of the U.S. dollar, in which Pioneer received a substantial percentage of its revenue. As a result, in 1982 the company lost money for the first time in its 44-year history.

In April 1982 President Ishizuka died suddenly, leaving Pioneer without direction at a critical juncture in its history. Since Nozomu Matsumoto felt that he was too advanced in years to reassume control, Seiya Matsumoto stepped in as the new president while Kanya Matsumoto became his second in command. The brothers faced a difficult situation. Given a lingering recession and consumers' continued indifference to disc technology, neither Pioneer's immediate prospects nor its long-term health was secure.

During the early 1980s the company added to its product line answering machines, dictating machines, cable TV equipment, and, in 1982, its successful first compact disc (CD) player. In 1983 Pioneer introduced a Laser-Karaoke device, which in effect allowed consumers to make their own home music videos; and in the following year, Pioneer began marketing the first CD players for automobiles. The combination of these innovations and Seiya Matsumoto's leadership was enough to restore Pioneer to profitability in 1983 and 1984, but 1985 ended in another deficit, emphasizing once again the critical role of laserdisc sales in the company's future. Pioneer had bet on laser, and after ten years of research, production, and marketing it had little to show for its daring.

During the late 1980s and early 1990s, however, the laserdisc market began to show improvement, as the cost of players decreased and a greater number of movies found their way onto disc format. The Pioneer CLD-100, introduced in 1989, was modestly priced and could play both video discs and CDs. Sales were up substantially, to almost 120,000 players in 1989. Pioneer remained committed as ever to the laser concept, spending $200 million in 1989 to buy DiscoVision Associates of California, a leading optical-disc research firm. The company also posted annual profits from 1986 through 1989.

The Transitional 1990s

An end to the Japanese economic boom in 1991 threw the country's economy into a lengthy downturn. Pioneer, like most Japanese electronics firms, was hurt by the difficult economic operating environment. The electronics firms also felt the effect of the high yen, which made Japanese exports more expensive overseas—as did high labor costs. In response, Pioneer and other firms shifted some of their production outside of Japan. Pioneer doubled the capacity of its audio equipment factory in the United Kingdom and set up a Mexican subsidiary to build car audio equipment for the North American market. In 1995 the company also established a subsidiary in Portugal to manufacture car audio equipment.

Still, in the mid-1990s Pioneer maintained two-thirds of its production in Japan, and despite its continued reputation for high-quality products, the high price tags of those products were increasingly being undercut by such rivals as Aiwa Co. Ltd. Thus, Pioneer was losing market share. The company ventured into the personal computer market in 1995 when it introduced the world's first Apple Macintosh clones. However, these high-priced machines quickly failed in the Japanese marketplace as consumers opted for cheap Windows-based PCs. These and other difficulties, including the continued failure of the laser disc to attract a mass audience, led Pioneer to post losses for the fiscal years of 1995 and 1996.

Soon after the end of the 1996 fiscal year, Seiya Matsumoto stepped aside as president, becoming company chairman, while Kaneo Ito, who had been in charge of the company's European sales network, became the new president. Pioneer soon embarked on a restructuring, aimed at reducing the workforce by nine percent, or about 650 jobs, and shifting more production to southeast Asia. Fortunately, Ito took over at a time when the company had already released or was developing some promising new products. Pioneer had introduced the world's first car navigation system into the Japanese market in 1990 and had a leading share of this rapidly growing sector in Japan. The company had also found success with its set-top boxes for cable and satellite TV. Moreover, in the development stages were high-picture-quality and thin-profile plasma displays for television and other applications.

In 1997 Pioneer introduced the PDP-501HD, the world's first high-definition 50-inch, wide-screen plasma display, aimed at the consumer market. Moreover, rather than stubbornly clinging to the fading laser disc technology, Pioneer joined with several other electronics manufacturers during this time in developing and marketing digital versatile disc (DVD) technology, which had the potential to supplant not only the laser disc but also the videocassette. Also, in mid-1996 the company established the Pioneer Music Group, Inc., a Franklin, Tennessee-based music label that was slated to specialize in rock, alternative, and Christian music.

Pioneer returned to profitability during the 1997 and 1998 fiscal years, in part because of the depreciation of the yen against the U.S. dollar. In 1997 Pioneer reorganized itself into three separate operating units: the Home Entertainment Company, which included both home audio and home video equipment; the Mobile Entertainment Company, which included car electronics and mobile communications equipment; and the Business Systems Company, which comprised business/industrial products. In May 1998 the Display Products Company was created as a fourth operating unit dedicated to business operations related to plasma and other types of displays. In August 1998 Pioneer announced a new strategy, called "Vision 2005," through which the company would focus on four key areas: DVD technology, display technology, digital home networks, and the development of new technologies. The company also set a goal of increasing revenues to ¥1.2 trillion (US$9 billion) by 2005. In conjunction with the Vision 2005 initiative, Pioneer introduced a new corporate logo in October 1998 that replaced the longstanding tuning fork logo. Thus began what might be dubbed the "post-laser-disc" era of Pioneer history.

Principal Subsidiaries

Tohoku Pioneer Electronic Corporation; Pioneer Video Corporation; Pioneer LDC, Inc.; Pioneer International Inc.; Shizuoka Pioneer Electronic Corporation; Pioneer North America, Inc. (U.S.A.); Pioneer Electronics (U.S.A.) Inc.; Pioneer New Media Technologies, Inc.; Pioneer Entertainment (U.S.A.) L.P.; Pioneer Electronics Technology, Inc. (U.S.A.); Pioneer Video Manufacturing Inc. (U.S.A.); Pioneer Industrial Components, Inc. (U.S.A.); Pioneer Electronics Service, Inc. (U.S.A.); Pioneer Electronics Capital Inc. (U.S.A.); Pioneer Speakers, Inc. (U.S.A.); Pioneer Music Group, Inc. (U.S.A.); Pioneer Digital Technologies, Inc. (U.S.A.); Pioneer Automotive Electronics

Sales, Inc. (U.S.A.); Pioneer International (Miami) Inc. (U.S.A.); Pioneer Electronics of Canada, Inc.; Pioneer Electronics de Mexico, S.A. de C.V.; Pioneer Manufacturing de Mexico, S.A. de C.V.; Pioneer Speakers, S.A. de C.V. (Mexico); Pioneer International Latin America, S.A. (Panama); Pioneer International Do Brazil, LTDA; Pioneer International Latin America, S.A. Agenda En Chile; Pioneer Electronics Eurocentre N.V. (Belgium); Pioneer Electronic (Europe) N.V. (Belgium); Pioneer Electronics Manufacturing N.V. (Belgium); Pioneer High Fidelity (G.B.) Ltd. (U.K.); Pioneer Electronics Technology (U.K.) Ltd.; Pioneer LDCE Ltd. (U.K.); Pioneer Electronics Deutschland GmbH (Germany); Pioneer France S.A.; Pioneer Electronics France S.A.; Pioneer Electronics (Italia) S.p.A. (Italy); Pioneer Electronics España S.A. (Spain); Pioneer Precision Technology S.A. (Spain); Pioneer Optical Disc Europe S.A. (Spain); Pioneer Electronics Benelux B.V. (Netherlands); Pioneer Electronics Denmark A/S; Pioneer Electronics Norge A/S (Norway); Pioneer Electronica Portugal Producao, S.A.; Pioneer Electronica A/O (Russia); Pioneer Electronic Poland Sp.zo.o; Pioneer Electronics Asiacentre Pte. Ltd. (Singapore); Pioneer Electronics (Singapore) Pte. Ltd.; Pioneer High Fidelity Taiwan Co., Ltd.; Pioneer Electronic (Taiwan) Corp.; Pioneer Technology (Malaysia) Sdn. Bhd.; Monetech Audio Sdn. Bhd. (Malaysia); Pioneer Electronics (Thailand) Co., Ltd.; Pioneer Manufacturing (Thailand) Co., Ltd.; Tohoku Pioneer (Thailand) Co., Ltd.; PT Monetech Audio (Indonesia); Pioneer Electronics (China) Ltd. (Hong Kong); Pioneer Electronics Technology (Hong Kong) Ltd.; Pioneer Electronics Trading (Shanghai) Ltd. (China); Pioneer Electronics Manufacturing (Shanghai) Co., Ltd. (China); Shanghai Pioneer Speakers Ltd. (China); Pioneer Electronics Australia Pty. Ltd.; Pioneer Gulf, Fze (United Arab Emirites).

Principal Operating Units

Home Entertainment Company; Mobile Entertainment Company; Business Systems Company; Display Products Company.

Further Reading

Flippo, Chet, "Pioneer Explores New Territory with PMG Label," *Billboard,* July 20, 1996, pp. 6+.

Hamilton, David P., "Pioneer Electronic, Hurt by Low-Cost Rivals, Pins Hopes on a New President, Restructuring," *Wall Street Journal,* May 21, 1996, p. C2.

Lewis, Jeff, "Pioneer's 'Vision 2005': $9B in Sales," *HFN,* August 31, 1998, p. 57.

McClure, Steve, "Five Japanese Companies Set to Launch DVD," *Billboard,* November 2, 1996, pp. 8+.

"Pioneer Cutting Work Force 16%," *Television Digest,* March 11, 1996, p. 15.

"Pioneer 'Early Retirement' Plan," *Television Digest,* August 26, 1996, p. 13.

"Pioneer Electronic: Still Committed to Videodiscs After a Wobbly Start," *Business Week,* January 24, 1983.

Schlesinger, Jacob M., "Pioneer Rethinks Quick Dismissal of 35 Managers," *Wall Street Journal,* February 2, 1993, p. A11.

The Spirit of Pioneer, Tokyo: Pioneer Electronic Corporation, 1989.

"To Encourage the Others," *Economist,* January 16, 1993, p. 66.

Weinberg, Neil, "A Pioneer That Lost Its Way," *Forbes,* October 21, 1996, pp. 174+.

—Jonathan Martin
—updated by David E. Salamie

◆Polaroid

Polaroid Corporation

549 Technology Square
Cambridge, Massachusetts 02139
U.S.A.
(781) 386-2000
Fax: (781) 386-3924
Web site: http://www.polaroid.com

Public Company
Incorporated: 1937
Employees: 10,011
Sales: $1.85 billion (1998)
Stock Exchanges: New York Pacific
Ticker Symbol: PRD
NAIC: 333315 Photographic & Photocopying Equipment
    Manufacturing; 333314 Optical Instrument & Lens
    Manufacturing; 339115 Ophthalmic Goods
    Manufacturing

Polaroid Corporation, founded on Edwin H. Land's belief that consumer markets should be created around inventions generated by scientific research, is a world leader in instant photography. The company manufactures and sells more than 50 types of film and more than 100 cameras and instant camera accessories. Instant photography products, since their 1948 debut, have consistently provided the bulk of Polaroid's income. Other operations, which the company announced in early 1999 that it may jettison, include sunglasses, graphic arts, glare-reducing polarizers, and holography.

Beginnings in Polarization Research

In 1926 Edwin Land's desire to create useful products based on scientific invention prompted him to pursue independent research on polarization rather than to return to Harvard after his freshman year. After creating a prototype synthetic polarizer in New York, Land returned to Harvard in 1929. A polarizing material selectively screens light waves. It could, for example, block waves of light that create glare while allowing other waves through. With the help of George Wheelwright III, a young Harvard physics instructor, Land obtained access to a laboratory and began producing small sheets of polarizing material. Land applied to patent this process in 1929, and a patent was granted in 1934. In June 1932, eager to explore the invention's practical applications, Land and Wheelwright abandoned their academic careers and founded Land-Wheelwright Laboratories, backed with Wheelwright's capital.

In 1933 the men incorporated their laboratory. Land-Wheelwright's staff—Land, Wheelwright, their wives, and a handful of other researchers—concentrated on developing polarizing material for no-glare car headlights and windshields. Enthusiasm for their work ran high, but commercial success eluded the Land-Wheelwright crew. Rebuffed by carmakers in Detroit, the company had no customers during the height of the Great Depression.

Photography giant Eastman Kodak provided the company's first financial break when it made a $10,000 order for photographic polarizing filters, later dubbed Polafilters. These plates, which consisted of a sheet of polarizing material sealed between two glass discs, increased contrast and decreased glare in photographs taken in bright light. Land-Wheelwright accepted the order and delivered the filters to Kodak. By this time, a friend, Professor Clarence Kennedy of Smith College, had dubbed the material "Polaroid," and the name was adopted. In 1935 Land negotiated with American Optical Company to produce polarized sunglasses. Such glasses could screen out glare rather than simply darken the landscape, and Land-Wheelwright contracted to begin production of Polaroid Day Glasses, a longtime source of revenue for Polaroid.

In 1937 Land formed Polaroid Corporation to acquire the operations that he and George Wheelwright had begun. Eight original shareholders fronted $375,000 to back Land and his projects. They invested in Land and his ideas, allotting him a voting trust of stock that gave him control of the company for the next decade. Wheelwright left the company in 1940 to become a navy lieutenant and never rejoined the company. Researchers had devised a number of commercial applications for Polaroid polarizing sheets—such as desk lamps, variable-density windows, lenses, and three-dimensional photographs called Vectographs—but most of these products never became significantly profitable.

Polaroid continued to court the major automakers, attempting to induce one of them to demonstrate its headlight system at the 1939 New York World's Fair. The carmakers all refused the project, but Chrysler agreed to run a Polaroid three-dimensional (3-D) movie at its display. Audiences dodged water that seemed to spray out of a garden hose into the crowd and gawked through Polaroid-made glasses of oppositely polarized lenses as an automobile appeared to dance itself together in the air above them. The public loved 3-D, but filmmakers were content with the magic of color and sound, and passed over the new technology.

In another unsuccessful marketing project, variable-density windows were installed on the observation car of the *City of Los Angeles.* Two polarized discs were mounted in the train wall; by means of a knob, passengers could turn the inner disk so that the window gradually became grayer until it was completely dark. As with the 3-D process, the novelty of polarized windows was not hugely successful.

Contributed to World War II Effort

In 1939 Day Glasses were the source of most of Polaroid's $35,000 profit. Although sales rose to $1 million in 1941, the company's 1940 losses had reached $100,000, and it was only World War II military contracts that saved Land and his 240 employees. By 1942 the wartime economy had tripled Polaroid's size. A $7 million navy contract to work on the Dove heat-seeking missile project was the largest contract Polaroid had ever had, though the bomb was not used during World War II. Polaroid produced a number of other products for the Armed Forces, including a device that determined an aircraft's elevation above the horizon, an infrared night viewing device, goggles, lenses, color filters for periscopes, and range finders.

Also during the war, the 3-D technology was employed in a machine-gunner training unit. Polaroid designed a trainer in which the student operated a life-size antiaircraft gun against the 3-D simulation of an attacking plane. Reconnaissance planes were equipped to take 3-D Vectographs, which provided relief maps of enemy territory. When viewed with polarized glasses, the 3-D pictures exposed contours of guns, planes, and buildings that camouflage obscured in conventional photographs. Vectographs were used in planning almost all Allied invasions, including that of Normandy. By the end of the war, in 1945, Polaroid's sales had reached $16 million. But as military contracts declined, so did staff, and Polaroid was down to about 900 employees, from a wartime high of 1,250. Sales fell to just $4 million in 1946 and were less than $2 million in 1947.

1948 Debut of Instant Photography Saved Company

By 1946 Land had realized that Polaroid Corporation was in deep trouble. Land also had come to believe that instant photography was Polaroid's only research line with potential to save the company. Land had first considered developing instant photography technology in 1943, when, on Christmas day, his three-year-old daughter asked to see the photographs her parents had taken earlier that day. Prompted by his daughter's query, Land conceived, in a flash, an instant, self-developing film and a camera that would process it. By 1946, however, the research on the film was far from complete. Nonetheless, Land announced early that year that the instant camera system would be demonstrated at the February 21, 1947 winter meeting of the Optical Society of America. Working around the clock, Polaroid scientists developed a working model of the system, which allowed Land to take an instant picture of himself at the Optical Society meeting. The photograph developed itself within a minute. The image of Land peeling back the negative paper from an instantly produced picture of himself made front page news in the *New York Times,* was given a full page in *Life* magazine, and was splashed across the international press.

It was an additional nine months before the camera was offered to the public via Jordan Marsh, Boston's oldest department store. The original camera, which weighed five pounds when loaded, sold for $89.75; film cost $1.75 for eight sepia-toned exposures. On the first day the camera was offered, demonstrators sold all 56 of the available units, and the cameras kept selling as fast as the factory could produce them. First-year photographic sales exceeded $5 million. By 1950 more than 4,000 dealers sold Polaroid cameras, when only a year earlier Kodak had virtually monopolized the U.S. photography market.

The 1950s were a decade of rapid expansion. Sales mounted, spurred on by an aggressive television advertising campaign. Instant photography could be demonstrated graphically on television. Black-and-white film was introduced in 1950 to an enthusiastic public. Enthusiasm quickly turned to ire, however, as the black-and-white images began to fade and disappear. Unable to develop a nonfading black-and-white film, Polaroid provided sponge-tipped tubes of a liquid polymer, which the consumers hand applied to each picture to set the image. This awkward process was not eliminated until 1963.

Despite the inconvenience, demand for instant photography held. To accommodate growing sales, Polaroid built a plant in Waltham, Massachusetts. The company's common stock was listed on the New York Stock Exchange in 1957. Polaroid formed its first international subsidiaries in 1959, in Frankfurt and Toronto. In 1960 it established Nippon Polaroid Kabushiki Kaisha in Japan and licensed a Japanese firm to produce two cameras for overseas sale.

During the 1960s Polaroid continued to offer improvements and variations on the original instant film and camera, though other products were also introduced. Polaroid's first color film was introduced in 1963, along with a pack-loading black-and-white film. In 1965 the inexpensive Swinger was pitched to teens. Selling for less than $20, the camera took only black-and-white pictures, sustaining the market for Polaroid black-and-white film. In 1966 the ID-2 Land Identification system was introduced. It produced full-color laminated cards in two minutes, allowing the company to provide instant driver's licenses and other photo identification cards. In 1967 Polaroid began construction on several new factories to boost production of cameras, film, color negatives, and chemicals. The company's stock split two for one in 1968. During the late 1960s Polaroid was outpacing other top stock market performers. In 1970 sales reached $500 million.

In October 1970 two black workers at Polaroid called upon other black employees to leave their jobs until Polaroid ceased all business in South Africa. Polaroid had no subsidiaries or investments in the country, but its products were distributed through Frank & Hirsch and some items were sold directly to the government. South African commerce accounted for less than 0.1 percent of the company's annual profits. Polaroid sent two black and two white employees to South Africa to assess the situation, and in 1971 the company decided to stop selling its products to the South African government. In addition, black workers at Frank & Hirsch would receive equal pay for equal work and be educated for promotion. Polaroid established a foundation to subsidize black education in South Africa, and made $25,000 in contributions to black cultural associations. Polaroid ended its association with Frank & Hirsch in 1977.

SX-70 Debuted in 1972

In 1972 the October cover of *Life* magazine featured a cluster of children grasping after a photograph whizzing out of the new SX-70 wielded by inventor Land. The SX-70 was the first integrated camera and film system, and the pictures developed outside the camera by themselves. The public eagerly purchased the camera. Despite the fact that sales in the early 1970s continued to grow at a rate of 20 percent per year, the tremendous expense of research, manufacturing, and marketing for the SX-70 caused earnings to fall. Financial analysts began to question Polaroid's stability. In 1974 Polaroid executives admitted that the company did not expect to make more than $3 a share that year. Actually, earnings were only 86 cents per share. Polaroid stock plummeted. By July 1974, just 26 months after the SX-70 was introduced, the stock had fallen from $149 to $14.

In 1975 Land turned the presidency of Polaroid over to Bill McCune, a senior vice-president who had been with the company since 1939 and had worked closely with Land on the development of the first instant camera and film. Manufacture of the SX-70 remained very costly, and numerous design features required modification. Yet Land was satisfied with the camera and wished to pursue research on Polavision, an instant motion picture system. McCune and others, however, favored improving the SX-70. Highly skeptical of Polavision, McCune wanted to base new product lines on market research, rather than following Land's method of creating a consumer demand for Polaroid's latest invention. Land introduced Polavision at the 1977 annual meeting, and a limited introduction followed. Although a scientific marvel, the instant films lasted only two and a half minutes and were silent. Videotaping was just hitting the market, and so Polavision was never a consumer success.

Land received his 500th patent and was inducted into the National Inventors Hall of Fame in 1977. Polaroid's corporate culture began to shift when McCune was voted chief executive

officer in 1980. While Land's entrepreneurial drive had created the company, a more diversified, market-oriented management was needed to continue to propel it. In 1982 Land retired fully, devoting his attention to research at the Rowland Institute for Science, which he had founded in 1965.

In 1976 Polaroid entered a costly and lengthy patent-infringement battle with Eastman Kodak Company. Kodak had been producing the negative component of Polaroid's black-and-white film since 1944, and its color negative since 1957. With the introduction of the Polaroid SX-70, though, Kodak terminated its partnership with Polaroid, and began its own instant-photography research. In 1976 Kodak introduced the EK-4 and EK-6 instant cameras and PR-10 instant film. Polaroid filed suit within a week, charging 12 patent infringements in camera film and design.

Legal preparations dragged on for five years, until the trial began in October 1981. Ten of the 12 original counts were pressed. After 75 days of testimony and three years of deliberation, U.S. District Court Judge Rya Zobel ruled that seven of the ten Polaroid patents were valid and had been infringed upon. As a result, Kodak's line of instant-photography products was terminated in 1986. When settlement talks began, Polaroid claimed about $6.1 billion in damages, lost sales, and interest. The case was not settled until 1991 and resulted in a payment by Eastman Kodak of $925 million.

Fended Off Hostile Takeover in Late 1980s

In August 1988 Shamrock Holdings offered to buy Polaroid at $40 a share plus 40 percent of the award from the Kodak settlement. Polaroid's board of directors rejected the offer, and soon after, the company sold 14 percent of its outstanding shares to an employee stock ownership program (ESOP). Shamrock charged that the ESOP was a form of management entrenchment, and sued. Delaware courts upheld Polaroid's position, and Shamrock raised its offer to $45 a share. Polaroid's board again rejected the offer and subsequently announced a $1.1 billion common stock buyback. Shamrock again sued Polaroid in February 1989 for management entrenchment, but Polaroid's tactics were again upheld. The fight against Shamrock was led by Chairman McCune and I. MacAllister Booth, who had become president in 1983 and CEO in 1985. The pair pruned Polaroid staff in the early 1980s and reorganized the company into three divisions: consumer photography, industrial photography, and magnetic media.

The first success reaped from this new marketing strategy was the Spectra, introduced in 1986. The upscale Spectra came out of market research indicating that instant camera users wanted better picture quality. Again responding to this desire, Polaroid introduced Hybrid IV, an instant film of near 35-millimeter quality, during the early 1990s. Polaroid also introduced a line of conventional film and videotapes starting in 1989. Marketing strategies also continued to become more sophisticated. In 1990 a $60 million advertising campaign emphasized new uses for instant cameras. Suggested uses included recording household items for insurance purposes or keeping a visual record of properties when househunting. In addition, the company cultivated its nonconsumer markets, which contributed at least 40 percent of photographic sales.

While Polaroid's product lines became more fully guided by market demand, Polaroid continued to be a research-and-development-driven company. By the early 1990s, the company had become the world market leader in instant photography and electronic imaging, and a major world manufacturer and marketer of conventional films, videotapes, and light polarizing filters and lenses. In addition to its instant photography products, Polaroid had by the early 1990s developed a presence in the medical imaging field, with such products as the 1993-released Helios medical laser imaging system, which produced a medical diagnostic image without chemical processing, and the Polaroid EMS Photo Kit, a camera specifically designed for the 35,000 emergency medical team (EMT) squads in the United States. A series of electronic imaging products were also developed for the business segment, including desktop computer film recorders, the Polaroid CI-5000 and CI-3000, and the CS-500i Digital Photo Scanner. In addition, Polaroid developed the ProCam, an instant camera earmarked for the business customer.

For the nonprofessional or amateur consumer, the long-awaited ''Joshua'' instant camera was introduced first in Europe in 1992, and then in the United States as ''Captiva'' in the summer of 1993. Captiva, indistinguishable in appearance from a 35-millimeter camera, took high-quality instant photos that were not ejected in the usual manner, but stored in the rear of the camera, which in turn contained a viewing window enabling the user to see the development of the last exposed frame. Because the photos were smaller than regular-sized 35-millimeter pictures, the camera appealed to those whose lifestyles favored a more compact and instant camera. ''HighDefinition'' instant film for the amateur photographer came on the market in 1992, further closing the gap in quality between 35-millimeter and instant film.

Troubles Mounted As the 1990s Continued

In the mid-to-late 1990s Polaroid faced an increasingly uncertain future. Overall sales were stagnant—the $2.15 billion figure of 1992 being repeated in 1997, before a more dismal result was announced for 1998: $1.89 billion. Demand for instant film was on the decline, in part because of the rapid growth of one-hour photo shops for conventional film, and the company's other forays were less than total successes. The Captiva had a very strong debut, but then sales dropped off and Polaroid cut back production. Booth retired in late 1995 and was replaced as chairman and CEO by Gary T. DiCamillo, who had been an executive at the Black & Decker Corporation, where he earned a reputation for cost-cutting, improving productivity, and rapidly developing new products. Soon after taking over, DiCamillo initiated a restructuring at Polaroid, which included a workforce cut of about 15 percent, or 1,570 jobs, and a charge of $247 million for 1995, leading to a net loss of $140.2 million for the year. DiCamillo also overhauled the company's management team, bringing in additional marketing and product development-oriented leaders from such firms as RJR Nabisco and Kraft Foods.

Further changes came in 1996 when Polaroid largely abandoned its venture into medical imaging, an area in which it had invested about $800 million, when it sold the bulk of its loss-making Helios unit to Sterling Diagnostic Imaging Inc. This sale led in part to a $33 million charge recorded in 1996, a year in which the company reported a net loss of $41.1 million.

The new management team at Polaroid concentrated on rolling out 30 to 40 new products each year, aiming to diversify the company's offerings. These included a disposable flashlight, alkaline batteries, and a new line of polarized sunglasses. In December 1997, meanwhile, Polaroid announced an additional workforce reduction of 15 percent, or about 1,500 jobs. The company took another restructuring charge of $323.5 million, resulting in a 1997 net loss of $126.7 million. During 1998 Polaroid announced additional job cuts of 600 to 700 employees, took a restructuring charge of $50 million, and posted a net loss of $51 million. The worldwide economic difficulties that began in 1997 proved particularly troublesome for Polaroid, which had long generated a significant portion of its revenue outside the United States. The hardest hit market for Polaroid was Russia, which had been the company's second largest market in 1995, accounting for $200 million in revenues; for 1998 Polaroid sold only about $25 million worth of goods in that economically troubled nation.

As Polaroid's red ink continued to flow, speculation about a possible takeover was rife. In addition, while DiCamillo had initially emphasized broadening the company's product mix when he came on board, he announced in early 1999 that he was considering selling four business units—sunglasses, graphic arts, glare-reducing polarizers, and holography—that had been key components of his diversification efforts. DiCamillo said that he wanted to focus the company on its core instant photography business. The emphasis would also be on the consumer market, with particular attention given to developing youth-oriented instant cameras, such as the I-Zone Instant Pocket Camera, which was a slender camera that produced miniature instant prints. The Pocket Camera had been a great success following its May 1998 debut in the Osaka region of Japan, and would be released in the United States in the summer of 1999. Other products the company was banking its future on included PopShots, the first instant one-time-use camera; and the JoyCam, a smaller, economically priced version of Polaroid's standard instant camera. The company was also attempting to win the race to develop the first digital camera with an instant print. But the larger question that especially clouded Polaroid's future was whether instant photography was becoming technologically obsolete.

Principal Subsidiaries

Polaroid A.G. (Switzerland); Polaroid A/S (Denmark); Polaroid Asia Pacific International Inc.; Polaroid Asia Pacific Limited; Polaroid Aktiebolag (Sweden); Polaroid Australia Pty. Limited; Polaroid do Brasil Ltda. (Brazil); Polaroid Canada Inc.; Polaroid Caribbean Corporation; Polaroid Contracting CV (Netherlands); Polaroid Espana, S.A. (Spain); Polaroid Europe Limited (U.K.); Polaroid Far East Limited (Hong Kong); Polaroid Foreign Sales B.V. (Netherlands); Polaroid Foundation; Polaroid Gesellschaft mit beschrankter Haftung (Germany); Polaroid Gesellschaft m.b.H. (Austria); Polaroid India Private Limited; Polaroid International B.V. (Netherlands); Nippon Polaroid Kabushiki Kaisha (Japan); Polaroid Malaysia Limited; Polaroid de Mexico S.A. de C.V.; Polaroid (Norge) A/S (Norway); Polaroid Oy (Finland); Polaroid Singapore Private Limited;

Polaroid (U.K.) Limited; Polaroid Memorial Drive LLC; Polaroid Partners, Inc.; Inner City, Inc.; PMC, Inc.; Polint, Inc.; PRD Capital Inc.; PRD Investment Inc.; PRD Management Limited (Bermuda); PRD Overseas Limited (Bermuda); Sub Debt Partners Corp.; Troon, Inc.

Further Reading

Alster, Norm, "Double Exposure," *Forbes,* September 14, 1992, pp. 408+.

Bailey, Steve, and Steven Syre, "In Hindsight, Perhaps Polaroid Should Have Sold," *Boston Globe,* October 22, 1998.

Blout, Elkan, "Polaroid: Dreams to Reality," *Daedalus,* spring 1996, pp. 39+.

Bulkeley, William M., "Polaroid, Emphasizing Marketing Push, Says Cheese: Instant-Camera Maker Hires Kraft's Posa to Rejuvenate Its Stagnant Brand," *Wall Street Journal,* November 5, 1996, p. B4.

Byrnes, Nanette, and Adrienne Hardman, "Cold Shower: Why Polaroid Shareholders Can Thank Roy Disney for His Aborted Takeover," *Financial World,* September 28, 1993, pp. 38–39.

Deutsch, Claudia H., "Touching Up a Faded Polaroid," *New York Times,* January 3, 1998, pp. D1, D2.

Dumaine, Brian, "How Polaroid Flashed Back," *Fortune,* February 16, 1987.

"Edwin Land: Inventor of Polaroid Camera," *Los Angeles Times,* March 2, 1991.

"Film Recorders (Overview of Four Evaluations of Desktop Film Recorders)," *PC Magazine,* May 14, 1991.

Hammonds, Keith H., "Why Polaroid Must Remake Itself—Instantly," *Business Week,* September 19, 1988.

Klein, Alec, "Polaroid Hopes New Cameras Click with Young Users," *Wall Street Journal,* February 4, 1999, p. B10.

——, "Polaroid May Sell Four Businesses Once Viewed As Key," *Wall Street Journal,* March 1, 1999, p. A10.

McElheny, Victor K., *Insisting on the Impossible: The Life of Edwin Land,* Reading, Mass.: Perseus Books, 1998, 510 p.

McWilliams, Gary, "A Radical Shift in Focus for Polaroid," *Business Week,* July 26, 1993, pp. 66–67.

——, "Larry, We Hardly Knew Ye," *Business Week,* December 27, 1993, p. 40.

Nulty, Peter, "The New Look of Photography: The Transition from Film to Electronic Imaging," *Fortune,* July 1, 1991.

Ozanian, Michael K., "Darkness Before Dawn," *Financial World,* June 6, 1995, pp. 42–45.

Palmer, Jay, "Spending Kodak's Money: Polaroid Uses Its Settlement Bounty to Sow Seeds of Future Growth," *Barron's,* October 7, 1991.

Pereira, Joseph, "Wall Street Sees a Turnaround Developing at Polaroid: Strong Reception for New Small Camera and Medical Devices Lifts Stock," *Wall Street Journal,* July 13, 1993, p. B4.

Polaroid Corporation: A Chronology, Cambridge, Mass., Polaroid Corporation, 1983.

"Polaroid Launches a Major Quality Initiative," *Modern Materials Handling,* April 1992.

"Polaroid Leads Peripherals Parade at Graphics Show," *PC Week,* March 16, 1992.

Rosenberg, Ronald, "Above Expectations: Strong Overseas Sales Lift Polaroid Income," *Boston Globe,* October 14, 1992.

"Sharper Focus," *Economist,* April 24, 1993, pp. 72–73.

Wensberg, Peter C., *Land's Polaroid: A Company and the Man Who Invented It,* Boston: Houghton Mifflin, 1987, 258 p.

Wurman, Richard Saul, *Polaroid Access: Fifty Years,* n.p.: Access Press, 1989.

—Elaine Belsito
—updated by David E. Salamie

The Providence Journal Company

75 Fountain Street
Providence, Rhode Island 02902
U.S.A.
(401) 277-7000
Fax: (401) 277-7889
Web site: http://www.projo.com

Wholly Owned Subsidiary of A.H. Belo Corporation
Incorporated: 1884 as The Providence Printing Company
Employees: 1,200
Sales: $359 million (1998 est.)
NAIC: 51111 Newspaper Publishers

The Providence Journal Company owns the *Providence Journal,* the longest continuously published daily newspaper in the United States. The *Journal*'s history goes back almost 180 years and includes several news publishing milestones, as well as four Pulitzer Prizes. Beginning in the late 1940s the company began to diversify, acquiring or starting up radio and TV stations, a printing business, cable television systems, and a cellular telephone network, many of which were sold off in the 1990s. Following its 1996 acquisition by the Dallas, Texas-based A.H. Belo Corporation, the *Journal* became part of a media conglomerate that owns 17 TV stations and seven newspapers.

Early Years

The Providence Journal Company traces its beginnings to January 3, 1820, when the *Manufacturers' & Farmers' Journal, Providence & Pawtucket Advertiser* was first published in Providence, Rhode Island. Founded at the urging of a group of local manufacturers, and published by "Honest" John Miller in association with a local bookseller, the paper's first issue announced that it would "be devoted to the support of the Manufacturing and American policy. It will be a medium of Scientifick, Manufacturing and Mercantile Information; and a faithful Reporter of the PASSING NEWS." Nine years later the paper expanded from two issues per week to six, changing its name to the *Providence Daily Journal and General Advertiser.*

Daily publication proved less profitable, however, and in 1838 John Miller was forced to sell out his remaining interest in the paper, which was purchased by Joseph Knowles and William L. Burroughs. Over the next few years ownership of the paper shifted as Burroughs sold his stake to George Danielson and Henry B. Anthony. The business was incorporated as the Providence Printing Company in 1884, the year both Anthony and Danielson died, with ownership of the stock going to their families. In 1885 the name was changed to the Providence Journal Company, and the company began publication of the *Providence Sunday Journal,* which would eventually bring the paper its largest circulation figures. During the Civil War a second edition was added, the *Evening Bulletin.* Several weekly and semiweekly papers were also started or acquired during the company's early years.

During the middle of the 19th century, the *Journal* had been strongly supportive of the Republican Party, coming to be known by the nickname "The Republican Bible." Under Danielson and Anthony, the latter elected U.S. Senator in 1858, the paper's support for Republican candidates and issues had been particularly enthusiastic. However, following the deaths of Danielson and Anthony, the paper began to take on a less biased perspective, and in 1886 published a series of criticisms of party boss Charles R. Brayton and his cronies. Two years later the *Journal* was officially drummed out of the fold at the Rhode Island Republican Party's state convention. The following day the paper published an editorial that officially declared its political independence, a position that has been maintained ever since.

Early on the *Journal* became noted for exploring new technologies, being one of the first newspapers to purchase "hot metal" Linotype machines to set type in 1889, and in 1903 acquiring wireless telegraph equipment to aid in news gathering. The first telegraph site was installed by radio pioneer Lee De Forest on nearby Block Island both to enable news gathering and to transmit text from the mainland to the island, where the Journal Company briefly published a daily newspaper. The company also installed wireless equipment at Rhode Island's Point Judith and aboard the steamer *Plymouth.* These operations were phased out after several years, following storm damage and financial losses.

Before the age of radio the Journal also "broadcast" sports events from a platform attached to the side of the paper's headquarters. A Journal staffer was handed a stream of wire reports through a window to give a play-by-play account to a crowd assembled in the street. The paper delayed the feed to its "megaphone man" just enough so that as the final moments of the game were described, newsboys could flood into the crowd with papers hot off the press that covered the event in its entirety.

World War I: The Journal *Backs Britain*

The paper gained particular notoriety during World War I, when its editor, the blustery, enigmatic Australian immigrant John Rathom, positioned the *Journal* firmly on the side of the Allies. During the years before American entry into the fighting, Rathom frequently published unique information about German and Austrian activities, to the extent that it was widely suspected that British intelligence was supplying the paper with information. Apparently this was actually the case, as Rathom had a secret contact in the British embassy in New York. The German government allegedly attempted to bribe Rathom to change the *Journal*'s position, to no avail. When the United States finally entered the war in 1917 on the side of the Allies, it was partially due to the efforts of Rathom and the *Journal* to stir up public sentiment against the Central Powers.

Several years later Rathom's ever-growing exaggeration of his and the *Journal*'s prewar achievements got him into trouble with the U.S. government. Following his move to publish an embellished account of his and the paper's efforts in a magazine, a letter in which he admitted his guilt was publicly released. Rathom remained editor until his death in 1923, despite this embarrassment.

In 1925 the paper became the first in the country to expand its coverage statewide, opening news bureaus that were located in such a way that, theoretically, no potential story was more than 20 minutes away. The paper also broadened its focus to treat the entire state as if it were a single metropolis. These changes were made under managing editor Sevellon Brown,

who was named editor in 1938. In 1937 the *Journal*'s only competing Providence-based daily, the *Star-Tribune*, went bankrupt and was sold at auction. Believing that the *Journal* was better off with competition, the Providence Journal Company purchased its rival and kept it running for four months. The company finally shut the *Star-Tribune* down, not wishing to cut into the *Journal*'s own readership. Since that time the *Journal* had no other Providence daily to compete with.

The paper won its first Pulitzer Prize in 1945, when chief editorial writer George W. Potter was honored for a series of essays. A second Pulitzer came in 1953, when the paper's entire editorial staff was recognized for local deadline reporting. Through a series of fortuitous coincidences, and with the help of established contacts, a bank robbery and hostage-taking situation were covered with astonishing thoroughness and speed. Only hours after the mid-day events had unfolded, the *Evening Bulletin* was on the streets with an edition that included detailed, accurate reporting and dramatic photographs.

Expanding Operations Through the 1980s

Beginning in the late 1940s, the Journal Company started to expand into other broadcast media, creating an FM radio station in 1948 and purchasing an AM station in 1954. Both of these were housed in Journal headquarters in Providence. With the dual impact of television and a depressed Rhode Island economy affecting newspaper circulation in the early 1960s, the Journal Company sought further ways to diversify. In 1962 the company formed a printing subsidiary, Providence Gravure, Inc., which eventually operated plants in four states that printed Sunday magazine sections and publications such as *TV Guide* and *Time*.

The Journal Company also entered the cable television arena, purchasing a small Westerly, Rhode Island-based cable system in 1968. The company organized a new subsidiary, Colony Communications, to manage this operation and develop others like it. Within a decade Colony was operating cable systems in almost 40 communities and serving more than 100,000 subscribers. The Journal Company entered television broadcasting directly in 1978 when it purchased WPHL in Philadelphia. Other television stations were later added in Tucson, Albuquerque, Santa Fe, and Louisville. The company was also quick to enter the pager and cellular telephone businesses, forming a new subsidiary called PJC Cellular in 1983.

The Providence Journal's history of technical innovation added a new chapter in 1985 when it became the first U.S. newspaper to use flexographic printing presses. This type of printing required much more precision from pressmen than the older letterpress and offset methods but used inks that did not rub off on readers' hands, allowed full-color printing, and caused significantly less waste of paper, at a time when newsprint costs were on the rise. After proving viable with the *Journal,* other papers soon followed suit and ordered flexographic presses.

In 1986 the *Journal* found itself in hot water after it published excerpts from wiretapped conversations dating from the 1960s, in defiance of a court ban. Despite the fact that the suppression order had been quickly rescinded, the U.S. Supreme Court found that the paper had erred in publishing the material and fined it $100,000, giving executive editor Charles

McC. Hauser an 18-month suspended sentence. The company also sold the Providence Gravure printing business in 1986, a year that saw corporate revenues reach $212.6 million.

1990s: Further Expansion and Public Stock Offering

In 1990 the Journal Company sold its cellular subsidiary to GTE Corporation for $750 million. Two years later the company, in association with the investment firm Kelso and Co., purchased a package of five television stations and several cable systems for $550 million from King Broadcasting. This deal put the total number of stations in the Journal Company's portfolio at nine, along with several others that it managed under Local Marketing Agreements. Over the next several years the company also made moves into cable broadcasting, investing in start-ups The TV Food Network and America's Health Network. Neither of these ventures made much headway, however.

In 1994 the *Journal* received a fourth Pulitzer Prize, for investigative reporting into corruption within Rhode Island's courts. (The paper had won its third Pulitzer in 1974, for an investigation by reporter Jack White into Richard Nixon's tax returns that resulted in the President paying $500,000 in back taxes.) In 1995 the company first began to offer the *Journal* on the Internet, via Prodigy's online network. After several disappointing years, the company moved for online independence, starting it own web site at projo.com.

Major changes were made to the newspaper in 1995. The *Bulletin*, which for some time had been merely a late edition of the morning *Journal*, was phased out entirely. The paper also dropped its Sunday magazine section, opting for the nationally syndicated *Parade* magazine. These moves were attributed to the surging price of newsprint and declining overall revenues. Also in 1995, the company sold its Colony Cablevision subsidiary to Continental Cablevision. The cable business, with 800,000 subscribers, was exchanged for 30 million shares of Continental stock.

In the spring of 1996, the Providence Journal Company went public, selling over $100 million worth of stock. While the company's board approved the offering, some members of the families who owned the paper expressed regret at entering the realm of public ownership. Still, the company needed the infusion of cash to help offset losses from declining advertising revenues at the paper and the two stalled cable networks in which the company had invested. In a move that was a surprise to many, three months after the stock offering the company was purchased for $1.54 billion in a friendly takeover by A.H. Belo, a Dallas, Texas-based news and television conglomerate. Among the parent's holdings were seven television stations and several newspapers, including the *Dallas Morning News*. Because both companies owned television stations in Seattle, one was exchanged for a station in another market. A year later the Journal Company's America's Health Network interest was sold, as its prospects for profitability remained distant.

In 1998 workers at projo.com won union representation, over the objections of the paper, which considered them production, rather than editorial, personnel. Members of the paper's news-gathering departments were represented by the Newspaper Guild, and the union had appealed to the National Labor Relations Board to force the paper to recognize the web site

workers' union affiliation and grant them the higher pay of editorial staff. At the 11th hour the paper backed down and met the union's demands.

In A.H. Belo's year-end earnings report for 1998, the parent company noted that the *Journal* had had an "outstanding" year, with "double-digit cash flow growth." Circulation of the daily *Journal* stood at nearly 170,000, with the Sunday edition at 244,000. In early 1999 the company received a new publisher and CEO when president Howard Sutton took over upon Stephen Hamblett's retirement. Hamblett had been CEO, publisher, and chairman since 1987 following the death of third-generation *Journal* publisher Michael Metcalf in a bicycle accident.

As it adapted to its place in the A.H. Belo fold, the Journal Company was getting back to focusing on what it had done best from the start, putting out a quality newspaper. Despite having slimmed down to a single, morning daily, and having halted the publication of its own Sunday magazine, the Providence *Journal* was still a highly regarded paper with extensive statewide coverage and a long tradition of integrity and innovation. With non-news interests reduced through divestment or their incorporation into the larger Belo portfolio, it appeared likely that the company could continue to adapt to the changes wrought by television and the Internet and maintain the *Journal*'s position among America's finest newspapers.

Principal Subsidiaries

The Providence Journal Newspaper Co.

Further Reading

"Belo Acquires Providence Journal Co.," *Editor & Publisher,* October 5, 1996, p. 13.

Brown, Rich, "Continental Buys ProJo Systems for $1.4 Billion," *Broadcasting & Cable,* November 28, 1994, p. 6.

Byrnes, Garrett D., and Charles H. Spilman, *The Providence Journal: 150 Years,* Providence, R.I.: Providence Journal Company, 1980.

Garneau, George, "Major Overhaul: Providence Journal Co. to Merge Evening Bulletin with Morning Journal," *Editor & Publisher,* April 8, 1995, p. 9.

——, "Union 'Invests' to Take a Peek at the Company's Finances," *Editor & Publisher,* October 22, 1994, p. 15.

Granger, Rod, "New TVFN Net Food for Thought," *Multichannel News,* April 19, 1993, p. 20.

Half a Century with the Journal, Providence, R.I.: Journal Company, 1904.

Higgins, John M., "ProJo's Colony: A Profile in Pragmatism," *Multichannel News,* February 10, 1992, p. 28.

Katz, Richard, "ProJo Takes Stake in Fledgling Health Network," *Multichannel News,* April 24, 1995, p. 26.

"Newspaper in Providence Is Fined for Violating Federal Court Order," *New York Times,* April 30, 1986, p. 23.

Noack, David, "Projo.com Goes Union, Settlement Avoids Ruling," *Editor & Publisher,* August 8, 1998, p. 9.

Peers, Martin, "Belo Adds 9 Stations in Big Buy," *Daily Variety,* September 27, 1996, p. 1.

Peterson, Iver, "Belo in $1.5 Billion Deal for Providence Journal Co.," *New York Times,* September 27, 1996, p. 2.

——, "Providence Journal Sale Raises Doubts on Autonomy and Hackles in Family," *New York Times,* March 10, 1997, p. 11.

Scardino, Albert, "A New Way to Print News," *New York Times,* November 23, 1985, p. 35.

—Frank Uhle

PSA Peugeot Citroen S.A.

75, avenue de la Grande-Armée
75116 Paris
France
(33) 1 40 66 55 11
Fax: (33) 1 40 66 54 14
Web site: http://www.psa-peugeot-citroen.com

Public Company
Incorporated: 1896 as Peugeot S.A.; 1924 as Société
    Anonyme Automobiles Citroen
Employees: 158,000
Sales: FFr 221.44 billion (US$41 billion) (1998)
Stock Exchanges: Paris OTC
Ticker Symbol: PEUGY (ADR)
NAIC: 336111 Automobile Manufacturing; 336312
    Gasoline Engine & Engine Parts Manufacturing;
    33639 Other Motor Vehicle Parts Manufacturing;
    336991 Motorcycle, Bicycle, & Parts Manufacturing;
    336999 All Other Transportation Equipment
    Manufacturing

PSA Peugeot Citroen S.A. is one of the big six European automotive manufacturers, producing passenger cars and light commercial and utility vehicles under the famous Peugeot and Citroen brand names, as well as motorbikes and scooters, and vehicles for military use. PSA, through subsidiaries Peugeot Citroen Motors, also produces car parts, and as such is one of Europe's largest suppliers of parts and motors to the automotive industry. PSA also develops and manufactures light machinery, high-tech equipment, and operates its own financial, freight, and distribution subsidiaries. In 1998 PSA reported sales of FFr 221.4 billion, or approximately US$41 billion. The company's automobile unit is the dominant player on the French market, just ahead of rival Renault. In France, Peugeot owns more than 30 percent of the market. Together with Ford Europe, Fiat, BMW, Daimler-Chrysler, and Renault, Peugeot is among the principal European automotive manufacturers, where it holds an 11.3 percent market share, and, among utility vehicles, the leading share of 17.4 percent.

PSA employs some 158,000 people, through operations in more than 100 countries. Fully 70 percent of the company's manufacturing is done outside of France. Nevertheless, Europe, and especially France, remain the company's chief focus. Almost all of PSA's sales are in Europe. France alone represents approximately 30 percent of Peugeot's car sales; total Europe sales account for some 90 percent of Peugeot's totals. However, the company has been making inroads in the Asian and Latin American markets, and has set targets to achieve 25 percent of annual sales outside of Europe at the turn of the century. More than 100 years after the founding of the original Peugeot motor company, the Peugeot family remains integral to the company's operations, with family members sitting on the company's board of directors and with the family's shareholding accounting for around 25 percent of the company's stock. Yet day-to-day operations have been led by chairman and CEO Jean-Martin Folz, who replaced longtime company leader Jacques Calvet in 1997.

Founding the French Automobile Industry in the 1890s

The Peugeot and Citroen names held a prominent position in the emerging French automotive industry of the 19th century. The Peugeot family was already among the country's prominent manufacturers, operating a textile mill in France's Alsace region. In the early part of the 19th century, the family turned to steel production, after Jean-Pierre and Jean-Frederic Peugeot invented the cold-roll method of manufacturing spring steel. The bicycle craze of the 1880s brought the family into wheeled vehicle production, as Armand Peugeot, grandson of Jean-Pierre and a cyclist himself, joined the family business. It was Armand Peugeot who would turn the Peugeot name into one of the most respected automotive manufacturers in the world.

Peugeot's success in the manufacture of machine tools resulted in his gaining recognition and influence, and many of his colleagues feared the risks entailed in devoting his complete resources to the manufacture of an automobile. However, this did not deter Peugeot. Production of the first Peugeot passenger vehicle—a three wheeled, steam-powered motoring car—was launched at the end of the 1880s. However, Peugeot quickly recognized the potential of the newly emerging internal combustion engine. In 1891 Peugeot traveled to Germany in search of the perfect twin-cylinder engine, resolved that he would not come back emptyhanded. Two months later he returned with the 525-cc version, which was being manufactured by Daimler for its own hand-built cars. This purchase, Peugeot told his colleagues, was the beginning of something "grand."

Peugeot's motor car would quickly make its mark, winning some of the world's first automobile races and establishing the Peugeot name among the top of the profession. Peugeot soon introduced a new type of automobile, the station wagon, before the turn of the century. Armand Peugeot was also credited with producing the world's first compact car, dubbed "Le Bébé" (the Baby), in 1905. Within 15 years Peugeot had established manufacturing facilities throughout France. The first Peugeot factories were established in Valentigney and Audincourt, and then in Lille and Sochaux. For a few years after the Sochaux plant was opened, production primarily involved the manufacture of trucks. The first of these to bear resemblance to modern trucks was the type 109 which, with a maximum load of three tons, could still reach 20 km/hr. Industrial vehicle production increased dramatically during World War I, but as the war ended it began to recede.

In the period leading up to the war Peugeot cars won many races, including the 1913 Indianapolis 500. During this time the company began producing a complete range of vehicles for all uses with one salient feature which would continue to distinguish its product line—its cars were sturdy and dependable vehicles with an excellent finish. Peugeot specialized mainly in the production of utilitarian models like the Bébé. The Quadralette engineered along the same lines as the Bébé and introduced at the Brussels Motor Show in 1920, subsequently led to the development of the model 5 CV which hit a record production figure of 83,000 chassis.

By then, a new name had appeared on the French automotive scene. André Citroen's father, a Dutch diamond merchant, had moved to Paris in the 19th century. André Citroen graduated from the Ecole Polytechnique, France's most prestigious university, in 1900 and turned to manufacturing. In 1913 Citroen established the company's precursor, the Citroen Gear Company, in 1913. In order to work smoothly, the teeth on the gears had the form of chevrons, the shape that became the emblem of the Citroen name. André Citroen soon began importing modern industrial working methods to France—during World War I, Citroen's introduction of mass production methods enabled the country to supply its war machine; Citroen himself turned production to munitions. These same production methods, inspired by Citroen hero Henry Ford, would later allow Citroen to produce economical cars in large quantities, and transform the automobile from an elite possession to a common consumer good in Europe. In 1916 M. Citroen began preparations to convert his Paris munitions factory on the Quai de Javel into a car factory. By the end of 1919, the factory was producing 30 cars a day.

The factory produced the Type A, appearing in June 1919, the first European car to be mass produced and the first low-cost car to be sold fully equipped (with, among other things, electric starter and lighting, hood, spare wheel, and tire). It was also the first car designed with the intention of reaching the popular market.

In 1920 Citroen's fame took off at rapid speed after the company won the fuel economy grand prix at Le Mans. As a result, the company greatly increased its rate of production; from a total of 2,810 cars built in 1919, the company had a production total of 12,244 in 1920.

The following year, Peugeot would make its own contribution to the automotive engine market, introducing the first diesel-powered passenger automobile. Peugeot continued to hand craft its automobiles, as Citroen moved its postwar production in two directions.

In 1921 production began on three types of "half-trucks," bearing the Citroen name and incorporating the B2 engine. The new truck type would accomplish the first vehicle crossing of the Sahara. This mission, led by Haardt and Audouin Dubreuil, left Algiers in December 1922 and arrived successfully in Timbuktu in February 1923. In the ensuing decades, Citroen gained world renown by participating in motor expeditions, rallies, and mass treks across desert landscapes in both Asia and Africa.

On the consumer site, Citroen was also innovating. In 1922 the company began offering credit sales, with repayments spread over 12 or 18 months. These arrangements helped to jump-start the popularization of the automobile throughout France. Also in 1922, the company presented the 5CV Type C, a model that contributed to the "democratization" of the automobile because it was economical and easy to drive—so easy, in fact, that it was dubbed the first "ladies' car." The model was mostly painted yellow; hence, its popular nickname was "petite citron," or little lemon.

Citroen first became known in foreign markets in 1921, when it exported a total of approximately 3,000 cars. This move sent the company on a long trek of expansion through numerous international territories throughout the century. André Citroen established the basis of a network of subsidiaries in Brussels, Amsterdam, Cologne, Milan, Geneva, and Copenhagen in 1924; the company exported a total of 17,000 vehicles during that year.

The year 1924 marked the official beginning of Automobiles Citroen. André Citroen founded the Société Anonyme Automobiles Citroen with a capital of FF 100 million. In the same year, the company presented the B10, the first automobile to have an all-steel body instead of the conventional mixed wood and steel construction. Made of cold-pressed panels welded together, the new body offered much better resistance to impact. Production increased in 1924 to 300 vehicles per day, for a total output that year of 55,387 automobiles.

In 1925 the company also shaped and welded its dealer network in France; the number of dealers increased from 200 in 1919 to 5,000 in 1925. The fame of Citroen continued to spread as Haardt and Audouin Dubreuil led their second mission, the Croisiere Noire, between October 1924 and July 1925. The Citroen Central African Expedition consisted of 16 men and eight half-trucks traveling a total of 20,000 kilometers from Colomb-Bechar (Algeria) to Antananarivo (Madagascar).

By 1928 Citroen's factories employed 30,000 workers and maintained a total production capacity of 1,000 vehicles per day; the company had 14 distributors in France and North Africa, ten subsidiary companies, and four factories in foreign countries. Overseas sales represented 45 percent of all French motor industry exports.

Peugeot would turn to the new automotive technologies in the late 1920s, yet remained committed to its tradition of hand-craftsmanship. The first "modern" Peugeot automobile, the 201, was introduced at the 1929 Paris Motor Show. This completely new car, which was originally fitted with an 1122-cc engine, earned Peugeot its reputation as a manufacturer of reliable vehicles. The 201 also inaugurated the company's system of model names, that would continue through the century, reaching the "x06" line in the late 1990s. What distinguished Peugeot from other car companies of its time was the number of technological developments that the company incorporated into its product designs year after year. Indeed, a steady stream of innovations formed the core of the company's history during its first century.

By 1932, for example, the company had produced the more refined 301 model, also available in a family version. The lines of the 201 and 301 had become more elegant and attractive, creating a distinctive style very much in keeping with the current trends of the time. In 1934 the first aerodynamic tests were conducted on the 301 model and Peugeot introduced the 401 model and the six-cylinder 601, but no other model could match the 201. Before the 201 finally went out of production in September 1937, 142,000 units had been produced. The aerodynamic series began in 1935 with the 402 prototype model, which had its headlights set behind the grill. It was with this model that the numbering system which Peugeot still uses today to identify its cars began. Peugeot launched the 302 model at the 1936 Paris Motor Show; this was a new and scaled-down version of the 402. Its most significant innovation was the use of the synchromesh gearbox, and it was also the first touring car fitted with a diesel engine.

After the crash of the New York Stock Exchange in 1929, Citroen, along with the rest of the world, entered an era of economic crisis. The company's yearly production fell in 1932 to 41,348 vehicles. Yet Citroen, like Peugeot, continued to introduce new automobile models and innovations. Milestones in the 1930s, nevertheless, included Citroen's first bus, a 22-passenger vehicle with all-steel bodywork and a six-cylinder engine, built at the Levallois factory in 1931. In 1932 the company announced the C4G and C6G, containing the first engines carried on soft mountings to eliminate vibration; a swan in flight between the double chevrons of the Citroen badge symbolized the advance.

Even as the Depression continued to dampen the high spirits of the French motor industry, André Citroen clung to his original thinking: the greater the number of products, the cheaper production becomes. In 1933 he set two goals: production of 1,000 vehicles per day, and the introduction of the new front-driven model developed by Citroen designer André Lefebvre.

The company announced the 7A in April 1934, the first of a line of Traction Avant models that were produced until 1957. The model had bold specifications: aerodynamic bodywork, unitary steel body with no chassis or running boards, all independent suspension, and hydraulic brakes.

M. Citroen's plans came to a standstill, however, when the company's financial difficulties led to an inability to pay its debts. In 1934 the French government asked the Michelin company, Citroen's principal creditor, to take financial control and refloat the company. Under the direction of Michelin, 8,000 layoffs took place. The company's production plummeted from 51,546 in 1934 to 29,101 in 1935. By that time, André Citroen was already ill; he died in 1935 of stomach cancer. Yet Citroen's legacy would remain that of a pioneer of the European motor industry—and the man most responsible for creating the automobile as a mass-consumer item in Europe.

Rebuilding in the Postwar Era

The loss of the company's independence, and the death of its founder, did not end Citroen's record of innovation. In 1936 Citroen conceived one of its all-time classics, the legendary 2CV (or "deux chevaux"). The idea was for a low-priced car with a very small engine, described by the design department as "four wheels under an umbrella." In 1939 the declaration of war prevented the company from announcing the 2CV. In May of that year, the company destroyed all of its 250 prototypes except one to maintain secrecy. In 1940 the Quai de Javel factory was bombed and Citroen's Belgian factory was partly destroyed. The company's production gradually fell to zero in 1943, partly due to management's refusal to comply with the demands of the Vichy government.

Peugeot, too, was crippled by the outbreak of the war. Production slowed during World War II and almost ground to a halt as a result of the damage incurred by Allied bombing. It picked up again immediately after the war with the 202 model, which had originally been introduced in 1938. This was replaced towards the end of 1947 by the 203 model, of which over 685,000 were built. With a unitary body and a 1300-cc 45 hp engine, this vehicle remained in production for almost 12 years without any major modifications.

On the Citroen side, production rebuilt slowly from 1,600 in 1945 to 12,600 in 1946. In 1948 the 2CV appeared at the Paris Motor Show. From October 1949 to the end of 1984, the company built over three million examples of the immensely popular and inexpensive vehicle. A cult developed around the 2CV, for it became something of a national symbol for the proletariat. Manifestations of popular enthusiasm for the 2CV included odes, sculptures, and water races (contestants removed the car's tires and floated the chassis on oil drums). As the company entered the 1950s, the demand for the 2CV stretched the delivery delay to six years.

In 1953 Citroen began decentralizing its production organization with the opening of the Rennes-la Barre Thomas factory in Brittany. It was not until the end of the 1970s, however, that the company achieved a balance between the Paris region and the provinces.

Citroen's design and development department pioneered a technical breakthrough in 1954: constant height hydropneumatic rear suspension. The system combined the actions of a gas and a liquid to achieve greatly improved road handling. In 1955 the company announced the DS19, with no front grille and a completely smooth nose. This model was revolutionary not only because of its aerodynamic shape, but also because of its technical features, including the newly developed hydropneumatic suspension. All major systems (gear change, clutch, steering, and brakes) were power operated. The model was an instant success: Citroen received 12,000 orders by the end of the first day.

In 1958 the factory of the Société Citroen Hispania at Vigo (Spain) began to produce 2CV vans for the Spanish market and for export. This gave the company representation in a market where imports were strictly limited by quotas. Also in 1958, the company announced the four-wheel drive 2CV Sahara, especially useful for oil exploration and mining teams in desert areas; the vehicle was capable of climbing a sandy, 40 percent slope fully laden. In 1959 a Citroen ID19 driven by Coltelloni, Alexandre, and Desrosiers won the Monte Carlo Rally; this led the company to its decision to participate in motor sports events in the years to come.

In April 1955 Peugeot began its association with the bus company Pininfarina. Since then, their cars have been produced with the marque of the Lion Rampant, first used on the modern 403. This car was given an 1800-cc 48 hp diesel engine in 1959. A more modern version of the 403 was launched in May 1960 and designated the 404. A total of 2.45 million of these models were built.

As Citroen entered the 1960s, the company expanded by establishing subsidiaries and signing joint ventures in foreign locations. In 1960, it reached an agreement with the Yugoslav Tomos concern for the assembly of the 2CV in Yugoslavia. In 1962 Citroen established sales companies in Montreal and Vienna. In 1963 the company set up a subsidiary in Chile for assembly and sales; it also reached an agreement with the Sedica company for the assembly of the 2CV and 3CV in Madagascar. In 1964 the Mangualde factory in Portugal came into operation to manufacture the 2CV; this move again allowed Citroen access to a market with severe restrictions on the import of fully assembled cars.

New Citroen models in the 1960s included the Ami 6, a model categorized as top-of-the-range, and the Dyane, a model categorized between the 2CV and Ami 6. In 1965 Citroen acquired the Panhard factory at Reims (France), a facility specializing in the manufacture of mechanical components for commercial vehicles. In 1967 after signing an industrial collaboration agreement for the production of common designs, Citroen took a majority shareholding in the company Berliet, the European Economic Community's largest producer of commercial vehicles.

Citroen underwent major reorganization the following year. Citroen SA, a holding company, was created to oversee the activities of Citroen, Berliet, and Panhard. Citroen SA gathered within its structure more than 20 subsidiary companies, including the Societe Anonyme Automobiles Citroen (handling production) and the Societe Commerciale Citroen (handling sales).

Citroen signed a technical and commercial agreement in 1968 with the Italian sports car company Maserati. It also signed an agreement with Fiat to set up a holding company, Pardevi, which would hold the majority of Citroen shares, and in which Fiat would have a 49 percent shareholding and Michelin, 51 percent. Under the terms of the agreement, Autobianchi models were to be sold through Citroen dealerships in France, Belgium, Switzerland, and Portugal; Citroens were to be sold through the Autobianchi dealerships in Italy.

Joining Forces in the 1970s

The Arab Oil Embargo of the 1970s and the resulting worldwide recession prompted Michelin to sell its Citroen holding to Peugeot. Peugeot was then eyeing international expansion to enable it to compete on a global scale. Two years later, the newly named PSA Peugeot Citroen SA purchased Chrysler's struggling European operations, including the Simca brand name. That name would soon be transformed to Talbot. The acquisition proved a disappointment, however, and the Talbot name disappeared in the 1980s.

Peugeot and Citroen, meantime, continued to be operated independently, with their own factories and distribution networks. The merging of the two companies took place over the following decades, especially under the leadership of Jacques Calvet, who took over as head of PSA in 1984. By 1998, Peugeot and Citroen, while retaining their brand identities, had nevertheless been streamlined into a more efficient organization, exemplified by the Citroen Xsara, a sedan featuring Citroen styling and Peugeot parts.

A new recession in the early 1980s propelled PSA into net losses; the company was also crippled by a weeks-long strike in its Parisian facilities. Yet the successful launch of a number of new models, including the popular Citroen BX and the luxury XM models, and the extension of the Peugeot 05 range, enabled a restructured PSA to emerge with profits of more than FFr 8 billion by the end of the decade. During the 1980s, also, PSA entered a number of new markets, including the fast-developing Pacific region, and particularly the Chinese market.

The European and world economies would contract yet again in the early 1990s. By then, the European auto market, facing the looming entry of Japanese carmakers, began taking on a new shape, as companies formed strategic partnerships, not only for sales and distribution, but for production as well, with many models sharing the same platforms among different makes. These moves helped PSA maintain its leading position in France, despite intense competition from French government-owned rival Renault, and kept PSA among the top automotive manufacturers in Europe.

PSA's balance sheet was further enhanced by the successful launches of new generation models, including the extended Peugeot 06 line and the highly successful Citroen Xantia and Xsara midrange sedans. In 1998 PSA put the finishing touches on the merging of the Citroen and Peugeot organizations, retaining the separate brand identities while merging production to a single operation. Closing out the year, PSA recorded sales of FFr 221.44 billion. A bustling European economy promised further sales expansion, even as PSA set its sights on increasing its international presence—the company's strategy for the year 2000 called for expanding its sales beyond Europe to 25 percent of total company sales.

Principal Subsidiaries

Automobiles Peugeot; Automobiles Citroen; Aciers et Outillage Peugeot; Cycles Peugeot; Engrenages et Reducteurs; Société de Constructions Mécaniques Panhard et Levassor; Gefco; Société de Crédit à l'Industrie Automobile-Socia; Société Financière de Banque-Sofib; Compagnie Générale de Crédit aux Particuliers-Credipar; PSA Wholesale Ltd.; Anglo French Finance Co., Ltd.; Peugeot Finance International NV; PSA Finance Holding; Societe Mecanique Automobile de l'Est (75%); Société de Construction d'Equipements, de Mecanisation et de Machines (SCEMM); Société Commerciale Citroen; Citroen Deutschland AG (Germany); Citroen Commerce AG (Germany); Citroen Hispania S.A. (Spain; 93%); Citroen Italia SpA (Italy; 96%); Comercial Citroen S.A. (Spain); Citroen (U.K.) Ltd.

Further Reading

Bardou, Jean-Pierre, *The Automobile Revolution: The Impact of an Industry,* Chapel Hill: University of North Carolina Press, 1982.

Bayley, Stephen, ''Where Did the Genius Go?'' *European,* August 21, 1997, p. 52.

Ducorroy, Regis, *Dates,* Neuilly-sur-Seine, France: Automobiles Citroen, 1991.

Greenhouse, Steven, ''Valiant Little Companion of the Road, Au Revior!'' *New York Times,* March 9, 1988.

Laux, James M., *In First Gear: The French Automobile Industry to 1914,* Liverpool: Liverpool University Press, 1976.

Lefebre, Pierre, *The New France,* London: Penguin, 1984.

Reynolds, John, *André Citroen: The Man and the Motor Cars,* Detroit: St. Martins Press, 1997.

Smith, Timothy K., ''Why a Little Car Won a Big Place in Europe's Heart,'' *Wall Street Journal,* July 11, 1984.

Tully, Shawn, ''A Battling Bureaucrat,'' *Fortune,* November 9, 1987, p. 86.

—updated by M.L. Cohen

Quill Corporation

100 Schelter Road
Lincolnshire, Illinois 60069-3621
U.S.A.
(847) 634-6650
Fax: (847) 634-5816
Web site: http://www.quillcorp.com

Division of Staples, Inc.
Incorporated: 1956 as Quill Office Supply Company
Employees: 1,300
Sales: $600 million (1998 est.)
NAIC: 45321 Office Supplies & Stationery Stores;
    454110 Mail-Order Houses

Quill Corporation is the largest and most successful direct marketer of office products in the United States. The company markets and sells an ever increasing number (approximately 15,000 at last count) of office supplies, including such items as file folders, calendars, computers, copiers, tax forms, storage boxes, file cabinets, fax paper, office furniture, and classroom and janitorial supplies. All of the company's products are sold at significantly discounted prices to schools, businesses, associations, institutions, and medical and professional offices throughout the United States. What is most unique about Quill Corporation is its ability to market and sell its products through a highly sophisticated system of print and electronic catalogues, supplemented by phone, fax, and web site sales support. In fact, Quill Corporation's web site has been ranked the number one office supplies web site, utilizing what is widely regarded within the industry as the most convenient and efficient online ordering system in the country.

Early History

Quill Corporation was the outgrowth of an idea by Jack Miller. Miller grew up on the north side of Chicago during the years when the city was still a strong mix of Eastern European ethnic groups. His father sold live poultry in a predominantly Polish-speaking area of the town, and became a successful small businessman through his efforts. Jack was pushed by his parents to attend college and, after graduating from the University of Illinois, the young man took a job as a door-to-door salesman of briefcases. By 1956 he had grown tired of peddling briefcases and started his own office supply business. Working out of a room near his father's poultry business, Jack sold office supplies to small firms throughout Chicago's north side. Lacking retail experience, the young entrepreneur relied on his door-to-door selling technique, and when customers phoned they would normally hear chickens squawking in the background as their orders were being taken.

By the end of his first month in business, Jack Miller had sold a mere $960 worth of office supplies. Nonetheless, he remained undeterred and was convinced that he could build a viable as well as profitable office supply business. Over the next year, the company grew steadily but slowly and, by the time his brother Harvey joined him in the business, the two men were able to pay themselves a salary of $90 per week. As the business continued to grow, the two brothers divided Chicago into halves, with Jack making calls to firms on the north side and Harvey making calls to firms located on the south side of the city. At the same time, they were able to move out of their father's poultry store and into their uncle Herb's basement, which served as their first office and warehouse.

By 1958 Quill Office Supply Company, named because of the original connection to the poultry store, moved once again into a more spacious 850-square-foot storefront, and then again in 1960 to an even larger warehouse and office space. The impetus behind the company's expansion was Jack and Harvey's original idea to send postcards and then fliers to current and potential customers notifying them of discounted office merchandise for sale. This method of selling office supplies, one of the first direct mail efforts in the industry, worked so well that the two men were soon spending more time on the phone filling orders than out selling their products door-to-door. The next step was a natural one. The Miller brothers glued together their first mail-order pamphlet complete with cut-out pictures from wholesale books, reduced their prices by 15 percent, offered to sell their supplies in bulk quantities direct from the manufacturer, and provided free delivery to all their customers.

By 1963 Quill Corporation had transformed itself into one of the first mail-order-only companies in the United States and, not surprisingly, celebrated by introducing its first big catalogue.

With such overwhelming success, the Miller brothers decided to arrange for a bank loan in order to finance a major expansion plan. A large portion of this money was used to purchase a two-story building that served as a new office and warehouse for the firm. Unfortunately, the company grew more slowly than expected, and repaying the loan turned out to be much more difficult than anticipated. When the loan was finally repaid, Jack and Harvey, who were now acting as president and treasurer, respectively, decided that any future expansion plans would be financed out of the company's profits and determined by its cash flow. This decision led the two men to examine Quill's operations and implement a policy that created a positive cash flow by turning over the company's receivables in less than one month and its inventory no less than ten times per year.

Growth and Expansion During the 1970s and 1980s

In 1974 Quill reported annual sales of $3.5 million. Arnold Miller, cognizant of the need to help his brothers Jack and Harvey, and perhaps even guilty of spending many years apart from his family working as a certified public accountant in California, joined the family business as secretary. At first, the three brothers shared the responsibility of decision-making for the company. As the firm grew, however, the responsibility and duties of each brother needed to be clearly delineated. Jack chose marketing, Harvey decided on operations, and Arnold volunteered to supervise the company's finances. The triumvirate worked well, and the company grew rapidly. As with any other organization, disagreement among the principals was nonetheless commonplace. In order to deal with the more divisive issues, a policy was implemented such that if all three of the brothers disagreed on a particular course of action then it was not undertaken.

Still, the best was yet to come for Quill Corporation. During the early and mid-1990s, the company's revenues skyrocketed, amounting to $180 million in 1986. Its mail-order business was the most successful within the office supplies market, with more than 40 million catalogues and flyers sent to a customer base of approximately 600,000 businesses and organizations, and listing more than 9,000 various office supplies and products. With business booming, the company's number of employees rose to over 850, providing some of the best customer service in the industry. During the entire decade of the 1980s, Quill Corporation made a commitment to numerous mailings of its catalogue and flyers each year—60 million pieces annually on average—

since Jack Miller was well aware of the fact that keeping customers constantly aware of its deep discounts was the only way to maintain a customer base that had little loyalty to office supply companies.

At the same time, however, a new and highly innovative breed of discount office supply warehouses arrived on the scene. The most successful and largest of the new deep-discount office supply firms was Office Depot, a company whose revenues by the mid-1980s had catapulted to over $300 million, surpassing Quill Corporation not only in sales but also in direct mail-order volume. With 80 stores in 15 states, Office Depot soon developed a reputation as one of the most aggressive discount price firms in the industry. While Quill sold its own brand of copy paper for $37.90 per case, Office Depot sold it for a little over $20. Other deep-discount office supply stores, such as BizMart, Office Club, and Staples, followed Office Depot's lead, and by the late 1980s Quill Corporation's growth in certain geographical markets had ground to a complete halt.

The Miller brothers were not the kind of businessmen to lose ground without a fight, so they went on the offensive. Jack Miller directed the campaign to regain the markets Quill had lost, and began with customer service. He focused on the training of pleasant telephone operators, whom he recognized as the company's front-line sales force. He strategically increased the number of targeted mailings to prospective customers, and introduced a new policy that guaranteed delivery of all company products within three to five days. Most importantly, Jack Miller focused on improving prices across the board. Under his direction, the company not only slashed prices for all its office supplies, but also streamlined and simplified its pricing strategy. By 1989 Quill Corporation was able to lower its prices for all products by nearly 15 percent, thereby reducing the firm's gross margins on average to a still healthy 30 percent. As a result, despite the competition from such firms as Office Depot and Staples, Quill Corporation continued to grow and prosper.

The 1990s and Beyond

During the early and mid-1990s, Quill Corporation remained under the direction of the Miller brothers. Confident of their ability to compete with the deep-discount office supply firms, the Miller brothers decided to make a foray into the retail store market and acquired Aaron's Office Furniture Warehouse, a small operation with five stores located in the Chicago metropolitan area. Jack Miller managed to successfully expand the operations of Office Furniture Warehouse, renamed Quill's Office Furniture, during the early years of the 1990s, and even opened another store by the end of fiscal 1994. Another strategic expansion involved the growth of the company's product line, when in 1995 the Miller brothers decided to carry a wide range of school supplies, such as crayons, rulers, audiovisual equipment, erasers, and other items to meet the needs of primary, secondary, and vocational students.

Much of the company's growth during these years was due to the result of an extremely important case heard before the U.S. Supreme Court. The state government of North Dakota had brought suit against Quill Corporation in order to force the out-of-state mail-order company to require that in-state customers pay taxes on their purchases. The litigation surrounding the case continued for a number of years and then, finally, the Supreme Court decided in favor of Quill Corporation. The majority opinion maintained that the North Dakota state government could not require the firm to collect taxes from in-state customers since Quill Corporation did not have any employees or retail stores located in the state. Customers flocked to buy Quill's products since they did not have to pay taxes on the purchases. Consequently, the Miller brothers decided to improve and upgrade their catalogue business, while selling off the office furniture stores purchased a few years earlier.

Then, without much warning or notice, the Millers decided to sell Quill Corporation to Staples, Inc., one of their traditional competitors, in the winter of 1998. All of the brothers were growing older, with Jack Miller set to celebrate his 69th birthday during the year. Many of the company's employees were taken by surprise, as well as industry analysts and other people working in the office supply products industry. According to Jack Miller, the three brothers had wanted to keep the operation a family business; however, there was not one member of the younger generation within the family who was willing to assume the responsibilities and duties necessary to maintain the company's success. In addition, the Miller brothers could not find a suitable candidate from the outside that they thought could direct the firm into the future. Consequently, the three aging entrepreneurs sold Quill Corporation, with sales of $600 million in 1997, to Staples, Inc. for $685 million in stock.

In 1998 Staples was operating 582 superstores throughout the United States, with a comprehensive line of office supply products ranging from copy paper to office furniture. The acquisition of Quill, which management decided to run as an operating division under the Quill name and logo, gave Staples access not only to an extremely successful direct-mail catalogue market, but also to a new and burgeoning Internet market that Quill was just starting to expand. Quill's $8 million in sales over the Internet alone in 1997 was clearly an indication of a huge future market for office supplies. Quill's extensive catalogue, database marketing abilities, brand equity, and delivery operation was one of the determining factors in Staples' decision to acquire one of its traditional rivals.

Quill Corporation's future seemed assured under the auspices of Staples, which reported revenues of $5 billion in 1998. The executives at Staples recognized what the Miller brothers had taken years to build, and were well aware of the potential profits that could result from careful management of the firm that started, humbly, in a poultry store.

Further Reading

Barrier, Michael, "Brother Act," *Nation's Business,* January 1989, p. 41.

Bulkeley, William, "Staples, Moving Beyond Superstores, Will Buy Quill for $685 Million in Stock," *Wall Street Journal,* April 8, 1999, p. B16.

Freeman, Laurie, "Frequent Mailings Keep Quill in Black Ink," *Advertising Age,* September 20, 1984, p. 9.

Harris, John, "The Battle of the Paper Clips," *Forbes,* May 14, 1990, p. 108,

Parr, Jan, "Quill's Miller Wields a Sharp Pencil," *Advertising Age,* October 17, 1998, p. S15.

"Quill Corporation Has Upgraded Its Corporate Web Site," *Purchasing,* February 11, 1999, p. 102.

Strazewski, Lea, "Three Direct Sellers Run the Office Party," *Advertising Age, May* 18, 1987, p. S18.

Troy, Mike, "Quill Purchase Gives Staples e-Presence," *Discount Store News,* April 20, 1998, p. 3.

—Thomas Derdak

Rand McNally & Company

8255 N. Central Park
Skokie, Illinois 60076-2970
U.S.A.
(847) 329-8100
Fax: (847) 673-0539
Web site: http://www.randmcnally.com

Private Company
Incorporated: 1856
Employees: 1,000
Sales: $200 million (1998 est.)
NAIC: 51113 Book Publishing; 511199 All Other
Publishers; 45411 Electronic Shopping & Mail-Order
Houses; 453998 All Other Miscellaneous Store
Retailers; 51121 Software Publishers

Rand McNally & Company, a leading U.S. publisher of travel books and electronic media for the travel industry, is perhaps best known for its maps and atlases, including the top-selling *Rand McNally Road Atlas,* a travel atlas which is updated every year. The company also creates such software as TripMaker and StreetFinder, and markets maps and globes for use in U.S. classrooms. Through its Transportation Data Management (TDM) operating unit, Rand McNally is the largest electronic publisher of information for the commercial transportation industry.

19th-Century Beginnings

Rand McNally & Company began in 1856 as a small printing business established on Chicago's Lake Street by company cofounders William Rand and Andrew McNally. In 1864 Rand and McNally bought the job printing department of the *Chicago Tribune* and began printing railroad tickets and timetables, but it was not for nearly another ten years that the first Rand McNally map would appear in the 1872 *Railway Guide.* Opting to expand the scope of its printed products, the company began producing globes and maps for schools in 1880.

By the end of the century, when Rand retired and sold his share of the company to McNally, the fledgling printing business had grown to employ a workforce of nearly 700. Andrew McNally died in 1904, and cofounder William Rand passed away the following year.

Map and Atlas Publishing Begins in 1907

Rand McNally began publishing road maps and road atlases in 1907 with the first photo-auto guide, which detailed the route of an automobile trip from Chicago to New York. The photo-auto guide consisted of directions for automobile drivers, along with accompanying photos to aid the traveler. The photos used in the company's subsequent Chicago-to-Milwaukee photo-auto guide would be taken by Andrew McNally II and his bride during their honeymoon in 1909.

In 1917 Rand McNally published the first road map to feature numbered highways. The numbering system, invented by a map draftsman named John Brink, eliminated the need for long names, which were difficult to depict on maps. Brink became the head of Rand McNally's new "Blazed Trails" department. In addition to producing the road maps, Rand McNally was also responsible for erecting many highway signs.

In the first of many partnerships between Rand McNally and the nation's oil companies, Rand McNally was hired in 1918 by the Gulf Oil Company to produce maps for a Gulf promotional campaign. The company also began producing educational materials for students. In 1922 Rand McNally published the first edition of *Goode's World Atlas,* named for its first editor, Dr. J. Paul Goode. The book became the standard geography text for U.S. high schools and colleges and would see its 19th edition published in the mid-1990s.

The first *Rand McNally Road Atlas* was published in 1924. By this time Rand McNally had completed publication of a complete set of numbered highway maps covering the United States, Canada, and Mexico. Among company milestones was the fact that in 1927 Rand McNally railroad maps were used by Charles Lindbergh for navigation over land during his historic flight across the Atlantic Ocean. In 1933 Andrew McNally II became president of the company. Under his leadership, an early foray into retail operations was realized when the first Rand McNally Map & Travel Store was opened in New York City in 1937.

Wartime Production

Demand for Rand McNally maps, particularly European maps, escalated during World War II. In fact, the company's presses began working 24 hours a day to meet orders, and that schedule continued throughout the war.

Aside from products for the war effort, the company also engaged in children's book publishing. During the 1940s Rand McNally published the works of noted children's author Marguerite Henry, whose bestselling children's books included *Misty of Chincoteague* and *King of the Wind*. In 1947 the company published *Kon-Tiki,* written by a relatively unknown Norwegian scientist, Thor Heyerdahl. The book became an international bestseller. Another Rand McNally printing specialty during this time involved tickets used in the transportation industry. In 1945 the company created a new ticket book with carbons that eliminated the previously bulky accordion-fold product used for airline and train tickets.

A third generation of McNallys continued the tradition of family leadership when Andrew McNally III became president of the company in 1948. The following year, Rand McNally entered the book manufacturing business on a full-scale basis with the purchase of the W.B. Conkey Company.

1950s–60s: Revolutions in Mapmaking

In 1952 Rand McNally moved its headquarters to the Chicago suburb of Skokie, to a newly constructed facility. New product development characterized the era, as the company's ticket division produced the first pressure-sensitive tickets, which eliminated the need for carbons in 1953. Moreover, Rand McNally became the first commercial mapmaker to utilize the scribing process to draft maps, a process that revolutionized mapmaking, during this time.

With the publication of the first full-color *Rand McNally Road Atlas* in 1960, the modestly successful publication became the world's most popular travel guide. Increased title production and demand for Rand McNally products prompted the 1962 construction of an additional book manufacturing plant. Over time this Versailles, Kentucky, plant was expanded to cover more than a million square feet and became one of the largest book manufacturing plants in the country. By the end of the 1980s the Versailles printing plant would be the largest maker of juvenile books in the United States.

In 1969 The Book Manufacturing Company, a subsidiary of the company, automated the process by which thumb indexes were cut and labeled for dictionaries and encyclopedias. In that year the company also published the first edition of *The New International Atlas* following a two-year, multimillion-dollar investment. The publication marked a new standard for U.S. mapmakers and enabled the company to overcome the traditional dominance of European mapmakers. In 1971 the company acquired a book manufacturing facility in Taunton, Massachusetts.

With the Arab oil embargo and higher oil prices in the early 1970s, the days of the free service station road map came to an end. As a result, Rand McNally began to place more importance on the merchandising of the *Rand McNally Road Atlas*. In 1974 Andrew McNally IV was named company president, becoming CEO as well four years later.

Technology Advances in the 1980s

In 1980 Rand McNally acquired Transportation Data Management (TDM), a small, technology-oriented company. This enabled Rand McNally to meld its enormous map database with a sophisticated electronic delivery system to provide routing and mileage information to the trucking and shipping industries. Focus on technology continued, as TDM introduced the computerized version of MileMaker, an online mileage and routing system for truckers and shippers which soon became an industry standard. By 1988 TDM was offering a PC-based Micro-MileMaker version of its MileMaker mileage and routing system that was previously available only as a mainframe or minicomputer package or on a timeshare basis. The PC-based system was aimed at smaller carriers who did not require a mainframe computer and who found timesharing too expensive.

During this time, Rand McNally's DocuSystems unit specialized in supplying airline and ground transportation tickets and baggage tags, along with other technologically complex documents for automated systems. DocuSystems pioneered the application of magnetic stripes onto automated ticket and boarding passes (ATBS) for United Airlines. The unit also developed an electronic ticketing system for airlines that used bar codes to detect ticket fraud, which was costing the airlines industry $200 to $500 million a year internationally. By the end of the 1980s DocuSystems had completed a series of strategic acquisitions to enhance the development of advanced capabilities in magnetic striping and baggage tags.

The company closed out the decade by expanding its chain of Map & Travel Stores, locating them in upscale malls and downtown areas. By 1994 there were more than 20 stores operating throughout the United States.

Acquisitions in the Early 1990s

In 1992 Rand McNally acquired Nicholstone Holdings Inc. of Nashville, Tennessee. Nicholstone specialized in book manufacturing, packaging, specialty printing, and binding, and produced computer software and documentation. This operation's capabilities in electronic publishing, multimedia printing, and packaging technology comprised the foundation of the Rand

---

McNally Media Services unit, which became a leading provider of digital packaging solutions for the software and entertainment industries.

In addition to the newly created Media Services group, Rand McNally's operations were organized into three other business groups: Book Services, which provided manufacturing services to other book and information publishers; DocuSystems, which specialized in transportation tickets and tags and other complex documents for automated systems; and Publishing, which encompassed the company's core geographic publishing business in travel, reference, education, and entertainment.

In 1993 Andrew McNally IV was named chairman, succeeding his father, Andrew McNally III, who became chairman emeritus. John S. Bakalar was appointed president, becoming the first non-family member to hold that position in the company's history. Bakalar also served as the company's chief operating officer. Also during this time, a fifth generation of McNallys joined the company, when Andrew McNally V began work in the company's Media Services Group in 1994.

Toward the end of 1993 the Versailles printing operation began to move to digital production. Many of the company's customers were equipped to submit digital files instead of the traditional mechanical-and-film materials used to create printing plates. In February 1994 Rand McNally and Eastman Kodak announced plans to install a direct-to-plate system to test the computer-to-plate system for long print runs. After completing a successful test period, Rand McNally purchased a full-time production system for installation in September 1995. A combination test site, production center, and showplace, the Versailles plant had grown from 300,000 square feet and 23 employees in 1962 to more than 1,000 employees and one million square feet.

In 1994 Rand McNally introduced the company's first consumer software product, TripMaker, to allow consumers to plan their trips on their home computers. The product demonstrated that Rand McNally had the ability to leverage its key assets into a new product that provided value to its customers, in spite of entering the market behind more technologically accomplished competitors.

Rand McNally had begun to convert its vast database resources into electronic form in 1989 when it hired Henry Feinberg to head its electronic systems division. Although TripMaker entered the CD-ROM market several years after Microsoft's Automap product, it surpassed Automap in sales in only two months. By 1995 Tripmaker accounted for a leading 32 percent market share, while Automap had fallen from more than a 50 percent market share to just 14 percent. Complementing TripMaker, which was designed to plan long vacations or business trips, Rand McNally introduced StreetFinder in 1995. StreetFinder focused on navigating in cities and became the market share leader in its category.

The company also launched its New Media Division to create and market consumer geographic products and services. Among the products to be offered later in the year was a full line of geographic software, including travel, reference, entertainment, and educational programs. The Media Services group acquired the software manufacturing, assembly, packaging, and order fulfillment facilities of DCA Ireland Ltd., based in Shannon, Ireland.

Challenges in the Late 1990s and Beyond

By the late 1990s, however, expansion at Rand McNally had been put in check. The privately held company, about which little financial information was made available, began to divest several of its operations. In January 1997 Rand McNally announced its intentions to sell its Book Services Group, which included the company's Versailles printing plant and another printing plant in Taunton, Massachusetts. A company spokesperson announced that Rand McNally would now concentrate on its core mapmaking business. The plants were sold to World Color Press, Inc., based in Greenwich, Connecticut, the third largest provider of print and digital information in the United States with 1995 revenues of $1.3 billion. Prior to the sale, Rand McNally was one of the three largest producers of hardcover books in the United States, and its Book Services Group accounted for $150 million of the company's estimated annual revenue of $500 million. The division had about 1,700 employees.

Also on the block were Rand McNally's Media Services division and DocuSystems. Within a couple of months Media Services was sold to McQueen, a Scottish software company, and DocuSystems was sold to a Chicago investment banking firm. That left Rand McNally with about 1,000 employees, down from 4,000 prior to the sales.

In April 1997 Rand McNally hired investment banking firm Goldman Sachs to explore its strategic options. By September, an announcement was made that controlling interest in the company would be sold to AEA Investors, Inc. In November of that year, the shareholders of AEA Investors, Inc. and the management of Rand McNally acquired a controlling interest in Rand McNally & Co. AEA was founded in 1969 by leading industrial families and chief executives of major corporations for the purpose of making investments in market-leading companies with attractive growth opportunities. Following the sale, the McNally family retired from active management in the company, with Andrew McNally IV remaining on the board of directors. Henry Feinberg was promoted from president of the company's publishing group to president and chairman of the entire company.

In December 1997 Rand McNally opened a new Internet travel store at www.randmcnallystore.com. This site offered consumers more than 3,000 products, including maps, travel guides, globes, software, games, and travel accessories.

At the end of the 1990s, the new streamlined Rand McNally was organized into seven divisions: Map and Atlas Publishing, Consumer Software, Educational Publishing, Rand McNally— TDM (Transportation Data Management), Map and Travel Stores, Allmaps (Canada), and Cartographic and Information Services.

With cash in hand Rand McNally was prepared to grow through strategic acquisitions. In November 1998 the company executed a letter of intent to acquire Thomas Bros. Maps, a privately held map publisher based in Irvine, California. The deal closed in the first quarter of 1999. Analysts had noted that the mapmaking industry was ripe for consolidation, and Thomas was considered one of the major regional players.

Principal Operating Units

Map and Atlas Publishing; Consumer Software; Educational Publishing; Rand McNally—TDM (Transportation Data Management); Map & Travel Stores; Allmaps (Canada); Cartographic and Information Services.

Further Reading

Borden, Jeff, "A Sale? IPO? The Borders Shift on Rand McNally Map," *Crain's Chicago Business,* February 10, 1997, p. 1.

Campbell, Ronald, "Irvine, Calif.-Based Thomas Bros. Technology Attracts Rand McNally," *Knight-Ridder/Tribune Business News,* November 15, 1998.

Goddard, Connie, "Rand McNally Returns to Children's Trade Market," *Publishers Weekly,* May 24, 1993, p. 51.

Hilts, Paul, "Rand McNally Moves to CTP," *Publishers Weekly,* September 11, 1995, p. 31.

Milliot, Jim, "Investors to Buy Rand McNally," *Publishers Weekly,* September 8, 1997, p. 12.

——, "Rand McNally Weighing Possible Sale of Company," *Publishers Weekly,* May 5, 1997, p. 11.

Navarrete, Angela, "Rand McNally's Dynamic Trip-Taking Duo," *PC World,* October 1998, p. 80.

Pack, Todd, "Rand McNally to Sell Book Services Group," *Knight-Ridder/Tribune Business News,* January 8, 1997.

"Rand McNally Acquires Nicholstone Holdings," *Publishers Weekly,* August 24, 1992, p. 32.

"Rand McNally Sells Its Printing Group," *Publishers Weekly,* January 13, 1997, p. 12.

"Rand McNally Starts New Media Div. for 'Geographic Software'," *Publishers Weekly,* April 18, 1994, p. 11.

"Rand Sale Done, Opens Internet Travel Store," *Publishers Weekly,* December 8, 1997, p. 10.

Schifrin, Matthew, "The Message, Not the Medium," *Forbes,* September 11, 1995, p. 86.

Weller, Sam, "Rand McNally Buys Thomas Bros.," *Publishers Weekly,* December 7, 1998, p. 16.

The Worlds of Rand McNally, Skokie, Ill.: Rand McNally, 1994.

Zarley, Craig, "The Mapmaker Markets a PC Package to Keep Long-Haul Truckers on Track," *PC Week,* December 8, 1987, p. 66.

—David Bianco

RHM

Ranks Hovis McDougall Limited

Chapel House
Liston Road
Marlow, Buckinghamshire SL7 1TJ
United Kingdom
(01) 628 478484
Fax: (01) 629 478404
Web site: http://www.tomkins.co.uk

Division of Tomkins PLC
Incorporated: 1899 as Joseph Rank Limited
Employees: 20,000
Sales: £1.80 billion (US$3.0 billion) (1998)
NAIC: 311422 Specialty Canning; 311423 Dried &
    Dehydrated Food Manufacturing; 311421 Fruit &
    Vegetable Canning; 311412 Frozen Specialty Food
    Manufacturing; 311211 Flour Milling; 311812
    Commercial Bakeries; 31192 Coffee & Tea
    Manufacturing; 311823 Dry Pasta Manufacturing;
    311999 All Other Miscellaneous Food Manufacturing

Ranks Hovis McDougall Limited (RHM) is the food division of Tomkins PLC, which acquired the company (then known as Ranks Hovis McDougall PLC) in 1992. A major food producer in the United Kingdom, RHM manages a federation of more than 20 subsidiary companies that also includes firms in Ireland, France, the Netherlands, and the United States. In addition to flour milling, the industry upon which RHM traces its roots back to Victorian England, the company is also involved in bread baking and cake making. Of increasing importance are RHM's partnerships with major customers; these include relationships to supply products and services to McDonald's and Pizza Hut restaurants and Marks & Spencer stores in the United Kingdom. Also among the companies that comprise RHM is The Red Wing Co., Inc., the largest manufacturer of private-label groceries in the United States.

Flour Milling Roots

Joseph Rank, the founder of the company, began in the milling business in 1875 by renting a small windmill. He lost money at first and had to take a cotenancy at West's Holderness Corn Mill. But he was soon able to recoup his losses and set enough money aside to expand his business. At this time competition from American and Hungarian flour was an issue for English millers. Rank explored new milling methods to improve his competitive position against these foreign imports. In 1885 he built a mechanically driven flour mill in Hull. By using steel rollers instead of mill stones, the mill was able to produce an impressive six sacks of flour an hour, up from one and a half. In 1888 he built another steel-roller plant in Lincolnshire, and soon after still another even more modern plant. This new plant, equipped with the best technology available, produced 20 sacks of flour an hour and was considered one of the finest flour mills in the country.

At the turn of the century Great Britain was plagued by malnutrition. The poor often lived on little more than bread and tea, and infant mortality was high. In 1901 military recruitment standards had to be lowered to find enough men to enlist for the Boer War: the new minimum height for recruits was reduced to five feet. Since bread was the staple of the country, Joseph Rank was challenged to increase productivity. He installed a plant that produced 30 sacks of flour an hour, and then another plant with a 40-sack-an-hour capacity. He also set up agencies to distribute his flour in parts of England where it previously had not been sold. In May 1899 Joseph Rank Limited was incorporated, and Joseph Rank became governing director, which he remained until his death in 1943.

In 1902 Rank made his first trip to the United States to see the wheat fields of the Midwest, determined to understand and conquer his competitors. Soon after his trip abroad, the company built mills in London and Cardiff. In 1912 a mill in Birkenhead was built to supply the needs of Ireland and northwestern England. Soon after that, the corporate headquarters was moved from Yorkshire to London.

During World War I, when starvation was a real threat to the people of Great Britain, Joseph Rank was asked to become a member of the Wheat Control Board. Frustrated by the government's inability to warehouse large quantities of wheat—distribution became chaotic as many ships carrying supplies were sunk—he relied much on his own resources and initiative to buy and store quantities of wheat and to increase the production capacity of his London mill. During the war years, the company employed 3,000 workers, many of them women who took on production jobs while men were away fighting the war. Despite his philosophy of personal initiative, Rank and his sons were known for public service, religious faith, and philanthropic work. In 1935 Joseph Rank received the Freedom of the City of Hull (the only public honor he ever accepted), in part because of a trust fund he had set up in Hull to help "poor persons of good character."

During the 1920s, the milling capacity in Great Britain exceeded the demand for flour. Nevertheless, Joseph Rank was able to expand into Scotland and consolidate and expand his operations in Ireland. He perceived the potential of new methods of transportation and communication very early, forming the British Isles Transport Company Limited to provide for the distribution needs of his company in 1920. In 1933 Ranks Limited became a public corporation. By this time Joseph Rank was in his eighties, but he was still actively involved in the business. His son Rowland was running his own business—the Mark Mayhew mill, which produced animal feed as well as flour, and which, after World War II, would be incorporated into the Rank company. His son James, who after his father's death in 1943 became chairman of the company, was employed during the war as the government's director for cereal imports. Joseph Rank, despite his age, also contributed to the war effort by working as a secret wheat buyer for the government to build up stocks in the year before the outbreak of war.

After World War II, James Rank, the new chairman, was joined by an associate of his government-service days, Cecil Loombe, who became a director. Their challenge was to reconstruct the mills devastated by bombing and to expand the company. A new mill in Gateshead was their first big postwar accomplishment.

In 1952 James Rank was succeeded by his brother Arthur as chairman. Under Arthur Rank, the company explored many new ventures and began to acquire a variety of small, family-owned agriculture and baking businesses. It was also during this period that the company's faith in quality control and research was firmly established. High standards of nutrition were set and maintained for both human and animal foods by testing in every phase of the production process. The legacy of these early efforts is RHM Technology Limited and its research center at High Wycombe, staffed by more than 200 scientists who continue to improve the nutritional value of the company's products as well as look for new food sources.

Acquired Hovis-McDougall in 1962 to Become RHM

In 1962, still under the leadership of Arthur Rank, Ranks Limited acquired the Hovis-McDougall Company and became

Ranks Hovis McDougall, Limited (RHM). In 1968 RHM made another important acquisition: the Cerebos food group, which brought with it a number of popular food brands as well as interests in France, Argentina, New Zealand, Australia, Canada, the United States, and South Africa. By 1969, after transforming the company from a flour mill to an international company with a variety of food interests, Arthur Rank was ready to hand over the chairmanship to his brother's son, whose name, like his grandfather's, was Joseph Rank.

Under Joseph Rank's leadership the company maintained its dedication to research. During the 1970s, the research center at High Wycombe prospered and undertook projects in crustacea farming cereal and seed production, wheat hybrids, and protein production from starch. By 1984 research had advanced to the point that the company was ready to undertake a joint venture with ICI, Britain's largest industrial company, to form Marlow Foods, a company dedicated to producing and promoting mycoprotein food—food made by industrial fermentation of wheat-derived products and noted for being high in protein and fiber and low in fat, as well as containing no cholesterol.

By the late 1970s, RHM and its competitor, Associated British Foods PLC, monopolized their industry. Each company was selling over 60 percent of the flour it milled to its own subsidiaries, thereby offsetting losses in its baking division. Unable to compete or sustain losses, many small independent bakeries closed.

Joseph Rank became president in 1981 and was succeeded as chairman by Sir Peter Reynolds. The company made a number of important acquisitions during the 1980s in the United Kingdom, the United States, and the Far East. The largest acquisition was the 1987 purchase of U.K.-based Avana Group, which was renamed Avana Bakeries Limited. After a career with the company that had begun in 1936, Joseph Rank retired in 1988, remaining an honorary president after his retirement.

RHM undertook an unusual advertising campaign in 1986—one designed not for consumers of its products, but rather for the financial press, to increase awareness of the company itself. The ads featured a variety of slogans, all of which emphasized the diversity of the company, including "We do not live by bread alone" and "We bakers like to have fingers in many pies."

An innovative accounting practice introduced in 1988 also drew attention to the worth of RHM (by this time known as Ranks Hovis McDougall PLC). In its 1988 annual report, RHM showed the value of all of its brands on its balance sheet. As intangible assets, brands are not usually counted on financial reports as part of a company's assets. Grand Metropolitan was the first company to ever put acquired brands on its balance sheet, in September 1988. RHM went even further by including acquired as well as internally developed brands. Brand accounting was somewhat controversial because procedures for calculation had not yet been standardized.

Late 1980s Marked by Takeover Battles

In 1988 much of RHM's energies were directed to fighting a hostile takeover attempt by Australia-based food concern Goodman Fielder Wattie Limited, of Australia, which owned 29.9 percent of RHM's shares (the financial press saw RHM's move to brand accounting, in part, as a way of discouraging such a takeover). After the Goodman Fielder bid was thwarted by British regulators, the Australian firm began negotiating with third parties to sell its RHM stake.

In April 1989, however, RHM made a surprising bid of US$2.4 billion for its former suitor, viewing the purchase of Goodman Fielder—at the time the largest food company in Australia and New Zealand—as a logical next step in its international expansion. Goodman Fielder quickly rejected the offer, even as RHM built up a 14.9 percent stake in Goodman. In May 1989 RHM dropped its bid, after Goodman Fielder sold its 29.9 percent stake in RHM to maverick Anglo-French financier James Goldsmith. Fearing that "Sir James" would attempt a takeover, RHM moved quickly to sell its stake in Goodman Fielder. But a Goldsmith takeover never materialized, and by early 1991 he had sold his entire RHM stake in the market, leaving the largest single stake in the company under five percent.

Meanwhile, RHM paid £80 million (US$144 million) to purchase the U.K. ready-to-eat cereal business of RJR Nabisco in 1988. The main brands acquired thereby were Shredded Wheat and Shreddies, which were manufactured in the United Kingdom and distributed throughout western Europe. RHM had great difficulty competing with U.S.-based cereal giant Kellogg Company, which, for example, claimed a market share of nearly 50 percent in the United Kingdom, compared to RHM's declining share of 15 percent. Facing a tough battle with Kellogg, RHM decided to exit from the cereal business, selling the unit to a joint venture of Nestlé S.A. and General Mills Inc. for £93 million (US$167 million) in mid-1990.

Acquired by Tomkins in 1992

RHM's profits and stock price were battered in the early 1990s by an economic recession, the continued decline in bread consumption in the United Kingdom, and the concomitant overcapacity in the bread-making industry. The company's weakness led to another hostile takeover bid, this time a £780 million (US$1.2 billion) offer from Hanson PLC, a company well-known for its takeovers that were quickly followed by asset sell-offs. Launched on October 5, 1992, the bid was rejected by the RHM board, which on October 16 announced a three-way demerger as a defense. The plan involved dividing the company into three separate units: a milling and baking group, a grocery products company, and a cake business.

In late October 1992, however, a white knight entered the scene in the form of Anglo-U.S. conglomerate Tomkins PLC, which bid £935 million (US$1.5 billion) for RHM, an offer accepted by the company's board and not challenged by Hanson. Tomkins—a diversified manufacturer of bicycles, handguns, industrial valves, and other products—was criticized by some analysts for having acquired too diverse an array of interests, but the acquisition of RHM seemed to prove the critics wrong. The renamed Ranks Hovis McDougall Limited, which became the food division of Tomkins, posted gains in operating profits each year from fiscal 1994 through fiscal 1998. RHM also remained largely intact after its acquisition by Tomkins, a development in sharp contrast to its likely fate had Hanson's hostile bid succeeded.

In 1995 Tomkins acquired Lyons Cakes, which two years later was integrated into Manor Bakeries Limited, an RHM subsidiary and the largest cake manufacturer in Europe. Also in 1997 RHM merged two of its subsidiaries—Tiffany Sharwood's Frozen Foods and Abercroft Cakes—to form RHM Frozen Foods Limited, a consolidation move aimed at lowering marketing costs for such brands as Mr. Kipling, McDougalls, and Sharwood's. RHM Frozen Foods held strong market positions in meat and pastry pies, ethnic ready-to-eat meals, individual cakes, and other desserts. In October 1997 Tomkins acquired Golden West Foods Limited for £35.6 million (US$54.1 million), gaining the leading supplier of products—buns, drinks, and sauces—and distribution services to the McDonald's fast-food chain in the United Kingdom. This addition to RHM bolstered the increasingly important area of partnerships for the company, which already had relationships with the Pizza Hut restaurant chain and the Marks & Spencer retail chain in the United Kingdom, as well as ownership of The Red Wing Co., Inc., the largest manufacturer of private-label grocery products—including ketchup, peanut butter, preserves, and jelly—in the United States.

Beginning in September 1996, following Tomkins's acquisition of industrial manufacturer Gates Corporation, Tomkins launched a disposal program to sell off nonstrategic businesses. Among the RHM companies sold were Carriage House Fruit Company Inc. and Chesswood Produce Limited, both jettisoned in 1998.

In May 1998 Tomkins paid £35.6 million (US$57.7 million) for Le Pain Croustillant Limited, a maker of specialty breads sold to major supermarket chains; Le Pain Croustillant subsequently became an RHM subsidiary. In March 1998 Tomkins acquired six flour mills in the United Kingdom from Kerry Group, an Irish food company, for £92 million (US$149 million). But in September of that year, U.K. regulators ruled that the purchase would give Tomkins too large a share of the domestic flour market and ordered the company to sell four of the six mills, allowing it to keep mills at Birkenhead and Cambridge. Despite this setback, the increasingly profitable Ranks Hovis McDougall appeared to be thriving in its role as the food division of Tomkins. RHM was likely to benefit from further add-on acquisitions funded by the deep pockets of its parent.

Principal Subsidiaries

Avana Bakeries Limited; British Bakeries Limited; R.F. Brookes Limited; Golden West Foods Limited; Holgran Limited; Le Pain Croustillant Limited; Manor Bakeries Limited; Overseal Foods Limited; Pasta Foods Limited; Rank Hovis Limited; RGB Coffee Limited; RHM Foods Limited; RHM Frozen Foods Limited; RHM Ingredients Limited; RHM Technology Limited; J.A. Sharwood & Co., Limited; Three Cooks Limited; Sofrapain (France); Gateaux Limited (Ireland); RHM Foods (Ireland) Limited; Ranks Meel B.V. (Netherlands); The Red Wing Co., Inc. (U.S.A.).

Further Reading

"Aiming for a Bigger Slice," *Grocer*, May 31, 1997, p. 44.
Braithwaite, Paul, "RHM Brands Facing Up to the Future," *Super Marketing*, November 20, 1992, pp. 26+.

Bray, Nicholas, "Tomkins Makes $1.5 Billion Bid for RHM, Topping Hanson Offer," *Wall Street Journal,* October 30, 1992, p. A7.

Carrington, Tim, and S. Karene Witcher, "U.K.'s Ranks Hovis Bids $2.4 Billion for Former Suitor," *Wall Street Journal,* April 25, 1989, p. A18.

de Jonquières, Guy, "Britain's Baking Industry Fights for Every Crumb," *Financial Times,* March 30, 1992, p. 17.

de Jonquières, Guy, and Richard Gourlay, "Searching for the Right Recipe," *Financial Times,* November 9, 1992, p. 15.

Forman, Craig, "Ranks Hovis Drops Bid for Goodman, May Sell Stake," *Wall Street Journal,* May 23, 1989, p. A15.

Gibson, Richard, "Venture of Nestle, General Mills Buys Cereal Line in U.K.," *Wall Street Journal,* July 24, 1990, p. B5.

" 'It Can't Be Done,' " *Frozen and Chilled Foods,* May 1998, pp. 23, 25–26, 29.

"Just Desserts for RHM," *Management Today,* December 1992, p. 13.

Lublin, Joann S., and S. Karene Witcher, "Goldsmith Buys 29.9% Ranks Hovis Stake," *Wall Street Journal,* May 19, 1989, p. A11.

"RHM: 1875–1975," London: Ranks Hovis McDougall, 1975.

Taylor, Roger, "Too Big for Its Own Good?," *Financial Times,* January 17, 1998, p. FTM5.

Urry, Maggie, "Kerry to Sell Spillers Mills to Tomkins," *Financial Times,* February 13, 1998, p. 26.

——, "Mandelson Order Tomkins to Sell Four Flour Mills," *Financial Times,* September 25, 1998, p. 26.

—updated by David E. Salamie

Where Service Quality is the Difference.

RSC
Rental Service Corporation

Rental Service Corporation

6929 E. Greenway Parkway, Suite 200
Scottsdale, Arizona 85254
U.S.A.
(602) 905-3300
(800) 441-3353
Fax: (602) 905-3400
Web site: http://www.rentalservice.com

Public Company
Incorporated: 1992
Employees: 2,600
Sales: $578.47 million (1998)
Stock Exchanges: New York
Ticker Symbol: RSV
NAIC: 532412 Construction, Mining, & Forestry
  Machinery & Equipment Rental & Leasing; 53249
  Other Commercial & Industrial Machinery &
  Equipment Rental & Leasing

Rental Service Corporation (RSC) is one of the largest equipment rental firms in the United States. For more than 50 years, RSC has provided equipment (ranging from electric hand tools, forklifts, and backhoes to post hole diggers and 100-foot telescopic boom lifts to earth-moving equipment, computerized and manned tool trailers, and mill supplies) for rental to the industrial, petrochemical, and construction industry, as well as to contractors and homeowners. The company also sells parts, supplies, and used rental equipment; distributes new equipment for manufacturers; and provides support services, including onsite maintenance and repair.

The rental equipment industry comprises more than 15,000 competitors engaged in the daily, weekly, or monthly rental of a wide range of equipment to virtually every segment of the economy. Industry size estimates range from $15 billion to $20 billion, with real growth rates variously estimated to be between ten percent and 20 percent per year. This growth stems from corporate America's increasing interest in outsourcing noncore business operations. This trend is being recognized by all indus-

try participants including rental chains; large equipment dealers; manufacturers such as Caterpillar, Deere, and Case; and private equity investors. The full size potential of the industry is not known, but it is estimated that more than 85 percent of the relevant equipment (i.e., backhoes, bulldozers, aerial lifts, air compressors, etc.) continues to be owned by the end user. Industry growth also is being complemented by the substantial improvement in the breadth, depth, and quality of rental equipment being offered by major industry competitors such as RSC, Hertz, National Equipment Services, Prime Service Inc., and U.S. Rentals. As a result of its rapid growth and local service nature, the rental business is highly fragmented and in the early stages of consolidation. The business has been dominated, traditionally, by ''Mom and Pop'' shops until such companies as Rental Service and industry leader United Rentals began acquiring them to take advantage of projected growth in the business as more and more companies decide to rent, rather than buy, equipment they do not need on a full-time basis.

Founding: 1992–95

The company was formed in 1992 in California. Because the company was private until 1996, little information is available regarding these first years in business. Since going public in 1996, however, the company has released information about its early financial history. Total revenue for 1993 reached $25.63 million, with a net loss of $294,000. Fiscal 1994 revenues grew to $41.82 million, and net income jumped to $1.98 million. In 1995 the company moved its headquarters to Arizona. Total revenue for the year reached $65.92 million, with a net income of $3.24 million.

First to Go Public: 1996

In September 1996 RSC was the first rental industry participant to go public, being traded on the NASDAQ. In the first day of trading, the stock shot from its initial opening price of $16 per share to $21.75. According to analysts, it was the sixth largest gainer in U.S. markets, and the 5.5 million shares went for $88 million, making it the largest initial public offering (IPO) in Arizona in 1996. U.S. Rentals, Prime Service, Hertz, and United Rentals soon followed suit with public offerings. By that time, the company had opened 25 locations and acquired 65 others, mostly concentrated in the Southeast. In 1996 total revenues climbed to $128.35 million, and net income dropped slightly to $2.72 million.

More Acquisitions: 1997

The following year, however, the company bounced back with a vengeance. In March 1997 the company acquired United Rentals & Sales Inc. of Jonesboro and Blytheville, Arkansas (not to be confused with industry leader United Rentals Inc. of Greenwich, Connecticut). The acquisition brought RSC its 100th and 101st locations added since the company's formation in 1992. The company also acquired Kastner Rentals of New Orleans, bringing the total acquisitions for calendar 1997 to five, comprising seven locations and with revenue of approximately $7.8 million. Early in April, the company made its sixth acquisition of the year, Cometect Inc. (dba Industrial Air Tool [IAT]) of Pasadena, Texas, for $32.6 million in cash and more than 189,000 shares of RSC stock. A market leader in the areas of onsite rental facility management, integrated tool room management services, and tool trailer rentals for industrial construction job sites, as well as a major supplier of maintenance, repair, and operating supplies to the petrochemical industry, IAT had estimated revenues for the fiscal year ending March 31, 1997 of $50 million from its four locations in Texas and Louisiana. The acquisition played a key role in RSC's new Industrial Division RSC and expanded the company's presence in the industrial marketplace.

In May of that year, the company moved from the NASDAQ to the New York Stock Exchange, increasing trading spreads on the company's stock and increasing volume nearly threefold. The next month's public offering sold some three million shares; some of the proceeds went to acquire Brute Equipment Co. (dba Foxx Hy-Reach) and Central States Equipment Inc. Foxx, which specialized in the rental and sale of aerial equipment to construction and industrial customers in Iowa and Illinois, was acquired for $32.7 million in cash, plus more than 284,000 shares of stock. Central, which specialized in the rental and sale of aerial equipment, ladders, and scaffolding in Kansas, Missouri, and Oklahoma, was purchased for $18 million in cash, plus more than 200,000 shares of stock. The two acquisitions expanded the company's geographic coverage into the Midwest, with five additional states, a combined eight locations, 80 employees, and revenues of approximately $32.4 million. More than 180 of Central's machines were used during construction of Station Casino's mammoth $300 million complex in Missouri. RSC also acquired D&D Rentals, with five locations in Tallahassee and Live Oaks, Florida; Stop Again

Rentals of Texarkana, Texas; Carter Rentals, with two location in Valdosta, Georgia; and Breedon Rental & Sales, with two locations in Van Buren and Russellville, Arkansas, bringing in companies with revenues totaling approximately $12.1 million. RSC signed eight additional letters-of-intent to acquire businesses having a combined 23 locations and revenues of approximately $41 million. The companies acquired had operations in Georgia, Pennsylvania, Maryland, Virginia, Delaware, Kansas, Missouri, Illinois, Tennessee, South Carolina, and Florida.

In December 1997 RSC announced it had executed a definitive agreement for Siems Rental & Sales Co. Inc. The 30-year-old independent equipment rental company added to RSC six locations in Maryland, Delaware, Pennsylvania, and Virginia, as well as annual revenue of approximately $18 million. In addition, RSC completed the acquisitions of Roesch Equipment Company, which operated one location in Urbana, Illinois, and had revenues of approximately $3.1 million, and Allen Equipment Inc., with one location in Franklin Park, Illinois, and revenues of approximately $2 million. Also that month, RSC acquired Denver-based Rent-It-Center Inc. (dba Center Rental & Sales Inc.) for a total purchase price of approximately $116.9 million in cash and more than 64,000 shares of stock. The acquisition of Center, one of the premier independent rental and sales companies in the industry, covering small tools through heavy equipment, brought 14 rental locations in Colorado, New Mexico, Texas, Kansas, Missouri, and Nebraska, and revenue of approximately $46 million. RSC's public offering that month consisted of some four million shares of common stock sold for approximately $24 million. For 1997, total revenues shot up to $261.26 million, a 103.5 percent increase over 1996 sales, and net income skyrocketed to $12.62 million, a 366.7 percent growth rate. By the end of the year, the company had more than 165 locations throughout the United States and Canada.

Still More Acquisitions: 1998–99

In January 1998 RSC completed acquisitions of Siems, R&M Rentals Inc., Panama City Rentals Inc., Frank Wilson's Rentals & Sales Co., and Ray E. Miller (dba Franklin Rent-All). The acquired companies brought to RSC a combined 14 locations in Arkansas, Delaware, Florida, Georgia, Maryland, Pennsylvania, South Carolina, Tennessee, and Virginia, and had combined revenues of approximately $26.6 million. The following month, the company acquired substantially all of the assets of JDW Enterprises, Inc. (aka Valley Rentals) for $93.6 million in cash and more than 435,000 shares of stock. The independent equipment rental company added clients in Arizona and New Mexico and revenues of some $41 million.

In April RSC completed the acquisitions of James S. Peterson Enterprises (dba Metroquip Rental Centers), T&M Rentals Inc., Rent-It Company Inc., and Southwest Rentals & Sales, altogether operating a combined nine locations in Minnesota, Nebraska, Indiana, Louisiana, and Missouri, with combined revenues of approximately $38.6 million. The following month, RSC bought Midwest Aerial Platforms Inc., with three locations in Illinois and Wisconsin and revenues of approximately $8.2 million. The acquisition expanded the company's presence in Illinois and brought it into its 26th state.

July 1998 saw the company make its first foray out of the U.S. market, and into the Canadian market, as RSC acquired

Alberta, Canada-based Fasco Rentals Ltd., which operated four locations in Edmonton and one in Bonnyville and had total revenues of approximately $3.9 million. In addition, the company picked up Sooner Rental & Supply Inc. and Barney Hurley Crane Service Inc., whose combined eight locations in Oklahoma and Illinois brought revenues near $6.3 million.

By the end of the year the company had acquired another 23 equipment rental companies, adding a total of 64 new locations as well as opening 20 new sites. The company's credit facility was expanded by $150 million, and total revenue for the year reached approximately $578.47 million.

In January 1999 the company announced that it had entered into a definitive merger agreement with Fort Lauderdale, Florida-based NationsRent, founded by James L. Kirk to consolidate the heavy equipment rental industry and funded in part by Wayne Huizenga, son Wayne, Jr., and Huizenga's brother-in-law Harris W. Hudson. The combined new company, RSC NationsRent, would bring together 375 locations across Canada and 38 states in the United States (244 of which were RSC's), creating the second largest company in the equipment rental industry, behind only Greenwich, Connecticut-based United Rentals Inc., which had about $1.5 billion in revenue in 1998. The merger/acquisition cost RSC an estimated $366 million. A few months later, United Rentals commenced a tender offer for all outstanding RSC shares at a price of $22.75 per share. The unsolicited offer was referred to the RSC board of directors for review and was rejected. The NationsRent-RSC merger would bring the total number of employees in the joint company to around 6,500. Although NationsRent stock dropped nearly 25 percent following the announcement, analysts indicated that it was not unprecedented, citing Viacom's purchase of Blockbuster Entertainment in 1994 as an example of similar occurrences. NationsRent itself had been on an acquisitions binge, buying Birmingham's Reliable Rentals, founded in 1987 by David Upton, in late 1998, as well as Rush Equipment in Pelham, Florida, and AA Rent Village in Tuscaloosa, Florida. NationsRent also was gearing up for a major branding campaign that would include a NASCAR sponsorship in 1999.

RSC's main rival, United Rentals, which became North America's largest rental equipment company in September 1998 when it bought U.S. Rentals for approximately $1.3 billion in stock and assumed debt, was not idle during this time either. It had been snapping up smaller competitors left and right and by March 1999 had 470 locations in its empire, throughout the United States and Canada.

By mid-1999, the top 100 competitors in the business, including RSC (of an approximate total 15,000 competitors), were estimated to hold only 17 percent of the full market, with no competitor holding more than a two percent market share. Therefore, as the 21st century neared, an outstanding growth opportunity existed for companies such as RSC, which possessed the management, systems, and financial resources to pursue consolidation aggressively.

Principal Subsidiaries

Center Rental & Sales; RSC Valley.

Further Reading

"*The Arizona Republic* AZ Inc. Column. The Arizona Republic," *Knight-Ridder/Tribune Business News*, April 9, 1999, p. OKRB99099013.

Balzer, Stephanie, "Rental Firm on $114 Million Buying Binge," *Business Journal—Serving Phoenix & the Valley of the Sun*, May 16, 1997, p. 1.

Bussey, Jane, "Miami-Based Equipment-Rental Company Considers Sale of Assets," *Knight-Ridder/Tribune Business News*, March 29, 1999, p. OKRB99088243.

Gilbertson, Dawn, "*The Arizona Republic* Taking Stock in Arizona Column," *Knight-Ridder/Tribune Business News*, April 13, 1999, p. OKRB99103011.

——, "Rental Service Corp. Stock Soars 36 Percent on First Day," *Knight-Ridder/Tribune Business News*, September 20, 1996, p. 920B0225.

——, "Scottsdale, Ariz.-Based Rental Service Corp. Is Target of Takeover Effort," *Knight-Ridder/Tribune Business News*, April 6, 1999, p. OKRB99096015.

——, "Scottsdale, Ariz.-Based Rental Service Corp. To Buy Rival Company," *Knight-Ridder/Tribune Business News*, January 22, 1999, p. OKRB9902201E.

Gladstone, Darren, "Windows CE Cements the Deal: Equipment Rental Company Taps Mobile Devices to Hasten Order Fulfillment," *PC Week*, April 5, 1999, p. 45.

"Hostile Bid Pressed by United Rentals," *New York Times*, April 14, 1999, p. C13.

Margolies, Dan, "Aerial Lift Equipment Firm Is Sold to Arizona Company," *Kansas City Business Journal*, May 16, 1997, p. 5.

McNair, James, "Equipment Rental Firms Caught in Merger Triangle," *Knight-Ridder/Tribune Business News*, April 5, 1999, p. OKRB990950AD.

——, "Fort Lauderdale, Fla., Equipment Rental Firm's Shares Slide," *Knight-Ridder/Tribune Business News*, March 19, 1999, p. OKRB990780A5.

——, "Fort Lauderdale, Fla., Scottsdale, Ariz., Leasing Firms to Merge," *Knight-Ridder/Tribune Business News*, January 21, 1999, p. OKRB990210FD.

Milazzo, Don, "NationsRent Merger Adds 17 State Stores," *Birmingham Business Journal*, February 8, 1999, p. 9.

"NationsRent Reaffirms Commitment to Complete 'Superior' Merger Transaction with Rental Service Corporation," *PR Newswire*, April 5, 1999, p. 4423.

Reimer, David M., et al., "Machinery Industry," *Value Line Investment Survey (Part 3—Ratings & Reports)*, February 5, 1999, p. 1301.

"Rental Service in $366 Million Deal for Rival," *New York Times*, January 22, 1999, p. C4.

"Rental Service Sues Two Rivals," *New York Times*, March 8, 1999, p. C20.

Sherer, Paul M., "Rental Service's Board Plans to Meet by Mid-April to Mull Unsolicited Offer," *Wall Street Journal*, April 6, 1999, p. A4.

Stieghorst, Tom, "Fort Lauderdale, Fla.-Based Firm Joins Another Equipment Rental Company," *Knight-Ridder/Tribune Business News*, January 21, 1999, p. OKRB990210A6.

"United Rentals Is Expected to Launch $560 Million Bid for Rental Service," *Wall Street Journal*, April 5, 1999, p. A4.

"United Rentals Makes Offer for Acquisition-Minded Rival," *New York Times*, April 6, 1999, p. C2.

—Daryl F. Mallett

Rooms To Go Inc.

11540 Highway 92 East
Seffner, Florida 33584
U.S.A.
(813) 623-5400
Fax: (813) 621-7766

Private Company
Incorporated: 1990
Employees: 3,310
Sales: $650 million (1998 est.)
NAIC: 44211 Furniture Stores

Rooms To Go Inc., a low- to mid-priced furniture store chain, has rapidly expanded to more than 60 stores since opening in 1990. *Furniture/Today* ranked Rooms To Go as one of the top four furniture stores in the United States, where in terms of sales the company is the fastest-growing furniture retailer. The privately owned company markets its products primarily in the southeastern United States and in 14 foreign countries. The company is organized around the concept of convenience, as implied by the "Rooms To Go" name. Company designers coordinate complete room sets, choosing colors, fabrics, styles, and furniture groupings, which are priced at a significant discount when purchased as a set. Rooms To Go promises customers the convenience of delivery within one week (typically), appealing to buyers who would rather not wait the many weeks or months it sometimes takes the competition to deliver. Chief competitors include Levitz, Kane's, Rhodes, and Roberds.

The company was founded by Jeffrey Seaman and his father, Morty Seaman. Both had worked in the retail furniture store of Jeffrey's grandfather, Julius Seaman, who founded a Woodbury, New York-based home furnishings company in 1934. While still in school, Jeffrey spent ten summers working for his grandfather, and after graduating from college he continued with the family business, becoming vice-president by the time he was 23. His father, Morty, an astute entrepreneur, was president of Seaman's at that time. In 1988 Seaman's Home Furnishings was taken over in a leveraged buyout by Kohlberg Kravis Roberts & Co. for $350 million, burdening the company with substantial debt. Jeffrey was only 28 at the time, but shouldered a large portion of the buying duties for the company, and along with his father developed an overseas program during Seaman's restructuring phase. According to Deena Van Steenburgh of *Furniture Retailer,* "Father and son stayed on board briefly as chief executive officer and president. But in February 1989, four months after a major financial restructuring designed to reduce the company's debt burden, Kohlberg Kravis Roberts replaced the Seamans with Matthew D. Serra, former president and CEO of the G. Fox division of May Department Stores." The company was crippled by debt until it emerged from bankruptcy in 1992.

1990: Fast Furniture

By then, Jeffrey Seaman had decided that it was time that he establish his own business. He envisioned a different merchandising approach and was anxious to combine his past experience in the furniture business with a new concept for a retail operation. Before he began developing his ideas he spent a significant amount of time researching various retail outlets across the country. He told Van Steenburgh: "I visited not only furniture retailers, but clothing retailers, toy retailers, and department stores. I was really impressed with The Limited and The Gap. I wanted my stores to look very 'Gappish'—uniform, colorful, interesting and open." He decided to adopt a slogan: "Buy a piece, save a little. Buy the room, save a lot!"

Seaman knew that he wanted to run at least a medium-sized business and would need a team of experienced help to do so. Comfortable with sharing authority and information, Seaman put together an impressive executive management team which included Gerard Benatar, former vice-president of furniture fashion at Macy's in New York and Barker Brothers in California; Jeff Finkel, former vice-president of real estate at Toys 'R' Us; and Harmon Jones, former director of construction for Bally Health Club and Spas. Seaman's impressive reputation within the industry persuaded the seasoned executives to accept the risk involved in starting up a new business. Morty Seaman, although not involved with the day-to-day operations of the business, assumed the role of advisor to his son, helping with strategic decisions, marketing, and some of the buying and planning. The elder Seaman told Van Steenburgh that Rooms To Go will succeed because his son is a ''born merchant'' with a simple business philosophy: ''work.'' For his part, Jeffrey Seaman has stated that the almost immediate success of the company could not have been possible without his father's input, according to an interview with Young Mi Kim in *High Points*.

Although the Florida market was intensely competitive, Jeffrey Seaman decided to locate his headquarters and first stores there because of the availability of good, affordable locations—and the desirable living environment. He knew that he wanted to open a lot of stores quickly, and planned to begin with approximately 18 in west and central Florida. Seaman hired Jeff Finkle to head the demographic searches and real estate acquisitions. Finkle was on the lookout for land or vacant stand-alone buildings near malls or areas with heavy shopping traffic, preferably in areas near other major retailers. Fourteen locations were targeted for 1991, including those in Tampa, Lakeland, Ft. Myers, Orlando, and Sarasota. The first store opened in Tampa in May 1991, and by the end of the year 13 more stores had opened, all located no more than 125 miles from the Lakeland warehouse, making prompt deliveries possible. Sales quickly met expectations, with the company netting $30 million in the first year.

As might be expected of a young businessman of the 1990s, Seaman knew from his prior experience at Seaman's that the design and implementation of an efficient computer system would be integral to the success of his new business. After presenting his business plan, Seaman hired a small Cambridge, Massachusetts software firm to help design and build a complex system that could adapt to a fast-growing business with a fast inventory flow, specifically designed to accommodate the delivery of complete rooms. The system took a year to write, ''but it was worth it,'' Seaman told Young Mi Kim, adding, ''Where the computer system at Seaman's cost millions, ours is more efficient and powerful and cost us a few hundred thousand.''

Recognizing that his talents in merchandising did not assure that he would make appropriate image and fashion decisions, Seaman turned to Gerard Benetar for fashion and design sense. Benatar and his team concentrated on the selection of stylish contemporary and transitional upholstery, case goods, accessories and lamps, and finally, the occasional pieces which are all combined to form room settings. Rooms To go purchased from High Point, Alexvale, Barclay, Bassett, Florida Furniture, Klaussner, Natuzzi, Palliser, Pilliod, and San Giacomo, among other domestic as well as international vendors. More than half of the company's case goods were designed by Seaman and his buyers on paper, involving them in a watchful attitude toward consumer trends. Working with short margins, Rooms To Go could offer savings to those customers who chose to buy rooms in packages. The company bought and sold large quantities of a few items, but offered rugs and other accessories to completely furnish a room. Rather than present a great variety of styles—or special orders—as most furniture retailers did, the company offered options on popular styles—enough to satisfy roughly 75 percent of customers who shopped in the mid-priced range.

The stores were designed so that customers could easily view all of the merchandise from any vantage point in the store. The interior architecture was well-lit, clean, and designed with mirrors and other elements that accentuated the feeling of bright, contemporary openness. Seaman and Benatar were aiming for an ambiance that appeared like a cross between Ikea and The Gap: lots of glass and an airy environment. They also focused on the arrangement of their displays, hiring display coordinators and teams assigned to particular stores. According to Young Mi Kim, Seaman wanted customers to enter a Rooms To Go store and avoid what he termed ''the shark attack.'' He explained: ''When a customer walks into a furniture store, she'll see six guys with ties that are too tight, ready to pounce.'' Seaman decided to concentrate efforts on making customers comfortable, including his policy of having staff members attired in colorful, casual golf shirts.

Innovative advertising was produced in-house to reflect the company's goals. Seaman deplored the strategy of fake sales (marking up prices, then advertising that furniture was marked down for sale) that he believed gave the industry a credibility problem. He contended that consumers feel ''ripped off'' by furniture retailers, some of whom have perpetual ''sales.'' He also recognized that consumers have come to expect buying at a bargain price. With that in mind, he decided to make it a company goal to convince customers that they would get great value from day one, and coined the motto,''no fake sales, no phony discounts, no delivery fairy tale—and assistance, not persistence, from the sales staff.''

1993: Rooms To Go Needed Room to Grow

By 1993 Rooms To Go had outgrown its 480,000-square-foot distribution center and headquarters in Seffner, Florida. The company added another 105,000 square feet to the center and hired 100 more employees to run it. They planned expansion of its 27 stores to reach 35 by the end of 1994. Seaman told Katherine Smith of the *Tampa Bay Business Journal* that ''he was somewhat surprised that the company already needs more room,'' acknowledging that Rooms To Go had been too conservative when it built the distribution center. Although the company image targeted a youthful audience, the prepackaged room concept had proven popular among snowbirds in Florida who apparently had better things to do than shop at numerous locations for furniture. The company succeeded in merchandising where competitors such as Dayton, Ohio-based Roberds, Inc. (offering a similar prepackaged concept) began reporting dropping profits. In preparation for more inventory to supply more stores, in 1995 Rooms To Go added an additional 185,000-square-feet of warehouse space to its Tampa International Center industrial building in Ybor City. By the early part of 1996, Rooms To Go had mushroomed into Florida's fastest-growing furniture retailer, and Seaman felt that the company had saturated that market. A new distribution center was opened in Atlanta to support the 25 new stores opening in the surrounding areas. While expanding into Atlanta, Georgia; Charlotte, North Carolina; and Chattanooga and Nashville, Tennessee, management also planned to expand its international sales operations.

1996: Global Expansion

Jeff Knott, former vice-president of Johnson & Johnson, and president of Jim Walter International Corporation of Tampa, was hired by Seaman to head the Rooms To Go international operations. Through licensing agreements with individuals or businesses, the company was soon selling its furniture in Turkey, Costa Rica, Honduras, Guatemala, and Columbia. Plans for a new venture into the Bahamas were realized in mid-1996. Seaman felt that there was a tremendous call for American products in the overseas market and anticipated a huge success abroad. A growing middle class in the Latin American region was contributing to a rise in home ownership and the demand for affordable furnishings—preferably American styles and labels. New trade opportunities with eastern Europe were also fueling a growing middle class in Turkey. Rooms To Go sponsored its licensees by helping them locate a space and laying out the stores for them, using tested company blueprints. Most of the international stores averaged 8,000 to 10,000 square feet, compared to the domestic scale of 18,000 to 25,000 square feet, which helped the new businesses keep overhead low. The company also helped with advertising abroad. Seaman explained to Carole Cancy of the *Tampa Bay Business Journal* that "We're letting them use our whole process," adding, "It's similar to franchising, [but] in franchising you have a little more control. We're assisting them, not commanding them."

1997: New Kids' Room Concept

Fort Lauderdale was chosen as the new testing ground for a spinoff concept that would exclusively handle children's furniture, including low-end, custom orders, and high-end brands such as Stanley. Since no other large chain was offering stores just for children's furniture, Rooms To Go was hoping to lure everyone who had children. Seaman explained: "What really convinced me we should do this was when I went shopping in GapKids, and I saw that there were three times as many people there as in the regular Gap next door," according to Cheryl Kane Heimlich of the *South Florida Business Journal*. At that time the only South Florida competitor specializing in that segment was the Miami-based retailer Falls Leather Gallery, who changed the name of their children's outlet to Kids & Teens Rooms. Falls Leather Gallery owner Eric Salem told Heimlich that "The Rooms To Go people are clever folks." He added, "They've watched the demographic studies and trends, and they know the youth market is a good market." Critics of the Rooms To Go expansion into the youth segment had misgivings concerning the company's ability to maintain its price point, suggesting that the quality of furniture sold at value prices would not stand up to the wear and tear of active children.

The first of the youth specialty stores, called Rooms To Go Kids, was opened in the Atlanta suburb of Marietta, Georgia. Making the most of its established customer base, the 8,000-square-foot youth store was attached to the existing Rooms To Go store, but was designed with a separate entrance. The stand-alone prototype featured 20 displays of bedroom sets, play tables, and other colorful pieces, accented by bright wallpapers, paint schemes, and complex curves and angles. Two more pilot stores were scheduled to open in Fort Lauderdale, Florida, and Duluth, Georgia, by the end of 1997. Noting that "selling" was probably the biggest difference between offering furniture for adult versus child use, the company concentrated on special training for its youth store salespeople. It was understood that more time would be needed in order to work with an entire family, explaining safety issues and home-assembly processes. The interiors focused on a comfortable environment with televi-

sions strategically placed throughout the store, featuring movies, news shows hosted by kids, and video games. Suppliers for the youth line included Stanley, Catalina, Lehigh, Sunny Mfg., and Rosalco, and the prices carried a broader range than in the adult furniture lines—package deals were also offered as in the adult category. By the time that plans were being made for an additional eight youth stores in the Florida market, Seaman and his managers had decided to increase the kids-store floor space to approximately 10,000 square feet. With the 1990s rise in the baby population the company expected the youth business to continue climbing for another decade or more.

Rooms To Go signed a 1997 joint venture agreement with Jusco Company, Ltd., a Japanese operator of department stores, supermarkets, and other businesses. The first Rooms To Go Kids store opened in Tokyo in 1998, with plans for full-line stores to open in the following year. Under the agreement Rooms To Go received royalties on sales and a buying fee. For its part, Rooms To Go helped Jusco develop its merchandise, 60 percent of which came from U.S. suppliers. If the venture proved successful enough, the company planned to expand throughout locations in Japan. According to Clint Engel of *Furniture Today*, "The Japanese stores will focus primarily on the middle to upper end of the Rooms To Go price spectrum," adding, "Japanese families live in much smaller houses than Americans but tend to spend more on individual pieces of furniture."

Expanding westward, Rooms To Go launched plans for a large store and youth store in Dallas, Texas, scheduled to open in 1999. A distribution center was on the drawing board to serve that market, which was expected to grow into several stores. The year 1998 was another good one for Rooms To Go, showing overall growth of 20 percent over 1997 revenues.

Poised for the next century, Seaman had a firm grip on the importance of brand building within the trade. He told Kimberley Wray of *HFN* that in the furniture industry, "the retailer has more opportunity than in almost any other business to build a brand because brands at the manufacturing level are virtually nonexistent. Think of Crate & Barrel on a busy day," he continued. "Do you think the customers recognize a single brand that Crate & Barrel carries? Can anybody in this room name one? Of course not. The customer is buying Crate & Barrel. That's the brand."

Further Reading

Allegrezza, Ray, "Great Rooms Go Casual," *HFN*, October 13, 1997, p. 32.

Cancy, Carole, "Furniture Chain Finds Room to Go Overseas," *Tampa Bay Business Journal*, May 3, 1996. p. 1.

——, "Rooms To Go May Be Going to Japan," *Tampa Bay Business Journal*, September 12, 1997, p. 1.

Engel, Clint, "Rooms To Go Adding 12 Stores," *Furniture/Today*, February 9, 1998, p. 1.

——, "Rooms To Go Opens 1st Kids Store in Georgia," *Furniture/Today*, March 1, 1997, p. 14.

——, "Westward Bound," *Furniture/Today*, December 1, 1997, p. 24.

"Florida-Based Rooms To Go Furniture Chain Spreads Across the South," *Knight-Ridder/Tribune Business News*, May 21, 1996, p. 5210201.

Gilbert, Daniela, "Here's Lookin' at You, Kid," *High Points*, October, 1997, p. 46.

Heimlich, Cheryl Kane, "Rooms To Go Testing Kids' Room Concept," *South Florida Business Journal*, January 17, 1997, p. 1.

Keefe, Robert, "Florida-Based Furniture Retailer Outgrows Its Expanded Warehouse," *Knight-Ridder/Tribune Business News*, September 8, 1995, p. 9080011.

Knight, Deena C., "America's Golden Boy," *Cabinetmaker*, July 4, 1997, p. 18.

Mi Kim, Young, "Blowing Them Away," *High Points*, October 11, 1993, p. 1.

"Rooms To Go Kids Undergoing Growth Spurt," *Kids Today*, January, 1998, p. 8.

Smith, Catherine Snow, "Fast Growing Rooms To Go Expanding," *Tampa Bay Business Journal*, March 4, 1994, p. 1.

Van Steenburgh, Deena, "Anatomy of a Young Upstart's Start-Up," *Furniture Retailer*, October, 1991, p. 32.

Wray, Kimberley, "Rooms To Go: How It Grows," *HFN The Weekly Newspaper for the Home Furnishing Network*, March 9, 1998, p. 19.

—Terri Mozzone

The Rottlund Company, Inc.

2681 Long Lake Road
Roseville, Minnesota 55113
U.S.A.
(651) 638-0500
Fax: (651) 638-0501

Public Company
Incorporated: 1973
Employees: 248
Sales: $160.83 million (1998)
Stock Exchanges: American
Ticker Symbol: RH
NAIC: 23311 Land Subdivision & Land Development;
    23321 Single Family Housing Construction; 23322
    Multifamily Housing Construction

Through its subsidiaries, The Rottlund Company, Inc. designs, builds, and markets detached single family homes and attached townhomes and villas in the Minneapolis-St.Paul, Minnesota; Des Moines, Iowa; Indianapolis, Indiana; southern New Jersey; and Naples-Ft.Myers, Orlando, and Tampa, Florida metropolitan areas. Rottlund homes are sold primarily through the company's own staff of sales personnel to a wide range of buyers. In 1998 the company celebrated 25 years in business. During that time it had grown from a small local builder into one of the top 60 home builders in the country, with an enormous, even dominant, presence in Minnesota.

Building the Name That Builds the Homes, 1970s

Rottlund was founded in 1973 by David Rotter and Ellroy "Roy" Lund. Within a short while, Bernard "Bud" Rotter also joined the firm. As small home builders, they initially built single family homes, one or two at a time, working and supervising all phases of construction. Roy was involved in directing the actual home construction. David took responsibility for managing production and operations. Bud was in charge of sales, land acquisition, and advertising. Thora Lund, Roy's wife, served as the office manager. At the start, the company chose to focus entirely on home building in the Minneapolis-St.Paul area. As the founders readily admitted in company literature, there were many ups and downs in the early days. There were times when orders for new homes outpaced the company's ability to deliver them in a timely fashion. Sometimes sporadic availability of building supplies and weather-related problems caused delays and unhappy customers. There were also times when building materials bought in quantity sat in storage awaiting a new construction project. Cash flow, too, was often strained.

By the mid-1970s Rottlund was known and respected for its commitment to understanding and meeting customer needs. The company began to realize that it needed to diversify the types of construction and be able to offer wider variety to a broader base of customers. By the end of the decade, the company was still building single-family homes, but the Rotter brothers and Lund had developed their long-term strategy that would prove to be a solid foundation on which to build the company through the next decade. To become a "brand name" company meant that they had to better understand not only their own customers, but also the broader trends in the market, including cultural distinctions and the effects of economic cycles on the building industry.

As the company grew in volume of homes being built, it was able to bring into the business the skills of local designers, managers and marketing people. Through their help, the company was able to seriously identify specific niches they could adopt. The new company philosophy was to study the market and identify the empty niches, foreseeing the trends in consumer demand. The company learned how to recognize customer tastes and coordinate styles and products within established building codes at the time achieving creative, personalized results for the customer.

One important need that the company identified was to have agreed upon expectations between the company and a given customer about timelines for completion and type and quality of materials and fixtures that would be used in a home-building project. If happy, satisfied customers were a goal, then communication had to be clear and concise. The company worked to better schedule all phases of the construction, coordinating all the subcontractors involved and allowing for the possibility of weather-related delays. This not only made for happier customers, but brought a cost-saving benefit to the company as well. The company reviewed all of its sales literature, particularly its use of industry jargon, and began to produce materials that were much simpler to read and more appealing in appearance. It also revised many of its forms and legal documents and the way it handled closings to make the process more understandable to the customer.

Challenges During the 1980s

In the early 1980s, the company learned a hard lesson when interest rates soared from eight to 16 percent. Rottlund's typical practice was to guarantee interest rates to its buyers at the time of a home purchase agreement. But as the overall U.S. economy changed so quickly and interest rates rose dramatically in a relatively short period, the company had to absorb much of the additional cost to still close on properties. While many of Rottlund's competitors were passing along the increased cost to customers by making forward commitments on mortgages from the secondary markets, Rottlund honored its original commitments to its customers. Although it was a costly lesson, Rottlund gained great respect from buyers, lenders, its subcontractors, and the larger community for honoring its rates.

In 1986 Rottlund developed a plan for success that set the tone for the entire company. The company would 1) be honest and straightforward and well-connected to the community; 2) have a diversified product line for long-term stability; 3) increase its use of modern technology; 4) find, hire, and keep employees who were committed, and 5) go public in 1992 to raise capital for national expansion. It was this final point of preparing for an initial public offering that consumed much of Rottlund's management team as the 1980s drew to a close. If the public offering was to be successful, the company had to be clearly defined and tightly managed. About this time, the company also made a significant investment to upgrade its technology systems, particularly its computer-assisted design (CAD) applications.

In 1988 Rottlund took a step toward diversifying its product line by moving into the construction of suburban townhouses. These proved to be cheaper to build and buy than detached houses since interest rates were continuing to remain in the double digits. For the next ten years, the company continued to build both types of homes in many different styles and sizes.

Going Public, Growing Large: The 1990s

By the early 1990s, Rottlund was far ahead of all other home builders. In 1993 alone, the company built 845 homes,

twice as many as Orrin Thompson, its closest competitor. Of the 845 homes built, 553 were multifamily homes and 292 were single-family homes. This level of production represented seven percent of the Twin Cities home construction market. As John Dierbeck, vice-president of sales, told Ingrid Sundstrom, "We grew because we did our business better and made people happy. Eventually we just broke away from the pack."

In February 1993, Rottlund announced that it was making plans to expand its operations into other markets. Having raised $6 million in its first public offering in October 1992, the company felt it was adequately capitalized to expand geographically. Initial market-testing was completed and company infrastructure was put in place to support the expansion. The company goal, simply stated, was to become a nationally known builder. Because they knew that building codes, housing needs, products, and costs differed from market to market, the Rotters developed new strategies to determine what housing needs were unmet in new markets it was considering, then planned accordingly. They set out to apply the same Rottlund philosophy, technology, and management style in cities beyond the Minneapolis-St. Paul area. Their expansion strategy called for initially bringing local designers, managers, and marketing people to the team who would give immediate recognition to the Rottlund name.

In August 1993, Rottlund formed North Coast Mortgage, Inc. as a wholly owned subsidiary to arrange financing for home buyers in the Minneapolis-St. Paul area (the subsidiary was sold five years later). In that same year, the company began home building operations in Naples-Ft. Myers, Florida, and Des Moines, Iowa. In 1994 they began home building operations in Indianapolis, Indiana, and Orlando and Tampa, Florida. To support those operations, the company established new divisions in those locations. Expansion also continued that year with over 180 homes built in the Des Moines area and nearly 60 homes in the Naples-Fort Myers, Florida market.

By the mid-1990s, Rottlund was being mentioned in national builder magazines and in real estate development circles and had a growing national reputation. Their customer base had broadened to include first-time buyers, customers moving up, and empty-nesters. The company had developed many styles of homes and branched out into atrium, villa, courtyard, and lodge-style homes. Moreover, Rottlund had become a specialist in developing neighborhoods or communities, not just building homes. The planned communities were designed to include convenient distances to schools and shopping, gardens, swimming pools, spas and exercise rooms, golf and other sports, hiking trails, and parks, all tailored to the lifestyle demands of the intended customer.

By the mid-1990s lower interest rates were adding stimulus to home-buying and boosting sales of homes. Rottlund expanded further. The company opened new divisions in Tampa and Orlando, Florida, and Indianapolis, Indiana, in 1995. In February 1996, Rottlund purchased the assets, including land, any work in progress, and the future contractual rights, to Kevin Scarborough, Inc., a New Jersey-based company for about $9.8 million. This positioned Rottlund well for expansion into the Delaware Valley of southern New Jersey.

In order to continue to respond to consumer preferences, the company further developed its internal marketing department to better utilize information which was now gathered from buyer profiles, focus groups, exit interviews at model sites, telephone surveys, and demographic databases. In the design department, the company moved to engage a number of unaffiliated architectural firms in addition to its in-house architectural staff.

In 1998 Rottlund Homes, a division of The Rottlund Company by that time, announced an agreement with Elim Care Inc. to develop the Cornerstone Commons of Plymouth, Minnesota, a senior retirement community. The cooperative effort boasted 82 spacious one- and two-bedroom apartment homes, and Cornerstone Assisted Living, which provided 50 apartment homes for people needing supportive services. Surrounding these units the company developed one-level walkout townhomes for use by the wider community of senior adults.

By then Rottlund had become the 59th largest home builder in the United States, having built and sold over 8,900 homes since its founding in 1973, with 6,500 of these being single-family homes and townhomes sold in the Minneapolis-St. Paul metropolitan area alone. At the close of 1998, the company owned or had options for over 2,100 home sites in communities under development and land for the development of over 2,000 additional planned home sites in proposed communities.

As of mid-1999 Rottlund, according to at least two leading trade publications, ranked among the top 100 builders in the nation. Given its commitments to quality and service, the company appeared to be in a very strong position to continue as a "name brand" builder well into the 21st century.

Principal Subsidiaries

Rottlund Homes of Iowa, Inc.; Rottlund Homes of Florida, Inc.; Rottlund Homes of Indiana, Inc.; Rottlund Homes of New Jersey, Inc.; and Rottlund Homes of Indiana Limited Partnership.

Further Reading

DePass, Dee, "Building a New Tradition: NW Business Pioneer," *Minneapolis Star Tribune,* March 3, 1996.

Dierbeck, John, ed., "25th Anniversary," *R + Vision* (Employee Newsletter), December 1998.

King, Mason, "Competition Hammers Builders Big and Small," *Indianapolis Business Journal,* November 10, 1997.

Mack, Linda, "The 7th Annual Star Tribune 100: Minneapolis' Largest Publicly Held Companies," *Minneapolis Star Tribune,* March 23, 1998.

"1998's Top 25 Builders Named in Twin Cities Metropolitan Area," *PR Newswire,* February 11, 1999.

"Rottlund Company Report," *Moody's Investor's Services,* November 21, 1998.

"Rottlund Reports Record Sales and Net Income for Third Quarter," *PR Newswire,* January 14, 1999.

"Rottlund Reports Revenues Jump 53%," *PR Newswire,* October 14, 1998, p. 1310.

Sundstrom, Ingrid, "Rottlund Breaks Away from the Pack," *Minneapolis Star Tribune,* March 28, 1994, p. 1D.

—J. D. Fromm

Rural/Metro Corporation

8401 E. Indian School Road
Scottsdale, Arizona 85281
U.S.A.
(602) 994-3886
Fax: (602) 481-3328
Web site: http://www.ruralmetro.com

Public Company
Incorporated: 1993
Employees: 12,250
Sales: $475.6 million (1998)
Stock Exchanges: NASDAQ
Ticker Symbol: RURL
NAIC: 621910 Ambulance Services, Air or Ground;
  922160 Fire Departments

Rural/Metro Corporation is one of the leading providers of health and safety services in the United States. The company is a diversified emergency services company providing "911" emergency ambulance and general transport services, fire protection and training services, and other safety and healthcare-related services and equipment to municipal, residential, commercial, and industrial customers. The company is one of the only multi-state providers of both ambulance and fire protection services in the United States and ranks as one of the largest private-sector providers of ambulance and fire protection services in the world, serving over 450 communities in 26 states, the District of Columbia, Canada, and Latin America.

The company was founded on the premise that many communities could benefit from innovative ways of delivering emergency services. As a private company, Rural/Metro was not bound by traditional ways of doing business. The company has a history of finding better, more efficient ways of managing personnel and resources, pursuing prevention as a key strategy, and providing better training for its employees.

Fire!—Founding "The Rural Fire Department," 1948–72

In 1948 in an unincorporated area north of Phoenix, Arizona, after watching his neighbor's house burn down one night "with no one there to officiate," newspaper reporter Louis A. Witzeman, following in the footsteps of Benjamin Franklin nearly two centuries before, secured pledges from his neighbors to pay him $10 a year for subscription fire protection. The 21-year-old Witzeman invested his last $900 and made a down payment on a fire truck. Thus began the "Rural Fire Department," a subscription fire service serving an area of about nine square miles. "There was no master planning or creative genius involved," says Witzeman. "It happened because I needed fire protection for my neighborhood and I was determined to get it." The first year in business, the company grossed $30,000.

"I never expected the company to grow so big," Witzeman says on the company's web site. "I just wanted to provide my neighborhood with fire protection. But soon I began to realize that I had really stumbled onto something. I found that the established ways of providing services were not as efficient as they could be. So Rural/Metro's cause became to look for new and better ways to do the job . . . for less money." In order to succeed, Rural/Metro had to be better than traditional services. Witzeman encouraged creativity, and explored different methods to exactly meet each of his client communities' particular needs. In fact, finding ways to deliver cost-effective service based on needs, rather than relying on traditional solutions, became Rural/Metro's primary ethic, which has remained with the company throughout its history.

By 1951 Rural had grown to three stations and several vehicles. Rural's firefighters were among the first in the country to receive extensive training in first aid, and put that training to work with the addition of an emergency rescue, first aid, and salvage unit. The company's dependable, cost-effective service resulted in Rural's first municipal fire contract with the city of Scottsdale, population 2,000, which remained in force until at least 1991, when the population had grown to 126,000.

In 1965 the company, noting that traditional red fire engines faded quickly in the Arizona sun and needed repainting often, began experimenting with white vehicles. A national study released in 1972 revealed that high-visibility ''lime yellow''—the color of tennis balls—was the most visible color under all weather conditions, and at night, and provided the greatest amount of contrast to environmental colors. Rural cast tradition to the wind and adopted the color.

In 1969 the company began providing ambulance and emergency medical services independent of its fire operations, and was covering several hundred square miles in Arizona's Maricopa, Pima, and Yuma counties, including the cities of Tucson and Yuma. Shortly thereafter, the company expanded into Tennessee, with the acquisition of the West Knoxville Fire Department, and five adjoining fire departments, and emergency medical and ambulance services grew into Texas and Florida.

Rural/Metro Growing Rapidly: 1970s–80s

The company grew significantly during the 1970s, through internal development and through acquisitions. As additional contracts were negotiated and more and more urban populations were being served, Rural changed its name in 1972 to Rural/Metro. In 1978, the company's 30-year anniversary, the company was featured on ''60 Minutes'' when Mike Wallace paid a visit to Arizona and aired a story on CBS which brought waves of good publicity for Rural/Metro. That year, Witzeman retired from his post as president, selling some 63 percent of the company to its employees, for $1 million, and retaining his chairmanship until 1980.

In 1985 Rural/Metro began requiring homeowners in Scottsdale, Arizona, to install in-home sprinkler systems, leading to a drop in fire losses by 1994 of 84 percent. In 1987 the company purchased the Arizona Medical Transport (AMT) ambulance company, and Rural/Metro became the largest provider of prehospital care and ambulance transportation in Arizona.

In 1988 the company brought in $50.25 million in revenue. That year a new president and CEO, Robert H. Manschot, was appointed. Holland-born Manschot, fluent in four languages and a veteran employee in nine countries, was previously a senior consultant and worldwide partner for The Hay Group and a manager for ITT Sheraton and Inter-Continental hotel chains. Vice-President of Emergency Services Tracy Skeen received the prestigious J. Walter Schaefer Memorial Award, given by the American Ambulance Association to the individual who exhibited the most exceptional leadership and guidance for the betterment of the ambulance industry as a whole.

By 1989 the company was posting $60 million in revenue, a more than 20 percent jump from the previous year, and had increased revenues every year for the previous decade. Rural/Metro was now serving the emergency needs of more than five million people in over 50 communities throughout the United States. The company held contracts with such companies as St. Louis, Missouri-based Monsanto Chemical Company and Idaho-based Potlatch Paper Company. Rural/Metro also managed an air tanker base at Fort Huachuca, Arizona, near Sierra Vista, for Monsanto's Wildland Fire Division, filling airline tanks with the latter's fire retardant, used to combat wildfires in Arizona and New Mexico; and also joined in a venture with Holland-based Smit Fire & Loss Prevention Company to provide offshore firefighting in the western hemisphere. In December of that year, Rural/Metro's emergency response team joined in fighting a fire burning on the 138,000 ton Norwegian tanker *Mega Borg*, in the Gulf of Mexico. They successfully extinguished the explosive blaze which killed four and injured 17, and kept the oil from leaking into the ocean.

The Roaring 1990s

In 1990, Rural/Metro responded to over 300,000 calls for assistance and annual revenues had grown to $65 million. A year later, in September 1991, the company joined with the Rotterdam International Safety Centre (RISC)—a joint venture between Smit International and Nederlandse Veiligheidsdienst—to form and operate a new company called RISC America. The new venture would provide sophisticated training for industrial, professional, and specialized firefighters and would operate fully-equipped emergency response teams available to respond anywhere in the world to combat unique emergency situations which required specific training and knowledge beyond the traditional firefighting realm, such as petrochemical and industrial fires. By the end of that year, the company operated ambulance/EMS services in over 30 communities throughout Arizona, Florida, Oregon, Tennessee, and Texas. Annual revenue in 1992 grew to $68.22 million, with a net income of $1.33 million.

The following year, in April, the company went public, with its stock being traded over the counter, and 29 percent of the company sold for some $22 million. A second public offering in July brought in another $19 million. That year, the company acquired the operations of four ambulance service providers and would go on to acquire more than 70 companies through 1998. Rural/Metro served more than 80 communities in nine states, including Arizona, Arkansas, Florida, Nebraska, New York, Ohio, Oregon, Tennessee, and Texas, and total revenue and net income grew again to $84.08 million and $2.69 million, respectively.

In 1994, the company responded to over 500,000 service calls and continued to set performance records, increasing both revenue (by 24 percent to $104.36 million) and income (by 76 percent to $4.73 million). The company additionally completed two further public offerings of common stock, and acquired the operations of eight ambulance service providers, including the stock of an ambulance service provider operating primarily in Lincoln and Omaha, Nebraska; and the assets of ambulance service providers operating in the Dallas, Texas metropolitan area and in several communities in Ohio.

By 1995 the company was the fourth largest private sector ambulance company. That year, it acquired EMS Ventures, a leading ambulance service provider in Gainesville and Augusta, Georgia, and Columbia, South Carolina; and LaSalle Ambulance Inc. in Buffalo, New York, one of four Rural/Metro companies to have received accreditation from The Commission on Accreditation of Ambulance Services. The company had grown to 800 ambulances, fire trucks, and wheelchair vans in more than 80 communities in the United States and was responding to half a million calls per year.

In 1996, under the direction of President James H. Bolin, Rural/Metro made 18 acquisitions, and was the largest provider of privatized fire protection in the United States, and one of the largest in ambulance services. The company was contracted by FedEx for airport rescue and firefighting services at the Memphis, Tennessee hub. That year, the company was declared Private Ambulance Provider of the Year by The Texas Department of Health, for the quality of its care and the community services the company performed. It also received the American Ambulance Association's Community Partnership Award.

Rural/Metro extended its reach in 1997 with 19 new acquisitions. New contracts in 1997 included airport firefighting and rescue services to the Municipal Airport of Morristown, New Jersey; Central Ohio Aerospace and Technology Center; John F. Kennedy International Airport in La Paz, Bolivia; Jorge Wilsterman International Airport in Cochabama, Bolivia; and Viru Viru International Airport in Santa Cruz, Bolivia; community fire services with North Tunica County Fire Protection in Tunica, Mississippi; fire protection, ambulance transportation, and rescue for Lockheed Martin Milan Army Ammunition Plant; emergency medical transportation in Aurora, Colorado; Gila Bend, Arizona; and Bellmead, Beverly Hills, Hewitt, Lacy-Lakeview, Northcrest, Robinson, Waco, and Woodway, Texas.

In 1998 the company entered into a joint venture in the greater Baltimore, Maryland and District of Columbia area, and a public/private alliance in the San Diego, California area. That year, Rural/Metro made 11 acquisitions, including Argentina-based Emergencias Cardio Coronarias, extending its reach into Central and South America. Ambulance services and fire protection services accounted for approximately 81 percent and ten percent, respectively, of the company's revenue for the fiscal year ended June 30, 1998. A number of miscellaneous services accounted for the remaining nine percent. For the first time in its history, although net income rose 48.7 percent to $475.6 million, the company's difficulties in absorbing its acquisitions led to lower profits ($7.5 million in net income, a 40.9 percent drop), layoffs, and an attempt by The International Brotherhood of Teamsters to unionize employees. John B. Furman took over as acting president and CEO.

As more and more government-run services continued to demonstrate inefficiency, continued privatization of these industries could similarly be expected. With its impressive 50-year history and continued growth, Rural/Metro appeared poised to dominate the industries in which it participated. Sales were expected to trend higher, with corresponding net income increases as the company sought to improve existing facilities and services into the 21st century.

Principal Subsidiaries

Aid Ambulance at Vigo County Inc.; American Medical Transport; Arizona Medical Transport; EMS Ventures of South Carolina Inc.; Physicians Ambulance Service Inc.; Rural/Metro Ambulance.

Further Reading

"After Gains of As Much As 116%, Bundy Is Back with Six New Picks," *Money*, September 1994.

"Ambulance Chasing," *Time*, December 9, 1996, p. 58.

Austin, Marsha, "Rival Biz Drives into Town; Ambulance Company Faces New Competition," *Denver Business Journal*, November 6, 1998, p. 1A.

Chiang, Melanie G., "Fast Mover: Rural/Metro Covers Ground in Fire, Ambulance Services," *Investor's Business Daily*, June 19, 1996.

Gilbertson, Dawn, "Arizona Emergency Services Firm Helps Out Phoenix Health-Care Company," *Knight-Ridder/Tribune Business News*, January 15, 1997, p. 115B1164.

Gonzales, Angela, "Company Makes Case for Attorney," *Business Journal—Serving Phoenix & the Valley of the Sun*, September 18, 1998, p. 1.

——, "On a Rescue Mission: Rural/Metro Tries to Douse Financial Fire," *Business Journal—Serving Phoenix & the Valley of the Sun*, September 18, 1998, p. 1.

——, "Rural/Metro Chases San Diego Job," *Business Journal—Serving Phoenix & the Valley of the Sun*, February 14, 1997, p. 1.

——, "Rural/Metro Fires Off $36M Offering," *Business Journal—Serving Phoenix & the Valley of the Sun*, April 5, 1996, p. 1.

——, "Rural/Metro Seeking to Enter Managed Care," *Business Journal—Serving Phoenix & the Valley of the Sun*, February 17, 1995.

Johnson, Hoyt, "Meeting the Need in a Better Way," *Scottsdale Scene*, September 1989.

Munk, Nina, "Making the Customer Pay," *Forbes*, February 13, 1995, p. 74.

Reagor, Catherine, "Scottsdale, Ariz.-Based Fire Protection Service Plans Real Estate Deal," *Knight-Ridder/Tribune Business News*, January 9, 1997, p. 109B0969.

Ruber, Ilana, "Rural/Metro Smokes Past Competition by Acquisition," *Business Journal—Serving Phoenix & the Valley of the Sun*, August 1, 1997, p. 1.

Schine, Eric, Richard S. Dunham, and Christopher Farrell, "America's New Watchword: If It Moves, Privatize It," *Business Week*, December 12, 1994, p. 39.

Trunnelle, Judy, "Top Directors' Fees of Arizona Public Companies," *Business Journal—Serving Phoenix & the Valley of the Sun*, July 3, 1998, p. 30.

Wiles, Russ, "Stock Takes a Dive at Rural/Metro Corp. of Scottsdale, Ariz.," *Knight-Ridder/Tribune Business News*, August 28, 1998, p. OKRB982400A.

—Daryl F. Mallett

Ruth's Chris Steak House

3321 Hessmer Avenue
Metairie, Louisiana 70002
U.S.A.
(504) 454-6560
Fax: (504) 454-9060
Web site: http://www.ruthschris.com

Private Company
Incorporated: 1965
Employees: 4,500
Sales: $225 million (1998 est.)
NAIC: 72211 Full-Service Restaurants

Ruth's Chris Steak House is an international chain of upscale restaurants. Various listings have placed Ruth's Chris among the best restaurants in the United States. The company runs Ruth's Chris Steak Houses in close to 70 locations, including four in Mexico and two in Taiwan. About half of the restaurants are run as franchises, and the company directly operates the others. Each restaurant has a unique decor, but all are similar in their menus, which feature corn-fed Midwestern beef steaks. Though other dishes are on the menu, steaks account for almost 90 percent of sales. Ruth's Chris beef is dry-aged in Chicago and then shipped twice weekly in large cuts to the restaurants. The steaks are cut into smaller portions at each restaurant, and cooked by a special process using a broiler heated to about 1,800 degrees Fahrenheit. This cooking method is consistent throughout the chain. The company is privately held by founder Ruth Fertel and her two sons.

Early Years

Ruth Fertel was born in 1927 and raised in Happy Jack, Louisiana. Her father sold insurance and her mother taught kindergarten. Fertel graduated from Louisiana State University in Baton Rouge at the age of 19 with a degree in chemistry and a minor in physics. She taught briefly at a junior college, and then married and began raising a family. In the early 1960s, Fertel found herself divorced and working as a lab technician to support her two teenage sons. She was making enough to get by, but not enough to send her sons to college. So Fertel began looking for another line of business. An advertisement for a local steak house somehow caught her eye. Although she had no experience in the restaurant business, Fertel decided to mortgage her house and buy Chris Steak House, a failed restaurant in a not too spiffy section of New Orleans. Chris Steak House had belonged to Chris Matulich, who operated the business for 35 years. He had sold the business, but took it over again when the new management went bankrupt. The steak house seated 60 people, had no parking lot, and was located near the New Orleans Fairgrounds racetrack. Against the advice of all the practical people she knew, Fertel borrowed $22,000 to buy Chris Steak House in May 1965. When Fertel opened for business a few weeks later, she was selling around 35 steaks a day, for close to $5 each. Fertel worked doggedly, cutting her own beef as well as cooking, waitressing, and doing the books. A few months after opening, Hurricane Betsy devastated New Orleans, and Fertel was left with no electricity and a cooler full of expensive raw meat. She turned the disaster to her advantage, cooking steaks for the relief workers and displaced people in the neighborhood. She was also able to keep the restaurant open on Fridays, as the bishop of the New Orleans diocese temporarily suspended meatless Fridays because of the loss of local fisheries in the storm. Fertel soon built a loyal customer base, and before long there were lines out the door. Fertel estimates that 90 to 95 percent of her customers were male, and her restaurant began to attract prominent local politicians and businessmen.

With the great popularity of the new Chris Steak House, Fertel opened a second one four blocks away. Chris Matulich, the original restaurant's first owner, sued Fertel to keep her from calling her second steak house by the name he had established. So Fertel simply added her first name, and the chain became Ruth's Chris Steak House. In 1975 Fertel's first restaurant burned down. Fertel relates in *Entrepreneur Magazine* that she called her bank in tears. But a man in the construction business happened to be in the bank at the time, and he assured Fertel he could erect a new restaurant for her in one week. He fulfilled his promise, and Fertel ended up with a much bigger restaurant—160 seats versus the old 60. She had no problem accommodating the crowd.

Growth Through Franchises in the 1970s and 1980s

Fertel worked tirelessly at her two New Orleans restaurants, and apparently had not thought of expanding into other markets. One of her devoted customers moved from New Orleans to Baton Rouge, yet still kept driving in to eat at Ruth's Chris. Finally he complained that the drive was too much, and asked if he could open a Baton Rouge franchise. Fertel claimed in a July 1997 *Restaurants and Institutions* article that she did not know anything about franchising, but that she let the customer have his wish because she was a good judge of people. The first franchise opened in Baton Rouge in 1976, and the chain began to grow. Franchisees paid an initial fee of $50,000, and then contributed six percent of gross sales back to Fertel's company. The earliest franchisees were friends or customers, and Fertel kept close control, spending time at each new restaurant to make sure it was operating up to her standards. Around the time she started franchising, Fertel perfected Ruth's Chris special broiler, a high-heat (1,800 degree) oven that seared the steaks. The franchised restaurants used this equipment as well, and basically followed the same menu. Though there were local variations, the overriding theme of the restaurants was good steak. Fertel insisted that each franchised restaurant buy its meat from her Chicago supplier, to keep quality consistent across the chain. Fertel also picked her markets carefully. In the early days, she was loathe to start a restaurant in a city without a professional football team. Her clientele continued to be overwhelmingly male, and football towns were the best bets for her kind of customer. Fertel also kept costs down by primarily moving new restaurants into existing locations. By taking over bankrupt restaurants, she avoided having to build from the ground up, and some of these failed restaurants had colorful histories. For example, the Ruth's Chris in Beverly Hills took the place of a restaurant that had been originally owned by Dean Martin, Frank Sinatra, and Sammy Davis, Jr.

By the early 1980s, Ruth's Chris was the only restaurant of its kind—an upscale steak house—that was growing through franchises. Fertel still kept close tabs on every aspect of the business, but as the chain grew to about a dozen restaurants, she had to find more experienced management. She hired Ralph J. Giardina, who was originally her banker, as president of the holding company she created for the chain, and in 1984 she hired Dan Earles as vice-president of operations. Earles had formerly managed a group of restaurants called Commander's Palace. Earles, Giardina, Fertel, and a group of seasoned staff spent a month on average at each restaurant that opened, making sure that the new restaurant conformed to the chain's standards. By 1987 there were 17 Ruth's Chris restaurants across the United States. Twelve were owned by eight franchisees, and the remainder were under Fertel's direct control. By that year the chain was the largest in the upscale steak house

market. Its closest competitors were the Palm, with ten restaurants, and Arnie Morton's, a seven-unit steak house group.

Planned Expansion in the Late 1980s

By 1987, sales for the 17-unit Ruth's Chris chain stood at nearly $22 million. Fertel's $22,000 investment had paid off in a big way. Not only had she put boundless energy into the running of her restaurants, but she made sure that franchisees delivered the same quality as the original steak house. Furthermore, despite growing national health concerns about fat, red meat, and high cholesterol, Fertel continued to serve huge steaks topped with butter. Meat and potatoes were classics, and she made no apologies for her menu. She was right: no bad news about steak seemed to dent Ruth's Chris. Over the years of expansion through franchises, the restaurants had gotten bigger. By the late 1980s, the average Ruth's Chris seated about 200 and drew close to 225 diners daily. In large cities, the average gross from a Ruth's Chris was about $2.5 million annually, while in smaller markets, annual sales were somewhere between $1 million and $1.5 million. The chain was a real moneymaker. A downturn in the oil-dependent economy caused some losses at individual restaurants in the late 1980s, such as the Houston Ruth's Chris. But the chain as a whole grew 10 to 15 percent in 1987, and Fertel herself took over the ailing Houston restaurant from its franchiser, sure that more good years were ahead.

Growth up to this point had been relatively slow, but in the late 1980s Fertel decided to expand the chain more aggressively. In 1987 Fertel made public her plans to add about a dozen restaurants to the chain over the next three years. By 1990, the Ruth's Chris chain had 28 locations. Sales were close to $60 million, in other words almost tripling in three years, and the planned expansion continued. Fertel was 65 in 1992, and claimed she was going into semi-retirement. This meant she was working only seven or eight hours a day, quite a cutback. Nevertheless, she was still central to the business, which had a corporate staff of only 11 people and no regional managers. The company opened its first two foreign locations in 1993, one in Taipei, Taiwan, and the other in Cancun, Mexico. The Taipei location was over a McDonald's, at what was said to be the busiest corner in the city. The Cancun Ruth's Chris opened in an upscale mall built by a local real estate developer, who also planned to open a Mexico City location. That same year, Ruth's Chris invaded Manhattan. New York was home to many famous steak houses, and Ruth's Chris settled into Midtown, hoping to be one more. This franchise was operated by a franchisee who already ran a Ruth's Chris in Weehawken, New Jersey.

By 1994 the chain had 43 units and sales had topped $100 million. At this point, the company announced it planned to double its number of restaurants over the next six to seven years but refrain from taking on new franchisees. Growth would come from new company-owned locations or from new restaurants opened by franchisees who were already running stores for the company. Fertel was also ready to step back from the day-to-day running of the company. Although she retained the post of chairman, in 1993 she hired Thomas Cangemi to run the chain as president and chief executive. His earlier business experience including running Dobbs International, an airline catering firm. The company also added regional vice-presidents around this time, a layer of management Ruth's Chris had formerly done without.

Increasing Competition in the 1990s

While Ruth's Chris announced it would take its growth a little more slowly, it did not really happen that way. It was not the only upscale steak house chain gambling on new markets, and competition began to be more noticeable. For instance, the year Ruth's Chris opened its New York City franchise, Morton's, a Chicago-based steak house chain, opened a New York restaurant just a few blocks away. One way upscale steak houses advertised was in airline in-flight magazines, since many of their customers were business travelers on expense accounts. Ruth's Chris touched off an imbroglio with the owner of a Dallas steak house in 1994 by implying in an article in a company publication that a listing of "America's Top 10 Steakhouses" used in one such airline in-flight magazine ad was bogus. The top ten listing came from an entity called the Knife & Fork Club of America. This was run by Dale Wamsted, who was the owner of Del Frisco's Double Eagle Steak House in Dallas. Not surprisingly, the Double Eagle was prominent in the Knife & Fork Club's listing. After a Ruth's Chris publication exposed the connection between Knife & Fork and Wamsted, Wamsted sued for libel. Ruth's Chris promptly countersued. Both sides dropped their suits in 1995, in a settlement which enjoined Wamsted from running his Knife & Fork Club ad again. Yet the listing game continued, with other clubs sponsored by groups of restaurants continuing to run "Top 10 Steakhouses" ads in in-flight magazines.

The chain's growth did not slow down in the late 1990s, as had been planned, but continued at its former pace. By 1995, the chain was doing $160 million in sales, with 48 restaurants. Franchisees opened Ruth's Chris restaurants in Portland, Oregon; in Indianapolis, Indiana; and in Mexico City in 1996, and the company opened its own restaurants in Tampa, Florida; Irvine, California; and Kansas City, Missouri. In 1997 the chain had 56 units; by 1998 there were ten more. For about six months of 1997, Ruth Fertel returned to the helm of her company as president and CEO. The president she had hired in 1993, Thomas Cangemi, resigned with no public comment, and Fertel came out of her semi-retirement to take over his duties. But Fertel turned 70 in 1997, and she was not willing to run the company again for long. By October 1997, a new chief executive had been installed. William L. Hyde took the job, leaving his position as president and chief operating officer of one of Ruth's Chris's major competitors, the Morton's Restaurant Group.

Fertel announced in 1997 that the company was considering going public. It was difficult to keep financing its own expansion, and a public offering might give the company a cash boost. The company bought back some of its units from franchisees, possibly because operating more of its own units would make the company more appealing to investors. Meantime, the company continued to add more units and upgrade existing ones.

The Future

Over the years, Fertel received dozens of awards from restaurant associations and business groups, recognizing her zeal and energy in building the Ruth's Chris chain. The chain had grown despite the popularity of many fad foods, including lighter, fancier fare. The success of the restaurant in cities across the nation and in exotic locales such as Hong Kong and Taipei, showed that the core product—good steak—had fans almost everywhere. The chain's projected sales for 1998 were $225 million, more than twice the figure of five years earlier. What remained to be seen was whether the chain would embark on a new course under new leadership and how a likely IPO might affect future growth.

Further Reading

Allen, Robin Lee, "Ruth Fertel: Tireless Entrepreneur," *Nation's Restaurant News,* September 21, 1992, p. 81.

Dailey, Patricia B., "Ruth Fertel: In Her Prime," *Restaurants & Institutions,* July 1, 1997.

Fabricant, Florence, "Steakhouse Chains Are Coming," *New York Times,* August 6, 1993, p. A21.

Frumkin, Paul, "Ruth's Chris Expansion Pads Lead over Segment," *Nation's Restaurant News,* July 6, 1987, p. 1.

Lamb, Sara, "Ruth's Chris Steak House Celebrates Ten Years in Mobile, Ala.," *Knight-Ridder/Tribune Business News,* September 12, 1995, p. 9120138.

McDowell, Bill, "Ruth's Chris Steak House," *Restaurants & Institutions,* August 1, 1994, p. 54.

"Never Give Up: Ruth's Chris Steak House," *Entrepreneur Magazine,* September 1997.

Nichols, Don, "Truth in Advertising?" *Restaurant Business,* August 10, 1996, p. 40.

Ruggless, Ron, "Del Frisco Files Libel Suit Vs. Ruth's Chris," *Nation's Restaurant News,* April 11, 1994, p. 3.

——, "Fertel Resumes Control of Day-to-Day Ops at Ruth's Chris," *Nation's Restaurant News,* March 10, 1997, p. 3.

——, "Ruth's Chris Names Hyde New Prexy, CEO," *Nation's Restaurant News,* October 6, 1997, p. 8.

"There's the Beef," *People,* October 20, 1997, p. 157.

Zacharias, Beth, " 'Serious Steaks' Still in Style," *Orlando Business Journal,* September 17, 1990, p. 1.

—A. Woodward

SAA (Pty) Ltd.

Airways Park
Johannesburg International Airport
Jones Road 1627
South Africa
+27-11-978-1763
Fax: +27-11-978-1862
Web site: http://www.saa.co.za

Private Company
Incorporated: 1934 as South African Airways
Employees: 10,000
Sales: R 5.68 billion (US$1.23 billion) (1997)
NAIC: 481111 Scheduled Passenger Air Transportation;
481211 Nonscheduled Chartered Passenger Air
Transportation

SAA (Pty) Ltd., better known as South African Airways, is the largest domestic carrier in South Africa, operating 575 domestic flights per week. Although troubled in the late 1990s, its status as a major global player is evidenced by a plethora of affiliations with the likes of American Airlines, Lufthansa, and Thai International.

1930s Origins

South African Airways was founded from the assets of Union Airways, a private carrier the Union of South Africa acquired on February 1, 1934. Its collection of several de Havilland and Junkers aircraft served to link Cape Town, Durban, and Johannesburg. This "Golden Triangle" would remain the company's hub center. SAA was soon flying "giant" Junkers Ju52 aircraft as far as Kenya.

World War II interrupted civil operations, which resumed in 1943 with the Lockheed Lodestar aircraft as primary carrier. SAA began "Springbok" (gazelle) service to England in November 1945 in conjunction with BOAC. The Johannesburg-London route had stops in Nairobi, Khartoum, and Tripoli. By 1947 SAA was flying several different types of aircraft, but in 1950 it was the Lockheed Constellation that cut flying time to England to 28 hours. In 1950 the DC-7 reduced this time further, and in 1953 SAA became the first pure jetliner operator outside England, leasing a Comet from BOAC.

Technological advancements in jet aircraft allowed SAA to expand its reach. Boeing's 707 allowed SAA to serve Europe nonstop (via Athens) in 1962. In 1969 it began flying to New York via Rio de Janeiro. The company's first Boeing 747s facilitated direct Johannesburg-London flights beginning in 1971. SAA added a weekly flight to Hong Kong in 1973.

In protest of apartheid, several African governments banned SAA from their airspace in 1963. This kept the carrier from overflying East Africa. SAA's transcontinental routes became longer and costlier as they had to follow the continent's west coast. U.S. anti-apartheid sanctions began in 1986. Years of isolation would make SAA unusually self-sufficient for its size, resulting in the development of considerable training and maintenance facilities.

South Africa entered a recession in 1989. Moreover, political instability and a horrendous drought fueled the crisis, and the country's inflation rate reached 15 percent. Under this backdrop of financial pressure, privatization of the airline became an earnestly considered option. Still, SAA ordered four costly 747s, deemed necessary to handle the long-range, west coast route to Europe.

Post-Apartheid Opportunities

SAA was made a division of Transnet, the South African government's holding company for transportation enterprises, on April 1, 1990, putting it in line for eventual privatization. While the Gulf War and a world recession were universally trying times for the civil aviation business, SAA experienced a fortunate turn of events in the early 1990s. At that time, world governments began lifting sanctions against South Africa after president Frederik de Klerk abolished apartheid and freed Nelson Mandela in February 1990. SAA rejoined the African tourism market in 1991 with resumed service to Nairobi and Kenya. Several other destinations in Africa and beyond opened up within a year. Soon 50,000 passengers a year were pouring in

Company Perspectives:

We will fly the spirit of our nation to the world and be a role model to our people. We embody the magic of free South Africa to host a safe, warm African experience.

from New York City alone; SAA also flew a Miami-Cape Town route. An agreement with Aeroflot came in November 1991.

SAA collaborated with Ukrainian operator Antau in 1992 to operate three Ilyushin Il-76 freighters. Although initially profitable (thanks in part to the relatively low salaries commanded by the Ukrainian pilots), the venture faltered due to the aircraft's unreliability. SAA converted an A300 (its first Airbus had been delivered in 1992) to haul freight on the same route, and discovered the Airbus used less than half the fuel. SAA also operated some of Antau's Antonov An-26 aircraft on domestic overnight express operations.

SAA entered into a code sharing agreement with American Airlines in November 1992. Other agreements followed as SAA withdrew from operating unprofitable international routes with its own equipment. However, it did continue to try new destinations and expand services where needed. SAA preferred to fly smaller planes (such as the Boeing 767, which it first tried in 1993) more frequently on long haul routes, rather than use ultrawide-body aircraft.

Thanks to its new routes, traffic grew 40 percent in 1992. SAA spent US$1.3 billion on new 747s and Airbus A320s to match the resulting demand through 1998. Still, the carrier failed to adapt quickly enough to avoid posting a loss of US$23 million in the fiscal year 1992–93. Political violence frightened many international travelers away from South Africa, and this segment was a vital source of income.

The lifting of South Africa's isolation also meant new competition from outside airlines. Moreover, the company also faced two domestic challengers, Comair and start-up Flitestar. Domestic fares were a fraction of those found in Europe, much to the dislike of SAA management.

Pathway to Privatization

Rather than try to serve every domestic destination, SAA concentrated on the trunk routes that warranted the use of its jets. SA Express, founded in 1994, and SA Airlink operated other regional routes with turboprops. Their cooperation brought new routes and more flights to the marketplace. SAA took a 20 percent interest in SA Express, the founders of which included a Canadian and a black South African. SA Airlink, independent of SAA, was established in 1992, though its origins dated back to 1978. Airlink, which had placed one of the region's most experienced black pilots in charge of flight operations, served as a type of training ground for SAA pilots hired under a national affirmative action program known as "Turnaround 2000."

However, the coming to power of the leftwing African National Congress in the mid-1990s dimmed hopes of SAA priva-

tization and other management reforms. Chief executive Michael F. Myburgh, who replaced Gerrit D. van der Veer in the spring of 1993, was able to trim 16 percent of the workforce in 1994, however. Bureaucratic wrangling also slowed the arrival of desperately needed Boeing 777 and 747 aircraft on order.

The carrier operated a truly unique, nostalgic flight when it dispatched a restored Douglas DC-4 (the last one ever built) to an air show in Oshkosh, Wisconsin, in July 1994. The plane had first seen SAA service in 1947; it was subsequently sold to the South African Air Force. The trip took 55 hours of flying time to cover nearly 10,000 miles. The 22 passengers paid more than US$6,000 each; they returned on a regular SAA jet from New York. SAA flew regional tours and chartered its Historic Flight, which operated other vintage aircraft such as the Ju52 and DC-3.

SAA managed a profit of US$72 million in 1995–96. It entered a code share agreement with Lufthansa in 1996, to the extent of cooperating in the areas of cargo, frequent flier programs, even airport lounges. Transnet also planned to open a network of travel agencies modeled on a Lufthansa program in Germany.

A New Look in 1997

In the late 1990s, SAA unveiled a dramatic new color scheme based on the colors of the flag, meant to evoke the richness of the country's landscape. The airline also moved its corporate headquarters from a high crime downtown area to the International Airport. By this time, SAA's worldwide network spanned 29 destinations from Japan to the Netherlands.

In spite of an increase in sales to R 5.68 billion, the fiscal year 1996–97 showed a record loss of R 323 million (US$45 million), thanks to a huge increase in the price of fuel (Johannesburg International had the world's highest fuel prices) and a 35 percent drop in the South African rand. Crime and a shortage of long haul aircraft were other hindering factors.

SAA was by then competing with 70 international and nine domestic airlines. Virgin Atlantic and British Airways, its archrival, had together reduced SAA's market share of profitable London traffic to 40 percent. Moreover, Comair had captured nearly a fifth of the domestic market. Its licensing agreement with British Airways allowed it to operate as a virtual clone, right down to aircraft livery and flight designators.

SAA introduced a "Frequent Freighter" program in 1997, designed to foster loyalty among shipping clients. It operated one Airbus A300, two Boeing 737s, and one 747 dedicated to freight, in addition to utilizing the cargo capacity of its passenger aircraft.

SAA appointed a new CEO in the summer of 1998 after the departure of Mike Myburgh. Coleman Andrews, a Stanford MBA, was credited with helping World Airways stave off bankruptcy in the early 1990s. He had also advised president Gerald Ford and had once run for lieutenant governor of Virginia. "We need to develop an airline which customers love and competitors fear," declared Andrews in SAA's in-flight magazine, *Sawubona*. Critics in *Finance Week* and the *Washington Post*, however, pointed out the more recent failing fortunes of World-

Corp., the parent group of World Airways, which itself seemed to face impending bankruptcy before Andrews's appointment. Andrews countered that he was not in direct control of that airline at the time.

The International Airline Passenger Association dubbed SAA the Best African Carrier in 1999, agreeing with *Executive Travel, Travel Weekly,* and the London *Evening Standard.* However, the service was not without its complaints, and absenteeism was a significant problem. Coleman's plan to rescue SAA focused on productivity and forecast layoffs. Coleman also wanted to standardize SAA's fleet for the first time in its history to save money on spare parts, maintenance, and training. He also planned to aggressively market the carrier's expertise in technical services.

Privatization had to await untangling financial problems at Transnet, which found itself R 4 billion (US$730 million) in debt in 1998. Part of the government's plans for SAA involved dismantling its various components. In 1997, the Johannesburg Airport, which had itself been a part of SAA, was transferred to another state enterprise, Airport Company SA, also in the process of privatization. In 1999 Transnet planned to unbundle SAA's business units: Technical, Cargo, and Passenger. It planned to sell up to 49 percent of the company; British Airways, Virgin, Singapore Airlines, Lufthansa, and other eminent airlines were considering investing. Andrews himself preferred a European carrier over a U.S. airline for hub/feeding possibilities.

In spite of SAA's considerable difficulties, signs of a new "African Renaissance" gave cause for hope. The World Tourism Organization ranked South Africa the 25th most popular tourist destinations in 1999. Hoping to offer "Africa's warmest welcome," SAA finally became independent of parent Transnet on March 31, 1999, under the name "SAA (Pty) Ltd."

Principal Subsidiaries

SA Express (49%); SA Alliance Air (Uganda; 40%).

Further Reading

Andrews, Coleman, "The Troubleshooter," *Airfinance Journal,* July/August 1998, pp. 22–23.

Birns, Hilka, and James Srodes, "Deflating SAA's New Mae West," *Finance Week,* June 25, 1998, pp. 17–19.

Collett, Naomi, "Agree to Disagree," *Airfinance Journal,* October 1997, pp. 46–48.

"The End of Aerial Apartheid," *Economist,* September 28, 1996.

Hill, Leonard, "A New Tail But an Old Story," *Air Transport World,* June 1997, pp. 40–43.

Kedrosky, Paul, "The Internet in Flight," *Forbes,* June 1, 1998, p. 32.

Keenan, Ted, "SAA's Privatisation Still on Runway," *Finance Week,* April 16, 1998, pp. 23–24.

Kjelgaard, Chris, "SAA Takes 767 on South African Lease," *Airfinance Journal,* October 1993, pp. 11, 13.

"Long Day's Journey. . .," *Air Transport World,* October 1994, pp. 143–44.

Marsh, Harriet, "South Africa: Missing the Tourist Bus?" *Marketing,* August 1, 1996, pp. 22–23.

Nelms, Douglas W., "The Springbok Springs Back," *Air Transport World,* February 1993, pp. 74–76.

Nevin, Tom, "Damned If You Do; Damned If You Don't," *African Business,* January 1998, pp. 13–16.

O'Lone, Richard G., "SAA Outlook Uncertain Despite End of Isolation," *Aviation Week and Space Technology,* October 11, 1993, pp. 37–39.

"SAA Adds Nine New Boeings to Fleet," *African Business,* February 1996, pp. 38–39.

"Teething Troubles," *Business Africa,* February 1, 1996, pp. 2–3.

Vandyk, Anthony, "From Trunks to Tertiaries," *Air Transport World,* September 1995, pp. 111–13.

—Frederick C. Ingram

Schneiderman's Furniture Inc.

8198 Elmer Road
Meadowlands, Minnesota 55765
U.S.A.
(218) 427-2131
(800) 220-2225
Fax: (218) 427-2223

Private Company
Incorporated: 1948
Employees: 190
Sales: $30 million (1998 est.)
NAIC: 44211 Furniture Stores

Schneiderman's Furniture Inc. is an independent furniture store chain founded in a remote rural area of northeastern Minnesota. The family owned and operated business has capitalized on its ability to adapt to the cyclical furniture market and provide superior service to customers. The company operates stores in the Twin Cities metropolitan area and in northern Minnesota.

Rural Roots: 1940s–70s

Max Schneiderman, a native New Yorker, labored for 21 years in the U.S. Steel mill in Duluth, Minnesota, before striking out on his own. Eager to escape the mill, he bought a general store in 1948 located in a sparsely populated area northwest of Duluth. But Schneiderman, his wife Edna, and their six children found a new set of difficulties.

The store's living quarters were without running water, and the store itself was thinly stocked and situated on a dirt road that was nearly impassable in the spring. To top it off, the establishment was associated with the deeds of its former owner—he had murdered three town board members over a beer license dispute and then killed himself. Customers avoided the place.

The whole family pitched in to make the operation work. Edna minded the township's post office, stationed in the store, and the children helped out where they could. Schneiderman capitalized on the movement toward modernization of rural homes and began stocking electrical and plumbing supplies.

The business received a boost when he purchased some of the closeout inventory of a wholesale hardware store for 20 percent below wholesale price. ''We could sell so many things way below what anyone could even touch,'' said Edna in a June 1988 *Corporate Report Minnesota* article by Jane Brissett, ''that it really kind of made his reputation.''

Schneiderman entered the furniture business by way of a barter agreement for a family sofa. In lieu of payment, Schneiderman began acting as a dealer for Duluth furniture wholesaler DeWitt-Seitz Company. He met customers at DeWitt-Seitz, showed the products, closed on the sale, and made deliveries. When the wholesaler shut its doors in the early 1960s, Schneiderman expanded his store to accommodate the inventory. By 1967 Schneiderman had made the shift from a general store carrying groceries and hardware to a furniture retailer.

Skeptics abounded. Some in the industry as well as some residents of the area doubted that Schneiderman could sustain a furniture store in such a remote region, but he persisted. He made sales and deliveries, measured floors for carpeting, and repaired television sets. Schneiderman, as he had with the general store, strove to carry good merchandise and sell at the lowest possible price. No sales, no advertising, and low overhead were his mantras. He would build seven additions to the store located in Elmer Township.

Economic Downturn on Home Turf Forces Change: 1980s

Although situated in the unincorporated township of Elmer, nearby Meadowlands—population of about 200—was the recognized location of Schneiderman's Furniture. Considered the middle of nowhere by some, the town was actually centrally located, at the hub of a number of small cities spread throughout northern Minnesota's Iron Range. The business also drew customers from the westernmost port cities of Lake Superior—Duluth, Minnesota, and Superior, Wisconsin.

The furniture store covered 30,000 square feet or about ten times its original size, by the early 1980s. A 40,000-square-foot warehouse sat across the road. Unfortunately, the local economy was in big trouble. The bottom had fallen out of the Iron Range's taconite industry, which produced a low-grade iron ore for steel production and provided high-paying jobs for Iron Rangers who frequented Schneiderman's Furniture store. Sales fell 15 percent in 1982; it was the first time in its history the company had failed to grow from one year to the next.

Larry and Russell Schneiderman—the youngest of the Schneiderman children, who bought the business from their parents in the mid-1970s—responded by establishing a second store across the highway from a major Duluth shopping mall. Schneiderman's Bed and Recliner, which opened in 1983, was a hit and siphoned additional business to the Meadowlands store. Encouraged by the success of the Duluth operation, the pair opened a third outlet the next year, this time in the Twin Cities metropolitan area. They chose another out-of-the-way location, a vacant furniture store in the Lakeville Mall.

Their new store was south of Minneapolis and St. Paul but close in proximity to some of the fastest-growing suburbs in the region. When the unit failed to bring in the traffic they had anticipated, the Schneiderman brothers realized they were not in northern Minnesota anymore. Advertising, not word-of-mouth referrals, ruled in the Twin Cities.

The Schneiderman brothers had done some advertising exploiting their father's name when they opened up in Duluth. The ads for the Lakeville store once again featured their dad and played off his "crusty-but-friendly" image. "Typical was the ad in which Max said, 'Don't plan on coming to my January mattress sale. I'm not having one.' The manufacturer was, however, and the store passed along the savings," wrote Brissett. Those early Schneiderman's campaigns were limited to newspapers and billboards.

Although advertising was a shift in strategy, the Schneidermans continued their tradition of holding the line on spending. Their 1986 advertising expenses were 3.9 percent of sales versus six percent on average for the nation's other furniture retailers.

The company also brought in a veteran of the Twin Cities furniture industry who helped facilitate the transition into the new market.

A fourth Schneiderman store, which opened in the affluent Minnetonka area in 1987, had something the three earlier stores did not: a good location. The store quickly proved to be the top store in terms of walk-in business. The store's genesis, though, was highlighted by tragedy as well as opportunity.

The opportunity arose when Thomasville, one of Schneiderman's largest furniture suppliers, began searching for a store to house a furniture gallery of their products in one of Minneapolis's western suburbs. The Schneidermans now had an understanding of the Twin Cities market and were ready to expand again. In addition, Russell Schneiderman, the younger of the two brothers, and his wife Monica were looking for a change: the couple were recovering from the loss of their young son to leukemia.

Russell's move to the Twin Cities to oversee the Minnetonka store was a significant change for the family business. The two brothers had worked side by side for years. Larry handled the financial end of the operation and Russell the floor, including design, selling, and floor setup. Both had worked in

the store as children, but responded to their chores in different ways. Larry had always planned to work for the family business and came on board full-time when he graduated from the University of Minnesota-Duluth with a degree in accounting. Russell, on the other hand, did not relish the thought of working in the furniture operation and moved toward a career in criminology, but in 1972 he gave the family business another try and found it suited him.

"He now works 60 hours a week as a hands-on manager at the Minnetonka store," wrote Brissett in 1988. "Once he called on a woman whose sofa had been delivered with a spot on it. Russell was on his hands and knees cleaning the sofa when her husband walked in. The man couldn't believe that the store owner would be in his house cleaning his sofa, but Russell says it's all in a day's work: 'If you're going to preach service, it's got to come from the top down.'" Under Russell's management, the Minnetonka store quickly matched the volume of the Lakeville operation.

In addition to the $500,000 investment in the new store, in 1987 the Schneidermans purchased the Lakeville Mall for $1 million. In 1988 they acquired warehouse space for the Twin Cities operations. In spite of all the activity down south, the Meadowlands store continued to be the largest revenue producer. Sales jumped 30 percent in 1987, aided by the addition of an 8,500-square-foot Thomasville Gallery.

Schneiderman's estimated sales were $7 million in 1987. By comparison, Minnesota's largest independent furniture dealer in the late 1980s was Gabberts, which had sales of $60 million. The smaller retailer carried less expensive lines than its larger counterparts, which among others included Dayton Hudson's Home Store.

The majority of Schneiderman's stores, unlike their more upscale competitors, were off the beaten track. In a positive vein, the outlying locations helped keep operating costs down. The company's bottom line also was aided by highly productive, loyal employees—the company instituted an employee profit-sharing plan in the late 1970s. Larry's wife Sheila, Larry's sister Karen Braun, and her husband Bob Braun also worked in the business. Last, Schneiderman's had a practice of keeping debt down and paying off borrowed funds quickly.

The profile of the retail furniture industry, once predominately family run operations such as Schneiderman's, was changing as mergers and acquisitions gobbled up small stores and independent dealers were pushed out of the market by larger competitors. Furthermore, the independents competed not only with other furniture retailers for the disposable income of consumers but with merchants offering desirable products and services such as new cars, vacations, and electronics.

Schneiderman's, however, bucked the tide and continued to grow. Jack Crahan, president of Flexsteel Industries, Dubuque, Iowa, and furniture supplier to Schneiderman's, said customer service was the key to the survival of the independent dealers still on hand. Services such as designer assistance and free delivery within 75 miles of the stores, plus a top-notch sales staff and competitive pricing—medium to good quality furnishings were discounted 25 to 35 percent from the suggested retail price—helped Schneiderman's keep pace with others in the industry.

Schneiderman's sales for 1989 were in the $12 to $15 million range, up from $9 million in 1988, according to a 1990 *Star Tribune* article by Ingrid Sundstrom. The company opened its fifth store, this time in the eastern metropolitan area of St. Paul, in 1990. The Roseville store was 26,000 square feet.

New Traditions Replace the Old: 1990s

The early 1990s were marked by the introduction of more and more sales, a considerable deviation from the founder's no sale policy. A 10,000-foot addition at the Meadowlands store was designated for special purchases in an effort to boost sales. Schneiderman's advertising budget had grown to six percent of sales.

Company President Larry Schneiderman said in a June 1994 *Corporate Report Minnesota* article that his "dad wouldn't have been offended" by the changes. Co-owner and Vice-President Russell Schneiderman demurred somewhat, "He'd say what my mom says: 'you guys are crazy. Why do you need the additional headaches of what you're doing?'"

Max Schneiderman's company reached $16 million in 1993. The company was growing at a good clip, with more stores and larger sales volume. The growth spurt included the addition of a furniture manufacturing business, purchased in 1990, as well as the construction of a corporate headquarters in Meadowlands. All the activity spread the brothers a little thin, though, and customer service slipped. The Schneidermans responded to the increasing number of complaints by adding a customer service department, upgrading the computer system, and hiring more workers to inspect, repair, refinish, and upholster their products. The company employed a total of 130 people.

The Meadowlands store remained the largest of the group in terms of size and sales revenue into 1994. Some customers traveled for 100 miles or more to shop there. The flagship store had a loyal following to be sure, but the Lakeville and Roseville operations were rapidly closing in on the sales leader.

Schneiderman's Furniture, over the years and beginning with the ads featuring Max, cultivated a reputation for quirky advertisements. An ad campaign in 1994 stirred up some political controversy as well as interest in their products. Rudy Perpich, Minnesota's unconventional former governor and Iron Range native, made a cameo appearance in a couple of Schneiderman's television commercials featuring "a couple of grumpy old guys talking about politics," Jack B. Coffman reported for the *St. Paul Pioneer Press*. The problem with these ads, according to political watchdogs, was that corporations cannot, in Minnesota, make direct contributions to political campaigns, and Perpich was expected to take another run for the governorship. A July 1994 *Star Tribune* editorial pointed out that corporations could hire whomever they wanted for their ads as long as the main purpose was to sell furniture. The brief appearance brought a lot of media attention to the business. The former governor and his wife had purchased their first dining room set at Schneiderman's some 40 years earlier.

The Schneiderman family business celebrated its 50th anniversary in 1998. Eighty percent of its revenue was now generated by the company's six Twin Cities units, but the business continued to be of major significance to its rural home. As the main industry in the area, Schneiderman's employed about 50 people in various aspects of the operation. The immediate region itself—Elmer Township and the city of Meadowlands combined—had a population of about 222.

By the late 1990s the only family member still at the Meadowlands location was brother-in-law Bob Braun. Karen Schneiderman Braun worked as a design consultant for the store. Larry Schneiderman joined his brother Russell in the Twin Cities in 1997 to better manage the rapid growth there. The founders also were gone. "Max measured for carpets until 1985, three years before his death. Edna sold furniture at the Meadowlands store until she retired in 1993," wrote Jane Brissett for the *Duluth News-Tribune* in 1998.

Furniture Futures

Schneiderman's Furniture, firmly entrenched in the Twin Cities market as it began its second 50 years, was positioning itself to capitalize on the shifting purchasing patterns of the baby boom generation. The company expanded its Roseville store, renovated two other Twin Cities stores, and was considering a ninth store for the near future.

Middle-aged boomers, who were a driving force in the U.S. economy, were buying more items for the hearth and home. The U.S. furniture and bedding market was $54.8 billion in 1997 and expected to continue to grow at a rate of five or six percent through the end of the millennium, according to a 1998 *Star Tribune* article by Janet Moore. General economic conditions—such as interest rates—also would continue to have an impact on the furniture industry. For example, furniture purchases traditionally rose and fell with the level of housing sales.

In the grand scheme of things, Schneiderman's Furniture was one of the smaller players in the industry. Its annual revenues were estimated to be $30 million. In the Twin Cities, Schneiderman's competed with stores such as Slumberland Furniture, the nation's 19th largest furniture seller, which had sales of $190 million. Locally based HOM Furniture had sales of $70 million.

National retailer J.C. Penney sold furniture in Schneiderman's market area, but the nation's largest furniture retailer, Heilig-Meyers of Richmond, Virginia, which had $1.7 billion in sales, did not. National chain stores had established a strong presence in many industries by the late 1990s, but regional operators still had the upper hand in the furniture business thanks to strong customer service and knowledge of local preferences. Schneiderman's Furniture had a tradition of knowing what their customers wanted and needed and supplying it, skills that would continue to serve them well into the next century.

Further Reading

Boxmeyer, Don, "Soaked, Sawed and for Sale," *St. Paul Pioneer Press*, November 15, 1997, p. 1A.
Brissett, Jane, "Big Store with Small-Town Roots," *Duluth News Tribune*, May 14, 1998, p. 1F.
——, "Schneiderman's Road Less Traveled," *Corporate Report Minnesota*, June 1988, pp. 60–64.

Brissett, Jane, and Patrick Kennedy, "Schneidermans Change Company, Keep Tradition of Risk Taking," *Corporate Report Minnesota,* June 1994, p. 17.

Coffman, Jack B., "Perpich Plays Coy in Commercial Gig," *St. Paul Pioneer Press,* July 8, 1994, p. 1B.

"Max Schneiderman Dies; Was Founder of Furniture Store," *Star Tribune* (Minneapolis), April 20, 1988, p. 6B.

Moore, Janet, "Turning the Tables, the Chairs, the Sofas . . .," *Star Tribune* (Minneapolis), November 15, 1998, 1D.

"Rudy's Back," *Star Tribune* (Minneapolis), July 16, 1994, p. 14A.

"Schneiderman's Furniture," *Corporate Report Fact Book 1999,* p. 570.

Sundstrom, Ingrid, "Down-Home Furniture Firm Is Thriving," *Star Tribune* (Minneapolis), May 6, 1990, p. 1D.

—Kathleen Peippo

S.C. Johnson & Son, Inc.

1525 Howe Street
Racine, Wisconsin 53403-2236
U.S.A.
(414) 260-2000
Fax: (414) 260-2133
Web site: http://www.scjohnson.com

Private Company
Incorporated: 1932
Employees: 13,000
Sales: $5 billion (1999 est.)
NAIC: 325611 Soap & Other Detergent Manufacturing;
325612 Polish & Other Sanitation Good
Manufacturing; 32562 Toilet Preparation
Manufacturing; 32532 Pesticide & Other Agricultural
Chemical Manufacturing; 326113 Unsupported
Plastics Film & Sheet Manufacturing

S.C. Johnson & Son, Inc. is one of the largest family-owned and family-managed companies in the United States and a leading manufacturer of home, personal care, and insect-control products. Long known colloquially as S.C. Johnson Wax (or simply Johnson Wax), its well-known products include Raid insecticides, Off! insect repellents, Glade air fresheners, Pledge furniture polish, Windex glass and surface cleaners, Ziploc storage bags, and Edge shaving gel. Johnson was founded in 1886 as a parquet flooring company and became one of the first U.S. corporations to expand worldwide, entering Great Britain in 1914. It sells its products in more than 100 countries. Still in family hands after more than a century, Johnson's strength is its ability to develop and market new products.

Parquet Flooring Business Led to Johnson Wax

In 1882 Samuel Curtis Johnson began selling parquet flooring made by the Racine Hardware Company in Racine, Wisconsin. Four years later, Johnson purchased the flooring business from the hardware company. The new organization had four employees and showed a first-year profit of less than $300.

Johnson's parquet customers often asked him about caring for their new floors. At that time shellac had been used for that purpose, but it tended to build up and peel off. Johnson created a product called Johnson's Prepared Wax to sell along with his flooring. The concept was borrowed from the European use of wax to care for old wooden floors. It was very successful, and Johnson began selling it even to people who had not bought his flooring. It was nationally advertised by 1888.

Samuel's son, Herbert F. Johnson, Sr., joined the firm in 1892, beginning a more than century-long tradition of family involvement in the business. By the following year the company was already experimenting with products such as wood dye, crack filler, and car wax. When the car wax proved to be popular, Johnson made a radiator cleaner. He was forced to buy back 900 Model T Ford radiators that were dissolved by the insufficiently tested product. This setback provided a valuable experience. Johnson Wax has given priority to top-rate research teams and chemists ever since.

As simple maple and oak flooring replaced the intricate parquet floors in the late 1800s, the company's diversification paid off. In 1898 sales of the floor wax and other woodcare products exceeded Johnson's flooring sales. Floor wax became Johnson's major product.

The company changed its formal name to S.C. Johnson & Son in 1906, when Herbert F. Johnson, Sr., became a partner. While continuing to add to their product line—Floor Renewer, Under-Lac, and Flat Color Finish—the company expanded overseas in 1914, when the British Johnson company was established. The company opened in Australia in 1917. Johnson discontinued the manufacture of parquet flooring, and the last shipment of it was made in 1917. Johnson concentrated on wax products and preservation products for cars, such as Hastee Patch and Self-Vulcanizer. S.C. Johnson died in 1919, and his son succeeded him as president. The three keys to Johnson Wax's continued success had been already established: international operations, chemical technology, and the use of advertising.

During this time, the company's innovations as an employer were also notable: it was one of the first U.S. companies to give paid vacations, a policy begun in 1900. With its 200 employees in 1917, S.C. Johnson Wax began one of the first profit-sharing

Company Perspectives:

In 1976, we formally stated our guiding philosophy in "This We Believe." In it, we express our beliefs in relation to the people to whom we are responsible and whose trust we must continue to earn. Employees: We believe our fundamental strength lies in our people. Consumers: We believe in earning the enduring goodwill of the people who use and sell our products and services. General Public: We believe in being a responsible leader in the free market economy. Neighbors and Hosts: We believe in contributing to the well-being of the countries and communities where we conduct business. World Community: We believe in improving international understanding.

programs in the country; the program in 1990 was the fifth oldest. It started offering group life insurance for employees also in 1917. In 1920 the Canadian Johnson company was formed. Throughout this decade, product offerings expanded, including enamel paints, carbon remover, weighted brushes for painters, and Kleen Floor and Restorer. Herbert F. Johnson, Jr., became president after his father's death in 1928. At that time, the company had 500 employees.

Wright-Designed HQ Unveiled in 1939

The French Johnson company opened in 1931, the same year in which sales began of one of Johnson Wax's longest-selling products, Glo-Coat Floor Finish. The product involved a colloid technology developed at Johnson Wax that freed it of the need for resins that caused yellowing. Glo-Coat became one of the most successful floor-care products of all time. In 1932 S.C. Johnson & Son was incorporated. The company's pension plan was initiated two years later, and product innovations continued. The most notable event of the decade, however, was the 1939 unveiling of the company's new office building, designed by Frank Lloyd Wright. An accomplishment in any era, it was particularly stirring at the close of the Great Depression, which Johnson weathered without laying off any employees. The Racine building continues to be headquarters for the company. In the late 20th century the company was still giving five percent of its pretax profits to charity, a tradition begun with the founder, who gave ten percent of his annual income to civic improvements.

By 1942 the company was concentrating its output on products for the war effort, while many employees were called upon to serve. Its contribution during World War II was marked by army and navy production awards. A Research & Development Tower was opened in 1950. The Lighthouse Resort for employees and retirees was unveiled in northern Wisconsin the following year.

The West German Johnson company was established in 1953. Samuel C. Johnson, great-grandson of the founder, joined the company in 1954. He headed the new-products department that was created the following year. Not long after, he produced his first new product within that division, an aerosol insecticide. His father, Herbert F. Johnson, Jr., sent him back to the lab, claiming

the insecticide was no different from others on the market. In 1956 Johnson came forward with Raid House & Garden Bug Killer; water-based, it was the first product that could be used on plants and in the home without killing the plants. Raid would become one of Johnson Wax's most profitable lines. Along with this breakthrough came Glade Air Fresheners, introduced the same year; they featured advanced technology in aerosol manufacturing. Insecticide products continued with Off!, an insect repellent first sold in 1957. Another very successful product, Pledge, came out in 1958. Herbert F. Johnson, Jr., became company chairman in 1958, and the presidency was assumed by the first nonfamily member, H. M. Packard.

In 1959 S.C. Johnson Wax established a presence in Italy, and this marked the start of a decade of international expansion: Chile, Switzerland, Sweden, and South Africa in 1961; Belgium, Japan, and the Netherlands in 1962; Norway, Austria, Spain, and Ghana in 1964; and Denmark, east Africa, Greece, Hong Kong, Singapore, and Thailand by 1968. Establishing an international base allowed Johnson Wax to manufacture its products from local materials for local markets; exporting the products would not have been profitable. In 1966 Packard became chairman and S.C. Johnson was named president.

Entered Personal Care Products in 1970

Johnson Wax entered the personal care product market in 1970, with the introduction of Edge, a shaving gel, which also went on to become a company mainstay. Penetrating eight more countries by 1972, the company recognized the need to slow its innovations in order to deal with its own growth. Johnson Diversified, Inc. (JDI), a wholly owned subsidiary, was formed in 1970. JDI began acquiring highly diversified companies, many of them recreational equipment manufacturers. In the early 1970s, 15 companies—ranging from Eureka Tent & Awning Company to Under Sea Industries—were acquired. William K. Eastham was elected president of S.C. Johnson & Son in 1972. Three years later the company eliminated chlorofluorocarbons, which had been linked to ozone layer damage, from its aerosol products worldwide; the move came three years before the U.S. government mandated their removal.

Gas prices and related mid-1970s economic circumstances made the company's diversification into recreational equipment costly. Five of the weaker companies were sold. During this time, there was a notable slowdown in the introduction of new products while Johnson Wax adjusted to its size and variety. JDI changed its name to Johnson Wax Associates (JWA) in 1977. After H.F. Johnson, Jr., died in 1978, S.C. Johnson took a sabbatical from his post as chairman and CEO in order to settle his father's estate; Eastham served as CEO in the interim. The company entered Egypt, Taiwan, and the Dominican Republic in 1979, but the decade was closing with lost momentum. Johnson Wax had introduced Agree conditioner and shampoo in 1977 and 1978. During that time, sales increased (to $1 billion by 1978) while profits declined. All consumer packaged goods saw sluggish profits during this time, and Johnson Wax had acquisitions and overseas expansions sapping profits in addition. While foreign markets accounted for 60 percent of the company's sales for a period during the late 1970s, the recession-affected U.S. dollar undercut this portion of earnings, and the company was faced with a call to change in the early 1980s.

Restructured in the 1980s

Raymond F. Farley became president in 1980, the same year S.C. Johnson resumed the CEO seat and began instituting needed reforms. In 1982 Johnson imposed a one-year wage freeze. It was the first time in 20 years that a wage freeze had been instituted without governmental exigency. He reduced the company's U.S. workforce by three percent with early retirement programs, then increased the research and marketing staffs. The company was restructured into four enterprise units: personal care, insecticides, home care, and commercial products. Units were organized to speed up the time between product idea and introduction, and new products were pouring forth by the mid-1980s. The advertising budget was nearly 70 percent higher in 1984 than in 1979, the research-and-development budget increased by 40 percent, and product price increases were reduced. Building on its consumer pest control products, S.C. Johnson & Son entered the market for commercial pest control in 1986 with the purchase of Bugs Burger Bug Killers.

One week before the October 1987 stock market plunge, JWA went public. Johnson called this move ''going public to stay private,'' since the offering created liquid assets needed for potential estate taxes, thus protecting the company's assets and its private status. At the time the family owned 90 percent of Johnson Wax, with employees holding the other ten percent. JWA was selling $250 million annually in the late 1980s, mostly fishing and other recreational gear, as well as ink-stamping equipment. JWA was the nation's largest producer of electric fishing-boat motors and a major seller of reels and lures. Sales at S.C. Johnson & Son, meantime, passed the $2 billion mark in 1987.

In late 1988, Farley became the second nonfamily member in Johnson's history to become chief executive. S.C. Johnson remained chairman. All four of his children were then involved with the company, with his eldest son, S. Curtis Johnson III, heading a venture-capital unit he induced his father to bankroll in 1983.

Tremendous Growth in the 1990s

In January 1990 Farley retired and was succeeded by Richard M. Carpenter, president and CEO. The 1990s were marked by a number of acquisitions and divestments, along with continued new product introductions and overseas expansion. In 1990 the company joined with a Ukrainian household production association to form S.C. Johnson Kiev Corporation, initially 80 percent owned by S.C. Johnson & Son but wholly owned by 1994. Although it got off to a rocky start, this venture reached profitability in 1995—after the collapse of the Soviet Union and the emergence of Ukraine as a sovereign nation. S.C. Johnson & Son found success making and marketing such products as Brillo dish detergent, Pronto furniture polish, and Duck toilet cleaner. Also in 1990 came the introduction of yet another successful new product, Glade Plug Ins, long-lasting fragrance dispensers which are plugged into electrical outlets; the product quickly gained the top position in the continuous-action air freshener category.

In late 1992 Carpenter retired and William D. George, Jr., who had headed the worldwide consumer products division, was appointed president and CEO. In January 1993 S.C. John-son & Son acquired Drackett Co. from Bristol-Myers Squibb Co. for $1.15 billion, a sum ten times larger than any previous company acquisition. Brands acquired therein included three that were either number one or two in their segment—Windex glass cleaners, Drano drain openers, and Vanish toilet bowl cleaner. Other brands gained included O-Cedar brooms and mops and Mr. Muscle hard-surface cleaners. The purchase bolstered the company's presence in household cleaners, which had already received a boost in 1992 from the debut of Toilet Duck and Bathroom Duck spray cleaners. It also, however, brought S.C. Johnson & Son into more direct competition with household cleaning giants Procter & Gamble Company and Clorox Company. Johnson Wax subsequently beefed up its global advertising budget, which by 1994 stood at about $500 million, or 14 percent of the company's $3.6 billion in revenues.

For antitrust reasons, S.C. Johnson & Son had to divest three Drackett brands within sectors in which the company was already very strong: Endust cleaning sprays, Behold furniture polish, and Renuzit air fresheners. A further divestment came in 1993 after the company decided to sell the bulk of its shampoo and lotion lines. In August of that year the Agree and Halsa brands were sold to Dep Corporation for $45 million. Less than a year later Dep sued S.C. Johnson & Son, charging it with changing its marketing of the two brands before the deal was closed, withholding sales information, and making false representations to Dep prior to the acquisition; and seeking recision of the deal plus $75 million in damages. Johnson Wax was the object of another lawsuit filed in 1997 that claimed that the company discriminated against blacks in its hiring and promotion policies. By 1997 William D. Perez, former head of the worldwide consumer products division, had become president and CEO of S.C. Johnson & Son.

In January 1998 Johnson Wax completed its second major acquisition of the decade when it purchased the DowBrands unit from Dow Chemical Co. for $1.13 billion. Added to the S.C. Johnson product portfolio were Ziploc plastic bags, Saran Wrap plastic wrap, and Fantastik cleaners. As with the Drackett acquisition, S.C. Johnson had to divest several acquired brands to gain antitrust muster, including Spray 'N Wash laundry-stain remover (Johnson already sold the Shout brand in this product category) and Glass Plus glass cleaner. The company also sold off the Yes laundry detergent and Vivid color-safe bleach lines. The acquisition of DowBrands brought an immediate 20 percent increase to company revenues, which grew from $4 billion in 1998 to more than $5 billion in 1999. Meantime, in February 1999, S.C. Johnson made a further withdrawal from the personal care sector through the sale of its dermatological skincare business—which was primarily made up of the Aveeno brand—to Johnson & Johnson for an undisclosed amount. S.C. Johnson had thus largely reduced its personal care line to the shaving sector, where the Edge for men and Skintimate for women brands were sector leaders.

By the late 1990s S.C. Johnson & Son was a broadly based consumer products giant, and this position was echoed in the company's decision in late 1998 to alter its logo and ads to say ''S.C. Johnson—A Family Company'' rather than ''S.C. Johnson Wax''—wax products being only a small part of the business. With its new image, S.C. Johnson entered the 21st century as an aggressively expanding firm, strongly committed to research and development and willing to pursue blockbuster acquisitions. It also remained firmly controlled by the Johnson family. S.C. Johnson remained chairman, while two sons held high posts: S. Curtis (Curt) Johnson, chairman of commercial markets, and H. Fisk Johnson, president of consumer products. A daughter, Helen Johnson-Leipold, had resigned her post as vice-president of personal and home care products in order to assume the chairmanship of the publicly held spinoff company Johnson Worldwide Associates, Inc.

Principal Subsidiaries

Johnson Venture Capital, Inc.; Prism Integrated Sanitation Management, Inc.; Whitmire Micro-Gen Research Laboratories Inc.; Ceras Johnson de Portugal, Lda.; Ceras Johnson Ltda. (Brazil); Johnson Company, Ltd. (Japan); S.C. Johnson (U.K.); La Johnson Francaise S.A. (France); Johnson Nederland B.V. (Netherlands); P.T. S.C. Johnson & Son (Indonesia) Ltd.; Johnson Wax (Egypt); Johnson Wax AG (Switzerland); Johnson Wax Consumer Products (Belgium); Johnson Wax GmbH (Germany); Johnson Wax Industrial Products (INNOCHEM) (Belgium); Johnson Wax Nigeria Limited; Johnson Wax Research and Development (U.K.); Johnson Wax S.p.A. (Italy); N.V. Johnson Wax Belgium S.A.; Johnson's Wax (East Africa) Ltd. (Kenya); Johnson's Wax Española, S.A. (Spain); Johnson's Wax Ltd. (Ghana); Johnsonwax del Ecuador S.A.; Korea Johnson Co., Ltd.; Quimica S.C. Johnson & Son Chilena S.A.C.I. (Chile); S.C. Johnson (Norway); S.C. Johnson & Son Colombiana S.A. (Colombia); S.C. Johnson & Son de Argentina S.A.I.C.; S.C. Johnson & Son (Hellas) E.P.E. (Greece); S.C. Johnson & Son, Inc. (Philippines); S.C. Johnson & Son, Limited (Canada); S.C. Johnson & Son, Ltd. (Thailand); S.C. Johnson & Son of South Africa (Pty.) Ltd.; S.C. Johnson & Son Pte. Limited (Singapore); S.C. Johnson & Son Pty. Ltd. (Australia); S.C. Johnson & Son, S.A. de C.V. (Mexico); S.C. Johnson & Son Taiwan Ltd.; S.C. Johnson & Son de Venezuela, C.A.; S.C. Johnson Company Limited (Cyprus); S.C. Johnson de Centroamerica S.A. (Costa Rica); S.C. Johnson Kiev Corp. (Ukraine); S.C. Johnson, Ltd. (Hong Kong); S.C. Johnson New Zealand Ltd.; Svenska Johnson's Vax AB (Sweden).

Further Reading

"Agree and Halsa Continue to Cause Problems for Dep Corporation," *Cosmetics International,* February 25, 1996, pp. 13+.

Benady, Alex, "Johnson Spend Is Biggest Ever," *Marketing,* November 4, 1993, p. 16.

Carrington, Tim, "Ukraine's Women Love These Two Firms," *Wall Street Journal,* February 6, 1992, p. A10.

"Dep Files Suit Against Johnson, Company Rumoured to Be Maybelline Target," *Cosmetics International,* March 25, 1994, pp. 1+.

Deveny, Kathleen, "As More Americans Declare War on Dirt, Cleaning-Product Firms Make Tidy Sums," *Wall Street Journal,* April 6, 1993, p. B1.

Dries, Mike, "S.C. Johnson to Build Warehouse, Distribution Center," *Business Journal- Milwaukee,* December 5, 1997, pp. 1+.

Ellis, James, "Sam Johnson Is 'Going Public to Stay Private,' " *Business Week,* December 5, 1988.

Fitzgerald, Kate, "How Johnson Will Gain with Drackett," *Advertising Age,* November 2, 1992, p. 13.

Gibson, Richard, "Bristol-Myers to Sell Drackett to S.C. Johnson: Wisconsin Firm Boosts Line of Household Products with $1.15 Billion Pact," *Wall Street Journal,* October 28, 1992, p. A3.

Henkoff, Ronald, "When to Take on the Giants," *Fortune,* May 30, 1994, pp. 111+.

Johnson, Samuel C., *The Essence of a Family Enterprise: Doing Business the Johnson Way,* Indianapolis: Curtis Publishing, 1988, 179 p.

Johnson Wax Magazine, December 1986.

Kaminski, Matthew, "Waiting Game Paying Off in Ukraine," *Financial Times,* July 25, 1995, p. 19.

McMenamin, Brigid, "Eroding Patent Rights," *Forbes,* October 24, 1994, p. 92.

Moss, Michael, "No One's Fall Guy, Johnson Wax Expert Barely Ever Slips," *Wall Street Journal,* August 7, 1996, p. A1.

Neff, Jack, "New Products Boosting Johnson, Categories," *Advertising Age,* September 15, 1997, p. 76.

Pierce, Lisa McTigue, "Line Plugs New Product into Top Spot," *Packaging* (Boston), March 1991, pp. 40+.

Schellhardt, Timothy D., "Race-Bias Suit at S.C. Johnson Raises Some Worker-Team Issues," *Wall Street Journal,* February 13, 1997, p. B7.

——, "This Office Building Is a Work of Art, Unless It's Raining," *Wall Street Journal,* February 18, 1997, p. A1.

Warren, Susan, "S.C. Johnson Seals Deal to Buy Ziploc and Other Brands from Dow Chemical," *Wall Street Journal,* October 29, 1997, p. A4.

—Carol I. Keeley
—updated by David E. Salamie

Sebastiani Vineyards, Inc.

389 Fourth Street East
Sonoma, California 95476
U.S.A.
(707) 938-5532
(800) 888-5532
Fax: (707) 935-1218
Web site: http://www.sebastiani.com

Private Company
Incorporated: 1904
Employees: 340
Sales: $200.9 million (1997)
NAIC: 31213 Wineries

One of the largest wineries in the United States, Sebastiani Vineyards, Inc. produces moderately priced table wines under a variety of labels, such as "Vendange," "Talus," "Sonoma Cask," "Heritage," "La Terre," and "Estates." A family-owned and -operated business, Sebastiani Vineyards developed into a major wine producer under the control of the founder's son, August Sebastiani, who focused on marketing inexpensive, jug wines. August Sebastiani's son Sam assumed the reins of control in 1980, but was fired six years later after attempting to transform the winery into a more upscale wine producer. Sam Sebastiani's younger brother Don, a former California legislator, took command in 1986 and during the course of the next decade tripled the winery's production volume. By the end of the 1990s, Sebastiani Vineyards was producing more than seven million cases of wine each year.

1895: Samuele Sebastiani Arrives in America

Sebastiani Vineyards began producing wine in 1904, when the patriarch of the family, Samuele Sebastiani, started a modest wine-producing business in Sonoma, California. A native of the Tuscany region in northern Italy, Sebastiani immigrated to the United States in 1895, arriving with the clothes on his back, a thorough understanding of how to produce wine, and little else. Young and poor, Sebastiani did what he could to provide food and shelter for himself in his new surroundings. He worked in gardens and performed other odd jobs until he saved enough money to buy a horse and a wagon. With the horse and wagon, Sebastiani hauled cobblestones from a quarry in Sonoma, cobblestones that were used to pave the streets of San Francisco, 40 miles to the south, and to lay the tracks for the city's famed cable cars. After nearly a decade of such work, Sebastiani had saved enough money to start a business truer to his heart. In 1904 he purchased a Sonoma vineyard and began producing his own wine, practicing a craft whose intricacies had been handed down through generations of Tuscans.

The land Sebastiani purchased had been operating as a vineyard for nearly 80 years before he purchased it in 1904. The vineyard's first owners were disciples of a sect whose origins were not far from Sebastiani's birthplace. In 1825 Franciscan monks residing at San Francisco Solano, a mission near Sonoma, enlisted the help of local Native Americans to clear the land for the vineyard. When Sebastiani began working the old Franciscan vineyard, he concentrated on producing Zinfandel, which he sold to familiar clientele. Sebastiani, using his horse-drawn wagon, delivered his Zinfandel to workers toiling at the Sonoma quarry, selling it by the cup and by the jug. Sebastiani worked at the vineyard until his death, establishing a legacy as one of the pioneers of northern California's wine country, destined to be the epicenter of wine production in the United States.

Second Generation Takes Over in 1952

Sebastiani's son, August, purchased the winery from his father's estate in 1952, and with his wife, Sylvia, developed the family business into one of the largest wineries in the United States. As a vintner, August Sebastiani displayed a talent for marketing his wines to a broad customer base, selling Sebastiani wines, as his father had, by the jug. He increased the winery's production volume a hundredfold during his nearly 30-year reign by tapping into the demand for table wines, relying almost exclusively on inexpensive wines marketed to the masses. August Sebastiani was the first vintner to market premium varietal wines in a magnum size. He introduced "Nouveau" Gamay Beaujolais to U.S. consumers and he created a blush wine known as Pinot Noir Blanc; two examples of Sebastiani labels

Company Perspectives:

The Sebastiani family has been making wine at its Sonoma Cask Cellars location since 1904. Our Sonoma Cask wines are the culmination of years of research and practical experience. The guiding philosophy behind the Cask winemaking program has always been to produce the best possible wines from grapes grown in Sonoma County. Flavor, balance and fidelity to the unique character of our viticultural area is our goal. We maximize quality, often at the expense of quantity.

that fueled the winery's rise during the latter half of the 20th century. By the end of his tenure in 1980, Sebastiani Vineyards ranked as the sixth largest table wine producer in the United States, controlling 3.9 percent of the market. His death in 1980 devolved stewardship of the winery to the third generation of Sebastianis and marked the beginning of a tumultuous, divisive decade for the Sonoma-based company.

August Sebastiani's eldest son, Sam J. Sebastiani, took control of the winery in 1980, assuming leadership at the age of 39. Under Sam Sebastiani's control, radical, sweeping changes were implemented that reflected a wholesale change in the winery's strategy. Sebastiani immediately led the winery away from its dependence on inexpensively priced jug wines and toward a new existence as a trendy upscale winery, capable of producing award-winning, high-quality wines. His objective for Sebastiani Vineyards, as he once wrote in an industry newsletter, was "to fall out of the top 10 from quantity, to the top 10 in quality," a dramatic shift in stance engendered by his vision that premium wines would be the choice of consumers in the years ahead. Sebastiani's prognosticative skills were laudable, prompting the publisher of the *Grape Intelligence Report* to remark, "[Sebastiani] saw that the days of jug wines were numbered in a worldwide shift toward premium wines," but Sebastiani's execution and timing led to difficult years for the winery.

Mid-1980s Troubles Lead to New Management

A number of factors conspired against Sebastiani's ambitious plan to upgrade the winery's image, particularly a worldwide grape glut that delivered a pernicious blow to the California wine industry. Also hampering Sebastiani's progress were increased competition from foreign wines, the growing popularity of California wine coolers, and a decrease in worldwide wine consumption. Further, Sebastiani Vineyards' mainstay business—the production of inexpensive table wines—was plagued by escalating production costs during the early 1980s, causing the winery's financial troubles to mount. Undaunted by declining sales, Sebastiani pushed ahead with his plans, systematically changing everything from labels to promotional techniques in effort to recast Sebastiani Vineyards as a premium wine producer. At one point, he offered to recall more than $2 million worth of lower-priced wine to blend it with private reserves. "If it's a choice of dumping the advertising and dumping the wine, you dump the wine," Sebastiani remarked, revealing his priorities for Sebastiani Vineyards' future. He continued to direct capital toward an aggressive and expensive

marketing campaign, despite declining sales, persisting with a program that struggled to identify the proper direction to pursue. Several marketing directors endeavored to find the appropriate image for the winery and failed, prompting Sebastiani and his wife, Vickie, to lead the marketing of Sebastiani Vineyards themselves. The couple traveled across the country, staging flamboyant wine tastings that proved highly successful. The peripatetic Sebastianis gained worldwide recognition for their winery, but back in Sonoma concerns were heightening as sales sagged. By 1985 Sebastiani Vineyards had slipped from being the sixth largest producer in the country to the eighth largest producer, while its market share had fallen from the nearly four percent earned by August Sebastiani to 2.3 percent. The stage was set for a family feud, a public rift between Sebastiani family members that centered on the prudence of Sam Sebastiani's vision.

On January 2, 1986, Sam Sebastiani received a letter from his mother, Sylvia, long a powerful figure at Sebastiani Vineyards and holder of 92 percent of the company's stock. While her husband developed the winery into one of the largest in the country, Sylvia Sebastiani exerted her own considerable influence over the company, regularly appearing at the winery to greet visitors and entertain guests. After August Sebastiani's death, Sylvia Sebastiani presided as the winery's board chairwoman, from which position she watched her son's dealings with the family business and grew increasingly displeased. In her letter, Sylvia Sebastiani noted that "the winery was being run very, very poorly" amid concerns about "incredibly high expenditures of money." The letter informed Sam Sebastiani that he and his wife, who served as the winery's director of food and wine, had been fired, a decision Sylvia Sebastiani said she reached in agreement with her daughter and fellow board member, Mary Ann Cuneo, and her other son, Don Sebastiani, a Sebastiani Vineyard board member and a representative of the Eighth District in California's state assembly. Concurrent with the ouster of her son and daughter-in-law, Sylvia Sebastiani announced she was stepping down as chairwoman to be replaced by her son Don. Mary Ann Cuneo's husband, Richard A. Cuneo, the winery's senior vice-president and secretary-treasurer, was named to replace Sam Sebastiani as president and chief executive officer on an interim basis.

Before the end of 1986, Don Sebastiani assumed full control over the winery, serving as both chairman and chief executive officer, with Cuneo serving under him as president. Under Don Sebastiani's control, the winery arrested its financial slide, bolstered by the strength of its biggest brand, "August Sebastiani Country Wines." The brand paid homage to the individual responsible for developing the winery into a major producer, a tribute Don Sebastiani sought to extend through his managerial approach by emulating his father's hallmark achievement: dramatically increasing production volume. During his first decade in command, Don Sebastiani increased the winery's production volume threefold, expanding at a pace that vaulted Sebastiani Vineyards past its competitors to reign as the quantitative champion of Bay Area wine producers. The company's growth was driven by the success of a full range of brands that positioned the winery in the most lucrative retail price categories. Sebastiani Vineyards' notable success was its "Vendange" brand, introduced in 1987. Marketed at the lower end of the price scale, the "Vendange" brand developed into the fastest-growing brand in the country by the early 1990s, helping Sebastiani Vineyards eclipse Sutter Home Winery Inc. in 1994 to rank as the largest winery in the Bay Area. The company, by this point, was registering an annual growth rate of approximately 15 percent, thanks to the growing demand for its ''Vendange'' brand and its super premium ''Sonoma Series'' brand. ''August Sebastiani Country Wines,'' holding sway as the company mainstay brand, was experiencing slower growth as the winery entered the mid-1990s, but a national promotional campaign—the largest in Sebastiani Vineyards' history—was launched in late 1994 to spur sales of the mid-priced, popular premium brand.

By the late 1990s, there were seven brands composing Sebastiani Vineyards' product line, each catering to mainstream consumer tastes and competing in different price categories. Annual sales in 1997 surpassed the $200 million mark for the first time, increasing more than 13 percent from the previous year's total. The $200.9 million in sales generated in 1997, drawn from the production of more than seven million cases of wine, was more than three times the total registered when Don Sebastiani first assumed leadership of the winery in 1986. Under his direction, Sebastiani Vineyards strengthened the mar-

ket recognition of its name, providing a decided advantage toward realizing future growth and market penetration. Although advancement at a pace commensurate with the past was not guaranteed, the roster of Sebastiani Vineyards brands appeared strongly positioned as the winery neared its centennial.

Principal Subsidiaries

Sebastiani Sonoma Cask Cellars.

Further Reading

Carlsen, Clifford, ''Sebastiani Vineyards Unseats Sutter Home for No. 1.,'' *San Francisco Business Times,* March 25, 1994, p. 21.
''Executive Profile: Don Sebastiani,'' *San Francisco Business Times,* December 4, 1998, p. 10.
Shandrick, Michael, ''Wine Family Feud Erupts; President Fired by Mom,'' *San Francisco Business Journal,* January 13, 1986, p. 1.
''What Holidays Mean to Them,'' *Beverage World,* October 1994, p. 22.
Winchester, Jay, ''Ripe for a Change,'' *Sales & Marketing Management,* August 1998, p. 81.

—Jeffrey L. Covell

Serta, Inc.

325 Spring Lake Drive
Itasca, Illinois 60143
U.S.A.
(630) 285-9300
Fax: (630) 285-9330
Web site: http://www.serta.com

Private Company
Incorporated: 1931 as Sleeper, Inc.
Employees: 2,100
Sales: $670 million (1998 est.)
NAIC: 33791 Mattress Manufacturing

Serta, Inc. is the second largest manufacturer and distributor of sleeping mattresses in the world, directly behind Sealy, Inc. Although the company has been in business since the early 1930s, it was during the 1990s that Serta grew to become one of the dominant firms in the industry. Serta has a list of accomplishments that would impress any industry analyst, including such significant achievements as: outperforming industry sales growth by more than two and a half times since the beginning of the 1990s; representing more than 30 percent of the total mattress manufacturers' growth, comprised of over 700 firms, since 1989; maintaining double digit sales increases from 1994 to the present, the only major mattress manufacturer to do so; and developing not only to become one of the leading mattress brands throughout Canada, but growing to become one of the largest suppliers to hotels, motels, and holiday resorts around the world. From 1989 to 1997, Serta reported that it had captured a 17 percent market share of the entire mattress industry. Not surprisingly, this kind of market dominance could only be achieved and sustained by means of an extensive network of 31 factories across the United States and Canada, as well as 23 manufacturing facilities located in such diverse countries as Venezuela, Taiwan, Saudi Arabia, New Zealand, Mexico, India, Iceland, and Chile.

Early History

Serta, Inc. was established during the worst years of the Great Depression. From the stock market crash in 1929 through the 1930s, the entire economy of the United States was hit by a depression of enormous magnitude. Family fortunes were lost overnight due to stock market losses; corporations and small businesses went bankrupt, farmers lost their farms because of foreclosures, many banks closed their doors to the public and, perhaps worst of all, numerous people lost their jobs and had no prospect of employment in the foreseeable future. President Coolidge maintained that the economy would correct itself sooner or later, and rejected requests from various interest groups to get the government involved in a strategy that would alleviate some of the economic hardship.

As prospects for a quick economic recovery, under the non-interventionist government strategy devised by Coolidge, were acknowledged by businessmen across the nation as unlikely, more and more independent small businesses began to form associations to strengthen the chances of their survival. One such association was a large group of independent mattress manufacturers who all agreed that their economic livelihood and future depended on their ability to compete with larger, well-established firms that combined brand-name recognition with significant amounts of money for advertising campaigns. Having debated the merits and demerits of working together, an assembly of 13 independent mattress manufacturers formally organized in 1931 and incorporated their businesses under one name, Sleeper, Inc.

The first decision made under the new flagship company was to establish strict guidelines for all of the products Sleeper, Inc. would manufacture, and then devise a strategy for marketing those products under an agreed-upon brand name. All of the independent businessmen that had formed the new company were thoroughly convinced that only a brand-name product could successfully compete with the larger mattress companies. Not wasting any time, therefore, Sleeper, Inc. quickly researched and developed its first brand-name mattress, Perfect Sleeper, in 1932. The first tuftless mattress ever made, the Perfect Sleeper was an immediate success. The combination of a nationally recognized brand-name mattress, along with an extensive network of companies committed to providing both retailers and consumers with high-quality products and services, meant that the independent mattress manufacturers that formed Sleeper, Inc. would survive the worst years of the Great Depression after all.

World War II and the Postwar Era

Just before U.S. entry into World War II in December 1941, the association of companies comprising Sleeper, Inc. voted to change the name of the company to Serta-Sleeper Associates. Not yet satisfied, they shortly afterward changed the firm's name again, this time to Serta, Inc. Thus christened, the company continued to increase sales of its brand-name mattresses, even though the war years demanded sacrifices on the part of consumers across the United States.

Serta, Inc. had done its homework during the 1930s and early 1940s, and was well-prepared for the dramatic increase in demand for consumer goods during the immediate postwar period. The company had previously initiated an intensive marketing research campaign to determine what kinds of products Americans were most likely to purchase. During the course of its research, the company found that consumers wanted to own recognizable brand-name items, not just any product on the market. In fact, Serta discovered that the vast majority of consumers would be more than willing to spend larger amounts of money for brand names that they knew and had come to trust, rather than pay less for products without brand-name recognition. This market research corroborated Serta's long-held belief that having a familiar and trustworthy brand name was imperative for its success.

As the market environment for consumer products developed at a hectic pace during the 1950s, with more and more products introduced by companies competing both for the attention and the buying power of U.S. consumers, Serta made the strategic decision to increase its advertising investment. In an attempt to heighten awareness within the general public, distinguish its products, narrow the consumer's choices, and make the shopping experience a more pleasurable activity, Serta was one of the first companies to advertise its products on such television programs as "The Bob Hope Show" and "The Tonight Show." Up to this time, radio and the print media were the two primary avenues for advertising Serta mattresses. But television helped the company to dramatically influence the public's preference for the Serta name.

The 1960s were good years for Serta. Sales increased steadily as the company's advertisements, especially on television, provided a high-profile visibility for its quality mattresses. In keeping with its tradition of conducting market research, Serta discovered that its mattresses were now one of the most recognizable consumer products in the United States. A culture of comfort had spread across the American landscape, and every item that contributed to a better, happier, and easier lifestyle was in greater and greater demand. Serta mattresses, of course, provided an individual with a sound and peaceful sleeping experience and, according to the company's advertisements, was worth the higher than normal market price. As sales increased, management decided it was an appropriate time to develop a strategic expansion plan for North America. Thus by the end of 1965, Serta had expanded its organization to include 39 plants and facilities across the United States and Canada, including new operations in Montreal, Toronto, Vancouver, and Winnipeg, as well as in Clear Lake, Iowa; Beloit, Wisconsin; Houston, Texas; and other U.S. cities.

Growth and Expansion During the 1970s and 1980s

Perhaps it was due to the sleepless nights caused by the disquieting Vietnam War, widespread civil unrest, or Watergate—whatever the case, the decade of the 1970s brought ever-increasing revenues to Serta. The company was selling its brand-name mattresses in record amounts across the United States, and management decided that a research and development department should be established with enough funds to conduct extensive research on sleep habits and new mattress technology. By 1976 the company's research and development personnel had developed the industry's first Pillow Soft mattress, designed specifically for people who had difficulty sleeping on a hard mattress. The Pillow Soft mattress, which combined elements of a firm spring mattress with a soft, pillow-like exterior, was one of the most successful products in the history of the company.

As sales continued to rise and the company's prospects looked more and more promising with each passing year, in 1980 management made the decision to implement a major overseas expansion program. The first stage involved the establishment of facilities in both Mexico and Puerto Rico, two counties in central America that had enough of a growing middle class to afford mattresses made by Serta. The second stage of the company's expansion effort was more complicated, and involved establishing a network of facilities both in Australia and Japan. Extensive market research was performed before company management had made the decision to expand into these two countries, but once made the effort was well worth it, with very promising revenues the first two years of operation, and the potential for larger revenues in the following years. During this time, of course, the company's research and development department was hard at work. In 1983 the department introduced a revolutionary continuous coil innerspring, and pioneered the use of convoluted foam in designing an improved version of the company's Perfect Sleeper line of mattresses.

The 1990s and Beyond

During the 1990s, Serta made a major capital investment to improve the equipment at its Research and Development center. State-of-the-art testing equipment such as the Comfort Sensor, which enabled engineers to measure pressure points on the body, contributed to the company's ability to translate ideas and concepts into industry innovations. This attention to research and development led to the introduction of the Serta Triple

Beam bed frame, widely regarded as the strongest and most durable in the industry, and the Perfect Night luxury mattress collection, which soon became Serta's most successful product to date. Astute enough to coordinate this major investment in research and development with a comprehensive marketing strategy, Serta in 1992 tripled its advertising investment. A year later, the company introduced one of the most successful advertising campaigns in the history of the industry with the tag line, "Serta: We Make The World's Best Mattress." The campaign was designed to play on the emotions of customers, while communicating the company's values of comfort, quality, and trust. What was most unique about this particular advertising campaign, however, was that it specifically targeted women, proven through the company's marketing research to be the primary buyers of mattresses for their households.

By the end of 1998, Serta had developed into a $670 million company, with 31 mattress factories and facilities throughout North America, and 23 plants and offices overseas. With its position as the second largest manufacturer of mattresses in the world quite secure, Serta is confident of and preparing to become number one in the industry.

Further Reading

Garau, Rebecca, "Firms Wonder, 'What's in a Name?'," *HFN,* October 7, 1996, p. 20.

——, "Luxury Bedding's Heyday: Not Just for the Rich and Famous Anymore," *HFN,* April 14, 1997, p. 21.

——, "Reach the Purse Via the Heart," *HFN,* October 7, 1996, p. 20.

——, "Serta's New Assertiveness: Aiming to Put More Sizzle in the Sell," *HFN,* March 17, 1997, p. 51.

Orenstein, Alison, F., "Bedding Debuts and Anniversaries," *HFN,* April 15, 1996, p. 32.

Rush, Amy Joyce, "Target Market," *HFN,* April 14, 1997, p. 59.

"Serta Lawsuit Claims Simmons Infringed on Mattress Patent," *Wall Street Journal,* June 24, 1998, p. B10.

—Thomas Derdak

Shorewood Packaging Corporation

277 Park Avenue
New York, New York 10172
U.S.A.
(212) 371-1500
Fax: (212) 752-5610
Web site: http://www.shorepak.com

Public Company
Incorporated: 1967
Employees: 2,700
Sales: $415.4 million (1998)
Stock Exchanges: New York
Ticker Symbol: SWD
NAIC: 322211 Corrugated & Solid Fiber Box
     Manufacturing; 322222 Coated & Laminated Paper
     Manufacturing; 322299 All Other Converted Paper
     Product Manufacturing; 323110 Commercial
     Lithographic Printing

Shorewood Packaging Corporation and its subsidiaries print and manufacture high-quality paperboard packaging for the cosmetics, home video, music, software, tobacco, toiletries, and general consumer markets in the United States, Canada, and China. Its specialized packaging consists principally of folding cartons and setup boxes for customers requiring sophisticated precision graphics.

Innovative Packager: 1967–89

Paul Bernard Shore and his brother Sam started Shorewood Press in New York City in 1948. This was a printing company that produced album covers for the music industry throughout the 1950s. In the 1960s Paul Shore invented the Shorepak, a record jacket printed directly on bleached paperboard instead of by gluing the album cover to the board. After the appearance of the Beatles' *Abbey Road* in 1968, the one-piece album jacket became the standard for the music industry.

Shorewood Packaging Corporation was founded in 1966 and incorporated in 1967, the year the firm opened a plant in Farmingdale, New York. Soon after, Shorewood formed a joint venture with CBS Records to package records in the United States and Canada. Shore purchased the CBS share of the U.S. company in the 1970s and opened a plant in LaGrange, Georgia, in 1979. Packaging for the music industry—including cassettes and, later, compact discs—accounted for almost all Shorewood's revenues until the 1980s. In 1980, however, Shore responded to slowing sales growth by entering other consumer products packaging. By 1986, when the firm went public, it also was producing packaging for several other industries, including videocassettes, foods, hosiery, tobacco, and cosmetics and toiletries. Shorewood acquired the CBS stake in its Canadian and British subsidiaries in 1985. It ended British operations in early 1992.

Shorewood claimed to be the largest manufacturer of packaging for the music industry when it went public. It owned plants in LaGrange and Roanoke, Virginia, and leased two in Farmingdale, New York, and one each in Los Angeles and Chicago, plus factories in Montreal and Toronto and in London and two other U.K. sites. Headquarters were in Farmingdale. Net sales had grown from $31.8 million in fiscal 1982 (the year ended July 28, 1982)—in which the company had net earnings of $1.2 million—to $77.9 million in fiscal 1987 (the year ended April 30, 1987), when net income reached $5.7 million. The long-term debt was $14.8 million at the end of fiscal 1987. In 1988 the company acquired another plant, in Andalusia, Alabama, with the purchase of Southeastern Box Corp. Shorewood's sales came to a record $139.3 million and its net earnings amounted to a record $16.2 million in fiscal 1990.

Shorewood Packaging enjoyed, at this time, a 40 to 45 percent market share of U.S. LP record, cassette, and compact disc packages. It also was the largest U.S. producer of packages for prerecorded videocassettes. In addition, it was providing high-quality, specialized packaging for an array of other customers, including Estee Foods, Pepperidge Farms, Liz Claiborne, Polaroid, and Turtle Wax. Its cigarette pack clients included Philip Morris and Brown & Williamson. Among the goods it was packaging were Close-Up toothpaste, Hanes hosiery, Capri cigarettes, Kodacolor film, and Old Spice deodorant.

Essential to Shorewood Packaging's success in the 1980s was its development of the JOSH system for printing many combinations of offset lithographic and gravure colors on both sides of paperboard on an integrated in-line web press system. Among "companies whose products have to be slick—with clean colors and interesting graphics—Shorewood has the edge," said an executive for the firm's largest shareholder in 1989, according to the *Wall Street Journal*. The company was a favorite on Wall Street at this time. Its stock, which traded at $4.50 a share (after a stock split) following the initial public offering, reached nearly $26 a share in 1989.

Diversification and Expansion in the 1990s

Shorewood Packaging's fiscal 1990 net income was not surpassed, however, until five years later. Although it remained the largest company for the music industry's album jacket and paper display needs in 1992, stock analysts saw a less promising future because of industry plans to replace the disposable long box for compact disks with a much smaller package. The firm's stock was trading as low as $7 a share. Sales to CBS Records had dropped from 38 to 18 percent of company revenues between fiscal 1987 and 1993, but the long box business still accounted for as much as $20 million of Shorewood's revenues of $184.1 million in the latter year.

In 1994 Shorewood Packaging shut down manufacturing operations at its original Farmingdale plant and the following year moved its headquarters from this Long Island community to midtown Manhattan. An official of the union local, which had had a contract with Shorewood since the company's inception, said Shorewood had asked workers to take a 65 percent cut in wages and benefits.

To maintain its position as the nation's largest folding carton company, Shorewood Packaging began acquiring rival firms, including Somerville Packaging Group, a unit of Cascade Paperboard International, for which it paid about $100 million in 1994. The appointment of Shore's son Marc as president of the firm in 1991 was credited with the transition to a more aggressive growth strategy. The Somerville acquisition enabled Shorewood's revenues to rise from $216.5 million in fiscal 1994 to $357 million in fiscal 1995, while its net income increased from $6.3 million to $22.5 million, although the long-term debt reached a record $160 million in early 1995. Securities analysts also praised the company for just-in-time delivery and improved engineering and proprietary technology. One recommended the stock because Shorewood "can print several different types of processes on the same line. You eliminate set-up times and it's cheaper, more accurate and a lot faster."

Somerville was an important supplier of cigarette packaging in the United States and also in Canada, where smoking was increasing after a large cut in cigarette taxes. Somerville also had increased its sales abroad, in part because of strong demand for hard flip-top packaging. With its acquisition the tobacco industry became Shorewood's main market, accounting for about 37 percent of its annual sales. The music industry now

was accounting for less than 25 percent but included as important customers were three of the six major record companies: BMG, Sony, and PolyGram. Another 1994 acquisition, Hemingway Packaging, put the parent company in a strong position in the production of cosmetic boxes. In addition, Shorewood began providing cigarette hard-pack boxes and cartons directly to China in 1995.

The production of sleeves for CD-ROM computer software also was a growing business for Shorewood. In 1995 the company opened a plant in Springfield, Oregon to produce these packages, with the objective of enhancing its service capabilities in both the software and home entertainment industries. The location of the plant reflected the fact that the Pacific Northwest was home to many of the leading software manufacturers. By 1998, through effective cross-selling, this facility also had generated increased production and sales of packaging for CD-ROM computer software and games at several of the company's East Coast facilities.

Paul Shore died in December 1995 and was succeeded as chairman and chief executive officer of Shorewood Packaging by his son Marc. Revenues and profits continued to be strong, with net income reaching $24.9 million and $26.3 million in fiscal 1997 and 1998, respectively. Operations in Canada accounted for 40 percent of the company's $415 million in revenue in fiscal 1998. Philip Morris was the leading customer that year, accounting for 25 percent of net sales. The long-term debt was $126.4 million at the end of the fiscal year.

In 1998 Shorewood Packaging completed a $45 million, 125,000-square-foot folding carton manufacturing plant in Guangzhou, China, to serve the Chinese market for cigarettes. The company then sold a 45 percent stake in the operation to Westvaco Corp., which paid about $25 million. Also in 1998, but late in the year, Shorewood purchased Queens Group, Inc. for about $129 million in cash and stock. This rival producer of high-quality printing and packaging for the home entertainment markets had annual sales of $148 million. Its acquisition raised Shorewood's manufacturing facilities to 16, employing about 3,700 people.

Shorewood Packaging in Fiscal 1998

Shorewood Packaging was, in fiscal 1998, supplying printed packaging products for many of the leading tobacco brands, including those ultimately sold in non-U.S. markets. The company believed itself to be the primary carton supplier to the Canadian tobacco industry, and tobacco customers accounted for 37 percent of net sales in the fiscal year. For its customers in the music and home entertainment industries, Shorewood was manufacturing compact disc packaging (including folders, booklets, and liners), prerecorded cassette packaging (including folders and sleeves), and other printed material and paperboard packaging. It had longstanding relationships with many of the major music production and distribution companies in the United States and in certain cases also had agreements, typically for five-year terms, to supply their packaging products. Shorewood also was manufacturing rigid setup boxes, principally for customers in the cosmetics and entertainment industries.

Although Shorewood Packaging generally was producing packaging from specifications, artwork, or film supplied by its customers, from time to time it was designing and developing new packaging concepts and structures requested by its customers. It was maintaining a research and development center located on the grounds of its Williamsburg, Virginia plant. The company also owned office and manufacturing space at Danville, Virginia, and Smiths Falls, Scarborough, and Brockville, Ontario, in addition to the aforementioned LaGrange, Roanoke, Andalusia, Springfield, and Guangzhou facilities. Leased facilities consisted of the Manhattan headquarters and office, manufacturing, and warehousing space in Redwood City, Los Angeles, and Santa Monica, California; Fairfield, Waterbury, and Watertown, Connecticut; LaGrange and Farmingdale; Chicago; Charlotte, North Carolina; and Brockville, Montreal, and Toronto, Canada.

Marc Shore owned nearly 19 percent of Shorewood Packaging's common stock in mid-1998, either outright or through estate or family-instrument partnerships. Ariel Capital Management, a shareholder since 1988, held 14 percent of the stock.

Principal Subsidiaries

Shorewood Acquisition Corp. of Delaware; Shorewood Asia Ventures Ltd. (Bermuda); Shorewood Corporation of Canada Limited (Canada); Shorewood Holographic Patterns, Inc.; Shorewood Packaging China Ventures Ltd. (Mauritius); Shorewood Packaging Company (Guangzhou) Ltd. (China); Shorewood Packaging Company of Illinois, Inc.; Shorewood Packaging Corp. of Canada, Ltd. (Canada); Shorewood Packaging Corporation of Alabama; Shorewood Packaging Corporation of Connecticut; Shorewood Packaging Corporation of Georgia; Shorewood Packaging Corporation of New York; Shorewood Packaging Corporation of Oregon; Shorewood Packaging Corporation of Virginia; Shorewood Packaging of California, Inc.; Shorewood Packaging of Delaware, Inc.; Shorewood Packaging of North Carolina, Inc.; Shorewood Technologies, Inc.; Shorewood Transport, Inc.; Shor-Wrap, Inc.; Shor-Wrap Packages of Canada, Ltd. (Canada); SPC Asia, Ltd. (Bermuda); SPC (Bermuda) Ltd. (Bermuda); SPC Company of New York, Inc.; SPC Company of Virginia, Inc.; SPC Corporation Limited (Canada); Toronto Carton Corporation Limited (Canada).

Further Reading

Benson, Barbara, ''Broader Product Line Packages Firm's Story,'' *Crain's New York Business,* September 5, 1994, p. 35.

Bernstein, James, ''Shorewood Packaging Shuts Down,'' *Newsday,* May 12, 1994, pp. A61–A62.

Breznick, Alan, ''CD Repackaging Puts Firm in a Box,'' *Crain's New York Business,* March 23, 1992, p. 39.

——, ''Packaging Firm Changing Tune,'' *Crain's New York Business,* September 6, 1993, p. 43.

Byrne, Harlan S., ''Not Boxed In,'' *Barron's,* November 7, 1994, p. 21.

Craig, David, ''Shorewood Packages Shout 'Buy Me,' '' *USA Today,* June 14, 1989, p. 3B.

Jeffrey, Don, ''Paul Shore, Packaging Innovator, Dies at 74,'' *Billboard,* December 23, 1995, pp. 10, 104.

Lichtman, Irv, ''Recording Boom Benefits Big 4 Fabricators,'' *Billboard,* July 9, 1988, pp. 3, 77.

''Shorewood Packing Goes Public,'' *Pulp & Paper,* December 1986, p. 35.

Steptoe, Sonja, ''Shorewood Packaging Caught the Eye of Wall Street; Now It Looks to Future,'' *Wall Street Journal,* December 11, 1989, p. C6.

—Robert Halasz

The Sierra Club

85 Second Street, Second Floor
San Francisco, California 94105-3441
U.S.A.
(415) 977-5500
Fax: (415) 977-5799
Web site: http://www.sierraclub.org

Nonprofit Company
Incorporated: 1892
Employees: 325
Sales: $52.88 million (1996)
NAIC: 813312 Environment, Conservation & Wildlife
Organizations; 511130 Book Publishers & Printing

The Sierra Club occupies a unique place in American culture. One of the most influential U.S. environmental activist groups, it has been supported by such legendary members as photographer Ansel Adams and founder John Muir. Though some picture it a bully, the group employs less extreme measures than Greenpeace and lacks the financial prowess of The Nature Conservancy.

Origins

California's Sierra Nevada mountains became the site of a mountaineering community in the last half of the 19th century. Legendary naturalist John Muir was active in promoting the creation of the Yosemite, Sequoia, and General Grant National Parks to protect the High Sierra from grazing sheep and other means of destruction.

Professor J.H. Senger, of the University of California, conceived a repository of maps and books of the area. By 1890 Senger and his students and colleagues had been discussing the idea of a "Sierra Club," with a headquarters in the remote, unspoiled Yosemite Valley. Muir, attorney Warren Olney, and artist William Keith began discussions at Keith's studio. Several professors from the University of California and Stanford, and other interested parties, soon joined the group, which counted 182 members at its inception. Olney drafted the club's articles of incorporation, which were signed in his law office on June 4, 1892. Muir was chosen as the first president.

The Sierra Club immediately began printing maps and newsletters, maintaining trails, and defeating legislation aimed at reducing Yosemite National Park's boundaries. The group also succeeded in lobbying to turn the Yosemite State Park over to the federal government, which incorporated it into the national park. At the time, however, exploring the area's rivers and mountains was the club's primary focus.

Hetch Hetchy and the 1910s:
The Sierra Club's First Major Controversy

A planned dam at Hetch Hetchy Valley to secure hydroelectric energy for the San Francisco community flared into a national controversy in 1910 that raged for a decade and left dividing scars. Hundreds of newspapers expressed (generally conservationist) opinions on the project and Congress held two sets of hearings on it.

Even one of the Club's founders, Warren Olney, who had been voted mayor of Oakland after receiving both Republican and Democratic nominations, felt the dam was necessary. He resigned from the club in the wake of the painful confrontation. The dam was built eventually.

John Muir died on Christmas Eve, 1914, crestfallen over the outcome of the Hetch Hetchy affair. Its memory produced a generation of more politically savvy leaders, however, and highlighted the need for better organized campaigns to save such wilderness areas. The Sierra Club's own reputation seemed enhanced by its role in the struggle, ensuring its influence in future public land management decisions. Part of Muir's legacy was the National Park Service, founded in 1916. Its first director, Stephen Mather, was a Sierra Club member. Thus began an era of cooperation with governmental agencies.

Joseph LeConte, son of one of the original founders, followed Muir as president in 1915. In the 1920s and 1930s the club continued the annual High Trips into the Sierra begun in 1901 and documented in *Bulletins*. They brought dozens of campers as new chapters sprouted up around California. Some were documented by legendary photographer Ansel Adams,

Company Perspectives:

To explore, enjoy, and protect the wild places of the earth; to practice and promote the responsible use of the earth's ecosystems and resources; to educate and enlist humanity to protect and restore the quality of the natural and human environment; and to use all lawful means to carry out these objectives.

who joined in 1919. He served as Sierra Club director from 1934 to 1971.

The Sierra Club helped turn the management of the Kings Canyon area away from the Forest Service, which allowed logging, and into the hands of the Park Service. The Kings Canyon National Park would escape much of the development of other national parks. When the Park Service plans recarved an existing road there, however, it highlighted a conflict between the club's goals of preserving nature and making it accessible.

In the 1940s chapters across the country came into being, not only in California but in the Northwest and New England. Membership stood at about 4,000. During World War II the club helped develop Army training materials for traversing mountainous terrain.

Postwar Building

The Sierra Club board updated its motto in 1951—''To explore, enjoy, and protect the Sierra Nevada and other scenic resources of the United States''—omitting the ''rendering accessible'' prerogative of the original version. The Sierra Club had 7,000 members at the time. One of the club's main concerns was the intense demand on timber brought about by postwar housing construction.

Dave Brower, a publicist for the Yosemite Park hospitality operator, became the club's first executive director in 1953—the beginning of professional Sierra Club staff. Already a volunteer, and a board member since 1941, he was hired to campaign against the Upper Basin project that threatened to place seven dams in the Colorado River basin.

Under Brower, the club boated observers along the rivers. Brower also testified before the U.S. House that Bureau of Land Reclamation engineers had simply miscalculated their water evaporation figures. As with Kings Canyon, they filmed trips through the area and produced a photo/text album, which included a chapter by legendary publisher Alfred A. Knopf. News magazines across the country began documenting the controversy unfolding at Dinosaur National Monument, which was saved, though at the expense of Glen Canyon. President Eisenhower was able to trigger dynamite in the canyon wall from the White House in 1963.

In 1960 The Sierra Club published the ambitious, large-format photo-and-text book *This Is the American Earth,* which sold well in spite of its steep $15 price. Other photo books followed in this unique program. Another innovation that would become ubiquitous in bookstores was the club's nature calendar, developed with Ballantine Books.

The Wilderness Act became law in 1964, though it still allowed mining. The Sierra Club championed the cause of a Redwood National Park on the northern California coast to protect some of the country's last virgin forests. The club published controversial open letters in national newspapers and by 1968 the beginnings of the park were in place.

A 1967 campaign to prevent dams in the Grand Canyon echoed The Sierra Club's earlier protests. The group produced three books as articles appeared in major consumer magazines. After running a confrontational ad in the *New York Times,* The Sierra Club found the IRS investigating and finally withdrawing its tax-exempt status.

The IRS action inflamed the press and the public. Club membership doubled in the next three years to 78,000. The group spent the rest of the decade fighting what it deemed inappropriately placed ski lodges and nuclear reactors. Its early vacillations on the latter issue allowed for the development of the Diablo Canyon nuclear power plant.

Brower began to receive criticism for turning too much of the club's attention to publications, which were now losing money. To promote them, he ran an ad in the *New York Times* that called for making the whole Earth a national park. The board did not appreciate the gesture, and within a few months he had been replaced by attorney Mike McCloskey as executive director. Brower later formed the Friends of the Earth.

Sierra Club in the Space Age

The Earth pictures taken from space in 1969 seem to have precipitated a shift in public perception, causing the planet to be seen as vulnerable, fragile, and unique in the universe. The National Environment Policy Act, which became law in January 1970, required impact studies for future federal projects. The Clean Air Act also was passed, the Environmental Protection Agency was created, and April 22, 1970 was designated the first Earth Day. For its part, The Sierra Club published a mass market activist's guide that sold 400,000 copies and began distributing a tip sheet from Washington.

The Sierra Club fought Walt Disney's plan for a massive ski resort in the Mineral King area of the Sierra Nevada range. In the process, it crossed paths, not for the last time, with Ronald Reagan, then governor of California. After a legal battle that extended to the U.S. Supreme Court, the proposed development was defeated.

Threatened coastlines and forest areas gave The Sierra Club more cause to rally in the 1970s. Logging, mining, and construction interests coveted pristine land, and others wanted to dissect national parks with motorized vehicles and power lines.

The energy industry—with its oil slicks, radioactive waste, and so on, became a particular concern of the 1970s. The club also challenged a Boeing proposal to build a supersonic aircraft similar to the Concorde, complaining of sonic booms and damage to the ozone layer. World population control also became a popular topic, discussed at a U.N. environmental conference in Stockholm in 1972.

The decade ended with a bang: the Alaska National Interest Lands Conservation Act doubled the national park system.

The Reagan Years

The Sierra Club motto was revised yet again in 1981 to reflect global concerns such as the newly revealed legacy of industrial pollution behind the Iron Curtain. The club also fought against development in the Amazon rain forest by lobbying the World Bank. Membership had reached 182,000 by this time.

Hoping to gain more sway with elected officials, the group began funding electoral campaigns in earnest (thanks to a 1974 campaign finance reform law), during a time that also saw the emergence of more radical groups such as Greenpeace. In 1980 the club donated $100,000 to various Democratic candidates for the U.S. and California legislatures who opposed Reagan's environmental policies. Ansel Adams died in 1984 while working on ''Manifesto of the Earth,'' a response to these policies.

Reagan's interior secretary, James Watt, was the bane of many a conservationist. He attempted to reopen the nation's most beloved natural sanctuaries to mining. Ironically, Watts and other Reagan appointees helped spark a renewed interest in environmental activism that doubled Sierra Club membership. Outrageous public comments finally cost him his job.

The club also lobbied in support of the Environmental Protection Agency's Superfund, allocated by Congress to clean up toxic waste sites. In 1985 the club bought a new office building in downtown San Francisco, where it kept its staff of 250. Two years later Michael Fischer was elected the club's fourth executive director.

The Earth-Friendly 1990s

One of The Sierra Club's main challenges, according to Fischer, was to remain responsive while avoiding the pitfalls of bureaucracy. It also sought to attract more minorities. Its San Francisco chapter established a gay and lesbian group. In 1992 the club's 625,000 members celebrated its 100th anniversary. The Sierra Club estimated its election budget that year at $1 million. Though membership growth slowed in the early 1990s, the group became more aggressively political. It lobbied hard to elect Democrat Ron Wyden to fill one of Oregon's senate seats in 1996 after the retirement of Senator Bob Packwood.

The group had begun endorsing credit cards, long distance service, stuffed animals, and other merchandising. It also stepped up its direct mailing efforts. The Sierra Club won a couple of favorable tax rulings regarding the sale of mailing lists and its Affinity Card royalties.

In the mid-1990s the club also focused its efforts on giant hog and poultry farms and their attendant pollution. Land conservation remained another important concern. In 1997 The Sierra Club proposed that after 100 years of commercial timber harvesting in national forests, the government should no longer allow the practice. Loggers argued that restrictions already had cost thousands of jobs and forced numerous mills out of business.

The Sierra Club sued the Environmental Protection Agency after its loosened medical waste controls. It also found itself on the opposite side of the courtroom. Bluebird Systems sued the group for $10 million after finding its web sites connected to the Bluebird local area network, as *Inc.* magazine reported.

A 1997 survey picked The Sierra Club as the most effective environmental lobby on Capitol Hill. The group spent $7 million on the 1998 elections, including advertising and its first get-out-the-vote campaign. Long a fixture on the national landscape of politics and the environment, The Sierra Club could be expected to continue into the next millennium the pursuit of its original cause: protecting and preserving the earth's natural resources.

Principal Subsidiaries

Sierra Club Foundation; Sierra Club Political Committee; Sierra Club Property Management, Inc.; Sierra Club Legal Defense Fund.

Further Reading

''Anti-Loggers Hit Trails in United States, Canada,'' *Wood Technology,* July/August 1997, pp. 18–19.

Carr, Clifton, and Tom Turner, *Wild by Law: The Sierra Club Legal Defense Fund and the Places It Has Saved,* San Francisco: Sierra Club Legal Defense Fund/Sierra Club Books, c. 1990.

Cohen, Michael P., *The History of the Sierra Club, 1892–1970,* San Francisco: Sierra Club Books, c. 1988.

Ember, Lois R., ''Environmentalists Regroup to Protect Their Agenda After Painful Defeats,'' *Chemical and Engineering News,* February 27, 1995, pp. 26–30.

Esterson, Emily, ''Bluebird's Unhappiness,'' *Inc.,* March 17, 1998, p. 20.

Forbes, Steve, ''Not a Bathtub,'' *Forbes,* March 23, 1998, p. 28.

Gilliam Ann, Ed. *Voices for the Earth: A Treasury of the Sierra Club Bulletin,* San Francisco: Sierra Club Books, 1979.

Hamilton, Joan, ''A Civil Society: Sierra Club Voted Most Influential,'' *Sierra,* January 1999, p. 11.

Hileman, Bette, ''Environmental Leaders Give EPA Mixed Reviews on Its Performance,'' *Chemical and Engineering News,* October 30, 1995, pp. 30–37.

Hjelmar, Ulf, *The Political Practice of Environmental Organizations,* Aldershot, England; Brookfield, Vt.: Avebury, 1996.

Hopkins, Bruce, ''Tax Court Opens Up New Fund-Raising Options,'' *Fund Raising Management,* September 1993, pp. 55, 58.

Jones, Holway, *John Muir and the Sierra Club: The Battle for Yosemite,* San Francisco: Sierra Club, 1965.

Kriz, Margaret, ''The Big Green Election Machine,'' *National Journal,* October 24, 1998.

McClure, Ronnie C., and Kenneth H. Silverberg, ''Tax Breather, Thanks to the Sierra Club,'' *Association Management,* December 1993, p. 26.

Nelson, Robert H., ''Tom Hayden, Meet Adam Smith and Thomas Aquinas,'' *Forbes,* October 29, 1990, pp. 94–97.

Schlossberg, Howard, ''Sierra Club Finds Direct Marketing Harder to Do, But Vows to Improve,'' *Marketing News,* March 29, 1993, p. 18.

Turner, Tom, *Sierra Club: 100 Years of Protecting Nature,* New York: Harry N. Abrams/Sierra Club, 1991.

Vanchieri, Cori, ''Burning Issues,'' *Hospitals and Health Networks,* March 5, 1998, p. 38.

Wexler, Robert A., ''Affinity Card Income Was Royalty, Not UBI,'' *Journal of Taxation,* November 1994, pp. 316–18.

—Frederick C. Ingram

Snell & Wilmer

L.L.P.
LAW OFFICES

Snell & Wilmer L.L.P.

One Arizona Center
Phoenix, Arizona 85004-0001
U.S.A.
(602) 382-6000
(800) 322-0430
Fax: (602) 382-6070
Web site: http://www.swlaw.com

Private Partnership
Founded: 1934 as Snell, Strouss & Salmon
Employees: 635
Sales: $92 million (1998 est.)
NAIC: 54111 Offices of Lawyers

With offices in Phoenix, Tucson, Salt Lake City, and Irvine, California, Snell & Wilmer L.L.P. is one of the western United States' largest law firms and the 110th largest firm in the country. Its 250-plus attorneys serve more than 8,000 clients, including multinational firms such as Ford, Toyota, and General Motors; Arizona-based firms such as Bank One Arizona and the Arizona Public Service Company; and individuals with a wide range of legal needs. Snell & Wilmer continues to play a major role in the development of modern Phoenix, while at the same time conducting a national practice. It also participates in Lex Mundi, an international association of law firms, to better represent its clients' interests overseas.

Origins

Frank L. Snell, Jr., and Mark Wilmer founded the law firm of Snell & Wilmer. Snell was born in Kansas City, Missouri, in 1899 and graduated in 1924 from the University of Kansas School of Law. After a few years of solo law practice in Miami, Arizona, Snell moved to Phoenix, where he established Snell, Strouss & Salmon in 1934 during the Great Depression.

Mark Wilmer was born in 1903 in East Troy, Wisconsin. After graduating from Georgetown University with his law degree, he practiced in Texas for two years before moving to Phoenix in 1931. In 1938 Wilmer left the Maricopa County Attorney's office, where he had prosecuted a local gambling operation, and joined Snell, Strouss & Salmon. To recruit a new lawyer for the busy firm, Frank Snell followed the advice of three Maricopa County Superior Court judges who said Wilmer was the state's best trial lawyer. Thus began a long partnership and friendship that lasted until both men died in 1994.

During World War II, Frank Snell demonstrated the leadership that made him one of the key players in the development of modern Phoenix. He initiated the "card room putsch" in which the city manager, police chief, and city magistrate—who together wielded undue control over city politics—resigned. Thus Phoenix no longer was off-limits to the military, the USO was reopened, and local leaders began the process to create a new charter government.

After the war, Joseph T. Melczer, Jr., James Walsh, and Edwin Beauchamp joined the firm. Around 1950 the firm decided to shorten its name from Snell, Wilmer, Walsh, Melczer & Beauchamp to Snell & Wilmer. Walsh left the firm to serve as a U.S. District Court judge, and Melczer became one of the state's premier lawyers for tax issues and estate planning.

The 1950s and 1960s

In the postwar period Frank Snell continued to make major contributions to Phoenix and Arizona as a lawyer and through his civic involvement. For example, in 1952 he helped create the Arizona Public Service Company (APS), the state's largest utility, from a merger of Central Arizona Light & Power Company and the Arizona Edison Company. Snell had served as an executive of the two predecessor firms from the mid-1940s. His law firm continued to provide outside counsel to APS into the 1990s.

In the 1950s Snell and a few others used an abandoned flight training building in Glendale to start the American Graduate School of International Management, often known as the Thunderbird School.

Meanwhile, Mark Wilmer represented Arizona in the complex water case *Arizona v. California.* For years Arizona had

425

Company Perspectives:

Our mission is to take a genuine interest in our clients, understand their objectives, and meet or exceed their expectations. We dedicate ourselves to these values. For our clients, we will work hard, provide superior legal services on a timely, effective, and efficient basis, and maintain the highest standard of professional integrity. For our firm, we will foster an enjoyable working environment based on open communication and mutual respect, and will encourage initiative, innovation, teamwork, and loyalty. For our community, we will continue our long tradition of service and leadership.

---

tried in vain to gain rights to Colorado River water. In 1953 Arizona filed a lawsuit against the California state government and seven California public agencies. Although California had more attorneys, Arizona had Mark Wilmer. From 1956 to 1958 Wilmer led the plaintiff's team in the trial held in San Francisco.

Based on Wilmer's discovery of an obscure 1928 congressional act, Arizona prevailed. In 1963 the U.S. Supreme Court ruled on appeal that Arizona was indeed entitled to Colorado River water, a landmark decision that opened the way for the Central Arizona Project and the state's tremendous population boom since that time. "The importance of this case to the people of Arizona cannot be overstated," said attorney Ed Hendricks in the summer 1995 *Arizona State Law Journal.* "If Arizona had lost, our State would not have had enough water to sustain its remarkable growth."

From 13 lawyers in 1958, the firm grew to 32 lawyers in 1968, but no women had yet joined the ranks of Snell & Wilmer.

The 1970s and 1980s

In 1972 Frank Snell decided to reduce his administrative role when the firm created its first executive committee, consisting of Mark Wilmer, Joseph Melczer, Don Corbitt, Richard B. Snell, and John T. Bouma. The firm made decisions to build a major national law firm, including expanded recruiting, community service, and legal education.

Meanwhile, two key developments in the 1970s tended to make the legal profession more business oriented. First, the U.S. Supreme Court decided that restrictions on professionals advertising violated the First Amendment's guarantee of free speech and also violated antitrust laws. Those decisions opened the floodgate of advertising by lawyers, dentists, doctors, and other professionals.

Then in 1979 Steven Brill began publishing the *American Lawyer* with articles about compensation and other internal affairs of the nation's major law firms. Many firms replaced compensation based on partner seniority to that based on ability to generate clients and build firm income. That led to more lateral hiring or "raiding" of experienced attorneys from other firms.

Not surprisingly, many law firms, including Snell & Wilmer, began to grow by leaps and bounds in the late 1970s and especially the 1980s. Much of that growth occurred under the leadership of John Bouma. Born in Fort Dodge, Iowa, Bouma graduated with a degree in political science from the University of Iowa in 1958 and then earned his law degree there. After serving two years in the military's Judge Advocate General Corps at Arizona's Fort Huachuca, in 1962 he joined Snell & Wilmer, then a 22-lawyer firm.

When Bouma joined the firm, Phoenix claimed about 440,000 residents, but by 1980 it had almost doubled its population to become the ninth largest city in the United States. Snell & Wilmer grew accordingly.

The law firm opened its Tucson branch office on October 1, 1988 and the following year merged with Tucson's oldest and largest firm, Bilby & Shoenhair. The combined firm with 213 lawyers operated under the name Snell & Wilmer. "There has been a strong tie between the two firms for many years," said John Bouma in the May 9, 1989 *Arizona Daily Star.* "Both organizations want to be able to serve our clients' expanding needs in the best and most efficient manner. The combined firms will have many of the most respected lawyers in the state in one organization and we're going to make a great team."

In 1989 Snell & Wilmer also started an office with five lawyers in Irvine, Orange County, California, the first time an Arizona law firm started a California branch. This move contradicted conventional wisdom, since California was heading into a bad recession. Snell & Wilmer stuck it out, however, and quickly expanded to have one of the ten largest law firms in Orange County.

In the 1970s and 1980s Snell & Wilmer hired its first women attorneys. Two women were part of the 51-lawyer firm in 1978, and by 1989 40 women made up about 20 percent of the rapidly growing firm's attorney ranks.

Snell & Wilmer's rapid expansion in the 1980s was influenced by the booming U.S. economy. From 1982 through 1990 Americans enjoyed 96 months of continuous economic growth, the largest peacetime expansion in the nation's history. According to the U.S. Census Bureau, the average real family income grew 15 percent from 1982 to 1989.

Developments in the 1990s

Snell & Wilmer in 1991 gained Mrs. Fields Original Cookies, Inc. as a new client. To serve the Utah-based cookie maker, the law firm opened a new branch office in Salt Lake City in 1991. Under the local leadership of Greg Nielsen, Snell & Wilmer recruited seven lawyers from the firm of Hansen and Anderson and hired others from three of Salt Lake City's oldest firms. By 1994 the Salt Lake City branch included 17 lawyers at its downtown office in the Broadway Centre. It was one of eight out-of-state law firms operating in Salt Lake City.

In 1993 Snell & Wilmer faced a major problem with its long-term client Arizona Public Service Company (APS). In 1993 APS, an account worth $3 million annually to the firm, considered dropping the law firm as its main outside counsel. A worker filed a lawsuit against APS because he felt he had not been selected for a job because earlier he had told APS about safety violations at its Palo Verde Nuclear Generating Station. In this "whistleblower" case, APS Executive Vice-President and CEO Jaron Norberg said in the August 13, 1993 issue of the *(Phoenix) Business Journal,* "The failure to provide certain items in the discovery process and the overall handling of the case was improper and ineffective." This case was significant in part because about two-thirds of Snell & Wilmer's work for APS concerned the nuclear plant. The two Snell & Wilmer attorneys who handled the whistleblower litigation were removed from that account, but APS decided to continue its longstanding relationship with the law firm.

In 1997 the *National Law Journal* named John Bouma as one of the nation's 100 most influential lawyers. It mentioned that Bouma was the past president of the State Bar of Arizona, the Arizona Bar Foundation, and the National Conference of Bar Presidents. He specialized in litigation and alternative conflict resolution involving antitrust, malpractice, and commercial law. He continued the tradition of Phoenix civic involvement set by Frank Snell by playing a major role in building new sports stadiums and a new science museum and expanding the Phoenix Art Museum. He served as a leader of the Phoenix Chamber of Commerce, Arizona Opera Company, and the Foundation for the Conservation of Arizona.

To serve clients' international needs, Snell & Wilmer became one of the founding members of Lex Mundi, a global association of independent law firms started in 1989 by Stephen McGarry. By 1998 Lex Mundi was the largest such association, with 10,500 lawyers in 145 law firms in more than 80 nations. Other law firm associations included Terralex and Commercial Law Affiliates.

"It (Lex Mundi) gives us the confidence to make referrals when our clients have needs outside the southwestern U.S.," said Snell & Wilmer attorney Rob Kinas in the June 11, 1998 *Arizona Business Gazette.* Lex Mundi's specialty committees also helped educate members on ongoing concerns such as international differences in ethics and law. Kinas also reported that Lex Mundi's web site (www.lexmundi.org) received more hits than any other online legal site. Some large law firms, however, including Chicago's Baker & McKenzie, chose to open multiple offices around the world instead of joining a group like Lex Mundi. A third globalization strategy for some law firms was to affiliate with one of the large international accounting firms.

In 1998 U.S. District Court Judge Thomas Brett upheld much of U.S. Bankruptcy Judge John H. Allen's decisions earlier in the decade by ruling that Snell & Wilmer was not entitled to some $500,000 from Bonneville Pacific, a Salt Lake City alternative-energy firm, for work done by attorney David Leta. But Brett also said the law firm might receive more than $70,000 for Leta's work for bankruptcy trustee Roger Segal.

In 1998 Snell & Wilmer received two honors or awards. The Arizona Best Practices Awards program, sponsored by the Arthur Andersen accounting firm, honored the law firm with a "Distinguished Achievement" award for "exceeding customer expectations." Snell & Wilmer was the nation's first law firm to receive this award from Arthur Andersen.

The second honor came when Kimm Walton, the author of *America's Greatest Places to Work with a Law Degree,* chose to include Snell & Wilmer as a firm attractive to new or junior associates. The author pointed out that Snell & Wilmer's clients included the Tucson Airport Authority, Honeywell, Del Webb, Intel, Mercury Marine, and Household International, which helped make it the nation's 110th largest law firm. Snell & Wilmer associates told Walton they enjoyed a family-friendly atmosphere in which they were encouraged to work at home if necessary. With computers and modern telecommunications, that policy was consistent with a major trend in many businesses.

Other Snell & Wilmer associates reported they liked the firm's decentralized management style that supported individual creativity, an open-door policy that improved communication between partners and associates, and "a lot of laughter in the halls." For example, every year the firm's annual retreat included videos and skits poking fun at the firm or its attorneys. That sense of humor helped Snell & Wilmer attorneys prepare for serious obstacles in the future.

In March 1999 Snell & Wilmer received a Governor's Arts Award for its long history of supporting Arizona's arts community. For example, it provided legal counsel in gaining lottery funding for the arts. The firm also had put together one of the state's largest photography collections and helped finance the restoration of Tucson's San Xavier Mission.

In the 1990s the legal profession faced major challenges, from little respect from the public, as seen in popular lawyer jokes, to a self-help consumer movement featuring standard legal forms on computer software and more legal information available on the Internet. Independent paralegals also offered certain services and tested the boundaries of the legal profession.

To improve the firm's efficiency, Chairman Bouma in 1994 announced that using standardized forms available on the computer would be a priority. One of the first law firms to use such an electronic forms bank, Snell & Wilmer by 1997 had about 3,000 forms available for all its major practice areas. Examples included litigation pleading forms, merger and acquisition confidentiality agreements, and loan forms for banking and real estate transactions. Although much time and effort was necessary to implement this program, in the long run it saved time for the firm's lawyers. This type of commitment to using technological solutions when appropriate helped the firm compete in a rapidly changing world.

Further Reading

Arizona Photographers: The Snell & Wilmer Collection, University of Arizona: Center for Creative Photography, 1990.

Campo-Flores, Arian, "We Are the World," *American Lawyer,* November 1998, pp. 124–27.

Costanzo, Joe, "Law Firm Wants Criticisms Stricken," *Deseret News,* June 20, 1996.

Fimea, Mike, "Staying in Good Company Law Firms Benefit from Affiliations," *Arizona Business Gazette,* June 11, 1998.

Funk, Marianne, "Bonneville Pacific Trustee Cuts Cash Flow to Lawyers, Others," *Deseret News,* December 2, 1992.

——, "Local Opportunities Blossom As National Law Firms Branch Out," *Deseret News,* April 3, 1994.

Giblin, Paul, "APS May Fire Snell & Wilmer After 41 Years," *(Phoenix) Business Journal,* August 13, 1993.

Marcus, Daniel R., "Electronic Forms Banks: Low-Tech, High-Yield," *American Lawyer,* November 1997.

Rozen, Leah, "A Hot Shot in Sun City," *American Lawyer,* July 1982, pp. 11–12.

Rubenstein, Bruce T., "Does Your Outside Counsel Ask for Your Feedback?," *Corporate Legal Times,* November 1997.

Schwartz, John, "Many Law Firms Chip Off Old 'Parents,' " *(Phoenix) Business Journal,* February 3, 1995, pp. 29–30.

Svejcara, Bob, "Bilby & Shoenhair Join State's Largest Law Firm, Snell & Wilmer," *Arizona Daily Star,* May 9, 1989, p. C1.

"Tribute to Frank Snell," *Arizona State Law Journal,* vol. 26 (winter 1994), pp. 917–23.

"Tribute to Mark Wilmer," *Arizona State Law Journal,* vol. 27 (summer 1995), pp. 411–22.

Walton, Kimm A., *America's Greatest Places to Work with a Law Degree,* New York: Harcourt Brace, 1999.

—David M. Walden

Solo Serve Corporation

1610 Cornerway Blvd.
San Antonio, Texas 78219
U.S.A.
(210) 662-6262
Fax: (210) 662-0938

Private Company
Incorporated: 1919 as Solo Serve Company
Employees: 1,000
Sales: $82 million (1998 est.)
NAIC: 45211 Department Stores

Solo Serve Corporation is a Texas-based chain of off-priced or discount retail stores offering a wide array of name-brand and other merchandise at prices substantially less than those found at department stores such as J.C.Penney's and Sears or specialty clothing stores. The company's stores are located throughout Texas and Louisiana, and sell such items as clothing for men, women, and children, fragrances and perfumes, hosiery, shoes and, in certain stores, a range of high-quality home furnishings. Yet over the past two decades, Solo Serve has experienced a host of financial and management difficulties, including filing for bankruptcy in 1994, and a notification by NASDAQ that the company stock could no longer trade on the exchange. Nonetheless, company owner-managers have not given up hope and, far from failure, Solo Save has fought its way out of bankruptcy and is looking forward to a more successful and profitable future.

Early History

Solo Serve Company was founded in 1919 by a group of investors interested in establishing a retail store that would meet the needs of people living in and around San Antonio, Texas. World War I was just ending, and the U.S. government had been encouraging its citizens to be cautious consumers, since many of the essential war materials such as rubber and tin were used by the Armed Forces to conduct operations in Europe. The state of Texas, with many people still living in a manner of the "Wild West," did not have access to the clothing and various other kinds of merchandise found in traditional department and spe-

cialty retail stores located on the East Coast or Midwestern states. A small group of businessmen decided it would be profitable, as well as meet the needs of many Texans, to open a retail store that sold a full range of merchandise. One of the most important decisions made by the original investment group was that the cost of items sold in the store would be at significantly discounted prices. This decision was made to attract the widest possible range of customers.

The store was a success from the day its doors opened for business. During the 1920s, as the store grew and its customer base expanded, women's clothing, men's clothing, and children's clothing were the most profitable merchandise sold. The state of Texas at this time in U.S. history was transformed from largely remote rural areas to a burgeoning, bustling conglomeration of modern cities with streetlights, automobiles, and symphony halls. Yet, in spite of the potential for even greater growth, the original investors made a commitment to serving the populace of San Antonio, thus the decision was made to concentrate on providing retail services in a highly localized area.

The store suffered significantly during the Great Depression of the 1930s. After the stock market crash of 1929, many people in Texas lost their jobs, small and big businesses went bankrupt, numerous banks were unable to pay their customers, and the farming and ranching communities, two of the most important components in the state's economy, were devastated by foreclosures. Not until Franklin Delano Roosevelt's election as president in 1932 was there a ray of hope that the economy might revive. When Roosevelt proclaimed a bank holiday and implemented sweeping reforms throughout the banking industry, and also initiated a government-led strategy to address the debilitating effects of the Depression, people from the state of Texas engaged in a collective sigh of relief. Yet the store was hit hard during these years, and forced not only to release employees from their jobs, but to cut back on the amount of merchandise offered to the public for sale.

World War II and the Prosperity of the Postwar Era

When the U.S. Pacific Fleet was surprised and attacked by the Japanese Air Force at Pearl Harbor, Hawaii, in December 1941, the original store in San Antonio, Texas, was still struggling to survive. The beginning of the war not only changed the course of almost every American, but also led to the revival of many businesses throughout the country. As manufacturing for wartime material increased, and as people went back to work after the lean years of the Great Depression, people were able to buy more goods than they had in the previous decade. The San Antonio store began to prosper once again, and management purchased large amounts of clothing, shoes, perfume, and other items for sale.

It was not until after the war was officially over, however, that the store began to profit from the servicemen returning from overseas and the rising demand for consumer goods which swept the country. U.S. industry had been rejuvenated by the war effort, and now every person who wanted a job was hired at a competitive wage. The store's buyers purchased up-to-date women's fashions, accessories, and shoes, as well as household furniture and appliances for those servicemen and their wives who were starting the "baby boom." Soon the store hired more employees, renovated the site initially purchased in 1919, and implemented an aggressive advertising campaign in the expanding community around San Antonio. As revenues shot up so did profits, and by the end of the 1950s the once small retail store had grown into one of the most successful businesses in San Antonio.

Having prospered throughout the 1950s, the store in San Antonio was ready to meet the challenges of the future. Changing demographics across the nation, including the exodus from urban areas to the newly created suburbs, significantly altered the way the retail business conducted its operations. The store in San Antonio saw its future in expanding, so management decided to open a new store to serve the growing population on the fringes of the city. Built to almost the same specifications as its original site, the store opened for business in May 1959, and sold the same items. The population around San Antonio continued to grow and the store grew with it. By the end of the 1960s, the company had doubled its revenues since the opening of the second store, and was ready to make another strategic expansion.

The 1970s and 1980s

The next 20 years were very good ones for Solo Serve Corporation. The two stores the company operated were performing so well during the entirety of the 1970s, with profits skyrocketing, the company's customer base increasing at a dizzying rate, and the number of employees burgeoning, that the revenues accrued were set aside to implement a major growth strategy. Management had decided by the end of the 1970s that it was an appropriate time to implement a comprehensive and thoroughgoing expansion program. One of the main reasons management made this decision was due to the rising popularity of large strip shopping centers and malls. Shopping malls were replacing the traditional stores normally found on the main retail street of every town across the United States, and management saw this growth as an opportunity to reap ever larger profits.

Confident in the future, management at Solo Serve opened three stores in 1981 alone, two more in San Antonio, and one in Austin, Texas. After a short year of reorganization and consoli-

dation, the company opened four new ones in 1983, including another store in Austin, two in New Orleans, and one in Baton Rouge, Louisiana. In September 1994, another store was opened for business in Mobile, Alabama. At this point, one would have thought that company management might slow down and make sure the expansion program was working well. However, the executives at Solo Serve continued their expansion at a hectic pace, and opened four new stores in 1985, including two additional stores in New Orleans, and one each in Corpus Christi, Texas, and San Antonio. By the end of the decade, three more stores were opened, thus bringing the total number of new stores to 16.

Growth and Retrenchment During the 1990s

Sales remained high, but profits slowed dramatically, and management considered the prospect of not building any new stores during the early years of the 1990s. The more influential members of the company's board of directors, however, pushed hard for a continuance of the expansion program. Not only did this group of directors win the debate, but they were even able to accelerate the growth process. Thus in 1990, Solo Serve Corporation opened six new stores in San Antonio, Houston, McAllen, and Austin, Texas. Five more stores were added in 1991, in El Paso, Houston, and Laredo, Texas. In 1992 Solo Serve management and its board of directors surprised even themselves—a total of 11 more stores were opened, with new locations such as Brownsville and Waco, Texas. With two more stores opened for business in 1993, the company counted 24 stores debuting to the public within four years. At the end of fiscal 1993, Solo Serve Company had a total of 43 stores in operation throughout Texas, Louisiana, and Alabama.

In order to fuel this heady growth, Solo Serve Corporation made its initial offering of public stock in April 1992. By trading its shares on the NASDAQ stock exchange management expected to raise significant amounts of revenue to continue the expansion plan. Sales of the company stock, though, were not as good as expected; as operating costs for the new stores began to increase, management at Solo Serve soon realized that its rapid growth strategy was backfiring. Increased competition, weakness in the apparel industry itself, and the inability of the company to procure certain discounted merchandise in the quantities it wanted and at the optimum time for sales led to dramatically decreasing revenues. As a result, on July 21, 1994 Solo Serve Corporation was forced to file for bankruptcy under Chapter 11 of the Bankruptcy Code. In 1995 General Atlantic Corporation, a holding company, purchased all of the company's preferred stock, and Solo Serve became a wholly owned subsidiary.

Net revenues and profits continued to decrease, however, and the financial condition of the company remained precarious. In April 1996, Solo Serve was finally able to climb out of bankruptcy, but suffered another setback when it was informed that its common stock would no longer be traded on the NASDAQ stock exchange, since it had fallen below the $1 minimum. From that time onward, the company began trading on the over-the-counter market. In 1997 and 1998, management at the company arranged to purchase all of the common stock and most of the preferred stock held by General Atlantic Corporation. This was done in order to regain control of the company's direction, and rebuild its core retail business in the stores operating throughout Texas and Louisiana.

During 1997 the company made a concerted effort to expand its product offering of brand name linens, bedding, glassware, furniture, and decorative accents. These products were in addition to the brand-name merchandise apparel sold to men, women, and children. Along with the expansion of its product line, the company also developed and implemented a special marketing campaign specifically oriented toward the socioeconomic background of the people that lived in the general area of each Solo Serve store. Despite these moves, management was forced to close a number of the stores and release their employees. At the end of fiscal 1998, Solo Serve Corporation was operating 27 stores, down from a high of 43 during the early 1990s.

Slowly, Solo Serve Corporation seemed to be inching its way back to financial stability. New management had been hired in 1997 and 1998 to evaluate all of the company's stores, close those that were underperforming, and open new ones in potentially lucrative markets. By December 1998, management had opened two new stores, and was planning to open two more by the year 2000. If the new management proved capable of exploiting genuine opportunities and new markets for its off-price retail stores, while keeping operating costs under control, Solo Serve Corporation stood a good chance of returning to profitability over the long term.

Further Reading

"Chain Store Sales Inch Up," *HFN,* August 31, 1998, p. 63.

Gunn, David, "Retailer-Supplier Alliance Targets 'Unsaleable' Losses," *Stores,* January 1999, p. 92.

Farrell, Nina, "Old Meets New," *HFN,* May 18, 1998, p. 26.

——, "Retailers Head to Market with a Social Agenda," *HFN,* October 5, 1999, p. 30.

Ross, Julie Ritzer, "Installations by Major Chains Highlight Growing Interest in Thin Client Systems," *Stores*, January 1998, p. 36.

Ryan, Ken, " 'Chains' Gains Make It a Memorable May," *HFN,* June 8, 1998, p. 1.

—Thomas Derdak

Soros Fund Management LLC

888 Seventh Avenue
New York, New York 10016
U.S.A.
(212) 262-6300
Fax: (212) 245-5154

Private Company
Founded: 1973
Employees: 125
Total Assets: $21.5 billion (1998 est.)
NAIC: 52591 Open-End Investment Funds

Soros Fund Management LLC runs a group of pools of money, called hedge funds, that trade in an array of financial instruments for the benefit of individuals and pension funds with the resources to take risks in the expectation of realizing great rewards. Soros Fund Management operates the Quantum Group of Funds, which had gross assets of $21.5 billion in 1998, more than any other hedge-fund group. So spectacularly did the company perform for its clients that $1,000 invested in 1969 with George Soros, the founder, would have been worth about $2.15 million in 1995 if all the dividends were reinvested. "No other investor has produced better results for such a long period," said *Business Week* in 1993.

Outwitting the Markets: 1969–80

Born in Hungary in 1930, George Soros avoided deportation and probable death in World War II because his Jewish family hid from the invading Germans. He moved to England in 1947 and graduated from the London School of Economics before becoming a trader for an investment bank. In 1956 he moved to New York City, where he became an analyst for European securities. He became a director of a new offshore fund in 1967 for the firm Arnhold & S. Bleichroeder.

In 1969 Soros started the Double Eagle Fund for Bleichroeder with $4 million in capital, including $250,000 of his own money. This hedge fund was also offshore, meaning its

nominal base was outside the United States, on the island of Curaçao in the Netherlands Antilles. This meant it was free from U.S. capital gains taxes and most federal regulations, but none of the investors could be Americans except Soros himself (who became a U.S. citizen in 1961). The minimum investment, in 1981, was $100,000.

Established in 1949, hedge funds got their name from their practice of buying stock on margin (that is, partially through a loan) and countering such an investing position (going long) by selling stock not already owned for delivery at a later date (selling short). They also used instruments such as options and futures contracts both to maximize their potential profits and to offset their risks. Another characteristic of hedge funds was that their managers were compensated mainly on the basis of performance rather than by a fixed percentage of the assets under management. Double Eagle traded in all financial markets, including currencies and commodities as well as stocks and bonds.

Soros and his assistant, Jim Rogers, left Bleichroeder in 1973 to start Soros Fund Management, a private partnership with only one employee, a secretary. The management team reserved for itself 20 percent of the profits from what was renamed the Soros Fund, with Soros receiving four-fifths and Rogers the remaining one-fifth. Soros's readiness to sell stocks short in a period of rising inflation and oil shortages enabled his fund to far outstrip the typical mutual fund. "We start with the assumption that the stock market is always wrong," Soros told a *Wall Street Journal* reporter in 1975. Soros Fund Management also looked beyond the United States; in 1971, for example, one-quarter of the fund's portfolio was invested in Japanese securities. Between the beginning of 1969 and the end of 1974, the fund roughly tripled in value, while the Standard & Poor's 500 stock index fell 3.4 percent.

The Soros Fund continued to realize spectacular returns in the second half of the 1970s. One perspicacious move was to get into technology- and defense-related issues long before the Reagan Administration military buildup. Between the end of 1969 and the end of 1980 the fund (which was renamed the Quantum Fund in 1979) gained 3,365 percent in value compared to 47 percent for the Standard & Poor's composite stock index. By the end of 1980—and after a year in which the fund doubled in value—the Quantum Fund was worth $381 million, and Soros's personal wealth was estimated at $100 million. Rogers left the firm that year. The cover story of the June 1981 issue of *Institutional Investor* called Soros "the world's greatest money manager."

Taking Aggressive Positions: 1981–92

Ironically, 1981 turned out to be Soros Fund Management's worst year, in which its fund, for the first and only time until 1996, lost money. Shares fell 22.9 percent, mainly because Soros, mistakenly thinking interest rates had peaked, took a heavy position in bonds. During what he later called an "identity crisis," in which he sought to extricate himself from day-to-day decision-making, investors withdrew one-third of the fund's assets.

Soros cut his staff to a few aides in September 1981 and turned over active management of most of the Quantum Fund to outside personnel. In 1983 he allotted management of half of the fund's money to Jim Marquez; the other half was in the hands of ten outside managers. Soros himself concentrated on macro analysis: world politics and its effects on monetary policies, plus changes in inflation, interest, and currency rates. By the end of 1983 the Quantum Fund had recovered its lost value.

Soros returned to active investing in 1984, and Marquez left the firm, his role eventually being filled by a team of four senior analysts/managers. In 1985 Soros leveraged the Quantum Fund's assets aggressively, taking positions worth more than its entire assets in support of his belief that the German mark and Japanese yen would rise against the U.S. dollar. The fund rose 122 percent in value that year, and its assets passed $1 billion. By now a dollar investment in the fund in 1969 was worth $164, after paying all fees and expenses. According to *Financial World,* Soros personally made $93.5 million in 1985. By the end of 1986 the Quantum Fund was worth $1.5 billion.

By contrast, the Wall Street stock market crash of October 1987 was a humbling experience for Soros, who was caught unprepared, He decided to sell large parts of the futures contracts of the Quantum Fund, but when the market recovered quickly, the fund lost $200 million in a single day and at least $350 million in all. The fund ended up 14 percent for the year, but Soros, increasingly absorbed in the political changes gripping Eastern Europe, again decided to withdraw from active management. Stanley Druckenmiller, hired in 1988, assumed the chief role the following year, with Soros as "coach." Half of all fees earned by Soros Management were allotted to the management team.

Between 1989 and 1993 the Quantum Fund, under Druckenmiller's direction, averaged annual gains of 40 percent in net asset value, higher than under Soros's own management. But Druckenmiller credited his boss. He told Jack D. Schwager, the author of *New Market Wizards* (cited in *Soros on Soros*), "Soros has taught me that when you have tremendous conviction on a trade, you have to go for the jugular. It takes courage to be a pig."

By this time the Quantum Fund had grown so large that in 1991 Soros established Quasar International Fund, to be run by 15 outside managers, though Soros was in charge of its currency trading. Quantum Emerging Growth Fund and Quota Fund were founded the next year. The former focused mainly on Asian and Latin American stocks, while the latter was a fund of funds, handled by ten outside managers. Quantum Realty Fund was established in 1993 and Quantum Industrial Holdings in 1994. Druckenmiller oversaw all these funds.

Soros Fund Management's readiness to "bet the farm" was put to the ultimate test in 1992, when Quantum Fund borrowed £5 billion and exchanged the currency for German marks, in support of the conviction that the British could not meet their commitment to maintain the value of the pound because it would require raising interest rates to a level that would throw their economy into deep recession. The British government spent £27 billion in a single day to support the pound but eventually gave up. The Quantum Fund made at least $1 billion from betting against the pound and perhaps another $1 billion in the Tokyo stock market and in trading the Italian lira and Swedish kroner. Quantum was the leading offshore fund that year, and four of the six best-performing funds were those of Soros Management. Soros himself, dubbed "the man who broke the Bank of England," earned at least $650 million that year, according to *Financial World.*

Those seeking Soros's investment philosophy were referred to his theory of "reflexivity" as set down in his 1987 book *The Alchemy of Finance.* He explained to Byron Wien in *Soros on Soros*, in less abstruse form: "The prevailing wisdom is that markets are always right. I take the opposite position. I assume that markets are always wrong. ... I am ahead of the curve. I watch out for telltale signs that a trend may be exhausted." Soros the philosopher had also become Soros the philanthropist: initiator of a network of 20 foundations encompassing Central and Eastern Europe.

Competing Against Its Own Reputation: 1993–98

Quantum Fund reported a 61.5 percent gain in 1993, earning for Soros, according to *Financial World*, $1.1 billion, making him the first American to earn more than $1 billion a year. (*FW* later upped this to $1.33 billion from Quantum Fund alone.) Of the other 100 biggest earners on Wall Street that year, nine were associated with Soros Fund Management. The following year, however, Quantum Fund had a return of only about 3.5 percent. Druckenmiller mistakenly forecast that the yen would keep falling against the dollar and took a large short position on the yen, also purchasing a large amount of Japanese stocks and selling Japanese bonds. The result was a loss of somewhere between $350 million and $800 million on a single day. Even so, Quantum did better than most of its hedge fund rivals, some of which suffered double digit losses that year.

Quantum Fund enjoyed a 39 percent gain, after fees, in 1995. Soros Fund Management had mixed results in 1996. Quantum Fund, with $7 billion of the company's $17 billion in gross assets, ended the year down 1.5 percent. Druckenmiller said he had again been wrong again on the Japanese economy and had mistimed his buying and selling of U.S. stocks. Quota Fund, however, which had $3 billion in its coffers, reported an 82 percent gain, and the five other Soros funds also were profitable, with Quasar International registering a 47.5 percent gain.

When the currencies of Thailand, Malaysia, Indonesia, the Philippines, and South Korea came under assault from speculators in the summer of 1997, Malaysian Prime Minister Mahathir Mohamad accused Soros and other money managers of deliberately destabilizing Asian regimes. Soros replied that his company's funds had made only minor trades in Southeast Asian currencies over the last two months. Druckenmiller added that Quantum had sold the Thai and Malaysian currencies short, but in the early spring, before the crisis. Ironically, he—and other Soros fund managers—bought as much as $1.8 billion worth of the Indonesian rupiah. "The IMF program [to support the currency] was as comprehensive as any I've seen," he explained, "but [Indonesian President] Suharto just reneged on it. I was naive about the level of corruption there," he told Riva Atlas.

Quantum Fund posted a 17 percent return in 1997, but this was only half the rate earned by the S&P 500. Druckenmiller mistakenly sunk money into Japanese stocks while selling bonds shorts, counting on an economic recovery that never occurred. Among U.S. stocks, Quantum had a heavy stake in two big losers—Newmont Mining Corporation and Waste Management Inc. Quota Fund, by contrast, enjoyed a 44 percent gain, after the 82 percent rise in 1996 and an incredible 159 percent jump in 1995. Quantum Emerging Growth Fund was up 22 percent, but Quasar International Fund grew by just eight percent, leading to a decision to take the management in-house.

Soros Fund Management had begun actively investing in Eastern Europe and the former Soviet Union in 1994. By the fall of 1997 more than $2.5 billion of the company's funds was invested in Russian businesses. Russia's 1998 financial crisis, consequently, was a severe blow to the firm, which lost most of its investment as stocks plunged 80 percent. Nevertheless, Quantum Fund ended the year up 12.4 percent.

By late October 1998, Quota Fund was down 13.6 percent for the year, and Nicholas Roditi, the London-based chief adviser to both Quota and to Quasar International Fund, took a medical leave. Quasar Emerging Growth Fund had dropped in value by 31 percent for the year by this time and consequently was closed for "corporate restructuring," as Soros put it. He proposed merging Quasar International Fund into Quantum Industrial Holdings, which had become his principal private equity investment vehicle. One of the managers of the latter fund was Soros's son Robert.

Soros Fund Management was reorganized in 1997 as a limited liability company with a three-man management committee consisting of Soros, Druckenmiller, and Gary Gladstein, the company's chief administrative officer. There were six funds with about $21.5 billion in gross assets in the summer of 1998. At the beginning of 1998, Quantum Fund had $5.54 billion in net assets; Quantum Emerging Growth, $1.82 billion; Quota, nearly $1.7 billion; and Quasar International, $1.21 billion. Shares of these funds were being traded in London. Soros's personal fortune was estimated at $5 billion in 1997.

Further Reading

Atlas, Riva, "Quantum Limp," *Institutional Investor,* March 1998, 58–65.

Beck, Ernest, "Soros Begins Investing in Eastern Europe," *Wall Street Journal,* June 1, 1994, p. A11.

Gilbert, Nick, "Soros: The Alchemist Loses His Touch," *Financial World,* November 6, 1994, pp. 38–42, 44–46.

Laing, Jonathan R., "Securities Fund Shuns Wall Street's Fashions, Prospers in Hard Years," *Wall Street Journal,* May 28, 1975, pp. 1, 23.

Morgenson, Gretchen, "Soros's Quantum Fund Losses in Russia Put at $2 Billion," *New York Times,* August 27, 1998, pp. D1, D4.

Pacelle, Mitchell, "Soros to Shut Down Hedge Fund," *Wall Street Journal,* October 27, 1998, p. C16.

Slater, Robert, *Invest First, Investigate Later: and 23 Other Trading Secrets of George Soros, the Legendary Investor,* Chicago: Irwin, 1996.

——, *Soros,* New York: Irwin, 1996.

Soros, George, *The Alchemy of Finance,* New York: Simon & Schuster, 1987.

——, *Soros on Soros,* New York: John Wiley & Sons, 1995.

Wallace, Anise, "The World's Greatest Money Manager," *International Investor,* June 1981, pp. 39–43, 45.

Weiss, Gary, and Gail E. Schares, "The Man Who Moves Markets," *Business Week,* August 23, 1993, pp. 50–55, 58, 60.

—Robert Halasz

Stevedoring Services of America Inc.

1131 Southwest Klickitat Way
Seattle, Washington 98134
U.S.A.
(206) 623-0304
Fax: (206) 623-0179
Web site: http://www.ssofa.com

Private Company
Incorporated: 1949 as Bellingham Stevedoring Company
Employees: 7,500
Sales: $850 million (1998 est.)
NAIC: 48832 Marine Cargo Handling

One of the largest stevedoring companies in the world, Stevedoring Services of America Inc. (SSA) provides the traditional services of a stevedore—loading and unloading ship cargo—and provides intermodal cargo-handling services, that is, transferring vessel-borne cargo to railroads and trucks, domestically and abroad. SSA is regarded as one of the first in the industry to expand beyond the traditional activities of a stevedore and develop itself into a full-service, cargo-handling company capable of warehousing cargo and moving cargo from ships to a variety of land-based transportation vehicles. The company's stevedoring operations started in the Pacific Northwest, expanded throughout the United States in later years, and spread internationally at a vigorous pace during the 1990s. Owned by the Smith and Hemingway families, SSA has been an aggressive acquirer during the 1990s as the stevedoring industry has consolidated. Operating at 150 locations worldwide, SSA handles every type of cargo and serves every major ocean carrier. By the end of the 1990s, SSA ranked as the 263rd largest private company in the United States, as calculated by *Forbes* magazine.

Pacific Northwest Origins

The corporate roots of SSA stretch back to 1880, but the company traces its origins to the year the Smith/Hemingway families started their legacy. In 1949 Fred R. Smith, the patri-

arch of the two families who would own and operate SSA for the remainder of the 20th century, formed Bellingham Stevedoring Company. A small, local stevedoring company based north of Seattle, Washington, Bellingham Stevedoring represented the foundation SSA was built on. Stevedoring companies traditionally coordinated the loading and unloading of ships, providing the equipment and serving as a labor broker at ports of call. Bellingham Stevedoring, in the 35 years separating its founding and the adoption of the SSA name, methodically expanded its operations on the West Coast. In 1952, Fred Smith made the first step outside Bellingham Bay by investing in a company called Southeast Stevedoring, which established the company's presence in Alaska. Two years later, Bellingham Stevedoring pushed south, acquiring Seattle Stevedoring from American Hawaiian Steamship Company. Henceforth known as Seattle Stevedoring, the Smith/Hemingway-controlled enterprise bolstered its presence in Washington State during the early 1960s, purchasing small stevedoring companies in the Puget Sound region. Between 1960 and 1963, the company acquired Everett Stevedoring Company, Olympia Stevedoring Company, and Twin Harbor Stevedoring Company, and established cargo-handling facilities at the Port of Tacoma and the Port of Port Angeles. Twenty years later, after completing further acquisitions, Seattle Stevedoring completed its expansion along the coastline. Between 1982 and 1983, the company acquired Brady Hamilton and Crescent Wharf and Warehouse, acquisitions that expanded services to all ports in Oregon and California. One year after this southward sweep, the company changed its name to Stevedoring Services of America.

Diversification Begins in the 1980s

Shortly after the name change, SSA reached a turning point in its history. From its founding to the 1980s, the company had evolved from a small stevedoring firm with a local focus to one of the largest regional stevedoring companies in the western United States. A more profound evolutional step awaited in the decade ahead, as the company not only continued to widen its geographic scope but also diversified beyond the traditional parameters defining a stevedoring firm. Historically, stevedores had served as the go-between for shippers and land-based transporters, providing the equipment and personnel—generally longshoremen—

to facilitate the transfer of goods from sea to land. As such, traditional stevedores were labor-brokers who operated port facilities, a description SSA sought to broaden. SSA led the way toward the development of a new, more sophisticated breed of stevedores by shaping itself into a full-service, cargo-handling company. SSA, in the years ahead, provided computerized cargo-tracking information, among other services, and it developed into an intermodal cargo handler. Intermodal cargo referred to cargo encased in containers that was moved via different modes of transportation, such as sea, truck, and rail, without being removed from its containers. SSA also led the way toward another industrywide trend: expansion through acquisition. The stevedoring industry, particularly during the 1990s, began to consolidate as larger stevedores acquired their smaller counterparts. Large shipping companies were beginning to develop their own stevedore operations, forcing the stevedore industry to respond by realizing the economies of scale engendered by consolidation. On both fronts—diversification and geographic expansion—SSA excelled, creating the dominant stevedoring company in the United States.

Although SSA had devoted itself to methodical expansion from the start of the Smith/Hemingway era, geographic growth began to occur at a decidedly more vigorous pace by the end of the 1980s. First, however, the company began to develop into a more comprehensive cargo handler, beginning its significant diversification under the management of F.D. ''Ricky'' Smith. Smith served as president from 1979 to 1991, before being promoted to chairman and chief executive officer, titles he would hold throughout the 1990s. Smith's promotion to the company's two most powerful posts in 1991 made room for the promotion of Jon Hemingway to president, the third generation of the Hemingway family to assume the office. Under the stewardship of these two individuals, SSA greatly increased its stature within the stevedoring industry.

In 1987, SSA established its first intermodal operations, joining Intermodal Management Services, Inc. to create Pacific Rail Services. Pacific Rail Services, organized as SSA's intermodal division, managed rail ramp operations, coordinating the transfer of containerized cargo from ship to train. Two years later, the company began its expansion drive, building on its formidable presence on the West Coast. SSA acquired Overseas Terminal Company, making it the largest stevedore and terminal operator in southern California. Also in 1989, the company completed its first eastward foray, acquiring Carolina Stevedoring, which operated in Charlestown, South Carolina; Savannah, Georgia; and Jacksonville, Florida. In the years ahead,

SSA's presence in the South Atlantic region would rival its dominant position on the West Coast.

Entering the 1990s, SSA was ready to build on the momentum established during the late 1980s and continue to diversify and expand, achieving nearly all its progress in both areas through acquisitions. The company ranked as one of the largest stevedoring companies in the United States by the early 1990s, strongly positioned on the West Coast and in the South Atlantic region. SSA operated more than a dozen shipping terminals that handled containerized cargo and other commodities, such as import steel, meal, fruit, export forest products, and agricultural goods. The company also stevedored various types of commercial and military cargo vessels that docked at SSA-operated terminals and facilities operated by other concerns. SSA's two subsidiaries were Pacific Rail Services, the company's intermodal division, and Crescent Warehouse, which ranked as one of California's largest operators of public marine storehouses.

In 1992 SSA renewed its expansion campaign, establishing operations on the East Coast. The company acquired a 50 percent interest in Delaware River Stevedores and started operations in Pennsylvania and New Jersey through a partnership with International Terminal Operating Company, Inc. The year's biggest acquisition was the purchase of Southeast Atlantic Cargo Operators (SEACO), a southeastern U.S. cargo handler with operations in Wilmington, Delaware; Charlestown, South Carolina; Savannah, Georgia; and Jacksonville, Florida. SEACO's addition to SSA's operations entrenched the company's position at ports first entered through the 1989 acquisition of Carolina Stevedoring. The push eastward, as perceived by the company, was a strategic necessity. ''In every maritime industry, consolidation is what's happening now,'' noted SSA's vice-president in May 1992. ''We just believe that we must expand to remain in the stevedoring business,'' he explained. The era of acquire or be acquired had begun, and SSA was intent on being the most active practitioner of the industrywide trend toward consolidation.

International Expansion in the 1990s

As SSA bolstered its domestic presence by expanding east, the company also looked overseas for growth. By mid-1992, the company was evaluating opportunities related to operating railyards or inland container depots in Malaysia and Thailand and had submitted bids for consulting work in Australia, Costa Rica, and Panama. Before the end of the year, SSA achieved progress in Thailand, winning a five-year contract commissioned by the State Railway of Thailand to operate the country's new container port 65 miles outside of Bangkok. More than any of its competition, industry observers claimed, SSA was concentrating on developing new technologies, including on-dock rail and electronic cargo tracking, while leading the industry in expanding domestically and internationally. Referring to SSA's investment in electronic data exchange systems that tracked cargo, Hemingway remarked, ''We're moving information just as much as we're moving cargo these days.'' The time when SSA could hope to succeed by solely serving as a labor broker was past. The 1990s required stevedores to provide more than their traditional services, and SSA, despite its lengthy ties to the past, was demonstrating an eager willingness to change with the times.

Although SSA steadfastly refused to divulge financial information, outside sources estimated the company was generating approximately $500 million in revenue during the early 1990s, making the company the largest stevedoring firm in the United States. SSA moved quickly toward the $1-billion-in-sales mark during the mid- and late 1990s by acquiring stevedores and other cargo-handling companies, particularly overseas. The company started its five-year contract in Thailand in June 1993, by which time several Central American countries had contracted with SSA to help them modernize their port operations. SSA's consulting services and its information services, which used computers to track cargo movement and to clear cargo through customs, were examples of the diversified range of marketable skills the company was benefiting from to succeed during the 1990s. In 1993, SSA also acquired New Zealand Stevedoring Company Limited, the largest stevedoring company in New Zealand, and, through a joint venture, began handling cargo throughout southern Africa.

By the end of 1994, SSA's resolute expansion in the midst of a consolidating industry was earning the company accolades from outside observers. A professor of port and marine transportation management at the University of Washington, in a December 1994 *Puget Sound Business Journal* article, referred to SSA as "probably the most significant success story in the independent stevedoring industry," praise that stemmed from the company's managerial acumen and its growing role as a worldwide stevedoring expert. Through a joint venture in Vietnam with Saigon Port, SSA began operating a trucking company and chassis leasing and repair operation, another example of the company's intermodal breadth. SSA also assisted the Chinese port of Tianjin design a container port, port development assistance that the company had also provided in India and Pakistan. SSA's most significant project in 1994 was a joint venture with Motores Internacionales S.A. to build and operate a container terminal near the city of Colon on the east end of the Panama Canal. The 16-month project cost $220 million, resulting in the Manzanillo International Terminal, regarded as one of the most efficient port facilities in the world. SSA dredged the channel, designed, financed, built, and marketed the terminal, and trained Panamanian employees for its operation.

Although SSA's international expansion was driven, in part, by diminishing opportunities to expand domestically, the company continued to find valuable acquisition candidates in the United States. In 1995, SSA purchased a large stevedoring firm named Ryan-Walsh, Inc., based in Mobile, Alabama. Specializing in handling forest products, Ryan-Walsh operated in 26 ports, maintaining a strong presence around the Gulf of Mexico, one of the few domestic regions SSA had yet to penetrate. Hemingway noted the importance of the Ryan-Walsh acquisition, remarking that it was "a very big thing for us . . . it really now makes us a nationwide company," before adding, "Our expansion in the United States is still a high priority."

Despite Hemingway's assurance that domestic expansion remained an important objective for the company, the bulk of SSA's activity during the latter half of the 1990s occurred on the international front. In 1995, the company formed a joint venture with Transportacion Maritima Mexcana, S.A. de C.V. to market and operate a container terminal in Manzanillo, Mexico. In 1996, the company acquired a 31 percent interest in Lotus Joint Venture Company, Ltd., a Vietnamese concern created to develop and operate a container terminal and warehousing operation in Saigon. In 1997, the company formed a joint venture named International Seaports as an organized entity to pursue its port development work in India and other Asian countries. The following year, SSA teamed with Orient Maritime Limited to develop and operate a terminal facility in Chittagong, Bangladesh.

As SSA prepared for the 21st century, the pattern of international expansion established during the 1990s was expected to continue. Overseas markets offered the greatest opportunities for growth, and SSA, with operations spanning the globe, stood well-positioned to take advantage of those opportunities as they emerged. Domestically, the company was expected to continue to develop its intermodal capabilities, such as the company's 1997 deal with Union Pacific. SSA's subsidiary Rail Terminal Services acquired the stock of Union Pacific Motor Freight from the Union Pacific railroad, which, under a ten-year contract, gave SSA control over 18 rail ramps across the country. With domestic expansion pointed in this direction, and the company's commitment to international expansion, SSA promised to be a leading stevedore in the century ahead.

Principal Subsidiaries

Ryan-Walsh, Inc.; Rail Terminal Services; Manzanillo International Terminal, Panama S.A.; Greystones Cargo Systems (South Africa); International Seaports Private Ltd. (India); Southern Cross Stevedoring (New Zealand).

Further Reading

Fabey, Michael, "National Stevedores Gobbling Up the Local Small Fry," *Philadelphia Business Journal,* May 18, 1992, p. 5.
Sansbury, Tim, "Stevedore Thinks It'd Be 'Cool' in St. Petersburg," *Journal of Commerce and Commercial,* September 1, 1995, p. 1A.
"Stevedoring Services of America," *Los Angeles Business Journal,* September 2, 1991, p. S7.
"Stevedoring Services of America," *American Shipper,* September 1991, p. 103.
Wilhelm, Steve, "SSA Expanding Presence in Far East, East Coast," *Puget Sound Business Journal,* June 18, 1993, p. 38.
——, "SSA Expands Again, Buys Alabama Stevedore Firm," *Puget Sound Business Journal,* May 5, 1995, p. 6.
——, "Waterfront Giant Expands Its Reach," *Puget Sound Business Journal,* June 5, 1992, p. 1.
——, "Waterfront Skill Carries SSA to Distant Shores," *Puget Sound Business Journal,* December 16, 1994, p. 1.

—Jeffrey L. Covell

Sunoco, Inc.

Ten Penn Center
1801 Market Street
Philadelphia, Pennsylvania 19103-1699
U.S.A.
(215) 977-3000
Fax: (215) 977-3409
Web site: http://www.sunocoinc.com

Public Company
Incorporated: 1890 as Sun Oil Company
Employees: 10,900
Sales: $8.58 billion (1998)
Stock Exchanges: New York Philadelphia
Ticker Symbol: SUN
NAIC: 211111 Crude Petroleum & Natural Gas
     Extraction; 211112 Natural Gas Liquid Extraction;
     32411 Petroleum Refineries; 48611 Pipeline
     Transportation of Crude Oil; 48691 Pipeline
     Transportation of Refined Petroleum Products; 42271
     Petroleum Bulk Stations & Terminals; 42272
     Petroleum & Petroleum Products Wholesalers; 23311
     Land Subdivision & Land Development; 483113
     Coastal & Great Lakes Freight Transportation

Sunoco, Inc. is one of the largest petroleum refiner-marketers in the United States. The company operates five refineries in the United States with total crude oil processing capacity of about 730,000 barrels per day. In the marketing arena, Sunoco sells gasoline under the Sunoco brand in 17 states, principally in the Northeast and Midwest. Other company activities include the worldwide sale of lubricants and petrochemicals, the operation of pipelines and terminals in the United States, and the production of metallurgical-grade coke for the steel industry. In the late 20th century, the company underwent a major restructuring, which included the divestment of its exploration and production operations, and the company changed its name from Sun Company, Inc. to Sunoco, Inc. in late 1998 as one of the final steps in that process.

Early History

Sunoco's beginnings go back to 1881, when Joseph Newton Pew, known as Newton Pew, and Edward Octavius Emerson incorporated Keystone Gas Company. Emerson was president, and Pew was the treasurer. Emerson, a 42-year-old banker, had the financial expertise and backing, while Pew, at 28, was just becoming known in the oil-and-gas real estate business, having traded in property and leases since the 1870s. Emerson and Pew's new company succeeded so well that within a year they incorporated Penn Fuel Company, the first supplier of natural gas to a major city, Pittsburgh, for home use as well as for industrial use. In the words of Pew's nephew J. Howard Pew, "When Newton Pew arrived in 1882, few Pittsburghers realized they were in need of natural gas. The Penn Fuel Company immediately embarked upon correcting this oversight by building gas pipelines to the city."

By 1884, the two men had sold their interest in the Penn Fuel Company and started The Peoples Natural Gas Company. Not too long after that, the partners got wind of substantial oil discoveries in Ohio. Pew sent his nephew, Robert Cunningham Pew, to investigate the possibility of securing leases in northwestern Ohio's oil fields. Under Pew and Emerson's direction, Robert spent $4,500 on two leases in Ohio's Findlay township. Robert Pew was left to manage the Ohio oil operations while Edward Emerson and Newton Pew focused their attention on the natural gas end of their business. By 1889, however, production in their Ohio oil fields grew so large that it could no longer be ignored. Pew and Emerson incorporated the Sun Oil Line Company in order to acquire the necessary pipelines, leases, storage tanks, and tank cars. The operation continued to grow to the point where, in 1890, Pew and Emerson thought it wise to consolidate their interests, and they incorporated Sun Oil Company of Ohio, in Ohio, with the stated intention of "producing petroleum, rock and carbon oil; transporting and storing same; refining, purifying, manufacturing such oil and its various products . . . ," getting Sun Oil off to a running start.

In 1894 Sun Oil, in a joint venture with Merriam and Morgan Paraffine Company of Cleveland, incorporated the Diamond Oil Company for the purpose of purchasing a refinery just outside Toledo for $22,200 from economically troubled Crystal

Oil Company. This plant refined the first oils that Sun Oil ever shipped. In 1895 Pew and Emerson bought out Merriam and Morgan's interest, and the refinery became entirely Sun Oil's. Not only did Sun Oil get its first refinery out of Diamond Oil; it adopted a diamond shape enclosing the words "Sun Oil" as the company trademark.

Both of Emerson and Pew's businesses were developing at a rapid pace. While Sun Oil continued to grow, The Peoples Natural Gas Company also prospered under the control of Emerson and Pew. In 1899, Pew bought out Emerson's stake in the Sun Oil Company and, by 1903, he had sold his own stake in The Peoples Natural Gas Company. In 1901 Pew reincorporated Sun Oil Company in New Jersey as Sun Company. Between 1899 and 1903 Newton Pew worked hard to help Sun Oil stand firmly on its own feet.

In 1901 the Spindletop well in Beaumont, Texas, spurting 100,000 barrels of oil a day for ten days, was the biggest oil strike yet. Newton Pew lost no time sending Robert Pew there. At that time, Beaumont was suffering from something akin to gold fever, except that Beaumont's gold was black. Within a month, Robert Pew had returned to Toledo, and Newton Pew sent Robert's brother, James Edgar Pew, in his stead.

J. Edgar Pew would become one of the most famous and respected oil men in the production end of the business. In the words of a retired Sun executive, J. Edgar Pew "was shrewd enough to see that you could make more money by drilling and producing the oil than by going around and buying it."

Pew bought 42 acres of land on the Neches River and erected storage tanks. In 1902, at a public auction, he bid $100,000 for the assets of the bankrupt Lone Star and Crescent Oil Company. His was the only bid of the day and it won the assets. The auction's terms, however, demanded an immediate down payment of at least 25 percent. When Pew went to the two local banks he'd been using, he found them closed for Decoration Day. As he kicked up dust on the streets of the town he saw his prize slipping away, until he spotted some men remodeling an old building to hold a new bank. Sun's reputation was already so well known, that a man inside the building wrote J. Edgar a check for $25,000 on the spot.

Meanwhile, Robert Pew observed that the key to Sun's success in its Texas endeavors lay in finding a way to move its Texas crude inexpensively to refineries, because the cost of transporting it over land was so high that it was out of the question. In October 1901, Newton Pew spent $45,000 for land on the Delaware River in Marcus Hook, Pennsylvania, and started building a refinery there to process the Texas crude. United Gas Improvement Company, of Philadelphia, Pennsylvania, was Sun's partner, with 45 percent of the venture. Five months later, in March 1902, the refinery received the first crude Sun sent out of Texas, delivered by Sun's first tanker, the S.S. *Paraguay.* In 1905 Sun transformed the *Thomas W. Lawson,* the world's largest schooner-rigged sailing ship, into an oil carrier.

Amidst all this, J. Howard Pew, Newton Pew's second son, began work at Sun. J. Howard Pew had finished both high school and college by the time he was 18. In 1901 the 19-year-old J. Howard began working in the Toledo, Ohio, refinery, experimenting with the heavy black residue from Sun's Texas

crude. In the new Marcus Hook refinery, the crude was developed into a lubricating oil, known as Sun Red Stock. By 1904 J. Howard Pew and his team of researchers had developed the first commercially successful petroleum asphalt. Sun had more than 100 trade-name products on the market by 1910.

In 1908, Joseph's third son, Joseph Newton Pew, Jr., joined the Sun staff in the purchasing department. He recalled that, about three months after he started, he asked his father for "a real job." According to Joseph, his father's response was, "Joe, you have been given your opportunity and it is up to you to make your job." Joe took those words to heart. He drove ox teams through the mud to get loads of pipe across West Virginia, laid mahogany roads in Venezuela, and spent five nights without sleep while bringing in a new well in Illinois.

By 1912 when Joseph Newton Pew, Sr., Sun's first president, died, his sons were already working together as a team. J. Howard became president at the age of 30; Joseph Newton Pew, Jr., became vice-president at 26.

J. Howard Pew took a business trip to Germany in 1915, a year after the beginning of World War I. He was shocked by Germany's air and naval strength and predicted with some accuracy the amount of damage Germany could inflict on Allied shipping, including oil tankers. When he returned to the United States, he authorized the beginning of Sun Ship, a shipbuilding facility on the Delaware River, south of Philadelphia. By 1917, when the United States became involved in the war, Sun Ship was able to slide its first freighter, the S.S. *Chester Sun,* into the water. By the end of World War I, Sun Ship had built three minesweepers and six tankers for the U.S. Navy.

Opened First Service Station in 1920

Before the war, Sun's place in the petroleum industry was in lubricating and industrial oils, and it sold oil directly to Philadelphia's United Gas Improvement Company (UGI). During the war, however, Sun severed its connections with UGI, and Sun was left with a huge supply of gas oil, the source of gasoline. The automobile industry had grown so rapidly that by 1918 more than six million vehicles moved over U.S. highways. Quickly shifting gears, Sun began to construct its first gasoline filling station in Ardmore, Pennsylvania, which opened in 1920. A diamond-shaped sign with a red arrow through it proclaimed Sun's Products. Since that day, Sun's trademark has not changed nor has the name of the gasoline, Sunoco.

In 1922 Sun Company once again reincorporated, as a Pennsylvania company, under the name Sun Oil Company (PA). Also in 1922, at the Marcus Hook refinery, Sun Oil set in motion its first high-pressure cracking units that enabled it to produce gasoline much more quickly. This expanded capacity allowed Sun Oil to increase its sales beyond the mid-Atlantic region.

Most other refiners at this time were adding tetraethyl lead to gasoline to kill engine knock. Sun Oil took a different track. It produced premium gasoline without adding lead. In 1927 Sun Oil introduced its only grade of gasoline, calling it Blue Sunoco, "The High Powered Knockless Fuel at No Extra Price." Blue dye was used in the gasoline so that motorists could identify it by its color, through the glass of the 1920s gravity-flow gasoline pumps.

In 1923 Sun Ship introduced the Sun Doxford diesel engine. In a few years Sun Ship became the largest U.S. manufacturer of large marine diesel engines. In 1931 it launched the world's first all-welded tanker, the S.S. *White Flash.* In 1931 Sun built the first long-distance petroleum products pipeline in the United States. This 730-mile pipeline stretched from Twin Oaks, Pennsylvania, through Syracuse, New York, to Cleveland, Ohio, with branch lines to cities in between.

The usual refining practice in the oil industry at the time was to heat the crude to such extreme temperatures that it became vaporous. The vapors were then condensed into gasoline and other products. This process yielded only about 40 percent highgrade fuel. The leftover 60 percent was a sludgy substance that could only be made into low-profit items. All this began to change in 1933, when Eugene Houdry, a Frenchman, made an appointment to see Arthur Pew, Newton Pew's oldest son.

Houdry was working on an invention that would get more gasoline out of every gallon, of a much higher octane. Most of his preliminary work had been done in France, and in Vacuum Oil Company's refinery in New Jersey. When Vacuum merged with Standard Oil Company of New York, however, Houdry's refining project was shelved. He had been trying to sell his refining process to other companies, but he had had no luck until he reached Sun Oil. Within an hour at the first meeting, Houdry and Arthur Pew struck a deal. Working in Sun Oil's Marcus Hook laboratory, Houdry developed a model that performed to perfection. Sun Oil then built Houdry's catalytic cracking plant at Marcus Hook refinery, ran it on trial for a year and a half in secret, then announced its success to the world in 1937.

Toward the end of World War II, when the gas needs of the United States were critical, the Marcus Hook refinery shipped more than 1.1 million barrels a month of 100-octane aviation gas. At the same time, Sun Ship built an average of one ship a week. The end of the war brought a sharp decline in U.S. ship construction, as foreign competition took business from U.S. commercial builders, Sun Ship included.

After the war, J. Howard Pew started grooming as his successor an outsider from Sun Oil's ranks. In 1947 Robert G. Dunlop became Sun Oil's first non-Pew president in 60 years. During his presidency, revenues grew sixfold and profits ninefold.

By the early 1950s, when car types began to vary, Sun Oil's one type of gasoline could no longer meet the differing octane needs of higher-compression engines, and Sun Oil's market share began to fall off. In 1956 Sun Oil opened its first custom-blending pump in Orlando, Florida; from five grades of gasoline, customers could select the one that best met their car's octane needs and the pump would mix it then and there. By 1958, Sun Oil had removed the last of the pump's flaws and was able to introduce six grades of custom blending to its entire market territory.

Dunlop's ability to make quick decisions led to Sun Oil's abundant Lake Maracaibo, Venezuela, oil discovery in 1957. Taking the advice of an advisory group, Sun Oil investigated this offshore site that ultimately had nearly 100 wells producing 450 million barrels of oil, 200 million of which were Sun Oil's

share. Sun's Venezuelan operations, known as VenSun, prospered until Venezuela nationalized its oil industry in 1975.

Sun Oil went on to establish the North Sea Sun Oil Company Ltd. in 1965. The next year, as a member of the Arpet group, Sun helped discover the Hewett gas field off England's coast, beginning Sun's history in offshore North Sea drilling.

Merged with Sunray DX in 1968

Bob Dunlop steered the company through the Sun Oil-Sunray DX Oil Company merger. Their courtship began in 1967 at an industry dinner in Midland, Texas, where Dunlop and Sunray chief Paul Taliafero were seated next to one another. Sun Oil operated primarily in the eastern United States and Sunray almost exclusively in the Midwest. Their refining and marketing regions added to each, complementing rather than competing. By every measurement Sun Oil was about twice the size of Sunray DX. The companies agreed to merge in 1968. A year and a half was spent planning the mechanics of the merger, which resulted in a company with 30,000 employees and more than $2 billion in assets. The merger turned Sun Oil into a huge corporation and changed the way the company would be run from that point hence.

All this time Sun Oil was working to develop what was called the world's first oil mine, Canada's Athabasca sands, on the Athabasca River. It was thought these sands held more recoverable oil than all of the oil in the Middle East. The problem was how to transport the sand to where the oil could be recovered or how to recover the oil onsite in such a far north location. Sun Oil finished construction of a refinery in 1967, intended to boil 45,000 barrels of oil out of the sand daily. The cost of such production was too high to compete with reigning low oil prices. Ten years later, however, when oil prices started climbing, Sun Oil's sands began to turn a profit.

Sun Oil constructed a $150 million operation in Yabuco, Puerto Rico, including an all-weather harbor and a 66,000-barrel-per-day refinery in 1969. In 1971 Sun Oil Company (PA) became simply Sun Oil Company.

In 1970, when Dunlop retired, H. Robert Sharbaugh became Sun Oil's new president. Attention was focused on pushing up the stock price and raising the cash dividend. Individual employees were given the opportunity to advance their own careers when a management-training school was founded. By 1974, Sharbaugh had been named CEO, and by 1975 he was chairman of the board. In 1975 Sharbaugh announced he would restructure the company into 14 decentralized operating units and two property companies, all of which would be controlled by a nonoperating parent company.

In 1976 Sun Oil Company changed its name to Sun Company, Inc., to portray the fact that it was involved in more businesses than just oil. That same year Theodore A. Burtis became Sun's new president. In 1978 Chairman Sharbaugh authorized the purchase of a large interest in Becton, Dickinson and Company, a medical supply firm, and it became obvious that Sharbaugh's vision for Sun differed from that of the board. In 1979 Theodore Burtis became Sun's new chairman.

In 1979 Sun, in an effort to redirect its company toward energy resources, made an acquisition in mining. This was Elk River Resources, Inc., which had mining operations in Kentucky and Virginia, with reserves of 186 million tons of coal in those states and in West Virginia. By 1983 this acquisition's production increased by almost 35 percent. Additional acquisitions expanded its coal reserves by 70 percent.

Acquired Texas Pacific Oil in 1980

In 1980 Sun bought all the domestic oil and gas properties of Texas Pacific Oil Company, a subsidiary of the Seagram Company, Ltd., for $2.3 billion. The acquisition brought to Sun properties with approximate average daily production of 32,000 barrels of crude oil and 104 million cubic feet of natural gas, as well as four million acres of unexplored land in the United States. In February 1982 Sun Ship was sold to Levingston Shipbuilding Company; it had not turned a profit in more than five years. Robert McClements, Jr., took over Burtis's duties as president in 1981, but Burtis remained CEO and chairman.

In 1982 when the People's Republic of China invited oil companies to help it develop its 3,000 miles of coastline, Sun was one of the first to jump in. In 1983 Sun was granted shares in exploration tracts in the Gulf of Beibu and the South China Sea. By 1984, a Sun-manned jack-up rig had been installed off Hainan Island in the Gulf of Beibu, and drilling began.

In 1984 Sun acquired the Exeter Oil Company for $76 million and some Victory Oil Company properties for $281 million. As McClements explained it, "The acquisitions reflect Sun's strategy of acquiring existing producing properties and, using its production know-how, quickly bringing them up to snuff." Within a short period of time Exeter's production climbed from 500 barrels a day to more than 1,000.

Burtis worked closely with McClements on strategic direction until McClements became CEO in 1985. That year Sun divested itself of its medical supply business. In 1986, the year the company celebrated its 100th anniversary, Sun continued to refocus on its core petroleum business by selling Sun Carriers, Inc., a motor freight transportation subsidiary, and Sun Distributors, Inc., a distributor of industrial products. The following year the company sold Standard Trucking Company. McClements added the chairmanship to his position as CEO that year, and Robert P. Hauptfuhrer was named president and chief operating officer.

Restructurings, 1988–98

Beginning in 1988, Sun entered a ten-year period marked by major restructuring initiatives. With oil prices on the decline in the late 1980s, Sun laid off employees and made the decision to exit from domestic oil and gas exploration and production. In November 1988 Sun spun off to its shareholders its subsidiary Sun Exploration and Production Company. As a result, McClements was once again appointed president of Sun, while Hauptfuhrer became chairman and CEO of the spinoff, which was soon renamed Oryx Energy Company. Simultaneous with these developments, Sun acquired Atlantic Petroleum Corporation for $513 million, which brought to Sun another refinery, a network of more than 1,000 Atlantic service stations (which

were soon rebranded under the Sunoco name), and a pipeline system.

In early 1991 Robert H. Campbell was appointed president and COO, with McClements remaining chairman and CEO. Later that year, another restructuring was begun, this one resulting in 1,000 job cuts and $100 million per year in pretax savings from streamlined operations. With the collapse of the real estate market, Sun also decided to divest its real estate business, Radnor Corp., a process that dragged on through the end of the decade.

By early 1992 Campbell was chairman, CEO, and president of Sun, following McClements' retirement. That year, Sun formally adopted a new strategic direction, which focused on value-added businesses: branded gasoline marketing, lubricants, chemicals, and logistics. Also in 1992 the company began to reduce its ownership interest in Suncor Inc., a Canadian affiliate that included the oil sands business. An initial public offering in March 1992 reduced Sun's stake from 75 to 68 percent; in May 1993 the stake was reduced again, to 55 percent, through a sale to a group of underwriters. Also in 1993 the company sold Cordero Mining Co., operator of a coal mine in Wyoming, to Kennecott Coal Company for $120.5 million.

In August 1994 Sun spent about $170 million to acquire a 177,000-barrels-per-day refinery in Philadelphia from Chevron U.S.A. Inc. This refinery was immediately adjacent to the refinery Sun had acquired with the 1988 acquisition of Atlantic Petroleum, and the two were combined into a single, more efficient refining complex. In 1995 this complex was linked directly to Sun's Marcus Hook Refinery via a 19-mile inter-refinery pipeline. In June 1995 Sun sold its remaining 55 percent interest in Suncor to a group of Canadian underwriters for $855 million.

Further restructuring moves came in 1996 as Sun continued to focus on the downstream side of the business. In September 1996 Sun sold its international oil and gas production business to Agip (U.K.) Limited, a part of Italy's ENI S.p.A., for $260 million in cash, thereby completing its exit from upstream activities. Just two months later, Sun bolstered its lubricants business through the purchase of the Kendall and Amalie lubricants unit of Witco Corporation. In December 1996 Sun departed from company tradition when it hired an outsider as company president for the first time. John G. Drosdick—who had previously served as president of two other major petroleum marketing firms in the United States, Ultramar Corporation and Tosco Refining Company—was named Sun president and COO, with Campbell retaining the chairman and CEO positions.

In 1997 Sun continued to restructure, particularly working to modernize its refineries and make them more efficient. The company was able by 1999 to cut its costs to refine a barrel of crude oil from $3.68 to $2. Sun appeared to be turning the corner on profitability as net income increased from $263 million in 1997 to $280 million in 1998, despite a revenue decline from $10.53 billion to $8.58. In a move perhaps symbolizing the end of the decade-long restructuring, the company changed its name in November 1998 to Sunoco, Inc., thereby adopting the well-known brand name. The company also made its first alterations to the Sunoco logo since 1954. With a new corporate image, heightened cost-consciousness, and a sharp focus on the downstream, Sunoco was well-prepared to defend its position as one of the largest independent U.S. refinery-marketers well into the 21st century.

Principal Subsidiaries

Helios Capital Corporation; Marine Investment Company of Delaware; Mascot Petroleum Company, Inc.; Mohawk Valley Oil, Inc.; Radnor Corporation; Sun Alternate Energy Corporation; Sun Altantic Refining and Marketing Company; Sun Canada Inc.; Sun Coal & Coke Company; Sun Coke Company; Sun Executive Services Company; Sun Geologic and Seismic, Inc.; Sun Ocean Ventures, Inc.; Sun Oil Argentina Limited; Sun Oil Argentina Limited S.A.; Sun Oil Company (U.K.) Ltd.; Sun Oil Export Company; Sun Oil International, Inc.; Sun Oil Shabwa Yemen Limited; Sun Oil (Thailand) Limited; Sun Oil Trading Company; Sun Pipe Line Company of Delaware; Sun Services Corporation; Sun Ship, Inc.; Sun-Del Services, Inc.; Sunoco Overseas, Inc.; The Claymont Investment Company; Triad Carriers, Inc.

Principal Operating Units

Sun Northeast Refining; Sunoco Northeast Marketing; Sunoco Chemicals; Sun Lubricants; Sunoco MidAmerica Marketing & Refining; Sunoco Logistics; Sun Coke.

Further Reading

Centennial Celebration: The Story of Sun Company, Radnor, Pa.: Sun Company, Inc., 1986.

Fan, Aliza, ''Sun Rises to Competitors' Challenge, Announces Ambitious Restructuring Plan,'' *Oil Daily,* June 14, 1995, pp. 1+.

Fox, Loren, ''Nimbler Sun Co.'s Restructuring Moves Spark Improved Earnings, Stock Price,'' *Wall Street Journal,* May 12, 1997, p. A9B.

Kovski, Alan, ''Sun to Rely on Acquisitions, Internal Growth to Continue on Path Toward Ambitious Goals,'' *Oil Daily,* May 11, 1998.

Roberts, William L., ''Sun Absorbs a Hit to Regain Its Footing,'' *Philadelphia Business Journal,* November 4, 1991, pp. 1+.

Sullivan, Allanna, ''Sun and Oryx Unveil Plans to Restructure,'' *Wall Street Journal,* October 4, 1991, p. A4.

Webber, Maura, ''Disappointed by Performance, Sun's CEO Remains Optimistic,'' *Philadelphia Business Journal,* December 13, 1996, pp. 1, 32.

——, ''Sun Co. Is Not Celebrating, but It Is Smiling,'' *Philadelphia Business Journal,* October 27, 1995, pp. 3, 17, 21.

——, ''Sun 'Outsider' Drosdick Is Shaking Things Up,'' *Philadelphia Business Journal,* May 2, 1997, pp. 1, 12.

——, ''Sun's Largest Restructuring Effort to Date Is Already Under Way,'' *Philadelphia Business Journal,* June 2, 1995, pp. 3+.

—Maya Sahafi
—updated by David E. Salamie

Svenska Cellulosa Aktiebolaget SCA

Box 7827
SE-103 97 Stockholm
Sweden
(08) 788 51 00
Fax: (08) 660 74 30
Web site: http://www.sca.se

Public Company
Incorporated: 1929
Employees: 32,082
Sales: SKr 61.27 billion (US$7.45 billion) (1998)
Stock Exchanges: Stockholm London
NAIC: 11311 Timber Tract Operations; 11321 Forest
    Nurseries & Gathering of Forest Products; 321113
    Sawmills; 321999 All Other Miscellaneous Wood
    Product Manufacturing; 322122 Newsprint Mills;
    32213 Paperboard Mills; 322213 Setup Paperboard
    Box Manufacturing; 322211 Corrugated & Solid Fiber
    Box Manufacturing; 322215 Nonfolding Sanitary
    Food Container Manufacturing; 322212 Folding
    Paperboard Box Manufacturing; 322291 Sanitary
    Paper Product Manufacturing

Svenska Cellulosa Aktiebolaget SCA (SCA for short) is one of Europe's leading forestry companies, specializing in absorbent hygiene products, corrugated packaging, and graphic papers. The company owns 4.4 million acres of productive forestlands, conducts sawmill operations, and uses equal amounts of recycled and fresh wood fibers in the products it makes—making it the largest collector and user of recycled paper in Europe. Founded in 1929 by the famed Swedish financier Ivar Kreuger, SCA initially served as a marketing organization for pulp producers in northern Sweden. After transforming itself from a holding company into an integrated forestry concern in 1954, SCA gradually expanded into the areas of newsprint and linerboard over the next two decades. In 1975 the company entered the consumer products field with the purchase of Mölnlycke AB, a manufacturer of fiber-based disposable hygiene products. This marked the start of SCA's increasing concentration on value-added products based on wood and its decreasing activity in traditional forestry products, such as pulp and low-grade paper. This development coincided in the 1980s and 1990s with SCA shifting some of its production from its Swedish homeland to the European mainland through a series of corporate acquisitions. In the 1990s SCA was also a major player in the trend toward worldwide forestry industry consolidation.

Formed in Late 1920s to Market Pulp

The roots of the establishment of SCA lie in the economic problems that hit the Swedish forestry industry in the 1920s. Forestry products, such as timber, pulp, and paper, were the country's largest export items, but their competitive position in the European market was damaged during the 1920s by the government's deflationary monetary policy that boosted the value of the krona. This coincided with strong competition from the U.S.S.R., which was dumping cheap timber products in Europe.

Faced with declining prices and profits, Swedish forestry companies were forced to hypothecate (pledge as security) their fixed assets and stocks to commercial banks when seeking loans. By the late 1920s, Svenska Handelsbanken, then Sweden's largest bank, feared that its lending position to the forestry industry was overexposed and sought ways to reduce its liabilities. It proposed that the Swedish financier Ivar Kreuger, who had gained a virtual monopoly over the production of matches worldwide, should take over its forestry industry holdings.

Kreuger was at first reluctant to accept the Handelsbanken's proposal since it would tie up capital, but, having recently bought several sawmill and pulp companies in the Sundsvall region in northern Sweden, he eventually saw possibilities in combining his forestry holdings with those of Svenska Handelsbanken. The merger would prevent cutthroat competition, reduce production costs, and consequently help raise and stabilize export prices. In addition, Kreuger would acquire several hydroelectric power stations as a result of the deal. His control over the power sources for the pulp and paper industry would also improve profitability.

Company Perspectives:

Qualitative growth and international expansion for Hygiene Products and Packaging.

In 1929 SCA was created with Svenska Handelsbanken selling its forestry shares to Kreuger's investment company, Kreuger & Toll, mainly on credit. SCA was designed to be a holding company to sell the pulp produced by its ten subsidiaries in northern Sweden. The companies that made up SCA included Bergvik & Ala, Skönvik, Sund, Trävaru Svartvik, Nyhamns Cellulosa, Torpshammars, Björknäs Nya Sågverks, Salsåkers Ångsågs, and Holmsund & Kramfors. The tenth company, Munksund, was added in 1934. SCA was Europe's largest forestry company, a position that it would maintain until the mid-1980s. At the time of its formation, it accounted for almost a third of Sweden's total pulp exports.

The SCA combine amounted to a loose confederation with each member company having its own president and board of directors as well as administrative control over finance, sales outside of pulp, and forest management. Svenska Handelsbanken retained its role as primary lender to SCA and most of its member companies, and their shares were hypothecated to the bank.

The first few years of SCA's existence were devoted to rationalizing its operations and constructing Europe's largest and most modern cellulose plant at Östrand. The large investment costs meant that the company did not pay a dividend for the years 1930 and 1931. The following year SCA faced its first serious crisis with the suicide of Kreuger, an event that triggered the collapse of Kreuger & Toll. The value of SCA's share capital dropped from SKr 100 million to SKr 4 million and Handelsbanken assumed control of SCA by purchasing its shares from the bankrupt investment company. Lacking experience in managing industrial concerns, Handelsbanken then sold most of its interest in SCA in 1934 to the Swedish industrialist Axel Wenner-Gren, the founder of the household appliance company Electrolux.

But Handelsbanken continued to play a supervisory role as the main creditor to SCA. The company's performance under the chairmanship of Wenner-Gren was lackluster, and Handelsbanken grew concerned about the company's ability to repay its debts. In 1941 the bank forced Wenner-Gren to sign an agreement that reduced the nominal share capital from SKr 30 million to SKr 10 million and converted SKr 40 million of the company's assets to new shares that would be held by Handelsbanken, thus giving it majority control over SCA. The timing of the deal was fortunate since the United States was threatening to place SCA on a trade blacklist and freeze its assets in the United States because of Wenner-Gren's suspected business ties with Nazi Germany. Handelsbanken's assumption of control prevented this from happening.

Handelsbanken used its controlling stake to carry out a reorganization of the company by consolidating the activity of each of its subsidiaries in the river valley where it was most dominant. It then decided to sell some of the subsidiaries to improve the company's financial position, with Bergvik & Ala and Hammarsforsens Kraft, a hydroelectric power company, being divested in 1943. Handelsbanken bought the remainder of Wenner-Gren's shareholding in SCA in 1947 and the company became a subsidiary of the bank.

Public, Integrated Forestry Firm Following World War II

The change in ownership coincided with a buoyant market for the forestry industry in the early postwar period, with prices hitting a peak during the Korean War boom of 1950–51. As a result, SCA finally managed to free itself from debt. In 1950 Handelsbanken decided the time was right to reap profits from its long-term involvement in SCA by introducing most of the company's shares on the Stockholm Stock Exchange. But SCA's ties with Handelsbanken have remained close ever since, with the bank continuing to act as prime lender to SCA and maintaining a representative on the board of directors.

Axel Enström, who became SCA president in 1950, charted a new corporate strategy by promoting closer cooperation among the company's various subsidiaries. This led to a full-scale merger of their activities in 1954, which transformed SCA from a holding company into a single integrated forestry concern.

During the 1950s and 1960s, SCA greatly expanded its activity from its traditional area of pulp and sawn timber into paper production, primarily newsprint and kraft paper, kraft liner, and corrugated board. Between 1959 and 1969, pulp production increased from 690,000 tons to 1.1 million tons, while paper production jumped from 160,000 tons to 600,000 tons, despite a reduction in the number of mills from 11 to eight. Revenues during this period climbed from SKr 375 million to SKr 825 million.

Moved into Value-Added Products in the Mid-1970s

The appointment of Bo Rydin as SCA president in 1972 marked the beginning of a new period for the company. In 1974 Rydin decided to diversify the company into value-added fiber-based products. A year later SCA purchased Mölnlycke, which had been founded in 1849 as a Swedish spinning and weaving business but had been transformed into a manufacturer of disposable hygienic products in the 1950s.

By 1979, when it celebrated its 50th anniversary, SCA's activities covered all segments of the forestry industry, from raw materials to consumer products. It was Europe's largest private forest owner with 1.7 million hectares (4.2 million acres) of forest land, equivalent to half the size of Switzerland, which provided 60 percent of the company's timber needs, a high level of self-sufficiency by international standards. Its six mills, which produced 1.3 million tons of pulp and 1.1 million tons of paper, were powered by the company's own hydroelectric stations run by the Bålforsens Kraft AB (BÅKAB) subsidiary. The mills were equipped with pulp and paper machinery produced by another SCA subsidiary, Sunds Defibrator. Pulp and paper accounted for half of SCA's sales of SKr 5.965

billion in 1979, and Mölnlycke was responsible for 30 percent of sales, with BÅKAB, Sunds Defibrator, and packaging companies making up the rest.

The 1980s were characterized by three major developments: a rapid increase in sales, growing internationalization through the purchase of several important European companies, and a reduced dependence on pulp and paper production combined with an emphasis on higher-value products. The company's diversification program during the early 1980s concentrated on increasing the number of its corrugated board operations in Sweden and the rest of Europe. Average annual output by these companies reached 750,000 tons by the mid-1980s, providing a captive market for 40 percent of SCA's production of linerboard, which is used as the outer surface of corrugated containers. SCA became Europe's largest linerboard producer in 1985 when it assumed majority ownership of Obbola Linerboard, a joint venture it had established with the U.S. St. Regis Paper Company in 1973.

Meanwhile, SCA was concentrating its pulp and paper production at four mills, with an average capacity of 300,000 tons, although its largest facility, the Ortviken newsprint plant, had a capacity of 600,000 tons. SCA then accounted for 25 percent of Sweden's total newsprint production. It also curtailed the production of pulp for outside consumers, its original business, with only five percent of its pulp being sold to third parties in the mid-1980s compared with 75 percent in the 1960s. This was designed to reduce its exposure to the sharp fluctuations in the world pulp market.

By the mid-1980s Mölnlycke had become the market leader for disposable consumer hygiene products—such as diapers and female hygiene goods—in Scandinavia and the Benelux countries and was Europe's leading supplier of disposable hygiene products to hospitals and industrial users. Bolstered by a cyclical upturn in the global forestry industry, SCA's sales almost doubled from SKr 6.7 billion in 1980 to SKr 12.6 billion in 1985, while profits before extraordinary items climbed from SKr 688 million to SKr 1.3 billion during the same period, reaching a peak of SKr 1.5 billion in 1984.

In 1987 SCA signaled its determination to expand beyond Scandinavia by raising SKr 1 billion through a new share issue to fund an acquisition spree for hygiene and packaging companies on the European continent. In January 1988 it purchased Peaudouce, France's leading disposable diaper producer, for SKr 2 billion in a move to strengthen Mölnlycke's market position in Europe and build up its consumer products sector, where profits were higher and more stable than in the traditional forestry products area.

Under its new president Sverker Martin-Löf, SCA then turned its attention to the corrugated board sector. It acquired Italcarta, Italy's largest corrugated board manufacturer, in July 1988, followed by a number of other corrugated board manufacturers, among them Bowater Containers, Belgium. With the Italcarta deal, SCA for the first time was consuming more linerboard than it was producing itself, thereby no longer having to sell linerboard on the open market. Its position as a net consumer of linerboard also would protect the company against a drop in demand.

While SCA was limiting its production of pulp and linerboard to in-house needs, it also decided to reduce its production of newsprint at the Ortviken facility in favor of lightweight coated paper. This move toward the production of high-quality printing paper was confirmed with the purchase of a majority shareholding in Laakirchen, an Austrian producer of magazine paper, in October 1988. The deal extended SCA's range to cover all grades of printing paper. Control of Laakirchen also made SCA a leading producer of tissue paper in Europe.

1990s Marked by Additional Acquisitions

The desire to broaden its international production base led to SCA's £1.05 billion purchase of the U.K. firm Reedpack in June 1990. The deal not only bolstered SCA's position as a leading European producer of corrugated boxes, but also made it a major producer of newsprint using recycled wastepaper. SCA's gradual shift from manufacturing newsprint from virgin fiber in Sweden to using recycled wastepaper gathered from Europe's cities reflected the increasing importance played by recycling in papermaking. The need to have access to wastepaper and to site manufacturing facilities close to consumers was one reason that SCA moved its operations near major population centers in Europe.

In late 1990 SCA turned its attention back to Sweden. It became the dominant shareholder in the country's third largest forestry concern, Mo och Domsjö (MoDo). The strategic alliance was forged to promote collaboration in printing, paper production, and joint investments in paper mills. Although SCA controlled slightly more than half of MoDo, there were no immediate plans to merge the two companies to form a concern that would rival Sweden's Stora, Europe's largest pulp and paper company, in size.

SCA's acquisition spree in Europe and the transformation of its product mix toward higher-value-added consumer products forced the company to divest some subsidiaries that were once considered central to its traditional activities in pulp and newsprint. In 1990 it completed the sale of its pulp machinery company Sunds Defibrator to Rauma-Repola in Finland. SCA also mortgaged half of its BÅKAB hydroelectric assets to the Swedish government-affiliated National Pension Funds to raise SKr 5 billion for new investments. In early 1991 it sold the tissue operations acquired from Laakirchen, as well as several units of Reedpack. SCA in 1992 exited from the energy sector entirely through the divestment of BÅKAB. These and other, smaller divestitures helped to ease the company's debt burden, which had increased substantially with the Reedpack acquisition. SCA's debt had reached 154 percent of equity in the wake of that purchase but by 1994 had been cut to 52 percent.

In late 1993 SCA entered into a joint venture with the South African Minorco and Mondi Paper groups to construct a massive £250 million (US$370 million) plant in Aylesford, England (just south of London), to make newsprint using recycled paper as the raw material. In 1994 the company entered into a preliminary agreement to acquire nearly 90 percent of Otor Holding, a leading French packaging company, but the sides were not able to reach a final agreement on terms. In late 1994 SCA took full control of a joint venture, Scott Health Care, it had set up with Scott Paper Co. of the United States in 1992. Philadelphia-based Scott Health Care specialized in adult incontinence and wound care products.

The worldwide paper industry began an era of intense consolidation in the mid-1990s. The trend was fueled by extreme downswings and upswings—extreme even for a typically volatile industry. During 1993–94 paper companies suffered through a severe downturn, with SCA's operating profit falling to SKr 2.17 billion in 1993 and to SKr 1.81 billion in 1994. During the next year the industry enjoyed one of its best years since World War II, and SCA saw its profits skyrocket to SKr 7.35 billion, while net sales nearly doubled from SKr 33.68 billion to SKr 65.32 billion. A significant portion of these increases, however, stemmed from the company's purchase of a 75 percent controlling stake in PWA, which had been the largest publicly traded pulp and paper company in Germany. SCA spent about SKr 7.5 billion (US$1.02 billion) in early 1995 through two separate transactions to gain the stake. This deal temporarily vaulted SCA past Stora into first place among European forest industries groups (later in 1995 Finland's two biggest forestry groups merged to form UPM-Kymmene Corp., a combination even larger than SCA-PWA). By late 1997 SCA had taken over PWA entirely. The acquisition of PWA significantly bolstered SCA's position in both packaging and tissues, while it also expanded SCA's activities into two new sectors: graphic and specialty decorative papers. The purchase, which was in large part debt financed, also increased SCA's debt load to about 70 percent of equity. The reason this ratio was not increased even more was that nearly simultaneous with its buyout of PWA, SCA sold its stake in MoDo since the alliance between the two Swedish firms was largely unsuccessful.

By mid-1996 the forestry industry had entered into another downturn, with pulp prices having fallen by nearly half from the level of late 1995. More consolidations and asset swaps followed. In late 1996 SCA swapped its French diaper brand Peaudouce for Kimberly-Clark's tissue plant in Prudhoe, England, and a ten-year license to use the Kleenex brand on tissue sold in the United Kingdom and Ireland. SCA also made a number of moves to beef up its packaging operations, aiming for a 20 percent share of the European corrugated board market. In 1996 the company acquired three Italian board producers. In August 1997 it spent SKr 970 million (US$122.6 million) to purchase the Italian packaging group Cochis. SCA in early 1999 paid SKr 2.6 billion (US$329.5 million) for the corrugated board business of the U.K. company Rexam and SKr 636 million (US$80.6 million) for Danapak Papemballage, the third largest corrugated board firm in Denmark. SCA also expanded aggressively in central and eastern Europe, spending about SKr 300 million (US$36.5 million) to open 14 packaging plants in the region. In early 1999 the company announced that it would double that investment over the next five years. At the end of 1998, SCA held 14 percent of the European corrugated board market.

SCA's results for 1998 were strong, with net sales of SKr 61.27 billion (US$7.45 billion) and operating profits of SKr 6.43 billion (US$781.8 million). At the time SCA touted itself as an integrated paper company with three key areas of activity: absorbent hygiene products, corrugated packaging, and graphic papers. In April 1999, however, SCA announced that it had entered into an agreement with MoDo to consolidate their fine paper operations into a new company that would initially be 50–50 jointly owned by the two companies but within two years be listed on the Stockholm Stock Exchange. Fine papers comprised a portion of SCA's graphic papers unit and consisted of three plants—in Stockstadt, Germany; Hallein, Austria; and Wifsta, Sweden—that produced coated and uncoated grades of fine paper for use in magazines and other materials requiring high printing quality, as well as uncoated fine paper for office applications. These assets would be combined with several MoDo plants to form the new MoDo Paper AB (MoDo itself would change its name prior to the exchange listing). MoDo Paper would be the third largest fine paper company in Europe with a market share of about 12 percent. This agreement was yet another step in the consolidation of the global forest products industry. SCA was likely to remain at the center of this continuing trend and participate in additional consolidating activities.

Principal Subsidiaries

SCA Forest and Timber AB; SCA Hygiene Products AB; SCA Hygiene Products AG (Germany); SCA Graphic Paper AB; SCA Fine Paper GmbH (Germany); SCA Packaging Holding BV (Netherlands); SCA Raw Materials and Logistics Europe N.V. (Belgium); AB SCA Finans; SCA Research AB; SCA Försäkrings-Aktiebolag.

Further Reading

Brown-Humes, Christopher, "SCA Tightens Grip on PWA," *Financial Times,* March 4, 1995, p. 11.

——, "Swedes Pull Out of Deal with French Packager," *Financial Times,* April 7, 1994, pp. 1, 18.

——, "Swedish Group's Deal Reinforces Its Paper Empire," *Financial Times,* January 6, 1995, p. 15.

Carnegy, Hugh, "SCA Buys Out Share of US Joint Venture," *Financial Times,* December 29, 1994, p. 14.

Marsh, Peter, "SCA to Boost Investment in Eastern Europe Packaging," *Financial Times,* March 9, 1999, p. 8.

McIvor, Greg, "SCA Offers DM550m for Remainder of PWA," *Financial Times,* August 15, 1997, p. 21.

McIvor, Greg, and Jonathan Ford, "Rexam Sells Corrugated Board Unit for £195m," *Financial Times,* December 22, 1998, p. 21.

Moore, Stephen D., "Cellulosa's Profit Fell 81% in Early 1992: Investors Are Undaunted by Swedish Pulp Firm's Setback," *Wall Street Journal,* June 12, 1992, p. A9B.

——, "Scandinavian Paper Firms Wrestle with Price Declines," *Wall Street Journal,* September 5, 1996, p. B8.

——, "Swedish Mills Seek Alliances Amid Recovery: SCA Joins Offering Blitz to Build Cash for Plan to Retool Paper Plants," *Wall Street Journal,* August 30, 1993, p. A5C.

Reier, Sharon, "Virgin No More: Why Sweden's Svenska Cellulosa Is Betting on Recycled Paper," *Financial World,* March 1, 1994, pp. 34+.

"SCA Focuses on Growth Through Acquisitions," *Paperboard Packaging,* November 1997, pp. 18+.

Utterström, Gustaf, *SCA 50 år: Studier kring ett storföretag och dess föregångare,* Sundsvall: SCA, 1979.

—John Burton
—updated by David E. Salamie

Tarmac

Tarmac plc

Hilton Hall
Essington
Wolverhampton, West Midlands WVII 2BQ
United Kingdom
(01902) 307407
Fax: (01902) 307408
Web site: http://www.tarmac.co.uk

Public Company
Incorporated: 1903 as Tar-Macadam (Purnell Hooley's Patent) Syndicate Limited
Employees: 24,369
Sales: £3.16 billion (US$4.91 billion) (1998)
Stock Exchanges: London
NAIC: 212312 Crushed & Broken Limestone; 212313 Crushed & Broken Granite Mining & Quarrying; 212319 Other Crushed & Broken Stone Mining & Quarrying; 23332 Commercial & Institutional Building Construction; 23411 Highway & Street Construction; 23491 Water, Sewer, & Pipeline Construction; 23499 All Other Heavy Construction; 23591 Structural Steel Erection Contractors; 324121 Asphalt Paving Mixtures & Block Manufacturing; 32731 Cement Manufacturing; 327331 Concrete Block & Brick Manufacturing; 32739 Other Concrete Product Manufacturing; 32732 Ready-Mix Concrete Manufacturing; 327991 Cut Stone & Stone Product Manufacturing; 54133 Engineering Services; 56121 Facilities Support Services

Tarmac plc is one of the leading heavy building materials and construction services groups in Europe, with additional operations in North America, southeast Asia, and the Pacific Rim. In the building materials sector, the company is a leading supplier of asphalt, crushed rock, sand, gravel, ready-mix concretes, mortars, specialist concrete, and precast concrete products. In construction, Tarmac is the largest building contractor in the United Kingdom, with additional operations in civil engineering, railway engineering, and major projects in the process, water, energy, and infrastructure sectors. In early 1999 Tarmac announced its intention to demerge these two business streams into two separately traded public companies, with the heavy building materials side retaining the Tarmac name.

Founded Through Invention of Tarmac

In 1901 the county surveyor of Nottingham, E. Purnell Hooley, noticed a dustless, unrutted patch of road as he was leaving an iron works. Inquiries revealed that a barrel of tar had burst and the spillage had been covered with slag. Immediately grasping its potential, Hooley began to experiment. A British patent for the process of mixing tar with slag was obtained in 1903, and by the middle of the year a length had been laid in an area where traffic was particularly heavy. In the following year a local newspaper, the *Newark Advertiser,* reported that the area was "as good today as when new." The new material was christened "tarmac."

In conjunction with John Parker, Hooley incorporated Tar-Macadam (Purnell Hooley's Patent) Syndicate Limited in June 1903 and became its chairman. Despite the support of the natural roadstone industry, for whom Hooley's invention was simply a profitable way of selling aggregate, the syndicate began to fail. An agreement with Alfred Hickman Ltd., a large iron works, forced Parker and Hooley to relinquish a large part of their holding in exchange for an injection of capital by Hickman. In 1905 Hickman took control and changed the syndicate's name to Tarmac Limited. Parker resigned, but Hooley was retained as a consultant on a large fee.

With increased use of automobiles at the beginning of the century, the road covering industry boomed. Unlike all its competitors, Tarmac Ltd. confined itself to one product: tarmac. When D.G. Comyn was made secretary in 1908, Tarmac was well established within the road building and slag industries. To raise capital for the expansion of its transport stock, the company was liquidated and the assets transferred to a new company. Tarmac Ltd. was reregistered under the same name in 1913.

Tarmac's profits fell by 25 percent during World War I, as a result of cuts in government road expenditure. Comyn's friendship with the head of the government's road board led to Tarmac's being given contracts to supply the crushed slag needed to build roads through French battlefields. Newly erected works in Yorkshire were handed over for military use, the acute labor shortage being compensated for by several hundred German prisoners of war.

By 1918 Tarmac was drawing up plans for large-scale expansion. The intention to build crushed-slag depots and adjacent tarmac plants on the south coast, owing to a fear of overproduction of slag in the northeast, was thwarted by the high cost of sea freight. Comyn was, however, generally optimistic about postwar demand, having determined government plans to increase road expenditure. In 1919 the company bought existing slag tips in the Midlands and erected new coating plants nearby. Tarmac's first natural stone quarry, Ffrith in North Wales, was acquired in 1919 but was never developed and was sold in 1951. In 1919 the company also began diversification within the construction industry. The acquisition of the patent on Vinculum, a process for binding the raw materials of concrete using waste slag dust, led to a contract to build houses in Wolverhampton and Birmingham, and the Vinculum division was established.

The 1920s began with extensive geographical and production capacity expansion. This heavy spending on acquisitions and expansion of railroad stock created a need for more capital. At the same time, prices of tarmac were falling despite a sharp increase in the cost of tar caused in large part by the occupation of the Ruhr, which was a major source of this substance. Comyn refused to raise the price of tarmac, believing that the company and his business connections were sufficiently established to survive a period of poor sales, while Tarmac's smaller competitors would fail. Comyn retired in 1926, because of ill health, in the only year that Tarmac made a loss, until 1992.

Expanded into Civil Engineering Between the Wars

Comyn's successor, Cecil Martin, reacted to the decline in sales by halving directors' salaries and reducing head office staff numbers by 20 percent. The company was reorganized and in 1929 a civil engineering division was established. It engaged in road construction and the building of military airfields. An experiment in shipping precoated tarmac from northeast plants to Gravesend was unsuccessful, and it was decided to revert to

Comyn's plans to build coating plants on the south coast. Preemption by Tarmac's largest rival, Crow Catchpole, which it later acquired, left Tarmac owning only three seaboard plants and with too much slag to dispose of. A series of convoluted deals with rival companies averted potentially crippling losses.

The early 1930s proved to be a stable period for Tarmac. A new product, Settite (bitumen macadam), believed to be superior to slag-based tarmac for road covering, was introduced in 1932. Diversifications into gravel and asphalt production were not successful, but were compensated for by the new spirit of camaraderie among mutually dependent industries. An important feature of this period was the price cooperation among blacktop producers. Whereas Comyn had sought to outwit his competitors, Martin favored a more amicable approach and was respected in the industry as a man of integrity. His efforts to help create a federation of slag producers in 1934 were rewarded eventually by a price agreement that guaranteed profits on the northeast slag plants. This brought new and lucrative contracts to the company.

By 1935 Tarmac's three divisions—roadstone, civil engineering, and Vinculum—were well established, although the company image was still predominantly that of a slag business. Whereas World War I had been difficult for Tarmac, World War II infused new life into the company. The occupation of France presaged the need for more airports in the United Kingdom, and Tarmac gained contracts from the U.S. Army and Air Force. Since military demand for tarmac was greater than for asphalt, the company's profits rose by more than 30 percent in the first year of the war, and by 43 percent in the second. By this time, the company had plants in northern England, north Wales, and Scotland, as well as a large transport stock. The increased mechanization of its plants compensated for the labor shortage. The civil engineering division won government contracts of £6 million and produced five million tons of road and runway material during the war. The Vinculum division also benefited from government demand for concrete blocks to build air raid shelters.

Despite steadily declining orders after August 1944, Tarmac anticipated an upsurge in demand as a result of the government's rearmament program. Tarmac consequently embarked on a £2 million program of reinvestment and development. New plants were commissioned in Yorkshire in 1949, existing plants were reconstructed and mechanized, and the transport stock was entirely replaced.

Postwar Expansion

In 1954 the company pursued considerable and risky expansion. A new iron foundry was being built in the northeast, and Tarmac proposed to build a massive works, including a wharf for ships of up to 3,000 tons, to deal with the slag produced. In the same year the company stepped up its transport conversion program, replacing railwagons with trucks. With the promise of a contract in 1956 to build Britain's first, eight-mile stretch of motorway, Tarmac was in need of capital. A rights issue raised £1 million to pay for this growth.

Cecil Martin decided to retire on his 65th birthday in 1957. No chairman was appointed during the period of reorganization that followed Martin's retirement, although his son, Robin, was made managing director of the roadstone division. It was decided to make Tarmac into a holding company with three main subsidiaries: Tarmac Roadstone, Tarmac Civil Engineering, and Tarmac Vinculum. Most of the group's profits came from Tarmac Roadstone. Robin Martin, who managed the subsidiary, had inherited a sound business, albeit one with geographical gaps and no natural stone resources.

A proposed merger of Tarmac and its largest rivals, Amalgamated Roadstone Corporation and Crow Catchpole—a large London-based tar distiller—broke down in 1958, but Tarmac bought Crow Catchpole the following year. With a toehold in London and the southeast, Tarmac entered another phase of growth. The acquisition of Tarslag, a major Midlands-based road materials company, marked Tarmac's first major quarrying venture, and the company rapidly became one of the three largest quarry owners in the Midlands. The consequent boost to Tarmac's construction activities led to the formation in 1960 of an industrial division. Further expansion was restricted during this period to allow the company to focus on internal restructuring and the formation of a series of localized construction teams.

Robin Martin became group managing director in 1963, when the worst winter weather in 100 years threatened to slow considerably the output of all Tarmac's divisions. Strains on finance and problems with integration of Tarmac's divided structure, coupled with government cuts in roadwork expenditure, dampened the optimism of the early 1960s. In anticipation of a decline in the availability of slag, Tarmac sought to strengthen its quarrying resources. The group's overdependence on slag sales was relieved by the acquisition, in 1966, of three large granite quarries in the north. Having secured the market for natural stone, Tarmac concentrated on procuring supplies of bitumen, its other main raw material. The opening in conjunction with Phillips Petroleum of Oklahoma of a refinery in Cheshire secured Tarmac's supply of bitumen. In 1968 the company merged with Derbyshire Stone and William Briggs, a large bitumen and building materials supplier and contractor in Scotland. Over the decade, group profits increased sixfold.

Diversified Further in the 1970s

With Tarmac's 1971 takeover of Limmer and Trinidad Limited, a London-based quarry products business with an asphalt lake in Trinidad, it became the largest road surfacing contractor and blacktop producer in the United Kingdom. The acquisition of Limmer marked the beginning of another period of diversification, particularly in Tarmac's quest to develop strength in the brick and concrete production markets. A growing need for a wider range of aggregates, including sand and gravel, and the acquisitions of several large hybrid companies, precipitated another company reorganization. The existing roadstone and bitumen divisions were renamed quarry products and building products, to reflect more accurately their activities. Two new divisions were formed from the construction division, and by the middle of the 1970s Tarmac was operating in five divisions: quarry products, building products, construction, properties and housing, and international. The regrouping reflected not only a new administrative strategy, but also an attempt to change Tarmac's image. Known traditionally as a road surfacing contractor and producer of blacktop, the company was keen to reaffirm its position as a broad-based construction and building materials producer.

The company's activities during the 1970s are difficult to evaluate. It was a period of dramatic expansion against a background of economic instability in Britain. The housing and properties division was established in 1974, following the acquisition of John McLean and Sons Limited, a leading housebuilder, the previous year. Within a few years, and without any major acquisitions, Tarmac became the third largest housebuilder in Britain. Eric Pountain, chairman of the Tarmac group, joined the company as chief executive of McLeans and became chief executive of the housing division. Under his leadership and with a policy of slow expansion and rigid financial controls, the housing division thrived. By the end of the decade one-third of Tarmac's profits came from housebuilding. The division became the management model for the rest of the company and set the precedent for the decentralization program at the end of the decade. The housing division prospered despite adverse economic conditions. The construction division continued its program of rapid expansion and diversification throughout the 1970s.

On the other hand, with the potential for growth in the United Kingdom restricted by the threat of recession, Tarmac began bidding for companies with established assets overseas. Having developed specialist construction skills in marine, soft, and rock tunneling with the takeovers of Mitchell Construction and Kinear Moodie in 1971, Tarmac seemed well placed to expand abroad. The new international division was set up to oversee the group's foreign projects. Few of the construction division's efforts on this front were successful, and it was not until the mid-1980s that the division began to recover from the ill effects of entering too many high-risk ventures abroad. The acquisition of the Holland Hannen and Cubitts construction company in 1976 was a cautionary event in Tarmac's history of foreign investment; Cubitts Nigeria, a failing African asset that had been overlooked at the time of acquisition, had to be sold off. It cost Tarmac £16 million.

Despite a successful joint venture with the Egyptian company Arab Contractors in 1977 to build a tunnel under the Suez Canal and participation in a long-term international consortium on an irrigation scheme in Peru, Tarmac withdrew from most of its overseas projects, having incurred several significant losses. By the end of the decade the performance of the construction division was threatening the stability of the Tarmac group. The company's growing dependence on its housing and quarry products divisions at a time when the almost static British economy was adversely affecting the construction industry precipitated a dramatic fall in share price in 1977.

Key Reorganization Launched in 1979

On balance, the events of the 1970s, although potentially disastrous for Tarmac, prompted the reorganization that made the company the largest in its field in the United Kingdom by the late 1980s. After a purge of top management in 1979, Eric Pountain was appointed chief executive of the Tarmac group. He had distinguished himself as director of the housing division and it generally was accepted that the growth of this division, despite an unfavorable economy, was almost entirely attributable to Pountain's management style and commitment to decentralization. He was the only director with previous experience as chief executive of a public company. He had joined Tarmac, he said, to make a big business work like a small business. Pountain's was an attitude strongly endorsed by Prime Minister Margaret Thatcher's government when it came to power in 1979. In 1985 Pountain was knighted, in recognition of his determination that Tarmac succeed despite the precarious economy of the early 1980s.

The most significant change at Tarmac under Pountain's leadership was the implementation of the decentralization program. Convinced that the company's difficulties in the previous decade were the result of poor management, Pountain implemented the strategy that made the housing division Britain's largest housebuilder ten years after its inception. Believing that divisional managers were better placed to assess prospective acquisitions than a board of directors, responsibility for growth and diversification was handed down to individual divisions. Decentralized organization clearly benefited the company, with profits increasing tenfold over the decade.

Reluctant to depend on domestic markets alone, and in view of the slow growth potential for the construction and quarrying industries in the United Kingdom, Tarmac in 1980 embarked on an expensive and ambitious program of acquisitions and development in the United States. The acquisition of the Hoveringham Group in 1981 marked the company's entry into the brick, tile, building block, and concrete markets. Hoveringham owned quarries in the United States and its takeover gave Tarmac a firm quarrying base in the United States. The £150 million acquisition of Lone Star Industries' ready-mix and concrete block plants in Florida in 1984, and the takeover of a large underwater limestone quarry at Pennsuco, gave Tarmac control of ten percent of Florida's total aggregate, or natural stone, output. With a source of stone assured, the company began buying ready-mix concrete and brick-building plants throughout the southern states. In 1986 Tarmac paid £263 million for a 60 percent share in Lone Star Industries, and the following year Tarmac America was established. Several smaller plant and quarry acquisitions followed, giving Tarmac a significant standing in the U.S. aggregates and concrete industries. Nevertheless, falling oil prices in Texas and severe weather conditions in Virginia in the late 1980s disrupted Tarmac America's activities and by the end of the decade the division represented only one-fifth of the group's total turnover.

Over the same period the housing division increased its output from 4,000 homes in 1980 to 11,000 in 1987, contributing with the quarry products division more than three-quarters of the group's turnover. Diversification within the building products division led to the creation of the industrial products division with roofing, construction, and oil interests in both the United Kingdom and the United States.

Sharp Downturn, Major Restructurings Marked the 1990s

By the late 1980s Tarmac's diversification strategy of the previous 20 years had given the company a leading presence in many industrial sectors. At the same time, however, the company's expansion into the U.K. housing market and its broad expansion in the United States turned nearly disastrous after the U.K. and U.S. construction markets collapsed in the late 1980s. The company's policy of decentralization also proved troublesome as central management was unable to respond quickly to the property recession and pull-back on land purchases for housing and commercial property joint ventures. The result was a 1992 pretax loss of £350.3 million, the largest ever recorded in the U.K. construction industry—a deep downfall from the heady days of 1988, when Tarmac posted pretax profits of £393 million. Early in that dark year of 1992, Neville Simms was appointed chief executive, having previously served as head of the construction division. Pountain remained nonexecutive chairman until early 1994, when John Banham took over that position.

Simms was charged with restructuring the company and fixing a balance sheet that had become dangerously debt-loaded. Tarmac's new strategy would involve a concentration on three core areas: housebuilding, construction, and quarry products. A number of peripheral businesses were sold off; by early 1994, 21 businesses had been divested, representing nearly £1 billion in turnover. Among the jettisoned operations were the commercial property development activities. By mid-1995 Tarmac also had exited from brick making. Through severe cost-containment efforts and the divestment program, the company was able to effect a substantial reduction in debt, cutting it from £677 million. The company also reinstated a greater degree of central control over investments by its units.

Tarmac's results improved to an aftertax loss of £58.8 million in 1993, followed by an aftertax profit of £74.7 million in 1994. Nonetheless, the company was barely profitable in 1995 and 1996, and even more dramatic changes were to come as management attempted to turn the group's fortunes around. In August 1995 Tarmac announced that it would sell its housebuilding division to concentrate on its building materials and other construction activities. Then in November of that year Tarmac and George Wimpey PLC, a U.K. housebuilding firm, reached an agreement on a £600 million asset swap, completed in March 1996, whereby Tarmac exchanged its housing division for Wimpey's quarrying and contracting businesses. Through this one deal, Tarmac was able to exit from a sector that had nearly caused its collapse, while at the same time bolster its two remaining core areas. Wimpey Minerals was one of the leading producers of U.K. construction materials and was the fifth largest aggregates producer and fifth largest coated stone producer in the United Kingdom. The unit also had significant operations in the United States, and smaller operations in the Republic of Ireland, the Czech Republic, the Middle East, and the Far East. Wimpey Minerals had revenues of £266.1 million and operating profits of £6.4 million in 1994. Wimpey Construction was one of the leading construction businesses in the United Kingdom, engaging in a wide range of building and civil engineering activities, with overseas activities in Canada and the Middle East. In 1994 the unit generated revenues of £667.7 million while posting an operating loss of £10.5 million. Soon after the swap, Tarmac cut more than 1,400 jobs from its workforce in a rapid rationalization of the merged businesses.

Tarmac returned to more robust profitability in 1997 and 1998, posting aftertax profits of £80.7 million and £92 million, respectively. Pressure from shareholders concerned over a falling stock price, coupled with a trend toward consolidation in the building materials industry, led to discussions in late 1998 between Tarmac and rival U.K. building materials firm Aggregate Industries about a merger to create one of the largest U.K. building materials companies. These talks made substantial progress, including a plan to spin off Tarmac's construction division following the merger, but in December 1998 the deal fell apart, due in part to disagreements over Simms's role in what would have been called Tarmac Aggregate International. The acrimonious end to the proposal led to further shareholder rancor.

Continuing to feel pressure to increase shareholder value, the company responded in February 1999 with an announcement of a proposed demerger of its two core areas—heavy building materials and construction services—into two separately traded public companies. Retaining the Tarmac plc name would be the heavy building materials unit, with Banham as nonexecutive chairman and Roy Harrison, head of the unit, becoming chief executive. Simms would serve as chairman and chief executive of the new construction services company. Tarmac would thus exit the 1990s a much slimmer and more focused company than the one that had entered the decade.

Principal Subsidiaries

GROUP CENTRE: Tarmac International (Investments) Limited; Tarmac International Holdings BV (Netherlands); Tarmac France (Jersey) Limited; Tarmac Industrial Products Limited; Tarmac France S.A. HEAVY BUILDING MATERIALS: Tarmac Heavy Building Materials UK Limited; Tarmac Roadstone Holdings Limited; Tarmac Minerals Limited; Tarmac Quarry Products Limited; Tarmac Topmix Limited; Tarmac Concrete Products Limited; Tarmac Topblock Limited; Tarmac Precast Concrete Limited; Richard Lees Limited; East Coast Slag Products Limited (51%); Midland Quarry Products Limited (50%); Cambrian Stone Limited (51%); Tarmac Routes et Carrières S.A. (France); Tarmac Materiaux de Construction S.A. (France; 95.3%); Soprefa S.A. (France); Etablissements Hecquet, S.A. (France); Tarmac Materiaux de Construction (Belgique) S.A. (Belgium); Ain Agglo SA (France); Tarmac Fleming Quarries Limited (Ireland); Tarmac Severokamen A.S. (Czech Republic; 73%); Tarmac Asphalt Hong Kong Limited (80%); Tarmac Pusheng Bitumen Concrete Co. Limited (China; 60%); Tarmac America, Inc. (U.S.A.); Wroclawskie Kopalnie Surowcow Mineralnych s.a. (Poland). CONSTRUCTION SERVICES: Tarmac Construction Limited; Tarmac Professional Services Limited; Crown House Engineering Limited; Sovereign Harbour Limited; Tarmac International Limited; The Expanded Piling Company Limited; Tarmac Construction Overseas Limited; Tarmac Construction (Contracts) Limited; Centrac Limited; Schal International Management Limited; Pasco International Limited; Stanger Limited; TPS Consult Limited; Tarmac Services Limited; Cimage Enterprise Systems Limited; TPS Consult Asia Limited (Hong Kong); Stanger Asia Limited (Hong Kong); Tarmac (PFI) Limited; Nord France Travaux Publics S.A. (France); Tarmac BTP S.A. (France); Tarmac Canada, Inc.

Further Reading

Davidson, Andrew, "Neville Simms," *Management Today,* March 1994, pp. 60–62.

Dyer, Geoff, "Ibstock Acquires Tarmac Brick," *Financial Times,* May 13, 1995, p. 8.

Earle, J.B.F., *Black Top: A History of the British Flexible Roads Industry,* Oxford: Asphalt & Coated Macadam Association, 1974.

——, *A Century of Road Materials: The History of the Roadstone Division of Tarmac Ltd.,* Oxford: Tarmac Ltd., 1971.

Pretzlik, Charles, "Advisers Try to Revive Tarmac Aggregate Deal," *Financial Times,* January 28, 1999, p. 32.

——, "Jealousy Ruins the Construction of a Special Relationship," *Financial Times,* December 16, 1998, p. 25.

——, "Tarmac Rationalises by Splitting Units," *Financial Times,* February 3, 1999, p. 28.

——, "Twin Roles for Simms After Tarmac Split," *Financial Times,* March 17, 1999, p. 21.

"Sir John Banham to Chair Tarmac," *Financial Times,* September 22, 1993, p. 21.

Taylor, Andrew, "Building Blocks But Not Houses," *Financial Times,* August 3, 1995, p. 20.

——, "Investors Test for Firm Foundations," *Financial Times,* November 8, 1996, p. 21.

——, "Preparing to Rebuild on More Substantial Foundations," *Financial Times,* April 28, 1993, p. 23.

——, "Reshaped Tarmac Returns to the Black," *Financial Times,* September 24, 1997, p. 24.

——, "Swap Lays Strong Foundations," *Financial Times,* November 16, 1995, p. 31.

——, "Tarmac and ARC to Merge Quarries," *Financial Times,* November 19, 1996, p. 24.

——, "Tarmac Mounts Swift Revamp," *Financial Times,* September 25, 1996, p. 30.

——, "Tarmac Sale Plan Deals New Blow to Housing Industry," *Financial Times,* August 3, 1995, p. 1.

——, "Tarmac's Recuperation at a Critical Point," *Financial Times,* November 3, 1993, p. 23.

——, "Tarmac Swaps Tiles for Bricks," *Financial Times,* October 23, 1993, p. 10.

——, "Wimpey and Tarmac Swap Asset Details," *Financial Times,* February 10, 1996, p. 8.

——, "Wimpey and Tarmac Swap Divisions," *Financial Times,* November 16, 1995, p. 27.

—Juliette Bright
—updated by David E. Salamie

Thyssen Krupp AG

August-Thyssen-Strasse 1
40211 Düsseldorf
Germany
(211) 824-1000
Fax: (211) 824-60000
Web site: http://www.thyssenkrupp.com

Public Company
Incorporated: 1999
Employees: 173,000
Sales: DM 70 billion (US$39 billion) (1999 est.)
Stock Exchanges: Frankfurt Düsseldorf London Swiss
NAIC: 23332 Commercial & Institutional Building
Construction; 23331 Manufacturing & Industrial
Building Construction; 331111 Iron & Steel Mills;
331221 Rolled Steel Shape Manufacturing; 331513
Steel Foundries; 33637 Motor Vehicle Metal
Stamping; 333921 Elevator & Moving Stairway
Manufacturing; 333922 Conveyor & Conveying
Equipment Manufacturing; 333512 Machine Tool
Manufacturing; 333319 Other Commercial & Service
Industry Machinery; 336211 Motor Vehicle Body
Manufacturing; 336399 All Other Motor Vehicle Parts
Manufacturing; 336611 Ship Building & Repairing;
54133 Engineering Services; 56121 Facilities Support
Services

Thyssen Krupp AG was created in March 1999 from the merger of two of Germany's oldest industrial giants, Thyssen AG and Fried. Krupp AG Hoesch-Krupp. The fifth largest company in Germany, Thyssen Krupp has five main divisions. Thyssen Krupp Steel is the fifth largest steelmaker in the world and specializes in carbon steel and stainless steel. Thyssen Krupp Automotive is one of the world's top ten auto suppliers, producing parts, components, assemblies, and systems for chassis, body, powertrain, and steering applications. Thyssen Krupp Industries produces elevators, escalators, and conveyors; metal-cutting machine tools; plastics machinery; and industrial bearings, rings, and other components. This division is also involved in shipbuilding and civil engineering. Thyssen Krupp Engineering plans and constructs chemical, cement, and other plants, and creates surface mining systems. Thyssen Krupp Materials & Services is involved in trading, industrial and building services, and project management.

Thyssen's Early History

Thyssen traces its origins to a steel plant in Bruckhausen near Hamborn on the Rhine, which started operations in December 1891 and later formed the core of the Thyssen empire. The plant was built by August Thyssen, a 50-year-old entrepreneur who had already built up a steel and engineering business called Thyssen & Co. August had worked in his father's banking business in Eschweiler and later as a manager-partner of a steel mill, called Thyssen, Fossoul & Co. In 1871, the year of Germany's first unification, he set up his own business at Mulheim in the Ruhr area with 35,000 talers and a paternal grant of the same sum. August Thyssen's business expansion in the 1880s included the purchase of large coal mines. He gradually bought into the Gewerkschaft Deutscher Kaiser coal pits and took the mining company over entirely in 1891. Thyssen & Co.'s Mulheim factories soon became unsuitable for August's expansion plans as the site was too small and lay too far away from a river, which he needed for transport. In 1889 he decided to build the steel plant at Bruckhausen, installing six furnaces using the modern Siemens-Martin technique, and a rolling mill with five trains for the first step. August also wanted to control his own crude steel supplies, building a plant in 1895 in Bruckhausen, which started operations two years later.

August's companies expanded quickly in the years leading up to World War I, securing their own coal and iron ore supplies. His drive for self-sufficiency made him buy into raw materials suppliers in France, North Africa, and Russia. By 1904, August's rolled steel production had hit 700,000 tons a year, putting him ahead of other producers in Germany. The demands made by Germany's military authorities during World War I buoyed Thyssen's business in the same way as other German industries, but Germany's defeat had catastrophic con-

452

sequences for the company. Its foreign property was confiscated, its plants in the Ruhr Valley were put temporarily under French control, and earnings were battered by the postwar hyperinflation.

August's shrunken business empire only became profitable again in late 1924. The octogenarian August concentrated on mechanizing production to cut costs, and initially resisted overtures from other German steel producers to form a cartel. However, Thyssen gave up its independence soon after August's death in 1926, joining four other coal and steel enterprises to form Vereinigten Stahlwerke AG (Vst). Thyssen made up more than a quarter of Vst's paid-up capital of 800 million reichsmarks and Fritz Thyssen became chairman of the supervisory board. Vst was decentralized in 1934; five steel mills in the western part of the Ruhr district were grouped into the August Thyssen-Hütte AG based in Duisburg.

Fritz Thyssen, the elder son of August, is remembered more for his association with Adolf Hitler than for his business skills. Frustrated by his father's long tenure at the head of the company, Fritz channeled his energies into right-wing politics aiming to subvert the Weimar Republic. He became an early supporter of the Nazi party. Fritz later fell out with the Nazis and recanted in a ghostwritten autobiography titled *I Paid Hitler*. He fled Germany in 1939, was captured in Vichy, France, and incarcerated from 1941 to November 1943 in a mental asylum and then until the end of the war in concentration camps. After World War II, Fritz's break with the Nazis was largely accepted by a denazification court, which fined him 15 percent of his German properties. At the end of 1948 he immigrated to Latin America.

Vst and Thyssen's main works, now ATH AG, fared just as badly under the Nazis. The Four Year plan of 1936, devised by Hitler to prepare Germany for war, restricted raw material supplies and made cost-effective production almost impossible. During the war years, ATH, like other German companies, became a supplier to war production, although in 1942 Nazi hard-liners accused the company of defeatism. In autumn 1944, Allied bombing raids destroyed many of ATH's factories, with production in its huge plants ceasing altogether.

Emerged Postwar As August Thyssen-Hütte

Worse was to follow. The victorious Allies allowed limited repairs at ATH's factories, and the first steel mills at Thyssen-Hütte, the main works of ATH, began operating again in October 1945 but only temporarily. In April 1946 the Allies agreed to stop reconstruction while they decided what to do with German industry, which they blamed for arming Hitler. In February 1948 the Allies decided to dismantle Thyssen-Hütte as part of their war reparations from Germany. Factories were detonated or stripped of machinery. The destruction of the Thyssen-Hütte and other works of Vst was only halted in November 1949 with the Petersberg Treaty, an agreement signed between the Allies and the new government of the Federal Republic of Germany. At the same time the Allies broke up the Vst group into 16 successor companies. They also separated the steel companies from their mining firms. All that remained of August Thyssen-Hütte AG was the core business of the former Thyssen Hütte at Hamborn. Nevertheless it restarted

its first blast furnace in 1951. Business improved once the Allies lifted steel production limits one year later.

In May 1953 August Thyssen-Hütte AG was relaunched as a public company with the successors of Fritz Thyssen as minority shareholders. Eventually, a consortium company belonging to the Fritz Thyssen family and the Commerzbank AG and Allianz AG insurance group was created and held a stake in Thyssen of more than 25 percent.

Thyssen's postwar history was dominated by two management board chairmen, Hans-Günther Sohl, who ran the company from 1953 to 1973, and his successor, Dieter Spethmann, who retired in 1991. Sohl rebuilt ATH as Germany's biggest steelmaker and Spethmann presided over its often difficult diversification into new product areas.

ATH flourished in the 1950s on booming steel demand, building new facilities to make flat rolled steel. The company invested some DM 700 million up to 1958 and spent DM 800 million alone on a new Beeckerwerth plant. Thyssen also expanded by buying up companies, taking over four major producers by 1968: Niederrheinische Hütte AG, Deutsche Edelstahlwerke AG, Phoenix-Rheinrohr AG, and Hüttenwerk Oberhausen AG. It also expanded into trading and services by buying into Handelsunion AG from 1960 onward. The future core of the Thyssen Handelsunion AG subsidiary, Handelsunion traded in steel, scrap metal and raw materials, and also offered transport services. Thyssen also forged alliances with other large German steel producers to make production more cost-effective, signing an agreement with Mannesmann in 1970 on steel pipe and rolled steel manufacturing.

Expanding steel output was still the ATH strategy at the beginning of the 1970s, when cheaper imports from newly emerging steel producing companies began to undercut European producers. Thyssen's steel production peaked at 17 million tons in 1974, the same year that the first major steel crisis hit world manufacturers. Like other German producers, Thyssen suffered from 1969 and 1973 revaluations of the deutsche mark, high wage costs, and the imposition of environmental controls. The oil price rise of 1973 delivered another blow to the industry as costs soared and demand shrank.

Thyssen Diversified in the 1970s and 1980s

Thyssen decided to scrap all plans to expand steelmaking capacity and to withdraw from sectors where competitors were undercutting the company's prices. Instead, Thyssen invested in streamlining production and in diversifying away from steel. In 1973–74, Thyssen took over Rheinstahl AG, the group's high technology engineering group which in 1976 was renamed Thyssen Industrie AG. In 1978 Thyssen bought a U.S. car components maker, The Budd Company.

However, these acquisitions initially caused problems. Rheinstahl had a number of steel mills, which increased Thyssen's capacity to 21 million tons a year. The company was forced to close nearly 30 plants in the Thyssen group between 1974 and 1980. The number working in Thyssen's West German steel plants decreased to fewer than 75,000 in 1979 from 85,000 five years earlier. Budd made money for Thyssen in the first two years after the takeover. The second oil crisis in 1979 pitched the U.S. economy into recession and caused heavy losses at Budd; the company only saw a turnaround in 1982. One of the biggest loss makers was Budd's railway equipment division; it had signed four large contracts in 1981 at fixed prices that never covered production costs. The division's workforce was cut to 700 from 2,500. Budd then concentrated on its core auto-components market, cutting its workforce from 21,500 in 1978 to fewer than 12,000 in 1986.

Thyssen's diversifications were continually dogged by the decline of the steel industry. Spethmann was determined to restructure Thyssen using the company's own financial resources. He opposed acceptance of subsidies such as those propping up rival state-owned steelmakers in Belgium, the United Kingdom, and France, but the near-collapse of steel prices forced Thyssen to accept European Community production quotas and subsidies in 1980. The steel crisis continued, however, forcing the creation of Thyssen Stahl AG in 1982 as an independent steel group, in a bid to find partners to help reduce costs. Spethmann made the first of many overtures to archrival Fried. Krupp GmbH for merging production but was rebuffed. Thyssen therefore imposed a tough program of cuts, with a reduction to the 1991 level of 11 million tons capacity from 16 million tons. Losses at Budd and at Thyssen Stahl forced the group to suspend dividend payments for two years in 1982. An improvement in the world economy prompted Thyssen to restart dividend payments at five marks a share, though losses at Thyssen Stahl continued until 1987.

In the 1980s, Thyssen linked its name to high-technology projects in the transport sector. It lead-managed a consortium developing the Transrapid train, capable of speeds of up to 500 kilometers an hour. The Transrapid was sold as a revolutionary form of transport running on a magnetic field rather than on wheels. The train had no engine on board and relied on electromagnetic motors in the track. Thyssen wanted to lay a Transrapid track from the northern port city of Hamburg to Munich in the south, but received government backing only for a smaller pilot track in North Rhine Westfalia state. The government was not entirely convinced that all of Transrapid's technical problems had been solved, and was worried about funding a white elephant project. A bitter row broke out before the government gave approval. Thyssen accused Bonn officials of trying to sabotage the project, which the company wanted to sell abroad.

Thyssen's image suffered in the 1980s when a book was published accusing Thyssen Stahl of malpractices in its treatment of Turkish guest workers. Thyssen successfully contested the book in court, however, and author Günter Wallraff had to delete passages from his bestseller, titled *At the Very Bottom.*

Declining Fortunes for Thyssen in the Early 1990s Led to Restructuring

Taking over Spethmann's chief executive post in 1991 was Heinz Kriwet, who presided over some of the company's darkest days. In the aftermath of the reunification of Germany, Thyssen reacted cautiously, shying away from buying into East Germany's decrepit steel industry. Instead, it concentrated on setting up 27 smaller ventures in the engineering and services sector, involving investments of some DM 500 million. It also signed another 40 cooperation deals with state-owned compa-

nies in the former communist country. The early years of the 1990s also saw Thyssen diversify again, through an entrance into the telecommunications industry, including the formation of an alliance with U.S. telecom firm BellSouth, with the partners hoping to grab a piece of an industry that was in the process of being deregulated in Germany.

Declining steel demand in the early 1990s had a major impact on Thyssen, leading to several years of declining profits before the company posted a net loss of DM 994 million for the 1992–93 fiscal year. During that year the company shed more than 7,000 jobs from its workforce as part of a rationalization program. Thyssen also began aggressively pursuing alliances with other companies in a near desperate attempt to cut costs and reduce losses. The most important of these was a linkup with Fried. Krupp AG Hoesch-Krupp, the new name for Fried. Krupp GmbH after it acquired ailing Rhineland steelmaker Hoesch AG through a hostile takeover. In 1995 Thyssen and Krupp merged their stainless steel operations in a joint venture called Krupp-Thyssen Nirosta, which was 60 percent owned by Krupp and 40 percent owned by Thyssen. Nirosta instantly became the largest stainless-steelmaker in the world, with annual capacity of 1.2 million metric tons and annual revenues of DM 4.5 billion (US$3.2 billion). In September 1995, meanwhile, two great-grandsons of Thyssen's founder, August Thyssen, sold their remaining stakes in the company, thereby severing the final ties between the Thyssen family and the company.

In March 1996 Kriwet took over as chairman of Thyssen, while Dieter Vogel, who had headed up the group's trading and services division, stepped into the chief executive slot. In August 1996 Vogel was arrested—along with nine other Thyssen executives—as part of an investigation into whether Thyssen executives had mishandled DM 73 million (US$49 million) in funds connected to the privatization of a former East German metals trading company. In late 1997 he was formally charged in connection with this investigation. For the year ending in September 1996, Thyssen reported a 36 percent decline in pretax profits. In response to these struggles, the company announced a major restructuring in late 1996 aiming for the withdrawal from or scaling back of activities in noncore areas, including long steel products, defense equipment, and coal and oil trading. Further, after failing in the summer of 1996 to forge a link in the telecommunications sector with Deutsche Bahn, the German national railway, Thyssen scaled back its involvement in that sector. In late 1997 Thyssen sold its stake in a German cellular-phone operator to Veba AG and RWE AG for DM 2.26 billion (US$1.26 billion). Also in 1997 Thyssen merged its shipbuilding operations with those of Preussag AG to form the largest shipbuilding concern in Germany, with annual sales of DM 3.5 billion (US$1.83 billion).

In March 1997 Krupp initiated a hostile takeover of Thyssen, which failed, but led to the late 1997 creation of Thyssen Krupp Stahl, a flat steel joint venture; additional negotiations then resulted in the March 1999 merger of the two companies to form Thyssen Krupp (these events are described in more detail below). Meantime, Thyssen finally appeared to have turned around its financial difficulties—sales were on the rise and net income was a very strong DM 2.19 billion by the 1997–98 fiscal year. The company's renewed focus was evident in its pursuit and completion of several significant acquisitions. In 1997

Thyssen acquired U.S.-based Copper and Brass Sales Inc., a leading trading and service center for nonferrous metals in North America. That same year, Thyssen paid US$675 million to acquire another U.S. firm, Giddings & Lewis Inc., the largest machine-tool maker in the United States. Giddings fit in well with Thyssen's already considerable auto-related operations, since the Fond du Lac, Wisconsin-based firm derived about 40 percent of its revenue from that industrial sector. In early January 1999 Thyssen, through its Thyssen Industries unit, purchased the North American elevator operations of Dover Corporation, including the Dover Elevator brand, for US$1.1 billion. Thyssen was already one of the top elevator firms worldwide, and with the addition of Dover Elevator became one of the top three or four companies in that area.

Krupp's Napoleonic Era Roots

The company that would eventually be known as Fried. Krupp GmbH, and then Fried. Krupp AG Hoesch-Krupp, was established on November 20, 1811, by Friedrich Krupp, member of a family of merchants whose roots in Essen can be traced back to 1587, and his two partners, brothers Georg Carl Gottfried von Kechel and Wilhelm Georg Ludwig von Kechel. They set up a factory for making English cast steel and products manufactured from it. There was a ready market for these products due to Napoleon's Continental Blockade, which prevented imports of cast steel from England. The two partners contributed the metallurgical knowledge, while Friedrich Krupp handled the commercial side and provided the necessary capital. When the steelmaking experiments of the two partners—and later of a third, Friedrich Nicolai—proved unsuccessful, Friedrich Krupp ran the factory on his own from 1816 onwards and developed a process for making high-quality cast steel on a factory scale. His products included cast steel bars, tanner's tools, coining dies, and unfinished rolls. In the years that followed, however, Friedrich Krupp failed to operate the factory at a profit. Competition was severe—particularly from Britain— and while Krupp's prices were too low, his production costs were too high. In addition, product quality varied because, owing to a lack of funds, Krupp occasionally had to use inferior raw materials. Only the family's considerable assets, which in the end were totally consumed, prevented the firm from going bankrupt. When Friedrich Krupp died in 1826, production had almost come to a standstill.

Therese Krupp, his widow, kept the firm going, supported by her relatives and her 14-year-old eldest son, Alfred. With only a few workers at first, the manufacture of cast steel continued. When in 1830 Alfred Krupp started to manufacture finished products, he was able to endorse these with his personal guarantee of quality. Output, however, remained at a low level.

Only after 1834 did the firm experience vigorous expansion. The lifting of customs barriers by the German Customs Union—an agreement between the German states, before their unification, to remove trade barriers between them and create a single economic entity—in 1834 boosted sales, and the purchase of a steam engine, financed by a new partner, helped to make production more cost efficient. Alfred Krupp endeavored above all to perfect the manufacture of high-precision rolls, which he later supplied additionally in rolling machines and rolling mills. Together with his two brothers he developed in the

early 1840s a mill for stamping, rolling, and embossing spoons and forks in one operation. Krupp took numerous journeys to find customers abroad, particularly in France, Austria, and Russia. A long sojourn in England enabled him to widen his knowledge of steelmaking and factory organization.

The firm's expansion did not follow a steady course, mainly because the market for rolls and rolling mills was limited. Further, there was no replacement market, since Krupp's rolls were virtually indestructible. The attempt to establish cutlery factories succeeded only in Austria, where in 1843 Krupp— together with Alexander Schoeller—founded the works at Berndorf near Vienna, which from 1849 onwards was managed by his brother Hermann. The search for new applications for his high-quality but expensive cast steel was unsuccessful at first. The general economic malaise which set in around 1846–47 hit the cast steel works badly. In April 1848 Alfred Krupp, now sole owner, could only save it from ruin by selling off personal assets and then by winning a major order from Russia for cutlery machinery.

Krupp Expanded into Railway Equipment and Cannon-Making in the 1850s

Around 1850 business started to pick up again. The burgeoning of the railways opened up a virtually unlimited market for Krupp's hard-wearing cast steel. Along with axles and springs, the firm's most important product in this field was the forged and rolled seamless railway tire. Invented by Alfred Krupp in 1852–53, this proved able to withstand the increasing track speeds without fracturing. In 1859 the breakthrough into cannon-making was achieved with an order from Prussia for 300 cast-steel cannon-barrel ingots.

To secure sales, Alfred Krupp sought new markets on other continents. He journeyed abroad, established agencies, and participated in international exhibitions. At the Crystal Palace Exhibition held in London in 1851, Krupp displayed a cast-steel cannon barrel which attracted great interest; for a cast-steel ingot weighing approximately 40 hundredweight he received the highest accolade, the Council Medal.

At an early stage Krupp introduced new, economic steelmaking processes, for instance the Bessemer process in 1862 as well as the open-hearth process in 1869. For products that had to be particularly tough, crucible steel remained his most important starting material. It was around this time that Krupp adopted a policy of acquiring ore deposits, coal mines, and iron works to secure the company's rapidly growing requirement of raw materials. With the swift expansion of the company—in 1865 the workforce totaled 8,248 and sales 15.7 million marks—it became necessary to delegate managerial tasks. In 1862 Alfred Krupp established a corporate body of management bearing joint responsibility for the affairs of the firm. His general directive of 1872 laid down the principles to be applied in running his enterprise as well as the social welfare policy to be pursued.

From the outset Alfred Krupp strove to create and maintain a loyal set of highly skilled employees. Only thus could he guarantee the high quality of his products. To alleviate the social problems caused by industrialization he introduced employee welfare schemes, at the same time enjoining his workers not to become involved in trade-union or social-democratic activity. As early as 1836 he set up a voluntary sickness and burial fund, which became a compulsory sickness and death benefit insurance scheme in 1853. In 1855 Alfred Krupp established a pension scheme and in 1858 a company-owned bakery that evolved into the employees' retail store. In 1856 the first hostels were built offering board and lodging to bachelor workers. The year 1861 saw the construction of the first company dwellings for foremen. Worker's housing estates, incorporating schools and branches of a retail store, followed in 1863, and from the early 1870s grew apace. In 1870 a company hospital was established.

In the years up to 1873 the firm continued to expand strongly. However, in the economic slump of 1874 it almost suffered financial collapse because Krupp had raised large bank loans without arranging adequate security. Thereafter the company entered a phase of steady development. The gunnery division was engaged in efforts to develop better field, siege, and naval guns. The divisions producing machinery components, shipbuilding material, and railway equipment were expanded. When Alfred Krupp died in 1887, the firm's employees numbered 20,200 and sales for 1887–88 amounted to 47.5 million marks.

Even during his lifetime Alfred Krupp was known as the Cannon King, mainly because during the Franco-Prussian War of 1870–71 Krupp's cast-steel guns had proved superior to the French bronze cannon. The way the firm presented itself to the public reflected the spirit of the times and for decades the manufacture of guns was given a prominence beyond its actual share of production. In fact, up to 1905 armaments generally accounted for less—and in some cases considerably less—than 50 percent of output; in the years leading up to World War I the proportion was between 50 and 60 percent.

Krupp Acquired Gruson Works and Germania Shipyard in the 1890s

Alfred's only son and heir, Friedrich Alfred Krupp, continued the expansion of the enterprise into a horizontally and vertically integrated concern. Entry into the production of armor plate at the behest of the Imperial Navy led in 1892–93 to the acquisition of the strongest competitor in this field, the Gruson works in Magdeburg. Production of armor plate was then concentrated in Essen while work in Magdeburg focused on the design and construction of plant and machinery.

At the urgings of his directors, as well as of Emperor Wilhelm II and the Imperial Navy, Krupp decided in 1896 to take over the Germania shipyard in Kiel. The plant was leased that year, and acquired in 1902. At this time Admiral Tirpitz, secretary of state for the Imperial Navy, introduced the program for the expansion of the German fleet under the Fleet Acts. The resultant boost to the German shipbuilding industry also benefited the Germania yard where, in addition to merchant vessels, warships clad in Krupp armor plating were now built. The year 1902 saw the building of the experimental submarine *Forelle*, forerunner of the U-boat. At the same time the company began producing diesel engines at the Germania yard, following the development of the first working diesel engine in 1897 by

Rudolf Diesel in collaboration with Krupp and Maschinenfabrik Augsburg.

The construction in 1897 of a large integrated iron and steel works at Rheinhausen strengthened the company's solid footing in iron and steel. A few years later the Thomas process was adopted there for the mass production of steel. Further ore and coal mines were acquired to cover the increasing raw materials requirements. Friedrich Alfred Krupp was particularly interested in the technology of steelmaking. He introduced scientific research into steel at Krupp and thus created the springboard for the successful development of special-steel production.

Friedrich Alfred Krupp expanded the employee welfare and benefit schemes, not only at Essen but also at the outlying works. He widened the scope of the health funds, built new housing estates, and created the Altenhof estate for retired and disabled workmen. He established educational and leisure amenities for his employees, in particular a lending library with numerous branches and an educational society.

During his lifetime Friedrich Alfred Krupp was caught in the crossfire of public debate. While to many he was a successful industrialist with a sense of national responsibility, his critics saw him as a capitalist entrepreneur who, through his links with the Imperial House and his support of the German Navy League, a nongovernment association formed to promote the strengthening of the German fleet, exerted influence on the country's naval policy in order to gain lucrative contracts for his company. The spectacular acquisitions of the Gruson works and the Germania yard readily lent themselves to such an interpretation.

In later literature too, Friedrich Alfred Krupp has been presented in controversial terms. New research has proven, however, that it was not he who initiated the program of naval expansion started in 1897–98. The main impetus came from Admiral Tirpitz and the circle of people close to Emperor Wilhelm II. Friedrich Alfred Krupp only acted in response to this policy.

When Friedrich Alfred Krupp died suddenly at the age of 48 in 1902, Bertha Krupp, the elder of his two daughters, inherited the company, which—as recommended in the will of the later owner—was converted into a stock corporation in 1903, when it became known as Fried. Krupp AG. Almost all the shares remained in the ownership of Bertha Krupp. When in 1906 she married Gustav von Bohlen und Halbach, counsellor to the Royal Prussian Legation at the Vatican, Wilhelm II as king of Prussia accorded Gustav the right to bear the name Krupp von Bohlen und Halbach and to pass on this name to his successors as owners of the company. After the wedding Gustav Krupp von Bohlen und Halbach was appointed to the supervisory board of Fried. Krupp AG, which he chaired from 1909 until the end of 1943.

In the years leading up to World War I, order books were healthy and the company continued to expand. By 1903 the workforce had increased to 42,000 and by 1913 to 77,000, with sales rising from 91.4 million marks in 1902–03 to 430.7 million marks in 1912–13. The increase in productivity mainly reflected the expansion of the Rheinhausen iron and steel works and the resultant fundamental reorganization of production in Essen.

In 1908 electric steelmaking was introduced at the Essen works. After a few years the company was making electric steels of such quality that they were able to partly replace high-grade crucible steel. Intensive research into alloying came to fruition in 1912 with the development of stainless chromium-nickel steels which, besides being resistant to corrosion, were also able to withstand the effects of acid and heat and were thus suitable for a wide range of applications.

The continuation and expansion of employee benefits and welfare remained key elements of corporate policy. Margarethe Krupp, the widow of Friedrich Alfred Krupp, established a domestic nursing service and provided the financial base for the Margarethenhöhe garden suburb. The company continued to build housing estates for its workers, these efforts being increasingly supplemented by independent housing associations closely linked to Krupp. Convalescent homes and a dental clinic were built, and the Arnoldhaus lying-in hospital was founded.

Krupp Increased Munitions Production During World War I

World War I brought an increase in armaments production and a further expansion of the company. In order to fulfill government contracts, munitions output was doubled in the first year of the war and by the third year it had reached more than five times its pre-1914 level. This output was achieved, particularly after 1916, by building huge new factories and increasing the workforce substantially. In November 1918 Krupp's employees totaled 168,000. Well-known products in these years were the 16.5-inch Big Bertha gun, 27 of which went into action in 1914; the merchant submarines *Deutschland* and *Bremen*, built at the Germania yard in 1915–16; and the long-barreled "Paris gun" with a range of 85 miles, of which seven were built.

Both at the time and in some of the subsequent literature the firm and the Krupp family were accused of having been the main beneficiaries of the war. More recent researchers have demonstrated how inaccurate a picture this was: compared with other companies only a relatively small portion of the profits initially earned were distributed to the shareholders, whereas the main part was invested in the new factory buildings which later were of little use. High personnel and welfare costs during but especially immediately after the war and the cost of converting to peacetime manufacture exhausted the company's substantial reserves. With the ending of hostilities the demand for armaments ceased. Under the Treaty of Versailles the company was prohibited from making ammunition, and cannon manufacture was allowed only to a limited extent. Krupp changed its production and embarked on the manufacture of locomotives, motor trucks, agricultural machinery, and excavators. The cost of reorganization, the wages for workers actually no longer needed, and the losses incurred through dismantling, inflation, and the dispute over the Ruhr River, when the government implemented a strategy of passive resistance to the occupation of the region by French and Belgian troops, plunged the company into a crisis in 1924–25 that threatened its very existence. Gustav Krupp von Bohlen und Halbach had no choice but to implement drastic cutbacks. Having initially refused for social reasons, he reduced the workforce within two years from 71,000 to 46,000. Unviable operations were closed down, production was streamlined, and newly launched but unprofitable mechani-

cal engineering activities were discontinued. Even then the company would not have overcome the crisis had it not been for the financial support it received from a combination of government agencies and banks.

Gustav Krupp von Bohlen und Halbach rejected the proposal of his directors that the Krupp works be closed down or incorporated in Vereinigte Stahlwerke, a combination of German steel companies, which was about to be established. He did, however, finally accept the suggestion made by Krupp director Otto Wiedfeld, who from 1922 until early 1925 was German ambassador to the United States, that the company be rehabilitated by selling a 50 percent shareholding to the British government. This plan had to be quickly abandoned, however, because the German government felt its policy of rapprochement with France might be jeopardized.

In the years that followed, the company gained a more stable footing, mainly by streamlining the fabricating operations and expanding the production of special steels. Between 1927 and 1929 a blast-furnace plant was added to the melting shops and rolling mills in the Borbeck district of Essen to form an integrated iron and steel works. One of the most modern in Europe, it enabled the production of special steel to be increased further. In 1926 Krupp introduced Widia sintered carbide, a product which, by virtue of exceptional hardness and wear resistance, brought a major breakthrough in tool engineering.

Close Alliance with Nazis: Early 1930s

The Great Depression, which first hit the world economy in 1929, brought this revival to an abrupt halt. The workforce, which by 1928 had risen to 92,300, fell back to 46,100 by 1932. Sales dropped from 577.5 million reichsmarks in 1928–29 to 240 million in 1931–32. After 1933 Germany experienced an economic upturn during which corporate policy at Krupp became closely entwined with the economic policy of the National Socialists. Governmental efforts to achieve self-sufficiency included the development of the country's iron ore deposits. The Renn process introduced by Krupp in 1929 permitted these inferior ores to be reduced economically. A coal conversion plant was built for producing petrol from coal. Increasing demand for rolled-steel products, especially for building the new autobahns, spawned the expansion of Krupp's structural engineering shops in Rheinhausen. Under the Four-Year Plan the state took increasing control of industry and at Krupp the production of locomotives, motor trucks, and ships was stepped up against the will of the company's directors. They wanted to give priority to the successful production of special steels and their fabrication for use in chemical process plant and other applications. In 1938, following the death of proprietor Arthur Krupp, son of Hermann Krupp, the Berndorf works near Vienna was incorporated in the concern. Krupp also expanded its shipbuilding activities by acquiring a majority shareholding in Deutsche Schiff-und Maschinenbau Aktiengesellschaft "Deschimag" in 1940–41. Sales rose from 809.6 million reichsmarks in 1937–38 to 1.1 billion in 1942–43; in the same period the number of employees rose from 123,400 to 235,000.

In the 1920s Krupp had, at the behest and later with the financial support of the German Reichswehr Office, undertaken design work of a military nature going beyond the tight restrictions imposed by the Treaty of Versailles. The resultant vehicles and equipment were manufactured in collaboration with other firms. In the 1930s work on the design and manufacture of armaments was stepped up, and during the war these activities were greatly intensified, controlled as they were by the state's grip on the economy. Weapons made up a much smaller proportion of total output than during World War I, however, because the manufacture of motor trucks, locomotives, bridges, ships, and especially submarines, continued at a high level.

Research has shown that in spite of claims to the contrary, Gustav Krupp von Bohlen und Halbach, president of the federation of German industry from 1931 to 1934, did not support Hitler or the Nazi party before they came to power. In keeping with his sense of national loyalty, however, he expressed his support for the state after Hitler's appointment as Reichskanzler.

At the end of 1943 the firm was reconverted into a sole proprietorship and transferred to Gustav's eldest son Alfried. The armaments authorities and semiofficial control committees were intervening more and more in industrial activity. Out of loyalty to his war-torn country Alfried endeavored to meet the demands imposed, though the lack of skilled workers, air raids, and the relocation of operations made this increasingly difficult. Like most of the armament factories in Germany during the war, Krupp used forced labor, as most of its workers had been called up for military service.

At the end of the war large areas of the works lay in ruins and much of what remained, like the iron and steel works in Essen-Borbeck, was compulsorily dismantled. The Gruson works and Berndorfer Metallwarenfabrik were expropriated by order of the Allies, and the Germania shipyard, also severely damaged by bombing, was dismantled and liquidated.

Gustav Krupp von Bohlen und Halbach was indicted for war crimes by the International Military Tribunal in Nuremberg but was found to be physically and mentally unable to stand trial. The suggestion made by the American, Russian, and French prosecuting counsels that his son Alfried be indicted in his place was rejected by the British prosecutor on the grounds that they were not conducting a game in which one player could be replaced by another. Nevertheless, Alfried Krupp von Bohlen und Halbach was put under arrest by the American occupying troops in Essen on April 11, 1945. His property was confiscated, and he was kept in prison until he was accused before a U.S. military court in 1947 together with members of the firm's senior staff. This was one of three trials against industrialists. Alfried Krupp von Bohlen und Halbach and his leading staff were accused of having planned and participated in a war of aggression, but were declared not guilty of these charges. Of the other charges of the indictment, criminal spoliation in occupied countries and promotion of slave labor, they were found guilty on July 31, 1948. In 1951 their prison terms were cut short and they were released. Two years later Alfried Krupp von Bohlen und Halbach resumed the management of his firm, which since 1945 had been under the control of the British military government.

Postwar Rebuilding of Krupp

The company's situation was perilous. On top of the losses already mentioned came the Allied divestment order under which Krupp was compelled to sever and sell its mining and steelmaking operations. The firm thus faced the loss of its raw materials base, in particular its vital steel interests. In 1951 Alfried Krupp von Bohlen und Halbach had declared that he would never again produce weapons. The object, therefore, was to shape a newly structured concern from the remaining manufacturing and engineering activities, comprising the locomotive and motor truck works, the Widia hard-metal plant, the forging and foundry shops, and the structural engineering operation in Rheinhausen. This restructuring was achieved in the years that followed. New markets were opened up in the developing countries for the engineering and construction of industrial plants. Together with Berthold Beitz, whom he had appointed as his chief executive at the end of 1953, Krupp contributed personally to this effort by making numerous order-winning trips abroad. The range of manufacturing and engineering activities was made as varied as possible in order to assure continuity of employment in the face of changing markets. In 1958 sales, including the coal and steel operations still subject to the divestment order, amounted to DM 3.3 billion, generated by a workforce of 105,200. Krupp had become the highest-revenue German company.

The Allied divestment order could only be complied with to a minor extent for lack of purchase offers. In 1960 Krupp therefore combined its remaining coal and steel operations and strengthened this base in 1965 through a merger with Bochumer Verein für Gusstahlfabrikation, a steel company in Bochum in which a majority shareholding had been acquired at the end of the 1950s. Krupp thus regained a position in the production of special steels, which it had lost with the dismantling of the Borbeck steel plant. In 1961 the company opened a plant in Brazil to make drop forgings for internal combustion engines and vehicles. In 1964 Krupp acquired a majority shareholding in Atlas-Werke AG, Bremen, including MaK Maschinenbau GmbH, Kiel.

In line with the general economic situation, the company followed a positive course into the mid-1960s, apart from a brief downturn in 1962–63. Nevertheless, until withdrawn in 1968, the divestment order prevented the company from developing a comprehensive long-term policy of corporate restructuring and investment. The financial crisis into which the company plunged in 1967 was largely triggered by the high level of supplier credits that had to be granted in the strongly expanding export business. As security for the banks, the federal and state governments provided guarantees, which, however, did not need to be taken up. The guarantees were subject to the condition that the sole proprietorship Fried. Krupp be converted into a stock corporation. This requirement dovetailed with the decision already taken by the owner to adapt the enterprise to the requirements of modern business and secure its future by changing its legal structure. In the terms of his will, Alfried Krupp von Bohlen und Halbach provided for the establishment of a nonprofit foundation. Since his son Arndt had renounced his inheritance before his father's death, leaving the way clear for the firm to be converted into a corporation, ownership of the late owner's private assets and the corporate property combined in the firm of Fried. Krupp was vested in the foundation. Alfried Krupp thus continued in modern form the idea formulated by his great-grandfather that ownership incurs social responsibility: the company would be run as a private-sector enterprise but its earnings used to serve the community at large.

Became Fried. Krupp GmbH in 1968

Alfried Krupp von Bohlen und Halbach died in July 1967. In 1968 the firm was entered in the Commercial Register as a limited-liability company, Fried. Krupp GmbH, with a capital stock of DM 500 million. Managerial responsibility was assigned to an executive board having the same powers as the management board of a stock corporation under German law. All shares in Fried. Krupp GmbH were placed in the ownership of the Alfried Krupp von Bohlen und Halbach Foundation, whose object was to preserve the company's coherence and to serve the public benefit. Berthold Beitz was chairman of the foundation's board of trustees. From 1970 to 1989 he was chairman of the supervisory board of Fried. Krupp GmbH. The foundation funded projects in Germany and abroad in the fields of science and research, education and training, public health, sports, literature, and the fine arts. Between 1968 and 1990 the foundation awarded grants totaling around DM 360 million.

In 1969 the coal mining assets were severed from the group and transferred to Ruhrkohle AG. Over the subsequent years activities in the engineering and construction of industrial plant were expanded, especially with the acquisition of Polysius AG and Heinrich Koppers GmbH. The steelmaking arm further strengthened its special-steel operations by acquiring Stahlwerke Südwestfalen AG.

In 1974 the state of Iran acquired a 25.04 percent interest in the stock capital of the steel subsidiary Fried. Krupp Hüttenwerke AG, strengthening the equity base. In 1976 Iran also acquired a 25.01 percent stake in Fried. Krupp GmbH, whose capital stock was increased to DM 700 million by the summer of 1978. Following the Iranian Revolution of 1979, these ownership interests were held by the Islamic Republic of Iran.

The 1980s saw the implementation of various restructuring schemes. Krupp sold off its interests in shipbuilding, an area of heavy losses. The steelmaking sector reduced its output of tonnage steel and in 1987–88 the plan to close the iron and steel works in Rheinhausen was met by a campaign of protest from the workforce. The works were kept in operation to a limited extent. At the same time Krupp further strengthened its activities in special steel—for example, by acquiring VDM Nickel-Technologie AG in 1989—as well as in mechanical engineering and electronics. In 1989 Gerhard Cromme became chairman and chief executive of Krupp. By 1990 the company, having successfully completed the restructuring, was back in the black and paid its first dividend in 16 years.

Completed Hostile Takeover of Hoesch in 1992

In 1991 Krupp secretly paid DM 500 million (US$294 million) to take a 24.9 percent stake in Hoesch AG, a neighboring and struggling steelmaker headquartered in Dortmund with a history dating back to the 1820s. Hoesch was having difficulty competing with its much larger rivals as the early 1990s were marked by overcapacity in steel throughout Europe. German steelmakers were particularly vulnerable because steel prices in that country were the highest in Europe. Krupp saw a

takeover of Hoesch as a great opportunity to rationalize the two companies' operations and cut costs. In December 1991 Krupp increased its stake in Hoesch to nearly 51 percent. Hoesch continued to resist being taking over, but by mid-1992 Krupp had won the battle and a merger of the two firms was backdated to January 1 of that year, creating Germany's second largest steel producer (trailing Thyssen).

The newly and cumbersomely named Fried. Krupp AG Hoesch Krupp—still headed by Cromme—had steelmaking capacity of around eight million metric tons and sales of about DM 28 billion (US$18.9 billion). The new Krupp had six divisions: steel, engineering, plant construction, automotive supplies, trade, and services. In January 1993 Krupp became a publicly traded company for the first time in its long history, though as late as the 1997–98 fiscal year the Alfried Krupp von Bohlen und Halbach Foundation still held a 50.47 percent stake while the Iranian government held 22.92 percent. The restructuring that followed the takeover of Hoesch including the shedding of more than 20,000 jobs and the closure of one of the combined company's two main integrated steel plants. Two years of heavy losses followed before Krupp posted a modest net profit of DM 40 million (US$29.2 million) for 1994.

The Long Road to the Thyssen-Krupp Merger

Following Krupp's 1994 takeover of Accial Speciali Terni, an Italian stainless steelmaker, the company in 1995 merged its enlarged stainless steel operations with those of Thyssen in the Krupp-Thyssen Nirosta joint venture, 60 percent owned by Krupp and 40 percent owned by Thyssen. In March 1997 Krupp launched a DM 13.6 billion (US$8 billion) hostile takeover bid of the larger Thyssen. This move led to fierce protests from workers fearful of another round of massive industrial layoffs, as had occurred after the Krupp takeover of Hoesch. When Cromme, dubbed the "job killer" because of those same layoffs, met with protesting workers he was pelted with eggs and tomatoes. With Thyssen's leadership resisting the attempted takeover, Krupp soon abandoned its hostile bid.

Nevertheless, Thyssen agreed to discuss with Krupp a merger of the two firm's flat steel operations, with the negotiations leading to the establishment in September 1997 of Thyssen Krupp Stahl AG, which was 60 percent owned by Thyssen and 40 percent owned by Krupp. Ekkehard Schulz, who had headed Thyssen Stahl, was named chief executive of the joint venture. The companies immediately announced that 25 percent of their flat steel workforce, or about 6,300 people, would lose their jobs as part of a restructuring.

Krupp and Thyssen were not finished with their dealmaking, however, and surprised many analysts in November 1997 with an announcement of a full merger of their entire companies. A key factor driving the merger was the increasing globalization of the world economy. The two industrial giants needed to be even larger in order to effectively compete on a global scale. After overcoming numerous hurdles, the companies consummated their union in March 1999 with the formation of Thyssen Krupp AG. Vogel, Thyssen's chief executive, still had the criminal charges hanging over him, and lost a battle to run the new company. Cromme and Schulz were named co-chief executives of the new company, which organized itself into six main divisions: Thyssen Krupp Steel, Thyssen Krupp Automotive, Thyssen Krupp Industries, Thyssen Krupp Engineering, and Thyssen Krupp Materials & Services. The company expected to slash annual costs by DM 1 billion (US$557 million) through the merger and intended to cut 2,000 of its 173,000 jobs. Revenues were estimated at DM 70 billion (US$39 billion). One other consequence of the merger was that the large stakes held by the main shareholders of Krupp were significantly diluted; the Alfried Krupp von Bohlen und Halbach Foundation held an initial 16.82 percent interest in Thyssen Krupp while the Iranian government held 7.64 percent. When combined—and these two parties sometimes had joined to block certain board initiatives at Krupp—they held about 24.5 percent of Thyssen Krupp, which was just less the 25 percent needed for a formal "blocking minority" per German law.

Principal Divisions

Thyssen Krupp Steel AG; Thyssen Krupp Automotive AG; Thyssen Krupp Industries AG; Thyssen Krupp Engineering AG; Thyssen Krupp Materials & Services AG.

Further Reading

Atkins, Ralph, "A Deal Forged from the Ashes of a Hostile Takeover," *Financial Times,* July 31, 1997, p. 28.

Bowley, Graham, "Thyssen, Krupp to Cut 6,300 Jobs," *Financial Times,* September 4, 1997, p. 36.

Brierley, David, "Battle for Thyssen Krupp," *European,* November 13, 1997, p. 26.

——, "Thyssen Steeled for the Fight," *European,* November 28, 1996, p. 24.

Burchardt, Lothar, "Zwischen Kriegsgewinnen und Kriegskosten: Krupp im Ersten Weltkrieg," *Zeitschrift für Unternehmensgeschichte,* Wiesbaden, 32, 1987.

Epkenhans, Michael, "Zwischen Patriotismus und Geschäftsinteresse: F.A.Krupp und die Anfänge des deutschen Schlachtflottenbaus, 1897–1902," *Geschichte und Gesellschaft,* Göttingen, 15, 1989.

Fisher, Andrew, "German Steelworkers Turn Heat on Banks," *Financial Times,* March 25, 1997, p. 26.

Gibson, Richard, Carl Quintanilla, and Brandon Mitchener, "Thyssen Agrees to Buy Giddings for $675 Million," *Wall Street Journal,* June 13, 1997, pp. A3, A12.

"Hunting Hoesch," *Economist,* October 19, 1991, pp. 86, 88.

James, Harold, *The German Slump: Politics and Economics, 1924–1936,* Oxford: Clarendon Press, 1986, 469 p.

"The King and Them," *Economist,* January 27, 1990, pp. 73 + .

Klass, Gert von, *Krupps: The Story of an Industrial Empire,* translated by James Cleugh, London: Sidgwick and Jackson, 1954.

Kohl, Christian, "A Global Vision for Steelmakers Thyssen, Krupp," *American Metal Market,* February 10, 1999, p. 8Λ.

Köhne-Lindenlaub, Renate, "Krupp," in *Neue Deutsche Biographie Bd. 13,* Berlin: Duncker Humblot, 1982.

Krupp: A Century's History of the Krupp Works 1812–1912, Essen: Krupp Works, 1912.

Lindemann, Michael, "How Cromme Engineered the Rebirth of a German Titan," *Financial Times,* March 14, 1996, p. 31.

——, "Thyssen Poised for Disposals After Setback in All Activities," *Financial Times,* January 31, 1996, p. 34.

Lindemann, Michael, and Quentin Peel, "Married Without a Honeymoon," *Financial Times,* May 19, 1994, p. 30.

Lindenlaub, Jürgen, and Renate Köhne-Lindenlaub, "Unternehmensfinanzierung bei Krupp, 1811–1848: Ein Beitrag zur Kapital-und Vermögensentwicklung," *Beiträge zur Geschichte von Stadt und Stift Essen,* Neustadt a.d. Aisch, 102, 1988.

Manchester, William, *The Arms of Krupp 1587–1968,* Boston: Little, Brown, 1968, 976 p.

Muhlen, Norbert, *The Incredible Krupps: The Rise, Fall and Comeback of Germany's Industrial Family,* New York: Henry Holt, 1959.

Nash, Nathaniel C., "Family Sells Last of Stake in Thyssen," *New York Times,* September 5, 1995, pp. D1, D7.

Norman, Peter, "Contrasting Response to Strategic Marriage," *Financial Times,* November 6, 1997, p. 34.

——, "Krupp-Thyssen Merger Mired in Rivalry," *Financial Times,* November 21, 1997, p. 26.

——, "Steel Groups Give in to Lure of Wedlock," *Financial Times,* November 5, 1997, p. 31.

——, "Thyssen and Krupp Outline Merger Gains," *Financial Times,* February 7, 1998, p. 17.

——, "Thyssen, Krupp Seek Breakthrough," *Financial Times,* January 5, 1998, p. 28.

——, "Thyssen Krupp Terms Agreed," *Financial Times,* September 12, 1998, p. 21.

——, "Troubles Just Starting for 'Krupp-Thyssen'," *Financial Times,* March 26, 1997, p. 28.

Parkes, Christopher, "Hauled Down the Merger Aisle," *Financial Times,* January 6, 1992, p. 13.

——, "Taking a Long-Term View of German Steel," *Financial Times,* April 21, 1992, p. 35.

Peel, Quentin, "Breaking Point for Nerves of Steel," *Financial Times,* February 25, 1993, p. 23.

Penson, Stuart, "Thyssen + Krupp = World's Largest Stainless Maker," *New Steel,* April 1995, pp. 58 + .

Reier, Sharon, "Krupp's Blitzkrieg," *Financial World,* December 10, 1991, pp. 26–28.

Roth, Terence, "Krupp, Hoesch Map Out Merger Plans," *Wall Street Journal,* October 22, 1991, p. A9C.

Schröder, Ernst, *Krupp: Geschichte einer Unternehmerfamilie,* Götingen: Muster-Schmidt Verlag, 1984, 103 p.

"Die Thyssen-Gruppe," *Usines et Industries,* December 1986.

Tinnin, David B., "Reforging an Old Steelmaker," *Fortune,* June 16, 1980, pp. 112 + .

Treue, Wilhelm, *Die Feuer Verlöschen nie. August Thyssen-Hütte, 1890–1926,* Düsseldorf: Econ-Verlag, 1966.

Treue, Wilhelm, and Helmut Uebbing, *Die Feuer Verlöschen nie. August Thyssen-Hütte, 1926–1966,* Düsseldorf: Econ-Verlag, 1969.

Turner, Henry Ashby, Jr., *German Big Business and the Rise of Hitler,* New York: Oxford University Press, 1985, 504 p.

Uebbing, Helmut, *Wege und Wegmarken: 100 Jahre Thyssen,* Berlin: Siedler, 1991, 348 p.

Wessel, Horst A., ed., *Thyssen & Co., Mulheim a.d. Ruhr: Die Geschichte einer Familie und Ihrer Unternehmung,* Stuttgart: F. Steiner, 1991, 227 p.

—Dieter Müller and Renate Köhne-Lindenlaub
—updated by David E. Salamie

Toho Co., Ltd.

1-2-1, Yuraku-cho
Chiyoda-ku
Tokyo 100-8415
Japan
(+81) 3-3591-1221
Fax: (+81) 3-3591-2414
Web site: http://www.toho-group.co.jp

Public Company
Founded: 1932
Employees: 1,474
Sales: ¥83.84 billion (US$927 million) (1998)
Stock Exchanges: Tokyo
NAIC: 51211 Motion Picture & Video Production; 51212
   Motion Picture & Video Distribution

Toho Co., Ltd. is one of the top Japanese filmmakers and one of the oldest in that country. Known worldwide for unleashing Godzilla in 1954, Toho has grown steadily to become a nearly US$1 billion international entertainment company.

Founding, 1932

Toho was founded in 1932. From the start, it faced serious competition in the entertainment industry, notably Shochiku Company Ltd., Japan's oldest cinema company, founded in 1895 to promote Kabuki theater. Undeterred, Toho wasted little time before producing some of Japan's top films. In 1954, the late Akira Kurosawa directed smash hit *Seven Samurai* for Toho, starring the late Toshiro Mifune. Kurosawa would go on to direct such movies as *The Hidden Fortress* (1958), *Yojimbo* (1961), and *Sanjuro* (1962). Other important directors, including Masaki Kobayashi (*Harakiri*, 1962; *Rebellion*, 1967) and Kihachi Okamoto (*Samurai Assassin*, 1965; *Sword of Doom*, 1966; *Kill*, 1968), worked for Toho as well. Actors who first signed with Toho and later went on to stardom included Kumi Mizuno (*Frankenstein Conquers the World*, 1965; and several Godzilla movies, 1965–99) and Haruo Nakajima, who made a

nice career, though his face was never seen until the 1970s, playing Gojira, or Godzilla.

In 1959 Toho released its 100th film, the three and a half hour epic *Nippon Tanjou* (*The Birth of Japan*). Known as the Japanese version of *The Ten Commandments*, the movie—directed by Hiroshi Inagaki—featured every major actor under contract to the studio, including Mifune, Mizuno, Ganjiro Nakamura, Hajime Izu, Akira Takarada, Akira Kubo, Eijiro Tono, Jun Tazaki, Yoshio Kosugi, Kyoko Kagawa, Akihito Hirata, and Takashi Shimura.

Calling All Monsters, 1954

Toho made another huge mark on the world when a giant prehistoric underwater lizard made his first appearance terrorizing Tokyo in 1954 in a Japanese movie called *Gojira*. Two years later, *Godzilla—King of the Monsters* appeared in the United States with new footage and featuring Raymond Burr (who went on to fame as detective Perry Mason). It was one of the first post-World War II Japanese films to commercially break through the U.S. market. Burr would reappear in *Godzilla 1985* (1985), commemorating the 30th anniversary of the lizard's debut.

In 1955 *Godzilla Raids Again* hit the world, but then Godzilla would not resurface for nearly eight years, when he began coming face-to-face with other famous monsters of filmland. Veteran monster King Kong put in an appearance in *King Kong tai Godzilla* (1963). Giant flying moth Mothra debuted when but a grub in *Mosura* (1962), and costarred with Godzilla in *Mosura tai Godzilla* (1964). Rodan, a prehistoric pterodactyl, appeared in *Radon* (1956) first, then costarred with Godzilla later in *Kaiju Daisenso* (1968). Ghidra, a three-headed monster from outer space, joined the lizard on screen in *Ghidorah Sandai Kaiju Chikyu Saidai no Kessan* (1964). Ebirah, an enormous lobster, appeared in *Nankai no Kai Ketto* (1966) and Godzilla's son debuted in *Gojira no Musuko* (1966). Other monster costars appeared throughout Godzilla's career, including a huge blob of sludge named Hedora (*Gojira tai Hedora*, 1971), Gigan (*Godzilla tai Gigan*, 1972), Megalon (*Gojira tai Megaro*, 1973), Mechagodzilla (*Gojira tai Meka-*

Gojira, 1974), and Biollante (*Gojira tai Biollante*, 1989). Just about everyone showed up in *Destroy All Monsters* (1968) for a monster mash.

The Case of the Disappearing Market, 1960–96

Toho continued attracting talent into the 1980s. The late director Juzo Itami debuted in 1984 with *The Funeral*, and filmed nine other movies—almost all starring his wife, Nobuko Miyamoto—including *Tampopo* (1985), *A Taxing Woman* (1987), and *The Gentle Art of Japanese Extortion* (1992).

The number of movie screens in Japan dwindled over the period from 1960 to 1990. By 1991 there were only about 2,000 screens in the entire country, some 600 of which were reserved exclusively for Japanese films, most of which were produced and/or distributed by Japan's Big Three: Toho, Shochiku, and Toei Co. Ltd. (which allied itself with Shochiku for greater distribution). At the time, Japan's film business resembled the U.S. market during the 1930s–40s, when five Hollywood-based studios controlled 70 percent of first-run theaters (in a market in 1946 which sold 4.7 billion tickets). The near-monopoly caused the Justice Department to force U.S. studios to sell off the theaters they owned and distributors to sell movies on a theater-by-theater/movie-by-movie basis.

The chokehold on the limited number of screens, and the split caused by the "cinema warfare" of Toho vs. Shochiku/Toei, made it very difficult for foreign filmmakers to show their movies at all, and *never* at both Toho *and* Shochiku/Toei theaters. U.S. blockbuster *Back to the Future II* opened on only eight theaters in Tokyo and 160 throughout Japan. Even giant Japanese corporations Sony (which owns Columbia Pictures) and Matsushita (which owns MCA) bowed to the iron grip of Toho and Shochiku. Matsushita began working with Shochiku to open video theaters in which to show its films. Sony, on the other hand, made a saber-rattling gesture of fighting back, opening its own independent theaters starting in 1984, but the 100-seat theaters were created to show mostly Japanese films, not intended for major international distribution.

In the spring of 1991, Time Warner Inc. allied with Osaka-based Nichii Co.—renamed MYCAL Corporation, one of Japan's largest retail companies—to construct 30 multiplex theaters in Japanese suburbs, each featuring six to 12 screens. With US$12.50 ticket prices, and with U.S. movie rentals bringing US$236 million from Japan, it was hoped the new theaters would capture more of the huge Japanese market. However, even Time-Warner located its theaters in areas where they would not directly compete with Toho- or Shochiku-owned theaters. By the end of 1991, Toho had turned total sales revenues of US$1.2 billion, while closest competitor Shochiku topped US$400 million. Toei allied with Saban Entertainment to produce the hit television series "Mighty Morphin' Power Rangers" and the subsequent movie. They also diversified into real estate.

In 1992 Toho—which then owned 158 theaters—sold the rights for a Godzilla movie to U.S. filmmaker TriStar. The following year, Steven Spielberg's *Jurassic Park*, with its computer-animated thunder lizards, was the most successful movie ever to date. Toei expanded slightly, building ten new theaters,

and creating Sun Stripe Pictures for coproduction of movies with U.S. companies. Nikkatsu went under in 1993.

Toho flexed its huge legal tail in 1994 when it swatted Kia Motor Co. with a lawsuit for using a giant monster lizard resembling Godzilla, clawing its way through power lines in its ads, along with the slogan, "There's only one thing more frightening to Japan. Aaaaaaaaaaaaaaaagh! A well-made car for under $9,000." The fact that Kia also supplied dealers with 25-foot-tall inflatable reptiles during the advertising campaign did not help. Toei and Saban allied that year with Italian broadcaster RTL Television to coproduce "V.R. Troopers" and "Cybertron," companion shows to "Power Rangers." Toei Animation allied with DIC Productions for domestic syndication and merchandising rights to the half-hour animated strip "Sailor Moon," a US$1.5 billion Japanese entertainment phenomenon featuring a 14-year-old female action hero.

The Death of Godzilla, 1995

In 1995 Toho made one last domestic Godzilla film, *Godzilla vs. Destroyer*, killing off the monster. Speculation abounded about whether this was truly the end of the great lizard, a media fascination surpassed only by the death of Superman in the same decade. Toho capped 1996 with US$953.8 million in total revenue and US$5.4 million net income.

Market Changes and the Resurrection of Godzilla, 1997

In 1997 television networks and book publishers moved visibly into movie production. *Mononoke Hime* (*Princess Mononoke*) was produced by Studio Ghibli Co.—one of two film production companies affiliated with Tokuma Shoten (Publishing) Co. (the other being Daiei Co.). Directed by one of Japan's best-loved animated filmmakers, Hayao Miyazaki (*My Neighbor Totoro*, 1993), *Mononoke*—distributed by Toho—made over US$108 million in its first seven weeks. Two previous Ghibli releases—*Pom Poko* (1994) and *Whispers of the Heart* (1995)—brought in US$22.8 million and US$16 million, respectively, making them huge successes. Disney consequently picked up Ghibli's list for worldwide distribution. Toei distributed Kadokawa Shoten (Publishing) Co.'s scifi feature *Evangelion* in 1997, which made nearly US$13.8 million in four months. Spielberg's *The Lost World: Jurassic Park* opened on more than 300 screens in Japan, along with a huge merchandising deal with MYCAL. Toho posted total revenue of US$905.4 million and net income of US$6.7 million.

By the end of 1998, over 153 million movie tickets were sold in Japan, topping the 150 million mark for the first time since 1986, and domestic box office revenues for the year reached an all-time record high of ¥193.4 billion (compared to the U.S. market in 1996: 1.3 billion movie tickets sold and US$26 billion in revenue). Things were looking up for the Japanese film industry as a whole.

This was not the case, however, for veteran film house Shochiku. In an attempt to diversify its holdings, and as a centenary celebration of its founding, Shochiku opened theme park Kamakura Cinema World in 1995. Dismantling part of its Ofuna Studio, the ¥15 billion park was a dismal failure, finally closing in December 1998. Father-and-son management team Toru and Kazuyoshi Okuyama were fired, and the company began moving away from production of "artsy" films, focusing more on commercially oriented movies. Shochiku lost over five percent of its workforce that year, and 6.3 percent of total revenue from 1997, falling to US$463.4 million, and posting a net loss of US$120.2 million. In an effort to revitalize itself, Shochiku began an extensive restructuring effort which included selling its headquarters building in Tokyo in February 1999 and naming Executive Vice-President Nobuyoshi Ohtani, a grandson of the company's founder, to the top post. The following month, the company announced cutbacks in its film production schedule, slashing the number of films to be produced in 1999 and 2000, to about five or six per year, with Shochiku veteran Yoji Yamada (the "Tora-san" series) directing most of them. Shochiku, in a bold move, also announced that it would abolish its block booking policy, allowing affiliated movie houses to show foreign movies as well as its own.

Toei was also struggling in 1998, cutting over seven percent of its workforce and posting total revenues of US$600.9 million, a 14.5 percent loss from the previous year. Net income climbed just over five percent to US$6.1 million. Toho, however, had a fabulous year, with hit movies for 1998 including *Odoru Daisosasen* (*Bayside Shakedown*), produced in affiliation with Fuji TV based on the latter's hit television police series. The company did reduce its own in-house production schedule, though, and began buying movies from other distributors, and commenced refurbishment of its affiliated movie houses.

Their big hit came that year when TriStar Pictures brought the 54-year-old lizard, and veteran of 22 Japanese films, back to the big screen in the United States with *Godzilla*, written by Dean Devlin and directed by Roland Emmerich, the duo behind blockbuster film *Independence Day*, starring Matthew Broderick. Since then, the company has been rolling in the proceeds. Godzilla's own web site appeared (www.godzilla.com) and the licensing frenzy began: toys, lunchboxes, action figures—all of which Toho had been producing for years—now hit the U.S. market with a vengeance, along with video games. Toho closed 1998 with total revenue of ¥83.84 billion (US$927 million), up 2.4 percent from 1997, with net income jumping 33 percent to US$4.5 million. The company also added dramatically to its

workforce, topping out at near 1,500 employees, a 178 percent growth rate.

By mid-1999 Toho had no plans to abolish its block booking system, but the Godzilla-sized monster Japanese filmmaker, standing tall in its industry like the Colossus of Rhodes, could be forced to as the Japanese market changed in the 21st century. Whether or not Toho changed its theater policy, Godzilla would return to the silver screen in December 1999 in *Godzilla Millennium*, propelling the lizard into another century of fame.

Principal Subsidiaries

Toho International Ltd.

Further Reading

Bailey, James, "Toho: No. 1 Japanese Distrib.," *Variety*, May 13, 1981, p. 255.

Darlin, Damon, "Godzilla vs. Kiamonster," *Forbes*, July 18, 1994, p. 18.

Dawkins, William, and Alice Rawsthorn, "Japanese Groups to Invest Up to ¥13BN in Paramount," *Financial Times*, May 14, 1996, p. 28.

Eisenstodt, Gale, "A Cozy Japanese Near Monopoly," *Forbes*, September 30, 1991, p. 52.

"Employ All Monsters," *People Weekly*, August 21, 1995, p. 17.

"First Fiscal Half Revenues Soar for Toho Entertainment Conglom.," *Variety*, October 19, 1988, p. 389.

"Godzilla to Bite the Dust," *New York Times*, July 16, 1995, p. 6.

"Japanese Domestic Rental Champs 1980," *Variety*, May 13, 1981, p. 256.

"Japan's Godzillas," *Economist*, April 11, 1987, p. 72.

Regelman, Karen, "The Green Giant of Japanese Showbiz," *Variety*, November 9, 1992, p. 43.

Segers, Frank, "Matsuoka: The Aristocrat of Nippon Film Industry," *Variety*, November 9, 1992, p. 43.

——, "Toho Leads Japan's First-Half Film Rentals to 8% Jump over 1984; Other Majors Way Down," *Variety*, August 7, 1985, p. 37.

Segers, Frank, and Ikuko Tani, "Toho Topper—Japan No Monopoly," *Variety*, May 4, 1983, p. 339.

Sterngold, James, "Does Japan Still Need Its Scary Monster?" *New York Times*, July 23, 1995, p. E1.

"Toho Co. (Japan)," *Wall Street Journal*, January 14, 1994, p. C6.

"Toho's Saturation Promo Blitz Bodes Big Biz for Kitty Picture," *Variety*, May 14, 1986, p. 28.

—Daryl F. Mallett

TOTO
TOTO LTD.

1-1, Nakashima 2-chome
Kokurakita-ku, Kitakyushu
Fukuoka 802
Japan
(093) 951-2707
Fax: (093) 922-6789
Web site: http://www.toto.co.jp

Public Company
Incorporated: 1917 as Toyo Toki Company, Ltd.
Employees: 11,257
Sales: ¥472.27 billion (US$3.18 billion) (1998)
Stock Exchanges: Tokyo
NAIC: 326191 Plastics Plumbing Fixtures Manufacturing;
    326199 All Other Plastics Product Manufacturing;
    327122 Ceramic Wall & Floor Tile Manufacturing;
    327991 Cut Stone & Stone Product Manufacturing;
    332998 Enameled Iron & Metal Sanitary Ware
    Manufacturing; 332913 Plumbing Fixture Fitting &
    Trim Manufacturing

TOTO LTD. is a leading Japanese manufacturer of plumbing products, including toilets, urinals, faucets, toilet seats, water heaters, and new ceramic materials; and system products, which include modular bathrooms, system toilets, modular kitchens, modular vanity cabinets, indoor and outdoor tiles, artificial marble countertops, and plastic and enameled cast-iron bathtubs. Though traditionally a business specializing in water-related household products, TOTO has further expanded its product line into nonhousehold projects such as those for hotels and offices. The company's overseas operations include sales companies and branches in China, Hong Kong, Singapore, South Korea, Taiwan, the United States, and Vietnam; and manufacturing companies in China, Germany, Indonesia, Malaysia, the Philippines, South Korea, Taiwan, Thailand, and the United States. Despite TOTO's increasing global presence, the vast majority of its sales are generated domestically.

Early History

The company was incorporated in 1917 as Toyo Toki Company, Ltd., in Kokura, Japan, with assets of ¥1 million. The company's inception took place during the *Taisho* era, a time of great social and economic change during which the Japanese economy grew and expanded, and the number of urban dwellers increased. As the demand for new, modern, urban housing increased, so did the demand for TOTO's ceramic products, and in 1920 the company introduced to its production facilities Japan's first tunnel kiln—a long narrow kiln with products carried on conveyors. Throughout the company's first half-century, TOTO's fortunes would parallel the growth and activity of the Japanese economy as a whole.

The company's growth was stifled in 1927 due to a serious economic depression that struck Japan as a result of over-extended capital investment and production. This was the beginning of extremely difficult times for TOTO. A financial panic followed the recession, and TOTO, along with most Japanese businesses, was forced to curtail production in the face of declining demand. The worldwide Great Depression, devaluation of the yen on world markets, and the removal of Japan from the gold standard all contributed to economic chaos. Moreover, in that same year a huge earthquake caused an even greater strain on Japan's economy. However, massive government expenditures on reconstruction helped TOTO survive extremely perilous times. In an effort to stimulate the economy, military expenditures were increased, reconstruction was accelerated again, and a period of military expansionism began, which did not stop until the end of World War II.

During the war years, despite the government's redirection of most Japanese industry to war production, TOTO continued to grow. In 1937 it had finished construction of a second sanitaryware manufacturing facility in Chigasaki. Still, conditions were difficult, as the Allied naval blockade had created extreme shortages in all raw materials, including coal, a basic ingredient needed by TOTO to fire its kilns. Moreover, in August 1945, the company as well as the entire city of Kokura, had just escaped total annihilation, since Kokura had been slated as the target of the second U.S. nuclear bomb. Because of extremely heavy cloud cover, however, and after three passes by the B-29 bomber carrying the bomb, the plane proceeded to its secondary target, Nagasaki.

Postwar Growth

At the end of the war, industrial production stood at about one-third that of prewar Japan; by 1965, manufacturing had risen to nearly four times that of the mid-1930s. The average family consumed 75 percent more goods and services than before the war, and during the 1950s and 1960s, TOTO began manufacturing new products, such as bath fittings. In 1964 TOTO ventured into the modular products field for the first time when it began manufacturing prefabricated bathrooms. The company kept pace with increased demand for its products by opening four more plants in the Kokura area, a plant in Shiga, and another located near the Chigasaki plant, which had been built before the war. By 1970, when Japan was experiencing water shortages, TOTO had developed a toilet that used only 1.6 gallons per flush. That year, the company also began manufacturing enamel baths and changed its name from Toyo Toki to TOTO LTD.

Along with the new product lines and name, came the development of new ceramics technologies. Traditional ceramics had several drawbacks, since they were inferior in weldability and workability. However, these problems were eliminated with the addition of silicon carbide, silicon nitride, and boron nitride into ceramic composition. The new ceramic compositions, a welcome improvement, were useful in the fields of engineering ceramics, given their thermal, wear, and corrosion resistances, as well as in electroceramics (in insulators or semiconductors).

During the years preceding the war, Japanese products had a general reputation for inferior workmanship and materials. As the scope of TOTO's markets and sales efforts expanded, an emphasis on total quality control became a priority. The development of an integrated quality-control system brought TOTO into a period of rapid growth and diversification of its product line. Sales grew as the company used the just-in-time method in both the ordering and delivery of raw materials it needed for production and in its sales program, by offering the same quick and timely response to the companies it supplied with products.

Most Japanese manufacturing had its roots in job-lot production, that is, producing a narrow range of products well and in great numbers. In its first 60 years of existence, for example, TOTO had concentrated on the production of a limited line of sanitary earthenware products. With mastery of the new and more efficient manufacturing techniques, sanitaryware would come to represent less than 20 percent of the company's total sales and production by the early 1990s.

Expanding Product Lines and Sales in the 1980s

In the 1980s, under the leadership of Hiroshi Shirakawa and then Yoshine Koga, TOTO took giant strides in expanding both its product line and sales organization. The company developed and maintained a network of retail sales locations that served the general public as well as designers, along with its traditional distribution to the home construction industry. New products, such as modular kitchens, vanity units, high-quality ceramic tile, water heaters, whirlpool bathtubs, high-tech toilets, "washlets" (microcomputer-controlled toilet seats with a warm-water washing feature), precision measuring tools, optical connectors, and magnetic discs contributed to explosive growth in sales in the 1980s. The increase in sales was met with the construction of almost completely automated production plants using both robotics and worker-free automated production lines.

Along with the growth of its product line, the company had begun overseas expansion of both its sales and manufacturing functions. In 1986 TOTO established the Cera Trading Company, the function of which was to import and market other manufacturers' plumbing products in an effort to expand TOTO's total market share. Beginning with the company's first joint venture with Kawasaki in 1986, resulting in the formation of the Nihron Yupro Corporation, TOTO was by the end of the 1980s doing business in France, Germany, Indonesia, Korea, Thailand, Hong Kong, Taiwan, and the People's Republic of China.

1990s: Expansion in the United States and China

Further overseas expansion came in the 1990s. TOTO entered the U.S. market in 1990 through the formation of a sales company called TOTO Kiki U.S.A., Inc. The main impetus for this move was the increasing numbers of U.S. communities that were instituting regulations mandating water-saving low-flush systems. TOTO's 1.6 gallons-per-flush toilets perfectly filled this burgeoning need. In 1992 TOTO expanded its U.S. presence with the opening of a facility for the manufacture of water-saving toilets, which was located in Atlanta and was operated through a newly formed subsidiary, TOTO Industries (Atlanta), Inc. The success of this venture led to the addition in 1996 of a second plant to the Atlanta operations. Also in 1996 TOTO established a third U.S. subsidiary—TOTO U.S.A., Inc.—which was set up to coordinate the company's U.S. activities.

China was a second market that TOTO targeted for significant expansion in the 1990s. The company began establishing manufacturing operations there, with the resulting products sold in China as well as exported to Japan and other countries. In fiscal 1994 the Beijing TOTO Co., Ltd. was established to produce toilets and other sanitaryware. In June 1996 Nanjing TOTO Co., Ltd. began production of cast-iron bathtubs, and one month later TOTO Dalian Co., Ltd. began making faucets. In 1995 TOTO set up TOTO (China) Co., Ltd. to coordinate the company's overall activities in that nation.

To further increase its line of new products, TOTO completed construction in 1991 of a new research and development laboratory at the Chigasaki plant. Among the new products that TOTO subsequently introduced was the Revlis (Silver) line of water-related products designed for senior citizens. People aged 65 and over in Japan were expected to increase from 15 percent of the population in 1990 to more than 20 percent by 2010 and to more than 30 percent by 2020, providing a solid basis for the Revlis line. Among the initial products in the line was an elevating toilet seat unit, which could be raised and lowered electrically. Another area of research was in developing a photocatalyst—a substance that changes its properties when exposed to light—that would repel water. Initially envisioned as an application to be used in bathroom tiles to prevent mildew and odors, TOTO's hydrophilic photocatalyst technology was first put to commercial use in a film for automobile side-view mirrors that ensured that mirrors were always clear, even in the rain or snow. This product was launched in April 1997 under the brand name Hydrotect.

Meanwhile, the 1991 end to the Japanese economic boom—which had peaked from 1986 to 1990—led to prolonged difficulties for TOTO. Most of the company's products were closely tied to the health of the construction industry in Japan, and the slumping economy drastically reduced the number of new housing starts. As a result TOTO's revenue growth slowed significantly, while net income figures were on the decline. The situation worsened during the fiscal year ending in March 1998 as the Japanese economy fell into recession during 1997. Housing starts fell another 21.6 percent in 1997, to 1.3 million units. TOTO's net sales thereupon fell from ¥472.27 billion in fiscal 1997 to ¥419.85 billion in 1998. Net income during this time fell from ¥11.87 billion to ¥3.42 billion. During 1998 TOTO announced that 1,000 jobs would be cut from its workforce by 2000 and that six factories would suspend production. That year, housing starts in Japan fell below 1.2 million units and renovations were down as well. Sales for fiscal 1999 fell another 13 percent, while TOTO posted a net loss of ¥21 billion, partly attributable to the workforce cuts, as an early retirement program led the company to dole out ¥15.5 billion in severance pay. While the Japanese economy continued in its weakened state in the late 1990s, TOTO was working hard to reduce its dependence on housing starts, an objective that was of vital importance to the company's future.

Principal Subsidiaries

TOTO Kiki (H.K.) Ltd. (Hong Kong); TOTO U.S.A., Inc.; TOTO Kiki U.S.A., Inc.; TOTO (China) Co., Ltd.; Royal TOTO Metal Co., Ltd. (South Korea); Kelim TOTO Co., Ltd. (South Korea); Taiwan TOTO Co., Ltd.; Nanjing TOTO Co., Ltd. (China); TOTO Dalian Co., Ltd. (China); Beijing TOTO Co., Ltd. (China); TOTO Beijing Co., Ltd. (China); TOTO Shanghai Co., Ltd. (China); Siam Mariwasa TOTO, Inc. (Philippines); The Siam Sanitary Fittings Co., Ltd. (Thailand); Siam Sanitary Ware Co., Ltd. (Thailand); TOTOKIKI (Malaysia) Sdn. Bhd.; P.T. Surya TOTO Indonesia; TOTO Industries (Atlanta), Inc. (U.S.A.); Bulthaup GmbH & Co. (Germany).

Further Reading

Beauchamp, Marc, "Toilets with Chips," *Forbes,* January 22, 1990, pp. 100+.

do Rosario, Louise, "Only in Japan," *Far Eastern Economic Review,* September 16, 1993, p. 64.

"Flush with Failure," *Economist,* August 29, 1998, p. 56.

Forbis, William H., *Japan Today: People, Places, Power,* New York: Harper & Row, 1975, 463 p.

Hane, Mikiso, *Japan: A Historical Survey,* New York: Charles Scribner's Sons, 1972, 650 p.

Hutton, Bethan, "Hi-Tech Answer to the Call of Nature: Japan's Toto Is Seeking Success in Export Markets—with the Electronic Toilet Seat," *Financial Times,* August 2, 1997, p. 15.

Johnson, Bradley, "U.S. Gets Bowled Over," *Advertising Age,* June 4, 1990, p. 8.

"May I Use Your Laboratory?," *Economist,* June 18, 1988, p. 78.

Schonberger, Richard J., *Japanese Manufacturing Techniques: Nine Hidden Lessons in Simplicity,* New York: Free Press, 1982, 260 p.

Wheeler, Claudia D., "Innovations in Antimicrobials: TOTO Takes Its Tiles into the Future," *Soap/Cosmetics/Chemical Specialties,* October 1994, pp. 54, 56.

—William R. Grossman
—updated by David E. Salamie

Tower Air

Tower Air, Inc.

JFK International Airport
Jamaica, New York 11430
U.S.A.
(718) 553-8500
(800) 34-TOWER; (800) 348-6937
Fax: (718) 553-4312
Web site: http://www.towerair.com

Public Company
Incorporated: 1982
Employees: 1,750
Sales: $483.82 million (1998)
Stock Exchanges: NASDAQ
Ticker Symbol: TOWR
NAIC: 481111 Scheduled Passenger Air Transportation;
    481212 Nonscheduled Chartered Freight Air
    Transportation

Tower Air, Inc. specializes in giving travelers good deals to about a dozen varied niche destinations, often ones of cultural interest. Although the New York-Tel Aviv market accounts for a quarter of its revenues, Tower has also flown charters to Mecca, while Greece, Italy, China, Japan, and Russia are some of its other destinations. The company has achieved low costs (just five cents per seat mile), allowing it to sell discount tickets without the restrictions required by other airlines. Tower keeps its giant planes filled with passengers, averaging load factors around 75 percent. Since inception Tower has preferred to stay in markets for the long term. It avoided fare wars by not supplying too many flights; most of its scheduled routes operated once per day or a few times per week. It was also careful not to overexpand as other budget carriers had in trying to compete with the majors. Scheduled operations accounted for half of Tower's business in the late 1990s. The company also flew freight and offered maintenance services.

1980s Origins

Morris K. Nachtomi, a 30-year veteran of Israeli state airline El Al, was one of the Tower Air's four founders. His family had immigrated to Israel shortly after it became independent. Following an early retirement from El Al, he and a few colleagues moved to New York to help Flying Tigers start its short-lived passenger line.

Nachtomi was also the first president of the passenger off-shoot of the Flying Tigers cargo line, Metro International Airways. When the Tigers abandoned the passenger business, Nachtomi bought the Tower name from Tower Travel Corporation, a travel agency offering packages to Israel and Western Europe that had been one of Metro International's clients.

After leasing charters, in November 1983 Tower Air began scheduled service on a leased Boeing 747. The first destination: Israel. Charters accounted for most of its business in the first few years. Charter operations gave Tower a ''heads-up'' to potential lucrative scheduled routes such as Paris (which it served through Orly, deemed better for the local market) and São Paulo. In refining its niches, the airline scheduled arrivals and departures to avoid rush hours.

Nachtomi became president in 1986 and was named chairman and CEO in 1989. After the Nachtomi Partnership bought out the other investors, his family then owned about three quarters of the stock.

Soaring Through the Persian Gulf War

Tower flew U.S. troops and cargo during the Persian Gulf War and was the second largest troop carrier, flying 300 sorties. Tower was the only foreign carrier to continue passenger service from Israel during the war, though lack of insurance prevented it from flying passengers to Tel Aviv. Thus, the airline flew civilian passengers out of Tel Aviv on the return trips of its military flights. Military charters typically provided one-fifth of revenue, though in 1991 they accounted for half.

Tower had two of its best years in 1990 and 1991, thanks to its responsiveness in canceling flights to match market conditions. Revenues in 1991, when Tower employed a little more than 500 employees, amounted to $245 million, up from 1990's $172 million. Tower attempted serving the German city of Cologne in May 1992. Scheduled service to Scandinavia was curtailed in the winter of 1992 as it was found unprofitable.

Tower simply did not subsidize money-losing routes. It also did not work with ticket consolidators for fear of becoming branded a commodity carrier.

While Tower hoped to build its presence in Europe and to initiate new service to South America, it eschewed opportunities in the former Soviet states, where it did not perceive the potential of profits. Moreover, the company did not see much potential for expansion in the United States, where it competed with a number of carriers under bankruptcy protection. In the early 1990s, Tower flew only between New York and Miami and San Juan in the domestic market.

At the time, Tower's fleet numbered only six Boeing 747s, which it spent $32 million to refurbish rather than invest hundreds of millions of dollars on the new MD-11 and A340 airliners it considered. The airline specialized in the bottom end of the market, and rather than sacrificing perquisites like in-flight meals and movies, Tower's passengers could expect less-frequent flights between destinations. The airline's New York-San Juan flights, for example, operated only on Saturdays. While this made the carrier less than ideal for business travelers, its New York-Paris business fare was only $299, one-third the price charged by the major carriers.

In the early 1990s Tower leased two buildings at JFK International Airport. One was a passenger terminal that the company spent $8 million to renovate. Tower planned to expand this terminal in the mid-1990s at a cost of another $6 million. The other building, Hangar 17, housed Tower's new corporate headquarters.

In 1993, Tower kept busy flying U.S. military personnel and cargo to support operations in Somalia. It was the first airline to fly troops into Mogadishu and also transported refugees for the United Nations during the conflict.

Initial Public Offering in 1993

Tower launched an initial public offering in 1993, with Nachtomi retaining about three-quarters of the shares. Tower Air took in $368 million in operating revenues in 1994. Scheduled passenger service rose 35 percent from 1993 to bring in more than half of the total, $206.6 million. Scheduled cargo operations accounted for $22.1 million, up 136 percent, while commercial and military charters were each worth about $67 million. The company's maintenance services brought in another $5 million, up 63 percent from the year before.

Revenues could have been higher, had the company flown any charters to Mecca that year. Troubles in Israel hurt sales there, and too much snow in New England impeded commuter traffic. Still, Tower was the third busiest airline at the John F. Kennedy Airport.

Unfortunately, Tower's operating expenses climbed even faster than revenues, to $46 million. A significant increase in marketing costs followed the launch of service to Ireland and India. The Bombay and New Delhi markets were in fact expected to surpass Tel Aviv within three years.

Tower chartered seven aircraft for the hajj (the Muslim pilgrimage to Mecca) in 1995. Painted in Air India and Garuda colors and staffed with their attendants, the flights were manned by Tower pilots and generated revenue based on block hours. Nachtomi told *Air Transport World* that year that flexibility was the key to keeping Tower's costs low. "Power by the hour" (PBH) leases on six of its aircraft charged the company only for block time that its planes were in use.

A similar system applied to pilots, represented by a union, who were paid at a lower hourly rate than other carriers, but generally were able to fly more hours. Tower kept the pilots on call around the clock, facilitating last-minute charters. Pilots were based in New York, Los Angeles, and Miami.

Half of Tower's employees in the mid-1990s worked part-time, and the company based cabin crews in Israel and India, also to match demand. The company made extensive use of outsourcing, often relying upon local travel bureaus rather than setting up its own offices in new markets. Tower only performed its own line maintenance and ground handling at JFK, where it had a supplier stock small parts at its hangar.

To guard against a possible scarcity of PBH-leased 747s, Tower maintained four of its planes on short-term leases while the other seven were owned, offering equity and associated depreciation and amortization benefits. Seating offered economy and business classes. The absence of a first class section and limited business seats allowed for a greater number of total seats, usually 470. By 1995, Tower's fleet had grown to 17, all Boeing 747s. This singular type fleet helped the company control maintenance costs.

Challenges in the Late 1990s

During this time, Tower began losing customers due to a public perception of poor service. In fact, the airline received an estimated ten times as many complaints as other airlines. Moreover, at the end of 1995, one of the carrier's planes skidded off a runway during an aborted take-off in a snow storm at JFK Airport. Although no fatalities occurred, Tower lost $5.2 million in the first half of 1996 and ranked fourth in the number of complaints per mile among leading U.S. airlines. Most budget airlines had faced such a perception challenge after the crash of a Valujet plane in May 1996. At the same time, major airlines kept lowering their fares. As a result, both volume and revenues fell among budget airlines, and Tower spent heavily on marketing to offset bad press, touting its safety record and own maintenance capacity in an advertising campaign to win back customers.

Under pressure from Delta, Continental, and American Airlines, the U.S. Department of Transportation (DOT) stripped Tower of its authority to fly to Brazil, transferring that entitlement to Continental and Delta. Undaunted, during the spring of 1997, Tower dedicated nine 747s to pilgrimages to Mecca. Still, Tower posted a loss of $4 million for the year on sales of $461.5 million.

In 1998, after a new U.S./France treaty, American Airlines, along with U.S. Airways, again challenged Tower Air service rights. However the DOT allowed Tower four additional Paris-New York flights, while U.S. Airways was cleared for daily Pittsburgh-Paris service. However, further expansion of Tower's French routes was soon challenged by several major U.S. carriers who charged the carrier had historically underutilized its routes. Tower also was granted permission to serve the Dominican Republic in 1999, a right it had been granted several years earlier but did not utilize at the time.

In the summer of 1998, Tower pilots voted for representation from the Air Line Pilots Association over the previously used Tower Air Cockpit Crew Association. Tower pilots were now flying 30 percent more flights than the previous summer, and salaries were rising in comparison to the major airlines. The company employed about 75 captains and 78 copilots in 1998.

Although commercial charter revenues fell in 1998, cargo and scheduled passenger service showed significant gains. Tower operated 18 747s in 1998, three of them dedicated to cargo. Most of the aircraft were more than 20 years old. Half of them were owned and half leased. In addition, the company leased two freighters to Fast Air Cargo in Miami. Tower won a USAF Air Mobility Command contract as part of the Civil Reserve Air Fleet, which also included FedEx and BAX Global.

Tower opened a new office at Los Angeles International Airport in the fall of 1998. With hajj charters booked through 2001 and its military business secure, the company seemed poised for more careful expansion.

Further Reading

Flint, Perry, "Life Beyond the Megacarriers," *Air Transport World,* June 1992, pp. 58–60.

Foster, Christine, "The Leaning Tower," *Forbes,* September 23, 1996, p. 40.

Galt, Jon, "Tower Air: Flying with an International Flair," *Airline Pilot Careers,* December 1998, pp. 20–26.

Lefer, Henry, "The 'Flexible Flier'," *Air Transport World,* June 1995, pp. 198–99.

"Passage to India," *Forbes,* August 14, 1995.

—Frederick C. Ingram

TransMontaigne Inc.

370 17th Street, Suite 2750
Denver, Colorado 80202
U.S.A.
(303) 626-8200
Fax: (303) 626-8228

Public Company
Incorporated: 1995 as TransMontaigne Oil Company
Employees: 566
Sales: $1.96 billion (1998)
Stock Exchanges: American
Ticker Symbol: TMG
NAIC: 42271 Petroleum Bulk Stations and Terminals;
213112 Support Activities for Oil & Gas Field
Operations; 486210 Pipeline Transportation, Natural
Gas; 486910 Pipeline Transportation, Gasoline &
Other Refined Petroleum Products

Denver-based TransMontaigne Inc. is a holding company that pursues business opportunities in the downstream sector of the petroleum industry. TransMontaigne's principal operating subsidiaries engage in pipelining, terminaling, storing, processing, and marketing refined petroleum products, chemicals, bulk liquids, natural gas, and crude oil in the mid-continent region of the United States, and in natural gas gathering and processing in the Rocky Mountain region. The company's subsidiary TransMontaigne Transportation Services owns and operates approximately 790 miles of pipeline and 31 terminal, storage, and delivery facilities in 19 states with a combined storage capacity of about 15 million barrels. Its three natural gas gathering and processing facilities are capable of combined throughput of approximately 94 million cubic feet of natural gas per day over 2,800 miles of pipeline. The company owns the NORCO, the Razorback, and the CETEX pipelines.

The Merger of a Private and a Public Company

Formed in 1977, the principal predecessor of Trans-Montaigne was a petroleum services firm based in Arkansas and run by Cortlandt Dietler, the company's first CEO. Unfortunately, little information covering this period of the company's history is available. In April 1995, management and certain institutional stockholders, led by Dietler, acquired control of the firm through a reverse merger in which the company's name became TransMontaigne Oil Company (later TransMontaigne Inc.). New management came on board and modernized the company at a cost of more than $20 million.

A little more than a year later, with annual revenues in excess of $300 million, TransMontaigne purchased Sheffield Exploration Company, a small exploration and production-focused public company based in Denver, via a paper trade that offered an efficient and low-cost means of going public. Sheffield had seen considerable growth in 1992 during a period of unstable gas prices as a result of its drilling operations in south Texas, a few select acquisitions in the Williston Basin (located in North Dakota and Montana), and revenue from its North Dakota gas processing plant, which had a throughput of 5.2 million cubic feet a day. In 1993, after purchasing a gas storage facility in Kansas, 11 gas gathering systems in Kansas and Oklahoma, and a processing plant in Oklahoma for $3.7 million, Sheffield doubled its capital investment budget to $1 million. After the 1996 merger with TransMontaigne, Sheffield became the sole surviving corporation, although 93 percent of the resulting TransMontaigne Oil Company was owned by the stockholders of the original TransMontaigne. The company sold off Sheffield's E & P assets and held onto its midstream operations in the Williston Basin. The new TransMontaigne began public trading in June 1996 with an initial offering of 3,500 shares. During the company's first year of operation, revenues increased to $533 million.

Outsourcing and Expansion: Mid- to Late 1990s

TransMontaigne's strategy involved capitalizing on the trend to outsource in the energy industry, doing for other companies what they no longer wanted to do for themselves. The company began acquiring pipelines, terminals, and storage facilities, then updating them to improve efficiency, lower costs, and boost throughput. In December 1996, Bear Paw Energy, a subsidiary of TransMontaigne, acquired the Koch Industries' Grasslands Facilities natural gas gathering, transmission, and

Company Perspectives:

The experienced, entrepreneurial personnel of Trans-Montaigne have propelled it into a dominant position as the refined petroleum products supply and distribution service provider in the four geographic regions in which it is currently active. The addition of new, strategically located facilities will enable TransMontaigne to further expand the supply and distribution network and scope of logistical services that it delivers to its customers, which include all major and independent refining and marketing companies. The procurement and consolidation of significant volumes of petroleum products at primary points of manufacture coupled with a "seamless" delivery system are the key components of TransMontaigne's corporate focus and capital utilization activities. In an increasingly complex energy market, TransMontaigne meets the needs of its customers, providing the required slate of petroleum products, when needed, where needed, and at the lowest effective cost.

certain processing plants, including about 2,500 miles of pipeline with a combined throughout capacity of 75 million cubic feet per day. The facilities, costing $71 million in cash, were located between TransMontaigne's existing North Dakota and Montana facilities and complemented the company's current activities in those states' Williston basin. They enabled the company to provide a complete service package to producers in North Dakota and Montana as well as to end-users of natural gas and natural gas liquids.

Other additions quickly followed. In February 1997, the company bought Mobil's Indiana fuel products terminal which connected to TransMontaigne's NORCO Pipeline and, through it, to several other Midwestern pipelines. This acquisition increased TransMontaigne's tank capacity by 1.2 barrels. At the same time, the company opened another 200,000-barrel terminal in South Bend, which also linked up to NORCO. Later in 1997, TransMontaigne completed the expansion and modernization of its Little Rock, Arkansas refined petroleum products truck terminal complex, which connected directly to the Texas Gulf Coast-originating TEPPCO pipeline. In November, it increased its systemwide tank storage capacity by nearly 70 percent with the purchase of the Houston-based Independent Terminal and Pipeline Co. The ITAPCO acquisition, which cost TransMontaigne about $32 million in common stock, was merged into its TransMontaigne Terminaling Inc. subsidiary. The terminal included 17 bulk liquid storage and distribution terminals located in eight states with a total tank capacity in excess of 3.3 million barrels. It brought the company's terminal and storage facilities to 27 and its tank capacity to 8.2 million barrels.

Prior to the acquisition of the ITAPCO Terminal Corporations and the Grasslands Facilities, TransMontaigne's revenues derived from its logistical petroleum services operating business segment, which consisted primarily of transporting, storing, terminaling, supplying, distributing, and from marketing refined petroleum products and to a lesser extent crude oil. Following ITAPCO, storage and terminaling of chemicals and other bulk liquids became a component of the company's logis-

tical petroleum operating business segment. Natural gas services had earlier become a separate operating business segment with the addition of the Grasslands Facility. Along with these changes, the company's revenue increased significantly, reaching slightly more than $1 billion in 1997.

In 1998 TransMontaigne went on to purchase a 225,000-barrel terminal and storage facility in Greenville, Mississippi, from Greenville Republic Terminal Inc., which it consolidated with its two other facilities in the area for a total combined tankage of 550,000 barrels. It also bought a 152,000-barrel Owensboro, Kentucky terminal from Marathon Oil Co. As TransMontaigne acquired, it also upgraded old facilities, frequently automating them so it could run operations with fewer employees than before.

In July 1998, it acquired the Southwest Terminal's terminaling, storage, and loading facilities at the Port of Brownsville, Texas, from Statia Terminals International N.V. for $6.5 million. Between August and January 1999, it acquired an approximately 20 percent interest in West Shore Pipeline Company in three separate purchases to become the second largest owner of West Shore. The pipeline, whose other owners included Citgo, Marathon, Equilon, Texaco, Amoco, Midwest, Mobil, and Exxon, was a 600-mile system that served about 55 locations, including four refineries, the Milwaukee and Chicago O'Hare airports, and 49 refined petroleum products truck terminals in the upper Midwest and Chicago area.

In the biggest in its series of terminal and other products-related purchases, in October 1998, TransMontaigne moved to double its total annual output of 84 million barrels and boost its assets to more than $800 million by purchasing Louis Dreyfus Energy Corp. for $161 million. The deal nearly doubled TransMontaigne's ten million barrel storage capacity by adding Louis Dreyfus's 24 terminals to TransMontaigne's 32 and expanded the company's presence into the Southeast. Louis Dreyfus Energy Corp., which was a major shipper on the Colonial pipeline that connected the Houston ship channel and major refining complexes to the New York Harbor, became TransMontaigne Product Services East Inc. Continuing its move eastward, in December TransMontaigne Terminaling Inc., another subsidiary of the company, purchased Sunoco's petroleum products terminal in Rensselaer, New York, and immediately leased it back to Sunoco.

In February 1997, it added a 200,000-barrel terminal in South Bend, also linked up to NORCO. By September 1998, its Transportation Services subsidiary had begun construction on three new facilities: the first phase of an expansion program on its NORCO Pipeline System; an additional 480,000 barrels of refined petroleum product tank storage at the company's Chicago area facilities; and a refined petroleum products terminal and storage facility north of Peoria, Illinois. The NORCO System connected to all major products pipelines in the midcontinent and to the TEPPCO and Explorer pipelines originating on the Gulf Coast. Through December 1998, TransMontaigne invested approximately $4 million in improvements and expansion of the ITAPCO Terminal and $25 million on its Grasslands facilities. In March 1999, it began plans with Colonial Pipeline Co. to build a barge facility on the Mississippi River that would improve Colonial's product delivery on that river and the Ohio.

Plans for the Future

The company's capital expenditure program contributed to a considerable increase in sales. Yet, TransMontaigne's 1998 profits suffered as a result of sharply higher income taxes that year. While the company's revenue approached $2 billion and operating income rose to $19.2 million from $9.9 million in 1997, taxes cut the company's net income 17 percent to $7.64 million from $9.17 million in 1997. In addition, the company's stock price edged downward to hit an all-time low. Capital expenditures for fiscal 1997 and 1998 totaled approximately $159 million, contributing to a negative cash flow from operations for 1998. That year TransMontaigne entered into a $500 million advance from its credit facility to refinance existing debt, fund the Louis Dreyfus acquisition, and prepare for future expenditures.

The original management and investor group led by Cortlandt Dietler still held about 80 percent of the outstanding shares, or about 50 percent of the company after a public offering in February 1997 that raised $63 million and paid for acquisitions and expansions. Plans for TransMontaigne's future in early 1999 were based on management's belief that fundamental structural changes and the trend toward outsourcing in the petroleum industry would continue to create opportunities for the company's growth as a service business. The gathering, processing, and marketing sector of the natural gas industry was in a consolidation phase, placing added stress on smaller companies to post solid returns. Oil and gas producers, which previously had operated their own natural gas gathering and processing operations, now sought to dispose of their downstream assets and facilities. TransMontaigne pursued its plan of strategic additions and expansion of facilities to improve its competitive position.

Principal Subsidiaries

TransMontaigne Transportation Services Inc.; TransMontaigne Pipeline Inc.; TransMontaigne Terminaling Inc.; TransMontaigne Product Services Inc.; TransMontaigne Holding Inc. (65%); Bear Paw Energy Inc.

Further Reading

Haines, Leslie, ''Critics Applaud Growth Genre,'' *Oil & Gas Investor*, May 1997, p. 82.
——, ''The Remarkable Year,'' *Oil & Gas Investor*, October 1993, p. 50.
Klann, Susan, ''There Is No Magic,'' *Oil & Gas Investor*, July 1997, p. 53.
Norman, James, ''TransMontaigne Builds U.S. Role with Dreyfus Purchase,'' *Platt's Oilgram News*, September 15, 1998, p. 1.

—Carrie Rothburd

Tropicana

Tropicana Products, Inc.

1001 13th Avenue East
Bradenton, Florida 34208
U.S.A.
(914) 747-4461
Fax: (914) 749-3983
Web site: http://www.pepsico.com

Division of PepsiCo, Inc.
Incorporated: 1947 as Manatee River Packing Company
Employees: 4,737
Sales: $1.93 billion (1997)
NAIC: 311311 Frozen Fruit, Juice, & Vegetable
    Processing

Tropicana Products, Inc. is the leading producer of chilled orange juice in the world. It also claims the top spot in the overall U.S. orange juice market, with a share of 33 percent, compared to archrival The Minute Maid Company's 24 percent (Ironically, Minute Maid is owned by PepsiCo, Inc.'s archrival The Coca-Cola Company). In the $2.45 billion U.S. chilled juice sector, Tropicana holds a commanding 39.8 percent share. The company was a pioneer in the not-from-concentrate, chilled orange juice sector, and accounts for more than 70 percent of U.S. not-from-concentrate sales. In North America, the company's main brands are Tropicana Pure Premium, Tropicana Season's Best, Dole juices, and Tropicana Twister. Internationally, Tropicana distributes its products in 23 countries, with the primary brands including Tropicana Pure Premium, Dole juices, Fruvita, Hitchcock, Looza, and Copella.

Founded by Sicilian Immigrant

The founder of Tropicana was Anthony T. Rossi, who was born in Messina, Sicily, in 1900, and had immigrated to the United States in 1921. Sailing from Naples, Italy, he landed in New York City with $30 in his pocket. He and four other friends came to the big city to make enough money to finance an adventure in Africa, where they planned to make a film. But Rossi found that he liked the United States and its money-making opportunities too much to leave, and the African expedition was quickly forgotten. After working in a machine shop, and as a cabdriver and chauffeur, in the late 1920s he purchased the first self-service grocery store in the country, the Aurora Farms market on Long Island, which he ran for 13 years.

In the early 1940s, longing to live in a climate similar to his native Sicily, Rossi—after first relocating in Virginia where he was a farmer—moved to Florida, settling in Bradenton, a small gulf coast town in Manatee County south of Tampa. He grew tomatoes on a 50-acre rented farm there, and also bought a cafeteria in downtown Bradenton, where his freshly prepared food proved popular. Dreaming of owning a chain of restaurants, he bought the Terrace restaurant in Miami Beach in 1944. Wartime gasoline rationing, however, crippled the Florida tourism industry, leading Rossi to exit the restaurant business.

The same week he sold his restaurant, Rossi embarked on a new venture, that of selling gift boxes of Florida citrus fruit to such department stores as Macy's and Gimbel's in New York City. Finding surprising success in this business, he moved in 1947 to Palmetto, a town just north of Bradenton, where he purchased the Overstreet Packing Company, renaming it the Manatee River Packing Company. Rossi was now able to buy his citrus directly from nearby growers rather than from retail supermarkets in Miami, cutting his costs and improving his product's freshness.

Rossi's gift boxes grew even more popular, and were soon being distributed across the country. He next expanded into selling jars of chilled fruit sections. But since only the largest fruit was selected for the boxes and the sections, Rossi needed to find a way to use the smaller fruit that was going to waste. He decided to squeeze the smaller oranges into juice, and ship it to the Northeast along with jars of fresh fruit sections, using specially modified refrigerated trucks. In 1949 the company moved to Bradenton and changed its name to Fruit Industries, Inc. That same year Rossi also entered the burgeoning market for frozen orange juice concentrate, purchasing an evaporator to extract the water from the juice. In addition, he registered "Tropicana" as a trademark and began using it on his fruit section and juice products, which proved so successful that he abandoned the marketing of the fruit gift boxes.

Company Perspectives:

Half a century ago, Italian immigrant Anthony Rossi established a small fruit packing business in Florida. The company he founded has grown to become the world's only global citrus juice business.

Personified brands, such as Speedy Alka Seltzer, were popular in the early television days of the 1950s, and Rossi joined the trend in 1951 when he commissioned the creation of "Tropic-Ana," a grass skirt- and lei-wearing, pigtailed girl balancing a large bowl of oranges on her head. The character provided an instantly recognizable symbol for the still-young company and helped establish it in the consumer market as Tropicana products began appearing in supermarket cases, mainly in the Northeast and Southeast. In 1953 the company moved to larger quarters, the former Florida Grapefruit Canning Plant in Bradenton, which served as the firm's headquarters into the late 1990s.

Pioneered Chilled Juice in 1954

The key event in the early years of the company came in 1954. That year Rossi, not wanting to be just one of a number of frozen juice concentrate producers, pioneered a flash pasteurization method that raised the temperature of freshly squeezed orange juice for a very short time, extending the juice's shelf life to three months while maintaining its flavor. This method—combined with American Can Company-commissioned packaging consisting of waxed paper cartons in half-pint, pint, and quart sizes—made possible the mass marketing of fresh chilled, not-from-concentrate juice into supermarkets and through home delivery services. Although Tropicana Pure Premium chilled orange juice quickly gained a following in much of the country, sales to New York City were particularly large, accounting for as much as 40 percent of overall sales in the 1960s and early 1970s.

Rossi now had a product that clearly distinguished his company from its competitors; he soon stopped offering Tropicana in frozen concentrate form. In 1957 he changed the name of the company to Tropicana Products, Inc. to reflect the increasing popularity of the brand. That same year Tropicana—not able to expand its truck fleet—began shipping orange juice from Florida to New York via an 8,000-ton ship the company had purchased, which it christened the SS *Tropicana*. Carrying at its peak use 1.5 million gallons of juice each week, the ship would land at Whitestone, Queens, where Tropicana had built a plant for receiving, packaging, and distribution. The *Tropicana* made its final orange juice voyage in 1961, and the company began relying exclusively on truck and rail transport.

In 1958 Tropicana Coffee made its debut. Marketed as a concentrated liquid in a push-button aerosol can, the product failed in part because it had a faulty valve which made it difficult to accurately shoot the liquid into a cup. In 1962 the citrus industry was rocked by one of its periodic freezes. More than one-third of the Florida orange crop was destroyed by a December freeze. Desperately in need of fruit, Tropicana boldly put processing equipment on a ship, which it anchored off the coast of

Mexico, a nation with a large and cheap orange crop. After some initial and profitable success in getting Mexican orange juice to the U.S. market, the Mexican government raised the price of oranges, scuttling the venture. Tropicana sold the ship and the equipment on board, losing $2 million in the process.

Went Public in 1969

Tropicana in the early 1960s began shipping more of its orange juice in glass bottles, aided by the company's development of a high-speed vacuum-packing method. With its base in sand-rich Florida, Tropicana took the next logical step of building its own glass plant, for the manufacture of the increasing amounts of glass bottles that were needed. The glass plant opened in 1964. Four years later the company became the first citrus industry company to operate its own plastic container manufacturing plant. Meantime, Tropicana in 1966 began selling its not-from-concentrate Florida orange juice overseas for the first time, shipping 14,000 cases of juice in glass bottles to France. The 1960s ended on another high note, when Tropicana Products, Inc. went public in 1969. Initially sold over the counter, the stock soon gained a listing on the New York Stock Exchange under the symbol TOJ. Revenues increased from $31.2 million in 1964 to $68.4 million by the end of the decade.

The infusion of capital from the stock offering set the stage for even more rapid growth at Tropicana. By 1973, in fact, revenues had reached $121.2 million, while net income grew nearly sixfold, to $10 million. Among the developments of the early 1970s was the launch of a company-owned train (the "Great White Train," later painted orange), which shipped bottles of juice from Bradenton to a distribution center in New Jersey. Continuing its moves to lessen its dependence on outside suppliers, Tropicana opened a box plant in 1972 and began making its own corrugated boxes. The following year Tropicana opened a new processing facility in Fort Pierce, Florida, a town on the Atlantic side of the state.

Although the so-called "orange juice wars" would not begin in earnest until the 1980s, a few skirmishes between Tropicana and Coca-Cola's Minute Maid took place in the 1970s. Coca-Cola in 1973 took direct aim at Tropicana's stranglehold on both the New York metropolitan area market and the chilled juice sector with the introduction into that area of Minute Maid chilled juice that had been reconstituted from frozen concentrate. This was the beginning of a long-running debate between the companies over which had the superior product. Tropicana contended that not-from-concentrate chilled juice was obviously superior since it was bottled (after being pasteurized) right out of the orange. Minute Maid argued that the concentrating process gave it the opportunity to blend the juice of oranges picked at different times of the year, thereby overcoming seasonal variations in orange taste and quality and giving the resultant juice a more consistent flavor and better overall quality. In any event, Minute Maid, backed by Coke's deep pockets, gained one edge—it quickly became the first nationally available chilled orange juice. The Tropicana-Minute Maid rivalry heated up further in 1975 when the former reentered the market for frozen concentrate.

By the mid-1970s, Tropicana had expanded its market range within the United States (though it still was not a national brand) and had gained a presence in the Bahamas, Bermuda, the West Indies, and several countries in Europe. Despite the Minute Maid entry into the chilled juice sector, Tropicana was the main beneficiary of the faster growth of chilled juice versus frozen concentrate. Whereas in the late 1960s chilled juice accounted for only 20 percent of the overall orange juice market, by the late 1970s it accounted for 31 percent. Tropicana was growing rapidly, with sales increasing 19 percent each year on average, reaching $244.6 million in fiscal 1977. Earnings were increasing 21 percent a year, standing at $22.5 million in 1977.

The health of Tropicana was reflected in an endless stream of suitors that attempted to woo the company in the 1970s. Among these were Philip Morris, PepsiCo (in an ironic twist), and Kellogg. On three separate occasions—in April 1974, June 1976, and July 1977—Tropicana and Kellogg, the cereal giant which sought to extend its breakfast offerings to include orange juice, agreed in principal to merge only to have Rossi walk away from the deal before it became final. Following the third failed Kellogg takeover, articles in the press focused on Rossi's inability to "let go"—the company founder still controlled 20 percent of Tropicana stock, dominated a more or less rubber-stamp board of directors, and held onto the positions of chairman, CEO, and president at the age of 77. Observers also worried about the company's lack of a succession plan. In October 1977 Rossi finally gave up the presidency, appointing to that post Kenneth A. Barnebey, an executive vice-president and director who had joined the company in 1955 as sales supervisor.

Purchased by Beatrice in 1978

In August 1978 Tropicana was finally sold to Beatrice Company for $490 million in cash and stock. The acquisition immediately ran into regulatory difficulties, and in 1980 a Federal Trade Commission (FTC) administrative law judge ruled that the purchase violated antitrust law because Beatrice could have expanded its own chilled juice brand—which had a market share of one percent—instead of buying Tropicana. The judge ordered Beatrice to divest Tropicana and pay to the government any Tropicana-derived profits. Following Beatrice's appeal, the FTC overturned the judge's ruling in 1983, finding that the acquisition was not illegal.

Barnebey headed up Tropicana Products following the acquisition but by 1982 Richard Walrack, a 30-year Beatrice veteran, had taken over as president of the Beatrice subsidiary (Rossi died in 1993 at the age of 92). Two important events in 1983 shook the orange juice industry and intensified the "orange juice wars." The Procter & Gamble Company (P&G) launched the Citrus Hill brand, offering both frozen concentrate and from-concentrate chilled juice. By 1984 the marketing power of P&G had quickly made Citrus Hill into a fairly strong third player. That year the declining frozen concentrate sector was led by Minute Maid's 25 percent share, with Citrus Hill holding seven percent and Tropicana four percent. Tropicana still held the top spot in the rapidly growing chilled juice sector with a 28 percent share, with Minute Maid claiming 18 percent and Citrus Hill nine percent. The second key event of 1983 was an orange freeze which forced Tropicana to raise the price of its not-from-concentrate chilled juice three times in quick succession. Amazingly, the company saw no drop-off in purchasing, as customers were clearly willing to pay a premium for what they perceived to be a superior prod-

uct—the not-from-concentrate juice. Funds from the higher prices were used to begin expanding the Tropicana brand outside of its strongholds in the Northeast and Southeast. Around this time, Tropicana—with the help of Beatrice—became more sophisticated in its marketing and product positioning. It rebranded its not-from-concentrate chilled juice Tropicana Pure Premium, while the from-concentrate version, which it had sold for a number of years, was first called Gold 'n Pure and then Tropicana Season's Best. Under Beatrice, Tropicana was also more aggressive about introducing new products, such as the 1985-debuted Tropicana Pure Premium HomeStyle orange juice, which featured added pulp.

Meanwhile the door to the Tropicana president's office became a revolving one, as Walrack resigned in June 1984 for "personal reasons," and his replacement—Wesley M. Thompson, who had been hired away from a Coca-Cola executive marketing position—did the same only nine months later. Stephen J. Volk, who had previously worked at PepsiCo, was named president in March 1985. Sales in the United States of chilled orange juice outpaced concentrate for the first time in 1986, as consumers continued to buy increasing amounts of convenience foods. Tropicana was well-positioned to take advantage of this trend.

Sold to Seagram in 1988

In April 1986 Beatrice was taken private through a $6.2 billion, highly leveraged buyout led by Kohlberg Kravis Roberts & Co. (KKR). Over the next two years, Beatrice was stripped of much of its assets to pay down debt. Tropicana was part of this asset sale; it was sold to The Seagram Company Ltd., the Canadian alcoholic beverage maker, for $1.2 billion in March 1988. By that time, Tropicana was a company with annual sales of $740 million and pretax profits of $100 million.

Under Seagram, Tropicana continued to expand within the United States, becoming a truly national brand for the first time. Also in an aggressive expansion mode, Minute Maid aimed squarely at Tropicana with the 1988 introduction of its own not-from-concentrate chilled juice brand, Minute Maid Premium Choice. Tropicana subsequently sued Coca-Cola over its advertising and packaging slogan for Premium Choice, which included the phrase "straight from the orange." Coca-Cola dropped the slogan rather than fight the suit. Despite the lawsuit, by 1990 Minute Maid had 11.7 percent of the not-from-concentrate, ready-to-serve orange juice market. That year, however, Tropicana edged past Minute Maid in the overall U.S. orange juice market, claiming 22.3 percent to its rival's 22.2 percent. The orange juice wars soon claimed their first victim when the top two orange juice brands proved to be too formidable competitors for even the likes of P&G, which discontinued the Citrus Hill brand in September 1992. Tropicana and Minute Maid were soon battling anew to gain share in the aftermath of Citrus Hill's withdrawal. Tropicana gained the initial upper hand, and by 1993 had extended its lead in the overall orange juice market to a somewhat comfortable 30.1 percent to 25.9 percent.

Even while it was ascending to the top spot, Tropicana continued to be beset by management turnover. Robert L. Soran, who had headed the company at the time of its acquisition by Seagram and continued as president afterward, was forced to resign in September 1991 following his failure to report to Seagram $20 million in cost overruns on construction projects in Florida, New Jersey, and California, according to Alix M. Freedman of the *Wall Street Journal.* In February 1992 William Pietersen, president of the Seagram Beverage Group, was named president of Tropicana as well. He resigned in January 1993 for "family considerations," with Myron A. Roeder taking over.

From the late 1980s through the mid-1990s, Tropicana expanded aggressively, both outside of its core orange juice products and outside of the United States. In 1988 the company introduced the Twister line of bottled and frozen juice blends; the "flavors Mother Nature never intended" were eventually to include apple-berry-pear, orange-peach, cranberry-raspberry-strawberry, and orange-strawberry-guava. Three years later, a low-calorie Twister Light line made its debut. By 1991 annual sales of the Twister lines reached $170 million. That year Tropicana Pure Premium was launched in Canada, the United Kingdom, Ireland, and France; Germany, Argentina, and Panama were added to Pure Premium's market area in 1994. Also in 1991 a joint venture between Tropicana and Kirin Brewery Company, Limited of Japan began importing and marketing orange juice in that country. In 1993 Tropicana introduced Grovestand orange juice, a ready-to-serve product that was touted to have the consistency and taste of fresh-squeezed juice. The company acquired Hitchcock, the number one premium fruit juice brand in Germany, from Deinhard & Company in 1994. By that time, about 12 percent of Tropicana's overall sales (which were about $1.3 billion in fiscal 1994) were generated from overseas markets, compared to just five percent in 1992. The company gained further overseas power through the May 1995 $276 million purchase of the global juice business of Dole Food Company, which had a strong presence in western Europe. Brands gained thereby were Dole juices in North America and Dole, Fruvita, Looza, and Juice Bowl juices and nectars in Europe. Tropicana then became known as Tropicana Dole Beverages, with Ellen Marram heading up the unit and Gary M. Rodkin serving as president of Tropicana Dole Beverages North America.

As the 1990s continued, Tropicana expanded further internationally, entering several more Latin American countries as well as Hong Kong and China. The company also scored a promotional coup in 1996 when the stadium for the Tampa Bay Devil Rays major league baseball team was named Tropicana Field. In 1997, in addition to celebrating its 50th anniversary, Tropicana began construction of a $17 million research and development center in Bradenton; opened its Midwest Distribution Center in Cincinnati, Ohio; launched Tropicana Pure Premium juice products into Portugal; introduced Tropicana Fruitwise Smoothies and Tropicana Fruitwise Healthy Fruit Shakes; and acquired Copella Fruit Juices Ltd., the leading producer and marketer of chilled apple juice in the United Kingdom.

Sold to PepsiCo in 1998

While Tropicana was expanding rapidly into a company with 1997 worldwide sales of $1.93 billion, Seagram was increasing its involvement in the entertainment industry. In May 1998 Seagram announced it would acquire PolyGram N.V., the world's largest music company, for $10.4 billion. To help fund the purchase, Seagram said it would divest Tropicana. Originally, Seagram planned to sell the unit to the public through an initial public offering. But with the IPO market not as attractive as it was earlier in the decade, Seagram struck a deal with PepsiCo, Inc., consummated in August 1998, whereby the juice business was sold to the beverage giant for $3.3 billion in cash. Tropicana became a division of PepsiCo, once again adopting the name Tropicana Products, Inc. Marram elected to pursue opportunities elsewhere, so Rodkin was named president and CEO of the company. One sign that Tropicana was poised for a bright future was an August 1998 Tropicana press release announcing that for the first time in U.S. history, sales of not-from-concentrate chilled orange juice had surpassed those of from-concentrate juice. In November 1998 the company announced that it had agreed to license the Tropicana brand name to Greene River Marketing, Inc. of Vero Beach, Florida, for use on ruby red fresh grapefruit. This marked the first time that the Tropicana name would appear in the produce section of supermarkets.

Further Reading

"Beatrice Foods: Adding Tropicana for a Broader Nationwide Network," *Business Week,* May 15, 1978, pp. 114–16.

Brennan, Peter, "Tropicana Tries Squeezing into Latin Markets," *Journal of Commerce,* December 27, 1995, pp. A1, 5B.

Buss, Dale D., "Fresh Markets for Tropicana," *Food Processing,* November 1996, pp. 53+.

Chen, Kathy, "Tea and Tropicana? Seagram Wants Juice to Be Chinese Staple," *Wall Street Journal,* January 2, 1998, pp. 1, 4.

"Coca-Cola Invades Tropicana's Market," *Business Week,* December 1, 1973, pp. 26, 28.

Cox, Meg, "Beatrice's Great Expectations for Tropicana Tempered by Host of Unforeseen Problems," *Wall Street Journal,* December 15, 1980, p. 27.

Dawson, Havis, "The Chill Leader," *Beverage World,* July 1997, pp. 46–47, 50, 52.

Dyslin, John, "New Beverage President Charts New Seas for Seagram," *Prepared Foods,* September 1993, pp. 13+.

"Fifty Years of Growth," Bradenton, Fla.: Tropicana Products, Inc., 1997, 27 p.

Freedman, Alix M., "Tropicana Officials Fired by Seagram Kept Quiet About $20 Million Overrun," *Wall Street Journal,* September 24, 1991, p. A4.

Freedman, Alix M., and Ed Bean, "Seagram to Buy Beatrice Unit for $1.2 Billion," *Wall Street Journal,* March 11, 1988, pp. 2, 12.

Gazel, Neil R., *Beatrice: From Buildup to Breakup,* Urbana: University of Illinois Press, 1990, 235 p.

Giges, Nancy, "Tropicana Puts Ad Squeeze on Foes," *Advertising Age,* June 14, 1984, pp. 1, 43.

Hwang, Suein L., "Seagram Is Set to Buy Dole's Juice Business," *Wall Street Journal,* January 5, 1995, pp. A3, A6.

——, "Seagram Ousts President at Tropicana, Seeks New Course As Juice Unit Sours," *Wall Street Journal,* October 5, 1992, p. B1.

Ingram, Frederick C., "Tropicana," *Encyclopedia of Consumer Brands,* volume 1, edited by Janice Jorgensen, Detroit: St. James Press, 1994, pp. 598–601.

Keefe, Robert, "Seagram's Tropicana Unit a Marketing and Fruit-Juice Powerhouse," *Knight-Ridder/Tribune Business News,* October 29, 1996.

King, Wayne, "Tropicana's Boss Finds His 'Crazy' Ways Work," *New York Times,* June 16, 1974.

Lawrence, Jennifer, "Coca-Cola to Shake Tropicana Juice," *Advertising Age,* May 23, 1988, pp. 3, 89.

Louis, Arthur M., "Tony Rossi Can't Let Go," *Fortune,* January 16, 1978, pp. 120–21, 124.

McCarthy, Michael J., "Squeezing More Life into Orange Juice: Premium Juice Is Focal Point of Fierce Battle," *Wall Street Journal,* May 4, 1989, p. B1.

O'Connell, Vanessa, "Seagram May Be About to Seek a Buyer for Tropicana," *Wall Street Journal,* May 18, 1998, p. B10.

Ono, Yumiko, "Tropicana Is Trying to Cultivate a Global Taste for Orange Juice," *Wall Street Journal,* March 28, 1994, p. B10.

Orwall, Bruce, and Eben Shapiro, "Seagram to Sell Tropicana Unit to Public," *Wall Street Journal,* May 22, 1998, pp. A3, A12.

"Pepsi's Sitting on Trop of the World After Making Juicy Deal with Seagram," *Beverage World,* August 15, 1998, p. 14.

Prince, Greg W., "Shoot for the Moon," *Beverage World,* December 1995, pp. 30, 32.

Recio, Irene, and Zachary Schiller, "They're All Juice Up at Tropicana," *Business Week,* May 13, 1991, p. 48.

Rossi, Sanna Barlow, *Anthony T. Rossi, Christian and Entrepreneur: The Story of the Founder of Tropicana,* Downers Grove, Ill.: InterVarsity Press, 1986.

Schiller, Zachary, and Gail DeGeorge, "What's for Breakfast? Juice Wars," *Business Week,* October 5, 1987, pp. 110, 115.

Shapiro, Eben, "Tropicana Squeezes Out Minute Maid to Get Bigger Slice of Citrus Hill Fans," *Wall Street Journal,* pp. B1, B10.

"Tropicana Goes It Alone," *Financial World,* May 22, 1974, p. 24.

"What Makes Rossi Run?," *Forbes,* November 15, 1971, pp. 50–51.

—David E. Salamie

Tupperware

Tupperware Corporation

14901 S. Orange Blossom Trail
Orlando, Florida 32837
U.S.A.
(407) 826-5050
(800) 858-7221
Fax: (407) 826-8268
Web site: http://www.tupperware.com

Public Company
Incorporated: 1946
Employees: 6,800
Sales: $1.08 billion (1998)
Stock Exchanges: New York
Ticker Symbol: TUP
NAIC: 422130 Sanitary Food Containers Wholesaling;
    326199 Kitchen Utensils, Plastics, Manufacturing

Tupperware Corporation, whose well-known Tupperware parties have spread to more than 100 countries, is one of the largest direct sellers in the world. Relying on independent consultants rather than employees for sales, the company generated more than $1 billion in revenues in 1998. Although Tupperware's mainstay for 50 years had been plastic food storage containers, in the 1990s the company expanded into kitchen tools, small appliances, and baby and toddler products. Although U.S. sales declined steadily in the 1980s and 1990s, international sales expanded, with the result that more than 85 percent of company revenues came from international business in the mid-1990s. The economic declines in the Far East and Latin America in the late 1990s left Tupperware with overall falling sales and an unsure outlook for the coming years.

Company Origins

Company founder Earl Tupper was an early plastics pioneer. The young inventor found work at DuPont in the 1930s without the benefit of a college education. By 1938 Tupper was ready to strike out on his own and devote himself to research in plastics.

That year he started his own company, leaving DuPont with only his experience and a discarded piece of polyethylene, remains from the oil refining process that no one had yet manipulated into a practical form. Tupper's fledgling company kept afloat by making plastic parts for gas masks in World War II, although Tupper continued to pursue his research with polyethylene. Tupper modified his own refining process, searching for more useful and appealing forms of plastic.

By 1942 Tupper had developed a plastic that was both durable and safe for food storage. The lightweight, flexible, and unbreakable material was also clear, odorless, and nontoxic. Tupper dubbed the new material Poly-T, and he further refined the product over the next few years. In 1946 he founded a new company, Tupperware, and began manufacturing food storage and serving containers with Poly-T. The containers were enhanced the following year with the unique Tupperware seal, an innovation that consumers would still find useful more than 50 years later. Tupper had gotten the idea for the airtight seal from a paint can lid.

Although Tupper quickly found department and hardware stores to carry his product, customers were harder to come by. Consumers were unfamiliar with the benefits of the new material and did not know how to operate the seal. Sales finally took off in the late 1940s when a few direct sellers of Stanley Home Products added Tupperware to their demonstrations. The products flourished with the direct selling approach because salespeople could explain the benefits of the plastic and personally demonstrate the seal to consumers. In addition, Stanley Home Products salespeople did not sell door to door, but rather sold their products at home parties. This method was particularly suited to Tupperware sales because homemakers felt they were getting advice from other homemakers who actually used the products.

Expansion in the 1950s–70s

The most successful early direct seller of Tupperware was Brownie Wise, a Detroit secretary and single mother. Tupper hired her in 1951 to create a direct selling system for his company. Within a few months Tupper had established the subsidiary

Company Perspectives:

Tupperware conducts its business through a single business segment, manufacturing and marketing a broad line of high-quality consumer products for the home. The core of Tupperware's product line consists of food storage containers which preserve freshness through the well-known Tupperware seals. Tupperware also has an established line of children's educational toys, serving products and gifts. The line of products has expanded over the years into kitchen, home storage and organizing uses with products such as Modular Mates containers, Fridge Stackables containers, OneTouch canisters, the Rock N'Serve line, Meals in Minutes line, Legacy Serving line and TupperMagic line, and many specialized containers. In recent years, Tupperware has expanded its offerings in the food preparation and servicing areas through the addition of a number of products, including double colanders, tumblers and mugs, mixing and serving bowls, serving centers, microwaveable cooking and serving products, and kitchen utensils.

Tupperware continues to introduce new designs and colors in its product lines, and to extend existing products into new markets around the world. The development of new products varies in different markets in order to address differences in cultures, lifestyles, tastes and needs of the markets.

Tupperware Home Parties, Inc. and had abandoned selling his products through retail stores. Wise's home party system used a sales force of independent consultants who earned a flat percentage of the goods they sold and won incentives in the form of bonuses and products. Wise, together with Gary McDonald, another Stanley veteran, created the Tupperware Jubilee, an annual sales convention that became famous and provided a format for the conventions of numerous direct-selling companies.

Sales skyrocketed, multiplying 25 times within three years. By the late 1950s Tupperware had become a household name. With almost no advertising, Tupperware had created phenomenal brand awareness. The company's rapid success can be attributed to its recruitment of almost 9,000 independent consultants by 1954, most of them women, and their enthusiastic spread of Tupperware parties.

Tupperware home parties provided an easy entrée into the workforce for women. Able to schedule the parties around their home and family responsibilities, women could earn extra cash and get together with friends and neighbors at the same time. In addition, the home party plan provided a milieu in which women were trusted as salespeople, unlike door-to-door sales, where women were not accepted at the time.

In 1958 Wise resigned from her vice-president position and Tupper sold the company to Rexall Drug. Despite the change in management the company continued to thrive. Throughout the 1960s and 1970s sales and earnings doubled every five years. The company had grown not only in the United States but also had entered and thrived in several foreign countries. Tupper-

ware's first venture outside the United States was to Canada in 1958. Tupperware parties were soon being thrown in Latin America, Western Europe, and Japan. International sales became a significant source of revenue for Tupperware in the 1970s, and Rexall Drug, which had become Dart Industries, had changed the subsidiary's name to Tupperware International.

Slipping Sales in the Early 1980s

Sales exceeded the half billion dollar mark in 1976. Four years later Dart Industries and Kraft Inc. merged, and the newly formed company looked to subsidiary Tupperware International to fuel its growth. Tupperware's growth slowed in the early 1980s, however, and by 1983 the subsidiary had cut seven percent from its sales and lost 15 percent from its earnings. Several factors contributed to the slip in sales and earnings. Competition had increased from Rubbermaid Inc., Eagle Affiliates, and other retail companies. In addition, an economic recovery had allowed many part-time sales people to find full-time work elsewhere, and the movement of women into the workforce had dried up the company's source for part-time labor and limited the time many women had to attend parties. The company exacerbated the labor problem, however, by not enticing people with higher commissions and by lowering the quality of their bonus prizes.

Sales continued to fall, slipping six percent in 1984, from $827 million to $777 million. Even worse, earnings plummeted 27 percent, to $139 million. The following year was no better: Sales dropped to $762 million and earnings declined to a mere $96 million. Tupperware finally took action, bringing in a new management team in 1985. K. Douglas Martin took over as president of Tupperware USA, and Dart and Kraft moved William L. Jackson from the company's Duracell battery division to the chairmanship of Tupperware. Having made significant improvements in the Duracell division, Jackson was expected to help turn Tupperware around.

Jackson immediately made several changes. To bolster slipping party attendance, he loosened the rules governing parties and allowed adaptations to the parties that would appeal to working women, such as shorter parties and parties thrown at the workplace. In addition, Jackson worked to improve Tupperware's training of its salespeople and eliminated any bonuses and sales incentives that appeared ineffective. Over the next couple of years Jackson instituted further changes. The company introduced its first catalog, which was sent out only in response to requests made to its toll-free number. In addition, national print and television advertising was stepped up to help counteract competition from Rubbermaid and other retail product lines. To improve the company's delivery speed, Tupperware built several new warehouses and a large distribution center.

New products in the mid-1980s helped boost both sales and company morale. In 1985 Tupperware introduced Ultra 21, a line of cookware to which market research had shown consumers would respond favorably. The company's new microwave cookware did very well and by 1987 had shown significant growth. Other products, including the company's traditional storage containers, struggled merely to maintain their sales figures.

Uneven Recovery in the Late 1980s and Early 1990s

In 1986 Dart and Kraft reversed their ill-fated merger. Dart renamed itself Premark International Inc., and former Kraft president Warren Batts took over as chair and chief executive officer. Tupperware apparently responded well to the change. Although the subsidiary posted a $58 million loss in 1986, its profits rose 48 percent in 1987.

Progress at Tupperware was uneven over the next several years. Sales in the United States continued to decline, although international business grew steadily. As a result, the proportion of U.S. to international sales gradually shifted until international sales accounted for more than half the company's revenues in 1992. That year, Tupperware's operations in the United States reported a loss of $22 million. In another management shift, Rick Goings, executive at direct sales leader Avon, took over as president of Tupperware in 1992.

In an effort to halt the decline in U.S. earnings, Tupperware cut costs and stepped up its sales force recruiting efforts. In addition, the company moved into direct mail, for the first time sending out unsolicited catalogs in 1992. Sales representatives provided names and addresses and paid Tupperware 65 cents for each catalog sent to one of their customers. Catalog customers then bought directly from their sales representatives. The company saw the catalog as yet another way to entice busy working women back into the Tupperware fold.

In 1993 the company was again enjoying profits in the United States, with earnings that year at $12.5 million. Sales also continued to grow internationally, helping improve the company's image on Wall Street. Shares of Premark International rose from $48 at the beginning of 1993 to $88 at the end of the year, due in large part to Tupperware's recovery.

Overall sales continued to improve in the mid-1990s, in part fueled by massive product introductions. Tupperware brought out approximately 100 new products between 1994 and 1996, including entire new product lines and specialty items catering to particular needs internationally, such as Kimono Keepers in Japan. As had been the case for the last decade, international sales growth outstripped that in the United States. Sales in the Far East and Latin America boomed, while sales in the United States improved slowly. As a result, by 1996, Tupperware relied on international business for 85 percent of its revenues and 95 percent of its profits.

Independence in 1996

Tupperware's finances continued to improve. By 1996 sales had reached 1.4 billion with earnings of $235 million. Premark International's food equipment and decorative product businesses were not faring quite as well: $2.2 billion in sales resulted in $168 million in earnings. Premark shares were trading well below competitors as a result, and management felt Tupperware was being held back by the company's other businesses. Consequently, in May 1996, Premark International spun off Tupperware, making it an independent public company. Premark shareholders received one share of Tupperware stock for each Premark share they held.

Wall Street responded positively to the spinoff; Tupperware shares began trading at $42 and soon rose to $55. Certain analysts sang the company's praises, including David Boczar, who told *Financial World,* "There is a perception of higher quality with Tupperware as well as the multifunctionality of the products, and also the nature of the distribution." He felt that the long-term prospects for the newly independent company were good.

The steady improvement in sales and earnings in the mid-1990s faltered in 1997. Revenues declined from a high of $1.37 billion in 1996 to $1.23 billion in 1997. Earnings plummeted 53 percent, from $175 million in 1996 to $82 million in 1997. Several factors had contributed to the decline. Domestically, a change in the company's sales plan led to a loss in its vital sales force. Quite a few sales representatives left Tupperware when the company raised the level of sales needed to qualify for a company minivan. Tupperware later renewed its recruiting efforts by offering subcompact company cars to sales representatives.

Internationally, the Asian economic crisis significantly affected Tupperware's performance, which relied on Japan alone for 12 percent of its sales in 1996. In addition, a third party vendor delayed Tupperware's delivery of products to its Japanese sales representatives, causing a major customer service problem. Although sales in the Far East continued to decline as the economic crisis there deepened, Tupperware hoped its expansion into India, Russia, and China in 1997 would offset the loss in sales.

In 1997 Tupperware experienced further discord with some of its U.S. consultants when it began enforcing a company policy prohibiting the sale of Tupperware online. The company's crackdown included cutting off from their distributors consultants who refused to shut down their web sites. Consultants with web sites resented the intrusion into how they ran their businesses, for as independent franchise owners, Tupperware consultants are not employees. By early 1998, however, only six web sites remained in operation from a high of almost 100 in 1996. Lawrie Hall, director of external affairs at Tupperware, explained the policy to *Fortune:* "We believe that the product-demonstration and customer services that our consultants offer face to face can't be adequately provided in an Internet environment." The following year, in a complete about-face from that position, Tupperware announced plans to sell merchandise over its own corporate web site.

Sales and earnings fell further in 1998. Revenues declined to $1.1 billion, a 21 percent decline since the company was divested from Premark two years earlier. Net income fell to $69 million, the company's lowest profits since its loss in 1992. Further erosion of the company's independent sales force in the United States was responsible in part for the decline in domestic sales. Internationally, slipping sales in Latin America and Japan posed the greatest threat to overall growth.

In the late 1990s Tupperware pursued several strategies to combat persistent declines in sales in the United States. Diversifying its distribution channels was one strategy. Tupperware had plans for selling over the Internet, through television infomercials, and at shopping mall kiosks. Diversifying its product line was another. Throughout the middle to late 1990s, Tupperware had been expanding into new product areas, including kitchen tools, small kitchen appliances, and children's products. Tupperware introduced a new sales technique in April 1998 with the "Demo in a Box." Consultants can purchase these boxes that come completely outfitted with recipes, apron, invitation inserts, video and audio training tapes, etc. Internationally, Tupperware continued to move into new geographic areas and to expand its independent sales force.

Although some analysts saw hope in the company's move into more traditional retail venues, overall confidence on Wall Street was low, as evidenced by the 63 percent decline in the company's stock price between 1997 and 1999. However, new products are introduced each month along with hostess incentives to keep interest high for customers to host/attend frequent parties and customer loyalty remains strong.

Further Reading

Badenhausen, Kurt, "Tupperware: No Party Pooper," *Financial World,* July/August 1997, pp. 20–22.

——, "Tupperware: Party On," *Financial World,* September 16, 1996, p. 24.

Daily, Jo Ellen, and Mark N. Vamos, "How Tupperware Hopes to Liven Up the Party," *Business Week,* February 25, 1985, pp. 108–09.

Fusaro, Roberta, "Tupperware to Sell on the Web," *Computerworld,* February 8, 1999, p. 8.

Hannon, Kerry, "Party Animal," *Forbes,* November 16, 1987, pp. 262–70.

Kinkead, Gwen, "Tupperware's Party Times Are Over," *Fortune,* February 20, 1984, pp. 113–20.

Marcial, Gene G., "Get Ready for a Tupperware Party," *Business Week,* May 9, 1994, p. 80.

Spiegel, Peter, "Party On," *Forbes,* May 3, 1999, p. 76.

"Tupperware Rolls Out Catalog Nationwide," *Catalog Age,* November 1992, p. 27.

Warner, Melanie, "Can Tupperware Keep a Lid on the Web?," *Fortune,* January 12, 1998, p. 144.

Weiner, Steve, "Waif Makes Good," *Forbes,* November 14, 1988, pp. 76, 80.

—Susan Windisch Brown

Tyco International Ltd.

The Gibbons Building
10 Queen Street, Suite 301
Hamilton HM11
Bermuda
(441) 292-8674
Fax: (603) 778-7342
Web site: http://www.tycoint.com

Public Company
Incorporated: 1962 as Tyco, Inc.
Employees: 87,000
Sales: $12.31 billion (1998)
Stock Exchanges: New York London Bermuda
Ticker Symbol: TYC
NAIC: 322221 Coated & Laminated Packaging Paper & Plastics Film Manufacturing; 32552 Adhesive Manufacturing; 326199 All Other Plastics Product Manufacturing; 33121 Iron & Steel Pipe & Tube Manufacturing from Purchased Steel; 332312 Fabricated Structural Metal Manufacturing; 332322 Sheet Metal Work Manufacturing; 332323 Ornamental & Architectural Metal Work Manufacturing; 332116 Metal Stampings; 332911 Industrial Valve Manufacturing; 332912 Fluid Power Valve & Hose Fitting Manufacturing; 332919 Other Metal Valve & Pipe Fitting Manufacturing; 332996 Fabricated Pipe & Pipe Fitting Manufacturing; 333414 Heating Equipment Manufacturing; 335931 Current-Carrying Wiring Device Manufacturing; 335929 Communications Wire & Cable; 334418 Printed Circuit Assembly; 334513 Instruments & Related Product Manufacturing for Measuring, Displaying, & Controlling Industrial Process Variables; 339112 Surgical Appliance & Supplies Manufacturing; 42161 Electrical Apparatus & Equipment, Wiring Supplies, & Construction Material Wholesalers; 561621 Security Systems Services

Tyco International Ltd. is a diversified manufacturing and service company, with four main operating groups: healthcare and specialty products, fire and security services, flow control, and electrical and electronic components. The healthcare and specialty products group manufactures and distributes disposable medical supplies and other specialty products and is involved in vehicle auction and reconditioning services. The fire and security services group is the world leader in the design, manufacture, installation, and service of fire detection, suppression, and sprinkler systems, as well as being the world leader in electronic security services. The flow control group makes and markets pipe, fittings, valves, meters, and related products that are used to transport, control, and measure the flow of liquids and gases. The electrical and electronic components group is involved in the manufacture and sale of electric and electronic connection devices and interconnection systems, printed circuit boards, steel electrical conduit, and undersea communications cable systems. Tyco has grown tremendously in the 1990s, with revenues increasing from $3.07 billion in fiscal 1992 to $12.31 billion in 1998; an aggressive program of acquisition during this period saw the company spend about $28 billion to purchase 110 companies.

Began in 1962 in High Tech

In 1960, with a science Ph.D. from Harvard, Arthur J. Rosenberg opened a research laboratory in Waltham, Massachusetts, and did experimental work for the government. Two years later Rosenberg incorporated Tyco, Inc. and branched into the commercial sector. He assembled a team of top researchers and Tyco developed high-tech products for the marketplace.

Tyco's early technological breakthroughs included a silicon carbide laser. This laser was the first blue-light laser and the first to fire a nonstop beam, all at room temperature. Other successful research projects led to the marketing of the Dynalux battery charger, a device that would never overcharge a battery. It had many industrial applications. Other advances came in fluid controls, microcircuitry, and fuel cell catalysts.

Rosenberg established an ambitious growth schedule for his company. To fill the gaps in its development and distribution

Company Perspectives:

Tyco focuses expansion efforts on specific market segments where we are, or can be, a global leader. We have an excellent record of maximizing opportunities in global markets. Our earnings per share growth is fueled by strong revenue gains combined with the relentless pursuit of efficiency.

network, Tyco began to acquire other companies. In 1965—the same year that the company changed its name to Tyco Laboratories, Inc.—Tyco began a spree of acquisitions that drastically changed the makeup of the company. In 1966 the company bought Industrionics Control, Inc., adding to other recent purchases of Mule Battery Manufacturing Company and Custom Metal Products, Inc. The next year, Tyco acquired the North American Printed Circuit Corporation, General Nucleonics Corporation, and Bytrex, Inc. In 1968 Electralab Electronics Corporation; Air Spec, Inc.; Explosive Fabricators Corporation; Dynaco Inc.; Coating Products, Inc.; and Digital Devices, Inc. were acquired. Accurate Forming Company, CBM Realty Corporation, Linear Corporation, Micro-Power Corporation, and Custom Products Inc. were added to the group in 1969. Tyco's sales increased from less than $1 million in 1963 to more than $41 million for all of its companies by 1969.

This dazzling growth, however, did not occur without complications. By the end of the 1960s, Tyco Laboratories needed a major reorganization to put its new units in order. The price of company stock had dropped dramatically from its peak in the mid-1960s, as Wall Street became disillusioned with high-tech companies. Tyco divested a number of unprofitable units in 1969, and assessed its corporate direction.

In 1970 the Tyco board quietly eased out founder Arthur J. Rosenberg, replacing him temporarily with Joshua M. Berman, a partner in the law firm Goodwin, Proctor, and Hoar, and a director of Tyco Laboratories. In September 1971 Ralph W. Detra took over as president, while Berman remained chairman and CEO. Detra resigned one year later, and Tyco was without a president until April 1973, when the Tyco board appointed Joseph P. Gaziano chairman, president, and CEO.

Acquired Simplex in 1974

Gaziano, a graduate of the Massachusetts Institute of Technology, had held a number of positions at the Raytheon Company before leaving in 1967 to run Prelude Corporation, a lobster-fishing concern. Gaziano launched a new era for Tyco Laboratories. During his tenure the company became much larger and more diverse, making acquisitions on a much grander scale than earlier. In January 1974 the stock of Tyco Laboratories was listed on the New York Stock Exchange, and four months later Gaziano completed Tyco's most ambitious acquisition thus far, the $22 million cash purchase of the Simplex Wire and Cable Company.

Simplex specialized in undersea cable, and had its beginnings when Charles A. Morss began manufacturing wire bird cages and fire screens at his firm, Morss and White, in the 1880s. As the revolution in electricity created new uses for wire products, the company adjusted its product lines to include insulated wire. In 1890 the firm changed its name to the Simplex Electrical Company, and it was incorporated five years later, focusing solely on the production of electrical cable. In 1900 Simplex laid the longest underwater telephone cable in the country, across the five-mile strait between Mackinaw City and St. Ignace, Michigan. The cable lasted 31 years beneath the frigid Great Lakes waters.

In the 1920s, a pair of Simplex scientists discovered that the proteins present in natural rubber were the cause of water absorption, and in 1926 patented a process to remove the proteins. The resulting Anhydrex cables were successfully marketed—lightweight, moisture-resistant cables.

During World War II, Simplex began producing submarine cable for the U.S. Navy and U.S. Coast Guard. By the end of the war, cable production had increased nearly fourfold. The company continued to do research for the military even after the war, and a location with greater security was acquired for the submarine-cable division. Located on the banks of the Piscataqua River in New Hampshire, the submarine-cable division became Simplex's flagship operation.

Throughout the 1950s and 1960s, Simplex grew due to technological developments in cable production. New products such as flexible pipeline and sodium conductor cables were introduced. In 1966 Simplex began offering installation of undersea cables for the first time.

While Simplex competed with such manufacturing giants as Western Union and Anaconda Wire and Cable in the conventional wire and cable markets, it had a lead in the underwater cable market. This specialization was one of the factors that made it attractive to Tyco Laboratories.

Acquired Grinnell in 1975

In September 1975, shortly after the Simplex acquisition, Tyco purchased the Grinnell subsidiary of International Telephone and Telegraph (ITT). Grinnell was the market leader in automatic sprinklers. ITT had been ordered by federal courts to divest the fire-protection-equipment and piping manufacturer on antitrust grounds. Tyco president Joseph Gaziano took the opportunity to purchase a well-established company at a reasonable price.

Originally founded in Providence, Rhode Island, in 1850 as the Steam and Gas Pipe Company, Grinnell operated with a member of the Grinnell family high in the corporate hierarchy until the late 1940s. The company began business installing Providence's original gas mains, then operated as a plumbing supplier. Before long its major product became the automatic sprinkling system, a product that was soon the market leader.

In 1892 the company was incorporated as the General Fire Extinguisher Company and grew steadily, manufacturing hydrant piping, steam and water heating equipment, iron fittings, brass products, and sundry mill supplies. In 1923 the company was reincorporated, while retaining the same name.

By 1929 humidifying equipment had been added to its product lines. On the eve of the Great Depression the company employed 4,000 people and had assets of almost $18 million. Over the next few years, however, the number of employees dropped to 2,650, and assets dropped to $12 million at the end of fiscal 1934. General Fire Extinguisher's stock traded at $7 per share in 1934, compared to $45 in 1930.

During World War II, the majority of the company's resources were applied to war production. In April 1944 General Fire Extinguisher changed its name to the Grinnell Corporation. War production had a rejuvenating effect on the company. By the end of 1944, Grinnell employed 6,000 workers and assets were up to $20 million.

In the 1950s, Grinnell diversified into the central station alarm business, which monitored burglar and fire alarms in subscribers' buildings 24 hours a day. In 1949 Grinnell bought a controlling interest in the Automatic Fire Alarm Company, an overseer of automatic fire-protection systems in New York City, Boston, and Philadelphia. In 1950 Holmes Electric Protective Company—which supplied burglar alarm services primarily to banks in New York City, Philadelphia, and Pittsburgh—was acquired. Three years later, Grinnell purchased a majority holding in the American District Telegraph Company, the largest central station alarm company in the United States.

In 1961 the U.S. Justice Department filed an antitrust suit against Grinnell and three subsidiaries, charging that the four companies had conspired to monopolize the central alarm business, and seeking to force the divestiture of the three subsidiaries—Holmes Electric Protective Company, Automatic Fire Alarm Company, and American District Telegraph. As a result of the trial in 1964, federal judge Charles E. Wyzanski ruled against Grinnell, and ordered that the company "cease and desist" from violating the Sherman Antitrust Act and divest all of its stock in the three central alarm companies; the judge also banned Grinnell's president, James D. Fleming, from corporate leadership. Grinnell appealed, charging that the judge both failed to comprehend the case, and was biased.

The controversial case found its way to the U.S. Supreme Court, where the ruling was upheld in 1966. In January 1968 Grinnell divested itself of the three subsidiaries, whose shares were spun off to Grinnell stockholders. Since the subsidiaries' earnings were never consolidated with Grinnell's, the company's balance sheet was not seriously affected. Indeed, Grinnell's own fire-protection and piping business had grown significantly in the 1960s.

In August 1969 Grinnell shareholders voted in favor of a merger with ITT, despite antitrust suits filed by the Justice Department to prevent the acquisition. The merger, however, was doomed. In 1971 federal courts, citing antitrust violations, gave ITT two years to divest itself of Grinnell. The deadline passed without a suitable bid, and ITT put the company under the stewardship of a court trustee in September 1973. After two losing years, Grinnell began to operate at a profit again, and was purchased by Tyco Laboratories.

Tyco paid $14 million and agreed to pay ITT 40 percent of Grinnell's net earnings for the next ten years, with a minimum payment of $28.5 million. At the time of the acquisition, Tyco's total sales were $58 million, overshadowed by its new subsidiary, Grinnell, whose turnover was $107 million.

Failed to Acquire Leeds & Northrup in Late 1970s

Tyco began its third major acquisition in November 1976 when it bought 13 percent of the Philadelphia-based process-control designer and manufacturer Leeds & Northrup Company. Through a press release Tyco announced its intention to buy more of Leeds & Northrup's stock. Leeds & Northrup filed suit in federal court, claiming that Tyco's press release was in effect an illegal tender offer and that Tyco had not filed the necessary documents with the Securities and Exchange Commission. Tyco agreed to halt its purchase of the stock temporarily, but over the next two years President and CEO Gaziano waged one of the most convoluted hostile takeover battles in corporate history.

Tyco's agreement to stop buying Leeds & Northrup stock was dependent on the latter company's continued independence. Leeds & Northrup President David Kimball began issuing new shares, and arranged for the Milwaukee-based Cutler-Hammer Inc. to buy nine percent of Leeds & Northrup stock as a hedge against further encroachment from Tyco. Gaziano protested, but could do little; Tyco was prevented by a court-approved agreement from gaining more than 19 percent of Leeds & Northrup until March 1978. In January 1978, Tyco gave up its attempt to acquire Leeds & Northrup, and sold its 19 percent interest to Cutler-Hammer for a $9.2 million profit.

Two months later Tyco bought 8.5 percent of Cutler-Hammer Inc., which now controlled 33.5 percent of Leeds & Northrup. By June, Tyco had 28.4 percent of the Cutler-Hammer shares. Gaziano then raised $25 million through debentures in the Eurodollar market, and increased Tyco's holding in Cutler-Hammer to 32 percent. Meanwhile, Koppers Inc., a chemical and engineering firm, accumulated 21 percent of the stock, erecting a formidable roadblock to Tyco's gaining a majority interest in Cutler-Hammer.

Joseph Gaziano responded by selling Tyco's 32 percent holding in Cutler-Hammer at a profit to the Eaton Corporation, a heavy equipment manufacturer that planned to merge with Cutler-Hammer, stipulating that Eaton would spin off the Leeds & Northrup shares to Tyco.

Eaton quickly made a tender offer of $261 million for the remaining Cutler-Hammer shares, a bid its board could not refuse, but at the last minute Cutler-Hammer sold the coveted 33.5 percent holding in Leeds & Northrup to General Signal Corporation. General Signal immediately announced its plan to merge with Leeds & Northrup. After a 20-month effort Gaziano failed to acquire Leeds & Northrup. "It just wasn't meant to be," he told *Forbes* magazine in 1978. Nevertheless, Tyco netted $12.9 million from the transactions.

Entered Packaging Through 1979 Purchase of Armin and 1981 Purchase of Ludlow

Gaziano continued to pursue his goal of making Tyco a $1 billion company by 1985. In September 1979 Tyco bought the Armin Corporation for $27 million. Armin was a leader in the production of polyethylene films, products used primarily in packaging.

Armin was incorporated as the Armin Poly Film Corporation in 1967 by Armin Kaufman, a Hungarian immigrant who had come penniless to the United States in 1955. The plastic film maker grew quickly and in 1969, Armin acquired Poly Version, Inc. and the E. Gluck Trading Company through stock exchanges. The Gluck acquisition represented a departure for the company from its main product line. Gluck made watches that sold in retail markets in the $10 to $50 price range under the Sutton, Chateau, Precision, Adventura, and Andre Rivalle labels. In 1975 digital watches with price tags ranging from $100 to $150 were introduced under the Armitron and Quasar label. These electronic watches were Armin's first attempt at manufacturing the timekeeping parts of watches themselves.

In the mid-1970s, over half of Armin's sales and about 70 percent of profits came from plastic films. New products such as film for sealing tapes, urethane foam sheet-molding compounds, and shrink wrap added to profits in the mid-1970s. Armin's Thermodynamics Corporation subsidiary, acquired in 1973, introduced a new Roto Extrusion process for its main product line—plastic pellets—promising better quality and lower costs.

Armin Corporation proved a profitable acquisition for Tyco Laboratories and Gaziano increased the company's share of the lucrative packaging market through the 1981 acquisition of the Ludlow Corporation, a manufacturer of packaging and other materials.

Ludlow dated back to 1868. The company was engaged in the import of jute from India for the manufacture of twines, carpet yarns, furniture webbing, cords, and other textile products at its Ludlow, Massachusetts, plant. In 1916 Malcolm B. Stone became president of Ludlow, and remained head of the corporation until 1957. Stone greatly expanded the operations of the company, buying a jute processing mill near Calcutta in 1920, giving Ludlow first choice of that country's jute crop.

In 1957 Austin B. Mason succeeded Stone. Mason, seeing that Ludlow's products were dependent on one commodity, jute, initiated a broad diversification program. Ludlow began producing paper specialties, including printed chart paper for scientific and military electronic equipment, coated papers, pressure sensitive papers, and gummed packaging paper products. Rubber and vinyl products for the automotive, shoe, and carpet industries also became a major part of Ludlow's product mix. By 1966 jute production, which had accounted for 90 percent of Ludlow's product lines ten years earlier, made up just 20 percent of sales.

In 1969 Ludlow entered the profitable mobile home market, a growing segment of the housing market at that time. Carpeting and home furnishings were added and, by 1971, made up more than half of Ludlow's sales. Ludlow's carpets, sold under the Ludlow and Walters label, were priced at the high end of the market. Ludlow's Forest Products subsidiary, based in Tennessee, produced a variety of nonupholstered furnishings. The company grew throughout the 1970s on the strengths of its diverse operations.

When Tyco Laboratories purchased Ludlow in 1981 for $97 million, Ludlow needed some streamlining. The company sold unprofitable units producing furniture, jute backing, textiles, and bags. Its specialty paper units enjoyed strong markets in medical applications and other technologically advancing fields.

Fort Increased Efficiency in the 1980s

In 1982 Joe Gaziano died suddenly at the age of 47. Tyco Laboratories entered a new period under the leadership of John F. Fort. Fort had risen through the ranks of the Simplex Wire and Cable Company, and was president of that firm at the time of the Tyco takeover. His style differed markedly from Gaziano's.

Fort disposed of Tyco's corporate jets and apartments, and trimmed the corporate staff to 35. Reining in the somewhat unwieldy conglomeration of businesses his predecessor had brought together, he divested such peripheral units as lawn furniture and latex. Fort organized Tyco's remaining subsidiaries into three main units: the fire protection and plumbing division, which consisted of Grinnell Corporation; the electronics division, made up of Simplex Wire and Cable and the Tyco Printed Circuits Group; and the packaging division, made up of Armin and Ludlow. Concentrating on making Tyco's existing businesses more profitable, Fort instituted a compensation program under which employees were rewarded in proportion to the profits their units generated.

Tyco made smaller acquisitions in the mid-1980s, including Micro-Circuit, Inc.; Hersey Products, Inc.; a water meter manufacturer, Atcor, Inc.; a pipe manufacturer; and 48 ITT production and distribution facilities worth $220 million. Following any such acquisition, Fort was ruthless about making the purchased firm more profitable, searching for ways to eliminate excess overhead and cut out unnecessary fat.

In 1987 Tyco's sales passed the $1 billion mark. Tyco paid $350 million in 1988 for the Mueller Company, a 132-year-old water and gas pipe manufacturer. The acquisition made Tyco a strong player in the area of flow control products, and this area soon became the company's fourth main unit, with the fire protection and plumbing division changed to a focus only on fire protection and the plumbing operations being subsumed into the new flow control division. This acquisition also built upon the 1986 purchase of Grinnell Flow Control from ITT. Sandwiched between these acquisitions was another important flow control buy, that of Allied Pipe & Tube Corporation, which was consummated in 1987. Another important deal came in 1990 when Tyco significantly bolstered its fire protection division through the purchase of Australia-based Wormald International Limited for $642.5 million in cash, stock, and a warrant. Wormald's marketing presence encompassed Australia, New Zealand, Asia, and Europe, heightening Tyco's international sales.

Kozlowski Quickened Acquisition Pace in the Mid-1990s

The early 1990s were a difficult period for Tyco thanks to the recession. Earnings were down despite the focus on cost containment, and the 1993 fiscal year saw the company post net income of a mere $1 million. Amidst these doldrums, the company leadership shifted in mid-1992 from Fort to L. Dennis Kozlowski, who had been with Tyco since the mid-1970s.

Kozlowski retained Fort's penchant for cost control but he slowly began to take a more aggressive approach to acquisitions—without ever pursuing a hostile bid and with two tough additional rules: an acquisition had to be immediately accretive to earnings and had to be twice as accretive to earnings as a stock buyback. The new leader also worked to build up Tyco's operations outside the area of fire and security services, its largest sector but one subject to the ups and downs of the U.S. construction market. At the same time, acquisition targets had to be complementary to an existing Tyco operation, however subtle that synergy might be. With this approach—and through spending $28 billion to acquire 110 companies from 1992 through 1998—Kozlowski was able to transform Tyco into a $12-billion-plus revenue giant with market leading positions in four areas: disposable and specialty products, fire and security services, flow control products, and electrical and electronic components. In reflection of an increased emphasis on the international market, the company changed its name to Tyco International Ltd. in 1993.

The first major acquisition of the Kozlowski era came in 1994 when Tyco paid $1.4 billion for Kendall International, a maker of disposable medical products with annual sales of $800 million. It was this purchase that transformed the packaging division into the disposable and specialty products division. This division was further bolstered in 1996 with the addition of five more companies, including Professional Medical Products, Inc., another disposable medical products maker, and Carlisle Plastics, a maker of plastic film. Also in 1996 Tyco added Thorn Security Group, a U.K. fire alarm and security system company.

In January 1997 Tyco abandoned a $4 billion bid to take over American Standard, a maker of air conditioners and bathroom fixtures. American Standard would have fit in well with Tyco's flow control division, but Tyco, keeping to its no-hostile-bids policy, walked away after the target's board rejected the offer. Undeterred, Tyco completed four major acquisitions over the remainder of 1997, adding one company to each of its divisions. Acquired in the area of disposable and specialty products was INBRAND, bought for $320 million, and a maker of disposable personal products such as adult incontinence products, feminine hygiene products, and baby diapers. By spending $850 million, Tyco secured the undersea cable-laying and maintenance operations of AT&T Corp. As part of the electrical and electronic components division, the AT&T unit was combined with Simplex to form Tyco Submarine Systems Ltd. In flow control, Tyco acquired Keystone International Inc. for $1.2 billion in stock. Houston-based Keystone was a world leader in the manufacture of valves, pipes, and other equipment used in the chemical, power, food/beverage, and petroleum industries. Tyco's largest acquisition to date was consummated in July 1997, when the company merged with ADT Limited, a Bermuda-based home security company, in a $5.4 billion transaction—a white knight deal that fended off a hostile takeover bid from Western Resources Inc. In this complicated transaction, a wholly owned subsidiary of ADT merged with Tyco International Ltd.; ADT thereupon changed its name to Tyco International Ltd.; and the wholly owned subsidiary that had merged with the former Tyco was renamed Tyco International (US), Inc. and became the U.S.

headquarters for the new Tyco, which was now domiciled in Bermuda for tax reasons. Tyco also added stock listings on the London and Bermuda exchanges to its NYSE listing. In addition to the number one electronic security service in North America and the United Kingdom, the ADT merger also brought Tyco, through ADT Automotive, the new area of vehicle auction services; this peripheral unit, which was small relative to other Tyco activities, was placed within the disposable and specialty products division.

In February 1998 Kozlowski turned down an offer to become president and eventual CEO of Raytheon Company. In April of that year Kozlowski told the *Financial Times* that he aimed to increase Tyco's non-North American revenue from 40 to 60 percent of the total within three years. Meantime, the Tyco executive did not slow down his company's pace of acquisition. In March 1998 Tyco closed on a $1.8 billion purchase of the Sherwood-Davis & Geck division of American Home Products. Sherwood-Davis was a leading maker of disposable medical products, including surgical sutures, catheters, and feeding tubes, and had annual revenues of about $1 billion. Three months later Tyco snapped up the Wells Fargo Alarm unit of Borg-Warner Corporation for $425 million. In October 1998 the company acquired United States Surgical Corporation (USSC) for about $3.17 billion in stock. USSC's complementary product line included disposable medical sutures, staples, and surgical items for minimally invasive operations. Yet another maker of disposable medical products was added in November 1998 when Tyco paid $460 million in cash for Graphic Controls Corporation. This spate of medical deals led Tyco to change the name of its disposable and specialty products division to healthcare and specialty products.

Tyco expanded its electronic security unit through the early 1999 purchases of Alarmguard Holdings, Inc. and Entergy Security Corporation, the latter paid for with $237 million in cash. In April of that year came Tyco's largest acquisition to date, that of AMP Incorporated, the world's leading manufacturer of electrical, electronic, fiber-optic, and wireless connection devices and interconnective systems. This was another white knight maneuver for Tyco, in that the $11.3 billion stock swap fended off AlliedSignal Inc.'s hostile bid to take over AMP. The addition of AMP was expected to help nearly double Tyco's revenues, which were projected to increase from $12.31 billion in 1998 to about $23 billion. Net income, which had already reached $1.18 billion in 1998, was projected to hit $2.3 billion in 1999. Kozlowski intended to continue Tyco's emphasis on highly strategic, carefully considered acquisitions, seeking only companies that fit within the company's four business areas. By sticking to this winning strategy, it seemed likely that Tyco could continue its astonishingly rapid rise to prominence—although finding attractive targets was also likely to prove increasingly difficult.

Principal Operating Units

HEALTHCARE AND SPECIALTY PRODUCTS: Accurate Forming; ADT Automotive; A&E Products; Armin Plastics; Carlisle Plastics, Inc.; Graphic Controls; Kendal Healthcare Products; Kendall International; Ludlow Coated Products; Ludlow Technical Products; Sherwood-Davis & Geck; Tyco Adhesives; Uni-Patch; U.S. Surgical. FIRE AND SECURITY SERVICES:

ADT; Alarmguard; Ansul; Atlas Fire Engineering; Automatic Sprinkler; Bon + Naga; CIPE; Fire Control; Fire Defender; Grinnell Corporation; Interco Alarms; Lintott Process System; Mather & Platt; Modern; National Fire & Security; O'Donnell Griffin; Olsen Engineering; OPPI; Quintrix Communications; SEPCI; Sonitrol; Thorn Security; Total Walther; Tyco Building Products; Tyco Engineering and Construction; Vigilant; Wormald Ansul (UK); Wormald Fire Systems. FLOW CONTROL: Allied Tube and Conduit; American Tube & Pipe; Anderson Greenwood; Bayard; Belgicast; Biffi; Canvil; Century Valve; Crosby; Debro Engineering & Presswork; Earth Tech; Glynwed Metals; Goliath Engineering; Grinnell; Hancock; Henry Pratt Company; Hindle Valves; J.B. Smith Co.; Intecva; James Jones; Keystone; Morin Actuators; Mueller Co.; Neotecha; Sempell; Star Sprinkler; T.J. Cope; Unistrut; Valvtron; Vanessa; Winn Valves; Yarway. ELECTRICAL AND ELECTRONIC COMPONENTS: Allied Tube & Conduit; AMP; The Rochester Corporation; Simplex Technologies; Tyco Printed Circuit Group, Inc.; Tyco Submarine Systems, Ltd.

Further Reading

Byrne, Harlan S., "One Hungry Tyke," *Barron's,* April 8, 1996, pp. 22–23.

Chakravarty, Subrata N., "Deal-a-Month Dennis," *Forbes,* June 15, 1998, pp. 66, 68.

Deutsch, Claudia H., "Finding the Profits (and Fun) in Mergers," *New York Times,* November 29, 1998, sec. 3, p. 4.

Green, Leslie, and J. Richard Elliot, Jr., "Cause for Alarm: The Story of the Anti-Trust Suit Against Grinnell Corp.," *Barron's,* May 30, 1966.

Johannes, Laura, "American Standard Rejects Tyco International's Offer," *Wall Street Journal,* January 14, 1997, pp. A3, A11.

——, "Tyco International Isn't Playing, It's Out on the Prowl," *Wall Street Journal,* January 17, 1997, p. B4.

——, "Tyco Plans to Acquire for $850 Million AT&T's Undersea Cable-Laying Unit," *Wall Street Journal,* April 14, 1997, p. B4.

——, "Tyco Will Acquire Alarm-System Unit of Borg-Warner," *Wall Street Journal,* April 21, 1998, p. B9.

Johannes, Laura, and Steven Lipin, "Tyco International, ADT in Merger Pact," *Wall Street Journal,* March 18, 1997, pp. A3, A14.

Lewis, William, "Tyco to Shift Focus Outside N. America," *Financial Times,* April 28, 1998, p. 32.

Lipin, Steven, "Tyco to Acquire Keystone International," *Wall Street Journal,* May 21, 1997, pp. A3, A6.

Lipin, Steven, and Gordon Fairclough, "Tyco Reaches Agreement to Buy AMP in Stock Swap Valued at $11.3 Billion," *Wall Street Journal,* November 23, 1998, pp. A3, A8.

Lublin, Joann S., and Jon G. Auerbach, "Tyco's CEO Refuses to Run Raytheon Co.," *Wall Street Journal,* March 5, 1998, p. A4.

Lublin, Joann S., and Mark Maremont, "A CEO with a Motto: 'Let's Make a Deal!,' " *Wall Street Journal,* January 28, 1999, pp. B1, B2.

Maremont, Mark, "Tyco Agrees to Buy Sherwood Division from American Home for $1.77 Billion," *Wall Street Journal,* December 22, 1997, pp. A3, A6.

——, "Tyco's Deal-a-Month Man," *Business Week,* January 27, 1997, p. 36.

Maremont, Mark, and Gordon Fairclough, "Accord with AMP Caps Months of Deal Making by Tyco," *Wall Street Journal,* November 24, 1998, p. B4.

Maremont, Mark, and Ross Kerber, "Tyco to Buy U.S. Surgical for $3.3 Billion in Stock," *Wall Street Journal,* May 26, 1998, p. A3.

Pasztor, Andy, "Water-System Gear Suit Draws Attention," *Wall Street Journal,* December 22, 1998, p. B7.

Thackray, John, "Tyco: The Operator," *Across the Board,* November 1991, pp. 21–23.

Waters, Richard, "ADT Agrees to Takeover by US Conglomerate," *Financial Times,* March 18, 1997, p. 27.

——, "Low-Tech but Riding High," *Financial Times,* March 18, 1997, p. 36.

—Thomas M. Tucker
—updated by David E. Salamie

Unigate PLC

Unigate House
Wood Lane
London W12 7RP
United Kingdom
(0181) 749 8888
Fax: (0181) 576 6071
Web site: http://www.unigate.co.uk

Public Company
Incorporated: 1959 as Unigate Limited
Employees: 28,243
Sales:£2.31 billion (US$3.86 billion) (1998)
Stock Exchanges: London
NAIC: 311611 Animal Slaughtering; 311613 Rendering
& Meat Byproduct Processing; 311512 Creamery
Butter Manufacturing; 311513 Cheese Manufacturing;
311514 Dry, Condensed & Evaporated Dairy Product
Manufacturing; 31152 Ice Cream & Frozen Dessert
Manufacturing; 311511 Fluid Milk Manufacturing;
311999 All Other Miscellaneous Food Manufacturing;
49311 General Warehousing & Storage; 48851
Freight Transportation Arrangement

Unigate PLC is a leading European fresh foods, dairy, and distribution company. Its largest business is that of fresh foods, which accounts for about 53 percent of operating profits and which manufactures value-added pork, bacon, and cooked meat products; as well as spreads, yogurt, desserts, cheese, and fruit juices. Unigate Dairies, responsible for about 29 percent of operating profits, is one of the largest milk processors in the United Kingdom, delivering milk to 1.3 million homes in addition to distributing fresh milk and cream to retailers and other channels. The dairy division also has butter and powdered milk operations. Wincanton Logistics, which generates about 18 percent of operating profits, is a leading supplier of logistics services to the U.K. distribution market. Unigate's evolution to its late 20th-century incarnation has been rather remarkable. The company, in its various forms, went from selling liquor in the mid-19th century to selling milk and baby food in the early 20th century, to becoming by 1991 a conglomerate that marketed goods and services ranging from turkeys to transportation to Mexican food. Through a host of divestments and acquisitions from 1992 through the remainder of the decade, Unigate shed its conglomerate status, emerging as a focused food and distribution group.

From Liquor to Milk

The history of Unigate goes back to 1882, when Charles Gates died and left his Guildford, Surrey grocer's shop to two of his sons, Charles Arthur and Leonard. The store primarily sold liquor; it was the local agent for Gilbey's wines and spirits and also sold beer. The Gates brothers added tea and coffee to their father's shelves. Then in 1885, according to a story that has become a part of company legend, they were seized by a violent fit of pro-temperance sentiment, vowed never to make money off the liquor trade again, and poured their entire stock of alcoholic beverages into the gutters of High Street, Guildford.

This left them without a source of livelihood, but it occurred to them that the cellars underneath the shop, as well as the yards and stables in back, could be converted into a dairy. They bought a milk separator and started West Surrey Dairy, purchasing milk from local farmers, selling the skim back to them for feeding pigs, and selling the cream to the prosperous citizens of Guildford. In 1888 the company changed its name to West Surrey Central Dairy Company Limited. Three more Gates brothers—Walter, William, and Alfred—and three of their sons joined the family business about this time.

It did not take long for the business to become successful enough to justify expansion. West Surrey Central Dairy bought creameries in Somerset, Dorset, and even Ireland. Its brown jugs of cream soon became famous throughout England, though the level of artistry on the label left something to be desired. According to one historian of the British dairy industry, they showed "a cow looking uncomfortably through a somewhat untypical four-barred gate, rather as if its neck had got stuck between the bars."

West Surrey Central Dairy entered the baby food business in 1904 when Dr. Killick Millard, medical officer of health for Leicester, asked it to supply powdered milk to help feed children of poor families. Four years later, its "Cow & Gate Pure

Company Perspectives:

Unigate is a European food and distribution group. It has over 28,000 employees and an annual turnover of £2.3 billion. Building on its strong financial position, the Group is pursuing expansion within Europe, both organically and by acquiring quality food and distribution businesses where it can add value. As it expands, Unigate is committed to consistent profitable growth as the means by which it can provide attractive returns to its shareholders, be a responsible employer and support the communities in which it operates.

English Dried Milk'' was first marketed on a large scale. The dried milk became widely popular despite the prevailing belief that breastfeeding was essential to a baby's health. In 1924 the company developed a special export version of its powdered milk, for feeding babies in tropical climates, which became very popular. In fact, an Indian nobleman once placed a rush order for two cases. It turned out, however, that he wanted to feed the milk to his racehorses.

In 1929 the company renamed itself after its popular Cow & Gate product line, becoming Cow & Gate Limited. During the 1930s it worked with scientists to develop specialized formulas to cater to infants with special needs. It came out with Frailac, a milk food for premature infants; Allergiac for babies sensitive to certain constituents of cow's milk; and a cereal food designed to start babies on mixed feeding at an earlier age.

On the corporate side, the company had gone public in 1918 under the chairmanship of Bramwell Gates, the son of Walter Gates. In the 1920s and 1930s, Cow & Gate expanded by acquiring dairies and creameries. Economic conditions were by no means easy in post-World War I Britain, and many of these acquisitions may have been salvages of struggling businesses. Cow & Gate began by purchasing Wallens Dairy Company of Kilburn in 1924 and added companies in Wales, Yorkshire, Lancashire, Cornwall, Devon, and Somerset over the next 15 years. In 1925 the company decided that its operations were large enough to justify setting up its own transportation subsidiary, and over the next seven decades that part of the company's operations (now known as the Wincanton Logistics) would become one of the nation's largest transport concerns.

Political uncertainty in Europe in the early 1930s convinced the Gates family to seek an overseas source of powdered milk as a way of safeguarding its export business. In 1933 Cow & Gate purchased a controlling interest in General Milk Products of Canada Limited. When World War II broke out in 1939, the British government banned all exports of food products, but Cow & Gate was able to keep its overseas markets supplied for the duration through its Canadian facilities.

Merged with United Dairies in 1959 to Create Unigate

Bramwell Gates retired in 1958 at the age of 83; he was replaced as chairman by Ernest Taylor. One of Taylor's first acts in office was to begin negotiating a merger with United Dairies, the nation's largest producer of dairy products. United was formed in 1917 when Wiltshire United Dairies, Metropolitan and Great Western Dairies, and Dairy Supply Company merged in an attempt to cope with distribution problems caused in the London market by the loss of men, vehicles, and horses to the war effort. In the late 1920s, United Dairies helped pioneer the sale of pasteurized milk in Britain. During the 1930s and into World War II it expanded into Scotland through the acquisition of dairies, and after the war it spread its presence to Wales, Liverpool, Cheshire, Birmingham, and Sherbourne.

The merger between Cow & Gate and United Dairies was consummated in 1959. The new company was reincorporated as Unigate Limited. Integration was not easy, however, and internal politics and rivalry between factions adhering to old-company loyalties continued to plague Unigate for years. In 1963 Unigate acquired Midland Counties Dairies and began buying up small grocery stores and restaurants soon thereafter, but otherwise the company moved slowly in the early 1960s as it tried to digest the merger.

Transformed into Conglomerate in the 1970s and 1980s

As milk consumption leveled off in the 1960s and began to decline as the decade ended, Unigate responded by increasing its nondairy businesses and its nonmilk product lines. In 1970 it announced plans to expand its retail activities, which included Kibby's supermarkets, Quids-In clothing shops, Uni-Wash laundrettes, and even some Kentucky Fried Chicken franchises. In 1973 it acquired Scot Bowyers, a meat-processing company. In 1975 it purchased Frigo, an American maker of Italian cheeses, and it acquired another U.S. specialty cheesemaker, Gardenia, in 1978.

Even so, Unigate's financial performance was sluggish through the early and mid-1970s and it continued to be bothered by political infighting, a sign that the merger was still not fully digested. So when John Clement became chief executive and chairman in 1977, he immediately set about knocking heads in the name of company unity. Over the next five years, Unigate lost a number of senior executives and Clement, a career dairyman, gained a reputation for autocratic rule. But he also put the company on solid financial footing and accelerated the process of diversifying its business.

One of Clement's first major acts as chairman was important in this regard. In 1979 Unigate parted with three-quarters of its manufacturing capacity when it sold 16 of its creameries to the Milk Marketing Board for £87 million. The sale lessened its presence in its traditional mainstay, but raised cash for acquisitions and paying off debt. In 1981 Unigate acquired Giltspur, a moving company; Turners Turkeys; and Casa Bonita, an American restaurant chain specializing in Mexican food. In 1984 it added another poultry processor, J.P. Wood. In 1985 it acquired Arlington Motor Holdings, followed by Colchester Car Auctions the next year, and added them both to the Wincanton Group. Also in 1986, it added the U.S. restaurant company Prufrock, which specialized in southern-style food through the Black-Eyed Pea chain.

In the mid- and late 1980s, however, some of these diversification moves were junked after they proved less than successful. In 1984 Clipper Seafoods, a struggling fish-products business, was sold off. Scot Bowyers was sold to Northern Foods in 1985. In 1987 Unigate divested several small engineering businesses that had been acquired with Giltspur. To complicate matters further, Unigate also began reinvesting in its milk business in 1987, acquiring the Middlesex dairy H.A. Job for £26 million. As of that year, it was still the U.K.'s leading milk supplier, despite relying on milk for less than one-third of its business.

The diversification of Unigate paid off in the early years of the 1980s, as the company's financial performance improved dramatically during the decade, with pretax profits more than doubling between 1981 and 1986, and its debt load steadily declining. But profits stagnated from 1987 through the end of the decade and Unigate's situation worsened in 1990 when recession hit. Clement was replaced as chief executive in October 1990 by Ross Buckland, who had headed up European operations for the Kellogg Company, the U.S. cereal giant. In December 1991 Clement was replaced as chairman by Brian Kellett.

Focused on European Food and Distribution in the 1990s

With Clement out of the picture, Buckland proceeded to deconglomerize Unigate, returning to a focus on food and distribution in the United Kingdom and Europe. The company raised more than £700 million via divestments through 1997. Disposals in 1992 included poultry processor J.P. Wood, sold to Hillsdown Holdings plc in February for £29.6 million; Giltspur International, sold in August to P&O Exhibition Services; and the Frigo and Gardenia cheese brands, sold in September to Stella Foods. In 1993 Unigate sold Arlington Motors to Lex Services PLC for £49.5 million in July and in September sold two businesses to Dalgety PLC for £30.4 million: Morton Foods, a supplier of batter and crumb coatings to the food industry, and W.J. Oldcare, which managed eight animal feed mills. In August 1994 Turners Turkeys was sold to Bernard Matthews P.L.C. for £18 million. During 1995 Unigate exited from the baby food business with the sale of its 29 percent stake in Nutricia, which raised £332 million; from the auto sector, through the US$62 million management-led buyout of National Car Auctions; and from the exhibitions business with the sale of Giltspur Inc. to the Dial Corp. for £40 million. The following year Unigate disposed of its restaurant operations by selling Black-Eyed Pea to DenAmerica Corporation (the largest franchisee of Denny's restaurants) for £42 million (US$65 million) and Casa Bonita to CKE Restaurants, Inc. for £27.1 million (US$42 million).

During the same period Unigate spent more than £400 million beefing up its foods, dairy, and logistics businesses, the three core units that would remain with the company by the end of the decade. The company made its first move into the European food sector in 1995, when it purchased two French firms: Prodipal, a maker of yogurts and desserts, and Vedial, a maker of spreads. In September 1996 Unigate paid £77.3 million for the U.K. and Italian margarine and spreads business of Kraft Foods International. Meantime, in 1994 Kellett died;

Buckland served as acting chairman until March 1995, when Ian Martin, a former executive with Grand Metropolitan PLC, took over as chairman.

Unigate's restructuring led to steady increases in pretax profits from fiscal years 1994 through 1998. It also left it in a strong position from which to make acquisitions. In May 1998 the company made a £1.59 billion bid to acquire Hillsdown Holdings—a holding company with interests in food, housebuilding, and furniture—but the proposal collapsed acrimoniously. In February 1999 Unigate acquired Fisher Quality Foods Limited, a leading U.K. supplier of sauces, dressings, and marinades, from the Albert Fisher Group PLC for £43 million. Meanwhile, Hillsdown had proceeded with a breakup plan, whereby it spun off its chilled convenience food subsidiary as Terranova. In March 1999 Unigate initiated a hostile £228.5 million takeover bid of Terranova, which was the part of Hillsdown it had wanted in the first place. After Unigate raised its bid to £274 million, Terranova's directors recommended that the bid be accepted. The pursuit of Terranova, as well as the purchase of Fisher Quality, made it clear that Unigate was ready to diversify again, but this time appeared to be much more selective, concentrating on building a wider base within its core food operations.

Principal Subsidiaries

Unigate (UK) Ltd.; Unigate Distribution Services Ltd.; Unigate Netherlands BV; Unigate Dairies Ltd.; St Ivel Westway Ltd.; St Ivel Ltd.; Malton Bacon Factory Ltd.; Stocks Lovell Ltd.; Fermanagh Creameries Ltd.; Wexford Creamery Ltd. (Ireland; 80%); Vedial S.A. (France); Société Laitière de la Vallée de l'Ourcq S.A. (France); Wincanton Ltd.

Principal Operating Units

Malton Foods; St Ivel UK; St Ivel Foods, Europe; Unigate Dairies; Wincanton Logistics.

Further Reading

Beddall, Clive, "Why Malton Is Now the Number One," *Grocer,* March 2, 1996, p. 16.

Bilefsky, Dan, and Alison Smith, "Unigate Makes £228m Bid for Terranova," *Financial Times,* March 17, 1999, p. 22.

Blackwell, David, "Dalgety Expands via Purchase of Two Unigate Subsidiaries," *Financial Times,* September 4, 1993, p. 8.

——, "Unigate Agrees to Buy Albert Fisher Division," *Financial Times,* January 20, 1999, p. 23.

Blackwell, David, and Antonia Sharpe, "Unigate Sells Nutricia Stake for Fl 745m," *Financial Times,* December 8, 1995, p. 20.

Carlino, Bill, "CKE Acquires Taco Bueno, Makes Push into Texas, Okla.," *Nation's Restaurant News,* September 9, 1996, pp. 1+.

Cull, Christian, "Full Day's Knight," *Grocer,* October 25, 1997, pp. 38–39.

Edgecliffe-Johnson, Andrew, "Unigate, Hillsdown Trade Recriminations," *Financial Times,* May 30, 1998, p. 19.

"Europe Is the Favoured Route for Unigate," *Grocer,* November 23, 1996, p. 12.

Maitland, Alison, "Unigate Chief Warns of Change," *Financial Times,* November 18, 1997, p. 26.

"Martin Takes Over Unigate Chair," *Financial Times,* March 10, 1995, p. 18.

Oram, Roderick, "Unigate Makes £65.1m Move into Continental Dairy Market," *Financial Times,* January 10, 1995, p. 19.

——, "Unigate to Buy Kraft UK and Italian Margarines for £77m," *Financial Times,* July 9, 1996, p. 17.

——, "Unigate to Cut 1,500 Dairy Staff As Milk Costs Soar," *Financial Times,* June 13, 1995, pp. 1, 22.

Ruggless, Ron, "DenAmerica Agrees to Acquire Black-Eyed Pea," *Nation's Restaurant News,* June 17, 1996, pp. 3+.

"Unigate," *Restaurant Business,* August 10, 1989, pp. 112+.

"Unigate Foods Hit Hard by Recession," *Super Marketing,* November 27, 1992, p. 17.

"Unigate Is Loaded with Cash but What Will It Buy?," *Grocer,* January 6, 1996, p. 8.

Urry, Maggie, "Unigate's Terranova Bid Nears Success," *Financial Times,* April 29, 1999, p. 29.

Willman, John, "Unigate Still Keen on Acquisitions," *Financial Times,* June 9, 1998, p. 22.

—updated by David E. Salamie

Union Pacific Corporation

1717 Main Street, Suite 5900
Dallas, Texas 75201-4605
U.S.A.
(214) 743-5600
Fax: (214) 743-5656
Web site: http://www.up.com

Public Company
Incorporated: 1969
Employees: 65,100
Sales: $10.55 billion (1998)
Stock Exchanges: New York
Ticker Symbol: UNP
NAIC: 482111 Line-Haul Railroads; 484122 General
    Freight Trucking, Long-Distance, Less Than
    Truckload; 551112 Offices of Other Holding
    Companies

Union Pacific Corporation (UP) is a holding company whose principal operating subsidiary is Union Pacific Railroad Company. UP's railroad business runs the largest rail system in the United States, with more than 36,000 miles of track crossing 23 states from the Midwest to the West and Gulf Coasts. Famed for its role in building a significant part of the country's first transcontinental railroad in 1869, UP survived early years of scandal and financial uncertainty to emerge by the late 1990s as the top U.S. railroad. UP's road to preeminence included the 1996 acquisition of Southern Pacific Rail Corporation, another firm with a rich history, including a prominent role of its own in the building of the transcontinental railroad. Union Pacific Corporation also owns—but is attempting to divest—Overnite Transportation Company, a leading U.S.-based general freight trucking company specializing in hauling less-than-truckload shipments. Overnite serves all 50 states and Canada and operates through 165 terminals.

Transcontinental Origins

Union Pacific came into existence in response to the widely held belief, fully formed by the 1850s, that the United States needed a rail link between its older, eastern states and the distant but rapidly growing states of the far West. Various proposals were made for northern, southern, and central routes, but the U.S. Congress could not agree on a plan. Following the South's secession from the United States in 1861 the remaining congressmen from the North quickly agreed upon a route, and U.S. President Abraham Lincoln finally signed the Pacific Railroad Act of 1862, urged on by military considerations as much as by those of economics. The act called for the creation of a public corporation, called Union Pacific Railroad Company, to build a railroad from Nebraska to the California-Nevada border and there to meet the Central Pacific, building east from Sacramento, California, and later linked with San Francisco. Later, the meeting place of the two railroads was set at Promontory Summit, Utah Territory. As amended by a second piece of legislation, the act specified that the company would be supported by a loan from the federal government of U.S. bonds, to be paid back in 30 years, and by the issuance of its own bonds and capital stock. Further, the company would receive land grants in the amount of 6,400 acres on alternating sides of every mile of track laid, a checkerboard swath of land across the middle of the country that would eventually total around 12 million acres of valuable minerals, grazing land, and metropolitan real estate. The government retained the right to inspect each section of track laid before releasing the allotted number of bonds, and it would keep two directors on UP's board, but the company was to be otherwise a venture of the private sector.

While the logic and value of a railroad across the western United States is obvious in the late 20th century, it was much less so in 1864. The men who became involved in the leadership of the UP—chiefly Thomas C. Durant and the Ames brothers, Oliver and Oakes—did so largely in order to make handsome profits off the railroad's hurried construction. Durant was the vice-president and dominant figure in the company's early years, and it was he and a handful of others who formed a construction company called Credit Mobilier of America (CMA) to receive contracts from UP for the building of its vast railroad. Estimates vary as to precisely how inflated these contracts were, but later congressional investigations left no doubt that the backers of CMA intentionally siphoned off far more of the UP's capital than was fair to its investors or good for its future financial health. The investigations of the early 1870s also revealed that the CMA principals bribed members of Congress with company stock.

Still, the railroad they built was a splendid success, and so vast a project might never have been undertaken without the promise of equally vast profits to be made. In five years the UP crews laid more than 1,000 miles of rail between Omaha, Nebraska, and Promontory Summit, Utah Territory, where on May 10, 1869, a golden spike completed the first transcontinental rail line. The railroad's completion supplied a critical impetus to the development of the American West, which to that time had been settled only on the Pacific Coast and in areas of unusual mineral wealth, such as Colorado. With the coming of the railroad, farmers, ranchers, and manufacturers were able to transport their goods to the great eastern metropolitan markets cheaply and quickly, and the West began to fill with pioneers. As the area's most significant railroad for almost 15 years, UP enjoyed rapid growth and excellent earnings for its scandal-ridden promoters, who were dominated from 1873 to the mid-1880s by financier Jay Gould.

Expanded During the 1870s

Gould's direction of UP was notable for two things. First, the railroad expanded considerably during the decade of the 1870s. Its main route from Omaha, Nebraska, to Ogden, Utah, was soon joined by a host of feeder lines extending into the neighboring territory, some of them of substantial length; and from its Ogden terminus the company acquired control of two new branches, the Utah and Northern running to Montana, and the Utah Central progressing in the general direction of Los Angeles, which it reached in 1901. More immediately significant was the 1880 annexation by the UP of one of its rivals, the Kansas Pacific. The Kansas line ran from Kansas City, Kansas, to Cheyenne, Wyoming, via Denver, Colorado, and although its finances were in even worse condition than UP's it added an important link to the company's Midwestern network. Finally, UP defended its transcontinental business by building a bridge to the Pacific Ocean through Idaho and Oregon, a system of new and existing lines that eventually fell under the aegis of UP's Oregon Short Line Railway Company. UP's original link to the ocean, the Central Pacific line to San Francisco, became a part of its most formidable rival, Southern Pacific, and was therefore lost to UP's purposes until late in the 20th century.

The second legacy of Jay Gould's years at UP was less beneficial. Beginning about 1875, Gould used the railroad's considerable income to pay an extremely high dividend on its common stock, of which he happened to own about two-thirds. As a result of Credit Mobilier's excessive construction contracts, UP was already badly overcapitalized and faced stiff periodic interest payments on its own bonds as well as an eventual lump sum reimbursement to the federal government of about $76 million of principal and interest on the latter's bond loan. Instead of taking prudent steps to provide for these liabilities, Gould bled UP of its cash flow, drove up the company's stock price by means of the huge dividends, and then sold the bulk of his shares in 1878 for a bulging profit. UP staggered on until 1884 with Gould and others of like persuasion in charge of its failing finances, at which time the company tried to make a fresh start under its newly elected president, Charles Francis Adams, Jr., a Bostonian of impeccable credentials and a scholar's grasp of the railroad business.

Went into Government Receivership in 1893

Adams faced a doubly difficult situation. UP's actual and reputed past sins made it nearly impossible to convince Congress and the public that the new president was in fact taking commendable steps toward reducing the company's debt and improving its efficiency. As a result, Adams's efforts were often thwarted, and UP continued to struggle under the burden laid upon it by its founders. At the same time, UP was by then no longer the sole provider of transcontinental rail service. Competition from three rival lines had cut severely into UP's operating income by the mid-1880s, further complicating Adams's task. The combination of looming government debt—due to mature in 1895—fresh competition in the market, and a skeptical legislative climate proved too much for the company when the financial panic of 1893 strained the U.S. economy to the utmost. In October of that year UP went into government receivership.

It was not until the end of 1895 that a satisfactory resolution of UP's debt was accomplished, during which interval the railroad lost many of its most important branch lines to local receiverships. In 1895 a reorganization committee representing UP's first-mortgage bondholders and backed by the New York investment banking house of Kuhn, Loeb and Company came up with a plan to foreclose on the railroad and sell its assets to a new company of the same name. The foreclosure sale was held in November 1897, and Kuhn, Loeb was able to raise the capital needed to pay off most of the government's $71 million in remaining debt and launch the new corporation on a solid financial basis. Quickly asserting himself on the UP's board of directors was an astute New York financier, Edward H. Harriman, who used his chairmanship of UP as the centerpiece of a remarkable railroad empire. Harriman was as brilliant a dealmaker as Jay Gould, but he also represented a new class of industrial magnate, one who was more interested in the construction of vast and durable business combines than in the clever manipulation of capital for immediate profit. Under Harriman's leadership, UP became one of the best run as well as one of the largest of U.S. railroads.

Harriman's Reign, 1898–1909, Brought Tremendous Growth

Harriman first set about retrieving the various pieces of UP lost during the receivership and soon reassembled the company's three basic networks: those running between Omaha and

Ogden, Ogden and the Pacific Northwest, and Ogden and Los Angeles. Between 1898 and Harriman's death in 1909, the UP increased its track miles from 2,000 to 6,000, and when the chairman became frustrated by UP's failure to gain control of the old Central Pacific run between Ogden and San Francisco's bay area, he wasted no time in buying up Central's owner, Southern Pacific (SP). SP was UP's chief rival and equal, the owner of three main routes between San Francisco and Portland, Oregon; San Francisco and Ogden; and San Francisco and the entire Southwest to New Orleans. SP also owned a series of steamship lines extending from California to Japan and Panama, and from New Orleans to New York. UP's purchase of 45 percent of SP's stock in 1901 for $90 million virtually merged the two giants of western rail transport into a single, monopolistic entity dominating the markets from Kansas City to San Francisco and Denver to New Orleans, Louisiana.

E. H. Harriman was a man of unlimited ambition. Shortly after sealing the Southern Pacific merger, he entered into a complicated series of maneuvers that resulted in the purchase by UP of a strong minority position in Northern Pacific, owner of vital Chicago connections operated by the Chicago, Burlington and Quincy Railroad. In turn, Northern Pacific and Great Northern Railroad became a part of a holding company known as Northern Securities Corporation, which was ordered dissolved by the U.S. Supreme Court in 1904. When the pieces of this gigantic, short-lived combination were sorted out, UP emerged as the owner of 20 percent of both Northern Pacific and Great Northern and a substantial amount of cash profit as well. With the proceeds of this wrangling, Harriman bought sizable shares of many of the other important railroads in the western United States, in particular the Illinois Central and the Atchison, Topeka and Santa Fe, the latter providing the UP-SP's sole competition in the Southwest. The empire of E.H. Harriman and UP-SP thus comprised large numbers of railroads, railroad stocks, steamship lines, increasingly valuable real estate holdings, and uncounted tons of coal, iron, and other minerals.

Harriman was a prudent administrator of his roads, reinvesting the bulk of their net income in extensive renovation and new rolling stock. In 1906, however, he began paying an unusually large dividend of ten percent, raising widespread accusations that Harriman was another profiteer out to gouge the public for his own benefit. The Interstate Commerce Commission (ICC) initiated an investigation into Harriman and UP that resulted in a 1913 decision by the U.S. Supreme Court that the company was inhibiting competition and must divest itself of its Southern Pacific holdings. Harriman did not live to see the UP thus reduced roughly to the size and shape it had been in 1900, the company's lines once again restricted to the three main routes between Omaha and Ogden, Ogden and the Northwest port cities, and Ogden and Los Angeles. Lost was the prized route between Ogden and San Francisco, but in the meantime UP had beefed up its branch system and added new lines between Portland and Seattle.

Although Harriman died in 1909, his family retained a powerful influence at the UP, Harriman's sons W. Averell Harriman and E. Roland Harriman sitting on the company's board for many years and both serving as chairmen. Furthermore, so successful was the elder Harriman that the company he left behind became a model for the railroad industry of financial

strength and unexcelled performance. From 1916's gross revenue of slightly more than $100 million, UP more than doubled sales to $211 million by 1923, where they remained for much of that prosperous decade. Earnings were steadily excellent in the 1930s and 1940s, an increasing portion of them in the 1930s generated by UP's oil and gas holdings and industrial real estate. A long-term problem for the railroad industry had by then made itself felt, however; truck and automobile traffic was eroding the railroads' share of both freight and passenger miles. This trend, which would intensify during much of the 20th century, was especially painful when the Great Depression of the 1930s curtailed the heavy industrial transport upon which the railroads had come to depend. UP revenues did not approach their former heights until World War II recharged the industrial economy after 1940, and in the early 1930s they barely topped $125 million annually.

Averell Harriman was chairman of UP for most of the 1930s, and did an excellent job of keeping expenses down during the lean years while also investing needed capital in technological developments such as the diesel locomotive. With the outbreak of World War II the Harrimans had little to worry about in the financial realm. The need to shuttle huge amounts of personnel and heavy equipment around the United States gave UP all the business it could handle, company employment nearly doubling to 60,000 and revenue pushing to more than $500 million by war's end. Between 1914 and 1944 alone, UP purchased 2,270 new locomotives, including a number of Big Boys, the world's largest steam locomotive designed for the most taxing Rocky Mountain routes. The end of the war in 1945 caused only a temporary drop in sales for UP, and by the early 1950s revenue was again exceeding $500 million annually and the company remained in generally excellent financial health.

Stepped Up Resource Development Activities in the 1960s

The next few years were not as kind, however. UP faltered in the late 1950s, its income, dividend, and stock price all falling between 1956 and 1961. Part of the problem lay in the rapid depletion of the company's best oil well, outside Los Angeles, and part in the continuing loss of railroad freight sales to the trucking industry. In response, UP restructured its holdings into three divisions—transportation, land development, and natural resources—and in the mid-1960s began a concentrated program of mineral, oil, and gas exploration. The reorganization into divisions helped UP pursue what had grown into three very distinct businesses, each one with the potential to add significant dollars to the company's bottom line. Only a small percentage of the railroad's 7.8 million acres of remaining land had been fully explored and utilized, but even so by 1967 the firm operated five oil and gas fields and was the owner of the world's largest known deposit of trona soda ash ore; vast reserves of coal; and sizable holdings of iron, titanium, and uranium. In a further step toward the exploitation of these resources, in 1969 UP acquired Champlin Petroleum Company and Pontiac Refineries from Celanese Corporation for $240 million, thus completing the formation of a fully integrated oil and gas business. Champlin would eventually operate three refineries, in Texas, Oklahoma, and California, and to ensure that its plants were kept busy UP also signed a joint-venture agreement allowing a subsidiary of Standard Oil Company of Indiana to drill for oil on its acreage, with UP getting royalties and retaining a quarter interest in whatever oil was found.

Overseeing this diversification at UP was chief executive officer Frank Barnett, the first CEO without intimate ties to the Harriman family to run the company in the 20th century. Barnett, who became CEO in 1967, had as his goal to develop equally strong transportation and nontransport divisions at UP. In 1969 UP established a holding company called Union Pacific Corporation, with Union Pacific Railroad Company becoming one of the subsidiaries of this holding company. With oil prices soaring after the oil crisis of 1973–74, UP's revenue quadrupled during the 1970s to $4 billion, more than half of which was provided in the late 1970s by the nontransportation businesses. The company's coal reserves also became more valuable during the energy-conscious 1970s, when UP upped its production tenfold. Less successful was the company's 13-year effort, begun in 1962, to win ICC approval of a merger with Chicago, Rock Island & Pacific Railroad (CRI&P) and thereby secure a valuable link between UP's Omaha terminus and both Chicago and St. Louis, Missouri. The merger was opposed by rivals of UP who feared the impact of its entry into Chicago, the nation's busiest rail center. The CRI&P subsequently ceased operations in 1980, and many of its lines were sold to other railroads, including the Missouri Pacific and the Missouri-Kansas-Texas Railroad.

Merged with Missouri Pacific and Western Pacific in 1982

In 1982 UP gained a Chicago gateway in another way. In a move reminiscent of E.H. Harriman's reign, the company took advantage of U.S. President Ronald Reagan's deregulation of the railroads to accomplish an important merger with the Missouri Pacific and Western Pacific railroads. Missouri Pacific operated some 11,500 miles of track in Texas, Oklahoma, and Missouri, and also provided the crucial bridge between Chicago and Omaha long sought by UP, along with three key gateways to Mexico; while Western Pacific operated a route between Ogden, Utah, and the bay area of San Francisco.

The merger was a major undertaking, and it signaled a new era of consolidation in the U.S. railroad industry. While the move would benefit all three partners in the long run, it also presented UP with a massive organizational problem. With suddenly bloated employee and management ranks and a doubling of track mileage, UP slipped to dead last in operating profitability among U.S. railroads in 1984, although profits were up nearly 30 percent. The company's problems were not helped by the steadily falling price of oil, which was especially hard on domestic producers trying to squeeze the last drop out of older oil wells; but its basic need was for a drastic pruning of its labor force. This was accomplished by Drew Lewis, U.S. secretary of transportation in the early 1980s and UP chairman starting 1987, and his railroad president, Michael Walsh, who together cut nearly 12,000 employees from UP's ranks. The cuts had resulted in far greater productivity from line workers as well as a more responsive management, whose ranks were thinned from nine administrative levels to only three. In another cost-saving move, Union Pacific Corporation in 1988 relocated its headquarters from New York City to Bethlehem, Pennsylvania.

Walsh resigned in 1991 to become CEO of Tenneco. He was succeeded by Richard K. Davidson.

Meanwhile, UP gave up trying to beat the truckers and instead joined them, buying Overnite Transportation Company, a national trucking company, in 1986 and stepping up its capacity for intermodal services. Union Pacific Corporation in 1987 combined its Champlin oil and gas unit with its Rocky Mountain Energy mineral unit to form Union Pacific Resources Group. In 1988 UP further expanded its railroad operations through the acquisition of the Missouri-Kansas-Texas. The following year the Harriman Dispatching Center opened in Omaha, providing a central location for all train dispatching. Also in 1989 UP acquired a 25 percent stake in the Chicago & North Western Railway (C&NW).

Concentrated on Railroad Operations in the Early to Mid-1990s

As the 1990s—a decade of intensified railroad consolidation—unfolded, Union Pacific Corporation increased its concentration on its railroad operations. In 1994 UP gained minority control of the C&NW, then acquired it outright the following year for $1.1 billion. UP subsequently had great difficulty integrating the C&NW, leading to service problems—including widespread delays for Midwest shippers—and an apology from UP management to its customers. Also in 1994 UP entered into a battle with Burlington Northern for control of the Atchison, Topeka & Santa Fe (the Santa Fe). UP's bid failed, and Burlington Northern and the Santa Fe merged in 1995 to form Burlington Northern Santa Fe, which thereby became the number one U.S. railroad. UP was able, however, to gain significant trackage rights from Burlington Northern as a merger concession.

Pennzoil Company, a major energy company best known for its motor oil, approached Union Pacific Corporation in 1995 about purchasing Union Pacific Resources, an overture that UP rejected. That year UP combined all of its natural resource operations into Union Pacific Resources, then sold a minority stake to the public. UP then sold its remaining 83 percent stake in 1996. It was during this period when it was divesting its noncore resources operations that Union Pacific made its boldest railroad acquisition yet in the consolidating 1990s: Southern Pacific.

Southern Pacific's Central Pacific Origins

The history of Southern Pacific begins with the efforts of Theodore D. Judah to build an earlier railroad, the Central Pacific. Judah was a Connecticut engineer experienced in railroad construction who moved to California in 1854 and immediately became absorbed by the possibility of a rail link between that state and the East. Not a financier, Judah lobbied Congress for help with his grand project, and around 1860 became acquainted with four ambitious businessmen from Sacramento. This quartet, whose members would go on to build and own the Southern Pacific, were Collis P. Huntington, proprietor of a large hardware store; Leland Stanford, lawyer and in 1861 governor of California; Charles Crocker, dry goods merchant; and Mark Hopkins, partner to Huntington. Along with Judah and a few other investors, the four promoters created the Central Pacific Railroad of California on June 28, 1861, and then set about finding the cash infusions that would be needed even to begin the mammoth construction project from Sacramento, California, to the East.

The bulk of these funds were eventually provided by the U.S. government, which under the terms of the railroad acts of 1862 and 1864 agreed to loan to Central Pacific a varying amount of government bonds for every mile of road built, depending on the difficulty of terrain traversed, and to grant it a checkerboard pattern of land on alternate sides of the railroad that would eventually total millions of acres of urban and range property. An important caveat deprived the railroad of most mineral rights to this land, a category generally interpreted by the courts to include oil. In addition to this federal aid, Central Pacific was empowered to sell stocks and bonds of its own, but in the early years few buyers for these could be found. The four original promoters were therefore continually scrambling for enough money to support the road's construction, which began in January 1863. To ease its chronic financial burden, Central Pacific persuaded municipalities to buy its bonds, threatening bluntly that if such support were not forthcoming the railroad would simply be built around the town in question, destroying its economic viability. In this way, Central managed to raise a substantial amount of money to complement its federal funds. However, as it became clear that the partners would succeed in their project, public optimism about the benefits thus gained was tempered by the realization that there would be one and only one major rail system in northern California.

Further blackening the reputation of the Central Pacific was the widespread belief that the promoters of the road were skimming profits. They awarded lucrative contracts to construction companies owned by themselves, contracts calling for payments in the form of both cash and Central Pacific stock and so liberal in terms that by the time the road was completed in 1869 the construction company was, in effect, its owner. The net result was that a railroad had been built over the Sierra mountains to Ogden, Utah, with government funds, but was now owned by four individuals.

Southern Pacific Supplanted Central Pacific by the 1880s

Once the road was finished the promoters decided to remain in the railroad business, foreseeing that with a modicum of effort they could establish a virtual monopoly over the state of California. They began an intensive campaign of acquisition and expansion, rapidly solidifying their hold on rail transport throughout the state's midsection. In particular, Central Pacific's attention was drawn to a new government railroad venture known as the Southern Pacific, chartered by Congress in 1866 to build rail lines from the San Francisco Bay area to San Diego, California, thence eastward to California's eastern boundary. The Central Pacific promoters gained control of this new road in 1868, recognizing that such a project would allow them to duplicate their construction profits and also grow to be the dominant railroad in the far West. In the following 15 years the Southern Pacific spread its myriad lines from Sacramento all the way to New Orleans, having effected a number of mergers in the process, and as early as 1877 the Central Pacific-Southern Pacific combination controlled 85 percent of all rail traffic in the state of California as well. In that year the combined companies

had sales of $22.2 million and a capital of $225 million, soon greatly enlarged by the additional tracks reaching out to Texas and New Orleans.

In 1884 the three remaining promoters—Hopkins having died in 1878—took steps to ensure their control of the rapidly expanding Southern Pacific. Having sold the bulk of their holdings in Central Pacific, which by then was clearly of secondary value, they formed a new corporation, Southern Pacific Company of Kentucky, with which they acquired all of the stock of the old Southern Pacific and its subsidiaries while agreeing to lease the use of Central Pacific's roads. This arrangement not only further concentrated their hold upon Southern Pacific, it also distanced the promoters from California's laws of incorporation, under which stockholders' liability was unlimited.

SP and its owners remained extremely unpopular for many years. The railroad's early bullying of municipalities, its discriminatory pricing, suspected trafficking in legislative votes by means of bribery, and monopoly power fueled popular resentment. Various legal remedies were attempted by the state of California, including the creation of a state Railroad Commission in 1876, but all were undermined by the Southern Pacific. In the 1890s the federal government also became increasingly involved in the regulation of railroads. The source of its concern was not only the public welfare but the more tangible fact that the transcontinental railroads owed the U.S. government a great deal of money, in the form of the 30-year bonds they had borrowed for construction and due to mature in the mid-1890s.

None of the roads, including Southern Pacific, had made provision for the repayment of these huge debts, operating income instead ending up in the hands of promoters. Partly in response to this crisis, the Interstate Commerce Commission (ICC) was created in 1887 as a federal agency charged with general regulation of the railroads; more specifically, by the mid-1890s it was clear that SP was unable to pay its debts and would require refinancing. So unpopular was the company in its home state of California that a San Francisco newspaper gathered 195,000 signatures—more than ten percent of the state population—on a petition asking the government to foreclose on the railway and to run it as a public service. This the government was disinclined to do, preferring to get its money back rather than enter the railroad business, and after long negotiations the debt was refunded until 1909 and SP was instructed to have it paid off by that date. As the Southern Pacific was by then already the largest railroad in the United States, with 7,300 miles of track, and a profitable company when managed properly, it was able to meet the new debt schedule and was by 1909 financially independent of the government.

SP Briefly Controlled by UP in the Early 20th Century

In 1901, shortly after the death of the last of Southern Pacific's founders had left the company vulnerable, the rival Union Pacific bought a controlling interest in the road and in effect merged the two great western rail systems. The railroad monopoly of California thus became part of an even larger corporate giant, stretching from Portland to New Orleans and Los Angeles to St. Louis, Missouri, and including a fleet of steamships traveling between California and the Far East and between New Orleans and New York. E.H. Harriman, Union Pacific's chairman, was a far more prudent administrator than the previous generation of rail magnates, and under his direction both the Union Pacific and Southern Pacific were run according to a conservative philosophy of low dividends, the reinvestment of income in capital improvements, and a tight lid on debt accumulation. As a result, SP was able to pay off the federal government while strengthening its physical assets and generally to grow into a mature, efficient corporation.

Congress and the U.S. populace were less interested in Harriman's skills than in the monopolistic status of his railroads. As two monopolies do not make a market, an ICC investigation was followed in 1911 by a federal antitrust suit against the Union Pacific-Southern Pacific combination. The Supreme Court agreed that the combine inhibited competition and in 1913 ordered the sale of SP stock, much of which ended up in the hands of the Pennsylvania Railroad. As of that date, then, the Southern Pacific Railroad was restored to the general configuration it had had before the 1901 merger, its three principal routes being those between San Francisco and Portland, San Francisco and Ogden, Utah, and San Francisco and New Orleans. A second antitrust action deprived SP of its Ogden lines for a number of years, but these were eventually restored. Other litigation forced Southern Pacific to give up most of the oil-producing land included in its original grants, oil falling under the rubric of mineral rights, as well as its timberland.

Southern Pacific survived, however, and enjoyed a decade of unbroken prosperity in the 1920s. Buoyed by a strong national economy and the rapid growth of its two main markets, California and Texas, Southern's net income steadily rose to its 1929 peak of $48 million, despite having lost to the ICC the right to fix its own freight rates. These results were misleading, however, for in the meantime the nature of U.S. transportation had undergone a fundamental change as great as that of the railroad itself. Truck and auto traffic trebled during the 1920s, and along with the airplane would soon wrest from the railroads most long-distance passenger service and many types of freight, except those bulk items for which rail transport is ideal. The impact of these changes was not really felt by SP until the Great Depression brought to an end the era of plentiful business for all; reeling from these double blows, SP watched its net decline to $4 million in 1931 and then disappear altogether for the next four years.

The age of railroads had come to an end, and under new President Angus McDonald the Southern Pacific began the long evolution needed if it were to survive in a truly competitive marketplace. The former monopoly became far more responsive to the needs of its customers, offering a much more flexible schedule of service and the use of the railroad's own short-haul trucking company, Pacific Motor Trucking Company. Although the latter was barred by law from competing with full-service truck lines it became an integral adjunct to SP's rail system, transporting goods between the rail depots and customer warehouses. SP also fought a well-publicized if losing battle for passenger business, offering low-priced tickets on a number of famous routes between California and the East. These efforts may well have kept the Southern Pacific name before the public eye, but it proved simply impossible to move passengers by rail as cheaply and directly as by car and airplane, and for many years passenger travel was a money-losing burden on all railroads.

Despite these generally gloomy developments, Southern Pacific remained a true giant among U.S. corporations. Its 1936 assets of $1.95 billion were exceeded by only two other U.S. industrial corporations; it retained ownership of millions of acres of land that would some day become extremely valuable; and with 16,000 miles of track and $200 million in annual sales, Southern Pacific was among the three largest U.S. railroads by any measure chosen. Although the industry as a whole faced new competition, SP itself continued to enjoy the benefits of its relatively uncrowded western territory, where only Union Pacific and Santa Fe offered any challenge to its supremacy. The company was thus well positioned to take advantage of the enormous upsurge in heavy freight caused by the outbreak of war in 1939. With every segment of the industrial economy straining to meet the requirements of war, the railroad entered a period of unprecedented prosperity. SP's net income reached an all-time high of $80 million in 1942 and remained strong for several years, despite a vigorous program of debt reduction and capital outlays for new rolling stock and track.

Postwar Prosperity for SP

Following the war, Southern Pacific settled into a long period of sedate good fortune. Business lost to the truckers and airlines was more than compensated by the overall economic growth of its western home. Passenger revenue continued to decline, except for commuter service, but under the regulatory regime of the ICC the railroads were ensured a living wage in the bulk freight business, and since neither mergers nor rate wars were permitted the competitive environment was stable and modestly profitable. Under Donald J. Russell, Southern Pacific's chief from 1952 through the mid-1960s, revenue rose from $650 million to $840 million, and the company expanded its trucking service as well as added a profitable oil pipeline along a segment of its track in the Southwest. Russell spent liberally on maintenance of track and rolling stock, and SP generally built a reputation as one of the country's soundest railroads, although the sheer size of its operations forced the company to incur debt for capital expenditures at a level higher than Wall Street thought prudent. The tremendous growth of California's population and agricultural production kept SP healthy, along with the rapid increase in intermodal—rail-to-truck and truck-to-rail—transport and a booming oil business in Texas and Louisiana. The latter portion of the SP system had been solidified years before by the acquisition in 1932 of the "cotton belt" lines extending northward to St. Louis from Dallas, Texas.

While SP's market area and rate structure were both fixed, it could and did increase efficiency by means of technological innovation and consequent labor cuts. By 1969 the entire railroad was under the guidance of a computerized information system which helped to cut down on idle cars and switching delays. By means of such changes Southern Pacific was able to reduce its labor force from 76,000 in the mid-1950s to 45,000 by 1970, while substantially increasing its volume of rail traffic. This trend continued; in 1990 SP employed about 21,000 workers.

In 1972 SP diversified into telecommunications. Using its existing network of microwave transmitters, the company became a carrier of long-distance telephone and data communications, first to large corporate users and later to the general public under the Sprint name. In 1979 it also bought Ticor, the largest title insurer in the United States. Neither venture was particularly successful, however. Telecommunications was a world all its own, one that demanded expertise and more capital than Southern Pacific could spare from its own vast physical plant; and the Ticor purchase had barely been signed when a severe recession all but killed the residential real estate market on which the title business depends. As a result, both companies were eventually sold off. In 1982 two of SP's chief rivals announced a potentially devastating merger—Union Pacific and Missouri Pacific (along with a third merger partner, Western Pacific) would soon form the largest rail combine since the days of E.H. Harriman.

The merger of Union Pacific and Missouri Pacific was made possible by U.S. President Ronald Reagan's deregulation of the railroad industry and presented Southern Pacific with grave problems. The new Union Pacific would be able to offer longer through service and lower rates than Southern Pacific in nearly every market area, and Southern Pacific immediately began casting about for a merger partner of its own. In 1983 Santa Fe Industries Inc. purchased Southern Pacific with the intention of merging SP with the Atchison, Topeka & Santa Fe Railway (known as the Santa Fe), one of SP's main competitors. The proposed merger elicited immediate opposition from government officials and Santa Fe's competition, and the Interstate Commerce Commission in 1987 blocked the Santa Fe-SP merger as anticompetitive. Robert Krebs, the chairman of Santa Fe Industries, was forced to sell one of his lines and chose SP, which he felt was the weaker of the two.

SP Acquired by Anschutz in 1988

In October 1988 Southern Pacific found a new home among the holdings of Denver billionaire businessman Philip Anschutz, whose Rio Grande Industries already owned the Denver and Rio Grande Western Railroad. Anschutz—who had used his political influence to help block the Santa Fe-SP merger—paid $1 billion for Southern Pacific, which thus became a part of Rio Grande Industries, a group of railroads that functioned as cooperating but distinct rail systems.

In the initial years after the purchase, SP suffered from declines in its traditional accounts in auto parts, lumber, and food; increased competition from UP and the Santa Fe; and more rigorous safety inspections in California, where SP trains were involved in two chemical spills in July 1991. SP continued to show operating losses after the merger and was profiting mainly from the proceeds of real estate sales. Its railroad operations were bolstered, however, by improving the quality of its service through heavy expenditures to maintain its track. As trade between the United States and Mexico increased in the early 1990s, SP was positioned to profit from it with its six Mexican gateways in California, Texas, and Arizona. The company's strategy appeared to be working as an operating loss of $347.7 million in 1991 had been reduced to $24.6 million in 1992. But in 1993, SP slid back to a loss of $149 million. Contributing to the loss was $14 million incurred from the settlement of a class-action lawsuit stemming from one of the 1991 derailments which had contaminated the Sacramento River with weed killer.

In the summer of 1993, Anschutz turned to a railroad company veteran, Edward Moyers, to assist in turning SP around. Moyers had retired after a very successful four-year stint at Illinois Central, where he cut its operating ratio (operating expenses as a percentage of revenues) from 98 percent to 71 percent. Anschutz hired Moyers as chief executive, and Moyers immediately focused on SP's operating ratio, which stood at 96.5 percent in 1993. In an effort to reduce SP's debt load, 30 million shares of common stock were offered to the public in August 1993. Although the initial offering price was estimated at $20 per share, the actual price of the shares as issued was $13.50. Still, that the offering was successful at all was attributed by many to the hiring of Moyers. Investor interest in Southern Pacific increased in the several months that followed, so that by February 1994, when a secondary stock offering of 25 million shares was initiated, they sold for $19.75 per share. Following these sales, Anschutz owned 41 percent of the shares outstanding.

Moyers started a multipronged strategy for revitalizing Southern Pacific. First, he worked to cut costs by reducing the employee ranks through a buyout program and a reorganization. In his first year, he reduced the labor force by more than 3,000 to about 19,000 jobs. Second, Moyers focused on service to SP's customers, putting pressure on his subordinates to improve the operations. This initiative saved a lucrative Georgia-Pacific account by increasing on-time Georgia-Pacific deliveries from 0 percent to 80 percent in three months. Overall, on-time deliveries were up by more than 50 percent in his first year. Moyers also sought to bolster Southern Pacific's equipment through the purchase of new locomotives, the rebuilding of existing locomotives, and better maintenance of both trains and track. Although SP was still in weak financial condition, Moyers had managed to make a number of improvements, and in February 1995 he once again retired. Moyers was succeeded as president and CEO by veteran railroader Jerry R. Davis.

Union Pacific-Southern Pacific Merged in 1996

By 1995, the consolidation that followed the deregulation of the railroad industry in the early 1980s had reduced the number of large, Class 1 railroads from 40 to 10. But the mergers were not over yet. In November 1995 Union Pacific filed an application with the ICC to acquire Southern Pacific in a $3.9 billion takeover. One month later the U.S. Congress abolished the ICC, creating the Surface Transportation Board (STB) as the new railroad industry oversight body. The UP-SP deal was fiercely opposed by the Justice, Transportation, and Agriculture departments and by such rival railroads as Kansas City Southern and Consolidated Rail. But in July 1996 the STB approved the merger, with the only major stipulation being that UP grant trackage rights to Burlington Northern Santa Fe over about 4,000 miles of track.

The combined UP-SP railroad, which would operate under the Union Pacific name, was once again the nation's largest, with more than 30,000 miles of track and about $10 billion in revenue. The merger was expected to result in $627 million in annual savings through the consolidation of operations. In late 1996 Lewis retired as chairman and CEO of Union Pacific Corporation, and was succeeded by Davidson, who had most recently been president and COO of the UP holding company.

Davidson was also named CEO of Union Pacific Railroad, while Davis became president and COO of the railroad.

Unfortunately, the integration of Southern Pacific into UP was no smoother than that of the Chicago & North Western. In fact it was far worse. Starting in the summer of 1997 and extending into 1998, Union Pacific's rail network suffered from gridlock, particularly along the Gulf Coast. By March 1998 delays in shipments had cost rail customers approximately $1 billion in curtailed production, reduced sales, and higher shipping costs. The STB in November 1997 ordered UP to temporarily open a part of its freight business in its Houston hub to Kansas City Southern. In February 1998 UP and Burlington Northern Santa Fe reached an agreement to create a joint dispatching center for their Gulf Coast operations, share ownership of line between Houston and New Orleans, and allow UP to use Burlington Northern tracks between Beaumont and Navasota, Texas, as needed, to bypass Houston congestion. In addition to its difficulties digesting SP, Union Pacific was also under fire for its safety record. Following three fatal accidents, a joint safety team was formed in August 1997 to review safety across the UP system. The team consisted of UP managers, union employees, and Federal Railroad Administration representatives. Meanwhile, UP moved its headquarters from Bethlehem, Pennsylvania, to Dallas in September 1997.

In May 1998 Union Pacific Corporation announced that it planned to divest its Overnite trucking unit through an IPO, in order to further focus on its core rail business. But the IPO was abandoned following a deterioration in market conditions. An attempt to find a third-party buyer failed as well. In the fourth quarter of 1998 the corporation recorded a $547 million charge to reflect an impairment in Overnite's goodwill, leading to a net loss of $633 million for the year, a loss that was also due to UP railroad's service problems and system congestion. Another outcome of the railroad's service difficulties was the August 1998 announcement of a plan to decentralize its railroad management. The railroad was reorganized into three regions—southern, based in Houston; northern, based in Omaha; and western, based in Roseville, California.

In September 1998 Ike Evans was named president and COO of Union Pacific Railroad, succeeding Davis, who became vice-chairman until his retirement in March 1999. Evans had previously been a senior vice-president at Emerson Electric Company, a manufacturer of electrical, electromechanical, and electronic products and systems. In July 1999 Union Pacific Corporation moved its headquarters again, this time landing in Omaha, where its main subsidiary, Union Pacific Railroad, was located. The corporation continued to look for an opportunity to divest Overnite through an IPO or sale to a third party and was likely to be busy assimilating Southern Pacific well into the 21st century.

Principal Subsidiaries

Overnite Transportation Company; Southern Pacific Rail Corporation; Union Pacific Railroad Company.

Principal Operating Units

Union Pacific Railroad; Overnite Transportation; Union Pacific Technologies.

Further Reading

"Back to Railroading for a New Era," *Business Week,* July 14, 1980.

Bailey, Ed H., *The Century of Progress: A Heritage of Service, Union Pacific, 1869–1969,* New York: Newcomen Society in North America, 1969, 24 p.

Barrett, Amy, "The Bull Pen: Union Pacific's Drew Lewis Says He's Fed Up with Politics," *Financial World,* January 8, 1991, pp. 24+.

Berman, Phyllis, and Roula Khalaf, " 'I Might Be a Seller, I Might Be a Buyer'," *Forbes,* February 3, 1992, pp. 86–87.

Byrnes, Nanette, "The Waiting Game," *Financial World,* September 13, 1994, pp. 32–34.

Cook, William S., *Building the Modern Union Pacific,* New York: Newcomen Society of the United States, 1984, 24 p.

Daggett, Stuart, *Chapters on the History of the Southern Pacific,* New York, Kelley, 1966.

Galloway, John Debo, *The First Transcontinental Railroad: Central Pacific, Union Pacific,* New York: Simmons-Boardman, 1950; reprint, Westport, Conn.: Greenwood Press, 1983.

Howard, Robert West, *The Great Iron Trail: The Story of the First Transcontinental Railroad,* New York: Putnam, 1962.

Huneke, William F., *The Heavy Hand: The Government and the Union Pacific, 1862–1898,* New York: Garland, 1985.

Kenefick, John C., *Union Pacific and the Building of the West,* New York: Newcomen Society of the United States, 1985, 18 p.

Klein, Maury, *Union Pacific: Birth of a Railroad,* New York: Doubleday, 1987.

——, *Union Pacific: The Rebirth, 1894–1969,* New York: Doubleday, 1990.

Kupfer, Andrew, "An Outsider Fires Up a Railroad," Fortune, December 18, 1989, pp. 133+.

Machan, Dan, "The Man Who Won't Let Go," *Forbes,* August 1, 1994, pp. 64–65.

Machalaba, Daniel, "A Big Railroad Merger Goes Terribly Awry in a Very Short Time," *Wall Street Journal,* October 2, 1997, pp. A1, A13.

——, "Union Pacific and Burlington Northern to Coordinate Some Train Dispatching," *Wall Street Journal,* February 9, 1999, p. A6.

——, "Union Pacific Reverses Course with Burlington Pact," *Wall Street Journal,* February 17, 1998, p. B4.

——, "Union Pacific to Reverse Centralization," *Wall Street Journal,* August 20, 1998, pp. A3, A9.

Machalaba, Daniel, and Anna Wilde Mathews, "Union Pacific Tie-Ups Reach Across Economy," *Wall Street Journal,* October 8, 1997, pp. B1, B17.

Machalaba, Daniel, and Asra Q. Nomani, "More Rail Deals May Be Down the Track," *Wall Street Journal,* July 5, 1996, p. A2.

Mathews, Anna Wilde, "Union Pacific's Burns Resigns Positions, Davidson, Davis Named to Succeed Him," *Wall Street Journal,* November 7, 1996, p. B10.

O'Reilly, Brian, "The Wreck of the Union Pacific," *Fortune,* March 30, 1998, pp. 94+.

Palmeri, Christopher, and Ann Marsh, "Can Drew Lewis Drive the Golden Nail?," *Forbes,* December 18, 1995, pp. 52+.

"Southern Pacific," *Fortune,* November 1937.

"SP's Strategy for Success," *Railway Age,* May 1993, pp. 31–32, 34, 36, 38.

Trottman, Nelson, *History of Union Pacific,* New York: Ronald Press, 1923.

"Union Pacific: The Story Behind the Statistics," *Railway Age,* December 1992, pp. 19–23.

Weber, Joseph, et al., "Union Pacific's Uphill Haul," *Business Week,* July 1, 1996, pp. 52, 54.

Welty, Gus, "Railroader of the Year: SP's Ed Moyers," *Railway Age,* January 1995, pp. 29–31.

——, "SP Battles Back to Respectability," *Railway Age,* November 1994, pp. 22–23, 25–26.

Willoughby, Jack, "The Rebuilding of Uncle Pete," *Forbes,* November 14, 1988.

Zellner, Wendy, "An Old Brakeman Faces His Ultimate Test," *Business Week,* October 6, 1997, pp. 110+.

———, "The Rails: Trouble Behind, Trouble Ahead," *Business Week,* November 24, 1997, pp. 40, 42.

Zellner, Wendy, and Kathleen Morris, "A Desperate Effort to Clear the Tracks," *Business Week,* March 2, 1998, p. 46.

—Jonathan Martin
—updated by David E. Salamie

United News & Media plc

Ludgate House
245 Blackfriars Road
London SE1 9UY
United Kingdom
(0171) 921-5000
Fax: (0171) 928-2728
Web site: http://www.unm.com

Public Company
Incorporated: 1918 as United Newspapers Ltd.
Employees: 18,150
Sales: £2.01 billion (US$3.12 billion) (1998)
Stock Exchanges: London
Ticker Symbol: UNEWY
NAIC: 51111 Newspaper Publishers; 51112 Periodical
Publishers; 511199 All Other Publishers; 51312
Television Broadcasting; 54187 Advertising Material
Distribution Services; 514191 On-Line Information
Services; 51411 News Syndicates; 51211 Motion
Picture & Video Production; 51212 Motion Picture &
Video Distribution

United News & Media plc (UNM) is a leading U.K.-based international media firm. Although the company's earliest roots are in the newspaper field, UNM's largest operating area is that of business services, which accounts for about 53 percent of overall revenues. The largest part of this division is Miller Freeman, which is the number one trade exhibition organizer in the world and a leading business magazine publisher, with strong positions in the United States, Europe, and Asia. Other business services operations include market research firms Audits & Surveys Worldwide Inc., Mediamark Research, and NOP Research Group; global newswire service, PR Newswire; and Visual Communications Group, a photographic image marketing group. UNM's second largest operating area is that of broadcasting and entertainment, which includes three Independent Television Network licenses in the United Kingdom, a 29 percent interest in the United Kingdom's Channel 5, and televi-

sion production and distribution activities. The third leg of the United News & Media empire is that of consumer publishing. This sector includes the remnants of the company's newspaper roots—the national U.K. papers the *Express* and the *Daily Star*—as well as advertising periodicals in the United Kingdom and the United States. UNM adopted its current name in 1995, before which it was known as United Newspapers plc.

Early History of United Newspapers

From the middle of the 19th century the newspaper industry had grown faster in the United Kingdom than in any other country in the world. Educational reform provided a literate readership interested in foreign affairs and domestic politics and rapidly improving road and rail links facilitated distribution throughout the country. The industrial revolution had created towns and cities that were able to provide a local newspaper with readers and advertisers. Advances in technology—Linotype and rotary presses, typewriters, telephones, and telegraphs—enabled local and national newspapers to operate profitably.

Politicians were quick to realize the great influence that newspaper editors had over the electorate, and from the 1850s onward there was a considerable interchange between the Parliament and Fleet Street, the traditional home of U.K. journalism. David Lloyd George, prime minister in the United Kingdom during World War I, was an adept user of the press and was not afraid to exercise his influence to negate the effects of a political crisis. When the *Daily Chronicle* employed as a military correspondent a stern critic of his policies, Lloyd George responded by calling together a group of Liberals to buy out the owners of the paper.

United Newspapers Ltd. was formed in 1918 by these supporters of the prime minister. The company bought two papers in the deal, of which the *Daily Chronicle* was the most important. The other paper, *Lloyd's Weekly News*, had been founded in 1842 and held the distinction of being the first newspaper with a circulation of one million readers. The board of United Newspapers soon began to publish a northern edition of the *Daily Chronicle* as a rival to the Conservative Lord Northcliffe's *Daily Mail* and also acquired the *Edinburgh Eve-*

Company Perspectives:

Our aim is to exploit fully our existing content, through established distribution channels and new media, and to invest boldly to develop new content and services to take advantage of the increased functionality of digital media.

ning News and the *Doncaster Gazette,* papers that carried on the strong Liberal tradition of Lloyd George and his politically minded associates.

In 1927 the company was sold for £2.9 million to the Daily Chronicle Investment Group, a joint venture of Liberal interests led by the Marquis of Reading, Sir David Yule, and Sir Thomas Catto. A covenant in the sales document restricted the owners to running the paper ''in accordance with the policy of Progressive Liberalism'' to further social and industrial reform, free trade, and ''other programmes of Liberal and Radical measures adopted by the Liberal party.''

Within a year United Newspapers was again in the hands of a new owner, William Harrison, a Yorkshireman who had trained as a solicitor in London. Although Harrison was a Conservative, he proclaimed that the group would continue to support Lloyd George and the Liberal cause. As chairman of the Inveresk Paper Company, Harrison bought a controlling interest in United Newspapers. The latter was then amalgamated with Provincial Newspapers Ltd., an umbrella organization taking in some 17 local newspapers that Harrison had acquired in the early and mid-1920s.

Harrison's belief in the regional market molded United's acquisition strategy for the next 50 years, but this strategy was also responsible for his downfall. In autumn 1929, 80 percent of the value of the shares in the Inveresk Paper Company was written off because of the Great Depression. In December Harrison resigned as chairman when it was revealed that Inveresk had debts of £2.5 million and that United Newspapers had no immediate means to pay for a £500,000 modernization program for the *Daily Chronicle.* Both companies were highly leveraged at a time when investment capital in all sectors of the economy was nearly impossible to secure.

The board of United Newspapers—led by Sir Bernhard Binder, founder of the chartered accountants Binder Hamlyn, and managing director Jack Akerman—was now facing a major crisis. Its solution was to merge the *Daily Chronicle* with the *Daily News* to produce a new title, the *Daily News and Chronicle.* In a move to provide finance for United's provincial press, 50 percent of the ownership of the new paper was sold to News and Westminster Ltd.

The mid-1930s were difficult for United Newspapers. It was a time of depression and mass unemployment, especially in United's marketplace, the north of England. Fears for the company's survival increased when Lord Rothermere announced his venture, Northcliffe Newspapers, with a stated aim of producing an evening paper in every city and metropolitan area served by United Newspapers. But in a move executed by Jack

Akerman and Sir Herbert Grotrian, who had replaced Binder as chairman, United Newspapers sold its 50 percent share in what—in June 1930—had become the *News Chronicle* for £500,000 and was instantly freed from its debt. The reaction from the City was ecstatic, and United's preference shares rose from one shilling sixpence to 25 shillings, as final proof that the crisis had been averted.

The war years were less difficult for United than they were for those newspaper groups that were based in heavily bombed Fleet Street. An increase in news was cruelly matched by newsprint rationing, distribution and communication problems, and government censorship. Although Sheffield and Hull suffered damage from Luftwaffe bombing comparable to that inflicted on London, presses in Scotland, Leeds, and the west country fared better, and United Newspapers was able to consolidate its success in these areas.

Drayton Took Over As Chairman in 1946

The next event of importance for the directors of United Newspapers occurred in the winter of 1946 with an invitation to dinner at the Hyde Park Hotel from Harold Charles Drayton. Drayton—always known as ''Harley''—was the epitome of the self-made man; born in rural Lincolnshire, he started his working life as a £1-a-week office boy and rose through the ranks of the City, eventually controlling the 117 Old Broad Street Group, a large and diverse empire of companies with worldwide interests.

Although Drayton described himself as almost uneducated, he was in truth an erudite and imaginative businessman. He realized that United Newspapers was holding assets of immense value, in the shape of offices and printing houses in the center of major towns and cities throughout the United Kingdom. Within a few weeks of the Hyde Park dinner, Drayton began negotiating with United Newspapers and eventually bought 500,000 shares, representing approximately one-third of the equity of the company. After several months as an ordinary board member, Drayton became chairman on New Year's Day 1948.

Years of steady but unspectacular profits for United followed, enlivened by a number of small and cautious acquisitions. Drayton realized that the directors of the company, three of whom were in their 70s, would soon have to be replaced. Two important additions were made to the board; significantly, they were both men who had risen through the ranks of Provincial Newspapers, a company associated with United that had been formed in 1930.

Ken Whitworth had been advertising manager of a group of local newspapers based in south London before joining the Royal Air Force in 1939. He returned from four years as a prisoner of war in Japan to prove his business worth as a member of several of Provincial's boards. William Barnetson had started as an editorial writer on the *Edinburgh Evening News* and swiftly rose to become editor. He demonstrated his management skills on the board of the Edinburgh paper and later on the board of Provincial. After the quiet years of the 1950s, when the United Kingdom struggled to recover from the ravages of World War II, United Newspapers entered the 1960s with the commercially minded Whitworth and the editorially gifted Barnetson as joint managing directors. With Harley Drayton as chairman it was to be the first golden age of United Newspapers.

United Newspapers entered the 1960s as a wealthy company with an established stable of widely read regional newspapers. It was to Barnetson's credit that he did not rush headlong into reckless expansion but instead formulated a cautious acquisition strategy that relied as much on the goodwill of competitors as on his own undoubted capacity for striking deals. United's move in 1963 to larger premises in Tudor Street was indicative of United's imminent emergence as a major player in the U.K. newspaper industry.

In 1963 the *Nelson Leader* and the *Colne Times,* both struggling Lancashire papers, were bought by United, which rationalized operations by transferring printing to its own under-derutilized plant at Burnley. Later in the same year United sold the 49 percent stake in the *Hull Daily News,* held by Provincial, for £1.7 million to Associated Newspapers. In November, United gave the *Edinburgh Evening News* to the Thomson group in exchange for two Sheffield papers, the *Telegraph* and the *Star.* For Thomson it meant the end of competition for its *Evening Dispatch* in Edinburgh and for United the loss of a fine paper was offset by the strengthening of its position in Yorkshire. This deal was followed by an agreement to sell United's *Yorkshire Evening News* for 20 percent of the equity of the far stronger Yorkshire Post Newspapers. Drayton adroitly realized that it was necessary to lose a battle, or at least to appear to lose a battle, to win the war. The purchase of the group of newspapers centered on the Blackpool office of the *West Lancashire Evening Gazette* and further consolidated United's position in the north of England.

Harley Drayton was succeeded as chairman by William Barnetson in April 1966. Barnetson followed Drayton's strategy and tactics when he sold the *Doncaster Gazette* to Yorkshire Post Newspapers in exchange for 49 percent of a new joint venture company, Doncaster Newspapers Ltd., which was set up to publish the *Doncaster Evening Post.* With Ken Whitworth's help as managing director, United introduced new economies in preparation for the company's greatest years of expansion.

The year 1969 started quietly with the acquisition of a group of weekly papers in north London. United then took the brave step of entering the periodicals market when Bradbury Agnew and Co., fearing hostile predators, offered its flagship *Punch,* the *Countryman,* and a number of printing houses to the company. During the tail end of the 1960s *Punch* had been suffering from a problem that was to recur with some regularity over the next 20 years. Seen as a magazine for dentist's waiting rooms, it found itself out of step with contemporary humor, but United worked closely with then editor William Davis to counter this problem.

While the deal with Bradbury Agnew was being finalized, United had begun to increase its shareholding in Yorkshire Post Newspapers. In October 1969 United acquired the total equity of the group in a transaction that was more of a mutually beneficial merger than a hostile takeover. In just one year United Newspapers had more than doubled in size.

The 1970s saw a further period of deliberate consolidation for United Newspapers. Under Lord Barnetson the company had become firmly established as one of the Big Four of the U.K. regional press, and acquisitions were designed to increase further its share of the local market. When Barnetson died in 1981 his successor David Stevens, later Lord Stevens of Ludgate, knew that if the group was to survive it would have to venture beyond traditional areas of interest and concluded that expansion abroad was vital. He instigated a process of rationalization that saw the closure of unprofitable papers in Sheffield, Doncaster, and Wigan and the sell-off of the group's printing interests.

Stevens's leadership of United coincided with the rise of the 1980s media magnates. Rupert Murdoch and Robert Maxwell did more than simply buy out the interests of the Astors, the Beaverbrooks, and the Rothermeres; they replaced the old-fashioned newspaper proprietor with an aggressive, profit-driven businessman who was prepared almost continually to buy and sell media interests. Stevens, with a public profile deceptively lower than that of his major competitors, ensured that United Newspapers did not lag behind.

Acquired Fleet Holdings in 1985

In January 1985 United Newspapers bought a 15 percent stake in Fleet Holdings, owner of the *Daily Express,* the *Sunday Express,* the *Star,* and the Morgan Grampian Group, from Robert Maxwell's Pergamon Press. When Lord Matthews, chairman of Fleet, refused to elect him to the board, Stevens initially launched a £223 million takeover offer in August 1985. This was well below the price of the company's shares at the time and was accepted by less than one percent of Fleet shareholders. The bid was subsequently raised to £317 million, significantly larger than the market value of United Newspapers itself. The skills Stevens had learned as a fund manager in the City enabled him to gain complete control of Fleet Holdings by October.

Express Newspapers gave United Newspapers its first national newspaper in 50 years, but the return to Fleet Street was to be far from easy. The *Daily Express* had been losing readers in the middle market and was further hit by the launch of *Today* in 1986. Numerous changes in editorial staff led to a confused editorial style and the paper's image problem was not helped by a steady turnover of advertising agencies.

Stevens initially reduced the number of regular employees from 6,800 to 4,700 and forced through new agreements with the national printing unions and the paper's own chapels. In the ensuing years to 1990, the number was further reduced to 1,700. Electronic production and direct input of copy to computers meant that the labor-intensive process of hot metal composition could be bypassed. A ban on secondary picketing, enforced by the Employment Acts of 1980 and 1982, further weakened the hold of the traditional printing unions, which had already been shaken by protracted strikes and violent demonstrations in Warrington and Wapping. These measures returned the newly acquired national papers to profitability, enabling Express Newspapers to embark on a program of investment to ensure the future viability of its newspapers. This strategy involved the utilization of the new print technology, investment in color presses, increased paginations, and reduced advertising proportions, with the clear aim of improving the papers' appeal to their target audiences. By 1990 there were strong indications of the success of this strategy, with all Express titles showing stable circulation and strong shares of their respective advertising markets. By the end of the 1980s the *Daily Express* and the *Daily Star* were, respectively, the fourth and sixth most popular daily titles in the United Kingdom. The *Sunday Express* was by far the biggest selling Sunday broadsheet paper and the fifth most popular of all national Sunday newspapers.

Diversified and Expanded Geographically in the 1980s and 1990s

Stevens's first major overseas acquisitions took place in the United States. Gralla, a family-run publisher of trade magazines and promoter of trade shows, was bought in 1983 for US$44 million. Miller Freeman, publisher of a number of medical and computer trade magazines, was the next U.S. acquisition, followed by PR Newswire, a corporate and financial news agency. In the domestic market, United took control of Link House Publications in a move that added the classified advertising paper *Exchange and Mart* to United's increasingly impressive list of titles.

Stevens also was determined to diversify into different markets. In 1987 Extel, a provider of financial and sporting information, was bought for £250 million. Benn Brothers plc, producer of directories and tax guides, was bought in 1987. In 1989 the *Daily Express* was the last national newspaper to leave Fleet Street, moving to the other side of the Thames River to new offices at Blackfriars Bridge.

By the beginning of the 1990s Lord Stevens had transformed United Newspapers from a publisher of regional U.K. newspapers to a diversified media group whose additional interests included the national U.K. papers *Express* and *Daily Star,* trade magazines, advertising publications, news services, and trade show activities. Geographically, the company had gained a considerable presence in the United States and was expanding certain business—most notably Miller Freeman and PR Newswire—into Asia. In 1995 this diversification was highlighted through the company changing its name to United News & Media plc.

Even more dramatic changes were in the cards for UNM during the remainder of the decade, under the continued direction of Stevens. In February 1996 a £2.9 billion (US$4.5 billion) merger joined the operations of UNM with those of MAI PLC—with the combined entity retaining the United News & Media name. MAI's interests included two television licenses in the United Kingdom for the Independent Television Network; a 29 percent stake in Channel 5, a national commercial broadcasting service in the United Kingdom that made its on-air debut in 1997; NOP Research Group, a market research company; and various financial services firms. MAI too had an agreement, also concluded in February 1996, with Time Warner to partner on a £225 million (US$344 million) Movie World theme park and film studio complex to be built just west of London. But it was the extension into television broadcasting, production, and distribution that made the MAI merger most attractive to UNM.

Within just a few years of this blockbuster deal, United News & Media made a series of acquisitions and divestments that further transformed the company. In late 1996 UNM bolstered its trade show operations through the £592.5 million (US$905 million) purchase of U.K.-based Blenheim Exhibitions and Conferences Ltd., which was soon integrated into Miller Freeman. This acquisition made UNM into the largest exhibitions group in the world. During 1997 United News acquired HTV, a Welsh independent television broadcaster; Telecom Library, a magazine publisher and trade show organizer in the United States; and Lemos Britto, a Brazilian trade show organizer.

In early 1998 UNM made a dramatic break from its past with the divestment of its regional newspaper business through three separate sales, totaling £450 million (US$700 million). In November of that same year, the company demerged the financial services businesses inherited from MAI into a separate public company called Garban plc. These moves left a more focused UNM, with three main business segments: business services, which included Miller Freeman, PR Newswire, and market research operations NOP and Mediamark Research; broadcasting and entertainment, which included the independent television licenses, the Channel 5 stake, and television show production and distribution activities; and consumer publishing, which included the *Express* and the *Daily Star* national U.K. newspapers and advertising periodicals in the United States and the United Kingdom. In the late 1990s more than half of the company's revenues were generated by business services, which was also UNM's most profitable sector.

At the turn of the century, United News & Media appeared likely to continue to make strategic acquisitions to bolster its core operations. Purchases made in early 1999 highlighted this strategy, while at the same time showing an ongoing interest in U.S. growth and an increasing interest in Internet-based opportunities. In January 1999 UNM—through PR Newswire—acquired NEWSdesk International, a leading European Internet distributor of corporate news for the high-tech industry. Two months later UNM acquired Audits & Surveys Worldwide Inc., a leading U.S. market research firm, and Continuing Medical Education, Inc., a provider of continuing medical education resources for U.S. physicians, including conferences and seminars, trade magazines, home study products, and web sites. In late April 1999 United News agreed to purchase CMP Media Inc. for US$920 million. The Manhassat, New York-based CMP's operations included the publication of such trade magazines as *Information Week, Computer Reseller News,* and *Electronic Engineering Times,* and the maintenance of 40 online web sites, including TechWeb and ChannelWeb. CMP was to be combined with Miller Freeman, creating one of the leading business-media groups.

Principal Subsidiaries

BUSINESS SERVICES: Miller Freeman PSNInc. (U.S.A.); Miller Freeman Asia Ltd. (Hong Kong); Blenheim Exhibitions and Conferences Ltd.; Miller Freeman BV (Netherlands); Miller Freeman, Inc. (U.S.A.); Miller Freeman plc; Groupe Miller Freeman SA (France); PR Newswire Association Inc. (U.S.A.); Visual Communications Group Ltd.; FPG International LLC (U.S.A.); Mediamark Research, Inc. (U.S.A.; 90%); NOP Research Group Ltd.; Audits & Surveys Worldwide, Inc. CONSUMER PUBLISHING: Express Newspapers plc; United Advertising Publications plc; United Advertising Publications, Inc. (U.S.A.). BROADCASTING AND ENTERTAINMENT: Anglia Television Ltd.; HTV Group Ltd.; Meridian Broadcasting Ltd.; Survival Anglia Ltd.; TSMS Group Ltd.

Principal Divisions

Business Services; Consumer Publishing; Broadcasting & Entertainment.

Further Reading

Davidson, Andrew, ''Lord Stevens,'' *Management Today,* March 1995, pp. 53–54, 56.

Gapper, John, ''Arculus Chooses a Tricky Moment to Go,'' *Financial Times,* February 14, 1998, p. 21.

——, ''United News Shares Slip on Demerger Plans,'' *Financial Times,* July 24, 1998, p. 24.

Great Britain, Monopolies and Mergers Commission, *EMAP plc and United Newspapers plc: A Report on the Proposed Transfers of Controlling Interests As Defined in Section 57(4) of the Fair Trading Act 1973 and of the Business of Publishing and Distributing Three Newspapers Owned by EMAP plc to United Newspapers plc,* London: HMSO, 1992.

Harverson, Patrick, and Raymond Snoddy, ''Express in £3Bn Merger Deal with TV Group MAI,'' *Financial Times,* February 9, 1996, p. 1.

Jenkins, Simon, *The Market for Glory: Fleet Street Ownership in the Twentieth Century,* London: Faber and Faber, 1986.

Newman, Cathy, ''Southnews Pays £47.5m for United Southern Arm,'' *Financial Times,* February 19, 1998, p. 21.

——, ''Three-Way Split for United Media Sale,'' *Financial Times,* January 8, 1998, p. 23.

——, ''United Sells Regional Titles for £450m,'' *Financial Times,* February 28, 1998, p. 18.

Parker-Pope, Tara, and Sara Calian, ''Joie de Screamer: Time Warner Plans More U.S.-Style Thrills for Europe,'' *Wall Street Journal,* February 14, 1996, p. B8.

Price, Christopher, ''Lord Stevens Prepares to Wind Down,'' *Financial Times,* November 13, 1996, p. 22.

——, ''United News Agreed Bid Values HTV at £371m,'' *Financial Times,* June 28, 1997, p. 20.

Rich, Motoko, ''United's Swift Move Wins Battle of Blenheim,'' *Financial Times,* October 16, 1996, p. 30.

Saatchi & Saatchi, *Top Fifty European Media Owners,* London: Saatchi & Saatchi Communications, 1989.

Schofield, Guy, *The Men That Carry the News: A History of United Newspapers Limited,* London: Cranford Press, 1975.

Snoddy, Raymond, ''Battle for Channel 5 Won by MAI and Pearson,'' *Financial Times,* October 28, 1995, p. 1.

——, ''Lord Stevens Looks to a Richer Future,'' *Financial Times,* April 10, 1995, p. 10.

——, ''TV Contestants on Their Marks,'' *Financial Times,* February 9, 1996, p. 15.

Snoddy, Raymond, Scheherazade Daneshkhu, and Alice Rawsthorn, ''MAI to Join Time Warner in £225m Film Theme Park,'' *Financial Times,* February 13, 1996, p. 1.

Taylor, A.J.P., ''Lloyd George: Rise and Fall,'' in *Essays in English History,* London: Hamish Hamilton, 1976.

—Andreas Loizou
—updated by David E. Salamie

US Airways Group, Inc.

2345 Crystal Drive
Arlington, Virginia 22227
U.S.A.
(703) 872-7000
Fax: (703) 872-5307
Web site: http://www.usairways.com

Public Company
Incorporated: 1937 as All American Aviation, Inc.
Employees: 41,393
Sales: $8.69 billion (1998)
Stock Exchanges: New York
Ticker Symbol: U
NAIC: 481111 Scheduled Passenger Air Transportation

US Airways Group, Inc. (formerly USAir Group, Inc.) is a holding company for several commercial airlines, of which US Airways (formerly USAir) is the largest. US Airways is a leading carrier of passengers in the eastern United States and the sixth largest airline in the country. It ranks first or second in departures at a number of important hubs, including Charlotte, Pittsburgh, Philadelphia, Baltimore/Washington International, Boston's Logan International, New York's LaGuardia, and Washington, D.C.'s Ronald Reagan Washington National. Through its fleet of nearly 400 jets, US Airways provides service to more than 100 airports in the United States, Canada, Mexico, France, Germany, Italy, the Netherlands, Spain, the United Kingdom, and the Caribbean. In addition to its flagship carrier, which generates about 90 percent of the company's operating revenues, US Airways Group also operates regional airlines under the US Airways Express, US Airways Shuttle, and other names. It also launched a low-cost, low-fare carrier in 1998, MetroJet.

Mail Delivery Origins

The company was originally incorporated in Delaware in 1937 as All American Aviation, Inc. by a glider pilot named Richard C. du Pont, of the Delaware du Ponts. On May 12, 1939, the airline began to deliver mail around the mountains of Pennsylvania and West Virginia. Since many communities did not have airstrips, the company devised a system employing hooks and ropes that enabled the mail plane to drop off one mailbag and pick up another without landing. Du Pont's method brought regular mail service to a number of once-isolated communities and was widely imitated. Later, All American began transporting passengers on its limited network. Despite the addition of more destinations the airline remained a small operation, serving many remote communities throughout the Alleghenies.

When the United States became involved in World War II, du Pont went to work on the Army's glider program in California. The mailbag snare he developed was adapted by the Army's Air Corps and used to rescue downed pilots behind enemy lines. Du Pont also helped to develop a glider that could be picked up by an already airborne airplane, a system that was used in the evacuation of Allied troops from the Remagen beachhead in Germany. Du Pont was killed in a glider crash in 1943.

After the war, All American Aviation changed its name to All American Airways; in 1953 the name was changed again to Allegheny Airlines. That same year the government chose Allegheny to operate shuttle services between smaller eastern cities and major destinations served by larger airline companies. Allegheny was provided a subsidy to operate these services to communities that otherwise would have had no air service.

The company experienced a period of healthy growth for several years in the 1950s and 1960s. The old DC-3s it was flying were replaced with new Convair 440s, Convair 540s, and Martin 202s. The operations and maintenance base was also relocated from Washington, D.C., to a modern complex in Pittsburgh. Allegheny began buying jets in 1966. In 1968 the company acquired Lake Central Airlines and in 1972 purchased Mohawk Airlines.

Concurrent with this steady growth, Allegheny was obliged to operate the government-assigned ''feeder'' services, but starting in 1967 Allegheny began subcontracting these routes to smaller

Company Perspectives:

The tools of a "Carrier of Choice" and "World-Class Global Carrier"—the aircraft, the information technology systems, the airports and training facilities—are in place. The issue before us is how we use those tools. If we use them in the months and years to come with the same skill and determination as we have used the tools available to us in the past three years, US Airways will define "World Class" in aviation, and that is precisely our intention.

independent carriers. The independents were able to make a profit on the routes because they had lower costs, they were not unionized, and their equipment was better suited for the rural "puddle jumper" routes, while the government was happy to release Allegheny from its obligations and discontinue the subsidies. Since the independents fed passengers mostly to Allegheny, the company itself had become a large regional airline.

Despite Allegheny's growth, passengers had a low opinion of the airline, which had acquired the nickname "Agony Air." The company's on-time record was poor, its customer service was described as unpleasant, and flight cancellations were common. In many cities the airline had a monopoly on air service, so there was little incentive to improve customer relations.

Emerged As USAir in 1979

Fortunately for Allegheny its chairman and president, Edwin Colodny, had previously served with the Civil Aeronautics Board (CAB). This experience provided him with the knowledge to acquire and protect the company's right to fly to certain destinations, and to successfully raise fares. Before any of his policies could be put into effect, however, the Airline Deregulation Act of 1978 was passed. Vigorously opposed to the passing of this act, Colodny argued that permitting all airlines to freely enter into any market would allow the larger airlines, with their vast resources, to raid markets served by smaller companies with the intention of driving them out of business. This did not happen. Instead, the larger airlines used their new freedom under deregulation to contend with each other, while regional operators such as Allegheny were virtually unaffected. Deregulation also provided new opportunities for regional airlines. For the first time, Allegheny was allowed to operate long-haul routes to Texas and the West Coast. With such an opportunity, the company clearly required an improvement upon its "Agony Air" reputation. Colodny decided to begin with a new name. He chose "USAir" over several other names, including "Republic Airlines" (which was later used by the old Minneapolis-based North Central Airlines). Allegheny officially became USAir on October 28, 1979.

Under the name USAir the company launched an advertising campaign in which it claimed to "carry more passengers than Pan Am, fly to more cities than American, and have more flights than TWA." This coincided with the inauguration of new routes to the Southwest, which were originally intended to prevent company jets from remaining idle during the traditional winter slump in the northeastern markets. In addition, USAir planned to implement a Pittsburgh-London route, but withdrew the application due to fears of "overambition." According to Colodny, "overexpansion is the most tempting of all possible sins of airline managements under deregulation. And, if overdone, it can result in a serious bellyache. In designing a route system, a carrier must limit its ego." As a result, the airline concentrated on consolidating its markets and strengthening its central Pittsburgh hub.

Colodny maintained that two-thirds of U.S. air travel was in markets of less than 1,000 miles, and USAir made it a point to concentrate on developing these local markets. The short duration of these flights, however, meant that the airplanes had to make more takeoffs and landings, which in turn increased maintenance costs. In the late 1980s the company flew DC-9s, B-727s, 737s, 757s, 767s, as well as several smaller aircraft for its express fleet subsidiaries. The average age of its 446 planes was nine years, one of the lowest averages in the industry.

The airline's on-time record significantly improved as a result of strict attention to scheduling and the "first flight of the day" standard, which prevented late starts from pushing back the whole day's schedule. The airline also perfected a system of efficient bad-weather maintenance. These measures contributed to what company officials claimed was the second lowest number of complaints to the CAB (Delta was first) based on passenger volume.

In order to remain competitive with other airline companies that were merging to form even larger companies, the USAir Group announced in December 1986 that it would be acquiring Pacific Southwest Airlines (PSA) for $400 million. The announcement surprised many industry analysts because USAir's predominantly East Coast airline network had few integration points with PSA, which was concentrated along the West Coast. First operated as a subsidiary of the USAir Group, PSA was later absorbed by USAir. The merger increased the amount of traffic on USAir by 40 percent and gave USAir landing rights in a number of cities on the West Coast.

Early 1990s Downturn

Nevertheless, USAir entered 1992 battered by a poor economy, as well as the fallout from a trouble-ridden merger with North Carolina-based Piedmont in 1987. The company had suffered three consecutive years of net losses (the largest in 1990, at $454 million), the forfeiture of many domestic routes, fierce price wars, and a series of staff reductions and wage freezes. Agis Salpukas, writing for the *New York Times,* declared: "USAir continues to bleed, but at a much slower rate. Costs have been cut, through a mix of layoffs, deferred orders of new planes and the closing of overlapping facilities." According to Salpukas, the company, if not yet sound financially, had nonetheless succeeded in refurbishing its public image. "No longer—or, at least, not so often—is the carrier referred to as Useless Air because of problems with flight delays, lost luggage and surly employees." Meanwhile Colodny retired in 1991, with Seth Schofield taking over as CEO.

On March 22, 1992, USAir suffered a tragedy when Flight 405, bound from LaGuardia to Cleveland, crashed into Flushing Bay within minutes after takeoff. Twenty-seven people, more than half of the flight's passengers, were killed. The crash, under investigation by the National Transportation Safety Board, was precipitated by a blustery snowstorm and problems involved in deicing planes at LaGuardia once they had been cleared for takeoff.

Following encouraging news from market analysts that USAir would bolster its East Coast presence with the acquisition of a minority stake in the Trump Shuttle (renamed USAir Shuttle) and major slot expansions at LaGuardia and Washington National, British Airways PLC (BA) announced in July 1992 that it had arranged to form a strong alliance with USAir and would purchase a 44 percent stake in USAir for $750 million. Colin Marshall, chief executive of the profitable BA, intended to create a dependable feeder market of overseas routes through the U.S. carrier. But American, United, and Delta Air Lines (the U.S. "Big Three") vigorously lobbied against the deal and demanded enhanced access to the British market if the deal was to be approved by the U.S. government. In December 1992 the purchase was blocked. In early 1993 BA and USAir restructured their agreement into a $400 million BA purchase of 25 percent of USAir. This investment/alliance, under which USAir gave up its London routes, received U.S. government approval. The government also approved a code-sharing arrangement that enabled the partners to offer their customers a seamless operation when they use both airlines to reach their destination.

USAir continued to be beset by its high-cost operating structure, and posted losses in 1993 and 1994, marking six straight years in the red. It was also the subject of bankruptcy speculation in the press. Under Schofield's plan to cut expenses by $1 billion a year and helped by a resurgent U.S. economy, USAir returned to profitability in 1995, posting net income of $119 million. In late 1995 Schofield, frustrated in his efforts to secure concessions from the company's pilots, suddenly announced his resignation. In January 1996 Stephen M. Wolf, former chief executive of United Airlines, came out of semiretirement to become chairman and CEO of USAir. Wolf quickly brought in a former colleague of his at United, Rakesh Gangwal, as president and chief operating officer.

Became US Airways in 1997

Wolf and Gangwal made the attainment of union concessions a key to the company's future. While negotiations continued, the company announced in November 1996 that the parent company would change its name to US Airways Group, Inc. and USAir would become US Airways, changes that took effect in February 1997. Around this same time, the company's alliance with BA fell apart after BA announced an alliance with American Airlines, with lawsuits following. The US Airways-BA code-sharing deal expired in March 1997. In late 1997 US Airways finally reached an agreement with the pilots' union on a five-year deal that established pay parity with the four largest U.S. carriers. With this concession in hand, the company was able to proceed with an order for 400 Airbus A320s, scheduled for delivery from 1998 through 2009. The new airplanes would

enable US Airways to continue as a major airline, rather than being forced to shrink into a regional one.

A newly revitalized US Airways made a host of strategic maneuvers during 1998. The company purchased full control of US Airways Shuttle, in which it had held a minority stake since 1992; launched the low-cost, low-fare MetroJet carrier to help it compete against Delta Express and Southwest Airlines, which had encroached into US Airways' core markets; reached an agreement with Airbus to purchase up to 30 widebody A330-300 aircraft for international flights; added to its transatlantic service with the debut of Philadelphia-London, Philadelphia-Amsterdam, and Pittsburgh-Paris runs; and, finally, entered into a marketing alliance with American Airlines involving linked frequent-flier programs and reciprocal airport lounge facility access. In May 1998 Gangwal became president and CEO of US Airways Group, with Wolf remaining chairman.

US Airways Group reported net income of $538 million in 1998, a reflection of its renewed strength. While the carrier had succeeded in cutting its high-cost structure and returned to the black, it faced severe challenges in a era of industry consolidation. Other major carriers were rapidly linking up through global alliances, and it seemed likely that US Airways would have to become more aggressive in this area if it wanted to remain a major carrier itself. By the late 1990s American Airlines had linked with both US Airways and BA, so it seemed possible that US Airways and BA would resurrect their partnership, perhaps creating an American-US Airways-BA trilateral alliance, which would certainly be a global airline power.

Principal Subsidiaries

US Airways, Inc.; US Airways Shuttle, Inc.; Allegheny Airlines, Inc.; Piedmont Airlines, Inc.; PSA Airlines, Inc.; US Airways Leasing and Sales, Inc.; USAir Fuel Corp.; Materials Services, Inc.; USAM Corp.

Further Reading

Alexander, Keith L., and Seth Payne, "USAir: This 'Dog' May Be Having Its Day," *Business Week,* June 21, 1993, pp. 74, 76.

Antonelli, Cesca, "US Airways Must Snare an Overseas Partner to Continue Profitable Path," *Pittsburgh Business Times,* April 17, 1998, p. 5.

Del Valle, Christina, "Brawl in the Cockpit at USAir," *Business Week,* September 25, 1995, p. 59.

Del Valle, Christina, Wendy Zellner, and Susan Chandler, "USAir's European Squeeze Play," *Business Week,* September 2, 1996, pp. 62–63.

Dwyer, Paula, et al., "Air Raid: British Air's Bold Global Push," *Business Week,* August 24, 1992.

Foust, Dean, Keith L. Alexander, and Aaron Bernstein, "USAir's Frightening Loss of Attitude," *Business Week,* June 6, 1994, p. 34.

Jennings, Mead, "Snowed Under: Growth of the British Airways-USAir Alliance Has Been Put on Hold As USAir Attempts to Put Its Own House in Order," *Airline Business,* April 1994, pp. 26+.

Kleinfeld, N.R., "The Ordinary Turned to Instant Horror for All Aboard USAir's Flight 405," *New York Times,* March 29, 1992.

Miller, James P., "US Air's Wolf Gives Gangwal the CEO's Job," *Wall Street Journal,* November 19, 1998, pp. A3, A14.

Salpukis, Agis, "USAir Discovers There Is Life After a Messy Merger," *New York Times,* January 19, 1992.

Shives, Robert, and William Thompson, *Airlines of North America,* Sarasota, Fla.: Crestline, 1984, 240 p.

Spiegel, Peter, "Can Heroes Work Miracles?," *Forbes,* April 6, 1998, pp. 53+.

"USAir's Seth Schofield Is Named Chairman," *Wall Street Journal,* May 14, 1992.

Velocci, Anthony L., "US Airways Accord Sets Stage for Growth," *Aviation Week and Space Technology,* October 6, 1997, pp. 35, 38–39.

Walker, Karen, "US Airways Cry Wolf!," *Airline Business,* August 1997, pp. 24+.

Whitaker, Richard, and Mead Jennings, "BA and USAir Forge a New Deal," *Airlines Business,* February 1993, pp. 20+.

Woellert, Lorraine, and David Leonhardt, "Pulling US Airways Out of a Dive," *Business Week,* September 14, 1998, pp. 131–32.

—John Simley
—updated by David E. Salamie

The Vons Companies, Incorporated

618 Michillinda Avenue
Arcadia, California 91007-6300
U.S.A.
(626) 821-7000
Fax: (626) 821-7933

Wholly Owned Subsidiary of Safeway Inc.
Incorporated: 1906 as Vons Grocery Company
Employees: 30,400
Sales: $5.41 billion (1996)
NAIC: 44511 Supermarkets & Other Grocery (Except Convenience) Stores; 45291 Warehouse Clubs & Superstores

The Vons Companies, Incorporated—wholly owned by Safeway Inc. since April 1997—is the second largest retail supermarket chain in southern California, trailing only Ralphs Grocery Co. The company has about 330 stores in southern California and in Nevada, under two main brands: Vons supermarkets and Pavilions stores, the latter of which are larger-format stores featuring wider selections of items and enhanced services.

Entrepreneurial Origins

Vons was created by Charles Von der Ahe, an entrepreneur instrumental in the development of the modern supermarket. Von der Ahe's first experience in the grocery business was as a delivery boy in Illinois. On the way to California, where he would eventually settle, Von der Ahe worked in several markets, observing merchandising techniques and customer buying patterns first hand. In 1906, with a total capital investment of $1,200, Von der Ahe opened a small grocery store named Von's Groceteria on the corner of Seventh and Figueroa in Los Angeles. Over the next few years, he opened additional stores, implementing a number of innovative strategies which fueled dynamic growth in his business. Von der Ahe was the first grocer to introduce cash-and-carry and self-service. In leasing his open storefronts to produce vendors and butchers, Vons also pioneered the combination store concept which would later lead to

his first supermarket. By 1929 the Vons Grocery Company numbered 87 stores.

Von der Ahe had the foresight to sell his stores to McMarr Stores in 1929, before the stock market crash decimated the value of commercial properties. McMarr would in turn eventually be purchased by Safeway. In the meantime, Von der Ahe enjoyed three years of retirement before being lured back into the grocery business by his sons Ted and Wil, who decided to open a new chain of Vons stores in the Los Angeles area. Von der Ahe helped his sons out with investment capital and industry expertise, and Vons stores began to multiply. The partnership culminated in the opening of a 50,300-square-foot food market in downtown Los Angeles in 1948. The prototype of the supermarket, this location boasted a number of innovative features which today are taken for granted, notably self-service produce, meat, and delicatessen departments. The store confirmed the Von der Ahe family's role as innovators in the retail food industry.

In 1960 Vons merged with Shopping Bag Food Stores, bringing the total number of stores under family management to 66. Particular emphasis was placed on understanding local markets and arranging shelf space accordingly, a practice that has continued to the present day. In 1967 the merger was challenged by the Federal Trade Commission. The case went all the way to the U.S. Supreme Court, which ordered Vons to divest itself of the Shopping Bag locations immediately. In 1969 Vons was bought out by the Household Finance Corporation, later Household International, which added the chain to its Household Merchandising division.

Dynamic Growth in the 1970s and Early 1980s

The expansion of Vons Stores into the San Diego area during the 1970s corresponded with a period of dynamic growth when the chain widened operations to include wholesale marketing to other retailers and fast-food chains. In the mid-1970s, Vons opened a series of mid-sized units called Value Centers, which sold food and drugs in one location. This "combo" concept would develop into Pavilions Stores in 1987. In the early 1980s, Vons expanded north into the Fresno area. In the same period, the company began to stress the importance of combining coupon promotions with in-store product demonstrations as a means of persuading more conservative customers to try new foods. Vons was among the first stores to operate its product promotion department as a profit center funded by fees from participating companies.

Vons scored a tremendous coup in 1984 when the company was designated the official supermarket of the Los Angeles Olympics. Under a deal worked out with the Olympic Committee, the chain agreed to provide food for more than 12,000 athletes, coaches, and trainers in the Olympic Village. Food worth $8 million was provided to the committee at cost for preparation by an independent foodservice organization. The balance, worth $2 million, was donated by the company. In return, Vons was guaranteed a number of exclusive merchandising and advertising opportunities. Store decor was changed to highlight the Olympic theme, and the Olympic logo was placed on a number of perishable items that were considered to have particular nutritional value.

Vons Regained Independence in 1986

In January 1986 top management in the Household Merchandising branch of Household International negotiated a $757 million leveraged buyout of their division. The deal, which was the largest retail buyout in the United States at the time, was masterminded by Roger E. Stangeland, who went on to become chairperson of the newly independent Vons Companies. Stangeland had been an executive at Household International since 1961, and had been responsible for Vons Stores since 1982. While the buyout successfully separated Vons from Household International, it also burdened the company with an unacceptable level of debt. Stangeland announced that reducing the debt-to-equity ratio would be a priority over the next few years. In the meantime, he added the ten-store Pantry chain to the Vons portfolio. He also charged William S. Davila, the company's president, with developing an expanded "combination store" concept. Started in 1986, the year of the leveraged buyout, the Pavilions subchain would number 28 stores by 1991.

At 75,000 square feet, the first Pavilions store was the company's largest to date. A combination store, Pavilions offered huge food and nonfood sections. Different departments were identified with banners and decked with white awnings which created the effect of tented "pavilions." Joe Raymond, a merchandising executive with Pavilions, described the concept as "breaking away from the pack." Important features included the plain white decor, designed to focus customer attention on the items on display. The store carried a greater selection of produce than comparable stores, and shoppers were invited to sample new products at a permanently staffed demonstration booth. In order to emphasize the freshness of the perishable goods, all food preparation was done in full view of the shopping public. At the same time, the nonfood area stressed value for money, with a large variety of health and beauty aids offered at discounts of up to 30 percent on average retail prices, and a professionally staffed pharmacy selling prescription drugs at discounts of up to 50 percent. In some areas, Pavilions competed directly with adjacent Vons stores, a situation that traditional marketing strategists would tend to avoid. Vons executives remained unruffled, however, articulating their belief that

if Pavilions did not go head-to-head with the older stores, a competitor certainly would.

In December 1986, Vons announced that a $700 million deal had been struck with Allied Supermarkets, Inc., a publicly listed Detroit retail and wholesale food marketer. The goal of the merger was to take Vons public while controlling the company's debt load. Roger Stangeland became chair and CEO of Vons, and William S. Davila was named president and COO. Since Vons had no ambitions to expand to the Midwest, Allied's Detroit assets were sold to members of the existing management. The merger achieved its goal; Vons went public on the New York Stock Exchange in early 1987.

Constantly in search of new merchandising techniques, Vons executives turned their attention to the ethnic composition of their customers in 1987. They observed that by 1990 an estimated 40 percent of southern California's population would be of Hispanic origin. In January 1987 the company opened its first Tianguis superstore in Montebello, California, designed to cater to the specific needs of Hispanic customers, especially first-generation immigrants. Tianguis, meaning marketplace in Aztec, denotes the place where the community met to shop and to socialize; commenting on the choice of name, CEO Stangeland said in August 1986 that Vons hoped to "position our stores as an important center in the community" and to "differentiate ourselves strongly from the competition." By 1991 the company was operating nine Tianguis stores throughout southern California and had plans to open two to three stores per year.

Tianguis differed from its predecessors in many ways. All advertising and store signs were bilingual, as were the stores' employees, hired from the local community. The produce section was greatly expanded to include a wide variety of Mexican herbs, fruits, and vegetables, while some product categories were eliminated completely. As in the Pavilions stores, meat preparation was done in front of customers. The grocery section included an extensive selection of Mexican imports, sharing shelf space with their U.S. counterparts. Distribution of imports was guaranteed through the early establishment of a subsidiary called Central de Abastos Internacional in 1986. To enhance the social aspect of the stores, aisles were widened to allow patrons to stop and chat. Diaper-changing rooms were installed at the back of each store since, in Vons President Davila's words, "shopping tends to be a family event for Hispanics." The introduction of the Tianguis stores was widely discussed in the industry. Vons had demonstrated once again its strength in adapting to the changing needs of the market before its competitors.

Purchased Safeway's Southern California Stores in 1988

On August 29, 1988, Vons took over 172 of Safeway's southern California operations, paying $297 million in cash and giving up 11.67 million shares of Vons common stock, leading to Safeway holding a more than one-third stake in Vons. As a result of this transaction, the number of stores under Vons control doubled, but the company's debt load also soared. In spite of its highly leveraged position, the company immediately embarked on an ambitious remodeling of the former Safeway stores, spending an average of $1.3 million on each location. Together with more efficient inventory control and labor scheduling, the remodeling was intended to increase per-store profitability, money that in turn would be used to pay off debt. A number of in-store innovations were also implemented, including an electronic coupon program and other cost-saving technology. The strategy worked. By November 1990, sales per square foot at the former Safeway stores had risen to $615 from an average of $447 at the time of the buyout. The industry average at the time was $550. Meanwhile, corporate finances also improved. Vons went from a $25 million loss in 1989 to a $50 million profit in 1990 and a $65 million profit in 1991. By 1991, the company's debt-to-total capitalization ratio had dropped to 60 percent. The company's financial position was also strengthened by a successful equity issue in 1991.

In January 1992 Vons acquired family-owned Williams Brothers Markets for $48 million in cash and a liability of $10 million on Williams Brothers' outstanding mortgages. The transaction was financed using Vons' existing revolving loan. Located in central California, the 18 Williams Brothers stores were well-known for their customer service and successful niche in marketing to local communities. As such, they integrated well with other stores in the Vons portfolio, while allowing Vons to expand further north.

During the course of the riots in Los Angeles in May 1992, several Vons stores were looted and burned. The cost of restoring the damaged properties, however, was largely covered by insurance. In the aftermath of the riots, attention was focused on the dearth of quality supermarkets in south central Los Angeles. Vons Companies announced that the chain would commit $100 million to developing markets in neglected areas over the next few years. Then in January 1993, an outbreak of food poisoning in Washington state that claimed the lives of three children was traced to hamburgers purchased at the Jack in the Box fast-food chain, which had purchased the meat tainted with the deadly E. coli bacteria from Foodmaker, parent company of Jack in the Box. Vons, as the meat processor for Foodmaker, was involved in the early stages of the investigation. After being commended by health authorities for its clean processing facility, Vons aided health authorities by tracing the source of the contaminated beef to one Foodmaker beef supplier. The incident had wide-ranging implications for United States Department of Agriculture inspection procedures, which were deemed inadequate.

In the early 1990s, Vons renewed a commitment to technological progress by announcing a dramatic increase in its Information Systems (IS) budget. IS initiatives were piloted in a number of metropolitan locations and included electronic shelf tags, which would be updated automatically when the checkout scanner price was changed. This system was intended to enhance customer service and decrease labor costs. The early 1990s also brought two new store formats: the warehouse-club-style Expo, a format abandoned in 1995; and Super Combo stores, which included banking services, catering facilities, a dry cleaner, photo processing, a pharmacy, as well as an expanded grocery section. Later in the decade the Super Combo format essentially was melded into the Vons and Pavilions formats, many of which included the added services and sections that were becoming increasingly common in grocery stores.

Overall, the early 1990s were difficult years for Vons not only because of the severe southern California recession but also as a result of a number of other factors: the heavy debt-load that was taken on to acquire the Safeway stores; the cost of acquiring William Brothers, remodeling 59 stores in 1993 alone, opening 12 new stores in 1993, and opening a new headquarters; the temporary closing of 45 stores due to damage from the 1994 Northridge earthquake; and the loss of some customers as a result of the Jack-in-the-Box food poisoning outbreak. Same-store sales fell two percent in 1992 and another nine percent in 1993. In response, Vons instituted a restructuring program in the third quarter of 1993, taking a $57 million charge for a cost-cutting program that involved a workforce reduction of about 15 percent, salary freezes, and other initiatives. Simultaneously, the company launched the Vons Value program, which began in January 1994 and featured 18,000 price reductions.

Continuing its recovery efforts, Vons spent $175 million in 1995 to open ten new stores and remodel 65 existing stores. The company also closed down a number of unprofitable stores and consolidated three distribution centers into two, while laying plans for a three-year, 15-unit expansion of the Pavilions subchain. Same-store sales fell 2.4 percent in 1994 and increased 3.5 percent in 1995, signaling a company on the rebound—having also been aided by the strengthening of the southern California economy.

Acquired by Safeway in April 1997

In 1996 Vons added 12 new stores to its chain, eight of them replacements for older units that were closed down and four of them bought from Smith's Food & Drug. Late in the year—as the company was laying plans to open 12 to 15 stores in 1997, six of them Pavilions, including the first San Diego stores for that format—Safeway offered to purchase the 65 percent of Vons it did not already own. The deal was completed in April 1997, with Safeway paying about $2.5 billion to complete the purchase, including $565 million in debt. Vons thereby became a wholly owned subsidiary of Safeway, but its 320 stores continued to operate under the Vons and Pavilions names. Shortly after completion of the deal, Safeway eliminated 240 administrative positions at Vons, representing 37 percent of the 650 Vons headquarters staff.

In February 1998 Vons contributed, along with several meatpackers and other companies, to a $58.5 million payment to Foodmaker to settle a lawsuit Foodmaker had filed in 1993 in connection with the Jack-in-the-Box food poisoning outbreak. In December 1998 Vons bought eight stores from the Ralphs chain and subsequently remodeled them and reopened them under the Vons banner. By January 1999 there were a total of 324 Vons and Pavilions stores. This number was likely to increase at a more rapid rate than in the past as Vons could now take advantage of the deeper pockets of its parent, which was the second largest grocery chain in North America, trailing only The Kroger Company.

Further Reading

Armstrong, Larry, ''Coupon Clippers, Save Your Scissors,'' *Business Week,* June 20, 1994, pp. 164, 166.
Deutschman, Alan, ''America's Fastest Risers,'' *Fortune,* October 7, 1991.

Duff, Mike, ''Superstores,'' *Supermarket Business,* January 1991.

Gutner, Todd, '' 'Focus on the Customer','' *Forbes,* August 2, 1993, pp. 45+.

''History of the Vons Companies, Inc.,'' Arcadia: Vons Companies, April 1992.

Jereski, Laura, ''Vons, Mired in California's Downturn, Draws Far More Negative Reviews Than Positive Ones,'' *Wall Street Journal,* December 30, 1993, p. C2.

McDermott, Terry, ''E. Coli Investigation Finds Vons Supplier,'' *Seattle Times,* February 23, 1993.

Tosh, Mark, ''Vons Is Fighting Sales Declines with Price Cuts, Staff Upgrades,'' *Supermarket News,* January 17, 1994, pp. 4+.

Weinstein, Steve, '' 'This Company Is Not Broken','' *Progressive Grocer,* July 1994, pp. 30–32.

Zwiebach, Elliott, ''Del Santo to Take Vons Helm,'' *Supermarket News,* May 1, 1995, pp. 4+.

——, ''Ready for Launch,'' *Supermarket News,* September 30, 1996, pp. 1+.

——, ''Safeway, Vons Are Poised to Benefit from Tie's Synergy,'' *Supermarket News,* December 23, 1996, pp. 1+.

——, ''Vons: Diversifying Formats for Diversified Needs,'' *Supermarket News,* April 7, 1986.

——, ''Vons' New Accent,'' *Supermarket News,* February 9, 1987.

——, ''Vons, Safeway Set to Tie Knot Tomorrow,'' *Supermarket News,* April 7, 1997, pp. 1+.

—Moya Verzhbinsky
—updated by David E. Salamie

Weyerhaeuser

Weyerhaeuser Company

33663 Weyerhaeuser Way South
Federal Way, Washington 98003
U.S.A.
(253) 924-2345
Fax: (253) 924-3543
Web site: http://www.weyerhaeuser.com

Public Company
Incorporated: 1900 as Weyerhaeuser Timber Company
Employees: 35,800
Sales: $10.77 billion (1998)
Stock Exchanges: New York Midwest Pacific
Ticker Symbol: WY
NAIC: 11311 Timber Tract Operations; 23321 Single
Family Housing Construction; 321113 Sawmills;
321211 Hardwood Veneer & Plywood Manufacturing;
321212 Softwood Veneer & Plywood Manufacturing;
321219 Reconstituted Wood Product Manufacturing;
32211 Pulp Mills; 322121 Paper (Except Newsprint)
Mills; 32213 Paperboard Mills; 322211 Corrugated &
Solid Fiber Box Manufacturing; 23311 Land
Subdivision & Land Development

Weyerhaeuser Company is the world's largest private owner of softwood timber and the world's largest producer of softwood lumber and market pulp. This diversified forest products company owns 5.1 million acres of timberland in the United States and license for 27 million acres in Canada. Weyerhaeuser also produces fine paper, containerboard, bleached paperboard, and a variety of wood products, and it is one of North America's leading recyclers of office wastepaper, newspaper, and corrugated boxes. The company is also involved in real estate development and construction, specifically single-family housing, residential lots, and master-planned communities.

Early History

Weyerhaeuser Timber Company, headquartered in Tacoma, Washington, was incorporated in 1900 as a joint venture in Pacific Northwest timber by James J. Hill, railroad magnate, and Frederick Weyerhaeuser, joint owner of Weyerhaeuser & Denkmann, a Midwestern lumber company that relied on forests in Wisconsin and Minnesota. Weyerhaeuser remained privately owned, primarily by the Weyerhaeuser family, until 1963.

Prior to World War I, the company was run by Frederick Weyerhaeuser. A German-born immigrant to the Midwest before the Civil War, his business philosophy evolved over his lifetime and became the operating philosophy for the new company. Weyerhaeuser felt that "the way to make money is to let the other fellow make some too."

Timber holdings doubled in the period preceding World War I. The company opened a sawmill to produce lumber and soon had the nation's first all-electric lumber mill, in 1915. Company plans to market lumber on the East Coast, using the new Panama Canal, were delayed until the end of World War I.

Although demand for lumber for railroad cars declined during World War I as steel was utilized, demand for lumber for military planes and other military uses increased. In the early days of the lumber mill, itinerant single men formed the core of the mill's laborers. Represented by the International Workers of the World (the Wobblies), they pushed for better working conditions, including an eight-hour work day. A struggle resulted, and labor unrest threatened the war effort. To ensure a steady supply of lumber for war material, the federal government established a union for the industry, something never done before or since. The union, the Loyal Legion of Loggers and Lumbermen, prevailed in its demand for the eight-hour day and 40-hour week. The hours changed the workforce; family men then constituted the core of workers in lumber.

The surplus of naval vessels at the end of the war allowed Weyerhaeuser to purchase ships at a reasonable cost to transport lumber to the East Coast through the Panama Canal. Weyerhaeuser Sales Company had been established in 1916 to promote this postwar expansion of markets.

Pioneered in Reforestation Beginning in the 1920s

John P. Weyerhaeuser, eldest son of the founder, led the company during the war and through the 1920s. He relied heavily, as had his father, on George Long, general manager from 1900 to 1930. Long, an early proponent of reforestation, approached the federal government before the war to lobby for cooperative forest fire prevention and for lower property taxes for timberland to make reforestation economically viable. This lobbying led to the Clark-McNary Act in 1924, which addressed these issues and expanded the national forest. The act also encouraged changes in taxation policies at the state level to promote reforestation. Weyerhaeuser responded by creating the Logged Off Land Company in 1925 to handle the sale of "logged off" land, to study reforestation, and to lobby at the state level for lower timberland taxes.

By the end of the 1920s Weyerhaeuser was the largest private owner of timber in the United States. At the beginning of that decade the company had produced its first national advertising campaign, promoting the lumber industry. By the decade's end the company's advertisements focused on the recently upgraded quality of its lumber, by trademarking and grademarking lumber, as well as by taking more care in handling the lumber during shipment to market.

The Great Depression produced hard times for the company, as few businesses or homes were being built. The depression in the lumber market would have been devastating if not offset by the company's diversification into pulp in 1931. By 1933 profits from pulp offset losses from lumber. The New Deal's Civilian Conservation Corps assisted in reforestation of logged off land during this period. State tax laws in the Pacific Northwest were amended to provide lower taxes for timberland, promoting reforestation. In 1940 the company started the first tree farm in the United States, near Gray's Harbor in Washington.

In 1935 the kidnapping of George Weyerhaeuser, the nine-year-old son of CEO John P. Weyerhaeuser, Jr., catapulted the Weyerhaeuser family to national attention. The Weyerhaeuser kidnapping ended happily, with the child safe, the ransom recovered, and the kidnappers apprehended. George Weyerhaeuser grew up to become president of his family's company.

In 1940 the company expanded its lumber business to include plywood and paneling. The Lend-Lease Program to assist the British prior to U.S. entry into World War II found Weyerhaeuser transport ships utilized to carry lend-lease material to the British in Egypt. During the war itself, the company served as an agent of the War Shipping Administration, directing 68 freighters and troop ships, of which two were sunk in combat.

Rapid technological and commercial changes in the lumber industry after the war affected Weyerhaeuser. The hand-operated whipsaw was replaced by the power chainsaw, and truck hauling replaced hauling by rail. Pent-up demand in construction, from the 1930s and early 1940s, led to greatly increased sales of lumber in this postwar era.

The company's organizational structure, highly informal and fraternal, was altered to accommodate rapid postwar expansion: more formal programs and reports were instituted, and subsidiaries were absorbed. A philanthropic foundation was established, and the Weyerhaeuser Real Estate Company replaced the Logged Off Land Company.

Diversified in the Postwar Era

Under the continued leadership of the Weyerhaeuser family, the company expanded into particle board production, plyveneer, hardboard, and hardwood paneling in the 1950s. Timberland holdings expanded beyond the Pacific Northwest for the first time, as land was purchased in Mississippi, Alabama, and North Carolina.

In 1958 Weyerhaeuser Sales Company, established in 1916, was absorbed into the parent company and Weyerhaeuser International S.A. was created to expand into foreign markets. With its increased diversification, the company in 1959 dropped "Timber" from its official name to become Weyerhaeuser Company and adopted its current trademark, a triangular tree over the word "Weyerhaeuser."

In 1960, for the first time in company history, the presidency of Weyerhaeuser passed out of the family to Norton Clapp. Under Clapp, the company went public in 1963. It expanded into the Japanese market as a result of surplus lumber involuntarily "logged" by Typhoon Frieda's 150-mile-per-hour winds in 1962. Weyerhaeuser's first overseas office was opened in Tokyo in 1963. In 1964 and 1965 European offices were opened in France and Belgium, respectively. The company acquired a wood products distribution firm in Australia, and it entered into a joint venture for bleached kraft pulp in Canada.

Clapp was succeeded as CEO in 1966 by George Weyerhaeuser, who served until 1988. Growth per year in the high-yield forestry program doubled, while the company contracted its first long-term debt. By the end of the 1960s annual sales exceeded $1 billion.

The 1970s were years of phenomenal growth, with sales surpassing the $2 billion mark in 1973. Sales doubled in five years and doubled again before the end of the decade. Weyerhaeuser entered the disposable diaper business in 1970; moved its corporate headquarters to Federal Way, Washington, in 1971; and centralized research in Tacoma in 1975. At the decade's end the company concluded an agreement with China to work there on the world's largest reforestation effort. In 1979 company sales were $4.4 billion.

If the 1970s were a boom decade, the early 1980s were a bust, with tight credit in housing leading to a depression in lumber similar to that of the 1930s. The volcanic eruption of Mount Saint Helens in May 1980 was also a blow to the company. Weyerhaeuser's Saint Helens Tree Farm was just below the mountain's dome, and the company lost 68,000 acres of timberland. Fortunately, the eruption took place on a Sunday, and fewer workers were in the path of the devastation. As a result of the eruption timberland values in the Northwest fell 75 percent. The company maintained dividends by diversifying into real estate and financial services. In 1986 Weyerhaeuser became the first U.S. forest products company listed on the Tokyo Stock Exchange and soon became the third most traded foreign stock there.

In response to difficult economic conditions, downsizing and economizing became company emphases in the 1980s. In one dramatic example, Weyerhaeuser instituted safety measures that reduced workers' compensation claims from $30 million to $10 million by 1990. To cut production costs still further, the company introduced a plantwide computer integrated manufacturing system.

Creighton Launched Reorganization and Restructuring in the Late 1980s

In 1988 John Creighton became president of Weyerhaeuser, and George Weyerhaeuser became chairman. Creighton reevaluated the company's diversification into areas outside of forest products. During the 1980s the company had become involved in insurance, home building, mortgage banking, garden products, pet supplies, and disposable diapers. While these businesses contributed greatly to the company's sales volume, they added very little to profits. As the head of Weyerhaeuser's nursery operations noted in the *Wall Street Journal* several years later, after the divestiture of his unit, ''Weyerhaeuser was darn good at growing trees, but they sure didn't know anything about garden supplies.''

Creighton reorganized Weyerhaeuser to focus the company's priorities and develop a coherent long-term strategy, selling off less profitable businesses and returning to a focus on forest products. As part of the restructuring program, Creighton altered the company's incentive system to reward each mill for profitability rather than the amount of product it manufactured. He also whittled Weyerhaeuser's product lines to concentrate on high-quality, higher-margin products such as white papers and high-grade lumber. By 1990 the company had sold or closed operations that had previously accounted for nearly $1 billion in sales. The loss of this revenue, however, affected virtually none of its profits.

As the restructuring program was gaining momentum in 1989, an economic recession loomed. After posting a record high of more than $10 billion in sales in 1989, Weyerhaeuser's sales dipped to $9 billion in 1990 and profits fell by 35 percent. The decline was attributed to decreased housing and other construction projects as banks grew more reluctant to lend money and, in addition, to an oversupply of pulp and paper in the market that lowered the price of paper. In 1991 the financial situation did not improve. Sales fell to $8.7 billion, and the company recorded a loss of $162 million compared to a profit of $565 million three years earlier.

Although significant, the losses suffered by Weyerhaeuser were not as large as those incurred by the rest of the forest industry. Beyond the damaging effects of the recession, other companies also sustained losses due to the protection of federal

timberlands that reduced their supply of wood. With 5.5 million acres of federal timberland cordoned off in the Pacific Northwest, lumber prices soared, and Weyerhaeuser was able to reap the benefits, harvesting timber on land it owned. This enviable position resulted in greater earnings for the company, and it was able to rebound from 1991's disastrous year. Profits in the first quarter of 1991 jumped 81 percent and, for the year, the company recorded earnings of $372 million. Also in 1991 Creighton added CEO responsibilities to his duties as president.

By 1992 the company had closed 50 plants—representing roughly 20 percent of its operating facilities—as part of its restructuring program, and it continued the divestiture of businesses that did not support the company's core business strategy. In 1993 Weyerhaeuser's diaper business was sold for $215 million; GNA Corp., Weyerhaeuser's consumer finance unit, was sold for $525 million, which represented the largest divestiture ever made by the company. In addition to shedding businesses that no longer fit the company, Weyerhaeuser strengthened its core businesses through the purchase of two pulp mills, several sawmills, and approximately 175,000 acres of timberland in Georgia from the Proctor & Gamble Company in 1992 for $600 million. The company also undertook a $1 billion modernization program to overhaul three of its largest paper mills—in Plymouth, North Carolina; Longview, Washington; and Kamloops, British Columbia.

Despite its large landholdings, Weyerhaeuser was not exempt from federal environmental regulations, and the company had to strike a deal with federal wildlife regulators to log in areas of Oregon inhabited by the endangered northern spotted owl. The company agreed in 1995 to leave corridors of larger, older trees, which the owls could use to move from Weyerhaeuser land to that of national forests. It was in large part through Creighton's leadership that the company began to shed its reputation as an inveterate clear-cutter, through such compromises. Creighton believed that it was in the company's long-term interest to take a more cooperative approach to environmental issues; he told *Business Week* in 1995: ''Although we own huge amounts of [private] timberland, to some degree we operate at the sufferance of the public.'' Another environmental concern that Creighton faced was that of salmon runs in the Pacific Northwest, which critics claimed were stilted up by heavy logging. Weyerhaeuser studied the effects of logging on 12 Northwest river basins, then formulated plans for minimizing the impact of future logging. In addition, in response to demands that chlorines be eliminated from the paper production process, Weyerhaeuser, as part of its paper mill modernization program, brought in new technology that enabled it to eliminate most chlorines from these mills.

Additions and Subtractions Continued in the Later 1990s

As the 1990s continued, Weyerhaeuser made additional moves that altered the company's operational makeup. The company bought 240,700 acres of timberland in the U.S. South in December 1995, then bought 661,200 acres in Mississippi and Louisiana and two sawmills early the following year. Later in 1996 Weyerhaeuser sold its facilities in Klamath Falls, Oregon, and 600,000 acres of forest to U.S. Timberlands for $309 million. This divestiture was part of a company strategy to return to its core Douglas fir processing activities, as the Klamath Falls acreage consisted mainly of ponderosa and lodgepole pine trees. In a further narrowing of the company's focus, Weyerhaeuser sold its mortgage company subsidiary and its Canadian chemical business in 1997. Also that year, the company made its first investment in the Southern Hemisphere, purchasing for $185 million a 51 percent interest in a joint venture in New Zealand that held 193,000 acres of fast-growing softwood timberlands.

In late 1997 Creighton retired and was succeeded as CEO and president by Steven R. Rogel, who became chairman as well in April 1999, taking over for the retiring George Weyerhaeuser. The appointment of Rogel, who had previously served as CEO and president of rival Willamette Industries Inc. of Portland, was a departure for Weyerhaeuser, which had never before chosen an outsider to run the company. Rogel had earned kudos for his tough-minded restructuring efforts at Willamette and was expected to focus on improving Weyerhaeuser's profitability, which had been on the decline since a peak in 1995 of $799 million. Rogel's focus on margins was likely to result in a further narrowing of Weyerhaeuser's interests; along these lines the company in early 1999 announced that it would table a proposed expansion of its pulp capacity and in April 1999 announced an agreement to sell its composite products business and a ply-veneer plant to SierraPine Limited. At the same time Weyerhaeuser was expected to increase its global presence, and in 1999 it opened plants in Mexico and in Wuhan, China, and acquired timberlands and sawmills in Australia through a limited partnership.

Principal Subsidiaries

Westwood Shipping Lines, Inc.; Weyerhaeuser Asia Ltd.; Weyerhaeuser Canada, Ltd.; Weyerhaeuser Financial Services, Inc; Weyerhaeuser Forestlands International, Inc.; Weyerhaeuser International Inc.; Weyerhaeuser Real Estate Company.

Principal Operating Units

Timberlands; Wood Products & Distribution; Pulp, Paper and Packaging; Real Estate.

Further Reading

Carlton, Jim, "Weyerhaeuser Outbids Georgia-Pacific to Acquire P&G Assets for $600 Million," *Wall Street Journal,* August 21, 1992, p. A3.

Erb, George, "Kudos for New CEO at Weyco," *Puget Sound Business Journal,* November 21, 1997, pp. 1+.

Ferguson, Kelly H., "Weyerhaeuser Focuses on Future with 'Minimum-Impact' Strategy," *Pulp and Paper,* September 1994, pp. 52, 55–56.

——, "Weyerhaeuser Paper Co.: Refocusing Redefines Major Industry Player," *Pulp and Paper,* January 1994, pp. 28–29.

Ferguson, Tim W., " 'Timmm Burrr!' Could Remain the Northwest's (Muffled) Cry," *Wall Street Journal,* July 9, 1991, p. A17.

Kimelman, John, "Weyerhaeuser: Not Too Late for the Timber Turnaround," *Financial World,* March 30, 1993, p. 22.

Lipin, Steven, "GE Capital to Buy GNA Corp. Unit of Weyerhaeuser," *Wall Street Journal,* January 7, 1993, p. A5.

Lubove, Seth, "Out of the Woods?," *Forbes,* March 22, 1999, p. 54.

Patrick, Ken L., "Weyerhaeuser Brings High-Tech Pulp Mill Online at Mississippi Complex," *Pulp & Paper,* December 1990, p. 79.

Richards, Bill, "Silver Lining: Owls, of All Things, Help Weyerhaeuser Cash in on Timber," *Wall Street Journal,* January 24, 1992, pp. A1, A6.

Swisher, Kara, "Weyerhaeuser Picks Rogel As New CEO, Recruiting Him from Rival Willamette," *Wall Street Journal,* November 18, 1997, p. B11.

Taylor, John H., "Rip Van Weyerhaeuser," *Forbes,* October 28, 1991, pp. 38–40.

Twining, Charles E., *F.K. Weyerhaeuser: A Biography,* St. Paul, Minn.: Minnesota Historical Society Press, 1997.

——, *Phil Weyerhaeuser, Lumberman,* Seattle: University of Washington Press, 1985.

Weyerhaeuser, George H., *"Forests for the Future": The Weyerhaeuser Story,* New York: Newcomen Society in North America, 1981.

Where the Future Grows, Tacoma, Wash.: Weyerhaeuser Corporation, 1989.

Yang, Dori Jones, "The New Growth at Weyerhaeuser," *Business Week,* June 19, 1995, pp. 63–64.

—Ellen NicKenzie Lawson and Jeffrey L. Covell
—updated by David E. Salamie

W.W. Norton & Company, Inc.

500 Fifth Ave.
New York, New York 10110
U.S.A.
(212) 354-5500
Fax: (212) 869-0856
Web site: http://www.wwnorton.com

Private Company
Incorporated: 1923 as People's Institute Publishing Co.
Employees: 400
Sales: $100 million (1997 est.)
NAIC: 51113 Book Publishers; 323117 Book Printing

W.W. Norton & Company, Inc. is an employee-owned publisher of trade books and college texts. Perhaps best known to college students for its Norton Anthologies, the company has published a diverse and well-respected mixture of academic and popular titles since it was founded more than 75 years ago.

Early History

W.W. Norton & Company began in 1923 as the not-for-profit People's Institute Publishing Co. William Warder Norton and his wife, M.D. Herter Norton, published in pamphlet form lectures delivered by others at the People's Institute, the adult division of Cooper Union in New York City. They initially ran the People's Institute Publishing Co. as a side venture, having come to New York from Columbus, Ohio, to work in the import-export business. Soon the demand for the lectures, some of which were delivered by the reigning intellectuals of the day, turned the Nortons into full-time publishers.

In 1925 Warder Norton spent six weeks in Europe, meeting publishers in England and on the continent. He bought the U.S. publishing rights to about 20 nonfiction titles that would be imported as unbound sheets and printed in the United States. He also arranged for an English-language version of Paul Bekker's *The Story of Music,* with his wife Herter doing the translation. Herter would later translate the poetry of German poet Rainier

Marie Rilke to widespread critical acclaim. *The Story of Music* was Norton's first music history title, a field in which the publisher would excel as its list expanded.

While in England Warder contacted philosopher Bertrand Russell, and they became friends. He acquired Russell's new work, *Philosophy,* the first of several of Russell's works that Norton would publish. As a result of Norton's trip, the company's first offerings had a distinctly European flavor and included such titles as John B. Watson's *Behaviorism,* which would become a classic in psychology, Franz Boas's *Anthropology and Modern Life,* John Cowper Powys's *The Meaning of Culture,* and Jose Ortega y Gasset's *The Revolt of the Masses.*

By 1929 Norton had 34 titles in print and a dozen employees. The firm survived the Great Depression in spite of having its bank account frozen for ten years by the failed Bank of the United States. The company's staff took pride in the quality of its list, and two successful titles published in the mid-1930s helped offset prior losses. They were *An American Doctor's Odyssey,* by Victor G. Heiser, and *Mathematics for the Millions,* by Lancelot Hogben. The former was the firm's first major bestseller and a main selection of the Book-of-the-Month Club, while the latter went on to sell more than 250,000 hardcover copies and remained in print as a Norton paperback.

Entered College Publishing, 1930

Norton's college department began by promoting the company's titles to university libraries and faculty. Warder Norton would also call on college professors and persuade them to write books for Norton to publish. In 1930 Norton became more seriously involved in college publishing when it acquired a substantial number of titles in print and under contract from textbook publisher F.S. Crofts. Crofts had previously obtained these titles from publisher Alfred Knopf. To these Knopf/Crofts titles Norton added books it had found in subjects such as history, literature, education, and foreign languages.

Around this time Norton also became more involved in publishing books on music and psychiatry. Up to this time most books on music history had been published in Germany, which had a near monopoly on music scholarship. With the rise of

Nazi Germany, however, many academics fled Europe and migrated to the United States. Norton published several titles on music history with an academic appeal. Then in 1941 it published Paul Henry Lang's *Music in Western Civilization,* a hybrid that sold well in the college and trade markets. Lang was a professor of music at Columbia University and, for a time, music critic of the *New York Herald-Tribune.* He became Norton's advisory editor in music and brought to the firm such market-leading textbooks as Joseph Machlis's *The Enjoyment of Music* and Donald J. Grout's *A History of Western Music.*

Norton began publishing important titles in psychiatry in 1932 with the publication of Franz Alexander's *The Medical Value of Psychoanalysis.* The next year it published Sigmund Freud's *New Introductory Lectures,* which would achieve long-lasting fame. Norton later became the U.S. publisher of the *Standard Edition of the Complete Psychological Works of Sigmund Freud.* In addition to publishing academic titles in psychiatry, Norton also published trade-oriented psychiatric works by authors such as Rollo May and Harry Overstreet that became bestsellers.

Published Western Civilizations, *1941*

In 1941 Norton's college department published *Western Civilizations* by Edward McNall Burns of Rutgers University. Within a year the book was recognized as an important history survey in the college market. As new editions were published, Norton introduced several firsts, including full-color illustrations and maps in the fifth edition. The sixth edition became the first survey text to be available in a two-volume paperback alternative to the single hardbound volume. With the publication of the 12th edition in the 1990s, the book continued to outsell most of its competitors.

During World War II paper and binding materials were in short supply. Norton was thinly staffed as many of its employees served in the armed forces. Warder Norton himself served as head of the Council of Books in Wartime, which was responsible for allocating scarce printing materials among all publishers. Late in 1945, shortly after the end of the war, Warder Norton died at the age of 54 following a brief illness.

Became an Employee-Owned Company, *1946*

Warder's death could have easily meant the end of the publishing company, but Herter Norton came up with a plan for the company to continue. She offered nearly all of her stock in the company to the firm's leading editors and managers. A Joint Stockholders Agreement was drawn up, entrusting ownership

of the firm to its employees. The agreement has remained in force for more than 50 years, and the number of shareholders has increased to include nearly all Norton employees. The agreement ensured Norton's independence; there is no market outside the company for its stock, and employees who have purchased shares must sell them back to the company or to other employees when leaving the firm.

Period of Expansion, *1950s*

Storer D. Lunt succeeded Warder Norton as the company's president from 1945 to 1957, when he became chairman until 1964. Norton's publishing program expanded in the 1950s, and the firm became more profitable. The college program went through a remarkable transformation when Norton began publishing the first of its Norton anthologies. These anthologies, with their innovative editorial and design standards, literally changed the way survey courses were taught. Perhaps the two most successful anthologies were those published for English survey courses, *The Norton Anthology of English Literature* and *The Norton Anthology of World Masterpieces.* The various Norton anthologies have sold more than an estimated 20 million copies.

The company's trade department also turned out an array of successful and influential titles during the 1950s and 1960s. These included *The Ugly American,* by William Lederer and Eugene Burdick; Betty Friedan's *The Feminine Mystique;* Dean Acheson's *Present at the Creation,* a political memoir; *Thirteen Days,* Robert F. Kennedy's posthumously published account of the Cuban Missile Crisis; and Joseph Lash's biography of Franklin and Eleanor Roosevelt, *Eleanor and Franklin,* which won a National Book Award.

Began Publishing Poetry and Paperbacks, *1960s*

In 1957 George C. Brockway became president of the company, serving until 1976. He was also chairman from 1971 to 1984.

During the 1960s Norton initiated a small but distinguished poetry program. The company would publish works by National Book Award winners A.R. Ammons, Stanley Kunitz, and Adrienne Rich, as well as former U.S. poet laureate Rita Dove.

The company also began a paperback publishing program and another in children's book publishing. While the latter did not survive the decade, the former proved quite successful and was closely allied with the company's college department. The paperback program began as the Norton Library, a series of reprint editions of little-known 19th-century novels. When these failed to sell well, the paperback program was expanded to include history, politics, and psychology. Other titles were drawn from Norton's already published hardcover editions, and acquisitions were made from other publishers, especially university presses.

The college department continued to be the principal engine in the company's growth. It strengthened its English list by publishing a series of Norton Critical Editions. It also became more heavily involved in subjects such as economics, political science, and the sciences. Competing against 12 other publishers, Norton won the right to publish the M.I.T. Introductory Physics series. Four texts in economics by Edwin Mansfield and an introductory psychology text by Henry Gleitman bolstered the college department's presence in the social sciences.

Sales Increased Fourfold, 1970s–90s

Donald S. Lamm, who had joined Norton in 1956 as a college sales rep, served as president from 1976 to 1994. He succeeded George Brockway as chairman in 1984. From the 1970s to the mid-1990s, Norton's sales increased fourfold. While the college department led the way, the company's trade department also contributed. College publishing added several important texts, including *American Government,* by Theodore J. Lowi and Benjamin Ginsberg; Hal R. Varian's *Microeconomics;* and *Macroeconomics,* by Robert E. Hall and John B. Taylor. The trade department added several academic authors to its list, including Nobel Prize-winning physicist Richard Feynman; Harvard paleontologist Stephen J. Gould; and historians such as Edmund S. Morgan, William S. McFeely, Jonathan Spence, and Peter Gay. McFeely's biography of Ulysses S. Grant won a Pulitzer Prize, and Gay's *Freud: A Life for Our Time* was a national bestseller.

The company's trade list became more eclectic as it introduced a variety of non-academic titles. Among the more successful titles were Martin Katahn's diet books and a series of mysteries from writer Walter Mosley that featured black detective Easy Rawlins. Norton also published *Helter Skelter,* an account of serial killer Charles Manson's family written by Vincent Bugliosi and Curt Gentry.

The company established Norton Professional Books in 1984. Its books were sold via catalogs and direct mail and were initially targeted for psychotherapists. Based in Evanston, Illinois, Norton Professional Books eventually expanded into architecture, design, and nautical science.

In the early 1990s Norton became more involved in international publishing. It created W.W. Norton & Company Ltd. in London, England, and established sales affiliations in several Far East countries. In 1994 W. Drake McFeely became president, and Donald Lamm was promoted to chairman. McFeely had joined Norton in 1976 and was most recently vice-president and associate director of the college department. In 1995 the company launched its web site, and in 1996 it published its first CD-ROM textbook.

At the start of 1996 Norton acquired Countryman Press, based in Vermont, to bolster its backlist. Countryman had a 23-year history and published a series of adventure guides for explorers, hikers, and bicyclists. It also had a mystery imprint, Foul Play Press, which Norton planned on continuing. It was

only the second acquisition in Norton's history, the first being Liveright Publishing Corporation in 1974.

Celebrated 75th Anniversary, 1998

As Norton celebrated its 75th anniversary in 1998, it could look back on a history of balance and stability. The employee-owned company was stable and profitable, taking in more than $100 million in annual revenues. Its last two years had shown record-breaking profits, and it had comfortably paid a $1 million advance to author Michael Lewis, who had left Norton after the success of his first book, *Liar's Poker.* Norton had achieved balance by carefully mixing trade and college publishing. It was guided by its founder's sense for publishing books of lasting value, or "Books That Live," his motto. Finally, the firm's employee ownership had given it unusual stability and promoted a high degree of loyalty.

Norton employees were entitled to buy stock in the company after working for the firm for three and a half years, and about half of the company's 400 employees owned stock in 1998. Approximately 50 to 60 percent of the stock was controlled by Norton's 14 directors.

The company's employee ownership would be an important factor in its ability to continue as a medium-sized independent publisher. It had no plans to grow through acquisitions but had broadened its offerings by taking on the distribution of books from other smaller publishers. In early 1999 the company announced a new imprint, Outside Books, a line of books about active living and the outdoors that would be published in association with *Outside* magazine. With its strong college department and expanding trade lines, Norton was likely to continue to prosper as an independent publisher.

Principal Subsidiaries

Norton Professional Books; W.W. Norton & Company Ltd. (U.K.).

Further Reading

"About W.W. Norton," http://www.wwnorton.com/about.htm, March 1, 1999.

Feldman, Gayle, "Seventy-Five Years of Norton's 'Books That Live,'" *Publishers Weekly,* June 29, 1998, p. 16.

Milliot, Jim, "Norton Acquires Vermont's Countryman Press," *Publishers Weekly,* January 29, 1996, p. 10.

"New Head for Norton: McFeely Is Appointed President," *Publishers Weekly,* May 23, 1994, p. 27.

"New Norton Line with 'Outside'," *Publishers Weekly,* March 15, 1999, p. 20.

Reid, Calvin, "Norton on the Web," *Publishers Weekly,* July 24, 1995, p. 11.

—David Bianco

INDEX TO COMPANIES

Index to Companies

Listings in this index are arranged in alphabetical order under the company name. Company names beginning with a letter or proper name such as Eli Lilly & Co. will be found under the first letter of the company name. Definite articles (The, Le, La) are ignored for alphabetical purposes as are forms of incorporation that precede the company name (AB, NV). Company names printed in bold type have full, historical essays on the page numbers appearing in bold. Updates to entries that appeared in earlier volumes are signified by the notation (**upd.**). Company names in light type are references within an essay to that company, not full historical essays. This index is cumulative with volume numbers printed in bold type.

American Land Cruiser Company. *See* Cruise America Inc.

American Learning Corporation, **7** 168

American Life Insurance Co., **III** 195–96

American Light and Traction. *See* MCN Corporation.

American Lightwave Systems, Inc., **10** 19

American Limestone Co., **IV** 33

American Limousine Corp., **26** 62

American Linseed Co, **II** 497

American Machine and Foundry Co., **II** 7; **III** 443; **7** 211–13; **11** 397; **25** 197

American Machine and Metals, **9** 23

American Machinist Press, **IV** 634

American Magnesium Products Co., **I** 404

American Maize-Products Co., 14 17–20; **23** 464

American Management Systems, Inc., 11 18–20

American Manufacturers Mutual Insurance Co., **III** 269, 271; **15** 257

American Materials & Technologies Corporation, **27** 117

American Media, Inc., 27 41–44

American Medical International, Inc., III 73–75, 79; **14** 232

American Medical Optics, **25** 55

American Medical Services, **II** 679–80; **14** 209

American Medicorp, Inc., **III** 81; **6** 191; **14** 432; **24** 230

American Melamine, **27** 317

American Merchandising Associates Inc., **14** 411

American Merchants Union Express Co., **II** 396

American Metal Climax, Inc. *See* AMAX.

American Metal Co. Ltd. *See* AMAX.

American Metal Products Company. *See* Lear Seating Corporation.

American Metal Products Corp., **I** 481

American Metals and Alloys, Inc., **19** 432

American Metals Corp., **III** 569; **20** 361

American Micro Devices, Inc., **16** 549

American Microsystems, **I** 193

American Milk Products Corp., **II** 487

The American Mineral Spirits Company, **8** 99–100

American Motorists Insurance Co., **III** 269, 271; **15** 257

American Motors Corp., I 135–37, 145, 152, 190; **II** 60, 313; **III** 543; **6** 27, 50; **8** 373; **10** 262, 264; **18** 493; **26** 403

American Movie Classics Co., **II** 161

American Multi-Cinema. *See* AMC Entertainment Inc.

American National Bank, **13** 221–22

American National Bank and Trust Co., **II** 286

American National Can Co., **III** 536; **IV** 173, 175; **26** 230

American National Corp., **II** 286

American National Fire Insurance Co., **III** 191

American National General Agencies Inc., **III** 221; **14** 109

American National Insurance Company, 8 27–29; **27 45–48 (upd.)**

American Natural Resources Co., **I** 678; **IV** 395; **13** 416

American Newspaper Publishers Association, **6** 13

American of Philadelphia, **III** 234

American Oil Co., **IV** 369–70; **7** 101; **14** 22

American Olean Tile Company, **III** 424; **22** 48, 170

American Optical Co., **I** 711–12; **III** 607; **7** 436

American Overseas Airlines, **12** 380

American Overseas Holdings, **III** 350

American Pad & Paper Company, 20 18–21

American Paging, **9** 494–96

American Paper Box Company, **12** 376

American Patriot Insurance, **22** 15

American Payment Systems, Inc., **21** 514

American Petrofina, Inc., **IV** 498; **7** 179–80; **19** 11

American Pfauter, **24** 186

American Phone Centers, Inc., **21** 135

American Photographic Group, **III** 475; **7** 161

American Physicians Service Group, Inc., **6** 45; **23** 430

American Platinum Works, **IV** 78

American Postage Meter Co., **III** 156

American Potash and Chemical Corporation, **IV** 95, 446; **22** 302

American Power & Light Co., **6** 545, 596–97; **12** 542

American Power Conversion Corporation, 24 29–31

American Premier Underwriters, Inc., 10 71–74

American Prepaid Professional Services, Inc. *See* CompDent Corporation.

American President Companies Ltd., III 512; **6 353–55**

American Printing House for the Blind, 26 13–15

American Protective Mutual Insurance Co. Against Burglary, **III** 230

American Publishing Co., **IV** 597; **24** 222

American Pure Oil Co., **IV** 497

American Radiator & Standard Sanitary Corp., **III** 663–64

American Railway Express Co., **II** 382, 397; **10** 61

American Railway Publishing Co., **IV** 634

American Re Corporation, III 182; **10 75–77**

American Record Corp., **II** 132

American Recreation Company Holdings, Inc., **16** 53

American Ref-Fuel, **V** 751

American Refrigeration Products S.A, **7** 429

American Republic Assurance Co., **III** 332

American Research and Development Corp., **II** 85; **III** 132; **6** 233; **19** 103

American Residential Mortgage Corporation, 8 30–31

American Resorts Group, **III** 103

American Rice, Inc., **17** 161–62

American River Transportation Co., **I** 421; **11** 23

American Robot Corp., **III** 461

American Rolling Mill Co., **IV** 28; **8** 176–77

American Royalty Trust Co., **IV** 84; **7** 188

American Rug Craftsmen, **19** 275

American RX Pharmacy, **III** 73

American Safety Equipment Corp., **IV** 136

American Safety Razor Company, III 27–29; **20 22–24**

American Saint-Gobain, **16** 121

American Sales Book Co., Ltd., **IV** 644

American Salt Co., **12** 199

American Satellite Co., **6** 279; **15** 195

American Savings & Loan, **10** 117

American Savings Bank, **9** 276; **17** 528, 531

American Sealants Company. *See* Loctite Corporation.

American Seating Co., **I** 447; **21** 33

American Seaway Foods, Inc, **9** 451

American Service Corporation, **19** 223

American Sheet Steel Co., **IV** 572; **7** 549

American Shipbuilding, **18** 318

American Skiing Company, 28 18–21

American Sky Broadcasting, **27** 305

American Smelting and Refining Co., **IV** 31–33

American Software Inc., 22 214; **25 20–22**

American Southern Insurance Co., **17** 196

American Standard Inc., III 437, 663–65; **19** 455; **22** 4, 6; **28** 486

American States Insurance Co., **III** 276

American Steamship Company, **6** 394–95; **25** 168, 170

American Steel & Wire Co., **I** 355; **IV** 572; **7** 549; **13** 97–98

American Steel Foundries, **7** 29–30

American Stock Exchange, **10** 416–17

American Stores Company, II 604–06; **12** 63, 333; **13** 395; **17** 559; **18** 89; **22** 37–40 (upd.); **25** 297; **27** 290–92

American Sugar Refining Company. *See* Domino Sugar Corporation.

American Sumatra Tobacco Corp., **15** 138

American Surety Co., **26** 486

American Systems Technologies, Inc., **18** 5

American Teaching Aids Inc., **19** 405

American Technical Services Company. *See* American Building Maintenance Industries, Inc. *and* ABM Industries Incorporated.

American Telephone and Telegraph Company. *See* AT&T.

American Television and Communications Corp., **I** 534–35; **II** 161; **IV** 596, 675; **7** 528–30; **18** 65

American Textile Co., **III** 571; **20** 362

American Thermos Bottle Company. *See* Thermos Company.

American Tile Supply Company, **19** 233

American Tin Plate Co., **IV** 572; **7** 549

American Title Insurance, **III** 242

American Tobacco Co., **I** 12–14, 28, 37, 425; **V** 395–97, 399, 408–09, 417–18, 600; **14** 77, 79; **15** 137–38; **16** 242; **18** 416; **27** 128–29. *See also* American Brands Inc. *and* B.A.T. Industries PLC.

American Tool & Machinery, **III** 420

American Tool Company, **13** 563

American Totalisator Corporation, **10** 319–20

American Tourister, Inc., 10 350; **13** 451, 453; **16 19–21**

American Tractor Corporation, **10** 379

American Trading and Production Corporation, **7** 101

American Transport Lines, **6** 384

American Trust and Savings Bank, **II** 261

American Trust Co., **II** 336, 382; **12** 535

American Twist Drill Co., **23** 82

American Ultramar Ltd., **IV** 567

American VIP Limousine, Inc., **26** 62

American Viscose Corp. *See* Avisco.

Heinrich Bauer North America, **7** 42–43
Heinrich Bauer Verlag, **23** 85–86
Heinrich Koppers GmbH, **IV** 89
Heinrich Lanz, **III** 463; **21** 173
Heinz Co. *See* H.J. Heinz Company.
Heinz Deichert KG, **11** 95
Heinz Italia S.p.A., **15** 221
Heisers Inc., **I** 185
Heisey Glasswork Company, **19** 210
Heiwa Sogo Bank, **II** 326, 361
Heizer Corp., **III** 109–11; **14** 13–15
HEL&P. *See* Houston Electric Light & Power Company.
Helados La Menorquina S.A., **22** 515
Helemano Co., **II** 491
Helen of Troy Corporation, 18 228–30
Helen's Arts & Crafts, **17** 321
Helena Rubenstein, Inc., **III** 24, 48; **8** 343–44; **9** 201–02; **14** 121
Helene Curtis Industries, Inc., I 403; **8 253–54; 18** 217; **22** 487; **28 183–85 (upd.)**
Helix Biocore, **11** 458
Hellefors Jernverk, **III** 623
Heller Financial, Inc., **7** 213; **16** 37; **25** 198
Hellman, Haas & Co. *See* Smart & Final, Inc.
Hellschreiber, **IV** 669
Helly Hansen ASA, 18 396; **25 205–07**
Helme Products, Inc., **15** 139
Helmerich & Payne, Inc., 18 231–33
Helmsley Enterprises, Inc., 9 278–80
Helmut Delhey, **6** 428
Helmuth Hardekopf Bunker GmbH, **7** 141
Help-U-Sell, Inc., **III** 304
Helvetia General, **III** 376
Helvetia Milk Condensing Co., **II** 486; **7** 428
Helvetia Schweizerische Feuerversicherungs-Gesellschaft St. Gallen, **III** 375
Hely Group, **IV** 294; **19** 225
Helzberg's Diamond Shops, **18** 60, 63
Hemelinger Aktienbrauerei, **9** 86
Hemex, **11** 458
Hemlo Gold Mines Inc., 9 281–82; 23 40, 42
Hemma, **IV** 616
A.B. Hemmings, Ltd., **II** 465
Henderson's Industries, **III** 581
Henderson-Union Electric Cooperative, **11** 37
Henijean & Cie, **III** 283
Henkel KGaA, III 21, 31–34, 45; **IV** 70; **9** 382; **13** 197, 199; **22** 145, 257
Henkel Manco Inc., 22 257–59
Henley Drilling Company, **9** 364
The Henley Group, Inc., I 416; **III 511–12; 6** 599–600; **9** 298; **11** 435; **12** 325; **17** 20
Hennessy Company, **19** 272
Henney Motor Company, **12** 159
Henredon Furniture Industries, **III** 571; **11** 534; **20** 362
Henri Bendel Inc., **17** 203–04
Henry Broderick, Inc., **21** 96
Henry Denny & Sons, **27** 259
Henry Grant & Co., **I** 604
Henry Holt & Co., **IV** 622–23; **13** 105; **27** 223
Henry I. Siegel Co., **20** 136
Henry J. Kaiser Company, Ltd., **28** 200
Henry J. Tully Corporation, **13** 531
The Henry Jones Co-op Ltd., **7** 577

Henry Jones Foods, **I** 437–38, 592; **7** 182; **11** 212
Henry L. Doherty & Company, **IV** 391; **12** 542
Henry Lee Company, **16** 451, 453
Henry, Leonard & Thomas Inc., **9** 533
Henry Meadows, Ltd., **13** 286
Henry Pratt Company, **7** 30–31
Henry S. King & Co., **II** 307
Henry S. Miller Companies, **21** 257
Henry Tate & Sons, **II** 580
Henry Telfer, **II** 513
Henry Waugh Ltd., **I** 469; **20** 311
Henry Willis & Co. *See* Willis Corroon Group Plc.
Henthy Realty Co., **III** 190
HEPCO. *See* Hokkaido Electric Power Company Inc.
Her Majesty's Stationery Office, 7 215–18
Heraeus Holding GmbH, IV 98–100, 118
Herald and Weekly Times, **IV** 650, 652; **7** 389, 391
Herald Publishing Company, **12** 150
Heralds of Liberty, **9** 506
Herbalife International, Inc., 17 226–29; 18 164
Herbert Clough Inc., **24** 176
Herbert W. Davis & Co., **III** 344
Herco Technology, **IV** 680
Hercofina, **IV** 499
Hercules Filter, **III** 419
Hercules Inc., I 343–45, 347; **III** 241; **19** 11; **22 260–63 (upd.); 28** 195
Hercules Nut Corp., **II** 593
Hercules Offshore Drilling, **28** 347–48
Hereford Paper and Allied Products Ltd., **14** 430
Herff Jones, **II** 488; **25** 254
Heritage Bankcorp, **9** 482
Heritage Communications, **II** 160–61
Heritage Federal Savings and Loan Association of Huntington, **10** 92
Heritage House of America Inc., **III** 81
Heritage Life Assurance, **III** 248
Heritage Media Group, **25** 418
Heritage National Health Plan, **III** 464
Heritage Springfield, **14** 245
Herman Goelitz, Inc., 28 186–88
Herman Miller, Inc., 8 251–52, **255–57**
Herman's World of Sports, **I** 548; **II** 628–29; **15** 470; **16** 457
Hermann Pfauter Group, **24** 186
Hermannshütte, **IV** 103, 105
Hermes Kreditversicherungsbank, **III** 300
Hermès S.A., 14 238–40
Herrburger Brooks P.L.C., **12** 297
Herrick, Waddell & Reed. *See* Waddell & Reed, Inc.
Herring-Hall-Marvin Safe Co. of Hamilton, Ohio, **7** 145
Hersey Products, Inc., **III** 645
Hershey Bank, **II** 342
Hershey Foods Corporation, I 26–27; **II** 478, 508, **510–12**, 569; **7** 300; **11** 15; **12** 480–81; **15** 63–64, **219–22 (upd.)**, 323; **27** 38–40
Hertel AG, **13** 297
Hertford Industrial Estates, **IV** 724
Hertie Waren- und Kaufhaus GmbH, V 72–74; 19 234, 237
Herts & Beds Petroleum Co., **IV** 566
Herts Pharmaceuticals, **17** 450

The Hertz Corporation, I 130; **II** 90; **6** 52, 129, 348–50, 356–57, 392–93; **V** 494; **9 283–85; 10** 419; **11** 494; **16** 379; **21** 151; **22** 54, 56, 524; **24** 9, 409; **25** 143
Hertz-Penske Leasing. *See* Penske Corporation.
Hervillier, **27** 188
Hespeler Hockey Inc., **22** 204
Hess Department Stores Inc., **16** 61–62; **19** 323–24
Hess Oil & Chemical Corp., **IV** 366
Hessische Berg- und Hüttenwerke AG, **III** 695
Hessische Landesbank, **II** 385–86
Hessische Ludwigs-Eisenbahn-Gesellschaft, **6** 424
Hesston Corporation, **13** 17; **22** 380
Hetteen Hoist & Derrick. *See* Polaris Industries Inc.
Heublein Inc., I 226, 246, 249, **259–61**, 281; **7** 266–67; **10** 180; **14** 214; **21** 314–15; **24** 140; **25** 177
Heuer. *See* TAG Heuer International SA.
Heuga Holdings B.V., **8** 271
Hewitt & Tuttle, **IV** 426; **17** 355–56
Hewitt Motor Company, **I** 177; **22** 329
Hewlett-Packard Company, II 62; **III** 116, **142–43; 6** 219–20, 225, **237–39 (upd.)**, 244, 248, 278–79, 304; **8** 139, 467; **9** 7, 35–36, 57, 115, 471; **10** 15, 34, 86, 232, 257, 363, 404, 459, 464, 499, 501; **11** 46, 234, 274, 284, 382, 491, 518; **12** 61, 147, 162, 183, 470; **13** 128, 326, 501; **14** 354; **15** 125; **16** 5, 139–40, 299, 301, 367, 394, 550; **18** 386–87, 434, 436, 571; **19** 515; **20** 8; **25** 96, 118, 151–53, 499, 531; **26** 177, 520; **27** 221; **28 189–92 (upd.)**
Hexalon, **26** 420
Hexatec Polymers, **III** 742
Hexcel Corporation, 11 475; **27** 50; **28 193–95**
Heyden Newport Chemical Corp., **I** 526
Heyer-Schulte, **26** 286
HFC. *See* Household Finance Corporation.
HFS Inc., **21** 97; **22** 54, 56
HG Hawker Engineering Co. Ltd., **III** 508
HGCC. *See* Hysol Grafil Composite Components Co.
HI. *See* Houston Industries Incorporated.
Hi Tech Consignments, **18** 208
Hi-Bred Corn Company, **9** 410
Hi-Lo Automotive, Inc., **26** 348–49
Hi-Mirror Co., **III** 715
Hi-Tek Polymers, Inc., **8** 554
Hibbett Sporting Goods, Inc., 26 189–91
Hibbing Transportation, **I** 448
Hibernia & Shamrock-Bergwerksgesellschaft zu Berlin, **I** 542–43
Hibernia Bank, **18** 181
Hibernian Banking Assoc., **II** 261
Hickman Coward & Wattles, **24** 444
Hickory Farms, Inc., 12 178, 199; **17 230–32**
Hickorycraft, **III** 571; **20** 362
Hicks & Greist, **6** 40
Hicks & Haas, **II** 478
Hicks, Muse, Tate & Furst, Inc., **24** 106
Hicksgas Gifford, Inc., **6** 529
Hidden Creek Industries, Inc., **16** 397; **24** 498
Higginson et Hanckar, **IV** 107

55–56, 219; **22** 78, 80; **23** 219; **24** 388; **25** 21, 85, 366; **28 308–13 (upd.)**

NetCom Systems AB, 26 331–33

Netherland Bank for Russian Trade, **II** 183

Netherlands Fire Insurance Co. of Tiel, **III** 308, 310

Netherlands India Steam Navigation Co., **III** 521

Netherlands Insurance Co., **III** 179, 308–10

Netherlands Trading Co. *See* Nederlandse Handel Maatschappij.

NetLabs, **25** 117

NetMarket Company, **16** 146

Netron, **II** 390

Netscape Communications Corporation, 15 320–22; 18 541, 543; **19** 201; **20** 237; **25** 18, 21; **26** 19; **27** 518

NetStar Inc., **24** 49

Nettai Sangyo, **I** 507

Nettingsdorfer, **19** 227

Nettle Creek Corporation, **19** 304

Nettlefolds Ltd., **III** 493

Netto, **11** 240

NetWest Securities, **25** 450

Network Associates, Inc., 25 119, **347–49**

Network Communications Associates, Inc., **11** 409

Neue Frankfurter Allgemeine Versicherungs-AG, **III** 184

Neue Holding AG, **III** 377

Neuenberger Versicherungs-Gruppe, **III** 404

Neuralgyline Co., **I** 698

Neuro Navigational Corporation, **21** 47

Neutrogena Corporation, 17 340–44

Nevada Bell Telephone Company, V 318–20; **14 345–47**

Nevada Community Bank, **11** 119

Nevada National Bank, **II** 381; **12** 534

Nevada Natural Gas Pipe Line Co., **19** 411

Nevada Power Company, 11 342–44; 12 265

Nevada Savings and Loan Association, **19** 412

Nevada Southern Gas Company, **19** 411

Neversink Dyeing Company, **9** 153

New America Publishing Inc., **10** 288

New Asahi Co., **I** 221

New Balance Athletic Shoe, Inc., 17 245; **25 350–52**

New Bedford Gas & Edison Light Co., **14** 124–25

New Broken Hill Consolidated, **IV** 58–61

New Century Network, **13** 180; **19** 204, 285

New City Releasing, Inc., **25** 269

New Consolidated Canadian Exploration Co., **IV** 96

New Consolidated Gold Fields, **IV** 21, 95–96

New CORT Holdings Corporation. *See* CORT Business Services Corporation.

New Daido Steel Co., Ltd., **IV** 62–63

New Departure, **9** 17

New Departure Hyatt, **III** 590

New England Business Services, Inc., 18 361–64

New England Confectionery Co., 15 323–25

New England CRInc, **8** 562

New England Electric System, V 662–64

New England Gas & Electric Association, **14** 124–25

New England Glass Co., **III** 640

New England Life Insurance Co., **III** 261

New England Merchants National Bank, **II** 213–14; **III** 313

New England Mutual Life Insurance Co., III 312–14

New England National Bank of Boston, **II** 213

New England Network, Inc., **12** 31

New England Nuclear Corporation, **I** 329; **8** 152

New England Power Association, **V** 662

New England Trust Co., **II** 213

New Fire Office, **III** 371

New Found Industries, Inc., **9** 465

New Galveston Company, Inc., **25** 116

New Guinea Goldfields, **IV** 95

New Halwyn China Clays, **III** 690

New Hampshire Gas & Electric Co., **14** 124

New Hampshire Insurance Co., **III** 196–97

New Hampshire Oak, **III** 512

New Hampton, Inc., **27** 429

New Haven District Telephone Company. *See* Southern New England Telecommunications Corporation.

New Haven Electric Co., **21** 512

New Hokkai Hotel Co., Ltd., **IV** 327

New Holland N.V., 22 379–81

New Horizon Manufactured Homes, Ltd., **17** 83

New Hotel Showboat, Inc. *See* Showboat, Inc.

New Ireland, **III** 393

New Jersey Bell, **9** 321

New Jersey Hot Water Heating Company, **6** 449

New Jersey Shale, **14** 250

New Jersey Tobacco Co., **15** 138

New Jersey Zinc, **I** 451

New London City National Bank, **13** 467

New London Ship & Engine, **I** 57

New Mather Metals, **III** 582

New Mitsui Bussan, **I** 507; **III** 296

New Nippon Electric Co., **II** 67

New Orleans Canal and Banking Company, **11** 105

New Orleans Refining Co., **IV** 540

New Plan Realty Trust, 11 345–47

New Process Company, **25** 76–77

New Process Cork Company Inc., **I** 601; **13** 188

New South Wales Health System, **16** 94

New Street Capital Inc., 8 388–90 (upd.). *See also* Drexel Burnham Lambert Incorporated.

New Sulzer Diesel, **III** 633

New Toyo Group, **19** 227

New Trading Company. *See* SBC Warburg.

New United Motor Manufacturing Inc., **I** 205

New UPI Inc., **25** 507

New Valley Corporation, 17 345–47

New Vanden Borre, **24** 266–70

New World Communications Group, **22** 442; **28** 248

New World Development Company Ltd., IV 717–19; 8 500

New World Entertainment, **17** 149

New World Hotel (Holdings) Ltd., **IV** 717; **13** 66

New York Air, **I** 90, 103, 118, 129; **6** 129

New York Airways, **I** 123–24

New York and Richmond Gas Company, **6** 456

New York and Suburban Savings and Loan Association, **10** 91

New York Biscuit Co., **II** 542

New York Central Railroad Company, **II** 329, 369; **IV** 181; **9** 228; **10** 43–44, 71–73; **17** 496

New York Chemical Manufacturing Co., **II** 250

New York City Transit Authority, **8** 75

New York Condensed Milk Co., **II** 470

New York Electric Corporation. *See* New York State Electric and Gas.

New York Evening Enquirer, **10** 287

New York Fabrics and Crafts, **16** 197

New York Gas Light Company. *See* Consolidated Edison Company of New York.

New York Glucose Co., **II** 496

New York Guaranty and Indemnity Co., **II** 331

New York Harlem Railroad Co., **II** 250

New York Improved Patents Corp., **I** 601; **13** 188

New York, Lake Erie & Western Railroad, **II** 395; **10** 59

New York Life Insurance Company, II 217–18, 330; **III** 291, 305, **315–17**, 332; **10** 382

New York Magazine Co., **IV** 651; **7** 390; **12** 359

New York Manufacturing Co., **II** 312

New York Marine Underwriters, **III** 220

New York Quinine and Chemical Works, **I** 496

New York Quotation Company, **9** 370

New York, Rio and Buenos Aires Airlines, **I** 115

New York State Board of Tourism, **6** 51

New York State Electric and Gas Corporation, 6 534–36

New York Stock Exchange, Inc., 9 369–72; 10 416–17

New York Telephone Co., **9** 321

The New York Times Company, III 40; **IV** 647–49; **6** 13; **15** 54; **16** 302; **19 283–85 (upd.); 23** 158

New York Trust Co., **I** 378; **II** 251

New York, West Shore and Buffalo Railroad, **II** 329

New York's Bankers Trust Co., **12** 107

New York-Newport Air Service Co., **I** 61

New Zealand Aluminum Smelters, **IV** 59

New Zealand Co., **II** 187

New Zealand Countrywide Banking Corporation, **10** 336

New Zealand Forest Products, **IV** 249–50

New Zealand Press Assoc., **IV** 669

New Zealand Sugar Co., **III** 686

New Zealand Wire Ltd., **IV** 279; **19** 154

Newark Electronics Co., **9** 420

Newco Waste Systems, **V** 750

Newcrest Mining Ltd., **IV** 47; **22** 107

Newell and Harrison Company. *See* Supervalu Inc.

Newell Co., 9 373–76; 12 216; **13** 40–41; **22** 35; **25** 22

Newey and Eyre, **I** 429

Newfoundland Brewery, **26** 304

Newfoundland Energy, Ltd., **17** 121

Newfoundland Light & Power Co. *See* Fortis, Inc.

INDEX TO INDUSTRIES

Index to Industries

ENGINEERING & MANAGEMENT SERVICES

ENTERTAINMENT & LEISURE

FINANCIAL SERVICES: BANKS

FINANCIAL SERVICES: NON-BANKS

FOOD PRODUCTS

FOOD SERVICES & RETAILERS

HEALTH & PERSONAL CARE PRODUCTS

INSURANCE

LEGAL SERVICES

MANUFACTURING

MATERIALS

MINING & METALS

PAPER & FORESTRY

PERSONAL SERVICES

PETROLEUM

PUBLISHING & PRINTING

REAL ESTATE

RUBBER & TIRE

NOTES ON CONTRIBUTORS

Notes on Contributors

BIANCO, David. Freelance writer.

BROWN, Susan Windisch. Freelance writer and editor.

BURGESS, Mary A. San Bernardino-based freelance writer; cofounder, Borgo Press.

COHEN, M. L. Novelist and freelance writer living in Paris.

COVELL, Jeffrey L. Freelance writer and corporate history contractor.

DERDAK, Thomas. Freelance writer and adjunct professor of philosophy at Loyola University of Chicago.

FROMM, J. D. Educator and author of teaching and planning resources.

HALASZ, Robert. Former editor in chief of *World Progress* and *Funk & Wagnalls New Encyclopedia Yearbook*; author, *The U.S. Marines* (Millbrook Press, 1993).

INGRAM, Frederick C. South Carolina-based business writer who has contributed to *GSA Business, Appalachian Trailway News,* the *Encyclopedia of Business,* the *Encyclopedia of Global Industries,* the *Encyclopedia of Consumer Brands,* and other regional and trade publications.

LEMIEUX, Gloria A. Freelance writer and editor living in Nashua, New Hampshire.

MALLETT, Daryl F. Freelance writer and editor; actor; contributing editor and series editor at The Borgo Press; series editor of SFRA Press's *Studies in Science Fiction, Fantasy and Horror*; associate editor of Gryphon Publications and for *Other Worlds Magazine*; founder and owner of Angel Enterprises, Jacob's Ladder Books, and Dustbunny Productions.

MOZZONE, Terri. Minneapolis-based freelance writer specializing in corporate profiles.

PEIPPO, Kathleen. Minneapolis-based freelance writer.

REGINALD, Robert. Professor, California State University, San Bernardino; founder and publisher, Borgo Press.

ROTHBURD, Carrie. Freelance technical writer and editor, specializing in corporate profiles, academic texts, and academic journal articles.

SALAMIE, David E. Part-owner of InfoWorks Development Group, a reference publication development and editorial services company.

UHLE, Frank. Ann Arbor-based freelance writer; movie projectionist, disc jockey, and staff member of *Psychotronic Video* magazine.

WALDEN, David M. Freelance writer and historian in Salt Lake City; adjunct history instructor at Salt Lake City Community College.

WERNICK, Ellen D. Freelance writer and editor.

WOODWARD, A. Freelance writer.